Encyclopedia of
Information
Systems and
Technology

Volume I

Ad Hoc–Fuzzy

Encyclopedias from the Taylor & Francis Group

Agropedia

Encyclopedia of Agricultural, Food, and Biological Engineering, Second Ed. (2 Vols.)
Edited by Dennis R. Heldman and Carmen I. Moraru   *Published 10/21/10*
Print: K10554 (978-1-4398-1111-5)   Online: K11382 (978-1-4398-2806-9)

Encyclopedia of Animal Science, Second Ed. (2 Vols.)
Edited by Duane E. Ullrey, Charlotte Kirk Baer, and Wilson G. Pond   *Published 2/1/11*
Print: K10463 (978-1-4398-0932-7)   Online: K10528 (978-0-415-80286-4)

Encyclopedia of Biotechnology in Agriculture and Food (1 Vol.)
Edited by Dennis R. Heldman, Dallas G. Hoover, and Matthew B. Wheeler   *Published 7/16/10*
Print: DK271X (978-0-8493-5027-6) Online: DKE5044 (978-0-8493-5044-3)

Encyclopedia of Pest Management (1 Vol.)
Edited by David Pimentel, Ph.D.   *Published 5/9/02*
Print: DK6323 (978-0-8247-0632-6) Online: DKE517X (978-0-8247-0517-6)

Encyclopedia of Plant and Crop Science (1 Vol.)
Edited by Robert M. Goodman   *Published 2/27/04*
Print: DK1190 (978-0-8247-0944-0) Online: DKE9438 (978-0-8247-0943-3)

Encyclopedia of Soil Science, Second Ed. (2 Vols.)
Edited by Rattan Lal   *Published 12/22/05*
Print: DK830X (978-0-8493-3830-4) Online: DKE5051 (978-0-8493-5051-1)

Encyclopedia of Water Science, Second Ed. (2 Vols.)
Edited by Stanley W. Trimble   *Published 12/26/07*
Print: DK9627 (978-0-8493-9627-4) Online: DKE9619 (978-0-8493-9619-9)

Business and Public Administration

Encyclopedia of Public Administration and Public Policy, Third Ed. (5 Vols.)
Edited by Melvin J. Dubnick and Domonic Bearfield   *Published 7/15/15*
Print: K16418 (978-1-4665-6909-6)   Online: K16434 (978-1-4665-6936-2)

Encyclopedia of Supply Chain Management (2 Vols.)
Edited by James B. Ayers   *Published 12/21/11*
Print: K12842 (978-1-4398-6148-6)   Online: K12843 (978-1-4398-6152-3)

Encyclopedia of U.S. Intelligence (2 Vols.)
Edited by Gregory Moore   *Published 12/19/14*
Print: AU8957 (978-1-4200-8957-8)   Online: AUE8957 (978-1-4200-8958-5)

Chemistry, Materials, and Chemical Engineering

Encyclopedia of Chemical Processing (5 Vols.)
Edited by Sunggyu Lee   *Published 11/1/05*
Print: DK2243 (978-0-8247-5563-8) Online: DKE499X (978-0-8247-5499-0)

Encyclopedia of Chromatography, Third Ed. (3 Vols.)
Edited by Jack Cazes   *Published 10/12/09*
Print: 84593 (978-1-4200-8459-7)   Online: 84836 (978-1-4200-8483-2)

Encyclopedia of Iron, Steel, and Their Alloys (5 Vols.)
Edited by George E. Totten and Rafael Colas   *Published 9/15/15*
Print: K14814 (978-1-4665-1104-0)   Online: K14815 (978-1-4665-1105-7)

Encyclopedia of Supramolecular Chemistry (2 Vols.)
Edited by Jerry L. Atwood and Jonathan W. Steed   *Published 5/5/04*
Print: DK056X (978-0-8247-5056-5) Online: DKE7259 (978-0-8247-4725-1)

Encyclopedia of Surface and Colloid Science, Third Ed. (10 Vols.)
Edited by P. Somasundaran   *Published 5/8/15*
Print: K20465 (978-1-4665-9045-8)   Online: K20478 (978-1-4665-9061-8)

Environment

Encyclopedia of Environmental Management (4 Vols.)
Edited by Sven Erik Jorgensen   *Published 12/13/12*
Print: K11434 (978-1-4398-2927-1)   Online: K11440 (978-1-4398-2933-2)

Encyclopedia of Natural Resources (2 Vols.)
Edited by Yeqiao Wang   *Published 7/23/14*
Print: K12418 (978-1-4398-5258-3)   Online: KE12440 (978-1-4398-5283-5)

Engineering

Dekker Encyclopedia of Nanoscience and Nanotechnology, Third Ed. (7 Vols.)
Edited by Sergey Edward Lyshevski   *Published 3/20/14*
Print: K14119 (978-1-4398-9134-6)   Online: K14120 (978-1-4398-9135-3)

Encyclopedia of Energy Engineering and Technology, Second Ed. (4 Vols.)
Edited by Sohail Anwar   *Published 12/1/14*
Print: K14633 (978-1-4665-0673-2)   Online: KE16142 (978-1-4665-0674-9)

Encyclopedia of Optical and Photonic Engineering, Second Ed. (3 Vols.)
Edited by Craig Hoffman and Ronald Driggers   *Published 6/1/15*
Print: K12323 (978-1-4398-5097-8)   Online: K12325 (978-1-4398-5099-2)

Medicine

Encyclopedia of Biomaterials and Biomedical Engineering, Second Ed. (4 Vols.)
Edited by Gary E. Wnek and Gary L. Bowlin   *Published 5/28/08*
Print: H7802 (978-1-4200-7802-2)   Online: HE7803 (978-1-4200-7803-9)

Encyclopedia of Biomedical Polymers and Polymeric Biomaterials (11 Vol.)
Edited by Munmaya Mishra   *Published 3/12/15*
Print: K14324 (978-1-4398-9879-6)   Online: K14404 (978-1-4665-0179-9)

Encyclopedia of Biopharmaceutical Statistics, Third Ed. (3 Vols.)
Edited by Shein-Chung Chow   *Published 5/20/10*
Print: H100102 (978-1-4398-2245-6)   Online: HE10326 (978-1-4398-2246-3)

Encyclopedia of Clinical Pharmacy (1 Vol.)
Edited by Joseph T. DiPiro   *Published 11/14/02*
Print: DK7524 (978-0-8247-0752-1)   Online: DKE6080 (978-0-8247-0608-1)

Encyclopedia of Dietary Supplements, Second Ed. (1 Vol.)
Edited by Paul M. Coates, Joseph M. Betz, Marc R. Blackman, Gordon M. Cragg, Mark Levine, Joel Moss, and Jeffrey D. White   *Published 6/25/10*
Print: H100094 (978-1-4398-1928-9)   Online: HE10315 (978-1-4398-1929-6)

Encyclopedia of Medical Genomics and Proteomics (2 Vols.)
Edited by Jürgen Fuchs and Maurizio Podda   *Published 12/29/04*
Print: DK2208 (978-0-8247-5564-5)   Online: DK501X (978-0-8247-5501-0)

Encyclopedia of Pharmaceutical Science and Technology, Fourth Ed. (6 Vols.)
Edited by James Swarbrick   *Published 7/1/13*
Print: H100233 (978-1-84184-819-8)   Online: HE10420 (978-1-84184-820-4)

Software, Networking, and Security

Encyclopedia of Information Assurance (4 Vols.)
Edited by Rebecca Herold and Marcus K. Rogers   *Published 12/21/10*
Print: AU6620 (978-1-4200-6620-3) Online: AUE6620 (978-1-4200-6622-7)

Encyclopedia of Information Systems and Technology (2 Vol.)
Edited by Phillip A. Laplante   *Published 10/15/15*
Print: K15911 (978-1-4665-6077-2)   Online: K21745 (978-1-4822-1432-1)

Encyclopedia of Library and Information Sciences, Third Ed. (7 Vols.)
Edited by Marcia J. Bates and Mary Niles Maack   *Published 12/17/09*
Print: DK9712 (978-0-8493-9712-7) Online: DKE9711 (978-0-8493-9711-0)

Encyclopedia of Software Engineering (2 Vols.)
Edited by Phillip A. Laplante   *Published 11/24/10*
Print: AU5977 (978-1-4200-5977-9)   Online: AUE5977 (978-1-4200-5978-6)

Encyclopedia of Wireless and Mobile Communications, Second Ed. (3 Vols.)
Edited by Borko Furht   *Published 12/18/12*
Print: K14731 (978-1-4665-0956-6)   Online: KE16352 (978-1-4665-0969-6)

Encyclopedia of
Information Systems and Technology

Volume I

Ad Hoc–Fuzzy

Edited by Phillip A. Laplante

CRC Press
Taylor & Francis Group
Boca Raton   London   New York

CRC Press is an imprint of the
Taylor & Francis Group, an **informa** business

AN AUERBACH BOOK

CRC Press
Taylor & Francis Group
6000 Broken Sound Parkway NW, Suite 300
Boca Raton, FL 33487-2742

© 2016 by Taylor & Francis Group, LLC
CRC Press is an imprint of Taylor & Francis Group, an Informa business

No claim to original U.S. Government works

Printed on acid-free paper
Version Date: 20151030

International Standard Book Number-13: 978-1-4987-5785-0 (Hardback)

Visit the Taylor & Francis Web site at
http://www.taylorandfrancis.com

and the CRC Press Web site at
http://www.crcpress.com

Encyclopedia of Information Systems and Technology

To the beloved dogs that I have had in my life: Ginger, Francis, Maggie, Teddy, and Henry, and those yet to come.

Encyclopedia of Information Systems and Technology

Editor-in-Chief
Phillip A. Laplante
Professor of Software Engineering, Great Valley School of Graduate Professional Studies, Pennsylvania State University, Malvern, Pennsylvania, U.S.A.

Editorial Advisory Board

Contributors

Azad Adam / *London, U.K.*

Ali Naser Al-Khwildi / *Commission of Media and Communications (CMC), Jadreiah, Iraq*

Sven Axsöter / *Department of Industrial Management and Logistics, Lund University, Lund, Sweden*

Mohamad Badra / *College of Technological Innovation, Zayed University, Dubai, United Arab Emirates*

Ricardo Baeza-Yates / *Barcelona Media Innovation Centre, Yahoo! Research, Barcelona, Spain*

Robert B. Batie Jr. / *Cyber Defense Solutions, Network Centric Systems, Raytheon Company, Largo, Florida, U.S.A.*

A. R. Bednarek / *University of Florida, Gainesville, Florida, U.S.A.*

Chuck Bianco / *IT Examination Manager, Office of Thrift Supervision, Department of the Treasury, Dallas, Texas, U.S.A.*

Galina Bogdanova / *Department of Mathematical Foundations of Informatics, Institute of Mathematics and Informatics, Bulgarian Academy of Sciences, Veliko Tarnovo, Bulgaria*

Gloria Bordogna / *Italian National Research Council, Institute for the Dynamics of Environmental Processes, Dalmine, Italy*

Terrence Brooks / *iSchool, University of Washington, Seattle, Washington, U.S.A.*

Christopher Brown-Syed / *Faculty of Continuing Education and Training, Seneca College, Burlington, Ontario, Canada*

Jason Burke / *SAS Institute, Cary, North Carolina, U.S.A.*

Carlos Castillo / *Yahoo! Research, Barcelona, Spain*

Glenn Cater / *Director, IT Risk Consulting, Aon Consulting, Inc., Freehold, New Jersey, U.S.A.*

Ranganai Chaparadza / *IPV6 Forum, ETSI-AFI, Berlin, Germany*

Ansuman Chattopadhyay / *Health Sciences Library System, University of Pittsburgh, Pittsburgh, Pennsylvania, U.S.A.*

Brian J.S. Chee / *School of Ocean and Earth Sciences and Technology (SOEST), University of Hawaii, Honolulu, Hawaii, U.S.A.*

Hsinchun Chen / *Department of Management Information Systems, University of Arizona, Tucson, Arizona, U.S.A.*

Jianhua Chen / *Computer Science Department, Louisiana State University, Baton Rouge, Louisiana, U.S.A.*

Marco Conti / *National Research Council (CNR), Pisa, Italy*

Marcelo Nogueira Cortimiglia / *Industrial Engineering Department, Federal University of Rio Grande do Sul, Porto Alegre, Brazil*

Kimiz Dalkir / *Graduate School of Library and Information Studies, McGill University, Montreal, Quebec, Canada*

Yan Dang / *Department of Management Information Systems, University of Arizona, Tucson, Arizona, U.S.A.*

Joanna F. DeFranco / *Pennsylvania State University, Malvern, Pennsylvania, U.S.A.*

Harry B. DeMaio / *Cincinnati, Ohio, U.S.A.*

Brian Detlor / *DeGroote School of Business, McMaster University, Hamilton, Ontario, Canada*

Andrew Dillon / *School of Information, University of Texas at Austin, Austin, Texas, U.S.A.*

Jianguo Ding / *School of Informatics, University of Skovde, Skovde, Sweden*

G. Reza Djavanshir / *Carey Business School, Johns Hopkins University, Baltimore, Maryland, U.S.A.*

Matt Dobra / *Department of Economics, Methodist University, Fayetteville, North Carolina, U.S.A.*

Marek J. Druzdzel / *School of Information Sciences and Intelligent Systems Program, University of Pittsburgh, Pittsburgh, Pennsylvania, U.S.A.*

Artur Dubrawski / *Robotics Institute, Carnegie Mellon University, Pittsburgh, Pennsylvania, U.S.A.*

Mark Edmead / *President, MTE Software, Inc., Escondido, California, U.S.A.*

Scott Erkonen / *Hot skills Inc., Minneapolis, Minnesota, U.S.A.*

Ben Falchuk / *Telcordia Technologies, Inc., Piscataway, New Jersey, U.S.A.*

Dave Famolari / *Telcordia Technologies, Inc., Piscataway, New Jersey, U.S.A.*

Roger R. Flynn / *School of Information Sciences and Intelligent Systems Program, University of Pittsburgh, Pittsburgh, Pennsylvania, U.S.A.*

Park Foreman / *Austin, Texas, U.S.A.*

Alejandro Germán Frank / *Industrial Engineering Department, Federal University of Rio Grande do Sul, Porto Alegre, Brazil*

Ulrik Franke / *Department of Information and Aeronautical Systems, Swedish Defense Research Agency (FOI), Stockholm, Sweden*

Curtis Franklin Jr. / *Senior Writer, NetWitness, Gainsville, Florida, U.S.A.*

José Antonio Garcia-Macias / *CICESE Research Center, Esenada, Mexico*

Antonio Ghezzi / *Department of Management, Economics and Industrial Engineering, Milan Polytechnic, Milan, Italy*

Lal C. Godara / *Australian Defence Force Academy, School of Electrical Engineering University College, University of New South Wales, Canberra, Australian Capital Territory, Australia*

Tandy Gold / *Independent Executive Consultant, Sanford, Florida, U.S.A.*

Steven D. Gray / *Nokia Research Center, Espoo, Finland*

Wendy Hall / *Intelligence, Agents, Multimedia Group, University of Southampton, Southampton, U.K.*

Monte F. Hancock Jr. / *Chief Scientist, Celestech, Inc., Melbourne, Florida, U.S.A.*

Chris Hare / *Information Systems Auditor, Nortel, Dallas, Texas, U.S.A.*

Kirk Hausman / *Assistant Commandant, Texas A&M University, College Station, Texas, U.S.A.*

Gilbert Held / *4-Degree Consulting, Macon, Georgia, U.S.A.*

Markus Helfert / *School of Computing, Dublin City University, Dublin, Ireland*

Paul A. Henry / *Senior Vice President, CyberGuard Corporation, Ocala, Florida, U.S.A.*

Rebecca Herold / *Information Privacy, Security and Compliance Consultant, Rebecca Herold and Associates LLC, Van Meter, Iowa, U.S.A.*

Francis Heylighen / *Free University of Brussels, Brussels, Belgium*

Randolph Hock / *Online Strategies, Vienna, Virginia, U.S.A.*

Javek Ikbal / *Director, IT Security, Major Financial Services Company, Reading, Massachusetts, U.S.A.*

Carrie L. Iwema / *Health Sciences Library System, University of Pittsburgh, Pittsburgh, Pennsylvania, U.S.A.*

Valentina Janev / *Mihajlo Pupin Institute, Belgrade, Serbia*

Gary G. Jing / *TE Connectivity, Shakopee, Minnesota, U.S.A.*

Leighton Johnson III / *Chief Operating Officer and Senior Consultant, Information Security and Forensics Management Team (ISFMT), Bath, South Carolina, U.S.A.*

Keith Jones / *Annapolis, Maryland, U.S.A.*

Paul B. Kantor / *School of Communication, Information and Library Studies, Rutgers University, New Brunswick, New Jersey, U.S.A.*

Leon Kappelman / *Information Technology and Decision Sciences Department, University of North Texas, Denton, Texas, U.S.A.*

Jessica Keyes / *New Art Technologies, Inc., New York, New York, U.S.A.*

Shafiullah Khan / *School of Engineering and Information Sciences, Computer Communications Department, Middlesex University, London, U.K.*

Joshua L. Kissee / *Instructional Technology Services, Information Technology Division, Texas A&M University, College Station, Texas, U.S.A.*

Walter S. Kobus Jr. / *Vice President, Security Consulting Services, Total Enterprise Security Solutions, LLC, Raleigh, North Carolina, U.S.A.*

Donald Kraft / *Department of Computer Science, U.S. Air Force Academy, Colorado Springs, Colorado, U.S.A.*

Mollie E. Krehnke / *Senior Information Security Consultant, Insight Global, Inc., Raleigh, North Carolina, U.S.A.*

Stephan Kudyba / *New Jersey Institute of Technology, Newark, New Jersey, U.S.A.*

Matthew Kwatinetz / *QBL Partners, New York, New York, U.S.A.*

Zhenhua Lai / *Department of Management Information Systems, University of Arizona, Tucson, Arizona, U.S.A.*

Sian Lun Lau / *Department of Computer Science and Networked Systems, Sunway University, Subang Jaya, Malaysia*

Ross A. Leo / *Professional Training and Development, University of Houston-Clear Lake, CyberSecurity Institute, Houston, Texas, U.S.A.*

Timothy F. Leslie / *Department of Geography and Geoinformation Science, George Mason University, Fairfax, Virginia, U.S.A.*

Shoshana Loeb / *Telcordia Technologies, Inc., Piscataway, New Jersey, U.S.A.*

Jonathan Loo / *School of Engineering and Information Sciences, Computer Communications Department, Middlesex University, London, U.K.*

Phillip Q. Maier / *Vice President, Information Security Emerging Technology & Network Group, Inovant, San Ramon, California, U.S.A.*

Franjo Majstor / *EMEA Senior Technical Director, CipherOptics Inc., Raleigh, North Carolina, U.S.A.*

Arun K. Majumdar / *VivoMind Research, Rockville, Maryland, U.S.A.*

Katherine Marconi / *Health Care Administration and Health Administration Informatics, University of Maryland, Adelphi, Maryland, U.S.A.*

Johan Marklund / *Department of Industrial Management and Logistics, Lund University, Lund, Sweden*

George G. McBride / *Senior Manager, Security and Privacy Services (SPS), Deloitte & Touche LLP, Princeton, New Jersey, U.S.A.*

Lowell Bruce McCulley / *IT Security Professional, Troy, New Hampshire, U.S.A.*

Lynda L. McGhie / *Information Security Officer (ISO)/Risk Manager, Private Client Services (PCS), Wells Fargo Bank, Cameron Park, California, U.S.A.*

Hermann Moisl / *Center for Research in Linguistics, University of Newcastle upon Tyne, Newcastle Upon Tyne, U.K.*

William Hugh Murray / *Executive Consultant, TruSecure Corporation, New Canaan, Connecticut, U.S.A.*

Nikolay Noev / *Department of Mathematical Foundations of Informatics, Institute of Mathematics and Informatics, Bulgarian Academy of Sciences, Veliko Tarnovo, Bulgaria*

David O'Berry / *Director of Information Technology Systems and Services, South Carolina Department of Probation, Parole and Pardon Services (SCDPPPS), Columbia, South Carolina, U.S.A.*

Kieron O'Hara / *Intelligence, Agents, Multimedia Group, University of Southampton, Southampton, U.K.*

Tero Ojanperä / *Nokia Research Center, Espoo, Finland*

Gabriella Pasi / *Department of Informatics, Systems and Communication, University of Studies of Milano Bicocca, Milan, Italy*

Keith Pasley / *PGP Security, Boonsboro, Maryland, U.S.A.*

Bonnie A. Goins Pilewski / *Senior Security Strategist, Isthmus Group, Inc., Aurora, Illinois, U.S.A.*

Christopher A. Pilewski / *Senior Security Strategist, Isthmus Group, Inc., Aurora, Illinois, U.S.A.*

Sean M. Price / *Independent Information Security Consultant, Sentinel Consulting, Washington, District of Columbia, U.S.A.*

Bernice M. Purcell / *School of Business Administration and Extended Learning, Holy Family University, Philadelphia, Pennsylvania, U.S.A.*

Viju Raghupathi / *Brooklyn College, City University of New York, New York, New York, U.S.A.*

Wullianallur Raghupathi / *Fordham University, New York, New York, U.S.A.*

James F. Ransome / *Cisco Systems, Santa Clara, California, U.S.A.*

John W. Rittinghouse / *Tomball, Texas, U.S.A.*

Ben Rothke / *International Network Services (INS), New York, New York, U.S.A.*

Jason W. Rupe / *Polar Star Consulting, LLC, Lafayette, Colorado, U.S.A.*

John C. Russ / *Department of Materials Science and Engineering, College of Engineering, North Carolina State University, Raleigh, North Carolina, U.S.A.*

Tefko Saracevic / *School of Communication and Information, Rutgers University, New Brunswick, New Jersey, U.S.A.*

Greg Schulz / *StorageIO Group, Stillwater, Minnesota, U.S.A.*

Suresh Singh / *Portland State University, Portland, Oregon, U.S.A.*

Ed Skoudis / *Senior Security Consultant, Intelguardians Network Intelligence, Howell, New Jersey, U.S.A.*

Floyd (Bud) E. Smith / *Writer, Oakland, California, U.S.A.*

John F. Sowa / *VivoMind Research, Rockville, Maryland, U.S.A.*

Dick Stenmark / *Department of Applied IT, IT University of Gothenburg, Gothenburg, Sweden*

D.E. Stevenson / *School of Computing, Clemson University, Clemson, South Carolina, U.S.A.*

E. Burton Swanson / *Anderson School of Management, University of California—Los Angeles, Los Angeles, California, U.S.A.*

M. Jafar Tarokh / *K.N. Toosi University of Technology, Tehran, Iran*

Christine B. Tayntor / *Writer, Cheyenne, Wyoming, U.S.A.*

Richard Temple / *AristaCare Health Services, South Plainfield, New Jersey, U.S.A.*

Charles Thompson / *Research Triangle Institute (RTI) International, Washington, District of Columbia, U.S.A.*

Wayne Thompson / *SAS Institute, Cary, North Carolina, U.S.A.*

James S. Tiller / *Chief Security Officer and Managing Vice President of Security Services, International Network Services (INS), Raleigh, North Carolina, U.S.A.*

Harold F. Tipton / *HFT Associates, Villa Park, California, U.S.A.*

Todor Todorov / *St. Cyril and St. Methodius University of Veliko Turnovo, and Department of Mathematical Foundations of Informatics, Institute of Mathematics and Informatics, Bulgarian Academy of Sciences, Veliko Tarnovo, Bulgaria*

Leyla Toumi / *Software Systems Research Laboratory (LSR-IMAG), National Center for Scientific Research (CNRS)/National Polytechnic Institute of Grenoble (INPG), Grenoble, France*

Don Turnbull / *School of Information, University of Texas at Austin, Austin, Texas, U.S.A.*

Sanja Vrane / *Mihajlo Pupin Institute, Belgrade, Serbia*

Nigel M. Waters / *Department of Geography and Geoinformation Science, George Mason University, Fairfax, Virginia, U.S.A.*

Jana Zabinski / *American National Standards Institute, New York, New York, U.S.A.*

Sherali Zeadally / *College of Communication and Information, University of Kentucky, Lexington, Kentucky, U.S.A.*

Yulei Zhang / *Department of Management Information Systems, University of Arizona, Tucson, Arizona, U.S.A.*

Encyclopedia of Information Systems and Technology

Contents

Volume I

Volume II

Encyclopedia of Information Systems and Technology

Topical Table of Contents

1. IT Fundamentals

2. Human-Computer Interaction

3. Information Assurance and Security, IT as a Profession

4. Information Management

5. Integrative Programming and Technologies

6. Mathematics and Statistics for IT

7. Networking

8. Programming Fundamentals

9. Platform Technologies

10. Systems Administration and Maintenance

11. System Integration and Architecture

12. Social and Professional Issues

13. Web Systems and Technologies

Preface

So, how does one go about building an encyclopedia? First you need a framework or body of knowledge to guide the commissioning of entries. There are several bodies of knowledge related to Information Systems and Technology that could have been used in organizing this *Encyclopedia*. But a consensus body of knowledge based on several of these was developed by Bill Agresti at Johns Hopkins University.[1] This body of knowledge is the one used in this encyclopedia. It defines the following key areas:

1. IT fundamentals,
2. human-computer interaction,
3. information assurance and security, IT as a profession,
4. information management,
5. integrative programming and technologies,
6. mathematics and statistics for IT,
7. networking,
8. programming fundamentals,
9. platform technologies,
10. systems administration and maintenance,
11. system integration and architecture,
12. social and professional issues, and
13. Web systems and technologies.

These areas, then, provide the organizational structure for this Encyclopedia.

Next is the formation of an Editorial Advisory Board. I am delighted and lucky to have recruited a Board who are both experts in their respective fields and friends. Together we identified and recruited expert authors to write these entries.

The task of finding authors was not easy. Teasing small entries for a dictionary is much easier than extracting substantial entries for an encyclopedia, and experts are always busy. Therefore, there were many false starts and stops, searches for new authors when necessary, and the need for constant encouragements. As the entries began to be delivered by the authors, peer reviews for the entries needed to be organized. Finding expert peer reviewers, who are also busy, wasn't always easy. The entries and review reports were then returned to the authors for revision, and in many cases, another round of reviews. The process was not dissimilar to editing a special issue of a scholarly journal, only magnified by a factor of 20. The final entries then needed to be edited by expert copy editors, then returned to the authors for another check. The editor-in-chief conducted one final check. It should be no surprise, then, the process from start to finish took four years.

I hope you are pleased with the result. This Encyclopedia is the result of the work of more than 200 expert contributors and reviewers from industry and academia across the globe. We tried to be as correct and comprehensive as possible, but of course, in a work of this grand scope, there are bound to be holes in coverage, as well as typographical, possibly even factual errors. I take full responsibility for these errors, and hope that you will contact me at eit@taylorandfrancis.com to notify me of any. The good news is that this Encyclopedia is a perpetual project – the online version will be updated regularly, and new print editions are anticipated. These updated versions allow for ongoing correction and augmentation of the Encyclopedia, and to keep pace with the rapid changes in Information Systems and Technology. My intention is to keep this Encyclopedia as relevant and fresh as possible.

The target readership for this Encyclopedia includes Information Systems and Technology professionals, managers, software professionals, and other technology professionals. I also expect the Encyclopedia to find its way into many library databases. Finally, I hope that this Encyclopedia will be added to the reading list for Information Science undergraduate and graduate students.

Phillip A. Laplante, Editor-in-Chief

Reference

1. Agresti, William W. An IT Body of Knowledge: The Key to an Emerging Profession, *IT Professional*, pp. 18–22, November/December, 2008.

Acknowledgments

Compiling an Encyclopedia is a massive effort, and the role of Editor-In-Chief is similar to that of the captain of an aircraft carrier – the captain merely articulates the mission of the ship and its destination and provides general guidance along the way – hundreds of others do the real work. This encyclopedia really did involve hundreds of people: contributors, reviewers, editors, production staff and more, so I cannot thank everyone personally. But some special kudos are required.

Collectively, I thank the authors of the entries and the reviewers – without them, of course, there would be no Encyclopedia. Members of the Editorial Advisory Board also provided a great deal of advice, encouragement, and hard work, and I am grateful to them for those. And there are many staff at Taylor & Francis in the acquisitions, editing, production, marketing, and sales departments who deserve credit. But I must call out some key individuals who guided me through this journey.

First, I want to thank senior acquisitions editor, John Wyzalek and production supervisor Claire Miller – I have worked with John and Claire on many projects and they have always provided wise guidance and kept me on task. Over the four years that were needed to solicit, develop, review, revise, and edit the entries, my development editor, Molly Pohlig has been my eyes, ears and hands. I am grateful for her enthusiasm and counsel. Finally, I have to, once again, thank my family for putting up with my physical presence but mental absence as I worked on this project in our family room over many days and evenings.

About the Editors

Phillip A. Laplante

Dr. Phillip A. Laplante is professor of Software and Systems Engineering at Penn State Universitys Great Valley School of Graduate Professional Studies. Previously, he was a professor and academic administrator at several colleges and universities. Prior to his academic experiences, Dr. Laplante worked as a professional software engineer for almost eight years. He was involved in requirements engineering and software delivery for such projects as the Space Shuttle Inertial Measurement Unit, commercial CAD software, and major projects for Bell Laboratories.

Dr. Laplante's research, teaching, and consulting focus on the areas of requirements engineering, software testing, project management, and embedded systems. He serves on a number of corporate and professional boards and is a widely sought speaker and consultant.

Dr. Laplante has written or edited 30 books, including three dictionaries and the *Encyclopedia of Software Engineering*, published by CRC Press/Taylor & Francis. He also edits the following Taylor & Francis Book Series: Applied Software Engineering, Image Processing, and What Every Engineer Should Know About.

He holds a BS degree in Systems Planning and Management, a Masters degree in Electrical Engineering, and a PhD in Computer Science, all from Stevens Institute of Technology. He also holds an MBA from University of Colorado. He is a Fellow of the IEEE and SPIE.

Encyclopedia of Information Systems and Technology

Volume I
Ad Hoc–Fuzzy
Pages 1–550

Ad Hoc–
Availability

Big Data–
Cellular

Cloud Computing

Communication–
Cybernetics

Data Analytics–
Data Mining:
Forensic

Data Mining:
Healthcare–
Decision

EDRMS–
Enterprise

Ethics–
Fuzzy

Ad Hoc Networks: Technologies

Marco Conti
National Research Council (CNR), Pisa, Italy

Abstract

This entry presents architectures and protocols for ad hoc networks—IEEE 802.11 and Bluetooth.

TECHNOLOGIES FOR AD HOC NETWORKS

The success of a network technology is connected to the development of networking products at a competitive price. A major factor in achieving this goal is the availability of appropriate networking standards. Two main standards are emerging for ad hoc wireless networks: the IEEE 802.11 standard for wireless local area networks (WLANs).[1] and the Bluetooth specifications. The Bluetooth specifications are released by the Bluetooth Special Interest Group (SIG)[2] (for short-range wireless communications).[3–5]

The IEEE 802.11 standard is a good platform for implementing a single-hop WLAN ad hoc network because of its extreme simplicity. Multihop networks covering areas of several square kilometers could also be built by exploiting the IEEE 802.11 technology. On smaller scales, technologies such as Bluetooth can be used to build ad hoc wireless body and personal area networks, i.e., networks that connect devices on the person, or placed around the person inside a circle with a radius of 10 m.

Here we present the architecture and protocols of IEEE 802.11 and Bluetooth. In addition, the performances of these technologies are analyzed. Two main performance indices will be considered: the throughput and the delay.

As far as throughput is concerned, special attention will be paid to the medium access control (MAC) protocol capacity,[6,7] defined as the maximum fraction of channel bandwidth used by successfully transmitted messages. This performance index is important because the bandwidth delivered by wireless networks is much lower than that of wired networks, e.g., 1–11 Mbps vs. 100–1000 Mbps.[8] Since a WLAN relies on a common transmission medium, the transmissions of the network stations must be coordinated by the MAC protocol. This coordination can be achieved by means of control information that is carried explicitly by control messages traveling along the medium (e.g., ACK messages) or can be provided implicitly by the medium itself using the carrier sensing to identify the channel as either active or idle. Control messages or message retransmissions due to collision remove channel bandwidth from that available for successful message transmission. Therefore, the capacity gives a good indication of the overheads required by the MAC protocol to perform its coordination task among stations or, in other words, of the effective bandwidth that can be used on a wireless link for data transmission.

The delay can be defined in several forms (access delay, queuing delay, propagation delay, etc.) depending on the time instants considered during its measurement.[6] In computer networks, the response time (i.e., the time between the generation of a message at the sending station and its reception at the destination station) is the best value to measure the quality of service (QoS) perceived by the users. However, the response time depends on the amount of buffering inside the network, and it is not always meaningful for the evaluation of a LAN technology. For example, during congested periods, the buffers fill up, and thus the response time does not depend on the LAN technology but it is mainly a function of the buffer length. For this reason, hereafter, the MAC delay index is used. The MAC delay of a station in a LAN is defined as the time between the instant at which a packet comes to the head of the station transmission queue and the end of the packet transmission.[6]

IEE 802.11 ARCHITECTURE AND PROTOCOLS

In 1997, the IEEE adopted the first WLAN, named IEEE 802.11, with data rates up to 2 Mbps.[9] Since then, several task groups (designated by letters) have been created to extend the IEEE 802.11 Standard. Task groups 802.11b and 802.11a have completed their work by providing two relevant extensions to the original standard.[1] The 802.11b task group produced a standard for WLAN operations in the 2.4 GHz band, with data rates up to 11 Mbps. This standard, published in 1999, has been very successful. There are several IEEE 802.11b products available in the market. The 802.11a

Encyclopedia of Information Systems and Technology, DOI: 10.1081/E-EIST-120043888

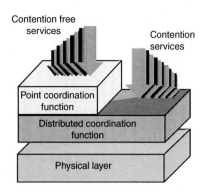

Fig. 1 IEEE 802.11 architecture.

task group created a standard for WLAN operations in the 5 GHz band, with data rates up to 54 Mbps. Among the other task groups, it is worth mentioning task group 802.11e (which attempts to enhance the MAC with QoS features to support voice and video over 802.11 networks) and task group 802.11g (which is working to develop a higher-speed extension to 802.11b).

The IEEE 802.11 standard specifies a MAC layer and a physical layer for WLANs (see Fig. 1). The MAC layer provides to its users both contention-based and contention-free access control on a variety of physical layers. Specifically, three different technologies can be used at the physical layer: infrared, frequency hopping spread spectrum, and direct sequence spread spectrum.[9]

The basic access method in the IEEE 802.11 MAC protocol is the distributed coordination function (DCF), which is a carrier sense multiple access with collision avoidance (CSMA/CA) MAC protocol. Besides the DCF, the IEEE 802.11 also incorporates an alternative access method known as the point coordination function (PCF). The PCF operates similarly to a polling system;[6] a point coordinator provides (through a polling mechanism) the transmission rights at a single station at a time. As the PCF access method cannot be adopted in ad hoc networks, in the following we will concentrate on the DCF access method only.

IEE 802.11 DCF

The DCF access method, hereafter referred to as Basic Access, is summarized in Fig. 2. When using the DCF, before a station initiates a transmission, it senses the channel to determine whether another station is transmitting. If the medium is found to be idle for an interval that exceeds the distributed interframe space (DIFS), the station continues with its transmission. (To guarantee fair access to the shared medium, a station that has just transmitted a packet and has another packet ready for transmission must perform the backoff procedure before initiating the second transmission). The transmitted packet contains the projected length of the transmission. Each active station stores this information in a local variable named network allocation vector (NAV). Therefore, the NAV contains the period of time the channel will remain busy (see Fig. 2A). [This prevents a station from listening to the channel during transmissions. This feature is useful to implement (among others) power-saving policies.]

The CSMA/CA protocol does not rely on the capability of the stations to detect a collision by hearing their own transmissions. Hence, immediate positive acknowledgments are employed to ascertain the successful reception of each packet transmission. Specifically, the receiver after the reception of the data frame: 1) waits for a time interval, called the short interframe space (SIFS), which is less than the DIFS; and then 2) initiates the transmission of an acknowledgment (ACK) frame. The ACK is not transmitted if the packet is corrupted or lost due to collisions. A cyclic redundancy check algorithm is adopted to discover transmission errors. Collisions among stations occur when two or more stations start transmitting at the same time (see Fig. 2B). If an acknowledgment is not received, the data frame is presumed to have been lost, and a retransmission is scheduled.

After an erroneous frame is detected (due to collisions or transmission errors), the channel must remain idle for at least an extended interframe space (EIFS) interval before the stations reactivate the backoff algorithm to schedule their transmissions (see Fig. 2B).

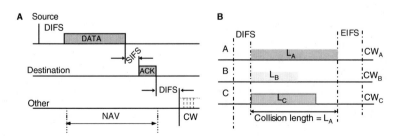

Fig. 2 IEEE 802.11 DCF: (**A**) a successful transmission, (**B**) a collision.

To reduce the collision probability, the IEEE 802.11 uses a mechanism (backoff mechanism) that guarantees a time spreading of the transmissions.

When a station S, with a packet ready for transmission, observes a busy channel, it defers the transmission until the end of the ongoing transmission. At the end of the channel busy period, the station S initializes a counter (called the backoff timer) by selecting a random interval (backoff interval) for scheduling its transmission attempt. The backoff timer is decreased for as long as the channel is sensed as idle, stopped when a transmission is detected on the channel, and reactivated when the channel is sensed as idle again for more than a DIFS. The station transmits when the backoff timer reaches zero. Specifically, the DCF adopts a slotted binary exponential backoff technique. The time immediately following an idle DIFS or EIFS is slotted, and a station is allowed to transmit only at the beginning of each Slot Time. (A slot time is equal to the time needed at any station to detect the transmission of a packet from any other station.) The backoff time is uniformly chosen in the interval $(0, CW - 1)$, defined as the backoff window, also referred to as the contention window. At the first transmission attempt $CW = CW_{min}$, and then CW is doubled at each retransmission up to CW_{max}. The CW_{min} and CW_{max} values depend on the physical layer adopted. For example, for the frequency hopping, CW_{min} and CW_{max} are 16 and 1024, respectively.[9]

An IEEE 802.11 WLAN can be implemented with the access points (i.e., infrastructure based) or with the ad hoc paradigm. In the IEEE 802.11 standard, an ad hoc network is called an independent basic service set (IBSS). An IBSS enables two or more IEEE 802.11 stations to communicate directly without requiring the intervention of a centralized access point or an infrastructure network. Due to the flexibility of the CSMA/CA algorithm, synchronization (to a common clock) of the stations belonging to an IBSS is sufficient for correct receipt or transmission of data. The IEEE 802.11 uses two main functions for the synchronization of the stations in an IBSS: 1) synchronization acquisition and 2) synchronization maintenance.

Synchronization Acquisition: This functionality is necessary for joining existing IBSS. The discovery of existing IBSSs is the result of a scanning procedure of the wireless medium. During the scanning, the station receiver is tuned on different radio frequencies, searching for particular control frames. Only if the scanning procedure does not result in finding any IBSS may the station initialize a new IBSS.

Synchronization Maintenance: Because of the lack of a centralized station that provides its own clock as common clock, the synchronization function is implemented via a distributed algorithm that shall be performed by all of the members of the IBSS. This algorithm is based on the transmission of beacon frames at a known nominal rate. The station that initialized the IBSS decides the beacon interval.

IEEE 802.11 DCF Performance

In this section, we present a performance analysis of the IEEE 802.11 basic access method by analyzing the two main performance indices: the capacity and the MAC delay. The physical layer technology determines some network parameter values relevant for the performance study, e.g., SIFS, DIFS, backoff, and slot time. Whenever necessary, we choose the values of these technology-dependent parameters by referring to the frequency hopping spread spectrum technology at a transmission rate of 2 Mbps. Specifically, Table 1 reports the configuration parameter values of the IEEE 802.11 WLAN analyzed in this entry.[9]

Protocol Capacity: The IEEE 802.11 protocol capacity was extensively investigated in Calì et al.[10] The main results of that analysis are summarized here. Specifically, in Calì et al.[10] the theoretical throughput limit for IEEE 802.11 networks was analytically derived, and this limit was compared with the simulated estimates of the real protocol capacity. This throughput limit was reached by establishing the maximum throughput that can be achieved by adopting the IEEE 802.11 MAC protocol and using the optimal timing of the backoff algorithm. The results showed that, depending on the network configuration, the standard protocol can operate very far from the theoretical throughput limit. These results, summarized in Fig. 3A, indicate that the distance between the IEEE 802.11 and the analytical bound increases with the number of active stations, M. In the IEEE 802.11 protocol, due to its backoff algorithm, the average number of stations that transmit in a slot increases with M, and this causes an increase in the collision probability. A significant improvement of the IEEE 802.11 performance can thus be obtained by controlling the number of stations that transmit in the same slot.

Several works have shown that an appropriate tuning of the IEEE 802.11 backoff algorithm can significantly increase the protocol capacity.[1,11–13] In particular, in Bianchi et al.[14] a distributed algorithm to tune the size

Table 1 IEEE 802.11 parameter values

Parameter value	t_{slot}	τ	DIFS	EIFS	SIFS	ACK	CW_{min}	CW_{max}	Bit rate
	50 μs	≤ 1 μs	2.56 t_{slot}	340 μs	0.56 t_{slot}	240 bits	8 t_{slot}	256 t_{slot}	2 Mbps

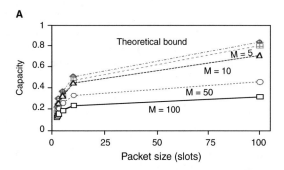

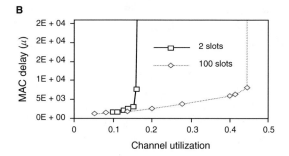

Fig. 3 IEEE 802.11 performance: (**A**) protocol capacity, (**B**) average MAC delay.

of the backoff window at run time, called Dynamic IEEE 802.11 Protocol, was presented and evaluated. Specifically, by observing the status of the channel, each station gets an estimate of both the number of active stations and the characteristics of the network traffic. By exploiting these estimates, each station then applies a distributed algorithm to tune its backoff window size in order to achieve the theoretical throughput limit for the IEEE 802.11 network.

The Dynamic IEEE 802.11 Protocol is complex due to the interdependencies among the estimated quantities.[11] To avoid this complexity, in Bruno et al.[13] a Simple Dynamic IEEE 802.11 Protocol is proposed and evaluated. It requires only simple load estimates for tuning the backoff algorithm. An alternative and interesting approach for tuning the backoff algorithm, without requiring complex estimates of the network status, has been proposed.[15–32] In this work a distributed mechanism is defined, called asymptotically optimal backoff (AOB), which dynamically adapts the backoff window size to the current load. AOB guarantees that an IEEE 802.11 WLAN asymptotically (i.e., for a large number of active stations) achieves its optimal channel utilization. The AOB mechanism adapts the backoff window to the network contention level by using two load estimates: the slot utilization and the average size of transmitted frames. These estimates are simple and can be obtained with no additional costs or overheads.

It is worth noting that the above mechanisms that tune the IEEE 802.11 protocol to optimize the protocol capacity also guarantee quasioptimal behavior from the energy consumption standpoint (i.e., minimum energy consumption). Indeed, in Bruno et al.[16] it is shown that the optimal capacity state and the optimal energy consumption state almost coincide.

MAC Delay:. The IEEE 802.11 capacity analysis presented in the previous section is performed by assuming that the network operates in asymptotic conditions (i.e., each LAN station always has a packet ready for transmission). However, LANs normally operate in normal conditions, i.e., the network stations generate an aggregate traffic that is lower (or slightly higher) than the maximum traffic the network can support. In these load

conditions, the most meaningful performance figure is the MAC delay (see section "Technologies for Ad Hoc Networks" and Conti et al.[6]). Two sets of MAC delay results are presented here, corresponding to traffic generated by 50 stations, made up of short (two slots) and long (100 slots) messages, respectively. Stations alternate between idle and busy periods. In the simulative experiments, the channel utilization level is controlled by varying the idle periods' lengths.

Fig. 3B (which plots the average MAC delay vs. the channel utilization) highlights that, for light load conditions, the IEEE 802.11 exhibits very low MAC delays. However, as the offered load approaches the capacity of the protocol (see Fig. 3A), the MAC delay sharply increases. This behavior is due to the CSMA/CA protocol. Under light-load conditions, the protocol introduces almost no overhead (a station can immediately transmit as soon as it has a packet ready for transmission). On the other hand, when the load increases, the collision probability increases as well, and most of the time a transmission results in a collision. Several transmission attempts are necessary before a station is able to transmit a packet, and hence the MAC delay increases. It is worth noting that the algorithms discussed in the previous section (i.e., service discovery protocol or SDP, AOB, etc.) for optimizing the protocol capacity also help prevent MAC delays from becoming unbounded when the channel utilization approaches the protocol capacity.[15]

IEE 802.11 Request to Send/Clear to Send

The design of a WLAN that adopts a carrier sensing random access protocol,[17] such as the IEEE 802.11, is complicated by the presence of hidden terminals.[18] A pair of stations is referred to as being hidden from each other if a station cannot hear the transmission from the other station. This event makes the carrier sensing unreliable, as a station wrongly senses that the wireless medium has been idle while the other station (which is hidden from its standpoint) is transmitting. For example, as shown in Fig. 4, let us assume that two stations, say S1 and S2, are hidden from each other, and both wish

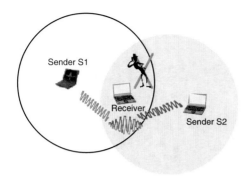

Fig. 4 The hidden stations phenomenon.

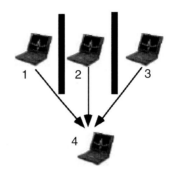

Fig. 6 Indoor scenario.

to transmit to a third station, named receiver. When S1 is transmitting to receiver, the carrier sensing of S2 does not trigger any transmission, and thus S2 can immediately start a transmission to receiver as well. Obviously, this event causes a collision that never occurs if the carrier sensing works properly.

The hidden stations phenomenon may occur in both infrastructure-based and ad hoc networks. However, it may be more relevant in ad hoc networks where almost no coordination exists among the stations. In this case, all stations may be transmitting on a single frequency, as occurs in the WaveLAN IEEE 802.11 technology.[19]

To avoid the hidden terminal problem, the IEEE 802.11 basic access mechanism was extended with a virtual carrier sensing mechanism, called request to send (RTS)/clear to send (CTS).

In the RTS/CTS mechanism, after access to the medium is gained and before transmission of a data packet begins, a short control packet, called RTS, is sent to the receiving station announcing the upcoming transmission. The receiver replies to this with a CTS packet to indicate readiness to receive the data. RTS and CTS packets contain the projected length of the transmission. This information is stored by each active station in its NAV, the value of which becomes equal to the end of the channel busy period. Therefore, all stations within the range of at least one of the two stations (receiver and transmitter) know how long the channel will be used for this data transmission (see Fig. 5).

The RTS/CTS mechanism solves the hidden station problem during the transmission of user data. In addition, this mechanism can be used to capture the channel control before the transmission of long packets, thus avoiding "long collisions." Collisions may occur only during the transmissions of the small RTS and CTS packets. Unfortunately, as shown in the next section, other phenomena occur at the physical layer making the effectiveness of the RTS/CTS mechanism quite arguable.

RTS/CTS Effectiveness in Ad Hoc Networks

The effectiveness of the RTS/CTS mechanism was studied in Vanni[20] in a real field trial. The main results of that study are summarized here. The testbed analyzed the performance of the TCP protocol over an IEEE 802.11 ad hoc network. To reduce the complexity of the study, static ad hoc networks were considered, i.e., the network nodes did not change their positions during an experiment. Both indoor and outdoor scenarios were investigated.

Indoor Experiments: In this case the experiments were performed in a scenario characterized by hidden stations. The scenario is shown in Fig. 6. Nodes 1, 2, and 3 are transferring data, via FTP, toward node 4. As these data transfers are supported by the TCP protocol, in the following the data flows will be denoted as TCP #i, where i is the index of the transmitting station.

In the analyzed scenario, a reinforced concrete wall (the black rectangle in the figure) is located between node 1 and node 2 and between node 2 and node 3. As a consequence, the three transmitting nodes are hidden from each other, e.g., nodes 2 and 3 are outside the transmission range of node 1; specifically, the ping application indicated no delivered packet. Node 4 is in the transmission range of all the other nodes.

Two sets of experiments were performed using the DCF mechanism with or without the RTS/CTS mechanism. In Table 2, the results of the experiments are summarized. Two main conclusions can be reached from these experiments:

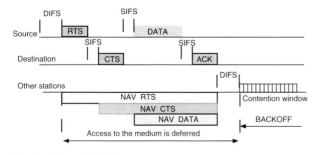

Fig. 5 The RTS/CTS mechanism.

Ad Hoc–
Availability

Table 2 Indoor results—throughput (Kbps)

	TCP#1	TCP#2	TCP#3	Aggregate
No RTS/CTS	42	29.5	57	128.5
RTS/CTS	34	27	48	109

1. No significant performance differences exist between adopting the RTS/CTS mechanism vs. the basic access mechanism only.
2. Due to the additional overheads of the RTS and CTS packets, the aggregate network throughput with the RTS/CTS mechanism is a bit lower with respect to the basic access mechanism.

These results seem to indicate that the carrier sensing mechanism is still effective even if transmitting stations are "apparently" hidden from each other. Indeed, a distinction must be made between transmission range, interference range, and carrier sensing range, as follows:

- The transmission range (TX_Range) represents the range (with respect to the transmitting station) within which a transmitted packet can be successfully received. The transmission range is mainly determined by the transmission power and the radio propagation properties.
- The physical carrier sensing range (PCS_Range) is the range (with respect to the transmitting station) within which the other stations detect a transmission.
- The interference range (IF_Range) is the range within which stations in receive mode will be "interfered with" by a transmitter and thus suffer a loss. The interference range is usually larger than the transmission range, and it is a function of the distance between the sender and receiver and of the path loss model.

Normally, the following relationship exists between the transmission, carrier sensing, and interference ranges: TX_Range $\leq$ IF_Range $\leq$ PCS_Range (e.g., in NS2 the following values are used: TX_Range = 250 m, IF_Range = PCS_Range = 550 m). The relationship among TX_Range, IF_Range, and PCS_Range helps in explaining the results obtained in the indoor experiments: even though transmitting nodes are outside the transmission range of each other, they are inside the same carrier sensing range. Therefore, the physical

carrier sensing is effective, and hence adding a virtual carrier sensing (i.e., RTS/CTS) is useless.

Outdoor Experiments: The reference scenario for this case is shown in Fig. 7. The nodes represent four portable computers, each with an IEEE 802.11 network interface. Two FTP sessions are contemporary active. The arrows represent the direction of the FTP sessions.

Several experiments were performed by varying the transmission, the carrier sensing, and the interference ranges. This was achieved by modifying the distance, d, between nodes 2 and 3. In all the experiments, the receiving node was always within the transmission range of its transmitting node—i.e., node 2(4) was within the transmitting range of node 1(3)—while, by varying the distance d, the other two nodes [i.e., the couple (3,4) with respect to the couple (1,2) and vice versa] could be:

1. In the same transmitting range (Exp #1);
2. Out of the transmitting range but inside the same carrier sensing range (Exp #2);
3. Out of the same carrier sensing range (Exp #3).

The achieved results, summarized in Table 3, show the following:

- *Exp #1*: In this case (all stations are inside the same TX_Range), a fair bandwidth sharing is almost obtained: the two FTP sessions achieve (almost) the same throughput. The RTS/CTS mechanism is useless as (due to its overheads) it only reduces the throughput.
- *Exp #3*: In this case the two sessions are independent (i.e., outside their respective carrier sensing ranges), and both achieve the maximum throughput. The RTS/CTS mechanism is useless as (due to its overheads) it only reduces the throughput.
- *Exp #2*: In the intermediate situation, a "capture" of the channel by one of the two TCP connections is observed. In this case, the RTS/CTS mechanism provides a little help in solving the problem.

The experimental results confirm the results on TCP unfairness in ad hoc IEEE 802.11 obtained, via simulation, by several researchers, e.g., see in Xu and Saadawi.[21] As discussed in previous works, the TCP protocol, due to flow control and congestion mechanisms, introduces correlations in the transmitted traffic that emphasize/generate the capture phenomena. This effect is clearly pointed out by experimental results presented in Table 4. Specifically, the table reports results obtained in the Exp #2 configuration when the traffic flows are either TCP or user datagram protocol (UDP) based. As shown in the table, the capture effect disappears when the UDP protocol is used.

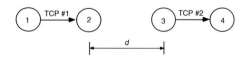

Fig. 7 Outdoor reference scenario.

Table 3 Outdoor results—throughput (Kbps)

	Exp#1		Exp#2		Exp#3	
	TCP#1	TCP#2	TCP#1	TCP#2	TCP#1	TCP#2
No RTS/CTS	61	54	123	0.5	122.5	122
RTS/CTS	59.5	49.5	81	6.5	96	100

To summarize, measurement experiments have shown that, in some scenarios, TCP connections may suffer significant throughput unfairness, even capture. The causes of this behavior are the hidden terminal problem, the 802.11 backoff scheme, and large interference ranges. We expect that the methods discussed in the section "IEEE 802.11 DCF Performance" for optimizing the IEEE 802.11 protocol capacity area are moving in a promising direction to solve the TCP unfairness in IEEE 802.11 ad hoc networks. Research activities are ongoing to explore this direction.

A TECHNOLOGY FOR WBAN ANDWIRELESS PERSONAL AREA NETWORK: BLUETOOTH

The Bluetooth technology is a de facto standard for low-cost, short-range radio links between mobile PCs, mobile phones, and other portable devices.[3–5] The Bluetooth SIG releases the Bluetooth specifications. Bluetooth SIG is a group consisting of industrial leaders in telecommunications, computing, and networking.[2] In addition, the IEEE 802.15 Working Group for WPANs has just approved its first WPAN standard derived from the Bluetooth specification.[22] The IEEE 802.15 standard is based on the lower portions of the Bluetooth specification.

The Bluetooth system is operating in the 2.4 GHz industrial, scientific, and medicine band. A Bluetooth unit, integrated into a microchip, enables wireless ad hoc communications of voice and data in stationary and mobile environments. Because the cost target is low, it can be envisaged that Bluetooth microchips will be embedded in all consumer electronic devices.

A Bluetooth Network

From a logical standpoint, Bluetooth belongs to the contention-free token-based multiaccess networks.[17] In a

Table 4 UDP vs. TCP performance (Exp #2)—throughput (Kbps)

	TCP traffic		UDP traffic	
	Flow #1	Flow #2	Flow #1	Flow #2
No RTS/CTS	123	0.5	83	84
RTS/CTS	81	6.5	77.5	68

Bluetooth network, one station has the role of master, and all other Bluetooth stations are slaves. The master decides which slave has access to the channel. The units that share the same channel (i.e., are synchronized to the same master) form a piconet, the fundamental building block of a Bluetooth network. A piconet has a gross bit rate of 1 Mbps. 1 Mbps represents the channel capacity before considering the overhead introduced by the Bluetooth protocols and polling scheme. A piconet contains a master station and up to seven *active* (i.e., participating in data exchange) slaves, contemporarily. Fig. 8 shows an example of two partially overlapping piconets. In the figure, we denote with M and S a master and a slave, respectively. Stations marked with P (Parking state) are stations that are synchronized with the master but are not participating in any data exchange.

Independent piconets that have overlapping coverage areas may form a scatternet. A scatternet exists when a unit is active in more than one piconet at the same time. (A unit can be master into only one piconet). A slave may communicate with the different piconets it belongs to only in a time-multiplexing mode. This means that, for any time instant, a station can only transmit on the single piconet to which (at that time) its clock is synchronized. To transmit on another piconet it has to change the synchronization parameters.

The complete Bluetooth protocol stack contains several protocols: Bluetooth radio, Baseband, link manager protocol, logical link control and adaptation protocol (L2CAP), and SDP. For the purpose of this entry, we will focus only on the Bluetooth radio, Baseband, and (partially) L2CAP protocols. A description of the Bluetooth architecture can be found in Bruno et al.[23]

Bluetooth radio provides the physical links among Bluetooth devices, while the Baseband layer provides a

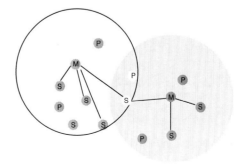

Fig. 8 Two partially overlapping piconets.

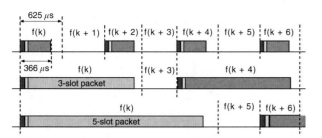

Fig. 9 One-slot and multislot packet transmission.

transport service of packets on the physical links. In the next subsections, these layers will be presented in detail. The L2CAP services are used only for data transmission. The main features supported by L2CAP are protocol multiplexing (the L2CAP uses a protocol type field to distinguish between upper layer protocols) and segmentation and reassembly. The latter feature is required because the Baseband packet size is smaller than the usual size of packets used by higher layer protocols.

A Bluetooth unit consists of a radio unit operating in the 2.4 GHz band. In this band are defined 79 different RF channels spaced 1 MHz apart. The radio layer utilizes as transmission technique the frequency hopping spread spectrum (FHSS). The hopping sequence is a pseudorandom sequence of 79-hop length, and it is unique for each piconet (it depends on the master local parameters). The FHSS system has been chosen to reduce the interference of nearby systems operating in the same range of frequency (e.g., IEEE 802.11 WLAN) and to make the link robust.[24,25] The nominal rate of hopping between two consecutive RF is 1600 hop/sec.

A time division duplex scheme of transmission is adopted. The channel is divided into time slots, each 625 μs in length, and each slot corresponding to a different RF hop frequency. The time slots are numbered according to the Bluetooth clock of the master. The master has to begin its transmissions in even-numbered time slots. Odd-numbered time slots are reserved for the beginning of slaves' transmissions. The first row of Fig. 9 shows a snapshot of the master transmissions.

The transmission of a packet nominally covers a single slot, but it may also last for three or five consecutive time slots (see the second and third rows of Fig. 9, respectively). For multislot packets, the RF hop frequency to be used for the entire packet is the RF hopping frequency assigned to the time slot in which the transmission began.

Bluetooth Piconet Formation

The Bluetooth technology has been devised to provide a flexible wireless connectivity among digital devices. Before starting a data transmission, a Bluetooth unit needs to discover if any other Bluetooth unit is in its operating space. To do this, the unit enters the inquiry

state. In this state, it continuously sends an inquiry message, i.e., a packet with only the access code. The inquiring unit can adopt a general inquiry access code that enables any Bluetooth device to answer the inquiry message or a dedicated inquiry access code that enables only Bluetooth devices belonging to certain classes to answer the inquiry message. During the inquiry message transmission, the inquiring unit uses a frequency hopping sequence of 32 frequencies derived from the access code. These 32 frequencies are split into two trains, each containing 16 frequencies. A single train must be repeated at least 256 times before a new train is used. Several (up to three) train switches must take place to guarantee a sufficient number of responses. As a result of this inquiring policy, the inquiry state lasts at most 10.24 sec. A unit can respond to an inquiry message only if it is listening to the channel to find an inquiry message, and its receiver is tuned to the same frequency used by the inquiring unit. To increase the probability of this event, a unit scans the inquiry access code (on a given frequency) for a time long enough to completely scan for 16 inquiry frequencies. Obviously, a unit is not obliged to answer an inquiring message, but if it responds it has to send a special control packet, the FHS packet, which contains its Bluetooth device address and its native clock.

After the inquiry, a Bluetooth unit has discovered the Bluetooth device address of the units around it and has collected an estimation of their clocks. If it wants to activate a new connection, it has to distribute its own Bluetooth device address and clock. This is the aim of paging routines. The unit that starts the paging is (automatically) elected the master of the new connection, and the paged unit is the slave. The paging unit sends a page message, i.e., a packet with only the device access code (DAC). The DAC is derived directly from the Bluetooth device address of the paged unit that, therefore, is the only one that can recognize the page message. After the paging procedure, the slave has an exact knowledge of the master clock and of the channel access code. Hence, the master and that slave can enter the connection state. However, a real transmission will begin only after a polling message from the master to the slave.

When a connection is established, the active slaves maintain the synchronization with the master by listening to the channel at every master-to-slave slot. Obviously, if an active slave is not addressed, after it has read the type of packet it can return to sleep for a time equal to the number of slots the master has taken for its transmission.

Most devices that will adopt the Bluetooth technology are mobile and handheld devices for which power consumption optimization is a critical matter. To avoid power consumption (caused by the synchronization), the Bluetooth specification has defined some power saving

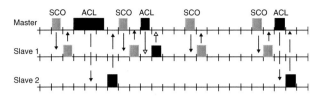

Fig. 10 Transmissions in a piconet.

states for connected slaves: Sniff, Hold, and Park Modes. We redirect the interested reader to Specification of the Bluetooth system[4] and Miller and Bisdikian.[5]

Bluetooth Scatternet

The Bluetooth specification defines a method for the interconnection of piconets: the scatternet. A scatternet can be dynamically constructed in an ad hoc fashion when some nodes belong, at the same time, to more than one piconet (interpiconet units). For example, the two piconets in Fig. 8 share a slave, and hence they can form a scatternet. The traffic between the two piconets is delivered through the common slave. Scatternets can be useful in several scenarios. For example, we can have a piconet that contains a laptop and a cellular phone. The cellular phone provides access to the Internet. A second piconet contains the laptop itself and several PDAs. In this case, a scatternet can be formed with the laptop as the interpiconet unit. By exploiting the scatternet, the PDAs can exploit the cellular phone services to access the Internet.

The current Bluetooth specification only defines the notion of a scatternet but does not provide the mechanisms to construct the scatternet.

A node can be synchronized with only a single piconet at a time, and hence it can be active in more piconets only in a time-multiplexed mode. As the interpiconet traffic must go through the interpiconet units, the presence of the inter-piconet units in all the piconets to which they belong must be scheduled in an efficient way.

The scatternet formation algorithms and the algorithm for scheduling the traffic among the various piconets are hot research issues, see Law et al.[26] and Zussman and Segall.[27]

Bluetooth Data Transmission

Two types of physical links can be established between Bluetooth devices: a synchronous connection-oriented (SCO) link, and an asynchronous connection-less (ACL) link. The first type of physical link is a point-to-point, symmetric connection between the master and a specific slave. It is used to deliver delay-sensitive traffic, mainly voice. The SCO link rate is 64 Kbps, and it is settled by reserving two consecutive slots for master-to-slave

transmission and immediate slave-to-master response. The SCO link can be considered as a circuit-switched connection between the master and the slave. The second kind of physical link, ACL, is a connection between the master and all slaves participating in the piconet. It can be considered as a packet-switched connection between the Bluetooth devices. It can support the reliable delivery of data by exploiting a fast automatic repeat request scheme. An ACL channel supports point-to-multipoint transmissions from the master to the slaves.

As stated before, the channel access is managed according to a polling scheme. The master decides which slave is the only one to have access to the channel by sending it a packet. The master packet may contain data or can simply be a polling packet (NULL packet). When the slave receives a packet from the master, it is authorized to transmit in the next time slot. For SCO links, the master periodically polls the corresponding slave. Polling is asynchronous for ACL links. Fig. 10 presents a possible pattern of transmissions in a piconet with a master and two slaves. Slave 1 has both a SCO and an ACL link with the master, while Slave 2 has an ACL link only. In this example, the SCO link is periodically polled by the master every six slots, while ACL links are polled asynchronously. Furthermore, the size of the packets on an ACL link is constrained by the presence of SCO links. For example, in the figure the master sends a multislot packet to Slave 2, which replies with a single-slot packet only because the successive slots are reserved for the SCO link.

A piconet has a gross bit rate of 1 Mbps. The polling scheme and the protocol control information obviously reduce the amount of user data that can be delivered by a piconet. The limiting throughput performances of a piconet were discussed in Bruno et al.[23] by analyzing a single master–slave link in which both stations operate in asymptotic conditions, i.e., the stations always have a packet ready for transmission. Here, the Bluetooth performances are analyzed under realistic traffic conditions where several slaves are active inside a piconet. In this case, the master must implement a scheduling algorithm to decide the slaves' polling order. The Bluetooth specification indicates as a possible solution the round robin (RR) polling algorithm: slaves are polled in a cyclic order. However, it has been shown [23] that, under unbalanced traffic conditions, the RR algorithm may cause (due to a large number of NULL packets) severe bandwidth wastage. Several authors have proposed new schedulers suitable for Bluetooth.[29–31] An effective scheduling algorithm, called efficient double-cycle (EDC), was proposed in Bruno et al.[23,28] EDC tunes the polling order to the network traffic conditions to limit the channel bandwidth wastage caused by the polling of empty stations. A detailed EDC specification through pseudocode can be found in Bruno et al.[23]

Due to space constraints, only a high-level description of EDC is provided here.

The EDC algorithm is based upon two main ideas. First, it is necessary to avoid NULL transmissions towards and from the slaves; furthermore, the fairness typical of a RR scheme should be preserved. These targets can be accomplished if the selection of the slave to be polled takes into consideration the master's knowledge of the traffic from and to the slaves. Hereafter, we indicate as uplink the link direction from the slaves to the master, and as downlink the link direction from the master towards the slaves.

For the downlink (i.e., master-to-slaves traffic), the master has a deterministic knowledge of the packets it has to send to each slave. In the other direction (uplink), the master does not have any knowledge; at most it can only estimate the probability that a slave will send a NULL packet. This probability can be estimated by exploiting the knowledge of each slave's behavior in the previous polling cycles.

An additional problem in guaranteeing fair and efficient scheduling in Bluetooth is caused by the coupling between the transmissions in uplink and downlink, i.e., a master-to-slave transmission implies also a polling of the slave and hence a possibly NULL transmission from the slave to the master. Therefore, it is not possible to remove a slave from the polling cycle without blocking, at the same time, the master's transmissions towards this slave (and vice versa). To introduce a (partial) decoupling in the scheduling of the transmissions in uplink and downlink, EDC introduces the idea of a double polling cycle: an uplink polling subcycle, $Cycle_{UP}$, and a downlink polling sub cycle, $Cycle_{DW}$. The main task of the scheduler is to identify the slaves eligible for the polling in $Cycle_{UP}$ and $Cycle_{DW}$, hereafter denoted as E(UP) and E(DW), respectively. E(DW) is computed by considering only the traffic from the master to the slaves, whereas E(UP) is computed by considering only the estimated slaves' activity, i.e., the traffic from the slaves to the master. Slaves that have no traffic to transmit (to the master) are removed from the eligible slaves during the $Cycle_{UP}$ while E(DW) contains only those slaves for which the master has packets to transmit. The distinction between the downlink and the uplink polling introduces a "fairness separation": in the downlink (uplink) subcycle fairness is guaranteed only in the downlink (uplink) direction, i.e., only the slaves with traffic in the downlink (uplink) are eligible for polling.

The scheduler defines the eligible slaves at the beginning of each polling cycle, and then it polls the slaves contained in E(DW) or in E(UP). During a cycle, a slave is polled at most once.

The scheduler has no problem defining the E(DW) set: it has a deterministic knowledge of the downlink traffic. On the other hand, for the uplink, it can only exploit the knowledge of the slaves' behavior in the

previous polling cycles. To this end, EDC uses the rate of null packets returned by a slave as an indication of that slave's transmission activity. Specifically, the basic behavior of EDC is derived from the backoff algorithms used in random access protocols. These backoff algorithms increase the time between transmission attempts when the number of consecutive collisions increases. In the EDC case, the number of consecutive NULL packets returned by a slave, say x, indicates its transmission requirements: the larger x is, the longer can be the polling interval for that slave. To implement this idea, EDC adopts a truncated binary exponential backoff algorithm. Specifically, a polling interval c_i and a polling window w_i are associated to each slave S_i. The values of these variables are updated as follows:

For each polling to S_i (in $Cycle_{UP}$ or in $Cycle_{DW}$), if S_i returns a NULL packet, c_i is increased by 1, otherwise it is set to 0.

After each polling to S_i, the polling window of S_i is set equal to $w_i = \min\{w_{max}, 2c_i\}$, where w_{max} is the maximum length (measured in number of polling cycles) of a slave polling interval.

After each polling cycle, $w_i = \max[0, w_i - 1]$.

In a polling cycle, a slave S_i is eligible only if $w_i = 0$.

Internet access via bluetooth: a performance evaluation study

Ubiquitous Internet access is expected to be one of the most interesting Bluetooth applications. For this reason, we evaluate here the scheduler impact on the performance experienced by Bluetooth slaves when they access remote Internet servers. Specifically, via simulation, we analyze a scenario made up of a Bluetooth piconet with seven slaves. Bluetooth slaves (through the master) download/upload data from/to remote Internet servers. In each slave of the piconet, the traffic [generated by either an FTP application or a constant bit rate (CBR) source] is encapsulated into the TCP/IP protocol stack, the L2CAP protocol, and the baseband protocol, and finally it is delivered on the Bluetooth physical channel. Large L2CAP packets are segmented into smaller packets before their transmission. The transmission of a new L2CAP packet cannot start until all fragments (generated during the.segmentation at the MAC layer) of the previous L2CAP packet have been successfully transmitted. The segmentation procedure is accomplished just before the transmission, in such a way as to maximize the amount of data conveyed by each baseband packet.[28]

Table 5 summarizes the details of the simulated scenario. For each slave, the direction of the data flow is indicated (downloading if data are retrieved from a remote Internet server or uploading if data are sent from

Table 5 Simulative scenario

	Data flow direction	Traffic type	Activity interval (sec)	Rate (Kbps)
Slave 1	Downloading	FTP—TCP	[0–90]	—
Slave 2	Downloading	FTP—TCP	[15–75]	—
Slave 3	Downloading	FTP—TCP	[30–75]	—
Slave 4	Downloading	CBR—UDP	[40–70]	30
Slave 5	Uploading	CBR—UDP	[45–70]	10
Slave 6	Uploading	CBR—UDP	[60–90]	5
Slave 7	Downloading	CBR—UDP	[65–90]	15

the slave towards the Internet), along with the application and the transport protocol adopted. The TCP version considered is the TCP-Reno.[30] In addition, by denoting with 0 the time instant at which each simulative experiment starts, the table reports the time interval in which each data flow is active (activity interval). The different activity intervals highlight the dynamic behavior of the scheduling algorithm. Finally, only for UDP flows, the table reports the source transmission rate.

Results reported here have been derived by assuming an ideal channel with no errors and using constant size packets—a TCP packet of 1024 bytes, a UDP packet of 500 bytes, and TCP ACKs of 20 bytes.

Fig. 11 shows the throughput for the TCP connection of Slave 1 when the scheduler adopts either the EDC or the RR algorithms. First, we can observe that EDC guarantees a throughput that is always (significantly) higher than that achieved with a RR scheduler.

Fig. 11 clearly shows the dynamic behavior of the EDC algorithm. In the first time interval, [0,15] sec, only Slave 1 is active, and hence the throughput obtained with EDC is more than twice that achieved with RR. This is expected since EDC adapts the polling rate to the sources' activity level. As the number of active sources increases, the difference between the RR and EDC performance decreases. The minimum distance between EDC and RR is achieved (as expected) when all sources are active. However, also in this case by adopting EDC, the Slave 1 performances are always better than those it achieves with RR. EDC exploits the inactivity periods of the CBR sources to increase the polling frequency of the TCP slaves. One may argue that the Slave 1 performance improvements are achieved

by decreasing the performance of the other flows inside the piconet. The results presented in Law et al.[26] indicate that this is not true. Indeed, those results show that EDC is fair as:

1. The three TCP flows, when active, achieve exactly the same throughput;
2. The throughput of each CBR flow is equal to the rate of the corresponding CBR source.

However, it must be pointed out that a small degree of unfairness may exist when EDC is adopted. Unfairness may exist among TCP flows depending on their direction (i.e., master-to-slave vs. slave-to-master). Specifically, experimental results[26] show that the TCP throughput slightly increases when the data packet flow is from the slave towards the master. This is due to the different polling rate (during $Cycle_{UP}$) to the slaves in the two cases. When the TCP data flow is from the master to the slave, the slave queue contains the acknowledgment (ACK) traffic. When the master sends a fragment of a TCP packet to the slave, it often receives a NULL packet from the slave (the ACK cannot be generated by the TCP receiver until the TCP packet is completely received); therefore, the polling interval for that slave increases, and the scheduler will avoid polling it for some successive uplink polling subcycles. This slows down the delivery of the acknowledgment traffic and as a consequence (due to TCP congestion and flow control mechanisms), also reduces the TCP data delivery rate. On the other hand, in the slave-tomaster scenario the slave queue contains the data traffic, and hence it is always highly probable to find a queued TCP packet when the master polls that slave (the TCP source is asymptotic). Therefore, in this scenario, the TCP connection is always eligible for polling in $Cycle_{UP}$ Furthermore, as soon as the ACK for the slave is generated, the master will serve it in the first available $Cycle_{DW}$, without introducing any additional delay.

To summarize, the results presented so far demonstrate that EDC significantly improves the throughput performance of TCP flows in a piconet, when compared to a RR scheduler. However, the decoupling of scheduler decisions between uplink and downlink can introduce some unfairness among data flows when the traffic in the two directions is correlated, as happens in a TCP connection.

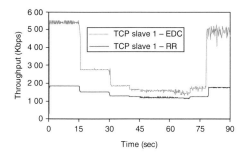

Fig. 11 TCP throughput of Slave 1 connection.

ACKNOWLEDGMENTS

This work was partially supported by North Atlantic Treaty Organization Collaborative Linkage Grant PST. CLG.977405 "Wireless access to Internet exploiting the IEEE 802.11 technology." The author thanks Giuseppe Anastasi, Raffaele Bruno, Enrico Gregori, and Veronica Vanni for fruitful discussions and their help in producing the results presented in this entry.

REFERENCES

1. *IEEE 802.11 WLAN. Available at:* http://grouper.ieee.org/groups/802/11/main.html.
2. Bluetooth Special Interest Group., Available at http://www.bluetooth.com/.
3. Bisdikian, C. An overview of the Bluetooth wireless technology. IEEE Commun. Mag. **2001**, *39* (12), 86–94.
4. *Specification of the Bluetooth System, Version 1.0B* December, 1999.
5. Miller, B.A.; Bisdikian, C. *Bluetooth Revealed*; Prentice Hall: New York, 2000.
6. Conti, M.; Gregori, E.; Lenzini, L. *Metropolitan Area Networks*; Springer-Verlag: New York, 1997.
7. Kurose, J.F.; Schwartz, M.; Yemini, Y. Multiple access protocols and time constraint communications. ACM Comput. Surv. **1984**, *16*, 43–70.
8. Stallings, W. *Local and Metropolitan Area Networks*; Prentice Hall: New York, 1996.
9. IEEE standard for Wireless LAN. In *Medium Access Control and Physical Layer Specification P802.11*; Institute of Electrical and Electronics Engineers, Inc., November 1997: See also IEEE P802.11/D10, Jan 14, 1999.
10. Calì, F.; Conti, M.; Gregori, E. Dynamic tuning of the IEEE 802.11 protocol to achieve a theoretical throughput limit. IEEE/ACM Trans. Netw. **2000**, *8*, 785–799.
11. Calì, F.; Conti, M.; Gregori, E. Dynamic IEEE 802.11: Design, modeling and performance evaluation. IEEE J. Select. Area. Commun. **2000**, *18*, 1774–1786.
12. Weinmiller, J.; Schláger, M.; Festag, A.; Wolisz, A. Performance study of access control in wireless LANs—IEEE 802.11 DFWMAC and ETSI RES 10 HIPERLAN. Mobile Netw. Appl. **1997**, *2*, 55–67.
13. Bruno, R.; Conti, M.; Gregori, E. A simple protocol for the dynamic tuning of the backoff mechanism in IEEE 802.11 networks. Comput. Netw. **2001**, *37*, 33–44.
14. Bianchi, G.; Fratta, L.; Oliveri, M. *Performance Evaluation and Enhancement of the CSMA/CA MAC Protocol for 802.11 Wireless LANs, PIMRC*; Taipei, Oct, 1996; 392–396.
15. Bononi, L.; Conti, M.; Gregori, E. *Design and Performance Evaluation of an Asymptotically Optimal Backoff Algorithm for IEEE 802.11 Wireless. LANs, HICSS-33*; Maui, Jan, 4–72000.

16. Bruno, R.; Conti, M.; Gregori, E. Optimization of efficiency and energy consumption in p-persistent CSMA-based wireless. LANs IEEE Trans. Mob. Comput. **2002**, *1* (1), 10–31.
17. Hammond, J.L.; O'Reilly, P.J.P. *Performance Analysis of Local Computer Networks*; Addison-Wesley Publishing: Company Reading, MA, 1988.
18. Tobagi, F.A.; Kleinrock, L. Packet switching in radio channels: Part II. IEEE Trans. Commun. **1975**, *23*, 1417–1433.
19. *PC Cards User's Guide Lucent Technology, WaveLAN IEEE 802.11;* Institute of Electrical and Electronics Engineers, Inc.: 1999.
20. Vanni, V. *Misure di prestazioni del protocollo TCP in reti locali Ad Hoc*; Computer Engineering Laurea ThesisPisa, 2002 (in Italian).
21. Xu, S.; Saadawi, T. Does the IEEE 802.11 MAC protocol work well in multihop wireless ad hoc networks?. IEEE Commun. Mag. **2001**, *39* (6), 130–137.
22. *WPA. N Task Group 1 IEEE 802.15,* Institute of Electrical and Electronics Engineers, Inc., http://www.ieee802.org/15/pub/TG1.html.
23. Bruno, R.; Conti, M.; Gregori, E. Architecture, protocols and scheduling algorithms. Cluster Comput. J. **2002**, *5* (2), 117–131.
24. Galli, S.; Wong, K.D.; Koshy, B.J.; Barton, M. Bluetooth technology: link performance and networking issues. In *European Wireless 2000*; Dresden, Germany, Sep 12–14, 2002.
25. Haartsen, J.C.; Zurbes, S. Bluetooth voice and data performance in 802.11 DS WLAN environment. *Technical Report Ericsson* 1999.
26. Law, C.; Mehta, A.K.; Siu, K.Y. A new Bluetooth scatternet formation protocol. ACM/Kluver Mobile Netw. Appl. J. (Special issue on ad hoc networks) **2003**, *8*(5), 485–498.
27. Zussman, G.; Segall, A. Capacity assignment in Bluetooth scatternets—analysis and algorithms. In *Networking 2002*; Pisa, Italy, May 19–24, 2002. LNCS 2345.
28. Bruno, R.; Conti, M.; Gregori, E. Wireless access to Internet via Bluetooth: performance evaluation of the EDC scheduling algorithm. 1st ACM Workshop on Wireless Mobile Internet, Rome, Italy, July 21; **2001**; 43–49.
29. Das, A.; Ghose, A.; Razdan, A.; Sarah, H.; Shorey, R. *Efficient Performance of Asynchronous Data Traffic Over Bluetooth Wireless Ad-hoc Network IEEE INFOCOM 2001*; Anchorage, AK, Apr 22–26, 2001.
30. Johansson, N.; Korner, U.; Johansson, P. Performance evaluation of scheduling algorithm for Bluetooth. In *IFIP Broadband Communications*; Hong Kong, Nov 10–12, 1999.
31. Kalia, M.; Bansal, D.; Shorey, R. *Data Scheduling and SAR for Bluetooth MAC. IEEE VTC 2000*; Tokyo, May 15–18, 2000.
32. Stevens, W.R. *TCP/IP Illustrated*; Addison Wesley: Reading, MA, 1994; *1*.

AES: Advanced Encryption Standard

Ben Rothke
International Network Services (INS), New York, New York, U.S.A.

Abstract

This entry presents the history and development of the advanced encryption standard (AES). Although the main advantages of AES are its efficiency and performance for both hardware and software implementations, it may not be easily implemented in large-scale nongovernmental sites, given the economic constraints of upgrading it, combined with the usefulness of the current Triple-DES (data encryption standard).

In the early 1970s, data encryption standard (DES) became a Federal Information Processing Standard (FIPS).[1] Under the Information Technology Management Reform Act (Public Law 104–106), the Secretary of Commerce approves standards and guidelines that are developed by the National Institute of Standards and Technology (NIST) for federal computer systems. These standards and guidelines are issued by NIST as FIPS for use government-wide. NIST develops FIPS when there are compelling federal government requirements, such as for security and interoperability, and there are no acceptable industry standards or solutions. This happened with little fanfare and even less public notice. In fact, in the late 1960s and early 1970s, the notion of the general public having an influence on U.S. cryptographic policy was utterly absurd. It should be noted that in the days before personal computers were ubiquitous, the force of a FIPS was immense, given the purchasing power of the U.S. government. Nowadays, the power of a FIPS has a much lesser effect on the profitability of computer companies given the strength of the consumer market.

Jump to the late 1990s and the situation is poles apart. The proposed successor to DES, the advanced encryption standard (AES), was publicized not only in the *Federal Register* and academic journals, but also in consumer computing magazines and the mainstream media. While IBM and the U.S. government essentially designed DES between them in what was billed as a public process, it attracted very little public interest at the time.

The entire AES selection process was, in essence, a global town hall event. This was evident from submissions from cryptographers from around the world. The AES process was completely open to public scrutiny and comment. This is important because, when it comes to the design of effective encryption algorithms, history has shown time and time again that secure encryption algorithms cannot be designed, tested, and verified in a vacuum.[2] In fact, if a software vendor decides to use a proprietary encryption algorithm, that immediately makes the security and efficacy of the algorithm suspect.[3] Prudent consumers of cryptography will *never* use a proprietary algorithm.

This notion is based on what is known as Kerckhoff's assumption. There are actually six assumptions. Dutch cryptographer Auguste Kerckhoff wrote La Cryptographie Militare (Military Cryptography) in 1883. His work set forth six highly desirable elements for encryption systems:

1. A cipher should be unbreakable. If it cannot be theoretically proven to be unbreakable, it should at least be unbreakable in practice.
2. If one's adversary knows the method of encipherment, this should not prevent one from continuing to use the cipher.
3. It should be possible to memorize the key without having to write it down, and it should be easy to change to a different key.
4. Messages, after being enciphered, should be in a form that can be sent by telegraph.
5. If a cipher machine, code book, or the like is involved, any such items required should be portable and usable by one person without assistance.
6. Enciphering or deciphering messages in the system should not cause mental strain and should not require following a long and complicated procedure.

This assumption states the security of a cryptosystem should rest entirely in the secrecy of the key and not in the secrecy of the algorithm. History has shown, and unfortunately, that some software vendors still choose to ignore the fact that completely open-source encryption algorithms are the only way to design a truly world-class encryption algorithm.

Encyclopedia of Information Systems and Technology, DOI: 10.1081/E-EIST-120046753

13

AES PROCESS

In January 1997, the NIST, a branch within the Commerce Department, commenced the AES process.[4] A replacement for DES was needed owing to the ever-growing frailty of DES. Not that any significant architectural breaches were found in DES, rather Moore's law had caught up with it. By 1998, it was possible to build a DES-cracking device for a reasonable sum of money.

The significance of the availability of a DES-cracking device to an adversary cannot be understated because DES is the world's most widely used, general-purpose cryptosystem. For the details of this cracking of DES,[5] see *Cracking DES: Secrets of Encryption Research, Wiretap Politics and Chip Design* by the Electronic Frontier Foundation (1998, O'Reilly & Assoc.).

DES was reengineered and put back into working order via the use of Triple-DES. Triple-DES takes the input data and encrypts it three times. Triple-DES (an official standard in use as ANSI X9.52-1998) is resilient against brute-force attacks, and from a security perspective, it is adequate. The X9.52 standard defines Triple-DES encryption with keys k_1, k_2, *and* k_3; k_3 as: $C = E_{k3} (D_{k2} [E_{k1} (M)])$ where E_k and D_k denote DES encryption and DES decryption, respectively, with the key k. So why not simply use Triple-DES as the new AES? This is not feasible because DES was designed to be implemented in hardware and is therefore not efficient in software implementations. Triple-DES is three times slower than DES; and although DES is fast enough, Triple-DES is far too slow. One of the criteria for AES is that it must be efficient when implemented in software, and the underlying architecture of Triple-DES makes it unsuitable as an AES candidate.

The AES specification called for a symmetric algorithm (same key for encryption and decryption) using block encryption of 128 bits in size, with supporting key sizes of 128, 192, and 256 bits. The algorithm was required to be royalty-free for use worldwide and offer security of a sufficient level to protect data for 30 years. Additionally, it must be easy to implement in hardware as well as software, and in restricted environments [i.e., smart cards, DSP, cell phones, field-programmable gate array (FPGA), custom ASIC, satellites, etc.].

AES will be used for securing sensitive but unclassified material by U.S. government agencies. It should be noted that AES (like DES) will only be used to protect sensitive but unclassified data. Classified data is protected by separate, confidential algorithms. As a likely outcome, all indications make it likely that it will, in due course, become the *de facto* encryption standard for commercial transactions in the private sector as well.

In August 1998, NIST selected 15 preliminary AES candidates at the first AES Candidate Conference in California. At that point, the 15 AES candidates were given much stronger scrutiny and analysis within the global cryptography community. Also involved with the process was the National Security Agency (NSA).

This is not the place to detail the input of the NSA into the AES selection process, but it is obvious that NIST learned its lesson from the development of DES. An initial complaint against DES was that IBM kept its design principles secret at the request of the U.S. government. This, in turn, led to speculation that there was some sort of trapdoor within DES that would provide the U.S. intelligence community with complete access to all encrypted data. Nonetheless, when the DES design principles were finally made public in 1992,[6] such speculation was refuted.

AES CANDIDATES

The 15 AES candidates chosen at the first AES conference are listed in Table 1.

A second AES Candidate Conference was held in Rome in March 1999 to present analyses of the first-round candidate algorithms. After this period of public scrutiny, in August 1999, NIST selected five algorithms for more extensive analysis (see Table 2).

In October 2000, after more than 18 months of testing and analysis, NIST announced that the Rijndael algorithm had been selected as the AES candidate. It is interesting to note that only days after NIST's announcement selecting Rijndael, advertisements were already springing up stating support for the new standard.

In February 2001, NIST made available a Draft AES FIPS[7] for public review and comment, which concluded on May 29, 2001.

This was followed by a 90-day comment period from June through August 2001. In August 2002, NIST announced the approval of FIPS 180-2, Secure Hash Standard, which contains the specifications for the Secure Hash Algorithm (SHA-1, SHA-256, SHA-384, and SHA-512).

DES Is Dead

It is clear that not only is the 56-bit DES ineffective, it is dead. From 1998, it is hoped that no organization has implemented 56-bit DES in any type of high-security or mission-critical system. If such is the case, it should be immediately retrofitted with Triple-DES or another secure public algorithm.

Although DES was accepted as an ANSI standard in 1981 (ANSI X3.92) and later incorporated into several American Banking Association Financial Services (X9) standards, it has since been replaced by Triple-DES.

Table 1 AES candidates chosen at the first AES conference

Algorithm	Submitted by	Overview[a]
CAST-256	Entrust Technologies, Canada	A 48-round unbalanced Feistel cipher using the same round functions as CAST-128, which use + — XOR rotates and four fixed 6-bit S-boxes; with a key schedule
Crypton	Future Systems, Inc., Korea	A 12-round iterative cipher with a round function using &	XOR rotates and two fixed 8-bit S-boxes; with various key lengths supported, derived from the previous SQUARE cipher
DEAL	Richard Outerbridge (U.K.) and Lars Knudsen (Norway)	A rather different proposal, a 6- to 8-round Feistel cipher that uses the existing DES as the round function. Thus, a lot of existing analysis can be leveraged, but at a cost in speed
DFC	Centre National pour la Recherche Scientifique, France	An 8-round Feistel cipher design based on a decorrelation technique and using + x and a permutation in the round function; with a 4-round key schedule
E2	Nippon Telegraph and Telephone Corporation, Japan	A 12-round Feistel cipher, using a nonlinear function that comprised substitution using a single fixed 8-bit S-box, a permutation, XOR mixing operations, and a byte rotation
FROG	TecApro International, South Africa	An 8-round cipher, with each round performing four basic operations (with XOR, substitution using a single fixed 8-bit S-box, and table value replacement) on each byte of its input
HPC	Rich Schroeppel, The United States	An 8-round Feistel cipher, which modifies 8 internal 64-bit variables as well as the data using + — x &	XOR rotates and a lookup table
LOKI97	Lawrie Brown, Josef Pieprzyk, and Jennifer Seberry, Australia	A 16-round Feistel cipher using a complex round function f with two S-P layers with fixed 11-bit and 13-bit S-boxes, a permutation, and + XOR combinations; and with a 256-bit key schedule using 48 rounds of an unbalanced Feistel network using the same complex round function f
Magenta	Deutsche Telekom, Germany	A 6- to 8-round Feistel cipher, with a round function that uses a large number of substitutions using a single fixed S-box [based on exponentiation on $GF(2^8)$], that is, combined together with key bits using XOR
MARS	IBM, The United States	An 8 + 16 + 8-round unbalanced Feistel cipher with four distinct phases: key addition and 8 rounds of unkeyed forward mixing, 8 rounds of keyed forward transformation, 8 rounds of keyed backward transformation, and 8 rounds of unkeyed backward mixing and keyed subtraction. The rounds use + — x rotates XOR and two fixed 8-bit S-boxes
RC6	RSA Laboratories, United States	A 20-round iterative cipher, developed from RC5 (and fully parameterized), which uses a number of 32-bit operations (+ — x XOR rotates) to mix data in each round
Rijndael	Joan Daemen and Vincent Rijmen, Belgium	A 10- to 14-round iterative cipher, using byte substitution, row shifting, column mixing, and key addition, as well as an initial and final round of key addition, derived from the previous SQUARE cipher
SAFER +	Cylink Corp., The United States	An 8- to 16-round iterative cipher, derived from the earlier SAFER cipher. SAFER + uses + x XOR and two fixed 8-bit S-boxes
SERPENT	Ross Anderson (U.K.), Eli Biham (Israel), and Lars Knudsen (Norway)	A 32-round Feistel cipher, with key mixing using XOR and rotates, substitutions using 8-key-dependent 4-bit S-boxes, and a linear transformation in each round
Twofish	Bruce Schneier et al., The United States	A 16-round Feistel cipher using 4-key-dependent 8-bit S-boxes, matrix transforms, rotations, and based in part on the Blowfish cipher

[a]From http://www.adfa.edu.au/~lpb/papers/unz99.html

Replacing a cryptographic algorithm is a relatively straightforward endeavor because encryption algorithms are, in general, completely interchangeable. Most hardware implementations allow plug-ins and replacements of different algorithms. The greatest difficulty is in the logistics of replacing the software for companies with tens or hundreds of thousands of disparate devices. Also, for those organizations that have remote sites, satellites, and so on, this point is ever more germane.

AES implementations have already emerged in many commercial software security products as an optional algorithm (in addition to Triple-DES and others). Software implementations have always come before hardware products due to the inherent time it takes to design and update hardware. It is generally easier to upgrade software than to perform a hardware replacement or upgrade, and many vendors have already incorporated AES into their latest designs.

Table 2 Five algorithms selected by NIST

Algorithm	Main strength	Main weaknesses
MARS	High-security margin	Complex implementation
RC6	Very simple	Lower security margin as it used operations specific to 32-bit processors
Rijndael	Simple elegant design	Insufficient rounds
Serpent	High-security margin	Complex design and analysis, poor performance
Twofish	Reasonable performance, high-security margin	Complex design

For those organizations already running Triple-DES, there are not many compelling reasons (except for compatibility) to immediately use AES. It is likely that the speed at which companies upgrade to AES will increase as more products ship in AES-enabled mode.

RIJNDAEL

Rijndael, the AES candidate, was developed by Dr. Joan Daemen of Proton World International and Dr. Vincent Rijmen, a postdoctoral researcher in the electrical engineering department of Katholieke Universiteit of the Netherlands.[8] Drs. Daemen and Rijmen are well-known and respected in the cryptography community. Rijndael has its roots in the SQUARE cipher,[9] also designed by Daemen and Rijmen.

The details on Rijndael are specified in its original AES proposal.[10] From a technical perspective,[11] Rijndael is a substitution-linear transformation network (i.e., nonFeistel) with multiple rounds, depending on the key size. Feistel ciphers are block ciphers in which the input is split in half. Feistel ciphers are provably invertible. Decryption is the algorithm in reverse, with subkeys used in the opposite order. Of the four other AES finalists, MARS uses an extended Feistel network; RC6 and Twofish use a standard Feistel network; and Serpent uses a single substitution-permutation network. Rijndael's key length and block size is either 128, 192, or 256 bits. It does not support arbitrary sizes, and its key and block size must be one of the three lengths.

Rijndael uses a single S-box that acts on a byte input in order to give a byte output. For implementation purposes, it can be regarded as a lookup table of 256 bytes. Rijndael is defined by the equation

$$S(x) = M(1/x) + b$$

over the field $GF(2^8)$, where M is a matrix and b is a constant.

A data block to be processed under Rijndael is partitioned into an array of bytes and each of the cipher operations is byte oriented. Rijndael's 10 rounds each perform four operations. In the first layer, an 8×8 S-box (S-boxes used as non-linear components) is applied to each byte. The second and third layers are linear mixing layers, in which the rows of the array are shifted and the columns are mixed. In the fourth layer, subkey bytes are XORed into each byte of the array. In the last round, the column mixing is omitted. Known as the key schedule, the Rijndael key (which is from 128 to 256 bits) is fed into the key schedule. This key schedule is used to generate the subkeys, which are the keys used for each round. Each subkey is as long as the block being enciphered, and thus, if 128-bit long, is made up of 16 bytes. A good explanation of the Rijndael key schedule can be found on the Edmonton Community Network.[12]

WHY DID NIST SELECT THE RIJNDAEL ALGORITHM?

According to the NIST,[13] Rijndael was selected due to its combination of security, performance, efficiency, ease of implementation, and flexibility. As clarified in the report by NIST (*Report on the Development of the Advanced Encryption Standard*), the fact that NIST rejected MARS, RC6, Serpent, and Twofish does not mean that they were inadequate for independent use. Rather, the sum of all benefits dictated that Rijndael was the best candidate for the AES. The report concludes that "all five algorithms appear to have adequate security for the AES." Specifically, NIST felt that Rijndael was appropriate for the following reasons:

- Good performance in both hardware and software across a wide range of computing environments
- Good performance in both feedback and nonfeedback modes
- Key setup time is excellent
- Key agility is good
- Very low memory requirements
- Easy to defend against power and timing attacks (this defense can be provided without significantly impacting performance)

PROBLEMS WITH RIJNDAEL

Although the general consensus is that Rijndael is a fundamentally first-rate algorithm, it is not without opposing views.[14] One issue was with its underlying architecture; some opined that its internal mathematics were simple, almost to the point of being rudimentary. If Rijndael were written down as a mathematical formula, it would look much simpler than any other AES candidate. Another criticism was that Rijndael avoids any kind of obfuscation technique to hide its encryption mechanism from adversaries.[15] Finally, it was pointed out that encryption and decryption use different S-boxes, as opposed to DES that uses the same S-boxes for both operations. This means that an implementation of Rijndael that both encrypts and decrypts is twice as large as an implementation that only does one operation, which may be inconvenient on constrained devices.

The Rijndael team defended its design by pointing out that the simpler mathematics made Rijndael easier to implement in embedded hardware. The team also argued that obfuscation was not needed. This, in turn, led to speculation that the Rijndael team avoided obfuscation to evade scrutiny from Hitachi, which had expressed its intentions to seek legal action against anyone threatening its U.S.-held patents. Hitachi claimed to hold exclusive patents on several encryption obfuscation techniques and had not been forthcoming about whether it would consider licensing those techniques to any outside party.[16] In fact, in early 2000, Hitachi issued patent claims against four of the AES candidates (MARS, RC6, Serpent, and Twofish).

CAN AES BE CRACKED?

Although a public-DES cracker has been built (it is an acceptable assumption to believe that the NSA has had this capability for a long-time) as detailed in *Cracking DES: Secrets of Encryption Research, Wiretap Politics and Chip Design,* there still exists the question of whether an AES-cracking device can be built.

It should be noted that after nearly 30 years of research, no easy attack against DES has been discovered. The only feasible attack against DES is a brute-force exhaustive search of the entire keyspace. Had the original keyspace of DES been increased, it is unlikely that the AES process would have been undertaken.

DES-cracking machines were built that could recover a DES key after a number of hours by trying all possible key values. Although an AES cracking machine could also be built, the time that would be required to extricate a single key would be overwhelming.

As an example, although the entire DES keyspace can feasibly be cracked in less than 48 hours, this is not the case with AES. If a special-purpose chip, such as an FPGA, could perform a billion AES decryptions per second, and the cracking host had a billion chips running in parallel, it would still require an infeasible amount of time to recover the key. An FPGA is an integrated circuit that can be programmed in the field after manufacture. They are heavily used by engineers in the design of specialized integrated circuits that can later be produced in large quantities for distribution to computer manufacturers and end users. Even if it was assumed that one could build a machine that could recover a DES key in a second (i.e., try 2^{55} keys per second), it would take that machine over 140 trillion years to crack a 128-bit AES key.

Given the impenetrability of AES (at least with existing computing and mathematical capabilities), it appears that AES will fulfill its requirement of being secure until 2030. But then again, a similar thought was assumed for DES when it was first designed.

Finally, should quantum computing transform itself from the laboratory to the realm of practical application, it could potentially undermine the security afforded by AES and other cryptosystems.

IMPACT OF AES

The two main bodies to put AES into production will be the U.S. government and financial services companies. For both entities, the rollout of AES will likely be quite different.

For the U.S. government sector, after AES is confirmed as a FIPS, all government agencies will be required to use AES for secure (but unclassified) systems. Because the government has implemented DES and Triple-DES in tens of thousands of systems, the time and cost constraints for the upgrade to AES will be huge.

AES will require a tremendous investment of time and resources to replace DES, Triple-DES, and other encryption schemes in the existing government infrastructure. A compounding factor that can potentially slow down the acceptance of AES is the fact that because Triple-DES is fundamentally secure (its main caveat is its speed), there is no compelling security urgency to replace it. Although AES may be required, it may be easier for government agencies to apply for a waiver for AES as opposed to actually implementing it. This is similar to those government agencies that applied for waivers to get out of the requirement for C2 (*Orange Book*) certification. With the budget and time constraints of interchanging AES, its transition will occur over time, with economics having a large part in it.

The financial services community also has a huge investment in Triple-DES. Because at present there is no specific mandate for AES use in the financial services community, and given the preponderance of Triple-DES, it is doubtful that any of the banking standards bodies will require AES use.

While the use of single DES (also standardized as X9.23-1995, Encryption of Wholesale Financial Messages) is being withdrawn by the X9 committee (see X9 TG-25-1999), this nonetheless allows continued use of DES until another algorithm is implemented.

But although the main advantages of AES are its efficiency and performance for both hardware and software implementations, it may find a difficult time being implemented in large-scale nongovernmental sites, given the economic constraints of upgrading it, combined with the usefulness of Triple-DES. Either way, it will likely be a number of years before there is widespread use of the algorithm.

REFERENCES

1. FIPS 46–3, http://csrc.nist.gov/publications/fips/fips46-3/fips46–3.pdf Reaffirmed for the final time on October 25, 1999.
2. Schneier, B. Security in the real world: How to evaluate security technology. Comput. Secur. J. **1999**, *15* (4), http://www.infosecuritymag.com.
3. Rothke, B. Free Lunch. In *Information Security Magazine*, February 1999, http://www.infosecuritymag.com.
4. http://csrc.nist.gov/encryption/aes/pre-round1/aes_9701.txt.
5. http://www.eff.org/descracker.html.
6. Coppersmith, Dan *the Data Encryption Standard and Its Strength against Attacks* IBM Report RC18613.
7. http://csrc.nist.gov/encryption/aes/draftfips/fr-AES-200102.html.
8. *Rijnadel,* http://www.baltimore.com/devzone/aes/tech_overview.html.
9. http://www.esat.kuleuven.ac.be/~rijmen/square/index.html.
10. http://www.esat.kuleuven.ac.be/~rijmen/rijndael/rijndaeldocV2.zip.
11. http://csrc.nist.gov/encryption/aes/round2/r2report.pdf.
12. http://home.ecn.ab.ca/~jsavard/crypto/co040801.htm.
13. http://csrc.nist.gov/encryption/aes.
14. Ferguson, N.; Kelsey, J.; Lucks, S.; Schneier, B.; Stay, M.; Wagner, D.; Whiting, D. Improved cryptanalysis of Rinjndael, http://www.counterpane.com/rijndael.html.
15. Twofish, *The Twofish Team's Final Comments on AES Selection,* http://www.counterpane.com/twofish-final.html.
16. http://www.planetit.com/techcenters/docs/security/qa/PIT20001106S0015.

BIBLIOGRAPHY

1. Savard, J. How Does Rijndael Work?, http://www.securityportal.com/articles/rijndael20001012.html.
2. Tsai, M. AES: An Overview of the Rijndael Encryption Algorithm, http://www.gigascale.org/mescal/forum/65.html.
3. Landau, S. Communications Security for the Twenty-first Century: The Advanced Encryption Standard and Standing the Test of Time: The Data Encryption Standard, http://www.ams.org/notices/200004/fea-landau.pdf; http://www.ams.org/notices/200003/fea-landau.pdf.
4. Schneier, B. *Applied Cryptography*; John Wiley & Sons: New York, NY, 1996.
5. Menezes, A. *Handbook of Applied Cryptography*; CRC Press: Boca Raton, FL, 1996.
6. Anderson, R. *Security Engineering*; John Wiley & Sons: New York, NY, 2001.
7. Brown, L. A Current Perspective on Encryption Algorithms, http://www.adfa.edu.au/~lpb/papers/unz99.html.

ANSI: American National Standards Institute

Jana Zabinski
American National Standards Institute, New York, New York, U.S.A.

Abstract

The American National Standards Institute is a private, nonprofit organization that oversees the standards and conformity assessment system in the United States.

INTRODUCTION

The American National Standards Institute (ANSI) is a private, nonprofit organization that oversees the standards and conformity assessment system in the United States, and represents the needs and views of U.S. stakeholders in standardization forums around the globe. ANSI's membership comprises government agencies, organizations, corporations, academic and international bodies, and individuals. The Institute represents the interests of more than 125,000 companies and 3.5 million professionals.

The ANSI approves standards that are developed by accredited organizations comprised of representatives of standard developing organizations (SDOs), government agencies, consumer groups, companies, and others. The Institute also accredits organizations that carry out product or personnel certification in accordance with requirements defined in international standards (see Fig. 1).

Standards ensure that the characteristics and performance of products are consistent, that the same definitions and terms are used, and that products are tested the same way. For example, standards ensure that libraries can share electronic card catalog information, and patrons can search those catalogs from connected computers with Internet access.

HISTORY

By the 20th century, the need for coordination among U.S. standards-setting groups became evident. In October 1918, three government agencies and five private sector organizations joined together to form a coordination body known as the American Engineering Standards Committee, the predecessor of what is now known as ANSI.

Today, the U.S. standardization community is comprised largely of nongovernmental SDOs and consortia; these groups are primarily supported by industry participation.

OVERVIEW OF THE U.S. STANDARDIZATION SYSTEM

Standardization encompasses a broad range of considerations—from the actual development of a standard to its promulgation, acceptance, implementation, and demonstration of compliance. A primary facilitator of commerce, standardization has become the basis of a sound national economy and the key to global market access.

Voluntary consensus standards serve as the cornerstone of the distinctive U.S. standardization system. These documents arise from an open process that depends on data gathering, a vigorous discussion of all viewpoints, and agreement among a diverse range of stakeholders. Thousands of individual experts representing the viewpoints of consumers, companies, industry and labor organizations, and government agencies at the federal, state, and local level voluntarily contribute their knowledge, talents, and efforts to standardization activities.

"Voluntary" refers only to the manner in which the standard was developed; it does not necessarily refer to whether compliance to a consensus standard is optional or whether a government entity or market sector has endorsed the document for mandatory use.

AMERICAN NATIONAL STANDARDS

The Institute oversees the creation, promulgation, and use of thousands of norms and guidelines that directly impact businesses in nearly every sector: from manufacturing and construction to agriculture, food service, software engineering, energy distribution, and more. Likewise, ANSI-accredited standards developers span the full gamut of industry sectors and services.

Encyclopedia of Information Systems and Technology, DOI: 10.1081/E-EIST-120044428

Fig. 1 ANSI Logo.

Though ANSI itself does not develop standards, the Institute facilitates the development of American National Standards, also known as ANS, by accrediting the procedures of standards developing organizations. ANSI accreditation signifies that the procedures used by these bodies meet the Institute's essential requirements for openness, balance, consensus, and due process. More than 200 active SDOs are accredited under the *ANSI Essential Requirements: Due process requirements for American National Standards.* Approximately 10,500 American National Standards carry the ANSI designation.

Hallmarks of the American National Standards process involve:

- Consensus by a group that is open to representatives from all interested parties
- Broad-based public review and comment on draft standards
- Consideration of and response to comments
- Incorporation of submitted changes that meet the same consensus requirements into a draft standard
- Availability of an appeal by any participant alleging that these principles were not respected during the standards-development process

For example, the National Information Standards Organization (NISO) develops and maintains standards for information systems, products, and services relating to bibliographic and library applications. NISO's standards span both traditional and new technologies, and address the full range of information-related needs, including retrieval, storage, and preservation.

Another ANSI-accredited standards developer, the Data Interchange Standards Association (DISA), writes standards that support e-commerce and business-to-business data exchange, from order processing to electronic payment. DISA also serves as the secretariat for the ANSI-Accredited Standards Committee (ASC) X12, which develops e-business exchange standards in XML and X12 EDI formats.

ANSI INVOLVEMENT IN INTERNATIONAL STANDARDS ACTIVITIES

In the international arena, ANSI promotes the use of U.S. standards abroad, advocates U.S. policy and technical positions in international and regional standards and conformity assessment organizations, and encourages the adoption of international standards as national standards where appropriate. The Institute is the official U.S. representative to the two major international standards organizations, the International Organization for Standardization (ISO) and, via the U.S. National Committee (USNC), the International Electrotechnical Commission (IEC). ANSI is also a member of the International Accreditation Forum.

Through ANSI, the U.S. has immediate access to the ISO and IEC standards development processes. ANSI and the USNC frequently carry U.S. standards forward to ISO and IEC where they are adopted in whole or in part as international standards. U.S. positions are developed by U.S. Technical Advisory Groups (TAGs) that have been accredited by ANSI or approved by the USNC. Participation in a U.S. TAG is open to all affected stakeholders.

On behalf of ANSI, NISO administers the U.S. TAG to ISO Technical Committee 46 (TC 46), *Information and Documentation.* TC 46 develops international standards relating to records management and museum documentation, as well as publishing, archiving, and indexing.

ASC X12 serves as the U.S. TAG administrator to ISO TC 154, *Processes, Data Elements and Documents in Commerce, Industry and Administration,* which supports international standardization activities in the field of industrial data. ISO TC 154 standards address business administration processes and information interchange between individual organizations.

CONFORMITY ASSESSMENT

On the other side of the standardization coin is conformity assessment, a term used to describe the evaluation of products, processes, systems, services, or personnel to confirm adherence to the requirements identified in a specified standard. In general, conformity assessment includes sampling and testing, inspection, supplier's declaration of conformity, certification, and management system assessment and registration. It can also include accreditation of the competence of those activities by a third party and recognition (usually by a government agency) of an accreditation program's capability.

Conformity assessment forms a vital link between standards that define product characteristics or requirements and the products themselves. It can verify that a particular product meets a given level of quality or safety, and it can provide explicit or implicit information about the product's characteristics, the consistency of those characteristics, and/or the performance of the product.

The ANSI's role in the conformity assessment arena includes accreditation of organizations that certify that products and personnel meet recognized standards. The ANSI-American Society for Quality National Accreditation Board serves as the U.S. accreditation body for management systems certification, primarily in areas such as quality (ISO 9000 family of standards) and/or the environment (ISO 14000 family of standards). ANSI also is involved in several international and regional organizations to promote the multilateral recognition of conformity assessments across borders to preclude redundant and costly barriers to trade.

The ANSI's accreditation programs themselves are created in accordance with international guidelines as verified by government and peer review assessments.

STANDARDS PANELS

Through its standards panel program, ANSI provides standards-based solutions to national and international priorities. Each of the Institute's panels engages a broad range of stakeholders in the coordination and harmonization of standards and conformity assessment activities relevant to the panel's area of focus.

In 2004, the ANSI Homeland Security Standards Panel supported a special project on private-sector emergency preparedness that had been requested by the 9/11 Commission. The panel continues to provide ongoing support for the Department of Homeland Security and other agencies.

At the request of the Office of Science and Technology Policy in the Executive Office of the President, ANSI launched the Nanotechnology Standards Panel to facilitate the development of standards for nanotechnology nomenclature and terminology; materials properties; and testing, measurement, and characterization procedures.

The Healthcare Information Technology Standards Panel is under contract with the Department of Health and Human Services to assist in establishing a national health IT network for the United States.

The Identity Theft Prevention and Identity Management Standards Panel is supporting all citizens in its efforts to facilitate the identification and development of standards to secure and protect personal information.

Launched in May 2007, the ANSI Biofuels Standards Panel is a cross-sector coordinating body established to promote the development and compatibility of standards and conformity assessment programs to support the large-scale commoditization of biofuels.

CONCLUSION

The ANSI provides the forum through which all affected stakeholders may cooperate in establishing, improving, and recognizing consensus-based standards and certification programs that are dynamically responsive to national needs. ANSI continues to be fully involved in its support of the goals of United States and global standardization and remains committed to enhancing the quality of life for all global citizens.

BIBLIOGRAPHY

1. American National Standards Institute official Web site, http://www.ansi.org.

Application Security

Walter S. Kobus, Jr.
Vice President, Security Consulting Services, Total Enterprise Security Solutions, LLC, Raleigh, North Carolina, U.S.A.

Abstract

The primary goal of application security is that it will operate with what the senior management has decided is a reasonable risk to the organization's goals and its strategic business plans. Second, it will ensure that the application, once placed on the targeted platforms, is secure.

Application security is broken down into three parts: (1) the application in development; (2) the application in production; and (3) the commercial off-the-shelf software (COTS) application that is introduced into production. Each one requires a different approach to secure the application. As with the Common Criteria ISO 15408, one must develop a security profile or baseline of security requirements and level of reasonability of risk.

APPLICATION SECURITY IN THE DEVELOPMENT LIFE CYCLE

In an ideal world, information security starts when senior management is approached to fund the development of a new application. A well-designed application would include at least one document devoted to the application's security posture and plan for managing risks. This is normally referred to as a security plan.[1] However, many application development departments have worried little about application security until the latter-day advent of Web applications addressing E-commerce. Rather than a firewall guarding the network against a threat, poor coding of Web applications has now caused a new threat to surface: the ability of hacking at the browser level using a Secure Socket Layer encrypted path to get access to a Web application and, finally, into the internal databases that support the core business. This threat has required many development firms to start a certification and accreditation program or at least address security requirements during the development life cycle.

SECURITY REQUIREMENTS AND CONTROLS

Requirements that need to be addressed in the development cycle are sometimes difficult to keep focused on during all phases. One must remember that the security requirements are, in fact, broken down into two components: (1) security requirements that need to be in place to protect the application during the development life cycle and (2) the security requirements that will follow the application into the targeted platform in the production environment.

SECURITY CONTROLS IN THE DEVELOPMENT LIFE CYCLE

Security controls in the development life cycle are often confused with the security controls in the production environment. One must remember that they are two separate issues, each with its own security requirements and controls. The following discussion represents some of the more important security application requirements on controls in the development life cycle.

Separation of Duties

There must be a clear separation of duties to prevent important project management controls from being overlooked. For example, in the production environment, developers must not modify production code without going through a change management process. In the development environment, code changes must also follow a development change management process. This becomes especially important when a code is written that is highly sensitive, such as a cryptographic module or a calculation routine in a financial application. Therefore, developers must not perform quality assurance on their own code and must have peer or independent code reviews.

Responsibilities and privileges should be allocated in such a way that it prevents an individual or a small group of collaborating individuals from inappropriately controlling multiple key aspects of any process or causing unacceptable harm or loss. Segregation is used to preserve the integrity, availability, and confidentiality of

Encyclopedia of Information Systems and Technology, DOI: 10.1081/E-EIST-120046702

information assets by minimizing opportunities for security incidents, outages, and personnel problems. The risk is when individuals are assigned duties in which they are expected to verify their own work or approve work that accomplishes their goals; hence, the potential to bias the outcome. Separation of duties should be a concern throughout all phases of the development life cycle to ensure there is no conflict of duties or interests. This security requirement should start at the beginning of the development life cycle in the planning phase. The standard security requirements should be that no individual is assigned a position or responsibility that might result in a conflict of interest to the development of the application. There are several integrated development tools available that help development teams improve their productivity, version control, maintain a separation of duties within and between development phases, create quality software, and provide overall software configuration management through the system's life cycle.

Reporting Security Incidents

During the design, development, and testing of a new application, security incidents may occur. These incidents may result from people granted improper access or successful intrusion into both the software and hardware of a test environment and stealing a new code. All security incidents must be tracked and corrective action taken prior to the system being placed into production. The failure to document, assess, and take corrective action on security incidents that arise during the development cycle could lead to the deployment of an application containing serious security exposures. Included are potential damage to the system or information contained within it and a violation of privacy rights.

These types of incidents need to be evaluated for the possible loss of confidentiality, loss of integrity, denial of service, and the risk they present to the business goals in terms of customer trust.

Security incidents can occur at any time during the development life cycle. It is important to inform all development project team members of this potential in the planning phase.

Security Awareness

Security awareness training must be required for all team members working on the development project. If a particular team member does not understand the need for the security controls and the measures implemented, there is a risk that the particular member will circumvent or bypass these controls and weaken the security of the application. In short, inadequate security awareness training may translate into inadequate protection

mechanisms within the application. The initial security briefing should be conducted during the planning phase, with additional security awareness, as appropriate, throughout the development life cycle. A standard for compliance with the security requirement is to review the security awareness training program to ensure that all project team members are aware of the security policies that apply to the development of the project.

Access

For each application developed, an evaluation must be made to determine who should be granted access to the application or system. A properly completed access form needs to be filled out by the development manager for each member who needs access to the development system and development software package. User identification and an audit trail are essential for adequate accountability during the development life cycle. If this security requirement has not been satisfied, there is a possibility that unauthorized individuals may access the test system and data, thereby learning about the application design. This is of special concern in applications that are sensitive and critical to the business operations of the organization. Access decisions for team personnel should be made at the assignment stage of the development project and no later than the planning stage of the development life cycle.

Determination of Sensitivity and Criticality

For every application that is going to be placed into the development and production environments, there must be a determination regarding the sensitivity of the information that will reside on that system and its criticality to the business. A formal letter of determination of sensitivity and criticality is required. This should be done prior to the approval stage of the application by the senior management because it will impact resources and money. The letter of determination of sensitivity is based on an analysis of the information processed. This determination should be made prior to any development work on the project and coordinated with the privacy officer or general counsel. The letter of criticality is used to evaluate the criticality of the application and its priority to the business operation. This document should be coordinated with the disaster and contingency officer. Both documents should be distributed to the appropriate information technology (IT) managers (operations, network, development, and security).

Applications that are sensitive and critical require more care and, consequently, have more security requirements than a nonsensitive or noncritical system. The improper classification of information or criticality in an "undetermined state" could result in the users not properly safeguarding information, inadequate security controls implemented, and inadequate protection and recovery mechanisms designed into the application or the targeted platform system.

Labeling Sensitive Information

All sensitive documentation must be properly labeled to inform others of their sensitive nature. Each screen display, report, or document containing sensitive information must have an appropriate label, such as *Sensitive Information* or *Confidential Information*. If labeling is incorrect or has not been performed, there is a risk that sensitive information will be read by those without a need to know when the application moves into production. Labeling should begin at the time that reports, screens, and so on are coded and continue through the system life cycle.

Use of Production Data

If production data is used for developing or testing an application, a letter specifying how the data will be safeguarded is required; and permission is needed from the owner of the data, operations manager, and security. Sensitive production data should not be used to test an application. If, however, production data must be used, it should be modified to remove traceability and protect individual privacy. It may be necessary to use encryption or hash techniques to protect the data. When the development effort is complete, it is important to scrub the hardware and properly dispose off the production data to minimize security risk. The risk of using production data in a development and test environment is that there might be privacy violations that result in a loss of customer and employee trust or violation of law. Development personnel should not have access to sensitive information.

Code Reviews

The security purpose of the application code review is to deter threats under any circumstance; events with the potential to cause harm to the organization through the disclosure, modification, or destruction of information; or by the denial of critical services. Typical threats in an Internet environment include:

- *Component failure.* Failure due to design flaws or hardware/software faults can lead to denial of service or security compromises through the malfunction of a system component. Downtimes of a firewall or false rejections by authorization servers are examples of failures that affect security.

- *Information browsing.* Unauthorized viewing of sensitive information by intruders or legitimate users may occur through a variety of mechanisms.
- *Misuse.* The use of information assets for other than authorized purposes can result in denial of service, increased cost, or damage to reputations. Internal or external users can initiate misuse.
- *Unauthorized deletion, modification, or disclosure of information.* Intentional damage to information assets that result in the loss of integrity or confidentiality of business functions and information.
- *Penetration.* Attacks by unauthorized persons or systems that may result in denial of service or significant increases in incident handling costs.
- *Misrepresentation.* Attempts to masquerade as a legitimate user to steal services or information, or to initiate transactions that result in financial loss or embarrassment to the organization.

An independent review of the application code and application documentation is an attempt to find defects or errors and to assure that the application is coded in a language that has been approved for company development. The reviewer shall assure that the implementation of the application faithfully represents the design. The data owner, in consultation with information security, can then determine whether the risks identified are acceptable or require remediation. Application code reviews are further divided into peer code reviews and independent code reviews, as follows:

- Peer code reviews shall be conducted on all applications developed whether the application is nonsensitive, sensitive, or is defined as a major application. Peer reviews are defined as reviews by a second party and are sometimes referred to as *walk-throughs*. Peer code review shall be incorporated as part of the development life cycle process and shall be conducted at appropriate intervals during the development life cycle process.
- The primary purpose of an independent code review is to identify and correct potential software code problems that might affect the integrity, confidentiality, or availability once the application has been placed into production. The review is intended to provide the company a level of assurance that the application has been designed and constructed in such a way that it will operate as a secure computing environment and maintain employee and public trust. The independent third-party code review process is initiated upon the completion of the application source code and program documentation. This is to ensure that adequate documentation and source code shall be available for the independent code review. Independent code reviews shall be done under the following guidelines:

Table 1 Confirmation that the application's information, integrity, and availability are assured

As the development project manager of XYZ application, I will need the following number of (NT or UNIX) servers. These servers need to be configured to store and process confidential information and ensure the integrity and the availability of XYZ application. To satisfy the security of the application, I need assurance that these servers will have a minimum security configured as follows:

Password standards

Access standards

Backup and disaster plan

Approved banner log-on server

Surge and power protection for all servers

Latest patches installed

Appropriate shutdown and restart procedures are in place

Appropriate level of auditing is turned on

Appropriate virus protection

Appropriate vendor licenses/copyrights

Physical security of servers

Implementation of system timeout

Object reuse controls

Please indicate whether each security control is in compliance by indicating a "Yes" or "No." If any of the security controls above is not in compliance, please comment as to when the risk will be mitigated. Your prompt reply would be appreciated not later than (date)

○ Independent third-party code reviews should be conducted for all Web applications, whether they are classified sensitive or nonsensitive, that are designed for external access (such as E-commerce customers, business partners, etc.). This

Table 2 Request for security

As the development project manager of XYZ application, I will need the assurance that the production network environment is configured to process confidential information and ensure the integrity and the availability of XYZ application to satisfy the security of the application. The network should have the following minimum security:

Inbound/outbound ports

Access control language

Password standards

Latest patches

Firewall

Configuration

Inbound/outbound services

Architecture provides security protection and avoids single point of failure

Please indicate whether each security control is in compliance by indicating a "Yes" or "No." If any of the security controls above is not in compliance please comment as to when the risk will be mitigated. Your prompt reply would be appreciated not later than (date)

independent third-party code review should be conducted in addition to the peer code review.

○ Security requirements for cryptographic modules are contained in FIPS 140-2 and can be downloaded at http://csrc.nist.gov/cryptval/140-2.htm. When programming a cryptographic module, one is required to seek independent validation of FIPS 140-2. One can access those approved vendors at http://csrc.nist.gov/cryptval/140-1/1401val2001.htm.

APPLICATION SECURITY IN PRODUCTION

When an application completes the development life cycle and is ready to move to the targeted production platform, a whole new set of security requirements must be considered. Many of the security requirements require the development manager to coordinate with other IT functions to ensure that the application will be placed into a secure production environment. Table 1 shows an example representing an E-mail message addressed to the group maintaining processing hardware to confirm that the application's information, integrity, and availability are assured.

A similar Email message could also be sent to the network function requesting the items in Table 2.

COMMERCIAL OFF-THE-SHELF SOFTWARE APPLICATION SECURITY

It would be great if all vendors practiced application security and provided their clients with a report of the security requirements and controls that were used and validated. Unfortunately, that is far from the case, except when dealing with cryptographic modules. Every time an organization buys an off-the-shelf software application, it takes a risk—risk that the code contains major flaws that could cause a loss in revenue, customer, employee privacy information, and so on. This is why it is so important to think of protecting applications using the defense-in-depth methodology. With a tiny hole in Web application code, a hacker can reach right through from the browser to an E-commerce Web site. This is referred to as *Web perversion*, and hackers with a little determination can steal digital property, sensitive client information, trade secrets, and goods and services. There are two COTS packages available on the market today to protect E-commerce sites from such attacks. One software program on the market stops application-level attacks by identifying legitimate requests, and another software program automates the manual tasks of auditing Web applications.

OUTSOURCED DEVELOPMENT SERVICES

Outsourced development services should be treated no differently than in-house development. Both should adhere to a strict set of security application requirements. In the case of the outsourced development effort, it will be up to technical contract representatives to ensure that all security requirements are addressed and covered during an independent code review. This should be spelled out in the requirements section of the Request for Proposal. Failure to pass an independent code review then requires a second review, which should be paid for by the contractor as a penalty.

SUMMARY

The three basic areas of applications security—development, production, and commercial off-the-shelf software—are present in all organizations. Some organizations will address application security in all three areas, while others only in one or two areas. Whether an organization develops applications for internal use, for clients as a service company, or for commercial sale, the necessity of practice plays a major role in the area of trust and repeated business. In today's world, organizations are faced with new and old laws that demand assurance that the software was developed with appropriate security requirements and controls. Until now, the majority of developers, pressured by senior management or by marketing concerns, have pushed to get products into production without any guidance of or concern for security requirements or controls. Security now plays a major role in the bottom line of E-commerce and critical infrastructure organizations. In some cases, it can be the leading factor as to whether a company can recover from a cyber-security attack. Represented as a major component in the protection of our critical infrastructure from cyber-security attacks, application security can no longer be an afterthought. Many companies have perceived application security as an afterthought, pushing it aside in order to get a product to market. Security issues were then taken care of through patches and version upgrades. This method rarely worked well, and in the end led to a lack of customer trust, reflecting negatively on the integrity of the development company. The practice of application security as an up-front design consideration can be a marketing advantage to a company. This can be marketed as an added feature so that, when the application is installed on an appropriately secure platform, it will enhance the customer's enterprise security program—not help to compromise it.

REFERENCES

1. NIST, *Guide for Developing Security Plans for Information Technology Systems Special Publication 800-16*: 1999.

Application Systems Development

Lowell Bruce McCulley
IT Security Professional, Troy, New Hampshire, U.S.A.

Abstract

This entry surveys some information security considerations pertinent to application systems development, reviews a number of areas related to application systems and the technical and organizational development environments, and describes a novel tool for incorporating security engineering into the application development process.

If carpenters built houses the way programmers build programs, the first woodpecker that came along would destroy civilization.
—*Weinberg's Second Law of Computer Programming*

Woodpeckers are just attempting to remove bugs.
—*Further commentary by Weinberg*

Jerry Weinberg was actually commenting on the state of the art in software engineering in the 1960s, not present-day security engineering, when he authored his second law. The fact that his comment is as pertinent to today's malicious hackers as it was to innocent practitioners of by-gone days illustrates the fundamental truth that security is an inherent attribute of well-designed information systems. His additional commentary points out that systems-engineering activities (e.g., debugging) destabilize systems, clashing with the security imperative for stable systems. This entry suggests that enlisting woodpeckers (or systems developers) in the security effort benefits both security and development. We posit that it is best to justify information security programs on economic issues in the management hierarchy by showing value from cooperating on technical issues in the project arena. The best way to benefit the development team and the entire organization is by working in harmony with development priorities, so we present several ways to do so.

We begin by surveying the existing state of the art in information security programs, in which we identify some things that do not work as well as they might. Economic factors are discussed as the fundamental drivers of management decisions about technology, applications systems, and security. We proceed to an examination of the nature of application systems and associated technologies, to better define our focus and the scope and bounds of our concerns. This leads to a review of the systems' development life cycle that applications follow, to understand how the development activities and security concerns change at different stages in the existence of applications systems. Finally,

we introduce an innovative approach to using a new security engineering tool in a way that generates value for the systems development process. We close by discussing the integration of that approach into the systems development life cycle, and identifying some potential directions for subsequent research and development.

STATE OF THE ART IN BUSINESS APPLICATIONS SYSTEMS SECURITY

A paradigm shift seems needed in our approach to securing business information systems.

The fundamental shift is to position security as a value enhancer throughout the application systems life cycle, especially the development engineering process. Application systems security would benefit from several effects of this shift, based on decades of experience developing critical systems. The reason is that business organizations often resist rather than promote security programs, on economic grounds. Application systems are the most important point of focus, because they are the *raison d'etre* for information systems (and thus for information security) in the business world. To successfully accomplish this, we must first understand several things, including economic factors, the nature of application systems and their life cycle, security drivers, and even historical context. This entry presents a framework and some tools to help integrate security into the application systems development process as a value enhancer.

Dr. Peter Tippett, CTO of TruSecure, wrote:

> For years, the focus of most security efforts has been centered on identifying and then fixing vulnerabilities in technology. The prevailing belief is that if a hole is found in the IT armor of an organization, it should be fixed immediately before it can be exploited by some cyber-deviant. While this approach sounds logical and effective, it is actually the beginning of a vicious cycle that occupies

Encyclopedia of Information Systems and Technology, DOI: 10.1081/E-EIST-120046706

vast amounts of time and wastes several millions of corporate, government, and consumer dollars every year.[1]

Dr. Tippett goes on to draw an analogy with healthcare, saying:

> The current approach to security would also have us inoculated for the most minor of illnesses, and protected against every possible cut, bruise, or blister…

which is both ineffective and impractical. Medicine has progressed beyond this piecemeal approach by taking a holistic view of the organism and by emphasizing prevention as the best cure. Unfortunately information security has not followed that model, at least not yet, but it suggests a framework to use as a model to improve our struggling InfoSec efforts. We need to extend our focus to view information systems as functional entities rather than collections of technical components, and to define and address security concerns in that holistic context. By doing so, we also have the opportunity to transform our security efforts from a costly burden into a valuable benefit.

Securing Web-based business-to-business E-commerce application systems poses new problems requiring a new approach to engineering security into the application systems development life cycle. A typical Web-based application utilizes external (e.g., Internet) connections from existing segmented network infrastructures that provide a layered defense-in-depth. The external connections are firewalled to protect an exposed demilitarized zone with hardened bastion hosts providing authorized services, monitored by intrusion detection systems (IDS), and isolated from the internal network by additional firewalls. No unnecessary ports are left open, and external network scans will find no vulnerabilities. This effectively isolates the internal systems from the uncontrolled external environment at the network infrastructure level, but at the application level things are different. By design, the Web server provides external connectivity to internal functions because that is the powerful advantage of E-commerce. However, this means that the external users are interacting with database and application servers that are not directly exposed through the infrastructure, but which may now be left exposed to attacks through the application design. The traditional approach of patching components when security vulnerabilities are found is no longer acceptable when those vulnerabilities may be discovered by attacks that disrupt databases critical to production scheduling or supply-chain ordering.

The reason for this situation is that today's integrated business information systems are highly evolved and complex systems of interdependent components structured in a logical organization, not a piecemeal collection of independent components to be patched and secured independently. As the complexity of our systems increases, the difficulty of finding and patching all the chinks in their armor becomes unmanageable. Worse, hidden dependencies arise that prevent recognition of vulnerabilities or prevent the application of patches, as well as obscuring responsibility for maintaining security. These factors all raise the cost of maintaining application systems security, which could be mitigated by more effective consideration of security when developing application systems.

For example, many systems affected by the Structured Query Language (SQL) Slammer worm were reportedly running applications that embedded the affected Microsoft server code. Some of the system owners may not have even known their system was running the Microsoft code as a dependency within another package, which raises the question of whether they or the third-party software vendor (TPSV) bore responsibility for applying the requisite security patches. Many customers turn to TPSVs because of limited technical resources, so they are dependent on the TPSV for support, including security issues associated with TPSV packages. TPSVs cannot blindly pick up patches from platform vendors and apply them to production systems at customer sites, because of risk that the patch may cause unforeseen and undesired side effects. The cost of qualifying vendor patches and applying them at customer sites is economically unpalatable for TPSVs, so it is unlikely that they will assume this role without some prodding. Potential liability exposure might be the necessary incentive, but reducing the required expense also would reduce the disincentive. Better engineering of security as a part of application systems development could provide this reduction.

The key to engineering security as a part of the application systems development process is to see security as an inherent attribute or characteristic of systems, not a separate feature. Basically, security is a way of expressing the robustness or fragility of systems. Information security concerns are described as confidentiality, availability, and integrity. When any of those is violated and expectations or requirements are not met, it is irrelevant whether they are broken by a malicious actor or the perversity of nature. Downtime, data corruption, and inappropriate disclosure are undesirable because they cause bad effects, not because they are caused by hostile adversaries. This definition makes security a feature that should be addressed within the established application systems development community, not parceled out for assignment to a separate organizational function. Information security practitioners can best promote improved practices by forming cooperative partnerships with application systems development organizations.

As a starting point, consider application security as a systems problem in which the overall security requirements and results are determined by the system environment. This is really another way of saying that appropriate security is accomplished by defense-in-depth, with the defense designed into overall system structure. The appropriate security is determined by application system requirements and implemented by making design tradeoffs and utilizing underlying host and network facilities. For example, consider a sensitive application that sends user identification documents and passwords unencrypted over a highly secure network using private protocols. Conventional information security practices might argue that an environment using unencrypted passwords should not be described as highly secure, but, in light of other design features, the cost of encryption is not justified by the value. Overall, the system is sufficiently secure, although one component may be less secure than it might possibly be. The successful security practitioner must understand how much security is enough, and how to accomplish that level of security cost-effectively. Exploiting existing processes in the application systems development organization is a good way to accomplish this, and this entry offers ways to do so.

ECONOMIC FACTORS

In the real world of business organizations, applications are the reason systems get built and deployed, to create and promote real economic value. Management decisions are driven most clearly by economic factors in the business world, but cost–benefit analyses are the underlying decisive factors in most sectors. There are complex psychological factors involved in accepting a certain cost in order to prevent risking an uncertain cost, so justifying the costs of information security programs on the basis of risk and cost avoidance can be difficult. It seems better to understand the forces that drive business initiatives and align security program justifications in harmony with them.

The fundamental issues that motivate the need for continued improvement in applications systems in business are nontechnical in nature. Economics is always the overriding priority, because even long-term strategic initiatives are undertaken in expectation of profitable returns on the investment. This gives systems associated with direct revenue producing activities a high stature, with those involved with handling money equally important (in many but not all companies, sales is more important than finance or operations). Systems dealing with cost containment and organizational overhead are not as high a priority, which may be significant to security program investments. Competitive advantage is a significant priority, because it generates economic benefits. Managers are always under pressure to reduce

costs, and schedule is a cost, so managers are also pressed to shorten delivery dates as much as possible. All of these factors work against an isolated information security program that presents a clearly measurable cost against benefits of uncertain economic value, and make it desirable to find ways to use security programs to add measurable value.

Costs of developing information systems are particularly difficult issues for most organizations, because of a number of inherent factors. Systems development is a highly specialized technical discipline that requires creative problem solving. The combination of discipline and creativity is not easily managed, leading to frequent schedule problems and associated budget overruns. Until a system is completed, the development results are not apparent, which forces management to expect success in large part based only on faith in the developers. These factors make development managers especially sensitive to issues that might affect schedule and costs. Security requirements introduce additional complexity and requirements into an already difficult development environment, so information security programs are often not embraced enthusiastically by systems developers. Using security initiatives to help facilitate meeting development schedules and budget requirements is a desirable alternative that improves teamwork.

Experience has consistently shown that the cost of fixing problems scales dramatically upward later in the application systems life cycle. Obviously, the cost of fixing a problem in design is much less than the cost of finding and fixing it once the system is built and in QA testing, and the cost of finding and fixing it once the system is in production use is even more. As a rough rule of thumb, the cost of fixing problems increases by an order of magnitude, or is about 1 times as much, for each stage later in the life cycle that the problem is found and fixed. Doing it right the first time is easiest and cheapest! This is really the fundamental drawback in the common approach to fixing security flaws as they are found in the field.

This phenomenon provides a great opportunity to turn the situation around and use security engineering to contribute positive value during the development process. By providing tools and techniques to identify and fix problems earlier in the system life cycle, security engineering can help to reduce the costs of those problems. For a simple example, buffer overruns frequently are the cause of vulnerabilities exploited by malicious adversaries, but they are also a cause of failures due to inadvertent errors, so they are undesirable because they cause a variety of problems. Thus, QA should and often does test for such scenarios. If QA is testing for buffer overruns, it will be much less expensive for developers to diligently avoid creating any that reach QA. That means using design and implementation techniques that prevent them and development tools that automatically recognize and test for them. This simple example shows good development engineering practice as well as purely information security considerations, but it illustrates the potential value that security engineering can provide by helping to reduce the cost of developing robust systems.

One major contributor to the cost escalation as problems are found and fixed later in the life cycle is the investment in schedule resources. Personnel and equipment have associated costs that must be accrued over time, so any extension of the schedule causes an increase in costs. This is a very important point for security practitioners to consider in their interaction with development organizations, because schedule is a very important and sensitive issue for developers. Any perception by the development team that security measures might cause delays or impede schedule progress is likely to lead to an adversarial relationship between the developers and the security practitioners. On the other hand, sensitivity to schedule issues and helpful cooperation in seeking to improve schedule performance will engender a much more positive relationship. Because many of the security concerns, especially those associated with availability and integrity, are also aspects of robust, reliable application systems, promoting good information security practices will contribute to improving quality without impacting schedule.

One particular issue around schedule may be of particular concern and an especially sensitive issue for the security practitioner to consider in certain development organizations. Software developers make a distinction between software prototypes, which are "quick and dirty" implementations used to explore design alternatives and evaluate their characteristics, and production-quality code that refines the chosen design alternative into a solid, robust implementation. A frequent issue is the pressure to take software prototypes to release prematurely, before refinements such as error checking or buffer bounds checking are added. A software development methodology referred to by terms, such as "rapid deployment" or "extreme development" has gained some vogue, based on alleged cost reductions realized from dramatic schedule reductions. This methodology purports to reduce time and cost spent in development by using a quick turnaround to reduce the cost of fixing only those problems that are found to occur in production operations (the argument is "why waste time designing problems that may never occur?"). This may simply hide costs by shifting them from development to operations or applications users, which is where the effects of production problems will be borne. The security risk is that such extreme development methodologies may be encouraging bad behavior (in slighting design and QA) for schedule rewards at the expense of introducing vulnerabilities that will only be recognized when they are exposed by operational incidents. These methodologies may have value to the

organization, but need to be scrutinized carefully for total life-cycle cost justifications. Security practitioners should be aware that such "bleeding edge" approaches are often extremely attractive to the creative technical personnel on development teams and that related issues (such as security compromises) may turn into political hot potatoes.

To summarize, the main factors that are the drivers for business applications of information systems are nontechnical and primarily economic in nature. Direct financial impacts, such as revenues and cost, are extremely important, and strategic issues, such as agility and competitive position, are also very significant. These needs motivate the need for applications systems and also shape the organizational environment and life cycle of such systems. Businesses will always want better systems sooner and cheaper, so anything contrary to those imperatives will be swimming against the tide. Information security practitioners need to align their efforts to promote these business priorities and position themselves in the mainstream of organizational efforts supporting those priorities in order to effectively accomplish the mission of protecting the information assets of the organization. One way to accomplish this is to take the role of collaborator and promoter or evangelist preaching value of security and cost of insecurity within the application systems development community.

APPLICATION SYSTEMS TECHNOLOGY BASE

It is important to remember that applications are the reason systems get built and deployed, to create and promote real business value. All the technology involved is simply a means to the end of delivering application functions to the users that benefit from their value. The systems environment, including the operating system kernel, utilities and administrative tools, user interfaces, software environments, network infrastructure and so on, is just the overhead required to deliver applications and realize the value that justifies their existence. Information systems security seeks to protect the components comprising the application systems environment for two basic reasons: 1) to keep them from being used to mount attacks; and 2) because they are needed by applications. Protecting those components is a means to the end of safeguarding business information assets, not an end in itself.

Business information assets exist within the context of information systems. Safeguarding those assets is accomplished by protecting the information systems that contain them. In seeking to do so, it is helpful to understand the nature of the information systems as well as the information assets we seek to protect. This section presents a discussion of information systems theory and practice, focused on some features of great practical importance to applications and security.

In the most general meaning, systems are a collection of functional elements organized in structure so that they interact to perform a particular function or task. Elements are often modular subsystems that can be viewed as independent systems themselves. Thus, a distributed application system may be comprised of network elements, such as hosts and servers, that are also individual systems operating in a network environment. The view of systems as a collection of subsystems that may be considered as independent systems themselves has some very important consequences that must be understood by the security practitioner concerned with systems security.

For one, a complex networked system may be a fragile assembly of robust components, because the structure and interactions of components are essential for the proper function of the system. The common approach of fixing security vulnerabilities as they are discovered has the effect of hardening the local components at the level of the patch, but not necessarily improving the security of the systems that incorporate those components. For example, a buffer overflow attack is a way of circumventing access controls on a hardened network. Using permitted traffic to carry malicious content through the controls on secured channels, in order to ultimately exploit an implementation flaw, allows the perpetrator to break containment and obtain unsecured access on a bastion host within a secured perimeter. Arguably, the implementation flaw could be said to make the network vulnerable instead of secure, but the vulnerability could be masked by filtering malformed traffic within the network instead of exposing the flawed implementation to potentially hostile input. The point is that the network system as a whole may be more or less vulnerable, independent of any one component.

Another consequence of viewing systems as a collection of subsystems is that it creates a hierarchical relationship in which it is essential to define the appropriate level of discussion in order to establish the scope and bounds of the system entities. This is extremely important for the development process, because the most common approach to developing information systems is to define modular functions that are subsequently refined and arranged in structures of increasing complexity. Managing this process and the resulting complexity is one of the major challenges in the field of business information systems, and especially in systems development. Failure to adequately meet this challenge may be the underlying cause of most security vulnerabilities.

One approach to managing this complexity is to view the hierarchical structure of information systems in an orderly sequence from a particular perspective. Two perspectives commonly encountered are top down and bottom up. Top-down design generates abstract systems design, broken down into software subsystems of programs and data structures. Bottom-up construction assembles physical resources into networks that run programs and communicate data. The software engineering process designs application systems from the top down and builds them from the bottom up.

Another way to express this is to consider that automated information systems exist at the intersection of a top-down perspective that describes abstract logical design and a bottom-up view of concrete physical implementation. The top-down approach deals with functional business information systems (e.g., payroll, order entry, etc.) and the bottom-up approach deals with programs and data on networked hardware and software systems.

This creates an ambiguity that commonly leads to confusion over which view is meant when referring to systems, for example, identifying systems for a security assessment. Do we mean the logical business function or the software and hardware that implement it? Evaluating access controls on a distributed ERP application is not the same as evaluating access controls on the networked servers hosting it. The security practitioner must clearly understand and communicate which perspective is intended when the context does not sufficiently identify the reference to make it unambiguous.

Information security practitioners need to take both views into account. Effective security programs must consider the value at risk, which can really only be determined based on the business functions expressed in the top-down perspective, and the cost of protecting the information assets, which depends on the implementation details embodied in the bottom-up view. The challenge is to secure applications by incorporating security as an integral part of the engineering process that develops and integrates both the top-down design and the bottom-up implementation of application systems.

There are also two phases of an application system's life during which different security concerns should be considered. Most commonly, application systems security is focused on the application during production operations, as this is when the application is performing its function of generating value (and thus, where it spends most of its lifetime). The development of application systems is generally considered separately, more as a production application of development tools and systems than in the context of the application being developed. This may minimize several important concerns. For one thing, security breaches during development may disclose or introduce vulnerabilities in the application itself ("dumpster diving" is an exploit that may target development documentation to identify vulnerabilities to be attacked in the application system product). For another thing, the development process may interact with production operations during design, testing, and deployment in ways that create or expose vulnerabilities in the production environment. For those reasons, application development should be considered in conjunction with the operational application systems by security practitioners concerned with the security of such systems. This is particularly challenging because the nature of development organizations and activities is distinctly different from production operations. It may be best to avoid tackling security issues in the development environment head-on and instead cooperatively team with developers to focus on improving security of the resulting application systems, while also seeking to indirectly improve development environment security (awareness and influence will be more effective with the developer personalities than with direct authority).

APPLICATION SYSTEMS COMPONENTS

Application systems may be comprised of a tremendous variety of components or subsystems, each of which introduces its own particular issues and concerns regarding security. In addition, the relationships and interactions among components also introduce further security complications. Developers who might be ignorant of security considerations may overlook or underestimate the importance of these issues. The security practitioner should be aware of the nature of major components that frequently comprise application systems, and have some acquaintance with the security issues that might be associated with them.

A superficial survey of the various components associated with applications systems is provided in this section, as an introduction to the many aspects that need to be considered both by application developers and security practitioners. The full range of components potentially comprising application systems includes hardware and firmware, operating system components (kernel, drivers, memory management), process management software (loader, scheduler, termination handler, core dumper), file system, command interpreter (shell), utilities, system runtime environment (environment variables, ports, configuration parameters), network protocol stacks, database software (e.g., SQL); user interfaces (graphical user interfaces [GUIs], command shells), help systems, runtime systems (language support libraries, object management systems), development tools (compilers, source management tools, profilers, debuggers, linkers, diagnostics), console management tools (backup utilities, remote administration packages, configuration management and remote deployment facilities, load managers, event loggers, tools, user account managers), and the organizational environment (management,

operations personnel, users, developers, vendor support staff, etc.).

The foundation for any system is the hardware used to implement it. Unfortunately, there are often features designed into the hardware to support security that are not utilized within the systems and application software. Sometimes the features are ignored by the software environment; others are more or less fully supported by the basic system software, but hidden or unutilized in other software components. Some hardware provides extremely flexible features that are normally utilized in a standard fashion, but can be used in other ways. This may camouflage security risks, because many users and technical staff may be unaware of the potential for alternative usages. An example is network interface cards (NICs) for Ethernet, which implement a media access control (MAC) address that is hard-coded by the manufacturer and encodes the manufacturer ID. However, the Ethernet chips used in some NIC cards allow the MAC address to be set to other arbitrary values by running software, which could introduce unrecognized security vulnerabilities in some systems.

Most intelligent hardware devices employ embedded firmware implementing the necessary system processing and control features. In the case of stand-alone network hardware, this firmware may embody the entire special purpose operating system required to install, configure, operate, maintain, and manage the device. General purpose computers incorporate firmware to extend basic hardware functions; for example, the NIC card MAC address functionality previously described is implemented by a combination of hardware and firmware. Differing firmware revision levels may introduce inconsistent security features, either fixing previously discovered vulnerabilities or introducing new ones. (A pseudo-scientific law of computer programming states that fixing any bug simply replaces it with two smaller bugs!) Firmware configuration management introduces potential security vulnerabilities. An example of the security vulnerabilities associated with firmware features would be the viruses that rewrite the firmware in the boot ROM to substitute virus code.

Operating system software provides functions to extend the basic hardware environment to provide more conveniently usable features for general purpose uses. The major operating system software consists of kernel implementing I/O facilities, memory management, CPU scheduling, device drivers, file system code, and process management (loader, scheduler, termination handler, and perhaps a core dumper). The basic facilities to support user authentication, authorization, and access control, or privileges and protections, are provided by operating systems functions. In addition, the associated command interpreters (or shell) and utilities may be considered part of the operating system, although the distinction between bundled and unbundled system components becomes very indistinct in this area. This feature is often exploited by intruders who replace bundled system components with modified versions to cover their tracks or introduce additional vulnerabilities. The operating system environment is often considered as separate and distinct from applications systems components, although it really is an essential element determining the fundamental security characteristics presented to the application system. Many security problems result from attacks that exploit vulnerabilities in applications or utilities to break out of the software function, to gain access to unintended and unrestricted operating systems capabilities. The capabilities exposed to such exploits are determined by how the application systems developers have utilized the underlying operating system features, but generally they are very significant concerns for the security practitioner.

Network protocols are an essential element of distributed systems, generally following the layered architecture made famous by the ISO Open System Interconnection protocol stack model. Internet protocols based on TCP/IP have become ubiquitous, but other protocol models still are used, although less widely. Many older protocols that once used an entirely proprietary stack have substituted TCP/IP for lower layers while retaining their distinct higher-level functional interfaces. There are many security concerns associated with network protocols. The criticality of their functions and their nature as communications media make them especially attractive targets for attacks, both as an end objective (e.g., denial of service, data theft) and as a stepping stone (e.g., worm vectors, relay systems). Because of this, network security is a separate specialized field, but the dependency on network protocols by distributed applications systems forces consideration of protocols as an important factor relevant to application security. The tight integration of network protocols with local I/O in some modern operating systems makes it easy to inject malicious input from remote sources. This is exploited by attacks, such as relatively low-level buffer overflows and higher-level cross-site scripting attacks. Network protocols are extremely flexible and must be carefully considered for potentially dangerous interactions with applications systems. This is one reason that it is imperative to ensure that any protocols received by a system must be properly handled (i.e., no unnecessary open ports listening for TCP/IP input, and all services on required ports properly configured for security).

GUIs are commonly used for interactive applications, utilities, and commands in modern systems. It is important to keep in mind that many systems incorporate software that uses command line interfaces, either because they were developed before GUIs were so common (legacy code), or because command lines are more convenient for expert users and automated scripting.

Such hidden nonGUI interfaces may provide targets for attackers, especially using network protocols to inject malicious input. Developers of new programs providing such interfaces for scripting convenience may assume that all input will come from local (and thus trusted) sources, and therefore not provide careful input validation and buffer checking, thus creating potential vulnerabilities to remote attackers or malicious local users. Because system designers frequently differentiate user interfaces as front-end GUIs from back-end processing of application business logic, this should be an area of particular concern for application systems security.

Database software, such as SQL processors, is an essential component of many application systems, and, as such, must be a major security concern. SQL packages may themselves be subsystems, including multiple components, and the interaction between these components may have important security implications. For example, the SQL Slammer worm exploited vulnerability in an SQL component interface in order to cause malicious commands to be executed by other system components. This vulnerability was present not only in stand-alone SQL servers, but also in embedded database components hidden within packaged application systems.

There is a help system provided with most modern application systems and GUIs, to provide context-specific assistance to the application users. This is not normally considered a security concern and has not been an attractive target for exploits. There is a slight possibility that the components used to provide application help could have vulnerabilities that might be subject to some attacks, but this seems fairly insignificant. A more significant concern might be the potential for inappropriate disclosure of information through context-specific help facilities, especially if the help facilities also provide an interface to remote diagnostic and support tools. In general, this area is probably not a major application systems security concern, but at the same time it should not be completely forgotten.

The run-time execution environment within a system consists of the various parameters that are used to set variable values controlling system functions; for example, the IP address of a networked host. Many of these configuration parameters are stored in some nonvolatile format (e.g., parameter files) and then used to initialize values for dynamic elements of the system. The configuration files may be read and interpreted by a script processor (e.g., through the command shell) or directly by the associated program itself. Sometimes the values are stored in environment variables to make them accessible over a longer period of time within the executing system environment. The contents of environment variables and configuration files are subject to attack and may provide avenues for exploits. These features are provided by the operating system and are subject to whatever access controls are implemented in that system and used by the developers of the particular features. An important issue regarding system privilege and protection mechanisms is that developers often find finely granular mechanisms cumbersome and inconvenient and thus may use shortcuts, such as elevated privilege or less protection, to reduce implementation efforts at the expense of security. Such features are usually considered internal details that are not exposed to external threats and thus may not be protected beyond "security through obscurity," which may leave vulnerabilities such as the potential for scripts to inject malicious commands (frequently executed with elevated privilege or undesirable account context). Also, inappropriate modification of these component values could well result in denial of service. The application systems security concerns associated with these features are certainly significant, but the relative obscurity of any vulnerabilities helps to moderate the priority of those concerns.

Modern software engineering seeks to abstract logical representations of function from the concrete (albeit virtual) resources used to implement those functions. As a consequence, application development tools such as object-oriented environments include extensive runtime support, which is often hidden even from the application developers. From a software engineering perspective, this is desirable as a means of hiding complexity, but from a security perspective this has the undesirable consequence of hiding dependencies and possible vulnerabilities. Object reuse is a major priority for reducing development costs, and this requires the most general and least constrained implementations. As a result, bounds and value checking may be compromised or complicated because the specific validation requirements often depend on the particular usage. It is not possible to effectively perform some validation (such as buffer size) external to the module or object using the values, but it may be more complicated to implement an effective check at the site of usage for arguments supplied externally by an invoking object or module. The security concerns in this area seem to be primarily focused on denial-of-service possibilities, although there should also be some awareness of dependencies on external vendors to provide secure components and eliminate vulnerabilities in their object management and compiler runtime systems. A related area of concern is the use of dynamic linked libraries in some systems, which provides a potential vulnerability for substitution of components incorporating malicious code in place of the original trusted components. This could be utilized by "root kits" installed to further exploit a compromised system. Application systems would be vulnerable to this exploit, although it may be more likely to target bundled host system components that are more widely known to attackers.

Management and operational support tools are essential components associated with any significant application systems, especially in a distributed network environment that may use "lights out" data center practices. The phrase "lights out" refers to data centers running 24/7 without being staffed 24/7, depending on automated management tools to allow remote administration by remote operations centers with online monitoring, or on-call operations personnel alerted using pagers. Event loggers, reporting and filtering tools, centralized monitors, and remote access to management consoles are all elements of the management systems used to support online operations for network systems delivering critical applications. These components are especially critical because they are vital to maintaining security of applications systems and are complex and subject to vulnerabilities themselves. The good news is that management systems are frequently supplied by major vendors who recognize the critical role of such systems and are committed to their security. The bad news is that such powerful management systems may introduce vulnerabilities, especially to application dependencies (the most common denial-of-service attacks are those inadvertently perpetrated by system and network administrators making mistakes during routine operations). Other management and operational support tools include backup utilities, load managers, deployment and configuration management tools, and user account managers. Such tools are obviously significant security concerns, but those concerns may not have received the same scrutiny for isolated functional utilities as they do for centralized console managers. For example, in small organizations or for less-visible applications, backups may be routinely performed but never tested. Failure modes need to be considered as potential security issues, so that a network glitch during a remote upgrade does not result in a complete denial of service (such considerations highlight the indistinct boundary between security and application design and implementation). The security practitioner concerned with application systems security needs to be very aware of and concerned about these tools, and may want to enlist operations and development staff to cooperatively review and address security implications in these areas.

As previously mentioned, applications systems development presents a unique environment with its own set of security considerations. Development tools include source management packages, compilers, linkers, profilers, debuggers, diagnostics, and many other utilities. In addition, developers and QA testers may need the ability to manipulate the running system environment in ways that production operations and ordinary users do not require (e.g., to set up or recover from specific test scenarios), and thus may be routinely granted access to use privileges that present security concerns. Because of this, development systems and accounts may be particularly attractive and valuable targets for attackers. There may also be vulnerabilities exposed in the development environment and process that are not present in production operations; for example, if samples of production data are used for testing without ensuring that appropriate protection is provided for sensitive content. This problem may be exacerbated once applications systems move to production, because problems during production may require access to sensitive data or even to production systems. Normally, a well-managed development organization will be effectively isolated from production to minimize security exposures, but this discipline comes at a cost and is especially subject to compromise when problems occur. Such situations require heightened awareness of security issues by all personnel involved (and, of course, entail a heightened stress level that makes everyone less receptive to reminders, highlighting the importance of cultivating routine awareness of good practice).

Finally, no application system functions in a vacuum. Application systems exist to serve human purposes in some form or fashion. The interactions with humans occur within an organizational environment and culture that defines the fundamental security context that must be considered by any effective practitioner. The organization includes management, users, operations personnel, developers, and external personnel, such as vendor support staff. Each has their own function and may place their job as a higher priority than security, so it is human nature that they may take shortcuts for convenience or intentionally or unintentionally compromise security in other ways. The security practitioner must remember that the goal of security is to protect the utility of systems to the organization, which requires promoting awareness of security considerations by all personnel. Most importantly, the practitioner must remember that the greatest utility is likely not the most secure system, but one with carefully considered security policies and practices that are appropriate to the system and organization. The reason for cooperatively integrating application systems security concerns into the development process is to properly establish the most appropriate security posture and to effectively implement it.

TECHNICAL CONCERNS FOR APPLICATION SYSTEMS

Some specific technical areas frequently cause security issues within application systems. This may be caused by the characteristics of the technical features involved (difficulty of use or complexity of feature), the nature of the use, or the limitations of application developers. Some particular concerns are input validation (filter for illegal values as well as protecting for buffer overflows), memory management (especially buffer overflow protection, but also stale data violating confidentiality, etc.), authentication/authorization/access (AAA) control (application implementations often trade strength for user convenience), session management (HTTP is stateless, so cookies are used to provide persistent context with extremely weak AAA), and configuration management (change control and QA to prevent insecure software in production). Security practitioners need to focus attention on these issues during design, development, and testing, to avoid the costly problems surfacing later in the life cycle. Designing sound solutions in these areas will help make implementation and testing easier, benefiting the entire team.

Application packages provided to third parties (including separate organizational entities within the same corporate umbrella) should specifically identify dependencies on platform and external package features in sufficient detail to understand security issues associated with those dependencies (including but not limited to potential denial-of-service attacks). Application providers should disclose such details and their clients or customers should insist on disclosure. Internally within development organizations, engineers should document, test, and monitor security of all dependency interfaces.

APPLICATION SYSTEMS DEVELOPMENT LIFE CYCLE

The existence of such application systems follows a very well-understood life cycle, initially determining and specifying functional requirements for the system to be implemented. This initial functional design phase moves into an implementation design phase, which determines the technical details that will be used to implement the system. The implementation design proceeds into a development process that further refines and arranges details of technical components to create the requisite functionality required by the initial functional specifications to answer business requirements. There is an iterative process of development and testing for both individual components and the entire system as implementation progresses, to assure satisfactory quality before release for production operations.

When the QA function determines that testing has found that requirements have been successfully met for satisfactory production operations, the application system is released for deployment to production. This stage of the systems development life cycle is sometimes called release engineering, for obvious reasons. Production deployment may be a simple transition of starting to use a new system, or it may require a very extensive process of parallel testing and progressive migration of critical functions onto the new implementation with pro-visions for falling back to previously used systems in the event of problems. The deployment into production requires updating configuration management systems used to control production systems, and often uses auto-mated tools to install the appropriate configuration on production systems automatically. There may be provi-sions for backing out of releases, especially in extremely critical production operations, to ensure that any new release does not cause unforeseen problems (e.g., the scale of production traffic may be difficult to reproduce in QA, leaving the potential for unrecognized problems caused by volume over time).

Upon the ultimate completion of production deploy-ment, the application system enters routine production operations and maintenance. During this phase, require-ments may evolve (e.g., rules for regulatory compliance may change slightly) and new or unusual situations may reveal flaws in the design or implementation that were not caught before release. These occurrences will require some maintenance upgrades to the production application system, so production operations are often referred to as the maintenance phase of the system development life cycle. Any changes will normally require appropriate testing before release, and should follow release engineering procedures similar to major new systems.

Security practitioners concerned with disaster recov-ery and business continuity planning need to be especially interested in the interaction of release engi-neering and deployment with configuration management and console operations tools. One powerful motivator for automating configuration changes and management is the impossibility of recovering to an unknown config-uration following any disaster! On a less dramatic scale, problems affecting routine system updates can have a costly ripple effect if the recovery from problems inter-feres with continuity of routine business operations. For example, if a network glitch interrupts the routine deployment of an automated update to a production server, the server may be left in an insecure state or simply unavailable until manual intervention restores a serviceable configuration. Preventing such situations (or recognizing and remedying them) is an opportunity to add value that will be beneficial to the entire organization.

Ultimately, the cycle ends when changing business requirements or technology motivate replacement or major enhancement of the production application sys-tem, and a new development cycle will be initiated, with deployment of the new system leading to replace-ment of its predecessor. Sometimes the functions provided by the application system will no longer be needed and the retirement of the system will not include any replacement. This situation can lead to legacy sys-tems becoming unused and forgotten but not removed,

with an increased risk that inattention will lead to insecurity.

INTEGRATING SECURITY INTO THE SYSTEMS LIFE CYCLE

The introduction to this entry discussed the historical approach of information security programs, focusing efforts and resources bottom up, on technical compo-nents rather than taking a holistic systems-oriented view of the problem. This approach is appropriate during the operational phase of the systems life cycle, but as the discussion about economic factors showed, retrofitting security with patches after system deployment is woe-fully expensive as well as fundamentally ineffective because of the nature of systems themselves. The para-digm shift suggested at the beginning of this entry focuses on integrating security into all phases of the sys-tems development life cycle as a way to provide more cost-effective improvements in application system security.

Treating security as a separate issue assigned to an isolated organizational unit creates a situation in which the security function too often ends up the antagonist of developers in the application systems development pro-cess. Because the development team goal is to ship the product as soon as possible, imposing security require-ments on the implementation design seems a costly impediment to achieving that goal. However, as we have seen, the development team and the information security practitioner share a common interest in deploying robust systems, because availability and integrity are funda-mental requirements for a functional system. Confidentiality is also a common interest, but based on separate business issues of competition, compliance, customer care (or privacy), which might be called the "four Cs" of confidentiality.

Benefits from including security in the entire system development life cycle start with the early top-down engineering design process, by helping to design robust systems more cost-effectively. As previously discussed, system development economics benefit greatly by meet-ing requirements earlier in the development process instead of reworking designs to fix shortcomings later. Presenting security requirements as metrics of robust quality early in the process motivates good practice in a cooperative rather than an antagonistic fashion. Throughout the development process, security considera-tions can be used to focus attention on critical aspects of the application system to improve product quality while avoiding costs for later patchwork. Overall, secu-rity can be an enabler of better performance by development teams, improving quality without impacting schedule, by better identifying and addressing critical concerns affecting robust quality.

Different stages in the application systems development life cycle have different security requirements and present different security challenges. Requirement documents and functional specifications are frequently housed on centralized document management or groupware systems, so security administration is not particularly challenging. Development hosts often present a particularly challenging technical environment, because creative systems developers are often inclined to push the limits both organizationally as well as technically. There is often friction between system administrators responsible for development systems and the developers using those systems, especially when powerful desktop workstations are used to facilitate development in a centrally managed network environment. Systems used for testing and quality assurance are usually much more cut-and-dried in their security requirements, because they normally should use environments identical to production as much as possible (exceptions should be clearly justified, perhaps by test management toolset requirements).

Deployment, or release engineering, is the interface and transition between development and production. Because they are responsible for moving system packages that have completed testing into production, security is a routine concern to which the users of these systems are well attuned. The security practitioner should keep in mind that these systems may not be monitored in the same way that production operations are monitored, although they would be high-value targets for an adversary seeking to inject malicious code into the production environment, or to simply disrupt production by causing unserviceable components to be released. Also, careful management of deployed configurations is an essential requirement for successful disaster recovery efforts, because it is impossible to recover to an unknown configuration.

The operations phase of the systems development life cycle is the usual focus of information security programs, so it is regarded as outside the scope of this entry except for one aspect. Failures occurring during production operations may require unusual diagnostic or emergency maintenance activities that force exceptions to normal operational security practices, or involve development or vendor personnel. These situations may cause unforeseen security implications, such as the potential exposure of confidential information contained in diagnostic files (e.g., core dumps) transmitted outside the normal security perimeter. Pressure to get corrections into production may lead to compromises in security, and such issues need to be carefully managed to ensure that such compromises are appropriate and not just convenient.

Security practitioners may find that system administrators and development managers share concerns over systems security issues, especially for development systems, and the most effective way to address those security concerns might be in the guise of organizational issues within the development team. For example, developers that use elevated privileges to bypass access control mechanisms during implementation may inadvertently introduce dependencies that are inappropriate to the production environment. These are subtle and costly problems, because they may not be discovered until much later in the QA process, or even after production release, necessitating costly correction efforts. Aligning security concerns with project management issues in this way, allows the practitioner to develop a recognition of the security function as supporting important values for the entire application systems development organization.

One way to classify security vulnerabilities is to identify the stage in the systems development life cycle in which the vulnerability is created, as a way to help in focussing appropriate attention on correcting vulnerabilities. This also allows defect tracking to assign responsibility if a flaw is discovered in the implementation. For example, input validation should be considered a design requirement, and thus included as a part of the functional specifications implemented in development. QA testing is commonly driven from functional specifications, so the discovery of a vulnerability because input validation is lacking might be a specification failure or a combination of implementation and testing failures. This feedback can be used for process improvement within the development organization, and may often be provided by defect tracking tools. Integrating security concerns into this feedback process is a way to align security efforts with the organizational efforts to continuously improve the development process and results.

INFORMATION CRITICALITY MATRIX TOOL FOR SECURITY EVALUATION

Disclaimer: The National Security Agency has neither reviewed nor approved the following material. It is purely the author's understanding of material obtained from a variety of sources, and his logical extensions of that material.

The InfoSec Assessment Methodology (IAM) developed by the National Security Agency (NSA) provides many useful features. One element of the IAM is particularly promising as a tool for improving application systems security and providing benefits of value to development schedules and results. This section will summarize the IAM, introduce the Information

Criticality Matrix used in the IAM, and suggest extensions of that matrix for use in application systems development.

One of the roles for the NSA is responsibility for information assurance for information infrastructures critical to U.S. national security interests, through the Information Assurance Directorate (IAD). One NSA/IAD program is the InfoSec Assessment Training and Rating Program (IATRP). According to the NSA Web site (http://www.nsa.gov/isso/iam/index.htm), NSA developed the IATRP, a two-part (training and rating) program, for the benefit of government organizations trying to raise their InfoSec posture in general or specifically trying to comply with the Presidential Decision Directive-63 requirement for vulnerability assessments. The IAM is a detailed and systematic way of examining information security programs.

The IAM framework specifically provides for customized extensions to accommodate particular situations having needs that do not fit or go beyond the standard IAM requirements, with the provision that any modifications does not reduce the level of assurance required to be IAM compliant. Much of the IAM codifies accepted practices, describing project organization, standard activities, required elements, and minimum performance expectations for acceptable results. A key feature is the use of a matrix to identify information and systems and structure measurement of the criticality of security for those components. Consistent with common information security practice, the IAM is primarily focused on the needs of operational organizations and their processes rather than their downstream products. This entry proposes extending the framework and techniques used in the IAM by applying them in coordination with the application systems life cycle.

To summarize the IAM, it provides a framework for projects evaluating information systems security programs. The purpose is to review the information system security posture of a specified operational system to assure that the security program is appropriate for the system requirements. It does not encompass technical vulnerability assessments, such as penetration testing or network mapping. There are three phases to the IAM: 1) the preassessment phase; 2) an onsite activities phase; and 3) a postassessment phase. The preassessment phase entails project planning and preparation, including organizational agreements, establishing the scope and bounds of the project, reviewing information about the systems being assessed, reviewing existing security program documentation, and planning and preparing for the onsite activities. The onsite activities gather data to explore and validate information from the preassessment phase and provide initial analysis and feedback to the organization responsible for the systems being assessed. The postassessment phase finalizes the analysis by incorporating results of the onsite activities with information provided during the preassessment phase, and produces a final report.

The IAM specifies a set of baseline categories that are normally reviewed by a compliant evaluation project, unless particular items are specifically excluded by agreement with the assessment client. Any categories that are omitted must be identified and justified, with the requirement that the omission does not reduce the level of assurance provided by the assessment. The standard IAM baseline information categories are InfoSec documentation, InfoSec roles and responsibilities, identification and authorization, account management, session controls, external connectivity, telecommunications, auditing, virus protection, contingency planning, maintenance, configuration management, backups, labeling, media sanitization/disposal, physical environment, personnel security, training, and awareness. Additional categories may optionally be added to accommodate specific requirements of the particular systems being evaluated (e.g., encryption), or to provide finer granularity. For example, incident response might be considered part of InfoSec roles and responsibilities and intrusion detection might be included under auditing, or they might be broken out as separate categories.

The purpose of the IAM is to ensure compliance with federal law mandating appropriate security for automated information systems at sensitive but unclassified (SBU) level or above. One purpose of the preassessment phase is to "identify subject systems, including system boundaries." This requires addressing both logical and physical systems, along the lines discussed in the section of this entry discussing application systems technology. Because a logical application system may encompass many physical systems, each of which processes a subset of the system information, it is very useful to have a means of establishing the security requirements for each individual component of the system. The subset may be a particular piece of information or a particular piece of physical equipment. In practice, the security requirements are determined by the nature of the information involved, so the equipment security requirements are derived from the security requirements of the information processed by the particular equipment. The "information criticality matrix" is a tool invented by Mr. Wilbur J. Hildebrand, Jr., NSA's Chief of InfoSec Assessment Services, for use in the IAM to determine the security requirements for particular items of information.

The "information criticality matrix" structures the determination of information security requirements by listing the information elements within the logical system and associated impact values for security attributes. The IAM uses confidentiality, integrity, and availability as the three required standard attributes, and requires that any change to this list be clearly documented. For example, one potential addition might be nonrepudiation, and it would be appropriate to justify the requirement for including it as a separate critical attribute. The result of this matrix provides an initial determination of information security requirements for the overall system, and also values to be used in further refinement of security requirements. The first refinement is the analysis of logical subsystems by selecting the entries for the specific information handled by those subsystems and using them to determine information security requirements for the subsystem. Another refinement is to determine the information security requirement for physical components, based on the information security requirements of all the information (or subsystems) processed by the component. These refinements provide the basis for evaluating whether the information security programs for the affected systems are appropriate for the security requirements of the information contained therein.

CRITICALITY MATRIX USE IN APPLICATION SYSTEMS DEVELOPMENT

The IAM criticality matrix provides a tool for initially determining information security requirements from a top-down logical systems perspective and then deriving security requirements for the bottom-up systems implementation. This can be productively applied to the development of application systems in several ways. One powerful extension would be to generalize the information resources evaluated using the criticality matrix to include functional processing components within the logical system design, so that the importance of particular software modules can be determined. This not only serves to focus security requirements, it provides value of great benefit to the systems development project in general, because availability and integrity measure, not just security requirements, but overall importance for the particular functions evaluated. The ability to better measure the importance of functional modules is very beneficial for the systems development project in general because it helps to guide project planning and management in areas, such as resource allocation, design attention, testing requirements, defect tracking, etc.

Another use of the criticality matrix to integrate security engineering into the application systems development process would be to focus more attention on addressing technical vulnerabilities (such as buffer overflows) in areas where they would affect critical components versus areas that are relatively less critical. In some environments, this might help guide management decisions about whether rapid prototyping is an appropriate tool or whether critical components might require additional development attention to ensure

appropriate production-quality systems are released for deployment. This provides another opportunity for security practitioners to develop a cooperative relationship as productive contributors generating value important to the application systems development team.

The criticality matrix could even be used to analyze the information security requirements of an application development project over the course of the system development life cycle, and thus to better focus efforts to provide appropriate security for systems used by development projects. Security requirements for systems housing functional specifications and design documents will be different from those of systems used for implementation development, testing, or deployment; and some of those security profiles may be different, depending on the security requirements of the application systems involved. The criticality matrix provides a tool to facilitate consistent evaluation of those security requirements, so that the development projects are neither burdened nor exposed inappropriately.

The criticality matrix can be used in different ways during different stages of the systems development life cycle. During application systems design, it can be used to set security and quality requirements for project features and for project planning and management. During development, it can be used to set appropriate standards for production implementation quality, source management, and feature completion. During QA, it can be used to focus test efforts most effectively, design test strategies, determine the scope and coverage of testing, and track defects according to importance and priority. In operations, it can guide configuration management and deployment planning, and rollout; prioritize bug tracking; and map defects into the systems development life cycle quality and security matrix to provide feedback for process improvement.

FUTURE DIRECTIONS

This entry has surveyed some information security considerations pertinent to application systems development, reviewed a number of areas related to application systems and the technical and organizational development environments, and described a novel tool for incorporating security engineering into the application development process. In the course of these topics, several suggestions for subsequent research and development were mentioned. This section reviews some possible directions for subsequent efforts.

There are a number of automated tools in use for managing systems development projects, automating testing, tracking defects, and configuration management and deployment. Incorporation of support for security engineering facilities, such as the criticality matrix, could be a useful enhancement to such tools. Similarly, intrusion detection systems and management console tools used for systems and network administration of production operations could be enhanced to use the IAM criticality matrix as a factor in prioritizing alerts for all events based on system criticality. It seems especially useful to have configuration management systems provide alerts for discrepancies, and management consoles to report those alerts, with severity settings keyed to the criticality of the subject system, as an adjunct to other IDS monitoring facilities. Undoubtedly, experience will suggest even more and better possibilities in the years ahead.

ACKNOWLEDGMENTS

The author would like to express grateful appreciation and thanks to Wilbur J. Hildebrand, Dr. Peter S. Tippett, and Jerry Weinberg.

REFERENCE

1.   http://turing.acm.org/technews/articles/2003-5/0312w. html#item8.

BIBLIOGRAPHY

1.   InfoSec assessment methodology, http://cisse.info/ CISSE%20J/2001/RKSm.pdf.
2.   Defect costs, http://www.cebase.org/www/AboutCebase/ News/top-10-defects.htmlhttp://www.jrothman.com/ Papers/Costtofixdefect.html.
3.   Systems development life cycle, http://www.usdoj.gov/ jmd/irm/life cycle/table.htm.

Artificial Intelligence

Jianhua Chen

Computer Science Department, Louisiana State University, Baton Rouge, Louisiana, U.S.A.

Abstract

Artificial intelligence (AI) is a multidisciplinary subject, typically studied as a research area within Computer Science. AI study aims at achieving a good understanding of the nature of intelligence and building intelligent agents that are computational systems demonstrating intelligent behavior. AI has been developed over more than 50 years. The topics studied in AI are quite broad, ranging from knowledge representation and reasoning, knowledge-based systems, machine learning and data mining, natural language processing, to search, image processing, robotics, and intelligent information systems. Numerous successful AI systems have been deployed in real-life applications in engineering, finance, science, health care, education, and service sectors. AI research has also significantly impacted the subject area of Library and Information Science (LIS), helping to develop smart Web search engines, personalized news filters, and knowledge-sharing and indexing systems. This entry briefly outlines the main topics studied in AI, samples some typical successful AI applications, and discusses the cross-fertilization between AI and LIS.

INTRODUCTION

This entry is about artificial intelligence (AI),[1–4] a multidisciplinary subject, typically studied within Computer Science. Ever since the dawn of civilization, humans have constantly asked questions regarding mechanisms of human intelligence. Human's abilities to think, reason, learn, act to achieve goals, adapt to changing environment, etc., which are central to intelligence, fascinated philosophers, scientists for centuries. There is a long history of human endeavor in unveiling the mystery of human intelligence and building artificial systems capable of doing smart things like humans do. The early works in understanding human intelligence focused on studying how humans "know" the world around them and how the human thinking and reasoning are performed. As early as 2300 years ago, Aristotle, a great Greek philosopher, studied the laws of thought and proper ways of reasoning. In his work "Prior Analytics,"[5] Aristotle defines syllogism, a kind of logical argument, which allows deduction of a valid conclusion from two given premises. For example, from the premises that "All men are mortal" (major premise) and "Socrates is a man" (minor premise), one can infer by syllogism that "Socrates is mortal." Over the long time after Aristotle, logicians such as Freg, Russell, Leibniz, Godel, Tarski, and others, have fully developed formal logic systems such as propositional logic and predicate logic, which formalize the thinking and reasoning process of humans. Moreover, such formal logic systems open up the possibility of being implemented on computational systems.

Endeavors of constructing mechanical/electronic artifacts to do calculation, concept manipulation, reasoning, and game playing can be found in many eras of human history. Such efforts contribute significantly to the foundations of AI. For more discussions on the foundations of AI, see section 1.1 in Russell and Norvig[1] and section 1.1 in Luger[2]. Around the twenty-sixth century B.C., the Chinese invented the abacus, the first mechanical tool in human history for performing arithmetic calculations (section 1.1.1 in Lugar[2]). Similar calculating equipments were also discovered in Roman relics, in India, and in Egypt from ancient times. In 1623, Wilhelm Schickard, a German mathematician, created a calculating clock for addition and subtraction. Soon after in 1642, the famous calculating machine Pascaline was created by Blaise Pascal, a great French philosopher and mathematician. Pascaline is capable of addition and subtraction with carries and borrows. Pascal noted,[6] "The arithmetical machine produces effects which approach nearer to thought than all the actions of animals." Gottfried Wilhelm Leibniz, a great German philosopher and mathematician, believed that human reasoning could be reduced to mechanical calculations of some kind, and thus one could use the calculation results to find out who is right and who is wrong in cases of conflicting opinions. He wrote,[7]

The only way to rectify our reasonings is to make them as tangible as those of the Mathematicians, so that we can find our error at a glance, and when there are disputes among persons, we can simply say: Let us calculate [calculemus], without further ado, to see who is right.

Encyclopedia of Information Systems and Technology, DOI: 10.1081/E-EIST-120043680

He envisioned that a machine could be devised for automatic derivation of scientific knowledge by deductive inference. In the late 1950s and early 1960s, amid the initial enthusiastic development of AI, Arthur Samuel developed[8] a computer program that learns to play the game of Checkers, which could learn to improve its game-playing skills by playing against a copy of itself, playing with human players, and storing good moves from Master game books. In 1997, IBM's Deep Blue Chess program,[9] with a combination of parallel processing, fast search, and AI ideas, scored a historical win against world Chess champion Kasparov.

As can be seen from these brief descriptions, the philosophical roots of AI can be traced back to over 2300 years ago. The past 200–300 years have witnessed a rapid development in mathematics and science. The formalization of mathematics and science has laid the intellectual foundations of AI. AI as a multidisciplinary area draws on the development in diverse disciplines in addition to philosophy and mathematics, including economics, psychology, linguistics, control theory and cybernetics, and neurosciences. In particular, the birth of the electronic computer in the 1940s was instrumental and crucial to making AI a viable distinctive scientific discipline within Computer Science. The availability of digital computers in late 1940s made it possible for researchers at that time to write computer programs for playing games, performing logical reasoning, and problem-solving. Researchers could then empirically study the computer's performance and analyze whether the computer demonstrated some kind of intelligence. In 1956, at Dartmouth College in Massachusetts, a two-month summer workshop was held[11] and attended by 10 prominent researchers of AI, including John McCarthy, Marvin Minsky, Claude Shannon, Arthur Samuel, Allen Newell, and Herbert Simon. The workshop was a milestone that signified the birth of AI—a name suggested by McCarthy and agreed by all the attendees of the workshop.

In the early 1950s, researchers and the general public were all fascinated by the possibilities made prominent by the advent of the electronic computer era. People asked numerous questions about whether computers could be intelligent, e.g., do things that used to require human intelligence, what is intelligence, what would it take for us to consider a computer to be intelligent. Objecting views were raised by many to the idea that indeed a computer could be intelligent, given sufficient storage memory and processing power. Alan Turing, a great British mathematician and considered by many as the founding father of Computer Science/AI, proposed in 1950[10] the famous Turing test. Turing proposed to replace the question "Can machines think" by the question of whether a digital computer can pass the Turing test. In the Turing test, a human interrogator converses in natural language with a computer and a human

participant, which are located in rooms separated from the interrogator. The questions from the interrogator and the answers from the computer/human participant are transmitted via online typed messages (similar to today's computer-relayed talk or instant messaging). After conversations for 5 min, the human interrogator needs to identify which one is the computer/human participant. According to Turing, a computer should be considered as "intelligent" if it passes the Turing test, i.e., if it fools the human interrogator over 30% of the time in many repeated trials. The central idea behind the Turing test is that a system is deemed intelligent if it can behave like humans. This conceptualization of intelligence (behaving like humans) makes it easier to discern intelligence because one does NOT need to know the inner workings of a system to judge whether the system is intelligent or not—it is sufficient to just look at the system's behavior. Turing predicted that by the year 2000, man could program computers with large storage capacities (109 units) so well that the computers would easily pass the test with an average human interrogator. Although his prediction was not realized, the discipline of AI certainly has achieved great advancement over the 58 years from the proposal of the Turing test.

After over 50 years of development, AI has become an industry and a gradually maturing subject. Theories of AI—computational theories of intelligence—have advanced significantly, with many flourishing research topic areas developed and numerous successful AI systems deployed in real-world applications. Today, we enjoy the great benefits of modern computer and information technology in our daily lives, many with important AI components. We have smart online shopping tools that can recommend suitable products catering to the specific preferences of customers; personalized message filtering tools that help to sort out spam e-mails; robots that perform (or assist doctors to perform) medical procedures with great precision; intelligent online information tools that allow us to know what is going on in the world with the click of a mouse and to obtain, create, and share knowledge efficiently. We have seen the great miracle of electronic computers and AI that our great intellectual pioneers have envisioned, and much more. Today, AI is more exciting than ever as a research area, playing an increasingly important role in the age of information technology. See Buchanan[11] for a brief account of AI history.

The rest of the entry is organized as follows. In the next section, the major topics of AI will be briefly described. Section on "Artificial Intelligence and Application" presents some sample applications of AI, along with a brief discussion of the impact of AI on LIS, and is followed by the conclusion. Readers interested to know more about the AI subject can consult leading text books[1–3] and other online sources.[4]

TOPICS OF STUDIES IN AI

In this section we survey some representative topics of AI study. Since AI is a very big and broad field, it is impossible to make a complete coverage of all topics of AI within the limited space of one entry. The omission of a topic in this entry is by no means an indication that the topic is not important.

Heuristic Search and Problem Solving

Heuristic search is a topic studied since the early days of AI. Researchers realized long ago that many AI problems could be viewed as a search problem. The concept of problem-solving as state space search was introduced in the 1950s.[12] In problem-solving, each possible scenario related to the task at hand is formulated as a state, and the entire collection of all possible states is called the state space, which contains the initial state of the problem, and the desired solution state (often called goal state). A state S has a number of neighboring states $N(S)$, which could be reached from state S in one step (by applying some state-transition operators). A state space could then be modeled as a (possibly weighted) graph with nodes representing states and edges connecting neighboring states. Given this view, solving a problem amounts to searching the state space (graph) to find a sequence of states that leads from the initial problem state to the goal state. For example, in computer checkers game-playing, each feasible board configuration constitutes a state in the search space. The initial state corresponds to the initial game board configuration and a board configuration in which the player (the computer) has won the game is one of the many goal states. A move of a piece in board configuration S transits it into a board configuration, which is a member of $N(S)$. The problem of playing the checkers game successfully against an expert human player is reduced to finding a sequence of moves (states) in response to the human player's moves such that the final state is a winning state for the computer.

For most search problems with real-world application, the search space is huge (or even infinite). Any blind exhaustive search method (such as breadth-first search and depth-first search) would suffer from combinatorial explosion that renders such search impractical. How to efficiently search the state space becomes a critical issue if we want to build useful AI applications. Heuristic search methods have been developed by AI researchers[13] to efficiently search the state space and overcome combinatorial explosion. Typical heuristic search methods are based on using a heuristic evaluation function h to guide the search process. The best-known heuristic search algorithm is perhaps the $A*$ algorithm[14] for searching a weighted graph for shortest path from the starting node ns to the destination node nd. The algorithm maintains a list of open nodes and a list of closed nodes. Each open node n corresponds to an existing partial path $\langle ns, \dots, n \rangle$, which could be extended into a path from ns to nd via n. For each open node, a measure $f(n) = g(n) + h(n)$ is used to estimate the length of the shortest path from ns to nd via n, where $g(n)$ is the actual length of the path $\langle ns, \dots, n \rangle$ and $h(n)$ is the heuristic estimate for the length of the shortest path $\langle n, \dots, nd \rangle$. The $A*$ algorithm always selects from the open list the node n with the lowest $f(n)$ value, considers the neighbors of node n for expanding the existing partial path in search for the shortest path from ns to nd. It has been shown[14,15] that if the heuristic function h is admissible, namely, $h(n)$ is always an underestimate of the actual length of the shortest path from node n to nd, then the $A*$ algorithm is optimal in that it is guaranteed to find the shortest path from ns to nd. Various improvements of the $A*$ algorithm have been proposed in the literature, including memory bounded $A*$ (MA) and simple memory bounded $A*$ (SMA), etc.

In using heuristic search for problem solving for specific applications, the design of the heuristic function h is a nontrivial task. One has to carefully analyze the specific problem at hand, formulate the search problem, and choose the h function by considering characteristics of the problem to be solved.

Knowledge Representation and Automated Reasoning

An intelligent agent must "know" the world around it, have knowledge about how to achieve goals (namely, what actions are needed to bring about a desired outcome), and can infer useful information from what it already knows in making intelligent decisions. Therefore, an intelligent agent should be a knowledge-based agent, with the ability to represent knowledge and perform automated reasoning from its knowledge.

Knowledge representation research (KR)[16] studies and develops formal systems for representing knowledge in a knowledge base, whereas automated reasoning research[17] focuses on finding efficient algorithms for inference from a given knowledge base represented in some formalization. These two areas of study are closely related.

Logic-based formalism is perhaps the most commonly used knowledge representation form in AI systems. See Genesereth and Nilsson[18] for more discussions of logical foundations of AI. Under a logic-based knowledge representation scheme, an intelligent agent's knowledge base is a set Δ of logical sentences in the representation logic language, and the inference problem faced by the agent becomes the problem of deriving logical consequences of Δ using valid inference rules of the logic. Propositional logic and first-order logic are most frequently used in practice for knowledge representation and reasoning.

When using logic as a tool for knowledge representation, one has to first define the syntax of the language for the logic, which specifies the basic symbols, logical connectives, and rules to formulate well-formed expressions (well-formed formulas) in that logic. For example, in propositional logic, the basic symbols are propositional symbols (typically represented by uppercase letters such as P, Q, R), each representing a proposition that can be true or false. The logical connectives in propositional logic include, ∧, ∨, and ¬. So if P, Q are propositional symbols, then P ∧ Q, P ∨ Q and ¬P are all well-formed formulas in the logic.

A logic must define the semantics of the language. Intuitively, semantics defines the "meaning" of well-formed formulas. The semantics of a logic defines the truth value of each formula for each possible world. The truth value for any well-formed formula in a possible world is obtained compositionally from the truth value of the basic proposition symbols in that possible world. For example, consider a propositional logic with two proposition symbols P and Q, where P stands for the proposition "John is a professor at Harvard" and Q denotes the proposition "John lives in Boston." Here we have totally four possible worlds: {TT, TF, FT, FF}, where each possible world spells out the truth value assignment for P and Q, in that world. For example, the possible world "TF" tells us that P is true and Q is false in this world. Thus, in this world, the well-formed formula "P ∧ Q" will be assigned the truth value "false (F)" because "P ∧ Q" is true in a possible world if and only if both "P" and "Q" are true in that world.

Once the semantics of a logic is defined, we can use logic for the purpose of reasoning, namely, we can ask the question, "can we derive conclusion φ given our knowledge base Δ"? This is the problem of checking whether φ is a logical consequence of Δ—whether φ is true in all possible worlds in which Δ is true. Automated reasoning is responsible for this task. Automated reasoning research aims at finding efficient, valid inference algorithms to support derivation of logical consequences. For automated reasoning in propositional logic and first-order logic, AI researchers pioneered by Alan Robinson have developed the resolution inference rule[19] and many of its variants. Since the logical reasoning problem in propositional logic is essentially reduced to the satisfiability (SAT) problem, which is known to be computationally hard, many heuristic methods have been developed, which aim to find efficient solvers for the SAT problem.[20–22] The development of resolution-based inference in first-order logic and the drive for a unified language for declarative knowledge representation and automated reasoning have led to the logic

programming technique, hallmarked by the language PROLOG.[23] In using PROLOG, one represents knowledge by a PROLOG program, and automated reasoning is carried out by the PROLOG interpreter that essentially performs resolution.

Researchers have developed a plethora of nonmonotonic logics for representing commonsense knowledge in the 1980s and 1990s. The idea is based on the observation that human commonsense knowledge is not well represented by propositional or first-order logic, so something new needs to be developed. Among the various frameworks proposed, we have Reiter's Default Logic,[24] McCarthy's circumscription,[25] etc. The studies on nonmonotonic logics and reasoning are closely related to the study of logic programming. Logics for dealing with time, events, knowledge, and belief have also been developed by AI researchers in order to more accurately model the real world. For example, situation calculus[26] and event calculus,[27] and temporal logic[28] as well as logic about actions[29] deal with time-, event-, action-related representation issues. Various logics on knowledge and beliefs[30] handle problems of representing (and reasoning about) beliefs and knowledge.

Knowledge representation studies involve not only developing formalisms (logic, etc.) for representing the real world, but also methodologies as to how to model the real world and represent the model within the chosen formalism. Generally speaking, decision on how to represent the world would require the identification of an ontology, which specifies the concepts (categories) for modeling the world and the taxonomy (inheritance hierarchy) relating the concepts. Other semantical relationships among concepts can also be included in an ontology. For example, when building an ontology for a university, we would identify concepts such as students, professors, courses, departments, employees, and staff. We can also organize the people in the university into a taxonomy (a tree) T with top node labeled as "person." The two children nodes below the root would be labeled by "student" and "employee," indicating a student is a person, and an employee is a person too. We could also identify other semantical relationships among concepts in this domain: for example, the relationship "enrolled-in" can be identified between "student" and "course," indicating that students take courses. This kind of ontology specification bears close similarity with Semantic Networks,[31] a representation scheme developed in early years of AI research. Clearly, tools supporting the construction and maintenance of ontologies are highly desirable. Ongoing research on knowledge representation appears to focus on developing formal systems and tools for representing and processing ontologies with applications in the Semantic Web.[32] This includes the studies of a unified knowledge representation framework based on XML, RDF, OWL (Web Ontology Language),[33] etc., and development of tools for extracting/

editing ontologies using the unified representation, and studies of inference procedures for query-answering with such representations. Some existing works investigate the problem of knowledge acquisition by agent with commonsense knowledge formalized by some logic.[34]

Machine Learning

An intelligent system must have the ability to learn new knowledge so as to adapt in an ever-changing world around it. Machine Learning[35,36] study focuses on developing computational theories and algorithms that enable computers to learn. Since the early years of AI development, many researchers have pursued the ideas of a learning machine, and the field of Machine Learning is now a quite matured subfield within AI. Machine learning is closely related to the fields of data mining[37] and pattern classification.[38]

A typical intelligent agent with learning capability could be modeled as consisting of a learning element, a knowledge base, and a performance element. The agent interacts with the outside environment by performing some tasks (by the performance element) in the environment, and getting experience through observing the environment and its feedback to the agent. The learning element of the agent learns useful knowledge from the experiences, such that the learned knowledge will enable the performance element to do better on the task in the future. For example, consider a computer program that learns to play the game of checkers. The performance element here is a component that plays the game by using an evaluation function f on board configuration features to choose the next move. The outside environment is another copy of the program itself, and the experience gained by the computer will be a sequence of games between the computer and its opponent, as well as the game outcomes (win, loss, or draw). The learning element of the system could be a least-mean square-based linear function learning algorithm, if we define the evaluation function f to be a linear function of the game board features. Arthur Samuel's Checkers program[8] has tested such set-ups.

Machine learning tasks can be classified as supervised, unsupervised, and reinforcement learning, depending on the kind of experience available to the learning agent. In supervised learning, the task is learning (an approximation of) a function f from a set of input–output pairs for f: $\{\langle x_1, f(x_1)\rangle, \ldots, \langle x_m, f(x_m)\rangle\}$. Here the experience is encoded in the supervision: the function values at the points $x_1, \ldots, x_m$. In the case of learning to classify Web pages as "interesting" or "uninteresting," the function value $f(x_i)$ for a Web page x_i will be just binary: 1 or 0 (denoting whether a Web page is interesting or uninteresting). In unsupervised

learning, we do not have a beneficial teacher providing the labels ($f(x_i)$) for each observed x_i, we can only identify the patterns present in the observed data $\{x_1, \ldots, x_m\}$. In some sense, unsupervised learning basically amounts to forming clusters from the data and thus identifying the inherent structures in the data. For reinforcement learning, the agent does get some feedback from the environment, but not in the form of direct supervision $f(x)$ for each observed instance x. Instead, the agent would perform a sequence of actions in the environment and then receive a "reinforcement" signal after performing the action sequence. For example, consider a robot exploring an open area with obstacles and trying to reach a specific goal location without bumping into the obstacles. Here we do not give specific supervisions as to what is the best move for each location—because such supervision may not be available anyway in practice. Instead, reinforcement signals could be assigned to reward or punish a sequence of actions. If the robot reached the target location through several moves without bumping into obstacles, it would get a positive reward. It would get a negative reward (punishment) when stumping into an obstacle.

Symbolic learning approaches represent the knowledge to be learned in symbolic forms such as decision trees, formulas in propositional logic, and logic programs, and learning often takes place in some form of symbolic manipulation/inference, loosely speaking. One popular learning algorithm is Quinlan's Decision Tree learning algorithm,[39] which constructs a decision tree from a set of training examples, in a top-down fashion. Each example is represented by a vector of attribute-value pairs, together with a class label for the example. In each step of the tree construction, the algorithm checks to see if the examples associated with the existing node are of the same class. If so, the node is a leaf node, and marked by the class name. Otherwise, the algorithm chooses the "most discriminating attribute" A to subdivide the examples associated with the node into disjoint subsets, and thus growing the tree. Then the tree construction process is applied recursively until the resulting subsets are "pure," namely, consisting of examples from one class. Various works have been done on learning Boolean functions, learning decision lists, and learning logic programs.

Artificial Neural Networks (ANNs)[40,41] follow a different approach to the learning task. ANN research was motivated by the desire to construct simplified mathematical, computational models that mimic the way human brain works, and hoping to achieve better performance on tasks requiring human intelligence. It is observed that human brains consist of large number of biological neurons, which are massively connected, each with relatively low switching speed in communications compared with the switching speed of electronic circuits. However, humans can perform, with amazing speed, complex cognitive tasks such as recognizing a familiar face, which is still a difficult task for computers in spite of their speed advantages. This suggests that the processing power of the human brain may come from its highly parallel mode of information processing, and the connection patterns among the neurons are crucial in making such massively parallel processing possible. The study of ANN models represents efforts in trying to simulate this model of human brains. An ANN consists of a number of simple processing units, called neurons, each capable of computing simple functions such as linear functions and threshold functions, and sigmoid functions. The neurons are interconnected with real-valued weights. Neural networks can be used to do predictions, to perform classification tasks, to approximate functions, and to find clusters in input datasets. Learning in ANN amounts to adjusting the numerical-valued weights that connect the neurons. Such learning could be supervised, unsupervised, or a hybrid of supervised and unsupervised. In the supervised learning, perhaps the most well-known learning algorithms are perceptron training algorithm for a single linear threshold unit, and the back-propagation algorithm for training multilayer feedforward networks. Neural networks have been used widely in many successful applications.

Genetic Algorithms (GAs)[42] are another distinctive family of methods for learning. GAs are search algorithms that are patterned after natural evolution. In using GA for learning, we are interested in searching for good solutions for a problem by selecting candidate solutions and recombining parts of candidate solutions guided by the mechanics of natural selection (survival of the fittest) and natural genetics (children inherit good traits from parents, with occasional mutations). GA maintains a current population of strings, each encoding a candidate solution to the problem. A fitness function f is defined as that which measures the merit of a string as a solution to the problem. The objective of GA is to search for the best string that maximizes the fitness value. GA applies the genetic operators reproduction, crossover, mutation to the existing population in generating the next population of candidate solutions. In the reproduction process, strings from the existing population are sampled with probabilities proportional to their fitness values. Crossover operations will produce two new strings from two parent strings by exchanging segments of the parents. And finally mutations may be applied to randomly alter one bit in a string. Through evolutions of strings from one generation to the next, GAs perform structured yet randomized search of the space of all possible strings, often efficiently, in looking for the optimal or near optimal solutions. Koza's genetic programming[43] further extends the idea of GA by evolving computer programs for problem solving. GA research is closely related to studies of Artificial Life and evolutionary computing.

Another type of machine learning is statistical learning,[44] utilizing probabilities and Bayesian theories for learning. In particular, graphical models aim at generating models represented as directed or undirected graphs with (conditional) probability tables attached to each node in the graph, and the entire graph captures joint distributions of a set of random variables. This includes learning Bayes Belief Networks[45] and learning (conditional) Markov Networks. Probabilistic Relational Models (PRMs) and related learning models have also been developed.

Natural Language and Speech Processing

An intelligent system must have the capability to communicate and interact effectively with the outside world. Effective communications include receiving information (in various forms) from the world, understanding such information, and sending out information in suitable forms understandable to the outside world. Natural language processing and speech processing address the problems involved for an intelligent computer to communicate with humans using natural (written or spoken) language such as English.

Natural language processing[46] research mainly handles the task of communicating with written natural language. The main topics studied include language understanding, language generation, and machine translation. The inputs to a natural language understanding system are written texts (articles, or paragraphs, or sentences) of some language, and the desired outputs are semantical structures represented in some form, which capture the semantic meanings of the inputs. Language generation handles the opposite side of the problem: Given semantic meanings to be communicated to the outside world, a natural language generator produces correct natural language sentences (paragraphs, articles) that convey the meanings accurately. Machine translation tackles the task of automated translating texts from the source language to the target language, say, from English to French.

In speech processing,[47] the tasks are speech understanding and speech generation. Clearly, the apparatus of natural language processing techniques can be used as components of a speech processing system. For speech understanding, the main hurdle is speech recognition, which requires the capability of converting the spoken language inputs into written texts (so that natural language understanding tools can be utilized subsequently). Similarly, for speech generation, the major task is to map written texts to speech utterance. Converting continuous speech signals to written text requires multiple steps, from the initial step of signal sequence segmentation, to the step of phoneme recognition, followed by the step of mapping phonemes to texts. Signal processing techniques are needed to handle speech signal noise removal and segmentation. Neural Networks and Hidden Markov Models are commonly used techniques for speech recognition and generation.[48] Speech recognition and generation techniques[49] are widely used in day-to-day applications, such as automated information systems in airlines and banks.

Natural language processing requires several important techniques. First, syntactical analysis tools such as parsers are necessary for analyzing the syntactical structures of sentences according to the language grammar—to find the subject, predicate, and the object in a sentence. Semantical analysis tools are needed to give semantic interpretation to the sentences. Contextual information and pragmatic background knowledge are also essential for semantic disambiguation (word meaning disambiguation, reference resolution, etc.). Thus, knowledge representation is also an important topic related to natural language processing.

Natural language processing is closely related to text-mining, which is an active area of study involving computer science and LIS. Text-mining aims to discover useful knowledge from large collections of textual documents, which can be seen as a generalization of natural language understanding. The studies in text-mining include text summarization, concept extraction, and ontology extraction.

Signal, Image Processing, and Robotics

The communications between an intelligent agent and the outside world can take various forms, such as visual and audio signals, in addition to utterances in natural language. Moreover, an intelligent agent should be able to act in the world and thus effecting changes to the world around it as well. Signal and image processing research develops techniques that support computer perception and understanding of information in image, audio, and other sensory forms (such as radio signals, infrared, and GPS signals). Robotics put together the techniques of AI study and build robots that can act intelligently, change the world, and achieve desired goals.

Although signal processing has been mostly studied by researchers in Electrical Engineering (EE), it has close connection to building fully autonomous intelligent agents. Image processing[50] and computer vision[51] are important topics in AI and EE. In image processing, the main task is image understanding, namely, to build a semantic model of a given imagery; and in computer vision, the main task is visual scene understanding, i.e., to building a model of the world (the perceived visual scene). Further extension of visual scene understanding would include understanding video streams (sequence of scenes). The "understanding" of a visual scene/image involves recognition of the objects present, the relevant photometry/geometry features of the objects, and the (spatial or other) relationships among the objects. To achieve the objectives of image/scene understanding, several stages of image processing operations are needed. Initial processing of images includes low-level operations such as smoothing to filter out noise in the image signals, edge detection, and image segmentation to decompose the image into groups with similar characteristics. These low-level processing operations are local computations and require no prior knowledge about the images for the particular application. The next stage processing involves object recognition, which requires isolating each distinctive object, determining the object's position and orientation (relative to the observer), and identifying the object shape. Objects are outlined by edges and described by a set of features, which are chosen by the designer of the image processing system. The feature could be shape-based (geometric features) or photometric features (such as textures, brightness, and shading). For this processing stage, the computations are not necessarily local; features for characterizing different objects could require computation involving the pixels of the entire image. Supervised learning or pattern classification[38] methods are typically used for object recognition. The problem of object recognition from images is still highly challenging: a good object recognition system must perform well in spite of variations in the input image. The variations include changing illumination of the image, different pose and orientation of the objects, and translation, scaling of the objects. We humans are very good at recognizing, for example, familiar faces even if the faces are varied by wearing eye glasses, putting on a hat, having a different facial expression, or being illuminated differently. But such variations are still very hard to handle by computers.

Robotics[52] studies the techniques for building robots, i.e., intelligent agents with capabilities to act in the physical world. The research in Robotics concerns with both the hardware and software aspects of robots. A robot possessed a set of sensors for perceiving its surrounding environment and a set of effectors (also called actuators) for effecting actions in the environment. For example, for a mobile robot such as the planetary rovers that explore the surface of Mars, it has range sensors for measuring distance to close-by obstacles and image sensors (cameras) for getting images of surrounding environment. It also has effectors such as wheels/legs, joints for moving around. Robots can be classified into three categories: 1) manipulators, which are robotic arms physically anchored at a fixed location, for example, garbage collection robot arms on the garbage van; 2) Mobile robots that move around using wheels, legs, etc.; and 3) hybrid—mobile robots with manipulators. In particular, there has been an increasing interest in building the so-called humanoid robots, which resemble humans in physical design and physical appearance.

The research problems studied in robotics call for utilization of all major AI techniques. A robot must be able to perceive its environment and represent the state of its environment in some knowledge representation form; it must be able to learn from its past experiences; it must be able to perform inference in making decisions about the correct move; it must be able to plan and act intelligently; it must be able to handle uncertainty; and it must be able to communicate effectively to teammates and human users. Robotic perception addresses the problem of constructing internal models/representations of the environment from the sensory signals of the robot. This includes the study on localization, i.e., locating the position of specific objects, on environment mapping which allows the robot to construct a map of its environment by observation and exploration. Robotic motion research concerns with the planning and control of robot moves by the effectors. Various control architectures have been proposed in the literature.

Robotics has found a wide range of successful applications in the real world. We will present some in the next section on AI applications.

AI APPLICATIONS

AI has found many successful applications in various sectors of the real world. Here we sample some of them. The online resource from Wikipedia[53] gives more samples.

Game playing. Since early days of AI, researchers have studied the problem of computer game playing using heuristic search methods and machine learning. Arthur Samuel's Checkers playing program pioneered the studies in this aspect. Along with the advances in computing power and AI research, many successful computer game playing systems have been developed that can compete at human master levels. TD-Gammon[54] is a neural network-based program that plays the game of Backgammon very well. The most well-known computer game player is perhaps the Deep Blue[9] Chess program from IBM. In a six-game match against world Chess champion Kasparov, Deep Blue achieved two wins, three draws, and one loss, thus overall it has won the match. Today there are many online computer game playing programs (chess, go checkers, backgammon, etc.) that people can play with and have fun. Almost all such game programs utilize ideas from AI in one way or the other.

Financial applications. Prominent financial firms in Wall Street have employed proprietary software systems for predicting stock-market trends and predicting stock prices for assisting mutual fund managers to boost investment returns. Although the details of such proprietary systems are held secret, it is known that at least a number of them used neural networks.

Medicine and health care. In more than 100 hospitals across the United States, nurses receive help from robotic "tugs"[55] that tow carts that deliver everything from meals to linens. Miniature robots have been used in surgery procedures for a number of diseases.[56] Data mining and machine learning techniques have been applied to find patterns of diseases and treatment effects of various medications from huge amounts of medical data. Intelligent medical imaging tools have been widely used to identify tumors/nodules from X-ray/CT-scan images for early detection and diagnosis of cancers. Moreover, computational biology combined with micro-array technology in biological sciences has enabled the medical scientists to quickly identify or pin-point the genes responsible for certain diseases.[57] The construction of large online medical knowledge bases and the availability of such medical knowledge to ordinary people contribute significantly to boost preventive care in public health.

Engineering and manufacturing applications. The ideas of heuristic search and GA have been widely used in solving optimization problems commonly seen in engineering applications such as job-shop scheduling and air traffic scheduling. In manufacturing, utilization of robotic arms at assembly lines is quite common, and such application enhances the productivity tremendously.

Environment protection. Remote-sensing techniques have been widely used for gathering information about the oceans, the atmosphere, the space, and the earth. It is a difficult task to process the huge amount of environment data and find trends in environment change so as to meet the challenge of climate change and global warming. AI methods such as image processing, pattern classification, and data clustering have been applied successfully for analyzing environment data to assist scientists in environment-related research.[58]

Space science explorations. Mobil robots have been used to explore the unknown terrains on Mars. According to the Mars rover's web page,[59]

NASA's twin robot geologists, the Mars Exploration Rovers, launched toward Mars on June 10 and July 7, 2003, in search of answers about the history of water on Mars. They landed on Mars January 3 and January 24 PST, 2004 (January 4 and January 25 UTC, 2004). The Mars Exploration Rover mission is part of NASA's Mars Exploration Program, a long-term effort of robotic exploration of the red planet.

After more than 4 years of geological surveying, the Mars Exploration Rover robots have ceased to communicate (November 11, 2008).

Intelligent information systems. AI research has significantly impacted the studies in LISs. Ideas in AI have been widely applied in information technology to build smart information systems. On the other hand, the explosive development of the Internet and the Web has fueled AI with many interesting and challenging research problems. Along with the challenges are the great opportunities to bring AI closer to ordinary people's day-to-day lives. Nowadays we take it for granted that we can find information about anything by using online search engines such as Google, Yahoo, or Microsoft Live. Millions of consumers utilize online shopping tools to buy services and products. Digital libraries are a commonplace, accessible to a much larger audience than before. What people probably did not realize is that behind all these nice and fascinating online tools and services (such as search engine and online shopping tools) there are important contributions of AI. For example, association rule mining and other AI methods are routinely used in many major online shopping Web sites so that related products can be recommended to consumers.

Intelligent information systems studies have developed a number of AI-based approaches in information extraction, indexing, and smart information retrieval. In information extraction, text-mining and natural language processing methods are developed to obtain semantical information from texts in the form of concepts and their relationships. Such information is then used for indexing the source texts to facilitate retrieval.[60] User profiles can be constructed by fuzzy clustering on user information-seeking behaviors (Web-click streams, etc.) to personalize the information service to individual users.[61] User information-seeking behavior includes not only current session Web-click streams of the user, but also previously logged Web search activities that help to model the user. Fuzzy rule, Neural Networks, and GA have been applied to adapt user queries for better retrieval performance.

There are continuous efforts in building large-scale commonsense knowledge bases and making information/knowledge in the collection accessible to ordinary people. The Wikipedia is one of such knowledge bases.[62] On the other hand, the studies in Semantic Web[32] aims at building large knowledge bases in formats such that the semantics (contents) of the information can be interpreted and processed by computers across the Web. Clearly, Semantic Web would promote knowledge sharing and intelligent query-answering beyond what the existing Web search engines would support. Along this line, the CYC project is another notable example.[63]

Many multimedia information retrieval systems have been constructed, resulting in various interesting applications such as music retrieval system[64] and video-clip retrieval system[65]. Image retrieval for security surveillance has been in practical use for quite some time.

Machine translation. Machine translation is one special type of intelligent information system service that supports automatic translation of texts from a source language to a target language. Today one can use machine translators at various online search engines, for example, Google. Although the performance is still not as good as that of human translators, machine translators are very useful in several ways. For one thing, human translators are highly specialized professionals and thus expensive to hire. Secondly, human translators would get tired and could not work as fast as computers. The common practice in using machine translation is to let the machines do the first (quick) cut of the translation and then let human translators polish the results produced by machines. This would greatly enhance the productivity of translation.

CONCLUSIONS

AI is an exciting research area. AI research is multidisciplinary in nature, drawing on advances in mathematics, philosophy, logic, computer science, information theory, control, cognitive science, and linguistics. The objective of AI is to understand the nature of intelligence and to build computer systems that behave intelligently. AI research covers a wide range of topics, many of which are briefly discussed in this entry. AI has found many successful applications that impact our daily life significantly. The entry samples some AI applications. AI and LISs have close connections, and cross-fertilization of research efforts between the two fields has been fruitful. Looking forward, we see great opportunities as well as challenges in realizing the dream of AI, which we embrace wholeheartedly.

ACKNOWLEDGMENT

This work was partially supported by NSF grant ITR-0326387.

REFERENCES

1. Russell, S.J.; Norvig, P. In *Artificial Intelligence: A Modern Approach*; 2nd Ed.; Prentice Hall: Upper Saddle River, NJ, 2003.
2. Luger, G.F. In *Artificial Intelligence: Structures and Strategies for Complex Problem Solving*; 6th Ed.; Addison Wesley: New York, NY, 2008.
3. Nilsson, N. In *Artificial Intelligence: A New Synthesis*; Morgan Kaufmann Publishers: San Mateo, CA, 1998.
4. http://en.wikipedia.org/wiki/Artificial_intelligence.

5. Jenkinson, A.J. (translator). **2007**, written at The University of Adelaide, Prior Analytics, eBooks @ Adelaide.

6. Pascal, B. In *Pensees de M. Pascal sur la Religion et sur quelques autre sujts*; Chez Guillaume Desprez: Paris, 1670.

7. Leibniz, G.W. In *The Art of Discovery* 1685; W 51.

8. Samuel, A. Some studies in machine learning using the game of checkers. IBM J. **1959**, (3), 210–229.

9. Hsu, F.-H. In *Behind Deep Blue: Building the Computer that Defeated the World Chess Champion*; Princeton University Press: Princeton, NJ, 2002.

10. Turing, A.A. Computing machinery and intelligence. Mind **1950**, *59*, 443–460.

11. Buchanan, B.G. A (very) brief history of artificial intelligence. AI Mag. **2005,** *26* (4), 53–60.

12. Newell, A.; Shaw, J.C.; Simon, H.A. Report on a general problem-solving program. Proc. Int. Conf. Inform. Process. **1959**, 256–264.

13. Pearl, J. In *Heuristics: Intelligent Search Strategies for Computer Problem Solving*; Addison-Wesley: New York, 1984.

14. Hart, P.E.; Nilsson, N.J.; Raphael, B. A formal basis for the heuristic determination of minimum cost paths. IEEE Trans. Syst. Sci. Cybernet SSC4 **1968**, (2), 100–107.

15. Dechter, R.; Judea, P. Generalized best-first search strategies and the optimality of *A**. J. ACM **1985**, *32* (3), 505–536.

16. Sowa, J.F. In *Knowledge Representation: Logical, Philosophical, and Computational Foundations*; Brooks/Cole Publishing Co.: Pacific Grove, CA, 2000.

17. In *Handbook of Automated Reasoning*; Robinson, A., Voronkov, A., Eds.; Elsevier Science B. V. and MIT Press: Amsterdam, The Netherlands, 2001.

18. Genesereth, M.; Nilsson, N. In *Logical Foundations of Artificial Intelligence*; Morgan Kaufmann Publishers: San Mateo, CA, 1988.

19. Robinson, J.; Alan, A. Machine-oriented logic based on the resolution principle. J. ACM **1965**, *12* (1), 23–41.

20. Marques-Silva, J.P.; Sakallah, K.A. GRASP: A new search algorithm for satisfiability. Proceedings of International Conference on Computer-Aided Design, Santa Clara, CA, **1996**; 220–227.

21. Zhang, H. SATO: An efficient propositional prover. Proceedings of International Conference on Automated Deduction (CADE-97), Springer-Verlag: London, U.K.

22. Zhang, L. Solving QBF with combined conjunctive and disjunctive normal form. Proceedings of Twenty-First National Conference on Artificial Intelligence (AAAI 2006), Boston, MA, July **2006**.

23. Kowalski, R. Predicate Logic as a Programming Language Proceedings IFIP Congress, North Holland Publishing Co.: Stockholm, Sweden, 1974; 569–574.

24. Reiter, R. A logic for default reasoning. Artif. Intell. **1980**, *13* (1–2), 81–132.

25. McCarthy, J. Applications of circumscription to formalizing common-sense knowledge. Artif. Intell. **1986**, *28* (1), 89–116.

26. Pirri, F.; Reiter, R. Some contributions to the metatheory of the situation calculus. J. ACM **1999**, *46* (3), 325–361.

27. Kowalski, R.; Sergot, M. A logic-based calculus of events. New Gen. Comput. **1986**, *4* (1), 67–95.

28. Emerson, E.A. In *Temporal and Modal Logic. Handbook of Theoretical Computer Science*; MIT Press: Cambridge, MA, 1990 Chapter 16.

29. Gelfond, M.; Lifschitz, V. Representing action and change by logic programs. J. Logic Program. **1993**, *17* (2-4), 301–322.

30. Chen, J. The generalized logic of only knowing that covers the notion of epistemic specifications. J. Logic Comput **1997**, *7* (2), 159–174.

31. Sowa, J.F. Semantic networks. In *Encyclopedia of Artificial Intelligence*; Shapiro, S. C., Ed.; Wiley: New York, 1987 revised and extended for the second edition, 1992.

32. Berners-Lee, T.; James, H.; Ora, L. The semantic web. Sci. Am. Mag. **2001**, *284* (5), 34–43.

33. http://www.w3.org/TR/owl-features/.

34. Kandefer, M.; Shapiro, S.C. Knowledge acquisition by an intelligent acting agent. Logical Formalizations of Commonsense Reasoning, Papers from the AAAI Spring Symposium Technical Report SS-07-05, Amir, E., Lifschitz, V., Miller, R., Eds.; AAAI Press: Menlo Park, CA, 2007; 77–82.

35. Mitchell, T. In *Machine Learning*; McGraw-Hill: New York, NY, 1997.

36. Bishop, C.M. In *Pattern Recognition and Machine Learning*; Springer: New York, NY, 2007.

37. Tan, P.; Steinbach, M.; Kumar, V. In *Introduction to Data Mining*; Addison-Wesley: New York, NY, 2006.

38. Duda, R.O.; Hart, P.E.; Stork, D.G. In *Pattern classification*; 2nd Ed.;Wiley: New York, NY, 2001.

39. Quinlan, J.R. Induction of decision trees. Mach. Learn. **1986**, *1* (1), 81–106.

40. Bishop, C.M. In *Neural Networks for Pattern Recognition*; Oxford University Press: Oxford, 1995.

41. Jain, A.K.; Mao, J. Artificial neural networks: A tutorial. IEEE Comput. **1996**, March, 31–44.

42. Goldberg, D.E. In *Genetic algorithms for search, optimization, and machine learning*; Addison-Wesley: New York, NY, 1989.

43. Koza, J.R. In *Genetic Programming: On the Programming of Computers by Means of Natural Selection*; MIT Press: Cambridge, MA, 1994.

44. Vapnik, V. In *Statistical Learning Theory*; Wiley-Interscience: New York, NY, 1998.

45. Pearl, J. In *Probabilistic Reasoning in Intelligent Systems*; Morgan Kaufmann Publishers: San Mateo, CA, 1988.

46. Allen, J.F. In *Natural Language Understanding*; 2nd Ed.; Benjamin Cummings: Melano Park, CA, 1987, 1994.

47. Deng, L.; O'Shaughnessy, D. In *Speech Processing: A Dynamic and Optimization-Oriented Approach*; Marcel Dekker Inc.: New York, 2003.

48. Rabiner, L.R. A tutorial on hidden Markov models and selected applications in speech recognition. Proc. IEEE **1989**, *77* (2), 257–286.

49. http://www.nuance.com/naturallyspeaking/legal/.

50. Chan, T.F.; Shen, J. (Jianhong). In *Image Processing and Analysis - Variational, PDE, Wavelet, and Stochastic Methods*; SIAM Publisher: Philadelphia, PA, 2005.

51. Davies, E.R. In *Machine Vision: Theory, Algorithms, Practicalities*; Morgan Kaufmann Publishers: San Mateo, CA, 2004.

52. Bekey, G. In *Autonomous Robots*; Massachusetts Institute of Technology Press: Cambridge, MA, 2005.

53. http://en.wikipedia.org/wiki/Category:Artificial_intelligence_applications.

54. Tesauro, G.; Sejnowski, T.J. A parallel network that learns to play backgammon. Artif. Intell. **1989**, *39* (3), 357–390.

55. Peter, T.A. Robot set to overhaul service industry. The Christian Science Monitor. February 28, **2008**. http://www.csmonitor.com/2008/0225/p01s01-usgn.html.

56. http://en.wikipedia.org/wiki/Robotic_surgery.

57. Schena, M.; Shalon, D.; Davis, R.W.; Brown, P.O. Quantitative monitoring of gene expression patterns with a complementary DNA microarray. Science **1995**, *270* (5235), 467–470.

58. Erotoz, L.; Steinbach, M.; Kumar, V. Finding clusters of different sizes, shapes, and densities in noisy, high dimensional data. Proceedings of SIAM Int. Conf. on Data Mining, San Francisco, CA, May 2003.

59. http://marsrovers.nasa.gov/overview/.

60. Punuru, J.; Chen, J. Extraction of non-hierarchical relations from domain texts. Proceedings of IEEE International Symposium on Computational Intelligence and Data Mining., Honolulu, HI, April 2007.

61. Martin-Bautista, M.J.; Kraft, D.H.; Vila, M.A.; Chen, J.; Cruz, J. User profiles and fuzzy logic for web retrieval issues. J. Soft Comput. **2002**, *6* (5), 365–372.

62. http://www.wikipedia.org.

63. Matuszek, C.; Witbrock, M.; Kahlert, R.; Cabral, J.; Schneider, D.; Shah, P.; Lenat, D. Searching for common sense: Populating Cyc from the web. Proceedings of the Twentieth National Conference on Artificial Intelligence, Pittsburgh, PA, July 2005.

64. Zhang, X.; Ras, Z.W. Sound isolation by harmonic peak partition for music instrument recognition. Fund. Inform **2007**, *78* (4), 613–628.

65. Proceedings of the 6th ACM International Conference on Image and Video Retrieval, CIVR, 2007; Sebe, N., Worring, M., Eds.; Amsterdam, the Netherlands, July 9–11 2007.

Artificial Neural Networks and Natural Language Processing

Hermann Moisl

Center for Research in Linguistics, University of Newcastle upon Tyne, Newcastle upon Tyne, U.K.

Abstract

This entry gives an overview of work to date on natural language processing (NLP) using artificial neural networks (ANNs). It is in three main parts: the first gives a brief introduction to ANNs, the second outlines some of the main issues in ANN-based NLP, and the third surveys specific application areas. Each part cites a representative selection of research literature that itself contains pointers to further reading.

INTRODUCTION

Two preliminary notes:

- Natural language processing (NLP) is here regarded as language engineering, that is, the design and implementation of physical devices that process human linguistic input in some application and not as cognitive modeling.
- The discussion is concerned solely with text. This is not meant to imply that speech processing is any sense less important in NLP than text processing— far from it. It is, rather, simply a consequence of space limits on this entry, which preclude consideration of what has become a research discipline in its own right.

ARTIFICIAL NEURAL NETWORKS

An artificial neural network (ANN) is an artificial device that emulates the physical structure and dynamics of biological brains. There are two broad approaches to such emulation. One approach regards ANNs as biological models that capture aspects of brain structure and dynamics as accurately as possible. The other sees ANNs as computational systems, which, although neurally inspired, can be developed in line with required computational properties without regard to biology. Historically, these two approaches have proceeded more or less independently, but with rapid advances in brain-imaging techniques and consequent improved understanding of the brain, there are clear signs of convergence. This discussion focuses on ANNs as computational systems.

ANNs were first proposed by McCulloch and Pitts[1] in 1943 and were developed throughout the 1950s and 1960s.[2,3] But, in 1969, Minsky and Papert[4] showed that there were computable functions that the ANN architectures of the time could not compute,[5] as a consequence of which ANN-based research activity diminished significantly. Some researchers persevered, however, and by the early 1980s interest in them had begun to revive.[6] In 1986, Rumelhart and McClelland published their now-classic *Parallel Distributed Processing*[7] volumes. Among other things, these proposed the backpropagation learning algorithm, which made it possible to train multilayer nets and thereby to overcome the computational limitations that Minsky and Papert had demonstrated. The effect was immediate. An explosion of interest in ANNs ensued, which continues today. This has generated a considerable variety of network architectures; details are available from numerous textbooks.[8–10]

ISSUES IN ANN-BASED NLP

Motivation

In general, a new technology is adopted by a research community when it offers substantial advantages over what is presently available. NLP has from the outset been dominated by a technology based on explicit design of algorithms for computing functions of interest and implementation of those algorithms using serial computers, an approach widely known as "symbolic NLP." It is only since the early 1980s that alternative technologies have been extensively used, among them ANNs. In what follows, we look briefly at the main advantages and disadvantages of ANNs relative to symbolic NLP.

Advantages

Of the various advantages referred to in the literature, the following two are arguably the most important:

Encyclopedia of Information Systems and Technology, DOI: 10.1081/E-EIST-120008648

- Function Approximation

It has been shown that certain ANN architectures, including widely used ones, can approximate any computable function arbitrarily closely.[11–14] The function f that a given ANN approximates is determined by its parameter values, or weights, and these parameter values are learned from a data set $D \subset f$. In principle, therefore, NLP functions can be approximated from data using ANNs, thereby bypassing the explicit design of algorithms for computing those functions.

Why should one want to dispense with explicit design? Looking back on several decades' work on symbolic NLP, and artificial intelligence (AI) more generally, some researchers have come to believe that a variety of problems are too difficult to be solved by algorithm design given the existing state of software technology[15] and have instead turned to function approximation techniques like ANNs. A, and probably the, chief advantage of ANN technology for NLP, therefore, is that it offers an alternative way of implementing NLP functions that symbolic NLP has thus far found difficult to implement.

- Noise Tolerance

Practical NLP systems must operate in real-world environments characterized by noise, which can for present purposes be taken as the presence of probabilistic errors in the data (e.g., spelling or syntax errors). A frequent criticism of symbolic AI/NLP systems is that they are brittle in the sense that noisy input, which the designer has not taken into account, can cause a degree of malfunction out of all proportion to the severity of the input corruption. The standard claim is that ANNs are far less brittle, so that the performance of an ANN-based system will "degrade gracefully" in some reasonable proportion to the degree of corruption.

Noise tolerance is a by-product of ANN function approximation. ANNs approximate a function from data by fitting a regression curve to data points, and the best approximation—the one that generalizes best—is not the curve that passes through the data points, but the one that best captures the general shape of the data distribution.[16,17] Most of the data points in a noisy environment will be at some distance from the regression curve; if the input corruption is not too severe, the regression model will place the corresponding output in or near the training data distribution.

Disadvantages

Scaling. Given some ANN architecture, the aim of learning is to find a set of connection strengths that will allow the net to compute a function of interest. Empirical results have repeatedly shown that the time required to train an ANN increases rapidly with the number of network connections, or network complexity, and fairly quickly becomes impractically long. The question of how ANN learning scales with network complexity is therefore crucial to the development of large nets for real-world applications. The answer is that learning is an NP complete or intractable problem—"We cannot hope to build connectionist networks that will reliably learn simple supervised learning tasks."[18]

This result appears to bode ill for prospects of scaling ANNs to large, real-world applications. It is all very well to know that, in theory, ANNs with suitable architectures and sufficient complexity can implement any computable function, but this is of little help if it takes impractically long to train them. The situation is not nearly as bad as it seems, however. The intractability result is maximally general in that it holds for all data sets and all ANN architectures. Although theoretically interesting, such generality is unnecessary in practice[19] and a variety of measures exist, which constrain the learning problem such that intractability is either delayed or circumvented. These include restricting the range of ANN architectures used,[19] developing mechanisms for determining optimal network complexity for any given learning problem such as network growing and pruning algorithms,[18] biasing the net toward data to be learned,[20,21] explicit compilation of knowledge into network weights,[22] preprocessing of inputs by feature extraction, where the features extracted reflect the designer's knowledge of their importance relative to the problem,[16] incremental training,[20] and transfer of weights from a net that has successfully learned a problem similar to the one of interest.[23,24]

Inscrutability. A network that has learned its training data and generalizes well realizes a desired behavior, but it is not immediately obvious how it does so; the set of connection strengths determine the behavior, but direct examination of them does not tell one very much. Because of this, ANNs acquired a reputation as "black box" solutions soon after their resurgence in the early to mid-1980s and have consequently been viewed with some suspicion, particularly in critical application areas like medical diagnosis expert systems where unpredictable behavior, or even the possibility of unpredictable behavior, is unacceptable. ANNs are, however, no longer the black boxes they used to be. Mathematical tools for understanding them have been developed,[13,14] and inscrutability has become less of a disadvantage in the application of ANNs.

Discussion

It needs to be stressed that the intention here is not to argue that ANN-based NLP is necessarily "better" than its symbolic counterpart in a partisan sense. They are alternative technologies, each with its strengths and weaknesses, and, in an NLP context, can be used pragmatically in line with one's aims. The present position with respect to NLP is that ANN-based systems, "while becoming ever more powerful and sophisticated, have not yet been able to provide equivalent (let alone alternative superior) capabilities to those exhibited by symbolic systems."[25]

ANN-Based NLP

NLP is historically intertwined with several other language-oriented disciplines, including cognitive science, AI, generative linguistics, and computational linguistics. In general, the interaction of these disciplines has been and continues to be important. It remains, however, that each discipline has its own research agenda and methodology, and it is possible to waste time engaging with issues that are simply irrelevant to NLP. Now, it happens that ANN-based research into natural language has been strongly cognitive science oriented. For present purposes, it is important to be clear about the significance of this for NLP.

The formalisms invented in the 1930s and 1940s to define computable functions were soon applied to modeling of aspects of human intelligence including, of course, language. There have been two main strands of development. One is based on automata and formal language theory and has come to be known as the "symbolic" paradigm. The other is based on ANNs and is known as the "connectionist" or "subsymbolic" paradigm. Until fairly recently, the symbolic paradigm dominated thinking about natural language in linguistics, cognitive science, and AI. It reached its apotheosis in the late 1970s, when Newell and Simon[26] proposed the physical symbol system hypothesis (PSSH), in which "physical symbol system" is understood as a physical implementation of a mathematically stated effective procedure, the prime example of which is the Turing machine. The PSSH was widely accepted as the agenda for future work in linguistics, cognitive science, and AI: In essence, the first two proposed cognitive virtual architectures, and the third implemented them. At this time, however, interest in ANNs was being revived by cognitive scientists who saw them as an alternative to the dominant symbolic paradigm in cognitive modeling, and a debate soon arose on the relative merits of the PSSH- and ANN-based approaches to cognitive modeling. The PSSH case was first put in 1988 by Fodor and Pylyshyn,[27] who labeled what we are here calling the symbolic as the "classical" position, and Smolensky[28] argued the ANN-based case;[29–32] between them they set the parameters for subsequent discussion.[33–43] The essentials of the debate are as follows.

The symbolist position (all quotations are from Fodor and Pylyshyn)[27] descends directly from the PSSH and thus proposes cognitive architectures, which compute by algorithmic manipulation of symbol structures; the mind is taken to be a symbol manipulation machine. Specifically, there are representational primitives—symbols. Being representational, symbols have semantic content (i.e., each symbol denotes some aspect of the world). A representational state consists of one or more symbols, each with an associated semantics,

in which 1) there is a distinction between structurally atomic and structurally molecular representations, 2) structurally molecular representations have syntactic constituents that are themselves either structurally molecular or structurally atomic, and 3) the semantic content of a representation is a function of the semantic contents of its syntactic parts, together with the syntactic structure.

Transformations of mental states "are defined over the structural properties of mental representations. Because these have combinatorial structure, mental processes apply to them by virtue of their form." Therefore,

if in principle syntactic relations can be made to parallel semantic relations, and if in principle you have a mechanism whose operation on expressions are sensitive to syntax, then it is in principle possible to construct a syntactically driven machine whose state transitions satisfy semantic criteria of coherence. The idea that the brain is such a machine is the foundational hypothesis of classical cognitive science.

The subsymbolic position (all quotations are from Fodor and McLaughlin)[28] defines cognitive models that are "massively parallel computational systems that are a kind of dynamical system." The primitives are subsymbols, which are like classical symbols in being representational, but unlike them in being finer-grained: they "correspond to constituents of the symbols used in the symbolic paradigm… Entities that are typically represented in the symbolic paradigm as symbols are typically represented in the subsymbolic paradigm as a large number of subsymbols." The difference between symbolic and subsymbolic models lies in the nature of the semantic content. The subsymbolic position distinguishes two semantic levels, the conceptual and the subconceptual: "The conceptual level is populated by consciously accessible concepts, whereas the subconceptual one is comprised of finer-grained entities beneath the level of conscious concepts." In classical models, symbols typically have conceptual semantics (i.e., semantics which correspond directly to the concepts that the modeler uses to analyze the task domain), whereas subsymbols in subsymbolic models have subconceptual semantics; the semantic content of a subsymbol in a subsymbolic ANN model corresponds directly to the activity level of a single processing unit in an ANN. Subsymbolic representations are, moreover, not operated on by processes, which manipulate symbol structures in a way that is sensitive to their combinatorial form because subsymbolic representations do not have combinatorial form. Instead, they are operated on by numeric computation. Specifically, a subsymbolic ANN model is a dynamical system whose state is a numerical vector of the activation values of the units comprising the net at any instant t. The evolution of the state vector is determined by the interaction of the input, the existing state of the system at t, and a set of numerical parameters corresponding to the relative strengths of the connections among units.

How do the symbolic and subsymbolic paradigms relate to one another as cognitive models? In the symbolist view,

> classical and connectionist [= subsymbolic] theories disagree about the nature of mental representations. For the former but not the latter, representations characteristically exhibit combinatorial constituent structure and combinatorial semantics. Classical and connectionist theories also disagree about the nature of mental processes: for the former but not the latter, mental processes are characteristically sensitive to the combinatorial structure of the representations on which they operate. These two issues define the dispute about the nature of cognitive architecture.

Now, any adequate cognitive model must explain the productivity and systematicity[44–46] of cognitive capacities. Symbolic models appeal to the combinatorial structure of mental representations to do this, but subsymbolists cannot: "Because it acknowledges neither syntactic nor semantic structure in mental representations, it treats cognitive states not as a generated set but as a list," and among other things lists lack explanatory utility. Because they cannot explain cognitive productivity and systematicity, subsymbolic models are inadequate as cognitive models; they may be useful as implementations of symbolically defined cognitive architectures, but this has no implications for cognitive science.

In the subsymbolist view, on the other hand, subsymbolic models refine symbolic ones rather than, as the symbolists maintain, implementing them. In a now-famous analogy, the relationship between symbolic and subsymbolic paradigms is likened to that which is obtained between the macrophysics of Newtonian mechanics and the microphysics of quantum theory. Newtonian mechanics is not literally instantiated in the world according to the microtheory, because fundamental elements in the ontology of the macrotheory, such as rigid bodies, cannot literally exist according to the

microtheory. In short, "in a strictly literal sense, if the microtheory is right, then the macrotheory is wrong." This does not, however, mean that Newtonian mechanics has to be eliminated, for it has an explanatory capacity, which is crucial in a range of sciences and branches of engineering and which a (strictly correct) quantum mechanical account lacks; such explanatory capacity is crucial in the subsymbolic view. Thus, cognitive systems "are explained in the symbolic paradigm as approximate higher-level regularities that emerge from quantitative laws operating on a more fundamental level"—the subconceptual—"with different semantics." Or, put another way, symbolic models are competence models that idealize aspects of physical system behavior, whereas subsymbolic models are performance models that attempt to describe physical systems as accurately as possible.

What are the implications of this debate for ANN-based NLP? First, the debate has forced a reexamination of fundamental ideas in cognitive science and AI, and, because much of the ANN-based research on NL is done within a cognitive science framework, ANN-based NLP cannot afford to ignore developments in the corresponding cognitive science work. This is not bland ecumenism, but a simple fact of life.

Second, notwithstanding what has just been said, it remains that the cognitive science focus of the debate can easily mislead the NLP researcher who is considering ANNs as a possible technology and wants to assess their suitability. The debate centers on the nature of cognitive theories and on the appropriateness of symbolist and subsymbolist paradigms for articulation of such theories. These issues, although intrinsically interesting, are orthogonal to the concerns of NLP as understood here. Cognitive science is concerned with the scientific explanation of human cognition, including the language faculty, whereas NLP construed as language engineering has no commitment to the explanation of any aspect of human cognition, and NLP systems have no necessary interpretation as cognitive models. The symbolist argument that the ANN paradigm is inadequate in principle for framing cognitive theories is, therefore, irrelevant to NLP, as are criticisms of particular ANN language-processing architectures in the literature on the grounds that they are "cognitively implausible," or fail to "capture generalizations," or do not accord with psycholinguistic data.

Third, once the need for cognitive explanation is factored out, the debate reduces to a comparison of standard automata theory and ANNs as computational technologies.[38] So construed, the relationship is straightforward. We have taken the aim of NLP to be design and construction of physical devices that have specific behaviors in response to text input. For design purposes, the stimulus–response behavior of any required device can be described as a mathematical

Ad Hoc– Availability

function (i.e., as a mapping from an input to an output set). Moreover, because the stimulus-response behavior of any physical device is necessarily finite, the corresponding input-output sets can also be finite, with the consequence that every NLP function is computable; in fact, the sizes of the I/O sets are specifiable by the designer and can, therefore, be defined in such a way as to make the function not only finite and therefore theoretically computable but also computationally tractable. As such, for any NLP mapping, there will be a Turing machine—a PSS—that computes it. But we have seen that certain classes of ANN are Turing equivalent, so there is no theoretical computability basis for a choice between the two technologies. The choice hinges, rather, on practical considerations such as ease of applicability to the problem in hand, processing efficiency, noise and damage tolerance, and so on.

And, finally, the debate has set the agenda for ANN-based language-oriented research in two major respects: The paradigm within the research is conducted, and the ability of ANNs to represent compositional structure. These are discussed in the following sections.

Research paradigms

The symbolist/subsymbolist debate has resulted in a trifurcation of ANN-based natural language-oriented research, based on the perceived relationship between PSSH- and ANN-based cognitive science and AI:

*   The symbolic paradigm[47,48] accepts the symbolist view of the position of ANNs relative to cognitive science. It regards ANNs as an implementation technology for explicitly specified PSS virtual machines and studies ways in which such implementation can be accomplished.
*   The subsymbolic paradigm[49–51] subdivides into what is sometimes called "radical connectionism," which assumes no prior PSSH analysis of the problem domain but relies on inference of the appropriate processing dynamics from data, and a position that in essence regards prior PSSH analysis of the problem domain as a guide to system design and/or as an approximate or competence description of the behavior of the implemented system. *Neural Networks and a New Artificial Intelligence*[42] exemplifies the radical position, and Smolensky, in a manner of speaking the father of subsymbolism, has in his various writings[28,52–54] taken the second.
*   The hybrid paradigm,[38,55–60] as its name indicates, is a combination of the symbolic and the subsymbolic. It uses symbolic and subsymbolic modules as components in systems opportunistically, according to what works best for any given purpose. A subsymbolic module might, for example, be used as a

preprocessor able to respond resiliently to noisy input, whereas the data structures and control processes are conventional PSS designs.

Interest in the hybrid paradigm has grown rapidly, and, to judge by relative volumes of research literature, it is now the most often used of the preceding three alternatives in engineering-oriented applications like NLP. It is not hard to see why this should be so. The hybrid paradigm makes full use of theoretical results and practical techniques developed over several decades of PSSH-based AI and NLP work, and supplements it with the function approximation and noise resistance advantages of ANNs where appropriate. By contrast, the symbolic and subsymbolic paradigms are in competition with established PSSH-based theory and/or methodology. On the one hand, the symbolic paradigm has yet to demonstrate that it will ever be superior to conventional computer technology as an implementation medium for PSS virtual machines. On the other, the subsymbolic paradigm essentially disregards existing PSSH-based NLP theory and practice and starts afresh. Of the three paradigms, therefore, it is the least likely to generate commercially exploitable systems in the near future, although it is the most intriguing in pure research terms.

Representation

The most fundamental requirement of any NLP system is that it be able to represent the ontology of the problem domain.[61–63] One might, for example, want to map words to meanings or strings to structural descriptions: Words, meanings, strings, and structures have to be represented in such a way that the system can operate on them to implement the required mapping. Most ANN-based NL work has been directly or indirectly concerned with this issue, and this section deals with it in outline.

There are two fundamentally different approaches to ANN-based representation:

*   Local representation: Given some set E of objects to be represented and a set N of network units available for representational use, a local representation scheme (or "local scheme" for short) allocates a unique unit or group of units $\in N$ for each object $e \in E$.
*   Distributed representation: Given the same sets E and N, a distributed representational scheme uses all the units $n \in N$ to represent each $e \in E$.

The difference is exemplified in the pair of representational schemes for the integers 0–7 shown in Fig. 1. In the local scheme, each bit represents a different integer, whereas in the distributed one all the bits are used to represent each integer, with a different pattern for each.

	Local	Distrib
1	0000001	0000001
2	0000010	0000010
3	0000100	0000011
4	0001000	0000100
5	0010000	0000101
6	0100000	0000110
7	1000000	0000111

Fig. 1 Local and distributed representational schemes.

Because, in the local scheme, each bit stands for one and only one integer, it can be appropriately labeled, but in the distributed scheme, no bit stands for anything on its own; no bit can be individually labeled, and each is interpretable only on relation to all the others.

Local and distributed schemes both have advantages.[41,61,64,65] Much of the earlier work used localist representation, and although the balance has now shifted to the distributed approach, significant localist activity remains.[47,66–69] In what follows, local and distributed approaches to the representation of primitive objects and of compositional structure in ANNs are discussed separately.

Local Representation.

Representation of Primitives. The local representation of primitive objects is identical to that in the PSSH approach: In a PSS, each object to be represented is assigned a symbol, and in local ANN representation, each object is assigned a unit in the net.

Representation of Structure. Local representation of primitive objects is straightforward, but representation of compositional structure is not. The difficulty emerges from the following example.[70] Assume a standard AI blocks world consisting of red and blue triangles and squares. A localist ANN has to represent the possible combinations. One unit in the net is allocated to represent "red," another for "blue," another for "triangle," and yet another for "square." If one wants to represent a "red triangle and blue square," the obvious solution is to activate all four units. Now represent "blue triangle and red square" using the same procedure. How can the two representations be distinguished? The answer is that they cannot, because there is no way to represent the different color-to-shape bindings in the two cases. In

other words, there is no way to represent constituency in a net like this. Localists have developed a variety of binding mechanisms to overcome this problem.[25,64,70,71]

Distributed Representation.

Representation of Primitives. In distributed ANNs, each primitive object is represented as a pattern of activity over some fixed-size group g of n units, or, abstractly, as a vector v of length n in which the value in any vector element v_i represents the activation of unit g_i, for $1 \leq i \leq n$. Such representation has significant advantages over the localist approach.[17]

Representation of Structure. The symbolist/subsymbolist debate made representation of compositional structure a major issue in ANN-based cognitive science on account of its explanatory capacity. The symbolists claimed that ANNs were incapable of representing structure, and for that reason dismissed them as inadequate for cognitive modeling. In response, adherents of ANN-based cognitive science have developed a variety of structure-representing mechanisms. But, as noted, NLP as construed here is not primarily interested in explanation, but in implementing mappings of interest, and many ANN architectures can implement any computable mapping without—as the symbolists observe— any recourse to compositional structure. Whatever its importance for cognitive science, therefore, is representation of compositional structure an issue for ANN-based NLP? The answer is that, in principle, compositional structure is not necessary for NLP, although it may be useful in practice. A discrete-time, continuous space dynamic system, such as a two-layer feedforward ANN with sigmoid activation function, may theoretically be capable of implementing any computable function, but, for some particular function, is finding the required weight parameters computationally tractable, and will network complexity have reasonable space requirements? It may well turn out that compositional structure makes implementation of certain NLP functions easier or indeed tractable; the need for compositional structure in ANN-based NLP is an empirical matter, and for that reason researchers need to be aware of the structuring mechanisms developed by ANN-based cognitive science.

Using a distributed ANN to represent compositional structure is difficult because arbitrarily complex structures have to be represented with a fixed-size resource (i.e., over some specific group of units). To see this, assume that the primitive objects in a given domain are represented as feature vectors. An ANN that uses distributed representations by definition uses all the available units for each vector. There would be no difficulty about individually representing "man," for

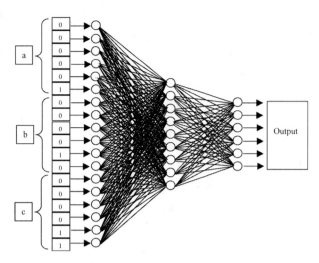

Fig. 2 A feedforward ANN for string processing.

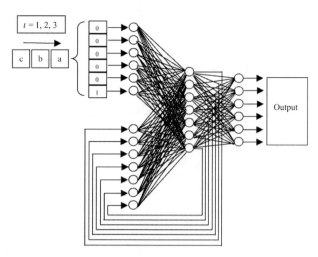

Fig. 4 A RANN for string processing.

example, or "horse." But how would the net represent "man" and "horse" at the same time? Even more difficult is the representation of relations, such as "man on horse." The problem, therefore, has been to find ways of overcoming this difficulty.

The crucial insight came from van Gelder in 1990.[72] He argued that distributed representations can be compositional but not necessarily in the sense intended within the PSSH paradigm. Van Gelder's article has become very influential in ANN-based cognitive science generally; its importance for present purposes lies in the distributed compositional representation, which it proposes and that underlies several distributed ANN-based representational mechanisms. Space limitations preclude a detailed account of it here. Suffice it to say that, as an alternative to the concatenative compositional representation used by symbolic cognitive

science, where the symbol tokens of an expression's constituents are spatially present in the compositional expression, van Gelder proposes nonconcatenative representation, where this is not the case. The importance of such nonconcatenative representation is that it breaks the link between abstract complexity and spatial representation size: because it does not require constituent tokens to be physically present in an expression token, it becomes possible in principle to represent abstract constituency relations over a fixed-size resource. What is needed in ANN terms are "general, effective, and reliable procedures"[73] to compose constituent tokens into and to decompose them from expression tokens represented over the representational units of the net. Several such nonconcatenative mechanisms have been proposed, chief among them tensor products,[74,75] recursive auto associative memories,[76–79] and holographic reduced descriptions.[73,80,81]

Sequential Processing

Text processing is inherently sequential in the sense that word tokens arrive at the processor over time. ANN-based work on NL has addressed this sequentiality[82,83] by using three main types of network architecture:

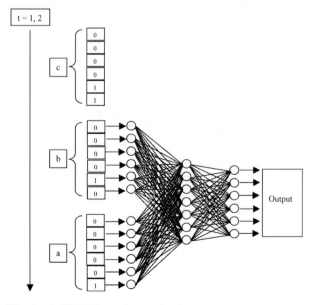

Fig. 3 A TDNN for string processing.

- Multilayer perceptrons (MLPs)
  MLPs are a feedforward architecture in which time is not a parameter: They map inputs to outputs instantaneously. MLPs consequently appear to be inappropriate for sequential processing. Nevertheless, the earlier ANN-based NL work used them for this purpose by spatializing time. Given a set of symbol strings to be processed, the MLP is given an input layer large enough to accommodate the longest string in the set, as in Fig. 2. This was unwieldy both because, depending on the input encoding scheme, it could result in large nets that take a long time to

train and because of the inherent variability in the length of NL strings. It is now rarely used.

- Time-delay neural networks (TDNNs)

A TDNN is an MLP whose input layer is a buffer k elements wide, as shown in Fig. 3. It processes input dynamically over time $t_0, t_1 \ldots t_n$ by updating the input buffer at each t_i and propagating the existing input values through the net to generate an output. The problem here is buffer size. For example, any dependencies in a string whose lexical distance is greater than the buffer size will be lost. In the limiting case, a buffer size equal to the input string length reduces to an MLP. TDNNs have been successfully used for finite state machine induction and in NLP applications.[84–86]

- Recurrent networks (RANN)

RANN use a fixed-size input layer to process strings dynamically. RANNs used for NL work are discrete-time, and input successive symbols in a string at time steps $t_0, t_1 \ldots t_n$, as in Fig. 4. The net's memory of sequential symbol ordering at any point in the input string is maintained in the existing state, which is fed back at each time step.

RANNs are dynamic systems that can be understood in terms of standard automata theory. A RANN that is driven through a trajectory in continuous-state space by a sequence of input signals is interpretable as an automaton driven through a trajectory in discrete space by an input symbol string, and the response of that RANN to a set of signal sequences as an automaton that defines a string set. Moreover, if the dynamics of the RANN are learned from input-output data rather than explicitly compiled into the net, then the RANN can be taken to have inferred an automaton that defines some language L or, equivalently, to have inferred the corresponding grammar.

There has been a good deal of work on the use of RANNs for grammatical inference, both for formal and for natural languages, and using a variety of RANN architectures.[82,87–100] The training of a simple recurrent network (SRN) as a finite state acceptor is paradigmatic: given a language L and a finite set T of pairs (a, b), where a is a symbol string and b is a Boolean that is true if $a{\in}L$ and false otherwise, train an SRN to approximate a finite state acceptor for L from a proper subset T' of T. The SRN, like various other RANN architectures used for grammatical inference, is a discrete-time, continuous-space dynamic system. To extract discrete computational states, the continuous ANN state space is partitioned into equivalence classes by using, for example, statistical clustering algorithms based on vector distance, and each cluster is interpreted as a single computational state. Any finite state machine extracted in this way is a possible computational interpretation of the RANN, but it is not unique, because the number of

states extracted depends on the granularity of the continuous-space partitioning and on the partitioning algorithm used.

Meaning Representation

There are some NLP applications, like document search, where the meaning of the text being processed is not an issue. In others, semantic interpretation of text is necessary but reasonably straightforward; an example would be an NL command interpreter for a database front end, where both the syntax of input strings and the semantic interpretations to which they are mapped are both well-defined and severely restricted relative to normal linguistic usage. However, when one moves to AI-oriented applications, such as (more or less) unrestricted NL understanding systems, semantic interpretation becomes a difficult and still largely unresolved problem. ANNs do not provide an easy solution, but they do offer a promising alternative to existing PSSH-based approaches.

Meaning is variously understood by different disciplines and by researchers within them. It does, however, seem uncontroversial to say that the meaning of NL linguistic expressions has to do with the denotation of states of the world and that semantic interpretation is a mapping from strings to denotations. That, in any case, is what is assumed here. PSSH-based AI and NLP systems have implemented the mapping by constructing system-internal representations of some aspect of the world—the "domain of discourse"—and then relating input strings to the representation.[101] How best to represent the world has become a research discipline in its own right—knowledge representation—and numerous formalisms exist. Some ANN-based work on semantic interpretation continues in the PSSH tradition in the sense that they use explicitly designed domain representations. Other work takes a radically different approach, however: Input strings are mapped not to explicitly designed representations of the world, which, inevitably, reflect a designer's analysis of what is significant in the task domain, but to representations that are learned from the world via transducers without designer intervention. At its most ambitious task, this line of research aims to embed NLP systems in robotic agents that not only receive inputs from an environment via, say, visual, acoustic, and tactile transducers, but also interact with and change the environment by means of effectors. The aim is for such agents to develop internal world representations by integrating inputs and internal states via self-organization based on adaptive interaction with the environment: "Concepts are thus the 'system's own,' and their meaning is no longer parasitic on the concepts of others (the system designer)."[102] In particular, agents would learn to represent the meanings of words and expressions from their use in specific environment-interactive situations. Work on this is proceeding,[42,43,102–112] although it must be said that, to keep experimental simulations tractable, the goal of real-world interaction is often reduced to explicitly designed microworlds reminiscent of ones like the famous SHRDLU in the PSSH tradition.

ANN-BASED NLP: AN OVERVIEW

ANN-based NL research[17,25,113–115] began, fairly slowly, in the early 1980s with articles on implementing semantic networks in ANNs,[116] visual word recognition,[117–119] word sense disambiguation,[120] anaphora resolution,[121] and syntactic parsing.[122–124] In 1986, Lehnert published an article[125] on the implications of ANN technology for NLP, an indication that this early work had by then attracted the attention of mainstream work in the field. Also in 1986 the *Parallel Distributed Processing* volumes[7] appeared, and these contained several chapters on language: McClelland and Kawamoto on case role assignment, McClelland on word recognition, and Rumelhart and McClelland on English past tense acquisition. All of these were to be influential, but the latter had an effect out of all proportion to the intrinsic important of the linguistic issue it dealt with. Rumelhart and McClelland presented an ANN that learned English past-tense morphology from a training set of (past tense/present tense) verb form pairs, including both regular ("-ed") and irregular formations. They regarded their net as a cognitive model of past tense morphology acquisition on the grounds that its learning dynamics were in close agreement with psycholinguistic data on past tense acquisition in children, and, because it was able to generalize the regular tense formation to previously unseen present tense forms after training, that what it had learned was an aspect of English morphology. Crucially, though, the net did this without reference to any explicit or implicit PSS architecture. This was quickly perceived as a challenge by symbolist cognitive scientists and became a test case in the symbolist versus subsymbolist debate outlined earlier. Pinker and Prince[126] made a long and detailed critique of the Rumelhart and McClelland model, in response to which the model was refined by a succession of researchers.[51,127–132]

From an NLP point of view, the chief importance of Rumelhart and McClelland's work and its successive refinements is not in its validity as a cognitive model but in the impetus that it gave to ANN-based NL research. It made 1986 a watershed year in the sense that the number of language-oriented articles has increased dramatically since then: disregarding speech and phonology on account of this entries focus on text

processing, there has been further work on a wide variety of topics, a representative selection of which follows:

General language acquisition: see also the preceding discussion of sequential processing.[41,89,90,133–135]
Morphology: see also the preceding discussion of past tense formation.[23,136,137]
Lexical category learning.[89,90]
Lexical semantics.[49,64,68,102–111,138–143]
Syntax and parsing.[41,49,89,90,115,144–154]
Sentence semantics.[49,155–159]
Metaphor interpretation.[160,161]
Text understanding.[49,162–164]
Language production.[49,50,140,165–168]
Dialog systems.[49,50]
Character recognition.[169–172]
Text classification.[173–176]
Data mining and text summarization.[177–181]
Text compression.[182]

REFERENCES

1. McCulloch, W.; Pitts, W. A logical calculus of the ideas immanent in nervous activity. Bull. Math. Biophys. **1943**, *5*, 115–133.
2. Medler, D. A brief history of connectionism. Neural Comput. Surv. **1998**, *1*, 61–101.
3. Taylor, J. The historical background. In *Handbook of Neural Computation*; Fiesler, E., Beale, R., Eds.; Institute of Physics Press: 1997.
4. Minsky, M.; Papert, S. In *Perceptrons*; MIT Press: 1969.
5. Pollack, J. No harm intended: A review of the *perceptrons* expanded edition. J. Math. Psychol. **1989**, *33*, 358–365.
6. Feldman, J.; Ballard, D. Connectionist models and their properties. Cogn. Sci. **1982**, *6*, 205–254.
7. In *Parallel Distributed Processing*; Rumelhart, D., McClelland, J., Eds.; MIT Press: 1986.
8. Ellacott, S.; Bose, D. In *Neural Networks*; International Thomson Publishing: 1996.
9. Rojas, R. In *Neural Networks: A Systematic Introduction*; Springer: 1996.
10. Haykin, S. In *Neural Networks: A Comprehensive Foundation,* 2nd Ed.; Prentice Hall: 1998.
11. White, H.; Hornik, K.; Stinchcombe, M. Multilayer feedforward networks are universal approximators. Neural Netw. **1989**, *2*, 359–366.
12. White, H. In *Artificial Neural Networks: Approximation and Learning Theory*; Blackwell: 1992.
13. Smolensky, P.; Mozer, M.; Rumelhart, D. In *Mathematical Perspectives on Neural Networks*; Lawrence Erlbaum: 1996.
14. Ellacott, S.; Bose, D. In *Neural Networks: Deterministic Methods of Analysis*; International Thomson Computer Press: 1996.

15. In *The Handbook of Brain Theory and Neural Networks*, Arbib, M., Ed.; MIT Press: 1995; 20.

16. Bishop, C. In *Neural Networks for Pattern Recognition*; Clarendon Press: 1995.

17. Moisl, M. NLP based on artificial neural networks. In *Handbook of Natural Language Processing*, Dale, R., Moisl, H., Somers, R., Eds.; Marcel Dekker: 2000.

18. Judd, J. Complexity of learning. In *Mathematical Perspectives on Neural Networks*, Smolensky, P., Mozer, M., Rumelhart, D., Eds.; Lawrence Erlbaum: 1996.

19. Baum, E. When are *k*-nearest neighbor and backpropagation accurate for feasible-sized sets of examples? In *Computational Learning Theory and Natural Learning Systems*, Hanson, S., Drastal, G., Rivest, R., Eds.; MIT Press: 1994.

20. Elman, J. Learning and development in neural networks: The importance of starting small. Cognition **1993**, *48*, 71–99.

21. Frasconi, P.; Gori, M.; Soda, G. Recurrent neural networks and prior knowledge for sequence processing: A constrained nondeterministic approach. Knowl.-Based Syst. **1995**, *8*, 313–332.

22. Omlin, C. Stable encoding of large finite state automata in recurrent neural networks with sigmoid discriminants. Neural Comput. **1996**, *8*, 675–696.

23. Gasser, M. Transfer in a connectionist model of the acquisition of morphology. In *Yearbook of Morphology 1996*, Baayen, H., Schroeder, R., Eds.; Foris: 1997.

24. Thrun, S.; Pratt, L. In *Learning To Learn*; Kluwer: 1997.

25. Dyer, M. Connectionist natural language processing: A status report. In *Computational Architectures Intregrating Neural and Symbolic Processes*, Sun, R., Bookman, L., Eds.; Kluwer: 1995; 391.

26. Newell, A. Physical symbol systems. Cogn. Sci. **1980**, *4*, 135–183.

27. Fodor, J.; Pylyshyn, Z. Connectionism and cognitive architecture: A critical analysis. Cognition **1988**, *28*, 3–71.

28. Smolensky, P. On the proper treatment of connectionism. Behav. Brain Sci. **1988**, *11*, 1–74.

29. Fodor, J.; McLaughlin, B. Connectionism and the problem of systematicity: Why Smolensky's solution doesn't work. In *Connectionism and the Philosophy of Mind*, Horgan, T., Tienson, J., Eds.; Kluwer: 1991.

30. Fodor, J. Connectionism and the problem of systematicity (continued): Why Smolensky's solution still doesn't work. Cognition **1997**, *62*, 109–119.

31. Smolensky, P. The constituent structure of connectionist mental states: A reply to Fodor and Pylyshyn. In *Connectionism and the Philosophy of Mind*, Horgan, T., Tienson, J., Eds.; Kluwer: 1991.

32. Smolensky, P. Connectionism, constituency, and the language of thought. In *Meaning and Mind. Fodor and His Critics*, Loewer, B., Rey, G., Eds.; Blackwell: 1991.

33. Clark, A. In *Microcognition: Philosophy, Cognitive Science, and Parallel Distributed Processing*; MIT Press: 1989.

34. In *Connectionism and the Philosophy of Mind*, Horgan, T., Tienson, J., Eds.; Kluwer: 1991.

35. Churchland, P.; Sejnowski, T. In *The Computational Brain*; MIT Press: 1992.

36. In *The Symbolic and Connectionist Paradigms: Closing the Gap*, Dinsmore, J., Ed.; Lawrence Erlbaum: 1992.

37. Clark, A. In *Associative Engines. Connectionism, Concepts, and Representational Change*; MIT Press: 1993.

38. Honavar, V.; Uhr, L. In *Artificial Intelligence and Neural Networks: Steps Toward Principled Integration*; Academic Press: 1994.

39. In *Mind as Motion. Explorations in the Dynamics of Cognition*, Port, R., van Gelder, T., Eds.; MIT Press: 1995.

40. In *Connectionism: Debates on Psychological Explanation*, Macdonald, C., Macdonald, G., Eds.; Basil Blackwell: 1995.

41. Elman, J.; Bates, E.; Johnson, M.; Karmiloff-Smith, A.; Parisi, D.; Plunkett, K. In *Rethinking Innateness. A Connectionist Perspective on Development*; MIT Press: 1996.

42. In *Neural Networks and a New Artificial Intelligence*, Dorffner, G., Ed.; Thomson Computer Press: 1997.

43. Clark, A. In *Being There. Putting Brain, Body, and World Together Again*; MIT Press: 1997.

44. Hadley, R. Systematicity in connectionist language learning. Mind Lang. **1994**, *9*, 247–273.

45. Niklasson, L.; van Gelder, T. On being systematically connectionist. Mind Lang. **1994**, *9*, 288–302.

46. Niklasson, L.; Sharkey, N. Systematicity and generalization in compositional connectionist representations. In *Neural Networks and a New Artificial Intelligence*, Dorffner, G., Ed.; Thomson Computer Press: 1997.

47. In *Connectionist Symbol Processing: Dead or Alive?*, Jagota, A., Plate, T., Shastri, L., Sun, R., Eds.; Neural Computing Surveys 1999; Vol. 2, 1–40.

48. Witbrock, M. The symbolic approach to ANN-based natural language processing. In *Handbook of Natural Language Processing*, Dale, R., Moisl, H., Somers, R., Eds.; Marcel Dekker: 2000.

49. Miikkulainen, R. In *Subsymbolic Natural Language Processing: An Integrated Model of Scripts, Lexicon, and Memory*; MIT Press: 1993.

50. Miikkulainen, R. Text and discourse understanding: The DISCERN system. In *Handbook of Natural Language Processing*, Dale, R., Moisl, H., Somers, R., Eds.; Marcel Dekker: 2000.

51. Dorffner, G. The subsymbolic approach to ANN-based natural language processing. In *Handbook of Natural Language Processing*, Dale, R., Moisl, H., Somers, R., Eds.; Marcel Dekker: 2000.

52. Smolensky, P.; Legendre, G.; Miyata, Y. Integrating connectionist and symbolic computation for the theory of Language. In *Artificial Intelligence and Neural Networks: Steps Toward Principled Integration*, Honavar, V., Uhr, L., Eds.; Academic Press: 1994.

53. Prince, A.; Smolensky, P. Optimality: From neural networks to universal grammar. Science **1997**, *275*, 1604–1610.

54. Smolensky, P.; Legendre, G. *Toward a Calculus of the Mind/Brain: Neural Network Theory, Optimality, and Universal Grammar*; MIT Press: Cambridge, MA: 2001.

55. Wermter, S. In *Hybrid Connectionist Natural Language Processing*; Chapman & Hall: 1995.

Ad Hoc–
Availability

56. Sun, R.; Bookman, L. In *Computational Architectures Integrating Neural and Symbolic Processes*; Kluwer: 1995.

57. Sun, R.; Alexandre, F. In *Connectionist-Symbolic Integration. From Unified to Hybrid Approaches*; Lawrence Erlbaum: 1997.

58. McGarry, K.; Wermter, S.; MacIntyre, J. Hybrid neural systems: From simple coupling to fully integrated neural networks. Neural Comput. Surv. **1999**, *2*, 62–93.

59. In *Hybrid Neural Systems*, Wermter, S., Sun, R., Eds.; Springer: 2000.

60. Wermter, S. The hybrid approach to artificial neural network-based language processing. In *Handbook of Natural Language Processing*, Dale, R., Moisl, H., Somers, R., Eds.; Marcel Dekker: 2000.

61. Sharkey, N. Connectionist representation techniques. Artif. Intell. Rev. **1991**, *5*, 143–167.

62. Sharkey, N.; Jackson, S. Three horns of the representational trilemma. In *Artificial Intelligence and Neural Networks: Steps Toward Principled Integration*, Honavar, V., Uhr, L., Eds.; Academic Press: 1994.

63. Sharkey, N.; Sharkey, A. Separating learning and representation. In *Connectionist, Statistical, and Symbolic Approaches to Learning for Natural Language Processing*, Wermter, S., Riloff, E., Scheler, G., Eds.; Springer: 1996.

64. Shastri, L. Structured connectionist models. In *The Handbook of Brain Theory and Neural Networks*, Arbib, M., Ed.; MIT Press: 1995.

65. Thorpe, S. Localized versus distributed representations. In *The Handbook of Brain Theory and Neural Networks*, Arbib, M., Ed.; MIT Press: 1995.

66. Feldman, J. Structured connectionist models and language learning. Artif. Intell. Rev. **1993**, *7*, 301–312.

67. Bookman, L. In *Trajectories through Knowledge Space. A Dynamic Framework for Machine Comprehension*; Kluwer: 1994.

68. Regier, T. In *The Human Semantic Potential*; MIT Press: 1996.

69. Feldman, J.; Lakoff, G.; Bailey, D.; Narayanan, S.; Regier, T.; Stolcke, A. L0: The first five years. Artif. Intell. Rev. **1996**, *10*, 103–129.

70. Bienenstock, D.; Geman, S. Compositionality in neural systems. In *The Handbook of Brain Theory and Neural Networks*, Arbib, M., Ed.; MIT Press: 1995.

71. Sun, R. Logics and variables in connectionist models: A brief overview. In *Artificial Intelligence and Neural Networks: Steps Toward Principled Integration*, Honavar, V., Uhr, L., Eds.; Academic Press: 1994.

72. van Gelder, T. Compositionality: A connectionist variation on a classical theme. Cogn. Sci. **1990**, *14*, 355–384.

73. Plate, T. Holographic reduced representations. IEEE Trans. Neural Netw. **1995**, *6*, 623–641.

74. Smolensky, P. Tensor product variable binding and the representation of symbolic structures in connectionist systems. Artif. Intell. **1990**, *46*, 159–216.

75. Legendre, G.; Miyata, Y.; Smolensky, P. Distributed recursive structure processing. In *Advances in Neural Information Processing Systems 3*, Touretzky, D., Lippman, R., Eds.; Morgan Kaufmann: 1991.

76. Pollack, J. Recursive distributed representations. Artif. Intell. **1990**, *46*, 77–105.

77. Chalmers, D. Syntactic transformations on distributed representations. Connect. Sci. **1990**, *2*, 53–62.

78. Callan, R.; Palmer-Brown, D. (S)RAAM: An analytical technique for fast and reliable derivation of connectionist symbol structure representations. Connect. Sci. **1997**, *9*, 139–160.

79. Adamson, M.; Damper, R. B_RAAM: A connectionist model which develops holistic internal representations of symbolic structures. Connect. Sci. **1999**, *11*, 41–71.

80. Plate, T. Holographic recurrent networks. In *Advances in Neural Information Processing Systems 5*, Giles, C., Hanson, S., Cowan, J., Eds.; Morgan Kaufmann: 1993.

81. Plate, T. A common framework for distributed representation schemes for compositional structure. In *Connectionist Systems for Knowledge Representation and Deduction,* Maire, F., Hayward, R., Diederich, J., Eds.; Queensland University of Technology: 1997.

82. Bengio, Y. In *Neural Networks for Speech and Sequence Recognition*; International Thomson Computer Press: 1996.

83. In *Sequence Learning: Paradigms, Algorithms, and Applications*, Sun, R., Giles, C. L., Eds.; Springer: 2001.

84. Clouse, D.; Giles, C.; Horne, B.; Cottrell, G. Time-delay neural networks: Representation and induction of finite-state machines. IEEE Trans. Neural Netw. **1997**, *8*, 1065–1070.

85. Bodenhausen, U.; Geutner, P.; Waibel, A. Flexibility through incremental learning: neural networks for text categorization. In *Proceedings of the World Congress on Neural Networks (WCNN)*; Lawrence Erlbaum Associates: 1993.

86. Bodenhausen, U.; Manke, S. A connectionist recognizer for on-line cursive handwriting recognition. In *Proceedings of the IEEE, International Conference on Acoustics, Speech, and Signal Processing*; IEEE: 1994.

87. Jordan, M. Attractor dynamics and parallelism in a connectionist sequential machine. In *Proceedings of the Eighth Conference of the Cognitive Science Society*; Lawrence Erlbaum Associates: 1986.

88. Servan-Schreiber, D.; Cleeremans, A.; McClelland, J. Learning sequential structure in simple recurrent networks. In *Advances in Neural Information Processing Systems 1*, Touretzky, D., Ed.; Morgan Kaufmann: 1989.

89. Elman, J. Finding structure in time. Cogn. Sci. **1990**, *14*, 179–211.

90. Elman, J. Distributed representation, simple recurrent networks, and grammatical structure. Mach. Learn. **1991**, *7*, 195–225.

91. Servan-Schreiber, D.; Cleeremans, A.; McClelland, J. Graded state machines: The representation of temporal contingencies in simple recurrent networks. Mach. Learn. **1991**, *7*, 161–193.

92. Pollack, J. The induction of dynamical recognizers. Mach. Learn. **1991**, *7*, 227–252.

93. Watrous, R.; Kuhn, G. Induction of finite-state languages using second-order recurrent networks. Neural Comput. **1992**, *4*, 406–414.

94. Zeng, Z.; Goodman, R.; Smyth, P. Discrete recurrent neural networks for grammatical inference. IEEE Trans. Neural Netw. **1994**, *5*, 320–330.

95. Horne, B.; Giles, C.; Lin, T. Learning a class of large finite state machines with a recurrent neural network. Neural Netw. **1995**, *8*, 1359–1365.

96. Frasconi, P.; Gori, M.; Maggini, M.; Soda, G. Representation of finite state automata in recurrent radial basis function networks. Mach. Learn. **1996**, *23*, 5–32.

97. Lawrence, S.; Fong, S.; Giles, C. Natural language grammatical inference: a comparison of recurrent neural networks and machine learning methods. In *Connectionist, Statistical, and Symbolic Approaches to Learning for Natural Language Processing,* Wermter, S., Riloff, E., Scheler, G., Eds.; Springer: 1996.

98. Tino, P.; Horne, B.; Giles, C.; Collingwood, P. Finite state machines and recurrent neural networks—Automata and dynamical systems approaches. In *Neural Networks and Pattern Recognition,* Dayhoff, J., Omidvar, O., Eds.; Academic Press: 1998.

99. Parekh, R.; Honavar, V. Grammar inference, automata induction, and language acquisition. In *Handbook of Natural Language Processing,* Dale, R., Moisl, H., Somers, R., Eds.; Marcel Dekker: 2000.

100. Omlin, C.; Giles, C. In *Symbolic Knowledge Representation and Acquisition in Recurrent Neural Networks: Foundations, Algorithms, and Applications*; World Scientific Publishing: 1999.

101. Poesio, M. Semantic analysis. In *Handbook of Natural Language Processing,* Dale, R., Moisl, H., Somers, R., Eds.; Marcel Dekker: 2000.

102. Dorffner, G.; Prem, E. Connectionism, symbol grounding, and autonomous agents. In *Proceedings of the 15th Annual Conference of the Cognitive Science Society*; Lawrence Erlbaum Associates: 1993.

103. Nenov, V.; Dyer, M. Perceptually grounded language learning: Part 1—A neural network architecture for robust sequence association. Connect. Sci. **1993**, *5*, 115–138.

104. Nenov, V.; Dyer, M. Perceptually grounded language learning: Part 2—DETE: A neural/procedural model. Connect. Sci. **1994**, *6*, 3–41.

105. Harnad, S. Grounding symbols in the analog world with neural nets. Think **1993**, *2*, 12–78.

106. Dyer, M. Grounding language in perception. In *Artificial Intelligence and Neural Networks: Steps Toward Principled Integration,* Honavar, V., Uhr, L., Eds.; Academic Press: 1994.

107. Srihari, R. Computational models for integrating linguistic and visual information: A survey. Artif. Intell. Rev. **1994–1995**, *8*, 349–369.

108. Harnad, S. Grounding symbolic capacity in robotic capacity. In *The Artificial Life Route to Artificial Intelligence: Building Embodied, Situated Agents,* Steels, L., Brooks, R., Eds.; Lawrence Erlbaum: 1995.

109. Jackson, S.; Sharkey, N. Grounding computational engines. Artif. Intell. Rev. **1996**, *10*, 65–82.

110. Sales, N.; Evans, R.; Aleksander, I. Successful naive representation grounding. Artif. Intell. Rev. **1996**, *10*, 83–102.

111. Bailey, D.; Feldman, J.; Narayanan, S.; Lakoff, G. Embodied lexical development. In *Proceedings of the 19th Annual Meeting of the Cognitive Science Society*; Stanford University Press: 1997.

112. Pfeifer, R.; Verschure, P. Complete autonomous systems: A research strategy for cognitive science. In *Neural Networks and a New Artificial Intelligence*, Dorffner, G., Ed.; Thomson International Computer Press: 1997.

113. Selman, B. Connectionist systems for natural language understanding. Artif. Intell. Rev. **1989**, *3*, 23–31.

114. Sharkey, N.; Reilly, R. Connectionist natural language processing. In *Connectionist Approaches to Natural Language Processing,* Reilly, R., Sharkey, N., Eds.; Lawrence Erlbaum: 1992.

115. Christiansen, M.; Chater, N. Connectionist natural language processing: The state of the art. Cogn. Sci. **1999**, *23*, 417–437.

116. Hinton, G. Implementing semantic networks in parallel hardware. In *Parallel Models of Associative Memory,* Hinton, G., Anderson, J., Eds.; Lawrence Erlbaum: 1981.

117. McClelland, J.; Rumelhart, D. An interactive activation model of context effects in letter perception: Part 1. An account of basic findings. Psychol. Rev. **1981**, *88*, 375–407.

118. Rumelhart, D.; McClelland, J. An interactive activation model of context effects in letter perception: Part 2. The contextual enhancement effects and some tests and enhancements of the model. Psychol. Rev. **1982**, *89*, 60–94.

119. Golden, R. A developmental neural model of visual word perception. Cogn. Sci. **1986**, *10*, 241–276.

120. Cottrell, G.; Small, S. A connectionist scheme for modeling word sense disambiguation. Cogn. Brain Theory **1983**, *6*.

121. Reilly, R. A Connectionist model of some aspects of anaphor resolution. In *Proceedings of the Tenth Annual Conference on Computational Linguistics*; ACL: 1984.

122. Small, S.; Cottrell, G.; Shastri, L. Towards connectionist parsing. In *Proceedings of the National Conference on Artificial Intelligence*; AAAI: 1982.

123. Fanty, M. In *Context-Free Parsing in Connectionist Networks TR 174*, Department of Computer Science, University of Rochester: 1985.

124. Selman, B.; Hirst, G. A rule-based connectionist parsing system. In *Proceedings of the Seventh Annual Meeting of the Cognitive Science Society*; Lawrence Erlbaum: 1985.

125. Lehnert, W. Possible implications of connectionism. In *Theoretical Issues in Natural Language Processing*; University of Mexico: 1986.

126. Pinker, S.; Prince, A. On language and connectionism: Analysis of a parallel distributed processing model of language acquisition. Cognition **1988**, *28*, 73–193.

127. MacWhinney, B.; Leinbach, J. Implementations are not conceptualizations: Revising the verb learning model. Cognition **1991**, *40*, 121–157.

128. Plunkett, K.; Marchman, V. U-shaped learning and frequency effects in a multi-layered perceptron: Implications for child language acquisition. Cognition **1991**, *38*, 43–102.

129. Daugherty, K.; Seidenberg, M. Rules or connections? The past tense revisited. In *Proceedings of the Fourteenth Annual Meeting of the Cognitive Science Society*; Lawrence Erlbaum: 1992.

130. Daugherty, K.; Hare, M. What's in a rule? The past tense by some other name might be called a connectionist net. In *Proceedings of the 1993 Connectionist Models Summer School*; Lawrence Erlbaum: 1993.

131. Plunkett, K.; Marchman, V. From rote learning to system building: Acquiring verb morphology in children and connectionist nets. Cognition **1993**, *48*, 21–69.

132. Marcus, G. The acquisition of the English past tense in children and multilayered connectionist networks. Cognition **1997**, *56*, 271–279.

133. Plunkett, K. Language acquisition. In *The Handbook of Brain Theory and Neural Networks*; Arbib, M., Ed.; MIT Press: 1995.

134. Seidenberg, M.; Allen, J.; Christiansen, M. Language acquisition: Learning and applying probabilistic constraints. In *Proceedings of GALA 1997: Language Acquisition: Knowledge Representation and Processing*; Sorace, A., Heycock, C., Shillcock, R., Eds.; University of Edinburgh: 1997.

135. Bates, E.; Elman, J.; Johnson, M.; Karmiloff-Smith, A.; Parisi, D.; Plunkett, K. Innateness and emergentism. In *A Companion to Cognitive Science*; Bechtel, W., Graham, G., Eds.; Basil Blackwell: 1998.

136. Hare, M.; Elman, J. Learning and morphological change. Cognition **1995**, *56*, 61–98.

137. Plunkett, K.; Juola, P. A connectionist model of English past tense and plural morphology. Cogn. Sci. **1999**, *23* (4).

138. Dorffner, G. Taxonomies and part–whole hierarchies in the acquisition of word meaning—A Connectionist Model. In *Proceedings of the 14th Annual Conference of the Cognitive Science Society*; Lawrence Erlbaum: 1992.

139. Dorffner, G.; Hentze, M.; Thurner, G. A Connectionist model of categorization and grounded word learning. In *Proceedings of the Groningen Assembly on Language Acquisition (GALA'95)*, Koster, C., Wijnen, F., Eds.; Center for the Study of Cognition: 1996.

140. Scheler, G. Generating English plural determiners from semantic representations: A neural network learning approach. In *Connectionist, Statistical, and Symbolic Approaches to Learning for Natural Language Processing*, Wermter, S., Riloff, E., Scheler, G., Eds.; Springer: 1996.

141. Scheler, G. Learning the semantics of aspect. In *New Methods in Language Processing*, Somers, H., Jones, D., Eds.; University College London Press: 1996.

142. Narayanan, S. Talking the talk *is* like walking the walk: A computational model of verbal aspect. In *Proceedings of the Annual Conference of the Cognitive Science Society*; Stanford: 1997.

143. Clouse, D.; Cottrell, G. Regularities in a random mapping from orthography to semantics. In *Proceedings of the Twentieth Annual Cognitive Science Conference*; Lawrence Erlbaum: 1998.

144. Waltz, D.; Pollack, J. Massively parallel parsing: A strongly interactive model of natural language interpretation. Cogn. Sci. **1985**, *95*, 1–74.

145. Hanson, S.; Kegl, J. PARSNIP: A connectionist network that learns natural language grammar from exposure to natural language sentences. In *Proceedings of the Ninth Annual Conference of the Cognitive Science Society*; Lawrence Erlbaum: 1987.

146. Howells, T. VITAL—A connectionist parser. In *Proceedings of the Tenth Annual Conference of the Cognitive Science Society*; Lawrence Erlbaum Associates: 1988.

147. Jain, A.; Waibel, A. Parsing with connectionist networks. In *Current Issues in Parsing Technology*, Tomita, M., Ed.; Kluwer: 1991.

148. Wermter, S.; Lehnert, W. Noun phrase analysis with connectionist networks. In *Connectionist Approaches to Natural Language Processing*, Reilly, R., Sharkey, N., Eds.; Lawrence Erlbaum: 1992.

149. Kwasny, S.; Johnson, S.; Kalman, B. Recurrent natural language parsing. In *Proceedings of the Sixteenth Annual Meeting of the Cognitive Science Society*; Lawrence Erlbaum: 1994.

150. Miikkulainen, R. Subsymbolic parsing of embedded structures. In *Computational Architectures Integrating Neural and Symbolic Processes*, Sun, R., Bookman, L., Eds.; Kluwer: 1995.

151. Tabor, W.; Juliano, C.; Tanenhaus, M. Parsing in a dynamical system: An attractor-based account of the interaction of lexical and structural constraints in sentence processing. Lang. Cogn. Processes **1997**, *12*, 211–271.

152. Henderson, J.; Lane, P. A connectionist architecture for learning to parse. In *Proceedings of 17th International Conference on Computational Linguistics and the 36th Annual Meeting of the Association for Computational Linguistics (COLING-ACL'98)*; University of Montreal: Canada, 1998.

153. Tabor, W.; Tanenhaus, M. Dynamical models of sentence processing. Cogn. Sci. **1999**, *23* (4).

154. Henderson, J. Constituency, context, and connectionism in syntactic parsing. In *Architectures and Mechanisms for Language Processing*, Crocker, M., Pickering, M., Clifton, C., Eds.; Cambridge University Press: 1999.

155. McClelland, J.; Kawamoto, A. Mechanisms of sentence processing: Assigning roles to constituents. In *Parallel Distributed Processing*, Rumelhart, D., McClelland, J., Eds.; MIT Press: 1986.

156. St. John, M.; McClelland, J. Learning and applying contextual constraints in sentence comprehension. Artif. Intell. **1990**, *46*, 217–257.

157. St. John, M.; McClelland, J. Parallel constraint satisfaction as a comprehension mechanism. In *Connectionist Approaches to Natural Language Processing*, Reilly, R., Sharkey, N., Eds.; Lawrence Erlbaum: 1992.

158. Wermter, S. A hybrid symbolic/connectionist model for noun phrase understanding. In *Connectionist Natural Language Processing*, Sharkey, N., Ed.; Kluwer: 1992.

159. Miikkulainen, R. Subsymbolic case–role analysis of sentences with embedded clauses. Cogn. Sci. **1996**, *20*, 47–73.

160. Wermter, S.; Hannuschka, R. A connectionist model for the interpretation of metaphors. In *Neural Networks and a New Artificial Intelligence*, Dorffner, G., Ed.; Thomson International Computer Press: 1997.

161. Narayanan, S. Moving right along: a computational model of metaphoric reasoning about events. In *Proceedings of the National Conference on Artificial Intelligence AAAI-99* AAAI: 1999 Orlando, FL.

162. Miikkulainen, R. Integrated connectionist models: Building AI systems on subsymbolic foundations. In *Artificial Intelligence and Neural Networks: Steps Toward Principled Integration*, Honavar, V., Uhr, L., Eds.; Academic Press: 1994.

163. Wermter, S.; Weber, V. SCREEN: Learning a flat syntactic and semantic spoken language analysis using artificial neural networks. J. Artif. Intell. Res. **1997**, *6*, 35–85.

164. Narayanan, S. Reasoning about actions in narrative understanding. In *Proceedings of the International Joint Conference on Artificial Intelligence IJCAI-99*; AAAI: Stockholm, 1999.

165. Ward, N. In *A Connectionist Language Generator*; Ablex: 1994.

166. Cottrell, G.; Plunkett, K. Acquiring the mapping from meaning to sounds. Connect. Sci. **1995**, *6*, 379–412.

167. Dell, G.; Burger, L.; Svec, W. Language production and serial order: A functional analysis and a model. Psychol. Rev. **1997**, *104*, 123–147.

168. Aretoulaki, M. Towards a hybrid abstract generation system. In *New Methods in Language Processing,* Somers, H., Jones, D., Eds.; UCL Press: 1997.

169. Basak, J.; Nikhil, R.; Pal, S. A connectionist system for learning and recognition of structures: Application to handwritten characters. Neural Netw. **1995**, *8*, 643–657.

170. Shustorovich, A.; Thrasher, C. Neural network positioning and classification of handwritten characters. Neural Netw. **1996**, *9*, 685–693.

171. Chiang, J.-H. A hybrid neural network model in handwritten word recognition. Neural Netw. **1998**, *11*, 337–346.

172. Lucas, S. Character recognition with syntactic neural networks. In *Handbook of Natural Language Processing,* Dale, R., Moisl, H., Somers, R., Eds.; Marcel Dekker: 2000.

173. Merkl, D. Text classification with self-organizing maps: Some lessons learned. Neurocomputing **1998**, *21*, 61–77.

174. Kaski, S.; Honkela, T.; Lagus, K.; Kohonen, T. WEB-SOM—Self-organizing maps of document collections. Neurocomputing **1998**, *21*, 101–117.

175. Wermter, S. Neural network agents for learning semantic text classification. Inf. Retriev. **2000**, *3*, 87–103.

176. Kohonen, T.; Kaski, S.; Lagus, K.; Salojarvi, J.; Paatero, V.; Saarela, A. Organization of a massive document collection. IEEE Trans. Neural Netw. **2000**, *11*, 574–585.

177. Merkl, D. Text data mining. In *Handbook of Natural Language Processing,* Dale, R., Moisl, H., Somers, R., Eds.; Marcel Dekker: 2000.

178. Winiwarter, W.; Schweighofer, E.; Merkl, D. Knowledge acquisition in concept and document spaces by using self-organizing neural networks. In *Connectionist, Statistical, and Symbolic Approaches to Learning for Natural Language Processing,* Wermter, S., Riloff, E., Scheler, G., Eds.; Springer: 1996.

179. Aretoulaki, M.; Scheler, G.; Brauer, W. Connectionist modeling of human event memorization with application to automatic text summarization. In *AAAI Spring Symposium on Intelligent Text Summarization*; Stanford: 1998.

180. König, A. Interactive visualization and analysis of hierarchical neural projections for data mining. IEEE Trans. Neural Netw. **2000**, *11*, 615–624.

181. Chen, C.; Honavar, V. Neural architectures for information retrieval and database query. In *Handbook of Natural Language Processing,* Dale, R., Moisl, H., Somers, R., Eds.; Marcel Dekker: 2000.

182. Schmidhuber, J.; Heil, S. Compressing texts with neural nets. In *Handbook of Natural Language Processing,* Dale, R., Moisl, H., Somers, R., Eds.; Marcel Dekker: 2000.

Ad Hoc– Availability

Assurance: Science of

Jason W. Rupe
Polar Star Consulting, LLC, Lafayette, Colorado, U.S.A.

Abstract

The subject of telecommunications and information technology (IT) reliability concerns is ultimately about assurance, the real intent of reliability in this field. This entry covers some basic definitions for a foundation, and some of the most important tools to use. Then, it separates into hardware, software, and data, as there are important differences to cover in each. Finally, it combines it all back together again to cover reliability concerns of systems, networks, services, and missions. The entry concludes with some of the related topics we can't forget, and important resources for finding out more. You'll find a lot of information mentioned here and some important ideas. Some of it is just to frame your thinking about reliability concerns, and, hopefully, you can see where the information applies in many more ways than we can describe in this short entry. In addition to seeing the risks and concerns, I hope you can equally come away with ideas for how to make the IT and telecommunications world more reliable.

INTRODUCTION: GENERALITIES

Why do we worry about reliability at all? Because the task of doing anything to scale requires it.

Much of the effort in scaling anything is really about improving its reliability. Operations costs are reduced by reducing rework, which is really about avoiding failures. So just about everyone has some role toward improving reliability in their daily lives. Hence, to build a solution, we have to judge the suitability of the parts of that solution, which is just another way of trying to estimate the reliability of things. The field of reliability is so broad and encompassing that it permeates our lives entirely, once we realize it. And, thus, it applies here.

But in this entry, we focus on the reliability aspects of information technology (IT) and telecommunications parts, subsystems, systems, and networks. We'll talk about the ideas that guide us to improve all relevant items in question, and to predict their suitability. We'll break down the concepts, and the ways we can think about the contributing technologies in hardware and software and data and networks. We'll discuss the methods and tools for understanding, improving, and estimating the suitability of equipment, systems, and solutions.

DEFINITIONS AND CONCEPTS

Reliability in its strictest sense is the probability that the item in question will perform for the intended duration of interest, say to age t. We are making the implicit assumption that the item in question is not repairable, or at least we are interested in its behavior up to when it

would otherwise be repaired. Therefore, we often talk about the reliability of components or parts, things that are replaced if possible, and either disposed of or at best recycled.

There are a few terms of convenience related to the strict sense of reliability. For convenience, we often talk about the mean time to failure. For a group of like items, we might think about mean time between failures. Those concepts, and the mean time to first failure for repairable or replaceable units in a system, are all terms of convenience. But as such, they are dangerous, because they are statistical means of data, or some estimate of that statistical mean. There is no such event as the average, and the distribution of failures matters a great deal here.

But we often use the term reliability to mean a whole lot of related ideas, bundled together in the general sense. That concept of reliability is really the entire scope of the assurance sciences, which this entry will cover, limited to the focus of this book of course, which is telecommunications and IT. In fact, it is common for people to say reliability when they really mean availability; but try to avoid that for clarity.

Availability is generally a proportion of time over which the item in question is functioning as intended. Implicit in this definition is that the item in question is repairable. Therefore, availability is usually applied to more complex items, such as systems, networks, services, and missions.

There is an easier way to think about availability, which usually is good enough. Realize that I said proportion of time, which raises questions, like from when to when? Here we have a choice, which amounts to

Encyclopedia of Information Systems and Technology, DOI: 10.1081/E-EIST-120052923

setting an initial condition or state for the item in question, and then some duration. In the absence of this information, we usually assume the initial state is unknown, and probabilistically in any state possible, the concept of steady state. It is easier just to think of it as though you were calculating the availability in some far future time, where you long forgot the initial condition of the item in question. And then we can simplify our thinking here to just consider availability to be the probability that the item in question is in a working state.

Maintainability is a general concept about how easy the item in question is to keep in a working state. Related to this concept is that of repairability, which is about how easy the item in question is to repair, which we sometimes measure in terms of the time to repair. Here you will hear about convenient concepts such as mean time to repair, which is as it sounds, the average time it takes to repair the item in question. A note on this subject however: use mean time to repair (mttr) at your own risk, because there is no such real event as average, and real events can vary far from that mttr you are considering. It is important to look at the distribution of repair times in any analysis, and work to reduce the variability as well as the statistical mean.

Survivability can almost be thought of as self-repair, but relies on the item in question, usually a complex system or network, to continue to function, or quickly recover to a functional state, after a failure event. We usually use this term in the context of a complex system or network in our field, so it applies to ideas similar to Automatic Protection Switching (APS) or fail over, where one part takes over for another like but failed one.

Related to this survivability concept is the idea of standby, because complex systems and networks rely on standby parts to enable survivability. There are different types of standby parts: hot, warm, and cold. Hot standby is for when the spare part is powered on, and ready to take over for the active part. In this state, it can fail just like the active part. In fact, we may even consider the parts here to really be in a load sharing configuration, where both (or all) parts are sharing the work load in some way. If you are familiar with link aggregation (LAG), a lag group is a good example of load sharing, as all links are carrying traffic, and if one link fails the rest continue to carry the traffic. Some systems have redundant power supplies, which is another example of how both units are likely sharing the load of supplying power. But if the hot standby unit is not sharing the work load, we can say it is at least powered on, and doing work sufficiently to think about it as behaving just like the active unit from a failure point of view.

Warm standby is similar to hot standby, but represents the situation where the standby unit is perhaps powered on, and maybe even state aware so that it can take over if the primary unit fails. But, in this state, it is not actively contributing to the work of the system, and is likely to be in a lower stress condition, where it has a lower probability of failure compared to an active component of the same age.

And last, we talk about a cold standby unit, where the standby unit sits in an inactive condition, waiting to be powered on to take over for the failed primary unit. A backup generator is a good example. It mostly sits there inactive at the datacenter, but ready to be turned on if the AC power feed from the utility were to ever drop below the power load.

Performability is a very useful concept, especially when applied to complex systems and networks. Some items in question don't just fail hard and completely, or otherwise work absolutely fine. Instead, they work to some varying degree. And depending on the use of the item in question, maybe that degraded performance still has value. We can think of the various states of the item in question being mutually exclusive, and complete, so that the item in question is in only one of these states at a time, and we can determine the probability that the item in question exists in one of those states. Using that state probability, and further acknowledging that the states each have a level of performance that we can define, we can then talk about the performance in each of these states. Perhaps the states and performance levels are not discrete, but that's okay. We can still talk about the probability distribution of the performance for the item in question. For a repairable system, availability is the same thing as performability, only we assume the performance is either 1 for fully functional, or 0 for fully failed. Performabilty only extends the idea of availability to account for levels of performance between fully functional and fully failed. That makes it a great concept when applied to networks, systems, missions, or even customer service level agreements (SLAs).

Just to close out these definitions, let's explicitly mention what kinds of items we are including in this idea of the item in question. We mentioned them already. Networks are as we usually define them in our world. And systems are usually a rack or box produced by an equipment vendor. It may contain cards or Network Interface Controllers or 10 Gigabit Small Form Factor Pluggables (XFPs) or other field replaceable units, which we often refer to as parts. Between the part and the system, we can talk about various levels of subsystems. This type of breakdown of the complex to its components is common, but here it should be done in a specific way, so that the effect of each part, how it contributes to the functions of the higher levels, and how support systems react to the failures, are all clearly defined. Fortunately, we usually build systems and networks in a way that follows the structure we seek. But, be careful; sometimes it is better to think of the fiber jumper and the XFPs on either side as a subsystem, as the failure of any of these three items results in the same impact on the system.

And each of these kinds of items serves some purpose, perhaps carrying out a specific time-bound mission, or meeting some SLAs associated with services being supported on the network.

UNDERSTANDING FAILURE TO AVOID IT

We seek to understand failure so that we can fix it, and avoid it in the future. We gain an understanding of failures through many mechanisms; but, for an operating network or system, we will focus on a few simple techniques and concepts in this entry. Let's start with root cause analysis (RCA); then move to failure modes, effects, and criticality analysis (FMECA); and finish with failure reporting and corrective analysis system (FRACAS).

RCA is about asking the basic question of why. I tell people they need to ask that question at least five times, and get a helpful answer each time. Doing this is important because you need options for addressing the cause. Some of these answers will be actionable, and others won't. Some of the actionable answers will be too expensive or difficult or unreliable to address, and others will be cheap and easy and reliable to address. And some of these answers may be in common across other failures, so addressing those issues gains the most advantage. Hence, you'll want to address the cause on several levels. First, fix the failure you analyzed, if it is not yet fixed. Then fix the cause of the failure so that failure doesn't recur there. Finally, fix the cause of that type of failure in all locations in which it is cost effective to do so. A bent fiber can be easily fixed. But look for the cause, which may be a poorly kept rack in need of some cable management, to help avoid the hands-in-plant failure mode. But don't just fix that one rack; look for other indicators of that problem, and fix them all; but fix the problem when it is cost-effective to do so. If doing some cable management risks bumping a fiber for a critical service, maybe we wait and ask for a maintenance window first, when priorities allow it. The same approach applies at all levels, and in all operations. Effective solutions lead to best practices.

FMECA is a good tool for documenting RCA, but be sure to capture all the information in our RCA for future reference. Consider using a FRACAS for capturing the information, or an equivalent information management system.

FMECA is but a method for discovering the modes of failure of an item in question, reduced to a manageable subsystem size, perhaps. In the early design phase, it can be applied through thought experiments and brainstorming, perhaps leveraging expert knowledge or past experience or even data collected on an earlier version of or subsystem related to the item in question. Once a prototype is established, it can be improved through applying any knowledge about the prototype. And once deployed, FMECA is an excellent way to capture field failure information.

The components of FMECA are just as described in its name, and usually it is best to capture the information in a grid table form or perhaps a tree or network diagram structure. Using RCA or brainstorming, as appropriate, capture the discovered failure modes down to the component or field replaceable unit level, as low a level as is meaningful. Then, using system knowledge, be sure to propagate the failure mode up through the subsystems, systems, and network impacts, which we document as the effect. Then, depending on how the overall network is used, and propagating that use down to each component, assign the criticality of the failure, usually in terms of impact to the mission, service, customer base, etc. Various practices for creating the criticality here have been used, with strengths and weaknesses for each. There is not enough space in this entry to explore these options, so pick one that enables fair comparison of the effects of each failure mode for each part in the whole scope of the study.

Finally, capture the RCA and FMECA information into a FRACAS or similar database or data management system. The information here must be referenced when analyzing future failure events, redesigning systems to perform better and more reliably, and when searching for early indications of increasing failure frequency in the network, for failure modes driven by degradation.

You may begin to notice a few things about the failures and causes in the data you captured. There may be a few ways to categorize the information, and maybe improve reliability. For one, we can likely categorize our results into categories of failure modes starting at a high level: hardware, software, configuration and design, human error, and external causes. And from there, we can dig into deeper details, and find some common causes to address. We might also discover that, depending on the age and condition of the system, the frequency of some failure modes varies. Typically, we can talk about at least three phases of the lifecycle of IT and telecommunications systems (and in other contexts for that matter): infant mortality, useful life, and wear out. During the early life of components, systems, and networks, there are quality problems in hardware, configuration problems in software, design problems at the system and network levels, and human error as operations personnel learn how to work with the new equipment. After some time, maybe six months to a year, the early failures are worked out of the system, and the rate of occurrence of failures drops and stabilizes over time. Here, random failures occur mostly, as long as special causes are addressed in a timely manner.

But after time, some wear out failure modes begin to appear, and become more prominent over time; this is the wear out phase. The age, condition, operation environment, and other factors can impact the frequency and appearance of these failure modes, and perhaps influence the approaches you choose to mitigate them.

When it comes to improving the reliability of a design, we are limited to a few simple approaches; most implementations are some combination or variant of these. First, we can be redundant, and that redundancy can be in hot, warm, or cold configuration. We can be redundant over time, by repeating or reworking what failed. We can be physically redundant, providing multiple copies of the failure prone unit at the same time. And we can use alternate resources to make up in part for the primary failure. Deeper, we can try to remove failure modes, maintain parts to proactively avoid failures, repair faster, change the items we use or the time of our use to lower risk, and work to reduce the rate of occurrence of failures. The complexity comes when we apply these techniques on multiple layers of complex systems and networks, then try to coordinate them.

BREAK DOWN THE STRUCTURE

It is most convenient to talk separately about hardware and software and systems and data as they all behave differently in terms of their reliability. We'll start with hardware, move to software, then discuss how data are handled in networks, followed by how all these come together into networks, and complete the structure with a discussion about services.

Hardware

Hardware is built up hierarchically. IT hardware has material that can break, and electronics that can fail, making up parts that are built into subsystems and systems to construct networks. Failure at the lower level has various impacts at the higher levels, with different reliability effects depending on usage. While a scratch on the case of a router won't matter to its ability to send bits through the Internet, an electrostatic discharge on a chip can cause a router to stop working completely, or even cause intermittent failures that are difficult to find.

The manufacturing of systems must be done with quality for the system to be reliable. This is but one way that the worlds of quality and reliability interplay. Poorly manufactured parts can be the cause of early failures, or premature failures. But quality parts used in a poor design, or manufactured with low quality into a system, can also result in early breakdowns. But high quality parts, made to specifications determined by an excellently engineered design, when manufactured into a system with high quality, can result in a highly reliable system, when used properly.

Lifetime behavior

Because the pattern has emerged often when examining failure data, we tend to talk about failures in terms of the phase of the life of the hardware. Because IT hardware is largely dominated by electronics failures, these phases line up well with electronic failure modes and causes. The phases are usually considered to be three: infant mortality, useful life, and wear out.

Infant mortality failures are those failures due to poor quality, which are premature, much earlier than expected, especially at such a high occurrence rate. Because poor part tolerance can be an indication of poor quality, some amount of parts or subsystem inspection and testing can help find and remove these causes of infant mortality.

Once the parts and system age beyond their early life, we usually experience a reduced rate of occurrence of failures, where the failures are mostly due to random causes. The random causes dominate this part of the system lifetime because the poor quality causes have by now been removed from the system, as their infant failures have occurred and the failed parts were replaced, and the system has not yet aged enough to have been worn out. This phase of life is usually indicated by a lower, relatively constant rate of occurrence of failures.

Later in the lifetime, the parts begin to wear out. Mechanical parts such as fans may have experienced particulate intrusion, and lubricants may age to become ineffective. Friction can wear out parts outside of tolerance, and vibration can further that friction degradation. After time, wear out takes over and completely fails the part, and the part may fail the system. Lasers, servos, capacitors, and other parts will physically degrade to a point where they no longer meet their intended function, and fail either catastrophically (such as a break), or slowly creep out of tolerance. In telecommunication cables, insulation can degrade rapidly in the natural temperature cycle and moisture exposure of the natural environment. Boards in electronics can even delaminate. Central offices and data centers are environmentally controlled to reduce the speed of this degradation, and to assure the control of outside causes of system stress that can cause performance degradation as well as physical degradation in parts.

These three phases of life for hardware are usually described together and depicted in what is referred to as the bathtub curve. Early in life, the hazard rate (or rate of occurrence of failures) is higher. Then, after a period of time, often 6 to 18 months for IT and telecommunications equipment, the hazard rate reduces to near its

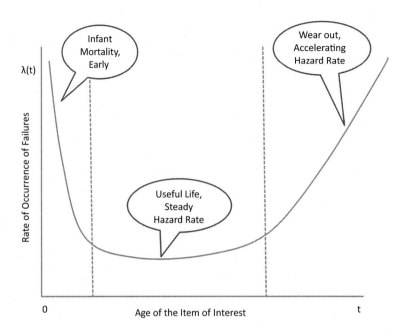

Fig. 1 Bathtub curve.

lowest level, and remains relatively constant (where failures are mostly due to external events and use). After much use, eventually either the equipment has met its useful life and is replaced by newer technology for service capability reasons, or it continues to be used until it begins to wear out. This period of life is indicated by a higher rate of occurrence of failures, which can accelerate as the item in question continues to age, and more competing risks become increasingly likely. Electronics wear out from material degradation and chemical processes, as do moving parts age due to friction. Small plastic parts can degrade, break or crack, and become less reliable; and at the system level these small problems can increase to where the system experiences higher hazard rates. Networks can even get complicated over time, pushing the limits of their intended use, and into usage conditions that result in higher hazard rates, even though no material within the equipment has physically broken.

Testing

For these reasons, system manufacturers will not only sample parts for quality before using them, but also test parts, subsystems, and systems in many ways: functional tests, burn-in, life tests, stress screening, and more.

Functional testing is just what you think it is, but remember it can happen at the part, subsystem, system, and network levels. Integration testing is a functional testing at a higher level. Acceptance sampling is usually associated with either visual inspection, or some type of measurement against a standard, which amounts to a simple test. But functional testing can be more involved. Keep in mind that functional testing will not usually

stress the item, so it may not be very effective at finding ways to improve the system's reliability. However, functional testing can test initial conditions, may still be an important part of the capability to test, and may be used in conjunction with other types of testing, which can be used to improve the reliability of the tested item, as well as future items to be produced.

When systems have the potential of experiencing infant mortality, we address these problems through burn-in. The process of burn-in is a period of time when the item in question is exercised in a way that simulates use, or is the same as use. In some cases, it may even be a usage at a higher level of stress, though usually not to the extreme. Electronic parts would be subjected to current, perhaps at higher temperatures or a higher voltage than would be its typical use environment, enough to find infant mortality failures. Because these types of tests take time, effort, money, space, power, etc., they are often implemented on subsystems or systems. Most every piece of IT equipment is at least burn-in tested, either as a completed system, or its field replaceable parts, or both.

Accelerated testing and screening take burn-in to the next level, for another purpose. While burn-in has as its goal to find infant mortality modes of failure, these accelerated tests are intended to find much more.

At the prototype stages of system development, we can accelerate testing to find faults in the design. We can apply FMECA results to start, developed through expert information and historical data from similar systems, to form an educated guess about the failure modes, and perhaps some estimate of the rate of occurrence of failures if the system were fully developed and deployed. But in cases in which we don't have enough knowledge, or need to support the knowledge we have with additional information for removing these modes of failure from the design, we can employ accelerated life testing (ALT). ALT can be applied to early prototypes to uncover failure modes, and this information can be fed back into the design process so that the design can be improved, and a more robust solution created. Because much IT equipment is deployed in controlled environments, and ALT can be expensive, it isn't always done. But for outside plant equipment, potentially deployed in harsh environments, some amount of ALT at the system or subsystem level is warranted, and its benefits are gained most at early steps in the development of a product or system. The environment under which the item in question will be used is a significant consideration; high stress environments can lead to accelerated degradation and early failures.

Indeed, even in deployed systems, manufacturing defects can get through normal testing (systems integration testing, burn-in, and more); therefore, at times, we push those conditions to an extreme level, and conduct what we call Accelerated Stress Screening (let's not abbreviate that one). This type of screening is often referred to as Environmental Stress Screening (ESS) or pushed even higher into Highly Accelerated Stress Screening, I suspect mostly to avoid the unfortunate abbreviation. But by any name, they are all basically the same thing: they are versions of putting the device, part, subsystem, or system into extreme conditions in a lab environment with the intent to reveal some weakness that otherwise could result in a postdeployment failure. Some of the best test equipment can push temperatures to extreme levels, up to and beyond the limits of the materials, but most importantly to do so under a fast cycling of temperatures, under extremes of dryness and moisture, under multiple dimensions of vibration (cyclical and random), with rapid parameter changes. Vibration tests, by the way, are great not only for stress testing and screening, but also for improving the design of packaging for shipping our equipment.

In addition to the many methods we have to improve hardware reliability, we have a huge number of methods for modeling and predicting the reliability of hardware. We should touch on a couple of important ones we often apply to the hardware component or system.

Lifetime data analysis is the field of statistics focused on failure data, with the intent often to predict lifetime, rate of occurrence of failures, and related important measures. Related to this field is that of Prognostics and Health Management, which is focused on using condition information related to failure, usually indirectly, to predict failure. Both are helpful for planning replacements and maintenance, and mostly to avoid failure conditions which can be very costly in some applications, including many IT and telecommunications services.

Utilizing statistical information about failures of components and systems, we can use methods like Markov models, renewal processes, Petri nets, and simulation to combine the small into the larger, on into network and system and service and mission. We will cover these capabilities a bit more later.

Software

Software reliability requires different concepts than hardware, because software behaves very differently. Software, once written, only changes if it is corrupt, or someone updates it. Failures due to software problems would be due to code being written incorrectly. Latent faults in software code will manifest as failures when code is executed with the parameters that exercise the latent fault, so changing use conditions matter a lot. This idea is similar to a flaw in the hardware that is stressed sufficiently at use, or in test, to become a failure in the infant mortality region, though not precisely the same idea.

For this reason, software is tested during its development, to allow correction before deployment, resulting in fewer field failures than otherwise. There is a wealth of research on various strategies for staffing teams of testing and development, not to mention automated testing tools that can assist and accelerate the software testing process. There are even quite a bit of models for predicting software reliability. Many of these software reliability prediction methods take information about the number of faults in the software, and the number of failures that the faults have caused, plus how many have been removed or known to remain, and how much of the software code and use cases have been covered, all to estimate the number of faults remaining in the software, and the amount of failures these faults may manifest in the field. This estimate is used for planning resources to reach a target software reliability at a release date, or to determine when the code is ready for release. If you are interested in learning more, a great place to start is the first models created by Littlewood and Musa. A classic reference to get started on the topic is the book by Musa et al.[1]

Software can experience random failures, due to misuse, and external causes. While testing can find some of these causes, and software can be designed to reduce these events, it isn't easy to predict all use conditions for the software. Especially today, there are so many more variables that lead to random software failures: applications are deployed in Clouds, distributed geographically and fragmented, utilized across the Internet or intranets, deployed on various operating systems, with different user tolerances for latency and accuracy.

Believe it or not, but software can also age. How does that happen? Well, software updates can introduce new errors, and errors can increase with each iteration, as more features are added, and new requirements expand so that the software itself contains more lines of code, and has more modes of failure and faults within.

Most of the efforts in research on software reliability focus on methods to create it better through tracking failures, using better methods, improved automated testing, and just about everything else that helps software development become more reliable. Software Reliability is an active area with a lot of development, though much of it appears to be evolutionary.

Data

Telecommunications and IT are often in the business of transmitting and storing data. The reliability of this handling of data therefore becomes important in many applications. We have several mechanisms for assuring data reliability. We can detect errors, and correct them. In transmission, some correction mechanisms are proactive in that redundant forms of information are sent in case of failure, and other mechanisms rely on retransmission of the information once a failure is detected. Because in this case information is being moved, we usually assume the source still has the information to retransmit; but that isn't always true, so figuring all this out can get a bit complicated. When transmitting, we can send information multiple times on the same connection, send in redundant ways on the same connection, send the same information over redundant connections over a network, or send it over redundant networks. In the storage of information, we usually rely on redundancy of the storage, either by some shared redundancy of storage, or duplicated, and often geographically distributed to guard against more failure modes. A lot of engineering decision goes in here.

Transmission Control Protocol (TCP) over Internet Protocol (IP), often written as TCP/IP, was designed with reliability in mind. Sure, we say IP is best effort, but TCP makes up for it through its reliable transport protocol. TCP has a reliability mechanism designed in it to allow acknowledgment of delivery, and timing for resends. If packets were sent but not acknowledged, the sending device can resend the packets, assuring delivery. TCP tries to infer the failure mode or degradation in the communication; therefore, it will back off its sending rate when the window is full, which means the agreed-to maximum number of unacknowledged packets have been sent. This condition results in slower transmission of information, which can be a detriment in some cases. Hence, engineers have designed solutions to address these issues.

Start with the single string of bits, say n of them. Let's say we want to detect when there is a bit error, say a 0 that gets detected as a 1, or vice versa. A simple

mechanism to achieve this want is the single parity-bit. For n bits sent, one bit indicates whether the sum of the $n-1$ bits is even or odd. That way, if a single bit is incorrect, the difference is detected. But not corrected, because we don't know which of the $n-1$ words is incorrect if the parity-bit doesn't match the sum, or if it is the parity bit that is incorrect. It could be any one of them, or three of them, or perhaps many more, or even the result of a register shift. In that event, our only choice is to discard the entire set of bits, perhaps the entire packet, and ask for a retransmission.

Note there are also options for detecting more than one error, which we will discuss in the context of error correction as well.

Sometimes resending packets just takes too long, and the purpose being served by those packets just can't wait for retransmission. So we consider proactive mechanisms. Forward Error Correction (FEC) is a mechanism for redundancy in data transmission and storage. By sending a few extra, specially defined bits, the message bits are checked, and potentially protected. Now is a good time to mention Hamming, the namesake of Hamming codes. By taking a set of bits, and completing calculations on subsets of these bits to create additional check bits, then sending the message and check bits, the receiver can perform calculations to determine whether the message bits are in error, and potentially to correct them. Two simple implementations of Hamming codes are referred to as single error correction and single error detection (SECSED) that requires 7 bits to carry 4 bits of message (therefore 3 check bits), and single error correction and double error detection (SECDED) which requires 8 bits to carry 4 bits of message (therefore 4 check bits). One can simply think of each check bit as the indicator of the sum of a subset of message bits as being even or odd. By selecting the message bits carefully to cover combinations well, the check bits can indicate one or more failures, and even correct for some of them. Good examples to help one understand the mathematics here are in the book by Shooman.[2]

As the complexity of these codes increases, which happens as we create more encoding schemes to create more reliable error detection and correction, their classification becomes important to understand. There are a wide range of options offered in the literature. But to keep it simple for the discussion of the reliability of these solutions, we can think of these methods as having the ability to detect a certain number of errors, and to correct for a number of errors less than or equal to the number that can be detected. After all, the first step in correcting an error is finding you have one.

Now consider more complex encodings, such as a byte of data, or, more generally, a codeword. We can then think of byte values that are more complex than a single bit, and, therefore, we have more complicated encoding possible, and more to check and correct for.

We must mention here the work of Reed-Solomon codes, which are for detecting and correcting codewords. Aside from working with more than just single bits, Reed-Solomon coding does pretty much the same thing we have already described: it provides error checking for message words through checksum words. Through some number of message words and a number of checksum words, an erred word can be found, and corrected. If I have two message words that can be digitized to a string of bits, and if I pad any shorter word with a number of 0 bits to make them the same length, then I can create a third word that is just the indicator of the sum of the two bits in each position of each word being even or odd. For example, if the first bit in word one is 0, and the first bit in word two is 1, then the first bit in the checksum word would be 1. Then when either message word goes missing, I can recreate it by checking the other message word and the checksum word. I know the first bit of word one is 0 because the first bits of both the second word and the checksum word are both 1. But if one of those three bits flips (goes 0 to 1 or 1 to 0), then I can only detect a problem. Will the real bit error reveal itself? Sorry, not this time.

This is also how RAID works for Reed-Solomon encodings. A great explanation for how this works, suitable for the computer scientist to understand and encode it, exists presently as a technical report by James Plank.[3]

Many of these solutions can be managed to address burst errors, or clusters of errors. If a storage system or transmission line is subject to likely clusters of failures, good engineers can create solutions to handle more than one error in the packet or codeword. By selecting the right encoding scheme for error detection and correction, strings of errors can be mitigated. But further, we can employ the idea of interleaving to do more. By changing the order of the bits, even spreading them out across words or even packets, we can still detect and correct burst errors using encoding schemes with low overhead, which detect only a small number of errors. If a string of five bit errors is spread across five different code words, and each code word only contains the one error, then we can detect and correct all of these bit errors with even a simple SECSED encoding.

The idea of n-modular redundancy is important here as well. We can proactively send multiple strings of complimentary bits across different links on a network, or even different networks.

Think of the possible combinations, and realize the engineering possibilities of using redundant transmission mediums in combination with the mechanisms described above. Analogously, by warehousing data in multiple locations, catastrophic events are less likely to impact our data (from loss of an entire disk array), or even our access to that data (from say a power outage).

Voting schemes are closely related to n-modular redundancy. In a simple configuration, three redundant sources of information can be managed through majority rule. But if you only have two, in the event of a disagreement, a tie breaker is required. But two is still helpful when the dominant failure mode is missing information. More complicated situations are rare, but can also be studied and considered for high reliability situations.

We can even extend these ideas to higher layers. We can use these same concepts to protect whole packets, and even sets of packets that are interleaved to avoid burst errors, and do more.

A common calculation for some of these types of protections is that of the k-out-of-n system.

BRING IT ALL BACK TOGETHER

Time to pull our heads out of the weeds a bit, and into the clouds, pun intended. Network design for reliability concerns (including all the *ilities* we've discussed and more) is about putting systems and parts together in ways that balance cost, performance, and reliability. Many of the approaches we discussed in other sections of this entry apply to enable us to build networks to meet reliability concerns.

Services as the Reason for it All

We have already discussed service reliability indirectly in the previous sections; but in IT and telecommunications, as ultimately a service oriented business, it is important to fully discuss the reliability aspects of services. SLAs are an advertised and contracted assurance of reliable performance, and are often applied to the network, though they are best when service oriented. The network supports the service, so the SLA must be translated to the network for design and life cycle management purposes.

Monitoring

Services and networks and systems are well supported through monitoring. High availability is assured in part through rapid repair and corrective actions. Availability is improved by any action that reduces downtime, and includes detection, notification, isolation and troubleshooting, and repair or replacement.

Communication networks have evolved over a great amount of time and generations. Through that evolution, these networks have become capable. We have several mechanisms to use to know how a network is performing (and therefore how reliable a service is), and its overall health (and therefore its reliability concerns).

MIB stands for Management Information Base, and technically refers to the database containing the network management information. However, we often refer to the measures one can obtain from network devices as MIBs.

The protocol for MIBs is Simple Network Management Protocol. Network devices are capable of monitoring and reporting on their condition, to a network management system. Much of these data are useful for knowing when equipment is stressed, potentially in a state of higher probability of failure. More directly, it can be the source of indication for service reliability problems, as network performance is a frequent failure mode for services.

When MIBS are not sufficient, we can utilize network probes or span ports to gather traffic for monitoring conditions or troubleshooting. Methods that send packets through networks with the intent of measuring performance can be useful too. Presently, technology exists to do much more, including gather all this information and more from network devices, archive it, report on it, and assist in deep dive troubleshooting when necessary. While many equipment vendors will have their own capabilities to offer, there are many best in class capabilities from vendors who specialize in network monitoring, which can provide broad, integrated solutions. There are even open development solutions.

Many of these best in class tools take the monitoring information to logical conclusions, offering predictions of network problems, assisted troubleshooting, anomaly detection, and identifying constraints to be addressed such as over utilized resources. From the data perspective, the basic set of statistics includes utilization, latency, jitter, packet loss, up time, and down time. All these can help operations maintain a network for high reliability and availability for the entire life cycle.

Design and Life Cycle

We mentioned previously the bathtub curve. It described from a failure perspective the life cycle of a product, system, or part. Hardware can have a failure behavior that follows a bathtub shape, somewhat. That shape can also be a reasonable description of software over time, when software experiences aging, which it can. Because of this changing failure behavior over the lifetime of an item, we have to manage the life cycle of items that are used for extended periods of time.

When we integrate the parts into systems, and the systems into networks, trouble can happen at the interfaces, where software and hardware meet, where systems communicate through data, etc. Variability happens, and designs must address that variability. While the tolerance of one design may be fine, and the design target of another design matches the first, the two designs will

together deliver a different tolerance, and that can translate into differences in performance of the system and network. These failures on the interfaces are tricky to find, and harder to eliminate, because two parts within specification may together make a system perform below its target, which can become a reliability problem.

IT and telecommunications disciplines have a definition for life cycle management which we will leave for other entries to discuss, but we will cover its overlap with reliability.

There is a demand side to the life cycle of a product or system, which dictates its necessary lifetime. Short lived purposes may not require devices with long lifetimes. But if the mission being supported is of a long duration, or the item of interest is to be reused many times, then its life cycle becomes a great concern. But even with short use duration items of interest, there is a life cycle of concern, because even these items must be created reliably, meet the intended function, and be disposed of so as to not cause further problems. Items of interest with longer use lifetimes must be maintained, and thus its components must also at times be replaced, repaired, or even augmented to serve evolving purposes. Life cycle management of a communication network is really about assuring the network continues to meet its intended purpose, even as that intent changes, for an often undefined duration.

In design, the life cycle must be considered along with cost, performance, and reliability concerns. At the first level of detail, maintenance decisions have to be made. That work involves planning the spare parts logistics and supply chain. The time to obtain a spare part, when needed, impacts repair time, but there is a cost of having hot redundant spare parts for all field replaceable units (such as plug in cards, PICs). So the entire spare logistics problem must be solved to manage cost and SLA goals. Fortunately, with a bit of modeling, such problems can be solved to at least be close to optimal. In addition, repairability concerns have to be considered in the selection of systems within the network.

Beyond sparing and repair logistics, we have to be concerned with the lifetime cost of such systems. At some point, technology will need to be replaced, either because performance is no longer where it needs to be to stay competitive in the market, or technology has evolved so that maintaining the old is no longer cost effective, or failures begin to occur at higher rates so that SLA concerns and maintenance costs become important concerns.

When engineered, networks and their systems must consider design margin as well. For example, line systems are designed for a needed reach between regeneration points. Lasers are selected as part of those line systems to transmit optical signals with sufficient design margins to maintain reliable communications.

However, lasers degrade over time, and fibers get disturbed and cut, leading to higher loss between regeneration points. Therefore, it is good to design a line system with enough margin to allow some degradation without loss of communication. If the margin is too small, then small degradations in the line system can begin to cause transmission errors, and communication failure. Sufficient margin will allow the line system to be robust to degradation in lasers and other components, and loss due to splices and connectors and bends. A large design margin will allow the line system to last longer, whereas a small design margin will either drive higher laser replacement rates later in life, or potentially require the line system to be replaced earlier. Designing this margin is tricky because the life cycle of the line system is full of unknowns such as the needed lifetime, the future maintenance costs, availability of spare parts in the far future, what competing technology changes will be available, and what competition will drive new applications for services over the line system. This uncertainty is the challenge of life cycle engineering.

Network Modeling

Network modeling, to cover it well, would take several books. Even covering the techniques and knowledge useful for modeling networks from a reliability concern perspective would take several books. Here are brief introductions of several relevant ideas and topics around modeling networks for reliability concerns. Remember, a network can be at most any scale. They can cover the planet (and into space), or be reduced to a single chip. The ideas here apply at any scale, when applied correctly.

We model networks for reliability concerns because we can't afford to build and fix bad networks, and we can't afford to experiment with them over long periods of time. While ALT is intended to improve components and systems so that they are more reliable, the network needs its compliment of modeling to design, plan, and engineer solutions with these components and systems so that services are met, products are serviceable, and networks are reliable. You can't apply ALT to an entire, large network, so we model the network instead.

We usually try to estimate the reliability of networks or services based on estimates of the reliability of parts. Telcordia provides useful but flawed part count methods which seek to account for complexity, variability in parts sources, environment conditions, and uncertainty in the rates of occurrence of failure. These methods allow for the incorporation of field failure information as well, for cases where parts and systems have been deployed before in similar use conditions. However, because such estimates are flawed, we usually have little confidence that these estimates are accurate; but they have value nonetheless.

- We can use these estimates to compare designs under the same assumptions of failure frequencies.
- Then we can conduct sensitivity analysis based on the uncertainty of these estimates, to understand extreme cases, and potential outcomes.
- From the sensitivity analysis, we can investigate which contributing factors need more certainty, and where we take the most risk with certain designs.
- Under certain assumptions, we can understand the risks associated with some design decisions (such as network topology, system configuration, etc.), and therefore make better design decisions.
- When planning a network that has been designed, we can determine how much spare capacity to begin with, and which types of network solutions are appropriate for the various services we intend to offer.
- By offering a given SLA, we can model network behavior to determine how well it can meet the guarantee.
- For special services and SLAs, we can determine what adjustments if any are necessary to meet the special services.
- When deciding how to offer new services, we can combine existing and future network elements and systems to determine how best to offer these new services, and what operations capabilities will be necessary.
- Planning for various contingencies, we can develop network solutions to help the network be more robust, and even contribute to Network Disaster Recovery (NDR) planning.
- And we can investigate for long term behaviors that we expect, want to avoid, or need to plan for throughout the life cycle of the network and its services.

Note that for each purpose (and there are many I didn't mention) we have a perspective. That perspective is the mission that must be met. And that mission will drive what gets modeled, what details are important to model, and what approach we take.

In most telecommunications and IT applications, communication is bidirectional, but not always. We usually model networks as bidirectional because they usually are. Some services and missions may be unbalanced, but still bidirectional. In cases where network elements handle one way communications, we usually have to model the matched pair which handles the communication in the other direction.

Furthermore, for these reasons, it is usually advantageous to have PICs or systems configured such that the failure of more than one link will impact both directions of a connection, rather than one direction on two different connections.

It is all too common, yet of little value, that networks are modeled as a series of nodes and links, where nodes can represent aggregations of equipment. I say this is of little value because at times these aggregations are entire data centers or central offices, yet the failure modes of these large scale systems are very complicated, not as simple as a node that fails or does not.

The right solution is to determine the FMECA information for each part and system, architect the solution through the equipment (including hardware, software, operations, everything), build up the effects at the appropriate level to reflect impact on the mission, and simplify series and parallel subsystems so that the model is reduced as much as possible. Then the resulting network, simplified yet still fully detailed, can be modeled with the right approach.

In network reliability research, some approaches will assume nodes are perfectly reliable, and some will assume links are perfectly reliable, while others will assume both can fail. (If the model assumes neither can fail, then you know it is not very useful.) Any of these three options can be sufficient for application to reality, by simple adjustment. If the approach assumes that links do not fail, then simply insert a node in the middle of a link that can fail, and the approach applies. If the approach assumes that nodes do not fail, then it gets

more complicated, but a node can be expanded into a set of links to model the appropriate behavior.

It is important to reduce your network model as much as you can to simplify estimation. Fortunately, we can perform series parallel reduction on parts of a network. For a simple example, line systems can usually be considered as a series system. Hence, under common assumptions, the reliability or availability of the line system can be modeled by multiplying the reliability or availability of the parts in that line system, as it is usually reasonable to assume the parts are failure-independent. Likewise, for a parallel system, we can often model a parallel system by multiplying the unreliability or unavailability of the parts to estimate the unreliability or unavailability of the parallel system, again assuming failure-independence (or accounting for the failure-dependence). Then we can convert by recalling the definition of reliability as being one minus unreliability, and availability as one minus unavailability.

See Fig. 2 for reliability or availability block diagrams of series and parallel systems, along with simple models of their reliabilities or availabilities. A reliability block diagram shows the system as functioning when there is a path through the diagram, usually left to right, which is not blocked by a failure. Availability block diagrams look the same, so context matters. The figure assumes availability is being calculated, but it applies to

Name	Diagram	Equation (Availability)
Series	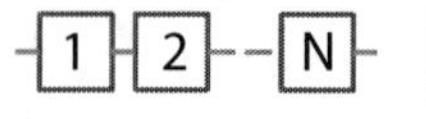	$A = \prod_{i=1}^{N} a_i = a_1 * a_2 * \ldots * a_N$
Parallel	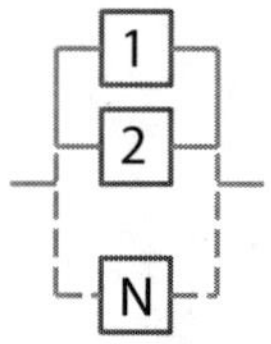	$A = 1 - \prod_{i-1}^{N} (1 - a_i)$
Bridge	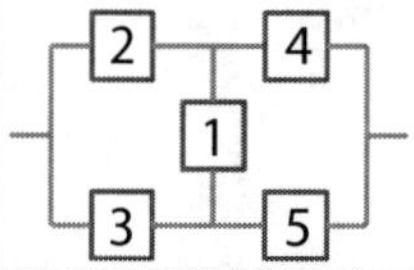	$A = a_1\big(1 - (1 - a_2)(1 - a_3)\big)\big(1 - (1 - a_4)(1 - a_5)\big)$ $+ (1 - a_1)(1 - (1 - a_2 a_4)(1 - a_3 a_5))$
K-out-of-N:Good	K-N:G	$A = \sum_{i=K}^{N} \binom{N}{i} a^i (1 - a)^{N-i}$ (for a all equal)
Tolerance	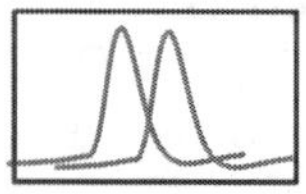	(Joint probability or convolutions of distributions usually required here.)

Fig. 2 Reliability or availability block diagrams, and models to accompany (reliability-independence of parts assumed).

reliability with suitable replacement of availability with reliability probabilities. A few more system structures are in the figure for use as well.

Network coherence is the idea that taking away any part of a network cannot improve its reliability. But there are cases where networks are not coherent! Take for example a circuit provisioned on a link that is less reliable than its alternative. At failure, the circuit is switched to a more reliable backup path. So from the perspective of that circuit, removing a part of the network makes it more reliable. For a less trivial example, consider that a given service is limited to a single path in a network due to congestion. But if a certain node fails, the traffic sourcing or terminating at that failed node will no longer be carried by the network, freeing capacity, potentially providing one or more additional paths for the given service to take, thus increasing its availability. Real communication networks can be non-coherent, so be careful with your assumptions.

When modeling networks or the services they provide, we have to consider the perspective of the mission in what we model. While that can drive more complicated situations than we describe here, which can change over time, we will limit our discussion to basics. It is common to model a single source (start) to terminal (end) connection through the network, allowing it to take any and all possible paths through the network, given the communication originating at a given node, and terminating at another. We can then expand this view to model a network connection from a given source node to any or each terminal node possible, or reversing the roles of source and terminal. And we can model the probability of a connection between all nodes in the network, such that the failure condition is when the network is divided. There can be more complicated versions. My favorite is to consider source and terminal nodes in pairs each, so that there can be two given source nodes, or two given terminal nodes. The modeling only complicates a bit, but the results are so much more useful for planning redundant connection points for high availability services.

When trying to determine the reliability concerns of a network, we usually have to rely on algorithms or heuristics.

- Start with series parallel reduction. Then if the simplified network is simple enough, represent it with a mathematical model, the mathematical definition of its structure function. If it is simple enough, a state enumeration of the parts may be possible.
- If there are subsystems in the network that can be modeled in isolation, but are more complicated than can be modeled well with series parallel reduction, then consider Markov models or renewal process models or Petri net models.

- If the network is complex, there are algorithms available that can define cut sets and path sets for networks. A simple approach is to use a depth first search of a network, starting at the source node, and finding all paths to the terminal node. Cut sets are just as useful, as they are the dual to path sets. But path sets may be more useful in cases where network capacity is being modeled with its failure behavior. Depending on the services being modeled, a small subset of the paths for a full network may be all that we need.
- If the network is complicated, such that we can't create a mathematical representation of the network after reductions, then we can consider Monte Carlo methods to simulate failure conditions of the network, and determine the reliability conditions of interest.

But because many telecommunications and IT networks require active switching to protect traffic in a failure, the number of paths that the service can take is limited. So we can usually create services with simplified models that we can handle without simulation. We can use the techniques covered above to build models of the few permitted paths through the network for any given source to terminal connection.

Where it may get complicated is when we have to account for more than just connectivity through the network. Considering reliability concerns of services and missions can involve constraints on capacity, timeliness, or other performance measures (perhaps inviting the need for a performability model). More complex modeling efforts become necessary in such cases, but nonetheless important to complete.

NETWORK DISASTER RECOVERY

While we have discussed many ways in which reliability concerns are important contributions to IT and telecommunications, we need to mention NDR in particular, as an important activity for any organization using or providing telecommunications or IT services. The activities outlined in this paper assist in NDR, but robust contingency planning must still take place. The guest editorial by Chen et al.[4] contains references to a good set of published articles that may be of interest to those getting started with their NDR plans.

STANDARDS

There are many relevant standards in IT and telecommunications that hold valuable contributions to reliability.

Of note and importance in our field are the many maintained by Telcordia.

In addition, and a great place to start simple for an organization looking to improve its operations, QuEST Forum[5] maintains TL9000 standards, with two important handbooks documenting measurement approaches and best practices: TL9000 Requirements Handbook (presently on release 5.5), and TL9000 Measurements Handbook (presently on release 5.0).[6]

CONCLUSION

In this brief entry, we covered many important considerations and topics in the area of IT and telecommunications reliability, but far from enough. Rather than pointing you to entire books and volumes for more, I'll only suggest a small next step, to look at a dated but relevant tutorial on this subject, with more of a modeling bend, but practical and full of useful bits nonetheless.[7]Additional resources are available on line, and many are free including those at scienceofnines.com.[8]

In engineering, and reliability concerns are no exception, details matter. From material selection to software architecture to data structure, all the details are important to address. Fortunately, reliability techniques apply to all these design and development issues, and that is a key reason we have such impressive telecommunications and IT achievements.

Networks and large scale systems are complicated, many layered things. Performance issues at one level manifest as failures at another. We can use many techniques, including improving the performance or robustness of a device, to improve the reliability of the system. This layered behavior is important to understand when providing IT and telecommunications services because the customers experience only the failures of services. All of the operations contribute.

I like to offer an alternate definition for reliability concerns that I think works better in most application areas, including this one: reliability is the study, management, and reduction of the variability in supply, including performance, to meet an uncontrolled demand. The variability in supply is not only driven by what we think of as traditional failures, but includes more complex issues which reveal as failures at higher levels.

The business of IT and telecommunications, for the entire life cycle, has reliability concerns as its primary goal. While it shares concern with performance and costs, reliability concerns are always there as well.

Have fun breaking things.

ACKNOWLEDGEMENT

Thank you to Polar Star Consulting, my customers, the IEEE, and the many colleagues and former coworkers who continue to share ideas and opportunities to break things so we can learn. Mostly, thank you to my family for letting me explore.

REFERENCES

1. Musa, J. D.; Iannino, A.; Okumoto, K. *Software Reliability*; McGraw-Hill: ISBN 0-07-044119-7.
2. Shooman, M. L. *Reliability of Computer Systems and Networks*; John Wiley & Sons, Inc.: ISBN 0-471-29342-3.
3. http://web.eecs.utk.edu/~plank/plank/papers/CS-96-332.pdf
4. Chen, C.-M.; MacWan, A.; Rupe, J. Network disaster recovery [Guest Editorial]. IEEE Commun. Mag. **2011**, *49* (1), 26–27.
5. http://questforum.org/
6. http://tl9000.org/handbooks/overview.html
7. Rupe, J. Assembling System/Network Reliability, Tutorial Notes of the 2003 Annual Reliability and Maintainability Symposium.
8. http://scienceofnines.com/

Availability of IS/IT

Ulrik Franke
Department of Information and Aeronautical Systems, Swedish Defense Research Agency (FOI), Stockholm, Sweden

Abstract

The entry introduces the concept of availability of information systems and information technology (IT). Starting from the definitions, it goes on to explain different ways to understand the concept, and how these have resulted in different scientific approaches over the years. Particular emphasis is given to the concept of service availability, and the corresponding notion of managing availability through Service Level Agreements. As IT service outages are very costly in modern society, the entry thoroughly introduces the economics of availability. The main formalisms for mathematical modeling of availability are also introduced.

INTRODUCTION

In modern society, information and communication technology (ICT) is becoming ubiquitous. Modern ICT is transforming our way of life; allowing us to work, buy things, educate ourselves, and meet our friends in ways not imagined two, or sometimes even one, decade ago. However, with these benefits comes an increased dependence on ICT. The consequences of outages – downtime – in ICT systems are becoming ever larger and more difficult to assess beforehand. ICT systems underpin our electricity distribution, the supply chains that bring food to our stores, the financial systems that let us use our money, the booking systems that let us travel, and so on. When these systems go down, modern society grinds to a halt.

The availability of information systems (IS) and information technology (IT) is a measure of the extent to which systems are able to perform their required functions at the time when they are needed. A typical measure is a percentage – a payment system, for example, might have 99.8% availability, roughly meaning that it fails to provide the required functionality 0.2% of the time. Clearly, maintaining high availability is a top priority in many different lines of business.

This entry aims to introduce and explain the concept of availability of IS and IT, including a few cases where this seemingly simple concept becomes more complicated. Furthermore, the reader should become acquainted with the basic statistics and modeling formalisms of availability, as well as some of the problems and questions that are open for research.

STEADY STATE AVAILABILITY ANALYSIS

A simple and widely used equation for availability is

$$A = \frac{MTTF}{MTTF + MTTR} \qquad (1)$$

where A denotes availability, MTTF denotes "Mean Time To Failure" and MTTR denotes "Mean Time To Repair". This equation is easy to interpret: the numerator is the time that the system *is* functioning (i.e., before it fails), and the denominator is that same time that the system *is* functioning plus the time it is *not* functioning (i.e., when it is being repaired). The quotient thus represents the functioning time as a fraction of all time. As MTTF approaches infinity or MTTR approaches zero, availability approaches 100%.

The concept of a system alternating between functioning and not functioning over time is illustrated in Fig. 1. In this case, MTTF can be calculated by summing the four TTFs and dividing by four, whereas MTTR can be calculated by summing the three TTRs and dividing by three.

It is important to note the use of the word "mean" in MTTF and MTTR. It means that the times used are averages over many cycles of operation and repair. If the system has reached a "steady state," that is, a state where the statistical distributions of time to failure and time to repair do not change with time, then Eq. 1 gives a good characterization of average system behavior over a period of time. The measure thus defined is referred to as *steady state availability*.

If, however, the system is not in a steady state, that is, if the statistical distributions of time to failure and time to repair do change with time, then Eq. 1 must be applied with caution. Old measurements of time to failure and time to repair may not be valid any more.

Encyclopedia of Information Systems and Technology, DOI: 10.1081/E-EIST-120053881

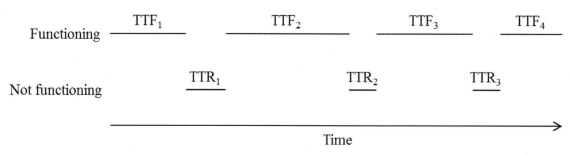

Fig. 1 A system alternating between functioning and not functioning over time.

Availability studied under these conditions is called *instantaneous availability*, that is, the probability that the system provides the required functionality at a given instant, rather than over a longer period of time.

Technical standardization bodies such as ISO[1] or ITU[2] often mention both aspects of availability in their standards. For example, the ISO/IEC 20000 (Information technology – Service management) defines availability as the "ability of a component or service to perform its required function at a stated instant or over a stated period of time".[1] In this entry, we will mostly concern ourselves with steady state availability.

AVAILABILITY OF HARDWARE, SOFTWARE, SYSTEMS, AND SERVICES

The steady state availability concept introduced in the previous section applies to all technical systems – light bulbs and computers alike. However, IS and IT have some special characteristics that set them apart from other technology in ways that are relevant for availability. Whereas a light bulb has just a single function – to provide illumination – modern IS are more complex. In particular, they are complex both in that they consist of many parts (hard drives, service buses, billing software, etc.), and in that they offer many different functions or services (storage of data in a database, access to the internet over the HTTP protocol, perform credit ratings on customers, etc.). How should availability be assessed in such a complex setting?

Indeed, it is possible to analyze many different aspects of IS and IT from an availability point of view. Hardware failure was once the most important reason behind outages. However, over the decades, the share of outages attributable to hardware has steadily fallen,[3] and in the 1980s, IT administration and software had become the main culprits.[4] In modern IS and IT, software failures and human errors have become the main reasons for outages.[5]

Software Reliability

The traditional scientific approach to studying software failures is found in the discipline of software reliability. Over the decades, many statistical models of software failures and failure rates have been developed, most often trying to describe how error-corrections and debugging efforts have affected the reliability of the resulting (imperfectly) debugged software. This is a mature and important field, and there are many good introductory and more advanced sources, for example, Pham.[6]

However, software reliability models are ill-posed to analyze some interesting and important aspects of IS and IT availability. To see this, we need to reconsider the "repair" word, familiar from MTTR, in the IS and IT context. Repairing a light bulb is straightforward – you spend a minute to exchange it for a new one. Repairing an information system, however, can mean different things. In software reliability, repairing a piece of software typically means fixing a bug. This is the work of programmers, and it is usually something that takes days, weeks, or months to complete, depending on complexity and priority. Once the software has been debugged, a new release is made. However, in the context of an enterprise information system such as an internet bank, repair means something else. If such a system experiences an outage, it has to come back up again, preferably in a matter of seconds, minutes, or hours, depending on complexity and priority. Bugs in the software engineering sense are rarely fixed at this stage – if software failure is to blame, the default strategy is most often a quick roll-back to the last working version. Bugs in the source code can then be fixed off-line. This kind of repair, which might more appropriately be called a *recovery* or a *restore*, is often the more relevant kind in order to analyze IS and IT availability in business operations. (This is sometimes called Mean Time to Restore Service – MTRS.) Therefore, it is not necessarily very enlightening to apply Eq. 1 to software failure and repair rates as found in the software reliability literature, if the goal is to support business operations with high availability requirements on IS.

Service Availability

These observations have had important consequences for availability modeling and analysis. System availability can still be modeled as a function of underlying hardware and software availability, but another paradigm has become increasingly popular over the years: service availability. This perspective ties right into the importance of IT for modern society – availability is not first and foremost evaluated from the perspective of software (or hardware) failure, but from the consequences of IT service failures. From this point of view, it is not interesting per se to analyze whether a particular hard drive crashes or a fiber optical cable is severed. The interesting questions are whether the data storage or communications services are interrupted. One way to express this change of perspective is to say that focus has shifted from the internal technical aspects of hardware or software failure to the external *consequences* of such failures – and their corresponding downtime – for the business operations supported. In the context of service availability, topics such as quality of service-aware service composition, user perceived availability, and component or architecture based availability assessment have become popular in the academic community.

The service-centric availability concept is enlightening in its focus on the consequences of downtime. It also readily offers an operationalization for anyone who wants to measure availability – the relevant downtime is the unavailability noticed by the business. A failure in a payment system that occurs without anyone noticing until the log is checked does not count as *service* downtime, even though there certainly was *system* downtime. Similarly, if a single system provides many services, some of which fail (e.g., off-site backup of data) while others remain up and running (e.g., local backup), service availability remains straightforward to asses, even though system availability becomes harder to define. In this way, a mature service catalog with appropriate granularity is a very helpful tool for availability analysis. However, some difficulties remain. If a service (e.g., an e-commerce payment system) is available to most customers, but not to all, should the service be assessed as available or not in the relevant interval of time? Surely, it does not make sense to equate unavailability to 1% of customers to unavailability to 100% of customers – but simply labeling a service with such availability problems "available" might have dire consequences. In this case, the service-centric availability concept does not offer any universal solution. However, it does offer the general insight that definitions of what constitutes available services should be made from the point of view of business operations.

Root Cause Analysis

As part of mature business continuity planning, it is prudent to analyze the causes of recorded service downtime. Such *root cause analysis* enables learning from past experience and, as such, contributes to better business continuity in the future. For example, if root-cause analysis reveals that a malformed message arriving through an integration solution caused a failure, then the external party that sent the message can be notified and/or better exception handling can be implemented in the integration platform. For nonrepairable systems, or for instantaneous availability analysis, this is conceptually straightforward. However, for steady-state analysis of repairable systems over a time interval, there need not be a unique root cause behind an outage. The malformed message can certainly be the immediate cause of failure – had it not occurred, neither would the failure. However, if service has not been restored after a few minutes of downtime, this might also be attributed to inadequate monitoring – had monitoring been in place, an automatic fail-over would have been completed by then. And indeed, if the requirements elicitation process had been sufficiently detailed about the message formatting requirements, the downtime would never have occurred.

The fact that there can be multiple root causes of IT service downtime is no reason not to conduct root cause analysis. On the contrary, this is a valuable practice. However, it does suggest that finding a (first) cause should not always be the end of the investigation. Indeed, while experts believe that lack of proper requirements and procurement practices are a top factor behind downtime,[7] such abstract root causes are not likely to show up in incident management logs. Availability analysts performing root cause analysis should take this into consideration.

SERVICE LEVEL AGREEMENTS (SLAS) AND AVAILABILITY

In modern IS and IT environments, business requirements are increasingly governed and managed "by contract",[8] namely by so called SLAs. Typically, such agreements cover a wide range of issues, including all kinds of quality aspects that the service-provider undertakes to deliver to the service-procurer. SLAs are not only used in dealings with external service-providers, but also increasingly within organizations, to formalize the agreements between the business and the (in-house) IT department. However, with the advent and increasing popularity of cloud computing, SLA management has become more important than ever, as these contracts increasingly become the only interface between the business and its IT support.

In terms of availability, a good SLA should reflect the needs of the business. Most often this is defined as a percentage, for example, 99.8%, reflecting steady-state availability over a time interval, as defined in Eq. 1. Sometimes, this is the *only* requirement on availability specified. This is not to be recommended. The reason is clear from Eq. 1: A given availability can be achieved by a lot of different combinations of MTTF and MTTR. For example, 99.8% availability 24 hours a day, 7 days a week means almost 18 hours of annual downtime. But clearly, there is a difference between a single 18 hour outage and some 200 separate 5 minute outages. Most companies would not be indifferent between these alternatives – shorter or fewer outages – even though the differences correspond to the same availability percentage. For example, the operator of an industrial plant with extensive supply chains, and a physical production process that is expensive to restart, probably prefers as few outages as possible even if they are longer, whereas a retailer for whom an 18 hour outage in the payment system the day before Christmas might mean the loss of the entire annual profit probably prefers as short outages as possible, even if they are many.[9]

To incorporate such considerations into an SLA, it is recommended to include constraints on the allowed time to service recovery (sometimes known as a Recovery Time Objective) as well as constraints on the number of service interruptions allowed. Together, two such constraints entails a worst-case availability in a time period, with the worst-case downtime being determined by the maximum number of outages allowed times the maximum outage duration allowed. Typically, the specified steady-state availability in the SLA should be better than this worst-case availability, in effect adding an additional constraint on the performance of the service-provider: every single outage cannot last for the longest acceptable duration.

Typically, other SLA objectives related to availability are also required. Recovery Point Objectives specifying the point to which data can be recovered are important for most lines of business, but the requirements can vary considerably. In a stock exchange trading system, each and every transaction made must be recoverable if the system crashes, whereas in a small business office environment, it might be enough to be able to recover yesterday's spreadsheets and text documents. Appropriate availability requirements must be based on a thorough understanding of the supported business operations.

PLANNED AND UNPLANNED DOWNTIME

When assessing availability, it is important to make sure that it is assessed with regard to the relevant operating time. For IT systems or services running continuously 24 hours a day, 7 days a week, the operating time is simply the same as calendar time, but for many services, this is not the case. Even an extremely availability-critical system such as a trading system on a stock exchange shuts down at the end of the trading day, only to reopen in the morning again. For such systems, it is straightforward to plan maintenance such as hardware or software upgrades to occur outside operating hours. Such *planned downtime* is required, at one point or another, for all systems and services. For services running continuously, redundant instances are required for upgrades, etc. Thus, one redundant system can be upgraded while another runs, and vice versa, maintaining the service without interruption.

Unfortunately, planned downtime sometimes leads to *unplanned downtime*, for example, if an upgrade takes longer than expected, or if an upgrade has been insufficiently tested before it is taken into operation. These are not uncommon scenarios, and insufficient change control or configuration management has been identified by experts as a top cause of unplanned downtime.[7] Therefore, it is prudent to add substantial safety margins to planned downtime, for example, when allocating service windows. Unfortunately, realistic testing of new configurations or upgrades to complex modern IS is not always possible in a test environment, making it virtually impossible to guarantee that a change will proceed without incident.

The risk of triggering unplanned downtime in relation to planned maintenance has important consequences for availability management. It is not uncommon to freeze the configuration of an IT system or an orchestrated set of IT services for the duration of particularly sensitive operations that must not suffer outages, such as during major product releases or transaction peaks such as Christmas in the retail sector. Here, it is interesting to observe a difference from traditional mechanical systems, where before sensitive operations old components can be changed for new ones earlier than they normally should. Such preventive maintenance before it is due is reasonable in systems where components wear out, and a new component is (almost always) better than an old one. However, software does not wear down as mechanical components do, leading to diametrically opposed practices in order to ensure high availability throughout a particular time interval.

THE ECONOMICS OF AVAILABILITY

So far, we have discussed availability from a *ceteris paribus* perspective: More is always better. However, in the real world all else is not equal, and trade-offs need

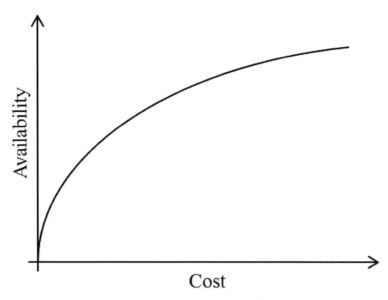

Fig. 2 The principle of diminishing returns on investment in availability.

to be made between the costs of achieving higher availability and the resulting benefits.

The Costs of Increasing Availability

The first component of such a trade-off is an understanding of the costs involved in achieving increased availability. There is no simple way to calculate these costs in the general case, though rules of thumb are sometimes proposed. What is clear, however, is that availability exhibits *diminishing returns*, i.e., when investing to increase availability; every percentage point will come at a greater cost than the last one. This conceptual relationship between investment and availability is illustrated in Fig. 2. A concrete example of what such a relationship might look like in practice is the Gartner rule of thumb that 99.3% availability for a "standard IT service" costs 2.15 times the cost of the standard service, whereas 99.81% availability costs 6.45 times the cost of the standard service.[10] While the exact figures should be taken with a large grain of salt, the fact that availability investments exhibit diminishing returns is indisputable.

Eq. 1 helps us understand the diminishing returns on availability investments. In order to increase A, Eq. 1 offers two possibilities: i) increase MTTF or ii) decrease MTTR. Any improvement in steady-state availability has to be the result of at least one of these. The standard (conceptual) way to increase MTTF is to build some kind of redundant solution with fail-over functionality – having two components rather than a single one. But for his method to double MTTF, a fail-over mechanism is needed for switching from one component to the other precisely when needed, and this comes at an additional cost, over and above the double component cost. (And

indeed it only works if there is no common cause of failure for both components.) So in general, there will be diminishing returns on investments in the increase MTTF strategy. Similarly, the standard (conceptual) way to decrease MTTR is to hire more people to do the repairs – having two system administrators rather than a single one to make systems repairs (or service recoveries) when needed. Doubling cost in this way might decrease MTTR by half – if the two repairmen can always work in parallel on a problem, and if it is never the case that one of them is idle while the other one is working. So in general, there will be diminishing returns on investments in the decreased MTTR strategy. These particular examples are simplified, but the principles hold true, and help explain the diminishing returns on availability investments.

How should we go about increasing availability? By increasing MTTF, by decreasing MTTR, or by a combination? This question is relevant to any decision maker, whether there is a fixed budget that should be spent so as to maximize availability, or if there is a fixed availability goal that should be reached at a minimal cost. Of course, this question typically cannot be answered in a precise way, because there is no reliable way of exactly predicting the availability that will result from particular investments. Nevertheless, it is a conceptually enlightening question to ask. The answer is that it depends on the prices of the two strategies. If we simplify a bit and assume that increasing MTTF translates to buying more or better technology, and that decreasing MTTR translates to hiring more or better personnel, then increasing MTTF will be a good strategy whenever technology is cheap, whereas decreasing MTTR will be a good strategy whenever labor is cheap. In microeconomic terms, the *technical rate of substitution* between technology

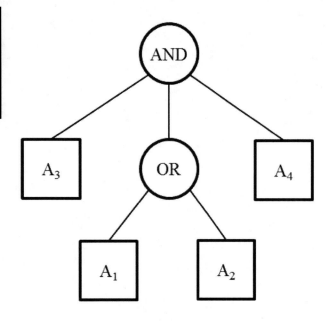

$$A_{tot} = A_3 A_4 (1 - (1 - A_1)(1 - A_2))$$

Fig. 3 The principle of a fault tree used to calculate system availability based on system component availabilities.

and labor should equal the *economic rate of substitution* between them.[11]

The Benefits of Increasing Availability

The second component of the trade-off is an understanding of the benefits of increased availability. The most important factor here is the outage costs: How much does an hour of downtime cost, or equivalently, how great is the benefit of preventing that outage? A straightforward but useful formula for calculating the average cost of an hour of downtime is the following:[12]

Employee costs/hour $*$ % Employees affected by outage

$+$ Average Revenue/hour $*$ % Revenue affected by outage

$=$ Estimated average cost of 1 hour of downtime   (2)

The idea is that the costs of downtime either come from lost productivity (employees who get paid but cannot work) or from lost revenue (sales that never happen). These kinds of calculations are the basis of estimates such as IBM's claim that IT systems downtime cost American businesses \$4.54 billion in 1996.[13] (It is surprisingly hard to find more up-to-date estimates of downtime costs that are not very limited in scope. Nevertheless, it is clear that downtime costs are large, and that they have most probably grown considerably during the last 20 years, as society has become ever more dependent on IT.)

It is important to note the word "average" in Eq. 2. Whereas the hourly salaries of employees are known and fixed, the hourly revenues are more difficult to assess. This contributes a lot to the uncertainty inherent in downtime cost calculations. In particular, even if an average hourly revenue is known (e.g., calculated based on last week, month, or year) this average may be way of the mark if there is a lot of variance. For example, hourly revenues in the retail sector can vary by more than a factor of 10, depending both on hour of the day, day of the week, or proximity to major holidays. Taking the variance of outage costs into account, rather than just focusing on averages, is important for prudent decision making with regard to availability.[9]

There is also another simplification involved in Eq. 2, worth noting. It assumes that outage costs scale linearly with the duration of the outage: On average, a two hour outage costs twice as much as a one hour outage and a ten hour outage costs ten times as much as a one hour outage. This is a good first approximation. However, there are clearly instances when this is not the case. Some IT systems have large fixed restart costs. Perhaps the best examples are industrial control systems, where every outage entails the halt and restart of a physical industrial process. If the fixed costs of a restart are sufficiently large, the difference between a one hour and two hour outage might not be so great. Other IT systems have snowball effects, where a short outage may go entirely unnoticed by customers, but a longer outage has severe consequences on brand goodwill and customer loyalty. Perhaps the best examples are payment systems or automated teller machines (ATMs), where a short outage typically just results in the customer swiping the card again, but a longer outage may prompt other customers standing in line to leave the store, or even drive customers to other banks. Again, there is no universal solution that fits all organizations. Decisions about what kind of availability profile to strive for need to be made from the point of view of the business operations that are supported by the IT services.[9]

Only when both the costs and benefits of availability investments are understood is it possible to make an enlightened trade-off between them.

MODELING FORMALISMS

The most straightforward way to model availability in complex systems is to use Fault Trees, a technique adopted from reliability engineering. A fault tree depicts a system composed of constituent components, each with an availability level of their own. The total availability of the system can then be calculated, depending on whether the components are redundant (the OR relation) or not (the AND relation). An example is given in Fig. 3.

Fault trees are logically equivalent to Reliability Block Diagrams, another formalism sometimes used. The fault tree formalism has proved to be a good method for rapidly and accurately approximating the availability of enterprise IS.[14]

However, the fault tree method assumes that the availabilities of components are *independent*. This is a simplifying and often useful assumption, but from an availability perspective, it can be wrong in two interesting ways. First, it is possible that there are *common cause failures*, i.e., that components do not fail independently of each other. Second, there are *repair interaction effects*, either because a common cause failure is repaired, thus affecting all affected components at once, or the repair time of one failed component is extended because all system administrators are occupied with the repair of another failed component. Modeling such more complex cases requires other formalisms. One possibility is to use Bayesian networks, where the influences of components on the availability of one another can be explicitly modeled in conditional probability tables.

Another possibility to model more complex systems is state models, where a system makes transitions between different states. A two component system requiring both components to be functioning in order to be available might for instance be modeled using three states: (i) two components functioning, (ii) one component functioning and one component not functioning, (iii) two components not functioning. Such a model can easily capture the impact of limited resources for repair. Typically, state space models are continuous-time Markov chains, meaning that steady state availability is readily found from the stationary distribution. Similarly, aspects of instantaneous availability can be studied by studying the transient behavior of the Markov chain.

Again, however, the Markov state-space models have some simplifying assumptions. The time spent in each state follows an exponential distribution. This is a mathematically convenient approximation, but empirical studies show that time to failure and time to repair typically follows other statistical distributions. For IT systems, TTF might be better modeled by a Weibull distribution,[15,16] and TTR by the log-normal distribution.[15,17] However, more realism comes at a price, as these models in practice depend on numerical simulations.

CONCLUSION

In modern society, availability of ICT is becoming increasingly important. This entry has introduced the concept of availability, with a particular emphasis on IT service availability, which is now an important part of the economy, and is becoming a top priority for companies that depend on cloud-based IT services.

Even though availability analysis is an old discipline with roots in reliability engineering, important challenges still remain. These include not least the economic aspects and trade-offs involved in decision making with regard to availability. There are efforts underway to turn this kind of "service level engineering" into a more mature discipline.[18] This work will certainly evolve over the years to come. So will the search for modeling formalisms and practices that balance the needs for simplicity and usability with the needs of decision makers to get appropriate analytical insights. A third important strand is empirical studies, which provide important insights into the state of the practice.

ACKNOWLEDGMENT

The author wishes to thank Dr. Johan König, who gave a number of useful comments on this entry.

REFERENCES

1. International Organization for Standardization. Information technology – service management – part 1: Specification. International standard ISO/IEC 20000-1:2005(E), International Organization for Standardization, December **2005**.
2. International Telecommunications Union. Final draft of revised recommendation e.800. Technical report, International Telecommunications Union, May 2008.
3. Genadis, T. C. A cost optimization model for determining optimal burn-in times at the module/system level of an electronic product. Intl J. Qual. Reliabil. Manag. **1996**, *13* (9), 61–74.
4. Gray, J. *Why Do Computers Stop and What Can Be Done About It?* Technical report, Tandem Computers Inc., June 1985.
5. Pertet, S.; Narasimhan, P. Causes of failure in web applications. Technical report, Parallel Data Laboratory, Carnegie Mellon University, CMU-PDL-05-109, 2005.
6. Pham, H. *Software Reliability*; Springer-Verlag: Singapore, 2000.
7. Franke U, Johnson P, König J, Marcks von Würtemberg L. Availability of enterprise IT systems: an expert-based bayesian framework. *Software Qual. J* **2012**, *20*(2), 369–94
8. Sallé, M.; Bartolini, C. Management by contract. In *Network Operations and Management Symposium*, 2004. IEEE/IFIP, *volume 1*; 787–800.
9. Franke, U. Optimal IT service availability: Shorter outages, or fewer? IEEE Trans. Network Serv. Manag **2012**, *9* (1), 22–33.

10. Malik, B.; Scott, D. *How to Calculate the Cost of Continuously Available IT Services*; Technical report, Gartner, Inc., November 2010.

11. Franke, U. Enterprise Architecture Analysis with Production Functions. In IEEE 18th International Enterprise Distributed Object Computing Conference (EDOC 2014), *2014*; 52–60.

12. Patterson, D. A. A simple way to estimate the cost of downtime. In Proceedings of the 16th Systems Administration Conf. LISA, **2002**; 185–188.

13. IBM Global Services. Improving systems availability. Technical report, IBM Global Services, 1998.

14   Närman P, Franke U, König J, Buschle M, Ekstedt M. Enterprise architecture availability analysis using fault trees and stakeholder interviews. *Enterpr. Inform. Syst* **2014**, *8*(1), 1–25

15. Schroeder, B.; Gibson, G. A. A large-scale study of failures in high-performance computing systems. Depend. Secure Comput. IEEE Trans. **2010**, *7* (4), 337–350.

16. Heath, T.; Martin, R. P.; Nguyen, T. D. Improving cluster availability using workstation validation. ACM SIGMETRICS Perform. Eval. Rev. **2002**, *30* (1), 217–227.

17. Franke, U.; Holm, H.; König, J. The distribution of time to recovery of enterprise IT services. IEEE Trans. Reliabil. **2014**, *63* (4), 858–867.

18. Kieninger, A.; Westernhagen, J.; Satzger, G. The economics of service level engineering. In System Sciences (HICSS), 2011 44th H*awaii International Conference*, **2011**; 1–10.

Big Data: Applications

Stephan Kudyba
New Jersey Institute of Technology, Newark, New Jersey, U.S.A.

Matthew Kwatinetz
QBL Partners, New York, New York, U.S.A.

Abstract

Data resources can provide value to organizations from the information that can be extracted from them. This extraction process involves querying data resources for particular variables at particular levels of aggregation in a particular format, and then initiating some type of analytic process. However, before conducting any of these activities, one essential task that underpins the information creation initiative, involves the creation of a conceptual model. In other words, whether you have terabytes of data or just a few thousand records, whether you are considering trends over the past few years or focusing on real-time data feeds, decision makers must determine what questions they are looking to answer with data and information.

By now you've heard the phrase "big data" a hundred times and it's intrigued you, scared you, or even bothered you. Whatever your feeling is, one thing that remains a source of interest is a clear understanding of just what is meant by the concept and what it means for the realm of commerce. Big data, terabytes of data, mountains of data, no matter how you would like to describe it, there is an ongoing data explosion transpiring all around us that makes previous creations, collections, and storage of data merely trivial. Generally, the concept of big data refers to the sources, variety, velocities, and volumes of this vast resource. We will describe the meaning of these areas to provide a clearer understanding of the new data age.

The introduction of faster computer processing through Pentium technology in conjunction with enhanced storage capabilities introduced in the early 1990s helped promote the beginning of the information economy, which made computers faster, better able to run state-of-the-art software devices, and store and analyze vast amounts of data.[1] The creation, transmitting, processing, and storage capacities of today's enhanced computers, sensors, handheld devices, tablets, and the like, provide the platform for the next stage of the information age. These super electronic devices have the capabilities to run numerous applications, communicate across multiple platforms, and generate, process, and store unimaginable amounts of data. So if you were under the impression that big data was just a function of e-commerce (website) activity, think again. That's only part of the very large and growing pie.

When speaking of big data, one must consider the source of data. This involves the technologies that exist today and the industry applications that are facilitated by them. These industry applications are prevalent across the realm of commerce and continue to proliferate in countless activities:

- Marketing and advertising (online activities, text messaging, social media, new metrics in measuring ad spend and effectiveness, etc.)
- Healthcare (machines that provide treatment to patients, electronic health records [EHRs], digital images, wireless medical devices)
- Transportation (Global Positioning System [GPS] activities)
- Energy (residential and commercial usage metrics)
- Retail (measuring foot traffic patterns at malls, demographic analysis)
- Sensors imbedded in products across industry sectors tracking usage

These are just a few examples of how industries are becoming more data intensive.

DESCRIPTION OF BIG DATA

The source and variety of big data involves new technologies that create, communicate, or are involved with data-generating activities, which produce different types/formats of data resources. The data we are referring to isn't just numbers that depict amounts, or performance indicators or scale. Data also includes less structured forms, such as the following elements:

- Web site links
- E-mails

Encyclopedia of Information Systems and Technology, DOI: 10.1081/E-EIST-120053826

- Twitter responses
- Product reviews
- Pictures/images
- Written text on various platforms

What big data entails is structured and unstructured data that correspond to various activities. Structured data entails data that is categorized and stored in a file according to a particular format description, where unstructured data is free-form text that takes on a number of types, such as those listed above. The cell phones of yesteryear have evolved into smartphones capable of texting, surfing, phoning, and playing a host of software-based applications. All the activities conducted on these phones (every time you respond to a friend, respond to an ad, play a game, use an app, and conduct a search) generate a traceable data asset. Computers and tablets connected to Internet-related platforms (social media, website activities, and advertising via video platform) all generate data. Scanning technologies that read energy consumption, healthcare-related elements, traffic activity, etc., create data. And finally, good old traditional platforms such as spreadsheets, tables, and decision support platforms still play a role as well.

The next concept to consider when merely attempting to understand the big data age, refers to velocities of data, where velocity entails how quickly data is being generated, communicated, and stored. Back in the beginning of the information economy (e.g., mid–1990s), the phrase "real time" was often used to refer to almost instantaneous tracking, updating, or some activities revolving around timely processing of data. This phrase has taken on a new dimension in today's ultra-fast, wireless world. Where real time was the goal of select industries (financial markets, e-commerce), the phrase has become commonplace in many areas of commerce today:

- Real-time communication with consumers via text, social media, e-mail

- Real-time consumer reaction to events, advertisements via Twitter
- Real-time reading of energy consumption of residential households
- Real-time tracking of visitors on a website

Real time involves high-velocity or fast-moving data and fast generation of data that results in vast volumes of the asset. Non-real-time data or sources of more slowly moving data activities also prevail today, where the volumes of data generated refer to the storage and use of more historic data resources that continue to provide value. Non-real time refers to measuring events and time-related processes and operations that are stored in a repository:

- Consumer response to brand advertising
- Sales trends
- Generation of demographic profiles

As was mentioned above, velocity of data directly relates to volumes of data, where some real-time data quickly generate a massive amount in a very short time. When putting an amount on volume, the following statistic explains the state of affairs: as of 2012, about 2.5 exabytes of data is created each day. A petabyte of data is 1 quadrillion bytes, which is the equivalent of about 20 million file cabinets' worth of text, and an exabyte is 1000 times that amount. The volume comes from both new data variables and the amount of data records in those variables.

The ultimate result is more data that can provide the building blocks to information generation through analytics. These data sources come in a variety of types that are structured and unstructured that need to be managed to provide decision support for strategists of all walks.[2]

BUILDING BLOCKS TO DECISION SUPPORT

You may ask: Why are there classifications of data? Isn't data simply data? One of the reasons involves the activities required to manage and analyze the resources that are involved in generating value from it. Yes, big data sounds impressive and almost implies that value exists simply in storing it. The reality is, however, that unless data can help decision makers make better decisions, enhance strategic initiatives, help marketers more effectively communicate with consumers, enable healthcare providers to better allocate resources to enhance the treatment and outcomes of their patients, etc., there is little value to this resource, even if it is called big.

Data itself is a record of an event or a transaction:

- A purchase of a product
- A response to a marketing initiative
- A text sent to another individual
- A click on a link

In its crude form, data provides little value. However, if data is corrected for errors, aggregated, normalized, calculated, or categorized, its value grows dramatically. In other words, data are the building blocks to information, and information is a vital input to knowledge generation for decision makers.[3] Taking this into consideration, the "big" part of big data can actually augment value significantly to those who use it correctly. Ultimately, when data is managed correctly, it provides a vital input for decision makers across industry sectors to make better decisions.

So why does big data imply a significant increase in the value of data? Because big data can provide more descriptive information as to why something has happened:

- Why and who responded to my online marketing initiative?
- What do people think of my product and potentially why?
- What factors are affecting my performance metrics?
- Why did my sales increase notably last month?
- What led my patient treatment outcomes to improve?

SOURCE OF MORE DESCRIPTIVE VARIABLES

Big data implies not just more records/elements of data, but more data variables and new data variables that possibly describe reasons why actions occur. When performing analytics and constructing models that utilize data to describe processes, an inherent limitation is that the analyst simply doesn't have all the pertinent data that accounts for all the explanatory variance of that process. The resulting analytic report may be missing some very important information. If you're attempting to better understand where to locate your new retail outlet in a mall and you don't have detailed shopper traffic patterns, you may be missing some essential descriptive information that affects your decision. As a result, you locate your store in what seems to be a strategically appropriate space, but for some reason, the traffic for your business just isn't there. You may want to know what the market thinks of your new product idea, but unfortunately you were only able to obtain 1000 responses to your survey of your target population. The result is you make decisions with the limited data resources you have. However, if you text your question to 50,000 of your target population, your results may be more accurate, or let's say, more of an indication of market sentiment.

As technology continues to evolve and become a natural part of everyone's lives, so too does the generation of new data sources. The last few years have seen the explosion of mobile computing: the smartphone may be the most headlining example, but the trend extends down to your laundry machine, sprinkler system, and the label on the clothing that you bought retail. One of the most unexpected and highest impact trends in this regard is the ability to leverage data variables that describe activities/processes. We all know that technology has provided faster, better computers—but now the trend is for technology to feed in the generation of never before seen data at a scale that is breathtaking. What follows are some brief examples of this.

The following illustrations depict the evolution of big data in various industry sectors and business scenarios. Just think of the descriptive variables (data resources) that can be analyzed in these contemporary scenarios as opposed to the times of the 1990s!

INDUSTRY EXAMPLES OF BIG DATA

Electioneering

In some recent political campaigns, politicians began to mobilize the electorate in greater proportion than ever before. Previously, campaign managers had relied unduly on door-to-door recruiting, flyering in coffee shops, rallies, and telemarketing calls. Now campaigns can be managed completely on the Internet, using social network data and implied geographic locations to expand connectivity between the like-minded. The focus is not just on generating more votes, but has extended to the ever-important fund-raising initiatives as well. Campaigners are able to leverage the power of big data and focus on micro-donations and the viral power of the Internet to spread the word—more dollars were raised through this vehicle than had been seen in history. The key function of the use of the big data allowed local supporters to organize other local supporters, using social networking software and self-identified zip code and neighborhood locations. That turned data resources *locational*, adding a new dimension of information to be exploited, polled, and aggregated to help determine where bases of support were stronger/weaker. Where will it go next? It is likely that in the not-so-distant future we will find voter registrations tagged to mobile devices, and the ability to circumvent statistical sampling polls with actual polls of the population, sorted by geography, demography, and psychographics. Democratic campaign managers estimate that they collected 13 million e-mail addresses in the 2008 campaign, communicating directly with about 20% of the total votes needed to win. Eric Schmidt (former CEO of Google) says that since 2008, the game has completely changed: "In 2008 most people didn't operate on (Facebook and Twitter). The difference now is, first and foremost, the growth of Facebook, which is much, much more deeply penetrated... you can run political campaigns on the sum of those tools (Facebook, YouTube, and Twitter)."[4]

INVESTMENT DILIGENCE AND SOCIAL MEDIA

"Wall Street analysts are increasingly incorporating data from social media and Internet search trends into their investment strategies."[5] The use of social media data is generally called unstructured data. In 2007, surveys showed that approximately 2% of investment firms used such data—today "that number is closer to 50%."[6] The World Economic Forum has now classified this type of data as an economic asset, and this includes monitoring millions of tweets per day, scanning comments on buyer sites such as Amazon, processing job offerings on TheLadders or Monster.com, etc. "Big data is fundamentally changing how we trade," said financial services consultant Adam Honore (adhonore, http://www.advancedtrading.com/Adam-Honore). Utilizing the number and trending features of Twitter, Facebook, and other media platforms, these investors can test how "sticky" certain products, services, or ideas are, in the country. From this information, they can make investment choices on one product vs. another—or on the general investor sentiment. This information does not replace existing investment diligence, but in fact adds to the depth and quality (or lack thereof sometimes!) of analysis.

Real Estate

Investment dollars in the capital markets are split between three main categories, as measured by value: bonds, stocks, and alternative assets, including real estate. Since bonds were traded, an informal network of brokers and market makers has been able to serve as gateways to information, given that many transactions go through centralized clearinghouses. In 1971, NASDAQ was the first stock market to go electronic, and as the information revolution continued, it soon allowed for any person around the world to sit at the hub of cutting-edge news, information, and share prices. After a particular tech-savvy Salomon Brothers trader left that company, he led the further digitization of data and constant updating of news to create a big data empire: Michael Bloomberg. Real estate, however, has been late to the game. To understand real estate prices in any given market has been more challenging, as many transactions are private, and different cities and counties can have significantly different reporting mechanisms and data structures. Through the late 1980s and 1990s, real estate was often tracked in boxes of files, mailed back and forth across the country. As cities began to go digital, a new opportunity was created. In the year 2000, Real Capital Analytics (http://www.rcanalytics.com) was founded by Robert White to utilize data mining techniques to aggregate data worldwide on real estate transactions, and make that data available digitally. Real estate research firms have many techniques to acquire data: programmatically scraping websites, taking feeds from property tax departments, polling brokerage firms, tracking news feeds, licensing and warehousing proprietary data, and more. All of these sources of data can be reviewed on an hourly basis, funneled through analysis,

and then displayed in a user-friendly manner: charts, indices, and reports that are sorting hundreds of thousands of daily data points.

Specialized Real Estate: Building Energy Disclosure and Smart Meters

Over 40% of energy use and carbon emissions in the United States come from existing buildings (http://www.eia.gov/consumption/commercial/index.cfm). To put this in perspective, if you combined the energy use and emissions output of all of the SUVs on the road in North America, this would be approximately 3%. So you can see that the use of energy by existing buildings is a very important piece of data. Until recently, this data has been held in many different databases for utilities across the country, with no central repository or easy means for reconciling these data sets. Today, three trends have picked up: 1) energy disclosure ordinances; 2) satellite heat map data; and 3) data warehousing aggregations based on smart meters. The amount of data needed here to control for effective information is staggering: any analysis must account for building size, use, geographic location, seasonality, climatic variation, occupancy, etc. In many of these cases, information is collected on a granularity of 1–15 minutes! That is for every building, in every city, in every state in the country: billions of data points *per day* (http://www.eebhub.org/).

Commerce and Loyalty Data

When you walk into your favorite retail outlet—be it clothing, jewelry, books, or food—there is nothing quite as gratifying as being recognized, your tastes being understood, and receiving personal service ("The usual, please!"). In the distant past, this probably meant a neighborhood shop where you literally were known by the salesperson. In the 1990s this was transformed into a "loyalty program" craze in which large-scale (franchised, national, international) retailers were able to tag your shopping to a digital ID card that they enticed you to use by offering discounts. But Internet commerce, under the thought leadership of Amazon, transformed this experience entirely. Once you are online, not only can a retailer track your purchases, but it can track what products you look at, things you plan to buy (wish lists), items you buy for others (registry), and even what pages you spend time on and for how long. This provides retailers with a competitive advantage: they can tailor your shopping experience and suggest new products. Witness Netflix recommendations, Pandora's preference algorithms, and LinkedIn's suggestion of who you might next want to connect with or apply for a job from. Moreover, it is not just information from their own site that these online merchants can now pull from—the trend has now reclaimed the point-of-sale data from brick-and-mortar stores as well. Retailers integrate physical data with online point-of-sale data, and can also view what other sites you visit, where else you make purchases, who makes purchases for you, and what "like-minded shoppers" may be in your network.

Crowd-Sourced Crime Fighting

In an effort to aid local policing efforts, policing has found a new ally: you! Over the last decade "hot spot" policing has become the effective leading strategy for reducing crime: take careful record of where crime occurs, measure density regions, and overwhelm the highest density regions with extremely quick and over-powering responses. However, this strategy still relies on actually being able to track all of the crime incidents—no small task, as the force's personnel have limited resources. Enter the crowd sourcing platforms. Some cities have created apps for mobile devices (or other interfaces) that allow individual citizens to upload information that indicates crimes they have witnessed (http://spotcrime.com/ga/augusta)! The upload contains the description of the crime, a geographic location, and a time stamp. As participation increases, so too do "eyes on the street," and the map is filled with the information needed to improve police performance.

Pedestrian Traffic Patterns in Retail

Thanks to some recent controversies, you probably already know that your cell phone allows you to be tracked at nearly any time of day, provided it is powered on. While privacy laws currently still protect you from being identified with this feature (without your opting in), new technologies are available to identify unique movements. Cell tower "repeaters" in strategic locations in malls and downtowns can track "unique cell phones" and their walking patterns. As a result, a mall owner might want to know how many people take the elevator vs. the stairs—and of the ones who take the elevator, do they ever walk by the store on the other side of it. Further, if they find a patron lingering in the leather goods section of the store for more than 12 minutes, but that customer does not stop at the cash register, they will send a text message advertisement promotion to the customer's phone before he or she leaves the store, offering a discount on—you guessed it—leather goods. This is only the beginning of this technology. Expect to see it deployed in cities to track crime patterns, the safety of certain intersections, and more (http://techcrunch.com/2007/12/14/path-intelligence-monitors-foot-traffic-in-retail-stores-by-pinging-peoples-phones/; http://

allthingsd.com/20111103/ex-googlers-raise-5-8-million-to-help-retailers-track-foot-traffic/).

Intelligent Transport Application

New applications being developed for smartphones pool voluntarily offered information from unique sources into a real-time database providing an instant advantage from the use of big data. Uber, a mobile phone-based transportation application, connects drivers (of limousines and taxis) with potential passengers. As each driver "opts in" to Uber from his or her phone, the phone sends a GPS signal update to the master Uber map. When a passenger is ready for a ride, the passenger turns on his or her Uber signal and effectively puts out an electronic thumb. Both passenger and driver receive an instant updated map with the potential matches to be found as moving dots across the map, with estimates of congestion (which influence pricing), as well as arrival information. In a similar fashion, Waze is a transport application for local drivers. When drivers get in their car, they turn on Waze, which utilizes the phone's GPS tracker, motion sensors, and built-in geographic road information (speed limits, lights, and stop signs) to estimate the level of traffic you are experiencing while driving. Waze then merges your information with all other local drivers' information, creating a real-time picture of road traffic. The application also allows for the reporting of police presence, traffic, accidents, and not-to-miss sights! In essence, this application creates a virtual cloud of self-reported big data.

DESCRIPTIVE POWER AND PREDICTIVE PATTERN MATCHING

As silos are broken down between traditional sources of data, aggregation of big data is allowing astounding predictive capabilities for the data scientist. One example comes from the MIT Media Lab, where a group used location data from mobile phones to estimate the number of shoppers at a particular department store on the biggest shopping day of the year: Black Friday. By combining this information with historical sales data, demographics of the trade region surrounding the department store, and other relevant factors (macroeconomic, weather, etc.), the team was able to predict retail sales on that day even before the department store itself could![2] Another example of the same practice comes from Farecast.com (now owned by Microsoft and accessed through Bing). By aggregating pricing information from all airlines and comparing it to historical information as well as statistically correlated databases that signal pricing, Farecast is able to accurately predict whether the price of a specific airline ticket will go up or down in the near, mid, or short term. At one point it even offered insurance to guarantee the accuracy of its information (http://www.upgradetravelbetter.com/2006/11/13/fare-guarantee-farecast-lets-you-insure-its-fare-predictions/)! Other examples of this approach include predicting housing price changes in the U.S. with publicly available web information[7] and the Center for Disease Control (CDC) using tweets (twitter.com) to predict the spread of disease, such as cholera in Haiti. In development today is the Square Kilometre Array (SKA), a telescope that is being designed to crunch 300–1500 petabytes of data a year. Just how much data is that? "If you take the current global daily internet traffic and multiply it by two, you are in the range of the data set that the SKA radio telescope will be collecting every day," says IBM researcher Tom Engbersen. "This is big data analytics to the extreme."[8]

Whatever way you may classify big data, whether it be new variable sources, larger volumes, closer to real-time activity, the mere availability of the resource doesn't necessarily imply greater value to organizations (http://qz.com/81661/most-data-isnt-big-and-businesses-are-wasting-money-pretending-it-is/). A few key elements that have to be present in order for big data to have signification value are: the data must contain relevant information corresponding to a particular process or activity, and the data must have quality. As in the short examples mentioned earlier, one must realize that simply because new data sources are generated in a particular process, it doesn't imply that it provides descriptive information on the impacts to measuring that process's performance. As far as quality goes, new data variables or more volumes of data must be a reliable and consistent resource to making better decisions. The process of maintaining data quality, variable consistency, and the identification of variables that describe various activities is a daunting task and requires not only competent analysts, but also the inclusion of subject matter experts and data experts. Remember, analytic techniques of all types are not self-generating methods for decision makers. Skilled professionals are essential to guide the process. Just consider some of the questions below regarding data that potentially describe processes:

- Do Twitter responses reflect accurate consumer sentiment toward events (was the tweet an overreaction or misinterpretation of the reported occurrence?)?
- Were survey questions interpreted correctly by responders?
- Do LinkedIn connections share the same business interests?
- Do Facebook friends share the same product interests?
- Do the demographics generated from credit card purchases truly reflect the profile of the consumer

purchasing the product (did younger consumers borrow parents' credit cards?)?

THE VALUE OF DATA

Simply crunching available data elements as they appear and drawing conclusions, whether it's big data or not, can yield suboptimal, even dangerous results to the decision-making process, and end up providing negative value to organizations rather than the assumed positive value. This last statement brings up a vital point to the realm of big data and value. When considering value, probably the most significant add to value that big data brings is the enhancement to the decision-making process to those who access it, manage it appropriately, and utilize it effectively. However, the concept of enhancing the decision-making process by leveraging data involves the widely encompassing realm of analytics and corresponding strategy. We use the phrase "widely encompassing" because the concept of analytics can include a vast variety of applications, depending on what you plan on doing with data. For simplicity's sake, this entry will focus primarily on the incorporation of business intelligence and mining applications in leveraging data sources.

CLOSING COMMENTS ON LEVERAGING DATA THROUGH ANALYTICS

Data resources can provide value to organizations from the information that can be extracted from them. This extraction process involves querying data resources for particular variables at particular levels of aggregation in a particular format, and then initiating some type of analytic process. However, before conducting any of these activities, one essential task that underpins the information creation initiative involves the creation of a conceptual model. In other words, whether you have terabytes of data or just a few thousand records, whether you are considering trends over the past few years or focusing on real-time data feeds, decision makers must determine what questions they are looking to answer with data and information. This process can be classified as a conceptual model. Consider using analytics to address the following scenario (e.g., what data variables and level of detail are needed to provide relevant information).

As a hospital administrator, you are looking to analyze those factors that impact the patients' satisfaction metric that describes their experience while being treated at your hospital.

No matter what industry you operate in, the bottom line to the decision-making process is that individuals must rigorously deliberate over what they are looking to better understand. Once this has been established, the process of leveraging data resources can be undertaken. That process then entails extracting the relevant data variables at corresponding levels of detail and initiating an analytic framework.

ETHICAL CONSIDERATIONS IN THE BIG DATA ERA

Before we go any further in describing the process of leveraging data assets, it is important to stress the adherence to sound ethical practices regarding the various facets of data acquisition, storage, and utilization. Some important concepts should be kept in mind when dealing with data resources, with a particular emphasis on data that describes individuals.

This entry does not promote or support heavy—or underhanded, controversial techniques in acquiring extensive personal data. Individuals should be made aware of how data is generated and gathered regarding their everyday activities, and privacy and security rules should be strictly adhered to. Ultimately, this entry adheres to the notion that the management of data resources and analytics should be conducted to yield positive outcomes for processes and individuals who interact with them.

REFERENCES

1. Kudyba, S. *Information Technology, Corporate Productivity, and the New Economy*; Quorum Books: Westport, Connecticut, 2002.
2. McAfee, A.; Brynjolfsson, E. Big data: The management revolution. Harvard Bus. Rev. October **2012**, 60–62.
3. Davenport, T.; Prusak, L. *Working Knowledge*. Harvard Business Review Press: Boston, MA, 2000.
4. Tumulty, K. *Twitter Becomes a Key Real-Time Tool for Campaigns*; Washington Post, April *26*, 2012.
5. What the experts say: Twitter guided trading. The Week, June 14, **2012**.
6. Cha, A. E. "Big Data" from social media, elsewhere online redefines trend-watching. Washington Post, June 6, **2012**.
7. Wu, L.; Brynjolfsson, E. The future of prediction: How Google searches foreshadow housing prices and quantities. ICIS 2009 Proc. 2009, paper 147. http://aisel.aisnet.org/icis2009/147
8. Peckham, M. IBM to help research and develop 'exascale' supercomputing telescope. Time Mag. April 2, **2012**. http://techland.time.com/2012/04/02/ibm-to-help-research-and-develop-exascale-supercomputing-telescope/

Big Data: Concepts, Technologies, and Applications

Bernice M. Purcell
School of Business Administration and Extended Learning, Holy Family University, Philadelphia, Pennsylvania, U.S.A.

Abstract

The term big data originates from the fact that the datasets used are so large that typical database systems are unable to capture, save, and analyze the datasets. While traditional database systems store only structured data, big data can include semistructured and unstructured data as well. The source of data for traditional database systems is stored transactions, whereas big data can be generated from web pages, social media, and sensors embedded in machinery and common devices. Storage and searches enabled by new technologies like Hadoop and No Structured Query Language (NoSQL) allow processing of enormous datasets. Big data impacts diverse industries such as healthcare, business, industry, and government. Big data has been enabled by cloud technology and is creating a need for new skill sets in the labor market.

INTRODUCTION

This entry covers the broad topic of big data. An explanatory definition of big data serves as an introduction. The concepts of volume, variety, and velocity, which are the acknowledged characteristics, are presented. Related to volume, variety, and velocity are growth of storage technology, advancements in data collection technology, and continual update of dynamic data.

The discussion of data sources introduces the formats of data as well as the breadth of data collection and storage technologies. The role of social media and the Internet of Things is broached at this juncture.

Big data technologies involve both hardware and software. The main hardware storage technologies used for big data are scale-out network attached storage (NAS) and object-based storage. Techniques for storage and processing include Hadoop and related software apps and NoSQL. Cloud computing technology also has an impact on big data and its usage.

The focus of the entry turns to uses of big data. Many industries use big data and are exploring additional capabilities. The industry segments examined are healthcare, retail, finance, industry, manufacturing, and public service. An analysis of impact on shifting jobs skills concludes the entry.

WHAT IS BIG DATA?

Traditional databases stored data in structured, relatively small datasets. With the advent of multimedia content, social media, and sensor-generated data, big data has come to dominate discussion in the database field. The term big data originates from the fact that the datasets used are so large that typical database systems are unable to capture, save, and analyze the datasets. Dataset size typically ranges from few dozen terabytes (TB) to several petabytes. Dataset size is influenced by business sector, software tools available in the sector, and average dataset sizes within the sector.[1]

Three terms most often used in discussion of big data are volume, variety, and velocity. Volume is associated with big data because of the amount of data contained within the dataset. Velocity means that the data is moving fast; that is, the data changes often. The term variety refers to the fact that the data is not uniformly structured; often the data is not structured at all.[2]

The volume of data continues to increase due to advances in storage and data capture technologies, which drive the costs of storage down. Data storage had been discussed in terms of TB (10^{12} bytes), but now is typically termed in petabytes (10^{15} bytes) with the expectation of zettabytes (10^{21} bytes) being the norm by the end of this decade. In terms of daily volume, Twitter generates in excess of 7 TB and Facebook 10 TB. Some large enterprises generate TB of data per hour. The volumes of data available to enterprises exceeds, in many cases, the ability of the enterprises to process, understand, and analyze the data.[3] Traditional data storage and processing means cannot accommodate this much data. Companies realize, however, that valuable data exists that they are not accessing or processing properly at present. The volume of data also impacts storage methodology—just having a great deal of storage space is not sufficient; an efficient means of storing the data to later find and process it is necessary.

The myriad forms of data stored and analyzed is the variety of data. Data comes from sensors, smart devices,

Encyclopedia of Information Systems and Technology, DOI: 10.1081/E-EIST-120050178

and social collaboration technologies. The format of the data ranges from traditional structured files to semistructured and unstructured data from web pages, web logs, clickstream data, and sensor data. Even social media, e-mail, and search indexes have been used as sources of data to be processed. Besides text, digital photos and videos are also considered valuable sources of data. It is estimated that as much as 80% of all available data is either semistructured or unstructured.[3] The variety of data necessitates new means of storing and processing data. Traditional databases stored primarily text data and some graphic files, but storage and processing changes as the types of data forms increase.

Conventional ideas of velocity refer to how quickly data arrives and is stored and the retrieval rate for the data. Big data changes the idea of velocity to the data inception point: how quickly is new data generated? To be competitive, a company needs to realize that data is in motion; if new data is available hourly, using data retrieved two days earlier does not give an accurate picture. Data is constantly being updated, so it needs to constantly be collected and re-collected from the data sources. The concept of streams computing used at IBM emphasizes continuously updated information. For example, a traditional query about people living in a New Jersey flood zone would be processed once with a set of static data, whereas a similar query in the streams computing paradigm would identify the present residents located in the flood zone, and the data would be updated continuously from available global positioning system (GPS) data.[3] Traditional data processing deals with static data and produces information that is essentially a still photo from one moment in the past. The velocity characteristic of big data means that a query will produce information from dynamic data yielding information that is up-to-the-minute and constantly updated. The most important thing to remember about velocity is that it means data is in motion, and much of it is always being updated.

A challenge presented by the volume, variety, and velocity of big data is veracity. How accurate is it? Traditional structured data is generally cleansed, that is, checked for accuracy. While data that are deemed less important are not checked (for example, middle initials), in general data quality is a priority when using structured data. The cost of cleansing big data, both in terms of money and time, is presently prohibitive. Big data is considered to presently have low value per byte because of its lack of perceived quality.[3] Cleansing structured data is relatively easy due to the fact that all elements in the files have the same exact structure, the volume of data to check is comparatively small, and the data is considered static. Perhaps as big data moves more into the mainstream and professionals develop more skill with collecting and storing big data, this situation may change. At present, however, the return on time and money spent to cleanse big data is too small to make verification practical.

SOURCES OF DATA

Data exists in one of three formats: structured, unstructured, or semistructured. Structured data is the data stored in traditional databases, and is formatted to allow storage and usage. When using structured data, every record has the same format as the others in the file. Unstructured data has no format and is stored exactly as collected. Semi-structured data has characteristics of both structured and unstructured data; the data has some common formatting, but is not entirely uniform.[4] Big data is usually unstructured or semi structured, although structured data can also be used in big data analysis. The sources of data are myriad and continue to grow each day. Major categories of the data sources are social media and the Internet of Things, which is discussed later.

Social Media

Social media outlets continue to grow and change. The once popular MySpace has given way to Facebook and its many capabilities and apps. Twitter allows anyone to voice their views, tell what they are doing, or comment on articles in 140 characters or less. YouTube videos can be entertaining, aggravating, or an informative evaluation of what is right (or wrong) with a product. Pinterest posts convey personal interests, including hobbies and favorite or recommended products and services. Even personal web pages can prove to be a source of data useful to organizations. The text, graphical, and video data available in these and other social media outlets provide an opportunity and a challenge to organizations—the data are out there, but need to be effectively found, collected, stored, and processed.

The Internet of Things

Many sources of big data are part of a phenomenon known as the Internet of Things. The Internet of Things is comprises sensors and actuators that are embedded in physical objects that provide data through wired and wireless networks. Doctors use pill-shaped cameras that send thousands of photos of patients' digestive tracks in diagnosing gastric problems. Sensors and satellites are used in diverse fields such as farming and traffic control. Sensors used in mining and drilling can aid in avoidance of damage and lower risk levels.[5]

Applications for the data gathered through the Internet of Things fall into two broad categories. The first category of data application is information and analysis, in which data gathered is used to generate information to aid in decision making regarding products and situations. Information and analysis applications include tracking behavior, enhancing situational awareness, and using sensor-driven decision analytics. Automation and control is the second application category and relates to decisions about process modification. Process optimization, resource consumption optimization, and complex autonomous system use are automation and control applications.[5]

Applications that track behavior are used to monitor the behavior of people, things, or data over time and locations. Auto insurance companies can install sensors into policy holders' cars in order to price the policy based upon the policy holder's driving behavior—both where the car is driven and how safely it is driven. Zipcar has used behavior tracking applications to facilitate short-term car rental to registered members, thus eliminating expensive car rental office locations and optimizing the company's profits. Use of radiofrequency identification (RFID) tags are embedded in products moving through supply chains to generate data to inform decision making about logistics. Advertising can be targeted to potential customers based upon location.[5] Many GPS units are now programmed to display local automated teller machines and convenience stores. The GPS units also may be equipped with features allowing the user to search for nearby restaurants or gas stations.

Enhancement of situational awareness enables decision makers to have real-time information about the environment to make immediate judgments. Video, audio, and vibration detectors can aid security personnel in detecting unauthorized access. Airline and trucking logistics decisions are enhanced with instantaneous data regarding weather, traffic, and vehicle location.[5] Highways are increasingly outfitted with electronic signage indicating traffic congestion and the estimated amount of time from the sign to major connecting routes. Car GPS units are programmed to generate and recommend alternative routes based upon up-to-the-minute traffic conditions. Radio stations offer subscribers the capability to receive updated traffic notices sent to subscriber smartphones, based upon sensors and video feeds from the subscriber's programmed daily route to work.

Sensor-driven decision analytics are applications that support longer-term decision making having a higher level of complexity. The healthcare industry has started experimenting with sensors in the monitoring and treatment of congestive heart failure. Patients' behavior and vital signs are tracked over time to aid both in the treatment of the individual patient and the accumulation of data. The accumulation of the data in turn will lead to more knowledge overall about the illness and will aid in decisions concerning treatment for the future. The oil and gas industries are implementing use of sensors in the exploration and development of oil and gas fields.[5]

As exploration and development move into new areas such as polar region exploration and new methods such as shale rock fracking, use of sensor data will become more commonplace.

Process optimization applications use sensors and actuators to gather data on ingredient mixtures, temperatures, and pressures, or the exact position of items on assembly lines, to make decisions on process improvement.[5] Decisions can be made based upon the data gathered that can reduce the number of errors, increase the overall product quality, or even inform changes that might need to be made at different times of the day or year that will increase productivity. Process optimization, in turn, will lead to improved quality product and a potential increase in revenue.

Optimized resources consumption applications use networked sensors and automated feedback mechanisms to affect change in utility usage patterns. Large manufacturers can closely monitor power usage in data centers to make decisions about computing load balancing and power-management.[5] Utilities are starting to adopt policies allowing customers with solar panels to sell excess energy the customer generates to the utility. Energy sell-back policies need sensor data and feedback mechanisms to track the amount of energy consumed by the customer and the amount generated and sold back.

Complex autonomous systems provide automated control in environments typified by great uncertainty. The unpredictability of the actions needed and the instantaneous need for the actions to occur depend upon quick processing of large amounts of data. The best example is collision avoidance systems under development and refinement in the auto industry. Automatic braking systems are already available in high-end automobiles. Research into networked vehicles using an automotive autopilot is dependent upon big data processing.[5] Lowering the cost of automatic braking systems, development of further collision avoidance systems, and movement toward automated cars requires immediate data processing capability in an on-board system.

Big Data Categories

Categories or domains of big data have been developed based upon the sources of data. Developers considered data characteristics or timeliness and flexibility inherent in the data based upon the source and pre-processing of the data. The categories or domains of big data are process-mediated data, machine-generated data, and human-sourced information.[6]

Process-mediated data is data created from business processes. The processes generating the data are well-defined and managed by the organization's information technology professionals. Process-mediated data is a representation of the legally-binding, present and historical position of the organization generating the data. Relational databases tend to be the repository of the data.[6] An example of process-mediated data would be sales transactions stored in a relational database. The data stored is a result of the business transaction for which the data is stored; the transaction is the process which generates the data.

Machine-generated data comes from sensors and machines recording measures and events. Data is generated both internally and externally to the organization storing and using the data. The processing platform for machine-generated data range from high-performance relational databases through NoSQL.[6] Machine-generated data is the data culled from the Internet of Things and would include oil-drilling sensor data through automobile computers.

Human-sourced information includes e-mails, blogs, text messages, and YouTube videos. Processing of human-sourced information requires use of Hadoop systems, content management systems, and related data stores.[6] The term information is used in this category because the domain contains data that has already been processed into information. Data is typically unprocessed, whereas information is data that has some degree of processing. The stored items in human-sourced information are not the words and the pixels, but rather the ideas that the e-mails, blogs, pictures, and videos convey. Therefore, human-sourced information is pre-processed data; the idea being conveyed contains what needs to be processed.

Summary

Big data is a data paradigm of major importance. Named in part for the size of its datasets, the characteristics that differentiate big data are its volume, variety, and velocity. Besides the traditional data files, big data is gathered from sources including social media and the Internet of Things. The three recognized domains of big data are process-mediated data, machine generated data, and human-sourced information. Combining traditional structured data and now abundantly available semistructured and unstructured data, big data presents opportunities and challenges to organizations. Development in the data storage and processing areas has been influenced by the challenges big data presents to organizations.

BIG DATA STORAGE TECHNOLOGIES

The character volume, variety, and velocity of big data influences the storage technologies utilized to store and process the data. Big data requires a large-scale storage environment capable of effective data retrieval. Two prominent technologies used for big data storage and processing are scale-out NAS and object-based storage systems. The use of cloud computing further leverages the benefits of big data to a larger number of organizations.

Scale-out NSA

Scale-out (or clustered) NAS is based upon the use of a massive number of computers serving only as storage devices connected to a network; the computers have no keyboards, mice, or monitors and are considered to be NAS devices. A number of NAS devices will be connected to a single NAS device called a NAS pod. The NAS pod is used to send data requests to the NAS devices attached to it and receive retrieved data from the NAS devices. Each of the NAS devices attached to the NAS pod contains different data collected and stored on the device. The NAS pod, in turn, is connected to other NAS pods. The group of NAS pods is connected by a switch to the network. When a data request is made, the same request goes to each pod, and in turn to each device.[4] The NAS devices have scaled-down operating systems, allowing the devices to function solely for the purpose of data retrieval. Access to the NAS devices is controlled by assigned Web address.[7] The use of parallel processing of the request and reduced size of the operating system yields an answer generated quickly from large inputs of data.

Object-Based Storage

Object-based storage systems differ from scale-out NAS by nature. Scale-out NAS is based upon the configuration of hardware, whereas object-based storage systems are differentiated by the means in which data is saved. Storage objects are the means by which data is stored in object-based storage. A storage object is a group of bytes on a storage device complete with methods for access, differentiating by characteristics, and security. A storage object is not set in size or structure and is, therefore, able to store various whole data structures, including files, database tables, and multimedia. Because data is stored in objects, the entire object is accessed, not just an individual file or structure. The storage method, therefore, makes access to the data faster.[8] The objects are able to be saved in sets of objects and distributed over a number of storage devices. Therefore, the grouping of the data into objects provides high capacity storage and throughput as well as scalability.[4]

Summary

Scale-out NAS and object-based storage are the two main storage technologies commonly used for big data. Scale-out (or clustered) NAS employs a massive number of computers serving only as storage devices connected to a network. The emphasis of scale-out NAS is, therefore, a large number of storage devices. Object-based storage is grounded in the concept of storage objects. A storage object is a group of bytes on a storage device complete with methods for access, differentiating by characteristics, and security. Rather than the number of storage devices, object-based storage uses the organization of the data to be stored.

BIG DATA STORAGE AND PROCESSING TECHNIQUES

The hardware platform used to store big data is only one part of the issue. The methodology for storing and analyzing the data is based upon a new paradigm for computing. The primary framework for storing and analyzing unstructured big data is Hadoop, while structured big data are processed using NoSQL.[4]

Hadoop

Hadoop is an open-source framework for use with distributed clustered file systems developed for large-scale data processing. Hadoop is grounded in the Google (distribute) File System (GFS) and a programming paradigm named MapReduce. MapReduce is further comprised of two main tasks—a mapper and a reducer.[3] Because Hadoop is open-source, it is readily available to anyone, as well as customizable. Users can adapt Hadoop to meet particular processing needs.

The Hadoop Distributed File System functions through breaking data into blocks. The blocks are distributed over clusters. To ensure both data availability and reduce possibility of data loss, the blocks of data are distributed redundantly over the clusters; that is, several copies of the same block of data will be stored in multiple places (at least on two different servers) over the network. Other benefits from the redundant storage of data are scalability and data locality. Data scalability means that data can be broken into smaller chunks for processing. Data locality means that data can be processed on the same server on which it is stored (which speeds processing). The default block size for Hadoop data is 64 Megabytes, although blocks are typically larger. In comparison, a traditional relational database stores data in blocks of 4–32 kilobytes. The data files in Hadoop are tracked by a special server called the Name-Node. The NameNode tracks the metadata (data about

the data, including its location on the servers) for all of the stored blocks of data. Due to the vital nature of this server, NameNode should be located on a robust server and regular backup procedures must be adhered to. Hadoop will work directly with the NameNode in storing and processing data blocks as needed.[3]

The MapReduce programming paradigm allows for use of hundreds or thousands of servers in a Hadoop cluster. The two tasks performed by Hadoop programs are mapping and reducing. The map task takes the data and converts it into tuples comprised of a key and a value. The key/value pairs produced by the map task become the input to reduce task, which takes the key/value pairs and reduces these down to the answer. A Hadoop MapReduce job is broken into several tasks that are managed by a JobTracker. The JobTracker communicates with the NameNode to discover where the necessary data for the tasks are located in the cluster. The map and reduce tasks are then scheduled on the cluster containing the data related to the particular tasks. In turn, TaskTrackers monitor the map and reduce tasks and send status information back to the JobTracker.[3]

Several application development languages have emerged that run on top of Hadoop to simplify program development. The most popular languages are Pig, Hive, and Jaql. Pig is designed to handle any kind of data and has a language component called PigLatin and a runtime environment. Hive is based upon Structured Query Language (SQL), so the learning curve is smaller than Pig. Jaql is a script-language for JavaScript Object Notation (JASON) and is inspired by several other programming languages.[3]

Pig was developed at Yahoo! to allow users to concentrate on analysis of large datasets rather than writing mapper and reducer programs. When using Pig, a data analyst will designate which datasets are to be loaded, then will give instructions on how to transform the dataset, and finally will specify that data either be dumped to a screen or stored to a file. Once the code is written, the runtime environment is used to run the program. The runtime environment offers three options: run embedded in a script, embedded in a Java program, or from the command line. Whichever method is chosen, the runtime environment translates the program into a series of mapper and reducer tasks. Although Pig has the advantage of simplifying use of Hadoop, users still need to learn the commands of the language.[3]

Hive also simplifies Hadoop, with the advantage that users experienced with SQL already know the commands, since Hive Query Language (HQL) is similar to SQL. However, HQL is limited in the number of commands it understands. Since it is based on SQL, Hive functions much like a relational database when processing. The exception that Hive is intended for long sequential scans and processing response time often takes minutes rather than the typical seconds in relational database processing.[3]

Jaql was given to the open source community by IBM and is able to process both structured and nontraditional data. Jaql's roots are in JASON, which is based upon use of name/value pairs and creation of ordered lists of values, both structures useful in Hadoop. Jaql is comprised of both a number of core operators and a large set of built-in functions.[3]

Pig, Hive, and Jaql are just three of the prominent languages used to ease the use of Hadoop. The choice of language is based upon the user's needs and abilities. A user who is experienced with SQL, and does not need to transform data extensively, would be best served by Hive. A user familiar with Javascript, and with using structured, semistructured, and unstructured data, could adopt Jaql. If a large amount of transformation is needed on large datasets, Pig would be the likely choice.

NoSQL

Big data can also be structured. Hadoop's strengths are for semistructured and unstructured data. When the data are structured but in extremely large datasets, other processing means are needed. The main method of structured big data analysis is use of NoSQL.

NoSQL is often characterized more by what it is not—either not only an SQL-based relational database management system (RDBMS) or not an SQL-based RDBMS. Traditional databases follow the RDBMS model, so NoSQL is considered either more than the RDBMS model, or different from the model. The RDBMS model is characterized by properties of atomicity, consistency, isolation, and durability, whereas NoSQL has the properties of Basically Available, Soft state, and Eventually consistent (BASE).[9]

In the RDBMS model, atomicity refers to the fact that an entire transaction must be completed; otherwise, none of it is completed and stored. Consistency means that a transaction brings the database from one state to another state (one with the transaction completed and stored). The property of isolation means that concurrent transactions are stored as if the transactions were completed serially, that is, one after another. Durability means that the transaction will remain unchanged after it is committed to the database. All of the RDBMS properties are based upon the transaction.

The NoSQL database model is based upon replicated data. Data is stored in part or in whole in several places in the database. The replication ensures that data is basically available; that is, at all times either all or part of the data is available for processing. The Soft state property refers to the fact that data is inconsistent and changeable. Eventually, consistent means that the data

will at some point in the future be consistent throughout all copies maintained in the database.[9]

Like Hadoop, NoSQL processes very large datasets, often tens or hundreds of TB or larger. While not as large as Hadoop datasets, the NoSQL datasets are stored and searched over a very large number of servers, employing full or partial data replication. The NoSQL method for processing data is called sharding, and employs a separate database run on each server and physical partitioning of data so each database has access to the data.[10] The process of sharding leads to the BASE properties of NoSQL, since sharding makes it impossible to guarantee that each copy of data is always identical. Each copy of data, however, will eventually be identical.

Sharding creates a loss of capabilities typically available in a RDBMS. The lost capabilities include joining data with distributed queries, completing distributed transactions, and changing the schema of the database. The partial functionality to compensate for loss capabilities is enabled by key/value pair support. Key/value pairs in NoSQL allow the user to use pre-joined data in tables and to program applications to work with online schema changes.[10] Therefore, the key/value pair used in Hadoop also enables the functionality of NoSQL.

One implementation of NoSQL is MongoDB. MongoDB is a document-orientated database. Whereas a RDBMS would be based on a row of data, MongoDB is based on a document. Documents have keys and values that are not fixed in size or type, as would be in a RDBMS. A document can actually be defined as an ordered set of keys with associated values. The use of documents and nonfixed keys and values enable scaling out, or partitioning data over several servers. The key/value pairs also make the querying of large structured datasets possible.[11]

Summary

Different techniques exist to enable the storage and processing of big data. The technique used depends upon the nature of the datasets. For large unstructured and semistructured datasets, Hadoop provides the means for storing and processing data based on the use of the MapReduce programming paradigm. For smaller, structured datasets, NoSQL allows for scaled-out storage and searching of data. Both Hadoop and NoSQL employ the use of key/value pairs.

BIG DATA AND CLOUD COMPUTING

Cloud computing is access to computing resources usually provided by an outside entity. The access to the on-demand cloud network requires little management effort by the business. Cloud computing provides access to technologies some organizations would not otherwise be able to afford. The scale-out NAS storage technology needed for big data storage and analysis is accessible through cloud computing to organizations that cannot invest in adoption of the technology.[12]

Several methods exist for providers to deploy cloud technology. The most common cloud service models that can impact big data usage are platform as a service (PaaS), infrastructure as a service (IaaS), hardware as a service (HaaS), and software as a service (SaaS).[12]

In the PaaS model, the cloud service provider makes technologies such as application design and development tools, application testing, versioning, integration, deployment, hosting, state management, and other related development tools available to clients.[12] The organization paying for the cloud service would be able to develop customized big data search programs using the application tools provided. The customer would expect the service provider to store data correctly and allow the organization's programmers to use their skills to develop customized searches.

Infrastructure as a service model entails that a client business pays on a per-use basis for use of equipment to support computing operations. The cloud service provider gives access to storage, hardware, servers, and networking equipment. Benefits that the organization gains through IaaS are financial flexibility, choice of services, business agility, cost-effective scalability, and increased security.[12] For an organization using IaaS to implement big data usage, the organization will have access to more storage capacity and faster data access than it could generally afford. The savings are particularly important for an organization that is not certain about the benefit of big data; IaaS provides a low-cost platform to experiment with the technology.

The basis of the HaaS idea is the model of time sharing on minicomputers and mainframes from the 1960s and 1970s. Hardware as a service provides an opportunity for the customer to license hardware directly from the service provider.[12] The licensing agreement eliminates the costs associated with storage hardware needed for big data implementation. The storage of the data, application creation, and searching would be performed by the client on the service provider's hardware.

Summary

Cloud computing essentially provides customers access to the platforms, infrastructure, and hardware needed to implement use of big data with a much smaller investment of funds and personnel. Organizations can experiment with big data storage and utilization technologies without making an expensive commitment. Smaller organizations can use big data without needing in-house experience. Cloud computing, therefore, opens the avenue of big data usage to a larger number of organizations.

USING BIG DATA

Different business sectors use big data in diverse ways. Decisions being made based on big data influence on everyday life. A research survey examined use of big data in companies world-wide. The researchers divided companies into nine distinct segments: healthcare, retail, finance, industrial, manufacturing, public services, utilities infrastructure, leisure, and media/public relations. Companies were classified by size, with mid-sized companies having fewer than 500 employees, large companies being between 500 and 5000 employees, and enterprises being companies with over 5000 employees. The researchers inquired about the use cases in each segment, and divided use cases into six distinct types: online archiving, staging structured data, utilization of streaming data, pre-processing data, combining data structure, and speed of processing.[6] Each segment used big data in unique ways based on needs and characteristics of the segment to lead to product innovations and operational improvements. Use cases also varied depending on the nature of the segment.

Healthcare Segment

The healthcare segment includes medical device and supply as well as pharmaceutical production. Healthcare companies responding to the big data survey were either enterprises (58.3% of respondents) or large companies (41.7% of respondents). The top use cases in the healthcare segment were combining data structure (22.9%), speed of processing (20.8%), and online archiving (20.8%).[6] The use cases are consistent with priorities in healthcare. Combining data structure is important due to the divergent forms of data shared: text in electronic medical records, graphic in radiologic files, graphic and text for several tests, and sensor data. Due to the critical nature of health information, speed of processing is essential to saving lives. Online archiving saves data for later use for patient care as well as research and development studies.

Several healthcare industry leaders are leading the way in implementation of big data. Kaiser Permanente has developed a computer system called HealthConnect which enables data exchange across a number of medical facilities to promote electronic medical record use. The system has already led to an improvement in cardiovascular disease outcomes and about $1 billion in savings, due to reduction in office visits and lab tests. Blue Shield of California and NantHealth have joined to develop an integrated system enabling healthcare providers to deliver evidence-based healthcare that is better coordinated and more personalized. AstraZenaca and HealthCre are conducting real-world studies of chronic illnesses and common diseases. Astmapolis' GPS-enabled tracker records inhaler usage by asthmatics to identify individual, group, and population trends to develop personalized treatments and spot prevention opportunities.[13]

Analysis of big data, called analytics, offers great promise in the pharmaceutical industry. The analytic technique of predictive modeling can be applied to studying biological processing and drugs based upon clinical data. Such study could identify molecules that can be developed into drugs targeting specific health problems. Big data analytics could lead to clinical trials with a better-selected population, making the trials smaller in number, shorter in time, less expensive, and more significant. Due to the velocity of big data and use of sensor data, clinical trials could be monitored in real time, allowing for quicker reaction to safety or operational signals needing attention or calling for adjustment. Collaboration among pharmaceutical companies, physicians, and contract research organizations can be enhanced by the easy flow of big data among the partners.[14]

Big data enables all of the preceding scenarios, but the costs can be prohibitive; therefore, the industry is moving slowly in the direction of big data analytics. Steps that are being undertaken now to expedite the scenarios in the future are management and integration of data among all research partners, more internal and external collaboration with a more open research and development area, and expedited portfolio decision making. Investment in miniaturized biosensors, remote-monitoring devices, and even smartphone apps will allow better research and development as well as better drugs. Some device ideas include smart pills that will both release drugs and relay patient data related to the patient's condition as well as smart bottles tracking drug usage.[14]

Retail Segment

Companies identified in the retail segment were consumer retailers as well as wholesalers and distributors. Enterprise companies were the largest category responding to the big data survey (52.4%) with large companies accounting for 42.9% of respondents and mid-sized companies accounting for 4.7% of responses. Speed of processing is the most prevalent use case in retail (28.3%), followed by combining data structure (21.7%).[6] Speed of processing is a key aspect of retail, since customers want their transactions to be processed as quickly as possible, whether the transactions are in a physical store or online. For online concerns, the availability of historic customer data can be used to suggest purchases as soon as a customer logs into the website. Combining data structure is relevant in planning; industry data combined with historical customer data can identify purchase trends.

The retail sector has recorded transactions for decades, but the unstructured data provided in the big data era will allow retailers to gain new insights into customer needs. The new sources of data for retailers are from the Internet of things and social media. The sources include RFID chips, location-based smartphone tracking, video and sensor capture of customer in-store behavior, and on-line searches and review. Three major areas in which big data can have a significant impact in retail are the supply chain, operations, and merchandising.[15]

Inventory management, returns management, and transport optimization are the key supply chain functions expected to be influenced by big data analysis. Real-time data on inventory can be enhanced by demand forecasting with the end result of a reduction in excess ordering and stockouts.[15] Real-time data can be tracked through transactions, as well as RFID chips, and demand forecasts can come from retail industry big data sources. Returns data can be used to generate product improvements.[15] Retailers have typically asked for the reason for returns, but the volume of data generated was previously too big to process productively. Big data processing can allow all of the return data to be processed to lead to possible improvements or product make-overs. The combination of inventory and return data, as well as store-specific sales data, will improve merchandise transport.

Operations management functions foreseen to be impacted are performance transparency and labor resource optimization. Data from individual stores including product analysis, store traffic, and employee performance can be analyzed to improve sales activities forecasts and identify best practices.[15] The product analysis and store traffic can be studied and refined so the products that sell well at each location can be determined and timed. Employee performance can lead to better scheduling of employees and better utilization of fulltime versus seasonal workers.

Assortment optimization and product placement are key functions impacted in merchandising. Data from video surveillance, smartphone tracking, and sensors are seen to have effect in product assortment and placement.[15] Data gathered will show which isles more customers visit, where customers stop and look, and what products customers look at but do not purchase. Retailers can then move products and be able to analyze whether the shift in location affected the volume of sales.

Big data can have other impacts upon retailers as well. Analytics can help retailers to improve merchandising and marketing strategies. Examples include location-based marketing by sending coupons to smart phones of customers nearby the store location, cross-selling or the sale of one product based upon purchase of another product, and customer segmentation based on social media and purchase history of an individual customer.[15]

Finance Segment

Finance, banking, and insurance companies comprise the finance segment as defined by the big data survey researchers. As with healthcare, only enterprise (61.0%) and large (39.0%) companies responded to the survey. Finance segment responses indicated that speed of processing (28.0%) was the largest use case, followed by pre-processing data (18.3%) and combining data structure (15.9%).[6] As with retail, customers and clients expect quick processing of transactions. Combining data structure in the finance segment not only aids product and service development but also data and information security.

Banking and financial markets are increasing use of big data and analytics to both gain competitive advantage and protect their assets. A survey conducted by IBM indicates a 97% increase in data and analytics use in two years. Data are generated from the huge volume of daily transactions as well as market conditions and customer preference data.[16]

Important uses of big data in the banking and finance sector are delivery of new products and services and the improvement of customer service and loyalty. Customer-centric products and services can be developed by analysis of data from market conditions and individual customer preferences.[16] For example, a customer's portfolio of products can be analyzed and compared to another customer's to see if a product in one portfolio would also be useful in the other. New products could be developed based upon historical data and contemporary market conditions.

A critical use of big data analysis to maintain the health of the sector is fraud detection. NYSE Euronext used big data analysis to examine trading patterns. The company developed a surveillance platform to detect suspicious patterns of trading activity to flag and investigate. The new algorithms in the platform increased speed by 99% and decreased needed resources by over 35%.[16] Faster detection of fraudulent activity coupled with a savings in resources will lead to a safer and more effective financial sector.

Industrial Segment

Aerospace and defense manufacturing, oil and gas production and refining, chemical manufacturing, and transportation and logistics organizations (airlines, trucking, and rail) are companies in the industrial segment. Speed of processing (22.4%) and combining data structure (20.4%) are key big data use cases, with pre-processing data and utilizing streaming data are tied for third dominant use cases (16.3%).[6] While speed of processing does not immediately seem of consequence in the industrial segment, use cases likely include failure warning systems and other such monitoring systems. Combining data structure is relevant due to the heavy use of sensor data. Pre-processing data is relevant when combining company data with publicly available or purchased research data for use with the organization's data. Streaming data is also important in industrial monitoring systems.

One major area of the industrial sector using big data for operational improvement is oil and gas production and refining. Big data has several applications in the oil and gas industry, including exploration and development, drilling and completions, and production and operations. The exploration and development includes the search for new resources and the preparation of new sites. Savings in labor and equipment costs are the main benefits big data brings to drilling and completions. Big data serves the production and operations areas through use of performance predictions based on past results.[17]

Exploration is enhanced by big data. Using enterprise data such as financial data and operational data in conjunction with real-time production data can lead to improvement in exploration operations, making exploration more efficient. Use of competitive intelligence generated by geospatial research, news feeds, and other syndicated information can lead to better assessment of acreage and can generate new prospective drilling sites.[17] By integrating the huge amounts of data already available from diverse sources, energy resources can be identified quicker and with less human effort.

The incorporation of geologic measurements and scientific models are used in the shale development to improve drilling operations. Engineering studies can be enhanced by big data through use of subsurface models to identify commercial prospects sooner and with a lower risk. A better understanding of the earth's subsurface is improved through use of big data leading to more affordability, safety, and sustainability in the drilling process.[17] Big data, therefore, improves the actual drilling process by examination of data gleaned during drilling and processing the data against models of the subsurface.

Production and operations are enhanced by use of predictive maintenance using big data. Predictive maintenance is the use of big data in predicting future performance based on historical results and the identification of sub-par production areas. Monitoring of huge numbers of shifting variables like pressure, temperature, volume, shock, and vibration can be used in prevention of equipment failure, thus decreasing downtime. Big data use also allows the optimization of field scheduling and improvement of shop floor maintenance planning.[17] Big data impacts the prediction of failure and improvement of planning, two areas that ensure better production and operations.

Manufacturing Segment

Researchers defined the manufacturing industry as all noncomputer or networking related manufacturing industries. Exactly half of the respondents from the manufacturing segment were enterprise companies, with 38.9% of respondents from large companies and the final 11.1% from mid-sized companies. Combining data structure (21.5%) was the largest use case in manufacturing, followed by speed of processing (20.3%) and utilization of streaming data (20.3%).[6] As in the industrial segment, combining data structure is important due to use of sensor data, and speed of processing due to data gathering through the manufacturing process. Utilization of streaming data is also based largely on use of sensors to gather data on the actual manufacturing process.

The U.S. manufacturing sector stores nearly 2000 exobytes of data, much of which is generated by sensors in the equipment owned and operated by the companies in their daily activities. Key areas of implementation of big data in manufacturing are research and development, production, and supply chain management. Product research and development is impacted by big data in product life cycle management by changing the way designers and engineers can test designs and in choice of parts and suppliers. Data used for design can include crowd-sourced data external to the company.[15]

Production and operations are improved through use of sensor data to detect wear on such equipment as industrial motors and drill bits, allowing for preventive maintenance. Food packages can be equipped with biosensors revealing contamination and spoilage. Performance dashboards are being developed that centralize machine and labor productivity tracking efficiency of processes. One manufacturing in the mineral products area used big data from sensors installed in the midzone of its kilns to monitor the temperature of lime mud, which indicates calcination. The data gathered about the heat profile allowed the operators to optimize the shape and intensity of the flame in the kiln, leading to a 5% increase in production.[15]

Supply chain optimization is another area in manufacturing that big data aids. One example is the manufacture of Boeing's 787 Dreamliner aircraft. Multiple delays from a number of suppliers of components for the aircraft led Boeing to develop a centralized production integration center containing data and live video feeds from suppliers around the globe. The data gleaned from the data and video feeds was synthesized and the impacts on the production schedules and costs were monitored, leading to improved supply chain performance.[15]

Public Services Segment

The public services segment is comprised of government, education, nonprofit entities, not-for-profit entities, and legal entities. Survey respondents from the public sector were mostly enterprises (52.6%), with 39.5% of responses coming from people in large companies and the final 7.9% from people in mid-sized companies. Use case in the public services segment indicates that 21.6% of the respondents' use cases centered on speed of processing, whereas combining data structure, pre-processing data, and online archiving each had 17.5% of the use cases.[6] All institutions in the public sector are heavily dependent upon data processing and retrieval, so speed of processing is important. The sector uses privately generated, purchased, and public data, so the data formats vary greatly making combining data structure relevant. Data is often processed before storage in public section institutions leading to the prominence of pre-processing data. Huge volumes of historical data storage make online archiving an important use case.

The National Archive and Records Administration is in the process of integrating digitally collected data with years-worth of traditionally archives materials. To accomplish the task, data in different structures must be stored together. Researchers at the Royal Institute of Technology in Sweden, the country's largest technical university, used big data technologies in an effort to better manage traffic congestion. Real-time sensor data were collected via vehicle GPS units, radar sensors from motorways, congestion patterns, and weather conditions. Analysis of the data was performed as collected to identify congestion spots and development recommendations for alternate routes. Vestas Wind Energy is moving to big data to improve its weather prediction wind library, which aids in site selection for new wind turbines. Big data use is anticipated to improve predictions to pinpoint smaller weather pattern grids; the previous grid size of 17×17 miles moved to 32×32 feet with use of fluid dynamics and is expected to be further refined.[18]

IMPACT ON JOB SKILLS

Because of the growing use of big data in business and industry, new jobs requiring specialized skills will need to be filled. The new skills are aggregated under the term analytics. Development of professionals with analytics skills means new approaches to data-intensive degree programs.[18] The 2013 IBM Institute for Business Value research study identified supply gaps in analytics personnel. The lack of analysis and interpretation of data into meaningful action was a key business challenge identified in the study. 36% of respondents cited the largest gap found as the ability to combine analytic skills with business knowledge. Other identified skills gaps were analytic skills (24%), data management skills (21%), and business skills (19%). The demand for data and analytics resources is forecasted to reach 4.4 million jobs world-wide by 2015, but only one-third of those positions are expected to be able to be filled.[19] Analytics skills in collecting, storing, processing, analyzing, and interpreting results will all be needed to facilitate productive use of big data.

CONCLUSION

Big data will play an increasingly important role in data sciences and daily life in the coming years. Increasing amounts of data are being stored in both traditional and unstructured forms due to declining storage technology costs as well as improvement and innovation in data processing and analysis techniques. New means of applying big data to everyday situations occur regularly and impacts are far-reaching. All sectors of business world-wide will continue to feel the impact of big data analysis for years to come. A major concern is the big data skills gap; a majority of jobs needing big data-related skills are expected to go unfilled due to the gap. The promise of big data applications should prompt job-hunters to seek the means to attain the skills. Educational institutions should invest in developing programs to develop the skills needed for big data jobs, and governments should emphasize the importance and expected need for such positions. Big data is a new technological disruption affecting the workforce. With jobs expected to exist in every economic sector, people need to learn data analytics skills to join the growing trend.

REFERENCES

1. Manyika, J.; Chui, M.; Brown, B.; Bughin, J.; Dobbs, R.; Roxburgh, C.; Byers, A.H. *Big data: The next frontier for innovation, competition, and productivity.* June 2011, Available from: http://www.mckinsey.com/Insights/MGI/Research/Technology_and_Innovation/Big_data_The_next_frontier_for_innovation
2. Gobble, M.M. Big data: The next big thing in innovation. Res. Technol. Manag. **2013**. *56* (1), 64–66.
3. Zikopoulos, P.C.; Eaton, C.; deRoos, D.; Deutsch, T.; Lapis, G. *Understandig Big Data: Analytics for Enterprise Class Hadoop and Streaming Data*; McGraw-Hill: New York, NY, 2012.
4. Purcell, B. Emergence of 'big data' technology and analyics. J. Technol. Res. **2013**, *4*, 1–7.
5. Chui M, Löffler M, Roberts R. The internet of things. *McKinsey Quart* **2010**, *2,* 1–9

6. EMA Inc. *Operationalizing the Buzz: Big Data; 2013*, 2013.
7. White, C.M. *Data Communications and Commputer Networks, A Business User's Approach*, 6th Ed.; Course Technology: Boston, MA, 2011.
8. Mesnier, M.; Ganger, G.R.; Riedel, E. Object-based storage. Commun. Mag. IEEE **2003**, *41* (8), 84–90.
9. *Oracle NoSQL Database.* 2011, Oracle: Redwood Shores, CA.
10. Hadoop and NoSQL technologies and the Oracle database. February **2011**, http://www.oracle.com/technetwork/database/hadoop-nosql-oracle-twp-398488.pdf.
11. Chowdorow, K. *MongoDB: The Definitive Guide.* 2nd Ed.; O'Reilly Media Inc.: Sebastopol, CA, 2013.
12. Purcell B. Big data using cloud computing. *J. Technol. Res* **2013**;*5*:4–11
13. Kayyali, B.; Knott, D.; Van Kuiken, S. *The Big-Data Revolution in U.S. Health Care: Accelertaing Value and Innovation*; McKinsey & Company: New York, 2013,
14. Cattell, J.; Chilukuri, S.; Levy, M. *How Big Data can Revolutionize Pharmaceutical R&D*; McKinsey & Company: New York, 2013.
15. Lund, S.; Manyika, J.; Nyquist, S.; Mendonca, L.; Ramaswamy, S. *Game Changers: Five Opportunities for U. S. Growth and Renewal*; McKinsey Global Institute: New York, 2013.
16. Turner, D.; Schroeck, M.; Shockley, R. *Analytics: The Real-World Use of Big Data in Financial Services*; IBM Global Services: Armonk, NY, 2013.
17. Hems, A.; Soofi, A.; Perez, E. *Drilling for New Business Value: How Innovative Oil and Gas Companies Are Using Big Data to Outmaneuver the Competition*; Microsoft, Inc.: Redmond, WA, 2013.
18. Federal Big Data Commission. *Demystifying Big Data: A Practical Guide to Transforming the Business of Government*; TechAmerica Foundation: Washington, DC, 2012.
19. Balboni, F.; Finch, G.; Rodenbeck Reese, C.; Shockley, R. *Analytics: A Blueprint for Value*; IBM Global Services: Armonk, NY, 2013.

BIBLIOGRAPHY

1. Chowdorow, K. *MongoDB: The definitive guide*, 2nd Ed.; O'Reilly Media Inc.: Sebastopol, CA, 2013.
2. Dadashzadeh, M. Big data and the Hobson's choice for IT management. Intl J. Manag. Inform. Syst. **2013**, *17* (4), 235.
3. Davenport, T.H.; Barth, P.; Bean, R. How big data is different. MIT Sloan Manag. Rev. **2012**, *54* (1), 43–46.
4. Manyika, J.; Hunt, D.; Nyquist, S.; Remes, J.; Malhotra, V.; Mendonca, L.; Auguste, B.; Test, S. *Growth And Renewal In The United States: Retooling America's Economic Engine*: McKinsey & Company: New York, 2011.
5. Morgan, D.M. Ramon, A.; Pranshu, G. Temporal data management in Nosql databases. J. Inform. Syst. Operat. Manag. **2012**, *6* (2), 1–7.
6. Ramanathan, S.; Sarulatha, N. Big data: A marketers perspective of emerging marketing approach. Intl J. Manag. Res. Rev. **2013**, *3* (5), 2872–2880.

Big Data: Structured and Unstructured Data

Arun K. Majumdar
John F. Sowa
VivoMind Research, Rockville, Maryland, U.S.A.

Abstract

Big data comes in two forms: the *structured* data intended for computer processing and the *unstructured* language that people read, write, and speak. Unfortunately, no computer system today can reliably translate unstructured language to the structured formats of databases, spreadsheets, and the semantic web. But they can do a lot of useful processing, and they are becoming more versatile. While we are still some distance away from the talking computer, HAL, in Stanley Kubrick's film *2001: A Space Odyssey*, this entry surveys the state of the art, the cutting edge, and the future directions for *natural language processing* that paves the way in getting us one step closer to the reality presented in that movie.

LIGHTWEIGHT AND HEAVYWEIGHT SEMANTICS

When people read a book, they use their background knowledge to interpret each line of text. They understand the words by relating them to the existing context and to their previous experience. That process of understanding is heavyweight semantics. But when Google reads a book, it just indexes the words without any attempt to understand what they mean. When someone types a search with similar words, Google lists the book as one of the "hits." That is lightweight semantics. The search engines use a great deal of statistics for finding matches and ranking the hits. But they do not do a deep semantic analysis of the documents they index or the search requests they match to the documents. The difference between lightweight and heavyweight semantics is in the use of background knowledge and models about the world and what things mean. The human brain connects all thoughts, feelings, and memories in a rich network with trillions of connections.

The semantic web is an attempt to gather and store human knowledge in a network that might someday become as rich and flexible. But that goal requires a method for representing knowledge: Fig. 1 is a *conceptual graph* (CG) that is part of the ISO 24707 Common Logic standard[1] and represents the sentence *Bob drives his Chevy to St. Louis.*

The boxes in Fig. 1 are called *concepts*, and the circles are called *relations*. Each relation and the concepts attached to it can be read as an English sentence: *The agent (Agnt) of driving is the person Bob. The theme (Thme) of driving is a Chevy. The destination (Dest) of driving is the city St. Louis. Bob possesses*

(Poss) the Chevy. The Chevy has attribute (Attr) old. For the semantic web, each of those sentences can be translated to a *triple* in the *Resource Description Format* (RDF). CGs and RDF are highly structured *knowledge representation languages*. They can be stored in a database or used as input for business analytics.

By itself, a CG such as Fig. 1 or the RDF triples derived from it represent a small amount of knowledge. The power of a knowledge representation comes from the interconnections of all the graphs and the supporting resources and processes:

1. *Ontology* is the study of existence. An ontology is the definition of the concepts and relations used to describe the things that exist in an application.
2. A *knowledge base* includes an ontology, the databases or graphs that use the definitions in it, and the rules or axioms that specify reasoning with the knowledge.
3. *Inference engines* process the rules and axioms to reason with and about the knowledge.
4. *Heuristics* use statistics and informal methods to process the knowledge in a variety of ways.

CGs and RDF are two notations for representing semantic information. There are many other notations, but they are all based on some version of formal logic combined with an ontology for the subject matter. Information represented in one notation can usually be translated to the others, but some information may be lost in a translation from a more expressive notation to a less expressive form.

A system with truly heavyweight semantics would use large amounts of all four resources. One of the

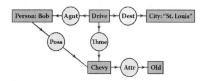

Fig. 1 A conceptual graph for *Bob drives his Chevy to St. Louis.*

heaviest is the Cyc project, which invested over a 1000 person-years of work in developing an ontology with 600,000 concept types and a knowledge base with 5 million rules and axioms. Cyc supplements that knowledge base by accessing facts from relational databases and the semantic web. Another heavyweight system is IBM's Watson,[2] which beat the world champion in the game of *Jeopardy!* IBM spent millions of dollars in developing Watson and runs it on a supercomputer with over 2000 CPUs.

The search engines that process billions of requests per day cannot use the heavyweight semantics of Cyc or Watson. But they are gradually increasing the amount of semantics for tagging web pages and interpreting queries. To promote common ontologies and formats, Google, Microsoft, and Yahoo! co-founded schema.org as a nonproprietary source of concept specifications. As an example, schema.org includes a concept called Job-Posting, which has the following related concepts:

```
baseSalary, benefits, datePosted,
educationRequirements, employmentType,
experienceRequirements, hiringOrganization,
incentives, industry, jobLocation,
occupationalCategory, qualifications,
responsibilities, salaryCurrency, skills,
specialCommitments, title, workHours
```

Any company that lists a job opening on a website can use these concept names to tag the information in the announcement. Search engines can then use those tags to match job searches to job announcements.

With less than a thousand concept types, schema.org has about 0.1% of Cyc's coverage of the concepts needed to understand natural language. It has an even smaller percentage of Cyc's axioms for doing automated reasoning. Instead, schema.org depends on the web masters to choose the concept types to tag the information on their web pages. This raises a chicken-and-egg problem. The search engines cannot use the tags to improve their results until a significant percentage of web pages are tagged. But web masters aren't going to tag their pages until the search engines begin to use those tags to direct traffic to their sites.

Social networks such as Facebook have more control over the formats of their pages. They provide the tools that their clients use to enter information, and those tools can insert all the tags needed for search. By controlling the tools for data entry and the tools for search, Facebook has become highly successful in attracting users. Unfortunately, it has not yet found a business model for increasing revenue. Their clients devote more time and energy communicating with their friends than with advertisers.

Methods for tagging web pages support a kind of semistructured or middleweight semantics. They do not provide the deep reasoning of Cyc or Watson, but they can be successful when the critical web pages are tagged with semantic information. The health industry is the most promising area for improving productivity and reducing cost by automation. But the huge bulk of information is still in unstructured natural language with few, if any, semantic tags. One of the greatest challenges for heavyweight semantics is to develop natural language processing (NLP) methods for automatically analyzing documents and inserting semantic tags. Those techniques are still at the research stage, but some of them are beginning to appear in cutting-edge applications.

COMMERCIALLY AVAILABLE NLP SYSTEMS

While we watched in amazement as the IBM's Watson supercomputer played *Jeopardy!* in a live TV broadcast, we realized that the field of NLP had passed a major milestone. The multiple supercomputing modules of Watson had access to vast troves of data: Big data, processed and used in real time for human-like natural language understanding, had finally taken a step away from science fiction into science fact. Table 1 in the Appendix shows that there are companies pursuing this very goal by using the cloud, which promises to provide the equivalent power of Watson's enormous supercomputing resources.

Science fiction had popularized NLP long before Watson: For example, the movie *2001: A Space Odyssey* featured a talking computer called HAL; on the popular 1960s television series *Star Trek,* the *Starship Enterprise* ship's computer would talk to Captain Kirk or his first officer Spock during their analyses. These dreams are getting one step closer to being fulfilled, even though that may still be well over a decade away. For example, the communicator used on *Star Trek* is now a reality as many of us have mobile audio-visual communicators— the miniaturizing of technology was science fiction then, and science fact now. Siri™, for Apple's iPhone™, is perhaps today's most well-advertised natural language understanding system and is swiftly becoming a household word: Behind it is a big data NLP analytics platform that is growing immensely popular in both the consumer and corporate environments. Siri has served to improve the efficacy by which things get done by combining voice and data spoken natural language technology: This improves overall performance for busy people on the go, and ultimately, therefore, contributes to a better bottom line. The miniaturization of computing power is continuing and now reaching into the realms of the emerging discipline of quantum computing, where it may be possible to have all possible worlds of contextual interpretations of language simultaneously available to the computer. However, before we reach out on the skinny branches onto quantum computing, let us consider the shift from typing to speaking and notice that this is essentially a social shift: For example, the shift in driving cars from holding a phone to hands-free talking, to hands-free dialing by speaking out the numbers, or now even asking for directions from the car's computer, we are already approaching the talking computer of the *Enterprise* in *Star Trek*.

For example, one of the business giants is Microsoft. Its business strategy has shifted into building socially consistent user experiences across their product lines such as Xbox Kinect™, Windows™ 8, and especially Windows Phone 8. This strategy will enable developers of "machine thinking" to build their applications into Microsoft products that will already provide the basic conversion of unstructured speech into structured streams of Unicode text for semantic processing. While Microsoft introduced its Speech Application Programming Interface in 1994, the company had not strategically begun to connect social media and semantic analyses with its tools. In 2006, Microsoft acquired Colloquis Inc., a provider of conversational online business solutions that feature NLP technology, and this technology has been improved upon and augmented for Microsoft products over 6 years ago. Not to be left out of the race to build market share by making it easier for humans and machines to communicate with each other, the Internet giant Google™ has pushed forward its agenda for advanced voice-and-data processing with semantic analytics as a part of its Android™ phone, starting with Google-411 service, moving to Google Voice Actions and others.

Nuance™ Corporation's SpeakFreely™ and their Clinical Language Understanding (CLU) system, which was used in IBM's Watson, enables a physician to simply talk about and describe the patient visit using a clinical medical terminology in conversational style. The CLU system is revolutionizing the electronic healthcare records industry by directly converting, at the source (the physician), all unstructured data into computable structured data.

In the Department of Defense and law enforcement markets, the Chiliad™ product called Discovery/Alert collects and continuously monitors various kinds of large-scale high-volume data, both structured and unstructured, and enables its users to conduct interactive, real-time queries in a conversational natural language along the lines of the conversation that Deckard, the role played by Harrison Ford, had with his photograph-analyzing computer in the movie *Blade Runner*, by Ridley Scott. Both Chilliad and SpeakFreely, while not consumer-oriented products, are harbingers of things to come: that conversationally advanced user interfaces based on full unrestricted natural language will become the de facto standard in the future. Which set of technologies is needed to achieve this is a race yet to be won.

Some companies are addressing specific market sectors. Google Glass™, for example, is focusing on the explosive medical information and health records market: data such as heart rate, calorie intake, and amount of time spent walking (or number of footsteps) can be collected for patients using various mobile apps, pedometers, heart monitors, as well as information contained in their medical records from other physicians. All of this amounts to a lot of data: very big data. And Google™ is betting on using its powerful cloud computing to perform, the same infrastructure that powers its successful web search engine, on the semantic and natural language data analytics domain to improve healthcare. A user-friendly dashboard will be ubiquitously accessed and displayed via Google Glass.

So what are the features that would be common to any big data natural language understanding?

Our viewpoint is that they possess the following characteristics:

1. *Seamless User Interfaces*—The application of advanced speech recognition and NLP for converting the unstructured human communications into machine-understandable information.
2. *A Diversity of Technologies*—The use of multiple forms of the state-of-the-art information organization and indexing, computing languages and models for artificial intelligence (AI), (the broad branch under whichnatural language understanding resides) as well as various kinds of retrieval and processing methods.
3. *New Data Storage Technologies*—Software such as Not Only SQL enables efficient and also interoperable forms of knowledge representations to be stored so that it can be utilized with various kinds of reasoning methods.
4. *Reasoning and Learning AI*—The integration of AI techniques so that the machine can learn from its own mistakes and build that learned knowledge into its knowledge stores for future applications of its own reasoning processes.
5. *Model-Driven Architectures*—The use of advanced frameworks depends on a diversified and large base of models, which themselves depend on the production of interoperable ontologies. These make it possible to engineer a complex system of heterogeneous components for open-domain, real-

time, real-world interaction with humans, in a way that is comfortable and fits within colloquial human language use.

The common theme in all of this: *The key to big data is small data*. Small data depends crucially on the development of very high quality and general models for interpreting natural language of various kinds: For example, the ability to handle short questions and answers is the key to handling big numbers of questions and answers, and this capability depends on good models. Unlike statistical systems that need big data to answer small data questions, the paradigm has become somewhat inverted.

Latest study[3] shows that over 50% of all medical applications will use some form of advanced analytics, most of which will rely on extraction of information from textual sources, compared with the paltry less than 10% today, and that most of the needed approaches to do this successfully will depend on a variety of models and ontologies for the various medical subfields. For example, the *2012 Understanding Healthcare Challenge* by Nuance™[4] corporation lists the following areas of growth: emergency medical responder/point-of-care documentation, access to resources, professional communications, pharm, clinical trials, disease management, patient communication, education programs, administrative, financial, public health, and ambulance/emergency medical services.

Traditionally, tools for business intelligence have been batch-oriented extract-transform-load data integration, relational data warehousing, and statistical analytics processes. These pipelined, rigid, time-consuming, and expensive processes are ill-suited to a conversational NLP interface, since they cannot adapt to new patterns without the aid of a programmer. Therefore, they are unsuited for the big data era. The world and its information are now resident within huge collections of online documents, and efforts at manual translation of knowledge, even crowdsourcing, are impractical since the humans would need to be perfectly rational, consistent, coherent, and systematic in their outputs. Today, search for key terms is still a domination approach to get results, but in reality, we want results as well-formed answers from knowledge bases that in turn have been built on text bases: The critical path in developing a successful natural language solution rests in the fundamental design decision matching between various available component technologies (either open source or from vendors), the application domain requirements, and the available models.

Next question: What drives big data NLP? There are five key points:

1. *Entity Identification*—This is needed to extract facts, which can then populate databases. Fact bases are critical to having the basic information needed for almost any kind of decision making. However, what kind of processing is needed and used to extract the salient, relevant facts (or in expert parlance, the *named entities* from free-form text)? What are the impediments to language variability and scalability, and what techniques work and which ones hold promise?

2. *Language Understanding*—The grammar and meaning of the words in a language are needed to extract information as well as knowledge from texts, which is not the same as extraction of facts. For example, business rules (while they also depend on the extraction of facts) tell you how a certain business process are to be operationalized, and the extraction of business rules can be used to automate or analyze a business. In the case of the law (as another domain), the capture of legal jurisprudence, for example, can be used to analyze for forensics in cases. However, how does one disentangle the real requirements for a text-information extraction engine? What are the costs, techniques, and methods that are the best in class in performance and scale?

3. *Causal and Explanatory Reasoning*—In almost any kind of analytics process—medical, financial, national security, banking, and customer service, there are processes that form dependent chains where one thing must happen before another. The ability of the computer to perform reasoning about what is going in a text depends on its ability to formulate scenarios of activities and to create explanations based on its understanding. This requires being able to reason, to make hypotheses (especially with ambiguous sentences as we shall show later on), and to formulate plans. All of these are components of the traditional research branches of AI.

4. *Voice and Data*—This is a huge industry that has grown from button-pushing interactions into conversational interactions. The kinds of systems used are pervasive in most customer support activities, from booking trains to planes and getting support for your computer. What makes the handling of voice and data, interactive speech, and media interfaces different for textual NLP and natural language understanding (NLU)? The key differentiator is that spoken language is most often broken up into islands of meanings with interjections, noise, and ambiguities in sound and content.

5. *Knowledge Representation and Models*—Models depend on ontologies, and in order to build an ontology, a method to represent knowledge must be chosen. Models apply to all the areas in (1) through (4), but add an entirely new dimension to big data: the ability to perform what-if reasoning to produce explanations and predications by handling language in terms of knowledge content, which includes facts,

information, rules, heuristics, feedback from the user, exploratory question answering (in which there are no "right" answers), and hypotheses. In speech systems, for example, knowledge-oriented NLP can look at the interactions across all of the islands of information and facts as they are spoken to derive the final meaning.

Given that we have presented some high-level points about NLP from a technical requirements perspective, without producing a 5-year course on natural language, we can now turn to the key business decision (and cost) factors in implementing a big data NLP/NLU system: namely, the technology approach (or strategy); the big data systems integration options; and finally, dealing with ambiguity and context, especially as it usually occurs in contextually dependent freely spoken language.

Technology Approach

A technology approach represents the choices made for handling big data NLP in an end-to-end, cradle-to-grave life cycle: knowledge representation, implementation language, and systems integration. A given technology approach will have a total cost of ownership for a specific capability, and this is a choice that is usually made as a consequence of a requirements process (which is often itself developed as a scenario of uses and use cases). For example, the needs of a system for call-center call routing where a user can listen to choices and respond by pressing a button to select the route to a human agent will have a simple template-based natural language generation and understanding component with a voice-and-data interface. However, a system for knowledge extraction may need to handle the complexities of natural language such as discourse representation, intratextual references, resolving analogies, metaphors and similes, or allegories into thematic, semantic knowledge structures and storing these for use in an interactive question answering module.

Each technology will depend on whether the data is unstructured, structured, or semistructured: For example, template-based methods work best when the data is regularly structured, such as text in the form of an invoice or the format of an address. For other types of text inputs, for example, when there is little background ontology available and the data is completely unstructured, statistical methods are favored. When good background resources and an ontology exist, the linguistic approach delivers superior results to the statistical approaches. The best is usually a hybrid combination of several approaches since data typically is partially a mix of unstructured, semistructured, and fully structured components. There are a number of basic technology

approaches, but the field is so diverse that a full compendium of the plethora of approaches would itself require many books to complete. However, from a bird's-eye viewpoint, the diaspora of technical approaches broadly falls into a few groups, which we have outlined as follows:

1. *Statistical (Mathematical) Methods*—These methods all use a number of mathematical equations and statistical properties of words and collections of texts. Algorithms that you may find out more about on the web that are representative of the mathematical approach have such names as Latent Semantic Analysis, Vector Space Methods, or Hidden Markov Models. While these terms refer to highly technical and detailed recipes for counting and ranking words and phrases in a text for analysis or indexing, they essentially do not require any background knowledge to work and so are fast to implement and very scalable.

2. *Template Methods*—These methods have been around since the 1960s. Templates are basically sentences with missing parts to be filled in. For example, take the simple sentence "The price is $10.00." This sentence can be made into a template by using variables denoted by the underline, "___ price is ___," so that whenever the sentence matches the exact same words, in the same order, then the price can be collected. This template can collect information such as "Book price is $9.00" and "Beans price is $1.75." A fancier form of templates is to use the so-called regular expressions that compile templates into very efficient computer programs (formally called finite state automata) that can process massive volumes of text that is semistructured with regular repeating patterns (like invoices, order processing, and addresses) at extremely high speed.

3. *Linguistic Methods*—These are the most sophisticated of approaches and generally need a background base of knowledge, ontology, a knowledge representation, and a variety of recipes by which text is assigned to concepts that identify the meanings. For example, models such as Discourse Representation Theory not only model the meaning of sentences but also how they relate to each other in paragraphs and the whole text. Other models, such as Rhetorical Structure Theory, express how the topics and focus of the text is related to the intent of the author to the reader. Linguistics methods also cover such things as what it means to interpret and answer a question, using a model of user questioning so that domains such as customer product servicing can be handled effectively by cataloging and storing all the questions that humans have answered and modeling these into the knowledge base of an automated system so that call-center costs can be

Big Data–
Cellular

saved. While it takes time to build linguistic models for NLP, they are the most powerful and the deepest of techniques with the highest potential payoffs and returns on investment.

Of course, these techniques are available for use in through a number of vendors, the newest of which are entering into the cloud-based model of Software as a Service. The vast majority of tools are provided by many of the familiar names in big business, such as IBM, SAS and others; however, there are many fast and high-growth opportunities in emerging niche markets, and these are served often by smaller high-tech startups. Table 1 in the Appendix provides a landscape of the types of companies that use NLP/NLU extensively and provides a quick-start guide for you to get out on the web to see what they're up to, what they provide, and what you can use if you are considering using this technology in an application.

Implementation and Systems Integration

Implementation choices boil down to either rolling out your own NLP system, which will usually have a very high cost, to choosing ready-made or open-source components and libraries of software and integrating their functionalities into a desired capability. The systems integration approach is the most cost-effective because, as an integrator, no research and development of the core components is needed; however, the burden falls on architecture and design as well as thoroughly understanding the pros and cons of software language choices (Java, C, C++, C#, Scala, Erlang, Prolog, Haskell, etc.) and integration approaches (CORBA, Java-RMI, TCP-sockets, etc.) for a target device set (iPhone, Android, laptop, desktop, web-services based, thick or thin client, etc.). In addition, there are several areas in which systems integration and testing will be highly domain dependent. For example, applications in medical informatics will need rich background data in the form of dictionaries, thesauri, ontologies, and databases that need to be coded and associated with the NLP strategy and technology approach. In the case of applications that serve a wider audience, for example, in customer relationship management and support, the requirements for powerful and seamless NLP are very high: I am sure I am not alone in stating that every once in a while I will encounter a so-called help system online or on the telephone that is still a far cry from the quality of help a real human provides.

As everyone knows, computers use 1s and 0s, so a programmer could string together the appropriate sequence of 1s and 0s to write any program: in reality, this would be rather impractical if not impossible to achieve as the program grows in size, complexity, and diversity of concepts and algorithms. Enter the evolution of programming languages and paradigms of

integration—all with the purpose of being able to write software at a higher level of complexity and hiding the fine-grained 1s and 0s that are, in the end, always produced to run on a given computer and operating system. Languages are constantly evolving from lower levels, being closer to the 1s and 0s, such as "Assembly" code to higher levels, with the newest languages, such as Scala™, that encapsulate cloud and large-scale concurrent programming concepts seamlessly. Some very high-level but older logical languages, such as Prolog, are seeing resurgence as new techniques and methods, as well as advancements in compiler design, have overcome the earlier limitations. Today, the most popular programming language is JAVA, followed by C/C++; and then others such as Python, Prolog, Lisp, Haskell, and Scala form their own niches. The main problem with mainstream languages like Java and C are that they are not designed for reasoning tasks: every reasoning algorithm has to be painstakingly written at a very low level, and therefore the costs are high. In contrast, and especially with present-day language designs for Prolog for NLP agent technologies and Scala as a backbone for cloud technologies, higher-level programming may soon be coming to the mainstream for NLP.

In the world of big data, and for the distribution of NLP tasks, the choice of language, such as Prolog or Scala or Java, and many other options can all benefit from the approach originally taken by Google and now available open source as Hadoop[5] as well as the precursor Grid Computing principles to build a cloud with NLP service components. For example, Epstein, regarding Watson, states:[6]

Early implementations of Watson ran on a single processor where it took 2 hours to answer a single question. The DeepQA computation is embarrassing parallel, however. Unstructured Information Management Asynchronous Scaleout (UIMA-AS), part of Apache Unstructured Information Management Architecture (UIMA), enables the scaleout of UIMA applications using asynchronous messaging. We used UIMA-AS to scale Watson out over 2500 compute cores. UIMA-AS handles all of the communication, messaging, and queue management necessary using the open Java Message Service standard. The UIMA-AS deployment of Watson enabled competitive run-time latencies in the 3–5 second range.

To preprocess the corpus and create fast run-time indices we used Hadoop. UIMA annotators were easily deployed as mappers in the Hadoop map-reduce framework. Hadoop distributes the content over the cluster to afford high CPU utilization and provides convenient tools for deploying, managing, and monitoring the corpus analysis process.

VivoMind™ Research, for example, believes in the IBM approach and is developing its own next-generation language and reasoning technologies by developing a state-of-the-art object-oriented Prolog language agent compiler (called Pi-Log™): after all, Prolog formed the critical NLP core of IBM's Watson.[7]

Ambiguity and Context

Natural languages are the most complex and sophisticated forms of communication and knowledge encapsulation, but today, it is not yet possible to program a computer in plain natural language. However, strides are being made that would enable one to program a computer in a controlled natural language.

The major problems facing the NLP and NLU systems integrator are that language is highly variable and flexible in use from one individual to the next. The freedom of language affords humans a wide variety of contexts: Context is all-important and context usually arises out of a situation. If I am at a billiard table, I can use the word *bank* as, "I banked it," in describing a shot; but if I am depositing money at an ATM, that same statement would mean something completely different. In online help systems, context-sensitive is particularly important. To restrict context, one approach is control what words a user can use. A controlled natural language would only understand language in a highly rigid form—but this can be learned by humans: for example, the medical language of radiology reports, or the controlled language of the Air Traffic Information System (ATIS) has been learned by humans and used by machines effectively. The choice in developing, buying, or using an NLP system faces the challenge of how to handle vague, ambiguous statements, or at the very least, in advising the user that the inputs were not handled or recognized. This can be tricky. Consider the following set of sentences from a computer's perspective:

1. Fruit flies like a banana and time flies like an arrow: is there a kind of insect called "time flies"?
2. I saw the man on the hill with a telescope: did the man have the telescope or was it the person watching the man on the hill?
3. He was a lion in the fight: how can human be an animal (of course, this is an analogy)?
4. He banked it: was it a billiard shot? a trip to the teller at bank? Or did he maneuver a plane?
5. She spilled the beans: did she vomit or did she tell the truth or did she spill beans literally?
6. John went through Harry to get to Paul: physically? Or what?
7. They were marketing people: were they in the slave trade or salespeople?
8. He sat down to eat and drink with a cigar: did he actually literally both eat and drink a cigar?
9. The man said that he did not do it: the man or someone else?
10. Nobody was found and no one came: murder or someone called "Nobody"?
11. This, that, and the other were the choices: choices of what? Apples? Bananas? Investments?

While these sentences are by no means exhaustive of the possibilities, the roadmap to success will be driven by very careful business use-case and scenario design to ensure that the NLP system can cope with ambiguous inputs and not lead into some sort of automation-surprise (like, for example, draining the users' accounts by some misconception in an online NLP banking system of the future).

Equally important is modality of interaction in language: spoken or written. The advent of the controlled "alphabet" (ASCII) for the computer keyboard is in evolution into a controlled "language" for spoken communications, (such as Siri™), and this means that the concept of NLP and NLU is tied in deeply with speech generation and recognition. For example, a template-based NLP system can trigger processing whenever it encounters the pattern "X costs Y dollars": So X can be apples, oranges, or land; and Y can be dollars, pesos, yen, or euros. But the computer has no understanding that this is a quantitative statement. The beauty of a controlled language system is that it has the simplicity of templates but also includes the component of knowledge representation for richer reasoning that basic template systems cannot provide. In contrast to quantitative data input, qualitative natural language data input is a particularly difficult area for computation since most qualitative descriptions are rich with adjectives and nuanced language. Today, the most aggressive efforts to develop systems that can understand qualitative viewpoints are the social mining NLP systems that attempt to understand user sentiment or market opinion.

FUTURE DIRECTIONS

Research projects worldwide are pioneering new NLP methods that promise to make major breakthroughs within the coming decade. Three projects that have already been used in significant applications illustrate the existing directions: the Cyc Project, which has developed the world's largest ontology; the IBM Watson Project, which beat the world champion in the *Jeopardy!* game; and the intelligent Prolog language-based agents at VivoMind™ Research, which use Stanford's CSLI Verb Ontology[8] that was a gift from IBM to Stanford for the public domain. These resources are being successfully used for mining materials science information from science and technology journals for a U. S. Department of Energy[9] program.

Table 1a   Technology platforms and vendors.

Platforms	Applications	Technology Sources
Cloud NLP Services	You design your application; the cloud API vendor provides all the algorithms. Cut down coding and total cost of ownership. Applications: • Social Network Mining • Open-Source Information Analyses • Blog, Website and News Analyses	**Alchemy**: http://www.alchemyapi.com/ **Nerd**: http://nerd.eurecom.fr/ **Ramp**: http://www.ramp.com/mediacloud **Bayes Informatics**: https://www.bayesinformatics.com/node/3 **Hakia**: http://company.hakia.com/semanticrank.html **Semantria**: http://www.semantria.com/ **Exalead**: http://www.3ds.com/products/exalead/products/exalead-cloudview/overview/ **Zemanta API:** http://www.zemanta.com/
NLP Application Services	Applications: • Market Intelligence • Sentiment Analysis • Social Opinion Mining • Trends Analyses • Continuous News Monitoring • Web-Site Monitoring	**Accenture Technology Labs:** http://www.accenture.com/Global/Services/AccentureTechnologyLabs/default.htm **Adaptive Semantics Inc.:** http://adaptivesemantics.com/ **Linguastat:** http://www.linguastat.com/ **Connotate:** http://www.connotate.com **Visible Technologies:** http://www.visibletechnologies.com/tru-pulse.html **RiverGlass:** http://www.riverglassinc.com/; **Fast:** http://www.fastsearch.com/ **Mnemonic Technology:** http://www.mnemonic.com **Chilliad:** http://www.chiliad.com **Crawdad Technologies:** http://www.crawdadtech.com/ **Lymbix:** http://www.lymbix.com/ **Northern Light:** http://www.northernlight.com **Nstein:** http://www.nstein.com **Recorded Future:** http://www.recordedfuture.com

Table 1b   Technology platforms and vendors.

Platforms	Applications	Technology Sources
NLP Solution Vendors	NLU solutions for various industries that use a variety of algorithms and methods in order to achieve performance, scalability, and results. Applications: • Social Network Mining • Open-Source Information Analyses • Blog, Website, and News Analyses • Market Intelligence • Sentiment Analysis • Social Opinion Mining • Trends Analyses • Continuous News Monitoring • Website Monitoring • Web Scraping	**Attensity:** http://www.attensity.com **Autonomy:** http://www.autonomy.com/ **BBN:** http://www.bbn.com/technology/knowledge/semantic_web_applications **Bitext:** http://www.bitext.com/ **Brainware:** http://www.brainware.com/ **Chilliad:** http://www.chiliad.com **ClearForest:** http://www.clearforest.com/ **Lextek International:** http://www.lextek.com/ **LXA Lexalytics:** http://www.lexalytics.com/ **NetOwl:** http://www.netowl.com/ **SAS:** http://www.sas.com/text-analytics/text-miner/index.htm **Lingpipe:** http://alias-i.com/lingpipe/ **Topic Mapper:** http://www.ai-one.com/
NLP Template-Based Sy	Keyword and key phrase extraction templates using word lists or thesauri. Applications: • Web Scraping • Key Term Extraction • Key Phrase Watch List Monitors	**Carrot:** http://project.carrot2.org/ **Kea:** http://www.nzdl.org/Kea/ **Sematext:** http://sematext.com/products/key-phrase-extractor/index.html **Maui:** http://code.google.com/p/maui-indexer/ **Keyphrase Extractor:** http://smile.deri.ie/projects/keyphrase-extraction

Table 1c Technology platforms and vendors.

Platforms	Applications	Technology Sources
NLP Toolkits	These vendors provide all the algorithms in the form of specific language application programming toolkits. Applications: • Medical Data Mining • Healthcare Records Analyses • Financial News Analyses • Extraction and Loading of Unstructured Text Into Databases • Customer Help and Support Systems	**Cognition**: http://www.cognition.com/ **Connexor**: http://www.connexor.com/ **Digital Reasoning**: http://www.digitalreasoning.com/solutions/ **Expert System**: http://www.expertsystem.net/ **Extractiv**: http://extractiv.com/ **IBM**: http://www.ibm.com/developerworks/data/downloads/uima/ **Ling-Join**: http://en.lingjoin.com/product/ljparser.html **Lingway**: http://www.lingway.com/ **Q-go**: http://www.q-go.nl/ **SAP**: http://www.sap.com/solutions/sapbusinessobjects/in dex.epx **Teragram**: http://www.teragram.com/oem/ **Temis**: http://www.temis.com **Vantage Linguistics**: http://www.vantagelinguistics.com/ **Xerox**: http://www.xrce.xerox.com/Research-Development/Document-Content-Laboratory
NLP Open-Source Tools	This is the classic build-versus-buy scenario. An Internet search resulted in many tool suites, and this is simply a sampling, not representative of the total available. Wikipedia list of open-source NLP tools: http://en.wikipedia.org/wiki/List of natural_language_processing_toolkits	**Stanford NLP–Stanford University (an Extensive tool suite, GPL)**: http://nlp.stanford.edu/software/index.shtml **Balie—Baseline Information Extraction (University of Ottawa, GNU GPL)**: http://balie.sourceforge.net/ **FreeLing (Universitat Politecnica de Catalunya, GNU LGPL)**: http://nlp.lsi.upc.edu/freeling/ **Gate—General Architecture For Language Engineering (Java, University of Sheffield, LGPL)**: http://gate.ac.uk/ **MALLET—Machine Learning for Language Toolkit (Java&x2014;University of Massachusetts—Common Public License)**: http://mallet.cs.umass.edu/ **NLTK—Natural Language Tool Kit**: http://nltk.org/ **Ellogon—Visual NLP (C + +, LGPL)**: http://www.ellogon.org/

Cyc has evolved into an open-source community with some domain-specific closed-source components, and the company is continuing to evolve. The history of Cyc and the lessons learned paved the way for us all.

Today, Watson requires a supercomputer to support its algorithms, but today's laptops are more powerful than the supercomputers of the 1990s. Before long, systems at the level of Watson will run on an ordinary server, then a laptop, and eventually a hand-held wizard. Perhaps these or other systems will lead to ultrasmart clouds of autonomous algorithms that "know" which NLP tasks they are best suited for. Perhaps groups of NLP processes can self-aggregate into useful workflows without programmer effort. New languages and algorithms may emerge. Perhaps the semantic web will

evolve into the cognitive cloud in the future. Several new startup companies (as shown in Table 1 in the Appendix) are already beginning to deliver fully cloud-based NLP solutions that eliminate the need to have a supercomputer at home.

What does the future hold for big data analytics here at VivoMind? We are building on the intelligent agent paradigm, which we believe will lead to ultrasmart clouds of autonomous algorithms that "know" which NLP tasks they are best suited for. In effect, the agents program themselves. We can use ordinary language to tell them what to do, not how to do it.

SCALA, the emerging new language that builds on the JAVA JVM, will also provide momentum into the cloud-based NLP approach: Multilingual NLP clouds and interoperability of intracloud NLP components as well as the emergence of the big data cognitive web are still very much in research phases with lessons learned from existing semantic web efforts that many see as the Cyc of yesteryear. We leave it to readers to develop the cognitive cloud of the future as a kind of world-covering software brain where questions, answers, and explanations can be synthesized on demand.

APPENDIX

Cloud-based NLP (Table 1a) is a fast-growing area and is a fast track for any company that has a unique solution to offer customers in the big data analytics arena without having a high up-front investment. According to McKinsey,[10] the market sizes are in the hundreds of billions of dollars for these areas of big data NLP.

There are many solutions vendors with customizable NLP solutions (Table 1b), in the form of reconfigurable applications and frameworks, which are at a higher level than just being components or developer tools sets. These applications can be rapidly configured for domain-specific tasks and can be quickly scaled to large volumes by replication of applications onto a server farm. The initial configuration costs are kept fairly low since the frameworks come with helper applications for rapid data ingestion.

At the simpler end of the spectrum, especially for specialty jobs, such as address processing and order processing where the format and layout of the text fits regular patterns, then the template-based methods are very hard to beat for speed and scalability. In the case of patterns of semistructured texts with a regular language, for example, the Air Traffic Information Systems dialogs, template-based systems are ideal for information extraction.

When proprietary know-how, trade secrecy, as well as sources and methods form the cornerstone of the business-use case, then it is hard to beat a good set of optimized commercial software developer toolkits and/ or open-source technologies for customized programming of an application or solution (Table 1c). Open-source tools are improving, and IBM's Watson used many open-source components. While we have provided a broad-strokes overview, there are many more companies and specialty component technologies on the market. Some, like the intelligent agent–based approaches like Connotate™, already have an early and strong lead with this very promising approach for scalable and distributed NLP.

REFERENCES

1. http://www.iso.org/iso/iso_catalogue/catalogue_tc/ catalogue_detail.htm?csnumber=39175.
2. http://www-03.ibm.com/innovation/us/watson/.
3. U. S. Hospital Health Data Analytics Market. http:// www.frost.com/c/10046/sublib/display-report.do? id=NA03-01-00-00-00-00.
4. http://www.nuance.com/landing-pages/healthcare/ 2012understandingchallenge/.
5. http://hadoop.apache.org/.
6. http://www.aaai.org/Magazine/Watson/watson.php.
7. http://www.cs.nmsu.edu/ALP/2011/03/natural-language- processing-with-prolog-in-the-ibm-watson-system/.
8. http://lingo.stanford.edu/vso/.
9. https://www1.eere.energy.gov/vehiclesandfuels/pdfs/ merit_review_2011/adv_power_electronics/ape032_ whaling_2011_o.pdf.
10. http://www.mckinsey.com/insights/mgi/research/ technology_and_innovation/big_data_the_next_frontier_ for_innovation.

Bioinformatics

Carrie L. Iwema
Ansuman Chattopadhyay
Health Sciences Library System, University of Pittsburgh, Pittsburgh, Pennsylvania, U.S.A.

Abstract

The field of bioinformatics sits at the intersection of biological science, computer science, and information science. It is a rapidly growing discipline that focuses on the development of tools for data management and analysis and assists with practical applications and determinations of significance. The purpose of this entry is to provide information specialists and librarians with a brief introduction to bioinformatics and an overview of established online resources that will be useful when assisting patrons with bioinformatics-related questions.

INTRODUCTION

The multidisciplinary field of bioinformatics integrates biological science, computer science, and information science. It developed because of vast amounts of data generated from the explosion in genetic sequencing experimentation. Because of this, it became necessary to create methods for accurately and succinctly storing, analyzing, and disseminating the exponential increase in biological data.

Bioinformatics is closely related to the fields of computational biology and systems biology, but they have distinct identities. Systems biology focuses on the integrative (as opposed to reductive) study of complex interactions in biological systems. Computational biology focuses on the development of efficient and accurate algorithms to support biological investigations. Bioinformatics focuses on the development of tools for data management and analysis and assists with practical applications and determinations of significance. Major research areas in bioinformatics include sequence alignment and analysis, gene identification and expression prediction, genome assembly and annotation, protein structure prediction and alignment, protein–protein interaction prediction, comparative genomics and proteomics, evolutionary modeling, image analysis, and mutation analysis, to name a few.

Successful biological research requires appropriate study design and careful data analysis in order to make a compelling case that supports (or refutes) a hypothesis. This is more easily accomplished using knowledge and data management databases and tools—i.e., bioinformatics resources.

Because the bioinformatics field is multidisciplinary and changing at such a rapid rate, it is impossible to fully cover all available resources and details. Thus, the purpose of this encyclopedia entry is to provide information specialists and librarians with a brief introduction to bioinformatics and an overview of established online resources that will be useful when assisting patrons with bioinformatics-related questions. This is not intended to be an entry on the basics of molecular biology or computer science. For more detailed explanations, please refer to the numerous bioinformatics textbooks available, such as those listed at the end of this entry, as well as the included online resources.

HISTORY

The field of bioinformatics is generally agreed to have originated in the 1960s thanks to the pioneering work of Margaret Dayhoff and her colleagues at the Protein Information Resource (PIR). In essence, they created the first annotated protein sequence database, although it was initially in print form.[1] As the amount of data grew, it became apparent that an electronic format was necessary, particularly for ease of searching and evaluation of the data.

The next phase in the history of sequence databases began in the 1980s with the advent of nucleotide sequence databases generated by the European Molecular Biology Laboratory (EMBL), GenBank for the National Center for Biotechnology Information (NCBI, part of the National Library of Medicine at the National Institutes of Health), and the DNA Databank of Japan (DDBJ). These three groups formed the International Nucleotide Sequence Database Collaboration, which agreed to share data, use a common format for data records, and have each database update only the records that were directly submitted to it. Records at all three sites are automatically updated every 24 hours.

The first complete genome of a live organism to be sequenced was the bacterium *Hemophilus influenza* by

Encyclopedia of Information Systems and Technology, DOI: 10.1081/E-EIST-120044665

The Institute for Genetics Research, started by Craig Venter.[2] He went on to create a private company, Celera Genomics, which used a whole genome shotgun strategy for sequencing large eukaryotic genomes. In contrast, the Human Genome Project (HGP), a large, federally funded consortium, used a clone by clone sequencing strategy. In 2001, the HGP[3] and Celera[4] simultaneously published the first complete sequence of the entire human genome, thereby signifying a major advance in the field of bioinformatics.

INFORMATION FLOW

Data enters the bioinformatics stream when a researcher deposits an experimental result into an archive. The data is annotated and curated before being released to the public archive and made available for analysis, including:

- Integration into other resources, such as organism-specific databases.
- Extraction of data subsets, such as identification of genes from a DNA sequence.
- Derivation of new information, such as translation of a presumptive amino acid sequence from a nucleotide sequence.
- Classification, such as grouping proteins by structure or function.
- Reannotation, such as providing links between original data entries that share a commonality.

ARCHIVAL VS. DERIVED DATABASES

Accessibility is the key element of sequence database utility. It is important to describe the distinction between archival (primary) and derived (secondary) databases in order to understand the nature of the data being accessed. Primary databases contain experimental results whereas secondary databases contain extrapolated results. GenBank is an example of an archival database that includes all sequence data submitted, meaning that there can be multiple entries for some loci. RefSeq is a derived database that provides only one example of each biological molecule limited to major organisms where sufficient data is available. This site provides a comparison of the two databases (http://www.ncbi.nlm.nih.gov/ books/bv.fcgi?rid=handbook.section. GenBank_ASM). In general, GenBank records are comparable to primary literature, whereas RefSeq records are comparable to review articles.

Examples of archived database contents include protein and nucleotide sequences, protein and nucleotide structures, organism-specific information, protein

expression patterns, metabolic pathways, interaction patterns, regulatory networks, and variations. Examples of derived database contents include sequence motifs, mutations and variations, relationships or classifications, bibliographic information, and Web site or database links.

The quality of information stored in databases is also of critical importance. If there are errors in the original data or in the annotations, there are obvious consequences for all subsequent conclusions using that data. Both archival and derived databases may be either automatically populated or manually curated and annotated. Annotation is the weakest link in the bioinformatics information flow process. Automated annotation is currently too limited, and manual annotation is very laborintensive and prone to human error. Nonetheless, data annotation is a very valuable and necessary part of the process that will hopefully improve in quality as the bioinformatics field continues to grow. With that in mind, it is important for researchers to always manually inspect the results they glean from using bioinformatics tools to make sure they make sense, and not just accept the data at face value.

MAJOR BIOINFORMATICS RESOURCE PROVIDERS

The bioinformatics field continues to grow, and with that expansion comes the ebb and flow of useful resources. The following three institutions have a track record for providing reliable databases and tools that are both useful and popular with bioinformatics researchers:

National Center for Biotechnology Information, http://www.ncbi.nlm.nih.gov/

NCBI was founded in 1988 as part of the National Library of Medicine, which is a branch of the National Institutes of Health in the United States. Along with the bibliographic archives PubMed and PubMed Central, NCBI houses the genome sequence archive GenBank. NCBI is a national resource for molecular biology information and provides free access to over 30 public databases, including Online Mendelian Inheritance in Man, the database of Genotype and Phenotype, and a searchable database of genes, Entrez Gene. NCBI also provides access to free bioinformatics tools such as Basic Local Alignment Search Tool (BLAST), a sequence similarity searching program. Research initiatives are in place to continually create new and better methods for storing and disseminating bioinformatics data. The resources provided by NCBI are used extensively and internationally and all at no cost to the user, which is a tremendous service not only to the scientific community but to the world.

European Bioinformatics Institute, http://www.ebi.ac.uk/

The European Bioinformatics Institute (EBI) is an academic research center that forms part of the EMBL (http://www.embl.org/) since 1992. EMBL-EBI is the European equivalent of NCBI. It hosts many major databases, including EMBL-Bank for nucleotide sequences, UniProt (formerly Swiss-Prot-TrEMBL) for protein sequences, and Ensembl for genomes. In addition, EMBL-EBI provides access to a variety of bioinformatics tools, services, and training.

University of California Santa Cruz Genome Bioinformatics Group, http://www.cbse.ucsc.edu/

The Genome Bioinformatics Group within the Center for Biomolecular Science and Engineering at University of California Santa Cruz (UCSC) is responsible for creating and maintaining the UCSC Genome Bioinformatics Web site, and in particular the UCSC Genome Browser, since the early 2000s. This particular resource is a popular tool in the bioinformatics field and is described later in this entry. The group provides additional tools, such as BLAT (fast sequence alignment), Gene Sorter (expression and homology), and VisiGene (virtual microscope for viewing in situ images).

BIOINFORMATICS RESOURCE IDENTIFICATION

There are already thousands of online bioinformatics resources available, with undoubtedly many more to come. One of the limiting factors of the field is the difficulty in navigating the vast array of resources and identifying the most appropriate tool (s) for the job. Three means of searching for bioinformatics resources are listed below.

Online Bioinformatics Resource Collection, http://www.hsls.pitt.edu/guides/genetics/obrc/

The Online Bioinformatics Resource Collection (OBRC) contains links and annotations for over 2000 bioinformatics databases and software tools. It was created in 2006 by the Molecular Biology Information Service for the Health Sciences Library System at the University of Pittsburgh.[5] The purpose of the manually curated OBRC is to bridge the gap between the rising information needs of biological and medical researchers and the rapidly growing number of online bioinformatics

resources. This freely available, searchable database arranges resources by categories and subcategories such as Structure Databases and Analysis Tools, Microarray, serial analysis of gene expression (SAGE), and other Gene Expression, and Enzymes and Pathways. The OBRC is the largest online collection of its kind and the only one with advanced search results clustering. It is a one-stop guided information gateway to the major bioinformatics databases and software tools on the Web.

Online Resource Finder for Lifesciences, http://orefil.dbcls.jp/

Online Resource Finder for Lifesciences, developed by Japanese computational biologists, it provides searches for online resources introduced in peer-reviewed papers in the life sciences.[6] A crawler automatically extracts all URLs listed in MEDLINE abstracts and full-text papers from BioMed Central open access journals and maintains them in a freely available, searchable database.

Nucleic Acids Research Bioinformatics Links Directory, http://bioinformatics.ca/links_directory/

The Bioinformatics Links Directory features curated links to molecular resources, tools, and databases culled from the annual Database issue and Web Server issue of the journal *Nucleic Acids Research* (NAR, http://nar.oxfordjournals.org/). NAR is a highly ranked open access journal that publishes articles on the biological, biochemical, physical, and chemical aspects of proteins and nucleic acids involved in nucleic acid interactions and/or metabolism. The freely available Bioinformatics Link Directory provides links to the resources themselves, as well as to the NAR-published articles about those resources.

DATABASES

The field of bioinformatics is dependent on the Internet for access to gene and protein sequences. Following is a list of well-established bioinformatics databases, including a brief description of and URL for each resource. They are categorized as One-Stop Gateways, Sequence, Gene-centric, Genome-centric, and Protein-centric. Be aware that this list is only a sampling of available resources. These particular resources were selected as representative and highly regarded bioinformatics databases and tools.

One-Stop Gateways

NCBI Entrez Gene, http://www.ncbi.nlm.nih.gov/
sites/entrez?db=gene

Entrez Gene is a freely available, gene-specific database
maintained by the NCBI. It focuses on completely
sequenced genomes; thus information on predicted or
known genes is not included. The database assigns
unique identifiers to each gene, allowing for easy
updates when new information becomes available. The
content of Entrez Gene includes, but is not limited to,
gene products and attributes, sequences, structure, map
location, citations, function, interactions, markers, phe-
notypes, homology, ontology, variation details, and
external database links. A key feature of the database is
that it links to additional relevant information about the
gene of interest within the other NCBI databases.
Thanks to a wealth of resources, Entrez Gene is a "one-
stop shop" for gene-centric information.

GeneCards, http://www.genecards.org/

GeneCards is searchable database that offers automatically mined genomic, proteomic, transcriptomic,
genetic, and functional information for known and predicted human genes. Developed and maintained by the
Crown Human Genome Center at the Weizmann Institute of Science, the information provided by GeneCards
includes gene function and expression, mutations and
single nucleotide polymorphisms (SNPs), protein–protein interactions, orthologies, related drugs and
compounds, disease relationships, and links to additional
resources that supply information on clones, antibodies,
expression assays, RNAi reagents, and recombinant proteins. Access to the database is free to academic
nonprofit institutions.

UCSC Genome Bioinformatics, http://genome.ucsc.
edu/

The UCSC (University of California, Santa Cruz)
Genome Bioinformatics site contains genome reference
sequence and draft assemblies. Sequences can be
explored using a number of tools, including the highly
regarded Genome Browser (see description later in this
entry). Blat maps a query sequence to the genome.
Gene Sorter displays a sorted table of genes of various
relationships such as genomic proximity, protein-level
homology, or gene expression profile similarity. Genome
Graphs permit upload and display of genome-wide data
sets. Table Browser retrieves information from the
Genome Browser annotation tables. Tutorials on the use
of the UCSC Genome Bioinformatics Web site are available through the genomics knowledge Web site
OpenHelix (http://www.openhelix.com/).

Sequence Databases

NCBI GenBank, http://www.ncbi.nlm.nih.gov/
Genbank/

GenBank is an annotated, noncurated genetic sequence
database compiling all publicly available nucleotide
sequences, including ribosomal RNA gene clusters,
mRNA sequences with coding regions, and segments of
genomic DNA with a single gene or multiple genes. It is
part of the International Nucleotide Sequence Database
Collaboration formed by GenBank at NCBI, the EMBL,
and the DDBJ. These three groups exchange information
daily, and GenBank reports a new release every 2
months. The database is designed to encourage access
to the most comprehensive and current nucleotide
sequence information. Many journals require sequence
information to be submitted to a database prior to publication; several options for submission to GenBank are
provided. As an archive of primary sequence data, Gen-
Bank may include multiple sequencing results for the
same loci.

NCBI RefSeq, http://www.ncbi.nlm.nih.gov/RefSeq/

The Reference Sequence database is a curated, nonredundant collection of DNA, RNA, and protein
sequences. As opposed to GenBank, RefSeq designates
a single example of each molecule and is limited to
major organisms with sufficient data. Records are
updated as new information is reported. RefSeq records
are intended to provide a comprehensive, stable dataset
for gene identification and characterization, genome
annotation, expression studies, comparative analyses,
and mutation and polymorphism analysis.

Gene-Centric Databases

TRED, http://rulai.cshl.edu/cgi-bin/TRED/tred.cgi?
process=home

The Transcriptional Regulatory Element Database
(TRED) is an integrated repository for *trans-* and *cis-*
regulatory elements in human, rat, and mouse that is
maintained by the Zhang Lab at Cold Spring Harbor
Laboratory. Annotation in TRED is a combination of
hand curation and automation. Both known and
unknown promoters are extracted from databases (e.g.,
GenBank) and assessed for accuracy. Each promoter is
then assigned a quality level based on supporting evidence reliability. In addition to extensive annotation and
curation, notable features of TRED include simple data
retrieval, on-the-fly sequence analysis tools, and information on transcription factor binding and regulation.

TRANSFAC, http://www.gene-regulation.com/

TRANSFAC, from BIOBASE, is a comprehensive cross-species database of eukaryotic *cis*-acting regulatory DNA elements and *trans*-acting factors and their experimentally proven binding sites. The database provides extensive information on transcription factors and their structures, functions, and expression patterns. TRANS-FAC includes a tool to automatically visualize gene-regulatory networks based on interlinked factors and gene entries in the database. A reduced functionality version is freely available to academic and nonprofit organizations; a paid subscription is required for access to additional tools.

Noncoding RNA

SILVA, http://www.arb-silva.de/

The SILVA databases are comprehensive ribosomal RNA databases developed and maintained by the Microbial Genomics Group at the Max Planck Institute for Marine Microbiology and collaborators in Germany. They are the official databases of the ARB software package which provides tools for analysis and handling of sequence information. SILVA contains manually curated information on aligned small and large subunit ribosomal RNA for eukaryotes, bacteria, and archaea.

RNAdb, http://research.imb.uq.edu.au/rnadb/

RNAdb is a comprehensive mammalian database containing sequences and annotations for noncoding RNAs (ncRNA). This includes microRNAs, small nucleolar RNAs, and larger mRNA-like ncRNAs. RNAdb is maintained by the Mattick group at the Institute for Molecular Bioscience . Originally thought of as part of "junk DNA," study of ncRNAs have become a hot topic of study in recent years as they may account for 98% of all genomic output in human.

High-Throughput Screening

ArrayExpress, http://www.ebi.ac.uk/microarray-as/ae/

ArrayExpress is a public repository of gene expression and other array, genome hybridization, and chip-on-chip data. Housed by the European Bioinformatics Institute, it aims to store MIAME -compliant data according to MGED standards (Minimal Information about a Microarray Experiment; Microarray and Gene Expression Data society). ArrayExpress consists of two databases, the Repository of Microarray and Transcriptomics Data and the Warehouse of Gene Expression Profiles. Data is available for browsing and for specific queries of experiments and expression profiles.

GEO, http://www.ncbi.nlm.nih.gov/geo/

The Gene Expression Omnibus (GEO) is an NCBI-based public repository for high-throughput experimental data. The database includes single and dual channel microarray-based experiments measuring genomic DNA (SNP, arrayCGH, and ChIP-chip), mRNA, miRNA, protein abundance, nonarray techniques like mass spectrometry peptide profiling, SAGE, and quantitative sequence data. GEO supports MIAME-compliant data submissions and provides navigation for querying, browsing, and retrieving gene expression information.

Genome-Centric Databases

NCBI Genomic Biology, http://www.ncbi.nlm.nih.gov/Genomes/

The Genomic Biology Web page from NCBI compiles a variety of genome-related tools and resources, including links to organism-specific pages that in turn link to additional species-relevant databases and Web sites.

NCBI Entrez Genome, http://www.ncbi.nlm.nih.gov/sites/entrez?db=genome

Another database from NCBI, Entrez Genome supplies views of genomes, integrated physical and genetic maps, complete chromosomes, and sequence maps with contigs. It is arranged in six organism groups (archaea, bacteria, eukaryotae, plasmids, viroids, and viruses) that include both complete chromosomes, plasmids, and organelles and draft genome assemblies. Also provided is a link to a form for submitting genome sequencing project information.

NCBI Map Viewer, http://www.ncbi.nlm.nih.gov/mapview/

NCBI's Map Viewer permits browsing of a subset of organisms in Entrez Genome. It provides for searching and viewing an organism's complete genome, chromosome map display, and zoom capabilities that allows users to control details down to the level of sequence data.

Ensembl, http://www.ensembl.org/

Ensembl is a software system that produces and maintains automatic annotation on selected eukaryotic genomes. It is a joint project between EMBL, EBI, and the Wellcome Trust Sanger Institute (WTSI: http://www.

Big Data–Cellular

sanger.ac.uk/). The Web site offers free access to all data and software from the project, which focuses on vertebrate genomes. Tools enable searching for nucleotide and peptide sequences, extracting and exporting sequences in text, html, or Excel formats, and customization.

UCSC Genome Browser, http://genome.ucsc.edu/goldenPath/help/hgTracksHelp.html

The UCSC Genome Browser is a tool for viewing and interpreting genome data. It displays the requested portion of a genome of interest along with numerous customizable aligned annotation tracks. The options include mapping and sequencing tracks (e.g., GC percent), phenotype and disease associations (e.g., RGD Human QTL), genes and gene prediction tracks (e.g., RefSeq Genes), mRNA and EST tracks (e.g., human ESTs), regulation (e.g., CpG islands), comparative genomics (e.g., conservation), variation and repeats (e.g., SNP arrays), and many more. These annotation tracks are based on UCSC-computed information from publicly available sequence data as well as contributed information from global collaborators. In addition to the availability of a thorough User Guide, additional tutorials and training materials are freely provided by OpenHelix (http://www.openhelix.com/downloads/ucsc/ucsc_home.shtml).

Protein-Centric Databases

UniProt, http://www.uniprot.org/

The Universal Protein Resource (UniProt) is a protein sequence and annotation data resource developed from collaboration between the EBI, the Swiss Institute of Bioinformatics (SIB), and the PIR. UniProt is composed of multiple databases: 1) UniProt Reference Clusters (UniRef), which provides clustered sets of sequences (pulled from the other UniProt databases) for sequence similarity searches; 2) UniProt Archive (UniParc), a nonredundant and comprehensive database containing publicly available protein sequences; and 3) UniProt Knowledgebase (UniProtKB), the primary collection of annotated and functional protein information. UniProtKB, in turn, consists of two sources: 1) UniProtKB/Swiss-Prot, containing reviewed, manually annotated information and 2) UniProtKB/TrEMBL, containing unreviewed, computationally analyzed information.

Structure

PDB, http://www.rcsb.org/

The Protein Data Bank (PDB) is an information portal to biological macromolecular structures. It is maintained by two members of the Research Collaboratory for Structural Bioinformatics (RCSB), Rutgers University, the San Diego Supercomputer Center and Skaggs School of Pharmacy and Pharmaceutical Sciences at the University of California, San Diego. The PDB is an international archive of information about the 3D structures of large biological molecules, including nucleic acids and proteins. It provides resources and tools for exploring the relationship between molecular structure and sequence, function, and disease. PDB is freely available and updated weekly.

MMDB, http://www.ncbi.nlm.nih.gov/Structure/MMDB/mmdb.shtml

The Molecular Modeling DataBase (MMDB) is the NCBI database for three-dimensional (3D) biomolecular structures. It consists of data from nuclear magnetic resonance and crystallographic experiments obtained from the PDB, which is updated weekly. As with all NCBI resources, the MMDB is cross-linked to sequence databases and bibliographic information. A 3D structure viewer, CN3D, provides interactive visualization of molecular structures. In addition, proteins with significantly similar substructures can be detected using a specialized algorithm, VAST.

Functional Domain

PROSITE, http://ca.expasy.org/prosite/

PROSITE is a database of protein families and domains on the Expert Protein Analysis System proteomics server from the SIB. It is based on the premise that proteins can be grouped into families based on sequence similarities. Proteins and protein domains within a particular family tend to derive from a common ancestor and share functional characteristics. Some protein regions are conserved over evolution, thereby providing a kind of signature for a protein domain or family. PROSITE contains signatures and structure/function information for over 1000 protein families.

Conserved Domains Database, http://www.ncbi.nlm.nih.gov/sites/entrez?db=cdd

The Conserved Domains Database is a collection of multiple sequence alignments for full-length proteins and specific domains. Curated by NCBI, it also contains over 12,000 protein domain models from outside sources such as Pfam and Simple Modular Architecture Research Tool (SMART) (see below). Proteins with similar domain architectures may be located using CDART, the Conserved Domain Architecture Retrieval Tool. Conserved domains in a specific protein sequence may be identified using the CD-Search service.

Pfam, http://pfam.sanger.ac.uk/

Pfam, from the Sanger Wellcome Trust Institute, is a database of protein families represented by hidden Markov models (HMMs) and multiple sequence alignments. It consists of both manually curated entries (Pfam-A) and automatically generated entries (Pfam-B). Pfam also creates clans, which are higher-level family groupings related by structure, profile-HMM, or sequence. Data is accessed by analyzing a protein sequence for Pfam matches, viewing Pfam families or clans, searching for protein sequence or structure domains, or by keywords.

SMART, http://smart.embl-heidelberg.de/

The Simple Modular Architecture Research Tool (SMART) supports the analysis of domain architectures and the identification and annotation of genetically mobile domains. It detects greater than 500 domain families found in chromatin-associated, signaling, and extracellular proteins and is available in two modes. Normal SMART uses proteomes from Swiss-Prot, SP-TrEMBL, and Ensembl. Genomic SMART uses proteomes from completely sequenced genomes—Ensembl for metazoans, and Swiss-Prot for all others. Normal mode contains redundancies, thus Genomic mode is better for finding exact domain counts or exploring domain architectures.

ANALYSIS TOOLS

In addition to databases, many online tools are available for analysis of genes and proteins. Here are a few used for Similarity and Homology Searching, Transcription Factor Binding Site Analysis, Multiple Sequence Alignment, Pattern and Profile Searching, and Protein Structure Prediction.

Similarity and Homology Searching

BLAST, http://blast.ncbi.nlm.nih.gov/Blast.cgi

The BLAST, from NCBI, rapidly searches sequences to identify regions of similarity. BLAST compares protein or nucleotide sequences to sequence databases and calculates match statistical significance. It is used to identify gene family members as well as infer evolutionary and functional relationships between sequences. Sequences may be searched by a specific species genome, by a basic BLAST program, or by a specialized BLAST program. Basic programs enable searching a nucleotide database by using a nucleotide query (blastn), searching a protein database by using a protein (blastp) or a translated nucleotide (blastx) query, and searching a translated nucleotide database using a translated nucleotide (tblastx) or a protein (tblastn) query. Specialized programs include, but are not limited to, finding conserved domains (cds) or domain architecture (cdart), searching for immunoglobulins (IgBLAST) or single nucleotide polymorphisms (snp), and aligning two sequences (bl2seq). BLAST is one of the most widely used bioinformatics programs based on its fast algorithm.

FASTA, http://www.ebi.ac.uk/Tools/fasta/index.html

FASTA, signifying "fast-all," at EBI is another program for fast and sensitive protein or nucleotide sequence similarity searching. It uses a substitution matrix to perform optimized searches for local alignments. FASTA is equivalent to BLAST when searching for highly similar sequences. Although BLAST is faster, FASTA may be better when searching for less similar sequences.

NCBI Blink, http://www.ncbi.nlm.nih.gov/sutils/blink.cgi?mode=query

BLink (BLAST Link) from NCBI displays the results of BLAST searches that have been precomputed for all protein sequences in the Entrez Protein database. These results permit users to quickly analyze similar sequences via graphical alignments, conserved protein domains and classes, 3D structures, and taxonomic trees. A variety of display and additional options are available for customized viewing. BLink is accessed by following the appropriate link within Entrez Protein records as well as from other pages that display protein information.

Transcription Factor Binding Site Analysis

Transcription Element Search System, http://www.cbil.upenn.edu/cgi-bin/tess/tess

The Transcription Element Search System is maintained by the Computation Biology and Informatics Laboratory at the University of Pennsylvania. It is a Web tool for predicting transcription factor binding sites in DNA sequences using site or consensus strings and positional weight matrices from TRANSFAC and other databases.

RNA Structure

Vienna RNA Websuite, http://rna.tbi.univie.ac.at/

The Vienna RNA Websuite is a comprehensive collection of tools for folding, design, and analysis of RNA sequence secondary structure. It is maintained by the Institute for Theoretical Chemistry at the University of Vienna. The RNA servers that comprise the websuite provide prediction of RNA–RNA interactions, folding of single and aligned sequences, analysis of RNA folding kinetics, and more.

Multiple Sequence Alignment

LALIGN, http://www.ch.embnet.org/software/LALIGN_form.html

LALIGN is a program that finds multiple matching sub-segments in two protein or DNA sequences. It was created and is maintained by EMBnet, a European molecular biology community. LALIGN allows for multiple input formats and either local or global alignment output.

ClustalW2, http://www.ebi.ac.uk/Tools/clustalw2/index.html

ClustalW2 is an automated multiple sequence alignment program for protein or DNA sequences maintained by EMBL-EBI. It is customizable and allows for multiple output formats.

T-Coffee, http://www.tcoffee.org/

T-Coffee is a collection of tools for computing, evaluating, and manipulating multiple alignments of protein, DNA, and RNA sequences. Developed by the Comparative Bioinformatics Group at the CRG in Barcelona, it is a freeware open source package provided through an international network of Web servers.

Pattern and Profile Searching

InterProScan, http://www.ebi.ac.uk/Tools/InterProScan/

InterProScan, from EMBL-EBI is a tool that helps identify protein domains, patterns, motifs, families, and functional sites. It combines different protein signature recognition methods from the InterPro consortium member databases into one resource.

Protein Structure Prediction

PredictProtein, http://www.predictprotein.org/

PredictProtein is a service for sequence analysis and prediction of functions and structures. It was developed by the Rost Lab at Columbia University. Upon submitting a protein sequence or alignment, PredictProtein returns multiple sequence alignments, sequence motifs, localization information, structural features, protein–protein interactions, functional annotations, and more.

FUTURE DIRECTIONS

As can be gleaned from the above listing of online databases and analysis tools, there are a large number of both broad and specialized bioinformatics resources available for researchers. Recently emerging is a push to combine or link some of the most important databases into a single information resource as well as create community-annotated resources in the form of Wikis. WikiProfessional, by KNEWCO (http://www.wikiprofessional.org/portal/) created a customizable "Concept Web" that promotes a unified view of the current state of knowledge on a topic.[7,8] This revolutionary trend with the use of Wikis to encourage communication and information sharing between researchers[9] includes the development of Wikis for gene function,[10] pathways,[11] and arrays.[12] It will be interesting to see whether these new resources that rely on community involvement to succeed become standards in the field.

Another trend for sharing information (data as well as news or other items of interest) is through the use of blogs. Many top journals offer their own blogs, such as *Science* (http://blogs.sciencemag.org/) and *Nature* (http://blogs.nature.com/). *Genome Technology Online* (http://www.genome-technology.com/issues/blog/) and *Open Helix* (http://www.openhelix.com/blog/) are also excellent resources for keeping up-to-date with bioinformatics-related news, tips, and trends. In addition, many privately run blogs often supply useful information as well as provide a forum for interaction between researchers and other interested parties.

The explosion of databases and analytic tools has reached such a critical mass that a new open access journal is to be published specifically on that topic: *DATABASE: The Journal of Biological Databases and Curation* (http://www.oxfordjournals.org/our_journals/databa/). According to the publisher, *Oxford Journals*, this journal "provides a platform for the presentation of novel ideas in database research surrounding biological information, and aims to help strengthen the bridge between database developers and users." The creation of a specific journal on the topic of databases themselves, as opposed to the "science" contained within databases, is a strong statement about the importance of these resources in their own right. This bodes well for the further development of methods to organize and index these bioinformatics tools in order to assist researchers with finding the resources they need.

CONCLUSION

Getting a question related to "bioinformatics" can be overwhelming for many librarians and information professionals, regardless of whether they have a scientific background or not. In addition to the actual bioinformatics databases and analytical tools, there are many resources available to assist information professionals with bioinformatics questions, including an issue of the *Journal of the Medical Library Association* devoted to expanding library roles in bioinformatics.[13] There is a strong network of science librarians that communicate through professional organizations such as the Science and Technology section of the Association of College & Research Libraries of the American Library Association (http://www.ala.org/ala/mgrps/divs/acrl/about/sections/sts/sts.cfm), the Biomedical & Life Sciences Division of the Special Libraries Association (http://units.sla.org/division/dbio/), the Genomics Working Group of the American Medical Informatics Association (http://www.amia.org/gen-wg/gen-wg-about), the Bioinformatics Special Interest Group of the American Society for Information Science and Technology (http://www.asis.org/SIG/bio.html), and the Molecular Biology & Genomics Special Interest Group of the Medical Library Association (http://medicine.wustl.edu/~molbio/).

The purpose of this encyclopedia entry is not to relate everything there is to know about the field of bioinformatics, as the subject is too vast and rapidly growing. Rather, the purpose is to provide definitions and a little background about the topic and provide a few key resources for help with locating bioinformatics-related information.

REFERENCES

1. *Atlas of Protein Sequence and Structure*; Dayhoff, M. O., Ed.; National Biomedical Research Foundation: Washington, DC, 1978; Vol. 5, Supplement 3.
2. Fleischmann, R.D.; Adams, M.D.; White, O.; Clayton, R.A.; Kirkness, E.F.; Kerlavage, A.R.; Bult, C.J.; Tomb, J.F.; Dougherty, B.A.; Merrick, J.M. Whole-genome random sequencing and assembly of *Haemophilus influenza Rd*. Science **1995**, *269* (5223), 496–512.
3. Lander, E.S. Initial sequencing and analysis of the human genome. Nature **2001**, *409* (6822), 860–921.
4. Venter, J.C. The sequence of the human genome. Science **2001**, *291* (5507), 1304–1351.
5. Chen, Y.B.; Chattopadhyay, A.; Bergen, P.; Gadd, C.; Tannery, N. The Online Bioinformatics Resources Collection at the University of Pittsburgh Health Sciences Library System—a one-stop gateway to online bioinformatics databases and software tools. Nucl. Acids Res. **2007**, *35*, D780–D785.
6. Yamamoto, Y.; Takagi, T. OReFiL: an online resource finder for life sciences. BMC Bioinformatics **2007**, *8* (1), 287.
7. Giles, J. Key biology databases go wiki. Nature **2007**, *445* (7129), 691–691.
8. Mons, B. Calling on a million minds for community annotation in WikeProteins. Genome Biol. **2008**, *9*(5), R89.
9. Hu, J.C. The emerging world of wikis. Science **2008**, *320* (5881), 1289–1290.
10. Huss, J.W.; Orozco, C.; Goodale, J.; Wu, C.; Batalov, S.; Vickers, T.J.; Valafar, F.; Su, A.I. A gene wiki for community annotation of gene function. PLoS Biol. **2008**, *6* (7), e175.
11. Pico, A.R.; Kelder, T.; van Iersel, M.P.; Hanspers, K.; Conklin, B.R.; Evelo, C. WikiPathways: Pathway editing for the people. PLoS Biol. **2008**, *6* (7), e184.
12. Stokes, T.H.; Torrance, J.T.; Li, H.; Wand, M.D. Array-Wiki: An enabling technology for sharing public microarray data repositories and meta-analyses. BMC Bioinformatics **2008**, *9* (suppl 6), S18.
13. Geer, R.C.; Rein, D.C. Building the role of medical libraries in bioinformatics. J. Med. Libr. Assoc. **2006**, *94* (3), 284–348.

BIBLIOGRAPHY

1. Barnes, M.R.; Gray, I.C. *Bioinformatics for Geneticists*; John Wiley & Sons, Inc.: West Sussex, England, 2003.
2. Baxevanis, A.D.; Davison, D.B.; Page, R.D.M.; Petsko, G.A.; Stein, L.D.; Stormo, G.D. In Current *Protocols in Bioinformatics*; John Wiley & Sons, Inc.: Hoboken, NJ, 2003.
3. Baxevanis, A.D.; Francis Ouellette, B.F. In *Bioinformatics: A Practical Guide to the Analysis of Genes and Proteins*; 3rd Ed.; John Wiley & Sons, Inc.: Hoboken, NJ, 2005.
4. Burgoon, L.D.; Zacharewski, T.R. Bioinformatics: Databasing and gene annotation. In *Methods in Molecular Biology: Essential Concepts in Toxicogenomics*; Mendrick, D. L., Mattes, W. B., Eds.; Humana Press: Totowa, NJ, 2008; Vol. 60, 145–57.
5. Campbell, A.M.; Heyer, L.J. *Discovering Genomics, Proteomics, and Bioinformatics*; 2nd Ed.; Pearson Education, Inc.: San Francisco, CA, 2007.
6. Claverie, J.M.; Notredame, C. *Bioinformatics for Dummies*; 2nd Ed.; Wiley Publishing, Inc.: Indianapolis, IN, 2007.
7. Lesk, A.M. *Introduction to Bioinformatics*; 2nd Ed.; Oxford University Press: New York, NY, 2005.
8. Mount, D.W. *Bioinformatics: Sequence and Genome Analysis*; 2nd Ed.; Cold Spring Harbor Laboratory Press: Cold Spring Harbor, NY, 2004.
9. O'Grady, T. Bioinformatics: a brief review of resources on the Web. C&RL News **2008**, July/August, 404–407.
10. Pevsner, J. *Bioinformatics and Functional Genomics*; John Wiley & Sons, Inc.: Hoboken, NJ, 2003.
11. Scherer, S. *A Short Guide to the Human Genome*; Cold Spring Harbor Laboratory Press: Cold Spring Harbor, NY, 2008.
12. Tramontano, A. *Introduction to Bioinformatics*; Chapman & Hall/CRC: Boca Raton, FL, 2007.
13. Zvelebil, M.; Baum, J.O. *Understanding Bioinformatics*; Garland Science: New York, NY, 2008.

Boolean Algebras

A.R. Bednarek
University of Florida, Gainesville, Florida, U.S.A.

Abstract

Boolean algebra, named after the 19th century mathematician and logician, George Boole, has contributed to many aspects of computer science and information science. In information science, Boolean logic forms the basis of most end-user search systems, from searches in online databases and catalogs, to uses of search engines in information seeking on the World Wide Web.

INTRODUCTION

In this entry, attention is focused on mathematical models of proven utility in the area of information handling, namely, Boolean algebras. Following some general comments concerning mathematical models, particular examples of Boolean algebras, serving as motivation for the subsequent axiomatization, are presented. Some elementary theorems are cited, particularly the very important representation theorem that justifies, in some sense, the focusing of attention on a particular Boolean algebra, namely, the algebra of classes, and applications more directly related to the information sciences are given.

Running the risk of redundancy, attention will be called to an often-repeated observation, but one of extreme importance in applications of mathematics to physical problems. Referring to Fig. 1, it is important to realize that when one constructs a mathematical model as a representation of a physical phenomenon, one is abstracting and, as a consequence, the model formulated is doomed to imperfection. That is, one can never formally mirror the physical phenomenon, and must always be satisfied with an imperfect copy. However, following the initial commitment to a model, the logic that one appeals to dictates the resultant theorems derived within the framework of the model. Of course, the depth of the theorems realized is limited by the sophistication of the model as well as the ingenuity of those who attempt to formulate the propositions within it. After theorems are derived within the framework of the model, they are interpreted relative to the physical situation that motivated the model.

It is not necessary to go very deeply into mathematics before facing the necessity of examining, in some detail, this cycle and developing a feeling for its power as well as its limitations. By way of example, almost any student of calculus encounters, in one form or another, the following problem:

The deceleration of a ship in still water is proportional to its velocity. If the velocity is v_0 feet per second at the time the power is shut off, show that the distance S the ship travels in the next t seconds is $S = (v_0/k)[1 - e^{-kt}]$, where k is the constant of proportionality.

HISTORY

The desired equation relating the distance traveled to the time is easily arrived at by means of the calculus. However, a close look at the solution reveals a few puzzling aspects. When does the ship stop? The conclusion is that it never stops. How far does it go? The conclusion is that it goes no further than v_0/k, that is, the distance it travels is bounded. Sympathy is due the beginning student of calculus who is puzzled by these observations, but, too often, we neglect to focus our attention on the source of the puzzlement. It really has nothing to do with the limit process that plays such an integral role in analysis, nor must we drag poor Zeno into the picture. This disturbing conclusion is not the consequence of any faulty mathematics, but is more directly related to the naïveté of the original model. If we say that the deceleration of a ship in still water (an idealization in itself) is proportional only to its velocity, then the conclusion that asserts itself is that the ship never stops but only goes a finite distance.

The usual remedy applied in such cases as the ship problem is to construct a more sophisticated model, that is, a model that takes into account more of the phenomena observed. For example, in the ship problem, the assertion that the deceleration is proportional only to the velocity might be amended to include friction in some way, resulting in an equation of greater complexity, the formulation and solution of which require a more general mathematical model. We might extend the preceding model to look like Fig. 2.

Encyclopedia of Information Systems and Technology, DOI: 10.1081/E-EIST-120008970

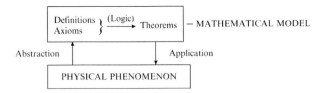

Fig. 1 Applying mathematics to physical problems.

The great power of mathematics lies in its ability to reflect several different phenomena at one time, and the theorems derived within the framework of a single axiomatization of these varied phenomena will, in turn, be applicable to each of them. However, the trade-off that exists between generalization and depth must constantly be kept in mind. That is, it should be remembered that it is difficult to prove deep theorems in very general models. But when axioms are added to the model, the phenomena that the model reflects begin to be delimited, and certainly one does not wish to undermine the real power of mathematics, that is, its ability to treat a variety of situations at the same time.

Examples

We now turn our attention to an examination of some of the particular examples of the model that is the principal concern of this entry, Boolean algebras. One must keep in mind that the common characteristics of these models are precisely those that will constitute the elements of our later axiomatization. To avoid infinite regress a certain level of sophistication on the part of the reader, if not actual mathematical experience, is assumed.

Example 1 (a finite algebra)

The system considered in this example consists of the two digits, 0 and 1, and two binary operations of multiplication, "$\cdot$," and addition, "$+$." The operations are defined by the multiplication and addition tables shown.

If x, y, and z are any *variables* that are allowed to assume one of the two values 0 or 1, then the structure defined earlier has an algebra possessing (among others) the following properties:

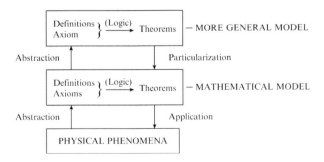

Fig. 2 Extending the model.

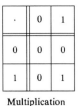

$\cdot$	0	1
0	0	0
1	0	1

$+$	0	1
0	0	1
1	1	1

Multiplication   Addition

Scheme 1 Multiplication and addition tables.

$$x \cdot x = x \qquad x + x = x \tag{1a}$$

$$x \cdot y = y \cdot x \qquad x + y = y + x \tag{1b}$$

$$x \cdot (y \cdot z) = (x \cdot y) \cdot z \qquad x + (y + z) = (x + y) + z \tag{1c}$$

$$(x \cdot y) + x = x \qquad (x + y) \cdot x = x \tag{1d}$$

$$x \cdot (y + z) = (x \cdot y) + (x \cdot z)$$
$$x + (y \cdot z) = (x + y) \cdot (y + z) \tag{1e}$$

Each of the aforementioned can be verified by a consideration of all the possible values of the variables.

If B is a collection consisting of the elements 0 and 1, and for each x in Bx' is defined by $x' = 1$ if $x = 0$, and $x' = 0$ if $x = 1$, then

$$x \cdot x' = 0 \qquad \text{and} \quad x + x' = 1$$
$$0 \cdot x = 0 \quad 1 \cdot x = x \quad \text{and} \quad 0 + x = x \quad 1 + x = x \tag{1f}$$

We let $[B; \cdot, +, {}']$ denote the system described in Example 1.

Example 2 (algebra of propositions)

The elements in this example are *propositions*, that is, statements to which it is possible to assign one of the truth values "true" or "false." Two propositions p and q are defined to be equal if and only if they have the *same* truth value. We consider the two logical binary operations of *conjunction* and *disjunction* as well as the unary (operating on a single proposition as contrasted with a binary operation, which operates on pairs of propositions) operation of *negation*. The conjunction of the propositions p and q is denoted by pq and is the proposition corresponding to that obtained by applying the logical connective "and." The conjunction is defined to be true only if both p and q are true. Otherwise it is false. The disjunction of p and q, denoted by $p + q$, is the proposition corresponding to that obtained by applying the logical connective "or." The proposition $p + q$ is false if and only if both p and q are false. The negation of p, denoted by $\bar{p}$, is the proposition having truth values opposite those of p. It corresponds to the logical statement, "It is false that p."

p	q	pq
T	T	T
T	F	F
F	T	F
F	F	F

p	q	$p+q$
T	T	T
T	F	T
F	T	T
F	F	F

p	$\bar{q}$
T	F
F	T

| | Conjunction | | Disjunction | | Negation |

Scheme 2   Conjunction, disjunction, and negation.

All of the aforementioned can be summarized well by employing "truth tables" that give the truth values of compound statements, realized by applying the operations discussed to the truth values of the component propositions.

One can verify that, in view of the definitions given, if p, q, and r are any propositions, the following statements hold.

$$pp = p \qquad p + p = p \tag{2a}$$

$$pq = qp \qquad p + q = q + p \tag{2b}$$

$$p(qr) = (pq)r \qquad p + (q + r) = (p + q) + r \tag{2c}$$

$$(pq) + p = p \qquad (p + q)p = p \tag{2d}$$

$$p(q + r) = pq + pr$$
$$p + (qr) = (p + q)(q + r) \tag{2e}$$

$$p\bar{p} \text{ is always false and } p + \bar{p} \text{ is always true} \tag{2f}$$

Denoting $p\bar{p}$ by 0 and $p + \bar{p}$ by 1 we have

$$0q = 0 \quad 1q = q \quad 0 + q = q \quad 1 + q = q$$

(*Note*: It is easy to see that $p\bar{p} = q\bar{q}$ and $p + \bar{p} = q + \bar{q}$ for any propositions p and q.)

We illustrate the employment of the truth table technique in the verification of part of the assertion in Eq. 2e, namely, that $p + (qr) = (p + q)(p + r)$.

Since the columns headed "$p + qr$" and "$(p + q)(p + r)$" have identical entries, the propositions $p + qr$ and $(p + q)(p + r)$ have the same truth value and are therefore equal.

p	q	r	qr	$p+qr$	$p+q$	$p+r$	$(p+q)(p+r)$
T	T	T	T	T	T	T	T
T	T	F	F	T	T	T	T
T	F	T	F	T	T	T	T
T	F	F	F	T	T	T	T
F	T	T	T	T	T	T	T
F	T	F	F	F	T	F	F
F	F	T	F	F	F	T	F
F	F	F	F	F	F	F	F

Scheme 3   Truth table for $p + (qr) = (p + q)(p + r)$.

The structure described in Example 2 is denoted in the sequel by $[\mathscr{P};, +, -]$.

Example 3 (algebra of sets)

The term *set* is taken as undefined and used synonymously with class, aggregate, and collection. The objects that constitute a set E are called the *elements* of E. To denote the logical relation of "being an element of E" we use the notation $x \in E$. This is read: "x is an element of E." The denial of this relation is symbolized by $x \notin E$.

The notation of $E = \{x | P(x)\}$ denotes the set E consisting of all x for which the proposition $P(x)$ is true. When the set under consideration is finite, it is often denoted by a simple listing of its elements; thus, $E = \{a,b\}$ is the set consisting of the elements a and b.

If $A = \{x | P(x)\}$ and there are no elements that satisfy the proposition $P(x)$, A is said to be the *empty set*. The empty (or *null*) set is denoted by ϕ.

If the sets E and F have the property that every element of E is an element of F, E is called a *subset* of F; this is denoted by $E \subset F$. If the set E is a subset of F, but F is not a subset of E, then E is said to be a *proper subset* of F, or F *properly contains* E. The empty set ϕ is a subset of every set.

Two sets E and F are *equal*, written $E = F$, if and only if $E \subset F$ and $F \subset E$.

Given two sets E and F, we define the *union*, denoted by $E \cup F$, by the set equation

$$E \cup F = \{x | x \in E \text{ or } x \in F\}$$

Similarly, the *intersection* of E and F, denoted by $E \cap F$, is defined by

$$E \cap F = \{x | x \in E \text{ and } x \in F\}$$

In general, consideration centers on subsets of a fixed set often referred to as the *universal set*. In particular, if X is the universal set, we let $\mathscr{P}(X)$ denote the set of all subsets of X. The set $\mathscr{P}(X)$ is often called the *power set* of X. If $E \in \mathscr{P}(X)$, then the *complement* of E, denoted by E', is defined as $E' = \{x | x \in X \text{ and } x \notin E\}$. If E and F are elements of $\mathscr{P}(X)$, that is, subsets of X, then the *difference* of the sets E and F, denoted by $E - F$, is the set defined by

$$E - F = \{x | x \in E \text{ and } x \notin F\}$$

It should be noted that $E - F = E \cap F'$.

It is often helpful to employ the schematics shown in Fig. 3 in visualizing the set-theoretic relations and operations defined earlier. The rectangular area represents the universal set X; subsets of X are denoted by areas within the rectangle.

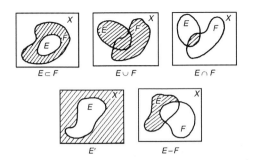

Fig. 3 Set-theoretic relations and operations.

Focusing our attention on a particular universal set X and its power set $\mathcal{P}(X)$, it is easy to verify the following properties (in no sense exhaustive) of the algebra of sets, where E, F, and G are arbitrary subsets of X.

$$E \cap E = E \qquad E \cup E = E \tag{3a}$$

$$E \cap F = F \cap E \qquad E \cup F = F \cup E \tag{3b}$$

$$E \cap (F \cap G) = (E \cap F) \cap G$$
$$E \cup (F \cup G) = (E \cup F) \cup G \tag{3c}$$

$$(E \cap F) \cup E = E \qquad (E \cup F) \cap E = E \tag{3d}$$

$$E \cap (F \cup G) = (E \cap F) \cup (E \cap G)$$
$$E \cup (F \cap G) = (E \cup F) \cap (E \cup G) \tag{3e}$$

$$E \cap E\prime = \phi \qquad\qquad E \cup E\prime = X$$
$$\phi \cap E = \phi \quad X \cap E = E \qquad \phi \cup E = E \quad X \cup E = E \tag{3f}$$

In the sequel we denote the preceding algebra of sets by $[\,\mathcal{P}(X);\, \cap,\, \cap,\, '\,]$.

Axiomatization

In the previous section we examined three structures possessing some common properties, namely, (1i), (2i), and (3i), where $i = 1, 2, 3, 4, 5, 6$. We abstract to construct the important mathematical (see Fig. 1) model called a *Boolean algebra*, named in honor of G. Boole who first studied it in 1847.[1,2]

Table 1 Boolean algebra and examples

Boolean algebra	Example 1	Example 2	Example 3
B	Set {0,1}	Set of all propositions	Set $\mathcal{P}(X)$ of all subsets of a fixed set X
$\wedge$	$\cdot$	Conjunction	Intersection
$\vee$	$+$	Disjunction	Union
$'$	$'$	Negation	Complementation
0	0	$p\bar{p}$	Empty set ϕ
1	1	$p + \bar{p}$	Universal set X

A *Boolean algebra* is a set B with two binary operations $\wedge$ (cap) and $\vee$ (cup) and a unary operation (complementation) satisfying the following axioms:

$$x \wedge x = x \text{ and } x \vee x = x \tag{4a}$$

$$x \wedge y = y \wedge x \text{ and } x \vee y = y \vee x \tag{4b}$$

$$x \wedge (y \wedge z) = (x \wedge y) \wedge z \text{ and } x \vee (y \vee z)$$
$$= (x \vee y) \vee z \tag{4c}$$

$$(x \wedge y) \vee x = x \text{ and } (x \vee y) \wedge x = x \tag{4d}$$

$$x \wedge (y \vee z) = (x \wedge y) \vee (x \wedge z) \text{ and } x \vee (y \wedge z)$$
$$= (x \vee y) \wedge (x \vee z) \tag{4e}$$

B contains *distinct* elements 0 and 1 such that

$$x \wedge x' = 0 \qquad\qquad \text{and} \quad x \vee x' = 1$$
$$0 \wedge x = 0 \quad 1 \wedge x = x \quad \text{and} \quad 0 \vee x = x \quad 1 \vee x = 1 \tag{4f}$$

This is by no means the only axiomatization possible,[3] but it is probably the one that is most commonly used.

To emphasize the relationship between the aforementioned axiomatization and the preceding particularizations, (Examples 1, 2, and 3) we identify in a tabular form the corresponding structural elements (Table 1).

We now prove a particular theorem to illustrate the generation of results within the framework of the model and their subsequent application.

Theorem. If $(B;\, \wedge,\, \vee,\, ')$ is a Boolean algebra, then for any x and y in B we have

$$x'' = x \tag{i}$$

$$(x \wedge y)' = x' \vee y' \tag{ii}$$

Proof. First of all we prove that every element has only one complement. Suppose $\bar{x}$ is an element such that $x \wedge \bar{x} = 0$ and $x \vee \bar{x} = 0$. Then

$$\bar{x} = \bar{x} \wedge 1 = \bar{x} \wedge (x \vee x') = (\bar{x} \wedge x) \vee (\bar{x} \wedge x')$$
$$= 0 \vee (\bar{x} \wedge x') = \bar{x} \wedge x'$$

but

$$x' = x' \wedge 1 = x' \wedge (x \vee \bar{x}) = (x' \wedge x) \vee (x' \wedge \bar{x})$$
$$= 0 \vee (x' \wedge \bar{x}) = (x' \wedge \bar{x})$$

and since $\bar{x} \wedge x' = x' \wedge \bar{x}$, we have $\bar{x} \wedge x'$. We then apply the preceding by demonstrating that $(x \wedge y) \wedge (x' \vee y') = 0$ and $(x \wedge y) \wedge (x' \vee y') = 1$, so that $(x \wedge y)' = x' \vee y'$.

 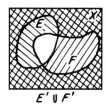

Fig. 4 Complement of intersection of two sets equals union of their complements.

$$(x \wedge y) \wedge (x' \vee y') = [(x \wedge y) \wedge x'] \vee [(x \wedge y) \wedge y']$$
$$= [(y \wedge x) \wedge x'] \vee [(x \wedge y) \wedge y']$$
$$= [y \wedge (x \wedge x')] \vee [x \wedge (y \wedge y')]$$
$$= [y \wedge 0] \vee [x \wedge 0] = 0 \vee 0 = 0$$
$$(x \wedge y) \vee (x' \vee y') = [(x \wedge y) \vee x'] \vee y'$$
$$= [(x \vee x') \wedge (y \vee x')] \vee y' = [1 \wedge (y \vee x')] \vee y'$$
$$= (y \vee x') \vee y' = (x' \vee y) \vee y'$$
$$= x' \vee (y \vee y') = x' \vee 1 = 1$$

An interpretation (application) of this theorem in Example 2 yields the fact that the negation of the conjunction of two propositions is the disjunction of the negations of each of them. For example, "it is false that x is a positive integer and x is greater than or equal to 5" is logically equivalent to the proposition "x is not a positive integer or x is less than 5."

An interpretation of the above in Example 2 yields the set-theoretic equation

$$(E \cap F)' = E' \cup F'$$

that is, the complement of the intersection of two sets is equal to the union of their complements, as shown in Fig. 4.

We describe very briefly some of the more significant results and developments in the theory of Boolean algebras. For a comprehensive treatment of the subject, see Birkhoff[3] and Halmos[4] and their bibliographies.

Every Boolean algebra can be made into a ring with identity in which every element is multiplicatively idempotent; that is, $x^2 = x$ for every x. This is accomplished by defining addition and multiplication as follows:

$$x + y = (x \wedge y') \vee (x' \wedge y) \text{ and } xy = x \wedge y$$

Because rings are more familiar and more carefully studied, many of the useful concepts can be translated into the context of Boolean algebras.

Conversely, if one starts with a ring with identity in which every element is idempotent (usually called a Boolean ring), defining $\wedge$ and $\vee$ by

$$x \wedge y = xy \quad x \vee y = x + y + xy$$

the Boolean ring is converted into a Boolean algebra.

Two Boolean algebras, B_1 and B_2, are said to be *isomorphic* if there exists a function $h: B_1 \rightarrow B_2$ that maps B_1 onto B_2 in such a way that distinct elements of B_1 are mapped onto distinct elements of B_2, and h preserves the operations; that is,

$h(x \wedge y) = h(x) \wedge h(y)$; $h(x \vee y) = h(x) \vee h(y)$; and $h(x') = h(x)'$.

If X is a compact Hausdorff space, then the class of sets that are both open and closed forms a Boolean algebra. A topological space is totally disconnected if the only components (maximal connected sets) are points. There is a very important *representation theorem* in the theory of Boolean algebras, the Stone Representation Theorem (M. H. Stone[5]). If B is a Boolean algebra, then a compact totally disconnected Hausdorff space S exists such that B is isomorphic to the Boolean algebra of all open–closed subsets of S.

An Application

We consider here one modest application of the preceding to switching theory. Switching theory is concerned with circuits composed of elements that can assume a finite number of discrete states, most commonly two states. These circuits are modeled as described earlier, and the models are analyzed. This is an idealization; the models neglect such characteristics as stability, temperature effects, and transition times. The theory of Boolean algebras has played an important role in the analysis of these models for circuits made of binary (two-state) devices.

A *switching function* is a rule by which the output of a composite circuit can be ascertained from the states of its components. If the variables x, y, and z denote switches and each switch can assume one of the states, open or closed (0 or 1), then the function $w = x \wedge y$ describes the output of a series circuit containing the switches x and y. Similarly, $t = x \vee y$ is a function describing a parallel circuit containing the switches x and y. These components, along with the negation function (x' is a switch that is open whenever x is closed and closed whenever x is open), allow the construction and analysis of complex circuits. This analysis can be carried out by the use of truth tables, and the circuits can be indicated by a diagram, as shown in Fig. 5.

With this interpretation it is readily seen that the above is a Boolean algebra. For example, the verification of axiom (Id) involves the observation that the circuits in Fig. 6 are equivalent.

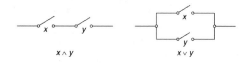

Fig. 5 Using switching functions to illustrate truth tables.

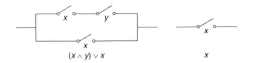

Fig. 6 Verification of axiom (Id) using switching functions.

After observing that it is indeed a Boolean algebra, the machinery of that algebra may be used to synthesize circuits, consider questions of realizability, minimize circuitry, and so forth. We can only hint at the possible applications.[6]

REFERENCES

1. Boole, G. *The Mathematical Analysis of Logic*; Cambridge, 1847.
2. Boole, G. *An Investigation of the Laws of Thought*; London, UK, 1854.
3. Birkhoff, G. *Lattice Theory*; Providence: RI, 1961; 155.
4. Halmos, P.R. *Lectures on Boolean Algebras*; Van Nostrand: Princeton, NJ, 1963.
5. Stone, M.H. The theory of representations for Boolean algebras. Trans. Am. Math. Soc. **1936**, *40*, 37–111.
6. Flegg, H.G. *Boolean Algebra and Its Application*; Wiley: New York, NY, 1964.

Big Data–
Cellular

Business Informatics

Markus Helfert
School of Computing, Dublin City University, Dublin, Ireland

Abstract

The rapid changes in recent years demand constant evaluation and modification of education programs. The following contribution summarizes some aspects of study programs in information systems (IS) and focuses on business informatics (BI). As a stream of IS, BI can be described as a method and model-centered approach focusing on business IS. The success of BI derives from the benefits that arise when business administration concepts are combined with computer science technologies and software engineering principles to form a coherent methodological approach. In addition, addressing the need for an innovative and cross-disciplinary study model to equip graduates with transformation skills we have developed a master's study program in BI. By discussing an example curriculum, this entry outlines the core elements of this program and gives direction for BI as a study domain.

INTRODUCTION

Many universities have offered various programs related to information systems (IS). However, the rapid changes of late demand constant evaluation and modification of education programs. These challenges include, for instance, the move toward programs, which are more applied and professionally orientated. The Bologna Declaration in Europe with its three-level study structure as well as the increasing pressure to ensure funding within most departments adds further pressure to many universities. Despite attempts being made to provide reference to curricula and guidelines, many universities and faculties struggle with the proper direction and design of the IS curricula.

Common reference curricula related to IS are, for example, the IS 2002: Curriculum Guidelines for Undergraduate Degree Programs in Information Systems; and the MSIS 2000: Model Curriculum and Guidelines for Graduate Degree Programs in Information Systems.[1,2] Although proposed for many years, several discussions and disagreement exist on the content and direction of IS curricula and IS as a discipline. A joint task force of the Association for Computing Machinery and Association of Information System is aiming at revising the IS 2002 undergraduate curriculum.[3] At the same time, we are experiencing decreasing enrolments in IS programs worldwide.[4]

To summarize aspects of the existing study programs in IS we focus on business informatics (BI). This entry aims to illustrate differences between BI and traditional IS study programs.[5] We structure the entry as following. First, we summarize the context of information technology (IT)- and IS-related study programs. Then we outline the main characteristics of BI. In addition,

we provide a generic framework for IS study programs. Finally, we present an overview of an example study program in BI—the European M.Sc. in Business Informatics at Dublin City University. We conclude the entry by outlining some key challenges of BI as a study domain.

CONTEXT OF IS STUDY PROGRAMS

One of the IS-related challenges at present is the increase in complexity and the growing interdependency between business aspects and IT. Organizational components like business strategy, rules, procedures, and processes, and the organization's application systems, including hardware, software, and databases, affect and influence each other. Any change in one of these components typically requires modifications in other components, whereas existing systems and structures often act as a constraint on organizations. As a consequence, the demand for graduates capable of analyzing complex information networks and project managers managing large IT projects is expected to increase. Therefore, subjects such as application integration, enterprise architecture, information management, and business process management are increasingly important.[6] In addition, claims that IT is no longer a source of strategic advantage indicate the move from technology-oriented jobs to more business-oriented roles. Universities are expected to provide, in addition to core knowledge of design and implementation of IS, a broad business and real-world perspective.

Graduates should show strong analytical and critical thinking skills as well as interpersonal communication and team skills. A further necessary area of expertise

Encyclopedia of Information Systems and Technology, DOI: 10.1081/E-EIST-120043667

for today's IT graduates is the international environment. In a decade that has seen the enlargement of the European Union and that globalized it, it is necessary for business and IT personnel to be competent to work in other countries and to work in multicultural teams. Graduates may need to understand how to manage geographically and ethnically diverse teams. Therefore, students should gain practical experience of studying and working abroad, by which they will be exposed to the business culture of another country. Spending time in another country offers many advantages: a chance to acquire new skills, to participate in multicultural teams, and to experience the benefits of cultural diversity.

BI AND IS

Traditionally, universities have focused on management and business studies as well as on computing, software engineering, and computer science. Computing and computer science (e.g., basic informatics) address technical and theoretical bases of IT and software systems. Business and management provide knowledge of the principal functions of management and focus on business operations and decision making (behavioral and organizational components). The combination of both disciplines, which include technical and social components, is generally described as IS. Terms such as management information systems (MIS), business information systems (BIS), or information systems and management (ISM) are also common.

Besides these courses, a growing number of universities, particularly in central and northern Europe, are offering undergraduate and postgraduate degrees in *business informatics*. The term seems well established in the German-speaking countries; however, it is often considered controversial. Indeed, BI stems from the literal translation of the German term "Wirtschaftsinformatik," but there seems a controversy about the characteristics of BI. BI is sometimes assumed to be equal to the broad area of IS, though some indications exist that BI has a stronger emphasis on engineering principles and methods.[7] To provide a foundation and to frame the subject in the IS discipline, in the following we outline the characteristics of BI.

Management-oriented IS programs sometimes lack consideration of a *methodological* combination of the theoretical work of computer science with a practical orientation toward designing systems and applications. This methodological focus is the area of BI, which complements traditional areas of IS that focus on *explaining* real-world scenarios. BI aims to engage constructively to develop solutions tailored to business problems. It takes an active role in aligning business strategy, corporate goals, business processes, and IT. The core element

of BI is a methodological approach to describe, explain, predict, and design information and communication systems. It involves the development of terminologies, models, and architectures that are explicit and sharable.

BI can be characterized as

- Interdisciplinary.[8]
- Focusing on business IS as socio-technical systems comprising both machines and humans.[9–12]
- Concerning the inception, development, implementation, maintenance, and utilization of business IS.[13,14]
- Describing the relationship between humans, business functions, information, and communication systems, and technology.[15]

BI can be summarized as a socio-technological and business-oriented subject with *engineering* penetration.[13] As a science discipline, BI is categorized as

- Applied science that studies real-world phenomena.
- Formal science that creates and applies formal description methods and models.
- An engineering discipline that systematically designs and constructs information and communication systems.[11]

The success of the subject derives from the benefits that arise when business administration concepts are integrated with computer science technologies and software engineering principles to form a coherent methodological approach. It centres on IS architectures and business processes and provides a systematic design and construction of organizational information and communication systems.

BI Subjects

In the following we present a framework for BI and IS for which we amalgamated prominent curriculum guidelines; an undergraduate and a graduate model curriculum predominantly referred to in the Anglophone area with one frequently referred reference curriculum in the German-speaking area.

- The model curriculum and guidelines for graduate degree programs in IS *(MSIS 2000).*[1]
- The latest version of the IS undergraduate model curriculum *(IS 2002).*[2]
- The recommendation for BI at universities *(BI recommendation).*[8]

The work of IS model curricula represent almost 30 years of experience in curriculum development. Started in the early 1970s by the Association for Computing

Machinery (ACM) other organizations, including Data Processing Management Association/Association of Information Technology Professionals(DPMA/AITP), International Federation for Information Processing (IFIP), and Association for Information Systems (AIS), have aided model curriculum development. The IS 2002 model curriculum is the latest version for an undergraduate IS curriculum, published by the ACM and AIS. IS 2002 includes detailed course descriptions and prescriptive advice on how to offer an IS undergraduate degree program. For our study we used the latest version of the IS 2002 undergraduate curriculum, although the existing version is now being reviewed by a joint ACM/AIS task force. The MSIS 2000 model curriculum was published by ACM and AIS as a guideline for master degree programs in IS. At a master's level, the curriculum is designed to accommodate students from a wide variety of backgrounds. It considers a set of interrelated building blocks, including foundational skills, core subjects, integration subjects, and career tracks. Emphasizing on career development skills, the curriculum includes oral, written, and presentation skills; people and business skills; and ethics and professionalism.

The model curricula are explicitly developed to include knowledge elements from three major computing disciplines: computer science, software engineering, and IS. It accumulates long experience in IS curriculum development and provides a coherent structure for a study program in IS. Thus, these model curricula seem to be appropriate, even though the model curricula are primarily based on the educational system and degree structures common to the United States and Canada, with limited acceptance and use outside of this area. The two-level educational structures underlying the curricula proved to be of advantage, as many European universities are restructuring their study programs toward a two-phase curriculum with bachelor and master degrees.

The third curricula we used, the recommendation for BI, is issued by the German Society for Informatics and the Association of University Professors of Management, Germany. It is aimed at providing common directions for education in BI at universities. In contrast to the MSIS curriculum, which provides a detailed recommendation for a curriculum, the BI recommendation is intended as a guideline and is focused on key qualifications and core subjects to be taught. The BI recommendation is mainly oriented toward a study program of nine semesters, leading to a degree of "Diplom-Wirtschaftsinformatik" (diploma/master level in BI).

To cluster subjects and to provide a list of taught subjects, we customized the framework in an iterative process involving expert opinion from 10 academics from different countries. The structure follows the proposed curriculum building blocks in the MSIS

curriculum. However, in order to accommodate particular subjects taught in some study programs, we added subject blocks of mathematics and logic, structural science, legislation, and economics, and business engineering, and included often taught business subjects, for example, logistics, procurement, and supply chain management. The list of career electives and domain-specific subjects presented here illustrates just some of the possible topics. The framework is presented in Table 1.

Architectural Focus of BI

In contrast to IS, BI appears to have a stronger focus on mathematics, logic, and structural science.[7] One reason for this could be the focus on the *systematic* construction and the application of methodological principles, which are often stated as typical for BI study programs. Indeed, mathematical principles are perceived as essential in order to systematically construct, formalize, and analyze models and architectures of IS.[16]

In this regard, business informaticians are often described as IS architects (in the sense of engineers) who are actively and systematically analyzing and designing business IS. Central to this is the subject "Information System Architecture." IS Architecture describes IS through various models and refer to both a dynamic view in the form of processes and the specification of the overall structure, logical components, and the logical interrelationships of a system.[17] The conceptual description of both views builds the methodological framework for understanding the alignment of software applications and information technologies, business processes, and the corporate strategy.[18] One example of an important architectural framework for BI is ARIS—architecture of integrated information systems.[19]

STUDY PROGRAM IN BI

In keeping with the points identified herein, we outline an example of a BI study program, introduced at Dublin City University—the European M.Sc. in Business Informatics. As an example, we provide an overview of the program in order to give guidelines for similar programs in BI.

The central focus of the proposed curriculum for BI is to qualify individuals to lead IS-related transformations of business. This enables them to apply technological solutions and develop IS architectures to solve business problems of organizations. With this goal in mind, the curriculum focuses on an engineering perspective and the integration of cultural studies. The program is intended for students who have achieved a

Table 1 Study framework

Informatics and fundamentals in engineering	Business and economics	IS	Integration and enterprise engineering	Informatics in action (representative)
Information and Communication Technology (hardware, software, networks, and communication technology) Programming and algorithms, data, and object structures *Mathematics and Logic* (analysis, linear algebra, numeric, logic) *Structural Science* (decision theory and methods for strategic decision making (e.g., risk analysis), statistics and quantitative models and methods, operations research, computational modeling, and simulation)	Accounting and financing Marketing, production, procurement, logistics Organization, human resources, and corporate management Legislation and economics	*Fundamentals of Information Systems* (types of IS, IS industry, IS relevant legal frameworks, management, and IS) *Principles of Business Information Systems* (principles of functional and process orientation and industry solutions) *Data Engineering* (data modeling and management, knowledge engineering, and business intelligence) *System and Software Engineering* (analysis, modeling, and design) Managing data communication and networking *Information Management* (information, knowledge, and people, project, and change management, IS/IT policy, and strategy, ethics, and privacy)	Business Engineering and IS Architecture Integrating IS Functions, Processes and Data Integrating IS Technologies and Systems	Academia and research Academic and research libraries Biochemistry and molecular biology Consulting Consumer health information Customer relationship management Data warehousing Decision making e-Government information Electronic commerce Electronic publishing Environmental management Financing and banking Healthcare information Human factors Insurance management Knowledge management Library services Logistics Multimedia technologies Project management Techniques of IT consulting Technology management

Source: From Helfert & Duncan.[7]

primary degree in computing, computer science, software engineering, or a comparable discipline. The program is designed to be completed in one calendar year of full-time study and consists of two taught semesters, followed by a third term consisting of a project of practical nature.

The curriculum has an emphasis on engineering principles, and includes a module on structural science, which encompasses management science, data

Big Data–
Cellular

Table 2 Curriculum overview

Semester 1	• Research skills/seminar topics	• Business process management
	• IS architecture	• Strategic management of IT
	• Structural science	• Business studies
Semester 2	• Supply chain management	• Sectoral applications of IS
	• Managing and working in an intercultural environment	• Regulation in IS
		• Project management
		• Managing change
Summer	Dissertation/project of practical nature	

Source: From Helfert & Duncan.[7]

engineering, and data mining. It also has a strong modeling component, and includes modules on IS architecture and business process management. The integrative perspective is provided by the supply chain management module. The program also covers the more traditional IS disciplines as in the strategic management of IT module. An overview of the general program structure is provided in Table 2.

In addition to the emphasis on engineering principles and core subjects of BI, the study program also supports the building of capabilities for managing transformations by aiming to expand transferable skills. In essence, transferable skills are those skills that having been learned in one context can then be applied in another. Typically these skills are based on modern teaching, learning, and assessment methods, and include

• Guided independent study and activity, with specialist input when appropriate.
• Recent or current popular case studies.
• Essay and report writing.
• Collaborative group work and discussions.
• Presentation of findings to the group as a whole.

In the final semester, students work on a project of practical nature. The general objective of this project is to allow students to draw on the theoretical knowledge gained over the taught element and to apply it in a practical setting in an international environment. The project of a practical nature gives students the opportunity to demonstrate their ability to analyze problems in the field of BI and draw conclusions according to scientific methods within a given timeframe.

SUMMARY AND CONCLUSION

This entry presented aspects of BI and illustrated a typical curriculum. We summarized some key requirements of IS graduates. In particular, graduates need a comprehensive understanding of behavioral aspects as well as software engineering, programming, and IT. Interpersonal and communication skills as well as problem-

solving and critical-thinking capabilities are essential for any IS and BI graduate.

The example curriculum as outlined herein comprises a balanced and interdisciplinary structure, which centres on engineering principles and focuses on transformation, models, and methods. The engineering penetration throughout the program is seen as one important characteristic, which differentiates this program from management-orientated IS degrees. In contrast to business administration programs, the production of information managers, often expected in practice, is not the objective of BI. As such, BI can complement the management-orientated stream of the IS discipline.

In conclusion, the BI approach appears to us to be innovative with regard to not only its interdisciplinary character, but also the engineering perspective and the integration of cultural studies and practical experience in an international setting equip graduates with essential transformation capabilities. Indeed, the focus on engineering principles in BI could play an important role in future education programs.

REFERENCES

1. Gorgone, J.; Gray, P.; Feinstein, D.L.; Kasper, G.M.; Luftman, J.; Stohr, E.A.; Valacich, J.S.; Wigand, R. Model curriculum and guidelines for graduate degree programs in information systems. Commun. Assoc. Inform. Syst. **2000**, *3* (1), 1–61.
2. Gorgone, J.; Feinstein, D.; Longenecker, H.E.; Topi, H.; Valacich, J.S.; Davis, G.B. Undergraduate information systems model curriculum update—IS 2002. Proceedings of the Eighth Americas Conference on Information Systems, Dallas, TX, 2002;.
3. Topi, H.; Valacich, J.; Kaiser, K.; Nunamaker, J.; Sipior, J.; Vreede, G.; Wright, R. Revisiting the IS model curriculum: Rethinking the approach and the process. Commun. Assoc. Inform. Syst. **2007**, *20* (11), 728–740.
4. Granger, M.; Dick, G.; Luftman, J.; Slyke, C.; Watson, R. Information systems enrollments: Can they be increased? Commun. Assoc. Inform. Syst. **2007**, *20* (41), 649–659.
5. Helfert, M.; Duncan, H. Business informatics and information systems—Some indications of differences in study programmes. Proceedings of UKAIS Conference 2005, Newcastle: U.K., 2005.

6. Traylor, P.S. Outsourcing. CFO Mag. **2003**, *19* (15), 24–25.

7. Helfert, M.; Duncan, H. Aspects on information systems curriculum: A study program in business informatics, International Federation for Information Processing (IFIP). In *The Transfer and Diffusion of Information Technology for Organizational Resilience,* Donnellan, B., Larsen, T., Levine, L., DeGross, J., Eds.; Springer: Boston, MA, 2006; Vol. 206, 229–237.

8. Appelrath, H.J. Rahmenempfehlung für die Universitätsausbildung in Wirtschaftsinformatik. Informatik Spektrum **2003**, *26* (2), 108–113.

9. Ferstl, O.K.; Sinz, E.J. *Grundlagen der Wirtschaftsinformatik*; 4th Ed.; Oldenbourg: München, Wien, 2001.

10. Retzer, S.; Fisher, J.; Lamp, J. Information systems and business informatics: An Australian German comparison. Proceedings of the 14th Australasian Conference on Information Systems 2003, Delivering IT and e-Business Value in Networked Environments, Lethbridge, N., Ed.; School of Management Information Systems, Edith Cowan University: Perth, Western Australia, 2003; 1–9.

11. König, W. Mitteilungen der Wissenschaftlichen Kommission Wirtschaftsinformatik. Profil der Wirtschaftsinformatik. Wirtschaftsinformatik **1994**, *36* (1), 80–81.

12. Heinrich, L.J. *Wirtschaftsinformatik—Einführung und Grundlegung*; 2nd Ed.; Oldenbourg: München, Wien, 2001.

13. Disterer, G.; Fels, F.; Hausotter, A. *Taschenbuch der Wirtschaftsinformatik*; 2nd Ed.; Carl Hanser Verlag: München Wien, 2003.

14. Scheer, A.-W. *Wirtschaftsinformatik—Referenzmodelle für industrielle Geschäftsprozesse*; 2nd Ed.; Springer: Berlin, 1998.

15. Heinrich, L.J. *Informationsmanagement—Planung, Überwachung und Steuerung der Informationsinfrastrukutr*; 7th Ed.; Oldenbourg: München, Wien, 2002.

16. Henderson, P. Mathematical reasoning in software engineering education. Commun. ACM **2003**, *46* (9), 45–50.

17. Foegen, M.; Battenfeld, J. Die Rolle der Architektur in der Anwendungsentwicklung. Informatik Spektrum **2001**, *5* (24), 290–301.

18. Zachman, J.A. A framework for information system architecture. IBM Syst. J. **1987**, *26* (3), 276–292.

19. Scheer, A.W. ARIS. *Handbook on Architectures of Information Systems*, Bernus, P., Mertins, K., Schmidt, G., Eds.; Springer: Berlin, 1998; 541–565.

**Big Data–
Cellular**

CDMA: Code Division Multiple Access Networks

Tero Ojanperä
Steven D. Gray
Nokia Research Center, Espoo, Finland

Tero Ojanperä
Steven D. Gray
Nokia Research Center, Espoo, Finland

Abstract

This entry provides an overview of various time division multiple access (TDMA) air interface systems including CDMA2000 and wideband code division multiple access.

INTRODUCTION

The promise of third generation is a world where the subscriber can access the WWW or perform file transfers over packet data connections capable of providing 144 Kbps for high mobility, 384 Kbps with restricted mobility, and 2 Mbps in an indoor office environment.[1] With these guidelines on rate from the International Telecommunications Union (ITU), standards bodies started the task of developing an air interface for their third generation system. In North America, the Telecommunications Industry Association (TIA) evaluated proposals from TIA members pertaining to the evolution of TIA/EIA-95B and TIA/EIA-136. In Europe, the European Telecommunications Standards Institute (ETSI) evaluated proposals from ETSI members pertaining to the evolution of Global Systems for Mobile Communication (GSM).

While TIA and ETSI were still discussing various targets for third generation systems, Japan began to roll out their contributions for third generation technology and develop proof-of-concept prototypes. In the beginning of 1997, the Association for Radio Industry and Business (ARIB), a body responsible for standardization of the Japanese air interface, decided to proceed with the detailed standardization of a wideband code division multiple access (WCDMA) system. The technology push from Japan accelerated standardization in Europe and the United States during 1997; joint parameters for Japanese and European WCDMA proposals were agreed. The air interface is commonly referred to as WCDMA. In January 1998, the strong support behind WCDMA led to the selection of WCDMA as the universal mobile telecommunications system (UMTS) terrestrial air interface scheme for FDD (frequency division duplex) frequency bands in ETSI. In the United States, third generation CDMA came through a detailed proposal process from vendors interested in the evolution of TIA/EIA-95B. In February 1998, the TIA committee TR45.5 responsible for TIA/EIA-95B standardization adopted a framework that combined the different vendors' proposals and later became known as CDMA2000.

For TDMA, the focus has been to offer IS-136 and GSM operators a competitive third generation evolution. WCDMA is targeted toward GSM evolution; however, enhanced data rates for GSM evolution (EDGE) allow the operators to supply IMT-2000 data rates without the spectral allocation requirements of WCDMA. Thus, EDGE will be deployed by those operators who wish to maintain either IS-136 or GSM for voice services and augment these systems with a TDMA-based high rate packet service. TDMA convergence occurred late in 1997 when ETSI approved standardization of the EDGE concept and in February 1998 when TIA committee TR45.3 approved the UWC-136 EDGE-based proposal.

The push to third generation was initially focused on submission of an IMT-2000 radio transmission techniques (RTTs) proposal. The evaluation process has begun in ITU[2] where Fig. 1 depicts the time schedule of the ITU RTT development. Since at the same time regional standards have started the standards writing process, it is not yet clear what the relationship between the ITU and regional standards is. Based upon actions in TIA and ETSI, it is reasonable to assume that standards will exist for CDMA2000, WCDMA, and EDGE and all will be deployed based upon market demands.

The entry is organized as follows: issues effecting third generation CDMA are discussed followed by a brief introduction of CDMA2000, WCDMA, and EDGE. A table comparing CDMA2000 and WCDMA is given at the end of the CDMA section. For TDMA, an overview of the IS-136-based evolution is given including the role played by EDGE.

CDMA-BASED SCHEMES

Third generation CDMA system descriptions in TIA and ETSI have similarities and differences. Some of the

Encyclopedia of Information Systems and Technology, DOI: 10.1081/E-EIST-120043953

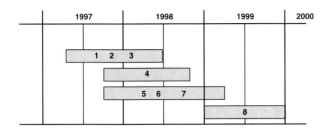

Fig. 1 ITU timelines: 1, 2, 3—radio transmission techniques (RTTs) request, development, and submission; 4—RTT evaluation; 5—review outside evaluation; 6—assess compliance with performance parameters; 7—consideration of evaluation results and consensus on key characteristics; 8—development of detailed radio interface specifications.

similarities between CDMA2000 and WCDMA are variable spreading, convolutional coding, and quadrature phaseshift keying (QPSK) data modulation. The major differences between CDMA2000 and WCDMA occur with the channel structure, including the structure of the pilot used on the forward link. To aid in comparison of the two CDMA techniques, a brief overview is given to some important third generation CDMA issues, the dedicated channel structure of CDMA2000 and WCDMA, and a table comparing air interface characteristics.

CDMA SYSTEM DESIGN ISSUES

Bandwidth: An important design goal for all third generation proposals is to limit spectral emissions to a 5 MHz dual-sided passband. There are several reasons for choosing this bandwidth. First, data rates of 144 and 384 Kbps, the main targets of third generation systems, are achievable within 5 MHz bandwidth with reasonable coverage. Second, the lack of spectrum calls for limited spectrum allocation, especially if the system has to be deployed within the existing frequency bands already occupied by the second generation systems. Third, the 5 MHz bandwidth improves the receiver's ability to resolve multipath when compared to narrower bandwidths, increasing diversity and improving performance. Larger bandwidths of 10, 15, and 20 MHz have been proposed to support highest data rates more effectively.

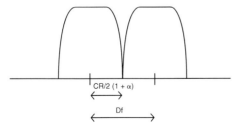

Fig. 2 Relationship between chip rate (CR), roll-off factor (α), and channel separation (D*f*).

Chip rate: Given the bandwidth, the choice of chip rate (CR) depends on spectrum deployment scenarios, pulse shaping, desired maximum data rate, and dual-mode terminal implementation. Fig. 2 shows the relation between CR, pulse shaping filter roll-off factor (α), and channel separation (D*f*). If raised cosine filtering is used, spectrum is zero (in theory) after $CR/2(1 + \alpha)$. In Fig. 2, channel separation is selected such that two adjacent channel spectra do not overlap. Channel separation should be selected this way, if there can be high power level differences between the adjacent carriers. For example, for WCDMA parameters minimum channel separation ($\mathbf{D}f_{min}$) for nonoverlapping carriers is $\mathbf{D}f_{min}$ = 4.096(1 + 0.22) = 4.99712 MHz. If channel separation is selected in such a way that the spectrum of two adjacent channel signals overlap, some power leaks from one carrier to another. Partly overlapping carrier spacing can be used, e.g., in micro cells where the same antenna masts are used for both carriers.

A designer of dual-mode terminals needs to consider the relation between the different clock frequencies of different modes. Especially important are the transmitter and receiver sampling rates and the carrier raster. A proper selection of these frequencies for the standard would ease the dual-mode terminal implementation. The different clock frequencies in a terminal are normally derived from a common reference oscillator by either direct division or synthesis by the use of a phase-locked loop (PLL). The use of a PLL will add some complexity. The WCDMA CR has been selected based on consideration of backward compatibility with GSM and primary domain controller (PDC). CDMA2000 CR is a direct derivation of the TIA/EIA-95B CR.

Multi-Rate: Multirate design means multiplexing different connections with different quality of service requirements in a flexible and spectrum efficient way. The provision for flexible data rates with different quality of service requirements can be divided into three subproblems: how to map different bit rates into the allocated bandwidth, how to provide the desired quality of service, and how to inform the receiver about the characteristics of the received signal. The first problem concerns issues like multicode transmission and variable spreading. The second problem concerns coding schemes. The third problem concerns control channel multiplexing and coding.

Multiple services belonging to the same session can be either time- or code-multiplexed as depicted in Fig. 3. The time multiplexing avoids multicode transmissions thus reducing peak-to-average power of the transmission. A second alternative for service multiplexing is to treat parallel services completely separate with separate channel coding/interleaving. Services are then mapped to separate physical data channels in a multicode fashion as illustrated in the lower part of Fig. 3. With this alternative scheme, the power, and

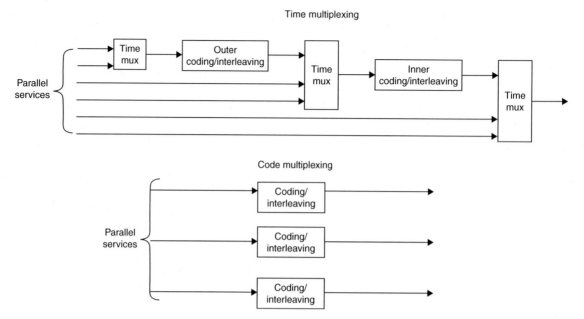

Time multiplexing

Code multiplexing

Fig. 3 Time and code multiplexing principles.

consequently the quality, of each service can be controlled independently.

Spreading and Modulation Solutions

A complex spreading circuit as shown in Fig. 4 helps to reduce the peak-to-average power and thus improves power efficiency.

The spreading modulation can be either balanced- or dual-channel QPSK. In the balanced QPSK spreading the same data signal is split into I and Q channels. In dual-channel QPSK spreading the symbol streams on the I and Q channels are independent of each other. In the forward link, QPSK data modulation is used in order to save code channels and allow the use of the same orthogonal sequence for I and Q channels. In the reverse link, each mobile station uses the same orthogonal codes; this allows for efficient use of binary phase-shift keying (BPSK) data modulation and balanced QPSK spreading.

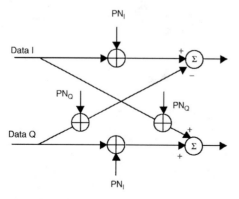

Fig. 4 Complex spreading.

Coherent detection in the reverse link: Coherent detection can improve the performance of the reverse link up to 3 dB compared to non-coherent reception used by the second generation CDMA system. To facilitate coherent detection a pilot signal is required. The actual performance improvement depends on the proportion of the pilot signal power to the data signal power and the fading environment.

Fast power control in forward link: To improve the forward link performance, fast power control is used. The impact of the fast power control in the forward link is two-fold. First, it improves the performance in a fading multipath channel. Second, it increases the multiuser interference variance within the cell since orthogonality between users is not perfect due to multipath channel. The net effect, however, is improved performance at low speeds.

Additional pilot channel in the forward link for beamforming: An additional pilot channel on the forward link that can be assigned to a single mobile or to a group of mobiles enables deployment of adaptive antennas for beamforming since the pilot signal used for channel estimation needs to go through the same path as the data signal. Therefore, a pilot signal transmitted through an omnicell antenna cannot be used for the channel estimation of a data signal transmitted through an adaptive antenna.

Seamless inter-frequency handover: For third generation systems, hierarchical cell structures (HCS), constructed by overlaying macro cells on top of smaller micro or picocells, have been proposed to achieve high capacity. The cells belonging to different cell layers will be in different frequencies, and thus an inter-frequency handover is required. A key requirement for the support of seamless inter-

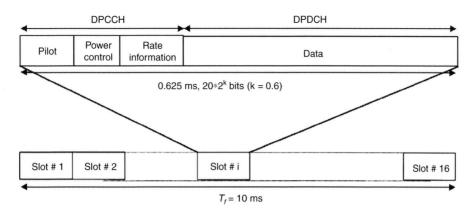

Fig. 5 Forward link dedicated channel structure in WCDMA.

frequency handover is the ability of the mobile station to carry out cell search on a carrier frequency different from the current one, without affecting the ordinary data flow. Different methods have been proposed to obtain multiple carrier frequency measurements. For mobile stations with receiver diversity, there is a possibility for one of the receiver branches to be temporarily reallocated from diversity reception and instead carry out reception on a different carrier. For single-receiver mobile stations, slotted forward link transmission could allow inter-frequency measurements. In the slotted mode, the information normally transmitted during a certain time, e.g., a 10 ms frame, is transmitted in less than that time, leaving an idle time that the mobile can use to measure on other frequencies.

Multi-user detection: Multiuser detection (MUD) has been the subject of extensive research since 1986 when Verdu formulated an optimum multiuser detector for additive white Gaussian noise (AWGN) channel, maximum likelihood sequence estimation (MLSE).[3] In general, it is easier to apply MUD in a system with short spreading codes since cross-correlations do not change every symbol as with long spreading codes. However, it seems that the proposed CDMA schemes would all use long spreading codes. Therefore, the most feasible approach seems to be interference cancellation

algorithms that carry out the interference cancellation at the chip level, thereby avoiding explicit calculation of the cross-correlation between spreading codes from different users.[4] Due to complexity, MUD is best suited for the reverse link. In addition, the mobile station is interested in detecting its own signal in contrast to the base station, which needs to demodulate the signals of all users. Therefore, a simpler interference suppression scheme could be applied in the mobile station. Furthermore, if short spreading codes are used, the receiver could exploit the cyclostationarity, i.e., the periodic properties of the signal, to suppress interference without knowing the interfering codes.

Transmit Diversity

The forward link performance can be improved in many cases by using transmit diversity. For direct spread CDMA schemes, this can be performed by splitting the data stream and spreading the two streams using orthogonal sequences or switching the entire data stream between two antennas. For multi-carrier CDMA, the different carriers can be mapped into different antennas.

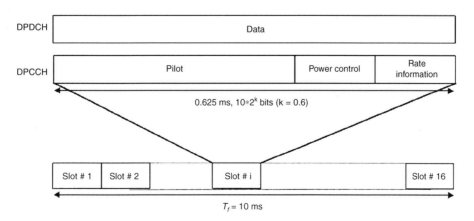

Fig. 6 Reverse link dedicated channel structure in WCDMA.

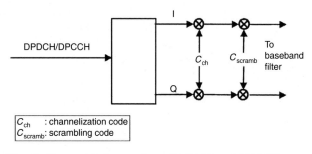

Fig. 7 Forward link spreading of DPDCH and DPCCH.

WIDEBAND CODE DIVISION MULTIPLE ACCESS

To aid in the comparison of CDMA2000 and WCDMA, the dedicated frame structure of WCDMA is illustrated in Figs. 5 and 6. The approach follows a time multiplex philosophy where the dedicated physical control channel dedicated physical data channel (DPDCH) provides the pilot, power control, and rate information and the DPDCH is the portion used for data transport. The forward and reverse DPDCH channels have been convolutional encoded and interleaved prior to framing. The major difference between the forward and reverse links is that the reverse channel structure of the DPCCH is a separate code channel from the DPDCH.

After framing, the forward and reverse link channels are spread as shown in Figs. 7 and 8. On the forward link orthogonal, variable rate codes, c_{ch}, are used to separate channels and pseudo random scrambling sequences, c_{scramb}, are used to spread the signal evenly across the spectrum and separate different base stations. On the reverse link, the orthogonal channelization codes are used as in the forward link to separate CDMA channels. The scrambling codes, c'_{scramb} and c''_{scramb}, are used to identify mobile stations and to spread the signal evenly across the band. The optional scrambling code is used as a means to group mobiles under a common scrambling sequence.

Spreading Codes

WCDMA employs long spreading codes. Different spreading codes are used for cell separation in the forward link and user separation in the reverse link. In the forward link Gold codes of length 2^{18} are truncated to form cycles of 2^{16} times 10 ms frames. In order to minimize the cell search time, a special short code mask is used. The synchronization channel of WCDMA is masked with an orthogonal short Gold code of length 256 chips spanning one symbol. The mask symbols carry information about the BS long code group. Thus, the mobile station first acquires the short mask code and then searches the corresponding long code. A short VL-Kasami code has been proposed for the reverse link to ease the implementation of MUD. In this case, code planning would also be negligible because the number of VL-Kasami sequences is more than one million. However, in certain cases, the use of short codes may lead to bad correlation properties, especially with very small spreading factors. If MUD were not used, adaptive code allocation could be used to restore the cross-correlation properties. The use of short codes to ease the implementation of advanced detection techniques is more beneficial in the forward link since the cyclostationarity of the signal could be utilized for adaptive implementation of the receiver.

Orthogonality between the different spreading factors can be achieved by tree-structured orthogonal codes whose construction is illustrated in Fig. 9.[5] The tree-structured codes are generated recursively according to the following equation,

$$C_{2n} = \begin{pmatrix} C_{2n,1} \\ C_{2n,2} \\ \vdots \\ C_{2n,2n} \end{pmatrix} = \begin{pmatrix} \begin{pmatrix} C_{n,1} & C_{n,1} \\ C_{n,1} & -C_{n,1} \end{pmatrix} \\ \vdots \\ \begin{pmatrix} C_{n,n} & C_{n,n} \\ C_{n,n} & -C_{n,n} \end{pmatrix} \end{pmatrix}$$

where C_{2n} is the orthogonal code set of size $2n$. The generated codes within the same layer constitute a set of

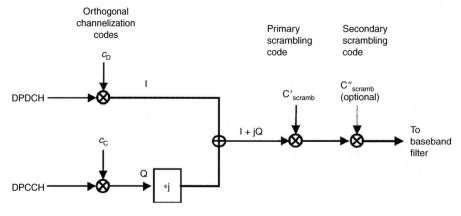

Fig. 8 Reverse link spreading for the DPDCH and DPCCH.

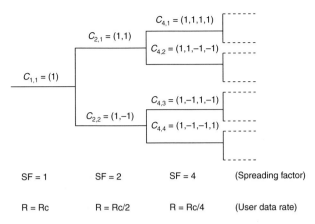

Fig. 9 Construction of orthogonal spreading codes for different spreading factors.

orthogonal functions and are thus orthogonal. Furthermore, any two codes of different layers are also orthogonal except for the case that one of the two codes is a mother code of the other. For example, code $C_{4,4}$ is not orthogonal with codes $C_{1,1}$ and $C_{2,2}$.

Coherent Detection and Beamforming

In the forward link, time multiplexed pilot symbols are used for coherent detection. Because the pilot symbols are user dedicated, they can be used for channel estimation with adaptive antennas as well. In the reverse link, WCDMA employs pilot symbols multiplexed with power control and rate information for coherent detection.

Multirate

WCDMA traffic channel structure is based on a single code transmission for small data rates and multicode for higher data rates. Multiple services belonging to the same connection are, in normal cases, time multiplexed as was depicted in the upper part of Fig. 3. After service multiplexing and channel coding, the multiservice data stream is mapped to one or more dedicated physical data channels. In the case of multicode transmission, every other data channel is mapped into Q and every other into I channel. The channel coding of WCDMA is based on convolutional and concatenated codes. For services with BER = 10^{-3}, convolutional code with constraint length of 9 and different code rates (between 1/2 – 1/4) is used. For services with BER = 10^{-6}, a concatenated coding with an outer Reed-Solomon code has been proposed. Typically, block interleaving over one frame is used. WCDMA is also capable of interframe interleaving, which improves the performance for services allowing longer delay. Turbo codes for data services are under study. Rate matching is performed by puncturing or symbol repetition.

Packet Data

WCDMA has two different types of packet data transmission possibilities. Short data packets can be appended directly to a random access burst. The WCDMA random access burst is 10 ms long, it is transmitted with fixed power, and the access principle is based on the slotted Aloha scheme. This method, called common channel packet transmission, is used for short infrequent packets, where the link maintenance needed for a dedicated channel would lead to an unacceptable overhead. Larger or more frequent packets are transmitted on a dedicated channel. A large single packet is transmitted using a single-packet scheme where the dedicated channel is released immediately after the packet has been transmitted. In a multipacket scheme, the dedicated channel is maintained by transmitting power control and synchronization information between subsequent packets.

CDMA2000

The dedicated channels used in CDMA2000 system are the fundamental, supplemental, pilot (Dedicated for the reverse link and common for the forward link.), and dedicated control channels. Shown for the forward link in Fig. 1 and for the reverse in Fig. 11, the fundamental channel provides for the communication of voice, low rate data, and signaling where power control information for the reverse channels is punctured on the forward fundamental channel. For high rate data services, the supplemental channel is used where one important difference between the supplemental and the fundamental channel is the addition of parallel-concatenated turbo codes. For different service options, multiple supplemental channels can be used. The code multiplex pilot channel allows for phase coherent detection. In addition, the pilot channel on the forward link is used for determining soft handoff and the pilot channel on the reverse is used for carrying power control information for the forward channels. Finally, the dedicated control channel, also shown in Fig. 10 for the forward link and in Fig. 11, for the reverse, is used primarily for exchange of high rate media access control (MAC) layer signaling.

Multicarrier

In addition to direct spread, a multi-carrier approach has been proposed for the CDMA2000 forward link since it would maintain orthogonality between the CDMA2000 and TIA/EIA-95B carriers.[6] The multi-carrier variant is achieved by using three 1.25 MHz carriers for a 5 MHz

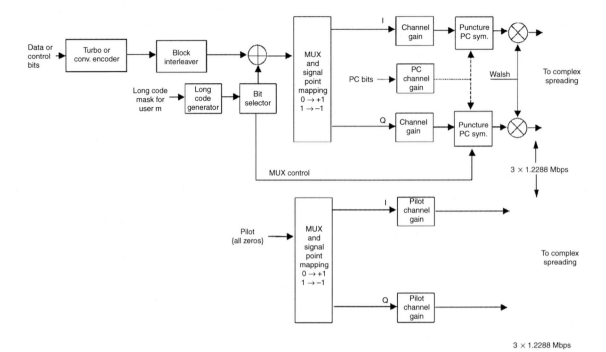

Fig. 10 Forward link channel structure in CDMA2000 for direct spread. (*Note:* dashed line indicates that it is only used for the fundamental channel).

bandwidth where all carriers have separate channel coding and are power controlled in unison.

Spreading Codes

On the forward link, the cell separation for CDMA2000 is performed by two M-sequences of length 3×2^{15}, one for I and one for Q channel, which are phase shifted by pseudo noise (PN)-offset for different cells. Thus, during the cell search process only these sequences are searched. Because there are a limited number of PN-offsets, they need to be planned in order to avoid PN-confusion.[7] In the reverse link, user separation is performed by different phase shifts of M-sequence of length 2^{41}. The channel separation is performed using variable spreading factor Walsh sequences, which are orthogonal to each other.

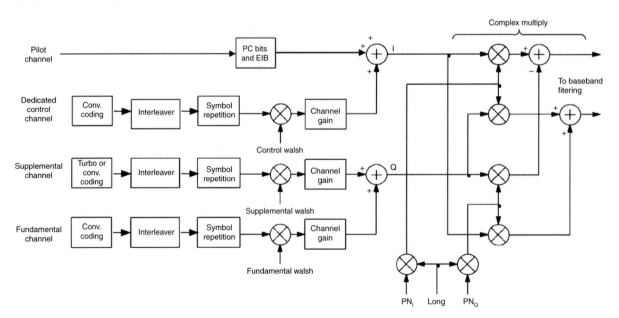

Fig. 11 Reverse link channel structure in CDMA2000.

Coherent Detection

In the forward link, CDMA2000 has a common pilot channel, which is used as a reference signal for coherent detection when adaptive antennas are not employed. When adaptive antennas are used, an auxiliary pilot is used as a reference signal for coherent detection. Code multiplexed auxiliary pilots are generated by assigning a different orthogonal code to each auxiliary pilot. This approach reduces the number of orthogonal codes available for the traffic channels. This limitation is alleviated by expanding the size of the orthogonal code set used for the auxiliary pilots. Since a pilot signal is not modulated by data, the pilot orthogonal code length can be extended, thereby yielding an increased number of available codes, which can be used as additional pilots. In the reverse link, the pilot signal is time multiplexed with power control and erasure indicator bit (EIB).

Multi-rate Scheme

CDMA2000 has two traffic channel types, the fundamental and the supplemental channel, which are code multiplexed. The fundamental channel is a variable rate channel which supports basic rates of 9.6 Kbps and 14.4 Kbps and their corresponding subrates, i.e., rate set 1 and rate set 2 of TIA/EIA-95B. It conveys voice, signaling, and low rate data. The supplemental channel provides high data rates. Services with different QoS requirements are code multiplexed into supplemental channels. The user data frame length of CDMA2000 is 20 ms. For the transmission of control information, 5- and 20 ms frames can be used on the fundamental channel or dedicated control channel. On the fundamental channel a convolutional code with constraint length 9 is used. On supplemental channels convolutional coding is used up to 14.4 kbps. For higher rates Turbo codes with constraint length 4 and rate 1/4 are preferred. Rate matching is performed by puncturing, symbol repetition, and sequence repetition.

Packet Data

CDMA2000 also allows short data burst using the slotted Aloha principle. However, instead of fixed transmission power it increases the transmission power for the random access burst after an unsuccessful access attempt. When the mobile station has been allocated a traffic channel, it can transmit without scheduling up to a predefined bit rate. If the transmission rate exceeds the defined rate, a new access request has to be made. When the mobile station stops transmitting, it releases the traffic channel but not the dedicated control channel. After a while it also releases the dedicated control channel as well but maintains the link layer and network layer connections in order to shorten the channel set-up time when new data needs to be transmitted.

Parametric Comparison

For comparison, Table 1 lists the parameters of CDMA2000 and WCDMA. CDMA2000 uses a CR of 3.6864 Mcps for the 5 MHz band allocation with the direct spread forward link option and a 1.2288 Mcps CR with three carriers for the multi-carrier option. WCDMA uses direct spread with a CR of 4.096 Mcps. The multi-carrier approach is motivated by a spectrum overlay of CDMA2000 carriers with existing TIA/EIA-95B carriers.[6] Similar to EIA/TIA-95B, the spreading codes of CDMA2000 are generated using different phase shifts of the same M-sequence. This is possible due to the synchronous network operation. Since WCDMA has an asynchronous network, different long codes rather than different phase shifts of the same code are used for the cell and user separation. The code structure determines how code synchronization, cell acquisition, and handover synchronization are performed.

TDMA-BASED SCHEMES

As discussed, TIA/EIA-136 and GSM evolution have similar paths in the form of EDGE. The UWC-136 IMT 2000 proposal contains, in addition to the TIA/EIA-136 30 kHz carriers, the high rate capability provided by the 200 kHz and 1.6 MHz carriers shown in Table 2. The targets for the IS-136 evolution were to meet IMT-2000 requirements and an initial deployment within 1 MHz spectrum allocation. UWC-136 meets these targets via modulation enhancement to the existing 30 kHz channel (136+) and by defining complementary wider band TDMA carriers with bandwidths of 200 kHz for vehicular/outdoor environments and 1.6 MHz for indoor environments. The 200 kHz carrier, 136 HS (vehicular/outdoor) with the same parameters as EDGE provides medium bit rates up to 384 Kbps and the 1.6 MHz carrier, 136 HS (indoor), highest bit rates up to 2 Mbps. The parameters of the 136 HS proposal submitted to ITU are listed in Table 2 and the different carrier types of UWC-136 are shown in Fig. 12.

Carrier Spacing and Symbol Rate

The motivation for the 200 kHz carrier is twofold. First, the adoption of the same physical layer for 136 HS (vehicular/outdoor) and GSM data carriers provides economics of scale and therefore cheaper equipment and faster time to market. Second, the 200 kHz carrier with higher order modulation can provide bit rates of 144

Big Data–Cellular

Table 1 Parameters of WCDMA and CDMA2000.

	WCDMA	CDMA2000
Channel bandwidth	5, 10, 20 MHz	1.25, 5, 10, 15, 20 MHz
Forward link RF channel structure	Direct spread	Direct spread or multi-carrier
Chip rate	4.096/8.192/16.384 Mcps	1.2288/3.6864/7.3728/11.0593/14.7456 Mcps for direct spread $n \times 1.2288$ Mcps ($n = 1,3,6,9,12$) for multi-carrier
Roll-off factor	0.22	Similar to TIA/EIA-95B
Frame length	10 ms/20 ms (optional)	20 ms for data and control/5 ms for control information on the fundamental and dedicated control channel
Spreading modulation	Balanced QPSK (forward link) Dual-channel QPSK reverse link) Complex spreading circuit	Balanced QPSK (forward link) Dual-channel QPSK (reverse link) Complex spreading circuit
Data modulation	QPSK (forward link) BPSK (reverse link)	QPSK (forward link) BPSK (reverse link)
Coherent detection	User dedicated time multiplexed pilot (forward link and reverse link), common pilot in forward link	Pilot time multiplexed with PC and EIB (reverse link) Common continuous pilot channel and auxiliary pilot (forward link)
Channel multiplexing in reverse link	Control and pilot channel time multiplexed I&Q multiplexing for data and control channel	Control, pilot fundamental, and supplemental code multiplexed I&Q multiplexing for data and control channels
Multi-rate	Variable spreading and multicode	Variable spreading and multicode
Spreading factors	4-256 (4.096 Mcps)	4-256 (3.6864 Mcps)
Power control	Open and fast closed loop (1.6 kHz)	Open loop and fast closed loop (800 Hz)
Spreading (forward link)	Variable length orthogonal sequences for channel separation. Gold sequences for cell and user separation	Variable length Walsh sequences for channel separation, M-sequence 3×2^{15} (same sequence with time shift utilized in different cells different sequence in I&Q channel)
Spreading (reverse link)	Variable length orthogonal sequences for channel separation. Gold sequence 2^{41} for user separation (different time shifts in I and Q channel, cycle $2^{16} \times$ 10 ms radio frames)	Variable length orthogonal sequences for channel separation, M-sequence 2^{15} (same for all users different sequences in I&Q channels), M-sequence 2^{41} for user separation (different time shifts for different users)
Handover	Soft handover Inter-frequency handover	Soft handover Inter-frequency handover

and 384 Kbps with reasonable range and capacity fulfilling IMT-2000 requirements for pedestrian and vehicular environments. The 136 HS (indoor) carrier can provide 2 Mbit/s user data rate with a reasonably strong channel coding.

Modulation

First proposed modulation methods were quaternary offset QAM (Q-O-QAM) and binary offset QAM (B-O-QAM). Q-O-QAM could provide higher data rates and good spectral efficiency. For each symbol, two bits are transmitted and consecutive symbols are shifted by $\pi/2$. An offset modulation was proposed, because it causes smaller amplitude variations than 16 QAM, which can

be beneficial when using amplifiers that are not completely linear. The second modulation B-O-QAM has been introduced, which has the same symbol rate of 361.111 ksps, but where only the outer signal points of the Q-O-QAM modulation are used. For each symbol, one bit is transmitted and consecutive symbols are shifted by $\pi/2$. A second modulation scheme with the characteristic of being a subset of the first modulation scheme and having the same symbol rate as the first modulation allows seamless switching between the two modulation types between bursts. Both modulation types can be used in the same burst. From a complexity point of view, the addition of a modulation, which is subset of the first modulation, adds no new requirements for the transmitter or receiver.

Table 2 Parameters of 136 HS.

	136 HS (vehicular/outdoor)	136 HS (indoor)
Duplex method	FDD	FDD and TDD
Carrier spacing	200 kHz	1.6 MHz
Modulation	Q-O-QAM	Q-O-QAM
	B-O-QAM	B-O-QAM
	8 PSK	
	GMSK	
Modulation bit rate	722.2 Kbps (Q-O-QAM)	5200 Kbps (Q-O-QAM)
	361.1 Kbps (B-O-QAM)	2600 Kbps (B-O-QAM)
	812.5 Kbps (8 PSK)	
	270.8 Kbps (GMSK)	
Payload	521.6 Kbps (Q-O-QAM)	4750 Kbps (Q-O-QAM)
	259.2 Kbps (B-O-QAM)	2375 Kbps (B-O-QAM)
	547.2 Kbps (8 PSK)	
	182.4 Kbps (GMSK)	
Frame length	4.615 ms	4.615 ms
Number of slots	8	64 (72 μs)
		16 (288 μs)
Coding	Convolutional	Convolutional
	1/2, 1/4, 1/3, 1/1	1/2, 1/4, 1/3, 1/1
	ARQ	Hybrid type II ARQ
Frequency hopping	Optional	Optional
Dynamic channel allocation	Optional	Optional

In addition to the originally proposed modulation schemes, quaternary offset QAM (Q-O-QAM) and binary offset QAM (B-O-QAM), other modulation schemes, CPM and 8-PSK, have been evaluated in order to select the modulation best suited for EDGE. The outcome of this evaluation is that 8 PSK was considered to have implementation advantages over Q-O-QAM. Parties working on EDGE are in the process of revising the proposals so that 8 PSK would replace the Q-O-QAM and Gaussian minimum shift keying (GMSK) can be used as the lower level modulation instead of B-O-QAM. The symbol rate of the 8 PSK will be the same as for GMSK and the detailed bit rates will be specified early in 1999.

Frame Structures

The 136 HS (vehicular/outdoor) data frame length is 4.615 ms and one frame consists of eight slots. The burst structure is suitable for transmission in a high delay spread environment. The frame and slot structures of the 136 HS (indoor) carrier were selected for cell coverage for high bit rates. The HS-136 indoor, supports both FDD and TDD duplex methods. Fig. 13 illustrates

the frame and slot structure. The frame length is 4.615 ms and it can consist of:

- 64 1/64 time slots of length 72 μs;
- 16 1/16 time slots of length 288 μs.

In the TDD mode, the same burst types as defined for the FDD mode are used. The 1/64 slot can be used for every service from low rate speech and data to high rate data services. The 1/16 slot is to be used for medium to high rate data services. Fig. 13 also illustrates the dynamic allocation of resources between the reverse link and the forward link in the TDD mode.

The physical contents of the time slots are bursts of corresponding length. Three types of traffic bursts are defined. Each burst consists of a training sequence, two data blocks, and a guard period. The bursts differ in the length of the burst (72 and 288 μs) and in the length of the training sequence (27 symbols and 49 symbols)

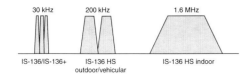

Fig. 12 UWC-136 carrier types.

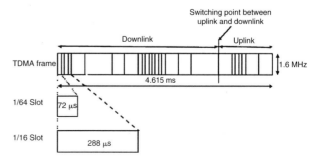

Fig. 13 Wideband TDMA frame and slot structure.

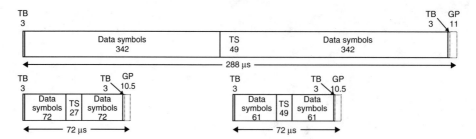

Fig. 14 Burst structure.

leading to different numbers of payload symbols and different multipath delay performances (Fig. 14). The number of required reference symbols in the training sequence depends on the length of the channel's impulse response, the required signal-to-noise ratio, the expected maximum Doppler frequency shift, and the number of modulation levels. The number of reference symbols should be matched to the channel characteristics, remain practically stable within the correlation window, and have good correlation properties. All 136 based schemes can use interference cancellation as a means to improve performance.[8] For 136 HS (indoor), the longer sequence can handle about 7 μs of time dispersion and the shorter one 2.7 μs. It should be noted that if the time dispersion is larger, the drop in performance is slow and depends on the power delay profile.

Multi-rate Scheme

The UWC-136 multirate scheme is based on a variable slot, code, and modulation structure. Data rates up to 43.2 Kbps can be offered using the 136 + 30 kHz carrier and multislot transmission. Depending on the user requirements and channel conditions a suitable combination of modulation, coding, and number of data slots is selected. 136 HS can offer packet switched, and both transparent and nontransparent circuit switched data services. Asymmetrical data rates are provided by allocating a different number of time slots in the reverse and forward links. For packet switched services, the radio link control (RLC)/MAC protocol provides fast medium access via a reservation based medium access scheme, supplemented by selective automatic repeat request (ARQ) for efficient retransmission.

Similar to 136 HS (outdoor/vehicular), the 136 HS (indoor) uses two modulation schemes and different coding schemes to provide variable data rates. In addition, two different slot sizes can be used. For delay tolerant packet data services, error control is based on a Type II hybrid ARQ scheme.[5] The basic idea is to first send all data blocks using a simple error control coding scheme. If decoding at the receiver fails, a retransmission is requested using a stronger code. After the second retransmission, diversity combining can be performed between the first and second transmissions prior to hard

decisions. This kind of ARQ procedure can be used due to the ability of the RLC/MAC protocol to allocate resources fast and to send transmission requests reliably in the feedback channel.[5]

Radio Resource Management

The radio resource management schemes of UWC-136 include link adaptation, frequency hopping, power control, and dynamic channel allocation. Link adaptation offers a mechanism for choosing the best modulation and coding alternative according to channel and interference conditions. Frequency hopping averages interference and improves link performance against fast fading. For 136 HS (indoor) fast power control (frame-by-frame) could be used to improve the performance in cases where frequency hopping cannot be applied, e.g., when only one carrier is available. Dynamic channel allocation can be used for channel assignments. However, when deployment with minimum spectrum is desired, reuse 1/3 and fractional loading with fixed channel allocation is used.

Time Division Duplex

The main discussion about the IMT-2000 air interface has been concerned with technologies for FDD. However, there are several reasons why time division duplex (TDD) would be desirable. First, there will likely be dedicated frequency bands for TDD within the identified UMTS frequency bands. Furthermore, FDD requires exclusive paired bands and spectrum is, therefore, hard to find. With a proper design including powerful FEC, TDD can be used even in outdoor cells. The second reason for using TDD is flexibility in radio resource allocation, i.e., bandwidth can be allocated by changing the number of time slots for the reverse link and forward link. However, the asymmetric allocation of radio resources leads to two interference scenarios that will impact the overall spectrum efficiency of a TDD scheme:

- Asymmetric usage of TDD slots will impact the radio resource in neighboring cells;

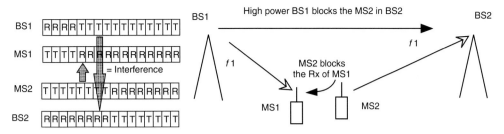

Fig. 15 TDD interference scenario.

- Asymmetric usage of TDD slots will lead to blocking of slots in adjacent carriers within their own cells.

Fig. 15 depicts the first scenario. MS2 is transmitting at full power at the cell border. Since MS1 has a different asymmetric slot allocation than MS2, its forward link slots received at the sensitivity limit are interfered by MS1, which causes blocking. On the other hand, since the BS1 can have much higher effective isotopically radiated power than MS2, it will interfere BS2's ability to receive MS2. Hence, the radio resource algorithm needs to avoid this situation.

In the second scenario, two mobiles would be connected into the same cell but using different frequencies. The base station receives MS1 on the frequency $f1$ using the same time slot it uses on the frequency $f2$ to transmit into MS2. As shown in Table 3, the transmission will block the reception due to the irreducible noise floor of the transmitter regardless of the frequency separation between $f1$ and $f2$.

Both TDMA- and CDMA-based schemes have been proposed for TDD. Most of the TDD aspects are common to TDMA- and CDMA-based air interfaces. However, in CDMA-based TDD systems, the slot duration on the forward and reverse links must be equal to enable the use of soft handoff and prevent the interference situation described in the first scenario. Because TDMA systems do not have soft handoff on a common frequency, slot imbalances from one BS to the next are easier to accommodate. Thus, TDMA-based solutions have higher flexibility. The frame structure for the wide band TDMA for the TDD system was briefly discussed in the previous section. WCDMA has been proposed for TDD in Japan and Europe. The frame structure is the same as for the FDD component, i.e., a 10 ms frame split into 16 slots of 0.625 ms each. Each slot can be used either for reverse link or forward link. For CDMA2000, the TDD frame structure is based on a 20 ms frame split into 16 slots of 1.25 ms each.

CONCLUSIONS

Third generation cellular systems are a mechanism for evolving the telecommunications business based primarily on voice telephony to mobile wireless datacomm. CDMA2000, WCDMA, and EDGE will be important technologies used to achieve the datacomm goal in light of events in TIA, ETSI, and ARIB. Standardization related to radio access technologies discussed in this entry were under way at the time of writing and will offer the European, United States, and Japanese markets both CDMA and TDMA third generation options. In comparing CDMA evolution, the European, United States, and Japanese based systems have some similarities, but differ in the CR and channel structure. In the best circumstances, some harmonization will occur between CDMA2000 and WCDMA making deployment of hardware capable of supporting both systems easier. In TDMA, the third generation paths of GSM and TIA/EIA-136 are through a common solution. This alignment will offer TDMA systems an advantage in possible global roaming for data services. In spite of the regional standards differences, third generation will be the mechanism for achieving wireless multimedia enabling services beyond the comprehension of second generation systems.

ACKNOWLEDGMENTS

The authors would like to thank Harri Holma, Pertti Lukander, and Antti Toskala from Nokia Telecommunications, George Fry, Kari Kalliojarvi, Riku Pirhonen, Rauno Ruismaki, and Zhigang Rong from Nokia Research Center, Kari Pehkonen from Nokia Mobile Phones, and Kari Pulli from the University of Stanford for helpful comments. In addition, contributions related to spectrum and modulation aspects from Harri Lilja from Nokia Mobile Phones are acknowledged.

Table 3 Adjacent channel interference calculation.

BTS transmission power for MS2 in forward link 1 W	30 dBm
Received power for MS1	−100 dbm
Adjacent channel attenuation due to irreducible noise floor	50–70 dB
Signal to adjacent channel interference ratio	−60 to −80 dB

Big Data–Cellular

REFERENCES

1. *Guidelines for Evaluation of Radio Transmission Technologies for IMT-2000, ITU-R M.1225;* 1998.

2. Special issue on IMT-2000: Standards Efforts of the ITU. IEEE Pers. Commun. **1997**, *4* (4), 8–40.

3. Verdu, S. Minimum probability of error for asynchronous gaussian multiple access. IEEE Trans. IT **1986**, *IT-32* (1), 85–96.

4. Monk, A.M.; Davis, M.; Milstein, L.B.; Helstrom, C.W. A noise-whitening approach to multiple access noise rejection—pt I: theory and background. IEEE J. Sel. Areas Commun. **1997**, *12* (5), 817–827.

5. Nikula, E.; Toskala, A.; Dahlman, E.; Girard, L.; Klein, A. FRAMES multiple access for UMTS and IMT-2000. IEEE Pers. Commun. **1998**, *5* (2), 16–24.

6. Tiedemann, E.G., Jr.; Jou, Y.-C.; Odenwalder, J.P. The evolution of IS-95 to a third generation system and to the IMT-2000 era. ACTS Summit, Aalborg, Denmark, Oct 7–9, 1997; 924–929.

7. Chang, C.R.; Van, J.Z.; Yee, M.F. PN offset planning strategies for nonuniform CDMA networks. VTC'97, Phoenix, AZ, May 4–7, 1997; 1543–1547.

8. Ranta, P.; Lappetelainen, A.; Honkasalo, Z.-C. Interference cancellation by joint detection in random frequency hopping TDMA networks. IEEE Intl. Conf. on Universal Personal Communications (ICUPC96), Cambridge, MA, Sept 29–Oct 3, 1996; 428–432.

Big Data–
Cellular

Cellular Systems

Lal C. Godara

Australian Defence Force Academy, School of Electrical Engineering University College, University of New South Wales, Canberra, Australian Capital Territory, Australia

Abstract
Cellular technology is a burgeoning field in wireless communications. Each cell contains a base station that communicates with mobiles in the cell by transmitting and receiving signals on radio links.

Big Data–
Cellular

CELLULAR FUNDAMENTALS

The area served by mobile phone systems is divided into small areas known as cells. Each cell contains a base station that communicates with mobiles in the cell by transmitting and receiving signals on radio links. The transmission from the base station to a mobile is typically referred to as downstream, forwardlink, or downlink. The corresponding terms for the transmission from a mobile to the base are upstream, reverse-link, and uplink. Each base station is associated with a mobile switching center (MSC) that connects calls to and from the base to mobiles in other cells and the public switched telephone network. A typical setup depicting a group of base stations to a switching center is shown in Fig. 1. In this section, terminology associated with cellular systems is introduced with a brief description to understand how these systems work.[1]

COMMUNICATION USING BASE STATIONS

A base station communicates with mobiles using two types of radio channels, control channels to carry control information and traffic channels to carry messages. Each base station continuously transmits control information on its control channels. When a mobile is switched on, it scans the control channels and tunes to a channel with the strongest signal. This normally would come from the base station located in the cell in which the mobile is also located. The mobile exchanges identification information with the base station and establishes the authorization to use the network. At this stage, the mobile is ready to initiate and receive a call.

A Call from a Mobile

When a mobile wants to initiate a call, it sends the required number to the base. The base station sends this information to the switching center that assigns a traffic channel to this call because the control channels are only used for control information. Once the traffic channel is assigned, this information is relayed to the mobile via the base station. The mobile switches itself to this channel. The switching center then completes the rest of the call.

A Call to a Mobile

When someone calls a mobile, the call arrives at the MSC. It then sends a paging message through several base stations. A mobile tuned to a control channel detects its number in the paging message and responds by sending a response signal to the nearby base station. The base station informs the switching center about the location of the desired mobile. The switching center assigns a traffic channel to this call and relays this information to the mobile via the base. The mobile switches itself to the traffic channel and the call is complete.

Registration

A mobile is normally located by transmitting a paging message from various base stations. When a large number of base stations are involved in the paging process, it becomes impractical and costly. It is avoided by a registration procedure where a roaming phone registers with an MSC closer to itself. This information may be stored with the switching center of the area as well as the home switching center of the phone. The home base of the phone is the one where it is permanently registered. Once a call is received for this phone, its home switching center contacts the switching center where the phone is roaming. Paging in the vicinity of the previous known location helps to locate the phone. Once it responds, the call may be connected as discussed previously.

Encyclopedia of Information Systems and Technology, DOI: 10.1081/E-EIST-120043846

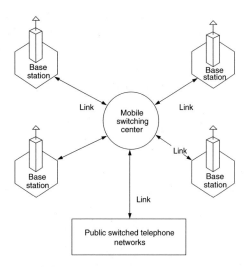

Fig. 1 A typical cellular system setup.

CHANNEL CHARACTERISTICS

An understanding of propagation conditions and channel characteristics is important for an efficient use of a transmission medium. Attention is being given to understanding the propagation conditions where a mobile is to operate and many experiments have been conducted to model the channel characteristics. Many of these results could be found in review articles[2–4] and references therein.

Fading Channels

The signal arriving at a receiver is a combination of many components arriving from various directions as a result of multipath propagation. This depends on terrain conditions and local buildings and structures, causing the received signal power to fluctuate randomly as a function of distance. Fluctuations on the order of 20 dB are common within the distance of one wavelength (Iλ). This phenomenon is called fading. One may think this signal as a product of two variables.

The first component, also referred to as the short term fading component, changes faster than the second one and has a Rayleigh distribution. The second component is a long-term or slow-varying quantity and has lognormal distribution.[5,6] In other words, the local mean varies slowly with lognormal distribution and the fast variation around the local mean has Rayleigh distribution.

A movement in a mobile receiver causes it to encounter fluctuations in the received power level. The rate at which this happens is referred to as the fading rate in mobile communication literature[7] and it depends on the frequency of transmission and the speed of the mobile. For example, a mobile on foot operating at 900 MHz would cause a fading rate of about 4.5 Hz,

whereas a typical vehicle mobile would produce the fading rate of about 70 Hz.

Doppler Spread

The movement in a mobile causes the received frequency to differ from the transmitted frequency because of the Doppler shift resulting from its relative motion. As the received signals arrive along many paths, the relative velocity of the mobile with respect to various components of the signal differs, causing the different components to yield a different Doppler shift. This can be viewed as spreading of the transmitted frequency and is referred to as the Doppler spread. The width of the Doppler spread in frequency domain is closely related to the rate of fluctuations in the observed signal.[2]

Delay Spread

Because of the multipath nature of propagation in the area where a mobile is being used, it receives multiple and delayed copies of the same transmission, resulting in spreading of the signal in time. The rms delay spread may range from a fraction of a microsecond in urban areas to on the order of 100 µs in a hilly area, and this restricts the maximum signal bandwidth between 40 and 250 kHz. This bandwidth is known as coherence bandwidth. The coherence bandwidth is inversely proportional to the rms delay spread. This is the bandwidth over which the channel is flat; i.e., it has a constant gain and linear phase.

For a signal bandwidth above the coherence bandwidth, the channel loses its constant gain and linear phase characteristic and becomes frequency selective. Roughly speaking, a channel becomes frequency selective when the rms delay spread is larger than the symbol duration and causes inter-symbol interference (ISI) in digital communications. Frequency-selective channels are also known as dispersive channels, whereas the nondispersive channels are referred to as flat-fading channels.

Link Budget and Path Loss

Link budget is a name given to the process of estimating the power at the receiver site for a microwave link taking into account the attenuation caused by the distance between the transmitter and the receiver. This reduction is referred to as the path loss. In free space the path loss is proportional to the second power of the distance; i.e., the distance power gradient is two. In other words, by doubling the distance between the transmitter and the receiver, the received power at the receiver reduces to one-fourth of the original amount.

For a mobile communication environment utilizing fading channels the distance power gradient varies and depends on the propagation conditions. Experimental results show that it ranges from a value lower than two in indoor areas with large corridors to as high as six in metal buildings. For urban areas the path loss between the base and the cell site is often taken to vary as the fourth power of the distance between the two.[2]

Normal calculation of link budget is done by calculating carrier to noise ratio (CNR), where noise consists of background and thermal noise, and the system utility is limited by the amount of this noise. However, in mobile communication systems, the interference resulting from other mobile units is a dominant noise compared with the background and man made noise. For this reason these systems are limited by the amount of total interference present instead of the background noise as in the other case. In other words, the signal to interference ratio (SIR) is the limiting factor for a mobile communication system instead of the signal to noise ratio (SNR) as is the case for other communication systems. The calculation of link budget for such interference-limited systems involves calculating the carrier level, above the interference level contributed by all sources.[8]

MULTIPLE ACCESS SCHEMES

The available spectrum bandwidth is shared in a number of ways by various wireless radio links. The way in which this is done is referred to as a multiple access scheme. There are basically four principle schemes. These are frequency division multiple access (FDMA), time division multiple access (TDMA), CDMA, and space division multiple access (SDMA).[9–20]

FDMA Scheme

In an FDMA scheme the available spectrum is divided into a number of frequency channels of certain bandwidth and individual calls use different frequency channels. All first generation cellular systems use this scheme.

TDMA Scheme

In a TDMA scheme, several calls share a frequency channel.[9] The scheme is useful for digitized speech or other digital data. Each call is allocated a number of time slots based on its data rate within a frame for upstream as well as downstream. Apart from the user data, each time slot also carries other data for synchronization, guard times, and control information.

The transmission from base station to mobile is done in time division multiplexmode, whereas in the upstream direction, each mobile transmits in its own time slot. The overlap between different slots resulting from different propagation delay is prevented by using guard times and precise slot synchronization schemes.

The TDMA scheme is used along with the FDMA scheme because there are several frequency channels used in a cell. The traffic in two directions is separated either by using two separate frequency channels or by alternating in time. The two schemes are referred to as frequency division duplex (FDD) and time division duplex (TDD), respectively. The FDD scheme uses less bandwidth than TDD schemes use and does not require as precise synchronization of data flowing in two directions as that in the TDD method. The latter, however, is useful when flexible bandwidth allocation is required for upstream and downstream traffic.[9]

CDMA Scheme

The CDMA scheme is a direct sequence (DS), spread-spectrum method. It uses linear modulation with wideband pseudonoise (PN) sequences to generate signals. These sequences, also known as codes, spread the spectrum of the modulating signal over a large bandwidth, simultaneously reducing the spectral density of the signal. Thus, various CDMA signals occupy the same bandwidth and appear as noise to each other. More details on DS spread-spectrum may be found in Pickholtz et al.[16]

In the CDMA scheme, each user is assigned an individual code at the time of call initiation. This code is used both for spreading the signal at the time of transmission and despreading the signal at the time of reception. Cellular systems using CDMA schemes use FDD, thus employing two frequency channels for forward and reverse links.

On forward-link a mobile transmits to all users synchronously and this preserves the orthogonality of various codes assigned to different users. The orthogonality, however, is not preserved between different components arriving from different paths in multipath situations.[14] On reverse links each user transmits independently from other users because of their individual locations. Thus, the transmission on reverse link is asynchronous and the various signals are not necessarily orthogonal.

It should be noted that these PN sequences are designed to be orthogonal to each other. In other words, the cross correlation between different code sequences is zero and thus the signal modulated with one code appears to be orthogonal to a receiver using a different code if the orthogonality is preserved during the transmission. This is the case on forward-link and in the absence of multipath the signal received by a mobile is not affected by signals transmitted by the base station to other mobiles.

On reverse link the situation is different. Signals arriving from different mobiles are not orthogonalized because of the asynchronous nature of transmission. This may cause a serious problem when the base station is trying to receive a weak signal from a distant mobile in the presence of a strong signal from a nearly mobile. This situation where a strong DS signal from a nearby mobile swamps a weak DS signal from a distant mobile and makes its detection difficult is known as the "near–far" problem. It is prevented by controlling the power transmitted from various mobiles such that the received signals at the base station are almost of equal strength. The power control is discussed in a later section.

The term *wideband CDMA* (WCDMA) is used when the spread bandwidth is more than the coherence bandwidth of the channel.[17] Thus, over the spread bandwidth of DS-CDMA, the channel is frequency selective. On the other hand, the term *narrowband CDMA* is used when the channel encounters flat fading over the spread bandwidth. When a channel encounters frequency selective fading, over the spread bandwidth, a RAKE receiver may be employed to resolve the multipath component and combine them coherently to combat fading.

A WCDMA signal may be generated using multicarrier (MC) narrowband CDMA signals, each using different frequency channels. This composite MC-WCDMA scheme has a number of advantages over the single carrier WCDMA scheme. It not only is able to provide diversity enhancement over multipath fading channels but also does not require a contiguous spectrum as is the case for the single carrier WCDMA scheme. This helps to avoid frequency channels occupied by narrowband CDMA, by not transmitting MC-WCDMA signals over these channels. More details on these and other issues may be found in Milstein[17] and references therein.

Comparison of Different Multiple Access Schemes

Each scheme has its advantages and disadvantages such as complexities of equipment design and robustness of system parameter variations. For example, a TDMA scheme not only requires complex time synchronization of different user data but also presents a challenge to design portable RF units that overcome the problem of a periodically pulsating power envelope caused by short duty cycles of each user terminal. It should be noted that when a TDMA frame consists of N users transmitting equal bit rates, the duty cycles of each user is $1/N$. TDMA also has a number of advantages.[9]

1. A base station communicating with a number of users sharing a frequency channel only requires one set of common radio equipment.
2. The data rate, to and from each user, can easily be varied by changing the number of time slots allocated to the user as per the requirements.
3. It does not require as stringent power control as that of CDMA because its interuser interference is controlled by time slot and frequency channel allocations.
4. Its time slot structure is helpful in measuring the quality of alternative slots and frequency channels that could be used for mobile-assisted handoffs. Handoff is discussed in a later section.

It is argued in Kohno et al.[14] that though there does not appear to be a single scheme that is the best for all situations, CDMA possesses characteristics that give it distinct advantages over others.

1. It is able to reject delayed multipath arrivals that fall outside the correlation interval of the PN sequence in use and thus reduces the multipath fading.
2. It has the ability to reduce the multipath fading by coherently combing different multipath components using a RAKE receiver.
3. In TDMA and FDMA systems, a frequency channel used in a cell is not used in adjacent cells to prevent cochannel interference. In a CDMA system it is possible to use the same frequency channel in adjacent cells and thus increase the system capacity.
4. The speech signal is inherently bursty because of the natural gaps during conversation. In FDMD and TDMA systems, once a channel (frequency and/or time slot) is allocated to a user, that channel cannot be used during non-activity periods. However, in CDMA systems the background noise is roughly the average of transmitted signals from all other users and thus a nonactive period in speech reduces the background noise. Hence, extra users may be accommodated without the loss of signal quality. This in turn increases the system capacity.

SDMA

The SDMA scheme, also referred to as space diversity, uses an array of antennas to provide control of space by providing virtual channels in angle domain.[18] This scheme exploits the directivity and beam-shaping capability of an array of antennas to reduce cochannel interference. Thus, it is possible that by using this scheme, simultaneous calls in a cell could be established at the same carrier frequency. This helps to increase the capacity of a cellular system.

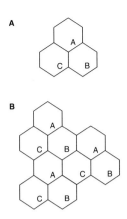

Fig. 2 (**A**) A cluster of three cells. (**B**) Channel reuse concept using a three-cell cluster.

The scheme is based on the fact that a signal arriving from a distant source reaches different antennas in an array at different times as a result of their spatial distribution, and this delay is utilized to differentiate one or more users in one area from those in another area. The scheme allows an effective transmission to take place between a base station and a mobile without disturbing the transmission to other mobiles. Thus, it has the potential such that the shape of a cell may be changed dynamically to reflect the user movement instead of used fixed size cells. This arrangement then is able to create an extra dimension by providing dynamic control in space.[19,20]

CHANNEL REUSE

The generic term, *channel*, is normally used to denote a frequency in FDMA system, a time slot in TDMA system, and a code in CDMA system or a combination of these in a mixed system. Two channels are different if they use different combinations of these at the same place. For example, two channels in a FDMA system

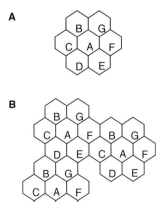

Fig. 3 (**A**) A cluster of seven cells. (**B**) Channel reuse concept using a seven-cell cluster.

use two different frequencies. Similarly, in TDMA system two separate time slots using the same frequency channel is considered two different channels. In that sense, for an allocated spectrum the number of channels in a system is limited. This limits the capacity of the system to sustain simultaneous calls and may only be increased by using each traffic channel to carry many calls simultaneously. Using the same channel again and again is one way of doing it. This is the concept of channel reuse.

The concept of channel reuse can be understood from Fig. 2 that shows a cluster of three cells. These cells use three separate sets of channels. This set is indicated by a letter. Thus, one cell uses set A, the other uses set B, and so on. In Fig. 2 this cluster of three cells is being repeated to indicate that three sets of channels are being reused in different cells. Fig. 3 shows a similar arrangement with cluster size of seven cells. Now let us see how this helps to increase the system capacity.

Assume there are a total of F channels in a system to be used over a given geographic area. Also assume that there are N cells in a cluster that use all the available channels. In the absence of channel reuse this cluster covers the whole area and the capacity of the system to sustain simultaneous calls is F. Now if the cluster of N cells is repeated M times over the same area, then the system capacity increases to MF as each channel is used M times.

The number of cells in a cluster is referred to as the cluster size, the parameter $1/N$ is referred to as the frequency reuse factor, and a system using a cluster size of N is sometimes also referred to as a system using N frequency reuse plan. The cluster size is an important parameter. For a given cell size, as the cluster size decreases, more clusters are required to cover the given area leading to more reuse of channels, and hence the system capacity increases. Theoretically, the maximum capacity is attained when cluster size is one, i.e., when all the available channels are reused in each cell. For hexagonal cell geometry, the cluster size can only have certain values. These are given by $N = i^2 + j^2 + ij$, where i and j are nonnegative integers.

The cells using the same set of channels are known as cochannel cells. For example, in Fig. 2, the cells using channels A are cochannel cells. The distance between cochannel cells is known as cochannel distance and the interference caused by the radiation from these cells is referred to as cochannel interference. For proper functioning of the system, this needs to be minimized by decreasing the power transmitted by mobiles and base stations in cochannel cells and increasing the cochannel distance. Because the transmitted power normally depends on the cell size, the minimization of cochannel interference requires a minimum cochannel distance; i.e., the distance cannot be smaller than this minimum distance.

In a cellular system of equal cell size, the cochannel interference is a function of a dimensionless parameter known as cochannel reuse ratio Q. This is a ratio of the cochannel distance D and the cell radius R, i.e.,

$$Q = \frac{D}{R}$$

For hexagonal geometry,

$$Q = \sqrt{3N}$$

It follows from these equations that an increase in Q increases the cochannel distance and thus minimizes the cochannel interference. On the other hand, a decrease in Q decreases the cluster size N and hence maximizes the system capacity. Thus, the selection of Q is a tradeoff between the two parameters, namely, the system capacity and cochannel interferences. It should be noted that for proper functioning of the system, the signal to cochannel interference ratio should be above a certain minimum value.[21]

CELLULAR CONFIGURATION

A cellular system may be referred to as a macrocell, a microcell, or a picocell system depending on the size of cells. Some characteristics of these cellular structures are now described.

Macrocell System

A cellular system with its cell size of several kilometer is referred to as macrocell systems. Base stations of these systems transmit several watts of power from antennas mounted on high towers. Normally there is no line of sight (LOS) between the base station and mobiles and thus a typical received signal is a combination of various signals arriving from different directions. The received signal in these systems experience spreading of several microsecond because of the nature of propagation conditions.

Microcell Systems

As cells are split and their boundaries are redefined, their size becomes very small. At a radius less than about a kilometer, the system is referred to as a microcell system. In these systems a typical base station transmits less than 1 W of power from an antenna mounted at a few meter above the ground and normally an LOS exists between the base and a mobile. Cell radius in microcell systems is less than a kilometer giving rms delay spread on the order of few tens of nanosecond compared with a few microseconds for macrocell systems. This impacts the maximum data rate a channel could sustain. For microcell systems maximum bit rate is about 1 Mbps compared with that of about 300 Kbps for macrocell systems.[8]

Microcell systems are also useful in providing coverage along roads and highways. Because the antenna height is normally lower than the surrounding buildings the propagation is along the streets and an LOS exists between the base and a mobile. When a mobile turns a corner, sometimes a sudden drop in received signal strength is experienced because of loss of LOS. Depending on how antennas are mounted on intersections and corners, various cell plans are possible. More details on these aspects may be found in Tripathi et al.[22] and references therein.

Picocell Systems

When cell sizes are reduced below about 100 m covering areas such as large rooms, corridors, underground stations, large shopping centers, cellular systems are sometimes referred to as picocell systems with antennas mounted below rooftop levels or in buildings. These in-building areas have different propagation conditions than those covered by macrocell and microcell systems, and thus require different considerations for developing channel models. Details on various models to predict propagation conditions may be found in Fleury and Leuthold.[4] Sometimes the picocell and microcell systems are also referred to as cordless communication systems with the term *cellular* identifying a macrocell system. Mobiles within these smaller cell systems are called cordless terminals or cordless phones.[23–25]

Providing in-building communication services using wireless technology based on cell shapes dictated by floors and walls, is a feasible alternative and offers many advantages. It is argued in Pandya[24] that RFs in 18-GHz band are ideal for such services because these do not penetrate concrete and steel structures, eliminating the problem of cochannel interferences. These frequencies offer huge bandwidth and require millimeter size antennas that are easy to manufacture and install.

Overlayed System

Small cell systems make very efficient use of the spectrum, allowing large frequency reuse resulting in an increased capacity of a system. However, these are not suitable for all conditions because of their large handoff requirement. A system of mixed cells with the concept of overlaying is discussed.[22,26-29] In this system a hierarchy of cells is assumed to exist. A macrocell system is assumed at the top of the hierarchy with smaller cells systems at its bottom. A mobile with high mobility is assigned to a macrocell system, whereas the one with a low mobility, to smaller cell systems. A design incorporating various combinations of different multiple access schemes reflects the ease of handoff and other traffic management strategies. A SDMA scheme has an important role to play in this concept, with various beams placed at the bottom of the hierarchy.

CHANNEL ALLOCATION AND ASSIGNMENT

Various multiple access schemes discussed in a previous section are used to divide a given spectrum into a set of disjoint channels. These channels are then allocated to various cells for their use. Channel allocation may be carried out using one of the three basic schemes, namely, fixed channel allocation, dynamic channel allocation, and hybrid channel allocation.[30]

Fixed Channel Allocation Schemes

In fixed channel allocation schemes, a number of channels are allocated to a cell permanently for its use such that these channels satisfy certain channel reuse constraints as discussed in the previous section. In its simplest form, the same number of channels are allocated to each cell. For a system with uniform traffic distribution across all cells, this uniform channel allocation scheme is efficient in the sense that the average call blocking probability in each cell is the same as that of the overall system. For systems where the distribution is not uniform, the call blocking probability differs from cell to cell, resulting in the call being blocked in some cells when there are spare channels available in other cells.

This situation could be improved by allocating channels nonuniformly as per the expected traffic in each cell or employing one of many prevailing channel borrowing schemes. One of these is referred to as a static borrowing scheme where some channels are borrowed from cells with light traffic and allocated to those with heavy traffic. Rearrangements of channels between cells are performed periodically to meet the variation in traffic load. In this scheme, the borrowed channels stay with the new cell until reallocated. There are other temporary borrowing schemes where a cell that has used all its channels is allowed to borrow a free channel from a neighbor provided it does not interfere with existing calls. The borrowed channel is returned to the original cell once the call is complete. Some temporary borrowing schemes allow any channel from a cell to be borrowed, whereas in others only nominated channels are allowed to be borrowed. Many borrowing strategies are available for selecting a channel, ranging from a simple scheme to pick the first available channel that satisfies the cochannel distance constraints to the one

that performs an exhaustive search to select a channel that yields maximum SIR and minimizes the future probability of call blocking.

Dynamic Channel Allocation Schemes

Fixed channel allocation schemes discussed thus far are simple to implement and are generally useful for relatively stable traffic conditions. These schemes are not very efficient for fast changing user distribution because they are not designed to adapt to short-term variations in traffic conditions. Dynamic channel allocation schemes are most suited for such situations. In these schemes, channels are not allocated to various cells but are kept in a central pool, and are assigned to calls as they arrive. At the completion of a call, the assigned channel is released and goes back to the pool. The process of channel assignment involves working out a cost of assigning a channel to a call and a channel with the minimum cost is chosen for the purpose. The various channel assignment schemes differ in the way the cost function is selected using various parameters of interest such as reuse distance, SIR ratio, and probability of call blocking. Some schemes base their assignment only on the existing traffic conditions in the service area whereas the others take the past and the present conditions into account.

Dynamic channel assignment schemes may be implemented centrally where a central controller assigns the channels to calls from the pool. The central controller is able to achieve very efficient channel assignment but requires high overhead. The channel assignment may also be implemented in a distributed manner by base stations where calls are originated. The channel implementation by base stations requires less overhead than that required by a central controller and is more suitable for microcell systems. The distributed channel assignment schemes can be divided into two categories. In one case each base station keeps detailed status information about existingavailable channels in its neighborhood by exchanging status information with other base stations. The schemes in this category may provide near optimum allocation but pay a heavy price in terms of increased communication with other base stations, particularly in heavy traffic. The other category of distributed channel assignment schemes uses simple algorithms that rely on mobiles to measure signal strength to decide the suitability of a channel.

Hybrid Channel Allocation Schemes

The fixed channel allocation schemes are efficient under uniformly distributed heavy traffic. On the other hand, the dynamic channel allocation schemes perform better under low traffic conditions with varying and nonuniformly distributed loads. The hybrid channel allocation schemes maximize advantages of both these schemes by dividing channels into fixed and dynamic sets. The channels in fixed sets are allocated as per fixed channel allocation strategies and those in the other set are free to be assigned to calls in a cell that has used all its allocated channels. The channels in this set are assigned as per the dynamic channel allocation procedures. Apparently, no optimum ratio of channels is assigned to two sets and the design parameter is dependent on local traffic conditions. More details on these and related issues may be found in Katzela and Naghshineh[30] and references therein.

HANDOFF

It is common for a mobile to move away from its servicing base station while a call is in progress. As the mobile approaches the cell boundary, the strength and quality of the signal it receives starts to deteriorate. At some stage, near the cell boundary, it receives a stronger signal from a neighboring base station than it does from its serving base station. At this point the control of the mobile is handed over to the new base station by assigning a channel belonging to the new cell. This process where a radio channel used by a mobile is changed, is referred to as handoff or handover.[22,25,29-32] When handoff is between two base stations as described earlier, it is referred to as intercell handoff. On the other hand, when handoff is between two channels belonging to the same base stations, it is referred to as intracell handoff. The situation arises when the network, while monitoring its channels, finds a free channel of better quality than that used by a mobile and decides to move the mobile to this new channel to improve the quality of channels in use. Sometimes, the network rearranges channels to avoid congestion and initiates intracell handoff.

Handoff is also necessary between different layers of overlayed systems consisting of microcells and macrocells. In these systems, the channels are divided into microcell channels and macrocell channels. When a mobile moves from one microcell to another and there is no available channel for handoff, a macrocell channel is used to meet the handoff request. This avoids the forced termination of a call. Later if a channel becomes available at an underlayed microcell, then the macrocell channel may be released and a microcell channel is assigned to the call by initiating a new handoff.

Forced termination of a call in progress is undesirable and to minimize it, a number of strategies are employed. These include reserving channels for handoff, using channel assignment schemes that give priority to a handoff request over new calls, and queuing the handoff request. The channel reservation and handoff priority scheme reduce the probability of forced termination by increasing the probability of blocking new calls. The queuing schemes are effective when handoff requests arrive in groups and there is a reasonable likelihood of channel availability in the near future.

The handoff is initiated when the quality of existing channels deteriorates below an acceptable threshold or a better channel is available. The channel quality is measured in terms of BER, received signal strength, or some other signal quality such as eye opening of radio signal that indicates signal to interference plus noise ratio.

For handoff initiation, the signal strength is used as an indication of the distance between the base and the mobile. For this reason, a drop in signal strength resulting from Rayleigh fading is normally not used to initiate handoff and some kind of averaging is used to avoid the problem. In some systems, the round trip delay between mobile and base is also used as an indication of the distance.

The measurement of various parameters may be carried out either at the mobile or at the base. Depending on where the measurements are made and who initiates the handoff, various handoff implementation schemes are possible including network-controlled handoff, mobile-controlled handoff, and mobile-assisted handoff.

Network-Controlled Handoff

In network-controlled handoff, each base station monitors the signal strength received from mobiles in their cells and makes periodic measurements of the received signal from mobiles in their neighboring cells. The MSC then initiates and completes the handoff of a mobile as and when it decides. The decision is based on the received signal strength at the base station serving the mobiles and base stations in neighboring cells. Because of its centralized nature, the collection of these measurements generates a large network traffic. This could be reduced to an extent by making measurements less frequently and by not requiring the neighboring base station to send the measurements continually. However, this reduces the accuracy. The execution of handoff by this method takes a few seconds and for this reason the method is not preferred by microcellular systems where a quick handoff is desirable.

Mobile-Controlled Handoff

Mobile-controlled handoff is a highly decentralized method and does not need any assistance from the MSC. In this scheme a mobile monitors the signal strength on its existing channel and measures signals received from the neighboring base stations. It receives BER and signal strength information from its serving base stations about uplink channels. Based on all this information, it initiates the handoff process by requesting the neighboring base for allocation of a low interference channel. The method has a handoff execution time on the order of 100 ms and is suitable for microcell systems.

Mobile-Assisted Handoff

In mobile-assisted handoff methods, as the name suggests, a mobile helps the network in the handoff decision making by monitoring the signal strength of its neighboring base stations and passing them to MSC via its serving base station. The handoff is initiated and completed by the network. The execution time is on the order of 1 second.

Hard Handoff and Soft Handoff

Handoff may be classified into hard handoff and soft handoff. During hard handoff the mobile can communicate only with one base station. The communication link gets broken with the existing base station before the new one is established and there is normally a small gap in communication during the transition. In the process of soft handoff, the mobile is able to communicate with more than one base station. It receives signals from more than one base station and the received signals are combined after appropriate delay adjustment. Similarly, more than one station receives signals from mobiles and the network combines different signals. This scheme is also known as macroscopic diversity and is mostly employed by CDMA systems.

Hard handoff, on the other hand, is more appropriate for TDMA and FDMA systems. It is also simple to implement compared with soft handoff. However, it may lead to unnecessary handoff back and forth between two base stations when the signals from two base stations fluctuate. The situation may arise when a mobile, presently being served, e.g., by Base 1, receives a stronger signal, from say Base 2 and is handed over to Base 2. Immediately after that it receives a stronger signal from Base 1 compared what it receives from Base 2, causing a handoff. This phenomenon, known as the ping-pong effect, may continue for some time and is undesirable because every handoff has a cost associated with it requiring network signaling of varying amount for authentication, database updates, circuit switching, and so on. This is avoided by using a hysteresis margin such that the handoff is not initiated until the difference between the signals received from the two base stations is more than the margin. For example, if the margin is Δ dB then the handoff is initiated when the signal

received by the mobile from Base 2 is Δ dB more than that from Base 1. More details on various handoff implementation issues may be found in Tripathi et al.,[22] Noerpel and Lin,[31] and Tekinay and Jabbari[33] and references therein.

CELL SPLITTING AND CELL SECTORIZATION

Each cell has a limited channel capacity and thus could only serve so many mobiles at a given time. Once the demand in that cell exceeds this limit, the cell is further subdivided into smaller cells, each new cell with its own base station and its frequency allocation. The power of the base station transmitters is adjusted to reflect the new boundaries. The power transmitted by new base stations is less than that of the old one.

The consequence of the cell splitting is that the frequency assignment has to be done again, which affects the neighboring cells. It also increases the handoff rate because the cells are now smaller and a mobile is likely to cross cell boundaries more often compared with the case when the cells are big. Because of altered signaling conditions, this also affects the traffic in control channels.

Cell sectorization is referred to the case when a given cell is subdivided into several sectors and all sectors are served by the same base station. This is normally done by employing directional antennas such that the energy in each sector is directed by separate antennas. This has the effect of increased channel capacity similar to cell splitting. However, it uses the same base station and thus does not incur the cost of establishing new base stations associated with the cell splitting. This helps in reducing the cochannel interference because the energy is directed in the direction of the sector that does not cause interference in the cochannel cells, particularly in cochannel cells in the opposite direction to the sector. As in the case of cell splitting, this also affects the handoff rate.

POWER CONTROL

It is important that a radio receiver receives a power level that is enough for its proper function but not high enough for this level to disturb other receivers. This is achieved with maintaining constant power level at the receiver by transmitter power control. The receiver controls the power of the transmitter at the other end. For example, a base would control the power transmitted by mobile phones and vice versa.

It is done by a receiver monitoring its received power and sending a control signal to the transmitter to control its power transmission as required. Sometimes a separate pilot signal is used for this purpose.

Power control reduces the near–far problem in CDMA systems and helps to minimize the interference near the cell boundaries when used in forwardlink.[12,13]

REFERENCES

1. Godara, L.C. Application of antenna arrays to mobile communications part I: performance improvement, feasibility and system considerations. Proc. IEEE **1997**, *85* (7), 1031–1062.
2. Phlavan, K.; Levesque, A.H. Wireless data communications. Proc. IEEE **1994**, *82* (9), 1398–1430.
3. Bertoni, H.L.; Honcharenko, W.; Maceil, L.R.; Xia, H.H. UHF propagation prediction for wireless personal communications. Proc. IEEE **1994**, *82* (9), 1333–1359.
4. Fleury, B.H.; Leuthold, P.E. Radiowave propagation in mobile communications: an overview of European research. IEEE Commun. Mag. **1996**, *34* (2), 70–81.
5. Lee, W.C.Y. *Mobile Communication Design Fundamentals*; John Wiley and Sons: New York, NY, 1993.
6. French, R.C. The effect of fading and shadowing on channel reuse in mobile radio. IEEE Trans. Veh. Technol. **1979**, *28* (3), 171–181.
7. Winters, J.H. Optimum combining for indoor radio systems with multiple users. IEEE Trans. Commun. **1987**, *COM35*, 1222–1230.
8. Andersen, J.B.; Rappaport, T.S.; Yoshida, S. Propagation measurements and models for wireless communications channels. IEEE Commun. Mag. **1995**, *33* (1), 42–49.
9. Falconer, D.D.; Adachi, F.; Gudmundson, B. Time division multiple access methods for wireless personal communications. IEEE Commun. Mag. **1995**, *33* (1), 50–57.
10. Raith, K.; Uddenfeldt, J. Capacity of digital cellular TDMA systems. IEEE Trans. Veh. Technol. **1991**, *40* (2), 323–332.
11. Lee, W.C.Y. Overview of cellular CDMA. IEEE Trans. Veh. Technol. **1991**, *40* (2), 291–302.
12. Gilhousen, K.S.; Jacobs, I.M.; Padovani, R.; Viterbi, A.J.; Weaver, L.A., Jr.; Wheatley, C.E., III On the capacity of cellular CDMA system. IEEE Trans. Veh. Technol. **1991**, *40* (2), 303–312.
13. Pickholtz, R.L.; Milstein, L.B.; Schilling, D.L. Spread spectrum for mobile communications. IEEE Trans. Veh. Technol. **1991**, *40* (2), 313–322.
14. Kohno, R.; Meidan, R.; Milstein, L.B. Spread spectrum access methods for wireless communications. IEEE Commun. Mag. **1995**, *33* (1), 58–67.
15. Abramson, N. Multiple access in wireless digital networks. Proc. IEEE **1994**, *82* (9), 1360–1370.
16. Pickholtz, R.L.; Schilling, D.L.; Milstein, L.B. Milstein, L. B. Theory of spread spectrum communications a tutorial. IEEE Trans. Commun. **1982**, *COM30* (5), 855–884.
17. Milstein, L.B. Wideband code division multiple access. IEEE J. Sel. Areas Commun. **2000**, *18* (8), 1344–1354.
18. Winters, J.H.; Salz, J.; Gitlin, R.D. The impact of antenna diversity on the capacity of wireless communication systems. IEEE Trans. Commun. **1994**, *42* (2/3/4), 1740–1751.
19. Godara, L.C. Application of antenna arrays to mobile communications. Part II: beam-forming and DOA considerations. Proc. IEEE **1997**, *85* (8), 1195–1247.
20. Mizuno, M.; Ohgane, T. Application of adaptive array antennas to radio communications. Electron. Commun. Jpn. Part I: Commun. **1994**, *77*, 48–59.
21. Rappaport, T.S. *Wireless Communications: Principles and Practice*; Prentice Hall: Englewood Cliffs, NJ, 1996.
22. Tripathi, N.D.; Reed, J.H.; Van Landingham, H.F. Handoff in cellular systems. IEEE Personal Commun. **1998**,; 26–37.
23. Padgett, J.E.; Gunther, C.G.; Hattori, T. Overview of wireless personal communications. IEEE Commun. Mag. **1995**, *33* (1), 28–41.
24. Pandya, R. Emerging mobile and personal communication systems. IEEE Commun. Mag. **1995**, *33* (6), 44–52.
25. Tuttlebee, W.H.W. Cordless personal telecommunications. IEEE Commun. Mag. **1992**, *30* (12), 42–53.
26. Freeburg, T.A. Enabling technologies for wireless inbuilding network communications four technical challenges, four solutions. IEEE Commun. Mag. **1991**, *29* (4), 58–64.
27. Pollinim, G.P. Trends in handover design. IEEE Commun. Mag. **1996**, *34* (3), 82–90.
28. Rappaport, S.S.; Hu, L.R. Microcellular communication systems with hierarchical macrocell overlays: traffic performance models and analysis. Proc. IEEE **1994**, *83* (9), 1383–1397.
29. Steel, R.; Whitehead, J.; Wong, W.C. System aspects of cellular radio. IEEE Commun. Mag. **1995**, *33* (1), 80–87.
30. Katzela, L.; Naghshineh, M. Channel assignment schemes for cellular mobile telecommunication systems: a comprehensive survey. IEEE Personal Commun. **1996**, *3* (3), 10–31.
31. Noerpel, A.; Lin, Y.B. Handover management for a PC network. IEEE Personal Commun. **1997**, *4* (6), 18–24.
32. Wong, D.; Lim, T.J. Soft handoffs in CDMA mobile systems. IEEE Personal Commun. **1997**, *4* (6), 6–17.
33. Tekinay, S.; Jabbari, B. Handover and channel assignment in mobile cellular networks. IEEE Commun. Mag. **1991**, *29* (11), 42–46.

Cloud Computing

Brian J.S. Chee
School of Ocean and Earth Sciences and Technology (SOEST), University of Hawaii, Honolulu, Hawaii, U.S.A.
Curtis Franklin, Jr.
Senior Writer, NetWitness, Gainsville, Florida, U.S.A.

Abstract

Clouds are, if anything, moving targets of misunderstood buzz words that seem to have caught the attention of industry journalists. Like its namesake, the concept of a cloud is nebulous and at the moment is changing faster than most of us can keep up. However, like rain clouds, cloud computing has the promise of providing a massive surge of growth in an industry that is struggling to grow up. This entry provides some historical background for the development of cloud technology, because the present day (and the future) cloud environments are built on the shoulders of the giants that came before them.

INTRODUCTION

In this entry, you'll learn about:

- History, or the mainframe revisited—It's amazing just how cyclical the information technology (IT) world is. We draw comparisons to how our experience with mainframes is helping to shape the emerging cloud marketplace.
- Abstraction layers and how they hide the gory details—It is said that great works are built on the shoulders of giants, and the road to Cloud City is the same. Abstraction layers have been developing and maturing over the years into a platform fit for the denizens of Olympus.
- Why scientific clusters, also known as high-performance computers, are both similar to and different from clouds—Clouds may have started as scientific computing tools, but the overall architecture has diverged to create a whole new technology. We take a hard look at what came before and how it has set the stage for Cloud City.
- Connections to the world and to data all have to happen seamlessly—If clouds are to be accepted, access to the clouds must be reliable and ubiquitous enough to drop off the radar of users. We discuss some of the changes happening that seem tailor-made for clouds.

IN THE BEGINNING

In the beginning was the mainframe and it was, if not good, at least straightforward. Users and staff alike knew precisely where input, output, and processing happened.

Think of the mainframe as the dense, hot core of what would become the computing universe we know now. In the (computing) moments just after the *Big Bang*, time-share and remote terminal services divorced input and output from processing, but it was still possible to walk down a hall, open a door, and point to the box doing the work. As early as 1960, though, computer scientists such as John McCarthy foresaw computing services that would be treated as a public utility. A decade later, networks and the Internet continued to make processing a more abstract piece of the computing pie.

Abstraction and a move toward computing as a public utility took a great step forward when the concept of Software as a Service (SaaS) was developed in the early 2000s. As the link between applications (or application components) and specific pieces of hardware continued to weaken, IT professionals searched for new ways to describe systems that resulted of disparate components coming together with no regard to the location of any single piece. The Internet has long been referred to as a *cloud*—named for the symbol used to represent the Internet in network diagrams—and has come now to encompass the trend toward SaaS and Web 2.0 as computing continues toward a disconnect from computing at physical locations. Cloud computing is, in many ways, a return to the centrally coordinated integration of the mainframe time-share era: The personal computer (PC) gave users the opportunity to strike back against the *glass house* and the elitism common to that day instead of allowing more cooperative integration of the new resource. Cloud computing is a counterreformation that brings with it the possibility of some very real performance wins for users and their organizations.

Cloud resources can also be described as part of a long line of technology advances that have further

Encyclopedia of Information Systems and Technology, DOI: 10.1081/E-EIST-120053809

159

distanced us from the details of running a data center. Science fiction author Arthur C. Clarke wrote about a global computing facility without shape and form—his characters simply used the *network* to communicate, play games, and do many other things, all without regard to what the operating system or central processing unit (CPU) was behind the scenes. People used only what they needed and paid for only what they used. It didn't matter where in the world (or the solar system, as Clarke proposed) you were; you could access your stored information regardless of whether you were using a private or a public terminal. This network was also ubiquitous, since even the monks at the top of a mountain as mentioned in the *Fountains of Paradise* had a terminal.

So what, precisely, is cloud computing? According to Carl Hewitt, in a paper published in 2008 by the Institute of Electrical and Electronic Engineers, cloud computing "is a paradigm in which information is permanently stored in servers on the Internet and cached temporarily on clients that include desktops, entertainment centers, table computers, notebooks, wall computers, handhelds, sensors, monitors, etc." That's a pretty thorough definition, but it may still be incomplete for our purposes, because it doesn't mention management, efficiency, delivery mechanisms, or the concept of abstraction. A more complete definition might be:

> Cloud computing is an information-processing model in which centrally administered computing capabilities are delivered as services, on an as-needed basis, across the network to a variety of user-facing devices.

This is the definition on which we will be basing the discussions in this entry. We will expand on some of the terms, but this is where we will begin.

For us to get to computing in a cloud, we first have to understand what, precisely, we are talking about. We will start with a discussion of key concepts that underlie cloud computing, then proceed to look at the specifics of cloud computing—and what it is that separates cloud computing from virtualization, clustering, and other forms of computing that separate processing from processors. Along the way, we'll be defining terms used in cloud computing discussions and looking at how and why organizations are using cloud computing for their critical applications.

COMPUTER SERVICES BECOME ABSTRACT

A computer system's functions and interactions with other systems can be visualized as a set of children's interlocking building blocks. A system architect starts with an imaginary pile of blocks of various colors and sizes, each color representing a different function or

process. The expectation is that pieces will lock together from bottom to top, and that they are of compatible sizes so they will form a solid wall when they are fitted into a structure. The concept of an abstraction layer is similar: It provides a way to connect two systems together without radically changing either. As a pleasant (and productive) side effect, abstraction layers can also be described as a way to hide architectural and programming details on either side of the interface.

Abstraction is a critical foundation concept for cloud computing because it allows us to think of a particular service—an application, a particular communication protocol, processing cycles within a CPU, or storage capacity on a hard disk—without thinking about a particular piece of hardware that will provide that service. Let's imagine abstraction applied to a task that has nothing to do with computers; we'll discuss the abstraction of going to the grocery store.

Pretend, for a moment, that you don't own any vehicles for transportation. Instead, you contract with service providers for transportation services. When you're ready to go to the grocery store, you pick up the telephone, dial a number, and tell the operator who picks up where you want to go. The operator, in turn, tells you when transportation will show up at your door. The telephone, telephone number, and the messages sent and received can be thought of as the program interface between you and the transportation service—they are part of a standard, consistent way of requesting transportation. Now, you wait the stated length of time and open your door to find a portal that leads you into a passenger compartment. Every time you request transportation, the portal and the passenger compartment look the same, but you'll never know whether the compartment sits inside an automobile, a bus, a luxury RV, or a yak-pulled cart. The fact is that the vehicle doesn't matter, because the passenger compartment, and transportation to your chosen destination, is all that's important.

When you reach the grocery store (within a time limit specified in the service-level agreement you have with the transportation company sign), the portal opens and you walk out into the store. When you've finished shopping, you place another call, and the same sort of transportation takes you back home (or to your next errand). For each trip, the transportation company is free to send whichever vehicle is available and can make the trip most efficiently, and you're never faced with the inefficiency of having an unused vehicle sitting around while you're doing things at home. Divorcing the transportation from the vehicle is what abstraction is all about. We'll come back to this abstract transportation example later on, but first let's look at just how abstraction has been applied to some common computing and network situations.

OSI Model

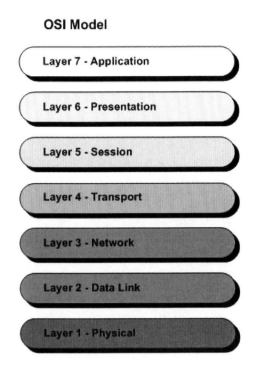

Fig. 1 The OSI model defines specific roles for hardware, software, and services that fall into seven distinct layers.

THE ISO-OSI MODEL: SEVEN LAYERS OF ABSTRACTION

The most commonly used abstraction layers in the computing world are found in the Open Systems Interconnection (OSI) seven-layer networking Basic Reference Model. This application of abstraction layers means that network equipment manufacturers (NEMs) no longer have to write software for specific pieces of equipment. In practice, this means that network adapter cards made by, say, 3Com, can connect via a standard cable to an Ethernet switch made by, say, Cisco. It also means that common communication applications such as e-mail and the World Wide Web can operate without having to be aware of which vendor made the network they are communicating across. The International Standards Organization (ISO) developed this seven-layer model, with each subsequent layer fitting into the next in a well-defined, standardized fashion. Very much like Russian *matryoshka* nesting dolls, the ISO seven-layer model separates the network communications path into layers that allow the NEMs to leverage a body of standardized work (see Fig. 1). This separation of roles has also led to the creation of an entirely new industry that concentrates their work on the manipulation of those middle layers for new and previously unknown services. These nested layers provide a way for specialization to work toward accomplishing a significantly more complex outcome by eliminating the need to constantly reinvent the wheel whenever a new network service is designed.

The OSI model provides for distinct roles for devices, services, and protocols that lie within each layer, and for specific ways in which the components in one layer interact with components in other layers. These carefully engineered roles and interactions not only make today's open networking possible, they provide a model for the kind of open yet highly structured architecture required for cloud computing to be possible. While the networking model is critical, however, it isn't the only sort of abstraction model required before we can understand cloud computing. Let's look next at the way in which Web servers and databases talk to one another to build popular applications on the Web.

OPEN DATABASE CONNECTION: THE ABSTRACT DATABASE

Another common abstraction model describes the way that Web servers connect to databases. The original database-to-Web connection wasn't developed by a standard committee, but by two programmers searching for a solution to a problem. Richard Chan and Jim Laurel owned a Honolulu-based computer equipment distribution firm called Aspect Computing. Their problem was how to leverage the new World Wide Web to allow customers to check stocking levels for their products. What they came up with became the foundation for the set of protocols that Microsoft and the standards committee would eventually name the Open DataBase Connection (ODBC) at some point after they purchased the technology from Aspect Computing. Originally called WebDB, this fundamental abstraction layer paved the way for many cloud services. Basically, instead of having to modify the web server directly through extensive Computer Generated Imagery calls specific to each data source, Richard and Jim utilized a set of functions to query various types of databases simply by changing a few configuration items (see Fig. 2).

Let's take a moment to think about the importance of what ODBC provides. In traditional database applications, the programmer writes an application in a language that is specific to the database management software. The piece of the application that makes it specific to a particular database is, in other words, an intrinsic part of the application. If the database manager is changed, the application has to be rewritten in order to remain functional. In the ODBC model, a common query language is used, and an external file provides the configuration information required to make the application work with a specific database. If the database management system changes, no modification is made to the application—the change happens in the external configuration file. It is, to be sure, an additional component for the overall application, but it is an additional

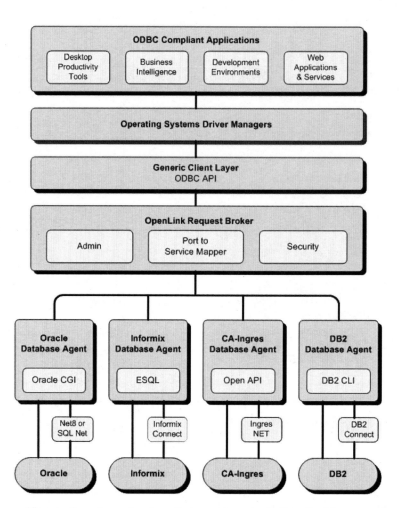

Fig. 2 ODBC defines a specific set of queries and actions that provide a standard method for an application to make use of any database (or set of databases) without requiring code customized for the individual database language.

component that makes programming easier and far more efficient for application developers.

OpenGL: ABSTRACT IMAGES

For a number of years the prevailing wisdom was that the additional components required for an open application model such as ODBC exacted a significant cost on the computing system—a cost so heavy that those applications requiring the highest performance weren't suitable for development on such a model. This wisdom was overturned by the rise of an abstraction model that enables some of the most critically high-performance computing around: graphics display processing (see Fig. 3).

OpenGL is a library of abstract layers that allows application and operating system programmers to write code for a standard graphics abstract layer, rather than for each new display adapter that might be released to the market. OpenGL is an important development for the computing industry because of the rapid pace at

which new display adapters are brought to market and the critical importance of graphical interfaces to the modern computer user experience.

OpenGL has been well accepted for several reasons. First, it has helped insulate application developers from a very rapidly changing marketplace. New graphics processors, and cards based on them, are brought to market frequently. OpenGL ensures that existing applications can take advantage of the latest hardware as soon as it reaches the market. Next, OpenGL is written in a way that allows it to use the most efficient algorithms for processing specific pieces of the graphical image. Some images are most efficiently dealt with in terms of individual pixels, or points of light within the picture. Others are more effectively considered in terms of lines, points, and other geometric components. OpenGL can do both. Finally, OpenGL began to be adopted as graphics processors were becoming more powerful, in many cases, than the basic CPU used in the computer. Even if OpenGL did require a processing tariff, it was barely noticed by users, and it meant a solid trade-off for the substantial benefits that OpenGL offered in other areas.

GEOMETRY PATH   **IMAGING PATH**

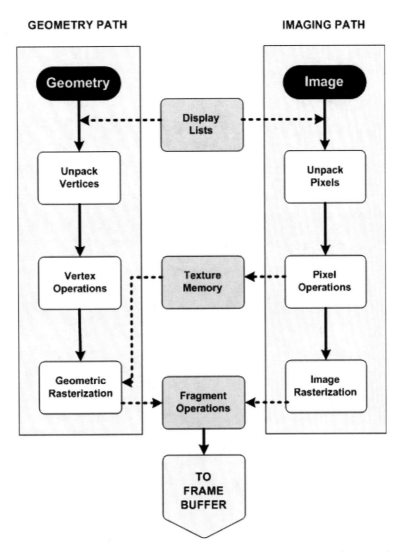

Fig. 3 OpenGL proved that an abstraction model can be fast enough to service the most performance-intensive parts of a computing platform—the graphic display components.

In OpenGL, we see an abstract model that has been accepted because it lowers the cost of applications, makes those applications available sooner and more widely than they might be otherwise, and provides a level of protection for investments against the horrors of rapid obsolescence.

These three examples of abstraction at various levels of computing—networking, applications, and user interface—demonstrate how software can be divorced from specific pieces of hardware when application development is in question. They also demonstrate the range of benefits that can accrue from considering the application a user handles as separate from the hardware and software infrastructure on which it runs. This abstraction from the computing angle is one side of the equation needed to get to cloud computing. The other side of the equation is abstraction of user demand, and that's what we'll look at next.

DEMAND ABSTRACTION

In order to visualize demand abstraction, we need to travel back in time a bit and learn from the systems created to support the glass houses of the mainframe elite. In those days, computing time was so expensive that systems administrators started charging a premium to users who wanted to go to the front of the line.

In the era when computing meant buying CPU time on a mainframe, users were forced to balance the health of their budgets versus actually being able to run programs within a reasonable amount of time. The balancing of low-priority and high-priority users was done through management services such as the Houston Automatic Spooling Priority, with faster queues costing more and slower queues costing less. Using Job Control Language (JCL) statements, users could tell the mainframe what kinds of resources their jobs needed, estimated time, libraries, and other parameters. Users with special project needs could go a bit further and, in some advanced cases, blow a ton of money to request a job queue that had its own initiator (each mainframe *CPU* had multiple initiators, which today would be called a virtual CPU core). To put this into perspective, the entire time-sharing option system, which at that time supported up to 32 simultaneous users, had a single initiator assigned to it. In those days, the infrastructure necessary to support time sharing was expensive enough that a whole market for data Private Branch Exchanges (think of these as phone systems for terminals) sprang up to allow hundreds or thousands of terminals to share the 32 *real* connections on the mainframe communications processor. A side benefit was the ability to switch between various time-share systems at each terminal, just like dialing a telephone.

The next, and most important, function of JCL was to allow users to request system resources in terms of memory, both temporary and permanent disk storage, print queues, punch queues, tape archiving, and dataset merging. If you had enough money and authority, you could even request access to specialized virtual machines that normally ran jobs of exceptionally high priority.

Why the emphasis on JCL? JCL was a very concise language set up to request resources from a computing facility when users had no knowledge of the resource's exact configuration. Users just made requests to this nebulous facility and ran their jobs. If this sounds familiar, it should: We've just reviewed one popular definition of a cloud. Demand abstraction in a cloud is exactly what users were doing with JCL back in the 1970s.

What are the differences, then, between the mainframe time-share computing of the 1970s and today's cloud computing? Some differences are trivial—Extensible Markup Language and middleware frameworks have replaced JCL on punchcards. Other differences are far more substantial: Today's clouds may be physically spread across the globe rather than just spread across a couple of IBM mainframes. One of the most important differences is that cloud computing uses the Internet, rather than private leased lines, for communications.

Why is that important? Well, in one sense, it's yet another layer of abstraction, since, without performing a series of trace-route operations, you have no way of knowing how the commands get from your workstation to the computer doing all the work (wherever that is). We should also point out that by treating the Internet as an abstraction layer, cloud computing can take place anywhere you have connectivity. Regardless of whether you're in your office, at home, or going mobile; you're now free to leverage cloud resources in a nearly constant fashion. So perhaps the change isn't the computing paradigm but rather the usage paradigm.

The point behind bringing this up is not to claim that there's nothing new in cloud computing, but to point out that some strategic, deployment, and management practices developed for mainframes may find new currency in the cloud environment. It's not that everything old is new again, but that the old can guide the new by lending their past elegance.

WHAT CAN YOU DO WITH A CLOUD?

One of the great difficulties in having short discussions about cloud computing is that clouds can look like so many different systems and do so many different things. Ultimately, the question, "What can you do with a cloud?" can only be answered with the question, "What can you imagine?" We'll talk about a number of things that individuals and companies are doing with clouds, but those examples will make a bit more sense if you start with some knowledge of where clouds got their start. Earlier, we said that clouds have a great deal in common with the mainframe time sharing of the 1960s and 1970s. That's quite true, but most of today's cloud infrastructures owe a great deal of their essential architecture to computer clusters.

The original clusters were a knee-jerk reaction by researchers starving for supercomputer time, but who were either too low on the priority list or too poor to actually get as much time as they needed. In their most basic sense, these clusters were systems that tied a number of inexpensive computers together into a single computing environment. They took advantage of the rapidly increasing power of small computers and promised researchers and technical computing customers near-supercomputing performance at near-PC prices. We see great similarities between the PC revolution, in how many sought out the PC as a less expensive way to ask business questions of their data, and the ways that scientists sought ways to ask the really hard computing questions of their data. The problem is that some of the problems in science are so computing-intensive that science has created massively parallel and expensive computing engines that have been out of the reach of all but the best-funded projects. The necessity for large amounts of computing for less well funded projects became the engine of creativity. One of the first successful projects in this direction was Beowulf.

Beowulf

In late 1993, Donald Becker and Thomas Sterling began sketching the outline of a commodity-based cluster system which they envisioned as a cost-effective alternative to large supercomputers. In early 1994, while working at the Center of Excellence in Space Data and

Information Sciences under the sponsorship of the High Performance Computing & Communications for Earth & Space Sciences project, they began work on Beowulf.

The initial prototype was a cluster computer consisting of 16 DX4 processors connected by channel-bonded Ethernet links. The machine was an instant success, and the idea of providing off-the-shelf commodity systems to satisfy specific computational requirements spread quickly through NASA and into the academic and research communities.

Although Beowulf took off like wildfire, it was still a long way from being a cloud. Beowulf laid the foundation for clustering a large number of inexpensive, off-the-shelf computers to provide high-performance computing cooperatively, but it was still a complex environment in which users had to write or rewrite their applications in terms of *parent* and *children* nodes, with the problem split into lots of smaller questions that were worked on as children node and the results compiled at the parent node. Quite a bit of skill was required in a variety of disciplines to break up larger questions into lots of smaller questions that could be handled by the commodity processors. Computing questions that could be solved nicely on traditional supercomputers didn't work anywhere near so well on the smaller PC platforms.

However, invention being the mother of invention, the developers leveraged their experience with traditional supercomputers and applied it to the smaller PC-based clusters. Key to their success was extension of the Message Passing Interface (MPI) abstraction layer that allowed the massively parallel applications to talk to each other effectively, providing the ability to have a master application spin off and control other applications, and then aggregate the results. Key to the success of the MPI abstraction layer is that it removed much of the complexity of writing for large-scale computing problems involved with passing data back and forth between parent and child nodes in the computing cluster.

Still to come were the abstraction of applications and hardware that is such an intrinsic part of true cloud computing, but these developments provided the foundation for a larger idea that was still years away. And what came next extended the idea even further.

Grid Computing

The basic concepts developed in Beowulf were taken much further by the folks at the Search for ExtraTerrestrial Intelligence project, who needed massive amounts of computing power to process their radio telescope data (to separate background noise from what they hoped would be a real signal of intelligent life). Their approach took advantage of the concept of *grid computing* and relied on legions of volunteers donating their screen saver time to help look for life *out there*.

According to Wikipedia, the free online encyclopedia:

> Grid computing is a form of distributed computing whereby a "super and virtual computer" is composed of a cluster of networked, loosely-coupled computers, acting in concert to perform very large tasks. This technology has been applied to computationally-intensive scientific, mathematical, and academic problems through volunteer computing, and it is used in commercial enterprises for such diverse applications as drug discovery, economic forecasting, seismic analysis, and back-office data processing in support of e-commerce and web services.

> What distinguishes grid computing from typical cluster computing systems is that grids tend to be more loosely coupled, heterogeneous, and geographically dispersed. Also, while a computing grid may be dedicated to a specialized application, it is often constructed with the aid of general purpose grid software libraries and middleware.

In the evolution of distributed computing systems (and cloud computing is, at the time of this writing, the ultimate expression of distributed computing), grid computing marks a middle step between clusters and clouds. Grids are far more widely dispersed than clusters, and the hardware tends to be somewhat more abstract (since the user doesn't know where the computer running the software is located). They also require a certain level of computing redundancy to be built in. The most famous grids have been built on the generosity of users around the world donating unused CPU cycles while their computers are idling on screen savers. It all sounds great, of course, but the programming techniques are radically different from other forms of programming, and both application developers and users must still be acutely aware that the application is running on a grid.

Virtualization

Another key piece in the march toward cloud computing has come with greater adoption of virtualized PC operating systems, starting with work done in the Linux community and leading to commercial versions by VMWare, Microsoft, and others. Taking a cue from the mainframe world, PC operating system architects applied those history lessons to allow full server systems to exist inside a virtual container on a host, thus allowing for more complete utilization of host system resources while maintaining control. Think of this as putting a house inside a big warehouse: It's complete, it's a full house, but it's connected to the outside world via the utility connections owned by the warehouse. Now, for the first time, an entire operating system, applications, and accessories can be packaged into a set of files that can be run in any compatible virtualized environment—an environment that for all intents and purposes looks and feels just like a non-virtualized environment. And these virtualized environments may house multiple virtualized machines to utilize hardware more efficiently and dramatically increase potential returns.

WHAT WOULD YOU LIKE IN YOUR CLOUD?

So far, we have seen why the abstraction (or separation) of function and system is the critical concept that underlies cloud computing, and that system design took several steps, from mainframes, to clusters, to grids, and finally to clouds. It's time to start answering the truly important question: What can you do with a cloud? We asked the question at the beginning of the section, then stepped aside and looked at history. No more teasing: Let's look at the practical side of clouds.

We've begun to define what a cloud is, but we haven't yet approached the question of what a cloud can do. This is in some ways a much more difficult question, because the answer can vary so widely from one cloud computing application to another. Do you need a word processing application to run on a workstation that is underpowered for today's most popular personal productivity software? A cloud application such as Google Docs could be your answer. Do you need a system that will allow a workgroup to collaborate on a project even though they're in different locations using different operating systems on their computers? Zoho has cloud applications to help make it happen. Does your start-up application provider business need to make an application available to an unknown number of customers without being forced to make an investment in massive start-up hardware costs? Amazon's cloud platform might be just the ticket. Does your company's business continuity plan call for off-site backup of critical data? You have a wide variety of storage cloud options to choose from. Each of these examples is different from the other, and yet each is a solid example of a cloud computer application. As we move forward, we'll look at the different types of applications and the consequences of choosing a particular one. First, however, let's consider the conditions that might lead a company or an individual to choose a cloud computing platform for a given application.

For some organizations, the decisions to move toward cloud computing starts with the most pedestrian sort of practical statement. "My IT staff is overextended, but I can't afford more staff and I still need to provide more services" is a common starting point, as are "The power bill for my data center is killing me" and "I can't afford the colocation charges to provide globally load-balanced applications—why can't I let someone else pay for the data centers around the globe?" Each of these is a good

reason to explore options for new computing solutions, and they are just three of hundreds of reasons why cloud computing has become such a hot topic in the IT world.

Cloud computing's flexibility in service delivery (and, generally, billing) makes it an ideal solution for companies faced with highly variable service demand or an uncertain financial environment. Let's look at a couple of examples of decisions to embrace different aspects of cloud computing from both large and small organizations.

Honolulu, Hawaii, is home to some of the most beautiful beaches and some of the most expensive electricity in the United States (as an example, the University of Hawaii paid something like $0.26/kilowatt-hour as of September 2009), and the university research community's thirst for supercomputer time is never-ending. Now, add to expensive electricity a growing push to make both new and existing facilities as *green* as possible. The trend toward building *green data centers* is no longer limited just to using better lighting or more efficient air conditioning, but extends to locating facilities in areas where both power and cooling have dramatically less impact on our world.

Rather than building a new series of data centers to meet research demand, the university began looking at cloud computing options for providing computing services to faculty and research staff. Microsoft has started opening a series of green data centers around the world to provide globally load-balanced services to both itself and to its customers. These centers are located in areas where inexpensive (and carbon-friendly) power sources are available, and they are usually situated where environment friendly cooling options are also available. One such Microsoft facility is located high in the mountains, where the year-round air temperature is cool enough to provide inexpensive cooling to the racks of computers housed there, and the center gets hydroelectric power directly from a nearby dam. Given the opportunity to save money, protect the environment, and still provide necessary computing services, the decision to move to the cloud was easy.

In another case, a small consulting firm based in Florida decided that it needed to look at options for a widely distributed group of employees and contractors to collaborate on projects. The owners looked at the cost of deploying and managing server-based systems based on Microsoft Windows and on Linux. The owners realized that maintaining the server required would demand either a dedicated employee or a substantial (for the consulting firm) contract with a service organization, and they decided to use Zoho as the firm's personal productivity and collaboration platform. For the firm's employees and contractors, the choice allowed the freedom of choosing the personal computing platform that suited them best (or, in some cases, that they already owned), and the security of knowing that work was stored on a managed remote cloud-based server. Zoho's use of Google Gears (a cloud computing service from a competing service provider) allowed employees to use personal productivity tools (such as a word processor) even where no connection to the Internet was available. For the firm's management, costs were contained while information security and organizational interaction were achieved.

As a third example, suppose a small company wanted to offer a set of services to Washington, DC area visitors around the time of the presidential inauguration. The owner recognized that if the company was successful, there would be a surge in traffic, data storage, and compute activity in the days leading up to the inauguration, with a drop-off following the event. While it was felt that the owner could be successful with the service, there were no resources to purchase a server and software, to deploy and maintain them, and then figure out what to do with it after the event—all for a project with a finite life span. Instead, the choice was made to deploy the service on the Amazon Elastic Compute Cloudof Amazon Web Services (AWS).

Using AWS allowed the owner to spend a small fraction of the money that would have been required to purchase and deploy hardware and software, and was thus able to concentrate all her resources on developing and marketing the service itself. While a successful service-based business might or might not stem from the inaugural project, the cloud-computing limit on capital expenses allowed her to proceed with a plan that might have remained simply a promising idea in an environment without clouds.

THE ANYTIME, ANYPLACE CLOUD

Now that *my server* can be anywhere in the world, can be managed from anywhere in the world, and can expand or contract on demand, why do we even think in terms of a server anymore? Once you've thought to ask this question, you've finally crossed the bridge into Cloud City.

While there are still legitimate strategic and tactical concerns that can make a self-hosted server and application the best solution for a particular organization, the fact is that in many cases you don't need to care about where you application lives or what your application is running on.

For example, it might have been years since you last thought in hard-dollar terms about *when* a job should run. This was a common consideration back in the days when mainframe computing was the only game in town, but it fell by the wayside as PCs and PC-based servers came to the fore. Now, you might agree to a service-level agreement that has your application running offshore in a lower-cost cloud farm up to a certain level of demand, and then automatically moves your application to higher-performance on-shore systems once demand crosses a certain threshold. The agreement might also include allowance for demand spikes exceeding your performance or bandwidth cap for a certain amount of time, with the expectation that the demand will shrink within a reasonable amount of time. These spikes might include surges in volume, memory, CPU time, and storage, with resources being determined by a formula instead of having specific limits. The best part of the cloud formula from your Chief Financial Officer's perspective? The odds are good that the agreement will mean you only pay for the higher performance for the period of time in which it is being used.

Abstraction, connection, and well-defined interfaces are the three components that combine to make cloud computing a viable option for a growing number of individuals and organizations.

Cloud Computing: Grids and HPCs (High-Performance Computers)

Brian J.S. Chee
School of Ocean and Earth Sciences and Technology (SOEST), University of Hawaii, Honolulu, Hawaii, U.S.A.
Curtis Franklin, Jr.
Senior Writer, NetWitness, Gainsville, Florida, U.S.A.

Abstract

This entry reviews computing grids and high-performance computing clusters—two critical precursors to cloud computing. You'll learn about the challenges in scheduling resources in each of these group computing situations, and how solving those problems laid the foundation for developing fully functional cloud computing.

INTRODUCTION

This entry covers:

- Grids versus high-performance computing versus clouds—We talk about how grids are not just potentially less expensive but can also be dramatically less reliable than a traditional high-performance computer (HPC). Both have their place in the world of scientific computing. Balancing the differences could mean the difference between a massive in-house investment or just leveraging corporate screen savers.
- Software differences in each platform—Just because you can do similar things on a grid and a traditional HPC doesn't mean the same applications will run on both right out of the box. Tweaks and tuning are a way of life for both, and you need to take into account those differences when writing for each.
- Examples of grids and HPC systems—We look at some of the success stories of both grids and HPCs, and we provide a bit more insight into which system is capable of doing various types of tasks.
- Job schedulers in HPCs as the beginning of a cloud description language, and why we should take a page from history—Managing job flow and shoehorning it into the available hardware resources is what it's all about. From mainframes to grids, to HPCs, making the most of your expensive hardware has always been the name of the game.

SCIENTIFIC COMPUTING AND ITS CONTRIBUTION TO CLOUDS

Grids, HPCs, and clouds often seem to be mentioned all in the same breath; they're all quite different and one size does *not* fit all. This entry looks closely at what each of these technology families are, and the sort of applications to which each may best be applied. There will be times when it seems we're diving rather deeply into one technology or another, but understanding the technology that underlies each of these terms, and learning the lessons to be gathered from deploying and managing grids and HPCs, will pay dividends when you start thinking about the best way to make cloud computing work for you and your organization.

DEFINING TERMS: GRIDS AND HPCS

Let's start by defining some key terms we'll be using in this entry. First, what is grid computing (or, to look at it from another direction, what is a computing grid)? We can begin by saying that a computing grid is the application of multiple computers working on a single problem at the same time. That's fine, as far as it goes, but that definition could apply to many things that aren't grids. What makes this computing collective a grid? Three terms fulfill in the necessary details: loosely coupled, geographically dispersed, and heterogeneous.

When computers are joined together for an application, they can be tightly coupled or loosely coupled. Tightly coupled systems generally share memory and other system resources, with the processors often linked

Encyclopedia of Information Systems and Technology, DOI: 10.1081/E-EIST-120053810

through a system bus or some other high-speed, short-distance network.

Think of tightly coupled computers as conjoined twins: One can't get very far without the other. Loosely coupled systems, on the other hand, are separate, autonomous computers that take directions from a central controller that breaks the problem into single-computer-sized packages, parcels the individual pieces out to members of the grid, and then accepts results and assembles them into answers. Loosely coupled computers are like fraternal twins that lead their own separate lives but can come together to work toward a single goal when asked nicely.

Grid computers are loosely coupled. They can be used for separate tasks until they are called upon to act as part of the grid—and they can often continue fulfilling their stand-alone responsibilities even when they are occupied with grid applications. This loose coupling allows for the next quality of the computing grid: geographic dispersal.

Since the members of a computing grid communicate through standard networks (or, most commonly, the Internet), it doesn't really matter where the constituent computers are located. It's as easy to have a computing grid that spans the globe as it is to have a grid in a single room. The dispersed grid is easier, in many ways; the electric power requirements are dispersed to many different power grids, and infrastructure problems that might take down a particular data center will usually affect only a small piece of the overall grid. With grid applications often designed to take advantage of unused central processing unit (CPU) cycles available on each constituent computer, grid computing tends to leave a shallow resource footprint across a very broad swath of a computing environment.

The computing environment that makes up a grid can be dispersed across more than just geography—it can cover multiple operating systems, as well. The heterogeneous nature of many grids increases both the performance and the robustness of the grid. Now, it must be noted that heterogeneity is an architectural possibility of a computing grid, not a requirement. Several grids make use of only a single type of computer. Whether the grid is made up of a single type of computer or a veritable *United Nations* of machines, the software that brings it together is a suite of resource controllers, data assemblers, client–computer applications, and a special class of software called *middleware* that glues it all together. We'll come back to middleware later, but first let's look at HPCs and how they do their work.

HPCs are similar to grids, in that they are loosely coupled computing environments, though they tend to be not quite so loosely coupled as grids. The reason for the difference in coupling *tightness* has to do with the nature of the communication between the different elements of the computing environment, and particularly between the central controller and the remote nodes that actually process data. Widely dispersed grids make extensive use of asynchronous communications, in which a computer sends out a message knowing that it will see a response eventually. It tends not to matter whether that response comes back in 200 milliseconds or 3 days. HPCs, given their emphasis on the best possible performance, are much more reliant on synchronous communication, in which messages are sent back and forth between two or more systems, with each computer waiting for a necessary response from another before it can continue processing.

The need for accurate synchronous communication means that HPCs tend to be centrally located, rather than highly dispersed, and connected via 10-gigabit Ethernet, Infiniband, or some other high-speed computer interconnection network rather than the Internet. Because of the nature of the communication requirement and the work that is done, HPCs are almost always made up of clusters of homogeneous computers, in which each constituent is precisely the same as every other constituent in the system.

All these performances tend to add up to some hefty numbers not only in performance but also in infrastructure costs. When the University of Texas at Abilene entered into a project in 2008 with Sun Microsystems to take the record for the world's largest supercomputer, the project ended up with $30 million in hardware costs alone. Some of the numbers were 62,976 CPU cores, 125 terabytes of memory, 1.7 petabytes of disk space, and 504 teraflops of performance, sucking down 3 megawatts of power and costing nearly a million dollars per year to run—not to mention the human resource costs to run this extremely specialized piece of equipment, and all these just to hold the record for a few short years. Rick Stevens, the associate director of the lab, has predicted that the system will be considered only moderate-sized system within just five years. He has, however, drawn an analogy to having a time machine that lets you look 5–10 years into the future of general-purpose computing.

SOFTWARE FOR GRIDS AND HPCS

The differences in software architecture make writing applications for grids and HPCs dramatically different. Learning to architect for this difference has been one of the many reasons why HPC/grid applications have tended to remain in the domain of research.

One of the key concepts in writing applications for grids, HPCs, or any other distributed computing systems is the idea of parent and child processes. In briefest terms, when a particular task has to be accomplished, it is analyzed to see whether it might fruitfully be broken up into smaller tasks. If breakup is possible, the distributed computing environment's controller breaks it up and sends each of the new, smaller tasks to another computer to be performed. The original task (the *parent*) then waits for data to be returned from each of the smaller tasks (the *children*) before it continues processing. The most important skill in writing effective code for a grid or an HPC is the ability to tell code how to break up larger tasks into smaller tasks so that parents are completed (and therefore report their results) as quickly as possible.

While traditional programming methods still apply, the change in writing for a parent and child environment can be likened to the learning curve a programmer had to go through when moving from stand-alone to networked applications. There's a whole new set of rules and a whole new set of tricks to learn as you optimize your code.

The biggest challenge is the overall architecture, for which you need to be prepared to think in terms of parent processes spawning children on what may be physically separate computing nodes, which may in turn spawn grandchildren under certain conditions. So now, instead of just worrying about endless loops, you have to wonder if your app will spawn too many children during its run and empty the resource hopper.

It may seem that grids and HPCs are the same thing from a programming point of view, but grids have wrinkles that tend to make life interesting for application developers. As we mentioned before, grids utilize asynchronous communications that now have to also learn about each individual node's resources and perhaps even figure out whether a given portion of the problem can actually be shoehorned onto a small node. Moreover, the communications pathways can be extremely variable and may have periods of no communications at all when a traveling node (such as a laptop computer) is offline for a while. As a result, grids usually need to work on smaller portions of a problem in which all of the data for a given process are downloaded to the individual node when the process is assigned to the node. In addition, the program needs to have the ability to be suspended cleanly as the grid client returns control back to the user. Keep in mind that many grid node systems are installed as screen savers, enabling those *idle* CPUs to become part of the overall grid cluster, so giving the machine back to the user is an important part of *playing nicely* in the grid world.

Overall, the problems that HPC and grid computing systems are designed to solve tend to be huge, but can be broken up into smaller, more manageable pieces. These problems also tend to be of high value in order to justify the huge amount of human resources necessary to create the complex application to take advantage of the environment. Problems such as weather modeling,

processing echo-return information for petrology surveys (looking for oil), gene folding, and ship or aircraft drag calculations are all excellent examples of HPC and grid cluster uses.

EXAMPLES OF GRID APPLICATIONS

It's one thing to talk about the way a system works. To get a better understanding of the differences between the platforms, let's look at some examples of the problems each is used to solve, and the ways in which each is deployed. We'll look first at a couple of applications of grid computing.

A Grid for the Stars

In 1999, at the University of California Berkeley, the Search for Extra-Terrestrial Intelligence (SETI) project folks carefully examined their computing needs and then looked at the budget they had and heaved a collective sigh of frustration. Scheduling time on the existing HPC clusters was prohibitively expensive, and the waiting list was sometimes measured in weeks or months. Another frustration they faced, as many academic projects did, was that many of their best students were foreign nationals, who couldn't use many supercomputer facilities because of their military funding. (Any sort of mixed-classification computing system in which classified materials are potentially processed is restricted to U.S.-cleared personnel only, even if the unclassified machine is physically separate from the system the foreign nationals want to use.) So with all these roadblocks in their way, what were the SETI people to do? The answer was to turn the HPC world on its head by changing the paradigm.

The SETI@home team published this overview on their blog:

> The UC Berkeley SETI team has discovered that there are already thousands of computers that might be available for use. Most of these computers sit around most of the time with toasters flying across their screens accomplishing absolutely nothing and wasting electricity to boot. This is where SETI@home (and you!) come into the picture. The SETI@home project hopes to convince you to allow us to borrow your computer when you aren't using it and to help us "... search out new life and new civilizations." We'll do this with a screen saver that can go get a chunk of data from us over the Internet, analyze that data, and then report the results back to us. When you need your computer back, our screen saver instantly gets out of the way and only continues its analysis when you are finished with your work.
>
> It's an interesting and difficult task. There's so much data to analyze that it seems impossible! Fortunately, the data

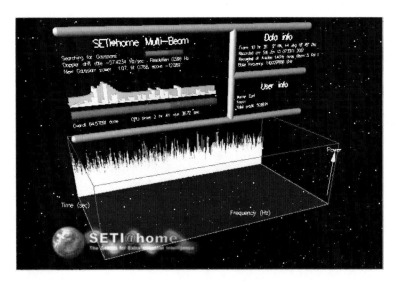

Fig. 1 While the grid computing goes on in the background, the screen saver displays the radio signal patterns that are currently being worked on.

analysis task can be easily broken up into little pieces that can all be worked on separately and in parallel. None of the pieces depends on the other pieces. Also, there is only a finite amount of sky that can be seen from Arecibo. In the next two years the entire sky as seen from the telescope will be scanned three times. We feel that this will be enough for this project. By the time we've looked at the sky three times, there will be new telescopes, new experiments, and new approaches to SETI. We hope that you will be able to participate in them too!

Translation: We can't afford to schedule a 2000-processor HPC cluster for a couple of years, so why not try to shoot for 100,000 nodes where we might lose 70% of the nodes over time? Let's make it hugely redundant to make up for the node loss. We then make it a screen saver with some cool eye candy (see Fig. 1) and voilá, nearly free supercomputer time for research. The idea worked well enough that Stanford and many others have all jumped on the bandwagon.

A Grid for Proteins

Medical researchers are investigating the effects on children of their parents' age and race at the time of their birth in order to better understand the proteins at work behind genetic disorders such as Huntington and Alzheimer's diseases. To understand the disorder, they need to simulate the protein folding process that occurs naturally in the body. Stanford University and associated project members have created a system called Folding@home, in which large numbers of volunteers install Folding@home screen savers. Each screen saver then downloads a small piece of the puzzle and works on a single portion of the huge dataset that the project is currently working on. When the screen saver is running, it chugs away on its small piece and then uploads

the results to a master server. It should be noted that because of the variable availability of these *nodes*, almost all grid projects have multiple nodes working on the same piece of the puzzle. That way, if a machine is turned off for a long weekend or is out for repair, they don't lose that little piece.

In the case of Folding@home, the total size of the dataset is known, as is the scope of the anticipated result. The problem for researchers was to get access to enough CPU time to crunch through the data that existed. According to the project's website, as of the first of January 2009, there were over a quarter-million CPUs working on the project. Folding@home is an extremely heterogeneous grid architecture, with client software for Microsoft Windows, Linux, Apple's Mac OS X, and the Sony Playstation 3 now available.

An example of the kind of problem being tackled by Folding@home is the following research as described by the team at Stanford University:

Combining Molecular Dynamics with Bayesian Analysis to Predict and Evaluate Ligand-Binding Mutations in Influenza Hemagglutinin
P. M. Kasson, D. L. Ensign, and V. S. Pande. *Journal of the American Chemical Society* (2009). Published online July 28, 2009.

Summary. The influenza virus infects people and animals by binding to complex sugar molecules on the surface of the respiratory tract. Bird viruses bind most strongly to bird cell-surface sugars and human viruses bind most strongly to human cell-surface sugars. As the swine-origin influenza virus has demonstrated, there is considerable overlap between the binding ability of human and pig viruses to cells of the other *host*. Changes to this binding affinity are one of the key components for viruses to make a jump between species, and it is difficult to predict the necessary mutations ahead of time. We would like to predict high-risk mutations to enable better surveillance and early control of potential interspecies transmission events. This work represents a first step in that direction, as we examine mutations to H5N1 avian influenza that alter ligand binding. We use Folding@Home as a powerful computational screen to evaluate mutations that will eventually require experimental testing to verify.

First launched in 2000, Folding@home is the most powerful distributed computing cluster in the world, and one of the world's largest distributed computing projects. Like all grid computing projects, however, the *secret sauce* involves breaking up the problem into a great many little pieces, which is also why such solutions aren't very useful for most *normal* business applications.

HPC IN *BLUE HAWAII*

In the world of high-performance academic research computing, the researcher uploads an application written specifically for a clustered/HPC environment. Each application consists of at least three pieces: the parent process that handles coordination of all the processes, the child applications that work on individual pieces, and a scheduler that allocates resources on a job-by-job basis. The real key to a successful HPC is a scheduler that *fits* the jobs into available resources to maximize the utilization of the cluster according to resource requests as each job is submitted to the system. If the scheduler is written properly, and the HPC environment is configured correctly, the clusters can be spread out over a geographic area among several cluster members controlled by the scheduler system. Now, at this point, you may be thinking that the environment has just moved from an HPC to a grid. While HPCs share much in common with grids, a major difference is that HPCs tend to be more homogeneous in makeup and child processes tend *not* to be duplicated, since HPCs tend to be dedicated to the purpose.

A very good example of HPC computing was the IBM SP2 called *Blue Hawaii,* which, architecturally, was the grandchild of the famous chess-playing *Deep Blue.* It was in learning this system that programmers experienced just how different HPC was from writing an application for a monolithic machine. With supercomputer time being horribly expensive and with long waiting lists for time, HPC programmers were and are motivated to wring as much performance as possible out of each CPU cycle. A common *Aha!* experience involved learning that looping was *unrolled* instead of nested. (Nested loops are like the Russian dolls that fit one inside another.) This technique was developed to open up the outer loop into multiple stacked single

loops so that more statements could be shoved into the CPU cache at a time. Similar to *pipelining* in the PC platform, programmers strove to learn additional details about the processor platform to *tune* their applications to fit more into the super-high-speed CPU cache and reduce the number of requests for instructions from the slower main random access memory (RAM).

Let's stop to think about this for a moment. Programming for multiple stacks, and unrolling rather than nesting loops, are all about maximizing system resource utilization. This is a theme we'll see repeatedly in virtually every technique and architecture we look at. Where HPCs are concerned, the reason for the optimization is speed, pure and simple. When we begin to look at cloud computing, the need for system optimization will be just as great, but the reason is based on economics rather than performance: System administrators want each piece of hardware to be utilized as close to 100% of the time as possible. Regardless of the motivation, the operating principles are the same: Build the architecture on a scheduling base that is able to optimize resource utilization without requiring users who are submitting jobs for processing to have any knowledge of the system.

In addition to optimizing CPU cache performance, programmers on *Blue Hawaii* took advantage of the way in which the CPU handles floating-point calculations. The SP2 was able to handle two calculations per cycle, so formula lines were tinkered with to make sure that exactly two floating-point requests were made per line. This is a solid illustration of the fact that a single optimization is rarely enough to ensure that computing resources are being used at top efficiency. Developers of schedulers, controllers, and middleware components must study, understand, and program for every system component their software touches in order to make the system perform efficiently.

SCHEDULING GRIDS AND HPCS

Both grids and HPCs have at their heart a job scheduler to control how the individual programs will run and best fit into the available resources. This scheduler must not only have knowledge of the program to be run, with algorithms for managing the way in which child and grandchild processes are spawned, but it must also have deep insight into the resources available on each member system of the computing environment. Obviously, there are many different ways of creating a piece of software with a set of functions as complex as those encapsulated in a scheduler. You need to think of a scheduler as a proxy for dozens, hundreds, or thousands of computing nodes. It has to handle authentication, resource allocation, and the actual run of the software.

There is an old saying about reinventing the wheel every time you need to make a trip, and that certainly applies to schedulers for both HPCs and grids. Two of the more commonly seen examples include one most often used in the grid computing world and another that's frequently seen in high-performance computing. The efforts by the Job Submission Description Language Working Group (JSDL-WG) are popular in the grid world, and the Maui Scheduler has become popular in the HPC world. JSDL-WG is a grid-oriented job control language that's independent of any programming language that might be used to create the jobs. JSDL can use EXtensible Markup Language (XML) to define different aspects of the job request, making it an open standard built on other open standards. This notion of open access will come to be a critical component of the move beyond grids to cloud computing.

The Maui Scheduler was developed in the 1990s as an open-source scheduling engine for high-performance computing clusters. Written to join groups of Unix computers together into cohesive high-performance systems, Maui allows administrators to set schedules and priorities, reserve resources for particular applications or pieces of applications, and perform other tasks that make systems more functional in a world where multiple simultaneous applications and competing priorities are the rule rather than the exception. Since the release of the Maui Scheduler, a commercial version of the software—Moab—has been developed, with support for additional operating systems (including Linux, Mac OS X, and Windows), a workload manager, cluster manager, and access portal, and resource management capabilities that aren't available in Maui. This pattern, of taking open-source software and building additional capabilities and components on it, is another direction that we'll see again in cloud computing. The Moab scheduler developed by the University of Utah Center for High Performance Computing built on the success of the Maui Scheduler to create Moab:

CHPC Software: Moab Scheduler

The Moab Scheduler is a software tool designed to allow flexible and near-optimal scheduling in a multiresource high-performance computing environment. Jobs are screened through a large number of administrator-configurable fairness policies and then prioritized based on factors such as job queue time, job expansion factor, and user CPU usage history. The Moab Scheduler maximizes control of system resources by allowing certain nodes to be reserved for specific users, groups, accounts, or projects and minimizes the amount of wasted computer resources by permitting anticipated downtime to be scheduled.

The Moab Scheduler is also an analysis/research tool. The Moab Scheduler collects a large number of statistics and can analyze this information to determine the effectiveness of the scheduling approach being used by Moab and the utilization of the resources available.

Source: From http://www.chpc.utah.edu/docs/manuals/software/moab.html

HOW GRID SCHEDULING WORKS

It should be obvious by now that the scheduler for either a computing grid or a high-performance computing cluster is a complex piece of software. When the software is moved to a cloud environment, it gets no simpler. As the software moves away from the cluster into larger grids and clouds, some people stop referring to it as a scheduler and begin to call it a broker, a reasonable label when the product is dealing with components that have their own intelligence and ability to make relatively simple decisions.

Let's take a look at the process of scheduling tasks in a computing grid as we set the stage for moving beyond clusters and grids into the computing cloud. Grid scheduling can be divided into three phases, consisting of 11 steps. The following are the authors' descriptions, but the steps and phases seem to be common to many scheduler efforts.

It should also be noted that the Open Grid Forum on environments such as the Open Grid Services Architecture has made a significant contribution toward creation of tools and standards for a common job management standard. Furthermore, IBM has been in the HPC game for a very long time, early on making a huge splash with their chess-playing HPC called *Deep Blue*. Much of IBM's work on scheduling and HPC job description languages are documented in a collection of documents called the Red Book series (http://www.redbooks.ibm.com).

Phase I: Resource Discovery

Step 1: Authorization filtering

Consider that the collection of nodes that make up a grid isn't much different from a hacker's botnet. (*Botnet* is short for *robot network;* in this case, the network consists of computers infected by hackers for the purpose of executing nefarious applications.) So it's probably for the best that modern grids include authentication before anyone can submit a job into the grid. It also makes sense that user profiles describe just what resources any authorized user is allowed to use. The approved resources may or may not include some sort of billing information if this isn't a volunteer grid. Billing information is often belittled by technical and scientific users as an unnecessary crutch for the *bean counters*, but properly allocating costs and allowing for capital recovery is a very real issue for most business (and many non-profit) organizations.

Since some sort of dataset access is also normally needed, the user profile might also include some credentials for one or more network-attached resources. An element of identity federation, or a single sign-on capability, is generally covered by the initial authorization filtering stage, allowing the user credentials presented for one computer within the cluster to serve as authenticating documents for every computer and application within the cluster.

Step 2: Application definition

In this step the user specifies a minimum set of resources for consideration by the scheduler. It would be counterproductive if, for instance, a job required nodes that could handle 64-bit word lengths but the scheduler kept trying to shove it onto older 32-bit nodes. This is where values such as RAM, scratch space (temporary disk storage), and specialized libraries are described in a job submission script supported by the scheduler. The rise of XML as a widely supported open standard for data interchange has made application definition a much more open and standards-based process for most clusters and grids. And although we speak of application definition in terms of user specification, in many cases the definition is generated by the application automatically, as it tells the environment what it needs in order to function successfully.

Step 3: Minimum requirement filtering

Based on the resources that an authenticated user is allowed to use (see Step 1), the scheduler attempts to find the first open slot that will fulfill the need. In small systems, this might be a pad and pencil, but in much larger systems it could involve nodes checking in periodically to update available resources. Regardless of the job and cluster size, it's all about matching needs to resources in such a way as to accommodate the needs of the users in a timely fashion.

Phase II: System Selection

Step 4: Information gathering

This stage is where politics can rear its ugly head. While the *best fit* for resources might exist on a particular set of hardware assets, business rules may force users into an alternative set of resources instead. This happens frequently in organizations such as universities, in which multiple departments have *contributed* to an institution-wide grid. In theory, all departments that contribute to the grid have equal access to its resources.

However, the *string* that many departments have attached to their participation in the grid is that during certain hours, researchers in that particular department *must* have priority over a particular subset of nodes. It should be pointed out that there exists a potential for resource changes by the time a job is actually submitted. A considerable amount of research is being done on predictive methods for resource allocation to create some sort of tuning feedback loop that will increase the accuracy of a predictive model over time, making gross time-block priority locks unnecessary to protect a department's authority over its own systems.

Step 5: System selection

The decision as to which nodes to use for a specific job varies in complexity, but a common thread has appeared in many scheduler development projects. Some methodologies that are commonly tossed around include Condor matchmaking, computational economies, and many others.

Condor matchmaking bases its operation on a classic scheme—the classified ad. Computing resources—the *sellers* in the analogy—advertise their services and capabilities through ClassAds, where they can also list the asking price for the resource. Users and applications—the *buyers* of the scheme—create their own ClassAds listing their requirements and preferences along with what they're willing to pay to have their requirements met. Condor matchmaking then goes through the ClassAds from buyers and sellers and makes the best matches based on the specifications given. The matchmaking is a one-time, static process though, as Condor continues to scan the environment to determine whether a better match might become available at any time.

Computational economies include a variety of techniques used to decide which processes will run on which resources. The techniques bring the principles of classic economics to bear on the problem in an attempt to get around the fact that both application-based methods and resource-based methods can lead to significant levels of system instability under certain circumstances. Using computational economies, resources and application pieces can constantly revalue themselves based on demand for their services and demand for their results, while the central scheduler constantly makes application deployment decisions based on the latest valuations. An economics-based system with constant review should mean that, at any given moment, the resources are being used most efficiently, while the application itself is operating at peak effectiveness.

Phase III: Job Execution

Step 6: Advance reservation

Reserving grid resources in advance may be as simple as blocking a collection of nodes within a particular department or as complex as an agent application watching and then placing holds on resources as they become available. Unfortunately, for most users, most long-term holds are the result of departments or managers blocking access to certain assets for significant lengths of time, *just in case*. While the desire to make sure that our scientists or our engineers can have unfettered access to resources that came from our budget, the truth is that the computational grid as a whole will operate far more efficiently (and most researchers and engineers will have far more productive encounters) if the scheduler is allowed to make decisions based on resource allocations and expenses.

Step 7: Job submission

If any of the steps we are discussing needs additional work, this is it. It's our opinion that if the Free and Open Source Software movement has an Achilles' heel, it is the attitude of rolling your own if you don't like how someone else does it. Just look at the number and variety of Linux distributions and you can begin to see why commercial (and closed) operating systems command the lion's share of the marketplace. This lack of standardization in the open-source grid world is where open source will again be left behind, as narrowly focused commercial efforts become a standard due to the lack of anything better.

Step 8: Preparation tasks

This step is where the rubber meets the road. As the job execution kicks off, resources such as datasets are moved into temporary storage and the parent process starts to populate information for each child to work on. As with anything, variety in temporary datasets may involve anything from little snippets of audio (a là SETI@home) to massive genomics databases. So, while most of us think of BitTorrent as a method for downloading illegal movies, it also happens to be a very efficient way of moving large files to a collection of hosts very quickly. File Transfer Protocol (FTP), secure copy, and secure FTP seem to be the current favorites, but Torrent is certainly being experimented with for large dataset distribution on grids.

Step 9: Monitoring progress

All good programmers build in error checking, and high-performance computing is no exception. Since high-performance computing is typically carried out in an asynchronous environment, there is great potential for a child to run out of data and sit idle unless the programmer has anticipated such a possibility and built in some sort of interrupt facility to notify the parent process that the child is now idle due to lack of data. Another good example is an application that *must* have all the pieces of the problem done in order to have valid results. So, if a child process should crash, it is better to end the entire run instead of having the rest of the processes continue running, finally producing a worthless run because one node is missing results.

Step 10: Job completion

What happens when the job is done? Do you ring a bell, send an e-mail, or do a file transfer of the results to a file in Timbuktu? This might also be where the program will need to write result codes into a file someplace. The important thing to remember is that the application *must* end and produce results of some sort—otherwise, it's not an algorithm, and therefore not a useful application at all.

Step 11: Cleanup

Do you trash the temporary datasets, or do you write them out to something more permanent? Where do the results go? Do you need to send a *close* transaction to an accounting system? It may not be very glamorous, but a good cleanup process means that your application cleanly closes down the use of a resource, rather than the system merely waiting for some sort of timeout to happen. The ideas and concepts in the material are drawn from J. M. Schopf's paper: July 2001 "GFD-1.4 Scheduling Working Group, Category: Ten Actions When Super Scheduling."

GRID VERSUS HPC VERSUS CLOUD

There are many reasons why you might choose to run an application on a grid rather than an HPC. Quite a few revolve around money, some revolve around availability, but both types of solution require massive amounts of computing power. Quite a few problems in this world just don't fit onto a monolithic computer system (one or more CPUs in a single computer) at a particular point in time. Moore's law ("The number of transistors that can be put on a chip doubles every 24 months") keeps us on our toes, since what didn't fit a year ago may fit today. However, we're talking about problems such as gene folding, analysis of seismic data for oil exploration, meteorology simulations, and so on—all applications that seemed out of reach for anyone just a few years ago, but that now are, through HPCs, grids, and computational clouds, within the reach of even the most underfunded research scientists.

To the frustration of many computer-industry historians, business clustering doesn't seem to have had a clear-cut inception, with a whole lot of people claiming the *first* or the *original* application. Let's just say that one or more folks must have looked at both grids and HPCs and saw an opportunity if they could be combined with the concept of a virtual machine.

When journalists first listened to a pitch by the folks in the Scyld Computing booth at the LinuxWorld 2003 Conference, their description of a business application cluster didn't sound very different from load balancing. However, the load balancing seen previously didn't have the ability to move applications from one physical machine to another. It also didn't have the ability to apply business rules to the process to allow lower-priority tasks to be suspended in order to let a higher-priority task to take over the physical machine. Scyld's example was of a company whose magnificent new widget is featured on CNN—suddenly, the traffic on their website explodes. Under normal circumstances the Web server would crash, but instead, lower-priority tasks are suspended so that the company website can take over multiple blades in the cluster. When the load subsides, the Web server shrinks back to its normal configuration and the lower-priority tasks are restarted. This was not unlike IBM's OS-VM and the way in which resources were allocated based on a complex set of business rules as demand and human intervention trigger dynamic reconfiguration of the systems. The difference, of course, was that Scyld could balance across huge numbers of individual computers, each running its own operating system and controlling its own resources.

Let's dissect the pieces and see why it is unlikely that this was a single Aha! moment for a single person. The key point is that all the technology had been around for a while and was now only being combined in novel ways to allow cloud computing to exist profitably within a corporate computing infrastructure. Because of this newness, the exact definition of cloud computing is a bit fuzzy as cloud computing and the industry develop. It's our belief that cloud computing, like all emerging technology, will most likely develop in stages.

Cloud Development Stage 1: Software as a Service and Web 2.0

Software as a Service (SaaS) and Web 2.0 trends set the stage for clouds. Existing users have started wondering why they really need to keep all their Web apps internal to the organization. As content management systems made inroads into replacing traditional websites, we saw an explosion of hosting sites catering to the latest craze.

We really think that SaaS, more than anything else, has got people saying "hmmmm…" Imagine a situation in which a manager has key services for the people, but is not paying for a data center to manage it. We also feel that the rapidly rising cost of energy has driven many a Chief Financial Officer to start asking if the organization really needs a data center, with all its inherent costs. If the programmers already use remote access instead of sitting at a physical computer, does it really matter where that server lives?

Cloud Development Stage 2: Hosted Virtualization

Hosted virtualization has become the "having your cake and eating it too" idea. Managers and system administrators have been using remote access to get to servers in the data center for years, so it sure isn't any different to point Microsoft's Remote Desktop Protocol over a virtual private network at a hosting site. As an indicator of just how fast virtualization has become mainstream, the way systems test engineers take systems out of a test drive has changed radically of late. Instead of downloading just the application and then going through a full installation, now we can download a fully set up virtual machine, with all the OS tweaking already done. So why not take that idea a bit further by prototyping your new servers in-house, and then, when they're debugged, push the virtual machine image to the hosting service.

Cloud Development Stage 2.5: Playing the *Energy Savings* Card

Latest spikes in the cost of energy have had a huge impact on the acceptance of virtualization. With everyone talking about recession punctuated by rising energy prices, suddenly maintaining your own datacenter isn't quite so cool anymore. Microsoft and Amazon apparently stumbled on a pretty good crystal ball, because they've been building data centers in areas with inexpensive green energy sources and cool-enough temperatures to reduce the cost of cooling these huge data centers. Remember, it doesn't matter where your data center is anymore.

It really hit home that virtualization is here to stay when we heard about an energy conservation program sponsored by Pacific Gas and Electric (PG&E) in northern California, under which PG&E offered dollar matching for consulting, purchase, and installation of virtualized environments (with a $2 million cap). The story we heard was that in some cases the company was able to shrink its server farm by a factor of 10, with electrical energy savings in the millions.

Cloud Development Stage 3: True Clouds

As with HPCs and grids, we'll soon be seeing a further level of abstraction in which the underlying operating system is no longer as important as being able to submit tasks into the cloud. Like HPCs and grids, clouds are going to need to be provisioned with some sort of job description language for resource requests and billing. It will be in the third stage that we'll most likely really start seeing things such as application rentals, or per-use licenses, appear on the market. We might even see application use billing become something like advertising click-through charges. We would even go as far as predicting that we might start seeing applications sold more along the lines of those sold in the Apple iPhone AppStore.

Key to the development of a true cloud environment will be the lessons learned by people in the grid and HPC world, combined with the lessons learned as virtualization keeps growing, hopefully mixed with some history lessons from the days of mainframe service bureaus. The job submission description systems have to mature and converge into some sort of industry standard; the development (or acceptance) of such a standard will be a critical moment in the development and survival of cloud centers.

Our vision for clouds is one in which the broker/agent/scheduler will shop for the best deal on a set of resources. As resource costs change over time (cheaper rates at night and on weekends, just like mobile phones), the cloud application agent will then move our tasks to the next cheapest set of resources, while continuing to shop for the best deal.

So is a grid a cloud? Is a cloud an HPC? We really think it's more a matter of standards. After all, a Web server, given the proper resources, could run on an HPC or a grid, and if the scheduler had the ability to detect load on, say, a Web server, it could react to that load and start up additional Web server nodes.

Our prediction is that cloud computing will, when the dust has fully settled, be made up of the best ideas of all its predecessors.

Finally, it will be market pressures that will force the competing technologies to standardize their efforts. It might finally be a 1000-lb gorilla that forces the change. On October 27, 2008, Microsoft unveiled its version of a cloud operating environment, and only time will tell whether Microsoft will do for cloud operating systems what it did for workstation operating systems.

The lessons learned from clusters and grids will stand us in good stead as we begin to understand what clouds can do for an organization and how they can be best deployed and managed within a corporate information technology structure.

Cloud Computing: History and Evolution

John W. Rittinghouse
Hypersecurity LLC, Tomball, Texas, U.S.A.

James F. Ransome
Cisco Systems, Santa Clara, California, U.S.A.

Abstract

This entry reviews the importance of knowing about the evolution of computing in order to get an appreciation of how we got into the cloud environment. It discusses how the rules computers use to communicate came about, and how the development of networking and communications protocols has helped drive the Internet technology growth. This, in turn, has driven even more changes in protocols and forced the creation of new technologies to mitigate addressing concerns and improve the methods used to communicate over the Internet.

It is important to understand the evolution of computing in order to get an appreciation of how we got into the cloud environment. Looking at the evolution of the computing hardware itself, from the first generation to the fourth generation of computers, shows how we got from there to here. The hardware, however, was only part of the evolutionary process. As hardware evolved, so did software. As networking evolved, so did the rules for how computers communicate. The development of such rules, or protocols, also helped drive the evolution of Internet software.

OVERVIEW

Establishing a common protocol for the Internet led directly to rapid growth in the number of users online. This has driven technologists to make even more changes in current protocols and to create new ones. Today, we talk about the use of Internet Protocol version 6 (IPv6) to mitigate addressing concerns and for improving the methods we use to communicate over the Internet. Over time, our ability to build a common interface to the Internet has evolved with the improvements in hardware and software. Using web browsers has led to a steady migration away from the traditional data center model to a cloud-based model. Using technologies such as server virtualization, parallel processing, vector processing, symmetric multiprocessing, and massively parallel processing (MPP) has fueled radical change. Let's take a look at how this happened, so we can begin to understand more about the cloud.

In order to discuss some of the issues of the cloud concept, it is important to place the development of computational technology in a historical context.

Looking at the Internet cloud's evolutionary development,[1] and the problems encountered along the way, provides some key reference points to help us understand the challenges that had to be overcome to develop the Internet and the World Wide Web (WWW) today. These challenges fell into two primary areas, hardware and software. We will look first at the hardware side.

HARDWARE EVOLUTION

Our present day lives would be different, and probably difficult, without the benefits of modern computers. Computerization has permeated nearly every facet of our personal and professional lives. Computer evolution has been both rapid and fascinating. The first step along the evolutionary path of computers occurred in 1930, when binary arithmetic was developed and became the foundation of computer processing technology, terminology, and programming languages. Calculating devices date back to at least as early as 1642, when a device that could mechanically add numbers was invented. Adding devices evolved from the abacus. It was a significant milestone in the history of computers. In 1939, the Berry brothers invented an electronic computer capable of operating digitally. Computations were performed using vacuum-tube technology.

In 1941, the introduction of Konrad Zuse's Z3 at the German Laboratory for Aviation in Berlin was one of the most significant events in the evolution of computers because this machine supported both floating-point and binary arithmetic. Because it was a "Turing-complete" device (According to the online encyclopedia Wikipedia, "A computational system that can compute every Turing-computable function is called Turing-complete

Encyclopedia of Information Systems and Technology, DOI: 10.1081/E-EIST-120053834

Fig. 1   The Harvard Mark I computer.
Source: From http://www.columbia.edu/acis/history/mark1.html (accessed January 2009).

(or Turing-powerful). Alternatively, such a system is one that can simulate a universal Turing machine."),[2] it is considered to be the very first computer that was fully operational. A programming language is considered Turing-complete if it falls into the same computational class as a Turing machine, meaning that it can perform any calculation a universal Turing machine can perform. This is especially significant because, under the Church–Turing thesis,[3] a Turing machine is the embodiment of the intuitive notion of an algorithm. Over the course of the next 2 years, computer prototypes were built to decode secret German messages by the U.S. Army.

First-Generation Computers

The first generation of modern computers can be traced to 1943, when the Mark I and Colossus computers (see Figs. 1 and 2) were developed,[4] albeit for quite different purposes. With financial backing from International Business Machines Corporation (IBM), the Mark I was designed and developed at Harvard University. It was a general-purpose electromechanical programmable computer. Colossus, on the other hand, was an electronic computer built in Britain at the end 1943. Colossus was the world's first programmable, digital, electronic, computing device. First-generation computers were built using hard-wired circuits and vacuum tubes (thermionic valves). Data was stored using paper punch cards. Colossus was used in secret during World War II to help decipher teleprinter messages encrypted by German forces using the Lorenz SZ40/42 machine. British code breakers referred to encrypted German teleprinter traffic as "Fish" and called the SZ40/42 machine and its traffic "Tunny."[5]

To accomplish its deciphering task, Colossus compared two data streams read at high speed from a paper tape. Colossus evaluated one data stream representing the encrypted "Tunny," counting each match that was discovered based on a programmable Boolean function. A comparison with the other data stream was then made. The second data stream was generated internally and designed to be an electronic simulation of the Lorenz SZ40/42 as it ranged through various trial settings. If the match count for a setting was above a predetermined threshold, that data match would be sent as character output to an electric typewriter.

Fig. 2   The British-developed Colossus computer.
Source: From http://www.computerhistory.org (accessed January 2009).

Fig. 3 The ENIAC computer.
Source: From http://www.mrsec.wisc.edu/.../computer/eniac.html (accessed January 2009).

Second-Generation Computers

Another general-purpose computer of this era was ENIAC (Electronic Numerical Integrator and Computer, shown in Fig. 3), which was built in 1946. This was the first Turing-complete, digital computer capable of being reprogrammed to solve a full range of computing problems,[6] although earlier machines had been built with some of these properties. ENIAC's original purpose was to calculate artillery firing tables for the U.S. Army's Ballistic Research Laboratory. ENIAC contained 18,000 thermionic valves, weighed over 60,000 pounds, and consumed 25 kilowatts of electrical power per hour. ENIAC was capable of performing 100,000 calculations a second. Within a year after its completion, however, the invention of the transistor meant that the inefficient thermionic valves could be replaced with smaller, more reliable components, thus marking another major step in the history of computing.

Transistorized computers marked the advent of second-generation computers, which dominated in the late 1950s and early 1960s. Despite using transistors and printed circuits, these computers were still bulky and expensive. They were therefore used mainly by universities and government agencies.

Fig. 4 The Intel 4004 processor.
Source: From http://www.thg.ru/cpu/20051118/index.html (accessed January 2009).

The integrated circuit or microchip was developed by Jack St. Claire Kilby, an achievement for which he received the Nobel Prize in Physics in 2000.[7] While congratulating him, U.S. President Bill Clinton wrote, "You can take pride in the knowledge that your work will help to improve lives for generations to come." It was a relatively simple device that Mr. Kilby showed to a handful of co-workers gathered in the semiconductor lab at Texas Instruments in 1958. It was just a transistor and a few other components on a slice of germanium. Little did this group realize that Kilby's invention was about to revolutionize the electronics industry.

Third-Generation Computers

Kilby's invention started an explosion in third-generation computers. Even though the first integrated circuit was produced in September 1958, microchips were not used in computers until 1963. While mainframe computers like the IBM 360 increased storage and processing capabilities even further, the integrated circuit allowed the development of minicomputers that began to bring computing into many smaller businesses. Large-scale integration (LSI) of circuits led to the development of very small processing units, the next step along the evolutionary trail of computing. In November 1971, Intel released the world's first commercial microprocessor, the Intel 4004 (Fig. 4). The 4004 was the first complete central processing unit (CPU) on one chip and became the first commercially available microprocessor. It was possible because of the development of new silicon gate technology that enabled engineers to integrate a much greater number of transistors on a chip that would perform at a much faster speed. This development enabled the rise of the fourth-generation computer platforms.

Fig. 5 Vannevar Bush's MEMEX.
Source: From http://www.icesi.edu.co/blogs_estudiantes/luisau-lestia (accessed January 2009).

Fourth-Generation Computers

The fourth-generation computers that were being developed at this time utilized a microprocessor that put the computer's processing capabilities on a single integrated circuit chip. By combining random access memory, developed by Intel, fourth-generation computers were faster than ever before and had much smaller footprints. The 4004 processor was capable of "only" 60,000 instructions per second. As technology progressed, however, new processors brought even more speed and computing capability to users. The microprocessors that evolved from the 4004 allowed manufacturers to begin developing personal computers small enough and cheap enough to be purchased by the general public. The first commercially available personal computer was the Micro Instrumentation Telemetry Systems Altair 8800, released at the end of 1974. What followed was a flurry of other personal computers to market, such as the Apple I and II, the Commodore Personal Electronic Transactor, the VIC-20, the Commodore 64, and eventually the original IBM PC in 1981. The PC era had begun in earnest by the mid-1980s. During this time, the IBM PC and IBM PC compatibles, the Commodore Amiga, and the Atari ST computers were the most prevalent PC platforms available to the public. Computer manufacturers produced various models of IBM PC compatibles. Even though microprocessing power, memory and data storage capacities have increased by many orders of magnitude since the invention of the 4004 processor, the technology for LSI or very-large-scale integration microchips has not changed all that much. For this reason, most of today's computers can still be categorized as fourth-generation computers.

INTERNET SOFTWARE EVOLUTION

The Internet is named after the Internet Protocol, the standard communications protocol used by every computer on the Internet. The conceptual foundation for creation of the Internet was significantly developed by three individuals. The first, Vannevar Bush,[8] wrote a visionary description of the potential uses for information technology with his description of an automated library system named MEMEX (see Fig. 5). Bush introduced the concept of the MEMEX in the 1930s as a microfilm-based "device in which an individual stores all his books, records, and communications, and which is mechanized so that it may be consulted with exceeding speed and flexibility."[9]

After thinking about the potential of augmented memory for several years, Bush wrote an essay entitled "As We May Think" in 1936. It was finally published in July 1945 in the *Atlantic Monthly*. In the article, Bush predicted: "Wholly new forms of encyclopedias will appear, ready made with a mesh of associative trails running through them, ready to be dropped into the MEMEX and there amplified."[10] In September 1945, *Life* magazine published a condensed version of "As We May Think" that was accompanied by several graphic illustrations showing what a MEMEX machine might look like, along with its companion devices.

The second individual to have a profound effect in shaping the Internet was Norbert Wiener. Wiener was an early pioneer in the study of stochastic and noise processes. His work in stochastic and noise processes was relevant to electronic engineering, communication, and control systems.[11] He also founded the field of cybernetics. This field of study formalized notions of feedback and influenced research in many other fields, such as engineering, systems control, computer science, biology, philosophy, etc. His work in cybernetics inspired future researchers to focus on extending human capabilities with technology. Influenced by Wiener, Marshall McLuhan put forth the idea of a *global village* that was interconnected by an electronic nervous system as part of our popular culture.

In 1957, the Soviet Union launched the first satellite, *Sputnik I,* prompting U.S. President Dwight Eisenhower to create the Advanced Research Projects Agency (ARPA) to regain the technological lead in the arms race. ARPA (renamed DARPA, the Defense ARPA, in 1972) appointed J. C. R. Licklider to head the new Information Processing Techniques Office. Licklider was given a mandate to further the research of the SAGE (Semi-Automatic Ground Environment) system. The SAGE system (see Fig. 6) was a continental air-defense network commissioned by the U.S. military and designed to help protect the United States against a space-based nuclear attack.[12] SAGE was the most ambitious computer project ever undertaken at the time, and it required over 800 programmers and the technical resources of some of America's largest corporations. SAGE was started in the 1950s and became operational

Fig. 6 The SAGE system.
Source: From United States Air Force Archives, retrieved from http://history.sandiego.edu/GEN/recording/images5/PDRM0380.jpg.

by 1963. It remained in continuous operation for over 20 years, until 1983.

While working at Information Processing Techniques Office, Licklider evangelized the potential benefits of a country-wide communications network. His chief contribution to the development of the Internet was his idea, not specific inventions. He foresaw the need for networked computers with easy user interfaces. His ideas foretold of graphical computing, point-and-click interfaces, digital libraries, e-commerce, online banking, and software that would exist on a network and migrate to wherever it was needed. Licklider worked for several years at ARPA, where he set the stage for the creation of the Advanced Research Projects Agency Network (ARPANET). He also worked at Bolt Beranek and Newman (BBN), the company that supplied the first computers connected on the ARPANET.

Fig. 7 An Interface Message Processor.
Source: From luni.net/wp-content/uploads/2007/02/bbn-imp.jpg (accessed January 2009).

After he had left ARPA, Licklider succeeded in convincing his replacement to hire a man named Lawrence Roberts, believing that Roberts was just the person to implement Licklider's vision of the future network computing environment. Roberts led the development of the network. His efforts were based on a novel idea of "packet switching" that had been developed by Paul Baran while working at Research And Development Corporation. The idea for a common interface to the ARPANET was first suggested in Ann Arbor, Michigan, by Wesley Clark at an ARPANET design session set up by Lawrence Roberts in April 1967. Roberts's implementation plan called for each site that was to connect to the ARPANET to write the software necessary to connect its computer to the network. To the attendees, this approach seemed like a lot of work. There were so many different kinds of computers and operating systems in use throughout the DARPA community that every piece of code would have to be individually written, tested, implemented, and maintained. Clark told Roberts that he thought the design was "bass-ackwards." (The art and science of hurtling blindly in the wrong direction with no sense of the impending doom about to be inflicted on one's sorry ass. Usually applied to procedures, processes, or theories based on faulty logic, or faulty personnel.)[13]

After the meeting, Roberts stayed behind and listened as Clark elaborated on his concept to deploy a minicomputer called an Interface Message Processor (IMP, see Fig. 7) at each site. The IMP would handle the interface to the ARPANET network. The physical layer, the data link layer, and the network layer protocols used internally on the ARPANET were implemented on this IMP. Using this approach, each site would only have to write one interface to the commonly deployed IMP. The host at each site connected itself to the IMP using another type of interface that had different physical, data link, and network layer specifications. These were specified by the Host/IMP Protocol in BBN Report 1822.[14]

So, as it turned out, the first networking protocol that was used on the ARPANET was the Network Control Program (NCP). The NCP provided the middle layers of a protocol stack running on an ARPANET-connected host computer.[15] The NCP managed the connections and flow control among the various processes running on different ARPANET host computers. An application layer, built on top of the NCP, provided services such as e-mail and file transfer. These applications used the NCP to handle connections to other host computers.

A minicomputer was created specifically to realize the design of the IMP. This approach provided a system-independent interface to the ARPANET that could be used by any computer system. Because of this approach, the Internet architecture was an open architecture from the very beginning. The IMP interface for the

IMP Architecture

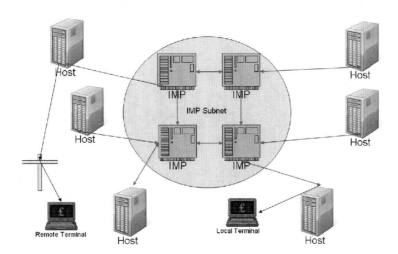

Fig. 8 Overview of the IMP architecture.

ARPANET went live in early October 1969. The implementation of the architecture is depicted in Fig. 8.

Establishing a Common Protocol for the Internet

Since the lower-level protocol layers were provided by the IMP host interface, the NCP essentially provided a transport layer consisting of the ARPANET Host-to-Host Protocol (AHHP) and the Initial Connection Protocol (ICP). The AHHP specified how to transmit a unidirectional, flow-controlled data stream between two hosts. The ICP specified how to establish a bidirectional pair of data streams between a pair of connected host processes. Application protocols such as File Transfer Protocol (FTP), used for file transfers, and Simple Mail Transfer Protocol, used for sending e-mail, accessed network services through an interface to the top layer of the NCP. On January 1, 1983, known as Flag Day, NCP was rendered obsolete when the ARPANET changed its core networking protocols from NCP to the more flexible and powerful TCP/IP protocol suite, marking the start of the modern Internet.

It was actually Robert Kahn and Vinton Cerf who built on what was learned with NCP to develop the TCP/IP networking protocol we use today. TCP/IP quickly became the most widely used network protocol in the world. The Internet's open nature and use of the more efficient TCP/IP protocol became the cornerstone of an internetworking design that has become the most widely used network protocol in the world. The history of TCP/IP reflects an interdependent design. Development of this protocol was conducted by many people. Over time, there evolved four increasingly better versions of TCP/IP (TCP v1, TCP v2, a split into TCP v3

and IP v3, and TCP v4 and IPv4). At the time of this writing, IPv4 is the standard protocol, but it is in the process of being replaced by IPv6, which is described later in this entry.

The TCP/IP protocol was deployed to the ARPANET, but not all sites were all that willing to convert to the new protocol. To force the matter to a head, the TCP/IP team turned off the NCP network channel numbers on the ARPANET IMPs twice. The first time they turned it off for a full day in mid-1982, so that only sites using TCP/IP could still operate. The second time, later that fall, they disabled NCP again for two days. The full switchover to TCP/IP happened on January 1, 1983, without much hassle. Even after that, however, there were still a few ARPANET sites that were down for as long as three months while their systems were retrofitted to use the new protocol. In 1984, the U.S. Department of Defense made TCP/IP the standard for all military computer networking, which gave it a high profile and stable funding. By 1990, the ARPANET was retired and transferred to the NSFNET. The NSFNET was soon connected to the CSNET, which linked universities around North America, and then to the EUnet, which connected research facilities in Europe. Thanks in part to the National Science Foundation's enlightened management, and fueled by the growing popularity of the web, the use of the Internet exploded after 1990, prompting the U.S. government to transfer management to independent organizations starting in 1995.

Evolution of Ipv6

The amazing growth of the Internet throughout the 1990s caused a vast reduction in the number of free IP addresses available under IPv4. IPv4 was never designed to scale to global levels. To increase available address space, it had to process data packets that were larger (i.e., that contained more bits of data). This resulted in a longer IP address and that caused problems for existing hardware and software. Solving those problems required the design, development, and implementation of a new architecture and new hardware to support it. It also required changes to all of the TCP/IP routing software. After examining a number of proposals, the Internet Engineering Task Force (IETF) settled on IPv6, which was released in January 1995 as RFC 1752. Ipv6 is sometimes called the Next Generation Internet Protocol (IPNG) or TCP/IP v6. Following release of the RFP, a number of organizations began working towards making the new protocol the *de facto* standard. Fast-forward nearly a decade later, and by 2004, IPv6 was widely available from industry as an integrated TCP/IP protocol and was supported by most new Internet networking equipment.

Finding a Common Method to Communicate Using the Internet Protocol

In the 1960s, 20 years after Vannevar Bush proposed MEMEX, the word *hypertext* was coined by Ted Nelson. Ted Nelson was one of the major visionaries of the coming hypertext revolution. He knew that the technology of his time could never handle the explosive growth of information that was proliferating across the planet. Nelson popularized the hypertext concept, but it was Douglas Engelbart who developed the first working hypertext systems. At the end of World War II, Douglas Engelbart was a 20-year-old U.S. Navy radar technician in the Philippines. One day, in a Red Cross library, he picked up a copy of the *Atlantic Monthly* dated July 1945. He happened to come across Vannevar Bush's article about the MEMEX automated library system and was strongly influenced by this vision of the future of information technology. Sixteen years later, Engelbart published his own version of Bush's vision in a paper prepared for the Air Force Office of Scientific Research and Development. In Englebart's paper, "Augmenting Human Intellect: A Conceptual Framework," he described an advanced electronic information system:

> Most of the structuring forms I'll show you stem from the simple capability of being able to establish arbitrary linkages between different substructures, and of directing the computer subsequently to display a set of linked substructures with any relative positioning we might designate among the different substructures. You can designate as many different kinds of links as you wish, so that you can specify different display or manipulative treatment for the different types.[16]

Engelbart joined Stanford Research Institute in 1962. His first project was *Augment,* and its purpose was to develop computer tools to augment human capabilities. Part of this effort required that he developed the mouse, the graphical user interface, and the first working hypertext system, named o**N**-**L**ine **S**ystem (NLS). NLS was designed to cross-reference research papers for sharing among geographically distributed researchers. NLS provided groupware capabilities, screen sharing among remote users, and reference links for moving between sentences within a research paper and from one research paper to another. Engelbart's NLS system was chosen as the second node on the ARPANET, giving him a role in the invention of the Internet as well as the WWW.

In the 1980s, a precursor to the web as we know it today was developed in Europe by Tim Berners-Lee and Robert Cailliau. Its popularity skyrocketed, in large part because Apple Computer delivered its HyperCard product free with every Macintosh bought at that time. In 1987, the effects of hypertext rippled through the industrial community. HyperCard was the first hypertext editing system available to the general public, and it caught on very quickly. In the 1990s, Marc Andreessen and a team at the National Center for Supercomputer Applications (NCSA), a research institute at the University of Illinois, developed the Mosaic and Netscape browsers. A technology revolution few saw coming was in its infancy at this point in time.

Building a Common Interface to the Internet

While Marc Andreessen and the NCSA team were working on their browsers, Robert Cailliau at European Organization for Nuclear Research (CERN) independently proposed a project to develop a hypertext system. He joined forces with Berners-Lee to get the web initiative into high gear. Cailliau rewrote his original proposal and lobbied CERN management for funding for programmers. He and Berners-Lee worked on papers and presentations in collaboration, and Cailliau helped run the very first WWW conference.

In the fall of 1990, Berners-Lee developed the first web browser (Fig. 9), featuring an integrated editor that could create hypertext documents. He installed the application on his and Cailliau's computers, and they both began communicating via the world's first web server, at info.cern.ch, on December 25, 1990.

A few months later, in August 1991, Berners-Lee posted a notice on a newsgroup called alt.hypertext that provided information about where one could download the web server (Fig. 10) and browser. Once this information hit the newsgroup, new web servers began appearing all over the world almost immediately.

Following this initial success, Berners-Lee enhanced the server and browser by adding support for the FTP

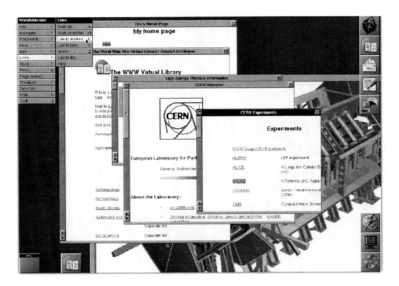

Fig. 9 The first web browser, created by Tim Berners-Lee.
Source: From http://www.tranquileye.com/cyber/index.html (accessed January 2009).

protocol. This made a wide range of existing FTP directories and Usenet newsgroups instantly accessible via a web page displayed in his browser. He also added a Telnet server on info.cern.ch, making a simple line browser available to anyone with a Telnet client.

The first public demonstration of Berners-Lee's web server was at a conference called Hypertext 91. This web server came to be known as CERN hypertext transfer protocol daemon (httpd), and work in it continued until July 1996. Before work stopped on the CERN httpd, Berners-Lee managed to get CERN to provide a certification on April 30, 1993, that the web technology and program code was in the public domain so that anyone could use and improve it. This was an important decision that helped the web to grow to enormous proportions.

In 1992, Joseph Hardin and Dave Thompson were working at the NCSA. When Hardin and Thompson heard about Berners-Lee's work, they downloaded the Viola WWW browser and demonstrated it to NCSA's Software Design Group by connecting to the web server at CERN over the Internet.[17] The Software Design Group was impressed by what they saw. Two students

from the group, Marc Andreessen and Eric Bina, began work on a browser version for X-Windows on UNIX computers, first released as version 0.5 on January 23, 1993 (Fig. 11). Within a week, Andreeson's release message was forwarded to various newsgroups by Berners-Lee. This generated a huge swell in the user base and subsequent redistribution ensued, creating a wider awareness of the product. Working together to support the product, Bina provided expert coding support while Andreessen provided excellent customer support. They monitored the newsgroups continuously to ensure that they knew about and could fix any bugs reported and make the desired enhancements pointed out by the user base.

Mosaic was the first widely popular web browser available to the general public. It helped spread use and knowledge of the web across the world. Mosaic provided support for graphics, sound, and video clips. An early version of Mosaic introduced forms support, enabling many powerful new uses and applications. Innovations including the use of bookmarks and history files were added. Mosaic became even more popular, helping further the growth of the WWW. In mid-1994, after Andreessen had graduated from the University of Illinois, Silicon Graphics founder Jim Clark collaborated with Andreessen to found Mosaic Communications, which was later, renamed Netscape Communications.

In October 1994, Netscape released the first beta version of its browser, Mozilla 0.96b, over the Internet. The final version, named Mozilla 1.0, was released in December 1994. It became the very first commercial web browser. The Mosaic programming team then developed another web browser, which they named Netscape Navigator. Netscape Navigator was later renamed

Fig. 10 Tim Berners-Lee's first web server.

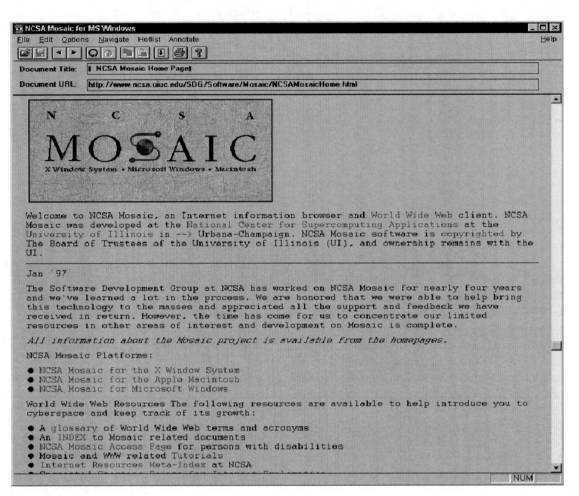

Fig. 11   The original NCSA Mosaic browser.
Source: From http://www.nsf.gov/od/lpa/news/03/images/mosaic.6beta.jpg.

Netscape Communicator, then renamed back to just Net-scape. See Fig. 12.

During this period, Microsoft was not asleep at the wheel. Bill Gates realized that the WWW was the future and focused vast resources to begin developing a product to compete with Netscape. In 1995, Microsoft hosted an Internet Strategy Day[18] and announced its commitment to adding Internet capabilities to all its products. In fulfillment of that announcement, Microsoft Internet Explorer arrived as both a graphical Web browser and the name for a set of technologies.

In July 1995, Microsoft released the Windows 95 operating system, which included built-in support for dial-up networking and TCP/IP, two key technologies for connecting a PC to the Internet. It also included an add-on to the operating system called Internet Explorer 1.0 (Fig. 13). When Windows 95 with Internet Explorer debuted, the WWW became accessible to a great many more people. Internet Explorer technology originally shipped as the Internet Jumpstart Kit in Microsoft Plus! for Windows 95.

One of the key factors in the success of Internet Explorer was that it eliminated the need for cumbersome manual installation that was required by many of the existing shareware browsers. Users embraced the "do-it-forme" installation model provided by Microsoft, and browser loyalty went out the window. The Netscape browser led in user and market share until Microsoft released Internet Explorer, but the latter product took the market lead in 1999. This was due mainly to its distribution advantage, because it was included in every version of Microsoft Windows. The browser wars had begun, and the battlefield was the Internet. In response to Microsoft's move, Netscape decided in 2002 to release a free, open source software version of Net-scape named Mozilla (which was the internal name for the old Netscape browser; see Fig. 14). Mozilla has steadily gained market share, particularly on non-Win-dows platforms such as Linux, largely because of its open source foundation. Mozilla Firefox, released in November 2004, became very popular almost immediately.

Fig. 12 The original Netscape browser.
Source: From http://browser.netscape.com/downloads/archive.

The Appearance of Cloud Formations—From One Computer to a Grid of Many

Two decades ago, computers were clustered together to form a single larger computer in order to simulate a supercomputer and harness greater processing power. This technique was common and was used by many IT departments. *Clustering*, as it was called, allowed one to configure computers using special protocols so they could "talk" to each other. The purpose was to balance the computational load across several machines, divvying up units of work and spreading it across multiple processors. To the user, it made little difference which CPU executed an application. Cluster management software ensured that the CPU with the most available processing capability at that time was used to run the code. A key to efficient cluster management was engineering where the data was to be held. This process became known as *data residency*. Computers in the cluster were usually physically connected to magnetic disks that stored and retrieved a data while the CPUs performed input/output (I/O) processes quickly and efficiently.

In the early 1990s, Ian Foster and Carl Kesselman presented their concept of "The Grid." They used an analogy to the electricity grid, where users could plug in and use a (metered) utility service. They reasoned that if companies cannot generate their own power, it would be reasonable to assume they would purchase that service from a third party capable of providing a steady electricity supply. So, they asked, "Why can't the same apply to computing resources?" If one node could plug itself into a grid of computers and pay only for the resources it used, it would be a more cost-effective solution for companies than buying and managing their own infrastructure. Grid computing expands on the techniques used in clustered computing models, where multiple independent clusters appear to act like a grid

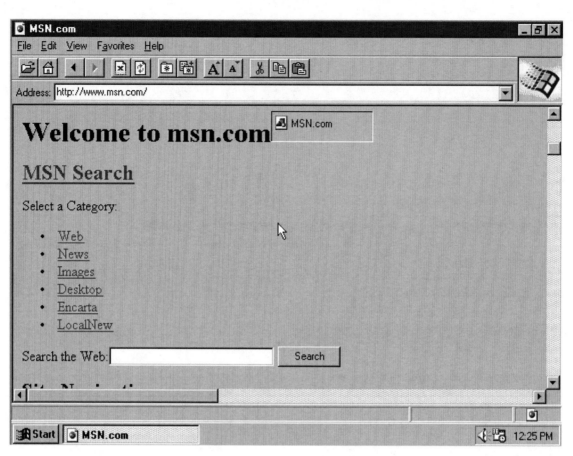

Fig. 13   Internet Explorer version 1.0.
Source: From http://www.microsoft.com/library/media/1033/windows/IE/images/community/columns/old_ie.gif (accessed January 2009).

simply because they are not all located within the same domain.[19]

A major obstacle to overcome in the migration from a clustering model to grid computing was data residency. Because of the distributed nature of a grid, computational nodes could be anywhere in the world. Paul Wallis explained the data residency issue for a grid model like this:

> It was fine having all that CPU power available, but the data on which the CPU performed its operations could be thousands of miles away, causing a delay (latency) between data fetch and execution. CPUs need to be fed and watered with different volumes of data depending on the tasks they are processing. Running a data-intensive process with disparate data sources can create a bottleneck in the I/O, causing the CPU to run inefficiently, and affecting economic viability.

The issues of storage management, migration of data, and security provisioning were key to any proposed solution in order for a grid model to succeed. A toolkit called Globus[20] was created to solve these issues, but the infrastructure hardware available still has not progressed to a level where true grid computing can be wholly achieved.

The Globus Toolkit is an open source software toolkit used for building grid systems and applications. It is being developed and maintained by the Globus Alliance[21] and many others all over the world. The Globus Alliance has grown into community of organizations and individuals developing fundamental technologies to support the grid model. The toolkit provided by Globus allows people to share computing power, databases, instruments, and other online tools securely across corporate, institutional, and geographic boundaries without sacrificing local autonomy.

The cloud is helping to further propagate the grid computing model. Cloud-resident entities such as data centers have taken the concepts of grid computing and bundled them into service offerings that appeal to other entities that do not want the burden of infrastructure but do want the capabilities hosted from those data centers. One of the most well known of the new cloud service providers is Amazon's Simple Storage Service (S3) third-party storage solution. Amazon S3 is storage for the Internet. According to the Amazon S3 website,[22] it provides a simple web services interface that can be

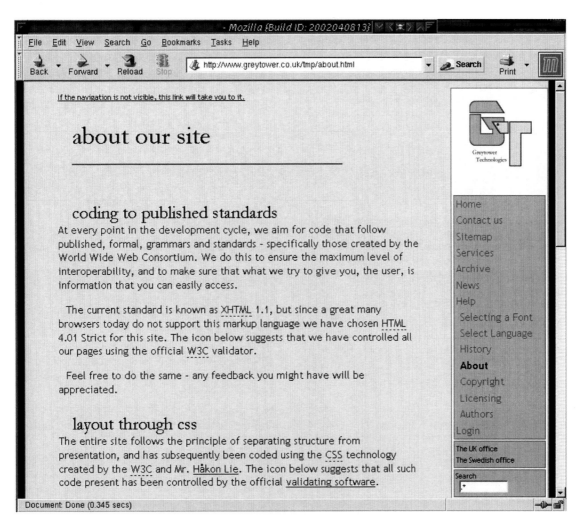

Fig. 14 The open source version of Netscape, named Mozilla.
Source: From http://browser.netscape.com/downloads/archive.

used to store and retrieve any amount of data, at any time, from anywhere on the web. It gives any developer access to the same highly scalable, reliable, fast, inexpensive data storage infrastructure that Amazon uses to run its own global network of web sites. The service aims to maximize benefits of scale and to pass those benefits on to developers.

In 2002, EMC offered a Content Addressable Storage (CAS) solution called Centera as yet another cloud-based data storage service that competes with Amazon's offering. EMC's product creates a global network of data centers, each with massive storage capabilities. When a user creates a document, the application server sends it to the Centera storage system. The storage system then returns a unique content address to the server. The unique address allows the system to verify the integrity of the documents whenever a user moves or copies them. From that point, the application can request the document by submitting the address. Duplicates of documents are saved only once under the same address, leading to reduced storage requirements.

Centera then retrieves the document regardless of where it may be physically located.

EMC's Centera product takes the sensible approach that no one can afford the risk of placing all of their data in one place, so the data is distributed around the globe. Their cloud will monitor data usage and automatically move data around in order to load-balance data requests and better manage the flow of Internet traffic. Centera is constantly self-tuning to react automatically to surges in demand. The Centera architecture functions as a cluster that automatically configures itself upon installation. The system also handles fail-over, load balancing, and failure notification.

There are some drawbacks to these cloud-based solutions, however. An example is a recent problem at Amazon S3. They suffered a "massive" outage in February 2008, which served to highlight the risks involved with adopting such cloud-based service offerings. Amazon's technical representative from the Web Services Team commented publicly with the following press release:

Early this morning, at 3:30am PST, we started seeing elevated levels of authenticated requests from multiple users in one of our locations. While we carefully monitor our overall request volumes and these remained within normal ranges, we had not been monitoring the proportion of authenticated requests. Importantly, these cryptographic requests consume more resources per call than other request types. Shortly before 4:00am PST, we began to see several other users significantly increase their volume of authenticated calls. The last of these pushed the authentication service over its maximum capacity before we could complete putting new capacity in place.

In addition to processing authenticated requests, the authentication service also performs account validation on every request Amazon S3 handles. This caused Amazon S3 to be unable to process any requests in that location, beginning at 4:31am PST. By 6:48am PST, we had moved enough capacity online to resolve the issue.

As we said earlier today, though we're proud of our uptime track record over the past two years with this service, any amount of downtime is unacceptable. As part of the post mortem for this event, we have identified a set of short-term actions as well as longer term improvements. We are taking immediate action on the following: (a) improving our monitoring of the proportion of authenticated requests; (b) further increasing our authentication service capacity; and (c) adding additional defensive measures around the authenticated calls. Additionally, we've begun work on a service health dashboard, and expect to release that shortly.

Sincerely,

The Amazon Web Services Team

The message above clearly points out the lesson one should take from this particular incident: *caveat emptor,* which is Latin for "Let the buyer beware."

SERVER VIRTUALIZATION

Virtualization is a method of running multiple independent virtual operating systems on a single physical computer.[23] This approach maximizes the return on investment for the computer. The term was coined in the 1960s in reference to a virtual machine (sometimes called a pseudo-machine). The creation and management of virtual machines has often been called *platform virtualization.* Platform virtualization is performed on a given computer (hardware platform) by software called a control program. The control program creates a simulated environment, a virtual computer, which enables the device to use hosted software specific to the virtual environment, sometimes called guest software.

The guest software, which is often itself a complete operating system, runs just as if it were installed on a stand-alone computer. Frequently, more than one virtual machine is able to be simulated on a single physical computer, their number being limited only by the host device's physical hardware resources. Because the guest software often requires access to specific peripheral devices in order to function, the virtualized platform must support guest interfaces to those devices. Examples of such devices are the hard disk drive, CD-ROM, DVD, and network interface card. Virtualization technology is a way of reducing the majority of hardware acquisition and maintenance costs, which can result in significant savings for any company.

Parallel Processing

Parallel processing is performed by the simultaneous execution of program instructions that have been allocated across multiple processors with the objective of running a program in less time.[24] On the earliest computers, a user could run only one program at a time. This being the case, a computation-intensive program that took X minutes to run, using a tape system for data I/O that took X minutes to run, would take a total of X + X minutes to execute. To improve performance, early forms of parallel processing were developed to allow interleaved execution of both programs simultaneously. The computer would start an I/O operation (which is typically measured in milliseconds), and while it was waiting for the I/O operation to complete, it would execute the processor-intensive program (measured in nanoseconds). The total execution time for the two jobs combined became only slightly longer than the X minutes required for the I/O operations to complete.

The next advancement in parallel processing was multiprogramming. In a multiprogramming system, multiple programs submitted by users are each allowed to use the processor for a short time, each taking turns and having exclusive time with the processor in order to execute instructions. This approach is known as "round-robin scheduling" (RR scheduling). It is one of the oldest, simplest, fairest, and most widely used scheduling algorithms, designed especially for time-sharing systems.[25]

In RR scheduling, a small unit of time called a time slice (or quantum) is defined. All executable processes are held in a circular queue. The time slice is defined based on the number of executable processes that are in the queue. For example, if there are five user processes held in the queue and the time slice allocated for the queue to execute in total is 1 second, each user process is allocated 200 milliseconds of process execution time on the CPU before the scheduler begins moving to the next process in the queue. The CPU scheduler manages this queue, allocating the CPU to each process for a time interval of 1 time slice. New processes are always added to the end of the queue. The CPU scheduler picks the first process from the queue, sets its timer to interrupt the process after the expiration of the timer, and then dispatches the next process in the queue. The process whose time has expired is placed at the end of the queue. If a process is still running at the end of a time slice, the CPU is interrupted and the process goes to the end of the queue. If the process finishes before the end of the time-slice, it releases the CPU voluntarily. In either case, the CPU scheduler assigns the CPU to the next process in the queue. Every time a process is granted the CPU, a context switch occurs, which adds overhead to the process execution time. To users it appears that all of the programs are executing at the same time.

Resource contention problems often arose in these early systems. Explicit requests for resources led to a condition known as deadlock. Competition for resources on machines with no tie-breaking instructions led to the critical section routine. Contention occurs when several processes request access to the same resource. In order to detect deadlock situations, a counter for each processor keeps track of the number of consecutive requests from a process that have been rejected. Once that number reaches a predetermined threshold, a state machine that inhibits other processes from making requests to the main store is initiated until the deadlocked process is successful in gaining access to the resource.

Vector Processing

The next step in the evolution of parallel processing was the introduction of multiprocessing. Here, two or more processors share a common workload. The earliest versions of multiprocessing were designed as a master/slave model, where one processor (the master) was responsible for all of the tasks to be performed and it only off-loaded tasks to the other processor (the slave) when the master processor determined, based on a predetermined threshold, that work could be shifted to increase performance. This arrangement was necessary because it was not then understood how to program the machines so they could cooperate in managing the resources of the system.

Vector processing was developed to increase processing performance by operating in a multitasking manner. Matrix operations were added to computers to allow a single instruction to manipulate two arrays of numbers performing arithmetic operations. This was valuable in certain types of applications in which data occurred in the form of vectors or matrices. In applications with less well-formed data, vector processing was less valuable.

Symmetric Multiprocessing Systems

The next advancement was the development of symmetric multiprocessing systems (SMP) to address the problem of resource management in master/slave models. In SMP systems, each processor is equally capable and responsible for managing the workflow as it passes through the system. The primary goal is to achieve *sequential consistency,* in other words, to make SMP systems appear to be exactly the same as a single-processor, multiprogramming platform. Engineers discovered that system performance could be increased nearly 10–20% by executing some instructions out of order. However, programmers had to deal with the increased complexity and cope with a situation where two or more programs might read and write the same operands simultaneously. This difficulty, however, is limited to a very few programmers, because it only occurs in rare circumstances. To this day, the question of how SMP machines should behave when accessing shared data remains unresolved.

Data propagation time increases in proportion to the number of processors added to SMP systems. After a certain number (usually somewhere around 40–50 processors), performance benefits gained by using even more processors do not justify the additional expense of adding such processors. To solve the problem of long data propagation times, message passing systems were created. In these systems, programs that share data send messages to each other to announce that particular operands have been assigned a new value. Instead of a global message announcing an operand's new value, the message is communicated only to those areas that need to know the change. There is a network designed to support the transfer of messages between applications. This allows a great number of processors (as many as several thousand) to work in tandem in a system. These systems are highly scalable and are called MPP systems.

MPP Systems

Massive parallel processing is used in computer architecture circles to refer to a computer system with many independent arithmetic units or entire microprocessors, which run in parallel.[26] "Massive" connotes hundreds if not thousands of such units. In this form of computing, all the processing elements are interconnected to act as one very large computer. This approach is in contrast to a distributed computing model, where massive numbers of separate computers are used to solve a single problem (such as in the SETI project, mentioned previously). Early examples of MPP systems were the Distributed Array Processor, the Goodyear MPP, the Connection Machine, and the Ultracomputer. In data mining, there is a need to perform multiple searches of a static database. The earliest MPP systems all used serial computers as individual processing units in order to maximize the number of units available for a given size and cost. Single-chip implementations of massively parallel processor arrays are becoming ever more cost effective due to the advancements in integrated-circuit technology.

An example of the use of MPP can be found in the field of artificial intelligence. For example, a chess application must analyze the outcomes of many possible alternatives and formulate the best course of action to take. Another example can be found in scientific environments, where certain simulations (such as molecular modeling) and complex mathematical problems can be split apart and each part processed simultaneously. Parallel data query is a technique used in business. This technique divides very large data stores into pieces based on various algorithms. Rather than searching sequentially through an entire database to resolve a query, 26 CPUs might be used simultaneously to perform a sequential search, each CPU individually evaluating a letter of the alphabet. MPP machines are not easy to program, but for certain applications, such as data mining, they are the best solution.

SUMMARY

In this entry, we stressed the importance of knowing about the evolution of computing in order to get an appreciation of how we got into the cloud environment. Examining the history of computing hardware and software helps us to understand why we are standing on the shoulders of giants. We discussed how the rules computers use to communicate came about, and how the development of networking and communications protocols has helped drive the Internet technology growth. This, in turn, has driven even more changes in protocols and forced the creation of new technologies to mitigate addressing concerns and improve the methods used to communicate over the Internet. The use of web browsers has led to huge Internet growth and a migration away from the traditional data center.

REFERENCES

1. Wallis, P. A Brief History of Cloud Computing: Is the Cloud There Yet? A Look at the Cloud's Forerunners and the Problems They Encountered, http://soa.sys-con.com/node/581838, 22 August 2008 (accessed January 2009).
2. http://en.wikipedia.org/wiki/Turing_complete (accessed March 2009).
3. http://esolangs.org/wiki/Church-Turing_thesis (accessed January 2009).
4. http://trillian.randomstuff.org.uk/~stephen/history (accessed January 2009).
5. http://en.wikipedia.org/wiki/Colossus_computer (accessed January 2009).
6. Shurkin, J. *Engines of the Mind: The Evolution of the Computer from Mainframes to Microprocessors*; W. W. Norton: New York, NY, 1996.
7. http://www.ti.com/corp/docs/kilbyctr/jackstclair.shtml (accessed January 2009).
8. http://en.wikipedia.org/wiki/Vannevar_Bush (accessed January 2009).
9. http://www.livinginternet.com/i/ii_summary.htm (accessed January 2009).
10. http://www.theatlantic.com/doc/194507/bush (accessed January 2009).
11. http://en.wikipedia.org/wiki/Norbert_Wiener (accessed January 2009).
12. http://www.computermuseum.li/Testpage/IBM-SAGE-computer.htm (accessed January 2009).
13. http://www.urbandictionary.com/define.php?term = Bass + Ackwards (accessed January 2009).
14. Heart, F.; Kahn, R.; Ornstein, S.; Crowther, W.; Walden, D. The interface message processor for the ARPA computer network. Proc. Spring Jt. Comp. Conf. **1970**, *36*, 551–567.
15. http://www.answers.com/topic/network-control-program (accessed January 2009).
16. Engelbart, D. Augmenting human intellect: A conceptual framework. In *A report for the Air Force Office of Scientific Research and Development*; October 1962.
17. Andreessen, M. *NCSA Mosaic Technical Summary*, 20 February 1993.
18. http://www.microsoft.com/windows/WinHistoryIE.mspx (accessed January 2009).
19. Wallis, P. Keystones and Rivets, http://it.toolbox.com/blogs/keystones-and-rivets/under standing-cloud-computing-22611 (accessed January 2009).
20. The reader is encouraged to visit http://globus.org/toolkit for more information.
21. http://www.globus.org (accessed January 2009).
22. The reader is encouraged to visit http://aws.amazon.com/s3.
23. Ou, G. Introduction to Server Virtualization, http://articles.techrepublic.com.com/ 5100-10878_11-6074941.html (accessed January 2009).
24. http://searchdatacenter.techtarget.com/sDefinition/0,,sid80_gci212747,00.html (accessed January 2009).
25. http://choices.cs.uiuc.edu/~f-kon/RoundRobin/node1.html (accessed January 2009).
26. http://en.wikipedia.org/wiki/Massive_parallel_processing (accessed January 2009).

Cloud Computing: Mobile Devices

John W. Rittinghouse
Hypersecurity LLC, Tomball, Texas, U.S.A.

James F. Ransome
Cisco Systems, Santa Clara, California, U.S.A.

Abstract

The cloud is becoming increasingly pervasive and mobile browsers are getting better every day, providing the ability to access the cloud and its applications. Organizations are deploying more and more software-as-a-service -based applications and, assuming they have enough bandwidth, there is no reason that mobile workers cannot access those applications on their devices with a browser that can actually fully handle web and cloud standards. This entry describes the mobile smartphones platforms, their operating systems, virtualization of these platforms, mobile collaboration applications, and future trends.

OVERVIEW

A December 2008 Informa Telecoms & Media study[1] estimated that there are over 4 billion connections to mobile devices worldwide—an astounding number when you realize that this figure represents 60% of the global population at the time. Of course, this does not mean that two out of every three people on Earth have a mobile phone. It is common in more than 60 countries, however, for one person to have two or more devices, even while there are no phones at all in some parts of the globe. In some countries, millions of people are now experiencing connectivity to the world for the first time through wireless technologies. It is changing their economic, social, and political fortunes forevermore.

The number of wireless users on 3G services continues to rise daily. Informa estimates that there are nearly 415 million 3G subscriptions to date, with 77% share of the 3G market on UMTS/HSPA1 networks or 320 million connections, and the remaining 95 million subscribed to the older Code Division Multiple Access Evolution-Data-DO2 technology. The number of commercial Universal Mobile Telecommunications System/High Speed Packet Access (HSPA) networks has risen to 258 in more than 100 countries, including 41 networks in 20 countries in the Latin America and Caribbean region. It is a foregone conclusion that HSPA and HSPA + 3 will complete with all prevailing mobile wireless technologies available. Telstra's commercial launch of HSPA +, reported peak theoretical downlink speeds of 21.6 Mbps. The 3G technology is more than capable of delivering the high-speed bandwidth that customers demand.[1]

If the cloud is becoming increasingly pervasive and mobile browsers are getting better every day, you may be asking yourself if you need anything more on your mobile device beyond a browser that can access the cloud. Can browser widgets provide enough functionality that you don't need applications on your device? What if you could get everything you need accomplished using simple widgets that leverage your mobile device-based browser to access the cloud? The potential impact on enterprise mobility is huge. While organizations are deploying more and more Software-as-a-Service (SaaS) applications, there is no reason mobile workers can't access those applications from their mobile devices, assuming they have enough bandwidth (i.e., 3G- or 4G-capable devices). All that is really required beyond such bandwidth is a browser that can actually handle all of the various SaaS-associated web standards. Imagine a future environment in which mobile device manufacturers will partner with multiple SaaS vendors to provide enterprises complete cloud-based computing solutions that work anywhere.

WHAT IS A SMARTPHONE?

The definition of a smartphone is not standardized and varies depending on who you ask. For most users, the consensus is that a smartphone is a mobile device that offers advanced capabilities beyond those offered by a typical mobile phone. Modern versions come with PC-like functionality. Many of the newer models have customized operating systems (OS) and associated software that provides a standardized interface. Nearly all smartphones have advanced features such as e-mail, Internet

Encyclopedia of Information Systems and Technology, DOI: 10.1081/E-EIST-120053838

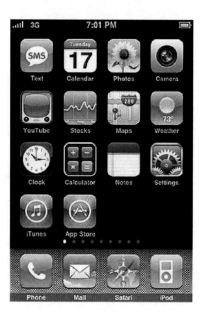

Fig. 1 The iPhone home screen.

access, instant messaging, etc. Smartphones are much more than just any other cell phones. They provide instant access to the web, which translates into immediate collaboration capability. Whether you are researching financial news to predict the stock market or looking for the perfect golf course to treat your client, it's on the Internet. Most smartphones allow you to sync data with your desktop computer. You can store and work on documents from your smartphone, and you can receive and reply to e-mails as they arrive in your inbox using real-time push e-mail.

Smartphone applications may be developed by the manufacturer of the device or by any other third-party provider or developer capable of accessing the open source OS. Other functionalities might include an additional interface such as a miniature QWERTY keyboard on the touch screen, built-in video and camera features, contact management, built-in navigation software, office document processing capability, and software for playing music and viewing video clips. Such smartphone capabilities transform the common cell phone into a mobile multimedia platform for your entertainment. They can store and display pictures, videos of friends and family, or even play live broadcasts of sports or movies.

Fig. 2 The message inbox for iPhone.

MOBILE OPERATING SYSTEMS FOR SMARTPHONES

Many regard the smartphone as a minicomputer with a phone. Most smartphones use an identifiable and open source OS, often with the ability to add user applications. This is a major factor differentiating smartphones from traditional mobile phones, which only support dedicated, proprietary applications. In the next few sections, we will take a look at several popular mobile devices and the OSs used with them.

iPhone

The Apple iPhone uses 3G technology, and its OS is based on the Darwin OS. Darwin forms the core set of components on which both the Mac OS X and iPhone OS are based. Darwin is compatible with Single UNIX Specification version 3 and Portable Operating System Interface (for Unix) applications and utilities. The iPhone touts features such as Global Positioning System (GPS) mapping, support for enterprise applications such as Microsoft Exchange, the new App Store, etc. The iPhone is a wide-screen mobile device very much like the iPod. It provides users a rich interface with HTML e-mail and an outstanding web browser. The iPhone home screen is shown in Fig. 1.

The iPhone lets you customize your home screen with applications and web clips of your choosing. You can arrange the icons any way you want or even create as many as nine home screens, each customizable to your needs. For example, if you check the same web site every day, you can create a web clip to access it directly from your home screen using a single tap of a finger. You can always press the home button to go back to your main home screen. iPhone supports rich HTML e-mail which allows you to see e-mail attachments in their original format. The iPhone supports more than a dozen file and image formats, including Portable Document Format, Microsoft Word, Excel, PowerPoint, and iWork attachments. Support for Microsoft Exchange Active-Sync gives you push e-mail that arrives automatically to your inbox, as shown in Fig. 2.

Google (Android)

Android is a software platform and OS for mobile devices that is based on the Linux kernel. It was originally developed by Google and later with the Open Handset Alliance (which is a group of more than 30 technology and mobile companies). The Android OS is the first complete, open, and free mobile platform. An Android Software Development Kit is available to help developers get started on new applications. Android allows developers to write managed Java code to control a

Fig. 3 The T-Mobile G1.

mobile device. Developers can distribute their applications to users of Android mobile phones. There is a marketplace called Android Market that enables developers to easily publish and distribute their applications directly to users of Android-compatible phones. The T-Mobile G1, shown in Fig. 3, is one of the better-known commercial offerings using Android.

Google has now released most of the Android code under the Apache license, a free software and open source license. Fig. 4 shows the major components of the Android OS.

Android developers have full access to the same framework application programming interfaces (APIs) used by the core applications. The architecture is designed to simplify reuse of components, so any application can publish its capabilities and any other application may then make use of those capabilities (subject to security constraints enforced by the framework). This same mechanism allows framework components to be replaced by the user. Underlying all applications is a set of services and systems, including:

1. A rich, extensible set of views that can be used to build an application (i.e., lists, grids, text boxes, buttons, and an embedded web browser)
2. Content providers that allow applications to access data from other applications or to share their own data
3. A resource manager to manage access to noncode resources such as localized strings, graphics, and layout files
4. A notification manager that enables all applications to display custom alerts in the status bar
5. An activity manager to manages applications and provide a common navigation stack

Every Android application runs in its own process, with its own instance of the Dalvik virtual machine (VM). The Dalvik VM is a major piece of Google's Android platform for mobile devices. It runs Java platform applications which have been converted into a compact Dalvik Executable (.dex) format suitable for systems that are constrained in terms of memory and processor speed.[2] Dalvik has been written so that a device can run multiple VMs efficiently. The Dalvik VM relies on the Linux kernel version 2.6 for

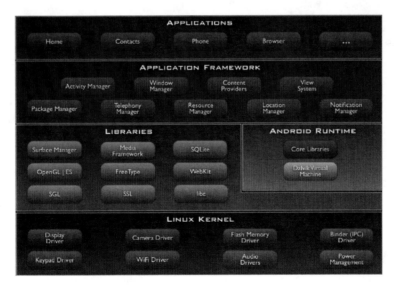

Fig. 4 Major components of the Android OS.
Source: From http://d.android.com/guide/basics/what-is-android.html.

Fig. 5 The Blackberry.

underlying functionalities such as threading, low-level memory management, and core system services such as security, memory management, process management, network stack, etc. The kernel acts as an abstraction layer between the hardware and the rest of the software stack.

Fig. 6 Windows mobile.

Blackberry

The BlackBerry solution consists of smartphones integrated with software that enables access to e-mail and other communication services. Developed by the Canadian company, Research In Motion (RIM), the BlackBerry is a wireless handheld device originally introduced in 1999 as a two-way pager. In 2002, RIM released their version of the smartphone, named Black-Berry. It supported push e-mail, mobile telephony, text messaging, internet faxing, web browsing, and other wireless information services. BlackBerry first made progress in the commercial marketplace by concentrating on enterprise e-mail. The BlackBerry has a built-in QWERTY keyboard, optimized for "thumbing" (the use of only the thumbs to type). System navigation is primarily accomplished by a scroll ball in the middle of the device (older devices used a track wheel on the side). This gives mobile users access to e-mail, phone, data, applications, games, and the Internet from a state-of-the-art smartphone, as shown in Fig. 5.

The BlackBerry offers an end-to-end encryption solution with two transport encryption options, Advanced Encryption Standard and Triple Data Encryption Standard for all data transmitted between their BlackBerry Enterprise Server and licensed BlackBerry smartphones. Private encryption keys are generated in a secure, two-way authenticated environment and are assigned to each BlackBerry smartphone user. Each secret key is stored only in the user's secure enterprise e-mail account and on the user's BlackBerry smartphone. Data sent to the BlackBerry is encrypted by the BlackBerry Enterprise Server using the private key retrieved from the user's mailbox. Next, the encrypted information is transported securely across the network to the smartphone, where it is decrypted using the key stored on the smartphone. Data remains encrypted in transit and is never decrypted outside of the corporate firewall.

Windows Mobile

Windows Mobile is a compact OS offering a set of basic applications commonly found on mobile devices. It is based on the Microsoft Win32 API. Devices that run Windows Mobile include pocket PCs, smartphones, portable media centers, and on-board computers for certain automobiles. Windows Mobile is designed to appear similar to desktop versions of Microsoft Windows. The platform supports third-party software development. Originally, Windows Mobile appeared as the pocket PC 2000 OS, then known as Windows Compact Edition (CE). Since then, Windows Mobile has been updated several times. The next planned release, Windows 7.0 was slated for the latter part of 2009. Fig. 6 shows what it was expected to look like.

Fig. 7 Clutter user interface.

Microsoft had projected in 2008 that it would see an increase of devices shipping with Windows Mobile from 11 to 20 million units. It missed its initial goal, selling only 18 million licenses, but even that number indicates the phenomenal growth of this market. Microsoft attributed the shortfall in its prediction to the delayed launch of some smartphone devices. Since then, Windows Mobile's market share as an OS for smartphones worldwide has fallen from 23% in 2004 to 12% in 2008.[3] Windows Mobile now has a worldwide smartphone market share of 14%. It is interesting to note that Microsoft licenses its Windows Mobile platform to four of the world's five largest mobile phone manufacturers—a strong testament to its popularity in the marketplace.

UBUNTU MOBILE INTERNET DEVICE

Ubuntu mobile internet device (MID) Edition is designed specifically for MIDs. Ubuntu MID is based on the popular Linux distribution Ubuntu. Ubuntu MID is highly flexible and customizable. It is an open source platform that is best suited to the kind of product differentiation that reaches target users in the mobile marketplace. MIDs generally have the following common features and attributes:

1. Small size/form factor, typically a 4–7-inch touch screen
2. Physical and/or virtual keyboard
3. WiFi, 3G, Bluetooth, GPS, WiMAX
4. 2–8-GB Flash or disk storage
5. 256 to 512 MB RAM (the more the better)
6. OpenGL 3D graphics support
7. USB, camera, headphone jack, speakers, microphone
8. Customizable (Flash or clutter[4]-based) user interface (see Figs. 7 and 8).

Ubuntu MID Edition has a suite of applications that work seamlessly to meet the needs of mobile users. Web applications such as Facebook, MySpace, YouTube, and Dailymotion are easily supported. Ubuntu MID needs no stylus—you navigate using a touchscreen. Just tap the screen or drag a finger for navigation and control. To launch applications, tap the application icon with your finger or tap menus and buttons to use them. You can swipe a web page to pan up, down, or

Fig. 8 Flash user interface.

Fig. 9 Ubuntu MID home screen.

sideways, and you can swipe a video, photo, song, or thumbnail page to move to the next or the previous one. Fig. 9 shows the home screen of Ubuntu MID.

In the next few pages we highlight some of the applications found in the default distribution of Ubuntu MID, to give you a feel for what capabilities exist on modern mobile devices and how they can enhance daily life, simply by facilitating collaboration via the Internet. When you first get the device running, it is important to set preferences such as time and date (see Fig. 10) and to perform any system updates to bring the version current with any releases or updates since your particular version was made available.

To update your system, simply tap the System menu and select the Update Manager. The application will start and display the "Starting Update Manager…" message as shown in Fig. 11.

Once the update manager starts, it will use your existing Internet connection and check with the update server to determine which applications on your system may need to be updated. You can even update the system itself using this tool. After checking with the server to see what may have changed, you will be presented with the screen shown in Fig. 12.

Simply click the green checkmark button to install updates. For the example in Fig. 12, five updates will be installed. The first part of the installation downloads the updates, as shown in Fig. 13.

The download will proceed and, depending on your connection speed, may take anywhere from a few seconds to minutes to complete. After the downloads complete, installation proceeds automatically. You may be asked to reboot the device to complete the install process.

Mobile users deal with office documents on a daily basis. Ubuntu MID offers an office document reader to read various document types such as. doc,. pdf,. xml, etc. The reader is shown in Fig. 14 displaying a .pdf file.

For users who need more than a read-only display of a document, Ubuntu MID also offers a complete mobile office solution, OpenOffice version 2.4 (see Fig. 15), which allows you to build presentations, spreadsheets, documents, etc. It is a very popular solution in the open source community.

Fig. 16 shows the editing of an. html document using OpenOffice. OpenOffice is the leading open source office software suite for word processing, spreadsheets, presentations, graphics, databases, etc. It is available in many languages and works on all common computer platforms. It stores data in an international open standard format, the ISO-approved Open Document Format,

Fig. 10 Setting the time and date on Ubuntu MID.

Fig. 11 The Ubuntu MID Update Manager.

Fig. 12 Installing updates.

and it can read and write files from other common commercial office software packages. It can be downloaded from the official web site[5] and used completely free of charge for any purpose.

The most recent versions of OpenOffice (version 3.0 and later) provide support for integrated e-mail and calendaring, using Thunderbird 2.0 for e-mail and Lightning for calendaring. Both of these products are available from mozilla.org and are also open source. Fig. 17 shows an inbox in OpenOffice e-mail.

For mobile users, traveling often involves downtime, sitting on a plane or in an airport or hotel lobby. FBReader is an ebook reader included with Ubuntu MID. FBReader works on Linux, Windows XP/Vista, FreeBSD, and various other Linux-based mobile OSs. FBReader is distributed under the terms of the GNU General Public License. It supports many ebook formats, such as fb2 ebook format, HTML, CHM, plucker, Palmdoc, zTxt, Text Compression for Reader, Rich Text Format, OpenReader, and plain text format. Direct reading from tar, zip, gzip, and bzip2 archives is also supported. FBReader can perform automatic library building, and automatic language and character encoding detection is also supported. Other features include:

1. Automatically generated contents table

Fig. 13 Downloading updates.

2. Embedded images support
3. Footnotes/hyperlinks support
4. Position indicator
5. Keeps the last open book and the last read positions for all opened books between runs
6. List of last opened books
7. Automatic hyphenation
8. Text search and full-screen mode, including screen rotation by 90, 180, and 270 degrees

An FBReader screen is shown in Fig. 18.

For those more inclined to chat using instant messaging, a full-featured IM client is provided, as illustrated in Fig. 19.

If you cannot find anyone to chat with, you can always use the Internet browser to visit your favorite web sites, listen to the radio, or watch videos on YouTube, Hulu, etc. The browser is very capable, supporting the most recent standards for a rich user interface. See Fig. 20.

MOBILE PLATFORM VIRTUALIZATION

Smart phones with rich and open OSs are growing in popularity, resulting in a market that is undergoing tremendous innovation and change. The pressure to reduce development costs and get phones to market faster has increased competitive pressure to deliver feature-rich phones to market faster and to migrate from proprietary OSs to open OSs without compromising the security of trusted services.

As mobile phones have become more powerful, beyond their basic phone functionality, phones now offer music, video, cameras, and built-in GPS capabilities. Rich applications are being built every day by a vibrant developer community utilizing the open OSs. As these capabilities have been developed, the mobile phone user's ability to include applications, pictures, videos,

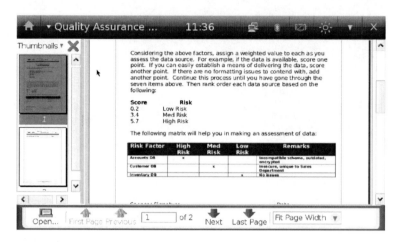

Fig. 14   The Ubuntu MID document reader.

music, e-mails, bank and credit card information, and personal information management (PIM) have all been combined to provide a much richer and more valuable experience into a persona that is portable and can be transferred seamlessly when upgrading to a new phone. The ability to protect and migrate personas will become an important purchasing decision. The risk of not securing and managing employee-owned devices if they contain confidential information is significant, and managing a wide variety of devices is complex in terms of both cost and security. Virtualization is a key enabling technology to address these issues.

Security is a serious issue for mobile handsets running an open source OSs. There are already a significant number of known viruses, and their numbers are growing fast for mobile phones but still lag far behind the number of known PC viruses. The mobile handset user is a roving agent in a wireless information technology (IT) world, and security is every bit as important as it is in the fixed-wire IT world. The frequent emergency security upgrades and patches common in the PC world, however, would be unacceptable to the average user of a mobile handset. Such an approach to security could stall the proliferation of smart and feature phones. Consequently, security must be designed in from day one of the handset's life cycle. Real-time virtualization solutions offer robust security via hardware-enforced memory isolation of partitions, isolating each OS from the others and preventing cross-corruption. In addition, specific partitions may be added and used to execute secure applications in small certifiable environments protected from the larger open environment or real-time operating system executing in other partitions. Security cannot be an afterthought.

A virtualization solution may be used to ease introduction of smart phone software functionality to an existing feature phone hardware platform, with minimal effort and cost. Virtualization-based solutions open up the phone software architecture to bring added functionality to both feature phones and smartphones in terms of service availability, security, and device management. Two examples of virtualization software being used on smartphones are discussed in the following sections.

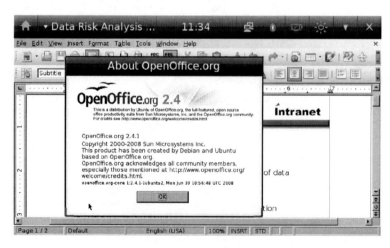

Fig. 15   Ubuntu MID OpenOffice.

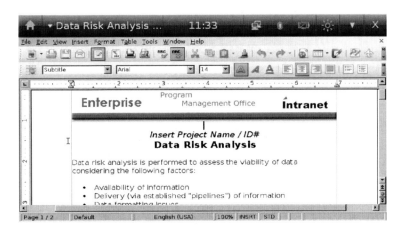

Fig. 16   Editing a document using OpenOffice.

Kernel-based Virtual Machine

Kernel-based Virtual Machine (KVM) is open source software that is a full virtualization solution for Linux on x86 hardware containing virtualization extensions (Intel VT or Advanced Micro Dynamics Virtualization (AMD-V)). KVM consists of a kernel module, kvm.ko, which provides the core virtualization infrastructure, and a processor-specific module, kvm-intel.ko or kvm-amd.ko, depending on the central processing unit manufacturer (Intel or AMD). KVM also requires a modified Quick Emulator,[6] although work is underway to get the required changes upstream. Multiple VM s running unmodified Linux or Windows images can be run using KVM. A wide variety of guest OSs work with KVM, including many versions of Linux, Berkeley Software Distribution, Solaris, Windows, Haiku, ReactOS, and the AROS Research Operating System. Each VM has private virtualized hardware: a network card, disk, graphics adapter, etc. The kernel component of KVM is included in Linux, as of the 2.6.20 kernel version.

KVM's performance is good, but not as good as that of some of the more mature products, such as VMware or VirtualBox. For example, network and graphics speeds are noticeably slower with KVM. In general, KVM performance can offer near-native speed, thanks to its use of Intel VT or AMD-V extensions. As an open source product, it is being very actively developed and is constantly improving.

VMWare

- VMware Mobile Virtualization Platform (MVP) is a thin layer of software that is embedded on a mobile phone to separate the applications and data from the underlying hardware. It is optimized to run efficiently on low-power, low-memory mobile phones. MVP is planned to enable handset vendors to bring phones to market faster and make them easier to manage.[7] VMware inherited the MVP software when it bought Trango Virtual Processors in October 2008. The technology serves much the same function as VMware's flagship server product, adding a flexible software layer onto hardware and making it easier to move applications from device to device.[8] MVP supports a wide range of real-time and rich OSs, including

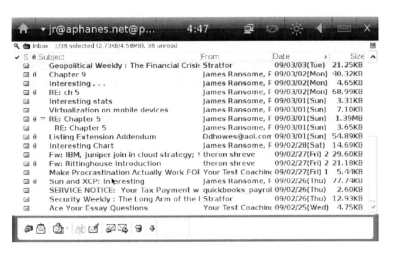

Fig. 17   OpenOffice e-mail in Ubuntu MID.

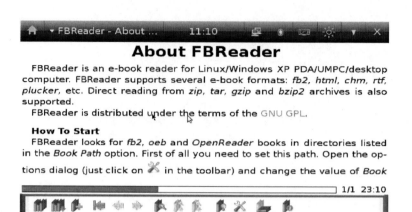

Fig. 18 FBReader.

Windows CE 5.0 and 6.0, Linux 2.6.x, Symbian 9.x, eCos, μITRON NORTi, and μC/OS-II.

VMware MVP benefits end users by being able to run multiple profiles (e.g., one for personal use and one for work use) on the same phone. Increasingly, handset vendors and carriers are migrating from proprietary OSs to rich open OSs so that their customers can choose from the widest selection of applications. With this transition to open OSs, however, protection of trusted services such as digital rights management, authentication, billing, etc., is becoming of increasing concern. VMware MVP allows vendors to isolate these important trusted services from the open OS and run them in isolated and tamper-proof VMs so that even if the open environment is compromised, the trusted services are not affected.

With VMware solutions, desktop and IT security administrators get the control and visibility they need to protect mobile data and prevent malicious code intrusion, while end users get the freedom and flexibility of "anytime, anywhere" access to their own familiar desktop environment. For virtual teams and telecommuters with a steady Internet connection, VMware View (formerly VMware Virtual Desktop Infrastructure) can be used to deliver remote access to server-based virtual desktop PCs through a secure network connection. Using VMware View, an organization can keep desktop images and sensitive information stored on servers behind the corporate firewall, eliminating the risk of a security breach as a result of laptop theft, allow remote access through a Web browser for maximum flexibility, or keep access limited to PCs with VMware View client software installed for maximum control, and can prevent data leakage and network intrusions with strong encryption, multifactor authentication, and access control policies for client-side USB devices.[9]

Mobile users with intermittent access to the Internet can use VMware (ACE) to deploy ACEs that workers can use on corporate-owned laptops, employee-owned PCs, or even iPods and USB memory sticks without putting sensitive corporate information at risk. VMware ACE clients are encapsulated inside a single file or "package," and ACE packages can be secured with strong encryption to protect the entire virtual desktop environment, not just specific files and folders. Administrators can set and enforce granular policies governing the lifespan of each ACE client package, the networks it can access, and the peripheral devices that can interface with it, with Active Directory integration for unified user authentication. The result is a scalable solution that

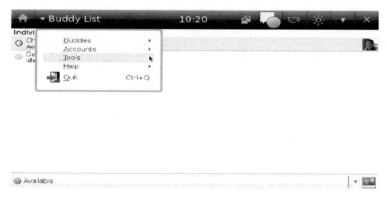

Fig. 19 Ubuntu MID instant messenger.

Fig. 20 Internet browsing on Ubuntu MID.

helps enhances the mobility of users while protecting access to valuable corporate information assets.[9]

COLLABORATION APPLICATIONS FOR MOBILE PLATFORMS

The growing popularity and power of mobile devices and the demand for business solutions and collaboration tools on mobile devices, along with Web 2.0 as a new platform for developing interactive applications across devices, has ushered in a new era for collaboration technologies—as can be seen in the advent of devices such as the Apple iPhone, the BlackBerry Storm touchphone, and the Google phone. The adoption of mobile collaboration services is not just a matter of design but also depends on factors such as mobile network coverage and pricing structures, all of which have been leveraged by these three phones, and others are on the way.

Mobile phones have evolved rapidly in the past few years, from specialized devices for voice communication to general-purpose computing devices that are able to run a rich variety of data applications. The latest mobile phones also provide a variety of networking options such as cellular, Bluetooth, WiFi, and WiMAX, which serve a range of coverage and bandwidth requirements. Mobile phones have now become the device of choice for people to keep in touch with family members, friends, and business partners. Current mobile phones allow people not only to make telephone calls but also to access e-mail and short messages, play games, share information, run video conferences, and coordinate business actions. Mobile phones are now equipped with faster processors, larger memory, and longer-life batteries. Many mobile phones today come with integrated position-tracking and camera features. Many of the software tools previously available in personal digital assistants, tablets, laptops, and desktop PCs have been ported to mobile phones, such as office and multimedia

applications. Today, many collaboration technologies are widely used, such as e-mail, instant messaging, data conferencing, workflow, wiki, and social networking systems.

Collaboration technologies based on mobile phones have unique advantages over laptops and desktop systems because they are lightweight and can fit into pockets or purses. They are truly mobile and can be connected all the time, which means you can take your desktop with you. Collaboration software on mobile hand-held devices provides the ability to be productive wherever you are. In this new era of mobile computing, the next generation of collaboration technologies on mobile phones is being developed to enable consumers to collaborate anytime, anywhere, using just their mobile phones. Although mobile collaboration technologies are still in their infancy and there is still significant room for progress, there have been several significant developments, such as the Cisco WebEx collaboration software, which has over 60% of the web collaboration conferencing software market,[10] being ported over to the iPhone[11]; the IBM Lotus Notes Traveler being extended to support a range of S60-based Nokia mobile phones built on the S60 third edition of the Symbian OS and providing a major alternative to Windows Mobile device support[12]; and Unison Technologies recently announcing its free unified communications software offering in a direct challenge to industry giants Microsoft and Google.[13]

FUTURE TRENDS

The real value of cloud computing is that it makes software and data available transparently and everywhere—including the mobile environment. Consumers of cloud computing services purchase computing capacity on demand and need not be concerned with the underlying technologies used to achieve server capabilities.

Computing resources are being accessed which are typically owned and operated by a third-party provider on a consolidated basis in data center locations. This stateless model facilitates much greater scalability than conventional computing and can be used in conjunction with virtualization to achieve maximum data center and computing resource utilization. One of the key elements of a stateless computing environment is a networked storage system that enables ubiquitous availability of software, making the cloud the ideal environment to enable mobile smartphone users to access its powerful computing power remotely.

Each day, more and more users connect to the Internet using their mobile devices. The mobile OS as an extension to the cloud is emerging as a value-added alternative to sophisticated and complex OSs such as Windows. New players such as Apple and Google are developing their mobile OSs to challenge Symbian and Windows Mobile. Mobile device hardware is too weak to run fully capable hardcore software such as Adobe Photoshop or Microsoft Office natively on a smartphone, which is why cloud computing will likely be the future model for of mobile computing. Cloud computing may prove to be an ideal strategy for reaping the full benefit of mobile devices, by allowing companies to essentially push their IT environment out to employees, rather than employees having to get access to the IT environment. In the future, cloud computing will also reduce the need for unnecessary full application overhead by using the mobile smartphone as a "dumb terminal" to leverage the powerful computing power of the cloud.

SUMMARY

Cloud computing for mobile devices is taking off with the expansion of high-speed wireless networks around the world. Mobile devices take data out of homes and offices and put them in our pockets, increasing the attractiveness of cloud computing as a model to connect end users with more than just the Internet and e-mail while they roam. This means that much of your vital data will be available not just at home, at the office, or in your wallet, but can easily be accessed by hooking up to the huge memory of the Internet cloud with a mobile device. Consumers are beginning to demand not only access to hotel and restaurant directions, airline reservations, weather reports, social networking sites, personal e-mail and instant messaging, but also full and secure access to their business applications at work or a business partner's site as well.

The cloud is becoming increasingly pervasive and mobile browsers are getting better every day, providing the ability to access the cloud and its applications. Organizations are deploying more and more SaaS-based

applications and, assuming they have enough bandwidth, there is no reason that mobile workers cannot access those applications on their devices with a browser that can actually fully handle web and cloud standards. In this entry we described the mobile smartphone platforms, their OSs, virtualization of these platforms, mobile collaboration applications, and future trends.

CLOSING COMMENTS

Cloud computing is in a period of strong growth, but cloud technology is still somewhat immature and will take another few years to mature. Development will probably be dominated by a select group of vendors, mostly technologically aggressive application development organizations. There will likely be proliferation of new vendors and then subsequent consolidation as cloud computing becomes appealing to more mainstream development organizations. As with any other technology going through a period of rapid growth, the stronger small players will survive and the weaker players will be driven out of the market. In the meantime, demand for interoperability and integration will likely drive a widely supported fabric of "intracloud" APIs that will be developed to link cloud-based systems across vendor platforms. This consolidation and integration, along with improved security, privacy, and governance enhancements, will broaden the appeal of cloud computing while building the trust of consumers, who will increasingly offload large portions of their IT infrastructure to third parties such as the SaaS providers described throughout this encyclopedia. The cloud is a hot topic, and it is not just IT personnel who will need to understand the benefits of cloud computing, but personnel across the entire business continuum. Many consumers and companies are missing out on the benefits of cloud computing because they do not fully grasp the concept of cloud computing; we hope this entry has improved your grasp.

REFERENCES

1. http://www.unstrung.com/document.asp?doc_id = 169641
2. Dalvik Virtual Machine, Wikipedia, (accessed March 2009).
3. Mclean, P. Microsoft Plans "Skymarket" Apps Store for Windows Mobile 7 in 2009, http://www.roughlydrafted.com/2008/09/01/microsoft-plans%E2%80%9Cskymarket%E2%80%9D-apps-store-for-windows-mobile-7-in-2009, RoughlyDrafted Magazine: San Francisco, CA, 1 September 2008 (accessed March 2009).
4. Clutter is an open source software library for creating fast, visually rich, and animated graphical user interfaces.
5. http://www.openoffice.org.

6. According to Wikipedia, "QEMU is a processor emulator that relies on dynamic binary translation to achieve a reasonable speed while being easy to port on new host CPU architectures," QEMU, Wikipedia, http://en.wikipedia.org/wiki/QEMU, (accessed March 2009).

7. http://www.vmware.com/company/news/releases/mvp.html.

8. http://bits.blogs.nytimes.com/2008/11/10/vmware-lends-virtual-hand-to-mobile-phone-crowd.

9. http://www.vmware.com/solutions/desktop/mobile.html.

10. http://www.pcmag.com/article2/0,4149,1418533,00.asp.

11. http://www.webex.com/iphone.

12. http://www.itwire.com/content/view/21856/1154.

13. http://www.channelinsider.com/c/a/Messaging-and-Collaboration/Unisons-Free-Unified-Communications-Software-Challenges-Microsoft-and-Google.

Cloud Computing

Cloud Computing: Security

John W. Rittinghouse
Hypersecurity LLC, Tomball, Texas, U.S.A.

James F. Ransome
Cisco Systems, Santa Clara, California, U.S.A.

Abstract

Virtualization is being used in data centers to facilitate cost savings and create a smaller, "green" footprint. As a result, multi-tenant uses of servers are being created on what used to be single-tenant or single-purpose physical servers. The extension of virtualization and virtual machines into the cloud is affecting enterprise security as a result of the evaporating enterprise network perimeter. In this entry, the importance of security in the cloud computing environment is presented, particularly with regard to the Software-as-a-Service environment and the security challenges and best practices associated with it.

OVERVIEW

Cloud service providers are leveraging virtualization technologies combined with self-service capabilities for computing resources via the Internet. In these service provider environments, virtual machines from multiple organizations have to be co-located on the same physical server in order to maximize the efficiencies of virtualization. Cloud service providers must learn from the managed service provider (MSP) model and ensure that their customers' applications and data are secure if they hope to retain their customer base and competitiveness. Enterprises are looking towards cloud computing horizons to expand their on-premises infrastructure, but most cannot afford the risk of compromising the security of their applications and data. For example, International Data Corporation (IDC) recently conducted a survey[1] (see Fig. 1) of 244 information technology (IT) executives/chief information officers (CIOs) and their line-of-business colleagues to gauge their opinions and understand their companies' use of IT cloud services. Security ranked first as the greatest challenge or issue of cloud computing.

This entry identifies current security concerns about cloud computing environments and describes the methodology for ensuring application and data security and compliance integrity for those resources that are moving from on-premises to public cloud environments. More important, this discussion focuses on why and how these resources should be protected in the Software-as-a-Service (SaaS), Platform-as-a-Service (PaaS), and Infrastructure-as-a-Service (IaaS) environments and offers security "best practices" for service providers and enterprises that are in or are contemplating moving into the cloud computing space. First, let's review the concepts of the three major cloud computing service provider models.

SaaS is a model of software deployment in which an application is licensed for use as a service provided to customers on demand. On-demand licensing and use relieves the customer of the burden of equipping a device with every application to be used.[2] Gartner predicts that 30% of new software will be delivered via the SaaS model by 2010.

PaaS is an outgrowth of the SaaS application delivery model. With the PaaS model, all of the facilities required to support the complete life cycle of building and delivering web applications and services are available to developers, IT managers, and end users entirely from the Internet, without software downloads or installation. PaaS is also sometimes known as "cloudware." PaaS offerings include workflow facilities for application design, application development, testing, deployment, and hosting, as well as application services such as team collaboration, web service integration and marshalling, database integration, security, scalability, storage, persistence, state management, application versioning, application instrumentation, and developer community facilitation. These services are provisioned as an integrated solution over the web.[3,4]

IaaS is the delivery of computer infrastructure (typically a platform virtualization environment) as a service. These "virtual infrastructure stacks"[5] are an example of the everything-as-a-service trend and share many of the common characteristics. Rather than purchasing servers, software, data center space, or network equipment, clients buy these resources as a fully outsourced service. The service is typically billed on a utility computing basis, and the quantity of resources consumed (and therefore the cost) typically reflects the level of activity.

Encyclopedia of Information Systems and Technology, DOI: 10.1081/E-EIST-120053836

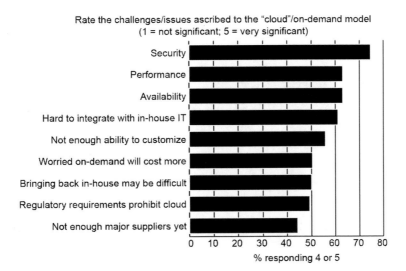

Fig. 1 Results of IDC survey ranking security challenges.
Source: From IDC Enterprise Panel, August 2008.

It is an evolution of web hosting and virtual private server offerings.[6]

Inspired by the IT industry's move toward SaaS, in which software is not purchased but rented as a service from providers, IT-as-a-Service (ITaaS) is being proposed to take this concept further, to bring the service model right to your IT infrastructure. The modern IT organization must run itself as a separate operation and become more strategic in operational decisions. Many organizations are in the process of transforming their IT departments into self-sustaining cost-center operations, treating internal users as if they were customers.

This transformation is not trivial and usually involves elements of project portfolio management, workflow reengineering, and process improvement. The transformation can take several years to be completed. Many large IT organizations have adopted the Information Technology Infrastructure Library framework to help with this transformation. Organizations can harness their help desks, avoid downtime resulting from unauthorized changes, and deliver better service to their internal customers simply by adopting best practices for managing service requests, changes, and IT assets. The adoption of ITaaS can help enterprise IT functions focus on strategic alignment with business goals. However, if efforts in this direction are poorly implemented, organizations risk further alienating their technical support staff from the rest of the organization—turning them into order takers for the enterprise rather than business advisers. When it is done properly, a customer-centric IT department increases productivity, drives up project success rates, and creates a higher profile for technology within the organization.

While enterprises cope with defining the details of cloud computing, the single, unifying theme is *service*. Cloud computing, on-demand applications, and managed

security are now perceived as part of an emerging ITaaS paradigm. Current industry buzz seems to reinforce the message that significant investments of capital, time, and intellectual resources are indeed being directed toward offering next-generation information and communication technology infrastructure, which may allow enterprises to outsource IT completely and confidently. Only time will tell if ITaaS is really on the edge of enterprise adoption. Many in the industry believe that the advent of developer platforms designed for the cloud will hasten this transition and, as a result, fewer enterprises will need to deploy middleware to manage patchwork-implemented business applications, legacy or otherwise. Infrastructure vendors are also jumping on this bandwagon. Amazon has been a pioneer, with the release of Amazon S3 (Storage-as-a-Service). With the maturation of virtualization technologies, the adoption of virtual infrastructure and storage-on-demand services will accelerate along with the SaaS model.

There are some key financial benefits in moving to an ITaaS model, such has not having to incur capital costs; having a transparent, monthly pricing plan; scalability; and reasonable costs of expansion. Operational benefits of ITaaS include increased reliability because of a centralized infrastructure, which can ensure that critical services and applications are monitored continually; software flexibility, with centrally maintained products that allow for quick rollout of new functionalities and updates; and data security, since company data can be stored on owner-managed premises, and backed up using encryption to a secure off-site data center.

Another service that is being discussed is the concept of Anything-as-a-Service (XaaS), which is also a subset of cloud computing. XaaS broadly encompasses a process of activating reusable software components over the network. The most common and successful example is SaaS. The growth of "as-a-service" offerings has been facilitated by extremely low barriers to entry (they are often accessible for free or available as recurring charges on a personal credit card). As a result, such offerings have been adopted by consumers and small businesses well before pushing into the enterprise space. All "as-a-service" offerings share a number of common attributes, including little or no capital expenditure since the required infrastructure is owned by the service provider, massive scalability, multitenancy, and device and location independence, allowing consumers remote access to systems using nearly any current available technology.

On the surface, it appears that XaaS is a potentially game-changing technology that could reshape IT. However, most CIOs still depend on internal infrastructures because they are not convinced that cloud computing is ready for prime time. Many contend that if you want real reliability, you must write more reliable applications. Regardless of one's view on the readiness of cloud computing to meet corporate IT requirements, it cannot be ignored. The concept of pay-as-you-go applications, development platforms, processing power, storage, or any other cloud-enabled services has emerged and can be expected to reshape IT over the next decade.

Other concerns plague IT executives. They fear their data won't be safe in the hands of cloud providers and that they won't be able to manage cloud resources effectively. They may also worry that the new technology will threaten their own data centers and staff. Collectively, these fears tend to hold back the cloud computing market that some perceive growing to nearly $100 billion in the next decade.

Although there is a significant benefit to leveraging cloud computing, security concerns have led organizations to hesitate to move critical resources to the cloud. Corporations and individuals are often concerned about how security and compliance integrity can be maintained in this new environment. Even more worrying, however, may be those corporations that are jumping into cloud computing that may be oblivious to the implications of putting critical applications and data in the cloud. This entry will answer the security concerns of the former and educate the latter.

Moving critical applications and sensitive data to public and shared cloud environments is of great concern for those corporations that are moving beyond their data center's network perimeter defense. To alleviate these concerns, a cloud solution provider must ensure that customers will continue to have the same security and privacy controls over their applications and services, provide evidence to customers that their organization and customers are secure and they can meet their service-level agreements, and that they can prove compliance to auditors.

CLOUD SECURITY CHALLENGES

Although virtualization and cloud computing can help companies accomplish more by breaking the physical bonds between an IT infrastructure and its users, heightened security threats must be overcome in order to benefit fully from this new computing paradigm. This is particularly true for the SaaS provider. Some security concerns are worth more discussion. For example, in the cloud, you lose control over assets in some respects, so your security model must be reassessed. Enterprise security is only as good as the least reliable partner, department, or vendor. Can you trust your data to your service provider? In the following paragraphs, we discuss some issues you should consider before answering that question.

With the cloud model, you lose control over physical security. In a public cloud, you are sharing computing resources with other companies. In a shared pool outside the enterprise, you don't have any knowledge or control of where the resources run. Exposing your data in an environment shared with other companies could give the government "reasonable cause" to seize your assets because another company has violated the law. Simply because you share the environment in the cloud, may put your data at risk of seizure.

Storage services provided by one cloud vendor may be incompatible with another vendor's services should you decide to move from one to the other. Vendors are known for creating what the hosting world calls "sticky services"—services that an end user may have difficulty transporting from one cloud vendor to another (e.g., Amazon's "Simple Storage Service" [S3] is incompatible with IBM's Blue Cloud, or Google, or Dell).

If information is encrypted while passing through the cloud, who controls the encryption/decryption keys? Is it the customer or the cloud vendor? Most customers probably want their data encrypted both ways across the Internet using Secure Sockets Layer protocol (SSL). They also most likely want their data encrypted while it is at rest in the cloud vendor's storage pool. Be sure that you, the customer, control the encryption/decryption keys, just as if the data were still resident on your own servers.

Data integrity means ensuring that data is identically maintained during any operation (such as transfer, storage, or retrieval). Put simply, data integrity is assurance that the data is consistent and correct. Ensuring the integrity of the data really means that it changes only in response to authorized transactions. This sounds good, but you must remember that a common standard to ensure data integrity does not yet exist.

Using SaaS offerings in the cloud means that there is much less need for software development. For example, using a web-based customer relationship management offering eliminates the necessity to write code and "customize" a vendor's application. If you plan to use internally developed code in the cloud, it is even more important to have a formal secure software development life cycle (SDLC). The immature use of mashup technology (combinations of web services), which is fundamental to cloud applications, is inevitably going to cause unwitting security vulnerabilities in those applications. Your development tool of choice should have a security model embedded in it to guide developers during the development phase and restrict users only to their authorized data when the system is deployed into production.

As more and more mission-critical processes are moved to the cloud, SaaS suppliers will have to provide log data in a real-time, straightforward manner, probably for their administrators as well as their customers' personnel. Someone has to be responsible for monitoring for security and compliance, and unless the application and data are under the control of end users, they will not be able to. Will customers trust the cloud provider enough to push their mission-critical applications out to the cloud? Since the SaaS provider's logs are internal and not necessarily accessible externally or by clients or investigators, monitoring is difficult. Since access to logs is required for Payment Card Industry Data Security Standard (PCI DSS) compliance and may be requested by auditors and regulators, security managers need to make sure to negotiate access to the provider's logs as part of any service agreement.

Cloud applications undergo constant feature additions, and users must keep up to date with application improvements to be sure they are protected. The speed at which applications will change in the cloud will affect both the SDLC and security. For example, Microsoft's SDLC assumes that mission-critical software will have a 3–5year period in which it will not change substantially, but the cloud may require a change in the application every few weeks. Even worse, a secure SLDC will not be able to provide a security cycle that keeps up with changes that occur so quickly. This means that users must constantly upgrade, because an older version may not function, or protect the data.

Having proper fail-over technology is a component of securing the cloud that is often overlooked. The company can survive if a non-missioncritical application goes offline, but this may not be true for mission-critical applications. Core business practices provide competitive differentiation. Security needs to move to the data level, so that enterprises can be sure their data is protected wherever it goes. Sensitive data is the domain of the enterprise, not the cloud computing provider. One of the key challenges in cloud computing is data-level security.

Most compliance standards do not envision compliance in a world of cloud computing. There is a huge body of standards that apply for IT security and compliance, governing most business interactions that will, over time, have to be translated to the cloud. SaaS makes the process of compliance more complicated, since it may be difficult for a customer to discern where its data resides on a network controlled by its SaaS provider, or a partner of that provider, which raises all sorts of compliance issues of data privacy, segregation, and security. Many compliance regulations require that data not be intermixed with other data, such as on shared servers or databases. Some countries have strict limits on what data about its citizens can be stored and for how long, and some banking regulators require that customers' financial data remain in their home country.

Compliance with government regulations such as the Sarbanes–Oxley Act, the GrammLeachBliley Act, and the Health Insurance Portability and Accountability Act, and industry standards such as the PCI DSS, will be much more challenging in the SaaS environment. There is a perception that cloud computing removes data compliance responsibility; however, it should be emphasized that the data owner is still fully responsible for compliance. Those who adopt cloud computing must remember that it is the responsibility of the data owner, not the service provider, to secure valuable data.

Government policy will need to change in response to both the opportunity and the threats that cloud computing brings. This will likely focus on the off-shoring of personal data and protection of privacy, whether it is data being controlled by a third party or off-shored to another country. There will be a corresponding drop in security as the traditional controls such as virtual local-area networks (VLANs) and firewalls prove less effective during the transition to a virtualized environment. Security managers will need to pay particular attention to systems that contain critical data such as corporate financial information or source code during the transition to server virtualization in production environments.

Outsourcing means losing significant control over data, and while this isn't a good idea from a security perspective, the business ease and financial savings will continue to increase the usage of these services. Security managers will need to work with their company's legal staff to ensure that appropriate contract terms are in place to protect corporate data and provide for acceptable service-level agreements.

Cloud-based services will result in many mobile IT users accessing business data and services without traversing the corporate network. This will increase the need for enterprises to place security controls between mobile users and cloud-based services. Placing large amounts of sensitive data in a globally accessible cloud leaves organizations open to large distributed threats—attackers no longer have to come onto the premises to steal data, and they can find it all in the one "virtual" location.

Virtualization efficiencies in the cloud require virtual machines from multiple organizations to be co-located on the same physical resources. Although traditional data center security still applies in the cloud environment, physical segregation and hardware-based security cannot protect against attacks between virtual machines on the same server. Administrative access is through the Internet rather than the controlled and restricted direct or on-premises connection that is adhered to in the traditional data center model. This increases risk and exposure and will require stringent monitoring for changes in system control and access control restriction.

The dynamic and fluid nature of virtual machines will make it difficult to maintain the consistency of security and ensure the auditability of records. The ease of cloning and distribution between physical servers could result in the propagation of configuration errors and other vulnerabilities. Proving the security state of a system and identifying the location of an insecure virtual machine will be challenging. Regardless of the location of the virtual machine within the virtual environment, the intrusion detection and prevention systems will need to be able to detect malicious activity at virtual machine level. The co-location of multiple virtual machines increases the attack surface and risk of virtual machine-to-virtual machine compromise.

Localized virtual machines and physical servers use the same operating systems as well as enterprise and web applications in a cloud server environment, increasing the threat of an attacker or malware exploiting vulnerabilities in these systems and applications remotely. Virtual machines are vulnerable as they move between the private cloud and the public cloud. A fully or partially shared cloud environment is expected to have a greater attack surface and therefore can be considered to be at greater risk than a dedicated resources environment.

Operating system and application files are on a shared physical infrastructure in a virtualized cloud environment and require system, file, and activity monitoring to provide confidence and auditable proof to enterprise customers that their resources have not been compromised or tampered with. In the cloud computing environment, the enterprise subscribes to cloud computing resources, and the responsibility for patching is the subscriber's rather than the cloud computing vendor's. The need for patch maintenance vigilance is imperative. Lack of due diligence in this regard could rapidly make the task unmanageable or impossible, leaving you with "virtual patching" as the only alternative.

Enterprises are often required to prove that their security compliance is in accord with regulations, standards, and auditing practices, regardless of the location of the systems at which the data resides. Data is fluid in cloud computing and may reside in on-premises physical servers, on-premises virtual machines, or off-premises virtual machines running on cloud computing resources, and this will require some rethinking on the part of auditors and practitioners alike.

In the rush to take advantage of the benefits of cloud computing, not least of which is significant cost savings, many corporations are likely rushing into cloud computing without a serious consideration of the security implications. To establish zones of trust in the cloud, the virtual machines must be self-defending, effectively moving the perimeter to the virtual machine itself. Enterprise perimeter security (i.e., firewalls, demilitarized zones, network segmentation, intrusion detection and prevention systems, monitoring tools, and the associated security policies) only controls the data that resides and transits behind the perimeter. In the cloud computing world, the cloud computing provider is in charge of customer data security and privacy.

SAAS SECURITY

Cloud computing models of the future will likely combine the use of SaaS (and other XaaS's as appropriate), utility computing, and Web 2.0 collaboration technologies to leverage the Internet to satisfy their customers' needs. New business models being developed as a result

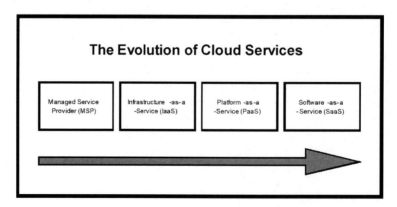

Fig. 2 The evolution of cloud services.

of the move to cloud computing are creating not only new technologies and business operational processes but also new security requirements and challenges as described previously. As the most recent evolutionary step in the cloud service model (see Fig. 2), SaaS will likely remain the dominant cloud service model for the foreseeable future and the area where the most critical need for security practices and oversight will reside.

Just as with an MSP, corporations or end users will need to research vendors' policies on data security, before using vendor services to avoid losing or not being able to access their data. The technology analyst and consulting firm Gartner lists seven security issues which one should discuss with a cloud-computing vendor:

1. **Privileged user access**—Inquire about who has specialized access to data, and about the hiring and management of such administrators.
2. **Regulatory compliance**—Make sure that the vendor is willing to undergo external audits and/or security certifications.
3. **Data location**—Does the provider allow for any control over the location of data?
4. **Data segregation**—Make sure that encryption is available at all stages, and that these encryption schemes were designed and tested by experienced professionals.
5. **Recovery**—Find out what will happen to data in the case of a disaster. Do they offer complete restoration? If so, how long would that take?
6. **Investigative support**—Does the vendor have the ability to investigate any inappropriate or illegal activity?
7. **Long-term viability**—What will happen to data if the company goes out of business? How will data be returned, and in what format?[7]

Determining data security is harder today, so data security functions have become more critical than they have been in the past. A tactic not covered by Gartner is to encrypt the data yourself. If you encrypt the data using a trusted algorithm, then regardless of the service provider's security and encryption policies, the data will only be accessible with the decryption keys. Of course, this leads to a follow-on problem: How do you manage private keys in a pay-on-demand computing infrastructure?[8]

To address the security issues listed above along with others mentioned earlier in the entry, SaaS providers will need to incorporate and enhance security practices used by the MSPs and develop new ones as the cloud computing environment evolves. The baseline security practices for the SaaS environment as currently formulated are discussed in the following sections.

Security Management (People)

One of the most important actions for a security team is to develop a formal charter for the security organization and program. This will foster a shared vision among the team of what security leadership is driving towards and expects, and will also foster "ownership" in the success of the collective team. The charter should be aligned with the strategic plan of the organization or company the security team works for. Lack of clearly defined roles and responsibilities, and agreement on expectations, can result in a general feeling of loss and confusion among the security team about what is expected of them, how their skills and experienced can be leveraged, and meeting their performance goals. Morale among the team and pride in the team is lowered, and security suffers as a result.

Security Governance

A security steering committee should be developed whose objective is to focus on providing guidance about security initiatives and alignment with business and IT strategies. A charter for the security team is typically one of the first deliverables from the steering committee. This charter must clearly define the roles and responsibilities of the security team and other groups involved in performing information security functions. Lack of a formalized strategy can lead to an unsustainable operating model and security level as it evolves. In addition, lack of attention to security governance can result in key needs of the business not being met, including but not limited to, risk management, security monitoring, application security, and sales support. Lack of proper governance and management of duties can also result in potential security risks being left unaddressed and opportunities to improve the business being missed because the security team is not focused on the key security functions and activities that are critical to the business.

Risk Management

Effective risk management entails identification of technology assets; identification of data and its links to business processes, applications, and data stores; and assignment of ownership and custodial responsibilities. Actions should also include maintaining a repository of information assets. Owners have authority and accountability for information assets including protection requirements, and custodians implement confidentiality, integrity, availability, and privacy controls. A formal risk assessment process should be created that allocates security resources linked to business continuity (BC).

Risk Assessment

Security risk assessment is critical to helping the information security organization make informed decisions when balancing the dueling priorities of business utility and protection of assets. Lack of attention to completing formalized risk assessments can contribute to an increase in information security audit findings, can jeopardize certification goals, and can lead to inefficient and ineffective selection of security controls that may not adequately mitigate information security risks to an acceptable level. A formal information security risk management process should proactively assess information security risks as well as plan and manage them on a periodic or as-needed basis. More detailed and technical security risk assessments in the form of threat modeling should also be applied to applications and infrastructure. Doing so can help the product management and engineering groups to be more proactive in designing and testing the security of applications and systems and to collaborate more closely with the internal security team. Threat modeling requires both IT and business process knowledge, as well as technical knowledge of how the applications or systems under review work.

Security Portfolio Management

Given the fast pace and collaborative nature of cloud computing, security portfolio management is a fundamental component of ensuring efficient and effective operation of any information security program and organization. Lack of portfolio and project management discipline can lead to projects never being completed or never realizing their expected return; unsustainable and unrealistic workloads and expectations because projects are not prioritized according to strategy, goals, and resource capacity; and degradation of the system or processes due to the lack of supporting maintenance and sustaining organization planning. For every new project that a security team undertakes, the team should ensure that a project plan and project manager with appropriate training and experience is in place so that the project can be seen through to completion. Portfolio and project management capabilities can be enhanced by developing methodology, tools, and processes to support the expected complexity of projects that include both traditional business practices and cloud computing practices.

Security Awareness

People will remain the weakest link for security. Knowledge and culture are among the few effective tools to manage risks related to people. Not providing proper awareness and training to the people who may need

them can expose the company to a variety of security risks for which people, rather than system or application vulnerabilities, are the threats and points of entry. Social engineering attacks, lower reporting of and slower responses to potential security incidents, and inadvertent customer data leaks are all possible and probable risks that may be triggered by lack of an effective security awareness program. The one-size-fits-all approach to security awareness is not necessarily the right approach for SaaS organizations; it is more important to have an information security awareness and training program that tailors the information and training according the individual's role in the organization. For example, security awareness can be provided to development engineers in the form of secure code and testing training, while customer service representatives can be provided data privacy and security certification awareness training. Ideally, both a generic approach and an individual-role approach should be used.

Education and Training

Programs should be developed that provide a baseline for providing fundamental security and risk management skills and knowledge to the security team and their internal partners. This entails a formal process to assess and align skill sets to the needs of the security team and to provide adequate training and mentorship—providing a broad base of fundamental security, inclusive of data privacy, and risk management knowledge. As the cloud computing business model and its associated services change, the security challenges facing an organization will also change. Without adequate, current training and mentorship programs in place, the security team may not be prepared to address the needs of the business.

Policies, Standards, and Guidelines

Many resources and templates are available to aid in the development of information security policies, standards, and guidelines. A cloud computing security team should first identify the information security and business requirements unique to cloud computing, SaaS, and collaborative software application security. Policies should be developed, documented, and implemented, along with documentation for supporting standards and guidelines. To maintain relevancy, these policies, standards, and guidelines should be reviewed at regular intervals (at least annually) or when significant changes occur in the business or IT environment. Outdated policies, standards, and guidelines can result in inadvertent disclosure of information as a cloud computing organizational business model changes. It is important to maintain the accuracy and relevance of information security policies, standards, and guidelines as business initiatives, the business environment, and the risk landscape change. Such policies, standards, and guidelines also provide the building blocks with which an organization can ensure consistency of performance and maintain continuity of knowledge during times of resource turnover.

Secure Software Development Life Cycle (SecSDLC)

The SecSDLC involves identifying specific threats and the risks they represent, followed by design and implementation of specific controls to counter those threats and assist in managing the risks they pose to the organization and/or its customers. The SecSDLC must provide consistency, repeatability, and conformance. The SDLC consists of six phases, and there are steps unique to the SecSLDC in each of phases:

- **Phase 1. Investigation:** Define project processes and goals, and document them in the program security policy.
- **Phase 2. Analysis:** Analyze existing security policies and programs, analyze current threats and controls, examine legal issues, and perform risk analysis.
- **Phase 3. Logical design:** Develop a security blueprint, plan incident response actions, plan business responses to disaster, and determine the feasibility of continuing and/or outsourcing the project.
- **Phase 4. Physical design:** Select technologies to support the security blueprint, develop a definition of a successful solution, design physical security measures to support technological solutions, and review and approve plans.
- **Phase 5. Implementation:** Buy or develop security solutions. At the end of this phase, present a tested package to management for approval.
- **Phase 6. Maintenance:** Constantly monitor, test, modify, update, and repair to respond to changing threats.[9]

In the SecSDLC, application code is written in a consistent manner that can easily be audited and enhanced; core application services are provided in a common, structured, and repeatable manner; and framework modules are thoroughly tested for security issues before implementation and continuously retested for conformance through the software regression test cycle. Additional security processes are developed to support application development projects such as external and internal penetration testing and standard security requirements based on data classification. Formal training and communications should also be developed to raise awareness of process enhancements.

Security Monitoring and Incident Response

Centralized security information management systems should be used to provide notification of security vulnerabilities and to monitor systems continuously through automated technologies to identify potential issues. They should be integrated with network and other systems' monitoring processes (e.g., security information management, security event management, security information and event management, and security operations centers that use these systems for dedicated 24/7/365 monitoring). Management of periodic, independent third-party security testing should also be included.

Many of the security threats and issues in SaaS center around application and data layers, so the types and sophistication of threats and attacks for a SaaS organization require a different approach to security monitoring than traditional infrastructure and perimeter monitoring. The organization may thus need to expand its security monitoring capabilities to include application- and data-level activities. This may also require subject-matter experts in applications security and the unique aspects of maintaining privacy in the cloud. Without this capability and expertise, a company may be unable to detect and prevent security threats and attacks to its customer data and service stability.

Third-Party Risk Management

As SaaS moves into cloud computing for the storage and processing of customer data, there is a higher expectation that the SaaS will effectively manage the security risks with third parties. Lack of a third-party risk management program may result in damage to the provider's reputation, revenue losses, and legal actions should the provider be found not to have performed due diligence on its third-party vendors.

Requests for Information and Sales Support

If you don't think that requests for information and sales support are part of a security team's responsibility, think again. They are part of the business, and particularly with SaaS, the integrity of the provider's security business model, regulatory and certification compliance, and your company's reputation, competitiveness, and marketability all depend on the security team's ability to provide honest, clear, and concise answers to a customer request for information (RFI) or request for proposal (RFP). A structured process and a knowledge base of frequently requested information will result in considerable efficiency and the avoidance of ad-hoc, inefficient, or inconsistent support of the customer RFI/RFP process. Members of the security team should be not only internal security evangelists but also security evangelists to customers in support of the sales and marketing teams. As discussed earlier, security is top-of-mind and a primary concern for cloud computing customers, and lack of information security representatives who can provide support to the sales team in addressing customer questions and concerns could result in the potential loss of a sales opportunity.

BC Plan

The purpose of BC/disaster recovery (DR) planning is to minimize the impact of an adverse event on business processes. BC and resiliency services help ensure uninterrupted operations across all layers of the business, as well as helping businesses avoid, prepare for, and recover from a disruption. SaaS services that enable uninterrupted communications not only can help the business recover from an outage, they can reduce the overall complexity, costs, and risks of day-to-day management of your most critical applications. The cloud also offers some dramatic opportunities for cost-effective BC/DR solutions.

Some of the advantages that SaaS can provide over traditional BC/DR are eliminating e-mail downtime, ensuring that email messages are never lost, and making system outages virtually invisible to end users no matter what happens to your staff or infrastructure; maintaining continuous telephone communication during a telecommunication outage so your organization can stay open and in contact with employees, customers, and partners at virtually any location, over any network, over any talking device; and providing wireless continuity for WiFi-enabled "smart" phones that ensures users will always be able to send and receive corporate e-mail from their WiFi-enabled devices, even if your corporate mail system, data center, network, and staff are unavailable.[10]

Forensics

Computer forensics is used to retrieve and analyze data. The practice of computer forensics means responding to an event by gathering and preserving data, analyzing data to reconstruct events, and assessing the state of an event. Network forensics includes recording and analyzing network events to determine the nature and source of information abuse, security attacks, and other such incidents on your network. This is typically achieved by recording or capturing packets long-term from a key point or points in your infrastructure (such as the core or firewall) and then data mining for analysis and re-creating content.[11]

Cloud computing can provide many advantages to both individual forensics investigators and their whole team. A dedicated forensic server can be built in the

same cloud as the company cloud and can be placed offline but available for use when needed. This provides a cost-effective readiness factor because the company itself then does not face the logistical challenges involved. For example, a copy of a virtual machine can be given to multiple incident responders to distribute the forensic workload based on the job at hand or as new sources of evidence arise and need analysis. If a server in the cloud is compromised, it is possible to clone that server at the click of a mouse and make the cloned disks instantly available to the cloud forensics server, thus reducing evidence-acquisition time. In some cases, dealing with operations and trying to abstract the hardware from a data center may become a barrier to or at least slow down the process of doing forensics, especially if the system has to be taken down for a significant period of time while you search for the data and then hope you have the right physical acquisition toolkit and supports for the forensic software you are using.

Cloud computing provides the ability to avoid or eliminate disruption of operations and possible service downtime. Some cloud storage implementations expose a cryptographic checksum or hash (such as the Amazon S3 generation of an MD5 hash) when you store an object. This makes it possible to avoid the need to generate MD5 checksums using external tools—the checksums are already there, thus eliminating the need for forensic image verification time. In today's world, forensic examiners typically have to spend a lot of time consuming expensive provisioning of physical devices. Bit-by-bit copies are made more quickly by replicated, distributed file systems that cloud providers can engineer for their customers, so customers have to pay for storage only for as long as they need. You can now test a wider range of candidate passwords in less time to speed investigations by accessing documents more quickly because of the significant increase in CPU power provided by cloud computing.[12]

Security Architecture Design

A security architecture framework should be established with consideration of processes (enterprise authentication and authorization, access control, confidentiality, integrity, nonrepudiation, security management, etc.), operational procedures, technology specifications, people and organizational management, and security program compliance and reporting. A security architecture document should be developed that defines security and privacy principles to meet business objectives. Documentation is required for management controls and metrics specific to asset classification and control, physical security, system access controls, network and computer management, application development and maintenance, BC, and compliance. A design and implementation program should also be integrated with the formal system development life cycle to include a business case, requirements definition, design, and implementation plans. Technology and design methods should be included, as well as the security processes necessary to provide the following services across all technology layers:

1. Authentication
2. Authorization
3. Availability
4. Confidentiality
5. Integrity
6. Accountability
7. Privacy

The creation of a secure architecture provides the engineers, data center operations personnel, and network operations personnel a common blueprint to design, build, and test the security of the applications and systems. Design reviews of new changes can be better assessed against this architecture to assure that they conform to the principles described in the architecture, allowing for more consistent and effective design reviews.

Vulnerability Assessment

Vulnerability assessment classifies network assets to more efficiently prioritize vulnerability-mitigation programs, such as patching and system upgrading. It measures the effectiveness of risk mitigation by setting goals of reduced vulnerability exposure and faster mitigation. Vulnerability management should be integrated with discovery, patch management, and upgrade management processes to close vulnerabilities before they can be exploited.

Password Assurance Testing

If the SaaS security team or its customers want to periodically test password strength by running password "crackers," they can use cloud computing to decrease crack time and pay only for what they use. Instead of using a distributed password cracker to spread the load across nonproduction machines, you can now put those agents in dedicated compute instances to alleviate mixing sensitive credentials with other workloads.[12]

Logging for Compliance and Security Investigations

When your logs are in the cloud, you can leverage cloud computing to index those logs in real-time and get the benefit of instant search results. A true real-time view

can be achieved, since the compute instances can be examined and scaled as needed based on the logging load. Due to concerns about performance degradation and log size, the use of extended logging through an operating system C2 audit trail is rarely enabled. If you are willing to pay for enhanced logging, cloud computing provides the option.

Security Images

With cloud computing, you don't have to do physical operating system installs that frequently require additional third-party tools, are time-consuming to clone, and can add another agent to each endpoint. Virtualization-based cloud computing provides the ability to create "Gold image" virtual machine (VM) secure builds and to clone multiple copies. When companies create a pool of virtualized servers for production use, they also change their deployment and operational practices. Given the ability to standardize server images (since there are no hardware dependencies), companies consolidate their server configurations into as few as possible "gold images" which are used as templates for creating common server configurations. Typical images include baseline operating system images, web server images, application server images, etc. This standardization introduces an additional risk factor: monoculture. All the standardized images will share the same weaknesses. Whereas in a traditional data center there are firewalls and intrusion-prevention devices between servers, in a virtual environment there are no physical firewalls separating the virtual machines. What used to be a multitier architecture with firewalls separating the tiers becomes a pool of servers. A single exposed server can lead to a rapidly propagating threat that can jump from server to server. Standardization of images is like dry tinder to a fire: A single piece of malware can become a firestorm that engulfs the entire pool of servers. The potential for loss and vulnerability increases with the size of the pool—in proportion to the number of virtual guests, each of which brings its own vulnerabilities, creating a higher risk than in a single-instance virtual server. Moreover, the risk of the sum is greater than the sum of the risk of the parts, because the vulnerability of each system is itself subject to a "network effect." Each additional server in the pool multiplies the vulnerability of other servers in the pool.[13] Gold image VMs also provide the ability to keep security up to date and reduce exposure by patching offline. Offline VMs can be patched off-network, providing an easier, more cost-effective, and less production-threatening way to test the impact of security changes. This is a great way to duplicate a copy of your production environment, implement a security change, and test the impact at low cost, with minimal start-up time, and it removes a major barrier to doing security in a production environment.[14]

Data Privacy

A risk assessment and gap analysis of controls and procedures must be conducted. Based on this data, formal privacy processes and initiatives must be defined, managed, and sustained. As with security, privacy controls and protection must an element of the secure architecture design. Depending on the size of the organization and the scale of operations, either an individual or a team should be assigned and given responsibility for maintaining privacy.

A member of the security team who is responsible for privacy or a corporate security compliance team should collaborate with the company legal team to address data privacy issues and concerns. As with security, a privacy steering committee should also be created to help make decisions related to data privacy. Typically, the security compliance team, if one even exists, will not have formalized training on data privacy, which will limit the ability of the organization to address adequately the data privacy issues they currently face and will be continually challenged on in the future. The answer is to hire a consultant in this area, hire a privacy expert, or have one of your existing team members trained properly. This will ensure that your organization is prepared to meet the data privacy demands of its customers and regulators.

For example, customer contractual requirements/agreements for data privacy must be adhered to, accurate inventories of customer data, where it is stored, who can access it, and how it is used must be known, and, though often overlooked, RFI/RFP questions regarding privacy must answered accurately. This requires special skills, training, and experience that do not typically exist within a security team.

As companies move away from a service model under which they do not store customer data to one under which they do store customer data, the data privacy concerns of customers increase exponentially. This new service model pushes companies into the cloud computing space, where many companies do not have sufficient experience in dealing with customer privacy concerns, permanence of customer data throughout its globally distributed systems, cross-border data sharing, and compliance with regulatory or lawful intercept requirements.

Data Governance

A formal data governance framework that defines a system of decision rights and accountability for information-related processes should be developed. This

framework should describe who can take what actions with what information, and when, under what circumstances, and using what methods. The data governance framework should include:

- Data inventory
- Data classification
- Data analysis (business intelligence)
- Data protection
- Data privacy
- Data retention/recovery/discovery
- Data destruction

Data Security

The ultimate challenge in cloud computing is data-level security, and sensitive data is the domain of the enterprise, not the cloud computing provider. Security will need to move to the data level so that enterprises can be sure their data is protected wherever it goes. For example, with data-level security, the enterprise can specify that this data is not allowed to go outside of the United States. It can also force encryption of certain types of data, and permit only specified users to access the data. It can provide compliance with the PCI DSS. True unified end-to-end security in the cloud will likely require an ecosystem of partners.

Application Security

Application security is one of the critical success factors for a world-class SaaS company. This is where the security features and requirements are defined and application security test results are reviewed. Application security processes, secure coding guidelines, training, and testing scripts and tools are typically a collaborative effort between the security and the development teams. Although product engineering will likely focus on the application layer, the security design of the application itself, and the infrastructure layers interacting with the application, the security team should provide the security requirements for the product development engineers to implement. This should be a collaborative effort between the security and product development team. External penetration testers are used for application source code reviews, and attack and penetration tests provide an objective review of the security of the application as well as assurance to customers that attack and penetration tests are performed regularly. Fragmented and undefined collaboration on application security can result in lower-quality design, coding efforts, and testing results.

Since many connections between companies and their SaaS providers are through the web, providers should secure their web applications by following Open Web

Application Security Project (OWASP)[15] guidelines for secure application development (mirroring Requirement 6.5 of the PCI DSS, which mandates compliance with OWASP coding practices) and locking down ports and unnecessary commands on Linux, Apache, MySQL, and PHP (LAMP) stacks in the cloud, just as you would on-premises. LAMP is an open-source web development platform, also called a web stack, that uses Linux as the operating system, Apache as the web server, MySQL as the relational database management system Rational Database Management System, and PHP as the object-oriented scripting language. Perl or Python is often substituted for PHP.[16]

Virtual Machine Security

In the cloud environment, physical servers are consolidated to multiple virtual machine instances on virtualized servers. Not only can data center security teams replicate typical security controls for the data center at large to secure the virtual machines, they can also advise their customers on how to prepare these machines for migration to a cloud environment when appropriate.

Firewalls, intrusion detection and prevention, integrity monitoring, and log inspection can all be deployed as software on virtual machines to increase protection and maintain compliance integrity of servers and applications as virtual resources move from on-premises to public cloud environments. By deploying this traditional line of defense to the virtual machine itself, you can enable critical applications and data to be moved to the cloud securely. To facilitate the centralized management of a server firewall policy, the security software loaded onto a virtual machine should include a bidirectional stateful firewall that enables virtual machine isolation and location awareness, thereby enabling a tightened policy and the flexibility to move the virtual machine from on-premises to cloud resources. Integrity monitoring and log inspection software must be applied at the virtual machine level.

This approach to virtual machine security, which connects the machine back to the mother ship, has some advantages in that the security software can be put into a single software agent that provides for consistent control and management throughout the cloud while integrating seamlessly back into existing security infrastructure investments, providing economies of scale, deployment, and cost savings for both the service provider and the enterprise.

Identity Access Management

Identity and access management (IAM) is a critical function for every organization, and a fundamental expectation of SaaS customers is that the principle of least privilege is granted to their data. The principle of least privilege states that only the minimum access necessary to perform an operation should be granted, and that access should be granted only for the minimum amount of time necessary.[17] However, business and IT groups will need and expect access to systems and applications. The advent of cloud services and services on demand is changing the identity management landscape. Most of the current identity management solutions are focused on the enterprise and typically are architected to work in a very controlled, static environment. User-centric identity management solutions such as federated identity management also make some assumptions about the parties involved and their related services.

In the cloud environment, where services are offered on demand and they can continuously evolve, aspects of current models such as trust assumptions, privacy implications, and operational aspects of authentication and authorization, will be challenged. Meeting these challenges will require a balancing act for SaaS providers as they evaluate new models and management processes for IAM to provide end-to-end trust and identity throughout the cloud and the enterprise. Another issue will be finding the right balance between usability and security. If a good balance is not achieved, both business and IT groups may be affected by barriers to completing their support and maintenance activities efficiently.

Change Management

Although it is not directly a security issue, approving production change requests that do not meet security requirements or that introduce a security vulnerability to the production environment may result in service disruptions or loss of customer data. A successful security team typically collaborates with the operations team to review production changes as they are being developed and tested. The security team may also create security guidelines for standards and minor changes, to provide self-service capabilities for these changes and to prioritize the security team's time and resources on more complex and important changes to production.

Physical Security

Customers essentially lose control over physical security when they move to the cloud, since the actual servers can be anywhere the provider decides to put them. Since you lose some control over your assets, your security model may need to be reevaluated. The concept of the cloud can be misleading at times, and people forget that everything is somewhere actually tied to a physical location. The massive investment required to build the level of security required for physical data centers is the prime reason that companies don't build their own data centers, and one of several reasons why they are moving to cloud services in the first place.

For the SaaS provider, physical security is very important, since it is the first layer in any security model. Data centers must deliver multilevel physical security because mission-critical Internet operations require the highest level of security. The elements of physical security are also a key element in ensuring that data center operations and delivery teams can provide continuous and authenticated uptime of greater than 99.9999%. The key components of data center physical security are the following:

- Physical access control and monitoring, including 24/7/365 on-site security, biometric hand geometry readers inside "man traps," bullet-resistant walls, concrete bollards, closed-circuit TV (CCTV), integrated video, and silent alarms. Security personnel should request government-issued identification from visitors, and should record each visit. Security cameras should monitor activity throughout the facility, including equipment areas, corridors, and mechanical, shipping, and receiving areas. Motion detectors and alarms should be located throughout the facilities, and silent alarms should automatically notify security and law enforcement personnel in the event of a security breach.
- Environmental controls and backup power: Heat, temperature, air flow, and humidity should all be kept within optimum ranges for the computer equipment housed on-site. Everything should be protected by fire-suppression systems, activated by a dual-alarm matrix of smoke, fire, and heat sensors located throughout the entire facility. Redundant power links to two different local utilities should also be created where possible and fed through additional batteries and UPS power sources to regulate the flow and prevent spikes, surges, and brownouts. Multiple diesel generators should be in place and ready to provide clean transfer of power in the event that both utilities fail.
- Policies, processes, and procedures: As with information security, policies, processes, and procedures are critical elements of successful physical security that can protect the equipment and data housed in the hosting center.

BC and DR

In the SaaS environment, customers rely heavily on 24/7 access to their services, and any interruption in access can be catastrophic. The availability of your software applications is the definition of your company's service

and the life blood of your organization. Given the virtualization of the SaaS environment, the same technology will increasingly be used to support BC and DR, because virtualization software effectively "decouples" application stacks from the underlying hardware, and a virtual server can be copied, backed up, and moved just like a file. A growing number of virtualization software vendors have incorporated the ability to support live migrations. This, plus the decoupling capability, provides a low-cost means of quickly reallocating computing resources without any downtime. Another benefit of virtualization in BC and DR is its ability to deliver on service-level agreements and provide high-quality service.

Code escrow is another possibility, but object code is equivalent to source code when it comes to a SaaS provider, and the transfer and storage of that data must be tightly controlled. For the same reason that developer will not automatically provide source code outside their control when they license their software, it will be a challenge for SaaS escrow account providers to obtain a copy of the object code from a SaaS provider. Of course, the data center and its associated physical infrastructure will fall under standard BC and DR practices.

The BC Plan

A BC plan should include planning for non-IT-related aspects such as key personnel, facilities, crisis communication, and reputation protection, and it should refer to the DR plan for IT-related infrastructure recovery/continuity. The BC plan manual typically has five main phases: analysis, solution design, implementation, testing, and organization acceptance and maintenance. DR planning is a subset of a larger process known as BC planning and should include planning for resumption of applications, data, hardware, communications (such as networking), and other IT infrastructure. DR is the process, policies, and procedures related to preparing for recovery or continuation of technology infrastructure critical to an organization after a natural or human-induced disaster.[18,19]

IS SECURITY-AS-A-SERVICE THE NEW MSSP?

Managed security service providers (MSSPs) were the key providers of security in the cloud that was created by Exodus Communications, Global Crossing, Digital Island, and others that dominated the outsourced hosting environments that were the norm for corporations from the mid-1990s to the early 2000s. The cloud is essentially the next evolution of that environment, and many of the security challenges and management requirements will be similar. An MSSP is essentially an Internet service provider (ISP) that provides an organization with some network security management and monitoring (e.g., security information management, security event management, and security information and event management, which may include virus blocking, spam blocking, intrusion detection, firewalls, and virtual private network [VPN] management and may also handle system changes, modifications, and upgrades. As a result of the. dot.com bust and the subsequent Chapter 11 bankruptcies of many of the dominant hosting service providers, some MSSPs pulled the plug on their customers with short or no notice. With the increasing reluctance of organizations to give up complete control over the security of their systems, the MSSP market has dwindled over the last few years. The evolution to cloud computing has changed all this, and MSPs that have survived are reinventing themselves along with a new concept of MSSP, which is now called Security-as-a-Service (SaaS)—not to be confused with Software-as-a-Service (SaaS), although it can be a component of the latter as well as other cloud services such as PaaS, IaaS, and MaaS.

Unlike MSSP, Security-as-a-Service does not require customers to give up complete control over their security posture. Customer system or security administrators have control over their security policies, system upgrades, device status and history, current and past patch levels, and outstanding support issues, on demand, through a web-based interface. Certain aspects of security are uniquely designed to be optimized for delivery as a web-based service, including:

- Offerings that require constant updating to combat new threats, such as antivirus and anti-spyware software for consumers
- Offerings that require a high level of expertise, often not found inhouse, and that can be conducted remotely. These include ongoing maintenance, scanning, patch management, and troubleshooting of security devices.
- Offerings that manage time- and resource-intensive tasks, which may be cheaper to outsource and offshore, delivering results and findings via a web-based solution. These include tasks such as log management, asset management, and authentication management.[20]

SUMMARY

Virtualization is being used in data centers to facilitate cost savings and create a smaller, "green" footprint. As a result, multitenant uses of servers are being created on what used to be single-tenant or single-purpose physical servers. The extension of virtualization and virtual machines into the cloud is affecting enterprise security as a result of the evaporating enterprise network perimeter—the de-perimeterization of the enterprise, if you will. In this entry, we discussed the importance of security in the cloud computing environment, particularly with regard to the SaaS environment and the security challenges and best practices associated with it.

REFERENCES

1. http://cloudsecurity.org/2008/10/14/biggest-cloud-challenge-security (accessed February 2009).
2. http://en.wikipedia.org/wiki/Software_as_a_service.
3. http://blogs.zdnet.com/Hinchcliffe/?p = 166&tag = btxcsim.
4. http://en.wikipedia.org/wiki/PaaS.
5. http://www.cbronline.com/article_feature.asp?guid=E66B8BF0-43BB-4AB1-9475-5884D82C897F.
6. http://en.wikipedia.org/wiki/IaaS.
7. http://www.infoworld.com/article/08/07/02/Gartner_Seven_cloudcomputing_security_risks_1.html (accessed February 2009).
8. http://en.wikipedia.org/wiki/Cloud_service#Cloud_storage (accessed February 2009).
9. Whitman, M.E.; Mattord, H.J. *Management of Information Security*; Thomson Course Technology: Stamford, Connecticut, 2004; 57.
10. http://www.eseminarslive.com/c/a/Cloud-Computing/Dell030509 (accessed February 2009).
11. http://www.bitcricket.com/downloads/Network%20Forensics.pdf (accessed February 2009).
12. http://cloudsecurity.org/2008/07/21/assessing-the-security-benefits-of-cloud-computing (accessed February 2009).
13. http://www.nemertes.com/issue_papers/virtulatization_risk_analysis.
14. http://cloudsecurity.org/2008/07/21/assessing-the-security-benefits-of-cloud-computing (accessed February 2009).
15. http://www.owasp.org/index.php/Main_Page (accessed February 2009).
16. http://www.webopedia.com/TERM/L/LAMP.html (accessed February 2009).
17. http://web.mit.edu/Saltzer/www/publications/protection/Basic.html (accessed February 2009).
18. http://en.wikipedia.org/wiki/Business_continuity_planning (accessed February 2009).
19. http://en.wikipedia.org/wiki/Disaster_recovery (accessed February 2009).
20. Security as a Service, http://en.wikipedia.org/wiki/Security_as_a_service (accessed February 2009).

Cloud Computing: Standards

John W. Rittinghouse
Hypersecurity LLC, Tomball, Texas, U.S.A.

James F. Ransome
Cisco Systems, Santa Clara, California, U.S.A.

Abstract

In Internet circles, everything eventually gets driven by a working group of one sort or another. A working group is an assembled, cooperative collaboration of researchers working on new research activities that would be difficult for any one member to develop alone. A working group can exist for anywhere between a few months or many years. Working groups generally strive to create an informational document, a standard, or find some resolution for problems related to a system or network. Most often, the working group attempts to assemble experts on a topic. Together, they will work intensively toward their goal. Working groups are sometimes also referred to as task groups or technical advisory groups. In this entry, we will discuss the Open Cloud Consortium and the Distributed Management Task Force as examples of cloud-related working groups. We will also discuss the most common standards used in cloud environments.

THE OPEN CLOUD CONSORTIUM

The purpose of the Open Cloud Consortium (OCC) is to support the development of standards for cloud computing and to develop a framework for interoperability among various clouds. The OCC supports the development of benchmarks for cloud computing and is a strong proponent of open source software to be used for cloud computing. OCC manages a testing platform and a test-bed for cloud computing called the Open Cloud Test-bed. The group also sponsors workshops and other events related to cloud computing.

The OCC is organized into several different working groups. For example, the Working Group on Standards and Interoperability for Clouds focuses on developing standards for interoperating clouds that provide on-demand computing capacity. One architecture for clouds that was popularized by a series of Google technical reports describes a *storage cloud* providing a distributed file system, a *compute cloud* supporting MapReduce, and a *data cloud* supporting table services. The open source Hadoop system follows this architecture. These types of cloud architectures support the concept of on-demand computing capacity.

There is also a Working Group on Wide Area Clouds and the Impact of Network Protocols on Clouds. The focus of this working group is on developing technology for wide area clouds, including creation of methodologies and benchmarks to be used for evaluating wide area clouds. This working group is tasked to study the applicability of variants of Transmission Control Protocol (TCP) and the use of other network protocols for clouds.

The Open Cloud Test-bed uses Cisco C-Wave and the University of Illinois at Chicago Teraflow Network for its network connections. C-Wave makes network resources available to researchers to conduct networking and applications research. It is provided at no cost to researchers and allows them access to 10G Waves (Layer-1 p2p) on a per-project allocation. It provides links to a 10GE (gigabit Ethernet) switched network backbone. The Teraflow Test-bed (TFT) is an international application network for exploring, integrating, analyzing, and detecting changes in massive and distributed data over wide-area high-performance networks. The TFT-bed analyzes streaming data with the goal of developing innovative technology for data streams at very high speeds. It is hoped that prototype technology can be deployed over the next decade to analyze 100-gigabit-per-second (Gbps) and 1000-Gbps streams.

Both of these products use wavelengths provided by the National Lambda Rail (NLR). The NLR can support many distinct networks for the U.S. research community using the same core infrastructure. Experimental and productions' networks exist side by side but are physically and operationally separate. Production networks support cutting-edge applications by providing users guaranteed levels of reliability, availability, and performance. At the same time, experimental networks enable the deployment and testing of new networking technologies, providing researchers national-scale test-beds without the limitations typically associated with production networks.

Encyclopedia of Information Systems and Technology, DOI: 10.1081/E-EIST-120053837

The Working Group on Information Sharing, Security, and Clouds has a primary focus on standards and standards-based architectures for sharing information between clouds. This is especially true for clouds belonging to different organizations and subject to possibly different authorities and policies. This group is also concerned with security architectures for clouds. An example is exchanging information between two clouds, each of which is Health Insurance Portability and Accountability Act-compliant, but when each cloud is administered by a different organization.

Finally, there is an Open Cloud Test-bed Working Group that manages and operates the Open Cloud Test-bed. Currently, membership in this working group is limited to those who contribute computing, networking, or other resources to the Open Cloud Test-bed. For more information on the OCC, the reader is encouraged to visit the OCC website.[1]

THE DISTRIBUTED MANAGEMENT TASK FORCE

According to their web site, the Distributed Management Task Force (DMTF)

> . . . enables more effective management of millions of information technology (IT) systems worldwide by bringing the IT industry together to collaborate on the development, validation, and promotion of systems management standards. The group spans the industry with 160 member companies and organizations, and more than 4000 active participants crossing 43 countries. The DMTF board of directors is led by 16 innovative, industry-leading technology companies. They include Advanced Micro Devices; Broadcom Corporation; CA, Inc.; Dell; EMC; Fujitsu; HP; Hitachi, Ltd.; IBM; Intel Corporation; Microsoft Corporation; Novell; Oracle; Sun Microsystems, Inc.; Symantec Corporation and VMware, Inc. With this deep and broad reach, DMTF creates standards that enable interoperable IT management. DMTF management standards are critical to enabling management interoperability among multi-vendor systems, tools and solutions within the enterprise.[2]

The DMTF started the Virtualization Management Initiative (VMAN). VMAN unleashes the power of virtualization by delivering broadly supported interoperability and portability standards to virtual computing environments. It enables IT managers to deploy preinstalled, preconfigured solutions across heterogeneous computing networks and to manage those applications through their entire life cycle. Management software vendors offer a broad selection of tools that support the industry standard specifications that are now a part of VMAN. This helps in lowering support and training costs for IT managers. Virtualization has enhanced the IT industry by optimizing use of existing physical resources and helping reduce the number of systems deployed and managed. This consolidation reduces hardware costs and mitigates power and cooling needs. However, even with the efficiencies gained by virtualization, this new approach does add some IT cost due to increased system management complexity.

Since the DMTF builds on existing standards for server hardware, management tool vendors can easily provide holistic management capabilities to enable IT managers to manage their virtual environments in the context of the underlying hardware. This lowers the IT learning curve, and also lowers complexity for vendors implementing this support in their solutions. With the technologies available to IT managers through the VMAN Initiative, companies now have a standardized approach to:

- Deploy virtual computer systems
- Discover and take inventory of virtual computer systems
- Manage the life cycle of virtual computer systems
- Add/change/delete virtual resources
- Monitor virtual systems for health and performance

Open Virtualization Format

The Open Virtualization Format (OVF) is a fairly new standard that has emerged within the VMAN Initiative. The OVF simplifies interoperability, security, and virtual machine life-cycle management by describing an open, secure, portable, efficient, and extensible format for the packaging and distribution of one or more virtual appliances. The OVF specifies procedures and technologies to permit integrity checking of the virtual machines (VM) to ensure that they have not been modified since the package was produced. This enhances security of the format and will help to alleviate security concerns of users who adopt virtual appliances produced by third parties. The OVF also provides mechanisms that support license checking for the enclosed VMs, addressing a key concern of both independent software vendors and customers. Finally, the OVF allows an installed VM to acquire information about its host virtualization platform and runtime environment, which allows the VM to localize the applications it contains and optimize its performance for the particular virtualization environment.

One key feature of the OVF is virtual machine packaging portability. Since OVF is, by design, virtualization platform-neutral, it provides the benefit of enabling platform-specific enhancements to be captured. It also supports many open virtual hard disk formats. Virtual machine properties are captured concisely using OVF metadata. OVF is optimized for secure distribution. It supports content verification and integrity checking based on industry-standard public key infrastructure and provides a basic scheme for management of software licensing.

Another benefit of the OVG is a simplified installation and deployment process. The OVF streamlines the entire installation process using metadata to validate the entire package and automatically determine whether a virtual appliance can be installed. It also supports both single-VM and multiple-VM configurations and packages containing complex, multitier services consisting of multiple interdependent VMs. Since it is vendor- and platform-independent, the OVF does not rely on the use of a specific host platform, virtualization platform, or guest operating system.

The OVF is designed to be extended as the industry moves forward with virtual appliance technology. It also supports and permits the encoding of vendor-specific metadata to support specific vertical markets. It is localizable—it supports user-visible descriptions in multiple locales, and localization of interactive processes during installation of a virtual appliance. This allows a single packaged virtual appliance to serve multiple markets.

STANDARDS FOR APPLICATION DEVELOPERS

The purpose of application development standards is to ensure uniform, consistent, high-quality software solutions. Programming standards are important to programmers for a variety of reasons. Some researchers have stated that, as a general rule, 80% of the lifetime cost of a piece of software goes to maintenance. Furthermore, hardly any software is maintained by the original author for its complete life cycle. Programming standards help to improve the readability of the software, allowing developers to understand new code more quickly and thoroughly. If you ship source code as a product, it is important to ensure that it is as well packaged and meets industry standards comparable to the products you compete with. For the standards to work, everyone developing solutions must conform to them. In the following sections, we discuss application standards that are commonly used across the Internet in browsers, for transferring data, sending messages, and securing data.

Browsers (Ajax)

Ajax, or its predecessor AJAX (Asynchronous Java-Script and XML), is a group of interrelated web development techniques used to create interactive web applications or rich Internet applications. Using Ajax, web applications can retrieve data from the server asynchronously, without interfering with the display and behavior of the browser page currently being displayed to the user. The use of Ajax has led to an increase in interactive animation on web pages. Despite its name, JavaScript and XML are not actually *required* for Ajax. Moreover, requests do not even need to be asynchronous. The original acronym AJAX has changed to the name Ajax to reflect the fact that these specific technologies are no longer required.

In many cases, related pages that coexist on a web site share much common content. Using traditional methods, such content must be reloaded every time a request is made. Using Ajax, a web application can request only the content that needs to be updated. This greatly reduces networking bandwidth usage and page load times. Using asynchronous requests allows a client browser to appear more interactive and to respond to input more quickly. Sections of pages can be reloaded individually. Users generally perceive the application to be faster and more responsive. Ajax can reduce connections to the server, since scripts and style sheets need only be requested once.

An Ajax framework helps developers create web applications that use Ajax. The framework helps them to build dynamic web pages on the client side. Data is sent to or from the server using requests, usually written in JavaScript. On the server, some processing may be required to handle these requests, for example, when finding and storing data. This is accomplished more easily with the use of a framework dedicated to process Ajax requests. One such framework, ICEfaces, is an open source Java product maintained by http://icefaces.org.

ICEfaces Ajax Application Framework

ICEfaces is an integrated Ajax application framework that enables Java EE application developers to easily create and deploy thin-client rich Internet applications in pure Java. ICEfaces is a fully featured product that enterprise developers can use to develop new or existing Java EE applications at no cost. ICEfaces is the most successful enterprise Ajax framework available under open source. The ICEfaces developer community is extremely vibrant, already exceeding 32,000 developers in 36 countries. To run ICEfaces applications, users need to download and install the following products:

- Java 2 Platform, Standard Edition
- Ant
- Tomcat
- ICEfaces
- Web browser (if you don't already have one installed)

ICEfaces leverages the entire standards-based Java EE set of tools and environments. Rich enterprise application features are developed in pure Java in a thin-client model. No Applets or proprietary browser plug-ins are required. ICEfaces applications are JavaServer Faces applications, so Java EE application development skills apply directly and Java developers don't have to do any JavaScript-related development.

Because ICEfaces is a pure Java enterprise solution, developers can continue to work the way they normally do. They are able to leverage their existing Java integrated development environments (IDEs) and test tools for development. ICEfaces supports an array of Java Application Servers, IDEs, third-party components, and JavaScript effect libraries. ICEfaces pioneered a technique called Ajax Push. This technique enables server/application-initiated content rendering to be sent to the browser. Also, ICEfaces is the one of the most secure Ajax solutions available. Compatible with Secure Sockets Layer (SSL) protocol, it prevents cross-site scripting, malicious code injection, and unauthorized data mining. ICEfaces does not expose application logic or user data, and it is effective in preventing fake form submits and Structured Query Language (SQL) injection attacks. ICEfaces also supports third-party application server Asynchronous Request Processing APIs provided by Sun Glassfish (Grizzly), Jetty, Apache Tomcat, and others.

Data (XML, JSON)

Extensible Markup Language (XML) is a specification for creating custom markup languages. It is classified as an extensible language because it allows the user to define markup elements. Its purpose is to enable sharing of structured data. XML is often used to describe structured data and to serialize objects. Various XML-based protocols exist to represent data structures for data interchange purposes. Using XML is arguably more complex than using JavaScript Object Notation (JSON) (described below), which represents data structures in simple text formatted specifically for data interchange in an uncompressed form. Both XML and JSON lack mechanisms for representing large binary data types such as images.

XML, in combination with other standards, makes it possible to define the content of a document separately from its formatting. The benefit here is the ability to reuse that content in other applications or for other presentation environments. Most important, XML provides a basic syntax that can be used to share information among different kinds of computers, different applications, and different organizations without needing to be converted from one to another.

An XML document has two correctness levels: *well-formed* and *valid*. A well-formed document conforms to the XML syntax rules. A document that is not well formed is not in XML format, and a conforming parser will not process it. A valid document is well formed and additionally conforms to semantic rules which can be user-defined or exist in an XML schema. An XML schema is a description of a type of XML document, typically expressed in terms of constraints on the structure and content of documents of that type, above and beyond the basic constraints imposed by XML itself. A number of standard and proprietary XML schema languages have emerged for the purpose of formally expressing such schemas, and some of these languages are themselves XML-based.

XML documents must conform to a variety of rules and naming conventions. By carefully choosing the names of XML elements, it is possible to convey the meaning of the data in the markup itself. This increases human readability while retaining the syntactic structure needed for parsing. However, this can lead to verbosity, which complicates authoring and increases file size. When creating XML, the designers decided that by leaving the names, allowable hierarchy, and meanings of the elements and attributes open and definable by a customized schema, XML could provide a syntactic foundation for the creation of purpose-specific, XML-based markup languages. The general syntax of such languages is very rigid. Documents must adhere to the general rules of XML, ensuring that all XML-aware software can at least read and understand the arrangement of information within them. The schema merely supplements the syntax rules with a predefined set of constraints.

Before the advent of generalized data description languages such as XML, software designers had to define special file formats or small languages to share data between programs. This required writing detailed specifications and special-purpose parsers and writers. XML's regular structure and strict parsing rules allow software designers to leave the task of parsing to standard tools, since XML provides a general, data model-oriented framework for the development of application-specific languages. This allows software designers to concentrate on the development of rules for their data at relatively high levels of abstraction.

JavaScript object notation

JSON is a lightweight computer data interchange format. It is a text-based, human-readable format for representing simple data structures and associative arrays (called objects). The JSON format is specified in Internet Engineering Task Force (IETF) Request for Comment (RFC) 4627. The JSON format is often used for transmitting structured data over a network connection in a process called serialization. Its main application is in Ajax web application programming, where it serves as an alternative to the XML format. JSON is based on a subset of the JavaScript programming language. It is considered to be a language-independent data format. Code for parsing and generating JSON data is readily available for a large variety of programming languages. The json.org website provides a comprehensive listing of existing JSON bindings, organized by language.

Even though JSON was intended as a data serialization format, its design as a subset of the JavaScript language poses security concerns. The use of a JavaScript interpreter to dynamically execute JSON text as JavaScript can expose a program to bad or even malicious script. JSON is also subject to cross-site request forgery attacks. This can allow JSON-encoded data to be evaluated in the context of a malicious page, possibly divulging passwords or other sensitive data. This is only a problem if the server depends on the browser's Same Origin Policy to block the delivery of the data in the case of an improper request. When the server determines the propriety of the request, there is no problem because it will only output data if the request is valid. Cookies are not adequate for determining whether a request is authorized and valid. The use of cookies is subject to cross-site request forgery and should be avoided with JSON. As you can see, JSON was built for simple tasks and can be useful, but there is some risk involved in using it—especially given the alternative solutions available today.

Solution Stacks (LAMP and LAPP)

LAMP

LAMP is a popular open source solution commonly used to run dynamic web sites and servers. The acronym derives from the fact that it includes **L**inux, **A**pache, **M**ySQL, and **P**HP (or Perl or Python) and is considered by many to be the platform of choice for development and deployment of high-performance web applications which require a solid and reliable foundation. The combination of these technologies is used primarily to define a web server infrastructure or for creating a programming environment for developing software. While the creators of these open source products did not intend for them all to work with each other, the LAMP combination has become popular because of its open source nature, low cost, and the wide distribution of its components (most of which come bundled with nearly all of the current Linux distributions). When used in combination, they represent a solution stack of technologies that support application servers.

Linux, Apache, PostgreSQL, and PHP (or Perl or Python)

The LAPP stack is an open source web platform that can be used to run dynamic web sites and servers. It is considered by many to be a more powerful alternative to the more popular LAMP stack. These advanced and mature components provide a rock-solid foundation for the development and deployment of high-performance web applications. LAPP offers SSL, PHP, Python, and Perl support for Apache2 and PostgreSQL. There is an administration front-end for PostgreSQL as well as web-based administration modules for configuring Apache2 and PHP. PostgreSQL password encryption is enabled by default. The PostgreSQL user is trusted when connecting UNIX. Many consider the LAPP stack a more secure out-of-the-box solution than the LAMP stack. The choice of which stack to use is made by developers based on the purpose of their application and the risks they may have to contend with when users begin working with the product.

STANDARDS FOR MESSAGING

You probably think you know what a messaging standard is. Unfortunately, the term *messaging* means different things to different people. So does the word *standard*. People may assume you are talking about networking when you begin discussing messaging standards. The term *messaging,* however, covers a lot of ground, and not all of it is specific to networking. For our purposes here, a *message* is a unit of information that is moved from one place to another. The term *standard* also is not always clearly defined. Different entities have differing interpretations of what a standard is, and we know there are open international standards, de facto standards, and proprietary standards. A true standard is usually characterized by certain traits, such as being managed by an international standards body or an industry consortium, and the standard is created jointly by a community of interested parties. The IETF is perhaps the most open standards body on the planet, because it is open to everyone. Participants can contribute, and their work is available online for free. In the following sections, we discuss the most common messaging standards used in the cloud—some of which have been used so much so that they are considered de facto standards.

Simple Message Transfer Protocol

Simple Message Transfer Protocol (SMTP) is arguably the most important protocol in use today for basic messaging. Before SMTP was created, e-mail messages were sent using File Transfer Protocol (FTP). A sender would compose a message and transmit it to the recipient as if it were a file. While this process worked, it had its shortcomings. The FTP protocol was designed to transmit files, not messages, so it did not provide any means for recipients to identify the sender or for the sender to designate an intended recipient. If a message showed up on an FTP server, it was up to the administrator to open or print it (and sometimes even deliver it) before anyone even knew who it was supposed to be receiving it.

SMTP was designed so that sender and recipient information could be transmitted with the message. The design process didn't happen overnight, though. SMTP was initially defined in 1973 by IETF RFC 561. It has evolved over the years and has been modified by RFCs 680, 724, and 733. The current RFCs applying to SMTP are RFC 821 and RFC 822. SMTP is a two-way protocol that usually operates using TCP port 25. Though many people don't realize it, SMTP can be used to both send and receive messages. Typically, though, workstations use Post Office Protocol (POP) rather than SMTP to receive messages. SMTP is usually used for either sending a message from a workstation to a mail server or for communications between mail servers.

Post Office Protocol

SMTP can be used both to send and receive messages, but using SMTP for this purpose is often impractical or impossible because a client must have a constant connection to the host to receive SMTP messages. The Post Office Protocol (POP) was introduced to circumvent this situation. POP is a lightweight protocol whose single purpose is to download messages from a server. This allows a server to store messages until a client connects and requests them. Once the client connects, POP servers begin to download the messages and subsequently delete them from the server (a default setting) in order to make room for more messages. Users respond to a message that was downloaded using SMTP. The POP protocol is defined by RFC 1939 and usually functions on TCP port 110.

Internet Messaging Access Protocol

Once mail messages are downloaded with POP, they are automatically deleted from the server when the download process has finished. Thus POP users have to save their messages locally, which can present backup challenges when it is important to store or save messages. Many businesses have compulsory compliance guidelines that require saving messages. It also becomes a problem if users move from computer to computer or use mobile networking, since their messages do not automatically move where they go. To get around these problems, a standard called Internet Messaging Access Protocol (IMAP) was created. IMAP allows messages to be kept on the server but viewed and manipulated (usually via a browser) as though they were stored locally.

IMAP is a part of the RFC 2060 specification, and functions over TCP port 143.

Syndication (Atom, Atom Publishing Protocol, and RSS)

Content syndication provides citizens convenient access to new content and headlines from government via RSS (Really Simple Syndication) and other online syndication standards. Governments are providing access to more and more information online. As web sites become more complex and difficult to sift through, new or timely content is often buried. Dynamically presenting "what's new" on the top of the web site is only the first step. Sharing headlines and content through syndication standards such as RSS (the little orange [XML] button, ATOM, and others) essentially allows a government to control a small window of content across web sites that choose to display the government's headlines. Headlines may also be aggregated and displayed through "newsreaders" by citizens through standalone applications or as part of their personal web page.

Portals can automatically aggregate and combine headlines and/or lengthier content from across multiple agency web sites. This allows the value of distributed effort to be shared, which is more sustainable. Press releases may be aggregated automatically from different systems, as long as they all are required to offer an RSS feed with content tagged with similar metadata. Broader use of government information online, particularly time-sensitive democratic information, justifies the effort of production and the accountability of those tasked to make it available.

- **Benefits:** Ability to scan headlines from many sources, all in one place, through a newsreader. Time-saving awareness of new content from government, if the RSS feed or feeds are designed properly. Ability to monitor new content from across the council, as well as display feeds on their own web site. Awareness of new content position councilors as guides to government for citizens. Ability to aggregate new content or headlines from across multiple office locations and agencies. This allows a display of "joined-up" government despite structural realities. Journalists and other locally focused web sites will be among the primary feed users.
- **Limitations:** Dissemination via syndication is a new concept to governments just getting used to the idea of remote online public access to information. Governments need to accept that while they control the content of the feed, the actual display of the headlines and content will vary. Popular RSS feeds can use significant amounts of bandwidth. Details on how often or when a feed is usually updated should be

offered to those grabbing the code behind the orange [XML] button, so they "ping" it once a day instead of every hour. Automated syndication requires use of a content management system. Most viable content management systems have integrated RSS functions, but the sophistication, ease of use, and documentation of these tools vary. There are three variants of RSS, as well as the emerging ATOM standard. It is recommended that a site pick the standard most applicable to their content rather than confuse users with different feeds providing the same content.

Rich Site Summary

Rich Site Summary (RSS) is a family of web feed formats used to publish frequently updated works—such as blog entries, news headlines, audio, and video—in a standardized format. An RSS document includes full or summarized text, plus metadata such as publishing dates and authorship. Web feeds benefit publishers by letting them syndicate content automatically. They benefit readers who want to subscribe to timely updates from favored web sites or to aggregate feeds from many sites into one place. RSS feeds can be read using software called a reader that can be web-based, desktop-based, a mobile device, or any computerized Internet-connected device. A standardized XML file format allows the information to be published once and viewed by many different programs. The user subscribes to a feed by entering the feed's Uniform Resource Identifier (URI) (often referred to informally as a Uniform Resource Locator (URL), although technically, those two terms are not exactly synonymous) into the reader or by clicking an RSS icon in a browser that initiates the subscription process. The RSS reader checks the user's subscribed feeds regularly for new work, downloads any updates that it finds, and provides a user interface to monitor and read the feeds.

Atom and Atom Publishing Protocol

The name Atom applies to a pair of related standards. The Atom Syndication Format is an XML language used for web feeds, while the Atom Publishing Protocol (AtomPub or APP) is a simple Hypertext Transfer Protocol (HTTP)-based protocol (HTTP is described later in this entry) for creating and updating web resources, sometimes known as web feeds. Web feeds allow software programs to check for updates published on a web site. To provide a web feed, a site owner may use specialized software (such as a content management system) that publishes a list (or "feed") of recent articles or content in a standardized, machine-readable format. The feed can then be downloaded by web sites that syndicate content from the feed, or by feed reader programs that allow Internet users to subscribe to feeds and view their content. A feed contains entries, which may be headlines, full-text articles, excerpts, summaries, and/or links to content on a web site, along with various metadata.

The Atom format was developed as an alternative to RSS. Ben Trott, an advocate of the new format that became Atom, believed that RSS had limitations and flaws—such as lack of ongoing innovation and its necessity to remain backward compatible—and that there were advantages to a fresh design. Proponents of the new format formed the IETF Atom Publishing Format and Protocol Workgroup. The Atom syndication format was published as an IETF "proposed standard" in RFC 4287, and the APP was published as RFC 5023.

Web feeds are used by the weblog community to share the latest entries' headlines or their full text, and even attached multimedia files. These providers allow other web sites to incorporate the weblog's "syndicated" headline or headline-and-short-summary feeds under various usage agreements. Atom and other web syndication formats are now used for many purposes, including journalism, marketing, "bug" reports, or any other activity involving periodic updates or publications. Atom also provides a standardized way to export an entire blog, or parts of it, for backup or for importing into other blogging systems.

A program known as a feed reader or aggregator can check web pages on behalf of a user and display any updated articles that it finds. It is common to find web feeds on major web sites, as well as on many smaller ones. Some web sites let people choose between RSS- or Atom-formatted web feeds; others offer only RSS or only Atom. In particular, many blog and wiki sites offer their web feeds in the Atom format.

Client-side readers and aggregators may be designed as standalone programs or as extensions to existing programs such as web browsers. Browsers are moving towards integrated feed reader functions. Such programs are available for various operating systems. Web-based feed readers and news aggregators require no software installation and make the user's feeds available on any computer with web access. Some aggregators syndicate web feeds into new feeds, e.g., taking all football-related items from several sports feeds and providing a new football feed. There are several search engines which provide search functionality over content published via these web feeds.

Web Services

REpresentational State Transfer (REST) is a style of software architecture for distributed hypermedia systems such as the World Wide Web (WWW). As such, it is not strictly a method for building "web services." The terms "representational state transfer" and "REST" were introduced in 2000 in the doctoral dissertation of Roy Fielding,[3] one of the principal authors of the HTTP specification.

REST refers to a collection of network architecture principles which outline how resources are defined and addressed. The term is often used in a looser sense to describe any simple interface which transmits domain-specific data over HTTP without an additional messaging layer such as (SOAP) or session tracking via HTTP cookies. These two meanings can conflict as well as overlap. It is possible to design a software system in accordance with Fielding's REST architectural style without using HTTP and without interacting with the WWW. It is also possible to design simple XML + HTTP interfaces which do not conform to REST principles, but instead follow a model of remote procedure call (RPC). Systems which follow Fielding's REST principles are often referred to as "RESTful."

Proponents of REST argue that the web's scalability and growth are a direct result of a few key design principles. Application state and functionality are abstracted into resources. Every resource is uniquely addressable using a universal syntax for use in hypermedia links, and all resources share a uniform interface for the transfer of state between client and resource. This transfer state consists of a constrained set of well-defined operations and a constrained set of content types, optionally supporting code on demand. State transfer uses a protocol which is client-server based, stateless and cacheable, and layered. Fielding describes REST's effect on scalability thus:

> REST's client-server separation of concerns simplifies component implementation, reduces the complexity of connector semantics, improves the effectiveness of performance tuning, and increases the scalability of pure server components. Layered system constraints allow intermediaries—proxies, gateways, and firewalls—to be introduced at various points in the communication without changing the interfaces between components, thus allowing them to assist in communication translation or improve performance via large-scale, shared caching. REST enables intermediate processing by constraining messages to be self-descriptive: interaction is stateless between requests, standard methods and media types are used to indicate semantics and exchange information, and responses explicitly indicate cacheability (Ibid).

An important concept in REST is the existence of resources, each of which is referenced with a global identifier (e.g., a URI in HTTP). In order to manipulate these resources, components of the network (user agents and origin servers) communicate via a standardized interface (e.g., HTTP) and exchange representations of these resources (the actual documents conveying the information). For example, a resource which is a circle may accept and return a representation which specifies a center point and radius, formatted in Scalable Vector Graphics (SVG), but may also accept and return a representation which specifies any three distinct points along the curve as a comma-separated list.

Any number of connectors (clients, servers, caches, tunnels, etc.) can mediate the request, but each does so without "seeing past" its own request (referred to as "layering," another constraint of REST and a common principle in many other parts of information and networking architecture). Thus an application can interact with a resource by knowing two things: the identifier of the resource, and the action required—it does not need to know whether there are caches, proxies, gateways, firewalls, tunnels, or anything else between it and the server actually holding the information. The application does, however, need to understand the format of the information (representation) returned, which is typically an HTML, XML, or JSON document of some kind, although it may be an image, plain text, or any other content.

REST provides improved response time and reduced server load due to its support for the caching of representations. REST improves server scalability by reducing the need to maintain session state. This means that different servers can be used to handle different requests in a session. REST requires less client-side software to be written than other approaches, because a single browser can access any application and any resource. REST depends less on vendor software and mechanisms which layer additional messaging frameworks on top of HTTP. It provides equivalent functionality when compared to alternative approaches to communication, and it does not require a separate resource discovery mechanism, because of the use of hyperlinks in representations. REST also provides better long-term compatibility because of the capability of document types such as HTML to evolve without breaking backwards or forwards compatibility and the ability of resources to add support for new content types as they are defined without dropping or reducing support for older content types.

One benefit that should be obvious with regard to web-based applications is that a RESTful implementation allows a user to bookmark specific "queries" (or requests) and allows those to be conveyed to others across e-mail, instant messages, or to be injected into wikis, etc. Thus this "representation" of a path or entry point into an application state becomes highly portable. A RESTFul web service is a simple web service implemented using HTTP and the principles of REST. Such a web service can be thought of as a collection of resources comprising three aspects:

• The URI for the web service

- The MIME type of the data supported by the web service (often JSON, XML, or YAML Ain't Markup Language, but can be anything)
- The set of operations supported by the web service using HTTP methods, including but not limited to POST, GET, PUT, and DELETE

Members of the collection are addressed by ID using URIs of the form <baseURI >/ <ID >. The ID can be any unique identifier. For example, a RESTFul web service representing a collection of cars for sale might have the URI:

```
http://example.com/resources/cars
```

If the service uses the car registration number as the ID, then a particular car might be present in the collection as:

```
http://example.com/resources/cars/yxz123
```

Simple Object Access Protocol

SOAP is a protocol specification for exchanging structured information in the implementation of Web Services in computer networks. It relies on XML as its message format and usually relies on other application-layer protocols, most notably RPC and HTTP for message negotiation and transmission. SOAP can form the foundation layer of a web services protocol stack, providing a basic messaging framework on which web services can be built.

As a simple example of how SOAP procedures can be used, a SOAP message can be sent to a web service-enabled web site—for example, a house price database—with the parameters needed for a search. The site returns an XML-formatted document with the resulting data (prices, location, features, etc.) Because the data is returned in a standardized machineparseable format, it may be integrated directly into a third-party site.

The SOAP architecture consists of several layers of specifications for message format, message exchange patterns (MEPs), underlying transport protocol bindings, message processing models, and protocol extensibility. SOAP is the successor of XML-RPC. SOAP makes use of an Internet application-layer protocol as a transport protocol. Critics have argued that this is an abuse of such protocols, as it is not their intended purpose and therefore not a role they fulfill well. Proponents of SOAP have drawn analogies to successful uses of protocols at various levels for tunneling other protocols.

Both SMTP and HTTP are valid application-layer protocols used as transport for SOAP, but HTTP has gained wider acceptance because it works well with today's Internet infrastructure; specifically, HTTP works well with network firewalls. SOAP may also be used over HTTPS (which is the same protocol as HTTP at the application level, but uses an encrypted transport protocol underneath) with either simple or mutual authentication; this is the advocated WS-I method to provide web service security as stated in the WS-I Basic Profile 1.1. This is a major advantage over other distributed protocols such as General Inter-ORB Protocol/Internet Inter-ORB Protocol or Distributed Component Object Model, which are normally filtered by firewalls. XML was chosen as the standard message format because of its widespread use by major corporations and open source development efforts. Additionally, a wide variety of freely available tools significantly eases the transition to a SOAP-based implementation.

Advantages of using SOAP over HTTP are that SOAP allows for easier communication through proxies and firewalls than previous remote execution technology. SOAP is versatile enough to allow for the use of different transport protocols. The standard stacks use HTTP as a transport protocol, but other protocols are also usable (e.g., SMTP). SOAP is platform-independent, language-independent, and it is simple and extensible.

Because of the verbose XML format, SOAP can be considerably slower than competing middleware technologies such as Common Object Request Broker Architecture (CORBA). This may not be an issue when only small messages are sent. To improve performance for the special case of XML with embedded binary objects, Message Transmission Optimization Mechanism was introduced. When relying on HTTP as a transport protocol and not using Web Services-Addressing or an Enterprise Service Bus, the roles of the interacting parties are fixed. Only one party (the client) can use the services of the other. Developers must use polling instead of notification in these common cases.

Most uses of HTTP as a transport protocol are made in ignorance of how the operation is accomplished. As a result, there is no way to know whether the method used is appropriate to the operation. The REST architecture has become a web service alternative that makes appropriate use of HTTP's defined methods.

Communications (HTTP, SIMPLE, and XMPP)

HTTP is a request/response communications standard based on a client/server model. A client is the end user, the server is the web site. The client making a HTTP request via a web browser or other tool sends the request to the server. The responding server is called the origin server. HTTP is not constrained to use TCP/internet protocol (IP) and its supporting layers, although this is its most popular application on the Internet. SIMPLE, the Session Initiation Protocol (SIP) for Instant Messaging (IM) and Presence Leveraging Extensions, is an IM and presence protocol suite based on SIP, and it is managed by the IETF. Like Extensible Messaging and Presence Protocol (XMPP), SIMPLE is an open standard. XMPP is also an open, XML-based protocol originally aimed at near-real-time, extensible IM and presence information (e.g., buddy lists) but now expanded into the broader realm of message-oriented middleware. All of these protocols are discussed in detail in the following paragraphs.

Hypertext Transfer Protocol

HTTP is an application-level protocol for distributed, collaborative, hypermedia information systems. Its use for retrieving linked resources led to the establishment of the WWW. HTTP development was coordinated by the WWW Consortium and the IETF, culminating in the publication of a series of RFCs, most notably RFC 2616 (June 1999), which defines HTTP/1.1, the version of HTTP in common use today.

HTTP is a request/response standard between a client and a server. A client is the end-user, the server is the web site. The client making a HTTP request—using a web browser, spider, or other end-user tool—is referred to as the user agent. The responding server—which stores or creates resources such as HTML files and images—is called the origin server. In between the user agent and origin server may be several intermediaries, such as proxies, gateways, and tunnels. HTTP is not constrained to using TCP/IP and its supporting layers, although this is its most popular application on the Internet. In fact, HTTP can be implemented on top of any other protocol; all it requires is reliable transport, so any protocol, on the Internet or any other network that provides reliable transport, can be used.

Typically, an HTTP client initiates a request. It establishes a TCP connection to a particular port on a host (port 80 by default). An HTTP server listening on that port waits for the client to send a request message. Upon receiving the request, the server sends back a status line such as "HTTP/1.1 200 OK" and a message of its own, the body of which is perhaps the requested resource, an error message, or some other information. Resources to be accessed by HTTP are identified using URIs (or, more specifically, URLs) using the http: or https URI schemes.

SIMPLE

SIP for IM and SIMPLE is an IM and presence protocol suite based on the SIP. Like XMPP, SIMPLE is an open standard. SIMPLE makes use of SIP for registering for presence information and receiving notifications when presence-related events occur. It is also used for sending short messages and managing a session of real-time

messages between two or more participants. Implementations of the SIMPLE-based protocols can be found in SIP softphones and also hardphones (In computing, a softphone is a software program for making telephone calls over the Internet using a general-purpose computer; a hardphone is a conventional telephone set.). The SIMPLE presence specifications can be broken up into core protocol methods, presence information, and the handling of privacy, policy, and provisioning.

The core protocol methods provide SIP extensions for subscriptions, notifications, and publications. The methods used, **subscribe** and **notify**, are defined in RFC 3265. **Subscribe** allows a user to subscribe to an event on a server. **Notify** is the method used whenever the event arises and the server responds back to the subscriber. Another standard, RFC 3856, defines precisely how to use these methods to establish and maintain presence. Presence documents contain information encoded using XML. These documents are transported in the bodies of SIP messages (RFC 3863 and RFC 4479 describe this procedure.). Privacy, policy, and provisioning information are needed by user agents to determine who may subscribe to presence information. A framework for authorization policies controlling access to application-specific data is defined in RFC 4745 and RFC 5025. SIP defines two modes of IM, the Page mode and the Session mode. Page mode makes use of the SIP method MESSAGE, as defined in RFC 3428. This mode establishes no sessions, while the Session mode based on the Message Session Relay Protocol (RFC 4975, RFC 4976) defines text-based protocol for exchanging arbitrarily sized content of any time between users.

Extensible Messaging and Presence Protocol

XMPP is an XML-based protocol used for near-real-time, extensible IM and presence information. XMPP remains the core protocol of the Jabber IM and Presence technology. Jabber provides a carrier-grade, best-inclass presence and messaging platform. According to a press release following its acquisition by Cisco Systems in November 2008, "Jabber's technology leverages open standards to provide a highly scalable architecture that supports the aggregation of presence information across different devices, users and applications. The technology also enables collaboration across many different presence systems such as Microsoft Office Communications Server, IBM Sametime, AOL AIM, Google, and Yahoo!"

Built to be extensible, the XMPP protocol has grown to support features such as voice-over-IP and file transfer signaling. Unlike other IM protocols, XMPP is an open standard. Like e-mail, anyone who has a domain name and an Internet connection can run the Jabber server and chat with others. The Jabber project is open source software, available from Google at http://code.google.com/p/jabber-net.

XMPP-based software is deployed on thousands of servers across the Internet. The IETF has formalized XMPP as an approved IM and presence technology under the name XMPP, and the XMPP specifications have been published as RFC 3920 and RFC 3921. Custom functionality can be built on top of XMPP, and common extensions are managed by the XMPP Software Foundation.

XMPP servers can be isolated from the public Jabber network, and robust security (via SASL and Transport Layer Security [TLS]) is built into the core XMPP specifications. Because the client uses HTTP, most firewalls allow users to fetch and post messages without hindrance. Thus, if the TCP port used by XMPP is blocked, a server can listen on the normal HTTP port and the traffic should pass without problems. Some web sites allow users to sign in to Jabber via their browser. Furthermore, there are open public servers, such as http://www.jabber80.com, which listen on standard http (port 80) and https (port 443) ports and allow connections from behind most firewalls.

STANDARDS FOR SECURITY

Security standards define the processes, procedures, and practices necessary for implementing a security program. These standards also apply to cloud-related IT activities and include specific steps that should be taken to ensure a secure environment is maintained that provides privacy and security of confidential information in a cloud environment. Security standards are based on a set of key principles intended to protect this type of trusted environment. Messaging standards, especially for security in the cloud, must also include nearly all the same considerations as any other IT security endeavor. The following protocols, while not exclusively specific to cloud security, merit coverage here. In the next few sections, we explain what they are and how they are used in the cloud environment.

Security (SAML OAuth, OpenID, SSL/TLS)

A basic philosophy of security is to have layers of defense, a concept known as *defense in depth*. This means having overlapping systems designed to provide security even if one system fails. An example is a firewall working in conjunction with an intrusion-detection system (IDS). Defense in depth provides security because there is no single point of failure and no single-entry vector at which an attack can occur. For this

reason, a choice between implementing network security in the middle part of a network (i.e., in the cloud) or at the endpoints is a false dichotomy.[4]

No single security system is a solution by itself, so it is far better to secure all systems. This type of layered security is precisely what we are seeing develop in cloud computing. Traditionally, security was implemented at the endpoints, where the user controlled access. An organization had no choice except to put firewalls, IDSs, and antivirus software inside its own network. Today, with the advent of managed security services offered by cloud providers, additional security can be provided inside the cloud.

Security Assertion Markup Language

Security Assertion Markup Language (SAML) is an XML-based standard for communicating authentication, authorization, and attribute information among online partners. It allows businesses to securely send assertions between partner organizations regarding the identity and entitlements of a principal. The Organization for the Advancement of Structured Information Standards (OASIS) Security Services Technical Committee is in charge of defining, enhancing, and maintaining the SAML specifications.[5] SAML is built on a number of existing standards, namely, SOAP, HTTP, and XML. SAML relies on HTTP as its communications protocol and specifies the use of SOAP (version 1.1). Most SAML transactions are expressed in a standardized form of XML. SAML assertions and protocols are specified using XML schema. Both SAML 1.1 and SAML 2.0 use digital signatures (based on the XML Signature standard) for authentication and message integrity. XML encryption is supported in SAML 2.0, though SAML 1.1 does not have encryption capabilities. SAML defines XML-based assertions and protocols, bindings, and profiles. The term SAML Core refers to the general syntax and semantics of SAML assertions as well as the protocol used to request and transmit those assertions from one system entity to another. SAML protocol refers to what is transmitted, not how it is transmitted. A SAML binding determines how SAML requests and responses map to standard messaging protocols. An important (synchronous) binding is the SAML SOAP binding.

SAML standardizes queries for, and responses that contain, user authentication, entitlements, and attribute information in an XML format.

This format can then be used to request security information about a principal from a SAML authority. A SAML authority, sometimes called the asserting party, is a platform or application that can relay security information. The relying party (or assertion consumer or requesting party) is a partner site that receives the security information. The exchanged information deals with a subject's authentication status, access authorization, and attribute information. A subject is an entity in a particular domain. A person identified by an e-mail address is a subject, as might be a printer.

SAML assertions are usually transferred from identity providers to service providers. Assertions contain statements that service providers use to make access control decisions. Three types of statements are provided by SAML: authentication statements, attribute statements, and authorization decision statements. SAML assertions contain a packet of security information in this form:

```
<saml:Assertion A... >
  <Authentication >
  ...
  </Authentication >
  <Attribute >
  ...
  </Attribute >
  <Authorization >
  ...
  </Authorization >
</saml:Assertion A >
```

The assertion shown above is interpreted as follows:

```
Assertion A, issued at time T by issuer I,
regarding subject S, provided conditions C are
valid.
```

Authentication statements assert to a service provider that the principal did indeed authenticate with an identity provider at a particular time using a particular method of authentication. Other information about the authenticated principal (called the authentication context) may be disclosed in an authentication statement. An attribute statement asserts that a subject is associated with certain attributes. An attribute is simply a name–value pair. Relying parties use attributes to make access control decisions. An authorization decision statement asserts that a subject is permitted to perform action A on resource R given evidence E. The expressiveness of authorization decision statements in SAML is intentionally limited.

A SAML protocol describes how certain SAML elements (including assertions) are packaged within SAML request and response elements. It provides processing rules that SAML entities must adhere to when using these elements. Generally, a SAML protocol is a simple request–response protocol. The most important type of SAML protocol request is a query. A service provider makes a query directly to an identity provider over a secure back channel. For this reason, query messages are typically bound to SOAP. Corresponding to the three types of statements, there are three types of SAML queries: the authentication query, the attribute query,

and the authorization decision query. Of these, the attribute query is perhaps most important. The result of an attribute query is a SAML response containing an assertion, which itself contains an attribute statement.

Open Authentication

Open Authentication (OAuth) is an open protocol, initiated by Blaine Cook and Chris Messina, to allow secure API authorization in a simple, standardized method for various types of web applications. Cook and Messina had concluded that there were no open standards for API access delegation. The OAuth discussion group was created in April 2007, for the small group of implementers to write the draft proposal for an open protocol. DeWitt Clinton of Google learned of the OAuth project and expressed interest in supporting the effort. In July 2007 the team drafted an initial specification, and it was released in October of the same year.

OAuth is a method for publishing and interacting with protected data. For developers, OAuth provides users access to their data while protecting account credentials. OAuth allows users to grant access to their information, which is shared by the service provider and consumers without sharing all of their identity. The Core designation is used to stress that this is the baseline, and other extensions and protocols can build on it.

By design, OAuth Core 1.0 does not provide many desired features (e.g., automated discovery of endpoints, language support, support for XML-RPC and SOAP, standard definition of resource access, OpenID integration, signing algorithms, etc.). This intentional lack of feature support is viewed by the authors as a significant benefit. The Core deals with fundamental aspects of the protocol, namely, to establish a mechanism for exchanging a user name and password for a token with defined rights and to provide tools to protect the token. It is important to understand that security and privacy are not guaranteed by the protocol. In fact, OAuth by itself *provides no privacy at all* and depends on other protocols such as SSL to accomplish that. OAuth can be implemented in a secure manner, however. In fact, the specification includes substantial security considerations that must be taken into account when working with sensitive data. With OAuth, sites use tokens coupled with shared secrets to access resources. Secrets, just like passwords, must be protected.

OpenID

OpenID is an open, decentralized standard for user authentication and access control that allows users to log onto many services using the same digital identity. It is a single-sign-on method of access control. As such, it replaces the common login process (i.e., a login name and a password) by allowing users to log in once and gain access to resources across participating systems.

The original OpenID authentication protocol was developed in May 2005 by Brad Fitzpatrick, creator of the popular community web site Live-Journal. In late June 2005, discussions began between OpenID developers and other developers from an enterprise software company named Net-Mesh. These discussions led to further collaboration on interoperability between OpenID and NetMesh's similar Light-Weight Identity protocol. The direct result of the collaboration was the Yadis discovery protocol, which was announced on October 24, 2005.

The Yadis specification provides a general-purpose identifier for a person and any other entity, which can be used with a variety of services. It provides a syntax for a resource description document identifying services available using that identifier and an interpretation of the elements of that document. Yadis discovery protocol is used for obtaining a resource description document, given that identifier. Together these enable coexistence and interoperability of a rich variety of services using a single identifier. The identifier uses a standard syntax and a well-established namespace and requires no additional namespace administration infrastructure.

An OpenID is in the form of a unique URL and is authenticated by the entity hosting the OpenID URL. The OpenID protocol does not rely on a central authority to authenticate a user's identity. Neither the OpenID protocol nor any web sites requiring identification can mandate that a specific type of authentication be used; nonstandard forms of authentication such as smart cards, biometrics, or ordinary passwords are allowed. A typical scenario for using OpenID might be something like this: A user visits a web site that displays an OpenID login form somewhere on the page. Unlike a typical login form, which has fields for user name and password, the OpenID login form has only one field for the OpenID identifier (which is an OpenID URL). This form is connected to an implementation of an OpenID client library. A user will have previously registered an OpenID identifier with an OpenID identity provider. The user types this OpenID identifier into the OpenID login form.

The relying party then requests the web page located at that URL and reads an HTML link tag to discover the identity provider service URL. With OpenID 2.0, the client discovers the identity provider service URL by requesting the eXtensible Resource Descriptor Sequence document (also called the Yadis document) with the content type **application/xrds + xml,** which may be available at the target URL but is always available for a target XRI. There are two modes by which the relying party can communicate with the identity provider: **checkid_immediate** and **checkid_setup.** In **checkid_immediate**, the relying party requests that the

provider not interact with the user. All communication is relayed through the user's browser without explicitly notifying the user. In **checkid_setup**, the user communicates with the provider server directly using the same web browser as is used to access the relying party site. The second option is more popular on the web.

To start a session, the relying party and the identity provider establish a shared secret—referenced by an associate handle—which the relying party then stores. Using **checkid_setup**, the relying party redirects the user's web browser to the identity provider so that the user can authenticate with the provider. The method of authentication varies, but typically, an OpenID identity provider prompts the user for a password, and then asks whether the user trusts the relying party web site to receive his or her credentials and identity details. If the user declines the identity provider's request to trust the relying party web site, the browser is redirected to the relying party with a message indicating that authentication was rejected. The site in turn refuses to authenticate the user. If the user accepts the identity provider's request to trust the relying party web site, the browser is redirected to the designated return page on the relying party web site along with the user's credentials. That relying party must then confirm that the credentials really came from the identity provider. If they had previously established a shared secret, the relying party can validate the shared secret received with the credentials against the one previously stored. In this case, the relying party is considered to be stateful, because it stores the shared secret between sessions (a process sometimes referred to as persistence). In comparison, a stateless relying party must make background requests using the **check_authentication** method to be sure that the data came from the identity provider.

After the OpenID identifier has been verified, OpenID authentication is considered successful and the user is considered logged in to the relying party web site. The web site typically then stores the OpenID identifier in the user's session. OpenID does not provide its own authentication methods, but if an identity provider uses strong authentication, OpenID can be used for secure transactions.

SSL/TLS

TLS and its predecessor, SSL, are cryptographically secure protocols designed to provide security and data integrity for communications over TCP/IP. TLS and SSL encrypt the segments of network connections at the transport layer. Several versions of the protocols are in general use in web browsers, e-mail, IM, and voice-over-IP. TLS is an IETF standard protocol which was last updated in RFC 5246.

The TLS protocol allows client/server applications to communicate across a network in a way specifically designed to prevent eavesdropping, tampering, and message forgery. TLS provides endpoint authentication and data confidentiality by using cryptography. TLS authentication is one-way—the server is authenticated, because the client already knows the server's identity. In this case, the client remains unauthenticated. At the browser level, this means that the browser has validated the server's certificate—more specifically, it has checked the digital signatures of the server certificate's issuing chain of Certification Authorities (CAs).

Validation does not identify the server to the end user. For true identification, the end user must verify the identification information contained in the server's certificate (and, indeed, its whole issuing CA chain). This is the only way for the end user to know the "identity" of the server, and this is the only way identity can be securely established, verifying that the URL, name, or address that is being used is specified in the server's certificate. Malicious web sites cannot use the valid certificate of another web site because they have no means to encrypt the transmission in a way that it can be decrypted with the valid certificate. Since only a trusted CA can embed a URL in the certificate, this ensures that checking the apparent URL with the URL specified in the certificate is an acceptable way of identifying the site.

TLS also supports a more secure bilateral connection mode whereby both ends of the connection can be assured that they are communicating with whom they believe they are connected. This is known as mutual (assured) authentication. Mutual authentication requires the TLS client-side to also maintain a certificate. TLS involves three basic phases:

- Peer negotiation for algorithm support
- Key exchange and authentication
- Symmetric cipher encryption and message authentication

During the first phase, the client and server negotiate cipher suites, which determine which ciphers are used; makes a decision on the key exchange and authentication algorithms to be used; and determines the message authentication codes. The key exchange and authentication algorithms are typically public key algorithms. The message authentication codes are made up from cryptographic hash functions. Once these decisions are made, data transfer may begin.

SUMMARY

In this entry we have discussed some of the more prevalent standards used in cloud computing. Although we have not analyzed each standard in depth, you should now have a feel for how and why each standard is used and, more important, an understanding of why they have evolved. Standards are important, to be sure, but most of these standards evolved from individuals taking a chance on a new innovation. As these innovative techniques became acceptable to users and implementers, more support for the technique followed. At some point, enough support was present to make the innovation be considered a "standard," and groups formalized protocols or rules for using it. Such a "standard" is used until more new innovation takes us elsewhere.

REFERENCES

1. http://www.opencloudconsortium.org/working-groups.html.
2. http://www.dmtf.org/about (accessed February 2009).
3. Fielding, R.T. *Architectural styles and the design of network-based software architectures*. Dissertation, University of California, Irvine, 2000. http://www.ics.uci.edu/~fielding/ pubs/dissertation/rest_arch_style.htm.
4. Schnier, B. http://www.schneier.com/blog/archives/2006/02/security_in_the.html, 15 February 2006 (accessed February 2009).
5. http://www.oasis-open.org/committees/ tc_home.php?wg_abbrev = security.

Cloud Computing: Virtualization versus

Brian J.S. Chee
School of Ocean and Earth Sciences and Technology (SOEST), University of Hawaii, Honolulu, Hawaii, U.S.A.
Curtis Franklin, Jr.
Senior Writer, NetWitness, Gainsville, Florida, U.S.A.

Abstract

There are significant differences between simple virtualization and cloud computing. In this entry, we will examine how they differ, and the criteria for determining which is the better solution in any given business situation.

INTRODUCTION

In this entry we will learn:

- What should be virtualized—There are some good fits and some not-so-good fits; it pays to do a bit of testing before jumping into the deep end.
- How to control cloud resources—There'll be no return on investment if one does not pay attention to maximizing cloud usage efficiently. It's going to be about learning from historical lessons.
- Virtualization as the key to building clouds—If clouds are to succeed, there will need to be a level of operating system (OS) agnostics, and virtualization will be the key to meeting the migration needs of enterprise users on their way to true clouds.
- How to manage the virtual machine and the cloud— The move from virtualization into a cloud will be about moving the virtual servers around within the collection of physical servers in order to maximize efficiency. Front-end management pieces are quickly developing to the point where even energy consumption can be taken into account.
- How to make the cloud pay for itself—How do one bill for cloud services when in some sort of shared tenant arrangement? Here we take a page from the mainframe world and are finally seeing the back-office financial aspect of clouds appearing.
- Development issues in the cloud—As paradigm shifts occur in the industry, so do changes in the techniques and methodologies of writing code. The cloud advantage is years of abstraction-layer development, which removes the "ball and chain" of low-level programming details.

VIRTUALIZATION AS THE FOUNDATION FOR CLOUDS

Regardless of whether one is going to build a mini-cloud in an existing data center environment or put applications into a full cloud, the environment the applications go into will be virtual. We've already seen how a virtual environment divorces the idea of computing resources from specific hardware (or instances of an OS); now, we'll look at what that can mean to the information technology (IT) operations for an organization. Next will come a set of questions that can be summarized as, "How virtual do you want to be?" It's one thing to create multiple virtual environments on a single piece of hardware in order to maximize the extent to which that hardware is used. It's quite another to spread a single virtual image across an undefined number of hardware resources in order to maximize the performance and availability of an application.

How does one know what to virtualize? The decision on which resources to virtualize generally comes down to a question of the resources already being used on various available servers, and where the organization needs to maximize return on investment and performance. If one were to look into the server closet of just about any medium-sized business, one'd find three or more physical machines running e-mail, file services, and Web services. Each physical server is typically dedicated to a single task, and each spends the majority of its time "idling," running at between 10% and 20% central processing unit (CPU) utilization, spinning its computational wheels while waiting for input or external processing to occur.

All those CPU cycles "going to waste" is probably an extravagance in modern business, and the hard-dollar costs associated with the servers can be a drag on a company's bottom line. Those physically separate

Encyclopedia of Information Systems and Technology, DOI: 10.1081/E-EIST-120053811

Cloud Computing

machines have software and hardware maintenance costs along with the human resource costs of remaining independent. Server OS software alone can become a significant expense when multiplied across an entire enterprise. In addition, the cost of the energy required to power and cool many separate servers has become considerable. When electricity was cheap, running multiple servers, each with twin 500-watt power supplies, wasn't a big deal. Today, however, as energy costs have skyrocketed, many companies have been forced to take a much harder look at overall company power loads.

Virtualization can provide cost savings on all fronts through upgrades to more efficient servers (some new servers have 95%-efficient power supplies, as compared to the 80%-efficient units common just a couple of generations ago), and, in most cases, easily combine all three of the servers mentioned earlier onto a single virtualized machine. The real icing on the cake is the ability to take a "snapshot" of virtual machines in any desired state and spin the image off to some kind of external storage.

The entire march from dedicated data centers to virtualization, external hosting, software as a service (SaaS), and now clouds is just a series of steps toward the eventual commoditization of data processing. The questions of whether an organization is ready to treat its various information assets as commodities or considers them "crown jewels" is at the core of the decision-making process that must be followed if virtualization or cloud computing is to be used as a successful IT strategy.

If the logical steps from single-purpose servers to virtualized applications to cloud computing are so smooth and straightforward, why not simply go straight into the cloud for all of an organization's needs? As we'll see, a number of ingredients keep the various computing types far more stratified in practice than they are in principle. While this is likely to change with time, managers and architects will need to keep the differences firmly in mind as they build applications for their organizations.

Sir Isaac Newton's remark about "standing on the shoulders of giants" is an apt description of how the computer industry works. A great example begins with Dr. Norman Abramson's DARPA-funded project called AlohaNET, which created a radio network that allowed students, faculty, and other staff at the University of Hawaii to connect to a time-share system on the university's BCC-500 central computer. It worked, but it had limitations in terms of congestion and collisions, which were later fixed by Robert Metcalf of the Xerox Palo Alto Research Center. This work led eventually, with the help of Intel and Digital Equipment Corporation, to Ethernet. Like a set of child's building blocks, ideas spawn new ideas to build something bigger and better over time. What made AlohaNET such a landmark technology was that it marked the first time that large numbers of users were connected by a single communications medium to a single large number computing system. It should also be noted that the Carrier Sense Multiple Access system proposed by Dr. Abramson was augmented with a collision detection system (CDMA/CD) by Xerox to increase the efficiency of the overall system and avoid many of the problems of collisions in the original DARPA project.

THE MISSING LINK BETWEEN VIRTUALIZATION AND CLOUDS

One of the chief factors complicating the decision on virtualizing or moving to the cloud is the handful of missing pieces in an overall control suite that makes application movement seamless. The true equivalent of what existed in Job Control Language, the comma-delimited mainframe control system that filled the days (and nightmares) of people who ran applications using punched cards on large IBM systems, hasn't arrived on the scene. It's not the punched cards that are missing; it's the control wrapper where environmental requirements for the application can be reported to the host system automatically that hasn't yet appeared. What's missing is a control layer that can convey resource requests to each cloud implementation in lieu of a human conversation. The job submission automation process is still a collection of incompatible systems with no existing method to move cloud jobs around automatically between clouds of varying flavors (Microsoft, Amazon, Google, etc.).

When users can submit applications to any system they have credentials for and not worry about installation issues, then we're at least in the neighborhood of a true cloud. It all needs to happen without human interaction. Something on this scale exists for desktop productivity applications, for which users can easily see data synchronized between desktop hard disks and storage located in the cloud through applications such as Dropbox and the Microsoft Mesh. On the server end, however, things are rather more complicated, and it's here that we'll focus our attention for most of the remainder of this entry.

VIRTUALIZATION: ABSTRACTION IN A BOX

Virtualization, as we've seen, is all about abstraction. In practical terms, this means figuring out the boundaries of abstraction layers and just how specific a developer needs to be in writing a new application.

An abstraction layer is a way of formalizing the OSI seven-layer model and choosing one of the layers (or even a slice from one of the layers) as the piece of the overall data processing puzzle that will be abstracted and virtualized. Make no mistake: Without abstraction (defining the services of a layer in terms of what they do and how they connect with the layers above and below them in the stack), virtualization (divorcing services from the hardware on which they run) just isn't possible. The ease and transparency with which this is possible plays a huge role in determining the success of virtualization (and, ultimately, cloud computing) projects.

For example, for all its faults, Windows successfully removed a huge amount of effort previously required to develop network applications. Microsoft's .NET framework went a great way toward creating a de facto standard with applications that, in theory, could cross between servers, to desktops, and then to mobile platforms. However, .NET certainly wasn't the first and certainly isn't the only framework of its kind. An entire flood of new toolkits, such as PHP, Python, Ruby on Rails, and others, are all about hiding the layers below. The ability to have a single line of code, rather than dozens, open a dialog window enables additional consistency and capabilities that had previously been rarely touched by programmers. These toolkits offer advanced capabilities to a wider design audience and provide a faster adoption curve because of their reduced learning curve. By eliminating the need for users or administrators to determine explicitly the machine on which a particular application (or piece of an application) will execute, these high-level toolkits made network service virtualization practical and widely accepted virtually overnight. What has been brought up time and again, however, is that these abstraction layers have almost become the flavor of the month. Conversion between systems obviously has to be taken into account as new systems are adopted.

Microsoft probably began the virtualization wars in earnest when their Virtual Server product was made a freely downloadable solution, a move that was closely followed by VMWare. While some observers focused on immediate product pricing and distribution strategies, what was really important was that both companies planted the seeds for much broader adoption of virtual machines when they made "type 2 hypervisor" products basically free.

A hypervisor (also called a virtual machine monitor) is software/hardware platform virtualization software that allows multiple OSs to run on a host computer at the same time.

- *Type 1 hypervisors* are installed onto bare metal or directly on the hardware platform. They run directly on the host's hardware to control it and also monitor guest OSs. This type thus represents the classic implementation of virtual machine architecture. And, by essentially eliminating the general-use OS, type 1

hypervisors actually offer better performance than the later type 2 systems.
- *Type 2 hypervisors* are software applications that run inside a conventional OS environment as a user or system space application. The main difference from type 1 hypervisors is that type 2 hypervisors run as normal users rather than as privileged "super-users." A very common application is as a "safe" workstation environment that is protected from outside attack.

Type 1 hypervisors have been available for some time, but they require significant effort to install and configure properly. Type 2 hypervisors, by taking advantage of the additional layer of abstraction provided by the underlying OS, are both less expensive and less labor-intensive to install, configure, and administer. Now that type 2 hypervisor systems are freely available, droves of users have rushed to develop virtual environments.

Why the rush? The widespread availability of type 2 hypervisors meant that system administrators and individual users could begin to experiment easily with virtualization. In many cases, the experiments led to acceptance of virtualization on at least a limited basis within the organization, as concerns about performance, administration costs, and stability were answered. The early experiments also sowed seeds for even greater virtualization acceptance as companies and users sought higher virtualized performance for lower costs.

Ironically, the search for higher performance drove the market back toward type 1 hypervisors, where now-experienced administrators could customize installations for optimal behavior, and software publishers, such as VMWare, Citrix, and Microsoft, could make some real profit. Some companies were able to import administration talent in order to begin their virtualization push with a type 1 hypervisor, and some organizations and users remained completely happy with a type 2 hypervisor. In most cases, however, organizations that eventually want to make the move to a fully virtualized type 1 environment to maximize performance start off with a type 2 hypervisor environment first to keep the cost of the learning curve down.

Interestingly enough, this mad rush to adoption has wedged open the licensing door at Microsoft with their Data Center Edition for Windows Server 2008. Lest we accidentally misinterpret Microsoft's "legalspeak," here's a paste from their website describing how the licensing works for this special version of Windows Server:

> Windows Server 2008 R2 Datacenter features Hyper-V, a flexible high-performance hypervisor-based virtualization technology.

In addition, Windows Server 2008 R2 Datacenter licenses include unlimited virtualization rights, meaning that you have rights to run an unlimited number of Windows Server instances on servers licensed with Windows Server 2008 R2 Datacenter. This gives you the benefits of virtualization while helping to reduce license management headaches and costs, thus helping you:

- Logically consolidate servers and streamline management.
- Reduce the cost associated with power, cooling, and data center space.
- Increase the availability of systems. (The quick migration feature enables to easily move running virtual machines between their physical hosts.)
- Reduce server sprawl by using multiple virtual machines hosted on a physical server.[1]

INSTANCES

Before we go further, we need to introduce a key piece of jargon. An individual running copy of a particular OS in a virtual environment is called an *instance*. On a single VMWare platform, for example, a company might have half a dozen instances of Windows Server running simultaneously, each instance hosting a separate set of applications. Regardless of whether one is running a type 1 or a type 2 virtual environment, all the instances of the OS will be resident in a single box. The ability to move virtual instances from box to box depending on demand is where the idea that would become clouds first arose.

As a historical note, this trend toward putting key pieces of code into hardware for speed reasons has happened several times during the history of computing. IBM had communications processors, network interface cards started adding intelligence to preprocess network packets, and graphic cards are now appearing with dozens of graphic processors. It just made sense for, first, VMWare and then Microsoft, to work directly with the CPU manufacturers to move some key virtualization code into hardware. Hyperthread-capable CPUs have become common, but, for the most part, they remain unused except on enterprise-grade servers. At this moment, most workstation OSs are unable to take advantage of these additions, but it's only a matter of time. What's most likely to happen is the implementation of a toggle similar to how Parallels (virtualization for workstations, but now a type 2 hypervisor) works on a Macintosh. Hit a key and the screen rotates like a cube to display the interface for a guest OS, leaving the host running in the background. Will we see type 1 hypervisors at the workstation? Only the market can tell.

The concept of treating multiple servers as a single virtualized entity only became practical once bare-metal installations of virtualized OSs became available and CPU manufacturers started adding hypervisor instructions directly to their base CPU code. The additional control over this high-wire balancing act was necessary to suspend an instance, and then move the entire program with state information to a new machine. In other words, a Web request could be stopped midway through and then continued on a new machine without anyone knowing. With this native hyperthreading support in place, a new instance of an OS with its hosted application could be launched (or, in the language of virtualization, *spawned*) whenever the demand for an application's services became greater than a single instance could support. Virtualization technology could now be used for dynamic demand balancing, spawning new application instances when needed to meet short-term requirements, and then shutting them down when the temporary surge in demand was over—all without direct and immediate human intervention.

Another huge leap in virtualization technology occurred when vendors started providing for de-duplication of application code across machines. Shared OS kernels became part of the computing landscape early in the development of virtualization, but now vendors started providing the intelligence to share application code across virtual machines, further reducing overhead. Instead of a full version of the OS for each virtual machine, portions were shared to cut down on the overhead for each virtual machine running. As the concept has continued to develop, storage virtualization is starting to offer de-duplication for common pieces (such as all the utilities in a typical OS install), further reducing the overall cost of the overhead for multiple instances of OSs and applications. As the cost of multiple instances of OSs went down (which happened as the knowledge of how to properly administer virtualized servers went up), companies became less reluctant to use virtualization as an alternative to reflexively buying new hardware every time a capacity crunch hit.

With these developments in common code sharing, mission-critical applications could move around in the virtual cluster and be assigned resources on the fly to respond to the massive surge of Web traffic caused by a product going viral because of unexpected success on YouTube or Oprah.

MANAGING INSTANCES

Virtual machine management was the next hurdle to overcome. Since neither was there a dedicated console for each server nor did each machine have an optical drive, peripheral sharing for system generation and/or

Cloud Computing

maintenance became necessary. Vendors such as Avocent, Raritan, Lantronix, Adder, and others that brought Internet Protocol keyboard/video/mouse sharing devices (IP KVMs) to market are now all bringing remotely mounted media to the data center. The ability to mount a disk image, spawning a new instance of an OS from a virtual disk image stored on a hard drive rather than from a physical CD-ROM, appeared almost simultaneously in management systems for blade servers and in virtual machine console applications. This critical ability became an overnight hit for remote management and automated demand balancing.

At the same time, the ability to launch some sort of a remote console for each virtual machine from a browser, eliminating the old "thick" console applications, allowed management to continue while OS instances were spawned. The growing reliance on abstraction layers and rapidly spawning OS instances led to an ironic problem, however: While abstraction layers exist to physically detach one layer from another, the layers can't become *too* detached or the entire system won't work.

One of the most common examples is also one of the most frustrating for system administrators: The local cursor used to control actions on a screen can become disconnected from mouse movement in the remote console, with the local and remote cursors never quite meeting. This is a particular problem with "thin" console applications that use a Web browser to provide a logical window into the operating environment of a remote server. This has almost always been an issue with how the remote machine was set up, but the problem has arisen time and again. While it is seldom fatal to an administration effort, it is a frustrating example of why IT professionals are still looking for improvements in virtual system administration applications.

Another massive change in the way servers are controlled has been the development of the service processor, which is a small computer piggybacking inside the server that is intended for environmental control of the main server. Under most circumstances, pressing the power button on a server is not really turning on the power supply directly; one is sending a signal to the service processor asking it to send power to the main server equipment. The service processor is also responsible for monitoring temperature, fan speed, voltage levels, intrusion sensors, and other hardware-oriented functions. In the case of some Dell blade servers, this management goes as far as being able to track power usage by blade or chassis, providing the potential for submetering in collocation services. Overall complexity and capabilities depend on the platform; in most blade servers, the service processor is also responsible for remote access. For its blade servers, Dell has an agreement with Avocent for IP KVM services, and SuperMicro has an agreement with Raritan. In both

cases, the service provides keyboard/video/mouse support to a remote computer over a network connection.

While remote console applications were being developed and deployed, network monitoring programs, such as HP Open View, OpenNMS, Packet Trap, Nagios, and UniCenter, started providing a deeper view into the virtualized environment. Instead of just monitoring the physical host, they started providing views to the virtualized host and provided additional information specific to the virtualized environment. Now, in addition to spawning instances automatically as demand increased, virtualization systems could provide accurate, real-time information to system administrators so they could tell when hardware capacities were close to being exceeded or software license counts were dangerously close to being full. At last, the tools were in place to all enterprises to fully virtualize many aspects of their server farm, using rack-mounted servers or blade servers to pack hundreds or thousands of virtual OSs into the space of a single 19-inch equipment rack. The use of blade servers has even started reaching into the medium-sized business realm with Hewlett-Packard's introduction of the C3000 series of blade server, nicknamed the "shorty." This smaller chassis can support four full-size blades or eight half-size blades. This branch office offering is typically configured with a storage blade and a couple of computing blades to handle branch office computing needs.

What happened when even virtual servers in the data center weren't enough to keep up with the rapidly growing demand for computing services? It was time, it seemed, to break out the clouds.

BEGINNING AND PERFECTING CLOUD COMPUTING

We've seen the growing movement toward abstraction in services and processes. We've seen the evolution of virtualization toward automatic spawning of instances when resource demand grows high. These have all been steppingstones that have set the stage for the next step: cloud computing. What, precisely, differentiates cloud computing from virtualization? Originally, the difference involved the location of the servers. Virtualization involved virtual OS instances on servers owned by (or provided through dedicated hosting agreements to) the organization. Cloud computing, on the other hand, was provided on servers located "in the cloud" of the Internet, at locations that weren't owned by, or even known by, the organization. In other words, computing resources don't have a specific location, but they're not in the organization data center.

We can begin with this definition of cloud computing: a set of services provided solely as a service, with no responsibility for or even knowledge of a server required by the service consumer. As enterprises have begun to explore cloud computing, the definition has broadened a bit. For now, let's take a look at cloud computing and the providers who make it happen.

What might a cloud service provider (CSP) look like? First, the cloud provider will want to stay well out of the "OS wars" that have consumed so many megabytes of blog and discussion group bandwidth for over 10 years now. In reality, the battle between Linux and Microsoft will continue for a long time to come, and the CSP will most likely need to have nodes for both OSs available for their customers. In some cases, the CSP will make certain OS-specific applications available to customers. In others, the CSP will make applications or functions available without ever letting the customer know which OS lies underneath the service provided. As we move toward true cloud providers, it will be irrelevant what the base OS is, since cloud applications should be able to move freely between different providers.

In order to keep their customers from being casualties in the OS wars, the CSP will need to have the equivalent of the scheduler in grids and high-performance computing to determine which base OS and resources are required for a particular job. This piece is not yet available from CSPs, though some are talking about putting it in place soon. The scheduler piece that is still missing is composed of two parts, which we'll call the *broker* and the *agent*. This idea for a path to better cloud computing is adapted from a description of high-performance computing (HPC)/grid scheduling in a paper by Jennifer M. Schopf of the Mathematics and Computer Science Division, Argonne National Laboratory.

A *broker* provides a public interface for external processes to talk to a cloud application, and an *agent* is a piece of code that goes shopping through the cloud for services or goods that the user application needs. Together, these two scheduler pieces reconcile the abstraction between layers and components that allows cloud computing to work in the first place. Successful scheduling as discussed here would allow for greater component abstraction, which means it would be easier for an application to be created from a large number of disparate pieces published by different CSPs.

Another missing piece in just about everything now published on public grids and clouds, and the key to successfully building complete applications from a large number of cloud-provided pieces, is the concept of *identity federation*. In identity federation, a user or enterprise provides its verified identity to the first organization providing a piece of the application chain. Other publishers and providers accept the verified identity from the first organization so the customer needs to log in only once to satisfy the identity requirements of many different software or service providers. Simply put, it answers the question of how to set up and use trust relationships between foreign organizations that are only loosely connected. How to set up business rules for automatic transactions and how to define a level of qualified trust for business partners still need to be answered. Web consumers today are using an early version at sites such as Amazon and UnitedMall. Credentials identifying individuals are passed from the umbrella site (Amazon or UnitedMall) to each partner online store providing discounts and special offers to UnitedMall or Amazon shoppers. Another example is how payment authorization is handled by PayPal, where payment requests are passed from the online store to PayPal and, once authorization is accomplished, payment credentials are passed back to the store.

UTOPIAN CLOUDS?

This may sound a bit utopian, but it's easy to look forward to a day when "agents" and "brokers" utilize something like a credit bureau to set up a level of financial trust. This financial trust would be used like a credit limit to set up boundaries on just how large a resource request an agent could make of a broker. In principle, and perhaps in practice, this sounds very much like what telephone companies do millions of times per second with calls transiting from one telco to another. With a business model and billing software already in place (and the billing software is truly the most difficult piece of the puzzle to fit into place), it's quite possible to imagine a telco morphing into a "cloud dating service" or perhaps a "cloud matchmaker" handling third-party agent and broker services. This third-party validation facility would be very similar to what happens when one uses a protected website. The user starts a connection to a website, which in turn starts the negotiation to establish a secure connection. The website has a set of credentials that is sent to the user's Web browser. The browser in turn sends those credentials to a third-party server called a *certificate authority*. The browser has already been sent a list of legitimate certificate authorities during its periodic updates, and all this happens via an encrypted conversation. If the website checks out against the certificate authority, the use gets an "All clear" to proceed with the encrypted conversation. It should be noted that while the most common use of certificate authorities is for secure socket layer Web conversations, the same certificate authority is used for a great number of encryption methodologies and technologies that require some sort of third-party validation of identity.

Did that sound too simple? It was. Did that sound too definitive? You bet. The rub is that cloud computing today is as nebulous as the name implies. At this moment, most cloud services don't sound much different from regular old SaaS, but marketing departments are using cloud-like buzzwords to describe upcoming opportunities. True cloud computing is going to require a whole lot of new standards and lots of thinking outside the virtualized box. The crystal ball we're peering into has a massive collection of applications that might not necessarily have a single purchase price. Instead, the cloud would handle usage billing, with the final bill consisting of CPU time, storage, application usage fee, and network transit fees. Late 2009 saw VMWare announce back-office cloud management coming out from behind the curtain. Instead of just market monsters, such as Amazon and Google, running clouds, it will be possible to handle the charge-backs necessary for something akin to "joint tenancy" billing for mini-clouds—the perfect role for small- to medium-sized Internet service providers as they morph to meet the changing market.

ACCOUNTING FOR CLOUDS

In a fully federated cloud, associated with every "cloud session" would be background accounting information, restrictions, a crypto key ring, and general preferences the user wants applied to the environment. There might also be different pricing for permanent prescience (always-available provisioning) covering specialized apps, such as agents and brokers, which might very well morph into something like a company telephone number. Perhaps we'll see business cards with a new information line that might read: "cloud://cheebert.honolulu.hi.us," which might then broker different information depending on who one is. If one is a friend who has previously been defined in the system, it might give my home phone number, but Joe Shmoe off the street would get routed to my general company information page. The public cloud broker might eventually be where Voice-over-IP, Web, instant messaging, and so on all combine for truly unified communications, where the broker would handle a much larger set of business rules to provide for automatic escalation of communications paths across multiple enterprises.

Security could potentially be high enough so that the line between public and private data would be simply a matter of credentials on a crypto key ring. After all, the world of classified processing has long had well-understood rules; for example, the National Industrial Security Program Operating Manual has well-defined procedures on how to mix users with different "need to know" and different classification levels, all separated into various "protection levels." If the Department of Defense can mix protection levels, why can't corporate

clouds? Especially if the cloud vendor has done a reasonable amount of due diligence to comply with whatever regulations may apply in a particular industry (i.e., Sarbanes-Oxley for publically traded corporations or HIPAA for the medical world).

Could this be a case of too many eggs in a single basket? Sure, but when we first connected corporations to the public Internet, we were also balancing risk against benefit. Clouds have the potential to allow IT groups to concentrate more on the bottom line instead of being slaves to the system update dance. Vendors, such as Coyote Point and F5, have gone to great lengths to address this need, with global load-balancing systems now able to start and stop virtual machines in geographically separated data centers.

A MATTER OF TRUST

If brokers become proxies for foreign trust relationships, clouds will be instigators for changing ideas of trust in the overall system as well. Historically, the Wang VS minicomputer system provided assigned credentials not only to users but also to programs. There was, for example, an application that presented users with totals of students in various class sections, their ethnicity, etc. An individual user, however, might not be allowed to see any specific information on individuals because of student confidentiality rules. The Wang VS program was given enough credentials to access to the student information database, but would only present the user with totals, not the contents of individual records. None of the reports that the user had access to would give any type of student details. The registrar who used the same program would present a different set of credentials and be able to get to an additional set of reports that would allow him to print class lists with names and student ID numbers.

The next step in the iterative growth process occurred when network credentials began to catch up to what users had available on the Wang computer. At a 1995 InfoWorld Identity Management System bake-off, IBM displayed an IBM Thinkpad that was running a virtualized mainframe and demonstrated how a gateway application provided a proxy into the "mainframe" so that an employee could have proxied access to mainframe information. In the identity management systems, templates were defined for roles, and in almost every case, the proxies were assigned to the roles rather than the individual. So, while back in August 2005, federation was only just being hinted at, today it needs to rise out of the stagnant waters of the standards committee backrooms if clouds are truly to fulfill their destiny.

SELF-PROVISIONED VIRTUAL SERVERS

Before we leave the topic of virtual servers, clouds, and the differences between them, we should take a brief look at some of the ideas that engineers are talking about in relation to virtual servers. The concept of self-provisioning virtual machines is being mentioned with increasing frequency by engineers at both VMWare and Microsoft. While it is as yet vaporware from both, it's unlikely to be far away. How might these self-provisioning servers work? The basic premise is a simple expansion of an ability we've already discussed for virtual machines. Sets of business rules would be set up to extend the basic ability to spawn new instances previously available in products such as VMotion from VMWare.

Previously, Vmotion could pause a noncritical server in order to reallocate resources when required to handle load spikes. This "contraction" of services left CPU and memory resources available to handle the surge in demand for another service or component. An ability to expand on demand, adding instances on additional hardware resources when surges hit, meets user need without starving, even temporarily, other applications or services. This step moves virtual machines one step closer to the "agents" and "brokers" just discussed as an important feature in forthcoming clouds.

Why can't a broker application in the virtualized system wait for requests and only when, say, a call center opens for the day, cause the start-up of the customer relationship management (CRM) virtual server? Maybe there will be something like a Web proxy, where the very first user of the day will have to wait longer for the Web request to populate the cache. Then each subsequent user no longer has to go out to the wide-area network for that particular Web page, since it can now come from local cache. The same concept could be used for a self-provisioning VM as long as business rules are intelligently set up to prevent a flip-flop effect as the VM pages in and out of the main system. We can do a portion of this using outside influences such as load balancers from F5 and Coyote Point. We can also script the provisioning according to predetermined scenarios, but it all has to be planned out in advance.

An early example is now available from both Microsoft in their System Center Virtual Machine Manager and from VMWare in their Virtual Center system. Both allow the extended application of business rules beyond just shifting resources, to automatically starting VMs upon detect of certain load conditions. Both vendors have also gone further into backup and restore, by allowing for failed servers to reappear automatically on other clusters through the application of restore rules that are set up beforehand. The gist is that consumers want to pay only for applications they're actually using, and if the call center isn't open for a third shift, then shut it down and save energy. Or, better yet, pay only for when one actually uses the CRM, since on-demand computing seems to be something that the people at SalesForce are hinting at for potential new pricing and usage models.

FROM VIRTUAL COMPUTING TO THE CLOUD

We've said throughout this entry that both virtual machines and cloud computing are all about abstraction layers. It's still virtualization if one can see details about the OS, especially if one still need to make accommodations for which OS is under it all. Once the OS details fade into the background, then that swirling mist around ones ankles might now be a cloud.

Users should be able to write or configure an application, test it on local resources, and then have an agent submit it to the CSPs. The great benefit of the cloud includes the ability to "rent" applications developed by others in order to meet rapidly changing needs. As an example, a rapidly growing company might find it advantageous to rent, say, a payroll application, submitting an "agent request" that would also include temporary credentials to a human resources cloud app so that they could access payroll data. In this case, the list of CSPs might include any of a number of financial clouds the company has vetted, with something like PayPal providing a financial proxy to actually transfer the funds for payroll. As the company grows, it could either expand its reliance on Web computing or develop custom applications to meet its unique needs exactly. In the most likely scenario, though, the company's forecast will include a hybrid approach, with basic services provided through cloud facilities and certain very specific components hosted on dedicated virtual machines that are very tightly integrated with the CSPs.

There has been a vision floating around in the world of science fiction about data processing facilities handled just like a utility: Rent the applications needed only for the time one uses them. One might have some in-house computing capability, but usage spikes could be off-loaded to the cloud as needed. This type of service is already being provided by a number of vendors, including Amazon, Google, and IBM. As the tools to integrate expansion capabilities into locally hosted applications improve and grow, it's not unreasonable to assume that overflow into the cloud will become a standard part of business continuity planning for most companies.

Our opinion is that the missing link is some sort of multiplatform computing abstraction layer that provides an identical development environment regardless of which platform or OS lies underneath.

Cloud Computing

It might be on just such a development system that we will start seeing something akin to the iPhone apps store, but for clouds.

DEVELOPING INTO THE CLOUD

An early example of what a cloud development environment might look like is the Adobe Integrated Runtime (AIR) environment. AIR has the pieces that a cloud development environment needs to have, including:

- XML-based resource requirement descriptors
- Ability to support multiple high-level object-oriented Web development systems (Java and Flash in AIR's case)
- Ability to support Internet, database, and hardware interfaces, all within an environment that doesn't seem to care if it's on a Windows or Linux environment (not included in first versions, but a publically stated goal of Adobe for the AIR environment)

This is not to say that AIR is already a fully realized cloud environment. Missing at the moment are cloud versions of the schedulers now found on HPCs and grids. The brokers need to be able to handle accounting proxies, data access proxies, auditing proxies, and financial proxies. We'll most likely see the cloud environment start with all the pieces in a single CSP; but, as the environment matures, we'll begin seeing specialized CSPs offering additional options.

CLOUDS: MINIMUM COMMITMENTS AND MAXIMUM LIMITS

Cloud computing will have tiered pricing as never before. This is already beginning to be put in place by many CSPs. Just as the service broker model could easily be based on existing telephone company business models, cloud computing pricing is going to start resembling mobile phone contracts, but with utilization spike allowances that will sound just like colocation facility bandwidth service agreements.

As cloud applications mature and cloud OSs migrate to more platforms, applications will be migrated from service provider to service provider by agent software, searching for the best rates for the amount of resources.

There may be broker nodes that will be the primary public point of contact, with agent nodes shopping around the globe as brokers change their rates over the workday. In an interesting "back to the future" way, this sounds just like what the old model used in dealing with service bureaus. Companies once had regular IT business models that included a requirement to shop around for some IT functions rather than upgrading just to handle occasional load spikes.

There are now PayPal accounts that can be used in hundreds of e-commerce sites all over the globe, and it's not a stretch to see a provider such as PayPal adding cloud information as part of the customer profile. As this model grows, perhaps eBay will provide "agent" applications for hire, using its internal cloud as the basis for a CSP business. These agents would definitely have some of their heritage from Web crawlers (a key component in the primary business model of cloud provider Google) but will also have a significant heritage component from a firm like PayPal, with its expertise in secure small transactions. This basis in existing well-understood technology an d business models means that broker services will become as commonplace as mobile telephone carriers—and as competitive.

In fact, service providers may be forced to demand minimum usage commitments just to stay profitable in light of "shoppers." Just as mobile phone providers often demand a minimum 2-year commitment if one wants the latest and greatest phone for free, CSPs could easily build their tier model on the notion of customer commitment. Do we predict that cloud computing may become the next supercommodity, like mobile phones? It's quite possible that the march of computing to commodity will drive the market to look very similar to this very familiar commodity market. Especially in light of the high cost of IT specialists, the high cost of energy, and the rapidly rising cost of colocation space driving the enterprise to look for new ways of doing business, cloud computing has benefits that we'll now explore in light of evolving business needs and models.

REFERENCES

1.   http://www.microsoft.com/windowsserver2008/en/us/ 2008-dc.aspx.

Communication Protocols and Services

William Hugh Murray
Executive Consultant, TruSecure Corporation, New Canaan, Connecticut, U.S.A.

Abstract

The information security manager is confronted with a wide variety of communications protocols and services. At one level, the manager would like to be able to ignore how the information gets from one place to another; he would like to be able to *assume* security. At another, he understands that he has only limited control over how the information moves; because the user may be able to influence the choice of path the manager prefers not to rely upon it. However, that being said, the manager also knows that there are differences in the security properties of the various protocols and services that he may otherwise find useful. This entry describes the popular protocols and services, discusses their intended uses and applications, and describes their security properties and characteristics. It compares and contrasts similar protocols and services, makes recommendations for their use, and also recommends compensating controls or alternatives for increasing security.

INTRODUCTION

We have so far trusted the dial-switched voice-analog network. It was operated by one of the most trusted enterprises in the history of the world. It was connection-switched and point-to-point. While there was some eavesdropping, most of it was initiated by law enforcement and was, for the most part, legitimate. While a few of us carefully considered what we would say, most of us used the telephone automatically and without worrying about being overheard. Similarly, we were able to recognize most of the people who called us; we trusted the millions of copies of the printed directories, and we trusted the network to connect us only to the number we dialed. While it is not completely justified, we have transferred much of that automatic trust to the modern digital network and even to the Internet.

All other things being equal, the information security manager would like to be able to ignore how information moves from one place to another. He would like to be able to assume that he can put it into a pipe at point A and have it come out reliably only at point B. Of course, in the real world of the modern integrated network, this is not the case. In this world the traffic is vulnerable to eavesdropping, misdirection, interference, contamination, alteration, and even total loss.

On the other hand, relatively little of this happens; the vast majority of information is delivered when and how it is intended and without any compromise. This happens in part despite the way the information is moved and in part because of how it is moved. The various protocols and services have different security

properties and qualities. Some provide error detection, corrective action such as retransmission, error correction, guaranteed delivery, and even information hiding.

The different levels of service exists because they have different costs and performance. They exist because different traffic, applications, and environments have different requirements. For example, the transfer of a program file has a requirement for bit-for-bit integrity; in some cases, if you lose a bit, it is as bad as losing the whole file. On the other hand, a few seconds, or even tens of seconds, of delay in the transfer of the file may have little impact. However, if one is moving voice traffic, the loss of tens of bits may be perfectly acceptable, while delay in seconds is intolerable. These costs must be balanced against the requirements of the application and the environment.

While the balance between performance and cost is often struck without regard to security, the reality is that there are security differences. The balance between performance, cost, and security is the province of the information security manager. Therefore, he needs to understand the properties and characteristics of the protocols so he can make the necessary trade-offs or evaluate those that have already been made.

Finally, all protocols have limitations and many have fundamental vulnerabilities. Implementations of protocols can compensate for such vulnerabilities only in part. Implementers may be faced with hard design choices, and they may make errors, resulting in implementation-induced vulnerabilities. The manager must understand these, so he will know when and how to compensate.

Encyclopedia of Information Systems and Technology, DOI: 10.1081/E-EIST-120046358

Communication–Cybernetics

PROTOCOLS

A protocol is an agreed-upon set of rules or conventions for communicating between two or more parties. "Hello" and "goodbye" for beginning and ending voice phone calls are examples of a simple protocol. A slightly more sophisticated protocol might include lines that begin with tags, like "This is (name) calling."

Protocols are to codes as sentences and paragraphs are to words. In a protocol, the parties may agree to addressing, codes, format, packet size, speed, message order, error detection and correction, acknowledgments, key exchange, and other things.

This section deals with a number of common protocols. It describes their intended use or application, characteristics, design choices, and limitations.

Internet Protocol

The Internet protocol (IP) is a primitive and application-independent protocol for addressing and routing packets of data within a network. It is the "IP" in TCP/IP, the protocol suite that is used in and defines the Internet. It is intended for use in a relatively flat, mesh, broadcast, connectionless, packet-switched net like the Internet.

IP is analogous to a postcard in the 18th century. The sender wrote the message on the one side of the card and the address and return address on the other. He then gave it to someone who was going in the general direction of the intended recipient. The message was not confidential; everyone who handled it could read it and might even make an undetected change to it.

IP is a "best efforts" protocol; it does not guarantee message delivery nor provide any evidence as to whether or not the message was delivered. It is unchecked; the receiver does not know whether or not he received the entire intended message or whether or not it is correct. The addresses are unreliable; the sender cannot be sure that the message will go only where he intends or even when he intends. The receiver cannot be sure that the message came from the address specified as the return address in the packet.

The protocol does not provide any checking or hiding. If the application requires these, they must be implied or specified someplace else, usually in a higher (i.e., closer to the application) protocol layer.

IP specifies the addresses of the sending or receiving hardware device; but if that device supports multiple applications, IP does not specify which of those it is intended for. (There is a convention of referring to all network addressable devices as "hosts." Such usage in other documents equates to the use of device or addressable device here. IPv6 defines "host.")

IP uses 32-bit addresses. However, the use or meaning of the bits within the address depends upon the size and use of the network. Addresses are divided into five classes. Each class represents a different design choice between the number of networks and the number of addressable devices within the class. Class A addresses are used for very large networks where the number of such networks is expected to be low but the number of addressable devices is expected to be very high. Class A addresses are used for nation, states and other very large domains such as .mil, .gov, and .com. As shown in Table 1, a zero in bit position 0 of an address specifies it as a class A address. Positions 1 through 7 are used to specify the network, and positions 8 through 31 are used to specify devices within the network. Class C is used for networks where the possible number of networks is expected to be high but the number of addressable devices in each net is less than 128. Thus, in general, class B is used for enterprises, states, provinces, or municipalities, and class C is used for LANs. Class D is used for multicasting, and class E is reserved for future uses.

You will often see IP addresses written as nnn.nnn.nnn.nnn.

While security is certainly not IP's long suit, it is responsible for much of the success of the Internet. It is fast and simple. In practice, the security limitations of IP simply do not matter much. Applications rely upon higher-level protocols for security.

Internet Protocol v6.0 (IPng)

IPv6 or "next generation" is a backwardly compatible new version of IP. It is intended to permit the Internet to grow both in terms of the number of addressable devices, particularly class A addresses, and in terms of quantity of traffic. It expands the address to 128 bits, simplifies the format header, improves the support for extensions and options, adds a "quality-of-service"

Table 1 IP network address formats

Network class	Description	Address class	Network address	Device address
A	National	0 in bit 0	1–7	8–31
B	Enterprise	10 in bits 0–1	2–15	16–31
C	LAN	110 in 0–2	3–23	24–31
D	Multicast	1110 in 0–3	4–31	
E	Reserved	1111 in 0–3		

Table 2 UDP datagram

Bit positions	Usage
0–15	Source port address
16–31	Destination port address
32–47	Message length (n)
48–63	Checksum
64–n	Data

capability, and adds address authentication and message confidentiality and integrity. IPv6 also formalizes the concepts of packet, node, router, host, link, and neighbors that were only loosely defined in v4.

In other words, IPng addresses most of the limitations of IP, specifically including the security limitations. It provides for the use of encryption to ensure that information goes only where it is intended to go. This is called secure-IP. Secure-IP may be used for point-to-point security across an arbitrary network. More often, it is used to carve virtual private networks (VPNs) or secure virtual networks (SVNs) out of such arbitrary networks. (VPN is used here to refer to the use of encryption to connect private networks across the public network, gateway-to-gateway. SVN is used to refer to the use of encryption to talk securely, end-to-end, across arbitrary networks. While the term VPN is sometimes used to describe both applications, different implementations of secure-IP may be required for the two applications.)

Many of the implementations of secure-IP are still proprietary and do not guarantee interoperability with all other such implementations.

User Datagram Protocol

User datagram protocol (UDP) is similar to IP—in that it is connectionless and offers "best effort" delivery service, and it is similar to TCP—in that it is both checked and application specific.

Table 2 shows the format of the UDP datagram. Unless the UDP source port is on the same device as the destination port, the UDP packet will be encapsulated in an IP packet. The IP address will specify the

Table 3 Sample UDP ports

Port number	Application	Description
23	Telnet	
53	DNS	Domain name service
43		Whois
69	TFTP	Trivial file transfer service
80	HTTP	Web service
119	Net News	
137		NetBIOS name service
138		NetBIOS datagrams
139		NetBIOS session data

physical device, while the UDP address will specify the logical port or application on the device.

UDP implements the abstraction of "port," a named logical connection or interface to a specific application or service within a device. Ports are identified by a positive integer. Port identity is local to a device, that is, the use or meaning of port number is not global. A given port number can refer to any application that the sender and receiver agree upon. However, by convention and repeated use, certain port numbers have become identified with certain applications. Table 3 lists examples of some of these conventional port assignments.

Transmission Control Protocol

Transmission control protocol (TCP) is a sophisticated composition of IP that compensates for many of its limitations. It is a connection-oriented protocol that enables two applications to exchange streams of data synchronously and simultaneously in both directions. It guarantees both the delivery and order of the packets. Because packets are given a sequence number, missing packets will be detected, and packets can be delivered in the same order in which they were sent; lost packets can be automatically resent. TCP also adapts to the latency of the network. It uses control flags to enable the receiver to automatically slow the sender so as not to overflow the buffers of the receiver.

TCP does not make the origin address reliable. The sequence number feature of TCP resists address spoofing. However, it does not make it impossible. Instances of attackers pretending to be trusted nodes have been reported to have toolkits that encapsulate the necessary work and special knowledge to implement such attacks.

Like many packet-switched protocols, TCP uses path diversity. This means some of the meaning of the traffic may not be available to an eavesdropper. However, eavesdropping is still possible. For example, user identifiers and passphrases usually move in the same packet. "Password grabber" programs have been detected in the network. These programs simply store the first 256 or 512 bits of packets on the assumption that many will contain passwords.

Finally, like most stateful protocols, some TCP implementations are vulnerable to denial-of-service attacks. One such attack is called *SYN flooding*. Requests for sessions, SYN flags, are sent to the target, but the acknowledgments are ignored. The target allocates memory to these requests and is overwhelmed.

Telnet

The Telnet protocol describes how commands and data are passed from one machine on the network to another over a TCP/IP connection. It is described in RFC 855. It is used to make a terminal or printer on one machine and an operating system or application on another appear to be local to each other. The user invokes the Telnet client by entering its name or clicking its icon on his local system and giving the name or address and port number of the system or application that he wishes to use. The Telnet client must listen to the keyboard and send the characters entered by the user across the TCP connection to the server. It listens to the TCP connection and displays the traffic on the user's terminal screen. The client and server use an escape sequence to distinguish between user data and their communication with each other.

The Telnet service is a frequent target of attack. By default, the Telnet service listens for login requests on port 23. Connecting this port to the public network can make the system and the network vulnerable to attack. When connected to the public net, this port should expect strong authentication or accept only encrypted traffic.

File Transfer Protocol

File transfer protocol (FTP) is the protocol used on the Internet for transferring files between two systems. It divides a file into IP packets for sending it across the Internet. The object of the transfer is a file. The protocol provides automatic checking and retransmission to provide for bit-for-bit integrity (see section "Services").

Serial Line Internet Protocol

Serial line internet protocol (SLIP) is a protocol for sending IP packets over a serial line connection. It is described in RFC 1055. SLIP is often used to extend the path from an IP-addressable device, like a router at an Internet service provider (ISP), across a serial connection (e.g., a dial-up connection) to a non-IP device (e.g., a serial port on a PC). It is a mechanism for attaching non-IP devices to an IP network.

SLIP encapsulates the IP packet and bits in the code used on the serial line. In the process, the packet may gain some redundancy and error correction. However, the protocol itself does not provide any error detection or correction. This means that errors may not be detected until the traffic gets to a higher layer. Because SLIP is usually used over relatively slow (56 KB) lines, this may make error correction at that layer expensive. On the other hand, the signaling over modern modems is fairly robust. Similarly, SLIP traffic may gain some compression from devices (e.g., modems) in the path but does not provide any compression of its own.

Because the serial line has only two endpoints, the protocol does not contain any address information; that is, the addresses are implicit. However, this limits the connection to one application; any distinctions in the intended use of the line must be handled at a higher layer.

Because SLIP is used on point-to-point connections, it may be slightly less vulnerable to eavesdropping than a shared-media connection like Ethernet. However, because it is closer to the endpoint, the data may be more meaningful. This observation also applies to point-to-point protocol (PPP).

Point-to-Point Protocol

PPP is used for applications and environments similar to those for SLIP but is more sophisticated. It is described in RFC 1661, July 1994. It is *the* Internet standard for transmission of IP packets over serial lines. It is more robust than SLIP and provides error-detection features. It supports both asynchronous and synchronous lines and is intended for simple links that deliver packets between two peers. It enables the transmission of multiple network-layer protocols (e.g., IP, IPX, and SPX) simultaneously over a single link. For example, a PC might run a browser, a notes client, and an e-mail client over a single link to the network.

To facilitate all this, PPP has a link control protocol (LCP) to negotiate encapsulation formats, format options, and limits on packet format.

Optionally, a PPP node can require that its partner authenticate itself using challenge handshake authentication protocol (CHAP) or password authentication protocol (PAP). This authentication takes place after the link is set up and before any traffic can flow (see sections "Challenge Handshake Authentication Protocol" and "Password Authentication Protocol").

HyperText Transfer Protocol

HyperText transfer protocol (HTTP) is used to move data objects, called pages, between client applications, called browsers, running on one machine, and server applications, usually on another. HTTP is the protocol that is used on and that defines the World Wide Web (WWW). The pages moved by HTTP are compound data objects composed of other data and objects. Pages are specified in a language called HyperText Markup Language, or HTML. HTML specifies the appearance of the page and provides for pages to be associated with one another by cross-references called hyperlinks.

The fundamental assumption of HTTP is that the pages are public and that no data-hiding or address reliability is necessary. However, because many electronic commerce applications are done on the WWW, other protocols, described further, have been defined, and implemented.

SECURITY PROTOCOLS

Much of the traffic that moves in the primitive TCP/IP protocols is public; that is, none of the value of the data derives from its confidentiality. Therefore, the fact that the protocols do not provide any data-hiding does not hurt anything. The protocols do not add any security, but the data do not need it. However, there is some traffic that is sensitive to disclosure and which does require more security than the primitive protocols provide. The absolute amount of this traffic is clearly growing, and its proportion may be growing also. In most cases, the necessary hiding of these data is done in alternative or higher-level protocols.

A number of these secure protocols have been defined and are rapidly being implemented and deployed. This section describes some of those protocols.

Secure Socket Layer

Arguably, the most widely used secure protocol is secure socket layer (SSL). It is intended for use in client–server applications in general. More specifically, it is widely used between browsers and web servers on the WWW. It uses a hybrid of symmetric and asymmetric key cryptography, in which a symmetric algorithm is used to hide the traffic and an asymmetric one, RSA, is used to negotiate the symmetric keys.

SSL is a session-oriented protocol; that is, it is used to establish a secure connection between the client and the server that lasts for the life of the session or until terminated by the application.

SSL comes in two flavors and a number of variations. At the moment, the most widely used of the two flavors is *one-way SSL*. In this implementation, the server side has a private key, a corresponding public key, and a certificate for that key-pair. The server offers its public key to the client. After reconciling the certificate to satisfy itself as to the identity of the server, the client uses the public key to securely negotiate a session key with the server. Once the session key is in use, both the client and the server can be confident that only the other can see the traffic.

The client side has a public key for the key-pair that was used to sign the certificate and can use this key to verify the bind between the key-pair and the identity of the server. Thus, the one-way protocol provides for the authentication of the server to the client but not the other way around. If the server cares about the identity of the client, it must use the secure session to collect evidence about the identity of the client. This evidence is normally in the form of a user identifier and a pass-phrase or similar, previously shared, secret.

The other flavor of SSL is *two-way SSL*. In this implementation both the client and the server know the public key of the other and have a certificate for this key. In most instances the client's certificate is issued by the server, while the server's certificate is issued by a mutually trusted third party.

Secure-HTTP

Secure-HTTP (S-HTTP) is a secure version of HTTP designed to move individual pages securely on the WWW. It is page oriented as contrasted to SSL, which is connection or session oriented. Most browsers (thin clients) that implement SSL also implement S-HTTP, may share key-management code, and may be used in ways that are not readily distinguishable to the end user. In other applications, S-HTTP gets the nod where very high performance is required and where there is limited need to save state between the client and the server.

Secure File Transfer Protocol

Most of the applications of the primitive FTP are used to transfer public files in private networks. Much of it is characterized as "anonymous"; that is, one end of the connection may not even recognize the other. However, as the net spreads, FTP is increasingly used to move private data in public networks.

Secure file transfer protocol (S-FTP) adds encryption to FTP to add data-hiding to the integrity checking provided in the base protocol.

Secure Electronic Transaction

Secure electronic transaction (SET) is a special protocol developed by the credit card companies and vendors and intended for use in multiparty financial transactions like credit card transactions across the Internet. It provides not only for hiding credit card numbers as they cross the network, but also for hiding them from some of the parties to the transaction and for protecting against replay.

One of the limitations of SSL when used for credit card numbers is that the merchant must become party to the entire credit card number and must make a record of it to use in the case of later disputes. This creates a vulnerability to the disclosure and reuse of the credit card number. SET uses public key cryptography to guarantee the merchant that he will be paid without his having to know or protect the credit card number.

Point-to-Point Tunneling Protocol

Tunneling is a form of encapsulation in which the encrypted package, the passenger, is encapsulated inside a datagram of the carrier protocol.

Communication–Cybernetics

Point-to-point tunneling protocol (PPTP) is a protocol (from the PPTP forum) for hiding the information in IP packets, including the addresses. It is used to connect (portable computer) clients across the dial-switched point-to-point network to the Internet and then to a (MS) gateway server to a private (enterprise) network or to (MS) servers on such a network. As its name implies, it is a PPP. It is useful for implementing end-to-end SVNs but less so for implementing any-gateway-to-any-gateway virtual private networks (VPNs).

It includes the ability to

- Query the status of Comm Servers
- Provide in-band management
- Allocate channels and place outgoing calls
- Notify server on incoming calls
- Transmit and receive user data with flow control in both directions
- Notify server on disconnected calls

One major advantage of PPTP is that it is included in MS 32-bit operating systems. (At this writing, the client-side software is included on 32-bit MS Windows operating systems dial up networking (rel. 1.2 and 1.3). The server-side software is included in the NT server operating system. See section L2TP.) A limitation of PPTP, when compared with secure-IP or SSL, is that it does not provide authentication of the endpoints. That is, the nodes know that other nodes cannot see the data passing between but must use other mechanisms to authenticate addresses or user identities.

Layer 2 Forwarding

Layer 2 forwarding (L2F) is another mechanism for hiding information on the Internet. The encryption is provided from the point where the dial-switched point-to-point network connects the ISP to the gateway on the private network. The advantage is that no additional software is required on the client computer; the disadvantage is that the data are protected only on the Internet and not on the dial-switched network.

L2F is a router-to-router protocol used to protect data from acquisition by an ISP, across the public digital packet-switched network (Internet) to receipt by a private network. It is used by the ISP to provide data-hiding servers to its clients. Because the protocol is implemented in the routers (Cisco), its details and management are hidden from the end users.

Layer 2 Tunneling Protocol

Layer 2 tunneling protocol (L2TP) is a proposal by MS and Cisco to provide a client-to-gateway data-hiding facility that can be operated by the ISP. It responds to

the limitations of PPTP (must be operated by the owner of the gateway) and L2F (does not protect data on the dial-switched point-to-point net). Such a solution could protect the data on both parts of the public network, but as a service provided by the ISP rather than by the operator of the private network.

Secure Internet Protocol

Secure Internet protocol (secure IP or IPSec) is a set of protocols to provide for end-to-end encryption of the IP packets. It is being developed by the Internet Engineering Task Force (IETF). It is to be used to bind endpoints to one another and to implement VPNs and SVNs.

Internet Security Association Key Management Protocol

Internet security association key management protocol (ISAKMP) is a proposal for a public-key certificate-based key-management protocol for use with IPSec. Because, in order to establish a secure session, the user will have to have both a certificate and the corresponding key, and because the session will not be vulnerable to replay or eavesdropping, ISAKMP provides "strong authentication." Moreover, because the same mechanism can be used for encryption as for authentication, it provides economy of administration.

Password Authentication Protocol

As already noted, PPP provides for the parties to identify and authenticate each other. One of the protocols for doing this is PAP (see also "Challenge Handshake Authentication Protocol"). PAP works very much like traditional login using a shared secret. A sends a prompt or a request for authentication to B, and B responds with an identifier and a shared secret. If the pair of values meets A's expectation, then A acknowledges B.

This protocol is vulnerable to a replay attack. It is also vulnerable to abuse of B's identity by a privileged user of A.

Challenge Handshake Authentication Protocol

CHAP is a standard challenge–response peer-to-peer authentication mechanism. System A chooses a random number and passes it to B. B encrypts this challenge under a secret shared with A and returns it to A. A also computes the value of the challenge encrypted under the shared secret and compares this value to the value returned by B. If this response meets A's expectation, then A acknowledges B.

Many implementations of PPP/CHAP provide that the remote party be periodically reauthenticated by sending a new challenge. This resists any attempt at "session stealing."

SERVICES

Telnet: File Transfer

FTP is the name of a protocol, but it is also the name of a service that uses the protocol to deliver files. The service is symmetric, in that either the server or the client can initiate a transfer in either direction, either can get a file or send a file, either can do a get or a put. The client may itself be a server. The server may or may not recognize its user, and may or may not restrict access to the available files.

Where the server does restrict access to the available files, it usually does that through the use of the control facilities of the underlying file system. If the file server is built upon the UNIX operating system and file system or the Windows operating systems, then it will use the rules-based file access controls of the file system. If the server is built upon the NT operating system, then it will use the object-oriented controls of the NT file system. If the file service is built on MVS, and yes that does happen, then it is the optional access control facility of MVS that will be used.

Secure Shell™

Secure Shell (SSH2) is a UNIX-to-UNIX client–server program that uses strong cryptography for protecting all transmitted data, including passwords, binary files, and administrative commands between systems on a network. One can think of it as a client–server command processor or shell. While it is used primarily for system management, it should not be limited to this application.

SSH2 implements Secure-IP and ISAKMP at the application layer, as contrasted to the network layer, to provide a secure network computing environment. It provides node identification and authentication, node-to-node encryption, and secure command and file transfer. It compensates for most of the aforementioned protocol limitations. It is now preferred to and used in place of more limited or application-specific protocols or implementations such as secure-FTP.

CONCLUSIONS

Courtney's first law says that nothing useful can be said about the security of a mechanism except in the context of an application and an environment. Of course, the converse of that law says that, in such a context, one can say quite a great deal.

The Internet is an open, not to say hostile, environment in which most everything is permitted. It is defined almost exclusively by its addresses and addressing schema and by the protocols that are honored in it. Little else is reliable.

Nonetheless, most sensitive applications can be done there as long as one understands the properties and limitations of those protocols and carefully chooses among them. We have seen that there are a large number of protocols defined and implemented on the Internet. No small number of them is fully adequate for all applications. On the other hand, the loss in performance, flexibility, generality, and function in order to use those that are secure for the intended application and environment is small. Moreover, as the cost of performance falls, the differences become even less significant.

The information security manager must understand the needs of his applications, and know the tools, protocols, and what is possible in terms of security. Then he must choose and apply those protocols and implementations carefully.

Communication–
Cybernetics

Complexity and Self-Organization

Francis Heylighen
Free University of Brussels, Brussels, Belgium

Abstract

This entry introduces some of the main concepts and methods of the science studying complex, self-organizing systems, and networks, in a nontechnical manner. Complexity cannot be strictly defined, it is only situated between order and disorder. A complex system is typically modeled as a collection of interacting agents, representing components as diverse as people, cells, or molecules. Because of the nonlinearity of the interactions, the overall system evolution is to an important degree unpredictable and uncontrollable. However, the system tends to self-organize, in the sense that local interactions eventually produce global coordination and synergy. The resulting structure can, in many cases, be modeled as a network, with stabilized interactions functioning as links connecting the agents. Such complex, self-organized networks typically exhibit the properties of clustering, being scale-free, and forming a small world. These ideas have obvious applications in information science when studying networks of authors and their publications.

INTRODUCTION

A new paradigm for scientific inquiry has been emerging: complexity. Classical science, as exemplified by Newtonian mechanics, is essentially reductionist: it reduces all complex phenomena to their simplest components, and then tries to describe these components in a complete, objective, and deterministic manner.[1,2] The philosophy of complexity is that this is in general impossible: complex systems, such as organisms, societies, or the Internet, have properties—emergent properties—that cannot be reduced to the mere properties of their parts. Moreover, the behavior of these systems has aspects that are intrinsically unpredictable and uncontrollable, and cannot be described in any complete manner. At best, we can find certain statistical regularities in their quantitative features, or understand their qualitative behavior through metaphors, models, and computer simulations.

While these observations are mostly negative, emphasizing the traditional qualities that complex systems lack, these systems also have a number of surprisingly positive features, such as flexibility, autonomy, and robustness, that traditional mechanistic systems lack. These qualities can all be seen as aspects of the process of self-organization that typifies complex systems: these systems spontaneously organize themselves so as to better cope with various internal and external perturbations and conflicts. This allows them to evolve and adapt to a constantly changing environment.

Processes of self-organization literally create order out of disorder.[1] They are responsible for most of the patterns, structures, and orderly arrangements that we find in the natural world, and many of those in the realms of mind, society, and culture. The aim of information science can be seen as finding or creating such patterns in the immense amount of data that we are confronted with. Initially, patterns used to organize information were simple and orderly, such as "flat" databases in which items were ordered alphabetically by author's name or title, or hierarchically organized subject indices where each item was assigned to a fixed category. Present-day information systems, such as the World Wide Web, are much less orderly, and may appear chaotic in comparison. Yet, being a result of self-organization, the Web possesses a nontrivial structure that potentially makes information retrieval much more efficient. This structure and others have been investigated in the science of networks, which can be seen as part of the sciences of complexity and self-organization.

The concept of self-organization was first proposed by the cyberneticist W. Ross Ashby[3] in the 1940s and developed among others by his colleague Heinz von Foerster.[4] During the 1960s and 1970s, the idea was picked up by physicists and chemists studying phase transitions and other phenomena of spontaneous ordering of molecules and particles. These include Ilya Prigogine,[1] who received a Nobel Prize for his investigation of self-organizing "dissipative structures," and Hermann Haken,[5] who dubbed his approach "synergetics." In the 1980s, this tradition cross-fertilized with the emerging mathematics of nonlinear dynamics and chaos, producing an investigation of complex systems that is mostly quantitative, mathematical, and practiced by physicists. However, the same period saw the appearance of a parallel tradition of "complex adaptive systems,"[6] associated with the newly founded

Encyclopedia of Information Systems and Technology, DOI: 10.1081/E-EIST-120043869

Santa Fe Institute for the sciences of complexity, that is closer in spirit to the cybernetic roots of the field. Building on the work of John Holland, Stuart Kauffman, Robert Axelrod, Brian Arthur, and other SFI associates, this approach is more qualitative and rooted in computer simulation. It took its inspiration more from biology and the social sciences than from physics and chemistry, thus helping to create the new disciplines of *artificial life* and *social simulation*. The remainder of this entry will mostly focus on this second, simulation-based tradition, because it is most applicable to the intrinsically social and cognitive processes that produce the systems studied by information science. Although the other, mathematical tradition sometimes uses the term "complex systems" to characterize itself, the labels of "nonlinear systems" or "chaos theory" seem more appropriate, given that this tradition is still rooted in the Newtonian assumption that apparently complex behavior can be reduced to simple, deterministic dynamics—an assumption which may be applicable to the weather, but not to the evolution of a real-world social system. Extending both traditions, the turn of the century witnessed a surging popularity of research into complex networks. This was inspired mostly by the growth of the World Wide Web and the models proposed by Watts and Strogatz,[7] and Barabasi and Albert.[8]

At present, the "science of complexity" taken as whole, is still little more than a collection of exemplars, methods, and metaphors for modeling complex, self-organizing systems. However, while it still lacks integrated theoretical foundations, it has developed a number of widely applicable, fundamental concepts and paradigms that help us to better understand both the challenges and opportunities of complex systems. This entry will try to introduce the most important of these concepts in a simple and coherent manner, with an emphasis on the ones that may help us to understand the organization of networks of information sources.

COMPLEX SYSTEMS

There is no generally accepted definition of complexity:[9] different authors have proposed dozens of measures or conceptions, none of which capture all the intuitive aspects of the concept, while they are applicable only to a very limited type of phenomena, such as binary strings or genomes. For example, the best-known measure, "Kolmogorov complexity," which is the basis of algorithmic information theory, defines the complexity of a string of characters as the length of the shortest program that can generate that string. However, this implies that random strings are maximally complex, since they allow no description shorter than the string itself. This contradicts our intuition that random systems

are not truly complex. A number of more complex variations of this definition have been proposed to tackle this issue, but they still suffer from the fact that they are only applicable to strings, not to real-world systems. Moreover, it has been proven that the "shortest possible" description is in general incomputable, implying that we can never be sure that we really have determined the true complexity of a string.

In spite of these fundamental problems in formalizing the notion of complexity, there are a number of more intuitive features of complex systems that appear again and again in the different attempts to characterize the domain.[2] One that is more or less universally accepted is that complexity must be situated *in between order and disorder*: complex systems are neither regular and predictable (like the rigid, "frozen" arrangement of molecules in a crystal), nor random and chaotic (like the ever-changing configuration of molecules in a gas). They exhibit a mixture of both dimensions, being roughly predictable in some aspects, surprising and unpredictable in others. This intermediate position, balancing between rigidity and turbulence, is sometimes called the "edge of chaos." A number of theorists have proposed that this precarious balance is precisely what is necessary for adaptation, self-organization, and life to occur, and that complex systems tend to spontaneously evolve toward this "edge."[6]

Another fundamental feature is that complex systems consist of many (or at least several) parts that are connected via their interactions. Their components are both *distinct* and *connected*, both autonomous and to some degree mutually dependent. Complete dependence would imply order, like in a crystal where the state of one molecule determines the state of all the others. Complete independence would imply disorder, like in a gas where the state of one molecule gives you no information whatsoever about the state of the other molecules.

The components of a complex system are most commonly modeled as *agents*, i.e., individual systems that act upon their environment in response to the events they experience. Examples of agents are people, firms, animals, cells, and molecules. The number of agents in the system is in general not fixed as agents can multiply or "die." Usually, agents are implicitly assumed to be goal-directed: their actions aim to maximize their individual "fitness," "utility," or "preference." When no specific goal can be distinguished, their activity still follows a simple cause-and-effect or condition–action logic: an agent will react to a specific condition perceived in the environment by producing an appropriate action. The causal relation or rule connecting condition and action, while initially fixed for a given type of agent, can in some cases change, by learning or evolutionary variation.

The environmental conditions to which an agent reacts are normally affected by other agents' activity. Therefore, an action by one agent will in general trigger further actions by one or more other agents, possibly setting in motion an extended chain of activity that propagates from agent to agent across the system. Such interactions are initially *local*: they start out affecting only the agents in the immediate neighborhood of the initial actor. However, their consequences are often *global*, affecting the system of agents as a whole, like a ripple produced by a pebble that locally disturbs the surface of the water, but then widens to encompass the whole pond.

Nonlinearity

The spreading of a wave is not a complex phenomenon, though, because its propagation is perfectly regular and predictable, and its strength diminishes as its reach widens. Processes in complex systems, on the other hand, are often *nonlinear*: their effects are not proportional to their causes. When the effects are larger than the causes, we may say that there is an amplification or *positive feedback*: initially small perturbations reinforce themselves so as to become ever more intense. An example is the spread of a disease, where a single infection may eventually turn into a global pandemic. Another example is the chain reaction that leads to a nuclear explosion. When the effects are smaller than the causes, there is a dampening or *negative feedback*: perturbations are gradually suppressed, until the system returns to its equilibrium state.

Interactions with positive feedback are very *sensitive to their initial conditions*: a change in that condition may be so small that it is intrinsically undetectable, yet result in a drastically altered outcome. This is called the *butterfly effect* after the observation that, because of the nonlinearity of the system of equations governing the weather, the flapping of the wings of a butterfly in Tokyo may cause a hurricane in New York. The non-observability of the initial perturbations means that the outcome is *in principle* unpredictable, even if the dynamics of the system were perfectly deterministic: no weather monitoring system can be so accurate that it senses all the movements of butterfly wings. This explains why weather forecasts cannot be truly reliable, especially for the longer term. Positive feedback will amplify small, random fluctuations into wild, unpredictable swings, making the overall behavior of the system chaotic. An illustration can be found in the erratic up-and-down movements of quotations on the stock exchange.

In spite of the omnipresence of fluctuations, most systems around us appear relatively stable and predictable. This is due to the presence of negative feedback, which suppresses the effects of such fluctuations. However, while negative feedback makes a system more predictable, it also makes it less controllable: if we try to change the state of such a system, we may find that our changes are counteracted, and that whatever we do,

the system always returns to its own "preferred" equilibrium state. Examples can be found in social systems where attempts from leaders or governments to change the behavior often are actively resisted so that they eventually come to nothing.

The dynamics of complex systems typically exhibits a combination of positive and negative feedbacks, so that certain changes are amplified and others dampened. This makes the system's overall behavior both unpredictable and uncontrollable. Moreover, such systems are normally open, which means that they exchange matter, energy and/or information with their wider environment. For example, an economy or ecosystem is dependent on the climate, and the amount of sunlight, rain, and heat that it produces. These in-going and out-going flows make the dynamics even more complicated, since we cannot know every external event that may affect the system. For example, a thriving economy or ecosystem may suddenly collapse because of the invasion by a foreign pest. Furthermore, the input of energy (such as sunlight) tends to feed amplification processes, so that they never reach the equilibrium that would otherwise follow the exhaustion of resources.

Modeling Complex Systems

For the above reasons, traditional deterministic models (such as systems of partial differential equations) of truly complex systems are in general impracticable,[10] if not in principle incomputable.[11] In nonlinear systems, simplifying the model by using approximations is dangerous as well. The common way to approximate the effect of complex interactions by reducing it to the "mean field" (i.e., the average effect of many discrete actions performed by independent agents) can actually lead to fundamental errors. For example, a differential equation representing the "mean field" effect may predict that a certain perturbation will die out because it is too small, while a computer simulation of the individual agents finds that its effect is amplified by positive feedback until it dominates the system.[12]

Because of these intrinsic difficulties with mathematical models, complexity researchers typically prefer computer simulations, which, while of course being approximations as well, are easier to manipulate, so that more different factors and variations of the model can be explored. Here, the system's evolution is traced step-by-step by iteratively applying the rules that govern the agents' interactions, thus generating the subsequent states of the system. Such simulations typically include a generator of random variations, to represent the effect of unpredictable perturbations. A typical setting is inspired by the Darwinian mechanism of natural selection, in which the rules that determine an agent's behavior are randomly "mutated" and sometimes recombined with the rules of another agent, after which the "fittest" or best performing agents or rules are selected to carry on, while the others are eliminated. To explore the possible behaviors of the system, many different "runs"—with different initial conditions or random variations during the process—of the simulation are performed. The main variable values for each run are collected. These results are then analyzed statistically to discover recurring trends.

This sometimes produces very robust results, in the sense that all runs, however, different in their initial behavior, eventually appear to converge to the same type of stable pattern. In the majority of cases, the outcomes can be classified into a relatively small number of distinct categories. This provides the researchers with a qualitative picture of the most likely results—and hopefully an insight into the factors that promote one outcome rather than another one. It is only exceptionally that no clear pattern can be discerned in the outcomes of the different simulation runs. The reason that complex systems in spite of their intrinsic unpredictability tend to settle into a relatively small set of recognizable behaviors is their inherent tendency to *self-organize*.

SELF-ORGANIZATION

Self-organization can be defined as the spontaneous emergence of global structure out of local interactions. "Spontaneous" means that no internal or external agent is in control of the process: for a large enough system, any individual agent can be eliminated or replaced without damaging the resulting structure. The process is truly *collective*, i.e., *parallel* and *distributed* over all the agents. This makes the resulting organization intrinsically *robust* and resistant to damage and perturbations.

As noted, the components or agents of a complex system initially interact only locally, i.e., with their immediate neighbors. The actions of remote agents are initially independent of each other: there is no correlation between the activity in one region and the activity in another one. However, because all components are directly or indirectly connected, changes propagate so that faraway regions eventually are influenced by what happens here and now. Because of the complex interplay of positive and negative feedbacks, this remote influence is very difficult to predict and may initially appear chaotic.

To explain the appearance of organization, we need to make one further assumption, namely that the outcome of interactions is not arbitrary, but exhibits a "preference" for certain situations over others. The principle is analogous to *natural selection*: certain configurations are intrinsically "fitter" than others, and therefore will be preferentially retained and/or multiplied during the

system's evolution. When the agents are goal-directed, the origin of this preference is obvious: an agent will prefer an outcome that brings it closer to its goals. For example, in a market, a firm will prefer the outcome that brings it more profit. In an ecosystem, an animal will prefer an outcome that brings it more food or that reduces its risk of being attacked by a predator. But even inanimate, physical objects, such as molecules or stones, have an inbuilt "preference," namely for the state that minimizes their potential energy. Thus, a stone "prefers" the stable state at the foot of a hill to an unstable state on the top. Here, "preference" simply means that the unstable state will sooner or later be abandoned, while the stable one will be retained.

Coevolution and Synergy

Given such a preference, it is clear why an individual agent tends to "organize" itself so as to settle down in its preferred situation. The problem is that what is best for one agent is in general not best for the other agents. For example, more profit for a firm generally means less profit for its competitors, and an animal safe from attack by a predator means a predator that goes hungry. However, interaction is in general not a *zero-sum game*: a gain by one party does not necessarily imply an equivalent loss by the other party. In most cases, an outcome is possible in which both parties to some degree gain. For example, a firm may increase its profits by developing a more efficient technology, which it then licenses to its competitors, so that they too become more productive. In that case, we may say that the interaction exhibits *synergy*: the outcome is positive for all parties; all involved agents "prefer" the outcome to the situation without the interaction.

In general, such a collective solution is still a compromise, in the sense that not all agents can maximally realize their preferences. Not all the stones can end up in the same, lowest, spot at the bottom of the hill, but they can all end up much lower than they were, by reducing the irregular hill to an even plain. Such a compromise reduces the tension or "conflict" between competing agents. (Such conflict would otherwise lead to instability as every action of the one, triggers a counteraction by the other). In that sense, we may say that the agents have *mutually adapted*; they have *coordinated* their actions so as to minimize friction and maximize synergy.

The achievement of this stable, synergetic state is in general a process of trial-and-error or variation-and-selection. Because agents are independent and interact locally, and because the dynamics of the system is unpredictable, they in general do not know what the effect of their actions on the other agents will be. They can only try out actions because they appear plausible, or even choose them at random, and note which ones bring them closer to their goals. Those actions can then be maintained or repeated, while the others are abandoned. This is the fundamental dynamics of natural selection. The main difference with traditional Darwinian evolution is that trial-and-error happens simultaneously on different sides: the agents *coevolve*, the one adapting to the other, until they mutually "fit."

From Local to Global Organization

To shift from local coordination to global organization, we just need to note that all interactions between all agents in the complex system will tend toward such a coherent, stable state, until they are all mutually adapted. This process generally accelerates because of a positive feedback. The reason is that if two or more agents have reached a mutually fit state, this defines a stable assembly to which other agents can now adapt, by trying to "fit" into the assembly as well. The larger the assembly, the more "niches" it has in which other agents can fit. The more agents join the assembly, the larger it becomes, and the more niches it provides for even more agents to join. Thus, the assembly may grow exponentially until it encompasses the global system.

This growth is typically faster when the agents are identical (e.g., molecules of the same substance) or similar (e.g., individuals from the same species), because the solution found by one agent will then suit the other agents as well, so that minimal further trial-and-error is needed once a good arrangement is locally found. This typically happens in processes of physical self-organization, such as crystallization, magnetization, or the emergence of coherent light in a laser.[5] When the agents are all different (e.g., species in an ecosystem), each in turn needs to explore in order to find its unique niche in an environment that continues to evolve, resulting in a much less explosive development.

In the case of identical agents, the global structure that emerges is typically uniform or regular, because the arrangement that is optimal for one agent is also the one optimal for the other agents. As a result, they all tend to settle into the same configuration. An example is a crystal, where all molecules are arranged at regular intervals and in the same orientation. In this case, self-organization produces a perfectly ordered pattern. In cases where the agents are diverse, like in an ecosystem or a market, the resulting structure is much more complex and unpredictable.

Global Dynamics

If we now consider the system as a whole—rather than the agents individually—we may note that the system too undergoes a process of variation. This can be seen as an exploration by the system of different regions of its state space, thus following an intricate trajectory. (The state space of the system is merely the Cartesian product of the state spaces of all its components).

Self-organization then means that the system reaches an *attractor*, i.e., a part of the state space that it can enter but not leave. In that sense, an attractor is a region "preferred" by the global dynamics: states surrounding the attractor (the attractor *basin*) are unstable and will eventually be left and replaced by states inside the attractor.

A nonlinear system has in general a multitude of attractors, each corresponding to a particular self-organized configuration. If the system starts out in a basin state, it will necessarily end up in the corresponding attractor, so that the long-term behavior can in principle be predicted (assuming we know what the attractor is, which is generally not the case). However, if it starts out in a state in between basins, it still has a "choice" about which basin and therefore which attractor it ends up in, and this will depend on unpredictable fluctuations. An attractor generally does not consist of a single state, but of a subspace of states in between which the system continues to move. The self-organized configuration, while more stable than the configuration before self-organization, is therefore in general not static but full of ongoing activity.

Self-organization can be accelerated by augmenting the initial variation that makes the system explore its state space: the more different states it visits, the sooner it will reach a state that belongs to an attractor. The simplest way to increase such variation is to subject the system to random perturbations, i.e., "noise." For example, if you shake a pot filled with beans, the beans will explore a variety of configurations, while tending to settle into the one that is most stable, i.e., where the beans are packed most densely near the bottom of the pot. Thus, shaking will normally reduce the volume taken in by the beans. This principle was called "order from noise" by the cyberneticist von Foerster[4] and "order through fluctuations" by the thermodynamicist Prigogine.[1]

Emergence

The pattern formed by the stabilized interactions, mutual "fittings," or "bonds" between the agents determines a purposeful or functional structure. Its function is to minimize friction between the agents, and thus maximize their collective "fitness," "preference," or "utility." Therefore, we may call the resulting pattern "organization": the agents are organized or coordinated in their actions so as to maximize their synergy.[5] However, such organization by definition imposes a *constraint* on the agents: they have lost the freedom to visit states outside the attractor, i.e., states with a lower fitness or higher friction. They have to obey new "rules," determining which actions are allowed, and which are not. They have lost some of their autonomy. The resulting mutual dependency has turned the collection of initially independent agents into an organization, i.e., a cohesive whole that is more than the sum of its parts. The goal of this "superagent" is to maximize overall synergy rather than individual utility. In a sense, the agents have turned from selfish individualists into conscientious cooperators. They have become subordinated (or "enslaved" in the terminology of Haken)[5] to the regulations of the collective.

This whole has *emergent* properties, i.e., properties that cannot be reduced to the properties of its parts. For example, a cell has the property of being alive, while the molecules that constitute it lack that property; gold has the properties of being shiny, malleable, and yellow, but these properties do not exist for individual gold atoms.[2] Rather than the parts individually, emergent properties characterize the pattern of interactions or relations between them. They typically include global or "holistic" aspects, such as robustness, synergy, coherence, symmetry, and function.

Different attractor regimes imply different properties for the system obeying that regime. For example, a circulating convection current may rotate clockwise or counterclockwise. Since it cannot be a priori predicted which attractor the system will end up in, the emergent properties of the whole cannot be derived from the properties of its parts alone. Once the attractor regime has stabilized, the behavior of the parts is rather regulated or constrained by the properties of the higher-level whole. This is called *downward causation*. For example, the correspondence between DNA triplets and amino acids in the genetic code is not determined by the chemical properties of the molecules that constitute DNA, but by evolutionary history producing a particular mechanism for "reading" DNA triplets in living cells. A random variation of that history might well have produced a different mechanism and therefore a different code. The languages that different people speak are not determined by the neurophysiology of their brain, but by the self-organization of shared lexicons and grammatical rules within a community of communicating individuals.

While the self-organized whole is intrinsically stable, it is still flexible enough to cope with outside perturbations. These perturbations may push the system out of its attractor, but as long as the deviation is not too large, the system will automatically return to the same attractor. In the worst case, the system is pushed into a different basin but that will merely make it end up in a different attractor. In that sense, a self-organizing system is intrinsically *adaptive*: it maintains its basic organization in spite of continuing changes in its environment. As noted, perturbations may even make the system more robust, by helping it to discover a more stable organization.

COMPLEX NETWORKS

The structure emerging from self-organization can often be represented as a network. Initially, agents interact more or less randomly with whatever other agents happen to pass in their neighborhood. Because of natural selection, however, some of these interactions will be preferentially retained, because they are synergetic. Such a preferentially stabilized interaction may be called a bond, relationship, or *link*. A link couples or connects two agents, in the sense that linked agents preferentially interact with each other. The different links turn the assembly of agents into a *network*. Within the network, the agents can now be seen as *nodes* where different links come together. Perhaps the most intuitive example is a social network, which links people on the basis of friendship, trust, or collaboration. Other well-known examples are the Internet, which connects computers via communication links, and the Web, which connects documents via hyperlinks. A more abstract example is the biochemical network that connects the molecules that react with each other within a cell in order to produce further molecules.

It is easy to define an abstract mathematical network. You just need a set N consisting of nodes n_i, and then select any subset L of links from the set of all possible connections between two nodes:

$$L = \{(n_i, n_j)\} \subset N \times N$$

However, complexity researchers have observed that "natural" (i.e., self-organized rather than artificially designed) or "complex" networks tend to exhibit a number of specific features: they are *scale-free, small-world*, and *clustering*. These features are defined statistically: certain configurations of links appear with a much higher probability than chance. We will try to explain these particular link distributions from the dynamics of self-organization of a network.

Random Networks

Let us assume that we start with a collection N of independent agents (future nodes of the network) that initially interact randomly, thus creating random links. This produces a *random network*, i.e., a network where the links have been selected by chance from the set $N \times N$ of all possible connections. Random networks have been extensively studied in mathematics. They exhibit the phenomenon of *percolation*: when links between randomly chosen nodes are added one by one, larger and larger subsets of N become connected into cohesive subnetworks. When more links are added, subnetworks will become connected to each other, defining a larger connected subset. When a certain threshold is passed, all subsets become connected so that there is now just a single connected network. It is said that the network *percolates*: imagine the links as tubes and a liquid being injected into one of the nodes; when the network percolates, the liquid will spread throughout the whole system, because any node is now directly or indirectly connected to any other node by an uninterrupted path or chain of links. Whatever happens in one node of the network can now in principle propagate to every other node in the network.

Small-World Networks

The maximum length of the shortest path connecting two nodes in a connected network is called the *diameter* of the network. If the diameter is small relative to the number of nodes, the network is said to be a *small-world network*. The notion derives from the "it's a small world" phenomenon in social networks: two people encountering each other will often find that they have one or more acquaintances in common. Studies of social networks have indicated that it is in general possible to find a short sequence of friend-of-a-friend links connecting two people. It has been estimated that on the scale of the world as a whole, two randomly chosen individuals are unlikely to be more than six such links removed from each other ("six degrees of separation").

Whereas random networks have the small-world property, the opposite applies to regular networks. An example of such a network is a two-dimensional lattice or grid, where each node is connected to its four direct neighbors (left-right-up-down), each of which is connected to its four neighbors, and so on. In a square grid of $100,000 \times 100,000 = 10$ billion nodes, the nodes at the opposite ends of a diagonal are 200,000 links apart. This is the diameter of the network. Compare this to the distance of a mere six links that apparently characterizes the world social network with its nearly 10 billion nodes! Regular networks, where nodes are linked according to strict, repetitive rules rather than random connections, are typically large-world networks. This means that a change in one node will normally take a very long time to propagate to the rest of the network. As a result, the network will be slow to react to perturbations or innovations.

We may conclude that complex networks are not regular. But they are not random either: their linking patterns do obey certain regularities, albeit not strictly. In fact, it has been shown that a regular network can easily be turned into a small-world network by adding a small number of randomly chosen links to the otherwise strictly constrained links.[7] These random links by definition do not care about the "distances" within the regular grid: e.g., they may directly connect nodes that

are otherwise 100,000 links apart. Such random links create "wormholes" or "shortcuts" between otherwise remote regions, thus bringing them suddenly within easy reach. As a result, a small number of random links added to a regular network spectacularly decreases the shortest path length between nodes.

Clustering

One of the nonrandom features that characterize complex networks is *clustering*. Clustering means that when A is linked to B, and B to C, then the probability is high (or at least much higher than could be expected in a random network) that A is also linked to C. In other words, two randomly chosen connections of B have a much higher than chance probability of being connected themselves.

The origin of this can best be explained by considering social networks. Here, the clustering property can be formulated as "the friends of my friends are (likely to be) my friends." In other words, friends tend to form a cluster or community in which everyone knows everyone. The reason is simple: when you regularly encounter your friends, you are likely to encounter their friends as well. More generally, if an agent A frequently interacts with an agent B, and B interacts with C, then the probability is high that A will sooner or later interact with C as well. If A and B have some similarity in aims that helps them to find synergy, and the same applies to B and C, then A and C are likely to discover a synergetic relationship as well.

Scale-Free Networks

A less intuitive feature of complex networks is that their distribution of links tends to follow a *power law*:[8] there are many nodes with few links, and few nodes with many links. More precisely, the number of nodes N with a given degree (i.e., number of links) K is proportional to a (negative) power of that degree:

$$N(K) \sim K^{-a}$$

(The values of the exponent a tend to vary between 1 and 3). A network that obeys a power law is called *scale-free*. When $a = 1$, N is inversely proportional to K: in other words, as the number of links goes up, the number of nodes with that number of links goes down proportionally.

This property has been established empirically, by counting the number of links in various networks, such as the Web or social networks. It turns out that a few nodes have an inordinate amount of links. They function as the *hubs* of the network, the central "cross-roads" where many different connections come together. The most common nodes, on the other hand, have just a few links. This means that nodes are strongly differentiated:

Communication–
Cybernetics

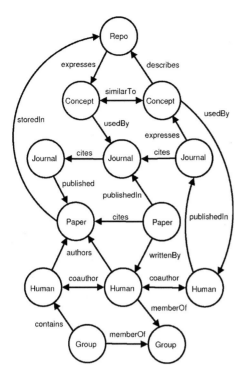

Fig. 1 A heterogeneous knowledge network, containing authors, concepts, and documents.

something that happens to a hub will have a disproportionately large influence on the rest of the network, while something that happens to an ordinary node may have little or no consequences. This has great practical implications: an innovation or perturbation that appears in a hub (e.g., a central network server, a high-visibility Web page, or a person who is known by many) may change the whole network in a short time, because it is immediately propagated far and wide. By identifying the hubs in a network, it becomes easier to manipulate its dynamics, for good or for bad. Obvious applications are the spread of computer viruses, contagious diseases, new ideas, or fashions.

Whereas clustering tends to increase distances in a network, by creating locally connected clusters that have few links outside the cluster, the presence of hubs has the opposite effect. Because hubs have a very large number of links they are likely to link into many different clusters, thus acting as shortcuts that reduce the distance between the clusters. But this also means that removing a hub may break the connections between otherwise remote regions of the network. This is a danger especially in communication networks such as the Internet, where the failure of a small number of hubs may split up the network into separate "islands" that no longer communicate with each other. Similar dangers exist in ecosystems where the disappearance of one or more key species—i.e., "hubs" on which many other species depend—may lead to a complete breakdown of the system.

Barabasi and Albert[8] have proposed a theoretical explanation for power-law distributions based on the mechanism of *preferential attachment*: new nodes joining the network preferentially establish links with nodes that already have a large number of links. They have shown that when the probability of linking to a node is exactly proportional to the number of links of that node, the resulting network obeys a power law with $a = 3$.

For a more general scenario for the self-organization of a complex network, consider a collection of agents that initially only interact locally with those that happen to pass in their neighborhood. Some of these interactions will be stabilized into enduring links. Once they have some links, the locality principle entails that agents are more likely to forge links with the "friends of their friends" than with randomly chosen others, thus promoting clustering. But agents that already have a high number of links also have many "friends of friends" (i.e., nodes two links away) and therefore they will be more likely to develop additional links within this two-step neighborhood or cluster. The more links an agent has, the larger its neighborhood, and therefore the larger the probability that it will receive even more links from within this neighborhood. Similarly, the larger the cluster, the more likely it is to receive random links from outside, thus extending the neighborhood outwards and linking it into other clusters. This determines a positive feedback, which leads to an explosive growth in the number of links. The agents that happen to be in the center of such a quickly growing cluster will become the hubs of the network.

APPLICATION TO KNOWLEDGE NETWORKS

Having reviewed key concepts typifying complex, self-organizing systems, and networks, we will sketch some possible applications of these ideas in the area of information science. Information science focuses on the knowledge that is available in the documents that are available in libraries and databases across the world. These documents are typically produced by authors or researchers who investigate a domain, building further on the results of other authors, and publishing their results in new papers or books that refer to these used sources. This knowledge producing system can be viewed as a very complex network, formed by the researchers, the concepts they use and the publications they produce. All the "nodes" of the network are linked directly or indirectly, by relations such as citation, collaboration, or information exchange. This complex system is intrinsically self-organizing: no individual or organization is in charge, or can decide in which direction knowledge should develop. Novel, globally available knowledge emerges out of the spontaneous, local interactions between the individual agents.

By applying the concepts and methods from the domain of complexity, we may hope to better understand the development and structure of this network. We can view it as a complex, adaptive system that generates new patterns (knowledge) through the complex, nonlinear interactions between multitudes of autonomous agents (individual scientists and organizations). This system has the structure of a heterogeneous network (Fig. 1), consisting of three basic types of nodes:[13] agents, i.e., the individuals or organizations who actively process and produce knowledge, containers, i.e., the documents, databases, or journals in which the produced knowledge is stored and made available to other agents, and concepts, i.e., the abstract elements of knowledge itself, which are typically represented as keywords.

There already exists some preliminary work on subnetworks of this encompassing network, such as collaboration networks between authors[14] or citation networks between documents. This research has found that they possess typical features of complex networks, such as being scale-free and small-world. For example, citation networks typically contain a small number of hubs ("citation classics") with very many links, while most publications only gather a few citations. Some of the most successful methods for information retrieval, such as the PageRank algorithm underlying the Google search engine, or the HITS method developed by Kleinberg,[15] implicitly use this network structure to identify the "hubs" of a hypertext network.

More interesting even than the static analysis of existing networks is the modeling of their evolution. We may assume that an information network will self-organize through the propagation of information between nodes across links, creating new links and nodes in the process. For example, assume that information is transferred from paper A to researcher B. After reading the paper, B may decide to get some more information linked to paper A, e.g., by contacting A's author, or reading some of A's references. These in turn may refer B to other authors or papers relevant for B's interests, and so on. Some of these additional sources may turn out to be particularly important for B's research, inspiring B to develop a new concept, published in the form of one or more papers. This process will create links (e.g., B may start collaborating with another author, or refer in new papers to papers discovered in this way) and nodes (e.g., new papers, new concepts, and new journals). Such links and nodes will tend to cluster around a small number of "hubs"—thus defining a new "community" of related authors, documents, and ideas.

The emergence of a new scientific domain is a good example of the self-organization of such a community of knowledge,[16] where people from initially diverse backgrounds find each other around a common interest, which gradually coalesces into a new paradigm. This process could be observed by mapping the network of authors, publications, and keywords in a particular domain at regular intervals (e.g., every 2–5 years), and analyzing it in terms of clustering, hubs, average distances, etc. The change of these features over time may show processes of self-organization taking place. A good theory of the self-organization of knowledge communities would propose a number of processes and parameters that allow us to predict where, when, and how such self-organization is most likely to take place. Such a theory would help us to find not only the presently most authoritative concepts, publications, or authors (hubs), but those that are likely to become so in the future. This would provide a very powerful instrument to uncover emerging trends and to direct attention and investment toward the most promising people, ideas, and information sources.

CONCLUSION

The science studying complex, self-organizing systems, and networks is still in its infancy. Yet, it already provides us with a powerful new perspective and a number of promising conceptual and modeling tools for understanding the complex phenomena that surround us, including organisms, the Internet, ecosystems, markets, and communities.

On the one hand, the complexity perspective reminds us to be modest in our aims: many phenomena in nature and society are simply too complex to be analyzed in the traditional scientific manner. Openness and nonlinearity make a complex system in principle unpredictable and uncontrollable: the tiniest internal or external perturbations can be amplified into global changes. Therefore, we will never be able to capture it in a complete and deterministic model. Still, agent-based computer simulations can help us to get an insight into the qualitative dynamics of the system, and to classify and delimit the likely scenarios for its further evolution.

On the other hand, the complexity perspective gives us new reasons for optimism: while we cannot truly control a complex system, it tends to self-organize to a state where it regulates itself. This state tends to increase the utility or fitness of the system's active components or agents, by coordinating their interactions so as to maximize synergy. The resulting organization is distributed over all the agents and their interactions, and thus much more robust and flexible than any centralized design. Moreover, it determines a number of emergent, global properties that cannot be reduced to the properties of the individual components. By understanding the underlying mechanisms, we may be able to facilitate and stimulate such self-organization, or to drive it in one direction rather than another.

One application of the complexity perspective is the analysis of complex networks, such as the World Wide Web, and the nonlinear processes that generate them. This has led to the identification of common statistical features of such networks: small-world, clustering, and scale-free link distributions. These notions promise a wealth of applications in the analysis of information networks, potentially helping us with the organization, management, retrieval, and discovery of relevant knowledge within masses of ill-structured and continuously changing data.

REFERENCES

1. Prigogine, I.; Stengers, I. *Order Out of Chaos;* Bantam Books: New York, NY, 1984.
2. Gershenson, C.; Heylighen, F. How can we think the complex? *Managing the Complex* Vol. 1: *Philosophy, Theory and Application*; Richardson, K., Ed.; Institute for the Study of Coherence and Emergence/Information Age Publishing: Charlotte, NC, 2005; 47–62.
3. Ashby, W.R. Principles of the self-organizing system. In *Principles of Self-organization*; von Foerster, H., Zopf, G. W., Jr., Eds.; Pergamon Press: New York, 1962; 255–278.
4. von Foerster, H. On self-organising systems and their environments. *In Self-Organising Systems*; Yovits, M. C., Cameron, S., Eds.; Pergamon Press: London, 1960; 30–50.
5. Haken, H. *Information and Self-Organization: A Macroscopic Approach to Complex Systems*; Springer-Verlag: New York, 2000.
6. Waldrop, M.M. *Complexity: The Emerging Science at the Edge of Order and Chaos*; Viking: London, 1992.
7. Watts, D.J.; Strogatz, S.H. Collective dynamics of small-world networks. Nature **1998**, *393*, 440–442.
8. Albert, R.; Barabasi, A.-L. Statistical mechanics of complex networks. Rev. Modern Phys. **2002**, *74*, 47–97.
9. Edmonds, B. What is complexity? The philosophy of complexity per se with application to some examples in evolution. In *The Evolution of Complexity*; Heylighen, F., Bollen, J., Riegler, A., Eds.; Kluwer: Dordrecht, 1999; 1–18.
10. Holland, J.H. Studying complex adaptive systems. J. Syst. Sci. Complex. **2006**, *19* (1), 1–8.
11. Levin, S.A. Complex adaptive systems: Exploring the known, the unknown and the unknowable. Bull. Am. Math. Soc. **2002**, *40* (1), 3–19.
12. Louzoun, Y.; Solomon, S.; Atlan, H.; Cohen, I.R. Modeling complexity in biology. Physica A: Statistical Mechanics and its Applications **2001**, *297* (1–2), 242–252.
13. Rodriguez, M.A. A multi-relational network to support the scholarly communication process. Int. J. Public Inform. Syst. **2007**, *1*, 13–29.
14. Newman, M. The structure of scientific collaboration networks. Proc. Natl. Acad. Sci. USA **2001**, *98*, 404–409.
15. Kleinberg, J. Authoritative sources in a hyperlinked environment. J. ACM **1999**, *46* (5), 604–632.
16. Wagner, C.S.; Leydesdorff, L. Network structure, self-organization, and the growth of international collaboration in science. Res. Policy **2005**, *34* (10), 1608–1618.

BIBLIOGRAPHY

1. Axelrod, R.; Cohen, M.D. *Harnessing Complexity: Organizational Implications of a Scientific Frontier;* Simon and Schuster: New York, NY, 2000.
2. Bar-Yam, Y. *Dynamics of Complex Systems*; Westview Press: Boulder, CO, 2003. http://necsi.org/publications/dcs.
3. Haken, H. *Information and Self-Organization: A Macroscopic Approach to Complex Systems*; Springer-Verlag: New York, NY, 2000.
4. Heylighen, F. The science of self-organization and adaptivity. In *Knowledge Management, Organizational Intelligence and Learning, and Complexity*; Kiel, L. D., Ed.; Eolss Publishers: Oxford, 2002. http://www.eolss.net. In: The Encyclopedia of Life Support Systems (EOLSS).
5. Holland, J.H. *Hidden Order: How Adaptation Builds Complexity*; Addison-Wesley: Reading, MA, 1996.
6. Kelly, K. *Out of Control*; Addison-Wesley: New York, NY, 1994.
7. Miller, J.H.; Page, S.E. *Complex Adaptive Systems: An Introduction to Computational Models of Social Life;* Princeton University Press: Princeton, NJ, 2007.
8. Newman, M.E.J. The structure and function of complex networks. SIAM Rev. **2003**, *45*, 167–256 http://arxiv.org/abs/cond-mat/0303516
9. Prigogine, I.; Stengers, I. *Order Out of Chaos;* Bantam Books: New York, NY, 1984.
10. Waldrop, M.M. *Complexity: The Emerging Science at the Edge of Order and Chaos*; Viking: London, 1992.

Communication–Cybernetics

Configuration Management

Leighton Johnson III
Chief Operating Officer and Senior Consultant, Information Security and Forensics Management Team (ISFMT), Bath, South Carolina, U.S.A.

Abstract
Configuration management (CM) is the process of managing and/or controlling changes made to hardware, software, firmware, and documentation of an information system, throughout the development and operational life of a system. In addition, source code management and version control are also part of CM. Since CM involves the entire realm of components and parts of any system, it is an integral part of the total system development life cycle for the system.

INTRODUCTION

Operating systems and other software applications had not been developed with security in mind. Software was developed with a focus on functionality and, in many cases, security-restricted functionality. However, as a result of damaging viruses or malware, and possible liability issues, software vendors, developers, and companies focus on incorporating security into their products.

Despite the efforts of the software vendors and developers to integrate security into their products, operating systems are typically installed with default configurations that may still be insecure. Additional efforts must be taken to disable unnecessary services and to enable security features of the necessary services. Safeguards must be incorporated to protect information systems and the confidentiality, integrity, and availability of the information system's data, information, and repositories that are operating on a network because systems are still susceptible to attack and/or compromise via well-known vulnerabilities and exploits.

System administrators utilize configuration management (CM) standards when designing access systems for users in order to mitigate risk in the organization's information technology (IT) infrastructure. Procedures and standards are usually developed by the software vendors, government agencies, and academic organizations for CM activities, actions, and events.

The benefits of an organization developing and implementing CM standards include, but are not limited to

- Decreasing the number of vulnerabilities and threats;
- Reducing the time required to research and develop appropriate security configurations for IT products;
- Reducing the amount of time and effort to service computer problems;
- Allowing smaller organizations and individuals that have limited resources to leverage outside resources to implement recommended best practice security configurations; and
- Preventing public loss of confidence or embarrassment due to compromised systems.

The CM process objectives are to

1. Define and establish structured methods and procedures to manage IT system changes once a baseline has been established;
2. Identify internal and external organizations, and define organizational roles and responsibilities relevant to the IT system CM process;
3. Define and establish organizational interfaces and information flow across interfaces to facilitate CM; and
4. Establish a configuration control board (CCB) to oversee and manage the CM process.

There are four basic stages to any CM process:

1. *Configuration identification*—Identifying and documenting the functional and physical characteristics of each configuration item (CI)
2. *Configuration change control*—Also known as change management—controlling changes to the CIs and issue versions of CIs
3. *Configuration status reporting and accounting*—Recording the processing of changes
4. *Configuration verification*—Also known as CM auditing—controlling the quality of CM procedures

CONFIGURATION IDENTIFICATION

Configuration identification is the process of defining and documenting the technical description of system components under CM control throughout the system's life cycle. Baseline design documents identify the

Encyclopedia of Information Systems and Technology, DOI: 10.1081/E-EIST-120045061

Communication–Cybernetics

Table 1 Configuration items that require management

Item	Type of change
Operating system configuration	Any change
Application configuration	Any change
Database configuration	Any change
Hardware	• Network devices • System • Peripherals ○ Replacing orders when new hardware is introduced
Network configuration	• Firewall • Router • Port (teaming, security) • Topology • Adding, updating, removing equipment or devices
Facilities management	The physical configuration of the data center, processing center, and network closet rooms • Power • Layout • Cooling system • Cabling, etc.

functional, physical, and performance characteristics of the IT system's CIs, and approved changes to the baseline constitute the configuration identification.

Configuration identification applies technical and administrative direction and surveillance that encompasses the following:

- Identify and document functional and physical characteristics of all CIs.
- Control all changes to CIs that constitute the baseline.
- Record and report on the status of all changes.

The CM process owner receives and evaluates change requests (CRs) from various input providers, establishes a disposition for the request (e.g., engineering change proposals (ECPs) or CRs), and records and reports on the status of all CRs and proposals. The CM process owner then provides inputs to the CCB that will be derived from the community of organizations that are responsible for life cycle management. Therefore, several items are required to produce the reports necessary to ensure that this management oversight is properly conducted.

Documentation

The IT system baseline configuration documents the functional, physical, and performance characteristics/features/behavior of the IT system CIs. In addition, over time, the baseline design will be modified to support new features, new software revisions, and new hardware as dictated and predicated by the CM process. Establishing the baseline configuration is a key input to CM implementation and control. A baseline configuration identifies a set of CIs, and associated attributes. Once the baseline is established, the appropriate documentation for each CI is placed under formal CM control. This baseline can be derived from multiple sources of data about the system such as

- The original purchase request and specifications of the system,
- The existing insurance/replacement identification data on the system,
- The business continuity/disaster recovery plan with its system inventories components, and
- Software vendors' automated baseline tools reports and outputs.

Configuration Items

A CI is an aggregation of hardware and software that satisfies an end user function and is designated for separate CM. CI identification will be used to establish and maintain a definitive base for control and status accounting of a CI throughout its life cycle. Table 1 reflects the standard CIs that are subject to CM control and oversight.

Inventory Management

The system hardware and software assets are purchased through various procurement channels. Details of design, orders, order status, order deliveries, quantities, serial numbers, and part numbers are captured during all phases of the procurement process. The purchase orders are reconciled against deliveries and equipment details in a centralized database.

A CM administrator is tasked with maintaining detailed information associated with the baseline design and site-specific designs, such as equipment or component location, rack location if mounted, etc. Table 2 outlines the details that are required to be captured, tracked, and audited. A configuration management database (CMDB) tool supports the automation of this task. A CMDB often contains data about managed resources like computer systems and application software, process artifacts like incident and change records, and relationships among them. The contents of the CMDB should

Communication–
Cybernetics

Table 2 CMDB fields

Field	Description
Configuration item name	Item name
Asset tag number	CI number
Asset owner	Who owns the CI
Manufacturer	Who created the item
Type	Kind of item
Serial number	CI serial number
Version number	CI version number, if necessary
Build number	Software build number, if necessary
Build/procurement date	When build/item was created or bought
Cost	Cost of item or build development
Location	Where is CI located
Environment data	External environmental data
Update type	Type of last CI updated
Update number	The change approval number
Update date	When was CI last updated
Change implementer	Who put the change/update in
Verified by	Who audited update

be managed by a CM process and serve as the foundation for other IT management processes, such as change management. Typical CMDB entry fields are listed in Table 2.

With the advent of ITIL® as a standard for IT service support and management, ITIL-based CMDBs are emerging as a prominent technology support tool for enterprise management solutions, services, and software.

Roles and Responsibilities

System owner

The core services and functions directly provided by the system owner are the overall CM of the IT system; allocation of funding resources; engineering, procurement management, and logistics support associated with the initial design and development; and configuration changes over the IT system life cycle.

Change control coordinator

The primary purpose of the change control coordinator (CCC) is to provide change control guidance to users, change initiators, and change implementers as well as to provide inputs and directions for CCB members and staff.

Change initiator

Change initiator is the initiator of the requested change or alteration to the CI.

Change implementer

Change implementer is the staff member or team that implements the suggested change to the CI.

Configuration control board

The CCB is the primary management organization responsible for ensuring that all CIs are maintained, changed, updated, or upgraded in an efficient and secure manner as to not allow inadvertent system failures due to improper changes to CIs.

System Requirements

Configuration architecture standards

CM requires a controlled and consistent IT architecture to be based on, as well as controlled and monitored changes to system architecture. The U.S. Government Federal Enterprise Architecture (FEA)[1] initiative provides one such standard, developed by the U.S. Office of Management and Budget and the Office of E-Government (E-Gov) and IT, the FEA Consolidated Reference Model—version 2.3, October 2007. Another standard used is the U.S. DOD Architecture Framework (DODAF),[2] DODAF Architecture Framework—version 1.5, April 23, 2007. The IT system under CM needs this controlled architecture to ensure the continued viability of each and every change as it is evaluated, implemented, tested, and approved. These architectures can be locally generated and controlled, formally created and controlled from an external third-party governance organization, or nationally or internationally mandated.

Automated mechanisms

Automated mechanisms should be employed within the CM framework for a few reasons such as

- To enforce access restrictions of the change agents (developers, installers, etc.) and
- To support auditing of the CM enforcement actions.

The CMDB provides this automated process and tools that minimize human error, increase data integrity, and decrease turnaround time for process execution. The CMDB tracks the CM of the baseline hardware, software, and configuration files. The CMDB also documents and tracks the status of CRs and ECPs. For security reasons, any changes that the fielded site configuration files to accommodate operational missions will not be stored by the CM tools.

CONFIGURATION CHANGE CONTROL

An effective configuration control is vital to baseline control, change management, and the program success. Configuration control justifies, evaluates, and coordinates the disposition of any proposed change. The implementation of all approved ECPs or CRs is managed through the CM change control process that identifies changes for a particular CI in the established or approved configuration baseline. A brief explanation of CM change control is provided here.

Change Initiation

Changes requested in the system are usually accomplished by one of the several means:

- Contacting the local IT helpdesk
- Submitting a CR form
- Submitting an ECP

Change Classes

Class criteria are defined to achieve desired visibility and change control. There are two major classes of changes that fall under CM. Class 1 changes affect the high-level CI design. All other changes are classified as Class 2.

Class 1

A Class 1 change is defined as any change that may affect

- The cost, schedule, and function of the CI over defined values;
- The interface compatibility between separate CIs; and
- A completed and tested CI after the baseline is established.

The CCB analyzes all Class 1 changes before implementation.

Class 2

A Class 2 change is any change that does not meet the Class 1 change criteria. Class 2 changes still do require CCB approval; however, this type of change is usually regarded as routine and would include activities such as printer installations, new desktop or workstation installations, etc.

Change Priority

All changes will be assigned a priority by the CCB chairperson. This priority level will assist in determining the level of effort and urgency needed to develop and field a change. Priority levels typically are routine or emergency.

Routine change

Routine changes have no immediate impact on the operation of the IT system and do not pose a safety concern for either the equipment or the personnel. An example

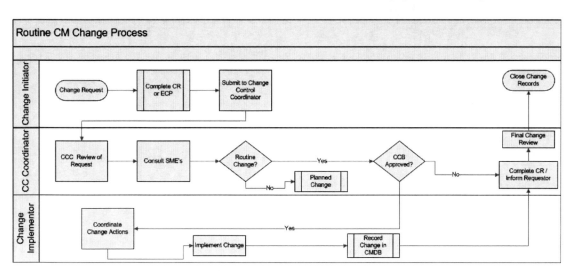

Fig. 1 Routine CM change process model.

of a routine priority is any change with minimal cost, performance, or schedule impact, such as a new printer installation on an existing network.

Emergency change

An ECP or CR will be given an emergency priority if it poses a situation that would render the equipment inoperable and unable to perform a mission or presents a safety hazard to personnel or equipment. An example of an emergency priority change is a replacement of a power circuit breaker center.

Fig. 1, routine CM change process, illustrates the steps to ensure that the appropriate level of attention is given to standard CM change procedures.

Step 1—Process initial change request

The change initiator drafts and then sends in, through the normal submittal methodology, the requested change to the system.

Step 2—Consult with subject matter experts

The CCC will consult with or be consulted by subject matter experts (SMEs) to determine the necessity of the changed request and ascertain any adverse implications of the request.

Step 3—CCC approval

The CCC will either approve or disapprove the CR/ECP. If disapproved, the CR/ECP will revert to the planned change process for further action, review, and planning. If there are no outside effects, then the CCC forwards the change item to the change control board for review and approval.

Step 4—Change control board approval

The change control board will either approve or disapprove the request for change (RFC). If disapproved, the CCB will cite the reasons for the disapproval and forward that decision to the change initiator and to senior management. If approved, the CCB will forward the change item to the installation/development organization for implementation once the update has been vetted.

Step 5—Configure/develop, test, accept

The SMEs/technical team, after receiving the approval from the CCB, will determine the technical inputs/requirements for updating the requested change. The SMEs/technical team members will develop the configuration/development initiative and prepare the initial change in the development environment. After determining that the update has passed the initial test cycle, the SMEs/technical team member will move the updated module to the user acceptance test environment where end users will have an opportunity to review/test and accept the change. On acceptance of the change from the end user, the SMEs/technical representatives will notify the CCB and the CCC to have the approved module moved into the quality assurance (QA) environment for security-based scan testing. This step will also provide the SMEs/technical representatives to fully regression test the module change in an environment that closely mimics the production environment to determine that there is no impact on the system. After successfully passing the QA test, the CCC prepares the module for release installation in the system's configuration update cycle.

Step 6—Record change

Once the requested change has been implemented, the CCC will update the status of the change in the CCC's CMDB tool.

Step 7—Close RFC

On completion of all change actions and documentation, the CCC will update the status of the change to completed and close the activity.

Configuration Control Board

The IT system CCB is a body of stakeholders who have vested interest in planning, designing, deploying, using, operating, maintaining, monitoring, and securing the functionalities or capabilities of the IT system. The CCB shall be governed and operated under a defined charter that is agreed to and accepted by all stakeholders.

CCB membership

IT system agency/unit/department senior executive will chair and conduct the business of the IT system CCB. The CCB is envisioned to be composed of representatives from the various cognizant units, departments, or organizations as defined. The membership is divided into voting and nonvoting categories:

1. Voting members are defined as usually the actual user organizations for the IT system.
2. Nonvoting members are defined as usually the IT support and other support staff for the organization.

This does not preclude nonvoting members from participating in CCB meetings, providing input, and expressing their views and analysis for consideration. Depending on the nature of an ECP/CR, a nonvoting member may be declared a voting member.

CCB charter

The CCB conducts/provides the following:

- Coordinate and conduct CCB meetings.
- Maintain the CM process.
- Classify CR type based on inputs and impact to the IT system mission.
- Review and determine disposition of CR/ECPs relative to resources available, severity priority, security threat/vulnerability, and type.
- Assign required resources for functional impact assessment (analysis, test, logistics, etc.).
- CR/ECP status review.
- CR/ECP analysis and test review.
- Implementation decision (yes/no).
- Request additional information from CR/ECP originator(s).
- Provide feedback to CR/ECP originator(s).
- Interface to external organizations.
- Project-manage CR/ECP life cycle (timelines, milestones, secure funding, coordination, etc.).
- Recommend configuration improvements, development, and test.
- Recommend/commission site configuration audits.
- Guidance and leadership to implement changes to the sites.
- Assist system owners plan future changes for the IT system.
- Interface to external user organizations, if necessary.
- Cooperation in technical investigations as required/requested from user/field staff.

CONFIGURATION STATUS REPORTING AND ACCOUNTING

Changes to an established baseline require in-depth analysis, evaluation, and detailed implementation reporting to ensure that the proper areas, software, hardware, and interfaces to other systems are all reviewed correctly, changed properly, all implementations are tested as well as vetted, and all appropriate baseline configuration documentation are actually and precisely updated during the CM process.

Typical areas that require this reporting and accounting include the following:

1. When CR/ECPs are submitted via the CM tool and distributed to the CCB by the CM administrator for preliminary review.
2. The reviews and evaluations by the IT support staff and the SMEs.
3. The CCB determinations, votes, and supporting documentation of the CR/ECP type and priority based on review.
4. If the board determines that further information is required, the originator is tasked with creating the additional informational documents and providing these to the CCB.
5. If the CR/ECP impacts other systems, then a liaison with appropriate organizations is scheduled to engage a broader audience (e.g., outside users, etc.) for discussion, analysis, and disposition with all meeting minutes, notes, and status reports providing inputs to this reporting activity.
6. Functional area staff members create and develop evaluations and propose fixes/resolution to address the CR/ECP. The evaluations and proposed solutions are documented and placed into the CM reporting mechanisms. These analyses and evaluations may require additional laboratory tests, technical feasibility assessments, and SME evaluations based upon the classification, priority, and extent of the proposed change.
7. CR/ECPs may be generated outside of the authority of the IT system CCB and introduced to the CCB for impact assessment. The CCB will review the CR/ECP and task functional areas within the CCB to assess the impact of the proposed solution(s) and provide a suspense date for the impact assessment. This may include one or all of the following evaluations: lab testing, engineering analysis, logistics, cost, schedule, etc.
8. Document the CCB "go/no go" decision on implementation.
9. The CR/ECP project team will develop, document, and execute an implementation plan and provide feedback to the change initiator. This plan and all supporting documentation is part of this CM stage.
10. The CCB will document the rationale for a "not to implement" decision and provide it to the change initiator.
11. Project team(s) provides status updates and raise issues that require CCB action.
12. CCC updates the CMDB with any changes that impact the baseline or site-specific configuration. This will include all relevant system documentation.

Modification Tracking

A historical record will be generated and maintained by the CM administrator using a CMDB for CR/ECPs.

Communication–Cybernetics

CRs/ECPs will be tracked and recorded with the following draft list of information:

1. Type of CR/ECP
2. CR/ECP number
3. Request title
4. Configurations affected
5. Final CCB decision and date
6. CI component identification
7. Number and location of the existing CI components affected by change
8. Technical POC information

For each CI component delivered to the organization/unit/department, the as-built history will be maintained (CMDB) with the information reflecting the retroactive installation (technology refresh) of newly designed components or modification history of existing baseline components.

CONFIGURATION VERIFICATION

The purpose and benefits of configuration verification and CM audits include the following:

- Ensure that the product design provides the agreed-to performance capabilities.
- Validate the integrity of the configuration definition documentation.
- Verify the consistency between a product and its configuration definition documentation.
- Ensure a known configuration as the basis for operation and maintenance instructions, training, spare and repair parts, etc.
- To confirm that adequate CM processes are in place to provide continuing control of established configurations at all phases of the system life cycle.

The historical record, maintained by the CM administrator, for CR/ECPs will be tracked and recorded. For each CI component delivered to the organization/unit/department, the as-built history will be maintained (CM tool) with information reflecting the retroactive installation (technology refresh) of newly designed components, or modification history of exiting baseline components.

Preparation and Conducting CM Verification and Audit

There are two widely used CM verification and audit processes: functional configuration audit (FCA) and physical configuration audit (PCA). Both audits will usually be conducted concurrently for each location with inventory of all major equipment as well as software and hardware

versions being recorded along with serial numbers for all of the equipment. For an FCA, SMEs are assigned based on the CIs to be reviewed. This also requires the technical documentation given in the following list; the operational requirements for training, logistics, safety, locations, and deployability; human factors involved in system; and governing statutory and regulatory standards. For the PCA, SMEs are assigned based on engineering, design, development activities, release criteria, manufacturing activities (if necessary), QA needs, and acceptance testing standards. Any shortages determined at the time of audit will be recorded and provided to the configuration management organization. The configuration installed will be documented in the CMDB for each location.

In the process of preparing for and conducting a configuration verification and audit, some of the documents necessary for review to ensure proper CM include

- Corporate acquisition strategy guidance
- Detailed system design documents such as
  - Functional requirements specifications
  - Software requirements specifications
  - Security requirements specifications
  - Operational requirements specifications
  - Use-case specifications

- Security certification and accreditation documents
- System approval forms—signed
- Contractual statements of work—if CI is externally created
- Facilities support documents, such as fire escape routes, if CI is facilities based
- CM plan
- Business continuity plan
- Contingency plan
- Disaster recovery plan
- Security oversight plan, if necessary
- Testing plan and results
- Drawings and equipment specifications
- CR/ECP documentation
- CMDB
- System interconnect/interface specifications
- System baseline documents

Detailed specifications for these types of audits are included in the available industry standards for Capability Maturity Model Integration and ISO 9000:2000, among others.

Expected CM audit topics will include

- Organization
  - Structure
  - Interfaces
  - Policies, plans, and procedures
- CI items

- o Documentation
- o Drawings
- o Libraries, repositories, and releases
- o Specifications
- o Standards and guidelines
- Configuration change control documentation
  - o CR/ECP process
  - o Evaluation of changes
  - o Approving changes
  - o Change release
  - o Change implementation
  - o Change testing
  - o CMDB
- Training
  - o Staff
  - o Subcontractor/supplier
  - o Customer

CM Verification Audit Results

The CM audit process is designed to

1. Ensure that CM policies are understood and being followed
2. Verify CM procedures exist and are adequate
3. Ensure that staff is following CM policies and procedures
4. Identify nonconformance with CM requirements and its effect on the CI
5. Assign corrective actions for nonconforming items to specific persons for resolution
6. Assure corrective actions are completed and reported

CONCLUSION

CM is a vital and necessary activity within any organization, which requires the identification and documentation of the product and/or service to produce consistent, repeatable, and reliable products and/or services throughout the system life cycle. There are a myriad of components to CM that require dedicated executive oversight, allocation of corporate resources (time, energy, and money), attention to detail, corporate guidance, and dedicated staff to successfully run and manage the CM program.

REFERENCES

1. *FEA Consolidated Reference Model—version 2.3*. U.S. Office of Management and Budget (OMB) and the Office of E-Government (E-Gov) and Information Technology (IT), October 2007.
2. *DODAF Architecture Framework version 1.5*. U.S. Department of Defense, April 23, 2007.

BIBLIOGRAPHY

1. MIL-HDBK-61A, *Configuration Management Guidance*. U.S. Department of Defense, February 7, 2001.
2. ANSI/EIA-649-1998, *National Consensus Standard for Configuration Management*, 1998.
3. EIA-649-A-2004, *National Consensus Standard for Configuration Management*, 2004.
4. ISO 10007, *Quality Management Systems—Guidelines for Configuration Management*, 2003.
5. ISO/IEC 27001:2005, *Information Technology—Security Techniques—Information Security Management Systems—Requirements*, October 2005.
6. NIST SP 800-70, *Security Configuration Checklists Program for IT Products: Guidance for Checklists Users and Developers*, May 2005.
7. NIST SP 800-64, *Security Considerations in the System Development Life Cycle*, Rev. 2, October 2008.

Cryptography

Javek Ikbal
Director, IT Security, Major Financial Services Company, Reading, Massachusetts, U.S.A.

Abstract

This entry presents some basic ideas behind cryptography. This is intended for audience evaluators, recommenders, and end users of cryptographic algorithms and products rather than implementers. Hence, the mathematical background will be kept to a minimum. Only widely adopted algorithms are described with some mathematical detail. We also present promising technologies and algorithms that information security practitioners might encounter and may have to choose or discard.

BASICS

What Is Cryptography?

Cryptography is the art and science of securing messages so unintended audiences cannot read, understand, or alter that message.

Related Terms and Definitions

A message in its original form is called the plaintext or cleartext. The process of securing that message by hiding its contents is encryption or enciphering. An encrypted message is called ciphertext, and the process of turning the ciphertext back to cleartext is called decryption or deciphering. Cryptography is often shortened to crypto.

Practitioners of cryptography are known as cryptographers. The art and science of breaking encryptions is known as cryptanalysis, which is practiced by cryptanalysts. Cryptography and cryptanalysis are covered in the theoretical and applied branch of mathematics known as cryptology, and practiced by cryptologists.

A cipher or cryptographic algorithm is the mathematical function or formula used to convert cleartext to ciphertext and back. Typically, a pair of algorithms is used to encrypt and decrypt.

An algorithm that depends on keeping the algorithm secret to keep the ciphertext safe is known as a restricted algorithm. Security practitioners should be aware that restricted algorithms are inadequate in the current world. Unfortunately, restricted algorithms are quite popular in some settings. Fig. 1 shows the schematic flow of restricted algorithms. This can be mathematically expressed as $E(M) = C$ and $D(C) = M$, where M is the cleartext message, E is the encryption function, C is the ciphertext, and D is the decryption function.

A major problem with restricted algorithms is that a changing group cannot use it; every time someone leaves, the algorithm has to change. Because of the need to keep it a secret, each group has to build its own algorithms and software to use it.

These shortcomings are overcome by using a variable known as the key or cryptovariable. The range of possible values for the key is called the keyspace. With each group using its own key, a common and well-known algorithm may be shared by any number of groups.

The mathematical representation now becomes: $E_k(M) = C$ and $D_k(C) = M$, where the subscript k refers to the encryption and decryption key. Some algorithms will utilize different keys for encryption and decryption. Fig. 2 illustrates that the key is an input to the algorithm.

Note that the security of all such algorithms depends on the key and not the algorithm itself. We submit to the information security practitioner that any algorithm that has not been publicly discussed, analyzed, and withstood attacks (i.e., zero restriction) should be presumed insecure and rejected.

A Brief History

Secret writing probably came right after writing was invented. The earliest known instance of cryptography occurred in ancient Egypt 4000 years ago, with the use of hieroglyphics. These were purposefully cryptic; hiding the text was probably not the main purpose—it was intended to impress. In ancient India, government spies communicated using secret codes. Greek literature has examples of cryptography going back to the time of Homer. Julius Caesar used a system of cryptography that shifted each letter three places further through the alphabet (e.g., A shifts to D, Z shifts to C, etc.). Regardless of the amount of shift, all such monoalphabetic substitution ciphers (MSCs) are also known as Caesar ciphers. While extremely easy to decipher if you know

Encyclopedia of Information Systems and Technology, DOI: 10.1081/E-EIST-120046715

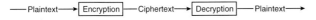

Fig. 1 Encryption and decryption with restricted algorithms.

how, a Caesar cipher called ROT-13 (N = A, etc.) is still in use today as a trivial method of encryption. Why ROT-13 and not any other ROT-N? By shifting down the middle of the English alphabet, ROT-13 is self-reversing—the same code can be used to encrypt and decrypt. How this works is left as an exercise for the reader. Fig. 3 shows the alphabet and corresponding Caesar cipher and ROT-13.

During the seventh century AD, the first treatise on cryptanalysis appeared. The technique involves counting the frequency of each ciphertext letter. We know that the letter E occurs the most in English. So if we are trying to decrypt a document written in English where the letter H occurs the most, we can assume that H stands for E. Provided we have a large enough sample of the ciphertext for the frequency count to be statistically significant, this technique is powerful enough to cryptanalyze any MSC and is still in use.

Leon Battista Alberti invented a mechanical device during the 15th century that could perform a polyalphabetic substitution cipher (PSC). A PSC can be considered an improvement of the Caesar cipher because each letter is shifted by a different amount according to a predetermined rule.

The device consisted of two concentric copper disks with the alphabet around the edges. To start enciphering, a letter on the inner disk is lined up with any letter on the outer disk, which is written as the first character of the ciphertext. After a certain number of letters, the disks are rotated and the encryption continues. Because the cipher is changed often, frequency analysis becomes less effective.

The concept of rotating disks and changing ciphers within a message was a major milestone in cryptography.

The public interest in cryptography dramatically increased with the invention of the telegraph. People wanted the speed and convenience of the telegraph without disclosing the message to the operator, and cryptography provided the answer.

After World War I, U. S. military organizations poured resources into cryptography. Because of the classified nature of this research, there were no general publications that covered cryptography until the late 1960s; and the public interest went down again.

During this time, computers were also gaining ground in nongovernment areas, especially the financial

sector, and the need for a nonmilitary cryptosystem was becoming apparent. The organization which is known as the National Institute of Standards and Technology (NIST), then called the National Bureau of Standards, requested proposals for a standard cryptographic algorithm. IBM responded with Lucifer, a system developed by Horst Feistel and colleagues. After adopting two modifications from the National Security Agency (NSA), this was adopted as the federal Data Encryption Standard (DES) in 1976.[1] NSA's changes caused major controversy, specifically because it suggested DES use 56-bit keys instead of 112-bit keys as originally submitted by IBM.

During the 1970s and 1980s, the NSA also attempted to regulate cryptographic publications but was unsuccessful. However, general interest in cryptography increased as a result. Academic and business interest in cryptography was high, and extensive research led to significant new algorithms and techniques.

Advances in computing power have made 56-bit keys breakable. In 1998, a custom-built machine from the Electronic Frontier Foundation costing $210,000 cracked DES in four and a half days.[2] In January 1999, a distributed network of 100,000 machines cracked DES in 22 hours and 15 minutes.

As a direct result of these DES cracking examples, NIST issued a request for proposals to replace DES with a new standard called the Advanced Encryption Standard (AES).[3] On November 26, 2001, NIST selected Rijndael as the AES.

Alphabet-Soup Players: Alice, Bob, Eve, and Mike

In our discussions of cryptographic protocols, we will use an alphabet soup of names that are participating in (or are trying to break into) a secure message exchange:

- *Alice*, first participant
- *Bob*, second participant
- *Eve*, eavesdropper
- *Mike*, masquerader

Ties to Confidentiality, Integrity, and Authentication

Cryptography is not limited to confidentiality only—it can perform other useful functions.

- *Authentication.* If Alice is buying something from Bob's online store, Bob has to assure Alice that it is indeed Bob's website and not Mike's, the masquerader pretending to be Bob. Thus, Alice should be able to authenticate Bob's website, or know that a message originated from Bob.

Fig. 2 Encryption and decryption with keys.

English Alphabet	A B C D E F G H I J K L M N O P Q R S T U V W X Y Z
Caesar Cipher (3)	D E F G H I J K L M N O P Q R S T U V W X Y Z A B C
ROT-13	N O P Q R S T U V W X Y Z A B C D E F G H I J K L M

Fig. 3 Caesar cipher (Shift-3) and ROT-13.

- *Integrity.* If Bob is sending Alice, the personnel manager, a message informing her of a $5000 severance pay for Mike, Mike should not be able to intercept the message in transit and change the amount to $50,000. Cryptography enables the receiver to verify that a message has not been modified in transit.
- *Nonrepudiation.* Alice places an order to sell some stocks at $10 per share. Her stockbroker, Bob, executes the order, but then the stock goes up to $18. Now Alice claims she never placed that order. Cryptography (through digital signatures) will enable Bob to prove that Alice did send that message.

Section Summary

- Any message or data in its original form is called plaintext or cleartext.
- The process of hiding or securing the plaintext is called encryption (verb: to encrypt or to encipher).
- When encryption is applied on plaintext, the result is called ciphertext.
- Retrieving the plaintext from the ciphertext is called decryption (verb: to decrypt or to decipher).
- The art and science of encryption and decryption is called cryptography, and its practitioners are cryptographers.
- The art and science of breaking encryption is called cryptanalysis, and its practitioners are cryptanalysts.
- The process and rules (mathematical or otherwise) to encrypt and decrypt are called ciphers or cryptographic algorithms.
- The history of cryptography is over 4000 years old.
- Frequency analysis is an important technique in cryptanalysis.
- Secret cryptographic algorithms should not be trusted by an information security professional.
- Only publicly available and discussed algorithms that have withstood analysis and attacks may be used in a business setting.

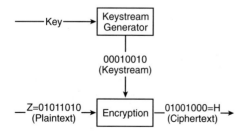

Fig. 4 Stream cipher operation.

- Bottom line: do not use a cryptographic algorithm developed in-house (unless you have internationally renowned experts in that field).

SYMMETRIC CRYPTOGRAPHIC ALGORITHMS

Algorithms or ciphers that use the same key to encrypt and decrypt are called symmetric cryptographic algorithms. There are two basic types: stream and block.

Stream Ciphers

This type of cipher takes messages in a stream and operates on individual data elements (characters, bits, or bytes).

Typically, a random-number generator is used to produce a sequence of characters called a key stream. The key stream is then combined with the plaintext via exclusive-OR (XOR) to produce the ciphertext. Fig. 4 illustrates this operation of encrypting the letter Z, the ASCII value of which is represented in binary as 01011010. Note that in an XOR operation involving binary digits, only XORing 0 and 1 yields 1; all other XORs result in 0. Fig. 4 shows how a stream cipher operates.

Before describing the actual workings of a stream cipher, we will examine how shift registers work because they have been the mainstay of electronic cryptography for a long time.

A linear feedback shift register (LFSR) is very simple in principle. For readers not versed in electronics, we present a layman's representation. Imagine a tube that can hold 4 bits with a window at the right end. Because the tube holds 4 bits, we will call it a 4-bit shift register. We shift all bits in the tube and, as a result, the bit showing through the window changes. Here, shifting involves pushing from the left so the rightmost bit falls off; and to keep the number of bits in the tube constant, we place the output of some addition operation as the new leftmost bit. In the following example, we will continue with our 4-bit LFSR, and the new leftmost bit will be the result of adding bits three and four (the feedback) and keeping the rightmost bit (note that in binary mathematics, $1 + 1 = 10$, with 0 being the rightmost bit, and $1 + 0 = 1$). For every shift that occurs, we look through the window and note the rightmost bit. As a result, we will see the sequence shown in Fig. 5.

1111.-> 0111 -> 0011 -> 0001 -> 1000 -> 0100 -> 0010 -> 1001 -> 1100 -> 0110 -> 1011 -> 0101 -> 1010 -> 1101 ->
1110 -> 1111
Keystream: 111100010011010 (Right-most bit through the window before repetition).

Fig. 5   4-bit LFSR output.

Note that after $2^{(N = 4)} - 1 = 15$ iterations, we will get a repetition. This is the maximum number of unique sequences (also called period) when dealing with a 4-bit LFSR (because we have to exclude 0000, which will always produce a sequence of 0000s). Choosing a different feedback function may have reduced the period, and the longest unique sequence is called the maximal length. The maximal length is important because repeating key streams mean the same plaintext will produce the same ciphertext, and this will be vulnerable to frequency analysis and other attacks.

To construct a simple stream cipher, take an LFSR (or take many different sizes and different feedback functions). To encrypt each bit of the plaintext, take a bit from the plaintext, XOR it with a bit from the key stream to generate the ciphertext (refer to Fig. 4), and so on.

Of course, other stream ciphers are more complex and involve multiple LFSRs and other techniques.[4] We will discuss RC4 as an example of a stream cipher. First, we will define the term S-box.

An S-box is also known as a substitution box or table and, as the name implies, it is a table or system that provides a substitution scheme. Shift registers are S-boxes; they provide a substitution mechanism.

RC4 uses an output feedback mechanism combined with 256 S-boxes (numbered $S_0 \ldots S_{255}$) and two counters, i and j.

A random byte K is generated through the following steps:

```
i = (i + 1) mod 256
j = (j + S₁) mod 256
swap (Sᵢ, Sⱼ)
t = (Sᵢ + Sⱼ) mod 256
K = Sₜ
```

Now, K XOR Plaintext = Ciphertext, and K XOR Ciphertext = Plaintext

Block Ciphers

A block cipher requires the accumulation of some amount of data or multiple data elements before ciphering can begin. Encryption and decryption happen on chunks of data, unlike stream ciphers, which operate on each character or bit independently.

Data encryption standard

The DES is over 25 years old; because of its widespread implementation and use, it will probably coexist with the new AES for a few years.

Despite initial concern about NSA's role in crafting the standard, DES generated huge interest in cryptography; vendors and users alike were eager to adopt the first government-approved encryption standard that was released for public use.

The DES calls for reevaluations of DES every 5 years. Starting in 1987, the NSA warned that it would not recertify DES because it was likely that it soon would be broken; they proposed secret algorithms available on tamper-proof chips only. Users of DES, including major financial institutions, protested; DES got a new lease on life until 1992. Because no new standards became available in 1992, it lived on to 1998 and then until the end of 2001, when AES became the standard.

DES is a symmetric block cipher that operates in blocks of 64 bits of data at a time, with 64-bit plaintext resulting in 64-bit ciphertext. If the data is not a multiple of 64 bits, then it is padded at the end. The effective key-length is 56 bits with 8 bits of parity. All security rests with the key.

A simple description of DES is as follows:[1]

Take the 64-bit block of message (M).
Rearrange the bits of M (initial permutation, IP).
Break IP down the middle into two 32-bit blocks (L & R).
Shift the key bits, and take a 48-bit portion from the key.
Save the value of R into Rold.
Expand R via a permutation to 48 bits.
XOR R with the 48-bit key and transform via eight S-boxes into a new 32-bit chunk.
Now, R takes on the value of the new R XOR-ed with L.
And L takes on the value of Rold.
Repeat this process 15 more times (total 16 rounds).
Join L and R.
Reverse the permutation IP (final permutation, FP).

There are some implementations without IP and FP; because they do not match the published standard, they should not be called DES or DES-compliant, although they offer the same degree of security.

Certain DES keys are considered weak, semiweak, or possibly weak: A key is considered weak if it consists of all 1s or all 0s, or if half the keys are 1s and the other half are 0s.[5]

Conspiracy theories involving NSA backdoors and EFFs DES-cracking machine notwithstanding, DES lives on in its original form or a multiple-iteration form popularly known as Triple-DES.

Triple-DES is DES done thrice, typically with two 56-bit keys. In the most popular form, the first key is used to DES-encrypt the message. The second key is used to DES-decrypt the encrypted message. Because this is not the right key, the attempted decryption only scrambles the data even more. The resultant ciphertext is then encrypted again with the first key to yield the final ciphertext. This three-step procedure is called Triple-DES. Sometimes, three keys are used.

Because this follows an Encryption > Decryption > Encryption scheme, it is often known as DES-EDE.

ANSI standard X9.52 describes Triple-DES encryption with keys k_1, k_2, k_3 as:

$$C = E_{k3}(D_{k2}(E_{k1}(M)))$$

where E_k and D_k denote DES encryption and DES decryption, respectively, with the key k. Another variant is DES-EEE, which consists of three consecutive encryptions. There are three keying options defined in ANSI X9.52 for DES-EDE:

The three keys k_1, k_2, and k_3 are different (three keys).
k_1 and k_2 are different, but $k_1 = k_3$ (two keys).
$k_1 = k_2 = k_3$ (one key).

The third option makes Triple-DES backward-compatible with DES and offers no additional security.

AES (Rijndael)

In 1997, NIST issued a request for proposals to select a symmetric-key encryption algorithm to be used to protect sensitive (unclassified) federal information. This was to become the AES, the DES replacement. In 1998, NIST announced the acceptance of 15 candidate algorithms and requested the assistance of the cryptographic research community in analyzing the candidates. This analysis included an initial examination of the security and efficiency characteristics for each algorithm.

NIST reviewed the results of this preliminary research and selected MARS, RC6™, Rijndael, Serpent, and Twofish as finalists. After additional review, in October 2000, NIST proposed Rijndael as AES. For research results and rationale for selection, see Weak DES keys: Appendix A.[5]

Before discussing AES, we will quote the most important answer from the Rijndael FAQ:

If you're Dutch, Flemish, Indonesian, Surinamer or South African, it's pronounced like you think it should be. Otherwise, you could pronounce it like reign dahl, rain doll, or rhine dahl. We're not picky. As long as you make it sound different from region deal.[6]

Rijndael is a block cipher that can process blocks of 128-, 192-, and 256-bit length using keys 128-, 192-, and 256-bits long. All nine combinations of block and key lengths are possible.[7] The AES standard specifies only 128-bit data blocks and 128-, 192-, and 256-bit key lengths. Our discussions will be confined to AES and not the full scope of Rijndael. Based on the key length, AES may be referred to as AES-128, AES-192, or AES-256. We will present a simple description of Rijndael. For a mathematical treatment, see Rijndael technical overview.[8,9]

Rijndael involves an initial XOR of the state and a round key, nine rounds of transformations (or rounds), and a round performed at the end with one step omitted. The input to each round is called the state. Each round consists of four transformations: SubBytes, ShiftRow, MixColumn (omitted from the tenth round), and AddRoundKey.

In the SubBytes transformation, each of the state bytes is independently transformed using a nonlinear S-box.

In the ShiftRow transformation, the state is processed by cyclically shifting the last three rows of the state by different offsets.

In the MixColumn transformation, data from all of the columns of the state are mixed (independently of one another) to produce new columns.

In the AddRoundKey step in the cipher and inverse cipher transformations, a round key is added to the state using an XOR operation. The length of a round key equals the size of the state.

Weaknesses and Attacks

A well-known and frequently used encryption is the stream cipher available with PKZIP. Unfortunately, there is also a well-known attack involving known plaintext against this—if you know part of the plaintext, it is possible to decipher the file.[10] For any serious work, information security professionals should not use PKZIP's encryption.

In 1975, it was theorized that a customized DES cracker would cost $20 million. In 1998, EFF built one for $220,000.[2] With the advances in computing power, the time and money required to crack DES has significantly gone down even more. Although it is still being used, if possible, use AES or Triple-DES.

Section Summary

- Symmetric cryptographic algorithms or ciphers are those that use the same key to encrypt and decrypt.
- Stream ciphers operate one bit at a time.
- Stream ciphers use a key stream generator to continuously produce a key stream that is used to encrypt the message.
- A repeating key stream weakens the encryption and makes it vulnerable to cryptanalysis.
- Shift registers are often used in stream ciphers.
- Block ciphers operate on a block of data at a time.
- DES is the most popular block cipher.
- DES keys are sometimes referred to as 64-bit, but the effective length is 56 bits with 8 parity bits; hence, the actual key length is 56 bits.
- There are known weak DES keys; ensure that those are not used.
- DES itself has been broken and it should be assumed that it is not secure against attack.
- Make plans to migrate away from DES; use Triple-DES or Rijndael instead of DES, if possible.
- Do not use the encryption offered by PKZIP for nontrivial work.

ASYMMETRIC (PUBLIC KEY) CRYPTOGRAPHY

Asymmetric is the term applied in a cryptographic system where one key is used to encrypt and another is used to decrypt.

Background

This concept was invented in 1976 by Whitfield Diffie and Martin Hellman[11] and independently by Ralph Merkle. The basic theory is quite simple: Is there a pair of keys so that if one is used to encrypt, the other can be used to decrypt—and given one key, would finding the other be extremely hard?

Luckily for us, the answer is yes, and this is the basis of asymmetric (often called public key) cryptography.

There are many algorithms available, but most of them are either insecure or produce ciphertext that is larger than the plaintext. Of the algorithms that are both secure and efficient, only three can be used for both encryption and digital signatures.[4] Unfortunately, these algorithms are often slower by a factor of 1000 compared with symmetric key encryption.

As a result, hybrid cryptographic systems are popular: Suppose Alice and Bob want to exchange a large message. Alice generates a random session key, encrypts it using asymmetric encryption, and sends it over to Bob, who has the other half of the asymmetric key to decode the session key. Because the session key is

small, the overhead to asymmetrically encipher/decipher it is not too large. Now Alice encrypts the message with the session key and sends it over to Bob. Bob already has the session key and deciphers the message with it. As the large message is enciphered/deciphered using much faster symmetric encryption, the performance is acceptable.

RSA Algorithm

We will present a discussion of the most popular of the asymmetric algorithms—RSA, named after its inventors, Ron Rivest, Adi Shamir, and Leonard Adleman. Readers are directed to RSA algorithm[12] for an extensive treatment. RSA's patent expired in September 2000, and RSA has put the algorithm in the public domain, enabling anyone to implement it at zero cost.

First, a mathematics refresher:

- If an integer P cannot be divided (without remainders) by any number other than itself and 1, then P is called a prime number. Other prime numbers are 2, 3, 5, and 7.
- Two integers are relatively prime if there is no integer greater than one that divides them both (their greatest common divisor is 1). For example, 15 and 16 are relatively prime, but 12 and 14 are not.
- The mod is defined as the remainder. For example, 5 mod 3 = 2 means divide 5 by 3 and the result is the remainder, 2.

Note that RSA depends on the difficulty of factoring large prime numbers. If there is a sudden leap in computer technology or mathematics that changes that, security of such encryption schemes will be broken. Quantum and DNA computing are two fields to watch in this arena.

Here is a step-by-step description of RSA:

1. Find P and Q, two large (e.g., 1024-bit or larger) prime numbers. For our example, we will use P = 11 and Q = 19, which are adequate for this example (and more manageable).
2. Calculate the product PQ, and also the product (P – 1) (Q – 1). So PQ = 209, and (P – 1)(Q – 1) = 180.
3. Choose an odd integer E such that E is less than PQ, and such that E and (P–1)(Q–1) are relatively prime. We will pick E = 7.
4. Find the integer D so that (DE – 1) is evenly divisible by (P – 1)(Q – 1). D is called the multiplicative inverse of E. This is easy to do: let us assume that the result of evenly dividing (DE – 1) by (P – 1)(Q – 1) is X, where X is also an integer. So we have X = (DE – 1)/(P – 1)(Q – 1); and solving for D, we get D = (X(P – 1) (Q – 1) + 1)/E. Start with X = 1

and keep increasing its value until D is an integer. For example, D works out to be 103.

5. The public key is (E and PQ), the private key is D. Destroy P and Q (note that given P and Q, it would be easy to work out E and D; but given only PQ and E, it would be hard to determine D). Give out your public key (E, PQ) and keep D secure and private.

6. To encrypt a message M, we raise M to the Eth power, divide it by PQ, and the remainder (the mod) is the ciphertext. Note that M must be less than PQ. A mathematical representation will be ciphertext = ME mod PQ. So if we are encrypting 13 (M = 13), our ciphertext = 13^7 mod 209 = 29.

7. To decrypt, we take the ciphertext, raise it to the Dth power, and take the mod with PQ. So plaintext = 29^{103} mod 209 = 13.

Compared to DES, RSA is about 100 times slower in software and 1000 times slower in hardware. Because AES is even faster than DES in software, the performance gap will widen in software-only applications.

Elliptic Curve Cryptosystems

As we saw, solving RSA depends on a hard math problem: factoring very large numbers. There is another hard math problem: reversing exponentiation (logarithms). For example, it is possible to easily raise 7 to the fourth power and get 2401; but given only 2401, reversing the process and obtaining 7^4 is more difficult (at least as hard as performing large factorizations).

The difficulty in performing discrete logarithms over elliptic curves (not to be confused with an ellipse) is even greater;[13] and for the same key size, it presents a more difficult challenge than RSA (or presents the same difficulty/security with a smaller key size). There is an implementation of elliptic curve cryptosystem (ECC) that uses the factorization problem, but it offers no practical advantage over RSA.

An elliptic curve has an interesting property: it is possible to define a point on the curve as the sum of two other points on the curve. Following is a high-level discussion of ECC.[13]

Example: Alice and Bob agree on a nonsecret elliptic curve and a nonsecret fixed curve point F. Alice picks a secret random integer A_k as her secret key and publishes the point $A_p = A_k^*F$ as her public key. Bob picks a secret random integer B_k as his secret key and publishes the point $B_p = B_k^*F$ as his public key. If Alice wants to send a message to Bob, she can compute $A_k^*B_p$ and use the result as the secret key for a symmetric block cipher like AES. To decrypt, Bob can compute the same key by finding $B_k^*A_p$ because $B_k^*A_p = B_k^*(A_k^*F) = A_k^*(B_k^*F) = A_k^*B_p$.

ECC has not been subject to the extensive analysis that RSA has and is comparatively new.

Attacks

It is possible to attack RSA by factoring large numbers, or guessing all possible values of (P − 1) (Q − 1) or D. These are computationally infeasible, and users should not worry about them. But there are chosen ciphertext attacks against RSA that involve duping a person to sign a message (provided by the attacker). This can be prevented by signing a hash of the message, or by making minor cosmetic changes to the document by signing it. For a description of attacks against RSA, see Attacks on RSA.[14] Hash functions are described later in this entry.

Real-World Applications

Cryptography is often a business enabler. Financial institutions encrypt the connection between the user's browser and web pages that show confidential information such as account balances. Online merchants similarly encrypt the link so customer credit card data cannot be sniffed in transit. Some even use this as a selling point: "Our website is protected with the highest encryption available." What they are really saying is that this website uses 128-bit secure sockets layer (SSL).

As an aside, there are no known instances of theft of credit card data in transit; but many high-profile stories of customer information theft, including theft of credit card information, are available. The theft was possible because enough safeguards were not in place, and the data was usable because it was in cleartext, that is, not encrypted. Data worth protecting should be protected in all stages, not just in transit.

SSL and TLS

Normal web traffic is clear text—your ISP can intercept it easily. SSL provides encryption between the browser and a web server to provide security and identification. SSL was invented by Netscape[15] and submitted to the Internet Engineering Task Force (IETF). In 1996, IETF began with SSL v3.0 and, in 1999, published Transport Layer Security (TLS) v1.0 as a proposed standard.[16] TLS is a term not commonly used, but we will use TLS and SSL interchangeably.

Suppose Alice, running a popular browser, wants to buy a book from Bob's online book store at bobs-books. com and is worried about entering her credit card information online. (For the record, SSL/TLS can encrypt connections between any two network applications and not web browsers and servers only.) Bob is aware of this reluctance and wants to allay Alice's fears—he wants to encrypt the connection between Alice's browser and bobsbooks.com. The first thing he has to do is install a digital certificate on his web server.

A certificate contains information about the owner of the certificate: e-mail address, owner's name, certificate usage, duration of validity, and resource location or distinguished name, which includes the common name (website address or e-mail address, depending on the usage), and the certificate ID of the person who certifies (signs) this information. It also contains the public key, and finally a hash to ensure that the certificate has not been tampered with.

Anyone can create a digital certificate with freely available software, but just like a person cannot issue his own passport and expect it to be accepted at a border, browsers will not recognize self-issued certificates. Digital certificate vendors have spent millions to preinstall their certificates into browsers, so Bob has to buy a certificate from a well-known certificate vendor, also known as root certificate authority (CA). There are certificates available with 40- and 128-bit encryptions. Because it usually costs the same amount, Bob should buy a 128-bit certificate and install it on his web server. As of this writing, there are only two vendors with wide acceptance of certificates: VeriSign and Thawte. Interestingly, VeriSign owns Thawte, but Thawte's certificate prices are significantly lower.

So now Alice comes back to the site and is directed toward a URL that begins with https instead of http. That is the browser telling the server that an SSL session should be initiated. In this negotiation phase, the browser also tells the server what encryption schemes it can support. The server will pick the strongest of the supported ciphers and reply back with its own public key and certificate information. The browser will check if it has been issued by a root CA. If not, it will display a warning to Alice and ask if she still wants to proceed. If the server name does not match the name contained in the certificate, it will also issue a warning. If the certificate is legitimate, the browser will:

- Generate a random symmetric encryption key.
- Encrypt this symmetric key with the server's public key.
- Encrypt the URL it wants with the symmetric key.
- Send the encrypted key and encrypted URL to the server.

The server will:

- Decrypt the symmetric key with its private key.
- Decrypt the URL with the symmetric key.
- Process the URL.
- Encrypt the reply with the symmetric key.
- Send the encrypted reply back to the browser.

In this case, although encryption is two-way, authentication is one-way only: The server's identity is proven to the client but not vice versa. Mutual authentication is also possible and performed in some cases. In a high-security scenario, a bank could issue certificates to individuals, and no browser would be allowed to connect without those individual certificates identifying the users to the bank's server.

What happens when a browser capable of only 40-bit encryption (older U. S. laws prohibited export of 128-bit browsers) hits a site capable of 128 bits? Typically, the site will step down to 40-bit encryption. But CAs also sell super or step-up certificates that, when encountered with a 40-bit browser, will temporarily enable 128-bit encryption in those browsers. Step-up certificates cost more than regular certificates.

Note that the root certificates embedded in browsers sometimes expire; the last big one was VeriSign's in 1999. At that time, primarily financial institutions urged their users to upgrade their browsers. Finally, there is another protocol called Secure HTTP that provides similar functionality but is very rarely used.

CHOOSING AN ALGORITHM

What encryption algorithm, with what key size, would an information security professional choose? The correct answer is: it depends. What is being encrypted, who do we need to protect against, and for how long?

If it is stock market data, any encryption scheme that will hold up for 20 minutes is enough; in 20 minutes, the same information will be on a number of free quote services. Your password to the *New York Times* website? Assuming you do not use the same password for your e-mail account, SSL is overkill for that server. Credit card transactions, bank accounts, and medical records need the highest possible encryption, both in transit and in storage.

Export and International Use Issues

Not long ago, exporting 128-bit web browsers from the United States was a crime, according to U. S. law. Exporting software or hardware capable of strong encryption is still a crime. Some countries have outlawed the use of encryption, and some other countries require a key escrow if you want to use encryption. Some countries have outlawed use of all but certain approved secret encryption algorithms. We strongly recommend that information security professionals become familiar with the cryptography laws of the land, especially if working in an international setting.[17]

Section Summary

- In asymmetric cryptography, one key is used to encrypt and another is used to decrypt.
- Asymmetric cryptography is often also known as public key cryptography.
- Asymmetric cryptography is up to 1000 times slower than symmetric cryptography.
- RSA is the most popular and well-understood asymmetric cryptographic algorithm.
- RSA's security depends on the difficulty of factoring very large (>1024-bit) numbers.
- Elliptic curve cryptography depends on the difficulty of finding discrete logarithms over elliptic curves.
- Smaller elliptic curve keys offer similar security as comparatively larger RSA keys.
- It is possible to attack RSA through chosen plaintext attacks.
- SSL is commonly used to encrypt information between a browser and a web server.
- Choosing a cipher and key length depends on what needs to be encrypted, for how long, and against whom.
- There are significant legal implications of using encryption in a multinational setting.

KEY MANAGEMENT AND EXCHANGE

In symmetric encryption, what happens when one person who knows the keys goes to another company (or to a competitor)? Even with public key algorithms, keeping the private key secret is paramount: without it, all is lost. For attackers, the reverse is true; it is often easier to attack the key storage instead of trying to crack the algorithm. A person who knows the keys can be bribed or kidnapped and tortured to give up the keys, at which time the encryption becomes worthless. Key management describes the problems and solutions to securely generating, exchanging, installing and storing, verifying, and destroying keys.

Generation

Encryption software typically generates its own keys (it is possible to generate keys in one program and use them in another); but because of the implementation, this can introduce weaknesses. For example, DES software that picks a known weak or semiweak key will create a major security issue. It is important to use the largest possible keyspace: a 56-bit DES key can be picked from the 256 ASCII character set, the first 128 of ASCII, or the 26 letters of the alphabet. Guessing the 56-bit DES key (an exhaustive search) involves trying out all 56-bit combinations from the keyspace. Common

sense tells us that the exhaustive search of 256 bytes will take much longer than that for 26 bytes. With a large keyspace, the keys must be random enough so as to be not guessable.

Exchange

Alice and Bob are sitting on two separate islands. Alice has a bottle of fine wine, a lock, its key, and an empty chest. Bob has another lock and its key. An islander is willing to transfer items between the islands but will keep anything that he thinks is not secured, so you cannot send a key, an unlocked lock, or a bottle of wine on its own.

How does Alice send the wine to Bob? See the answer at the end of this section.

This is actually a key exchange problem in disguise: How does Alice get a key to Bob without its being compromised by the messenger? For asymmetric encryption, it is easy—the public key can be given out to the whole world. For symmetric encryption, a public key algorithm (like SSL) can be used; or the key may be broken up and each part sent over different channels and combined at the destination.

Answer to our key/wine exchange problem: Alice puts the bottle into the chest and locks it with her lock, keeps her key, and sends the chest to the other island. Bob locks the chest with his lock, and sends it back to Alice. Alice takes her lock off the chest and sends it back to Bob. Bob unlocks the chest with his key and enjoys the wine.

Installation and Storage

How a key is installed and stored is important. If the application does no initial validation before installing a key, an attacker might be able to insert a bad key into the application. After the key is installed, can it be retrieved without any access control? If so, anyone with access to the computer would be able to steal that key.

Change Control

How often a key is changed determines its efficiency. If a key is used for a long time, an attacker might have sufficient samples of ciphertext to be able to cryptanalyze the information. At the same time, each change brings up the exchange problem.

Destruction

A key no longer in use has to be disposed of securely and permanently. In the wrong hands, recorded ciphertext may be decrypted and give enemy insights into existing ciphertext.

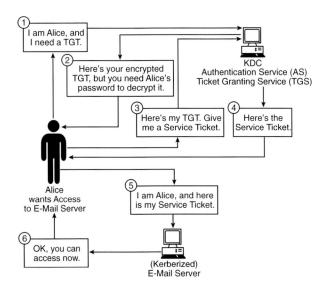

Fig. 6 Kerberos in operation.

Examples and implementations of PKI

A public key infrastructure (PKI) is the set of systems and software required to use, manage, and control public key cryptography. It has three primary purposes: publish public keys, certify that a public key is tied to an individual or entity, and provide verification as to the continued validity of a public key. As discussed before, a digital certificate is a public key with identifying information for its owner. The CA "signs" the certificate and verifies that the information provided is correct. Now all entities that trust the CA can trust that the identity provided by a certificate is correct. The CA can revoke the certificate and put it in the certificate revocation list, at which time it will not be trusted anymore. An extensive set of PKI standards and documentation is available.[18] Large companies run their own CA for intranet/extranet use. In Canada and Hong Kong, large public CAs are operational. But despite the promises of the "year of the PKI," market acceptance and implementation of PKIs are still in the future.

Kerberos™

From the comp.protocol.kerberos FAQ:

> Kerberos; also spelled Cerberus. *n.* The watchdog of Hades, whose duty it was to guard the entrance—against whom or what does not clearly appear; it is known to have had three heads.
> —*Ambrose Bierce The Enlarged Devil's Dictionary*

Kerberos was developed at MIT in the 1980s and publicly released in 1989. The primary purposes were to prevent cleartext passwords from traversing the network and to ease the log-in process to multiple machines.[19]

The existing version is 5—there are known security issues with version 4. The three heads of Kerberos comprise the key distribution center (KDC), the client, and the server that the client wants to access. Kerberos 5 is built into Windows 2000 and later, and will probably result in wider adoption of Kerberos (notwithstanding some compatibility issues of the Microsoft implementation of the protocol[20]).

The KDC runs two services: authentication service and ticket granting service (TGS). A typical Kerberos session (shown in Fig. 6) proceeds as follows when Alice wants to log on to her e-mail and retrieve it.

1. She will request a ticket granting ticket (TGT) from the KDC, where she already has an account. The KDC has a hash of her password, and she will not have to provide it. (The KDC must be extremely secure to protect all these passwords.)
2. The TGS on the KDC will send Alice a TGT encrypted with her password hash. Without knowing the password, she cannot decrypt the TGT.
3. Alice decrypts the TGT; then, using the TGT, she sends another request to the KDC for a service ticket to access her e-mail server. The service ticket will not be issued without the TGT and will only work for the e-mail server.
4. The KDC grants Alice the service ticket.
5. Alice can access the e-mail server.

Note that both the TGT and the ST have expiration times (default is 10 hours); so even if one or both tickets are captured, the exposure is only until the ticket expiration time. All computer system clocks participating in a Kerberos system must be within 5 minutes of each other and all services that grant access. Finally, the e-mail server must be kerberized (support Kerberos).

Section Summary

- Key management (generating/exchanging/storing/installing/destroying keys) can compromise security.
- Public key cryptography is often the best solution to key distribution issues.
- A public key infrastructure is a system that can manage public keys.
- A certificate authority is a PKI that can validate public keys.
- Digital certificates are essentially public keys that also include key owner information. The key and information are verified by a CA.
- If an entity trusts a CA, it can also trust digital certificates that the CA signs (authenticates).
- Kerberos is a protocol for eliminating cleartext passwords across networks.

- A TGT is issued to the user, who will use that to request a service ticket. All tickets expire after a certain time.
- Under Kerberos, tickets are encrypted and cleartext passwords never cross the network.

HASH FUNCTIONS

A hash function is defined as a process that can take an arbitrary-length message and return a fixed-length value from that message. For practical use, we require further qualities:

- Given a message, it should be easy to find the hash.
- Given the hash, it should be hard to find the message.
- Given the message, it should be hard to find another (specific or random) message that produces the same hash.

Message Digests

A message digest is the product of a one-way hash function applied on a message: It is a fingerprint or a unique summary that can uniquely identify the message.

MD2, MD4, and MD5

Ron Rivest (the R in RSA) designed all of these. All three produce 128-bit hashes. MD4 has been successfully attacked. MD5 has been found weak in certain cases; it is possible to find another random message that will produce the same hash. MD2 is slower, although no known weaknesses exist.

Secure hash algorithm

The secure hash algorithm (SHA) was designed by NIST and NSA, and is used in the digital signature standard, officially known as the secure hash standard and is available as FIPS-180-1.[21]

The existing SHA produces a 160-bit hash and is also known as SHA-1. There are additional standards undergoing public comments and reviews that will offer 256-, 384-, and 512-bit hashes. The draft standard is available.[16] The proposed standards will offer security matching the level of AES. The draft is available as FIPS-180-2.[22]

Applications of Message Digests

Message digests are useful and should be used to provide message integrity. Suppose Alice wants to pay $2000 to Eve, a contract network administrator. She types an e-mail to Bob, her accountant, to that effect. Before sending the message, Alice computes the message digest (SHA-1 or MD5) of the message and then sends the message followed by the message digest. Eve intercepts the e-mail and changes $2000 to $20,000; but when Bob computes the message digest of the e-mail, it does not match the one from Alice, and he knows that the e-mail has been tampered with.

But how do we ensure that the e-mail to Bob indeed came from Alice, when faking an e-mail source address is notoriously easy? This is where digital signatures come in.

Digital Signatures

Digital signatures were designed to provide the same features of a conventional ("wet") signature. The signature must be nonrepudiable, and it must be nontransferable (cannot be lifted and reused on another document). It must also be irrevocably tied back to the person who owns it.

It is possible to use symmetric encryption to digitally sign documents using an intermediary who shares keys with both parties, but both parties do not have a common key. This is cumbersome and not practical.

Using public key cryptography solves this problem neatly. Alice will encrypt a document with her private key, and Bob will decrypt it with Alice's public key. Because it could have been encrypted only with Alice's private key, Bob can be sure it came from Alice. But there are two issues to watch out for: 1) the rest of the world may also have Alice's public key, so there will be no privacy in the message; and 2) Bob will need a trusted third party (a certificate authority) to vouch for Alice's public key.

In practice, signing a long document may be computationally costly. Typically, first a one-way hash of the document is generated, the hash is signed, and then both the signed hash and the original document are sent. The recipient also creates a hash and compares the decrypted signed hash to the generated one. If both match, then the signature is valid.

Digital Signature Algorithm

NIST proposed digital signature algorithm in 1991 to be used in the Digital Signature Standard and the standard issued in May 1994. In January 2000, it announced the latest version as FIPS PUB 186-2.[23] As the name implies, this is purely a signature standard and cannot be used for encryption or key distribution.

The operation is pretty simple. Alice creates a message digest using SHA-1, uses her private key to sign it, and sends the message and the digest to Bob. Bob also uses SHA-1 to generate the message digest from the message and uses Alice's public key on the received message digest to decrypt it. Then the two message digests are compared. If they match, the signature is valid.

Finally, digital signatures should not be confused with the horribly weakened "electronic signature" law passed in the United States, where a touch-tone phone press could be considered an electronic signature and enjoy legal standing equivalent to an ink signature.

Message Authentication Codes

Message authentication codes (MACs) are one-way hash functions that include the key. People with the identical key will be able to verify the hash. MACs provide authentication of files between users and may also provide file integrity to a single user to ensure files have not been altered in a website defacement. On a web server, the MAC of all files could be computed and stored in a table. With only a one-way hash, new values could have been inserted in the table and the user will not notice. But in a MAC, because the attacker will not know the key, the table values will not match and an automated process could alert the owner (or automatically replace files from backup).

A one-way hash function can be turned into a MAC by encrypting the hash using a symmetric algorithm and keeping the key secret. A MAC can be turned into a one-way hash function by disclosing the key.

Section Summary

- Hash functions can create a fixed-length digest of arbitrary-length messages.
- One-way hashes are useful: given a hash, finding the message should be very hard.
- Two messages should not generate the same hash.
- MD2, MD4, and MD5 all produce 128-bit hashes.
- SHA-1 produces a 160-bit hash.
- Encrypting a message digest with a private key produces a digital signature.
- Message authentication codes are one-way hashes with the key included.

OTHER CRYPTOGRAPHIC NOTES
Steganography

Steganography is a Greek word that means sheltered writing. This is a method that attempts to hide the existence of a message or communication. In February 2001, *USA Today* and various other news organizations reported that terrorists are using steganography to hide their communication in images on the Internet.[24] A University of Michigan study[25] examined this by analyzing two million images downloaded from the Internet and failed to find a single instance.

In its basic form, steganography is simple. For example, every third letter of a memo could hide a message. And it has the added advantage over encryption that it does not arouse suspicion: often, the presence of encryption could set off an investigation; but a message hidden in plain sight would be ignored.

The medium that hides the message is called the cover medium, and it must have parts that can be altered or used without damaging or noticeably changing the cover media. In case of digital cover media, these alterable parts are called redundant bits. These redundant bits or a subset can be replaced with the message we want to hide.

Interestingly, steganography in digital media is very similar to digital watermarking, where a song or an image can be uniquely identified to prevent theft or unauthorized use.

Digital Notary Public

Digital notary service is a logical extension of digital signatures. Without this service, Alice could send a digitally signed offer to Bob to buy a property; but after property values drop the next day, she could claim she lost her private key and call the message a forgery. Digital notaries could be trusted third parties that will also time-stamp Alice's signature and give Bob legal recourse if Alice tries to back out of the deal. There are commercial providers of this type of service.

With time-sensitive offers, this becomes even more important. Time forgery is a difficult if not impossible task with paper documents, and it is easy for an expert to detect. With electronic documents, time forgeries are easy and detection is almost impossible (a system administrator can change the time stamp of an e-mail on the server). One do-it-yourself time-stamping method suggests publishing the one-way hash of the message in a newspaper (as a commercial notice or advertisement). From then on, the date of the message will be time-stamped and available for everyone to verify.

Backdoors and Digital Snake Oil

We will reiterate our warnings about not using in-house cryptographic algorithms or a brand-new encryption technology that has not been publicly reviewed and analyzed. It may promise speed and security or low cost, but remember that only algorithms that withstood documented attacks are worthy of serious use—others should be treated as unproven technology, not ready for prime time.

Also, be careful before using specific software that a government recommends. For example, Russia mandates the use of certain approved software for strong encryption. It has been mentioned that the government certifies all such software after behind-the-scenes key escrow. To operate in Russia, a business may not have any choice in this matter, but knowing that the government could compromise the encryption may allow the business to adopt other safeguards.

REFERENCES

1. Data Encryption Standard (DES). http://www.itl.nist.gov/fipspubs/fip46-2.htm.
2. Specialized DES cracking computer. http://www.eff.org/descracker.html.
3. Advanced Encryption Standard (AES). http://csrc.nist.gov/publications/fips/fips197/fips-197.pdf.
4. Schneier, B. In *Applied Cryptography*, 2nd Ed.; John Wiley: New York, NY, 1995.
5. Weak DES keys: Appendix A. http://www.ietf.org/rfc/rfc2409.txt.
6. AES selection report. http://csrc.nist.gov/encryption/aes/round2/r2report.pdf.
7. Rijndael developer's site. http://www.esat.kuleuven.ac.be/~rijmen/rijndael/.
8. Rijndael technical overview. http://www.baltimore.com/devzone/aes/tech_overview.html.
9. Rijndael technical overview. http://www.sans.org/infosecFAQ/encryption/mathematics.htm.
10. PKZIP encryption weakness. http://www.cs.technion.ac.il/users/wwwb/cgi-bin/tr-get.cgi/1994/CS/CS0842.ps.gz.
11. Diffie, W.; Hellman, M. New directions in cryptography. IEEE Trans. Inf.Theory **1976**, *IT–22*, 644–654.
12. RSA algorithm. http://www.rsasecurity.com/rsalabs/rsa_algorithm/index.html.
13. Paper on elliptic curve cryptography. ftp://ftp.rsasecurity.com/pub/ctryptobytes/crypto1n2.pdf.
14. Attacks on RSA. http://crypto.stanford.edu/~dabo/abstracts/RSAattack-survey.html.
15. SSL 3.0 protocol. http://www.netscape.com/eng/ssl3/draft302.txt.
16. TLS 1.0 protocol. http://www.ietf.org/rfc/rfc2246.txt.
17. International encryption regulations. http://cwis.kub.nl/~frw/people/koops/lawsurvy.htm.
18. IETF PKI working group documents. http://www.ietf.org/html.charters/pkix-charter.html.
19. Kerberos documentation collection. http://web.mit.edu/kerberos/www/.
20. Kerberos issues in Windows 2000. http://www.nrl.navy.mil/CCS/people/kenh/kerberos-faq.html#ntbroken.
21. Secure Hash Standard (SHS). http://www.itl.nist.gov/fipspubs/fip180-1.htm.
22. Improved SHS draft. http://csrc.nist.gov/encryption/shs/dfips-180-2.pdf.
23. Digital Signature Standard (DSS). http://csrc.nist.gov/publications/fips/fips186-2/fips186-2-change1.pdf.
24. *USA Today* story on steganography. http://www.usatoday.com/life/cyber/tech/2001-02-05-binladen.htm#more.
25. Steganography study. http://www.citi.umich.edu/techreports/reports/citi-tr-01-11.pdf.

Cyberforensics

Keith Jones
Annapolis, Maryland, U.S.A.

Abstract

Beginning in the 1980s, cyberforensics is a multidisciplinary field that facilitates the review of data sets to generate a factual or opinion-based presentation to stakeholders. Cyberforensics found its roots from investigations of cybercrimes and branched into nearly every facet of professional and personal lives. Cyberforensics consists of five key phases: acquisition, storage, identification, analysis, and presentation. This entry reviews the five key phases and introduces the history of the field, the tools, and additional resources.

INTRODUCTION

Found in the legal and IT industries, cyberforensics is the acquisition, storage, identification, analysis, and presentation of facts and opinions drawn from the review of the digital data sets collected (see Fig. 1). It is a subset of the cybersecurity field, and lies in the reactive review of the data sets collected after a triggering event warrants such analysis as opposed to the proactive security tasks generally associated with cybersecurity (see Fig. 2).

DIGITAL MEDIA TYPES

There are a large number of digital media types that a forensic investigator may encounter in any investigation. The list here is not intended to be exhaustive, as new devices are released daily that find their way into an investigation. Some of the types of devices that are encountered are as follows:

- Desktops
- Laptops
- Servers
- Network file system shares
- Tablets
- Smart phones
- External hard disks
- Flash devices (such as camera, extra phone storage, and USB flash drives)
- Network devices (such as firewalls and wireless access points)
- Cloud accounts (such as e-mail accounts and online storage)
- Virtual machines

Depending on the listed media types, a different acquisition and analysis process must be appropriately applied. The type of acquisition and analysis of a network device may not be appropriate for a desktop computer. Similarly, acquiring a virtual machine could be easier than acquiring a server computer system by the nature of how virtual machines are stored on the hard drive.

The next section will discuss the different acquisition methods for different types of computer media.

ACQUISITION

The acquisition of data can occur for nearly any given data set. A large number of acquisitions occur because a desktop, laptop, or server computer system is involved in an investigation. Typically, the data is acquired using a method known as bit-for-bit forensic imaging. This type of imaging starts at the beginning of the computer media—in this case the hard drives and any external hard drives associated with the computer—and copies every bit into a file on a separate hard drive until the end of the hard drive is encountered. This is repeated for every hard drive device found in the computer system. This is often referred to as forensically imaging a computer system. (Note if a computer contains a redundant array of inexpensive disks (RAID), a different method of acquisition may be employed in order to read the data quickly, without needing to reassemble every bit in the RAID manually or using third party software.)

Forensical imaging produces the *best copy* or *golden copy* and is the best-evidence image representing the first copy of the data of the original evidence. In this case, an image is simply a very large file representing the original computer hard drive. It is imperative that this copy is not altered in any way. This copy is traditionally stored away, while a working copy is used

Encyclopedia of Information Systems and Technology, DOI: 10.1081/E-EIST-120048609

Communication–Cybernetics

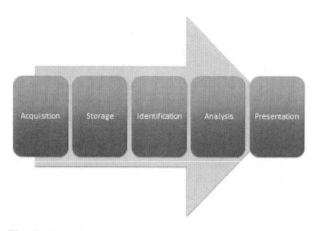

Fig. 1 Cyberforensics procedure.

during the analysis of the data. Using this method, a worst-case mistake that could write to the working copy would not be detrimental to the investigation as one could make a new working copy from the best-evidence copy and start over from the beginning.

Other types of acquisition are not as straightforward as forensically imaging the original evidence. Sometimes other data sets require different methods to acquire the data. For example, a company may have a large networked file system share containing all of the data relevant to a particular event. It may be infeasible or even impossible to forensically duplicate the device providing the file share. Perhaps, the only way to acquire the data is by using a logical copy. A logical copy is the same type of copy any Microsoft Windows user completes when they drag and drop files from one place to another. However, a logical copy can be complemented by collecting the file metadata, the information about the file such as the time and date stamps, along with the data of the files. In addition, a number of forensic tool vendors provide a method to capture logical data such as these into logical image files to complement the types of files used to fully forensically image a computer system.

Smart phones present a particular challenge to a forensic investigator during the acquisition phase. First,

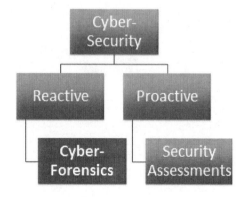

Fig. 2 CyberSecurity.

there are a large number of phone manufacturers. Second, each manufacturer produces a large number of phones with different features and internal hardware. An iPhone is not the same internally as a typical Android-based phone. The acquisition of data from smart phones usually requires a specialized set of hardware. There is a connector that is specific to the phone. Moreover, there is a protocol for each phone the data collector must follow in order to accurately record data. This may seem simple, but with the sheer number of different types of phones in the market, this is a very tricky endeavor.

Cloud accounts are typically more difficult to collect compared with the traditional forensic image of a computer system because data must be accessed using the protocol of that cloud account. Sometimes, a cloud account may not have a protocol to collect data that a forensic investigator may use. Other times, such as an online e-mail account, an investigator is fortunate because a mail software package may be used to copy all of the e-mails into a file that can be processed for further review. The number of types of cloud accounts is enormous and will not be listed in this entry. It is important to take away the fact that with every type of account, there is, in theory, a specialized acquisition method associated with that type of data.

Even without a full forensic duplication the investigator can place the first copy of the data set from the original evidence in the best-evidence category and any subsequent copies as working copies.

STORAGE

The aforementioned best-evidence copy of the data should be stored in a tamper-proof area. Not only is it important for the data to be unaltered, but it is also important to protect the confidentiality of the data collected. When a person possesses the forensic image from a computer system it is the same as that person possessing the original computer system. The original computer system could contain company intellectual property, personally identifiable information, or potential health information about the owner or other individuals.

Using defense in depth, it is wise to save the data using a form of encryption. Encryption will allow an investigator to transport the data safely. During transport, any accidental disclosure or loss will not be as detrimental to the data's owner as it would be encrypted, in theory, with a difficult-to-guess password or an unavailable certificate.

As the best evidence is used, it is typically checked in and out of evidence storage using a method to track who accessed the evidence and when.

IDENTIFICATION

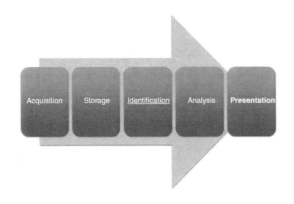

The identification of computer data ranges from the generic, such as *phone data*, when referencing a whole data set, to the specific, such as "a file containing registry entries from Microsoft Windows." Identification is usually accomplished automatically using a forensic suite of tools, which employs several methods to match the data with the correct type listing.

The most commonly used data identification forensic tool is signature matching, which compares the beginning and the end of a file to a known file type. For example, Microsoft Office documents typically have the hexadecimal phrase at the beginning of the file:

D0 CF 11 E0 A1 B1 1A E1 00

If this phrase is encountered in a file, it is reasonably safe to assume Microsoft Office is used to open and analyze the file. This type of identification dates back to the *file* command on Unix systems, which uses a file called a *magic file* containing numerous signatures for files the command can detect.

Identification extends beyond simply signature matching files. For example, one could identify all of the deleted files from a forensic image because a hard drive's unallocated space is acquired in the process. Further, an investigator may even carve a potential deleted file from unallocated space by using signature matching and identifying where a file may begin, end, and select all of the data in between.

Once all of the data have been identified, one proceeds to the analysis phase.

ANALYSIS

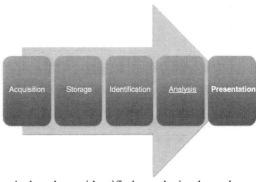

Once it has been identified, analysis depends on the type of data. For example, a forensic image of a desktop system will contain deleted files, while a logical copy of the same system will not. The following types of analyses could take place on any given system depending on the investigation at hand.

Internet History Review

This includes a review of the Internet browsing cache, history files, and remnants of websites visited that may be on the analyzed computer system. Because website data is routinely downloaded by the major web browsers, some websites the computer browsed could be reconstructed and viewed. In addition, an index to the remnants downloaded is usually kept by the browser in order to speed subsequent access to the same website and that file can be reviewed. In some web browsers, this file may be referred to as a *history file*.

Deleted File Review

Files that are deleted from a file system are not in fact lost forever. If the portion of the hard drive that contains a deleted file, which is now referred to as unallocated space, has not been overwritten with new data, then the old data may be resurrected. This is because file system access is typically slow, and operating systems do not wipe the data from a deleted file in a standard file deletion event because the time it would take to delete a file would be high. Instead, the file is marked as deleted and the space that was once occupied is now available as unallocated space, ready for a new file to be written.

Data Exfiltration Review

The question that is forefront in most investigations is whether or not data was copied from the computer to another destination. This is called *data exfiltration* in the cyberforensics industry. If data is copied from a company server to an attacker's computer system, it is exfiltrated from the company network. This plays an important role in security breaches or an insider that has *gone bad* because important information from an organization may be copied to a computer not owned by the company. By the sheer nature of computer data, multiple copies can be quickly created and disseminated from that point. Imagine a company with important intellectual property on their network share. Once an attacker or an insider copies that information to their computer system and disseminates it, it could cause the company stock price to fall as their manufacturing process is now in the public domain. Many cases require that any signs of data exfiltration be reported in the presentation phase.

System Logs Review

Microsoft Windows and Unix systems contain system logs. These system logs contain information such as logon and logoff events, permission changes, failed logon attempts, and much more. Reviewing such system logs gives the investigator a clearer picture regarding what happened on the system, if they are available. One such event where they may not be available is if the investigator is reviewing the system logs for events from long ago. Some logs *rollover*, overwriting the log information from long ago with newer log event information from real time. Therefore, it is important for the investigator to acquire the system logs for review sooner rather than later.

Registry Review

Microsoft Windows saves the system state and configuration in a facility called the Microsoft Windows Registry. To an investigator, this is one of the best logs available for analysis. Even though the system uses the registry as configuration storage, an investigator can view it as a large log file for review. The system registry contains multiple areas that an investigator can review to determine facts about the system. The system registry can contain anything from the system's internet protocol address, when it was shut down, what users logged in from the Windows domain, to documents last opened by a user on the system. The Windows registry is useful to almost every type of investigation imaginable.

File System Review

The file system is likely the best place to uncover evidence. As most machines are acquired using the full forensic duplication technique described previously, the file system is all that is available to the investigator at the beginning of the analysis phase. Each review discussed previously starts with the file system, and the relevant files are subsequently discovered in order to perform the respective review. Files that are not deleted and those that have been deleted can be reconstructed from the full forensic image in order to undergo analysis. In a logical copy, it is important to remember that deleted files are not available for analysis.

File Fragment Review

Files that have been deleted and partially overwritten by new files are called *file fragments*. File fragments are still important to some investigations even though the whole file cannot be reconstructed from the unallocated area of the file system. The reason a number of file fragments are important is because it attempts to prove that files once existed on the file system. Sometimes, the mere existence of a particular file, such as company intellectual property on a non-company system, is enough to show data exfiltration, which is all the stakeholders may care about. File fragments are typically found through the previously mentioned data carving methods.

Recycle Bin History Review

Specific to Microsoft Windows is the Recycle Bin. It is the trash can icon on the desktop where the user may move files in order to delete them. This adds an additional spot the deleted files are stored before they are truly deleted from the file system. The Recycle Bin stores the data in case the users change their mind about deleting the files and desire to move them back to their file system. Inside the Recycle Bin there is an index record, or also referred to as a history record, of the files that were deleted, where they originally existed, and when they were deleted. Perhaps, the case under investigation is the deletion of files after a court order was written to prevent such activity. The Recycle Bin history record could be used to prove that data was deleted even though the legal court order prevented the user from doing so. In this case, if proven, the user could be in trouble for breaking a court order.

Prefetch File Review

Microsoft Windows, in its desire to load programs quickly, prefetches executables and they are stored in a prefetch directory. Therefore, it is sometimes possible to see what files were executed on the system. If it is claimed that a subject did not run a program, the prefetch directory may hold the truth to that claim.

Scheduled Jobs Review

Micorosoft Windows and Unix allow for a user to schedule jobs to run. It is common for an attacker to

Fig. 3 Forensic analysis.

schedule their malicious tools to run periodically in the future. By examining the scheduled jobs file or directory, an investigator may detect a malicious user running programs not native to the machine. Windows store the data in *AT* files, while Unix stores the data in *cron* files.

USB Activity Review

The Microsoft Windows registry, as previously discussed, holds information about the system configuration. Parts of the registry are dedicated to maintaining a list of USB devices plugged in. For the system, it needs to know the information for subsequent usage, while for the investigator these sections of the registry will be similar to a log file. Tools are available to automatically parse the Windows registry and extract the history of USB activity. This type of analysis is useful when determining if data was exfiltrated or if other sources of data, such as an unknown USB device, could be pertinent to the case. If a file is zipped and a USB storage device is plugged into the system not long after, it is a safe bet that further analysis may uncover data exfiltration.

Volatile Memory Review

Volatile memory review has now become popular. Before a machine is shutdown, it is possible to extract the contents of memory in order to analyze it for running processes, open files, and other useful activity. The tools and analysis techniques for volatile memory analysis require a working knowledge of computers, specifically with respect to how data is stored in memory. When the machine is shut down, this memory disappears because it is volatile. Therefore, it is important to acquire the data before the machine changes state, such as being shutdown to perform a full forensic duplication as already described. Many artifacts, which were once only available on the file system, can be pulled from memory.

Hash Matching Review

A numerical hash can represent every file. A hash is a mathematical calculation of the contents of the file. No two files, in theory, will generate the same hash unless those files are exactly the same. A hash can be thought of as a *digital fingerprint* of a file. The most common hash algorithm used in cyberforensics is the MD5 hash. The MD5 hash is a 128-bit number generated from the contents of the file. If one bit is different between the content of the files, the MD5 hash of each will be different. Using this tool, investigators are able to quickly rule out all known system files using a software library called the NIST Software Reference Library (NSRL) distributed from the National Institute of Standards and Technology (NIST). This library contains millions of files known as normal system and program files and an investigator can rule out *hits* between analyzed files and files found in the NSRL. This makes the investigator much more efficient because they must analyze only the files that do not exist in the NSRL. Further, known bad files, such as malware, may have a MD5 hash that will show up in the investigator's data. Even if the MD5 shows up 100 times in the data, only one analysis must be completed on one of the 100 files because all of the other files are the same. Hashes are a very effective toolkit for discovering duplicate information.

Keyword Search Review

Often, keywords that are important to an investigation are known to the investigator. For example, a keyword or phrase from an important company document is already known. In this case, the investigator can instruct his tools to search for the keyword or phrase in every file in the evidence. This way, the investigator has much less to review and can review just the keyword or phrase hits in their data. Keyword searching is commonplace in cyberforensics.

Back to the topic of generic analysis, the analysis of data typically falls into two different types of categories: deterministic and probabilistic (see Fig. 3).

Deterministic Analysis

The majority of forensic analysis falls into deterministic analysis. Deterministic analysis typically uncovers facts. For example, if a file exists on a system, it is a deterministic fact that it exists. However, stating who put the file on the system would most likely be formed as a probabilistic opinion. Many proposed court experts make the mistake of taking probabilistic opinions and applying them as though they were facts in a deterministic manner. Examples of deterministic facts are as follows:

- The file was on the computer system.
- A phone call was made to 555-555-5555.

- The user "asmith" surfed the web on July 1, 2014.

Examples of probabilistic facts and opinions not to be confused with deterministic facts are as follows:

- Bob put the file on the computer system.
  - How does one know it was Bob who put the file?
- Bob made the phone call to 555-555-5555.
  - How does one know it was Bob who made the call?
- The user "asmith" surfed the web on July 1, 2014, because I know that program and that is how it works.
  - How does one know that is what occurred? More testing must be done of the proposed tool and published in order to be convincing.

Probabilistic Analysis

Probabilistic analysis uncovers the confidence of the fact or opinion being presented. For example, during an analysis, it may be a near 0% chance that a phrase would show up randomly on a hard drive. One would come to that opinion by applying the scientific method to a number of hard drives to derive the probability distribution of each possible character on the computer system and then applying the probabilities with the proper statistical mathematics to the data discovered in the case. For example, if it is found that a bit has a 50% chance of a 0 and 50% chance of a 1, any character could be randomly generated as a 1/256th chance as any other character. As soon as the phrase becomes larger, the probability of the phrase randomly appearing on a hard drive becomes much smaller.

Probabilistic analysis is a new type of computer forensics and is being written as this text was being published.

PRESENTATION

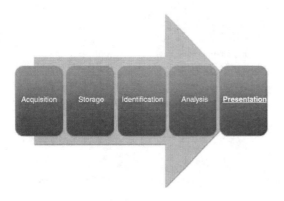

Presentation of forensic findings is usually accomplished in one or more of the following ways:

- Verbally
- Visually (with graphics)
- In a written report
- In an actual presentation (such as a PowerPoint (PPT) file)
- Verbal and written testimony for court

Typically, the user of the information determines the presentation. In some cases, the information is used in court and a report, verbal testimony in the form of a deposition, and a final testimony in court are warranted. In other cases, the consultant's end client uses the information and only a verbal account is needed.

This phase ends the traditional cyberforensics investigation. At any time an investigation can uncover evidence where the investigator must start at *Acquisition* and begin fresh for the new piece of evidence. Once the investigator has consumed all the pieces of evidence, the cyberforensics investigation concludes. Routinely, many cases do not finish due to lack of funding, time, manpower, or a combination of factors.

HISTORY

Computer forensics began in approximately the early 1980s when personal computers became more affordable for the home user. As computer use grew exponentially in the 1990s, so did computer crime. Computer crime was the main force behind using computer forensics for nearly 20 years until the 2000s. As computers found their way into civil lawsuits in the 2000s, the U. S. Government mandated that electronic data be discussed between litigating parties. A U. S. law was introduced in 2006 enforcing such action in civil disputes. Many states followed the federal law's lead, and hence cyberforensics was everywhere. Cyberforensics outside of the criminal arena became very common.

During 2005–2015, two main forces were driving cyberforensics: cybercrime and the legal profession. Cybercrime was concentrating on the crime involving data breaches, while the legal profession pushes much more generic investigations, depending on the conflict at hand. Cyberforensics is often referred to as *e-discovery* in the legal profession. The difference between e-discovery and cyberforensics is the scope of data. E-discovery concentrates on finding the wheelbarrow of hay from a hay stack, while cyberforensics typically concentrates on the needle from the wheelbarrow of hay. Cyberforensics uses fact and opinions, while e-discovery involves the production of many documents relevant to the litigation.

TOOLS

There are a number of tools used in computer forensics. This list is not meant to be exhaustive.

Autopsy by Brian Carrier

Autopsy is one of the only fully featured suites of cyberforensic tools available as open source. The tool is easy enough to use that an investigator can learn the trade for little to no cost, but a more advanced investigator can also use its powerful interface. A number of the analysis techniques described in this text can be performed using this tool. The missing feature from this tool is the ability to acquire data, but it is able to import data acquired by other tools, including the open source DD imaging tool.

Volatility by the Volatility Foundation

The Volatility framework is written in Python and uses the in-depth knowledge of the authors to parse memory to extract investigative leads a layman investigator may not know how to do manually. The project is also featured in a full-length in-depth memory forensics book about how to use the framework, what it does, and the magic behind the scenes.

XWays by XWays Software Technology AG

XWays is another fully feature tool suite of forensic tools. XWays is a commercial toolkit, which means it is not freely available. XWays is a really powerful toolkit that requires the user to be first familiar with cyberforensics before using it. Once an investigator is fully familiar with cyberforensics, XWays is one of the most powerful tools available to examine the data at a granular level.

EnCase by Guidance Software

EnCase is a toolkit that has been on the market for a long time and is very well known. EnCase allows an investigator to traverse through full forensic duplications with ease, as if they were loaded in Windows Explorer. EnCase forensic duplication format is the number one type of format acquisitions are stored as.

Forensic Tool Kit (FTK) by AccessData

FTK is most likely the second oldest tool available to an investigator. It comes with many tools, including FTK Imager, which allows an investigator to acquire evidence in many different formats, including the EnCase format. FTK itself works well for a novice investigator because it uses many analysis steps listed throughout this text and makes the results available to the user. FTK is also useful to an advanced investigator who wants to view the output quickly without having to reconstruct much data manually.

Internet Examiner Toolkit (IXTK) by SiQuest

IXTK is a specialized tool used to examine internet history artifacts. The newest version identifies and catalogs a number of different file types and allows the investigator to view them by selecting the type, which is a real time saver compared with older traditional methods.

NetAnalysis by Digital Detective

NetAnalysis is a tool similar to IXTK which allows an investigator to select deleted or readily available internet history artifacts from a computer system. The tool produces a report that the investigator can review and mark up for further analysis or presentation reasons.

RESOURCES

- http://www.sleuthkit.org:
  The home of Autopsy
- http://www.volatility-foundation.org:
  The home of the Volatility Framework
- http://www.x-ways.net:
  The home of XWays
- http://www.encase.com:
  The home of EnCase
- http://www.accessdata.com:
  The home of FTK
- http://www.siquest.com:
  The home of IXTK
- http://www.digital-detective.net:
  The home of NetAnalysis
- http://en.wikipedia.org/wiki/Computer_forensics:
  An informative article on cyberforensics
- http://en.wikipedia.org/wiki/MD5:
  An informative article on the MD5 hash algorithm

CONCLUSION

As a relatively young discipline, cyberforensics is an industry full of opportunities for participants and end stakeholders. Nearly everything in the world is run electronically from cars to computers, and cyberforensics examines data to paint the story of when and where events occurred. Data most laymen may think is lost can be recovered and reviewed by a trained investigator

Communication–
Cybernetics

in cyberforensics. The industry continues to grow and evolve.

BIBLIOGRAPHY

1. Carrier, B. *File System Forensic Analysis*, 1st Ed.; Addison-Wesley Professional: March 27, 2005.

2. Hale Ligh, M.; Case A.; Levy J.; Walters, A. *The Art of Memory Forensics: Detecting Malware and Threats in Windows, Linux, and Mac Memory*, 1st Ed.; Wiley: July 28, 2014.

3. Jones, K.; Bejtlich, R.; Rose, C. *Real Digital Forensics*; Addison-Wesley Professional: October 3, 2005.

Cybernetics

Christopher Brown-Syed
Faculty of Continuing Education and Training, Seneca College, Burlington, Ontario, Canada

Abstract

Cybernetics is the study of communication and control in animals and machines. Associated with computing and with information theory, it can be thought of as one of several approaches that constitute an even broader field, sometimes called the "systems sciences." While cybernetics is often associated with machine intelligence, or with hybrid systems with both human and machine components, its principles can be applied to any system, from a single cell system to entire human societies. Cybernetics suggests that every communications system is also a control system. Moreover, it demonstrates that systems of communication and control are similar in animals and in machines. Its major contributions include the notion of a linkage between communication and control, the idea of "feedback," and the idea of using logically separate communication channels for information content, that is, for messages themselves and for signals that control the system. Pioneered by Norbert Wiener, cybernetics represents a departure from earlier and concurrent information theory, because it emphasizes ways to modify the behavior of a system, while it is operating.

INTRODUCTION

With the 1948 publication of Wiener's seminal works, *Cybernetics; Or Control and Communication in the Animal and the Machine*,[1] and *The Human Use of Human Beings; Cybernetics and Society*,[2] interest in the approach developed rapidly, cybernetic principles became incorporated into the broader disciplines of systems-thinking, computing, and information theory, and became widely shared and applied. Wiener's autobiography[3] and his collected works[4] provide insights into the contexts in which he developed the approach. People who called themselves "cyberneticians" also adopted the concepts and methods of other schools of thought. By the mid-1960s, one author could refer to cybernetics as "a miscellany of loosely related activities."[5]

Consequently, the term has sometimes been used ambiguously in the literature. However, almost all practitioners of cybernetics sharecommon notions of communication and control, and recognize the importance of feedback in achieving desired outcomes. Several have sought to apply cybernetic principles to the solution of social problems.

Cybernetics can perhaps best be thought of as an approach to the study of complex systems, based upon several accepted notions; among them, the relationship between communication and control, the central importance of information in providing feedback, and the notions of emergent properties, and of purposive action or goal-directedness (teleology). Of these, perhaps the most essential or distinguishing feature of the approach is its focus upon the concept of "feedback."

The term cybernetics was first used in its modern context by the mathematician Norbert Wiener (1894–1964) to provide a focus on the studies arising from the information theory of Ralph Hartley (1888–1970), Claude Shannon (1916–2001), Warren Weaver (1894–1978), and their successors, which emphasized communication, control, and the importance of feedback, and demonstrated how electrical circuits could be used for computing. In his treatise, *The Computer and the Brain*, John Von Neumann (1903–1957) made explicit comparisons of information processing in the computers of the day and the human nervous system and brain as then understood. The titles of Wiener's seminal works include: *Cybernetics: Control and Communication in the Animal and the Machine*, *The Human Use of Human Beings: Cybernetics and Society*, and *God and Golem Inc.* These exemplify some of the threads of future discourse in the field.

The term "cybernetics" itself has been traced to Plato's *Laws*, and derives from the Greek κυβερνήτης, meaning "helmsman," or "steersman." The Latin *gubernator* and the English "governor" are equivalents.[6] The master of a ship sets and monitors its course, and takes corrective actions by comparing the actual to desired progress toward a destination, applying feedback to maintain the homeostasis, or stability, of a system. The system in question may be a computer or communications system, an organization, or even a nation. A wide array of derivative terms, such as "cyborg" and "cyberspace," has emerged, mostly reinforcing the notion that cybernetics is a discipline primarily concerned with communication and control.

Encyclopedia of Information Systems and Technology, DOI: 10.1081/E-EIST-120043868

From a cybernetic point of view, signals, messages, or information, passed along a communications channel, result in some outcome which involves a change of state within a system, and perhaps to its external environment. Through feedback mechanisms, that outcome can be monitored and additional messages sent to achieve a desired result.

For example, an electric wire running to a household lamp has an on/off switch but nothing to monitor its own effectiveness. When the switch is closed, current flows to the lamp, and it either illuminates or fails to go on. There is no feedback mechanism in a simple electrical circuit. A thermostat, however, involves a feedback mechanism. The temperature sensor in the thermostat keeps the furnace connected until a desired temperature is reached. The process of monitoring the temperature, and keeping the furnace going until the desired temperature is reached, is a feedback process.

Cybernetic principles have been widely applied in various engineering contexts, and have demonstrated everyday uses. Any communication pathway involving a transmitter, a message, and a receiver can be thought of as a "communications channel." In order to handle feedback continuously, and without confusion, Wiener and his colleagues realized that more than one channel of communication would be desirable. Otherwise, the messages containing the information and those controlling the system could interfere with one another.

An effective communications system needs one channel to exchange informational messages, and another to convey the messages which control the operation of the system itself. This principle underlies many of today's Internet communications protocols, such as the File Transfer Protocol (FTP). An FTP connection consists of a "data connection" and a "control connection."[7] They can be thought of as two communications channels— one through which files are exchanged and the other which allows users to start, monitor, and stop the process. Without the second channel, it would be difficult to stop a process, such as a lengthy file download, or even to tell how much of the file had been transferred successfully. It would be hard to attract the other computer's attention.

HISTORY AND DEFINITIONS

Arriving at a single comprehensive definition for the term "cybernetics" is complicated by the fact that central to this approach is the concept of "feedback" or, more generally, of "circularity." The computing term "recursion" is sometimes used in this context. A recursive program is one which uses its own outputs as inputs, or which "calls itself" in an iterative fashion. This notion has been applied to the discipline itself.

Those who consider themselves cyberneticians must necessarily apply the approach to their own work. Thus, the field is in constant revision. Furthermore, cybernetics itself can be thought of as a complex and open system, drawing upon parallel or concurrent developments in a range of allied fields, and those fields themselves are constantly evolving. In return, cybernetic principles and insights have had an impact in a wide range of studies. By the admission of the American Society for Cybernetics, each cybernetician advances his or her own view of the discipline and benefits reciprocally.

Although the term evokes immediate associations with the theory of communication, computing and artificial intelligence, and with mathematical and engineering approaches, humanists and social scientists have contributed to the field's development since its inception. Early cybernetic contributions were made not only by engineers like Norbert Wiener, computer scientist John Von Neumann, Claude Shannon, founder of "information theory," and systems analyst Anthony Stafford Beer (1926–2002), but also by the anthropologists Margaret Mead (1901–1978) and Gregory Bateson (1904–1980), the biophysicist Heinz von Foerster (1911–2002), and by Ludwig von Bertalanffy (1901–1972), who founded General System Theory (GST). The mathematicians and computer scientists Alan Turing (1912–1954) and Alonzo Church (1903–1995) made significant contributions. Turing's work was directly involved both with cryptanalysis and with artificial intelligence, and Church was long associated with the *Journal of Symbolic Logic*.

Marshall McLuhan (1911–1980), historian of culture and technology, saw cybernetics as a means of exploring societal complexities. Wiener describes his involvement with Vannevar Bush (1890–1974), John Von Neumann (1903–1957), Warren Weaver, and others, in the introduction to *Cybernetics*, noting a key conference held at Princeton during the winter of 1943–1944, and the contributions made by Arturo Rosenblueth Stearns (1900–1970), and other Mexican physiologists, cardiologists, and mathematicians from the United States and Mexico.[8] Rosenblueth was to collaborate with Wiener for much of the next decade. Thus, connections between the biological and computing sciences were being established, even while efforts at improving mechanisms of control were being focused upon the war effort; upon such immediate problems as perfecting signaling systems, improving the accuracy of gunnery, and similar engineering concerns.

Numerous definitions of the discipline appear on Web pages of the American Society for Cybernetics, where it is characterized as an interdisciplinary study, involving the key notions of "systemic dynamicity; homeostasis around a value; and recursive feedback." The Society's Web document, *Defining Cybernetics*, outlines perspectives of several of its past and existing members.[9] According to Francisco Varela, a "first-order cybernetics" would involve "the cybernetics of observed systems," while a "second-order cybernetics" would consist of the "cybernetics of observing systems," that is, the analysis of the inquiry itself. Thus, Larry Richards can characterize it as "a way of thinking about thinking," and Humberto Maturana as "the art and science of human understanding," while Gordon Pask describes it as "the art and science of manipulating defensible metaphors." Physicist André-Marie Ampère (1775–1836) had suggested *cybernétique*, as a term for "the sciences of government."[9]

Essentially, writers in the field agree on the centrality of the notions of communication and control, of the central role of information (sometimes thought of as "detectable differences"), and of recursion or feedback. In the words of Heinz von Foerster (1911–2002), a founder of the school of thought, "Should one name one central concept, a first principle, of cybernetics, it would be circularity."[9]

Because a theory of signs underlies any study of their exchange, the discipline is also related to semantics and semiology. There is also considerable overlap among the domains of Information Theory and Informatics, and the broader field of "systems thinking," as conceived by Ludwig von Bertalanffy (1901–1972), Anatol Rappaport (1911–2007), and their colleagues and successors, which deals with notions of self-organizing systems, complexity, and goal-directedness (teleology).

Like the GST of von Bertalanffy, and like systems analysis in general, cybernetics attempts to deal with all systems, both living and nonliving. As a result, those active in the field and the activities they undertake overlap considerably with approaches taken in related fields of inquiry. This complicates any study of the literature of cybernetics, and any attempt to define the boundaries of cybernetics as a system of thought. One need not be involved with computing to practice a cybernetic approach. It can be applied to economics, to the governance of societies, to almost any aspect of societal or natural systems and their environments. Biofeedback, a popular subject during the 1960s and 1970s, will serve as an example. Embraced by advocates of a "new age" or "counterculture," the biofeedback of the day involved monitoring one's own brain-waves, and attempting to use them to achieve meditative states. There is also considerable overlap between cybernetics and "informatics," including its subfield of "social informatics."

Major threads of discussion in the cybernetics literature have involved the study of automata, stochastic processes, machine intelligence, analyses of the human nervous system and cognition, and more concrete engineering problems such as disambiguation of signals, the functions of symbols, and error detection and correction. Cybernetics is not only concerned with quantities of information exchanged, but also with the contents and contexts of messages.

RELATIONSHIPS WITH OTHER APPROACHES

Ludwig von Bertalanffy's GST, and subsequent evolutions of it, exhibits a close kinship to cybernetics, as defined by Wiener. In particular, the "systems-thinking" movement of the latter twentieth century sought to find similarities among the various sciences, and even, occasionally, to reconcile the humanities with those sciences. The notions of open versus closed systems, of goal-directedness or teleology, and of emergent properties characterize the GST approach. Emergent properties are higher-order ones exhibited by entire systems, rather than by their individual components. GST and cybernetics both emerged during a period at which, in von Bertalanffy's words, notions were appearing in all sciences "like wholeness, holistic, organistic, gestalt, etc."[10]

Cybernetics and other "systems-thinking" approaches are concerned with dynamic systems which interact with their environments, and which use information to control their courses. Another important implicit idea is that of "teleology," or goal-directedness. While past events shape current decisions, future goals can inform them, that is, provide direction. Yet another is the notion of "emergent properties." As systems grow more complex, they display characteristics which their component parts, examined separately, do not. As well, the notion of "self-organizing" systems is important both in cybernetics and in the systems-thinking movement generally. With emergence, argues this school of thought, come new capacities for "self-organization."[11]

Other examples of systems-thinking approaches include the "viable systems" models of Stafford Beer (1926–2002), the "appreciative systems" of Sir Geoffrey Vickers (1894–1982), and the Soft Systems Methodology introduced by Peter Checkland (1930–), and still being enhanced and applied. The use of models, and mathematical logic, also characterizes cybernetic approaches. There is, therefore, considerable overlap among the domains of Information Theory and Informatics, and of "systems-thinking," as conceived by Ludwig von Bertalanffy, Anatol Rappaport (1911–2007), and their colleagues and successors in the International Society for the Systems Sciences.

CYBERNETICS AND SOCIETY

The communication scholar Marshall McLuhan (1911–1980), speaking in Washington DC at a foundational conference organized by the newly established American Cybernetic Association in 1964, ventured that what he called the "cybermation" of society represented a democratizing force. Focusing on the centrality of the notion of feedback,[12] McLuhan suggested that in an automated world, actions and their effects occurred simultaneously, and that the holistic aspects of cybernetics bespoke a trend away from the specialization which characterized the industrial age, toward a post-industrial one in which actions and their consequences were immediately connected and felt across society as a whole. McLuhan saw the impact of "cybermation" as far greater than previous innovations, such as the wheel, the printing press, or telecommunications, predicting widespread transformations in the organization and governance of the economic system, and of society as a whole.

That McLuhan found the cybernetic approach promising should not be surprising, since his own work was indebted to that of historian Harold Innis (1894–1952), who advocated a "cyclical" approach to history, reminiscent of the "circularity" central to cybernetics. The Institute of Electrical and Electronics Engineers(IEEE), through a series of published conference proceedings on Systems, Man, and Cybernetics, continues to emphasize social as well as engineering applications.

PHILOSOPHICAL, ETHICAL, AND RELIGIOUS ASPECTS

In *The Human Use of Human Beings*,[4] which was written with broad audiences in mind, and *God and Golem, Inc.*,[13] Wiener raised awareness of some ethical and metaphysical problems posed by machine intelligence. There is a larger question as well, that if nature, the environment, or the universe is considered to be a system, can it be said to have a goal and a governor, or is it self-governing?

Less than a decade after Wiener had proposed the term "cybernetics," demonstrable job loss as a result of what some perceived as "runaway" technology was raising concern over the automation of industrial processes. Citing rising unemployment due to automation, and attendant ethical concerns, Wiener addressed some of these concerns in, *God and Golem, Inc.* In this apologia for his new science, Wiener criticizes what he takes to be religious opposition, and advances a secular view of history. Its title alludes to the legend of the Golem, in which Rabbi Judah Loew, of Prague (1525–1609), or sometimes, another master, brings an artificial human to life. (cf. Psalm 139:16, "Your eyes beheld my unformed substance." According to the legend, an understanding master replicates God's creative act, bringing life to a human figure formed of earth, as was Adam. However, the problem of controlling the creature leads to its eventual destruction).

Wiener suggests a potential for conflict between cybernetics and religion or metaphysics. Alan Turing had suggested that a machine that behaved in a way indistinguishable from a human could be considered intelligent. That problem could become acute, if intelligent systems were to become self-aware.

Any philosophical discussion about synthetic intelligence must grapple with the mind–body dualism raised centuries earlier by René Descartes (1596–1650).

Though their professional concerns did not always coincide, both the philosophers Bertrand Russell (1892–1970) and Ludwig Wittgenstein (1989–1951) rejected metaphysics, and their work was much in keeping with the post-war intellectual climate in the West. In that milieu, machine intelligence could be seriously considered, setting aside as irrelevant any "ghosts in the machine" like the "soul" or "spirit." Russell's "logical positivism," and Wittgenstein's investigations concerning language, and the work of other British analytical philosophers, also raised practical questions that would become relevant in the pursuit of machine intelligence. Another British philosopher Gilbert Ryle (1900–1976) had popularized the phrase "ghost in the machine,"[14] and Arthur Koestler (1905–1983), who was directly involved in the early development of GST, took it up.[15] Writing about cybernetics in 1966, Jagjit Singh resolved to use the term "to denote an interdisciplinary inquiry into the nature and physical basis of human intelligence, with the object of reproducing it synthetically."[16] Singh goes on to stress the connection between "the complexity of a system and the language used" to describe it. Singh recognized that messages in any language could be ambiguous. Inspired by the work of British analytical philosophers, he notes objections to logical positivism and semiotics raised by the existentialist philosophers of the day, notably Jean-Paul Sartre (1905–1980), whose nominalist theory of language suggested that words were almost completely personal and subjective. Moreover, Singh notes the importance of cultural diversity, and the grave errors caused by mistranslation. If systems could not be described, at least to machines, by means of a common vocabulary, machine intelligence would be difficult to achieve. This problem will be evident to anyone who uses the "search engines" of the early 21st century. Words are often ambiguous, even within the same languages, and the contexts in which they are used are of critical importance. As well, Singh points out the connection, at the level of basic thermodynamic laws, between information and its physical media, crediting cybernetics with the quest for ever more efficient ways of encoding and transmitting complicated messages.[17]

In turn, cybernetics and the quest for machine intelligence have attracted the attention of philosophers, especially since developments in computing and programming languages have made artificial intelligence realizable. For philosophers, these developments cast a new light upon the "mind–body" problem which has been debated for centuries, inspiring numerous philosophical investigations, one accessible example being *The Mind's I*, by Hofstadter and Dennett.[18]

IDEOLOGICAL INFLUENCES

Writers in the Soviet Union had initially opposed cybernetics on philosophical grounds, considering it a possible Western pseudo-science, and a possible rival to dialectical materialism, but they had accepted it by the end of the 1950s, and even established a cybernetics group within the Soviet Academy. This was in part due to their recognition of the need to automate industrial processes and accounting.

The cybernetic approach was justified within a Marxist–Leninist framework, in part because it appeared to be a mechanism to explain human communication without recourse to metaphysics, and which could also investigate its economic influences. Moreover, there was an immediate need to advance the science of computing, stimulated by Russia's Cold War rivalries with the West. As well, the cybernetic notion of circularity or feedback bore some resemblance to the concept of "reflection" or "self-study," which was considered essential to the emergence of socialist society.[19] Especially during the 1960s and 1970s, cybernetics received significant attention in the Soviet Union not only within engineering and communications, but also within the broader context of Marxist–Leninist philosophy. Many Soviet publications issued during the period deal with social as well as engineering issues, in part because of the ideological necessity of framing all scientific investigation within the broader context of the socialist endeavor.

ROBOTICS, HUMAN–MACHINE INTERFACES, AND ASSISTIVE TECHNOLOGIES

Over the decades since its inception, the term "cybernetics" has been associated with automata, semantics, signal disambiguation, and the development of practical communications and control systems, for example, in "railway cybernetics." More theoretical works have dealt with computational philosophy, cognition, and the application of concepts derived from computing to the study of the human nervous system and the function of the brain. There are practical implications of cybernetic theorems in medical informatics, the development of artificial limbs or assistive devices, and robotics in general. Numerous publications of the IEEE and the American Society for Cybernetics reflect these and similar areas of concern. While such publications may not refer directly to cybernetics, its approaches and tenets are often assumed. (IEEE transaction series of note include *IEEE Transactions on Signal Processing*, and *IEEE Transactions on Systems, Man, and Cybernetics*, among others.)

If the mechanisms of communication and control are similar in the animal and the machine, it should be possible to link the two. Von Neumann noted the similarity between the systems of communication and control in computers and the brain in 1958.[20] James R. Newman's seminal article, "Computing Machinery and Intelligence," has been widely reprinted.[21]

Steve Mann's *Cyborg: Digital Destiny and Human Possibility in the Age of the Wearable Computer* arose from his experiments in assistive technologies.[22] Among these, Mann proposed linking medical life-sign monitors to environmental controls such as heating and air conditioning, or even to emergency medical services, and described his work with small video capture devices linked to computers, that could help people organize their lives. Text-to-speech and voice command recognition have already made significant inroads into everyday life. Direct interfaces between the brain and prosthetic or environment control devices are already being applied to assist people with disabilities on an experimental basis.

Von Neumann's classic work *The Computer and the Brain* drew comparisons between the human brain and the computers of his time. Since then, considerable advances have been made, both in computing and in neuroscience. It is now possible to consider seriously the potential, not only for using the human nervous system to control artificial limbs, but also for linking the brain directly to computers, communications systems, and ultimately, to other human brains and to the vast storehouse of recorded knowledge residing in the Internet.

Proponents of such interfaces foresee a world in which individual self-actualization will increase by unlimited degrees, but dystopian views, such as those which characterize science fiction's "Matrix," and Star Trek's "Borg" society, populated by humans turned to drones by connectivity, remind us of Wiener's original dictum: every communications technology is also a control mechanism. The specter of mind-control clouds the bright horizon of individual and societal empowerment envisaged by McLuhan.

Major threads of discussion in the cybernetics literature involve automata, stochastic processes, machine intelligence, analyses of the human nervous system and cognition, and more concrete engineering problems such as disambiguation of signals, the functions of symbols, and error detection and correction. These are concerns, not only with quantities of information exchanged, but also with the contents of messages.

Communication–
Cybernetics

THE PREFIX "CYBER"

The prefix "cyber," occurring in terms like "cyberspace," "cyberpunk," and "cybrarian," has increasingly been applied broadly in science fiction and in the popular media, in depictions of virtual reality, role-playing games, artificial intelligence, and social networking. The term "cyberspace" has been used as a synonym for the global Internet, or applied to activities or services associated with it. The terms "cyberwarfare" and "cybercrime" occur in defense and law enforcement contexts, while "cyberspace" is a term commonly used in the mass media in social networking contexts, or as a synonym for the Internet itself. At the time of writing, at least 500 titles in the Library of Congress catalog used the term "cyberspace" in the context of the Internet.

Since communication, on this view, always implies control, and always involves information exchange and feedback as a regulator, the appearance of terms like "cybercrime," "cyber-terrorism," and "cyberwarfare" are predictable. By manipulating information about a battlefield, or an economy, combatants can react to extreme events, and can influence an enemy's actions by denying crucial information, or by manipulating it.

Because Wiener's initial definition linked communications with control, this more restrictive usage of the prefix, "cyber," remains valid, though its repeated usage may lead to misconceptions of the broader discipline of cybernetics. The popularly conceived possibility of a "cyborg" as a composite entity made up of biological and mechanical components is presumed in Wiener's original formulations. Wiener, Von Neumann, Alan Turing, Alonzo Church, and others emphasized the similarity, if not the identity, between information processing in animals and machines. Investigations of the brain, and advances in micro- and nanotechnology, have made direct interfaces between biological and mechanical systems possible, though the art of applying them is in its infancy.

Do these neologisms have anything to do with cybernetics as a discipline? The application of cybernetic principles to the study of social networking seems particularly promising. In the networking environment of the early 21st century, actions such as the posting of photographs or audiovisual material, text messages, Weblog entries, or feeds from commercial news media can achieve universal and instantaneous distribution, and invite immediate responses. As well, the network behaves as a self-organizing system, with peer pressure playing a large role in governing behavior. The messages carried over the network modify one another, reinforcing and rejecting, providing the sort of collaborative creating milieu that cybernetics, in its most optimistic formulations, predicts. While its eventual outcomes remain to be seen, social networking, and the Internet itself, appear to exemplify self-organizing systems, with technical, economic, and societal components. Cybernetics, viewed as the study of communication, control, and circularity, seems particularly well suited to its investigation.

CYBERNETICS AND LIBRARIANSHIP

For librarianship, perhaps the most applicable of Wiener's insights was his recognition of the implicit link between communication and control. Wiener's dictum, "[e]very communications technology is a control technology," has deep consequences for social informatics. It implies that every new information and communications medium, such as the Internet, necessarily increases social or economic advantages for those who have access to it, and concurrent disadvantages for those who do not. At least one contemporary writer has used the term "cyber-capitalism" in a critique of current developments in networking.[23] Therefore, the very existence of public libraries and open-source software becomes essential to the goal of narrowing the "digital divide" and to rectifying global information disparities. As well, the increasingly evident similarity of processes of control and communication in the animal and the machine, and the broader societal implications of discoveries about human and machine intelligence, have practical implications for information retrieval.

A "cybrarian" is perhaps best defined as a librarian who uses digital resources. *The Cybrarian's Manual*, an American Library Assoiciation publication, edited by Pat Ensor, both suggests and typifies this usage.[24] This is not a work of fundamental research, but rather an anthology of articles, most outlining techniques and practices.

However, certain sections of the *Cybrarian's Manual* are pertinent here, because they trace historical developments in science fiction that introduce the "cyber" prefix, or pose ethical problems associated with machine intelligence, or with cybernetics and society.

FURTHER INFORMATION

The annual conference agendas of the American Society for Cybernetics, http://www.asc-cybernetics.org, provide a means of tracking current investigations, as do the Principia Cybernetica Web[24] and the IEEE, http://www.ieee.org. The journal *Kybernetes*[25] and the relatively new series *IIAS Transactions on Systems Research and Cybernetics*[26] are also of note. The related International Society for the Systems Sciences maintains a site at http://isss.org/world/index.php.

CONCLUSION

The principles of cybernetics, viewed as the study of control and communication, have influenced thinkers not only within the fields of computing, electrical engineering, informatics, and artificial intelligence, but also in a broad range of social-scientific disciplines, and from across the political spectrum. In particular, the notion of feedback has become as deeply imbedded in fields as diverse as medicine and management that its origins in the seminal investigations of Norbert Wiener may easily be overlooked. From initial experiments, aimed at exploring communication and control in biological and mechanical systems to observations about the operations of whole societies, cybernetic-thinking has become infused into the fabric of the systems sciences. Perhaps most importantly, systems science approaches, such as cybernetics, offer ways of dealing with complex situations, by reference to a few simpler models, and to connect the concept of "information" itself with the physical processes involved in its storage, communication, and control.

In the context of library and information science, which turns increasingly to automated means and digital communications, the observation that every communications mechanism must also be a control mechanism carries with it serious implications for the employment of emerging technologies, and the bridging of the digital divide. Moreover, the linking of human and machine intelligence, whether through the perfection of intelligent computer systems or through the development of assistive technologies, holds great promise for librarianship's endeavor of locating, organizing, and disseminating information, and assisting in the creation of new knowledge for a broad range of clients and contexts.

REFERENCES

1. Wiener, N. *Cybernetics, Or, Control and Communication in the Animal and the Machine*; Technology Press: Cambridge, MA, 1948.
2. Wiener, N. *The Human Use of Human Beings; Cybernetics and Society*; Houghton Mifflin: Boston, MA, 1950.
3. Wiener, N. *I Am a Mathematician, the Later Life of a Prodigy; An Autobiographical Account of the Mature Years and Career of Norbert Wiener and a Continuation of the Account of His Childhood in Ex-Prodigy*; MIT Press: Cambridge, MA, 1970.
4. Wiener, N. *Collected Works with Commentaries*; MIT Press: Cambridge, MA, 1976.
5. Singh, J. *Great Ideas in Information Theory, Language and Cybernetics*; Dover Publications: New York, 1966; 4.
6. Dechert, C.R. The development of cybernetics. In *The Social Impact of Cybernetics*; Dechert, C. R., Ed.; Simon and Schuster: New York, NY, 1966; 11–38.
7. Network Working Group, In *RFC 959: Tile Transfer Protocol, October 1985 (Obsoletes RFC 765)* http://www.faqs.org/rfcs/rfc959.html (accessed January 2009).
8. Wiener, N. In *Cybernetics, Or, Control and Communication in the Animal and the Machine*; Technology Press: Cambridge, MA, 1948; 14–16.
9. American Society for Cybernetics, In *Defining Cybernetics*. http://www.asc-cybernetics.org/foundations/definitions.htm (accessed January 2009).
10. von Bertalanffy, L. *General System Theory, Foundations, Development, Applications*; G. Braziller: New York, NY, 1968.
11. Vickers, C.G. *Control, stability, and choice* [Unpublished manuscript]. University of Toronto Faculty of Applied Science and Engineering: 1956 Vickers, Geoffrey, Sir, 1894.
12. McLuhan, H.M. Cybernation and culture. In *The Social Impact of Cybernetics*, Dechert, C. R., Ed.; Simon and Schuster: New York, NY, 1966; 95–108.
13. Wiener, N. *God and Golem, Inc.: A Comment on Certain Points Where Cybernetics Impinges on Religion*; MIT Press: Cambridge, MA, 1964.
14. Ryle, G. *The Concept of Mind*; Penguin Books: Harmondsworth, Middlesex, U.K., 1949.
15. Koestler, A. *The Ghost in the Machine*; Arkana: London, U.K., 1967.
16. Singh, J. *Great Ideas in Information Theory, Language and Cybernetics*; Dover Publications: New York, NY, 1966; 5–7.
17. Singh, J. *Great Ideas in Information Theory, Language and Cybernetics*; Dover Publications: New York, NY, 1966; 79–83 and passim.
18. Hofstadter, D.R.; Dennett, D.C. *The Mind's I: Fantasies and Reflections on Self and Soul*; Basic Books: New York, 1981.
19. Kirschenmann, P.P. *Information and Reflection: On Some Problems of Cybernetics and How Contemporary Dialectical Materialism Copes with Them*; Reidel: Dordrecht, the Netherlands, 1970.
20. Von Neumann, J. *The Computer and the Brain*; Yale University Press: New Haven, CT, 1958.
21. Newman, J.R. Computing machinery and intelligence. Mind **1950**, *49*, 433–460 (Published under the title "Can a Machine Think," in volume 4 of *The World of Mathematics*, Newman, J. R., Ed.; 2099–2123, Simon & Schuster (1956). Reprinted in 2000, and in *The Philosophy of Artificial Intelligence*, Margaret, B., Ed.; Oxford University Press: New York, 1990).
22. Mann, S. *Cyborg: Digital Destiny and Human Possibility in the Age of the Wearable Computer*; Doubleday: Toronto, ON, Canada, 2001.
23. Laxer, J. *The Undeclared War: Class Conflict in the Age of Cyber Capitalism*; Penguin: Toronto, ON, Canada, 1999.
24. Ensor, P. *The Cybrarian's Manual 2*; American Library Association: Chicago, IL, 2000.
25. Principia Cybernetica Web. http://pespmc1.vub.ac.be/
26. IIAS Trans. Syst. Res. Cybern.: Int. J. Int. Inst. Adv. Stud. Syst. Res. Cybern. 2001 A list of IIAS publications is available at http://www.iias.edu.

Data Analytics

Stephan Kudyba
New Jersey Institute of Technology, Newark, New Jersey, U.S.A.

Abstract

The primary initiative in leveraging the value of data resources lies in the realm of analytics. This term, however, encompasses a wide variety of methodologies that can provide descriptive, comparative, and predictive information for the end user. The present entry will provide a brief background and description of some noteworthy analytic approaches as applied to more historical, structured data and include references to big data issues along the way. The area of big data and analytics will be addressed in greater detail in the real-time and continuous analysis section at the end of the present entry.

Analytic methods can range from simple reports, tables, and graphics to more statistically based endeavors to quantitative-based methods. We provided some analytic approaches according to some commonly referred to categories. Regardless of the techniques deployed, the end result of an analytic endeavor is to extract/generate information to provide a resource to enhance the decision-making process.

1. Spreadsheet applications (also facilitated by vendor software packages)
   a. Data/variable calculations, sorting, formatting, organizing
   b. Distribution analysis and statistics (max, min, average, median, percentages, etc.)
   c. Correlation calculation between variables
   d. Linear and goal programming (optimization)
   e. Pivot tables (an intro to online analytic processing (OLAP) and business intelligence (BI))
2. BI
   a. Query and report creating
   b. OLAP
   c. Dashboards
3. Multivariate analysis (also part of BI)
   a. Regression (hypothesis approach)
   b. Data mining applications (data-driven information creation)
      • Neural networks
      • Clustering
      • Segmentation classification
      • Real-time mining
4. Analysis of unstructured data
   a. Text mining
5. Six Sigma
6. Visualization

The type of analytic approach is generally dictated by the objective of what the user of the analysis requires, and where the objective and overall initiative needs to be clearly defined to achieve the most effective and informative results. This problem definition process generally involves the selection of a performance metric and identification of variables that impact that metric. Once the scope of the analytic endeavor (problem definition) has been established, then corresponding data resources must be managed (variables selected at a particular level of detail) and analysis can begin. The remainder of this entry will provide an overview of some of the aforementioned analytic methods mentioned.

INTRODUCTION TO THE CONCEPT OF ANALYTICS

One of the initial stages of any analytic endeavor is the incorporation of an investigative study of a data resource. In other words, before a report is generated or quantitative modeling is conducted, an analyst needs to better understand what's in a data file. This investigative process involves conducting a distribution analysis of various data variables, perhaps calculating maximum, minimum, and variance metrics such as standard deviations. This provides a descriptive character of what the data variables are composed of and renders additional analysis more robust, as it identifies the presence of such issues as data bias or skew, outliers, and even errors in data resources.

Encyclopedia of Information Systems and Technology, DOI: 10.1081/E-EIST-120053827

Time	Performance Metric	Marketing Source	Source Traffic Location
Hour	Clicks	Paid, Generic	Town
Day	Bounce	search	County
Month	Conversions	Mobile device	State
	Cost	Banners	
		Referral site	

BUSINESS INTELLIGENCE

Reports

The focus of the present entry involves the utilization of BI applications (e.g., OLAP, dashboards, and mining) to extract actionable information from all types of data to enhance the decision-making process. One of the most basic levels of this approach is the creation of business reports that incorporate sequel-related queries of data resources to extract variables that describe a business scenario. The introduction of big data involves additional requirements to this process; namely, when devising the parameters of the report to be created, the decision maker now must consider new variables that impact that conceptual report. The volume of data that must be processed must also be considered, and finally, the currency of the report (e.g., how often a report must be updated to provide adequate information for the decision maker). However, as simple as the process of generating a report may be, creating one that provides essential information to those that receive it may be a quite complex task.

Consider a request by an Internet marketing department to produce an analytic report that depicts the performance of various Internet marketing tactics that drive traffic to a company's landing page. Although this initiative appears to be straightforward and simplistic in nature, one must consider all the variables that comprise the area to be analyzed, along with the needs of the user of the report.

Some dimensions and variables that could be included in this analysis would involve:

Platforms such as Google Analytics provide robust functionality to accomplish extensive report generation in the e-commerce spectrum. When conducting customized analytics (tailored analytics to a specific company's activities) data experts and analysts must apply due diligence to acquire that information that provides a strategic advantage in the marketplace. This involves the storage, processing, management, and ultimate analysis of data resources that describe a particular process.

Well-designed reports that incorporate all the pertinent and available variables that describe a business activity can be an important source of information to decision makers (see Fig. 1). However, the limitation of information creation at the report level is that the user often scans a report, assimilates the information, and quickly thinks of alternative business scenarios that are essential to providing more robust information regarding a process or activity. The report is limited to its existing level of data aggregation and variables depicted. The next step to analysis or BI involves the application of OLAP, which gives users the flexibility to view and analyze multiple scenarios of a business process. Before we describe the application of OLAP functionality that leverages large data resources and

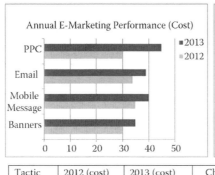

Tactic	2012 (cost)	2013 (cost)	Change	Tactic	2013 Conv
PPC	30,000	44,000	46%	PPC	22%
Email	34,000	39,000	15%	Email	20%
Mobile	35,000	40,000	14%	Mobile	42%
Banner	30,000	34,000	13%	Banner	16%

Fig. 1 Annual report of e-marketing cost and conversions.

Table 1 Hypothetical data recording national sales activities

Salesperson	Product Category	City/Area	Customer Industry	Units	Sales
KDE	ETL	NY	Finance	90	$45,000
SEF	Reporting	NY	Insurance	80	$24,000
CHT	Analytics	Boston	Finance	10	$20,000
HHT	Database	Phili	Retail	55	$41,250
GGN	Database	Atlanta	Manufact	65	$48,750
THT	ETL	DC	Retail	18	$9,000
TTW	ETL	Phili	Retail	42	$21,000
AHY	Analytics	Chicago	Retail	30	$60,000
FDO	Reporting	San Fran	Manufact	39	$11,700
JJT	Reporting	Chicago	Finance	42	$12,600
GHI	ETL	NY	Transport	32	$16,000
BDE	Analytics	DC	Transport	71	$142,000
PEC	Reporting	NY	Finance	26	$57,045
LYJ	Database	Chicago	Insurance	52	$39,000
KIP	Analytics	San Fran	Insurance	75	$150,000
OBN	Database	NY	Retail	53	$39,750
ERB	Database	San Fran	Manufact	93	$69,750
SEN	Reporting	LA	Retail	17	$5,100
JJR	ETL	NY	Retail	96	$48,000
WNS	ETL	Phili	Manufact	32	$16,000
DHK	Reporting	Boston	Finance	26	$7,800
TRN	Reporting	Boston	Transport	30	$9,000
RGH	Database	Phili	Retail	54	$40,500
MMR	Database	Atlanta	Retail	46	$34,500
SJP	ETL	Atlanta	GPU	80	$40,000

addresses currency of data, consider the more simplistic spreadsheet application of Pivot Tables.

PIVOT TABLES

A simplistic version of OLAP that many users can quickly relate to includes the use of pivot tables in a spreadsheet environment. Pivot tables leverage data in a flat, spreadsheet file to present alternative scenarios that describe a business activity. Through basic spreadsheet functionality, users can quickly generate a table view of

Table 2 Sales by product category by city

ETL (Extract Transfer and Load)

New York	$61,000
DC	$9,000
Philadelphia	$37,000
Atlanta	$40,000
Total	$195,000
Reporting	
New York	$81,045
San Francisco	$11,700
Chicago	$12,600
Boston	$16,800
Los Angeles	$5,100
Total	$127,245

relevant variables at a particular level of aggregation. For example, a spreadsheet of data that describes a software company's sales activities can include numerous rows according to corresponding variables. Hypothetical data recording national sales activities of branches across the country is illustrated in Table 1.

With a simple pivot function, Table 2 could be calculated with ease.

Dynamic Reporting through OLAP

Pivot tables are similar to OLAP in that they provide a multidimensional view of an activity. Enterprise OLAP provides greater scale to the analytic process, as it provides the platform to address multiple levels of aggregation of data resources, can depict updated views as source data is updated, and can process extremely large volumes of data. With this flexibility, OLAP can help decision makers investigate information addressing

General Cube Inputs

Time	Descriptive Variables	Performance Metrics
Daily	Demographics	Sales
Weekly	Behavioral	Response rate
Monthly	Strategic	Operational
Quarterly	Process related	Units

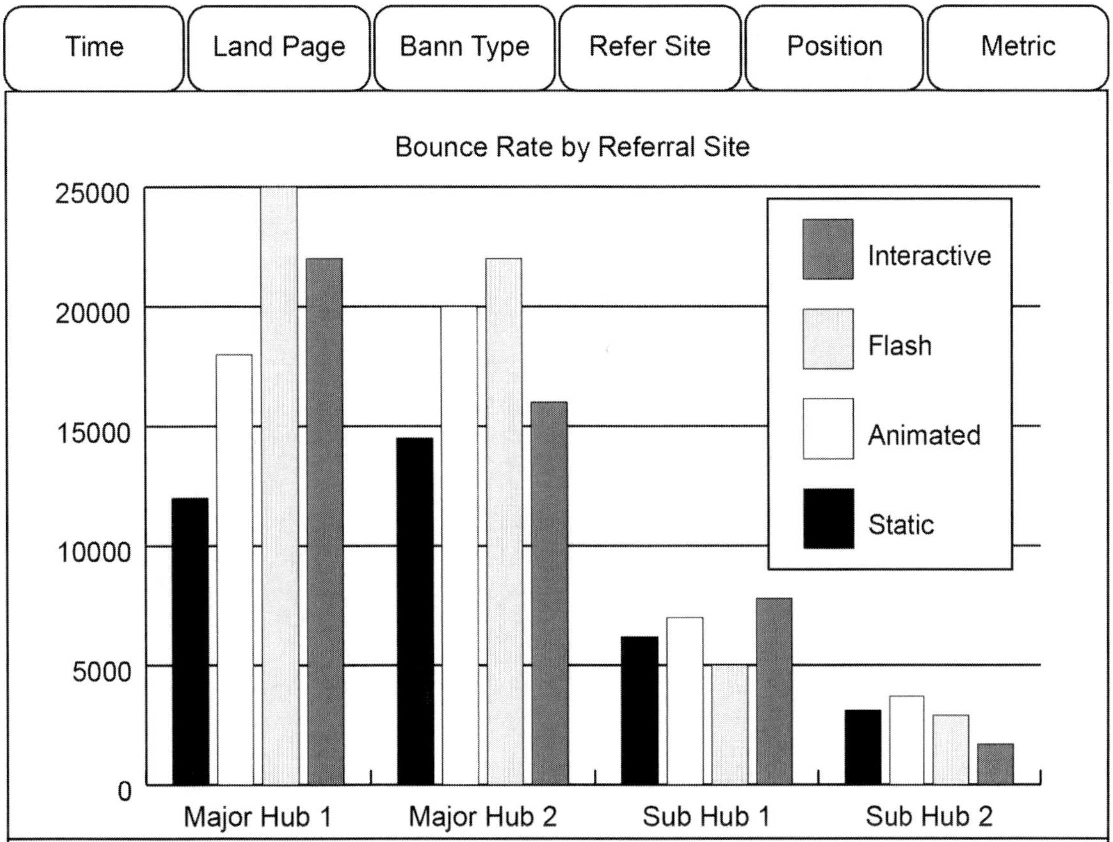

	Major Hub 1	Major Hub 2	Sub Hub 1	Sub Hub 2	Total
Static	12000	14500	6200	3100	35800
Animated	18000	20000	7000	3700	48700
Flash	25000	22000	5000	2900	54900
Interactive	22000	16000	7800	1700	47500
Total	**77000**	**72500**	**2000**	**11400**	**186900**

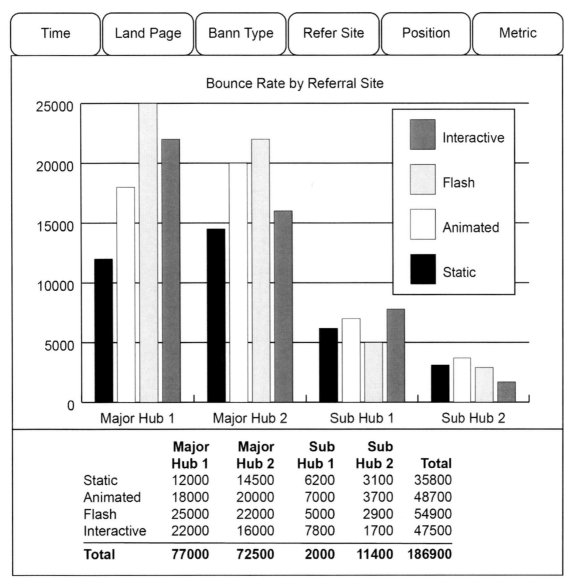

Fig. 2 Banner performance multidimensional cube.

multiple descriptive scenarios regarding an operation's activity, therefore enhancing the knowledge generation process and overall ability to generate effective strategic conclusions. The diversity of information views involves various dimensions of time, performance metrics, and descriptive variables.

These inputs must be organized to provide information (variables at levels of detail) that describes a business scenario in order to facilitate decision support for the end user. Consider the graphical view of a cube in Fig. 2.

Fig. 2 depicts an illustration of an OLAP cube that facilitates analytics of banner Internet marketing tactics. The cube presents a multidimensional view of the variables that describe the activities involved in banner advertising. The platform gives the analyst the ability to query data variables from different levels of detail and in different combinations, through both numeric data and visualization. The tabs at the top of the graphic depict the variables that are available to be analyzed. The scenario depicted illustrates the bounce rate (number of bounces) according to different types of referral sites where the various banner styles (static, animated, flash, and interactive) are displayed.

Users have the ability to change variable views from different perspectives, including:

Time (hourly, daily, quarterly)
Landing page (social media, home, custom landing design)
Banner type (static, animated, etc.)
Referral site (main hub, MSN, Yahoo; subhub, complementary site)
Position (banner position, top, middle, bottom)

These perspectives can be analyzed according to pre-defined metrics, including bounce, views, click-throughs, and conversions. By navigating the different dimensions of the cube, the analyst can quickly identify strengths and weaknesses in different banner advertising initiatives. OLAP enhances the decision makers' ability to more fully understand the attributes that comprise the activities of banner advertising.

So what about big data, you say? Remember, big data entails not only volume of data but also the new variables (sources of data). Both these factors are considered when conducting analytics. In other words, a conceptual model must be generated that best describes the attributes of a desired process (entity to be better understood), and then data corresponding to those variables must be applied to that analytic framework. Big data adds complexity to the generation of the conceptual model as it introduces new descriptive variables that may not have been available or incorporated in the traditional structure of the particular process. The value of big data follows the basic concepts just mentioned; however, it can provide even greater value to the user by providing more robust models that provide greater descriptions and understanding of what affects process performance. In the banner ad scenario, perhaps the new variable that must be added to provide more insightful information to decision makers regarding the effectiveness of their e-commerce advertising is the source of where traffic is coming from regarding the technological platform. In other words, is traffic coming from mobile devices, laptops, or tablets? When considering big volumes and velocities of data in an OLAP environment, methods such as parallel processing and map reduction of data resources must be considered.

OLAP provides a robust source of BI to decision makers, as it can leverage data resources including big data volumes and provides a platform that offers a flexible, accurate, and user-friendly mechanism to quickly understand what has happened and what is happening to a business process. The multidimensional framework will give users the power to view multiple scenarios of a given process, such as the following:

- What is the bounce rate if I utilize a specific type of landing page?
- Where are my highest conversion rates coming from?
- Is there seasonality according to day of the week or month of the year for my traffic?

The key to a valuable OLAP cube involves the combination of a few factors. One of these relates to the concept mentioned earlier, namely, that a cube must effectively describe a business scenario. The conceptual model that is used to build the cube must include noteworthy variables (relevant) with an appropriate detailed format that give users true BI. The next major factor is filling the cube with accurate, current, and consistent data. Deficiencies in either of these areas can quickly render the analytic method useless for decision making.

Analytics at a Glance through Dashboards

In today's ultra-fast, ultra-competitive information-based economy, it seems that the more senior a manager you may be, the less time that is available for investigation and drilling around multidimensional cubes. Often the level of analytics is filtered down to a few insightful reports, ongoing insights absorbed in the marketplace, and the access to real-time dashboards that display key performance indicators (KPIs) relevant to a particular process. These dashboards are designed to provide decision makers with a feedback mechanism as to how an organization is performing. The key elements of dashboards are the delineation of relevant KPIs to a particular process, timeliness of their readings (currency of information), and finally, a user-friendly visual that provides the decision maker with a clear way of determining whether a process is operating successfully or not. The more traditional visual platform resembles that of an odometer in an automobile, where color schemes of performance reflect that of traffic lights (e.g., green, all is well; yellow, caution; and red, something is wrong and needs to be investigated). However, dashboard technology is quickly evolving where styles can include combinations of a variety of visuals (bar, line, pie charts) according to designated scales and are being utilized by decision makers at all levels in an organization.

The key to the effectiveness of a dashboard design involves its connection to the process at hand and use for decision making. Displays must be simple to understand and interpret. Just as a simple graphic display must adhere to design conventions (e.g., coherent color scheme, axis labeling, and scale), so too must dashboard design, which adds complexity to the process as it combines various visual elements. The true key to a successful dashboard is evident by its effectiveness in providing timely, easy-to-understand decision support of a corresponding process. Dashboards that are too busy (include too many visuals), that are difficult to interpret, can quickly become omitted from an analyst's arsenal of decision support information.

Consider the dashboard example in Fig. 3. The various graphic displays are clearly delineated from one another (separate sections) and are clearly labeled. Also, the design includes different visual displays, so the information presentation does not appear to overlap or include a blended view. Finally, complementary but distinctly different KPIs give the decision maker a well-rounded view of a human capital management application in this case.

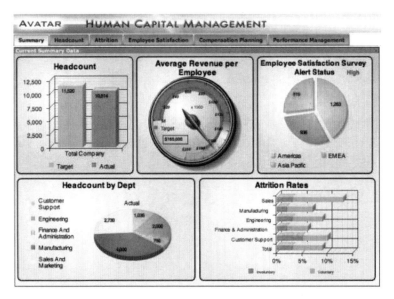

Fig. 3 Clearly designed employee analytic dashboard.
Source: From http://www.dashboards-for-business.com/dashboards-templates/business-intelligence/business-intelligence-executive-dashboard; Domo, Inc., http://www.domo.com.

Robust BI and Drill-Down behind Dashboard Views

Dashboards provide an instantaneous mechanism to analyze the performance status of a process. Organizations with extensive analytic capabilities through BI applications can have OLAP cubes that can be quickly drilled into from a dashboard KPI that provides descriptive analytics of underlying variables that underpin the KPI. A prime example of an e-commerce-based KPI is the bounce rate on a landing page for an organization, especially when a new marketing initiative has been launched. Perhaps an organization has initiated an Internet marketing campaign with banners listed on various complementary referral sites. A red signal indicating a higher-than-acceptable bounce rate would provide decision makers with a timely analytic alert mechanism to investigate the source of the problem. A real-time cube or report could quickly depict which referral site may be the greatest source of misdirected traffic.

Not all dashboard displays need to be real time, where a simple refresh of data on an interim basis provides decision makers with an accurate indication of whether a process's performance is adequate. However, the big data era involving high velocity of streaming data resources often requires a real-time dashboard visual of a given process to provide users with a quick view of variable impacts on KPIs.

DATA MINING AND THE VALUE OF DATA

As we've illustrated in the BI section (e.g., reporting, OLAP, and dashboards), a primary approach to generating value from data resources is to manage it into useful information assets (e.g., building conceptual models and viewing data according to level of details according to variables that describe a process). The next step in the valuation process is to generate a higher level of knowledge through the information created from data. Data mining involves the application of quantitative methods (equations and algorithms), along with forms of statistical testing that process data resources, which can identify reliable patterns, trends, and associations among variables that describe a particular process. Techniques such as segmentation classification, neural networks, logistic regression, and clustering, to name a few, incorporate the use of algorithms and code or mathematical equations to extract actionable information from data resources.

Why Things Are Happening

Data mining can provide decision makers with two major sources of valuable information. The first refers to descriptive information, or the identification of why things may be occurring in a business process. This is done through the identification of recurring patterns between variables. Cross-sectional graphic displays can add significant information to decision makers to illustrate patterns between variables. Fig. 4 provides a simple graphical view that illustrates an ad spend vs. dollar revenue elasticity curve as identified in the mining process. The figure depicts that a recurring pattern exists between the two variables, and that a direct relationship is prominent, where an increase in ad spend yields an increase in product revenue. Many non-mining-centric analysts would quickly raise the point that

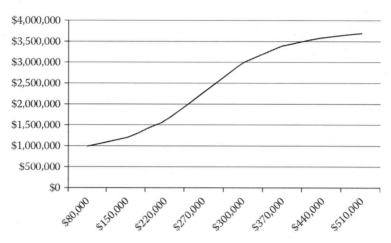

Fig. 4 Advertising spend vs. revenue curve.

this information is not noteworthy, given the natural relationship between the two variables (e.g., the more spent on advertising, the more sales that are generated); however, this criticism is quickly dispelled when posing the question: If ad spend is increased by 5% from $200,000, what is the expected increase in revenue? It is difficult to answer without the use of mining.

Mining methods can yield insightful patterns as to demographic and behavioral attributes of consumer response to marketing initiatives, the impacts of process components on performance metrics, and many more. Following are a few prominent applications where mining is often utilized:

- Consumer propensities
- Marketing and advertising effectiveness
- E-commerce initiatives
- Fraud detection
- Worker and team performance
- Pricing policies
- Process-related applications (throughput, workflow, traffic analysis)
- Healthcare-related areas (outcomes measurement, treatment effectiveness)
- Risk assessment

What Is Likely to Happen

The other main source of information where mining provides value to decision makers is in the deployment of mining results. The patterns that have been identified are often embedded in an equation or algorithmic function, often referred to as the model, which can be used to perform a "what if" analysis or estimate expected results based on inputs. In other words, if I market my product to a particular market segment defined by demographics, what is my expected response rate? Or, is a particular activity (e.g., credit card use) likely to be fraudulent? If the analysis is based on a time series

approach, mining models can provide forecasts for product sales. The analyst in this case needs to make assumptions as to expected input values.

Real-Time Mining and Big Data

The evolution of the big data era has increased the utilization of the concept of real-time or streaming mining approaches. More traditional streaming mining involves the creation of models through analyzing a data sample or historical data of a given process. The resulting model then becomes a function that can be used to process streaming or real-time incoming data, and corresponding actionable outputs are generated in real time as well. Streaming mining addresses the big data concept of velocity and volume of data and is incorporated in processes where timely results are needed to improve strategies. Streaming mining applications are commonly applied in

- Website traffic analysis for real-time online marketing
- Fraud detection for online transactions
- Financial market risk and trading

The real-time and continuous analytic section described later in this entry provide more detailed descriptions and applications in this area.

Some big data sources (e.g., sensor and satellite producing entities) with extreme velocity and volume sometimes render the ability to extract a sample that represents the entire data source as difficult, to say the least. In these instances, the ability to create optimized quantitative models to process this streaming data is limited. Techniques such as multisampling[1] and the implementation of self-optimizing quantitative techniques that learn as data is encountered have evolved to address this issue.

Analysis of Unstructured Data and Combining Structured and Unstructured Sources

Up to this point, this entry has dealt with analytics of structured data. The big data era, however, largely involves the incorporation of unstructured data resources that need to be analyzed in order to identify actionable information that enhances strategic initiatives. Text mining addresses the analytics of textual data (words, phrases, messages, e-mails, etc.). At a high level of description, text analytics seeks to create structure from unstructured sources. It does this by processing various unstructured forms and classifies them into particular categories. Processing is generally based in mathematics or linguistics.

In the realm of the vastly growing utilization of electronic communication, which includes texting, tweeting, leaving content on social media, e-mailing, etc., one can quickly see the possible value that exists in deploying analytic techniques to extract information that describes responses to marketing initiatives and product and service offerings, reactions to news and events, and general consumer behavior and sentiment.

An example involving the analysis of both structured and unstructured data for informative decision support is evident when examining patients' electronic health records to better understand treatment outcomes and patient diagnosis.

More structured physiological data (e.g., blood sugar levels) can be combined with unstructured data (e.g., physician comments on treatment) to better understand a patient's status. Analytic techniques such as semantic mining can be applied in this situation to extract actionable information.

SIX SIGMA ANALYTICS

Still many other analytic approaches exist outside the realm of BI applications. More intensive user-generated analytics include Six Sigma-based initiatives. The core of Six Sigma is a philosophy and focus for reducing variability in process operations. It involves process definition and the incorporation of an array of statistical analytic methods to measure the performance of various attributes.[2] Classic Six Sigma is underpinned by the DMAIC methodology, which is an acronym for the following:

Define: Process attributes and project objectives.
Measure: Identify relevant data variables and measure performance of the process.
Analyze: Identification of sources of unacceptable variances.
Improve: Initiate strategic tactics to address causes of variance.
Control: Establish metrics to measure performance for ongoing feedback and take appropriate actions to address shortcomings of process.

The initial three steps to the methodology clearly depict classic analytics as they involve the definition of the problem objective and corresponding use of statistics and techniques to analyze the performance of the process. In the big data era, new sources of descriptive variables and volumes can enhance the application of Six Sigma across processes and industries. Consider the latest evolution of the healthcare industry that has involved an aggressive adoption of information technologies to underpin the vast processes that exist in a healthcare provider's operations in treating patients.

Activity time stamps are commonplace for many processes in healthcare organizations that simply record when an activity of a subprocess begins and ends. This data is available at the patient level of detail. This seemingly trivial data element yields great significance in its facilitation of conducting analytics. Consider the activity of a patient checking in to an emergency room (ER).

The entire process of checking in to an ER to being diagnosed is composed of various subcomponents (Table 3). Variability or breakdowns in throughput in any of these subcomponents can adversely increase waiting times for patients, which can result in poor customer satisfaction ratings and the subpar outcome of the patient's well-being. A DMAIC scenario is provided to illustrate the analytic initiative.

In the ER scenario provided, the process has been defined (e.g., tracking the time to patient disposition from checking in to an ER), and the [D]/define step for DMAIC has been addressed. The next step is to create data variables that describe the various subcomponents of the process and measure corresponding performance rates.

Data Analytics–
Data Mining:
Forensic

Table 3 Subcomponents of ER Throughput

Activity	Time	Duration	% Change	Alert
Check in at ER	2:00 a.m.			
Move to Triage	2:20 a.m.	20 min.	5%	
Information Collection	2:28 a.m.	8 min.	10%	
MSE by Physician	2:42 a.m.	14 min.	12%	
Disposition of Patient	3:15 a.m.	33 min.	85%	XXX

Market Share

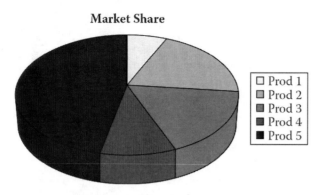

Fig. 5 Pie chart depicting market share.

- Patient checks in to ER
- Patient is moved to triage, where nurse is assigned and patient is moved to bed
- Nurse collects patient information (medical history)
- Medical service examination (MSE) is performed by a physician and tests are ordered
- Test results are received and patient disposition (admitted to hospital or sent home) is conducted

Time stamps of corresponding subcomponents to the process are generated and stored, where duration of each of the subcomponents must be measured. In this case, the healthcare service provider has a historic perspective of measuring the process and has calculated the previous quarter's average duration for all the subcomponents. The next step is to analyze existing performance (average for the prevailing month) to identify any significant changes to the baseline. Table 3 depicts a significant change (variance) in the duration of finishing the MSE to receiving lab results for patient disposition. Statistical techniques considering variance measurement are incorporated at the analytic stage to determine the level of significance, and therefore a need to implement the improve (I) stage. Here the analyst drills down into details of the process of ordering, conducting tests, and receiving results and communicating them back to the ER. At this stage, another, more detailed DMAIC study can be conducted to determine the factors that cause a high time duration from ordering to receiving test results to occur. Once this is accomplished, the decision maker can then formulate a strategic plan to address bottlenecks affecting the process (e.g., add radiology staff, adjust technology platform that communicates information in the test ordering process, implement an activity scheduling system). Once strategic initiatives have been implemented, the final step, control (C), follows to monitor effectiveness of the strategic endeavor and overall performance of the process.[3]

The combination of available data (e.g., simple but voluminous sources of activity time stamps) in conjunction with a project and process definition and analytics enhances efficiency and organizational outcomes.

AN OFTEN OVERLOOKED SECTOR OF ANALYTICS (POWER OF THE SIMPLE GRAPHIC)

Although many think of analytics as crunching numbers through an array of techniques and interpreting metrics to support decision making, analytics are greatly enhanced by the incorporation of an often taken-for-granted application of visual displays. Just think of having to analyze tables and columns of pure numbers when reviewing analytic reports. The process can quickly become mundane and even painful. In the host of analytic applications described and for numerous additional analytic methods, there is a common denominator to a successful endeavor, and that is the use of graphics to disseminate information. A simple view of a well-designed graphic can provide the decision maker with a clear presentation of extensive analytic results in a comprehendible manner.

To successfully leverage graphics, a few key points need to be considered. Before you become intrigued with robust colors and images that quickly draw you to generate dramatic conclusions about a particular process, take a step back and increase your understanding of what the information is actually portraying. In other words:

1. Analyze the titles and legends.
2. Take notice of the scale of the axis.
3. Understand the graphic/chart method used.

When you fully understand the variables that are depicted in the graphic, what the type of graphic focuses on, and the scale of the axis, only then can the analyst begin to generate effective interpretations. In the following section, a variety of graphical styles are listed with some simple descriptions of when they should be used. Keep in mind that when considering graphics in a big data era, the most significant elements are real-time graphics that provide analysts with a streaming view of processes. The real-time streaming visualization of data actually becomes a dashboard that analysts can monitor to observe variances in KPIs in relation to some event.

Graphic Types

Fig. 5 illustrates the classic pie chart that depicts how a whole unit is divided among some subcomponents (pieces of an established pie). Market share is a prime example for pie charts, where share can be delineated

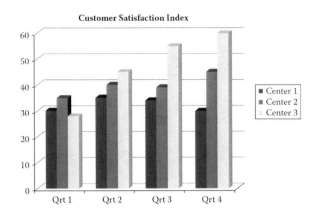

Fig. 6 Bar chart (comparative view of multicomponent process).

by product lines, regions, industry competitors, etc. Pie charts have limitations when considering negative values.

Despite the seemingly simplistic bar chart depicted in Fig. 6, the visual actually incorporates a number of important elements in the realm of analytics. The graphic depicts a comparative view of a multicomponent process (call centers in this case) in a time series setting (quarterly views). With a quick glance, the analyst can make inferences regarding relative performance (customer satisfaction) of three different call centers over time. Bar charts are more appropriate in depicting quantities or amounts of select variables.

Bar charts are also often used to illustrate variable distributions (percentages of ranges or categories of a given variable). Fig. 7 depicts a categorical age variable and the amount of data that exists in selected ranges. This gives analysts a better understanding of the dimensions of a given data variable, and in this case enables them to determine if there is any age skew or bias (high percentage of one age range relative to the population). In conducting market research, a variable distribution view enables the researcher to determine if a target market is included in a data resource.

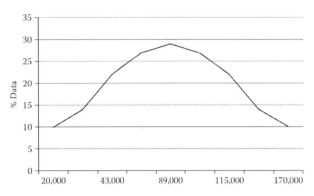

Fig. 8 Line chart of continuous variable distribution of mall traffic.

Variable distribution analysis can often include visuals via line graphs that are useful in illustrating scenarios involving continuous variables. Fig. 8 illustrates the continuous data variable of mall foot traffic for a given day according to retailers.

Time series line charts provide users with a visual of potential seasonality in processes. Fig. 9 depicts the classic holiday effect in retail as is seen in the repetitive bump in sales in Q4.

Another type of chart involves the scatter plot that is commonly used to illustrate correlations between variables, where simple plots of individual data points are depicted. Fig. 10 depicts data points depicting correlations between employee performance and training received.

A rather insightful chart style is the bubble chart. The bubble graphic enables analysts to depict three-dimensional scenarios in a coherent fashion by incorporating bubble size to illustrate variable attributes. Fig. 11 depicts the multidimensional scenario of organizational team performance according to workload and team size.

Yet another graphic style that has increased in importance over the evolution of the big data era is the use of maps. Map visuals are generally utilized when an analysis involving location is emphasized; however, location can also refer to a process location. Applications such as traffic analysis or population analytics are common

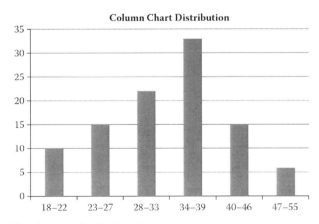

Fig. 7 Age distribution chart.

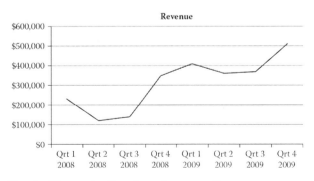

Fig. 9 Time series line charts for seasonality.

Data Analytics–Data Mining: Forensic

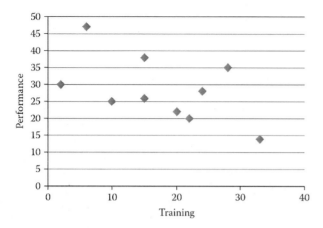

Fig. 10 Scatterplot for correlations.

examples. Traffic can refer to website activities, vehicular, consumer, or some type of designated activity.

In a simple web traffic visual, a map can illustrate cross sections of time and area of a web page that are receiving high user traffic. This can provide strategists with actionable information to more effectively apply online marketing tactics (e.g., display banners in hot spots on a particular page at a particular time).

Civil engineering can leverage heat maps by incorporating Global Positioning System data to investigate hot areas of traffic incidents (congestion, accidents) and optimize new designs to alleviate existing trouble areas and in designing new roadways.

Fig. 12 provides a standard heat map where "hot colors" depict more intense activity. In this case, the hotter areas depict areas where job vacancies are difficult to fill.

Map visuals are particularly applicable in the big data era, when real-time, high-velocity analytics and voluminous sources are involved. Applications that leverage big data include geovisualization that involves the analysis of geographic-specific flows of data and bioinformatics and sensor output in the healthcare spectrum. For example, the healthcare industry is increasingly utilizing streaming sensor data generated by

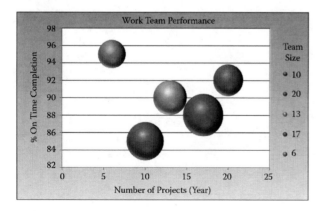

Fig. 11 Bubble chart depicting workforce team performance.

various treatment and diagnostic technologies. For diagnosis (Magnetic Resonance Imaging), these data describe the characteristics of a patient. Visual displays of this source are essential to extract information on trouble areas for patients. As big data sources emerge, the application of heat maps should become a common visual technique for providing analysts with a mechanism to enhance strategic initiatives.

This concludes our section on visual analytics. The following section provides a more technical description of data management and analytic concepts in a high-volume, big data environment. Event stream processing (ESP) can be utilized for analyzing streaming big data in motion, where this technique is often utilized as a front end for historical analytics as well.

REAL-TIME AND CONTINUOUS ANALYTICS[4]

Complex event processing (CEP) refers to systems that process or analyze events closer to the creation of those events, prior to storage. Some definitions refer to CEP events from the "event cloud" because it is not always defined where events will be published into CEP for processing and whether they will be ordered or not. This is very different from traditional analytics, or historical analytics, where data is first stored persistently (usually in a database) before it is analyzed or processed. CEP systems reduce latency times of analyzing data, usually referred to as events, by analyzing or processing the data before it is stored. In fact, sometimes, this form of analytics is done as a front end to historical analytics in order to aggregate (or reduce) raw data before storing it persistently for further analytics. This combination of CEP and front-ending historical analytics (as depicted in Fig. 13) can be a very powerful, multistage approach to analyzing data for actionable intelligence and consequently acting on intelligence sooner than otherwise possible, which can sometimes create new business opportunities than otherwise possible.

The term *complex* in CEP sometimes creates confusion relative to what it refers to. CEP systems analyze events that are published into them and create derived (or synthetic) events that represent some transformation of the events that were published into them. These derived events usually represent an aggregated view over time of many input events, and hence are referred to as complex events. While the name *CEP* is relatively new, the science of systems analyzing events in motion (before they are stored) has been around for some time. This science of analyzing events in motion consisted largely of two types of processing models. The first type was more rule based, both inference and event, condition, action. The second type of systems were based

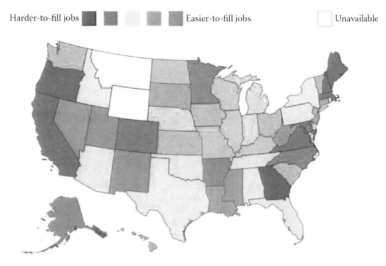

Fig. 12 Heat map that illustrates areas of hard-to-fill job vacancies.
Source: From Wanted Analytics, http://www.wantedanalytics.com.

more on the concept of continuous queries, were mostly relational in nature, and they analyzed (or processed) events that were published into them as event streams. These systems tended to focus on processing high volumes of events in very low latencies, therefore creating new opportunities around leveraging actionable intelligence in very small time frames from the event occurrences. Systems that utilize continuous queries to analyze events in motion are referred to as ESP, even though many of these systems have product names that include CEP. So ESP can be viewed as a type of CEP system that utilizes continuous query models to analyze event streams in motion. Having made this initial distinction between rules-based and continuous query-based CEPs, there has been a blending of these approaches over time, and at least one rather prominent rules-based engine has focused on low-latency applications such as algorithmic trading in capital markets. The remainder of this section will focus on continuous query-based CEPs, which we will refer to as ESP.

As mentioned earlier, ESP systems are usually architected to handle large volumes of events with very low latencies, which is why a lot of these systems focused on capital markets, where front office trading, risk, and

position management systems needed to make decisions in milliseconds, or more likely today, microseconds. These systems process financial market data from real-time financial feeds (such as trades, quotes, and orders) where the volumes could reach millions of events per second. ESP systems are being applied across many markets and applications, including personalized marketing, trading systems, operational predictive asset management, fraud prevention, and even cyber security.

The continuous annual growth of data, much of this being computer generated, has spawned the evolution of new methods to be able to analyze all of this data, and ESP helps fill that need by analyzing large volumes of raw data (or event streams) and looking for actionable intelligence. This actionable intelligence is usually aggregated events, and hence a significant level of data reduction by ESP systems can be done before it makes its way to the more traditional historical analytics. This form of multistage analytics helps keep up with the growth of data and enables actionable intelligence to be obtained in lower latencies, hence enabling opportunity. ESP systems will sometimes find patterns or other aggregations of events that are directly actionable, and other times they find aggregations of events that need to be analyzed further before they become actionable.

This multistage analytics approach is also very useful, given that the type of analytics done by ESP is quite different from traditional statistical-based analytics. Historical analytics typically works on a static data set at rest and applies complex algorithms and searches that can be very statistical in nature. ESP models, however, are much more additive and data transformational in nature. ESP models are often referred to as continuous queries because they essentially query data in motion, where the resultant set of the queries is continuously being updated. For this type of processing, it is

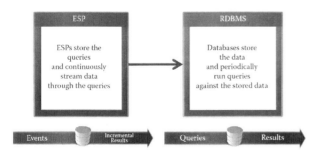

Fig. 13 Event processing and front-ending historical analysis for faster decision making.

Data Analytics–
Data Mining:
Forensic

important that the queries are additive in nature. In other words, when a new event comes in, these queries typically update the retained state of the queries without having to reread all the events already processed.

These continuous queries can be modeled as directed graphs where input event streams are published into the top of the graph, and each subsequent node in the graph performs transformations on the events it receives. The nodes of the graph can be thought of as windows with operators and retention policies. So each node performs a transformation on each event it gets, producing zero, one, or more resultant events that are retained in the window for a defined period of time or volume, and are passed on to the sibling nodes connected to that window. The nodes come in various forms, including relational, procedural, and rules. Relational nodes include all the primitives of Structured Query Language, such as joins, aggregates, projections, and filters. Most ESP systems also support pattern matching, which is a rule-based window that allows one to specify event patterns of a temporal nature. For example:

Event-A **Followed-by** (within 2 minutes) *Event-B* **Followed-by** (within 1 minute) **Not** *Event-C*

where we are looking for an event pattern such that *Event-A* occurs, and that is followed within 2 minutes by *Event-B* occurring, which in turn is not followed by the occurrence of *Event-C* for the next minute.

Procedural nodes, or windows, typically allow one to write event stream handlers using some procedural language (like C + +) to process the events from the event streams that are input into that node or window. So one can model continuous queries as one or more directed graphs of data transformation nodes that work in parallel to produce continuous results in very low latencies.

Fig. 14 is an example of a very simplistic ESP continuous query where event streams are published into the continuous query via source windows. Once each event is absorbed into the source window, it makes its way to any connected windows or subscribers. Every window type that is not a source window is referred to as a derived (or synthetic) window because they have an associated operator that transforms each event coming into it to zero, one, or more resultant events. In our simple example, we show window types filter, join, and procedural. The terminology (such as windows) is not standardized across ESP systems, but the basic concepts around continuous queries and their node types hold true. ESP continuous queries are data transformation models that continuously query event streams as they flow through the ESP where each window or operator in the flow could retain an event state that represents some period of latest events. One can model very powerful continuous queries that can reduce data into something immediately actionable or at least more relevant for further historical or predictive analytics.

VALUE OF DATA AND ANALYTICS

We began this entry by stressing the importance of analytics as an essential component to deriving value from data, where the era of big data adds intensity to the concept, as it adds new dimensions to the equation. Regardless of the source of data, its value is not realized unless it provides some resource to a strategic endeavor. Rarely does a decision maker reference a data source

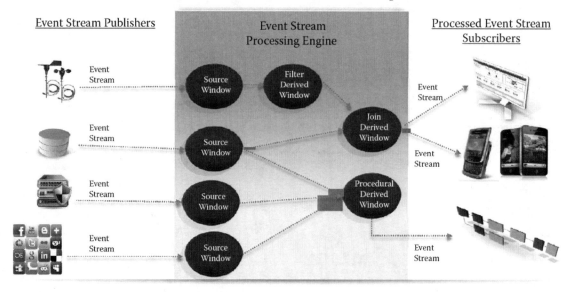

Fig. 14 ESP continuous query.

without first formulating a reason to do so. Once the conceptual need is defined, only then can data provide value.

The conceptual need involves the quest to better understand a process with the goal of enhancing its efficiency, productivity, or profitability. Simply analyzing random data and coming up with associations between variables may actually generate negative returns since the analytic process requires time and resources, and the result may not add meaningful information.

Consider the growing data resource in the area of sports. More variables (variety) and real-time downloads of various athletic activities at corresponding events (velocity and volume) may seemingly provide great value to understanding various attributes of different athletes and sports teams. However, in order to truly generate value for decision making, a conceptual model must be created. Consider the quest to better understand what leads a team to achieve a winning record. An analysis of corresponding data could yield the following result: a basketball team is more likely to win a game the more 3-point shots they make.

At first glance, this may seem to be very valuable information, but the revelation proves limited at best when looking to make a strategic decision. What does a coach do in leveraging this associative pattern—encourage players to take more shots from the 3-point zone? Does he change practice to intensify skills for increasing 3-point percentages for players? And if so, what happens to the team's performance from the 2-point zone, and does a reduction in 2-point conversions decrease the likelihood of winning a game despite an increase in 3-point shots? In the case at hand, does the variable of number of 3-point shots really add descriptive value to what leads to a team's success? Perhaps more appropriate variables that can provide strategic action could entail:

Team practice data (frequency, drills, duration)
Player descriptions (height, speed, position, age)
Type of offensive and defensive tactics

Identifying patterns among these types of variables empowers a coach (decision maker/strategist) to implement strategic initiatives that impact a performance metric or defined objective—winning.

Efficiency, Productivity, and Profitability

The concept of value also extends to three often cited benchmarks in the realm of commerce: efficiency, productivity, and profitably. One should note that although the three terms appear synonymous, there are noteworthy differences among them, so when seeking to succeed in strategic endeavors, decision makers must clearly understand the entire initiative from the perspective of these three concepts.

Analytics of all types naturally address the quest for enhancing efficiencies of corresponding processes. Enhancing efficiency naturally leads to cost reduction for the defined process; however, simply increasing efficiency for a particular activity does not necessarily imply an increase in productivity and profitability at the organizational level. Consider a marketing department for a small retailer that depends on more traditional mail order initiatives to generate sales. The department could consistently achieve increased efficiency in the process of creating printed marketing materials, generating addresses, and mailing literature to the market. These efficiencies could be achieved by implementing new printing technologies, data-based endeavors, etc. However productivity as measured by response rate or increased product sales may not necessarily increase. Perhaps traditional mail is no longer the most effective marketing medium for the type of product, given the evolution of e-marketing tactics and the adoption of smartphones and electronic communication by consumers, or perhaps the target market has changed its behavior and a different segment is actually more appropriate for the product. What may actually transpire for this endeavor is an efficient process that yields decreased productivity for the organization (deploying resources and achieving decreased returns).

Just as analytics were utilized to better understand what drives wasteful activities for the mail order marketing initiative, so too should they be utilized for such endeavors as better understanding overall marketing effectiveness and target marketing. Simply put, strategic endeavors must incorporate a bigger picture than simple processes, which provides a segue to the third concept of value, which involves profitability. Profitability must be included in any endeavor where productive and efficient strategies must make sense on a cost and revenue basis.

Investment in Internet advertising has grown dramatically over the past years, partially because of the cost-effectiveness of some tactics; however, the latest growth of this sector has also resulted in increased costs, a variable that needs to be monitored. A core tactic to e-marketing is search engine optimization for websites, an initiative that is ongoing and incurs costs of continuous management (verbiage of meta-tags, frequency of key phrases, reciprocal links). These costs must be considered in the overall spectrum of e-commerce initiatives. So when leveraging big data feeds involving site traffic relative to page layouts and cross-selling tactics, costs of an entire space need to be managed to understand profitability.

This introduces an important issue in the big data era. Big data is not free and involves technological infrastructure (servers, software) for data management along with labor resources (analytic and technical minds) to leverage this complex resource. Organizations must therefore fully understand how big data resources may impact their operations. Just because new volumes and velocities of data exist doesn't imply that the resource will be a value to every organization. An important concept to keep in mind to estimate this value is answering the question: Will new data resources help an organization better understand its process performance or marketplace?

With new resources come new ideas that leverage them. The evolving big data era in conjunction with new information technologies has introduced an opportunity for organizations to create new markets. Through analytics, big data is transformed into information that provides value by enhancing decision-making capabilities through knowledge generation. Organizations can better understand those processes essential to their operations. The concept of the creation and dissemination of information goes beyond value to organizations as it extends to individuals. Insightful information derived from big data generated from wireless sensor devices can be made available to consumers that may provide beneficial value to them. Consider a wireless device (body sensor) manufacturer that extracts information from users that may enable them to estimate and offer optimized fitness programs on a personalized basis, thus augmenting the value of the product device to existing consumers and adding value to new prospects. As the big data, analytic, and communication era continues to evolve, innovative initiatives that involve information creation in areas previously untapped can prove to be a bold new market.

The big data era requires the analyst to more intensely exhaust data resources that may provide descriptive elements of a given process as new varieties of data variables evolve. Analysts must also consider whether a process must be monitored in a real-time environment (velocity/volume) in order to uncover strategic insights in the information creation and decision-making process. There is little doubt that the job of analyst has become more important and also more complex.

REFERENCES

1. Rajaraman, A.; Ullman, J. Mining data streams. In *Mining of Massive Data Sets*; Cambridge University Press: Cambridge, MA, 2011; 129–132.
2. Pande, P.; Neuman, R. *The Six Sigma Way: How GE, Motorola, and Other Top Companies Are Honing Their* Performance; McGraw Hill: New York, NY, 2000.
3. Kudyba, S.; Radar, R. Enhancing data resources and business intelligence in healthcare. In *Healthcare Informatics: Increasing Efficiency and Productivity*; Taylor & Francis: Boca Raton, FL, 2010.
4. Baulier, J. (contrib.). *Real Time and Continuous Analytics*; SAS: Cary, NC.

BIBLIOGRAPHY

1. Kudyba, S.; Hoptroff, R. Data Mining and Business Intelligence: A Guide to Productivity; IDEA Group Publishing: Hershey, Pennsylvania, 2001.

Data Analytics: Architectures, Implementation, Methodology, and Tools

Wullianallur Raghupathi
Fordham University, New York, New York, U.S.A.

Viju Raghupathi
Brooklyn College, City University of New York, New York, New York, U.S.A.

Abstract

Big data analytics is transforming the way companies use sophisticated information technologies to gain insight from their data repositories to make informed decisions. Big data analytics and applications are at a nascent stage of development, but the rapid advances in platforms and tools can accelerate their maturing process.

OVERVIEW

With the storage and maintenance of very large or big data sets of structured and unstructured data, companies are starting to use big data analytics to analyze and gain insight to make informed decisions.[1–3] This entry discusses big data analytics, followed by a description of the architecture, frameworks, and tools. An outline of the implementation methodology is then provided. This is followed by a discussion of the key challenges. An ongoing prototype research project using big data analytics in the mining of the unstructured information in cancer blogs is also described. Finally, conclusions are offered.

INTRODUCTION

The big data phenomenon has spread rapidly across the spectrum of industries and sectors.[3–5] It typically describes the incredibly large volume of data that is collected, stored, and managed. This large volume of being analyzed to gain insight to make informed decisions.[6–8] To this end, big data analytics is emerging as a subdiscipline of the field of business analytics involving the application of unique architectures and platforms, technologies, unique programming languages, and open-source tools. The key underlying principle is the utilization of distributed processing to address the large volume and simultaneous complexity and real-time nature of the analytics.[9–12]

Very large data sets have existed for decades—the key difference is the emergence of the collection and storage of unstructured data primarily from the social media. The data gathered from unconventional sources, blogs, online chats, emails, sensors, tweets, and information gleaned from nontraditional sources, such as social media, pictures, audio and video multimedia that use web forms, mobile devices, scanners, and so on, hold the potential to offer different types of analytics, such as descriptive, predictive, and prescriptive. From a comparative perspective, big data did exist in 1960s, 1970s, 1980s, and 1990s, but it was mostly structured data (e.g., numerical/quantitative) in flat files and relational databases. With the emergence of the Internet and the rapid proliferation of web applications and technologies, there has been an exponential increase in the accumulation of unstructured data as well.[13] This has led to an escalating and pressing opportunity to analyze this data for decision-making purposes.

For example, it is universal knowledge that Amazon, the online retailer, utilizes big data analytics to apply predictive and prescriptive analytics to forecast what products a customer is likely to purchase. All of the visits, searches, personal data, orders, and so on are analyzed using complex analytic algorithms.[14] Likewise, from a social media perspective, Facebook uses analytics on the data collected via the users' accounts. Google is another example of a company that analyzes the whole breadth and depth of data collected by tracking the searches.[14] Examples can be found not only in Internet-based companies, but also in industries, such as banking, insurance, healthcare, and others, and in science and engineering.[15–17] Recognizing that big data analytics is here to stay, we next discuss the primary characteristics.

Encyclopedia of Information Systems and Technology, DOI: 10.1081/E-EIST-120053828

Data Analytics–Data Mining: Forensic

BIG DATA ANALYTICS

Like big data, the analytics associated with big data is also described by three primary characteristics: volume, velocity, and variety (http://www-01.ibm.com/software/data/bigdata/). There is no doubt data will continue to be created and collected, continually leading to an incredible *volume* of data. Second, data being accumulated at a rapid pace and in real time. This is indicative of *velocity*. Third, gone are the days of data being collected in standard quantitative formats and stored in spreadsheets or relational databases. Increasingly, the data in multimedia format and unstructured. This is the *variety* characteristic. Considering the volume, velocity, and variety, techniques have also evolved to accommodate these characteristics to scale up to the complex and sophisticated analytics needed.[8,18] Some practitioners and researchers have introduced a fourth characteristic: *veracity*.[14] The implication of this is data assurance. That is, both the data and the analytics and outcomes are error-free and credible.

Simultaneously, the architectures and platforms, algorithms, methodologies, and tools have also scaled up in granularity and performance to match the demands of big data.[19,20] For example, big data analytics is executed in distributed processing across several servers (nodes) to utilize the paradigm of parallel computing and a divide and process approach. It is evident that the analytics tools for structured and unstructured big data are very different from the traditional business intelligence (BI) tools. The architectures and tools for big data analytics have necessarily to be of industrial strength. Likewise, the models and techniques, such as data mining and statistical approaches, algorithms, visualization techniques, and others, have to be mindful of the characteristics of big data analytics. For example, the National Oceanic and Atmospheric Administration uses big data analytics to assist with the climate, ecosystem, environment, and weather forecasting and pattern analysis, and commercial translational applications. NASA engages big data analytics for aeronautical and other types of research.[14] Pharmaceutical companies are using big data analytics for drug discovery, analysis of clinical trial data, side effects, and reactions. Banking companies are utilizing big data analytics for investments, loans, customer demographics, and others. Insurance and healthcare providers and media companies are other industries that use big data analytics.

The 4Vs are a starting point for any discussion on big data analytics. Other issues include the number of architectures and platforms, the dominance of the open-source paradigm in the availability of tools, the challenge of developing methodologies, and the need for user-friendly interfaces. While the overall cost of the hardware and software is declining, these issues have to be addressed to harness and maximize the potential of big data analytics. We next delve into the architectures, platforms, and tools.

ARCHITECTURES, FRAMEWORKS, AND TOOLS

The conceptual framework for a big data analytics project is similar to that for a traditional BI or analytics project. The key difference lies in how the processing is executed. In a regular analytics project, the analysis can be performed with a BI tool installed on a stand-alone system, such as a desktop or laptop. Since big data is large by definition, the processing is broken down and executed across multiple nodes. While the concepts of distributed processing are not new and have existed for decades, their use in analyzing very large data sets is relatively new as companies start to tap into their data repositories to gain insight to make informed decisions. Additionally, the availability of open-source platforms, such as Hadoop/MapReduce on the cloud, has further encouraged the application of big data analytics in various domains. Third, while the algorithms and models are similar, the user interfaces are entirely different. Classical business analytics tools have become very user-friendly and transparent. On the other hand, big data analytics tools are extremely complex, programming intensive, and need the application of a variety of skills. As Fig. 1 indicates, a primary component is the data itself. The data can be from internal and external sources, often in multiple formats, residing at multiple locations in numerous legacy and other applications. All this data has to be pooled together for analytics purposes. The data still in a raw state and need to be transformed. Here, several options are available. A service-oriented architectural approach combined with web services (middleware) is one possibility. The data continues to be in the same state, and services are used to call, retrieve, and process the data. Data warehousing is another approach wherein all the data from the different sources are aggregated and made ready for processing. However, the data unavailable in real time. Through the steps of extract, transform, and load (ETL), data from diverse sources are cleaned and made ready. Depending on whether the data are structured or unstructured, several data formats can serve as inputs to the Hadoop/MapReduce platform.[18,21]

In the next stage in the conceptual framework, several decisions are made regarding the data input approach, distributed design, tool selection, and analytics models. Finally, to the far right the four typical applications of big data analytics are shown. These include queries, reports, online analytic processing, and data mining. Visualization is an overarching theme across the four applications. A wide variety of techniques and technologies have been developed and adapted

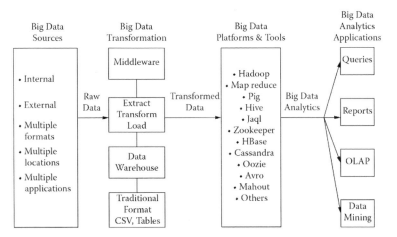

Fig. 1 An applied conceptual architecture of big data analytics.

to aggregate, manipulate, analyze, and visualize big data. These techniques and technologies draw from several fields, including statistics, computer science, applied mathematics, and economics.[22,23]

Hadoop

The most significant platform for big data analytics is the open-source distributed data processing platform Hadoop (Apache platform), initially developed for routine functions, such as aggregating web search indexes. It belongs to the class of NoSQL technologies (others include CouchDB and MongoDB) that have evolved to aggregate data in unique ways. Hadoop has the potential to process extremely large amounts of data mainly by allocating partitioned data sets to numerous servers (nodes) that individually solve different parts of the larger problem, which are then integrated back for the final result.[14,20] It can serve either as a data organizer or as an analytics tool. Hadoop offers a great deal of potential in enabling enterprises to harness the data that is difficult to manage and analyze. Specifically, Hadoop makes it possible to process extremely large volumes of data with varying structures (or no structure at all). However, Hadoop can be complex to install, configure, and administer, and individuals with Hadoop skills are difficult to find. Furthermore, organizations are not ready to embrace Hadoop completely.

It is generally accepted that there are two important modules in Hadoop:[24,25]

1. *The Hadoop Distributed File System (HDFS).* This facilitates the underlying storage for the Hadoop cluster. When data for the analytics arrives in the cluster, HDFS breaks it into smaller parts and redistributes the parts among the different servers (nodes) engaged in the cluster. Only a small chunk of the entire data set resides on each server/node, and it is conceivable that each chunk is duplicated on other servers/nodes.

2. *MapReduce.* Since the Hadoop platform stores the complete data set in small pieces across a connected set of servers/nodes in distributed fashion, the analytics tasks can be distributed across the servers/ nodes too. Results from the individual pieces of processing are aggregated or pooled together for an integrated solution. MapReduce provides the interface for the distribution of the subtasks and then the gathering of the outputs.[18,20,21] MapReduce is discussed further below.

A major advantage of parallel/distributed processing is graceful degradation or the capability to cope with possible failures. Therefore, HDFS and MapReduce are configured to continue to execute in the event of a failure. HDFS, for example, monitors the servers/nodes and storage devices continually. If a problem is detected, it automatically reroutes and restores data onto an alternative server/node. In other words, it is configured and designed to continue processing even in light of a failure. In addition, replication adds a level of redundancy and backup. Similarly, when tasks are executed, MapReduce tracks the processing of each server/node. If it detects any anomalies, such as reduced speed, going into a hiatus, or reaching a dead end, the task is transferred to another server/node that holds the duplicate data. Overall, the synergy between HDFS and MapReduce in the cloud environment facilitates industrial strength, scalable, reliable, and fault-tolerant support for both the storage and the analytics.[18,20]

It is reported that Yahoo! was an early user of Hadoop.[14] Its key objective was to gain insight from the large amounts of data stored across its numerous and disparate servers. The integration of the data and the application of big data analytics was mission critical. Hadoop appeared to be the perfect platform for such an endeavor. Yahoo! is apparently one of the largest users of Hadoop and has deployed it on thousands of servers/ nodes. The Yahoo! Hadoop cluster apparently holds huge "log files" of user-clicked data, advertisements, and lists of all Yahoo! published content. From a big data analytics perspective, Hadoop is used for a number of tasks, including correlation and cluster analysis to find patterns in the unstructured data sets.

Some of the more notable Hadoop-related application development-oriented initiatives include Apache Avro (for data serialization), Cassandra, and HBase (databases), Chukka (a monitoring system specifically designed with large distributed systems in view), Hive (provides ad hoc Structured Query Language (SQL)-like queries for data aggregation and summarization), Mahout (a machine learning library), Pig (a high-level Hadoop programming language that provides a data flow language and execution framework for parallel computation), Zookeeper (provides coordination services for distributed applications), and others.[18,20] The key ones are described below.

MapReduce

MapReduce, as discussed above, is a programming framework developed by Google that supports the underlying Hadoop platform to process big data sets residing on distributed servers (nodes) in order to produce the aggregated results. The primary component of an algorithm would *map* the broken up tasks (e.g., calculations) to the various locations in the distributed file system and consolidate the individual results (the *reduce step*) that are computed at the individual nodes of the file system. In summary, the data mining algorithm would perform computations at the server/node level and, simultaneously, in the overall distributed system to summate the individual outputs.[20] It is important to note that the primary Hadoop MapReduce application programming interfaces are mainly called from Java. This requires skilled programmers. In addition, advanced skills are indeed needed for development and maintenance.

In order to abstract some of the complexity of the Hadoop programming framework, several application development languages have emerged that run on top of Hadoop. Three popular ones are Pig, Hive, and Jaql. These are briefly described below.

Pig and PigLatin

Pig was originally developed at Yahoo! The Pig programming language is configured to assimilate all types of data (structured/unstructured, etc.). It comprises two key modules: the language itself, called PigLatin, and the runtime version in which the PigLatin code is executed.[24] According to Zikopoulos et al.,[20] the initial step in a Pig program is to *load* the data to be subjected to analytics in HDFS. This is followed by a series of manipulations wherein the data converted into a series of mapper and reducer tasks in the background. Finally, the program *dumps* the data on the screen or stores the outputs at another location. The key advantage of Pig is that it enables the programmers utilizing Hadoop to focus more on the big data analytics and less on developing the mapper and reducer code.[20]

Hive

While Pig is robust and relatively easy to use, it still has a learning curve. This means the programmer needs to become proficient.[20] To address this issue, Facebook has developed a runtime Hadoop support architecture that leverages SQL with the Hadoop platform.[24] This architecture is called Hive; it permits SQL programmers to develop Hive Query Language (HQL) statements akin to typical SQL statements. However, HQL is limited in the commands it recognizes. Ultimately, HQL statements are decomposed by the Hive Service into MapRaduce tasks and executed across a Hadoop cluster of servers/nodes.[20] Also, since Hive is dependent on Hadoop and MapReduce executions, queries may have a lag time of up to several minutes in processing. This implies Hive may not be suitable for big data analytics applications that need rapid response times, typical of relational databases. Finally, Hive is a read-based programming artifact; it is therefore not appropriate for transactions that engage in a large volume of write instructions.[20]

Jaql

Jaql's primary role is that of a query language for Java-Script Object Notational (JSON). However, its capability goes beyond JSON. It facilitates the analysis of both structured and nontraditional data.[20] Pointedly, Jaql enables the functions of select, join, group, and filter of the data that resides in HDFS. In this regard, it is analogous to a hybrid of Pig and Hive. Jaql is a functional, declarative query language that is designed to process large data sets. To facilitate parallel processing, Jaql converts high-level queries into low-level queries consisting of MapReduce tasks.[20]

Zookeeper

Zookeeper is yet another open-source Apache project that allows a centralized infrastructure with various services; this provides for synchronization across a cluster of servers. Zookeeper maintains common objects required in large cluster situations (a library). Examples of these typical objects include configuration information, hierarchical naming space, and others.[20] Big data analytics applications can utilize these services to coordinate parallel processing across big clusters. As described in Zikopoulos et al.,[20] one can visualize a Hadoop cluster with >500 utility services. This necessitates a centralized management of the entire cluster in the context of such things as name services, group services, synchronization services, configuration management, and others. Furthermore, several other open-source projects that utilize Hadoop clusters require these types of cross-cluster services.[20] The availability of these in a Zookeeper infrastructure implies that projects can be embedded by Zookeeper without duplicating or requiring constructing all over again. A final note: Interface with Zookeeper happens via Java or C interfaces presently.[20]

HBase

HBase is a column-oriented database management system that sits on top of HDFS.[20] In contrast to traditional relational database systems, HBase does not support a SQL. The applications in HBase are developed in Java very similar to other MapReduce applications. In addition, HBase does support application development in Avro, REST, or Thrift. HBase is built on concepts similar to NameNode (master) and slave nodes in HDFS and JobTracker and TaskTracker slave nodes in MapReduce. A master node manages the cluster in HBase, and regional servers store parts of the table and execute the tasks on the big data.[20]

Cassandra

Cassandra, an Apache project, is also a distributed database system.[14] It is designated as a top-level project modeled to handle big data distributed across many utility servers. It also provides reliable service with no particular point of failure (http://en.wikipedia.org/ wiki/ Apache_Cassandra). It is also a NoSQL system. Facebook originally developed it to support its inbox search. The Cassandra database system can store 2 million columns in a single row. Similar to Yahoo!'s needs, Facebook wanted to use the Google BigTable architecture that could provide a column-and-row database structure; this could be distributed across a number of nodes. But BigTable faced a major limitation—its use of a master node approach made the entire application depend on one node for all read-write coordination—the antithesis of parallel processing.[14] Cassandra was built on a distributed architecture named Dynamo, designed by Amazon engineers. Amazon used it to track what its millions of online customers were entering into their shopping carts. Dynamo gave Cassandra an advantage over BigTable; this is due to the fact that Dynamo is not

dependent on any one master node. Any node can accept data for the whole system as well as answer queries. Data is replicated on multiple hosts, creating stability and eliminating the single point of failure.[14]

Oozie

Many tasks may be tethered together to meet the requirements of a complex analytics application in MapReduce. The open-source project Oozie to an extent streamlines the workflow and coordination among the tasks.[20] Its functionality permits programmers to define their own jobs and the relationships between those jobs. It will then automatically schedule the execution of the various jobs once the relationship criteria have been complied with.

Lucene

Lucene is yet another widely used open-source Apache project predominantly used for text analytics/searches; it is incorporated into several open-source projects. Lucene precedes Hadoop and has been a top-level Apache project since 2005. Its scope includes full text indexing and library search for use within a Java application.[20]

Avro

Avro, also an Apache project, facilitates data serialization services. The data definition schema is also included in the data file. This makes it possible for an analytics application to access the data in the future since the schema is also stored along with it. Versioning and version control are also added features in Avro. Schemas for prior data are available, making schema modifications possible.[20]

Mahout

Mahout is yet another Apache project whose goal is to generate free applications of distributed and scalable machine learning algorithms that support big data analytics on the Hadoop platform. Mahout is an ongoing project, evolving to include additional algorithms (http:// en.wikipedia.org/wiki/Mahout). The widely used core algorithms for classification, clustering, and collaborative filtering are implemented using the map/reduce paradigm.

Streams

Streams deliver a robust analytics platform for analyzing data in real time.[20] Compared to BigInsights, Streams applies the analytics techniques on data in motion. But like BigInsights, Streams is appropriate not only for

Table 1   Outline of big data analytics methodology

Stage 1   Concept design
- Establish need for big data analytics project
- Define problem statement
- Why is project important and significant?

Stage 2   Proposal
- Abstract—summarize proposal
- Introduction
  - What is problem being addressed?
  - Why is it important and interesting?
  - Why big data analytics approach?
- Background material
  - Problem domain discussion
  - Prior projects and research

Stage 3   Methodology
- Hypothesis development
- Data sources and collection
- Variable selection (independent and dependent variables)
- ETL and data transformation
- Platform/tool selection
- Analytic techniques
- Expected results and conclusions
- Policy implications
- Scope and limitations
- Future research
- Implementation
  - Develop conceptual architecture
    - Show and describe component (e.g., Fig. 1)
    - Show and describe big data analytic platform/tools
  - Execute steps in methodology
  - Import data
  - Perform various big data analytics using various techniques and algorithms (e.g., word count, association, classification, clustering, etc.)
  - Gain insight from outputs
  - Draw conclusion
  - Derive policy implications
  - Make informed decisions

Stage 4
- Presentation and walkthrough
- Evaluation

structured data but also for nearly all other types of data—the nontraditional semistructured or unstructured data coming from sensors, voice, text, video, financial, and many other high-volume sources.[20]

Overall, in summary, there are numerous vendors, including Amazon Web Services (AWS), Cloudera, Hortonworks, and MapR Technologies, among others, who distribute open-source Hadoop platforms.[14] Numerous proprietary options are also available, such as IBM's BigInsights. Further, many of these are cloud versions that make it more widely available. Cassandra, HBase, and MongoDB, as described above, are widely used for the database component. In the next section, we offer an applied big data analytics methodology to develop and implement a big data project in a company.

BIG DATA ANALYTICS METHODOLOGY

While several different methodologies are being developed in this rapidly emerging discipline, a practical hands-on methodology is outlined here. Table 1 shows the main stages of such a methodology. In stage 1, the interdisciplinary big data analytics team develops a concept design. This is a first cut at briefly establishing the need for such a project since there are trade-offs in terms of cheaper options, risk, problem-solution alignment, and so on. Additionally, a problem statement is followed by a description of project importance and significance. Once the concept design is approved in principle, one proceeds to stage 2, which is the proposal development stage. Here, more details are filled. Taking the concept design as input, an abstract highlighting the overall methodology and implementation process is outlined. This is followed by an introduction to the big data analytics domain: What is the problem being addressed? Why is it important and interesting to the organization? It is also necessary to make out a case for a big data analytics approach. Since the complexity and cost are much higher than those of traditional analytics approaches, it is important to justify its use. Also, the project team should provide background information on the problem domain and prior projects and research done in this domain.

Both the concept design and the proposal are evaluated in terms of the 4Cs:

- *Completeness*: Is the concept design complete?
- *Correctness*: Is the design technically sound? Is correct terminology used?
- *Consistency*: Is the proposal cohesive, or does it appear choppy? Is there flow and continuity?
- *Communicability*: Is the proposal formatted professionally? Does the report communicate the design in easily understood language?

Next, in stage 3, the steps in the methodology are fleshed out and implemented. The problem statement is broken down into a series of hypotheses. Please note these are not rigorous as in the case of statistical approaches. Rather, they are developed to help guide the big data analytics process. Simultaneously, the independent and dependent variables are identified. In terms of analytics itself, it does not make a major difference to classify the variables. However, it helps identify causal relationships or correlations. The data sources as outlined in Fig. 1 are identified; the data collected (longitudinal data, if necessary), described, and transformed to make it ready for analytics. A very important step at this point is platform/tool evaluation and selection. For example, several options, as indicated previously, such as AWS Hadoop, Cloudera, IBM BigInsights, are available. A major criterion is whether the platform is available on a desktop or on the cloud. The next step is to apply the various big data analytics techniques to the data. These are not different from the routine analytics. They are only scaled up to large data sets. Through a series of iterations and *what if* analysis, insight is gained from the big data analytics. From the insight, informed decisions can be made and policy shaped. In the final steps, conclusions are offered, scope and limitations are identified, and the policy implications discussed. In stage 4, the project and its findings are presented to the stakeholders for action. Additionally, the big data analytics project is validated using the following criteria:

- Robustness of analyses, queries, reports, and visualization
- Variety of insight

- Substantiveness of research question
- Demonstration of big data analytics application
- Some degree of integration among the components
- Sophistication and complexity of analysis

The implementation is a staged approach with feedback loops built in at each stage to minimize risk of failure. The users should be involved in the implementation. It is also an iterative process, especially in the analytics step, wherein the analyst performs *what if* analysis. The next section briefly discusses some of the key challenges in big data analytics.

CHALLENGES

A big data analytics platform must support, at a minimum, the key functions necessary for processing the data. The criteria for platform evaluation may include availability, continuity, ease of use, scalability, ability to manipulate at different levels of granularity, privacy and security enablement, and quality assurance.[14,26] Additionally, while most of the presently available platforms are open source, the typical advantages and limitations of open-source platforms apply. They have to be shrink-wrapped, made user-friendly, and transparent for big data analytics to take off. Real-time big data analytics is a key requirement in many industries, such as retail, banking, healthcare, and others.[12] The lag between when data is collected and processed has to be addressed. The dynamic availability of the numerous analytics algorithms, models, and methods in a pull-down type of menu is also necessary for large-scale adoption. The in-memory processing, such as in SAP's Hana, can be extended to the Hadoop/MapReduce framework. The various options of local processing (e.g., a network, desktop/laptop), cloud computing, software as a service, and service-oriented architecture web services delivery mechanisms have to be explored further. The key managerial issues of ownership, governance, and standards have to be addressed as well. Interleaved into these are the issues of continuous data acquisition and data cleansing. In the future, ontology and other design issues have to be discussed. Furthermore, an appliance-driven approach (e.g., access via mobile computing and wireless devices) has to be investigated. We next discuss big data analytics in a particular industry, namely, healthcare and the practice of medicine.

BIG DATA ANALYTICS IN HEALTHCARE

The healthcare industry has great potential for the application of big data analytics.[27–31] From evidence-based

Data Analytics—
Data Mining:
Forensic

to personalized medicine, from outcomes to reduction in medical errors, the pervasive impact of big data analytics in healthcare can be felt across the spectrum of healthcare delivery. Two broad categories of applications are envisaged: big data analytics in the business and delivery side (e.g., improved quality at lower costs) and in the practice of medicine (aid in diagnosis and treatment). The healthcare industry has all the necessary ingredients and qualities for the application of big data analytics—it is data intensive, requires critical decision support, is outcomes based, requires improved delivery of quality healthcare at reduced costs (in this regard, the transformational role of health information technology, such as big data analytics applications is recognized), and so on. However, one must keep in mind the historical challenges of the lack of user acceptance, lack of interoperability, and the need for compliance regarding privacy and security. Nevertheless, the promise and potential of big data analytics in healthcare cannot be overstated.

In terms of examples of big data applications, it is reported that the Department of Veterans Affairs (VA) in the United States has successfully demonstrated several healthcare information technology and remote patient monitoring programs. The VA health system generally outperforms the private sector in following recommended procedures for patient care, adhering to clinical guidelines and achieving greater rates of evidence-based drug therapy. These achievements are largely possible because of the VA's performance-based accountability framework and disease management practices enabled by electronic medical records and HIT.[6,32] Another example is California-based Kaiser Permanente, an integrated managed care consortium that connected clinical and cost data early on, thus providing the crucial data set that led to the discovery of Vioxx's adverse drug effects and the subsequent withdrawal of the drug from the market.[6,33] Yet another example is the National Institute for Health and Clinical Excellence, part of the UK's National Health Service (NHS), pioneering the use of large clinical data sets to investigate the clinical and cost effectiveness of new drugs and expensive existing treatments. The agency issues appropriate guidelines on such costs for the NHS and often negotiates prices and market access conditions with pharmaceutical and medical products industries.[6] Further, the Italian Medicines Agency collects and analyzes clinical data on the experience of expensive new drugs as part of a national cost-effectiveness program. The agency can impose conditional reimbursement status on new drugs and can then reevaluate prices and market access conditions in light of the results of its clinical data studies.[6]

BIG DATA ANALYTICS OF CANCER BLOGS

In this section, we describe our ongoing prototype research project on the use of the Hadoop/MapReduce framework on the AWS for the analysis of unstructured cancer blog data.[31] Health organizations and individuals, such as patients, are using blog content for various purposes. Health and medical blogs are rich in unstructured data for insight and informed decision making. While the present applications, such as web crawlers and blog analysis, are good at generating statistics about the number of blogs, top 10 sites, and others, they are not advanced/useful or scalable computationally to help with analysis and extraction of insight. First, the blog data growing exponentially (volume); second, they are posted in real time and the analysis could become outdated very quickly (velocity); third, there is a variety of content in the blogs; and fourth, the blogs themselves are distributed and scattered all over the Internet. Therefore, blogs in particular and social media in general are great candidates for the application of big data analytics. To reiterate, there has been an exponential increase in the number of blogs in the healthcare area, as patients find them useful in disease management and developing support groups. Alternatively, healthcare providers, such as physicians, have started to use blogs to communicate and discuss medical information. Examples of useful information include alternative medicine and treatment, health condition management, diagnosis–treatment information, and support group resources. This rapid proliferation in health- and medical-related blogs has resulted in huge amounts of unstructured yet potentially valuable information being available for analysis and use. Statistics indicate health-related bloggers are very consistent in posting to blogs. The analysis and interpretation of health-related blogs are not trivial tasks. Unlike many of the blogs in various corporate domains, health blogs are far more complex and unstructured. The postings reflect two important facets of the bloggers and visitors: individual patient care and disease management (fine granularity) to generalized medicine (e.g., public health).

Hadoop/MapReduce defines a framework for implementing systems for the analysis of unstructured data. In contrast to structured information, whose meaning is expressed by the structure or the format of the data, the meaning of unstructured information cannot be so inferred. Examples of data that carry unstructured information include natural language text and data from audio or video sources. More specifically, an audio stream has a well-defined syntax and semantics for rendering the stream on an audio device, but its music score is not directly represented. Hadoop/MapReduce is sufficiently advanced and sophisticated computationally to aid in the analysis and understanding of the content of health-related blogs. At the individual level (document-level analysis), one can perform analysis and gain insight into the patient in longitudinal studies. At the group level (collection-level analysis), one can gain insight into the patterns of the groups (network behavior, e.g., assessing the influence within the social group), for example, in a particular disease group, the community of participants in an HMO or hospital setting, or even in the global community of patients (ethnic stratification). The results of these analyses can be generalized.[31] While the blogs enable the formation of social networks of patients and providers, the uniqueness of the health/medical terminology comingled with the subjective vocabulary of the patient compounds the challenge of interpretation.

Discussing at a more general level, while blogs have emerged as contemporary modes of communication within a social network context, hardly any research or insight exists in the content analysis of blogs. The blog world is characterized by a lack of particular rules on format, how to post, and the structure of the content itself. Questions arise: How do we make sense of the aggregate content? How does one interpret and generalize? In health blogs in particular, what patterns of diagnosis, treatment, management, and support might emerge from a meta-analysis of a large pool of blog postings? How can the content be classified? What natural clusters can be formed about the topics? What associations and correlations exist between key topics? The overall goal, then, is to enhance the quality of health by reducing errors and assisting in clinical decision making. Additionally, one can reduce the cost of healthcare delivery by the use of these types of advanced health information technology. Therefore, the *objectives* of our project include the following:

1. To use Hadoop/MapReduce to perform analytics on a set of cancer blog postings from http://www.the-cancerblog.com
2. To develop a parsing algorithm and association, classification, and clustering technique for the analysis of cancer blogs
3. To develop a vocabulary and taxonomy of keywords (based on existing medical nomenclature)
4. To build a prototype interface
5. To contribute to social media analysis in the semantic web by generalizing the models from cancer blogs

The following levels of development are envisaged: first level, patterns of symptoms, management (diagnosis/treatment); second level, glean insight into disease management at individual/group levels; and third level, clinical decision support (e.g., generalization of patterns, syntactic to semantic)—informed decision making. Typically, the unstructured information in blogs comprises the following:

Blog topic (posting): What issue or question does the blogger (and comments) discuss?

Disease and treatment (not limited to): What cancer type and treatment (and other issues) are identified and discussed?

Other information: What other related topics are discussed? What links are provided?

What Can We Learn from Blog Postings?

Unstructured information related to blog postings (bloggers), including responses/comments, can provide insight into diseases (cancer), treatment (e.g., alternative medicine, therapy), support links, and so on.

1. What are the most common issues patients have (bloggers/responses)?
2. What are the most discussed cancer types (conditions)? Why?
3. What therapies and treatments are being discussed? What medical and nonmedical information is provided?
4. Which blogs and bloggers are doing a good job of providing relevant and correct information?
5. What are the major motivations for the postings (comments)? Is it classified by role, such as provider (physician) or patient?
6. What are the emerging trends in disease (symptoms), treatment, and therapy (e.g., alternative medicine), support systems, and information sources (links, clinical trials)?

What Are the Phases and Milestones?

This project envisions the use of Hadoop/MapReduce on the AWS to facilitate distributed processing and partitioning of the problem-solving process across the nodes for manageability. Additionally, supporting plug-ins are used to develop an application tool to analyze health-related blogs. The project is scoped to content analysis of the domain of cancer blogs at http://www.thecancerblog.com. Phase 1 involved the collection of blog postings from http://www.thecancerblog.com into a Derby application. Phase 2 consisted of the development and configuration of the architecture—keywords, associations, correlations, clusters, and taxonomy. Phase 3 entailed the analysis and integration of extracted information in the cancer blogs—preliminary results of initial analysis (e.g., patterns that are identified). Phase 4 involved the development of taxonomy. Phase 5 proposes to test the mining model and develop the user interface for deployment. We propose to develop a comprehensive text mining system that integrates several mining techniques, including association and clustering, to effectively organize the blog information and provide decision support in terms of search by keywords.[31]

CONCLUSIONS

Big data analytics is transforming the way companies are using sophisticated information technologies to gain insight from their data repositories to make informed decisions. This data-driven approach is unprecedented, as the data collected via the web and social media is increasing by the second. In the future, we will see rapid, widespread implementation and use of big data analytics across organizations and the industries. In the process, the challenges highlighted above need to be addressed. As it becomes more mainstream, issues such as guaranteeing privacy, safeguarding security, establishing standards and governance, and continually improving the tools and technologies would garner attention. Big data analytics and applications are at a nascent stage of development, but the rapid advances in platforms and tools can accelerate their maturing process.

REFERENCES

1. Franks, B. *Taming the Big Data Tidal Wave*; John Wiley & Sons: New York, NY, 2012.
2. Gobble, M. Big data: The next big thing in innovation. Res. Technol. Manag. **2013**, *56*, 64–65.
3. McAfee, A.; Brynjolfsson, E. Big data: The management revolution. Harvard Bus. Rev. **2012**, *90* (10), 61–68.
4. Davenport, T.H., Ed. *Enterprise Analytics*; FT Press, Pearson Education: Upper Saddle River, NJ, 2013.
5. EIU. *Big Data—Lessons from the Leaders*; Economic Intelligence Unit: 2012.
6. Manyika, J.; Chui, M.; Brown, B.; Buhin, J.; Dobbs, R.; Roxburgh, C.; Byers, A.H. *Big Data: The Next Frontier for Innovation, Competition, and Productivity*; McKinsey Global Institute: 2011.
7. Mehta, A. *Big Data: Powering the Next Industrial Revolution*; Tableau: Seattle, WA, 2011.
8. Russom, P. *Big Data Analytics*; TDWI Best Practices Report, 2011.
9. Kumar, A.; Niu, F.; Re, C.Hazy: Making it easier to build and maintain big-data analytics. Commun. ACM **2013**, *56* (3), 40–49.
10. Oracle. *Oracle Information Architecture: An Architect's Guide to Big Data*; 2012.
11. Raden, N. *Big Data Analytics Architecture—Putting All Your Eggs in Three Baskets*; Hired Brains, Santa Fe, NM, 2012.
12. SAP AG. Harnessing the Power of Big Data in Real-Time through In-Memory Technology and Analytics. In *The Global Information Technology Report*. World Economic Forum, 2012; 89–96.
13. Nair, R.; Narayanan, A. *Benefitting from Big Data Leveraging Unstructured Data Capabilities for Competitive Advantage*. Boozandco: New York, NY, 2012.
14. Ohlhorst, F. *Big Data Analytics: Turning Big Data into Big Money*; John Wiley & Sons: New York, NY, 2012.
15. Connolly, S.; Wooledge, S. *Harnessing the Value of Big Data Analytics*; Teradata: Dayton, OH, 2013.
16. Srinivasan, N.; Nayar, R. *Harnessing the Power of Big Data—Big Opportunity for Retailers to Win Customers*; Infosys, 2012.
17. White, D.; Rowe, N. *Go Big or Go Home? Maximizing the Value of Analytics and Big Data*; Aberdeen Group, 2012.
18. Zikopoulos, P.C.; deRoos, D.; Parasuraman, K.; Deutsch, T.; Corrigan, D.; Giles, J. *Harness the Power of Big Data—The IBM Big Data Platform*; McGraw-Hill: New York, NY, 2013.
19. Ferguson, M. *Architecting a Big Data Platform for Analytics*; Intelligent Business Strategies: Cheshire, UK, 2012.
20. Zikopoulos, P.C.; Eaton, C.; deRoos, D.; Deutsch, T.; Lapis, G. *Understanding Big Data—Analytics for Enterprise Class Hadoop and Streaming Data*; McGraw-Hill; New York, NY, 2012.
21. Sathi, A. *Big Data Analytics*; MC Press Online LLC, 2012.
22. Courtney, M. Puzzling out big data. Eng. Technol. **2013**, *7* (12), 56–60.
23. HP. *Information Optimization—Harness the Power of Big Data*; 2012.
24. Borkar, V.R.; Carey, M.J.; Li, C. Big data platforms: What's next? XRDS **2012**, *19* (1), 44–49.
25. Mone, G. Beyond hadoop. Commun. ACM **2013**, *56* (1), 22–24.
26. Bollier, D. *The Promise and Peril of Big Data*; The Aspen Institute, Communications and Society Program: Washington, DC, 2010.
27. Burghard, C. *Big Data and Analytics Key to Accountable Care Success*; IDC Health Insights: Framingham, MA, 2012.
28. Fernandes, L.; O'Connor, M.; Weaver, V. Big data, bigger outcomes. J. AHIMA **2012**, 38–42.
29. IBM. *IBM Big Data Platform for Healthcare*; Solutions brief, June 2012.
30. jStart. *How Big Data Analytics Reduced Medicaid Readmissions*; A jStart case study: 2012.
31. Raghupathi, W. Data mining in health care. In *Healthcare Informatics: Improving Efficiency and Productivity*; Kudyba, S., Ed.; Taylor and Francis: Boca Raton, FL, 2010; 211–223.
32. Dembosky, A. Data prescription for better healthcare. Financ. Times **2012**, *19*.
33. Savage, N. Digging for drug facts. Commun. ACM, **2012**, *55* (10), 11–13.

Data Analytics: Mutivariate Temporal Data

Artur Dubrawski
Robotics Institute, Carnegie Mellon University, Pittsburgh, Pennsylvania, U.S.A.

Abstract

This entry demonstrates a big data analytics approach designed to support discovering and leveraging informative patterns in large-scale multidimensional temporal data of transactions. This type of data is abundant in many domains of human activity. The approach can be adjusted to specific application scenarios. It provides a few instances of societally and commercially beneficial use of the proposed approach. These examples leverage comprehensive screening of large databases for multiple aspects of change, which in turn may help explain existing events and carry forthcoming information.

INTRODUCTION

Many of the important big data sets encountered in practice assume the form of a record of transactions. Each entry in such data typically includes date and time of an event (such as a nonprescription drug purchase transaction or a record of a repair of a vehicle) and a potentially large number of descriptors characterizing the event (e.g., the type, dose, and quantity of the medicine sold or the model year, make, configuration, and description of failure of the vehicle). Time-stamped transactional data can be used to answer various questions of practical importance. Typical applications leverage the temporal aspect of data and include detection of emergence of previously unknown patterns (such as outbreaks of infectious diseases inferred from unusually elevated volume of sale of certain kinds of drugs in a region or new shopping behaviors developing among specific demographic niches of a customer base), prediction of future occurrences of particular types of events (such as imminent failures of equipment or qualitative changes of monitored business processes), and explanation of patterns or events of specific interest (What is special about the particular cluster of customer data? Can we assess and scope geographically and demographically the potential impact of a newly detected escalating crisis?).

In this entry, we show a few examples of practical application of an intuitively structured approach to tackling these types of questions. The approach consists of two fundamental steps, which conceptually combine data mining and machine learning paradigms:

1. Extraction from data of a possibly very large set of features that, hypothetically or based on application domain expertise, may be informative for the task at hand

2. Use of the extracted features to learn probabilistic models capable of answering posed business questions, while automatically identifying subsets of features that enable the optimal performance at the task at hand

With the exception of some applications where the informative features are known in advance and are readily available in source data, it is often desirable to allow the first step to be highly comprehensive, even exhaustive if possible, to avoid missing potentially useful features. The second step aims to mitigate the resulting complexity and to identify manageable subsets of features that yield practically realizable and effective models.

Large scales of comprehensive searches across potentially highly multidimensional data impose special requirements on the computational feasibility of the proposed process to make it practical. It is often possible to addresses this challenge by using cached sufficient statistics approach. The sufficient statistics data structures store a limited and controllable amount of information about data that is needed to very quickly compute all estimates necessary for analyses or statistical inference. There is usually a one-time computational setup cost involved in creating the sufficient statistics cache, and a memory storage requirement; but as soon as that is done, data-intensive analytic algorithms can retrieve the needed precomputed information from rapidly accessible intermediate storage instead of reaching out to the source databases. We sometimes observe orders-of-magnitude speedups of information retrieval operations when using such caches to support advanced analytics of large data.[1] It is worth noting that the use of cached statistics does not preclude leveraging infrastructural efficiencies of distributed computing systems and

Encyclopedia of Information Systems and Technology, DOI: 10.1081/E-EIST-120053830

Data Analytics–
Data Mining:
Forensic

algorithms. In fact, they can be used jointly for additional improvements of scalability.

The next sections of this entry showcase a few examples of practical applications of the proposed approach. They involve multidimensional transactional data with a temporal component and illustrate a subset of possible types of business questions that can be asked against such types of data. They also show examples of how the input data can be featurized to allow learning of effective predictive models. The first of these examples involves monitoring the status of public health. It relies on a massive-scale screening through multivariate projections of records of outpatient hospital visits to detect statistically significant spatiotemporal increases in the number of patients reporting with similar symptoms and disease signs. The enabling idea is to use cached sufficient statistics to support exhaustive searches across millions of hypotheses and sort them according to their statistical significance. Looking at the most significant detections, public health officials can focus their attention and investigative resources on the most unusual escalations that may be indicative of emerging outbreaks of disease.

The second example looks at mining high-frequency data collected at the bedside of intensive care patients to predict imminent episodes of acute deterioration of their health. The multivariate baseline data is decomposed spectrally and compressed to form a compact but still highly multidimensional model of typical variability of vital signs characteristics obtained from patients who are not in crisis. The new observations are processed in the same way, and their principal component projections are monitored using a control-chart approach for any statistically significant departures from the expectation. These departures are considered as potentially informative of the near-future deteriorations of health. They serve as inputs to a machine-learning algorithm that uses a representative set of annotated examples of health crises to learn how to predict their future onsets.

The third example employs a similar control-charting approach to event detection; however, it uses a bivariate temporal scan, instead of the univariate cumulative sum (CuSum) chart, to extract potentially informative events from large amounts of bank transaction data. Some of these events are then automatically selected by a classification model trained to anticipate upcoming spending sprees by the bank customers.

The fourth and final application example looks at a few challenges of predictive informatics when it is used to support management of fleets of expensive, complicated equipment. The featuring of high-frequency data from vibration monitoring subsystems is achieved by computing a set of temporal derivatives of increasing orders. It can yield remarkably accurate predictors of onset of uncertain vibration exceedence events. It helps detect the opportunities for preventive maintenance of aircraft before faulty conditions actually set in. Another look at the same application context, but using a multi-stream analysis, demonstrates the ability of a big data approach to dismiss a number of probable false alerts. Some apparent mechanical faults recorded by the in-flight aircraft health-monitoring systems can be therefore classified as benign artifacts, highly explainable by the particular conditions of flight.

EXAMPLE APPLICATION: PUBLIC HEALTH

One of the societally important applications of modern analytics is to support surveillance of public health. Multiple efforts have been staged over the past decade, primarily in developed countries, to leverage statistical data mining to monitor relevant and digitally available information. It includes records of patients reporting to emergency rooms with particular sets of symptoms, volumes of daily sales of certain types of nonprescription medications, lab test requests, ambulance requests, and so forth.[2–6] Any excessive activity manifesting in a subset of such multivariate spatiotemporal data may indicate an emerging disease outbreak. The key benefit that can be provided by big data analytics is the ability to automatically and comprehensively screen the incoming data for escalations that cannot be confidently explained as random fluctuations consistent with historical trends. They likely represent an emerging threat. Computational scalability of modern event-detection algorithms allows for large-scale screenings with a small number of constraints, giving public health officials a timely and complete view of possible challenges. Being situationally aware, they can validate the most significant detections and mitigate emerging crises before they escalate and impact a substantial number of people.

Modern biosurveillance systems will soon benefit from electronic health records and related developments to enable highly specific, granular analyses of data. Comprehensive reporting of individual disease cases with multiple descriptive details (reported symptoms and signs, treatment, patient demographics, relevant medical history, outcomes, etc.), especially from regions where such detailed information was never recorded, will allow multiple beneficial uses of the resulting data. The potential scope includes but is not limited to highly specific syndromic surveillance of infectious diseases, monitoring of populationwide trends of chronic diseases, detection of emerging new health threats, forecasting demand on healthcare resources, tracking long-term trends in disease evolution and effectiveness of treatment, enabling scientific discovery, and other similar objectives.

However, many existing public health information systems are subject to various limitations, including spotty coverage, large latencies in data reporting, low resolution and uncertain quality of data when it is available, limited analytic capacity at local and country levels, and so forth. These limitations are further exacerbated by underdevelopment, lacking infrastructure, and limitations of available resources (human and financial), often found in developing countries. And often the developing countries are where the health challenges with a potential worldwide impact emerge first. Their discovery, mitigation, and containment at or near geographic origins are certainly desirable objectives. Luckily, the emergence of universally accessible communication technology has been shown to mitigate some of the challenges. It allows deploying practical and affordable biosurveillance systems even in rural areas of developing countries without substantial information technology infrastructure.

One example of such system, the Real-Time Biosurveillance Program (RTBP), involves an application of the event detection technology to multivariate public health data in Sri Lanka.[7] The system relies on simple and affordable cell phones to convey the contents of comprehensive and accurate hand-written records of outpatient visits. This information goes to a central data repository for monitoring, detection of emerging outbreaks of diseases, as well as visualization, drill-downs, and reporting. RTBP has been found practical and effective at rapid and reliable detection of emerging spatiotemporal clusters of disease and at monitoring dynamics of chronic diseases. Its setup required minimal investments in infrastructure, relying on standard cell phone technology to digitize and relay patient visit data (symptoms, signs, demographics, preliminary diagnoses, and treatments) collected at rural (infrastructure-deprived) healthcare facilities from the field to decision makers. The system dramatically reduced data-reporting latencies (from weeks to within 24 hours), allowed collection of high-resolution information (down to the individual case level, and with multiple dimensions) with much more detail than preexisting solutions and at a fraction of their cost. The included comprehensive statistical analysis toolkit has been designed for rapid processing and highly interactive visualizations of the results of statistical analyses, drill-downs, rollups, and various types of reporting, making the RTBP a complete business intelligence solution that enhanced situational awareness of public health analysts and managers. Big data analytics has been the key enabler of effective and comprehensive handling of daily aggregates of 25 data attributes of various arities, yielding almost 100,000 unique conjunctive combinations of attribute-value pairs represented in data, with a theoretical size of the full contingency table in excess of 10^{12} cells.

The analytic component of RTBP relies on the capability of large-scale screening for subsets of data that show statistically significantly increased numbers of current patients. The method of choice is a bivariate temporal scan.[8] It considers, for instance, the number of children with bloody stools arriving this week from the southern outskirts of the city as the target query, and compares that number against a baseline activity such as the current week's count of patients from the southern suburbs less the number of those in the target group, as well as against counts of target and baseline groups observed in the past. The resulting four numbers fill a two-by-two contingency table, and a statistical test of its uniformity is performed (typically, either Fisher's exact or χ^2 test is used). Upon appearance of an unusually high number of patients who belong to the target group, when compared with the size of the corresponding baseline population and with the target and baseline counts observed during historical reference periods, the resulting p-value of the test will be low. The RTBP massive screening algorithm tries a very large number of target queries and produces the list of findings sorted by their p-values from the most to the least anomalous. The cached sufficient statistics framework allows such large-scale searches to complete fast enough for practical, often interactive use.[9]

RTBP has been extensively validated on historical epidemiological data. Within seconds of loading the data, the analysts could find emergence of leptospirosis in Sri Lanka (Fig. 1). Its interactive spatiotemporal analysis tracks probabilities of an outbreak of any named disease or any cluster of cases sharing similar symptoms (thick line in time series display). When tried on historical data, it detected emergence of clusters of leptospirosis in 2008 and 2009 weeks before they were originally recognized by the officials (who did not have a capable surveillance tool at their disposal at the time). Dashed lines in the time series plot depict the temporal distribution of daily volumes of patients diagnosed with the disease. The alert signal highlights a few periods of unusually high activity of the disease that are automatically flagged by the statistical scanning algorithm. The corresponding geospatial snapshots of the observed diagnosed case distributions for two periods of the highest escalation are shown in the maps. Circles with the radii proportional to the number of cases depict spatial distribution of the disease. The events of 2008 impacted primarily central-eastern provinces of the country. The outbreak of 2009 has primarily affected the capital region and the city of Colombo.[4]

Dengue fever outbreaks in Sri Lanka in 2009 and 2010 are thought to be the worst in history. The one in 2009 amounted to 35,007 recorded cases and 346 deaths. An instance of RTBP would have issued warnings in early 2009 about that year's event, when dengue cases just began to escalate, and it would have continued to issue alerts throughout the period of escalated activity of disease. RTBP early warnings would have

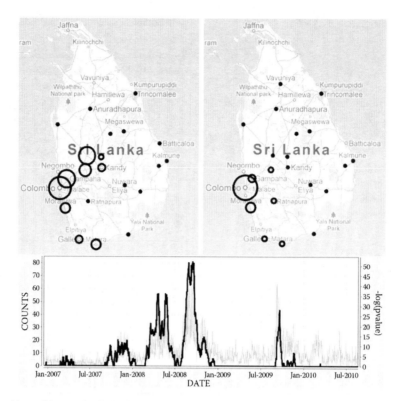

Fig. 1 Retrospective tracking of leptospirosis in Sri Lanka.

given health officials valuable time to stage responses and to reduce the impact of the crises.

In Fig. 2, temporal distribution of daily nationwide counts of dengue cases is plotted with dashed lines. Moving average (aggregated monthly) of cases of all reportable diseases excluding dengue is shown with thin solid line, and the RTBP alert signal for dengue is plotted as solid black. RTBP event detection algorithm is sensitive to unusual escalations of dengue activity that could not be explained by simple means such as the overall increase of the number of reported sick patients. Using non-dengue disease counts as a baseline helps mitigate the impact of irrelevant data such as occasional fluctuations in the healthcare system throughput or reporting flaws, allowing for a reduction in the false alert rate. It is interesting to see a side effect of using such a baseline that manifested in the summer of 2009. During one of the periods of peak dengue activity, its alert signal briefly went down because the baseline

counts escalated as well. That was due to an independent but simultaneous outbreak of another disease. Newer methods (such as Disjunctive Anomaly Detection algorithms introduced by Sabhnani, Dubrawski, and Schneider[10]) can identify coinciding events that affect overlapping subpopulations.

Besides the originally intended goal to detect emergence of notifiable diseases, the system has also shown utility in tracking progression of chronic ailments. For instance, it enabled discovery of a gender division pattern among hypertension patients. The condition is apparently two to three times more prevalent in Sri Lankan female patients than in males. The extent of the difference had not been known to the health officials in the country before their use of this technology.

Extensive field validation of RTBP in Kurunegala region of Sri Lanka revealed several dimensions of its remarkable utility. It offers a qualitatively better timeliness of reporting and analysis than any of the preexisting systems because the input data are collected almost instantaneously (worst case, daily) as opposite to 4–8 week latencies experienced before. It provides a much higher resolution and much more detail in data, leveraging case-level information as opposite to weekly-by-disease aggregates. It also offers unparalleled maintainability and cost-effectiveness. The total costs of operation are lower than with the previously used paper-based notifiable disease reporting systems (attainable 30% cost avoidance). Last but not least, it comes with capable analytic software that empowers epidemiologists

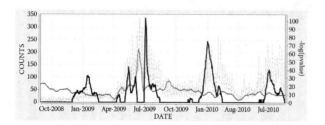

Fig. 2 Dengue fever outbreaks in Sri Lanka in 2009 and 2010 are thought to be the worst in history.

and public health officials with up-to-date information about the current status and trends in health of populations in their areas of responsibility, enabling rapid responses to emerging crises before they escalate—a capability that had not been available to them before.

EXAMPLE APPLICATION: CLINICAL INFORMATICS

Clinical information systems collect and process various types of data to fulfill multiple objectives that include supporting diagnostic and treatment decisions, scientific research and discovery, clinical trials, surveillance of trends in response to therapies, detection of adverse events in clinical practice, as well as many business functions such as auditing of insurance claim reconciliation practices and fraud detection, to name a few. Many of such data sets assume the familiar form of logs of transactions, or they can be transformed to take such form. Richness, variety of types and form factors, and abundance of the clinical data, combined with multiplicity of potentially beneficial uses of the information it may contain, create tremendous opportunities for application of big data analytics.

One of the many important goals of clinical informatics is to equip physicians and nurses with surveillance tools that will issue probabilistic alerts of upcoming patient status escalations sufficiently in advance to allow taking preventive actions before the undesirable conditions actually set in. A recent study[11] conducted a successful preliminary validation of an approach using high-frequency vital signs data (such as electrocardiogram signals, blood pressure, oxygen content, and similar waveform data measured at O(125 Hz) frequencies) typically collected at the bedside of intensive care patients. To generate potentially informative events from vital signs, each measurement channel was first segmented into sequences of k consecutive observations. Then, Fourier transformation was performed to obtain spectral profiles of each segment of the raw signal. Multiple spectral profiles, extracted from periods of observation that were considered medically benign (no crises), were then assembled to form a k-dimensional flat table. Principal component analysis was then applied to this table, and the top p components were considered further. Those p components formed a null space spectral model of the expected normal dynamics of the given vital sign. One null space model was built for each measurement channel separately. Each newly observed set of k consecutive measurements could then be processed through Fourier transformation and projected onto the p principal components of the corresponding null space model. Over time of patient observation, those projections produced p time series

per measurement channel. Then, a control chart can be applied (in particular, Lonkar et al.[11] used the CuSum chart[12]) to each of these time series and mark the time stamps at which CuSum alerts were raised. These alerts mark moments when the observed spectral decomposition of a vital sign does not match what is expected on the basis of the distribution of medically uneventful data. Each of potentially hundreds of such events may be informative of near-future deteriorations of health. Predictive utility of each type of the automatically extracted events was quantified using training data, which contained the actual health alerts in addition to the vital signs.

To accomplish the task, an exhaustive search across all pairs of CuSum event types (inputs) and alert types (outputs) was performed, where the big data analytics technology (in particular, the T-Cube cached sufficient statistics data structure[13]) provided the enabling efficiency. In this manner, input–output pairs with high values of the lift statistic were identified. Lift estimates the ratio of conditional probability of, in this case, observing a specific type of a health crisis, given the recently observed CuSum event of a particular type, to the prior probability of observing the same type of health crisis at any time (irrespective of the presence or absence of any prospective indicators). Under null hypothesis of no relationship between the health crises and detected leading CuSum events, lift should equal 1.0. Input–output pairs with lifts significantly greater than 1.0 can be expected to enable prediction of health status alerts.

In a preliminary study,[11] the authors found a few promising indicators of tachycardia episodes with lifts significantly greater than 1.0 and prediction lead times ranging from tens of minutes to a couple of hours. Then, they used a subset of these indicators as inputs for a machine-learning classifier that revealed cross-validation-based recall of 85% at 4.85% false-positive rate, and the area under the receiver operating characteristic curve score of 0.857. Fig. 3 depicts an example result obtained in one patient with the presented method. The positive exceedance CuSum events (depicted with light gray spikes, their moving average frequency shown in dark gray in the top diagram) were obtained from one of the principal components of the blood pressure signal. The spikes in the bottom diagram indicate critical tachycardia episodes to be predicted. As can be seen, the frequency of indicator events visibly escalates a few hours prior to the onset of tachycardia occurring shortly past the 20-hour mark of this intensive care unit stay. The same early warning signal is raised again before a period of persistent tachycardia starting at about the 60-hour mark. The accuracy and specificity of these candidate early warnings has been validated as potentially valuable by practicing cardiologists.

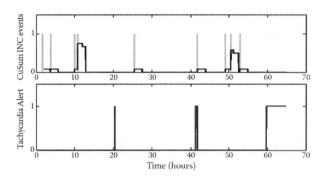

Fig. 3 Frequency (dark gray in the top diagram) of candidate indicators (light gray) typically increases ahead of the onset of tachycardia events (bottom diagram).

EXAMPLE APPLICATION: FINANCE

The preceding examples above used either multivariate aggregation of the raw data or oddities among spectrally decomposed dense waveforms to identify relationships that may carry predictive power. In a separate case study, we looked at predicting changes in behavior of retail bank customers. We used a scalable implementation of temporal scan algorithm[8] to screen highly multidimensional bank transactions to detect recent changes in spending behaviors of customers. We stratified these data according to a variety of criteria such as age bracket, gender, education, affluence of home neighborhood, and so forth. The algorithm first detects temporal change points in the individual customer's activity by comparing it with their historical records as well as with the current and historical activity of relevant peer groups. The algorithm considered more than 230 different types of such points resulting from multiple stratification criteria mentioned earlier and from multiple time scales of sought behavioral shifts. Detected changes that could not be explained by random fluctuations of data are then considered as possible predictors of future events such as, for example, 1 day credit card spending sprees. Machine learning can be used to automatically select the empirically most useful set of such candidate indicators. Fig. 4 presents a

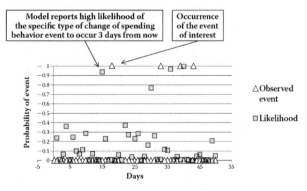

Fig. 4 A big data analytics model can accurately predict 1 day spending sprees 3 days ahead of their occurrence.

temporal distribution of events of interest (to be predicted ahead of time, outlined triangles) and likelihood scores produced by the trained model (tone squares). The result has been obtained for one of the bank customers whose data were not used for training the model. This model was specifically tailored to forecast spending sprees supposed to occur 3 days ahead, and in the shown example it is indeed remarkably accurate at returning elevated likelihoods at this exact interval before the actual occurrences of these events. Cumulative performance at predicting this particular type of spending behavior, measured across several thousand test customers, provides the bank with the attainable positive yield on the order of hundreds of thousands of dollars per annum, net of the costs of processing false detections that occur at the rates that allow desirably precise identification of the events of interest.

EXAMPLE APPLICATION: MANAGEMENT OF EQUIPMENT

Typically, more than 5% of the budget of a developed country is spent on the maintenance and repair of equipment and structures,[14] and yet too often, less than a satisfactory proportion of the inventory is fully available for its intended use. For instance, 2010 mission capability rates of fighter fleets in the U. S. Air Force varied between 52% and 67%.[15] Managers of expensive equipment must carefully monitor processes that impact their supply chains to ensure the required availability and to control the costs of fleet sustenance. If logistics assumptions are violated, perhaps due to an inadvertent introduction of a batch of faulty spare parts or a change of equipment operating conditions, an unexpected surge of demand on maintenance and supply may develop, reducing availability and escalating costs of operations. In practice, complexities of the underlying processes often make it difficult for managers to recognize emerging patterns of failures before they make a substantial impact. Only when equipment readiness statistics are significantly affected will the notice be taken. Additional costs are often incurred due to expediting root-cause investigations and implementing temporary solutions to mitigate the shortages. The ability to discover early indicators of such crises is the key to their effective and prompt mitigation.

The Collective Mind Trending Tool[16] aims to provide such capability. It is designed to notify fleet managers about emergence of one or more of a huge variety of possible problems substantially earlier than was possible before, and to enable pragmatic prioritization of investigative efforts according to the statistical significance of the detections. It has been validated in one of the U. S. Air Force jet aircraft fleets. Comprehensive statistical

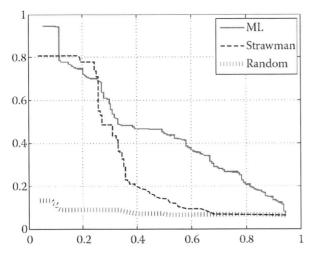

Fig. 5 Precision (vertical axis)–recall (horizontal axis) characteristic of the model trained to predict vibration exceedences using dynamical features of the observed vibrations (solid line) substantially outperforms a simpler technique that uses time since previous exceedence (dashed line).

searches for fleetwide patterns of escalated maintenance activity yielded 10–20% improvement in accuracy of monthly watch lists of potentially problematic components while mitigating the "we do not know what we do not know" challenge. Similar automated statistical analyses help identify unexpected failure patterns in individual "bad actor" components and in individual aircraft. Early detection of systematic failures revealed avoidable replacements of parts. The resulting value of these avoided exchanges across this particular fleet of aircraft is estimated at $18 million per annum.

The structure of a typical maintenance log of equipment fleet has a striking resemblance to the log of outpatient visits at hospital emergency rooms. Both types of data consist of records of time-stamped transactions with multiple categorical descriptors characterizing each entry. Patient demographics is analogous to the aircraft configuration data, clinical information to the history of use, signs and symptoms to the noticed malfunction modes and their circumstances, preliminary diagnoses and applied treatments to the records self-diagnostic information and repair attempts undertaken, and so forth. The complexities of maintenance data can, however, exceed the levels known in public health domains. Typical equipment maintenance logs we have analyzed would consist of 14–54 data attributes of various arities (besides time), 0.5–6.5 million unique conjunctive combinations of properties, and the theoretical capacity of the corresponding contingency tables ranging between 10^{25} and 10^{93} cells. Comprehensive analyses of such data would not be possible without scalability provided by big data analytics.

Maintenance logs are just one type of data collected about fleets of expensive equipment. Modern aircraft,

for instance, produce extensive amounts of self-diagnostic information through the built-in structural, electrical, software, and electronic integrity monitoring systems. These additional streams of data create new opportunities for big data analytics. For example, correlating fault messages logged by the built-in test system with recent maintenance history can be used to quantify effectiveness of repairs and to identify possible unexpected side effects of configuration changes or upgrades.

One of common diagnostic modalities onboard modern aircraft are vibration sensors. Excessive vibrations are responsible for premature fatigue of structures and could shorten useful life of mechanical and electrical subsystems and components, as well as cause faults in electronics. We have evaluated the potential utility of big data analytics in processing vibration amplitude data collected with a particular type of sensor onboard more than 300 reasonably homogeneous aircraft over a prolonged period of exploitation, and in a wide range of flight regimes. The data have been featurized by computing dynamic characteristics (such as temporal derivatives of increasing orders) from the time series of specific vibration frequency channels. The resulting set of multiple numeric features was then fed to a machine-learning classifier (in particular, a Random Forest model was used[17]) with the binary output labels formed by the presence or absence of the actual vibration exceedence alerts during a period of 10–40 flying hours into the future. We hypothesized that many types of mechanical changes in aerospace structures begin relatively slowly and could be manifested in early stages by relatively miniscule changes in the observed patterns of vibrations, before they escalate to a level that requires alerting flight crews as well as ground mechanics of a possible problem. If we were successful at reliably predicting imminent vibration alerts a few good flight hours ahead of the onset of the actual crises, it would enable preemptive maintenance of the aircraft before flight safety was compromised and before significant repairs were required. It would allow improved reliability and safety of flight, while reducing the costs of maintenance.

Fig. 5 shows the results of cross-validation of alternative approaches to predicting vibration exceedences recorded by one particular type of onboard sensor. The horizontal axis reflects the recall rates of the vibration alerts that actually took place, while the vertical axis shows the correct prediction rates. The hash line depicts performance of a random predictor, the dashed line uses time since the last exceedence as the only input feature, and the solid line is our method of choice that learns to predict future alerts from multiple dynamical characteristics of the observed vibrations. At the 50% recall rate, which is when half of all actual exceedences recorded after 10 and before 40 flight hours from now are correctly predicted by the algorithm, almost 50% of the

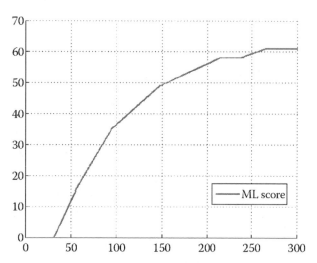

Fig. 6 Operating characteristic of the preventive maintenance model. Vertical axis: Number of flights during which vibration alerts would be avoided. Horizontal axis: Number of additional maintenance actions.

early warnings are correct (truly positive). This accuracy is about 2.5 times higher than that of an alternative that simply leverages the sequential character of occurrences of the vibration exceedences. The utility of the proposed machine-learning approach is even more evident at higher recall rates. If the user requires that 70% of all events are announced 10–40 flight hours ahead of their actual onset, the performance of the strawman method cannot be distinguished from random, but about one-third of the alerts (4 times the baseline) issued by the machine-learning model are correct.

How does this performance translate to operational benefits? Fig. 6 provides a characteristic with respect to one variety of pragmatic criteria. The horizontal axis denotes the number of preventive inspections triggered by machine-learning-generated early warnings, and the vertical axis corresponds to the number of flights that originally were plagued with the particular vibration exceedences that the preventive maintenance would have helped avoid. This analysis assumes that the existing operating procedure requires the ground crew to perform

an inspection and associated maintenance after each flight with at least one instance of such vibration alert. The use of early warnings allows performing it before these flights. We assume that such action would eliminate vibration exceedances that would have happened during the next flight, as well as any other exceedances if they form a sequential cluster (for the sake of this exercise, the cluster is assumed terminated when the gap between the last exceedence in the existing cluster and the next event is greater than or equal to 20 flying hours). Hence, the benefits of early warnings are measured with the number of flights for which vibration alerts could have been avoided when using the machine-learning-based prognoses. These benefits increase, and the associated flight safety risk decreases, along the vertical axis of the graph in Fig. 6. The cost of this operating procedure is measured with the number of preventive maintenance episodes that will need to be conducted in response to the early warning alerts. It is depicted along the horizontal axis of the graph. Subsequent points along the characteristic result from varying the sensitivity threshold of the machine-learning predictor at which the preemptive alerts are triggered. The higher the sensitivity the more alerts, leading to higher rates of recall of the actual imminent problems and potentially to a greater number of false positives. The optimal set point can be determined dynamically, for example, based on the current availability of technical personnel. In this case, the personnel capacity will translate to a hard limit of the number of preventive inspections that could be conducted in the specific amount of time, and the characteristic will translate that to the corresponding expected reduction in the number of flights with vibration alerts. Note that the preventive maintenance, if effective, would eliminate the need of postflight maintenance normally triggered by the in-flight alerts. Alternatively, a desirable operating set point could be obtained by establishing a specific cost/benefit tradeoff. For instance, responding to the 150 strongest machine-learning alerts would have eliminated 50 flights that would involve vibration exceedence alerts. This proposal may be feasible as long as the value of the avoided flight safety risk plus the improvement of equipment availability compensates the increased effort of the maintainers plus the cost of the expended consumable resources.

Similar experimental setups can be used to support human understanding of processes and patterns manifested in complex temporal data. Let us take as an example of the familiar aircraft vibration alerts. As indicated earlier, high standards of flight safety enforce thorough processing of each alert issued during flight and require ground crew technicians to investigate root causes in order to isolate and fix failures if they are in fact present. However, luckily, in practice, many such alerts cannot be linked to any identifiable technical

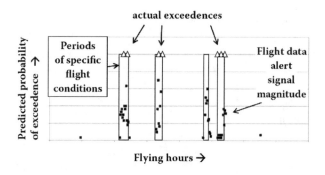

Fig. 7 Machine-learning model identifies vibration exceedances that are explainable by the specific flight conditions and likely do not indicate a technical fault.

issue. A valid hypothesis states that at least some of them could be triggered by specific flight conditions as opposite to actual failure modes. If we were able to produce a model that could reliably correlate occurrences of certain types of vibration exceedences with specific flight regimes, such alerts could be potentially dismissed as "fake failures," allowing substantial savings of troubleshooting efforts by the ground crew technicians. To test the concept, we have built such models for the fleet of aircraft considered earlier.

An example result is shown in Fig. 7. The model trained to predict a certain type of in-flight alerts using a 60-dimensional vector of flight parameters (pressures, angles, engine parameters, status of subsystems, declared phase of flight, etc.) produces a signal (plotted in solid squares) that temporally overlaps three out of four times with the bursts of vibration exceedances (outlined triangles) recorded during this flight. In addition, elevation of the predictive signal coincides with the aircraft being in a specific flight regime, which after expert evaluation was found to be a plausible explanation of these alerts. Plausibly explainable alerts would not require troubleshooting follow-ups by ground crews, saving time and money and keeping the aircraft available for the next flight without delay. This is one of many examples of the ability of big data analytics to find useful explanations of the observed phenomena when the complexities and the amounts of the underlying raw data make it extremely difficult for humans to process and comprehend.

SUMMARY

We have demonstrated a big data analytics approach designed to support discovering and leveraging informative patterns in large-scale multidimensional temporal data of transactions. This type of data is abundant in many domains of human activity. Our approach can be adjusted to specific application scenarios by customizing the featurization of the source data and by selecting the appropriate machine-learning algorithms to provide predictive capabilities. We have shown a few instances of societally and commercially beneficial use of the proposed approach. These examples leverage comprehensive screening of large databases for multiple different aspects of change, which in turn may help explain current events and carry information about the future.

ACKNOWLEDGMENTS

This material is based upon work supported by the National Science Foundation under award number 0911032. Many thanks to Michael Baysek, Lujie Chen, Gilles Clermont, Madalina Fiterau, Roman Garnett, Xuewei He, Peter Huggins, Yogi Koasanto, Katsuji Kurihara, Ming Liang, Rajas Lonkar, Saswati Ray, Maheshkumar Sabhnani, Norman Sondheimer, Nuwan Waidyanatha, and Yiwen Xu for contributing information that inspired this text.

REFERENCES

1. Moore, A.; Lee, M. Cached sufficient statistics for efficient machine learning with large datasets. J. Artif. Intel. Res. **1998**, *8*, 67–91.
2. Burkom, H.S.; Murphy, S.; Coberly, J.; Hurt-Mullen, K. Public health monitoring tools for multiple data streams. Morbid. Mortal. Week. Rep. **2005**, *54* (Suppl.), 55–62.
3. Dubrawski, A. Detection of events in multiple streams of surveillance data. In *Infectious Disease Informatics and Biosurveillance*; Zeng, D., Chen, H., Castillo-Chavez, C., Lober, W., Thurmond, M., Eds.; Dordrecht Heidelberg: New York: Springer, London, 2010.
4. Dubrawski, A.; Sabhnani, M.; Fedorka-Cray, P.; Kelley, L.; Gerner-Smidt, P.; Williams, I.; Huckabee, M.; Dunham, A. Discovering Possible Linkages between Foodborne Illness and the Food Supply Using an Interactive Analysis Tool. 8th Annual Conference of the International Society for Disease Surveillance, 2009. Available online at http://thci.org/syndromic/conference2010/09abstracts.aspx
5. Rolka, H.; Burkom, H.; Cooper, G.F.; Kulldorff, M.; Madigan, D.; Wong, W.K. Issues in applied statistics for public health bioterrorism surveillance using multiple data streams: Research needs. Stat Med. **2007**, *26* (8), 1834–1856.
6. Wong, W.K.; Cooper, G.F.; Dash, D.H.; Levander, J.D.; Dowling, J.N.; Hogan, W.R.; Wagner, M.M. Bayesian biosurveillance using multiple data streams. Morbid. Mortal. Week. Rep. **2005**, *54* (Suppl.), 63–69.
7. Waidyanatha, N.; Sampath, C.; Dubrawski, A.; Prashant, S.; Ganesan, M.; Gow, G. Affordable system for rapid detection and mitigation of emerging diseases. Intl J. E-Health Med. Commun. **2011**, *2* (1), 73–90.
8. Roure, J.; Dubrawski, A.; Schneider, J. A study into detection of bio-events in multiple streams of surveillance data. In *BioSurveillance 2007, Lecture Notes in Computer Science 4506*, Zeng, D., et al. Eds.; 2007; pp. 124–133.
9. Sabhnani, M.; Dubrawski, A.; Waidyanatha, N. T-Cube Web Interface for Real-time Biosurveillance in Sri Lanka. 8th Annual Conference of the International Society for Disease Surveillance, 2009. Available online at http://thci.org/syndromic/conference2010/09abstracts.aspx
10. Sabhnani, M.; Dubrawski, A.; Schneider, J. *Searching for Complex Patterns Using Disjunctive Anomaly Detection*. ISDS Annual Conference Proceedings 2012. Available online at: http://www.syndromic.org/uploads/files/Searching for Complex Patterns Using Disjunctive.pdf
11. Lonkar, R.; Dubrawski, A.; Fiterau, M.; Garnett, R. Mining intensive care vitals for leading indicators of adverse

health events. Emerg. Health Threats J. **2011**, *4*, 11073, DOI: 10.3402/ehtj.v4i0.11073.

12. Basseville, M.; Nikiforov, I.V. *Detection of Abrupt Changes: Theory and Application*; Prentice-Hall: Englewood Cliffs, N. J., 1993.

13. Dubrawski, A. The role of data aggregation in public health and food safety surveillance. In *Biosurveillance: Methods and Case Studies*; Kass-Hout. T., Zhang, X., Eds.; Taylor & Francis: Boca Raton, FL, 2010.

14. McGrattan, E.R.; Schmitz Jr., J.A. Maintenance and repair: Too big to ignore. Fed. Reser. Bank MI Quarter. Rev. **1999**, *23* (4), 2–13.

15. Shackelford, M.D.; Carlisle, H.J. Presentation to the House Armed Services Committee Subcommittee on Tactical Air and Land Forces. U. S. House of Representatives, March 15, 2011.

16. Dubrawski, A.; Sondheimer, N. Techniques for Early Warning of Systematic Failures of Aerospace Components, 2011 IEEE Aerospace Conference, Big Sky, MT, March 2011.

17. Breiman, L. Random forests. Mach. Learn. **2001**, *45* (1), 5–32.

Data Mining

Monte F. Hancock, Jr.
Chief Scientist, Celestech, Inc., Melbourne, Florida, U.S.A.

Abstract

The purpose of thisentry is to provide the reader with grounding in the fundamental philosophical principles of data mining as a technical practice. The reader is then introduced to the wide array of practical applications that rely on data mining technology. The issue of computational complexity is addressed in brief.

GOALS

After you have read this entry, you will be able to define data mining from both philosophical and operational perspectives, and enumerate the analytic functions data mining performs. You will know the different types of data that arise in practice. You will understand the basics of computational complexity theory. Most importantly, you will understand the difference between data and information.

INTRODUCTION

Our study of data mining begins with two semi-formal definitions:

Definition 1. Data mining is the principled detection, characterization, and exploitation of actionable patterns in data. Table 1explains what is meant by each of these components.

Taking this view of what data mining is we can formulate a functional definition that tells us what individuals engaged in data mining do.

Definition 2. Data mining is the application of the scientific method to data to obtain useful information. The heart of the scientific approach to problem-solving is rational hypothesis testing guided by empirical experimentation.

What we call science in the present times was referred to as natural philosophy in the 15th century. The Aristotelian approach to understanding the world was to catalog and organize more-or-less passive acts of observation into taxonomies. This method began to fall out of favor in the physical sciences in the 15th century, and was dead by the 17th century. However, because of the greater difficulty of observing the processes underlying biology and behavior, life sciences continued to rely on this approach until well into the 19th century. This is why the life sciences of the 1800s are replete with taxonomies, detailed naming conventions, and perceived lines of descent, which are more a matter of organizing observations than principled experimentation and model revision.

Applying the scientific method today, we expect to engage in a sequence of planned steps:

1. Formulate hypotheses (often in the form of a question)
2. Devise experiments
3. Collect data
4. Interpret data to evaluate hypotheses
5. Revise hypotheses based upon experimental results

This sequence amounts to one cycle of an iterative approach to acquiring knowledge. In light of our functional definition of data mining, this sequence can be thought of as an over-arching data mining methodology.

A BRIEF PHILOSOPHICAL DISCUSSION

Somewhere in every data mining effort, you will encounter at least one computationally intractable problem; it is unavoidable. This has technical and procedural implications, but it also has philosophical implications. In particular, since there are by definition no perfect techniques for intractable problems, different people will handle them in different ways; no one can say definitively that one way is necessarily wrong and another right. This makes data mining something of an art, and leaves room for the operation of both practical experience and creative experimentation. It also implies that the data mining philosophy to which you look when science falls short can mean the difference between

Encyclopedia of Information Systems and Technology, DOI: 10.1081/E-EIST-120053843

Table 1 Definitive   data mining attributes

Attribute	Connotations
Principled	Rational, empirical, objective, and repeatable
Detection	Sensing and locating
Characterization	Consistent, efficient, and tractable symbolic representation that does not alter information content
Exploitation	Decision making that facilitates action
Actionable Pattern	Conveys information that supports decision making

success and failure. Let's talk a bit about developing such a data mining philosophy.

As noted above, data mining can be thought of as the application of the scientific method to data. We perform data collection (sampling), formulate hypotheses (e.g., visualization, cluster analysis, and feature selection), conduct experiments (e.g., construct and test classifiers), refine hypotheses (spiral methodology), and ultimately build theories (field applications). This is a process that can be reviewed and replicated. In the real world, the resulting theory will either succeed or fail.

Many of the disciplines that apply to empirical scientific work also apply to the practice of data mining: assumptions must be made explicit; the design of principled experiments capable of falsifying our hypotheses is essential; the integrity of the evidence, process, and results must be meticulously maintained and documented; outcomes must be repeatable; and so on. Unless these disciplines are maintained, nothing of certain value can result. Of particular importance is the ability to reproduce results. In the data mining world, these disciplines involve careful configuration management of the system environment, data, applications, and documentation. There are no effective substitutes for these.

One of the most difficult mental disciplines to maintain during data mining work is reservation of judgment. In any field involving hypothesis and experimentation, preliminary results can be both surprising and exhilarating. Finding the smoking gun in a forensic study, for example, is hitting pay-dirt of the highest quality, and it is hard not to get a little excited if you smell gunpowder.

However, this excitement cannot be allowed to short-circuit the analytic process. More than once I have seen exuberant young analysts charging down the hall to announce an amazing discovery after only a few hours' work with a data set; but I don't recall any of those instant discoveries holding up under careful review. I can think of three times when I have myself jumped the gun in this way. On one occasion, eagerness to provide a rapid response led me to prematurely turn over results to a major customer, who then provided them (without review) to their major customer. Unfortunately, there was an unnoticed but significant flaw in the analysis that invalidated most of the reported results. That is a

trail of culpability you don't want leading back to your office door.

THE MOST IMPORTANT ATTRIBUTE OF THE SUCCESSFUL DATA MINER: INTEGRITY

Integrity is variously understood, so we list the principal characteristics data miners must have.

- **Moral courage.** Data miners have lots of opportunities to deliver unpleasant news. Sometimes they have to inform an enterprise that the data it has collected and stored at great expense does not contain the type or amount of information expected.
- Further, it is an unfortunate fact that the default assessment for data mining efforts in most situations is "failure." There can be tremendous pressure to produce a certain result, accuracy level, conclusion, etc., and if you don't: Failure. Pointing out that the data do not support the desired application, are of low quality (precision/accuracy), and do not contain sufficient samples to cover the problem space will sound like excuses, and will not always redeem you.
- **Commitment to enterprise success.** If you want the enterprise you are assisting to be successful, you will be honest with them; will labor to communicate information in terms they can understand; and will not put your personal success ahead of the truth.
- **Honesty in evaluation of data and information.** Individuals that demonstrate this characteristic are willing to let the data speak for itself. They will resist the temptation to read into the data that which wasn't mined from the data.
- **Meticulous planning, execution, and documentation.** A successful data miner will be meticulous in planning, carrying out, and documenting the mining process. They will not jump to conclusions; will enforce the prerequisites of a process before beginning; will check and recheck major results; and will carefully validate all results before reporting them. Excellent data miners create documentation of sufficient quality and detail that their results can be reproduced by others.

WHAT DOES DATA MINING DO?

The particulars of practical data mining "best practice" will be addressed later in great detail, but we jump-start the treatment with some bulleted lists summarizing the functions that data mining provides.

Data mining uses a combination of empirical and theoretical principles to connect *structure* to *meaning* by

- Selecting and conditioning relevant data
- Identifying, characterizing, and classifying latent patterns
- Presenting useful representations and interpretations to users

Data mining attempts to answer these questions:

- What patterns are in the information?
- What are the characteristics of these patterns?
- Can meaning be ascribed to these patterns and/or their changes?
- Can these patterns be presented to users in a way that will facilitate their assessment, understanding, and exploitation?
- Can a machine learn these patterns and their relevant interpretations?

Data mining helps the user interact productively with the data

- *Planning* helps the user achieve and maintain situational awareness of vast, dynamic, ambiguous/incomplete, disparate, multi-source data.
- *Knowledge* leverages users' domain knowledge by creating functionality based upon an understanding of data creation, collection, and exploitation.
- *Expressiveness* produces outputs of adjustable complexity delivered in terms meaningful to the user.
- *Pedigree* builds integrated metrics into every function, because every recommendation has to have supporting evidence and an assessment of certainty.
- *Change* uses future-proof architectures and adaptive algorithms that anticipate many users addressing many missions.

Data mining enables the user to get their head around the problem space

Decision Support is all about helping users make the best choices:

- Enabling users to group information in familiar ways
- Controlling Human Machine Interface complexity by layering results (e.g., drill-down)
- Supporting user's changing priorities (goals, capabilities)

- Allowing intuition to be triggered ("I've seen this before")
- Preserving and automating perishable institutional knowledge
- Providing objective, repeatable metrics (e.g., confidence factors)
- Fusing and simplifying results (e.g., annotate multi-source visuals)
- Automating alerts on important results ("It's happening again")
- Detecting emerging behaviors before they consummate (look)
- Delivering value (timely, relevant, and accurate results)

Some general application areas for data mining technology are:

- Automating pattern detection to characterize complex, distributed signatures that are worth human attention and recognize those that are not
- Associating events that go together but are difficult for humans to correlate
- Characterizing interesting processes not just facts or simple events
- Detecting actionable anomalies and explaining what makes them different and interesting
- Describing contexts from multiple perspectives with numbers, text, and graphics
- Accurate identification and classification—add value to raw data by tagging and annotation (e.g., automatic target detection)
  - Anomaly, normalcy, and fusion—characterize, quantify, and assess normalcy of patterns and trends (e.g., network intrusion detection)
- Emerging patterns and evidence evaluation—capturing institutional knowledge of how events arise and alerting users when they begin to emerge
- Behavior association—detection of actions that are distributed in time and space but synchronized by a common objective: connecting the dots
- Signature detection and association—detection and characterization of multivariate signals, symbols, and emissions
- Concept tagging—ontological reasoning about abstract relationships to tag and annotate media of all types (e.g., document geo-tagging)
- Software agents assisting analysts—small footprint, fire-and-forget apps that facilitate search, collaboration, etc.
- Help the user focus via unobtrusive automation

  Off-load burdensome labor (perform intelligent searches, smart winnowing)

Post smart triggers or tripwires to data stream (anomaly detection)

Help with workflow and triage (sort my in-basket)
- Automate aspects of classification and detection
  o Determine which sets of data hold the most information for a task
  o Support construction of ad hoc on-the-fly classifiers
  o Provide automated constructs for merging decision engines (multi-level fusion)
  o Detect and characterize domain drift (the rules of the game are changing)
  o Provide functionality to make best estimate of missing data
- Extract, characterize, and employ knowledge
  o Rule induction from data and signatures development from data
  o Implement non-monotonic reasoning for decision support
  o High-dimensional visualization
  o Embed decision explanation capability in analytic applications
- Capture, automate, and institutionalize best practices
  o Make proven enterprise analytic processes available to all
  o Capture rare, perishable human knowledge and distribute it everywhere
  o Generate signature-ready prose reports
  o Capture and characterize the analytic process to anticipate user needs

WHAT DO WE MEAN BY DATA?

Data is the wrapper that carries information. It can look like just about anything: images, movies, recorded sounds, light from stars, the text in a book, the swirls that form your fingerprints, your hair color, age, income, height, weight, credit score, a list of your likes and dislikes, the chemical formula for the gasoline in your car, the number of miles you drove last year, your cat's body temperature as a function of time, the order of the nucleotides in the third codon of your mitochondrial DNA, a street map of Liberal Kansas, the distribution of IQ scores in Braman Oklahoma, the fat content of smoked sausage, a spreadsheet of your household expenses, a coded message, a computer virus, the pattern of fibers in your living room carpet, the pattern of purchases at a grocery store, the pattern of capillaries in your retina, election results, etc. In fact: A *datum* (singular) is any symbolic representation of any attribute of any given thing. More than one datum constitutes *data* (plural).

Nominal Data vs. Numeric Data

Data come in two fundamental forms—nominal and numeric. Fabulously intricate hierarchical structures and relational schemes can be fashioned from these two forms.

This is an important distinction, because nominal and numeric data encode information in different ways. Therefore, they are interpreted in different ways, exhibit patterns in different ways, and must be mined in different ways. In fact, there are many data mining tools that only work with numeric data, and many that only work with nominal data. There are only few (but there are some) that work with both.

Data are said to be *nominal* when they are represented by a name. The names of people, places, and things are all nominal designations. Virtually all text data is nominal. But data like Zip codes, phone numbers, addresses, social security numbers, etc. are also nominal. This is because they are aliases for things: your postal zone, the den that contains your phone, your house, and you. The point is the information in these data has nothing to do with the numeric values of their symbols; any other unique string of numbers could have been used.

Data are said to be *numeric* when the information they contain is conveyed by the numeric value of their symbol string. Bank balances, altitudes, temperatures, and ages all hold their information in the value of the number string that represents them. A different number string would not do.

Given that nominal data can be represented using numeric characters, how can you tell the difference between nominal and numeric data? There is a simple test: If the average of a set of data is meaningful, they are numeric.

Phone numbers are nominal, because averaging the phone numbers of a group of people doesn't produce a meaningful result. The same is true of zip codes, addresses, and Social Security numbers. But averaging incomes, ages, and weights gives symbols whose values carry information about the group; they are numeric data.

Discrete Data vs. Continuous Data

Numeric data come in two forms—discrete and continuous. We can't get too technical here, because formal mathematical definitions of these concepts are deep. For the purposes of data mining, it is sufficient to say that a set of data is *continuous* when, given two values in the set, you can always find another value in the set between them. Intuitively, this implies there is a linear ordering, and there aren't gaps or holes in the range of

Nominal to Numeric Coding of Data

Name	Class	Feature 1 (habitat)	Feature 2 (diet)	Feature 3 (integument)	Feature 4 (morphology)	Feature 5 (life cycle)
Bill	primates	land	omnivore	skin w/o feathers	biped no wings	live birth
Bubbles	fishes	sea	omnivore	scales	no wings, non biped	eggs w/o meta
Rover	domestic	land	carnivore	skin w/o feathers	no wings, non biped	live birth
Ringo	bugs	land	herbivore	exoskeleton	wings, non-biped	egss w. meta
Chuck	bacteria	parasitic	other	other	no wings, non biped	other
Tweety	birds	land	omnivore	skin with feathers	wings, biped	eggs w/o meta

Original Nominal Data

Within each column, establish a mapping to some numeric code for each nominal value. For example, in column 2, Class, we code mammals as "1" and non-mammals as "2":

Name	Class	Feature 1 (habitat)	Feature 2 (diet)	Feature 3 (integument)	Feature 4 (morphology)	Feature 5 (life cycle)
1	1	2	3	1	3	1
2	2	1	3	3	4	3
3	1	2	2	1	4	1
4	2	2	1	4	1	2
5	2	3	4	5	4	4
6	2	2	3	2	2	3

Final Coding: Categories mapped to numeric representations

Fig. 1 Nominal to numeric coding of data.

possible values. In theory, it also implies that continuous data can assume infinitely many different values.

A set of data is *discrete* if it is not continuous. The usual scenario is a finite set of values or symbols. For example, the readings of a thermometer constitute continuous data, because (in theory), any temperature within a reasonable range could actually occur. Time is usually assumed to be continuous in this sense, as is distance; therefore sizes, distances, and durations are all continuous data.

On the other hand, when the possible data values can be placed in a list, they are discrete: hair color, gender, quantum states (depending upon whom you ask), headcount for a business, the positive whole numbers (an infinite set) etc., are all discrete.

A very important difference between discrete and continuous data for data mining applications is the

matter of error. Continuous data can presumably have any amount of error, from very small to very large, and all values in between. Discrete data are either completely right or completely wrong.

Coding and Quantization as Inverse Processes

Data can be represented in different ways. Sometimes it is necessary to translate data from one representational scheme to another. In applications this often means converting numeric data to nominal data (*quantization*), and nominal data to numeric data (*coding*).

Quantization usually leads to loss of precision, so it is not a perfectly reversible process. Coding usually leads to an increase in precision, and is usually reversible.

There are many ways these conversions can be done, and some application-dependent decisions that must be made. Examples of these decisions might include choosing the level of numeric precision for coding, or determining the number of restoration values for quantization. The most intuitive explanation of these inverse processes is pictorial. Notice that the numeric coding (Fig. 1) is performed in stages. No information is lost; its only purpose was to make the nominal feature attributes numeric. However, quantization (Fig. 2) usually reduces the precision of the data, and is rarely reversible.

Numeric to Nominal (Quantization)

Original Values	After Quantization	Nominal Categories
$ 3245	$ 5000	A
$ 6187	$ 5000	A
$ 12876	$ 15000	B
$ 22453	$ 25000	C
$ 23855	$ 25000	C
$ 36786	$ 35000	D
$ 43732	$ 45000	E
$ 46666	$ 45000	E

Quantization Bins:

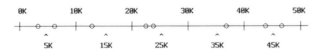

Fig. 2 Numeric to nominal quantization.

● - ● - ● - ● - ● - ● - ● - ● - ● - ● - ● - ● - ● - ● - ● - ● - ● - ● - ● - ●
This pattern conveys NO INFORMATION because it exhibits no variation.

Fig. 3 Noninformative pattern.

A Crucial Distinction: Data and Information Are Not the Same Thing

Data and information are entirely different things. Data is a formalism, a wrapper, by which information is given observable form. Data and information stand in relation to one another much as do the body and the mind. In similar fashion, it is only data that are directly accessible to an observer. Inferring information from data requires an act of interpretation which always involves a combination of contextual constraints and rules of inference.

In computing systems, the problem "context" and "heuristics" are represented using a structure called a domain ontology. As the term suggests, each problem space has its own constraints, facts, assumptions, rules of thumb, and these are variously represented and applied.

The standard mining analogy is helpful here. Data mining is similar in some ways to mining for precious metals:

- **Silver mining.** Prospectors survey a region and select an area they think might have ore, the rough product that is refined to obtain metal. They apply tools to estimate the ore content of their samples and if it is high enough, the ore is refined to obtain purified silver.

- **Data mining.** Data miners survey a problem space and select sources they think might contain salient patterns, the rough product that is refined to obtain information. They apply tools to assess the information content of their sample and if it is high enough, the data are processed to infer latent information.

However, there is a very important way in which data mining is not like silver mining. Chunks of silver ore actually contain particular silver atoms. When a chunk of ore is moved, its silver goes with it. Extending this part of the silver mining analogy to data mining will get us into trouble. The silver mining analogy fails because of the fundamental difference between data and information.

The simplest scenario demonstrating this difference involves their different relation to *context*. When I remove letters from a word, they retain their identity as letters, as do the letters left behind. But the information

● ● ●   - - -   ● ● ●   ● ● ●   ● ● ●   ● ● ● | ● ● ● | ● ● ● | ● ● ●   ● ● ●
S   O   S   S   S   S   S   S | O | O | O   S
This pattern conveys information BY VIRTUE of its variation (called <u>Modulation</u>)

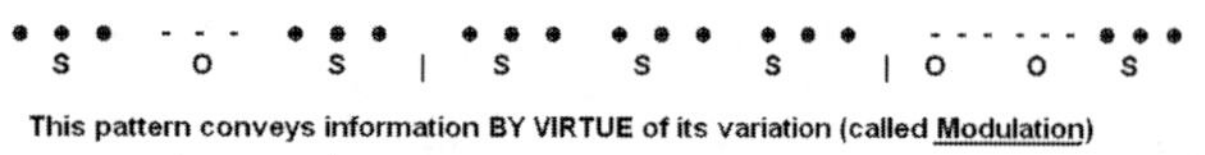

Fig. 4 Informative modulation pattern.

conveyed by the letters removed and by the letters left behind has very likely been altered, destroyed, or even negated.

Another example is found in the dependence on how the information is encoded. I convey exactly the same message when I say "How are you?" that I convey when I say "Wie gehts?," yet the data are completely different. Computer scientists use the terms *syntax* and *semantics* to distinguish between representation and meaning, respectively.

It is extremely dangerous for the data miner to fall into the habit of regarding particular pieces of information as being attached to particular pieces of data in the same way that metal atoms are bound to ore. Consider a more sophisticated, but subtle example:

A Morse code operator sends a message consisting of alternating, evenly spaced dots and dashes (Fig. 3).

This is clearly a pattern but other than manifesting its own existence, this pattern conveys no information. Information Theory tells that us such a pattern is devoid of information by pointing out that after we've listened to this pattern for a while, we can perfectly predict which symbol will arrive next. Such a pattern, by virtue of its complete predictability is not informative: a message that tells me what I already know tells me nothing. This important notion can be quantified in the Shannon Entropy (see glossary). However, if the transmitted tones are varied or modulated, the situation is quite different (Fig. 4).

This example makes is quite clear that information does not reside within the dots and dashes themselves; rather, it arises from an interpretation of their inter-relationships. In Morse code, this is their order and duration relative to each other. Notice that by removing the first dash from O = - –, the last two dashes now mean M = - -, even though the dashes have not changed. This *context sensitivity* is a wonderful thing, but it causes data mining disaster if ignored.

A final illustration called the *Parity Problem* convincingly establishes the distinct nature of data and information in a data mining context.

The Parity Problem

Let's do a thought experiment (Fig. 5). I have two marbles in my hand, one white and one black. I show them to you and ask this question: Is the number of black marbles even, or is it odd?

Naturally you respond *odd*, since one is an odd number. If both of the marbles had been black, the correct answer would have been *even*, since 2 is an even number; if I had been holding two white marbles, again the correct answer would have been *even*, since 0 is an even number.

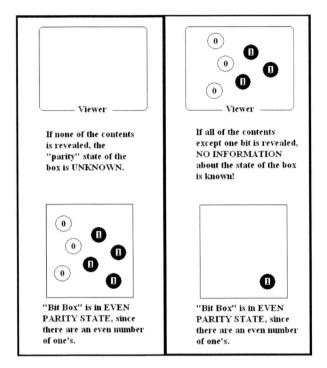

Viewer

If none of the contents
is revealed, the
"parity" state of the
box is UNKNOWN.

Viewer

If all of the contents
except one bit is revealed,
NO INFORMATION
about the state of the box
is known!

"Bit Box" is in EVEN
PARITY STATE, since
there are an even number
of one's.

"Bit Box" is in EVEN
PARITY STATE, since
there are an even number
of one's.

Fig. 5   The parity problem.

This is called the Parity Two problem. If there are N marbles, some white (possibly none) and some black (possibly none), the question of whether there are an odd number of black marbles is called the Parity-N Problem, or just the Parity Problem. This problem is important in computer science, information theory, coding theory, and related areas.

Of course, when researchers talk about the parity problem, they don't use marbles, they use zeros and ones (binary digits = bits). For example, I can store a data file on disc and then ask whether the file has an odd or even number of ones; the answer is the parity of the file.

This idea can also be used to detect data transmission errors: if I want to send you 100 bits of data, I could actually send you 101, with the extra bit set to a one or zero such that the whole set has a particular parity that you and I have agreed upon in advance. If you get a message from me and it doesn't have the expected

- Information can be <u>irretrievably</u> distributed!
    - 0010100110... 1 (The Parity Problem)
        - <u>No subset of the features</u> contains any information at all!

- Information is usually "bound" in cliques rather than individual features. Therefore...
    - *...the best feature set is often not
    the set of best features.*

"As a coach, I play not my eleven best, but my best eleven." - Knute Rockne

Fig. 6   Feature sets vs. sets of features.

parity, you know the message has an odd number of bit errors and must be resent.

Five Riddles about Information

Suppose I have two lab assistants named Al and Bob, and two data bits. I show only the first one to Al, and only the second one to Bob. If I ask Al what the parity of the original pair of bits is, what will he say? And if I ask Bob what the parity of the original pair of bits is, what will he say?

Neither one can say what the parity of the original pair is, because each one is lacking a bit. If I handed Al a one, he could reason that if the bit I can't see is also a one, then the parity of the original pair is even. But if the bit I can't see is a zero, then the parity of the original pair is odd. Bob is in exactly the same boat.

Riddle one. Al is no more able to state the parity of the original bit pair than he was before he was given his bit and the same is true for Bob. That is, each one has 50% of the data, but neither one has received any information at all.

Suppose now that I have 100 lab assistants, and 100 randomly generated bits of data. To assistant 1, I give all the bits except bit 1; to assistant 2, I give all the bits except bit 2; and so on. Each assistant has received 99% of the data. Yet none of them any more is able to state the parity of the original 100-bit data set than before they received 99 of the bits.

Riddle two. Even though each assistant has received 99% of the data, none of them has received any information at all.

Riddle three. The information in the 100 data bits cannot be in the bits themselves. For, which bit is it in? Not bit 1, since that bit was given to 99 assistants, and didn't provide them with any information. Not bit 2, for the same reason. In fact, it is clear that the information cannot be in any of the bits themselves. So, where is it?

Riddle four. Suppose my 100 bits have odd parity (say, 45 ones and 55 zeros). I arrange them on a piece of paper, so they spell the word "odd." Have I added information? If so, where is it? (See Fig. 6).

Riddle five. Where is the information in a multiply encrypted message, since it completely disappears when one bit is removed?

Seven Riddles about Meaning

Thinking of information as a vehicle for expressing *meaning*, we now consider the idea of "meaning" itself. The following questions might seem silly, but the issues they raise are the very things that make intelligent computing and data mining particularly difficult. Specifically, when an automated decision support system must infer the "meaning" of a collection of data values in order to correctly make a critical decision, "silly" issues of exactly this sort come up… and they must be addressed.

For our purposes, the most important question has to do with context: does meaning reside in things themselves, or is it merely the interpretation of an observer? This is an interesting question I have used (along with related questions in axiology) when I teach my Western Philosophy class. Here are some questions that touch on the connection between meaning and context:

Riddle one. If meaning must be known/remembered in order to exist/persist, does that imply that it is a form of information?

Riddle two. In the late 18th century, many examples of Egyptian hieroglyphics were known, but no one could read them. Did they have meaning? Apparently not, since there were no "rememberers." In 1798, the French found the Rosetta Stone, and within the next 20 or so years, this "lost" language was recovered, and with it, the "meaning" of Egyptian hieroglyphics. So, was the meaning "in" the hieroglyphics, or was it "brought to" the hieroglyphics by its translators?

Riddle three. If I write a computer program to generate random but intelligible stories (which I have done, by the way), and it writes a story to a text file, does this story have meaning before any person reads the file? Does it have meaning after a person reads the file? If it was meaningless before but meaningful afterwards, where did the meaning come from?

Riddle four. Two cops read a suicide note, but interpret it in completely different ways. What does the note mean?

Riddle five. Suppose I take a large number of tiny pictures of Abraham Lincoln and arrange them, such that they spell out the words "Born in 1809"; is additional meaning present?

Riddle six. On his deathbed, Albert Einstein whispered his last words to the nurse caring for him. Unfortunately, he spoke in German, which she did not understand. Did those words mean anything? Are they now meaningless?

Riddle seven. When I look at your family photo album, I don't recognize anyone, or understand any of the events depicted; they convey nothing to me but what they immediately depict. You look at the album, and many memories of people, places, and events are engendered; they convey much. So, where is the meaning? Is it in the pictures, or is it in the viewer?

As we can see by considering the questions above, the meaning of a data set arises during an act of interpretation by a cognitive agent. At least some of it resides outside the data itself. This external content we normally regard as being in the domain ontology; it is part of the document context, and not the document itself.

DATA COMPLEXITY

When talking about data complexity, the real issue at hand is the *accessibility* of latent information. Data are considered more complex when extracting information from them is more difficult.

Complexity arises in many ways, precisely because there are many ways that latent information can be obscured. For example, data can be complex because they are unwieldy. This can mean many records and/or many fields within a record (dimensions). Large data sets are difficult to manipulate, making their information content more difficult and time consuming to tap.

Data can also be complex because their information content is spread in some unknown way across multiple fields or records. Extracting information present in complicated bindings is a combinatorial search problem. Data can also be complex because the information they contain is not revealed by available tools. For example, visualization is an excellent information discovery tool, but most visualization tools do not support high-dimensional rendering.

Data can be complex because the patterns that contain interesting information occur rarely. Data can be complex because they just don't contain very much information at all. This is a particularly vexing problem because it is often difficult to determine whether the information is not visible, or just not present.

There is also the issue of whether latent information is actionable. If you are trying to construct a classifier, you want to characterize patterns that discriminate between classes. There might be plenty of information available, but little that helps with this specific task.

Sometimes the format of the data is a problem. This is certainly the case when those data that carry the needed information are collected/stored at a level of precision that obscures it (e.g., representing continuous data in discrete form).

Finally, there is the issue of data quality. Data of lesser quality might contain information, but at a low level of confidence. In this case, even information that is clearly present might have to be discounted as unreliable.

COMPUTATIONAL COMPLEXITY

Computer scientists have formulated a principled definition of *computational complexity*. It treats the issue of how the amount of labor required to solve an instance of a problem is related to the size of the instance (Fig. 7).

For example, the amount of labor required to find the largest element in an arbitrary list of numbers is directly proportional to the length of the list. That is, finding the

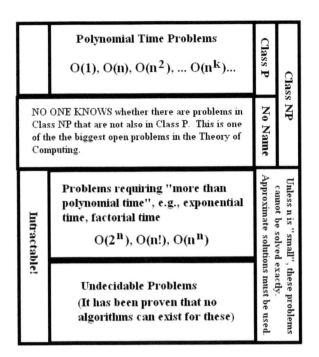

The Hierarchy of Computational Complexity

Fig. 7 The hierarchy of computational complexity.

largest element in a list of 2000 numbers requires twice as many computer operations as finding the largest element in a list of 1000 numbers. This *linear* proportionality is represented by O(n), read "big O of n," where n is the length of the list.

On the other hand, the worst-case amount of labor required to sort an arbitrary list is directly proportional to the square of the length of the list. This is because sorting requires that the list be rescanned for every unsorted element to determine whether it is the next smallest or largest in the list. Therefore, sorting an arbitrary list of 2000 numbers items requires four times as many computer operations as sorting a list of 1000

numbers. This *quadratic* proportionality is represented by $O(n^2)$ read "big O of n squared," where n is the length of the list.

Lots of research has been conducted to determine the Big O complexity of various algorithms. It is generally held that algorithms having polynomial complexity, $O(n^p)$, are tractable, while more demanding Big O complexities are intractable. The details can't be addressed here, but we do note that many data mining problems (optimal feature selection, optimal training of a classifier, etc.) have a computational complexity that is beyond any polynomial level. In practice, this means that data miners must be content with solutions that are good enough. These are referred to as *satisficing solutions*.

Problems that are very computationally complex in their general case may fall into a class of problems referred to as *NP-Hard*. These problems, which have no known efficient algorithmic solutions, are frequently encountered in data mining work. Often problems in a domain are arranged in a hierarchy to help system architects make engineering trades (Fig. 8).

Some NP-Hard Problems

- **The Knapsack Problem.** Given cubes of various sizes and materials (and hence, values), find the highest value combination that fits within a given box.
- **The Traveling Salesman Problem.** Given a map with N points marked, find the shortest circuit (a route that ends where it starts) that visits each city exactly once.
- **The Satisfiability Problem.** Given a boolean expression, determine whether there is an assignment of the variables that makes it true.
- **The Classifier Problem.** Given a neural network topology and a training set, find the weights that give the best classification score.

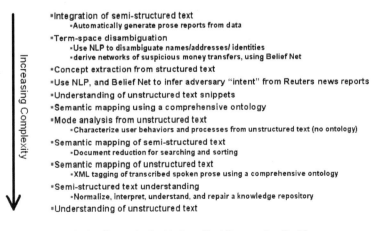

Complexity Hierarchy for Various Text Processing Problems

Fig. 8 Complexity hierarchy for various text processing problems.

Some Worst-Case Computational Complexities

- Determining whether a number is positive or negative: $O(1)$ = constant time
- Finding an item in a sorted list using binary search: $O(\log (n))$
- Finding the largest number in an unsorted list: $O(n)$
- Performing a Fast Fourier Transform: $O(n*\log (n))$
- Sorting a randomly ordered list: $O(n^2)$
- Computing the determinant of an n-by-n matrix: $O(n^3)$
- Brute-force solution of Traveling Salesman Problem: $O(n!)$

SUMMARY

The purpose of this entry was to provide the reader with a grounding in the fundamental principles of data mining as a technical practice. Having read this entry, you are now able to define data mining from both a philosophical and operational perspective, and enumerate the analytic functions data mining performs. You know the different types of data that arise in practice. You have been introduced to the basics of computational complexity theory, and the unavoidable presence of intractability. Most importantly, you have considered the important differences between data and information.

Now that you have been introduced to some terminology and the fundamental principles of data mining, you are ready to continue with a summary overview of data mining as a principled process.

Data Analytics—
Data Mining:
Forensic

Data Mining: Big Data

Wayne Thompson
SAS Institute, Cary, North Carolina, U.S.A.

Abstract

There are so many complex problems that can be better evaluated with the rise of big data and sophisticated analytics in a distributed, in-memory environment to make better decisions within tight time frames. The underlying optimization methods can now solve problems in parallel through co-location of the data in memory. The data mining algorithms are vastly still the same; they are just able to handle more data and are much faster.

BIG DATA

Big data is a popular term that describes the exponential growth, availability, and use of information, both structured and unstructured. Big data continues to gain attention from the high-performance computing niche of the information technology market. According to International Data Corporation (IDC),[1] "the amount of information created and replicated will surpass 1.8 zettabytes (1.8 trillion gigabytes), growing by a factor of nine in just five years. That's nearly as many bits of information in the digital universe as stars in the physical universe."

Big data provides both challenges and opportunities for data miners to develop improved models. Today's massively parallel in-memory analytical computing appliances are no longer hindered by the size of data to be analyzed. A key advantage is that you are able to analyze more of the population with a broad range of classical and modern analytics. The goal of data mining is generalization. Rather than relying on sampling, you can isolate hard-to-detect signals in the data, and you can also produce models that generalize better when deployed into operations. You can also more readily detect outliers that often lead to the best insights. You can also try more configuration options for a specific algorithm, for example, neural network topologies including different activation and combination functions, because the models run in seconds or minutes instead of hours.

Enterprises are also moving toward creating large multipurpose analytical base tables that several analysts can use to develop a plethora of models for risk, marketing, and so on.[2] Developing standardized analytical tables that contain thousands of candidate predictors and targets supports what is referred to as model harvesting or a model factory. A small team of analysts at Cisco Systems build over 30,000 propensity-to-purchase models each quarter. This seasoned team of analysts has developed highly repeatable data preparation strategies along with a sound modeling methodology that they can apply over and over. Customer dynamics also change quickly, as does the underlying snapshot of the historical modeling data. So the analyst often needs to refresh (retrain) models at frequent intervals. Analysts need the ability to develop models in minutes, if not seconds, vs. hours or days (Fig. 1).

Using several champion and challenger methods is critical. Data scientists should not be restricted to using one or two modeling algorithms. Model development (including discovery) is also iterative by nature, so data miners need to be agile when they develop models. The bottom line is that big data is only getting bigger, and data miners need to significantly reduce the cycle time it takes to go from analyzing big data to creating ready-to-deploy models.

Many applications can benefit from big data analytics. One of these applications is telematics, which is the transfer of data from any telecommunications device or chip. The volume of data that these devices generate is massive. For example, automobiles have hundreds of sensors. Automotive manufactures need scalable algorithms to predict vehicle performance and problems on demand. Insurance companies are also implementing pay-as-you-drive plans, in which a Global Positioning System (GPS) device that is installed in your car tracks the distance driven and automatically transmits the information to the insurer. More advanced GPS devices that contain integrated accelerometers also capture date, time, location, speed, cornering, harsh braking, and even frequent lane changing. Data scientists and actuaries can leverage this big data to build more profitable insurance

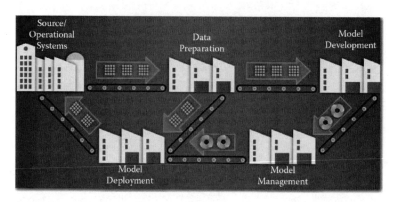

Fig. 1 Analytics is moving out of research and more into operations.

premium models. Personalized policies that reward truly safe drivers can also be written.

The smart energy grid is another interesting application area that encourages customer participation. Sensor systems called synchophasers monitor in real time the health of the grid and collect many streams per second. The consumption in very short intervals can be modeled during peak and off-peak periods to develop pricing plan models. Many customers are "peakier" than others and more expensive to service. Segmentation models can also be built to define custom pricing models that decrease usage in peak hours. Example segments might be "weekday workers," "early birds, home worker," and "late-night gamers."

There are so many complex problems that can be better evaluated with the rise of big data and sophisticated analytics in a distributed, in-memory environment to make better decisions within tight time frames. The underlying optimization methods can now solve problems in parallel through colocation of the data in memory. The data mining algorithms are vastly still the same; they are just able to handle more data and are much faster.

DATA MINING METHODS

The remainder of this entry provides a summary of the most common data mining algorithms. The discussion is broken into two subsections, each with a specific theme: classical data mining techniques and machine learning (ML) methods. The goal is to describe algorithms at a high level so that you can understand how each algorithm fits into the landscape of data mining methods. Although there are a number of other algorithms and many variations of the techniques, these represent popular methods used in real-world deployments of data mining systems.

Classical Data Mining Techniques

Data mining methods have been developed largely by contributions from statistics, ML, artificial intelligence, and database systems. By strict definition, statistics is not data mining. Statistical methods were being used long before the term *data mining* was coined to apply to business applications. In classical inferential statistics, the investigator proposes some model that may explain the relationship between an outcome of interest (dependent response variable) and explanatory variables (independent variables). Once a conceptual model has been proposed, the investigator then collects the data with the purpose of testing the model. Testing typically involves the statistical significance of the parameters associated with the explanatory variables. For these tests to be valid, distributional assumptions about the response or the error terms in the model need to be correct or not be violated too severely. Two of the most broadly used statistical methods are multiple linear regression and logistic regression.

Multiple linear regression and logistic regression are also commonly used in data mining. A critical distinction between their inferential applications and their data mining applications is in how one determines suitability of the model. A typical data mining application is to predict an outcome, a target in data mining jargon, based on the explanatory variables, inputs, or features in data mining jargon. Because of the emphasis on prediction, the distributional assumptions of the target or errors are much less important.

Often, the historical data that are used in data mining model development have a time dimension such as monthly spending habits for each customer. The typical data mining approach to account for variation over time is to construct inputs or features that summarize customer behavior for different time intervals. Common summaries are recency, frequency, and monetary value. This approach results in one row per customer in the model development data table.

An alternative approach is to construct multiple rows for each customer, where the rows include customer

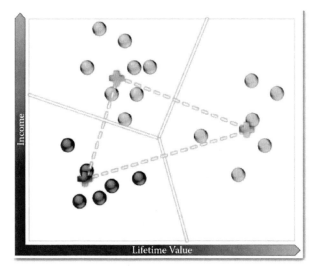

Fig. 2 k-Means cluster analysis cross symbols represent the cluster centroids.

behavior for previous months. The multiple rows for each customer represent a time series of features of the customer's past behavior. When you have data in this form, you should use repeated measures or time series cross-sectional models.

Predictive modeling (supervised learning) techniques enable the analyst to identify whether a set of input variables is useful in predicting some outcome variable. For example, a financial institution might try to determine whether knowledge of an applicant's income and credit history (input variables) helps predict whether the applicant is likely to default on a loan (outcome variable). Descriptive techniques (unsupervised learning) enable you to identify underlying patterns in a data set.

Model overfitting happens when your model describes random noise or error instead of the true relationships in the data. Albert Einstein once said, "Everything should be as simple as it is, but not simple." This is a maxim to abide by when you develop predictive models. Simple models that do a good job of classification or prediction are easier to interpret and tend to generalize better when they are scored. You should develop your model from holdout evaluation sources to determine whether your model overfits. Another strategy, especially for a small training data set, is to use k-fold cross-validation, which is a method of estimating how well your model fits based on resampling. You divide the data into k subsets of approximately the same size. You train your model k times, each time leaving out one of the subsets that is used to evaluate the model. You can then measure model stability across the k holdout samples.

k-Means Clustering

k-Means clustering is a descriptive algorithm that scales well to large data.[3] Cluster analysis has wide application, including customer segmentation, pattern recognition, biological studies, and web document classification. k-Means clustering attempts to find k partitions[4] in the data, in which each observation belongs to the cluster with the nearest mean. The basic steps for k-Means are

1. Select k observations arbitrarily as initial cluster centroids.
2. Assign each observation to the cluster that has the closest centroid.
3. Once all observations are assigned, recalculate the positions of the k centroids.

Repeat steps 2 and 3 until the centroids no longer change (Fig. 2). This repetition helps minimize the variability within clusters and maximize the variability between clusters. Note that the observations are divided into clusters so that every observation belongs to, at the most, one cluster. Some software packages select an appropriate value of k. You should still try to experiment with different values of k that result in good homogeneous clusters that are relatively stable when they are applied to new data.

You should try to select input variables that are both representative of your business problem and predominantly independent. Outliers tend to dominate cluster formation, so consider removing outliers. Normalization is also recommended to standardize the values of all inputs from a dynamic range into a specific range. When using a distance measure, it is extremely important for the inputs to have comparable measurement scales. Most clustering algorithms work well with interval inputs. Most k-Means implementations support several dimension-encoding techniques for computing distances for nominal and ordinal inputs.

After you group the observations into clusters, you can profile the input variables to help further label each cluster. One convenient way to profile the clusters is to use the cluster IDs as a target variable and then use a decision tree and candidate inputs to classify cluster membership.

After the clusters have been identified and interpreted, you might decide to treat each cluster independently. You might also decide to develop separate predictive models for each cluster. Other popular clustering techniques include hierarchical clustering and expectation maximization (EM) clustering.

**Data Analytics–
Data Mining:
Forensic**

Table 1 Sample data layout for market basket analysis

User ID	Artist Name	Song Title
WayneT223	Black Eyed Peas	"Let's Get It Started"
WayneT223	Coldplay	"Viva La Vida"
WayneT223	Aerosmith	"Crazy"
Stephen707	Black Eyed Peas	"Let's Get It Started"
Stephen707	Amy Winehouse	"Valerie"

ASSOCIATION ANALYSIS

Association analysis (also called affinity analysis or market basket analysis) identifies groupings of products or services that tend to be purchased at the same time or purchased at different times by the same customer. Association analysis falls within the descriptive modeling phase of data mining. Association analysis helps you answer questions such as the following:

- What proportion of people who purchase low-fat yogurt and 2% milk also purchase bananas?
- What proportion of people who have a car loan with a financial institution later obtain a home mortgage from that institution?
- What percentage of people who purchase tires and wiper blades also get automotive service done at the same shop?

At a minimum, the data for association analysis contains the transaction ID and an item (Table 1).

In the example data, let's assume that the transactions are from listeners of Pandora. The items represent the artist and the song. You can develop rules that are based on listener preferences for artists or songs. Association rules are based on frequency counts of the number of times that items occur alone and in combination in the transaction record. Confidence and support are important measures that evaluate the strength of the associations.[5] Using the rule A== >B, the confidence for the association rule is the conditional probability that a transaction contains item B, given that the transaction already contains item A. Confidence for the association rule A== >B can be expressed mathematically as the following ratio:

$$\frac{transactions\ that\ contain\ both\ items\ A\ and\ B}{transactions\ that\ contain\ item\ A}$$

The level of support indicates how often the association combination occurs within the transaction database. In other words, support quantifies the probability of a transaction that contains both item A and item B. Support for the association rule A== >B can be expressed mathematically as the following ratio:

$$\frac{transactions\ that\ contain\ both\ items\ A\ and\ B}{all\ transactions}$$

Expected confidence for the rule is another important evaluation criterion. It is the proportion of all transactions that contain item B. The difference between confidence and expected confidence is a measure of the change in predictive power due to the presence of item A in a transaction. Expected confidence indicates what the confidence would be if there were no relationship between the items. Expected confidence for the association rule A== >B can be expressed mathematically as the following ratio:

$$\frac{transactions\ that\ contain\ item\ B}{all\ transactions}$$

A final measure is lift, which is the ratio of the rule's confidence to the rule's expected confidence. In other words, lift is the factor by which the confidence exceeds the expected confidence. Larger lift ratios tend to indicate more interesting association rules. The greater the lift, the greater the influence item A has on the likelihood that item B will be contained in the transaction.

You want to isolate interesting rules that have not only high confidence but also reasonable support and lift values greater than one. A rule might be: "If a user listens to the Black Eyed Peas, there is a 28% confidence that she will also listen to Coldplay." A support value of 1.5% indicates how frequently this combination of songs appears among all user listening transactions.

Association rules should not be interpreted as direct causation. Association rules define some affinity between two or more items. You can develop rules of a predefined chain length among the set of items. This example rule has a chain length of two.

The network plot in Fig. 3 displays rules for the various artists. The maximum number of artists in a rule (chain length) was set to two. The plot has been filtered to include only rules that have a confidence of two and a support of one. Although they are a bit hard to see, the color and thickness of the lines indicate the confidence of a rule. The color and size of the nodes indicate the counts. There are some very nice clusters of artists based on genre, artist type, and artist hotness. For example, Beyoncé, Mariah Carey, and Britney Spears are connected. You can develop rules for a sample of historical transactions as done here, and then score future listeners to produce recommendations of artists (or songs) that a new user might want to hear.

Association discovery can be extended to sequence analysis for time stamps. An example sequence rule might be: "Of customers who purchased an iPhone, 15% of them will purchase an iPad Mini in the next 6 months."

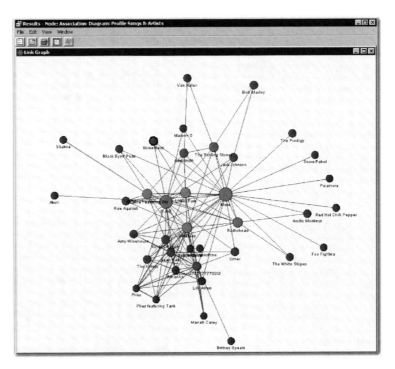

Fig. 3 Network plot of artist listening rules derived from market basket analysis.

Multiple Linear Regression

Multiple linear regression models the relationship between two or more inputs (predictors) and a continuous target variable by fitting a learner model to the training data. The regression model is represented as:

$$E(y) = \beta_0 + \beta_1 x_1 + \beta_2 x_2 + \cdots + \beta_k x_k$$

where $E(y)$ is the expected target values, xs represent the k model inputs, β_0 is the intercept that centers the range of predictions, and the remaining βs are the slope estimates that determine the trend strength between each k input and the target. Simple linear regression has one model input x.

The method of least squares is used to estimate the intercept and parameter of the equation that minimizes the sums of squares of errors of the deviations of the observed values of y from the predicted values of $\hat{y}$. The regression can be expressed as:

$$\hat{y} = b_0 + b_1 x_1 + b_2 x_2 + \cdots + b_k x_k$$

where the squared error function is:

$$\sum (Yi - \hat{Y}i)^2.$$

Multiple linear regression is advantageous because of familiarity and interpretability. Regression models also generate optimal unbiased estimates for unknown parameters. Many phenomena cannot be described by linear relationships among the target variables and the input variables. You can use polynomial regression (adding power terms, including interaction effects) to the model to approximate more complex nonlinear relationships.

The adjusted coefficient of determination (adjusted R^2) is a commonly used measure of the goodness of fit of regression models. Essentially, it is the percentage of the variability that is explained by the model relative to the total variability, adjusted for the number of inputs in your model. A traditional R^2 statistic does not penalize the model for the number of parameters, so you almost always end up choosing the model that has the most parameters. Another common criterion is the root mean square error (RMSE), which indicates the absolute fit of the data to the actual values. You usually want to evaluate the RMSE on holdout validation and test data sources; lower values are better.

Data scientists almost always use stepwise regression selection to fit a subset of the full regression model. Remember that the key goal of predictive modeling is to build a parsimonious model that generalizes well on unseen data. The three stepwise regression methods are as follows:

- Forward selection enters inputs one at a time until no more significant variables can be entered.
- Backward elimination removes inputs one at a time until there are no more nonsignificant inputs to remove.
- Stepwise selection is a combination of forward selection and backward elimination.

Data Analytics—
Data Mining:
Forensic

Stepwise selection has plenty of critics, but it is sufficiently reasonable as long as you are not trying to closely evaluate the *p*-values or the parameter estimates. Most software packages include penalty functions, such as Akaike's information criterion or the Bayesian information criterion, to choose a best subset of predictors. All possible subset regression combination routines are also commonly supported in data mining toolkits. These methods should be more computationally feasible for big data as high-performance analytical computing appliances continue to get more powerful.

Shrinkage estimators, such as the least absolute shrinkage and selection operator (LASSO),[6] are preferred over true stepwise selection methods. They use information from the full model to provide a hybrid estimate of the regression parameters by shrinking the full model estimates toward the candidate submodel.

Multicollinearity occurs when one input is relatively highly correlated with at least another input. It is not uncommon in data mining and is not a concern when the goal is prediction. Multicollinearity tends to inflate the standard errors of the parameter estimates, and in some cases the sign of the coefficient can switch from what you expect. In other cases, the coefficients can even be doubled or halved. If your goal is model interpretability, then you want to detect collinearity by using measures such as tolerances and variance inflation factors. At a minimum, you should evaluate a correlation matrix of the candidate inputs and choose one input over another correlated input based on your business or research knowledge. Other strategies for handling correlated inputs include centering the data or redefining the suspect variable (which is not always possible). You can also generate principal components that are orthogonal transformations of the uncorrelated variables and capture *p*% of the variance of the predictor. The components are a weighted linear combination of the original inputs. The uncorrelated principal components are used as inputs to the regression model. The first principal component explains the largest amount of variability. The second principal component is orthogonal to the first. You can select a subset of the components that describe a specific percentage of variability in the predictors (say 85%). Keep in mind that principal components handle continuous inputs.

Regression also requires complete case analysis, so it does not directly handle missing data. If one or more inputs for a single observation have missing values, then this observation is discarded from the analysis. You can replace (impute) missing values with the mean, median, or other measures. You can also fit a model using the input as the target and the remaining inputs as predictors to impute missing values. Software packages also support creating a missing indicator for each input, where the missing indicator is 1 when the corresponding input is missing, and 0 otherwise. The missing indicator

variables are used as inputs to the model. Missing values trends across customers can be predictive.

Multiple linear regression is predominantly used for continuous targets. One of the best sources for regression modeling is by Rawlings.[7] Other important topics addressed include residual diagnostics and outliers.

Logistic Regression

Logistic regression is a form of regression analysis in which the target variable (response variable) is categorical. It is the algorithm that is most widely used in data mining to predict the probability that an event of interest will occur. Logistic regression can be used to estimate fraud, bad credit status, purchase propensity, part failure status, churn, disease incidence, and many other binary target outcomes. Multinomial logistic regression supports more than two discrete categorical target outcomes.

For logistic regression, the expected probability of the event outcome is transformed by a link function to restrict its value to the unit interval. A linear combination of the inputs produces a logit score (the log odds of the event). Maximum likelihood is used to estimate the values of the parameters. Fig. 4 shows a partial listing of the maximum likelihood estimates along with the absolute regression effect estimates from a stepwise logistic regression that classifies home equity loan applicants as good or bad.

Some of the candidate inputs that are selected by the stepwise model to classify bad debt status are occupational category (JOB), number of recent credit inquires (NINQ), value of current property (VALUE), amount of loan request (LOAN), and debt-to-income ratio (DEBT-INC). Some of the inputs have missing values, so they were imputed (replaced) using either the mode (most frequently occurring value) or the median. These estimates have a prefix of *IMP* to indicate that they are imputed by the software. Logistic regression also requires complete case analysis; otherwise, any observation that has one or more missing values is discarded from the analysis.

The exponential of a parameter estimate provides an odds ratio. The odds ratio can be thought of as the increase in the primary odds, with being a bad debt applicant associated with a change of one unit in each input. The absolute value indicates the magnitude or relevance of a model effect. For example, the absolute value of 0.535 for the JOB category SALES ranks 14th out of all model effects. The color indicates the sign of the coefficient.

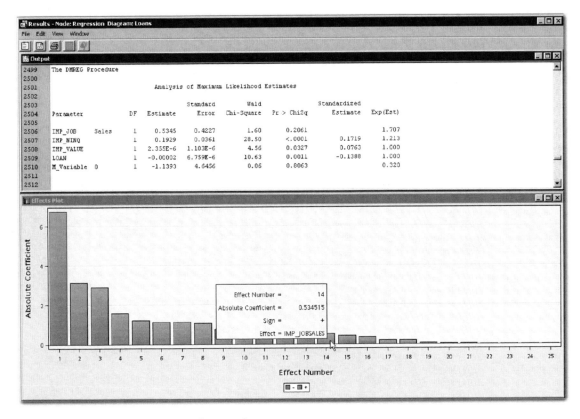

Fig. 4 SAS Enterprise Miner logistic regression sample output.

Decision Trees

A decision tree is another type of analytic approach developed independently in the statistics and artificial intelligence communities. The tree represents a segmentation of the data that is created by applying a series of simple rules. Each rule assigns an observation to a segment based on the value of one input. One rule is applied after another, resulting in a hierarchy of segments within segments. The hierarchy is called a tree, and each segment is called a node. The original segment contains the entire data set and is called the root node of the tree. A node with all its successors forms a branch of the node that created it. The final nodes are called leaves. For each leaf, a decision is made and applied to all observations in the leaf. The type of decision depends on the context. In predictive modeling, the decision is simply the predicted value or the majority class value.

The decision tree partitions the data by recursively searching for candidate input variable thresholds at which to split a node and choosing the input and split point that lead to the greatest improvement in the prediction. Classification and regression trees,[8] chi-square automatic interaction detector,[9] and C5.0 are the most well-known decision tree algorithms. Each of these algorithms supports one of several splitting criteria, such as the following:

- Variance reduction for interval targets (CHAID)
- *f*-Test for interval targets (CHAID)
- Gini or entropy reduction (information gain) for a categorical target (CART™ and C5.0)
- Chi-square for nominal targets (CHAID)

These algorithms also offer control over how to handle missing values, the depth of the tree, the leaf size, pruning, and many other options.

The decision (classification) tree in Fig. 5 displays the results of classifying patients as having one of two types of heart disease. The classification is based on data such as age, alcohol use, blood pressure, and maximum heart rate. For explanatory purposes, a very simple decision tree was grown by partitioning 50% of the data into a training source and 50% into a validation source. Decision trees, like other predictive modeling algorithms, can overfit the data. Validation data is incorporated by the algorithm to automatically prune the decision tree to a simpler fit.

The top-level root node shows that 55.64% of 133 patients in the training data have type 1 heart disease and 44% have type 2 heart disease. The incidence of heart disease patients in the training and validation data is approximately the same because a random sample that is stratified by the target is used prior to growing the tree. The initial split that best separates the two types of heart disease is based on the discrete predictor

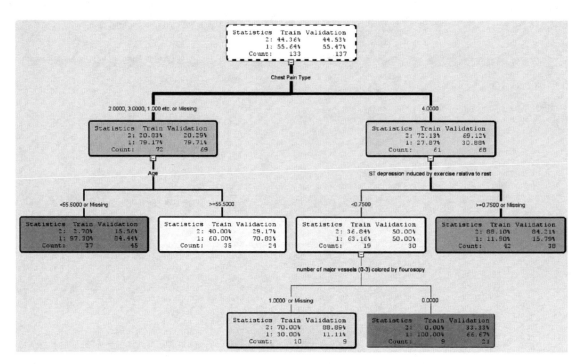

Fig. 5 Illustration of a decision tree for classifying two types of heart disease.

chest pain type. Patients with type 4 chest pain have a 72.13% incidence of type 2 heart disease. Otherwise, the patients tend to have type 1 heart disease. The nodes that result from the chest pain split have essentially the same distribution of chest pain types for both the training and validation data. Large differences in the target distribution indicate an unstable split, which is not the case here. If the training and validation numbers are out of sync, you should consider overriding the tree with a manual split by using one or more of the following methods: using an interactive decision tree, collecting more representative data, and modifying the splitting criteria. The remainder of the tree shows the additional successive splits that are of heart disease based on age, depression levels, and the number of major vessels

colored by fluoroscopy. The terminal leaves (unsplit data) result in the final classification (decision) for all patients in each respective leaf. This simple decision tree was grown interactively. Decision trees provide many advantages, but as with any easy-to-use modeling algorithm, they have their disadvantages (Table 2).

A common strategy for potentially enhancing the predictive ability of regression models is to first stratify the data using a decision tree and then fit a separate regression model (or other predictive algorithm) in each leaf. This practice is often called stratified modeling, with the resulting model being a hybrid model. The stratified model sometimes solves the problem of nonadditivity. Dividing the population into segments can be more representative of the population. Typically, a small decision

Table 2 Decision tree advantages and disadvantages

Advantages	Disadvantages
Enables interpretation of a model as a sequence of if-then-else rules, especially for smaller trees.	Large decision trees can be hard to interpret.
Handles missing values as separate new values or via surrogate (backup) splitting rules.	Can be unstable. Small changes in the underlying data can result in an entirely different decision tree.
Accounts for interaction effects. One tip is to export the node ID variable from a decision tree as an input to another model that represents interaction effects.	Uses a step function that can have large errors near boundaries. These errors can result in poor prediction performance for complex nonlinear patterns.
Works well with high-dimensional data.	Uses less data after each split (this can also be advantageous).
Often used for variable selection and easily ignores redundant variables.	
Supports categorical and continuous targets and inputs.	

Neural Network Terms

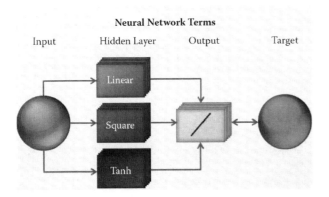

Fig. 6 Simple neural network with one hidden layer and three hidden units.

tree is grown interactively by the user. The algorithm can help suggest splits, or you can impose your business experience to define a splitting rule. Separate regression models are then developed in each leaf. For example, rather than continuing to grow a decision tree, you may want to define a single splitting rule, such as the chest pain split shown in Fig. 5, and then use another modeling technique to model the observations in each node.

Machine Learning

ML algorithms are quantitative techniques used for applications that are focused on classification, clustering, and prediction and are generally used for large data sets. ML algorithms also focus on automation, especially the newer methods that handle the data enrichment and variable selection layer. The algorithms commonly have built-in data handling features such as treating missing values, binning features, and preselecting variables. The term *data mining* has been around for at least two decades. Data mining is the application of statistics, ML, artificial intelligence, optimization, and other analytical disciplines to actual research or

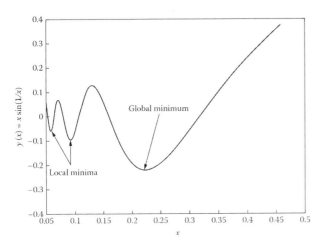

Fig. 7 Example of local vs. global minimum for a simple function.

commercial problems. Many ML algorithms draw heavily from statistical learning research. Characterizing the distribution of variables and the errors from models was central in the works of Fisher, Karl Pearson, and other seminal thinkers in statistics.

Neural Networks

Artificial neural networks were originally developed by researchers who were trying to mimic the neurophysiology of the human brain. By combining many simple computing elements (neurons or units) into a highly interconnected system, these researchers hoped to produce complex phenomena such as intelligence. Although there is controversy about whether neural networks are really intelligent, they are, without question, very powerful at detecting complex nonlinear relationships in high-dimensional data.

The term *network* refers to the connections of the basic building blocks called neurons.[10] The input units contain the values of the predictor variables. The hidden units do the internal, often highly flexible nonlinear computations. The output units compute predictions and compare these with the values of the target. A very simple network, such as that in Fig. 6, has one input layer that is connected to a hidden unit, which is then connected to an output unit. You can design very complex networks—software packages naturally make this a lot easier—that contain perhaps several 100 hidden units. You can define hidden layers that enable you to specify different types of transformations.

The primary advantage of neural networks is that they are extremely powerful at modeling nonlinear trends. They are also useful when the relationship among the input variables (including interactions) is vaguely understood. You can also use neural networks to fit ordinary least squares and logistic regression models in their simplest form.

As with most predictive modeling algorithms, you should be careful not to overfit the training data, which is easy to do with neural networks. Choosing the number of hidden layers and neurons is hard, so it is best to start with simple networks. You should start with simple networks and progressively build and evaluate the benefit of more complex network topologies. Most neural network modeling packages support preliminary runs. Using preliminary runs is highly advisable because it prevents your network from converging to local minima instead of a global minimum. Local minimum is where the network gets trapped in a suboptimal solution instead of finding the true global minimum. A local minimum is analogous to a situation, where if you start on the side of a mountain and walk downhill, you may find only the local low point, not necessarily the global low point (Fig. 7).

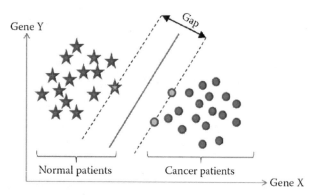

Fig. 8 SVMs find the hyperplane that best separates the data classes.

Neural networks are also often referred to as black boxes; even though they are extremely good at prediction, they are often hard to understand. Like regression analysis, neural networks require you to first replace (impute) missing values before you train the network. The most popular ML algorithm today is deep learning neural networks. These new generation neural networks have highly deep and complex architectures that address the issue of local minima by adding unsupervised layer-wise pretraining of deep architectures.

Support Vector Machines

Support vector machines (SVMs) are a powerful ML technique for classification and regression.[11] They work by finding a hyperplane that best splits the target values. The gap (margin) is the largest distance between the borderline data points or what are called the support vectors (see the grey stars and dots) (Fig. 8). New data points are scored based on their position in the decision on the boundary where only the support vectors values are needed.

Naturally, many data are not so easily separable. Patients might fall in the margin or the data may be very nonlinear. To handle nonlinearity, SVMs introduce a kernel trick, which maps the inputs to a higher-dimensional space to enable separation of the classes (Fig. 9).

SVMs are good at classifying both simple and complex models. Unlike neural networks, they avoid local minima and overfitting.

Ensemble Models

Ensemble models are now standard in data mining because they perform extremely well on large complex data and because they are automated. *Ensemble* stems from the French word together that means "all the parts considered." One ensemble approach is to use multiple modeling methods, such as a neural network and a decision tree, to obtain separate models from the same training data set. The component models from the complementary modeling methods are averaged to form the final model.

Ensemble models tend to work best when the individual models disagree with one another. Combining linear models often leads to the same model solution. Decision trees are weak learners and are very unstable when presented with new data, but they are excellent candidates for an ensemble model. *Bagging*[12] is a common ensemble algorithm, in which you do the following:

1. Develop separate models on *k* random samples of the data of about the same size.
2. Fit a classification or regression tree to each sample.
3. Average or vote to derive the final predictions or classifications.

Boosting[13] goes one step further and weights observations that are misclassified in the previous models more heavily for inclusion into subsequent samples. The successive samples are adjusted to accommodate previously computed inaccuracies. *Gradient boosting*[14] resamples the training data several times to generate results that form a weighted average of the resampled data set. Each tree in the series is fit to the residual of the prediction from the earlier trees in the series. The residual is defined in terms of the derivative of a loss function. For squared error loss and an interval target, the residual is simply the target value minus the predicted value. Because each successive sample

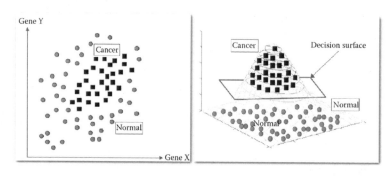

Fig. 9 SVMs handle nonlinearity by mapping the data into a higher-dimensional space using kernel tricks.

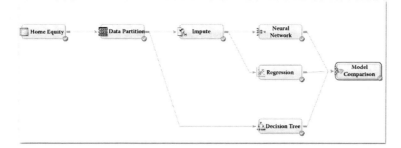

Fig. 10 SAS Enterprise Miner process flow analysis. The model comparison node provides a common framework for comparing the predictions from modeling tools.

is weighted according to the classification accuracy of previous models, this approach is sometimes called *stochastic gradient boosting*.

Random forests are my favorite data mining algorithm, especially when I have little subject knowledge of the application. You grow many large decision trees at random and vote over all trees in the forest. The algorithm works as follows:

1. You develop random samples of the data and grow k decision trees. The size of k is large, usually greater than or equal to 100. A typical sample size is about two-thirds of the training data.
2. At each split point for each tree you evaluate a random subset of candidate inputs (predictors). You hold the size of the subset constant across all trees.
3. You grow each tree as large as possible without pruning.

In a random forest you are perturbing not only the data but also the variables that are used to construct each tree. The error rate is measured on the remaining holdout data not used for training. This remaining one-third of the data is called the out-of-bag sample. Variable importance can also be inferred based on how often an input was used in the construction of the trees.

Model Comparison

It is very important to compare models that are developed from the same algorithm across challenger methods to help ensure that you select a sound model that is useful for scoring and also provides useful insights (Fig. 10). It is important to incorporate the following three partitioned data sources into your model building efforts:

Training data, which are used for preliminary model fitting

Validation data, which are used to access the adequacy of the model. For example, validation data can be used

to stop a neural network, determine the best subtree for a decision tree, or select the final subset of inputs from a stepwise regression.

Test data, which are used to obtain a final, unbiased estimate of the generalization error of the model.

You should also develop stratified random samples to preserve the ratio of rare target events, such as fraud or other important strata variables such as cluster codes, geography, and time.

Fig. 11 provides model comparison statistics for logistic regression, decision tree, and neural network models each of which is used to classify home equity loans as good or bad. The misclassification chart (see Fig. 11, top left) displays how often the model correctly classified good applicants (0) and bad applicants (1) in the validation data. The misclassification chart (also called a confusion matrix) is often reported in table format. The decision tree is selected as the best model based on minimizing the misclassification rate in the validation data. The overall misclassification rate for the decision tree is 11.74% in the validation data (see Fig. 11, top right). The misclassification rate is also comparable in the test data set (not shown). The lift or gains chart (Fig. 9, bottom left) shows the cumulative lift for each model using the validation data. Lift is calculated as the ratio between the results obtained with the predictive model and those using no model. You can also think of lift as how well the model captures the target event (bad credit applicants) across the ranked scored applicants relative to the random model. The scores have been sorted from high to low and grouped into 10 deciles. We expect the random baseline model to capture 10% of the bad credit applications in each decile. The decision tree model captures about 35% more bad credit applicants in the second decile (35/10 = 3.5). The cumulative lift is comparable for all three models at about the fourth decile and beyond. Cumulative response and model lift are often used in targeted marketing campaigns to determine an appropriate depth of file for targeting customers.

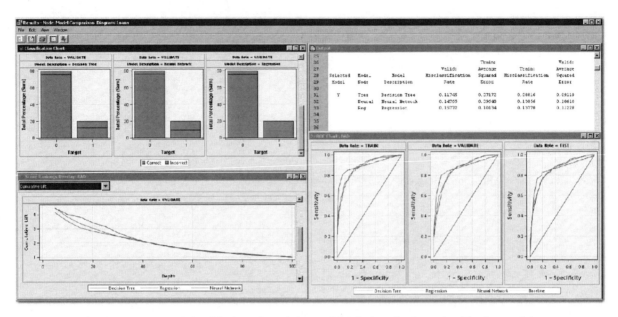

Fig. 11 Misclassification chart, cumulative lift chart, fit statistics, and ROC chart for three classification models.

All these comparison statistics are based on a default posterior probability of 0.5. Any applicant with a score above 0.5 is classified as a bad credit applicant. You might want to modify the cutoff (especially for rare events) to see how this modified cutoff affects the decisions. The receiver operating curve (ROC) (Fig. 11, bottom right) displays sensitivity vs. 1 − specificity (the true positive rate vs. the positive rate for each model).

- Sensitivity (true positive rate): $100*D/(C + D)$
- Specificity (true negative rate): $100*A/(A + B)$
- Sensitivity (true positive rate): $100*D/(C + D)$
- Specificity (true negative rate): $100*A/(A + B)$

Because the true positive rate and false positive rate are both measures that depend on the selected cutoff value of the posterior probability, the ROC is calculated for all possible cutoff values. Each point on the curve represents cutoff probabilities. Points closer to the lower left represent higher cutoff probabilities. Points closer to the upper right correspond to lower cutoff points. The extreme points (1, 1) and (0, 0) represent rules in which each case is classified as an event (1) or a nonevent (0). Models that push upward and more to the left have stronger discriminatory power.

Text Analytics

Text analytics encompasses tools, solutions, and processes aimed at getting the most out of your unstructured text. That text may come from myriad sources—both informal sources such as online complaints, emails, and social media comments, and formal sources such as patent documents, inspection reports, and warranty claims. Regardless of origin, you want to understand and use both the global themes and patterns contained in the collection as a whole, as well as detect the isolated comment buried in a single phrase of a single document that is hidden within tens of thousands of documents.

Text analytics can be viewed from two perspectives. On the one hand, it may involve recognizing patterns across an entire collection of documents, so that we can apply these patterns to make decisions on new documents. This process is called text mining and requires an entire collection of data in order for the patterns to emerge. Another perspective of text analytics comes from realizing that we understand a lot about language and the way things are written. Given the right tool and the knowledge of what we are trying to identify, we can write rules based on the syntax and grammar of the sentences to extract key information and apply them to vast collections. We refer to this process as knowledge engineering.

	Predicted Nonevent	Predicted Event
Nonevent (good applicant)	True negative (A)	False positive (B)
Event (bad applicant)	False negative (C)	True positive (D)

In the end, both approaches are important and useful and can be combined to greatly benefit the business analyst. While many companies are just concerned with storing and preserving textual content, the savvy business analyst is looking to automatically leverage text analytics to improve business models and to gain insight that would not otherwise be apparent. The following list is not exhaustive but represents the kinds of projects many business analysts modeling with text accomplish:

- Gain an understanding of what their customers are saying in emails, chat rooms, social media, call center data, and surveys. This can occur with drill-down, as in learning what differences there may be between what your high-profit customers are writing and what your low-profit customers are saying.
- Monitor patterns and trends in a textual warranty report in order to indicate when issues in the field or in a call center are becoming a serious problem and need intervention.
- Build a statistical model using text, possibly in addition to other qualitative and quantitative variables, to predict fraud, churn, upsell opportunity, and so on.
- Determine public sentiment toward their new product or any aspects of their product.

- Analyze your company in comparison with your competition by using public comments on social media sites.
- Organize and classify your documents so that they are easily explored and found by your user base.

Accessing the documents

Text analytics requires several important components to enable the analyst to reach these goals. The first component is providing access to the documents. These documents may be contained within a directory on your computer's file system, in SAS data sets, other third-party databases, across the web on html pages, or other kinds of document management systems. In addition, the documents may be stored in a variety of formats, such as MS Word, PDF, html, xml, or plain text. Tools to reach this data and extract the relevant text for analysis are important. Once the documents are accessible, referenced by a table that perhaps contains additional metadata about the documents, such as demographic information about the author and time stamps, the real text analytics can begin.

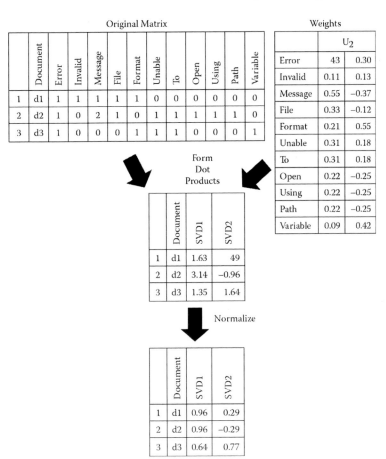

Fig. 12 A data set representation of a document collection and the results of the singular value decomposition.

Learning from the collection: Text mining

Text mining involves translating the unstructured text to a table form so that either a text-specific algorithm or any one of the traditional data mining algorithms can be used.

From text to data set

The best approaches to text mining require complex language-specific functionality for creating features from text. The simplest approach is to tokenize the text and use terms as features for your data set, but extraction of more complex features can also be important, such as using parts-of-speech tags and other linguistic elements as features. In addition, users typically apply stop lists to eliminate noise terms and synonyms lists to map terms that mean the same thing together. Another nice technique is to use a statistical spelling correction feature that will help you assign improperly spelled terms to their intended spelling. The end result is a quantitative representation of the collection where each row of the data set represents a document and the extracted features become the variables for the data set. The entries in the cells of this data set are weighted frequencies of the feature counts within each document. See the original matrix in Fig. 12 for an example.

Dimension reduction with singular value decomposition

When the term by document matrix is created, it may have hundreds of thousands of variables, and it will be very sparse, since any one document contains very few of the features in the corpus. As a result, this augmented document goes by the term *data set*, which needs to be reduced as input to traditional data mining algorithms. This is accomplished with a matrix factorization

approach known as the singular value decomposition (SVD). The SVD algorithm discovers a weight matrix, shown as weights in Fig. 12, that allows any document to be projected into a much smaller dimensional space. In the example, the end result is a two-dimensional representation of each. The final reduced matrix for mining maintains the information in the original data set but compresses it into a much smaller form.

Exploratory models

With text mining, you can use the patterns that are found across the collection to enhance exploratory analysis in the following ways:

- Clustering: Document clustering separates your documents into mutually exclusive sets. There are many algorithms that can be used once the SVD has been applied. Two common approaches are hierarchical clustering, which shows relationships between clusters and subclusters, and a mixed Gaussian model approach, which assumes that a collection of Gaussian distributions generated the data. For both approaches, you can interpret the discovered clusters by reporting on the terms that characterize them.
- Topic modeling: Another approach that is similar to clustering is topic modeling. Topics are more flexible than clusters because they allow documents to contain or be associated with many topics. One approach to topic modeling rotates the SVD vectors of weights (described earlier in Fig. 12) in order to more clearly distinguish what subset of terms contribute the most to each dimension. The terms associated with the highest weight become the automatic label for the discovered topic. An example is shown in Fig. 13. Another popular approach to topic models involves latent Dirichlet allocation. This approach assumes that the topics were generated from a generative

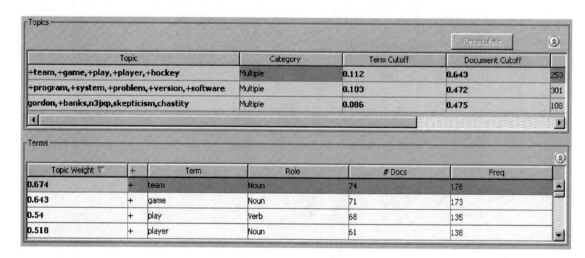

Topics					
Topic	Category	Term Cutoff	Document Cutoff		
+team,+game,+play,+player,+hockey	Multiple	0.112	0.643	253
+program,+system,+problem,+version,+software	Multiple	0.103	0.472	301
gordon,+banks,n3jxp,skepticism,chastity	Multiple	0.086	0.475	108

Terms					
Topic Weight ▽	+	Term	Role	# Docs	Freq
0.674	+	team	Noun	74	176
0.643	+	game	Noun	71	173
0.54	+	play	Verb	68	135
0.518	+	player	Noun	61	138

Fig. 13 Detected topics and the term weights for the first topic.

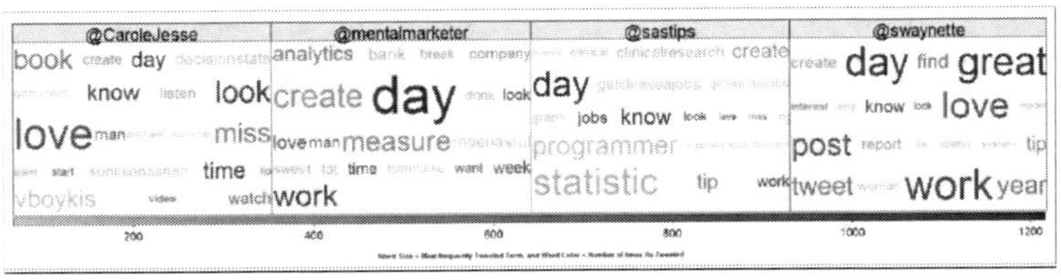

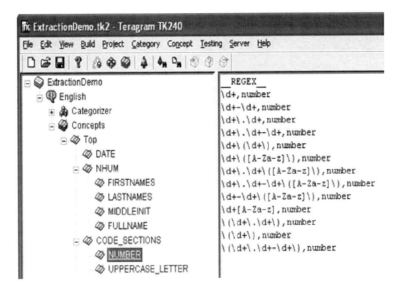

Fig. 14 Profile of terms commonly used by four tweeters.

process and that the parameters of that generative process are then optimized to fit the training data.

- Trending and profiling: Another technique that is important in exploratory analysis is the ability to explore the relationships between the text in your documents and any other variable associated with your document. For instance, you might want to report on how complaints written by women differ from those written by men, or if a time stamp on your collection exists, you can indicate what terms are trending over time. Fig. 14 profiles four different tweeters by reporting on the terms each tweeter tends to use.

Predictive models

With labeled textual training data, predictions can be made to do such things as automatically separate documents into categories or predict an interval-valued variable such as profit. Once the SVD transformation is done, these tasks can be done with standard data mining models such as regression models, decision trees, neural networks, and other models discussed in earlier sections.

In addition, models designed specifically for the text can be applied. One example is an inductive rule learning algorithm. This approach has the benefit of providing learning rules that are interpretable and useful for categorizing documents. The rules are simply formed from the presence or absence of terms and are marked as significant based on a test such as the chi-square test. An example of such a rule might be "patriot" and "revolution" and not "football" and not "missile." This might be a good predictor that a document that satisfies this rule is about an American Revolution patriot and not a football team or a missile.

Digging deeper with natural language: Knowledge engineering

While text mining attempts to leverage the entire collection to learn patterns, another important approach for text analytics is to have a domain specialist write linguistic rules for identifying and extracting important information from individual documents. The rules are not derived from a text collection, but rather are created by a specialist who understands the goals of the analysis. As a result, an analyst may write linguistic rules that empower a "classification engine" that automates the organization and retrieval of textual content for people in various divisions of your organization. An

Fig. 15 A tool for extracting content from natural language text.

example of a tool that allows a user to create these rules is shown in Fig. 15.

Sentiment analysis is a second goal that often benefits from this user-driven approach. The domain expert writes natural language rules in order to analyze the written sentiment directed toward such things as your company or your company's products or services. The solution helps you to determine if the expressed attitudes are generally positive or negative and helps to determine in what ways they are positive or negative.

Combining approaches

The best text analytics no doubt leverages both of these approaches. On the one hand, a domain expert may custom design a rule that then becomes an important feature in a statistically based text mining model. On the other hand, a statistical model may inform a domain specialist as to what rules he or she may write. The end result is more effective text analytics.

REFERENCES

1. IDC digital universe study. *Sponsored by EMC*, June 2011.
2. Chu, R.; Duling, D.; Thompson, W. Best Practices for Managing Predictive Models in a Production Environment. In *Proceedings of the SAS Global **2007** Conference*. SAS Institute: Cary, NC, 2007.
3. Hartigan, J. A. *Clustering Algorithms*; Wiley: New York, NY, 1975.
4. McQueen, J. Some methods for classification and analysis of ultivariate observations. In *Proceedings of 5th Berkeley Symposium on Mathematical Statistics Probability*; **1967**; Vol. 1, pp. 281–297.
5. SAS Enterprise Miner 12.1. *On-Line Reference Help*; SAS Institute: Cary, NC, 2012.
6. Tibshirani, R. Regression shrinkage and selection via the lasso. J. R Statis. Soc. B **1996**, *58* (1), 267–288.
7. Rawlings, J. O. *Applied Regression Analysis: A Research Tool*. Wadsworth: Belmont, CA, 1988.
8. Breiman, L.; Friedman, J. H.; Olshen, R. A.; Stone, C. J. *Classification and Regression Trees*. Wadsworth International, Belmont, CA, 1984.
9. Kass, G. V. An exploratory technique for investigating large quantities of categorical data. *Appl. Statis.* **1980**, *29* (2), 119–127. (Standard reference for the CHAID algorithm Kass described in his 1975 PhD thesis.)
10. Bishop, C. M. *Neural Networks for Pattern Recognition*; Oxford University Press: Oxford, 1995.
11. Vapnik, V. *The Nature of Statistical Learning Theory*; Springer-Verlag: New York, NY, 1995.
12. Breiman, L. Bagging predictors. Mach. Learn. **1996**, *24*, 123–140.
13. Schapire, R. E.; Freund, Y. *Boosting: Foundations and Algorithms*; MIT Press: Cambridge, MA, 2012.
14. Friedman, J. H. Greedy function approximation: A gradient boosting machine. Ann. Statis. **2001**, *29* (5), 1189–1232.

BIBLIOGRAPHY

1. Neville, P. Growing trees for stratified modeling. Comput. Sci. Statist. **1999**, *30*. (Extends the ideas of Sonquist, et al. and Alexander and Grimshaw for more independent variables and more types of models.)

Data Mining: Forensic Analysis

Monte F. Hancock, Jr.
Chief Scientist, Celestech, Inc., Melbourne, Florida, U.S.A.

Abstract

The practical purpose of this entry is to characterize the information to be collected and organized during the Data Evaluation Step of a data mining spiral. Rather than developing these ideas in prose from which the reader must extract actionable chunks, the material is presented as a topically organized checklist of questions to be addressed. This entry also describes some techniques for conducting the preliminary analysis of domain data; that is, analysis which is performed before the Feature Extraction Step. The aspect that distinguishes this genre from others is that here we are searching data for instances of unknown patterns; patterns that are not well characterized, and for which representative examples are not available.

GOALS

After you have read this entry, you will understand supervised and unsupervised data mining methods as they relate to each other. You will understand how data clustering is an unsupervised data mining process. You will have seen examples of the formulation of objective functions, and a hierarchical architecture for unsupervised processing. You will be familiar with the fundamentals of multilayer perceptron neural networks (NN). You will have seen how text mining can be used to build sensitive and specific search applications.

Examples

- Motion Pattern Analysis
  - Vehicle traffic (Kirchhoff applies, because matter is conserved.)
  - Network traffic (Kirchhoff does not apply, because information is not conserved.)
- Data Clustering
- Document Analysis
  - Steganography
- Clique detection
  - Network analysis
  - Collaborative filtering
- Fraud and Abuse
  - Money laundering
  - Network intrusion detection
- Time Series Analysis
  - Forecasting
  - Market prediction
  - Customer acquisition/attrition prediction
- Finite State Modeling
  - Processes with random elements (hidden Markov model)
  - Behavior modeling
- Process Optimization, Scheduling, and Planning
  - Constrained optimization
  - Resource management
- Change Detection/Anomaly Processing

INTRODUCTION

The approach taken in this entry is more descriptive than pedagogical. While supervised learning can be treated as a special case of the regression problem, unsupervised learning covers an application space much too broad to be covered by any single theory. However, we will establish a metaphor for unsupervised architectures that casts them as realizations of supervised learning, where training examples have been replaced by working hypotheses captured in an *objective function*.

With this metaphor in view, we will describe the fundamentals of unsupervised learning though carefully chosen case studies and examples that highlight the various design and development considerations for this genre.

GENRE OVERVIEW

This genre consists of problems whose solutions are instances of unsupervised learning. Techniques such as supervised learning rely on having labeled examples of target patterns. For unsupervised learning, the data input is a set of unlabeled feature vectors (no ground truth).

The goal of unsupervised learning is fundamentally the same as the goal of supervised learning: the

Encyclopedia of Information Systems and Technology, DOI: 10.1081/E-EIST-120053814

Data Analytics—
Data Mining:
Forensic

357

detection, characterization, and exploitation of actionable patterns in data.

Is it even possible to construct an application to search for unknown patterns? The answer to this depends upon what *unknown* means in the problem domain. Supervised learning *knows* target patterns in the sense that it has examples that can be used for modeling. These are *known unknowns*: we are certain they really exist, and we can more or less precisely characterize them.

But supervised learning is not designed to address the problem of *unknown unknowns*: phenomena of uncertain existence and nature, not heretofore observed, characterized, or necessarily even hypothesized.

Fortunately, saying that we don't have specific examples or a precise characterization of a target pattern does not mean that we know *nothing* upon which to base a search. If that were the case, we wouldn't recognize a target pattern if we found one.

It is possible in many search applications to form reasonable hypotheses about what some target patterns might look like, even though specific examples are not available. In this sense, supervised learning may be likened to a police officer who familiarizes himself or herself with photographs in a blotter. Unsupervised learning is like the partner, who relies on hypothetical descriptions created by a *profiler*. Discovery in the first case is done by matching suspects with a set of known examples, and in the second by matching suspects with a set of hypothesized properties.

RECOMMENDED DATA MINING ARCHITECTURES FOR UNSUPERVISED LEARNING

Unsupervised learning architectures have three functional components:

1. Unlabeled feature vectors (training set)
2. An objective function (measures the performance or quality of a model)
3. A learning algorithm that uses vigilance parameters and the output of the objective function to modify the model (incrementally updates the model)

A training set for unsupervised learning is just like a training set for supervised learning, except that the vectors do not have ground truth labels.

An objective function for a system accepts as input the state of the system, and assigns to it a measure of quality. It is a scoring mechanism. Suppose, for example, that the system is a chess game. A simple objective function might count the number of pieces a player has taken from his opponent. A more sophisticated objective

function could incorporate measures derived from the configuration of pieces on the board, look-ahead to possible future states, etc.

Learning algorithms range from the mindlessly simple (e.g., Monte Carlo methods), to the tremendously complex (e.g., simulated annealing). The purpose of a learning algorithm is to make changes to the model being developed so that its performance (i.e., quality as determined by application of the objective function) attains a level that makes it a usable model.

To determine the type and magnitude of changes to make during learning, training algorithms must have notions of significance that make sense in the problem domain. This information is supplied by one or more vigilance parameters. A *vigilance parameter* is a threshold of some sort that is used to determine when things are sufficiently similar/different, good/bad, right/wrong, and so on, for a decision to be made. For example, if a police officer is looking for a tall suspect, does someone who is $5'10''$ qualify? If he is looking for a tall building, do six stories suffice?

Fig. 1 reiterates the general learning architecture for supervised learning on the left, and shows the general learning architecture for unsupervised learning on the right. It is the intentional parallelism seen here that allows us to understand unsupervised learning by noting its similarities and differences with supervised learning.

The box at the top of the unsupervised learning loop (evaluate and learn), is the learning algorithm. It uses the output of the objective function (the box at the bottom of the learning loop) to make an inference about the present model, and updates it. The model has two parts: the parameters $(p_1, p_2, ..., p_k)$ of the objective function; and the inferred symbols $x_1, x_2, ..., x_M$.

There are no ground truth tags in the unsupervised scenario. Instead, there are property tags x_j inferred by the learning algorithm. These can be numbers, names, vectors, URLs, documents, complex structures, pieces of code—instances of whatever it is the unsupervised learning process is attempting to associate with the training vectors.

EXAMPLES AND CASE STUDIES FOR UNSUPERVISED LEARNING

We now apply the metaphor of Fig. 1 to implement an unsupervised learning application using what is usually regarded as a supervised learning paradigm (a multilayer perceptron).

For this example, a set of unlabeled feature vectors is provided. It is desired to aggregate these into clusters of vectors that are similar to each other to facilitate categorization for subsequent processing. We formulate the

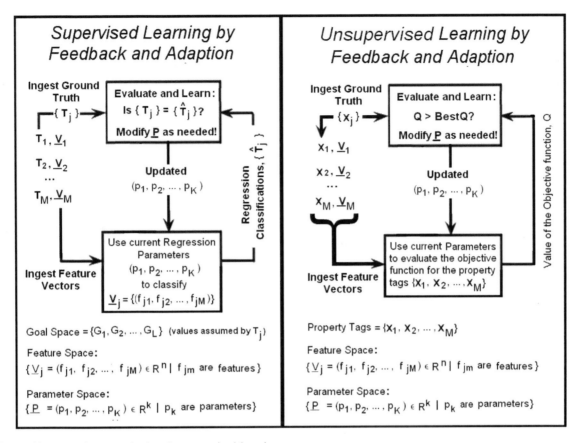

Fig. 1 Architectures for supervised and unsupervised learning.

following unsupervised learning process by selecting the three fundamental components of unsupervised learning:

1. *Unlabeled feature vectors (training set)*

    We already have a data set. The standard data preparation methods are applied as needed (e.g., segmentation divides the data into disjoint calibration, training, and validation sets; gaps are repaired; data are normalized, etc.)

2. *An objective function (measures the performance or quality of a model)*

    Because we don't know anything about the problem space from which these data come, there aren't any *a priori* formulae or heuristics to use as a basis for clustering. Therefore, we fall back on the metric properties of Euclidean space, and formulate our own definition for what good clustering might mean in terms of distances in feature space.

Here are some distance-based properties of good clustering of numeric data:

- **Property 1**—Clusters that are more tightly packed are better than clusters that are loose.
- **Property 2**—Vectors are less likely to be assigned to the wrong cluster when the clusters are far apart.

- **Property 3**—Each vector should be close to its own cluster, and far from the others.

These must now be turned into an objective function that can be efficiently evaluated. Rather than perform a large number of point-to-point distance computations, we compute the centroid (center of gravity = average) for each cluster by averaging its member vectors coordinate-wise. The centroid of cluster J will be the vector:

$$\mu_J = \frac{1}{L_J} \sum_{k=1}^{L_J} (v_{Jk1}, v_{Jk2}, ..., v_{JkN})$$

Here μ_J is the centroid of cluster J; it is a vector having N components. L_J is the number of vectors in cluster J; N is the number of features in a feature vector; and v_{Jki} is the ith feature of vector k of cluster J.

Define a metric for each property:

- **Metric 1**—A = Intra-cluster distance: the sum of the distances from each vector in a cluster to its centroid. Smaller is better.
- **Metric 2**—E = Inter-cluster distance: the sum of the distances from each vector to the centroids of clusters of which it is not a member. Larger is better.

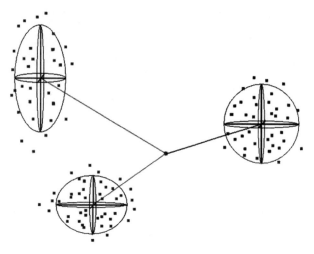

Fig. 2 Component metrics for clustering quality.

- **Metric 3**—C = Centroid distance: the sum of the distances between all the centroids. Larger is better.

These can be rolled up into a single number whose value increases when any of these metrics gets better. When better means larger, the metric goes into the numerator. When better means smaller, the metric goes into the denominator:

$$D = \frac{CE}{A + 0.1}$$

The 0.1 is an arbitrarily chosen small number that is added in the denominator to avoid division by zero, which happens if all the vectors are at the same location (usually due to some data conditioning error).

This is our designer objective function. It is an abstract measure of clustering quality, so particular values don't mean much. But larger values mean better quality, and that is all that matters here. The various component metrics can be seen later on (Fig. 2).

3. A learning algorithm that uses vigilance parameters and the output of the objective function to modify the model (incrementally updates the model). We decide to use my favorite learning method: LUCK.

Monte Carlo methods conduct repeated trials of random instantiations of the model being developed. This is an undirected search of the model's parameter space for settings that optimize the objective function. The process is simple:

a. Initialize the model by assigning valid values to its parameters.
b. Ingest the best model parameters seen so far.
c. *Jiggle* the best model parameters by applying a random adjustment to them (e.g., if they are real numbers, add or subtract a tiny value from each one).
d. Apply the objective function to the *jiggled* model.
e. Run the entire training set using the jiggled model, and evaluate the objective function on the resulting clustering. If it is better than the best clustering, the jiggled model becomes the new best model. If not, it is discarded.

Steps 1–4 are repeated, producing occasional incremental improvements in model quality. Each repetition is one *training epoch*. If the objective function is well-chosen and efficiently computable, it can be repeated

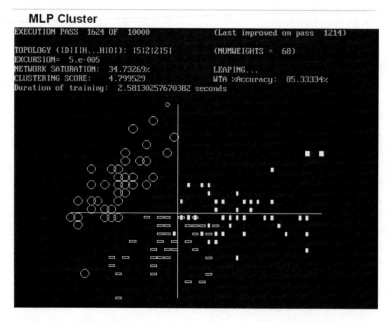

Fig. 3 Unsupervised clustering applied to Fisher iris data.

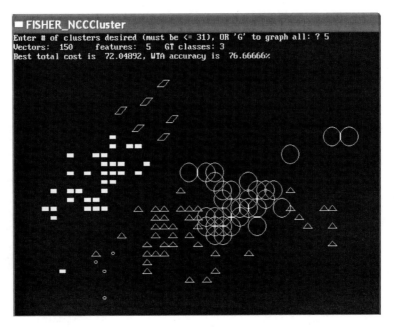

Fig. 4 Output of deterministic clustering.

many times at a reasonable computational cost. The incremental improvements on an epoch are usually small, but a million small improvements can produce a high quality model.

This unsupervised clustering method was applied to the Fisher iris data, giving the result depicted graphically in Fig. 3. The vigilance parameter required by this application is the number of clusters to create. The value used for this run was 5.

The model form used was a three-layer neural network; it ingested the feature vectors and assigned them to clusters. During a Monte Carlo run, it was the weights of this neural network that were randomly *jiggled* to vary the model. As these weights varied, the neural network would give higher and lower values for the objective function value, D. Over many epochs, this allowed the neural network to find weight settings that maximized D, resulting in a good clustering.

Ground truth is known for this problem, so it is possible to check the results of the unsupervised clustering (which did NOT use the ground truth). This was done by assigning all vectors in an inferred cluster, the actual ground truth of most of its members. This is the so-called *majority rule*, and is often used in applications. This gives an accuracy score of 85.3% for this run.

Notice that 1624 epochs were run. During an epoch, all 150 patterns in the Fisher set are processed. Even so, the total execution time, including disc input/output (I/O), was 2.58 seconds. With an implementation this efficient, it is possible to run millions of training epochs per hour, providing fairly good coverage of the parameter space.

It is important to note that there is nothing special about using a neural network here. Any paradigm that has sufficient representational power could be used (e.g., a polynomial of sufficiently high-degree). Principled paradigm selection is a deep subject; however, in applications the choice is usually made empirically.

For comparison, Fig. 4 shows the output of a deterministic clustering routine, that is, it has no random element, and always gives the same clustering. It used the same vigilance parameter setting (five clusters). Its result does not align as well with the actual ground truth, and there is nothing that can be done about this. Since it is deterministic (rather than trained), its result cannot be improved by additional processing.

Case Study: Reducing Cost by Optimizing a System Configuration

This case study describes a project to determine the optimal placement of hundreds of vehicle tracking signposts around a city to facilitate tracking and timing of municipal buses. A signpost is a small, stationary radio installed near the roadway that periodically transmits its "ID number." This transmission is picked up by passing buses and sent back to a tracking center, which knows the location and ID number of all the signposts. In this way, a precise position and time for buses is obtained inexpensively and can be monitored by the tracking station. Optimizing this system is an unsupervised learning problem because it is based not upon labeled examples, but upon domain heuristics that characterize a good model in terms of its properties. Sampling is used to create candidate models that are then evaluated using an objective function. Many Monte Carlo epochs incrementally produce a good model.

Hundreds of signposts would be required for adequate bus location and schedule tracking, and to support emergency call-in. Each signpost required a site-survey, installation, and servicing, at a cost of thousands of dollars each. Any significant reduction in the number of signposts that did not compromise system requirements would result in substantial savings. A placement strategy had been prepared manually by a group of municipal transportation experts; this configuration was used as the starting point for the data mining modeling effort.

The work for this effort was carried out almost entirely by a custom-built unsupervised learning application. It used a Monte Carlo simulation very similar to that described above. During each epoch, it simulated a full 24-hour day of buses running the city's 65,000 miles of bus routes. Each epoch used different locations for the signposts.

An *ad hoc* objective function was designed that totaled the vehicle speed and location error of the system moment-by-moment. These metrics were chosen because they were the basis for testing goals called for in the system requirement specification.

When the time allotted to simulation epochs was completed (nearly 200 hours of continuous machine time), the best placement scenario for the signposts was output. It reduced the number of signposts required in the model created by the human experts by approximately 75%, saving hundreds of thousands of dollars on labor and hardware on this fixed-price municipal program.

The simulation model used for this optimization project was so successful that a graphical user interface was added, and it was turned over to the municipality for use as a route planning tool.

Case Study: Stacking Multiple Pattern Processors for Broad Functionality

This case study describes a prototype constructed to monitor network traffic for suspicious behavior. Suspicious behavior might be the introduction of a known threat (e.g., a virus that has been seen before), or just changes in system operation that indicate that something unusual is going on.

The approach used was to implement a hierarchy of intelligent applications, each designed to perform a very specific task in the detect-assess-react cycle. Since these tasks are of different types, different kinds of machine reasoners were used for each component.

Operationally, the system activates only levels of the hierarchy needed for an adequate response to the perceived threat. The prototype had three subnetworks being monitored; the user could inject a particular attack process that was unknown to the system.

This Cognitive Intrusion Detection (CID) prototype is supposed to detect elevated activity levels on the network, and activate successively more intelligent applications up the hierarchy until the top level actually automatically retrains the bottom level detector to stop this attack process from gaining entry in the future (Fig. 5).

Multiparadigm Engine for CID

A layer-by-layer description of the CID components follows; refer to Fig. 5.

Layer 1: Data reduction layer

It is in this layer that raw packet data are conditioned for ingestion by the system. For example, it is here that packets are rolled up into sessions. The system processes these sessions.

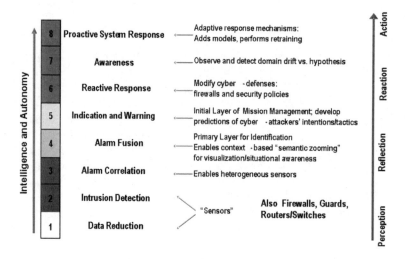

Fig. 5 CID model.

The prototype is merely reading pre-sessionized data from disc. It would be far too complicated to incorporate a sessionizer into a demo, and would not add anything to the demonstration of the eight-layer architecture.

This system is using real session data. The basic data contain no attack sessions: they consist of normal sessions only. The demo does, however, allow the operator to inject real attack sessions into the data stream so that the response of the system can be observed.

The architecture for the prototype assumes a network having three separate subnetworks. Each subnetwork is processed independently, illustrating that the eight-layer architecture can be distributed in a natural way.

Layer 2: Intrusion detection layer

It is in this layer that CID engines process the sessions. The prototype has three real, trained nearest-neighbor classifiers (one for each subnetwork). The classifiers were trained separately on slightly different data sets. This illustrates the fact that the eight-layer architecture can have multiple, diverse imbedded CIDs.

Layer 3: Correlation layer

It is in this layer that the reporting results from all the subnet CIDs are brought together, along with system performance information. For this prototype, the correlator is ingesting synthesized subnetwork packet loading information, and statistics on e-mail traffic for each subnetwork. In practice, any measurable operational phenomena could be processed in layer 3.

The prototype correlator uses a real, fully parametric rule base to implement a fuzzy correlation. This correlation merges disparate pieces of evidence to develop estimates of the likelihood that the system is in various operational modes (e.g., nominal vs. intruded). The rule sets create Conclusion Justification Reports, which are written to the display for review by the operator.

Layer 4: Fusion layer

It is in this layer that all the information generated by layers 1–3 is brought together in an intelligent join, which is interpreted by a real, operational Bayesian Belief Network (BBN).

This layer is also responsible for checking support data; to illustrate this, the prototype simulates access of a database of known attack phenomenology. Synthesized results are passed back to the system, and are used in subsequent processing.

The prototype's BBN consists of 11 nodes in four levels. These nodes correspond to components of the system state variable, and logically partition this variable into modes that are mutually exclusive within each level. Default prior conditional probabilities are specified at initialization time; these are updated dynamically as the system transitions through various states to yield optimized assessments of system state.

Layer 5: Indications and warnings

It is in this layer that alerts and status are developed based upon notifications from the layers below.

This layer is only invoked when the layer 4 (fusion) determines there are indications the system might have been compromised (based upon system behavior, whether the CIDs detected an intrusion or not).

The prototype's decision engine for layer 5 is just a case statement that selects from among several reasonable alert and warning messages, based upon information for the layers below. In practice, it would probably be a knowledge-based expert system (KBES) or a decision tree.

Layer 6: Reactive response

It is in this layer that the alert and status information from layer 5, along with information from earlier layers is reviewed, and hypotheses are developed about the system state. These hypotheses are expressed in the form of an option list, from which subsequent layers may select courses of action.

The prototype's decision engine for layer 6 is just a case statement that selects from among several reasonable options for action, based upon information for the layers below. In practice, it would probably be a KBES or a decision tree.

Layer 7: Awareness

It is in this layer that the system reasons about the network state, and selects actions from those presented by layer 6, or decides that no action is required. These actions are bound into a system level action plan which is passed to layer 8 for implementation.

The prototype's decision engine for layer 7 is just a case statement that selects from among several reasonable options for action, based upon information for the layers below. In practice, it would probably be a KBES or a decision tree.

Layer 8: Proactive response

It is in this layer that the system-level action plan developed in layer 7 is carried out. Any action the system is capable of performing can be commanded from this layer. For the prototype, there are three actions that are

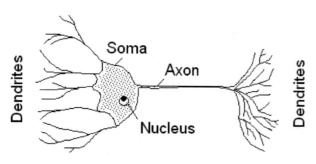

Fig. 6 A biological neuron.

supported: do nothing, close/watch a port, or retrain a CID.

When layer 4 determines that there has been a network attack by reviewing system behavior and checking a database of known attacks, but the attack session was not detected by the subnet CID, it will retrain the CID. It retrieves the sessionized data from the attack sessions (e.g., by using the database information), constructs a training set, and retrains the failed CID dynamically as the system runs. This prototype actually implements the retraining capability, illustrating the fact that the 8-layer architecture supports self-awareness and online self-correction.

TUTORIAL ON NNS

NN as the basis for a computing paradigm (both supervised and unsupervised) have been around since the work of McCulloch and Pitts (1943), and perhaps longer. The neural approach has had a colorful history, and has been successfully applied to some very hard problems. One of the first generally acknowledged commercial applications was the use of one-layer NNs for time-domain noise cancellation on long-distance phone lines. This is an unsupervised application, because the machine is not trained on examples of noise types; rather, it dynamically adapts its response to previously unseen line noise as it occurs.

The Neural Analogy

The human brain has tremendous processing capability. If this capability has a physiological basis, it might be possible to build artificial analogs of the human brain that exhibit some of its processing characteristics. Of course, it is entirely possible that this function follows form approach will not work; we can try it anyway.

The human brain appears to consist of many billions of small processing elements (living neurons) that are organized into cortices, lobes, and hemispheres, and highly-interconnected to form a massively parallel device (Fig. 6).

Artificial NN are constructed to mimic this brain architecture. Artificial NN are highly-interconnected networks of simple artificial processing elements called neurons (Fig. 7) that have been organized (trained) in such a way that their stimulus/response patterns solve domain problems.

So, while the conventional approach to hard problems has led to the development of sophisticated compute-bound single-processor systems with few inputs and outputs, the neural approach has led to the development of primitive I/O bound multiprocessor systems with many inputs and many outputs.

Artificial Neurons: Their Form and Function

Some (but not all) artificial neurons are direct analogs of biological neurons. The Threshold Logic Unit (TLU) is one such commonly used analog and will serve as the basis for the following discussion. The TLU is in many ways archetypal; it appeared early in the history of the field, and most other artificial neuron architectures have formal and functional characteristics, very much like those of the TLU. A direct comparison of the TLU with a biological neuron shows clearly the structural and functional similarity of the two.

The TLU (Fig. 7) emulates the biological neuron in both form and function. Input stimulation (in the form of numeric data rather than ions) arrives at the TLU, where each datum is multiplied by a weighting factor to simulate the various dendritic sensitivities (e.g., their electrical resistances, or gains). Just as an electrical charge obeys the superposition principle in accumulating on the cyton, the TLU sums the weighted inputs, and applies a response function.

If a threshold check determines that the resulting transformed weighted sum is sufficiently high, the TLU fires, forwarding its transformed weighted sum for processing by other neurons. Notice that the simulation of dendrite action in the TLU is performed by the computation of the dot product of the input data with the input weights. It is, therefore, a correlation measurement. For the TLU of Fig. 7, note that if the response function is $R(t)$, then: $N(x, y) = R(ax + by)$.

In order to perform useful work, both biological and artificial neurons must be arranged in networks so that they can process and forward information. Infinitely many arrangements (topologies) are possible, but layered architectures occur frequently in nature and

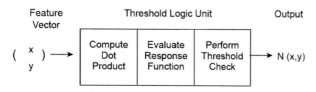

Fig. 7 Functional block diagram of an artificial neuron.

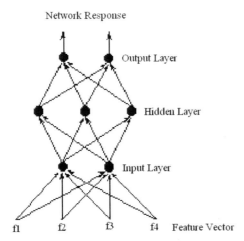

Fig. 8   A multilayer neural network.

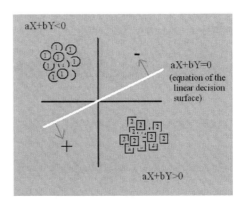

Fig. 10   A decision line in feature space.

artificial neural work. In a layered architecture, neurons are organized into successive layers, with layer N receiving its input from layer $N-1$, and forwarding its output to layer $N + 1$. In artificial NN, layers are usually either one or two dimensional arrays of artificial neurons. The layer which receives raw input data from the world is called the input layer. The layer which dumps its output back out to the world is called the output layer. All other layers have no direct contact with the world, and are called hidden layers (Fig. 8).

Using NN to Learn Complex Patterns

One of the fundamental application problems in computing today is the development of systems that can carry out the rapid, reliable, automatic recognition and classification of complex patterns.

Artificial NN are naturally suited to solving pattern classification problems through machine learning. The TLU of Fig. 9 has two input weights, a and b, and its response function is the identity function, $R(d) = d$, where $d = ax + by$ is the dot product of the input ordered pair (x, y) with the vector of input weights $(a,$

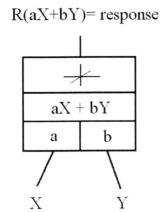

Fig. 9   A threshold logic unit.

$b)$. A firing threshold of minus infinity is assumed, so the neuron will always produce an output. This single artificial neuron, viewed as a one-layer neural network, is a linear classifier which assigns positive values to points in one half-plane and negative values to points in the other. With properly chosen values of a and b, it would discriminate between the two clusters shown in Fig. 10. The values of a and b are determined during training, and will depend upon the application.

The 1-neuron network just described can ingest any pair of numeric features and render a linear classification decision. It could, for example, be used to classify computers as good or bad, where x is cost and y performance. For any particular candidate computer, measurements of the two features x and y would be made, the feature vector (x, y) formed, and the neuron allowed to render its decision. This decision will appear at the neuron's output as either a positive or negative number. To consider more than two features, additional input weights must be used, and the dot product becomes longer, say $d = ax + by + cz + ew$ for four features.

A more general problem is the assignment of a phenomenon to one of several classes based upon its feature vector. For example, it might be desirable to classify a seismic event into one of several possible categories, based upon a suite of numeric features obtained through direct measurement. For such a problem, it is natural to build a neural network with the same number of output neurons as there are classification categories. After training (to obtain the correct input weights), the neural network can be shown newly measured feature vectors, and the output neuron producing the highest response will correspond to the machine's classification decision. Further, the relative magnitudes of the output responses can sometimes be used to develop a network confidence factor, and catch-22 output neurons can be used to flag I-Don't-Know answers, or classify to subcategory.

Of course, few interesting problems yield to a linear classifier. It has been shown that artificial NN with

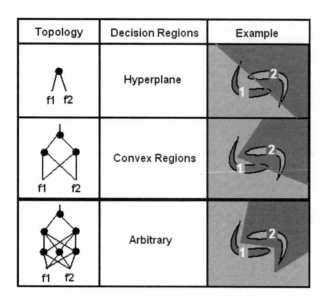

Topology	Decision Regions	Example
f1 f2	Hyperplane	2 1
f1 f2	Convex Regions	2 1
f1 f2	Arbitrary	2 1

Fig. 11 Complex networks supporting complex decision regions.

multiple layers can solve arbitrarily complex, but well-posed, classification problems (Fig. 11).

For problems too hard to attack directly, learning machines provide an implementation strategy that gives results that are as good as the developer's ability to collect examples.

Text mining takes a different approach to unsupervised learning. Text mining technology has two broad components: *syntactic* methods, and *semantic* methods. Syntactic methods are those that base their processing only on the representation of information in text: grammar, vocabulary, and term statistics. The simplest of these are so-called *bag of words* methods, which rely entirely on relative word frequencies, ignoring word order entirely.

Syntactic methods are based upon the assumption that particular words are chosen to say specific things about particular topics, and that by tabulating these

correlations and co-occurrences, it is possible to indirectly infer the text's latent information.

Semantic methods are those that base their processing on information content: aspects of *meaning* such as context, word order, document externals, denotative and connotative definitions of terms, and structure of discourse. Semantic methods are much more sophisticated and computationally expensive. They might use combinations of grammatical processing to parse a block of text, lexicons to assign meaning to words, and ontologies to recognize and assign meaning to phrases, figures of speech, idioms, and perhaps even similes, metaphors, and other analogies.

Semantic methods generally require the use of a *domain ontology*: a structure that enumerates and characterizes all domain entities, and gives the facts, rules, and processes governing their operations and interactions. An ontology is a comprehensive, high-fidelity domain model. They are difficult and expensive to construct.

Syntactic methods, being statistical in nature, can be used without any understanding of the actual meaning of a document. In fact, when using bag of words methods, it is often not even necessary to understand the language involved as long as terms can be reliably identified and counted. However, this can be a problem for inflected languages.

When semantic methods are used, it is often in conjunction with, and subsequent to, the application of syntactic processing. This presents an opportunity to understand text using both structure and meaning by building a hybrid syntactic/semantic application. An obvious architecture for such an application would be to cascade the functionality by first applying inexpensive syntactic methods, and invoking the more expensive (Fig. 12).

MAKING SYNTACTIC METHODS SMARTER: THE SEARCH ENGINE PROBLEM

Suppose we have a collection of documents, $\mathbf{D} = \{d_1, d_2,\dots, d_M\}$. Each document is composed of character strings, which we call terms. Most terms will be words, but some will be numbers or more complex symbols, such as 12/25/2011.

Consider the search engine problem: locating a document or set of documents based upon a list of search terms (in this context, these are often referred to as keywords). Assuming that the search will be using an exact match (usually referred to as a hard match) on the search terms to identify documents of interest, what list of keywords is best?

A bit of thought suggests that this problem is analogous to the clinical screening problem: when screening

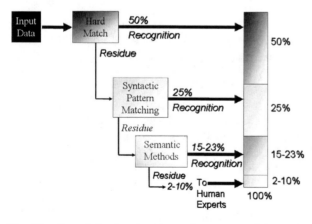

Fig. 12 Cascaded functionality of a syntactic/semantic application.

for a particular disease or disease group in the general population, what set of tests is best? In the clinical context, the measures of accuracy used for such a *disease search* are *sensitivity* and *specificity*.

- **Sensitivity**—The proportion of persons with the condition who test positive.
- **Specificity**—The proportion of persons without the condition who test negative.

In the search engine problem, a search having a high sensitivity will be able to identify instances of the desired pattern. It will have a high detection rate. A search having a high specificity will be able to identify (and therefore, reject) instances that do not have the pattern. It will have a low false alarm rate. These are exactly the characteristics desired: a good search result is one that has all of what you want and none of what you do not want.

There are many ways our hard match search engine could be implemented. Here are three simple bag of words strategies:

- **Implementation 1**—A document is returned if, and only if, it contains every term in the keyword list.
- **Implementation 2**—A document is returned if it contains at least *N* of the terms in the keyword list, where *N* is a user-adjustable parameter.
- **Implementation 3**—A document is returned if it contains any of the terms in the keyword list.

The stringent match criterion of Implementation 1 will probably give few false alarms, but will also miss many good documents. It is specific, but not sensitive. The loose match criterion of Implementation 3 will probably return most good documents—along with many false alarms. It is sensitive, but not specific.

Implementation 2 is a compromise that falls between these extremes. However, it requires that the user provide a search-specific tuning parameter that they probably cannot estimate accurately. It is a step in the right direction, but a step that the user cannot take.

Additional analysis is required. Thinking again about sensitivity and specificity as they relate to keyword selection, two facts are seen:

- A keyword is *good* for a given document if that document uses it multiple times, because a term that a document uses frequently is likely to be related to what the document is actually about. This will make a search more sensitive to those documents most likely to be relevant.
- A keyword is *good* if it is in documents that are about the topic of interest, but not in documents about unrelated topics. This will enable the search to

detect and ignore irrelevant documents, making a search more specific.

These two considerations suggest a way to calibrate search terms by assigning each one a numeric weight that is determined by its effect on sensitivity and specificity. Moreover, these weights can be computed *a priori* by the search engine, and need not be provided by the user.

The perfect keyword would occur many times in the documents I want and nowhere else. That probably won't be the case for most keywords, but we can still create a metric that measures how close a particular keyword comes to this standard of perfection for a particular document.

A Submetric for Sensitivity

Recall that our entire collection of documents is $\mathbf{D} = \{d_1, d_2, \ldots, d_M\}$. We form the set of all terms that occur anywhere in any document; call it $\mathbf{W} = \{w_1, w_2, \ldots, w_L\}$.

Define:

$$T_i(w_j) = \text{number of times term } w_j \text{ occurs in document } i$$

From this, it is possible to compute the total number of times a term occurs, counting multiplicities, in the entire collection $\mathbf{D}$ by adding the occurrences in each document:

Total count of occurrences of term

$$w_i = \sum_{k=1}^{M} T_k(w_i)$$

To measure a keyword's sensitivity to a specific document, we compute the proportion of all occurrences of a term that are in that one document. This is called the *term frequency* for that term and document. The term frequency (*TF*) for term *j* in document *i* is:

$$TF_{ij} = \frac{T_i(w_j)}{\sum_{k=1}^{M} T_k(w_j)}$$

This is the number of times w_j appears in document *i* divided by the number of times w_j appears in all documents, and *M* is the number of documents in the entire collection.

The term frequency is a number between 0 and 1 inclusive. It is zero for documents in which the term does not occur. If there are lots of documents, *TF* will be a very small number for most terms and it will be a larger number for rare terms. If a term occurs in only

Part of speech	Examples
Adverbs	quickly, as
Articles	a, an, the
Conjunctions	and, but, however
Interjections	hooray, ouch
Prepositions	on, over, beside
Pronouns	she, you, us

one document, its *TF* will be 1 for that document, and 0 for all other documents.

A Submetric for Specificity

To incorporate a metric component that will keep precision high, we must measure how common a term is across the entire set of documents. Terms that occur in lots of documents will not be very discriminating for any particular document. This is the reason that certain parts of speech are poor standalone search terms:

We will return to this concept when we discuss stopwords below.

The specificity of a search term for a corpus **D** of documents measures whether the occurrence of that term is concentrated in a small percentage of the documents, or found in many of the documents. A natural way to measure this is to compute the proportion of all documents that contain the term.

Define:

$A(w_j, d_i) = 1$ if term w_j occurs in document d_i, 0 if it does not

The total number of documents among the M documents in $\mathbf{D} = \{d_1, d_2, \dots, d_M\}$ that contain term w_j is then given by:

$$DocCount(w_j) = \sum_{k=1}^{M} A(w_j, d_i)$$

Then the proportion of all documents that contain the term is given by the document frequency (DF) for w_j:

$$DF(w_j) = \frac{DocCount(w_j)}{M}$$

The*DF* is a number between 0 and 1 inclusive. It is 1 if the term occurs in every document and it will be smaller number for terms that occur in few documents. If a term occurs in no documents, its *DF* will be 0 for all documents.

Combining the Submetrics to Obtain a Single Score

A good search term w_j for a document d_i will have a large *TF* and a small *DF*. These can be combined into a single metric by taking a ratio where the *large = good* submetric *TF* is in the numerator, and the *small = good* submetric *DF* is in the denominator.

To avoid carrying around a quotient of fractions that is four lines high, it is customary to write this quotient as a product of *TF* with the reciprocal of *DF* referred to as the Inverse Document Frequency (*IDF*). A term's *IDF* value is usually quite a bit larger than its *TF* values, so it is customary to take the logarithm of *DF* to control its magnitude so that it doesn't overwhelm *TF*:

$$\log(\text{IDF}) = \log\left(\frac{M}{DocCount(w_j)}\right)$$

Since there is no need to compute *DF* for terms that do not occur in any document in **D**, *DocCount* (w_j) will always be at least 1.

Combining the sensitivity enhancing *TF* submetric with the specificity enhancing submetric log (IDF), we obtain:

$$\begin{aligned} \text{TF.IDF} &= \big(TF(w_j, d_i)\big)\big(IDF(w_j)\big) \\ &= TF(w_j, d_i) \log\left(\frac{M}{DocCount(w_j)}\right) \end{aligned}$$

The TF. IDF score for a term is a numeric measure of how specific and sensitive that term will be as a keyword for documents on topics associated with the term. The embedded period in the name is a reminder that this is the product of *TF* and *IDF*. (The log is usually taken using to the base 2, but the base doesn't really matter.)

Some important observation can now be made:

1. TF. IDF can be pre-computed for every term in a document by just counting terms and performing a couple of quick calculations. It boils down to computing some term and document histograms and taking log-normalized ratios. This can be done efficiently and quickly even for large, dynamic collections of documents. When documents are added or removed from the corpus, updating the term score is accomplished by adjusting the frequencies for the affected terms.

2. Because this computation is performed by the search engine at the document repository, the user need not provide weights or thresholds for a search. They simply have to choose salient keywords, which will then be TF. IDF, weighted by the search engine.

Fig. 13 The first few entries of a stop-word list.

3. The search engine doesn't necessarily need to look at all the words in a document to determine whether to return it on a search. By sorting the TF. IDF terms scores within a document, the search engine can match on only the best keywords within each document—those with the highest TF. IDF values. These will be the most sensitive and discriminating terms in that document, so in theory, this will give both high sensitivity and high precision.

Putting It All Together: Building a Simple Search Engine

Given what has been done to this point, describing a step-by-step process for building a simple search engine is relatively easy.

It is assumed that a corpus of documents is to be searched using keywords. The goal is to conduct a document retrieval application that will return documents based upon a list of search terms supplied by the user.

Note: Single-word search terms only; no multiword phrases for our simple engine.

Step 1

Prepare three word lists: a spell-check list, a stop-word list, and a synonym list, and use them as follows:

The spell-check list is just a large word list. A good one to start with is the *Orchy Word List*, which is available free online. It contains over 100,000 English words.

To perform a naive spell-check for a term, locate the term in the spell-check list. If it is present, assume it is correctly spelled. If the term is not present, either discard the search term, or replace it with a near-match from the spell-check list.

A *stop-word* is a word that serves only a structural purpose (e.g., a, the), so it will never be helpful in a

search. Lists of stop-words can be found on the Internet (Fig. 13).

Before using the search terms passed by the user, remove any that are in the stop-word list. These contribute nothing to our simple search.

The synonym list will be used to allow the search engine to provide a limited *search by concept* capability. Instead of requiring the user to select exactly the right search term in exactly the right form (e.g., plural/singular, present/past tense), append the synonyms for each search term to the search term list passed by the user.

Synonym lists are available free on the internet (e.g., a public-domain version of Roget's Thesaurus).

Note: To really make this search fast, apply spell-check and stop-wording to all the documents in the corpus.

Step 2

For each document, compute the TF. IDF scores for the words it contains (Fig. 14).

Step 3

Place the N keywords having the highest TF. IDF scores for each document into a keyword table for the documents. It is the terms in this table, rather than the document itself, that will be matched. In Fig. 15, N = 10.

If you want to try to assign some kind of meaning to terms, then a lexicon must be created (Fig. 16).

The Objective Function for This Search Engine and How to Use It

Document retrieval is done by evaluating an objective function based upon the TF. IDX scores for the search terms, as follows:

1. Spell-check the search terms passed by the user.
2. Remove search terms that are in the stop-word list
3. Append search term synonyms to the search term list if a pseudo-semantic search-by-concept capability is desired.
4. Step through each of the rows in the document keyword table (Fig. 15). For each document, retrieve the terms from the search term list that are also in the document's keyword table entry. Place the matching terms into what we will call a *match list* for that document.
5. For the terms that are in the match list for a document, sum the TF. IDF scores from the TF. IDF table (Fig. 14). This gives the *match score* for this document, and completes the computation of the objective function for this document.

	A	B	C	D	E
1	word	Doc	TF	IDF	TF.IDF
2	bilingual	195	0.1411378	4.56087	0.6437111
3	fram	92	0.1187613	2.809603	0.333672
4	nomex	1697	0.1419402	7.60589	1.079582
5	coalescing	1076	6.32E-02	5.995955	0.3791798
6	resurface	893	5.36E-02	6.50678	0.3489578
7	jelepla	761	0.130189	7.60589	0.9902033
8	apartheid	307	7.04E-02	4.56087	0.3212107
9	mcduck	620	5.34E-02	7.60589	0.4064215
10	saurophaga	1852	0.1610622	7.605392	1.224941
11	lough	1882	8.75E-02	4.660953	0.408042
12	jai	712	0.1654027	4.469898	0.7393329
13	entrusted	1712	0.1184784	5.995955	0.7103908
14	repeaters	1281	0.1214953	6.219098	0.7555909
15	deficient	1125	9.31E-02	5.040443	0.469225
16	schmidt	254	5.17E-02	6.50678	0.3361322
17	americans	104	2.70E-02	7.605392	0.2055511
18	transcribed	670	0.1553293	5.120486	0.7953617
19	segregating	836	2.90E-02	6.912245	0.2001229
20	abashidze	782	7.27E-02	7.60589	0.552955
21	sacrificed	1192	0.1490607	5.995955	0.893761
22	pollenizers	104	0.1186048	7.605392	0.9020362
23	padishah	1758	7.04E-02	7.60589	0.5357256
24	estonian	1691	8.87E-02	7.60589	0.6742831
25	intensity	935	0.1315638	3.916513	0.5152712
26	concubine	400	0.1337654	7.605392	1.017338
27	phoebastria	54	0.1150292	7.60589	0.8748993
28	tularemia	1506	0.1612902	6.912245	1.114877
29	valenciana	80	0.1425678	7.605392	1.084284
30	struggle	382	0.1372798	3.116757	0.4278679
31	kalighat	1030	0.139699	7.60589	1.062535
32	sentiment	236	6.01E-02	4.309556	0.2591332
33	parsecs	1766	4.08E-02	5.659482	0.2306857
34	connection	35	0.1294118	2.904913	0.37593

Fig. 14 Computation of TF.IDF scores.

	A	B	C	D	E	F	G	H	I	J	K	L
1	Document	Term	key1	key2	key3	key4	key5	key6	key7	key8	key9	key10
2	1	1906 San Francisco	1906	1908 in literat	1910 in literature	Aftershock	Amadeo Giannini	18-Apr	Arnold Genth	Bancroft Librar	Carnegie Ins	Correlation
3	2	1923 Great Kanto e	1923	1960	Akagi	Anarchism	Bombing of Tokyo	Boso Peninsu	Chiba	Enoshima	Firestorm	Geologic fault
4	3	1970 Ancash earthc	1970	Aija	Ancash Region	Andes	Avalanche	Belgium	Callej&oacut	Chimbote	Deposit (ged	Earthquake
5	4	1976 Tangshan eart	1556	1556 Shaanxi	1900	1920	1923	1927	1976	2004 Indian Oc	About.com	Aftershock
6	5	1980 eruption of Mo	1980	1981	2004 volcanic ac	Airport	Alaska	Alfalfa	Altitude	Animal	Apple	10-Apr
7	6	1985 Mexico City e	1985	20	Alan Garc&iacut	Earthquake	Epicenter	Fault line	Felipe Gonz&	Jaime Lusinchi	José	Mexico City
8	7	2001 Gujarat Eartho	2001	Ahmedabad	Bhuj	Earthquake	Gujarat	India	Intraplate ear	26-Jan	Mumbai	Plate tectonics
9	8	2003 UB313	(55565) 2	(55637) 2002	(87269) 2000 O	20000 Varuna	2003	2003 EL61	2003 UB313	2004 XR190	2005	2005 FY9
10	9	2004 Chuetsu Earth	1995	2004	2005	200 Series Sh	Chubu region	Earthquake	East Japan F	Great Hanshin	Heisei	Hokuriku region
11	10	2004 Democratic Na	2000 Der	2003 invasion	2004	2004 Republic	2004 U.S. preside	2008 Democr	9/11 Commis	Abortion	Abu Ghraib	Acclamation
12	11	2004 Indian Ocean	Thailand	Kata Noi Bea	1556 Shaanxi ea	1737	1755 Lisbon earth	1952	1957	1960	1970 Bhola	1 E1 m
13	12	2005 Kashmir earth	1906 Sar	1935	2001 Gujarat Ea	2004 Indian Oc	2005	2006	ABC News	AFP	Afghanistan	Aftershock
14	13	2005 Lake Tangany	2005	African Great	Angola	Burundi	Burundian Civil W	5-Dec	Democratic F	Earthquake	East Africa	Epicentre
15	14	2005 Sumatra earth	1833	1861	1964	2004 Indian Ocea	2005 Sumatr	AUD	2-Apr	Australia
16	15	Aardvark	1766	Aardvark (disa	Africa	Afrikaans	Afrosoricida	Animal	Ant	Anteater	Armadillo	Australasia
17	16	Abidjan	1990s	1 E9 m&sup2	2002	2004	Abengourou	Aboisso	Accra	Adiaké	Africa	Agboville
18	17	Abkhazia	16th cent	1950s	1960s	1980s	1989	1990s	1991	1992	1994	1996

Fig. 15 Document keyword table.

	A	B	C	D	E	F	G	H	I	J	K	L	M	N
1	Persian	CULTURE			Cat	Cat breeds	Cat show	Chinchilla	Domestic	Grooming	Himalayan	Iran	Pedigree	Persian Empire
2	Pelican	ANIMAL		Australia		American	White Pelic	Antarctica	Bestiary	Bird	Booby	Brown Peli	Carolus Lir	Chordate
3	Acholi language	CULTURE				Acholi peo	Acholiland	Back vowe	Central vov	Close-mid	Close vowe	Eastern St	Front vowe	Gulu District
4	Proton	NATURAL				Acid	Acid-base	Alpha parti	Antimatter	Antiparticl	Antiparticl	Antiproton	Atom	Atomic nucleus
5	Saint Petersburg	PLACE	1918			1924	1941	1943	1944	1959	1970	1979	1989	1991
6	Clarinet	CULTURE				1690	1812	1839	1910s	1930s	1940s	19th centu	2006	20th century classical music
7	Snake	ANIMAL				Adam and	Adaptive ra	Adder	American	Anaconda	Anacondas	Anal spurs	Andhra Pra	Aniliidae
8	Arctic Circle	PLACE		Alaska		Antarctic C	Arctic	Arctic Circ	Axial tilt	Canada	Circle of la	Circumpola	Dalton Hig	Degree (angle)
9	Plate tectonics	TECHNOL	1960s			20th centu	Africa	African Pla	Aleutian Is	Alfred Weg	Alps	Antarctic P	Antarctica	Appalachian Mountains
10	New Zealand	PLACE		.nz		13th centu	15th centu	1616	1642	1643	1769	1840	1841	1845
11	Mouse	ANIMAL				Arthur Den	Biology	Bird-of-pre	Brain		Cancer	Carolus Lir	Cat	Cells
12	Asparagus	FOOD				Abensberg	Adam Ferr	Amino aci	Aphrodisia	Apicius	Asparagac	Asparagal	Asparagine	Asparagus (disambiguation)
13	Theatre	PLACE			Acting	Actor	Alexander	Antonin Ar	Aristotle	Ballet	Bertolt Bre	Black com	Broadway	California
14	Wombat	ANIMAL		Africa			Australia	Australian	Breastfeed	Cartilage	Chordate	Climate ch	Crepuscula	Cyperaceae
15	Palace of Westminster	PLACE	1834			1974	2005	Airey Neav	Ancient Gr	Ancient Ro	Anglo-Sax	Anston	Arthur Wel	1st Duke of Wellington
16	Maseru	PLACE				1871	1884	1966	Basotho	Basutolan	Caledon R	Camptown	Candle	Carpet
17	Yuri Gagarin	PERSON	1934			1943	1955	1957	1960	1961	1968	1986	Afterburne	12-Apr
18	Norway	PLACE		.bv	.no	.sj	1066	11th centu	1349	1387	1450	1537	17th century	
19	Ancient Egypt	PLACE	1000 BC			10th miller	1160s BC	11th centu	1250s BC	1300	1300 BC	1400 BC	1500 BC	1550s BC
20	Iguanodon	ANIMAL	1822			1878	1882	Alphonse	Briart	BBC	Barremian	Belgium	Bernissart	Brussels
21	Turkish Republic of North	PLACE		.nc.tr		1960 Treat	1963	1964	1967	1974	1975	1983	1 E9 m&s	2004
22	Saint Lucia	PLACE		.lc		1500	1660	1663	1667	1814	1924	1958	1962	1979
23	Nagaland	PLACE				2001	Alichen-M	Andaman	Andhra Pra	Arunachal	Assam	Baptist	Bengali	Bihar
24	Persian Gulf	PLACE	1960s			1980	1988	1991	Arab	Arabian Pe	Arabian Se	Arabic lan	Arvand/Sh	Bahrain
25	Sweet potato	FOOD			Agricul	Alcohol	Americas	Annual pla	Archaeolo	Binomial n	Burundi	Caribbean	Carolus Lir	China
26	Crocodile	ANIMAL				1807	Afric	Alligator	Alligatorid	American	American	American		Asia

Fig. 16   Lexicon of keyword terms.

6. Return to the user the N documents having the highest match scores. Sort them in order of decreasing score so the best choice is at the top of the list.

That's it. You have used text mining to construct an objective function that implements a customized search engine for your set of documents, **D**.

Note: The technique described here can be applied to data mining in any problem domain where fast search upon subpatterns is desired. This includes image search, graph search, and many other domains. This is obvious once you realize that TF. IDF is really just a statistical feature extraction method.

SUMMARY

Having read this entry, you now understand supervised and unsupervised mining methods as they relate to each other. You understand data clustering as an unsupervised mining process. You have seen examples of the formulation of objective functions, and a hierarchical architecture for unsupervised processing. You are familiar with the fundamentals of multilayer perceptron NN. You have seen how text mining can be used to build sensitive and specific search applications.

Data Mining: Healthcare

Katherine Marconi
Health Care Administration and Health Administration Informatics, University of Maryland, Adelphi, Maryland, U.S.A.
Matt Dobra
Department of Economics, Methodist University, Fayetteville, North Carolina, U.S.A.
Charles Thompson
Research Triangle Institute (RTI) International, Washington, District of Columbia, U.S.A.

Abstract

Current practices and today's information technology investment and strategic decisions can either promote or limit tomorrow's successes. This entry discusses the types of big health data and its impact on patient, provider, and organizational health decision making. The entry ends by discussing possible future trends and threats to using big data to improve the delivery of health services.

INTRODUCTION

Big data has many attributes that apply to the large electronic sources of health data being created, managed, and analyzed by healthcare providers, health organizations, and patients and their families. Data from genetic mapping, pharmaceutical tracking, public health reporting, digital x-rays, computerized axial tomography scans and laboratory results, payer and provider data, insurance claims data, and consumer online behavior adds up to petabytes of information. What makes this data so exciting is that big data has the potential to improve individual and population health, make the business of healthcare more cost-effective, and lead to new treatments of chronic and infectious diseases. In healthcare, the success of enterprisewide electronic information will be measured by its contributions to improvements in individual and population health.

We are in an era of availability of health data that enables us to transform the data to usable health information and devise better ways to manage individual and population health outcomes. But the ability to combine data into large and useful information remains a significant challenge and will take unexpected twists and turns before its full potential is realized. Current practices and today's information technology (IT) investment and strategic decisions can either promote or limit tomorrow's successes. In this entry, we discuss the types of big health data and its impact on patient, provider, and organizational health decision making. The entry ends by discussing possible future trends and threats to using big data to improve the delivery of health services.

Some view data[1] as being "big" because it is just ahead of the culture and time period's methods of data storage and analysis. Big data combines information from different sources and is analyzed to change our practices; it should improve patient outcomes and improve the nation's healthcare delivery system. This concept of rethinking health information is not a new one. In 1854, John Snow,[2] a founder of epidemiology, modernized methods of how we investigate and treat epidemics, specifically the transmission of cholera. He collected data in a new way, combined it with nonhealth information, and thought differently about it. Although his information covered slightly less than 200 sick individuals, by mapping their location along with the locations of noninfected individuals and the London water supply, he produced "big data" for that time period. He identified the source of a cholera epidemic, how it could be stopped, and introduced us to population-based health. John Snow pictured commonly available information differently and stopped an epidemic from spreading (Fig. 1).

Sources of today's big health data can be grouped onto four categories based on American Informatics Management Association informatics domains:

- data associated with the delivery of clinical care
- public health survey and surveillance information
- genetic and medical research–related information
- healthcare-consumer-driven information

Big data is not simply drawn from each of these sources; it relates information among them in new ways. It also links to other available social and economic information. For example, it may involve linking traditional health information with nonhealth information, such as sales volume, to track patient behaviors or health conditions. Health managers, as they plan enterprisewide IT systems, need to consider these external

Fig. 1 Spot map of deaths from cholera in Golden Square area, London, 1854.
Source: Adapted from Snow.[3]

and internal sources of information that are available for their decision making.

Another modern example can be found in the genetic mapping of the 20,000–25,000 human genes and the underlying billions of DNA pairs. The National Institutes of Health (NIH) 1000 Genomes Project has made the data freely available on the web for research, the equivalent of "30,000 standard DVDs".[4] Because of the Human Genome Project, we now have screening tests available for a variety of inherited diseases and many potential avenues for advancing treatment. It is a model for shared medical research information that is available to others for further analyses.

Thus, the core principle of big data in health is the ability to combine large amounts of information using different analytic methods to improve clinical and related service delivery decision making. But we should also be aware that because big data influences how we make decisions, it may lead to changes in our organizations' structures and cultures. Big data necessitates working in clinically led teams, rather than the traditional physician-driven care model. It involves sharing of primary medical information among researchers, public health agencies, patients (consumers), and health services. Big data is changing the way we share health information and deliver healthcare.

TYPES OF BIG HEALTH DATA

Combining clinical, public health, research, and consumer health data into meaningful information is challenging. Medical decision making is very complex, and recording it involves textual information, not just coding. While common data definitions for clinical conditions are in place, such as the *International Classification of Diseases*, 9th Revision, Clinical Modification (ICD-9-CM) for diagnosis coding, there are gray areas that require further clarification and consensus such as definitions of individual characteristics in research studies and different versions of Health Level Seven International messaging standards. The many available software systems to choose from also add to this complexity.

There are policy issues of confidentiality and privacy, where individual information needs to be pooled for analysis without identifying the person. At the same time, there is the need to protect business-sensitive information in a very competitive and regulated medical environment. While these issues exist in other industries, they are magnified in healthcare and have become barriers to realizing the potential of big data. Clinical services, public health, medical research, and consumer-driven information share these common barriers to contributing to care improvement.

CLINICAL SERVICES DATA

For healthcare providers to realize the potential for clinical data to improve their practice and patient outcomes, their organizations must have the technology and capacity to relate information from a number of data sources, including unstructured data and visual information. Not only is this data large, but organizations must be able to acquire it, store it, and analyze it in real time to produce meaningful information for clinical decision making. In this context, meaningful information means results that are easily understood by clinicians, support staff, and administrators (depending on the system).

Clinical Decision Support Systems (CDS) layer on the analytic software to translate clinical data into real-time information for clinical decision making. They apply rules to patient care information to indicate contradictions in care or other outliers. The rules may be a combination of medical expertise and analysis of past illness, diagnoses, and treatment patterns. For CDS to improve care, the system must be acceptable to clinical providers and easily fit into the complex patient—provider workflow of organizations. In one example where the fit was not completely thought through by system implementers and users, information from a CDS, bypassed the nursing information and had the potential to lead to medication errors. As an Agency for Healthcare Research and Quality whitepaper indicates, the timing and ownership of CDS systems are essential to their success.[5]

Clinical big data, however, is not only useful for individual patient care; it also makes the individual part of a population. For relatively rare conditions, where previously a specialist might ask one or two colleagues for a second opinion, large clinical data sets give the provider (or clinician) the ability to review treatments for additional patients with similar diagnoses, giving them additional data for clinical decision making. It also provides a base of information for monitoring disease trends, service usage, and quality of care. The National Notifiable Disease Surveillance System operated by the Centers for Disease Control and Prevention (CDC) is a good example. Symptoms are documented in an electronic health record (EHR) at the clinical encounter level, and a diagnosis is coded and entered into a database. The ability to view, aggregate, and analyze this data enables public health practitioners to monitor the occurrence and spread of diseases. As in the John Snow example, clinical data leads to population health management.

To improve quality of care and to change care patterns, big clinical data is impossible without building comprehensive EHRs, longitudinal health records of an individual's health. Comprehensive EHRs include diagnoses, problem lists, present and past medications, results of tests, and treatments from different units and facilities that are accessed by individuals. They form the basis of CDS and other analytic systems. While the

percentage of physicians adopting some form of EHR doubled between 2008 and 2011, this percentage still is only 55%.[6] Reports from State Health Information Exchanges also show limited progress in information sharing among hospitals and physician practices, but the information frequently is limited to demographics and pharmaceutical information.

This limited data collection and sharing is apparent in the Beacon Community Program grantees.[7] The federal government funded them to provide prototypes of electronic medical record systems. They are important pilot projects for comprehensive EHRs, but most focus on linking information for specific diseases, such as diabetes, heart disease, or asthma or partial health facility functions, rather than the comprehensive data needed to cover patient care that encompasses many different conditions at different health facilities. Fig. 2 summarizes the current clinical uses of electronic clinical information as described by physicians. The figure indicates the variety of functions that EHRs contribute to as they become more common and comprehensive.

If one looks at all of the certified health IT systems approved through the federal EHR technology program, it is a time of experimentation and flowering of platforms to create large clinical health data systems. The Office of the National Coordinator for Health Information Technology's[6] (2012) certified Health IT Product List provides a myriad of systems meeting meaningful use requirements. The systems are needed to promote data standardization that will allow data exchange (interoperability) among organizational entities and their many IT systems. A software company executive states that with any type of acquisitions companies can have "from 50 to 70 business systems alone".[8] Multiple EHRs need to be integrated into a manageable number of systems that are interoperable, thus easily transferring information from one system to another.

Healthcare managers today have many options in planning their enterprisewide EHR solutions. Managers may choose to opt for commonly used systems, such as Wextler Medical Center's use of the Elderly Pharmaceutical Insurance Coverage system in its four hospitals to link facility functions, including its inpatient system, emergency room system, revenue cycle system, patient scheduling, and operating room system.[9] Others have opted to build interoperability among existing systems and on integrating CDS systems within them. A good example of interoperability can be found in the work of Health Information Exchanges that are creating interfaces among different physician and hospital electronic systems, allowing exchange of patient data to facilitate efficient healthcare delivery.

Of importance in choosing EHRs with big data in mind, providers and administrators of clinical services need to decide how to store the large amounts of data available to them in forms that facilitate their real-time

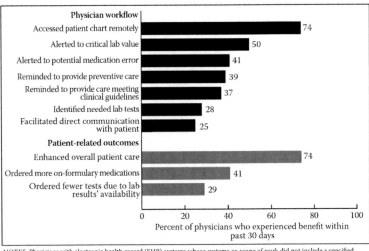

NOTES: Physicians with electronic health record (EHR) systems whose systems or scope of work did not include a specified capability responded not applicable. These responses are included in the denominator for percentages. Data represent office-based physicians who reported having adopted EHR systems (55% of sample). The sample includes nonfederal, office-based physicians and excludes radiologists, anesthesiologists, and pathologists. SOURCE: CDC/NCHS, Physician Workflow study, 2011.

Fig. 2 Percentage of physicians whose EHRs provided selected benefits: United States, 2011.
Source: From http://www.cdc.gov/nchs/data/databriefs/db98.htm.[6]

analyses for quality improvement. Some of the key management decisions to enable these systems to produce big data include the availability of standardizing for different order sets; security, multiple clinical services, and clinician teams within facilities; enterprise management; imaging software development; and linking to analysis and knowledge management applications. The National Institute of Standards and Technology's[4,10] user-centered design provides one process to guide organizations through these decision-making processes.

The federal government has provided both support and constraints for the growth of electronic medical records and big data. Meaningful Use requirements, which are tied to federal Medicare and Medicaid Incentive Payments, are facilitating this development through the definition and required reporting of health measures and usability standards, such as pharmaceutical interaction checks.[11] Meaningful Use has three phases that are being phased in through 2015: Stage 1 is data capture and sharing basic clinical information; Stage 2 focuses on capturing and sharing advanced clinical processes; and Stage 3 captures improvements in quality, safety, and efficiency. Because it is being implemented in different phases, it can be used as a guide for the development of comprehensive EHRs.

Because Meaningful Use focuses on the development of a limited set of common measures that must be reported to the federal government, it may focus providers on meeting federal standards rather than on developing a comprehensive EHR that meets their own needs. Additionally, the construction of usability standards for healthcare data is lagging behind other federal health EHR standards and requires further development, and federal rules for patient consent and information

sharing need to be reconsidered, given this emerging era of big data.

The federally driven Accountable Care Organizations (ACOs) have potential to link patient care among organizations through EHRs. They can provide new opportunities for amassing the wealth of health information available into large data sets for clinical decision making. Funding for ACOs is tied to patient care across different services, necessitating EHRs that can be used to analyze populations of patients, rather than just individuals. No matter which direction the organization of clinical health services takes, EHRs are the wave of the future. In *What's Ahead for EHRs: Experts Weigh In,* The California Health Foundation[12] discusses the next generation of EHRs: innovative systems that facilitate the use of large pools of information. Their report and a review of current health big data efforts show that we are only in the initial stages of using big data to improve health outcomes.

PUBLIC HEALTH SURVEY AND SURVEILLANCE INFORMATION

Public health information systems range from those that store individual health information for public health surveillance, such as immunization or infectious disease reporting, to real-time alert systems for drug interactions, disseminating research findings, and reporting unlikely clusters of unknown or rare conditions. The focus of this information is on protecting the public's health, rather than individual health. Information from health surveillance systems, such as CDC's Notifiable Diseases reporting, and surveys, such as the National Interview Health Survey, has existed for decades. But as pointed out by experts in this area, their information often is not linked or interoperable among reporting organizations, including the cities and states involved in the surveillance systems. The growth of public health information has outpaced our capacity for storage, interpretation, and use. Similar to clinical care, it is an area where coordinated efforts are needed among health facilities and with city, state, and federal health agencies.

An early 21st century World Health Organization (WHO) surveillance system is a potential model for future worldwide surveillance. During the severe acute respiratory syndrome epidemic, the WHO created a virtual laboratory model using the phone, video, and Internet to monitor and respond to the outbreak. With today's advanced technology, efforts can go beyond this and allow for even quicker reporting, analyses of information, and responding to unusual health events.

One recent example of analyses of a large set of information for improving population health was published in the September 21, 2012, *Morbidity and Mortality Weekly Report*. By combining time-trend rat inspection information with census data that covered a population of 770,000 individuals and approximately 35,000 residences in 12 Bronx, New York, neighborhoods, New York City was able to estimate the prevalence of rats, a known health risk.[13] To realize the full potential of this information as big data, the city might consider linking this data with neighborhood clinics and other surveillance information.

The U.S. government is taking some steps to grapple with its diverse health incident disease reporting systems. BioSense 2.0 is an effort by the CDC to reduce the costs and increase the feasibility of state and local data systems that will communicate with each other. The Food and Drug Administration[14] is undertaking a similar effort to monitor product safety—the Sentinel Initiative to pool existing resources so that large amounts of data can be processed to quickly produce needed information. It also is supporting a Virtual Laboratory Environment to produce innovative analytics for using the information currently available throughout the United States.

Both policy and resource issues need to be addressed to make large sets of public health data available for linkage and analysis to improve population health. First is the flow of information between and among cities, states, and the U.S. government. Data sharing and linkage with each other and with other surveillance information is limited because of a lack of data standardization, structured ways to get clinical information into EHRs, nonuse of standard health information exchange protocols, and the privacy and security required for records that identify individuals. Additionally, updating historical surveillance and survey systems requires resources frequently not available to state and local health agencies. These are not insignificant barriers and need to be considered when prioritizing future forays by public health into big data.

MEDICAL RESEARCH DATA

Within the medical research community a huge amount of information exists, but it is tied to specific grants and institutions. Tension exists between the pull to share information for quicker development of new treatments and the need to patent information to protect profits. At the national level, The NIH has a number of disease-based initiatives to share information for use in further research. Besides its Genomes Project, for example, the National Heart, Lung, and Blood Institute,[15] NIH has developed the Cardiovascular Research Grid and the Integrating Data for Analysis, Anonymization, and Sharing initiatives to enable researchers to easily store and share information. It not only uses technology to store information but also emphasizes communication and education about the system. The success of the Cardiovascular Research Grid and other efforts will be measured in their ability to advance prevention, diagnosis, and treatment beyond the individual research results and meta-analyses that we see today.

Medical research also is advancing in its use of big data through mathematical modeling. Pharmaceutical companies are using predictive modeling to design new drug formularies and to modify existing ones. From creating mathematical models for neurology clinical trials, to characterizing the genetic determinants of heroin abuse, and to geomapping infectious diseases spread, disease modeling is an important medical research tool.

Once again, common definitions, data standardization, and advanced analytical software will facilitate sharing of huge data sets among researchers. The PhenX project led by RTI International and funded by the National Human Genome Research Institute[16] is one example of how to plan and produce big data for genetic research and ultimately impact public health.[16] Genetics and epidemiological research are being integrated to provide researchers with high quality and low burden measures that can be included in genome-wide association studies and other types of studies. With large population studies producing large amounts of information about exposure to potential carcinogens, weak causal relationships, such as the association of environmental factors with genetic characteristics, now can be studied. But barriers to pooling data and the meta-analysis of existing studies include lack of common exposure measures and associated analytics. The PhenX project is producing a toolkit to solve these barriers; it is stretching the science of medical research analytics.

A 2010 Position Statement on Data Management and Sharing signed by 17 organizations from five countries highlights the policy and political barriers that need to be overcome for big data in medical research to reach its full potential.[17] The agreement points to the current complexity of country policies and procedures for sharing research information and it defines the principles by which such data sets can be used by others to improve the public's health. Signatories include NIH, Agency for Healthcare Research and Quality, and the Bill and Melinda Gates Foundation. *A Call for Action on Health Data from Eight Global Agencies,* including the WHO, states similar principles for the timely sharing across countries of "health financing, health workforce, service access and quality, intervention coverage, risk factors, and health status" information. Its principles center on "developing a common data architecture, strengthening performance monitoring and evaluation, and increasing data access and use".[18]

These agreements show that the major public and foundation funders of medical research agree on the principles of data sharing. However, the mechanics of storing and accessing data sets still are being worked out. In a 2011 conference, participants stressed that the technological systems for research repositories exist; it is the impact of data sharing on research careers, intellectual property, and profits that must be agreed to. This is especially true in the pharmaceutical industry, where big health data is a reality.

CONSUMER-CENTERED INFORMATION

Patient-driven care is a commonly used concept in health services. The Institute of Medicine (IOM) defines patient-centered care as: "Health care that establishes a partnership among practitioners, patients, and their families (when appropriate) to ensure that decisions respect patients' wants, needs, and preferences and that patients have the education and support they need to make decisions and participate in their own care."[19] Its meaning can vary but its underlying concept is that individuals manage their health status by actively seeking information about their health and that they and providers communicate with each other. These efforts, along with capturing and analyzing consumer-driven health information, are caught up in the lack of comprehensive EHRs and connected surveillance systems. Because most health services IT efforts focus on EHRs and other electronic records attached to organizations, rather than tied to consumers, the development of comprehensive longitudinal health records remains a challenge. While consumer-accessible medical records and information is recognized as important, the business models for organization and analyses still need development.

In a 2011 survey, CDC reports that less than 50% of people use the Internet to learn about health information. Less than 10% communicate with providers by e-mail.[20] Security and privacy concerns are a major factor in limiting this interaction. But there is a huge potential for big data analyses of consumer-driven information. This potential includes not just Internet information patterns but usage of remote patient monitoring for conditions such as diabetes or asthma and other electronic devices.

One model for the analysis of consumer Internet behavior can be found in a 2003 National Cancer Institute funded study. Researchers Bader and Theofanos[21] partnered with Ask Jeeves to analyze the feasibility of measuring cancer hits on Ask.com. Their analysis showed the types of cancers queried and the types of content queried, such as symptoms or treatment. Their methodology forms a framework for today's much larger Internet-driven health data analyses. Not addressed in their article is how this information then could be used to improve consumer searches—the purpose of big health data. A more recent article by Socha et al.[22] maps information about users of a library-based phone health literacy service with Census information. The authors found that combining information can identify geographic areas and populations that the phone service is not reaching.

Another source of big data is remote patient monitoring. Remote patient monitoring, which produces real-time information not just for individual behavior but for patterns of behavior and associated treatments, is expected to more than double by 2016—from a $8.9 billion to a $20.9 billion market.[23] The data produced requires systems that can handle large amounts of information, especially if visual imaging is remotely transmitted, but not only is detection of illness made easier for consumers, it also presents opportunities for analyzing areas of business growth.

For healthcare executives, now is the time to lay out strategies for the roles that consumers will play in their organization's service delivery electronic interactions. At one end of the spectrum, consumers can be made part of a clinical "shared decision-making" process. A paper by Swan[24] shows how consumer involvement might be achieved. They are educated about their options and listened to regarding their wishes for clinical procedures. In the middle, there will at least be opportunities for communication and questioning of medical personnel using mobile phone texting and other electronic devices. At the opposite end of the spectrum, consumers can be viewed more passively as readers of web information on health, with companies then analyzing and shaping where their information comes from. Health organizations need to define how they will interact with their public before they consider their IT systems.

At the least, they should have plans for the analyses of their market's Internet behaviors that can be used to build new consumer services, attract new patients, and retain existing ones. The websites of large health organizations, such as Kaiser Permanente and the Cleveland Clinic, contain a wealth of medical information waiting to be mined for consumer use patterns. These organizations also allow patients to use the Internet to access their medical information and to interact with physicians, providing opportunities for analyses and improvements in their business processes.

CREATING ANALYTICAL TOOLS THAT DELIVER INFORMATION FOR CLINICAL AND BUSINESS DECISION MAKING

Big data in health must draw from multiple IT platforms and multiple types of information, ranging from text to disease coding and billing information. Health organizations first need to resolve these types of IT issues so that analytics can be created to produce real-time and useful information. A number of software tools are available for large data sets. Some are specific to one area of health, such as CDC software for analyzing specific surveillance and survey data sets; others are not specific.

Choosing one or more analytical tools starts with common definitions. One of the more complex areas in healthcare that must be made manageable before EMRs and big data sets can be built is getting clinical data into the EHR, such as through the use of clinical order sets. In a case study on CDS Systems, Clinovations[25] started with approximately 1300 computerized provider order entry sets that physicians used in six hospitals. Through a consensus process with the clinicians (that also could have been augmented with statistical modeling of order set data) all clinicians were given a chance to develop standard order sets. The result was 354 electronic order sets for use in an EMR and CDS system.

Big data also requires a skilled analytic workforce that combines research and statistical skills frequently found at universities, large public health agencies, and consulting organizations in addition to clinical staff involved in the delivery of health services. Thus, an unlikely combination of health data management and software skills, statistical analyses, experienced medical care, and data literacy is needed. In essence, while discussions of the big data workforce frequently concentrate on data scientists or analysts, a team approach is required in healthcare. The combination of medical knowledge, engineering, computer science, and communication is too rare a skill set for an organization to depend on in one person. For the healthcare executive to release teams for this work means considering the

time, staffing, and resources that must be devoted not just to information storage but to end uses including analytical and decision-making processes. It requires ensuring that clinical and other patient staff have time built into their schedules for adapting clinical decision-making systems to their institution's needs.

There are broad trends in data analysis software that are likely to provide lasting value to health analytics. For example, Software for the Statistical Analysis of Correlated Data (SUDAAN®) is widely used for survey data, MATLAB® is a powerful tool used for structural modeling, EViews is popular among people interested in analyzing time-series data, MapReduce/Hadoop are a Java-based combination frequently used for data-mining applications, and Statistica and JMP are increasingly used. Other specific applications' main purpose is the displaying of data, such as geographic information systems software. In smaller practices and specific health clinics, Microsoft Office tools Excel and Access are frequently used for data analysis. While Access is capable of limited data mining and Excel is capable of basic statistical analysis, neither is a robust replacement for a dedicated software package or for storing big data sets.

For clinical and health business data sets, Statistical Analysis System (SAS) and Statistical Product and Service Solutions (IBM/SPSS) often are the analytical software of choice, whereas among researchers the usage of SPSS lags far behind that of Stata and SAS. For example, in a study analyzing the use of statistical packages across three health journals in 2007–2009, Dembe et al.[26] found from articles mentioning the statistical programs used that, 46% used Stata and 42.6% used SAS, while only 5.8% used SPSS. Robert Muenchen's research[27] indicates that among academics, a wide variety of biomedically targeted statistical programs, most notably Stata and R, are quickly increasing in market penetration.

SAS, SPSS, Stata, and R are examples of how each analytical package has different costs and advantages. The pricing agreements they have vary with the different software publishers. R, as open-source software, is free. Pricing for Stata 12 varies by the version; for example, one of the cheapest versions that can be purchased allows datasets with up to 2047 variables and models with up to 798 independent variables, with a more expensive version allowing for datasets with up to 32,797 variables and models with up to 10,998 independent variables. The licenses for SPSS and SAS, on the other hand, are annual licenses. The pricing of SPSS is generally such that many of the statistical tools that are included in the full versions of SAS and Stata require the purchase of additional modules that can quickly inflate the purchase cost of SPSS.

In addition to the cost advantage, R and Stata benefit from their easy and relatively rapid extensibility. While the capabilities of each of these software packages has increased over time, the user bases of both R and Stata contribute extensively to the computational power of these software packages through the authorship of user-written add-ons. As a result, Stata and R users generally do not have to wait for the new, cutting-edge techniques to be incorporated into the base version of the software—many have already been written by users, and those with an understanding of the programming languages can script their own.

While Stata and R have an advantage in cost and extensibility, the relative strengths of SAS and SPSS are in the analysis of big data. Using Stata and R is far more memory intensive than SPSS or SAS. This advantage, however, is quickly disappearing with developments in computing, particularly the move from 32 bit Windows to 64 bit Windows. Recent extensions to R further reduce this limitation, allowing data sets to be analyzed from the cloud. Related to this, SAS and SPSS also have an advantage in the actual modeling of big data, particularly in the realm of data mining. SPSS Modeler (formerly Clementine) and SAS Enterprise Miner offer a full suite of data-mining techniques that are currently being developed by R users and are mostly absent from Stata.

Some of these modules are essential to many health scientists, including modules for dealing with survey data, bootstrapping, exact tests, nonlinear regression, and so on. R is always no more expensive than SPSS and SAS; and in the long run, Stata is usually cheaper than SPSS and SAS. These very different costing structures show the time and expertise needed in choosing analytical software.

User-friendliness is certainly one of the many concerns when considering statistical programs. There are likely to be large differences across purposes of what defines user-friendly, in particular between academic and health business settings. As a result, the criteria for user-friendliness is likely to differ across purposes; while decision makers in a corporate setting are likely to view the quality of the graphical user interface as the most important element of a software's user-friendliness, academics will typically view the ease of coding as contributing the most to ease of use.

SUCCEEDING IN A BIG DATA CULTURE

As discussed in the beginning of this entry, the success of big data in healthcare will be judged by its ability to integrate health and nonhealth information and produce real-time analyses that improve patient outcomes, overall population health, and related business processes. Big data takes the paper-based quality improvement mantra of Plan, Do, Study, Act and brings it into the electronic age.[28] This will mean continual changes in the way medicine is practiced and services and research projects are managed, and in every aspect of healthcare delivery. Big data has the potential to change the relationship of consumers and the industry.

The McKinsey Institute Big Data Study points out that the U.S. healthcare system is at a crossroad. It must develop comprehensive EHRs, standardize the way information is collected, and turn it into useful information. If information is able to be standardized and shared, it then can influence patient care and health outcomes. One story that shows how pervasive change must be in our health culture is the transforming effect of patient satisfaction data on health services. We often think of the outcomes of healthcare in terms of patient health and illness severity. But another dimension is patient satisfaction with a facility's services—its cleanliness, the friendliness of staff, and the food that is served. When one hospital set up an ongoing system for measuring and monitoring these dimensions, it was able to make practice changes that raised abysmal patient satisfaction rates. The system led to efforts to instill a culture of service throughout the organization, affecting staff from cleaning crews to surgeons. The facility may not have been able to compete on specialty services with other area faculties, but because it can use data for continuous quality improvement, it can now compete using positive patient experiences as a competitive marketing tool.

As further development occurs in this facility and it is able to link patient satisfaction experiences with patient and care characteristics, it will realize the potential of big data. Similarly, when surveillance data is routinely linked with census and environmental information, the potential for using this information to pinpoint and act upon population health issues greatly increases. Health in present times is a business, with government public health agencies also adopting common business practices. Big data in healthcare, when it is available electronically, has the potential to make healthcare more efficient and effective.

REFERENCES

1. McKinsey Global Institute. Big data: The next frontier for innovation, competition, and productivity, **2011**, Retrieved from http://www.mckinsey.com/insights/mgi/research/technology_and_innovation/big_data_the_next_frontier_for_innovation.
2. University of California–Los Angeles (UCLA) (n.d.) John Snow, http://www.ph.ucla.edu/epi/snow.html.
3. Snow, J. Snow on Cholera; Oxford University Press: London: Humphrey Milford, 1936. Copied from http://www.cdc.gov/osels/scientific_edu/SS1978/Lesson1/Section2.html.
4. NIST. 1000 genes project data available on Amazon cloud. NIH News, 2012, Retrieved from http://www.nih.gov/news/health/mar2012/nhgri-29.htm.

5. Berner, E.S. Clinical decision support systems state of the art. Agen. Healthcare Res. Qual. **2009**, Retrieved from http://healthit.ahrq.gov/images/jun09cdsreview/09_0069_ef.html.

6. National Center for Health Statistics, CDC, HHS. Physician adoption of electronic health record systems: United States, 2011. NCHS Data Brief, Retrieved from http://www.cdc.gov/nchs/data/databriefs/db98.htm (accessed July 2012).

7. Tucker, T.; Chasan, E. The financial-data dilemma. Wall St. J. **2012**, B4.

8. Office of the National Coordinator for Health Information Technology. Beacon community program, **2012b**, Retrieved from http://www.healthit.gov/policy-researchers-implementers/beacon-community-program.

9. Guerra, A. Phyllis Teater, Associate V. P./CIO Wextler Medical Center at The Ohio State University, Retrieved from http://healthsystemcio.com/2012/07/06 (accessed July 2012).

10. NIST. NIST guide to the process approach for improving the usability of electronic medical records. U. S. Department of Commerce. NISTIR 7741, 2010, Retrieved from http://www.nist.gov/itl/hit/upload/Guide_Final_Publication_Version.pdf.

11. CMS. An introduction to the Medicare EHR incentive program for eligible professionals, **2015**. Retrieved from https://www.cms.gov/Regulations-and-guidance/Legislation/EHRIncentivePrograms/downloads/Beginners_Guide.pdf.

12. California Health Foundation. What's ahead for EMRs: Experts weigh in. Retrieved from http://www.chcf.org/search?query = what's%20ahead%20for%20ehrs&sdate = all&se = 1 (accessed February 2012).

13. CDC. Evaluation of a neighborhood rat-management program—New York City, December 2007–August 2009. MMWR Weekly. **2012**, *61* (37), 733–736.

14. Food and Drug Administration. FDA's Sentinel Initiative, **2012**, Retrieved from http://www.fda.gov/Safety/FDAsSentinelInitiative/ucm2007250.htm.

15. National Heart, Lung, and Blood Institute. The Cardio-Vascular research grid, **2013**, Retrieved from http://www.cvrgrid.org/.

16. Hamilton, C.E.; Strader, L.C.; Pratt, J.G.; Maiese, D.; Hendershot, T.; Kwok, R.K.; Hammond, J.A.; Huggins, W.; Jackman, D.; Pan, H.; Nettles, D.S.; Beaty, T.H.; Farrer, L.A.; Kraft, P.; Marazita, M.L.; Ordovas, J.M.; Pato, C.N.; Spitz, M.R.; Wagener, D.; Williams, M.; Junkins, H.A.; Harlan, W.R.; Ramos, E.M.; Haines, J. The PhenX Toolkit: Get the most from your measures. Am. J. Epidemiol. **2011**, *174* (3), 253–260. Retrieved from http://aje.oxfordjournals.org/content/early/2011/07/11/aje.kwr193.full.

17. Welcome Trust, The Position Statement on data management and sharing, **2010**, Retrieved from http://www.wellcome.ac.uk/About-us/Policy/Policy-and-position-statements/WTX035043.htm.

18. Chan, M.; Kazatchkine, M.; Lob-Levyt, J.; Obaid, T.; Schweizer, J.; Sidibe, M.; Veneman, A.; Yamada, T. Meeting the demand for results and accountability: A call for action on health data from eight global health agencies. PLoS Med **2010**, *7* (1), e1000223. Retrieved from http://www.plosmedicine.org/article/info%3Adoi%2F10.1371%2Fjournal.pmed.1000223.

19. Institute of Medicine (IOM). *Crossing the quality chasm: A new health system for the 21st century*; National Academies Press: Washington, DC, 2001, Available at http://nap.edu/catalog/10027.html.

20. CDC.QuickStats: Use of health information technology among adults aged ≥18 years—National Health Interview Survey (NHIS), United States, 2009 and 2011. Weekly **2012**, *61* (32), 638. Retrieved from http://www.nist.gov/itl/ssd/is/big-data.cfm (accessed August 2012).

21. Bader, J.L.; Theofanos, M.F. Searching for cancer information on the Internet: Analyzing natural language search queries. J. Med. Internet Res. **2003**, *5* (4), e31. Retrieved from http://www.ncbi.nlm.nih.gov/pmc/articles/PMC1550578/.

22. Socha, Y.M.; Oelschegel, S.; Vaughn, C.J.; Earl, M. Improving an outreach service by analyzing the relationship of health information disparities to socioeconomic indicators using geographic information systems. J. Med. Lib. Assoc. **2012**, *100* (3), 222–225. Retrieved from http://www.ncbi.nlm.nih.gov/pmc/articles/PMC3411259/.

23. Lewis, N. Remote patient monitoring market to double by 2016. Informat. Week HealthCare Retrieved from http://www.informationweek.com/healthcare/mobile-wireless/remote-patient-monitoring-market-to-doub/240004291 (accessed July 2012).

24. Swan, B. Emerging patient-driven health care models: An examination of health social networks, consumer personalized medicine and quantified self-tracking. Intl J. Environ. Res. Pub. Health **2009**, *6* (2), 492–525. Retrieved from http://www.mdpi.com/1660-4601/6/2/492/htm.

25. Clinovations. Case study: electronic health records + clinical decision support. **2013**, Retrieved from http://www.clinovations.com.

26. Dembe, A.E.; Partridge, J.E.; Geist, L.C. Statistical software applications used in health services research: Analysis of published studies in the U. S. BMC Health Ser. Res. **2011**, *11*, 252. Retrieved from http://www.biomedcentral.com/1472-6963/11/252/abstract.

27. Muenchen, R.A. The popularity of data analysis software. PMCID, PMC3411259, **2012**. Retrieved from http://r4stats.com/articles/popularity/.

28. Institute for Healthcare Improvement (IHI). Science of improvement: How to improve. Retrieved from http://www.ihi.org/knowledge/Pages/HowtoImprove/ScienceofImprovementHowtoImprove.aspx (accessed April 2011).

BIBLIOGRAPHY

1. CDC. National health interview survey, **2015**. Retrieved from http://www.cdc.gov/nchs/nhis.htm.

2. Office of the National Coordinator for Health Information Technology. Certified health IT product list. **2012a**, Retrieved from http://oncchpl.force.com/ehrcert/EHRProductSearch?setting=Inpatient.

Data Mining: Knowledge

Monte F. Hancock, Jr.
Chief Scientist, Celestech, Inc., Melbourne, Florida, U.S.A.

Abstract

The practical purpose of this entry is to present data mining methods for inferring knowledge from data, and embedding it in decision support applications. The issue of uncertainty in reasoning systems will be addressed, and a proven protocol for conducting knowledge acquisition from domain experts will be presented.

GOALS

After you have read this entry, you will understand the fundamentals of using data mining methods to develop applications for both structural reasoning (e.g., decision trees) and nonstructural reasoning (e.g., expert systems). You will be familiar with the practical considerations involved with reasoning under uncertainty. You will know a concrete methodology for conducting structured knowledge-acquisition interviews of domain experts, and capturing their heuristics in executable form. You will be aware of some techniques for rule induction and optimization of heuristic systems.

INTRODUCTION TO KNOWLEDGE ENGINEERING

Knowledge Engineering (KE) is the general term used to refer to the discipline of obtaining human knowledge, and embedding it in software applications. It includes all aspects of the principled, formal manipulation of knowledge, including structured interview methods, knowledge extraction from data, knowledge representation, and the architecture, design, implementation, validation, and maintenance of knowledge-based systems (KBS).

KE is best understood as a generally applicable problem-solving methodology rather than just another tool in the data mining suite. Virtually all well-designed, nontrivial data mining applications will have some embedded knowledge and a knowledge component for making best use of domain data. This embedded knowledge often serves to validate and fuse mining results derived by other means. It is the functionality that stands closest to the human user, and is the ideal means for vetting, preparing, and explaining the results of data mining processes to the user.

For most data mining applications that don't interact directly with a user, embedded knowledge is implicit; it is inserted here and there into the application as needed. In this section, we focus on data mining projects that are very knowledge intensive—those for which knowledge is the core of the solution, rather than merely an adjunct to some other paradigm.

The Prototypical Example: Knowledge-Based Expert Systems

Conventional software development methodologies often represent a functional design in terms of data and control flows. These methodologies, and the block diagrams they produce, are not natural for representing state-oriented, knowledge-based software for three reasons:

1. Knowledge-based applications behave more like state machines than procedural systems. Rather than execute predetermined sequences of routines to service previously defined use cases, they transition from belief-state to belief-state as facts are received and evidence is accumulated. Control flow in these systems tends to be very simple, and doesn't vary much from problem instance to problem instance. Knowing the control flow of a KBS tells you little about the system, and doesn't advance the design process much at all. This is why it is possible to build generic expert system shells that can be deployed in disparate problem domain

   Summarizing this point: Procedural applications derive their power from their structure; this structure implements a (usually complex) sequence of carefully planned steps that mirror the structure of the problem domain. Knowledge-based applications have trivial, domain agnostic structures; they derive their power from their embedded knowledge.

Encyclopedia of Information Systems and Technology, DOI: 10.1081/E-EIST-120053815

2. Knowledge-based software (as the name suggests) is knowledge intensive rather than data intensive. In conventional procedural applications, data is volatile and in motion (input/output [I/O], parameter passing, etc.). Conventional applications operate by moving and transforming data.

   Knowledge, however, is usually stable and stationary. KBS solve problems by undergoing state changes rather than transforming data. The results they produce are decisions, not transformed data. These decisions are representations of the final belief-state of the KBS following its review and adjudication of the facts provided as evidence.

   Summarizing this point: Data flows are secondary to the operation of KB applications, and do not depict salient information about their operation.

3. Conventional procedural applications freely mix data and control (branch on data, call with arguments, inline case statements, etc.), while KB applications strictly segregate data and control. This is essential to preserving the simplicity of the inferencing architecture and making the embedded knowledge maintainable and extensible.

For these three reasons, and others, the use of data and/or control flows to represent the operation of KB applications produces design documents that are not very informative. Therefore, the design of KB applications and systems should focus on the following components.

1. Characterizing the knowledge to be used
2. Selecting the inferencing mechanism to employ
3. Designing the human–machine interface (HMI)

If the problem being addressed was amenable to crisp, high-precision evaluation using some closed-form expression, a KB approach would not even be used. Knowledge-based methods are used when such *a priori* formulae do not exist; therefore, their output is usually a list of options ranked by confidence rather than a single, firm answer.

In this sense, KB applications are not deterministic (i.e., two well-informed human experts can disagree). This makes complete specification of the problem solution difficult, which introduces schedule risk if a *waterfall* methodology is used. For this reason, a spiral methodology is typically used for the development of KB applications. Here is a notional example appropriate for KB application development:

Spiral methodology for knowledge-based application development

1. Collaborate with users/domain experts to characterize the problem.

2. Identify other domain expert(s), a chief expert, and resource materials.
3. Write a knowledge acquisition plan (KAP), schedule spirals, and prototypes.
4. Characterize the legacy environment and determine the method to deploy application.
5. Execute KAP and conduct structured interviews with users and domain experts.
6. Select solution approach:
   • Characterize HMI
   • Characterize inference engine (forward-chaining, Dempster–Shafer, etc.)
7. Create development environment:
   • Create inference engine software
   • Create HMI software
   • Create knowledge representation mechanism
8. Develop first prototype
9. Expert critique and peer review of prototype
10. Upgrade prototype using new/amended/corrected knowledge.
11. Iterate steps 9 and 10 **until requirements are satisfied or resources are exhausted**

This approach is sometimes referred to as *rapid prototyping*. This methodology proceeds by creating successively more complete versions of the final application as experts and developers interact. The prototyping is considered *rapid* because the calendar time between spirals is kept short (~30–60 days), and the foundational software structure is completed in step 8. Prototype evaluation and extension steps 9 and 10 are focused on knowledge exploitation, and the HMI.

Inference Engines Implement Inferencing Strategies

Reasoning can be conducted in a variety of ways. The reasoning method chosen for a particular problem is called an *inferencing strategy*. The inferencing strategy defines what knowledge and facts will be used, and how they will be used to produce conclusions for the user.

If inferencing is thought of as being a step-by-step process of deriving conclusions using evidence, it is clear that this can be done in two distinct ways: first, we can reason *forward* from facts to conclusions; or second, we can reason *backward* from conclusions to facts. The former is called forward chaining, and the latter, backward chaining. These two approaches appear in many guises, and the methodology actually used is sometimes a matter of semantics (Fig. 1).

Forward chaining

We want to classify Socrates as either mortal or immortal. We are given two facts: All men are mortal, and

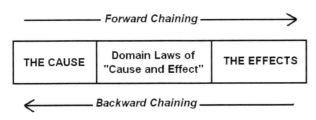

Fig. 1 Forward and backward chaining inference engines.

Socrates is a man. We apply a transitivity property of sets. If x is a member of A and A is contained in B, then x is a member of B. Using this property, we move from the facts *forward* to the conclusion: Socrates is mortal. Forward chaining is analogous to *direct proof* in mathematics.

Backward chaining

We want to decide whether our patient has the measles, or the mumps. We have three facts: body temperature is elevated, red spots are present, and no glands are swollen.

Our domain ontology has a fact table giving symptomology:

- Measles will present with red spots, elevated body temperature, and sensitivity to light.
- Mumps will present with elevated body temperature, difficulty swallowing, and swollen glands.

We begin with the hypothesis that the correct conclusion is mumps. Looking *backward* toward the symptomology that would precede this diagnosis, we see a poor match with our given facts. We then try the hypothesis that the correct conclusion is measles. Looking *backward* toward the symptomology that would precede this diagnosis, we have a good (but not perfect) match with our given facts.

The hypothesized conclusion that allows us to most effectively reason *backward* to our facts is the preferred one: measles. Backward chaining is analogous to *indirect proof* in mathematics (e.g., proof by contradiction).

The inferencing strategy to use is determined by the type of problem. Thinking of facts and conclusions as being placed into a graph, it is usually best to reason in the direction that has the lowest *branching factor*. For example, it is possible to solve a quadratic equation by backward chaining, which amounts to guessing answers until you find one that works. But there are an infinite number of guesses to check, so the backward branching factor is infinite. On the other hand, using the quadratic formula, one can reason from the coefficients in the problem *forward* to the one, unique solution in a few steps.

COMPUTING WITH KNOWLEDGE

Knowledge-based applications are white box state machines because they rely on an understanding of domain internals. In making decisions using knowledge, the application transitions from state to state, where each state is characterized by a set of beliefs. The final set of beliefs is the final state of the application, and is the application's recommended decision.

This is completely different from decision making by a domain-agnostic regression machine, such as a neural network or support vector machine, which is pure black box input-compute-output calculation. The differences between these reasoning paradigms drive the functional differences between the two approaches.

Some of the advantages of white box, KB computing over black box domain agnostic regression are:

- It allows principled, domain-savvy synthesis of circumstantial evidence.
- It copes well with ambiguous, incomplete, or incorrect input.
- It enables justification of results in terms domain experts use.
- It facilitates good pedagogical helps.
- It solves the problem like a human, so it is comprehensible to domain experts.
- It generally degrades gracefully as difficulty of problem instances increases.
- It can grow in power with experience (either by manual or by automatic extension).
- It preserves perishable human expertise.
- It allows efficient incremental upgrade, adjustment, and repurposing.

Graph Methods: Decision Trees, Forward/ Backward Chaining, Belief Nets

Graph-based methods for reasoning are structural methods: they represent knowledge explicitly as a formal structure (usually a graph, table, or ordered list), and perform reasoning by navigating the structure. Attention here will be restricted to graphs, which have mathematical richness sufficient to encode any computable relation among domain elements (e.g., entities and facts).

There are several formalisms for principled reasoning that are based upon graphs. Graphs are mathematical structures consisting of vertices (also called nodes) that are connected by edges (also called links). In general, the edges do not have a direction associated with them; they just indicate that two vertices are related. A connected graph that has edges with directions and contains no loops (also referred to as a Directed Acyclic Graph) is called a tree (Fig. 2).

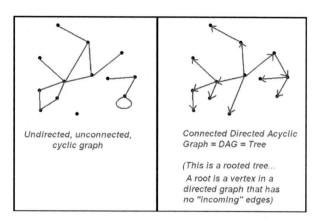

Fig. 2 Cyclic and acyclic graphs.

Graphs are very general mathematical objects that can be used to represent all kinds of useful, real-world relationships, including correlation, causation, source/ sink, priority, implication, and many more. This allows knowledge engineers (KEs) to use graphs (and the data structures that encode graphs) as a knowledge representation scheme. Because graphs can be stored as data, new knowledge can be incorporated into an application by updating a data structure. Further, knowledge encoded in a graph can be shared among users, saved, and passed along to forthcoming generations of users.

This type of knowledge encoding can be made actionable by thinking of domain processes as *sequences of states* that can be modeled and predicted. If domain facts and conclusions are placed into a graph where the edges represent evidentiary relevance within the process

Stage 1: toss the unfair coin.

Outcomes: **"H" , "T"**

p(H) = 3/4, p(T) = 1/4

Stage 2: draw a chip from an urn as follows:

i) if the coin toss was "H", draw from Urn I
ii) if the coin toss was "T", draw from Urn II

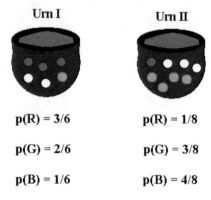

Urn I	Urn II
p(R) = 3/6	p(R) = 1/8
p(G) = 2/6	p(G) = 3/8
p(B) = 1/6	p(B) = 4/8

Fig. 3 Two-stage coin toss experiment.

(e.g., by cause and effect, or merely correlation), forward and backward chaining can be used to look at paths between them: we *reason over the graph*. The resulting decisions can be quantified by attaching probabilities or levels of confidence to the edges between vertices; these are accumulated as the graph is traversed, and used to compute beliefs or confidence factors once inferencing is complete.

An obvious example is a decision tree describing a multistage experiment. Consider the following simple two-stage experiment.

Stage 1

This stage involves a single toss of an unfair coin. The coin is unfair because the probability of heads is f, and the probability of tails is ¥.

Stage 2

This stage involves selecting a single poker chip from one of two urns. Urn I has three red chips, two green chips, and one blue chip. Urn II has one red chip, three green chips, and four blue chips (Fig. 3).

- Stage 1 of the experiment: A person tosses an unfair coin one time.
- Stage 2 of the experiment: If the result of the coin toss is heads, the person draws one poker chip from Urn I. If the result of the coin toss is tails, the person draws one poker chip from Urn II.

The outcome of the two-stage experiment is the color of the poker chip drawn. There are clearly three possible outcomes: red, green, or blue. We ask: What is the probability that we end up with a red chip? A decision tree can be used to model and predict elements of this experiment.

In this type of analysis, it is customary to use upper case letters to denote events (e.g., H = the toss produced heads), and p to denote probabilities (e.g., $p(H)$ = probability of the event heads = f). When it is desired to consider the probability of several events occurring together, these are placed in a comma separated list:

$p(A, B, C)$ = *probability that the events A, B, and C all happen.*

A decision tree for the two-stage experiment will begin with a node having two edges emanating from it: one for each of the two possible outcomes for Stage 1. It is often helpful to annotate the edges with the probability that that edge will be the one traversed out of the previous vertex.

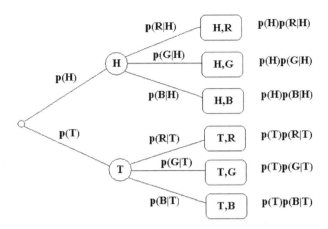

$$p(R) = p(H,R) + p(T,R) = p(H)p(R|H) + p(T)p(R|T)$$

$$p(G) = p(H,G) + p(T,G) = p(H)p(G|H) + p(T)p(G|T)$$

$$p(B) = p(H,B) + p(T,B) = p(H)p(B|H) + p(T)p(B|T)$$

Fig. 4 Decision tree with expressions.

The vertical bar character (| or pipe) is used to denote a conditional probability: the probability that an event will occur given the fact that some other event has occurred. In the case of our experiment, the conditional probability that a red chip will be drawn, given the fact that the coin toss was heads is:

$P(R|H) = $ *probability of red given heads* $= 3/6$

Notice that the conditional probability that a red chip will be drawn, given the fact that the coin toss was tails is:

$p(R|T) = $ *probability of red given tails* $= 1/8$

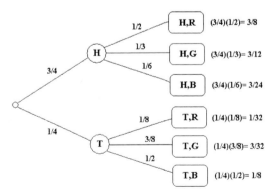

$p(R) = p(H,R) + p(T,R) = p(H)p(R|H) + p(T)p(R|T) \quad = (3/8)+(1/32)= 13/32$

$p(G) = p(H,G) + p(T,G) = p(H)p(G|H) + p(T)p(G|T) \quad = (3/12)+(3/32)= 11/32$

$p(B) = p(H,B) + p(T,B) = p(H)p(B|H) + p(T)p(B|T) \quad = (3/24)+(1/8)= 8/32$

Fig. 5 Decision tree with substituted values.

Filling out a two-tiered graph for this two-stage experiment yields Fig. 4.

The laws of probability show that the probability of taking a particular path through the decision tree is just the product of the probabilities of the edges in the path (the *path product*):

$p(H, R) = $ the probability of getting a red chip by tossing heads $= p(H)\, p(R|H)$

$p(H, G) = $ the probability of getting a red chip by tossing tails $= p(H)\, p(R|T)$

Obviously, the probability of ending up with a red chip will be the sum of the distinct ways this can occur, as indicated by the expressions in Fig. 4. This is sometimes referred to as the Decomposition Theorem.

The key observation in all this is that you can compute the probabilities of outcomes for multistage experiments if you can compute the probabilities for each stage, which is often straightforward. By substituting the easily computable numeric values for each stage into the decision tree, Fig. 5 is obtained.

The answer to our question is $p(R) = 13/32$ (probably not what someone would guess!). This is all pretty intuitive. What is not so obvious is that it is possible to reason backwards through a decision tree.

Now consider this question: suppose we ended up with a red chip. What is the probability that the coin toss came up heads or tails? If a general method can be determined for answering *reversed* questions like this, it can be used to interchange the roles of cause and effect in inferencing. Not only will it be possible to determine the likely outcomes from initial conditions, but it will also be possible to determine the likely initial conditions that gave rise to an observed outcome.

The method we seek was developed by the Reverend Thomas Bayes in the latter part of the 18th century. Accordingly, it is named Bayes' rule. It explains how to interchange the order of an outcome and a condition, that is, given all the $p(A|B)$ values, compute the $p(B|A)$ values (Fig. 6).

Using Bayes' theorem, we can answer our second question: If the final outcome is red, what are the probabilities of heads and tails on the coin toss (Fig. 7)?

This method is widely used in predictive modeling applications. For example, if years of historical data tell us the probability that a certain bond goes down when stock S goes up, Bayes' rule can reverse this to estimate the probability that stock S goes up when this bond goes down. Much more can be said on this topic in a probability and statistics course.

Bayesian Belief Networks

In any inferencing problem involving uncertainty, it is the joint probability distribution of the facts we want to model: $p(A, B, C, \ldots, N)$. Bayesian belief networks

Bayes' Rule

$$p(A \mid B) = \frac{p(A,B)}{p(B)} = \frac{p(B \mid A)p(A)}{p(B)}$$

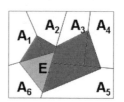

$$p(A_i \mid E) = \frac{p(E \mid A_i)p(A_i)}{p(E)} = \frac{p(E \mid A_i)p(A_i)}{\sum_i p(E \mid A_i)p(A_i)}$$

- Based on definition of conditional probability
- $p(A_i|E)$ is posterior probability given evidence E
- $p(A_i)$ is the prior probability
- $P(E|A_i)$ is the likelihood of the evidence given A_i
- $p(E)$ is the preposterior probability of the evidence

Fig. 6 Bayes' rule.

(BBNs) represent what is known about this distribution using a graph. Each node in the graph is a variable, and edges explicitly model probabilistic relationships between the variables. This provides a computational architecture for computing the impact of evidence on beliefs.

BBNs are a graph-based framework for representing and analyzing models involving uncertainty. They are used for intelligent decision aids, data fusion, intelligent diagnostic aids, automated free text understanding, and data mining. They arose from the cross-fertilization of ideas between the artificial intelligence, decision analysis, and statistics communities.

The interest in BBNs has increased dramatically since the mid-1990s, when computationally viable methods became available for implementing them. Other factors were the development of easy-to-use commercial software, and a growing number of creative applications. The principal difference between a BBN and other knowledge representation and probabilistic analysis tools are:

- BBNs handle uncertainty in mathematically rigorous, yet simple way.
- BBNs can easily be visualized as graphs (Fig. 8).

The capabilities of BBNs:

- BBNs naturally support reasoning with uncertain and incomplete evidence.
- BBNs can reason both forward and backward.
- BBNs model the domain in terms of cause and effect, which is very intuitive to human experts.
- BBNs force us to think about all the relationships among the facts, and allow us to model these relationships explicitly and objectively.
- BBNs provide a mathematically rigorous way of applying evidence consistently. They are deterministic, nonmonotonic, and insensitive to the order of updating.
- BBNs can be generalized to include temporal reasoning.
- BBNs provide an inferencing architecture that reduces computational complexity.

The presence of an edge in a BBN is an explicit statement of a direct causal relationship between the connected nodes. The absence of an edge in a BBN is an explicit statement of the lack of a direct causal relationship between the unconnected nodes. BBNs and decision trees are strongly related, but as implementation formalisms for probabilistic reasoning, BBNs have a number of advantages (refer to Table 1):

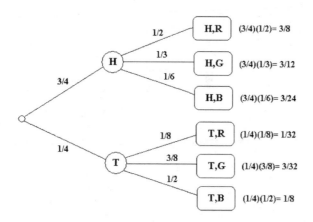

By Bayes' Theorem, we can reason backward:

$$p(H|R) = p(R|H)p(H) / p(R) = (3/8) / (13/32) = 12/13$$

$$p(T|R) = p(R|T)p(T) / p(R) = (1/32) / (13/32) = 1/13$$

Fig. 7 Decision tree applying Bayes' theorem.

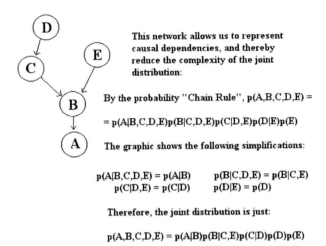

This network allows us to represent causal dependencies, and thereby reduce the complexity of the joint distribution:

By the probability "Chain Rule", p(A,B,C,D,E) =

= p(A|B,C,D,E)p(B|C,D,E)p(C|D,E)p(D|E)p(E)

The graphic shows the following simplifications:

$$p(A|B,C,D,E) = p(A|B) \qquad p(B|C,D,E) = p(B|C,E)$$
$$p(C|D,E) = p(C|D) \qquad p(D|E) = p(D)$$

Therefore, the joint distribution is just:

$$p(A,B,C,D,E) = p(A|B)p(B|C,E)p(C|D)p(D)p(E)$$

Fig. 8 Graph of a Bayesian belief network.

Nongraph Methods: Belief Accumulation

Nongraph-based methods for reasoning represent knowledge implicitly as functions. These functions are usually a collection of rules with an adjudicator, a regression function, or clauses with a resolution method. They perform reasoning by function evaluation. A good example is the multilayer perceptron.

Attention here will be restricted to systems that reason by using *heuristics*: terse rules of thumb, usually obtained from human experts, and apply evidence (facts) in discrete units to adjust confidence in one or more plausible solutions. These systems are also referred to as expert systems, rule-based systems, and production systems. They implement the classical "Perry Mason" sort of forensic reasoning that combines all the evidence in a principled way to arrive at a resolution that is consistent and coherent with all the evidence taken together.

Not all truth is created equal. In the real world, every piece of evidence has a pedigree. This pedigree includes, among other things, the credibility (nature and status) of the source, means of transmission, timeliness, precision, topical relevance, method of interpretation, and effectiveness of conformation with other evidence. None of these elements comes with a guarantee of perfect fidelity, so reasoning by evidence accumulation is

inherently uncertain in the sense that even valid reasoning can produce *untrue* conclusions. We begin with a couple of common definitions for reasoning strategy:

Monotonic reasoning strategies are those that assume that the truth values of facts do not change during the reasoning process. Of course, in actual practice, particularly when reasoning under uncertainty, facts may be revised, updated, or even contradicted as evidence is collected. These changes can require the withdrawal of previous assertions and amendment of subsequently drawn conclusions. Reasoning strategies supporting both the assertion and withdrawal of facts are said to be *nonmonotonic*.

Reasoning under *uncertainty* occurs when asserted facts are imprecise, incommensurable (can't be made consistent), incomplete, and/or false. Imprecision is inherent in all measurements, but the more important aspect of uncertainty is the presence of outright misrepresentation of information, whether accidentally through error, or intentionally by action of an adversary. Uncertainty can be thought of in two ways:

1. **Uncertainty is unavoidable.** Uncertainty exists in the input, processing, and output of all real-world systems. On the input side, decision support tools use a variety of techniques for capturing uncertainty (e.g., statistics and fuzzy logic). During reasoning, uncertainty is best managed by selecting modeling paradigms that intrinsically handle the type of uncertainty presented by the problem at hand.

2. For example, uncertainty arising from the inability to precisely measure problem variables is wellhandled by maximizing estimation margins, suggesting the use of Support Vector Machines, while uncertainty arising from the inherent inability to predict human actions is wellhandled by formalisms that directly model biased indeterminism such as BBN and KBS. On the output side, uncertainty is handled by providing metric adjuncts that represent the certainty/support of the result. Examples are interval estimates, likelihoods, and confidence factors.

3. **Uncertainty should be modeled.** If multiple models or stages contribute to the output of a decision

Table 1 Advantages of BBN over decision trees

Decision trees	BBN
● Require that the edges exiting each node are disjoint and exhaustive.	● Do not require that the edges exiting each node be disjoint or exhaustive.
● Require that values are known for all relevant features.	● Do not require that values are known for all relevant features.
● Reason *forward* by computing sums of path products.	● Reason both *forward* and *backward* by using the probability calculus.
● Compute probabilities of outcomes based upon certain knowledge of the evidence.	● Compute beliefs of outcomes based upon uncertain knowledge of the evidence.
● Represent assumptions about independence with the probabilities used.	● Represent assumptions about independence with the network topology.

support sequence, each must estimate its own uncertainty so the conclusion can be properly annotated for the user. Good design of such applications often includes not only measures of confidence, but also Conclusion Justification Reports that explain the reasoning of the application.

4. For decision support systems to be trusted by human users, they must be able to estimate the quality of their outputs and be able to explain them in the language of the user. When conclusion justification processes are automated, they provide decision support functionality that provides the user with a recommendation, a numeric measure of confidence (in the user's own terms), and the reasoning used to arrive at these conclusions.

INFERRING KNOWLEDGE FROM DATA: MACHINE LEARNING

Humans continue throughout their lives to expand their cognitive power by assimilating their experiences, in a yet unknown way. In light of this analogy, it makes sense to make the following empirical definition of machine learning:

Machine learning is any process that automatically characterizes experience in a manner that improves the machine's performance. While observation may be regarded as a collection process, the act of organizing experience is a process involving a complex mix of cognitive operations, including hypothesis generation and testing, simulation, planning, and assessment.

Machine learning is the automatic organization of execution history into machine resident structures in such a way that machine performance is improved. Under this definition, machine learning is something a machine does, not something that is done to the machine. Machine learning is distinguished from programming in exactly the same way that human learning is distinguished from hard-wired animal instinct.

While this definition is imperfect, it does capture the fundamental point: learning is a matter of behavior, not composition. Learning must be more than just the accumulation of bulk information; a small expert system with the ability to automatically create new and useful rules should be called a learning machine; a conventional database, of whatever size, probably should not.

Note: Collecting data is no more learning than pasting text is writing.

Machine reasoning is the principled estimation of belief vectors. Machine reasoners use symbols to represent concepts, and consistently organize these symbols within a system according to the rules governing the domain. As a cognitive task, learning builds on itself. This must be done in an order that insures fundamental facts and methods are in place before more advanced extensions are addressed. Learning is assessed empirically: a system can claim to have learned a datum when it can produce it *and* can claim to have learned a method when it can perform it.

Both humans and machines learn new things by relating them to things they already know. A dictionary provides a good example: it defines unknown words in terms of (hopefully) known words, so they can be understood.

Learning Machines

There are some very good reasons for building machines using adaptive methods. Development of conventional software requires detailed knowledge of the problem domain, while development with learning machines consists more of training than programming. Risk and expense can sometimes be reduced by relying more on real-world examples than the guidance of human experts.

There are many problems for which no closed-form algorithmic solutions are practical, or even known. Learning machines can develop usable solutions for some of these. Machines, which are only programmed, often don't cope well with ambiguity or incomplete information. Learning machines can be more robust.

Machines don't mind dull, repetitious work. They never ask for a raise, retire, or take time off. They can be put anywhere or everywhere. They are not protected by Occupational Safety and Health Administration standards. If machines can be trained to act as smart assistants to overloaded human experts, they multiply the human resource. When a machine focuses the human's attention on the 50% of the problem that is hard (and interesting), and handles the other 50% that is easy (and boring), the human–machine pair is twice the human alone. Also, learning machines that can explain their reasoning can be used as training tools for new personnel. And machines tend to be consistent and unbiased (but not necessarily predictable).

Machines cannot learn from experience unless they have experiences. To make this possible, a learning machine developer will typically program a learning machine shell having (at least) three components: an I/O interface, inferencing mechanism (s), and training algorithm (s). This novice system is much like John Locke's Tabula Rasa—a blank slate upon which experience writes. Having been endowed with these components, the shell can be apprenticed in the problem domain to its master.

To train, the novice learning machine applies its ignorant inferencing mechanism to the feature vectors in the training set, producing an output for each one. Some of these outputs will be correct, and some incorrect. The training algorithm compares these outputs with the correct associations in the training set, and makes adjustments to the parameters used by the inferencing mechanism. The extended repetition of this process allows the learning machine to incrementally improve its performance in terms of scope, accuracy, and confidence.

Of course, there is no free lunch. Learning machines can discover things about the problem domain that their developers didn't know (it has happened to me!), but those things will always be seen in retrospect, to have been implicit in the training set. If they were not, the machine was not learning, it was hallucinating.

How does the learning algorithm know what adjustments to make to the decision parameters to improve system performance? That is the question upon which most researchers in the field spend the bulk of their time.

There are many approaches. Some rely on gradient searches, some rely on recursion, and there are even so-called genetic algorithms that invoke mutation and natural selection to evolve learning machines that can solve a given problem. Each technique has its strengths and weaknesses.

The question becomes, "What does knowledge look like?" Before a learning machine can be built, a scheme for representing domain knowledge must be formulated. This knowledge representation problem is one of the fundamental problems of intelligent system design. As machines learn, they bind domain knowledge into fundamental units of a type corresponding to the learning machine paradigm selected by the developer.

KBS, as they exist today, were invented by Dr. Edward Feigenbaum of Cornell University in the 1960s, though the use of heuristics has been around as long as the IF statement. KBS captures expert-level human knowledge in executable rules. These rules are strictly segregated from other code, and codify experts' intuitive approach to the domain problem.

Using Modeling Techniques to Infer Knowledge from History

Knowledge can often be inferred from electronic sources by data modeling techniques. This generally takes the form of rule induction: automatically detecting semantic patterns in data and characterizing them in the form of heuristics.

Data modeling engines operate on data to provide two basic types of decision support: they help the system obtain domain understanding; and, they enable appropriate user action. Underlying these operations are various *pure reasoners*. Each *pure reasoner* has an architecture that is driven by the type of reasoning it must perform:

- **Classifiers.** Classifiers ingest a list of attributes, and determine into which of finitely many categories the entity exhibiting these attributes falls. For the integrated learning problem, classifiers would be used to identify the components of a complex plan.
- **Estimators.** Estimators ingest a list of attributes, and assign some numeric value to the entity exhibiting these attributes. The estimation of a probability or a risk score is an example of this type of reasoning. For integrated learning, the assessment of information value and cost is an estimation problem.
- **Semantic mappers.** Semantic mappers ingest text (structured, unstructured, or both), and fill in a data structure that gives meaning to the text. For integrated learning, this capability is needed to understand (segment, parse, interpret, store) the dialogue between human and machine during the observation phase of learning. Semantic mapping generally requires some kind of domain ontology.
- **Planners.** Planners ingest a scenario description, and formulate an efficient sequence of feasible actions that will move the domain to the specified goal state. Next-event prediction (What step should follow this one?) is an example of this type of reasoning.
- **Associators.** Associators sample the entire corpus of domain data, and identify relationships among entities. Automatic clustering of data to identify coherent subpopulations is a simple example. A more sophisticated example is the forensic analysis of travel records to infer the planning components of a trip.

Integration of pure reasoners

Problems are often hard because their solution cannot be readily obtained by a single pure reasoner, and the integration of multiple pure reasoners is problematic. A system able to automatically handle a wide range of user questions would integrate certain aspects of each of the five pure reasoners described earlier. In fact, even pair-wise combinations of pure reasoners can provide benefit (e.g., integrating a classifier with a semantic mapper yields a system that can categorize entities, and justify its reasoning.)

Some intuitive formalism

A bit more rigor will be added in a later section (Mathematizing Human Reasoning), but we are now ready for an intuitive and formal description of how heuristic reasoning might be implemented.

The user wants to make best use of information. This has several aspects. First, he will want to establish minimum levels of belief that he feels are necessary to trade one proposed action against another. Second, he will want the ability to dynamically adjust the weight given by his tools to each factor that contributes to a decision.

User-directed dynamism is achieved in different ways, depending on the reasoning scheme being used. In the case of BBNs, for example, it can be achieved by making the node probability tables editable.

Let b_j be a numeric value in [0,1] expressing how much a potential solution satisfies constraint j, and let d_j be a numeric value in [0,1] expressing how much a potential solution violates constraint j. A final decision can be made by adjudicating (combining in a principled way) the satisfaction and dissatisfaction scores. The type of adjudication is determined by the expression that combines the beliefs and disbeliefs collected as the rules fire. Such an evidence-combining rule is sometimes called an *aggregation rule*.

- Satisfaction = expression that aggregates all the beliefs, b_j
- Dissatisfaction = expression that aggregates all the disbeliefs, d_j
- Then, the solution score = Satisfaction–Dissatisfaction.

An overall measure of how well a solution simultaneously satisfies all constraints can be generated by subtracting the dissatisfaction score from the satisfaction score. With proper normalization, this scoring method can be made to yield solution scores that lie within a desired range. Common choices are [−1, + 1] and [0%, 100%].

This approach to simulation modeling of a set of hypotheses by aggregating positive and negative contributions of elements of a work plan has many advantages, the principal ones being:

1. It is quantitative, systematic, and extensible.
2. It is computationally efficient.
3. It can be made independent of the order in which factors are considered.
4. It makes explicit the effect of each piece of evidence on the final conclusion.
5. It is closer to the way human experts actually solve problems than to structural methods like decision trees and belief networks.
6. It explicitly addresses the manner in which positive and negative evidences interact.
7. By using our confidence in each piece of evidence to weigh the beliefs and disbeliefs during aggregation, we obtain a natural, quantitative way to incorporate the effect of uncertainty into our reasoning.
8. It allows objective and consistent adjudication of many pieces of evidence.
9. Using a smooth aggregation rule allows the solution score to serve as an objective function for mathematically optimizing the set of heuristics.

This last advantage is tremendously important, because it shows that heuristic systems can be made *trainable* by numerical optimization of the solution score. Genetic algorithms, Monte Carlo methods, and Gradient Descent can be used in this way to enable a heuristic system to learn by experience. During a maintenance training session, an updated training set is collected, and the b_j and d_j are adjusted to optimize the solution score in a supervised learning mode.

Performed as part of periodic maintenance, this reweighting of the heuristics adjusts the system for changes in domain processes. This kind of self-updating ability is an aspect of *future proofing*: making a system robust to changes in the problem domain.

Domain Knowledge the Learner Will Use

Learning is a process requiring the integration of new knowledge with old. Therefore, learning requires a representation scheme and repository for knowledge. The representation must be rich enough to support knowledge from any source and of any type; the repository must be organized for efficiency, extensibility, and, as much as possible, independence from idiosyncrasies of the domain.

Domain knowledge exists in documents, electronic form (databases, data warehouses, etc.), and in the minds of human experts. At a high level, the domain knowledge needed to support machine reasoning must be collected into an ontology consisting of static and dynamic components.

It is not possible here to delve into the details of constructing and using domain ontologies, but it is useful to know something about the types of structures and information that ontologies might contain. To this end, we present a notional table of contents for a domain ontology:

The static component consists of three corpora, and the dynamic component consists of two corpora:

The components of a static domain ontology

1. Static Linguistic Knowledge:
   a. A term taxonomy (hierarchical glossary)
   b. Synonym list (terms that can be equated to reduce size of vocabulary)
   c. Stopword list (terms used in smooth discourse, but which carry no information)
   d. Phrase/structure grammar for the domain
2. Static Spatio-temporal Rules:
   a. Hard temporal constraints (time zones, calendars, etc.)
   b. Hard spatial constraints (maps, etc.)
3. Constraint Base:
   a. Logistical rules (equipment, site protocols)

b. Resource databases (databases, web pages, etc.)

c. Personnel databases (names, contact information, skill sets, experience)

The components of a dynamic domain ontology

1. Dynamic Linguistic Knowledge:
   a. State of discourse (goals, user and system state vectors, etc.)
   b. Segmented
   c. latest discourse (topics, concepts, etc.)
2. Dynamic Hypotheses:
   a. Hypothesized plan (what the system thinks it is observing)
   b. Facts now known with high confidence
   c. Facts hypothesized
   d. Facts needed but unknown
   e. Planned actions (classifiers to run, simulations to perform, etc.)

Inferring domain knowledge from human experts

In developing knowledge from human experts during the knowledge acquisition interview, the KEs must get three things: the expert's *rules* (heuristics, tip-offs, associations), the expert's *methods* (means of reasoning in the domain), and the expert's *confidences* (subjective assessment of the evidentiary value of each element of information).

You can't just ask an expert for these. Rare is the expert possessing a detailed, formal understanding of his/her own thought processes. However, approximations of these can be elicited during a structured knowledge acquisition interview.

Frankly, data mining and automated decision support systems constitute a psychological double threat to the domain expert. First, from their perspective, you are asking them to give you the keys to their kingdom so you can build a system that will make them obsolete. Second, you believe that what they do is simple enough that any nonexpert off the street (you) can automate it. Of course, neither of these perceptions is accurate; nevertheless, the experts must be won over. They must understand that everyone knows they cannot be replaced. They must be shown unreasonable deference. They will not be indifferent to you: they usually become either powerful advocates or invincible adversaries.

Some general guidelines for interacting with experts:

1. The KEs must be open, childlike, and empathic.
   a. This is essential to avoid appearing to be a threat. You are the student; the domain expert is the master. If you start acting like a peer, they'll stop talking to you.

2. Interviews must be with one expert at a time.
   a. Isn't it more efficient to interview multiple domain experts together? NO. It is incredibly wasteful. For, if experts regard themselves as peers, the interview will turn into a one-upmanship barrage of war stories, with the experts interacting more with each other than with you. Or, if an expert is subordinate, they will merely parrot what the highest present authority says; talking to them privately later will not get them to tell you otherwise. In both cases, you have wasted your experts.
3. A Chief Expert must be designated.
   a. Different experts will approach the same problem in different ways—sometimes very different. Someone with acknowledged technical authority must be chosen to help you harmonize disparate accounts, or you will end up building a schizophrenic system. (Don't laugh: I've seen it.)
4. Interviews should be 2-on-1: one to direct, one to write.
   a. Three people should attend each interview: two interviewers, and one domain expert (DE). Only one of the interviewers interacts with the DE; the other takes copious notes, and keeps their eyes and ears open. After the interview, the two interviewers can do a debrief, going through the notes and making sure that everything has been correctly documented.
5. Regular contact with frequent follow-up is essential.
   a. Don't let the DEs forget that you exist. Find ways to keep them engaged (e.g., suggest that they be invited to design walkthroughs and prototype demonstrations). If you need expert help and your main contacts are not available, you'll need some backups.
6. "Cut Metal" ASAP
   a. Get a first prototype out quickly. This shows you are real. It might not be much more than some screen mock-ups hung together by a case statement, but that's ok. You can get useful feedback on your HMI concept, and ask for additional suggestions. Be sure to explicitly incorporate and comment on how the advice of the domain expert(s) drove your work.

The structured knowledge acquisition interview consists of a sequence of discourses, each designed to elicit a particular kind of knowledge from the expert. For best results, the expert should not be given a prebriefing explanation of the discourses. Some of the discourse techniques include:

A.
Stream of consciousness monologues

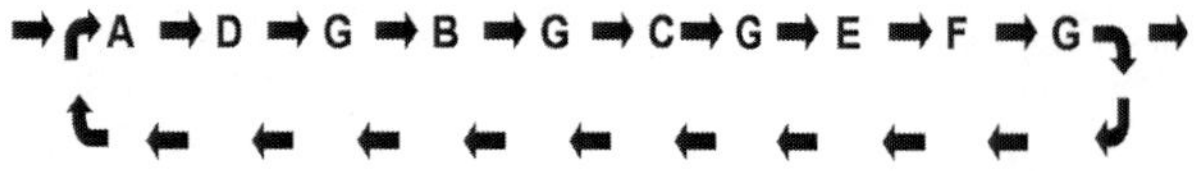

→ A → D → G → B → G → C → G → E → F → G →

Fig. 9   Structured knowledge acquisition interview flow.

B.
Visualization (scenario walkthroughs, seeing the solution, etc.)
C.
Prioritization
D.
Standard scenarios
E.
Standard anomalies
F.
Single-factor variations
G.
Opinionated regurgitation

These are applied according to a sequence typified in Fig. 9.

- **Stream of consciousness monologue.** The domain expert is asked to think silently for 60 seconds about the problem domain. They then express their thoughts in terse phrases (two or three words) as long as they can until they *run out*. These phrases are collected and analyzed after the interview for the presence of key words, jargon, acronyms, which ideas were mentioned first, which are ideas were repeated, what seemingly important ideas were left out, etc. By the way: I've never met an expert who could do this for more than two minutes before "running out"!
- **Visualization.** The domain expert mentally walks through a work day. Set them up by saying, "You just arrived. You have your coffee, and you sit down at your desk. Then what?" They describe step-by–step precisely what they see and do. The interviewer can interrupt and add elements, such as, what types of problems might arise here?
- **Prioritization.** To determine the relative significance of domain elements, and flush out hidden rules, priorities, and assumptions; pose hypothetical dilemmas that force a hard choice. "If you are in situation A, and can only use one tool, which tool will it be?"
- **Standard scenarios.** Ask the domain expert to set up and describe the nominal, day-to-day situations that arise in the domain, and how they are addressed.
- **Standard anomalies.** Once the domain expert has described a normal day, find out what *unusual* might mean: "Let's assume that everything is normal; what sorts of unusual things or conditions might arise? How are these addressed?"
- **Single-factor variations.** Recount for the domain expert a normal scenario, but toggle some element:

"Suppose we are in normal situation A, but condition B is *not* present? Can this happen? Does it happen? What then?"
- **Opinionated regurgitation.** In interviews of this type, domain experts tend to speak in categorical terms. They might generalize, leave out special cases, etc. To identify these, recap the last segment of the interview in hard, black and white terms. The interviewer says, "Ok, every single day always begins with scenario A, and is then always followed by scenario B and never some other scenario." At this point, the domain expert will jump in and say, "Well, sometimes…," and lay out the various allowable conditions that cause deviations that are still within the range of normal activity.

These techniques are very effective at flushing out hidden assumptions, rules, constraints, biases, and so on, that the domain expert might not think to mention, and the knowledge expert won't know to ask about. They work best if the domain expert is not aware of the underlying method behind your madness.

How do interview questions turn into embedded knowledge?

Most knowledge derived from domain experts during structured interviews is encapsulated in heuristics represented as structured constructs: case statements, if-then-else structures, and so on. This example pretty much tells the tale:

What the Expert Says:

KE: What evidence makes you certain an animal is a primate?

KE: If it's a land animal that'll eat anything…but it bears live young and walks upright, etc.

KE: Any obvious physical characteristics?

DE: Yes, no feathers, of course, or wings, or any of that. Well, then, it's got to be a primate.

KE: So, ANY animal which is a land-dwelling, omnivorous, skin-covered, unwinged featherless biped which bears live young is necessarily a primate?

DE: Yes.

KE: Could such an animal, be, say, a fish?

DE: No, it couldn't be anything but a primate.

What the KE hears:

If (f1,f2,f3,f4,f5) = (land, omni, feathers, wingless biped, born alive) Then primate and (not fish, not domestic, not bug, not germ, not bird)

Writing on a Blank Slate

Consider a categorical approach to computational perception after the fashion of Kant in his *Critique of Pure Reason*[1]; one that is plastic in accordance with Locke's *tabula rasa* described in *An Essay Concerning Human Understanding*.[2] He said that the mind is a blank slate (*tabula rasa*) upon which experience writes. Such an approach to system building can be realized mathematically in various ways (BBNs, Dempster–Schafer). This will be discussed further.

Before interaction with expert knowledge or domain data, the learning machine must be endowed with a cognitive form for which a software architecture can be created. Even after the software structure is in place, the machine is merely a collection of empty containers for collecting and interpreting experience.

It is the KE's task to formulate a cognitive form appropriate to the decision support needs of the user, and infer from it a software architecture that will support its operation. This cognitive form includes (from lower level to higher level):

Low

1. A domain symbolic representational scheme
2. A domain lexicon
3. Instances of domain-appropriate data structures
4. A collection of fact templates (relations on data) as object-oriented-objects with methods
5. A collection of information templates (relations on facts)
6. A collection of knowledge templates (relations on information elements)
7. A catalog of domain user goal patterns
8. A catalog of reasoning patterns
9. A domain inferencing calculus
10. A domain generative grammar
11. A trainable nonmonotonic reasoner that can handle uncertainty

High

Because these elements initially have form but no content: they are a *tabula rasa*. When instantiated (populated with content), they constitute a domain ontology.

How is the content to be derived? There are two ways:

1. Knowledge can be manually placed into the application by direct encoding. This is the approach used by groups developing machines that emulate complex human behaviors (Wolfram Alpha, IBM's Watson, Cyc).

2. Knowledge can be learned by experience. Adaptation that produces useful change requires evaluation of experience in a context supported by domain knowledge. This suggests an effective architecture for computational perception will be hierarchical, knowledge intensive, and built around multiple heterogeneous adaptive reasoners using dynamic information structures.

Mathematizing Human Reasoning

While propositional and predicate logic are powerful reasoning tools, they do not mirror what human experts actually *do*. Either do decision trees, Bayesian analysis, neural networks, or support vector machines.

Pose a problem for a human expert in their domain, and you will find, even given no evidence, that they have an *a priori* collection of beliefs about the correct conclusion. For example, a mechanic arriving at the repair shop on Tuesday morning already holds certain beliefs about the car waiting in Bay 3 before they know anything about it. As the mechanic examines the car, they will update their prior beliefs, accruing *bias* for and against certain explanations for the vehicle's problem. At the end of the initial analysis, there will be some favored (belief = large) conclusions, which will be tested, and thus accrue more belief and disbelief. Without running decision trees, applying Bayes' theorem, or using margin maximizing hyperplanes, they will ultimately adopt the conclusion they most believes is true. It is this *preponderance of the evidence* approach that best describes how human experts actually reason; and it is this approach we seek to model.

Bias-based reasoning (BBR) is a mathematical method for automating implementation of a belief-accrual approach to expert problem solving. It enjoys the same advantages human experts derive from this approach; in particular, it supports automated learning, conclusion justification, confidence estimation, and natural means for handling both nonmonotonicity and uncertainty.

Dempster–Shafer reasoning is an earlier attempt to implement belief-accrual reasoning, but suffers some well-known defects (Lotfi paradox, constant updating of parameters, monotonic, no explicit means for uncertainty). BBR overcomes these.

Using Facts in Rules

For simplicity and definiteness, the reasoning problem will be described here as the use of evidence to select one or more possible conclusions from a closed, finite list that has been specified *a priori* (the classifier problem).

Expert reasoning is based upon facts (colloquially, interpretations of the collected data). Facts function as both indicators and contra-indicators for conclusions. Positive facts are those that increase our beliefs in certain conclusions. Negative facts are probably best understood as being exculpatory: they impose constraints upon the space of conclusions, militating against those unlikely to be correct. Facts are salient to the extent that they increase belief in the truth, and/or increase disbelief in untruth.

A rule is an operator that uses facts to update beliefs by applying biases. In software, rules are often represented as structured constructs such as if-then-else, case, or switch statements. We use the if-then-else in what follows.

Rules consist of an antecedent and a multipart body. The antecedent evaluates a Boolean expression; depending upon the truth-value of the antecedent, different parts of the rule body are executed. The following is a notional example of a rule. It tells us qualitatively how an expert might alter his or her beliefs about an unknown animal should he or she determine whether or not it is a land-dwelling omnivore:

If (habitat = land) and (diet = omnivorous)
    Then
        Increase Belief (primates, bugs, birds)
        Increase Disbelief (bacteria, fishes)
    Else
        Increase Disbelief (primates, bugs, birds)
        Increase Belief (bacteria, fishes)
    End Rule

If we have an *Increase Belief* function, and a *Decrease Belief* function ("aggregation functions," called AGG), many such rules can be efficiently implemented in a looping structure:

In a data store:

$T_j (F_i)$ truth-value of predicate j applied to fact F_i

bias $(k,j,1)$ belief to accrue in conclusion k when predicate j true

bias $(k,j,2)$ disbelief to accrue in conclusion k when predicate j is true

bias $(k,j,3)$ belief to accrue in conclusion k when predicate j false

bias $(k,j,4)$ disbelief to accrue in conclusion k when predicate j is false

Multiple rule execution in a loop:

If $T_j (\mathbf{F}) = 1$ Then if predicate j true for $\mathbf{F_i}$
    For k = 1 to K for conclusion k:
        Belief (k) = AGG(B(k,i),bias (k,j,1)) true: accrue belief bias (k,j,1)
        Disbelief (k) = AGG(D(k,i),bias (k,j,2)) true: accrue disbelief bias (k,j,2)
    Next k
    Else
    For k = 1 TO K for conclusion k:

        Belief (k) = AGG(D(k,i),bias (k,j,3)) false: accrue belief bias (k,j,3)
        Disbelief (k) = AGG(B(k,i),bias (k,j,4)) false: accrue disbelief bias (k,j,4)
    Next k
    End If

This creates a vector B of beliefs (b (1), b (2),…, b (K)) for each of the conclusions 1, 2, …, K, and a vector D of disbeliefs (d (1), d (2), …, d (K)) for each of the conclusions 1, 2, …, K. These must now be adjudicated for a final decision.

Clearly, the inferential power here is not in the rule structure, but in the knowledge held numerically in the biases. As is typical with heuristic reasoners, BBR allows the complete separation of knowledge from the inferencing process. This means that the structure can be retrained, even repurposed to another problem domain, by modifying only data; the inference engine need not be changed. An additional benefit of this separability is that the engine can be maintained openly apart from sensitive data.

Summarizing—thinking again in terms of the classifier problem:

When a positive belief heuristic fires, it accrues a bias $\beta > 0$ that a certain class is the correct answer; when a negative heuristic fires, it accrues a bias $\delta > 0$ that a certain class is the correct answer. The combined positive and negative biases for an answer constitute that answer's belief.

After applying a set of rules to a collection of facts, beliefs and disbeliefs will have been accrued for each possible conclusion (classification decision). This ordered list of beliefs is a *belief vector.* The final decision is made by examining this vector of beliefs, for example, by selecting the class having the largest belief–disbelief difference (but we will formulate a better adjudication scheme).

Problems and Properties

There are two major problems to be solved; these are, in a certain sense, inverses of each other:

1. The adjudication problem—reasoning forward from biases to truth: What is the proper algorithm for combining accrued positive and negative biases into an aggregate *belief vector* so that a decision can be made?

2. The learning problem—reasoning backwards from truth to biases: Given a collection of heuristics and tagged examples, how can the bias values to accrue, β_{kl} and δ_{jl}, be determined?

Conventional parametric methods (e.g., Bayesian inferencing), compute class likelihoods, but generally do not explicitly model negative evidence. Rather, they increase likelihoods for competing answers. They are inherently batch algorithms, performing their analysis after all evidence has been presented. They have the good characteristic that they are capable of directly modeling the entire joint distribution (though this is rarely practical in actual practice). Their outputs are usually direct estimates of class probabilities.

BBR does not model the entire joint distribution, but begins with the assumption that all facts are independent. This assumption is generally false for the entire population. We have found that this is effectively handled by segmenting the population data into strata within which independence holds approximately; rules are conditioned to operate within particular strata.

BBR supports both batch and incremental modes. It can roll up its beliefs after all evidence has been collected, or it can use an incremental aggregation rule to adjust its bias with respect to each class as evidence is obtained.

Desirable properties for a BBR:

1. Final conclusions should be independent of the order in which the evidence is considered.

2. The aggregation rule should have compact range, for example, it must have no gaps, and there must be a maximum and minimum bias possible.

3. A bias of zero should mean that evidence for and against an answer are equal.

SUMMARY

Having read this entry, you understand using fundamental data mining methods to infer and embed knowledge in decision support applications. You are familiar with methods for dealing with uncertainty in reasoning applications, and know how to conduct effective knowledge acquisition interviews with domain experts.

REFERENCES

1. Kant, E. *Critique of Pure Reason*; Cambridge University Press, 1999 (Trans. by P. Guyer and A. Wood).
2. Locke, J. *An Essay Concerning Human Understanding*; Prometheus Books, 1995.

Data Mining: Process

Monte F. Hancock, Jr.
Chief Scientist, Celestech, Inc., Melbourne, Florida, U.S.A.

Abstract

The purpose of this entry is to provide the reader with a deeper understanding of the fundamental principles of data mining. It presents an overview of data mining as a process of discovery and exploitation that is conducted in spirals, each consisting of multiple steps. A Rapid Application Development (RAD) data mining methodology is presented that accommodates disruptive discovery and changing requirements.

GOALS

After you have read this entry, you will be able to explain the more complex principles of data mining as a discipline. You will be familiar with the major components of the data mining process, and will know how these are implemented in a spiral methodology. Most importantly, you will understand the relative strengths and weaknesses of conventional and RAD development methodologies as they relate to data mining projects.

INTRODUCTION

Successful data mining requires the cultivation of an appropriate mindset. There are many ways that data mining efforts can go astray; even seemingly small oversights can cause significant delays or even project failure. Just as pilots must maintain situational awareness for safe performance, data miners must remember where they are in their analysis, and where they are going. All of this demands a principled approach implemented as a disciplined process.

The alternative to using a disciplined process is often expensive failure. "Data mining boys love their analytic toys"; directionless analysts can spend infinite time unsystematically pounding on data sets using powerful data mining tools. Someone who understands the data mining process must establish a plan: there needs to be a "Moses."

There also needs to be a "Promised Land." Someone familiar with the needs of the enterprise must establish general goals for the data mining activity. Because data mining is a dynamic, iterative discovery process, establishing goals and formulating a good plan can be difficult. Having a data mining expert review the problem, set up a reasonable sequence of experiments, and

establish time budgets for each step of analysis will minimize profitless wandering through some high-dimensional wilderness.

There is still some disagreement among practitioners about the scope of the term *data mining*: Does data mining include building classifiers and other kinds of models, or only pattern discovery? How does conventional statistics fit in? There is also disagreement about the proper context for data mining: Is a data warehouse necessary? Is it essential to have an integrated set of tools? However, there is general agreement among practitioners that data mining is a process that begins with data in some form and ends with knowledge in some form.

As we have seen, data mining is a scientific activity requiring systematic thinking, careful planning, and informed discipline. We now lay out the steps of a principled data mining process at a high level, being careful not to get lost in the particulars of specific techniques or tools.

In computer science, development methodologies that repeat a standardized sequence of steps to incrementally produce successively more mature prototypes of a solution are referred to as *spiral methodologies*. Each cycle through the sequence of steps is one spiral.

An enterprise is any entity that is a data owner (DO) having an operational process. This includes businesses, government entities, and the World Wide Web. The following is an overview of a data mining project as a process of directed discovery and exploitation that occurs within an enterprise.

DISCOVERY AND EXPLOITATION

As a process, data mining has two components: discovery and exploitation.

Encyclopedia of Information Systems and Technology, DOI: 10.1081/E-EIST-120053812

Discovery is an analytic process, for example, determining the few factors that most influence customer churn. Exploitation is a modeling process, for example, building a classifier that identifies the customers most likely to churn based upon their orders last quarter. We can characterize these functionally by noting that, during discovery, meaningful patterns are detected in data, and characterized formally, resulting in descriptive models. During exploitation, detected patterns are used to build useful models (e.g., classifiers).

- Discovery
  - Detect actionable patterns in data
  - Characterize actionable patterns in data
- Exploitation
  - Create models
  - Interact with the enterprise

Depending on the complexity of the domain, the discovery process will have some or all of the components shown in Fig. 1.

Once the discovery process has provided the necessary insight into how the data represent the domain, exploitation begins. It will have some or all of the major components in Fig. 2, and might use some of the techniques suggested there.

This inclusive view of data mining is a bit broader than that presently held by some, who reserve the term data mining for what is here called the discovery component. They would refer to our exploitation component as predictive modeling. The broader view is taken here for three reasons:

1. The broader conception of data mining appears to be the direction things are headed in business intelligence circles, driven in part by tool vendors who continually increase the scope of their integrated data mining environments.
2. Some of the same tools and techniques are used for both discovery and exploitation, making discrimination between them somewhat subjective anyway (Are we exploiting yet?).
3. More and more, analysts want to engage in both discovery and exploitation using data mining tools and methods, going back and forth between the two during a project. Distinctions between discovery and exploitation are blurred in such situations.

Though an inclusive view of data mining is taken here, it should not be inferred that the distinction between discovery and exploitation is unimportant. For the purpose of managing a data mining project, selecting the right techniques, and keeping track of what we're doing now is essential to proper project management.

The data mining process will now be described as a sequence of steps, each having a specified purpose. The purpose, order, and content of each step are expressed in terms general enough to encompass those outlined in the well-known competing process standards.

Data mining projects are undertaken to solve enterprise problems. Some of these problems can be considered solved when insight is gained (e.g., What are the indicators of impending default?); others are solved only when this insight is made actionable by some application (e.g., Automatically predict default!). It is the difference between a question mark and an exclamation point: the descriptive models developed during the

Data selection (defining the sampling frame)

Data cleansing

- Common data problems (outliers, gaps, time, consistency, collisions, imbalance)
- Identifying/handling outliers (statistical methods)
- handling missing fields (weak fill values, degapping, gap masking)
- handling temporal problems (aging, cycling, trends, non-stationarity, etc.)
- checking consistency (semantic filtering)
- handling class collisions
- handling class imbalance (replication, decimation)
- other

Data representation

- data syntax (precision, scale, format)
- nominal vs. numeric trades
- coding (nominal to numeric data)
- quantization (numeric to nominal data)

- **Feature extraction and transformation**
  - data registration
  - data normalization
  - feature synthesis
- **Feature enhancement**
  - feature salience (discriminating power of a feature)
  - feature independence (information contribution of a feature)
  - information-theoretic transforms (making information more accessible)
- **Data division**
  - sampling
  - stratifying
  - segmenting (creating training, calibration, validation, and holdback sets)
- **Configuration management**
  - nomenclature and naming conventions
  - documenting the workflow for reproducibility

Components of the Discovery Process

Fig. 1 Components of the discovery phase.

```
          Paradigms Selection                          •  Model Evaluation (objective function)
                 -what it is, when to use it, how to create      -   accuracy (% correctness,
                  it, how to use it                                  precision/recall, RMS, etc.)
                 -neural networks (perceptrons, hopfield         -   lift curve
                  nets, recurrent nets, etc.)                    -   confusion matrices
                 -knowledge-based expert systems                 -   ROI
                 -radial basis functions                         -   other
                 -adaptive logic networks                   •  Model Deployment
                 -nearest-neighbor classifiers                   -   Web-based SOA, ASP
                 -support vector machines                        -   API, plug-ins, linked objects, file
                 -decision trees, belief nets                        interface, etc.
                 -others                                         -   other
          Test Design                                       •  Model maintenance
          Model Construction                                     -   retraining, stationarity
                 -training (e.g., NN)                            -   changing the feature set
                 -construction (e.g., KBES)                          (adding/subtracting features)
          Meta-Schemes Development                               -   other
                 -bagging
                 -boosting

                          Components of the Exploitation Process
```

Fig. 2   Components of the exploitation process.

discovery phase address the "?", and the predictive models produced during the exploitation phase bring about the "!".

It is the enterprise goal that determines whether both discovery and exploitation are pursued for a particular data mining project. Typically, analysts and researchers want to discover, while managers and practitioners want to exploit.

Discovery is a prerequisite to exploitation. Sometimes though, there is sufficient knowledge of the domain to begin exploitation without undertaking an extensive discovery effort. This is the approach taken, for example, by expert system developers who build intelligent applications using the knowledge already possessed by domain experts (DEs). Either way, every well-designed data mining effort includes an inquiry into what is already known about the domain.

ELEVEN KEY PRINCIPLES OF INFORMATION-DRIVEN DATA MINING

Included here to round out this introduction to data mining as a process are some foundational principles of the data mining process. Overlooking any one of them can lead to costly data mining project failure; ignore them at your peril. These are so important that we list them together for ready review before moving on to detailed treatments:

1. In order of importance: choose the right people, methods, and tools
2. Make no prior assumptions about the problem (begin as a domain agnostic)
3. Begin with general techniques that let the data determine the direction of the analysis (funnel method)

4. Don't jump to conclusions; perform process audits as needed
5. Don't be a one widget wonder; integrate multiple paradigms so the strengths of one compensate for the weaknesses of the other
6. Break the problem into the right pieces; divide and conquer
7. Work the data, not the tools, but automate when possible
8. Be systematic, consistent, and thorough; don't lose the forest for the trees.
9. Document the work so it is reproducible; create scripts when possible
10. Collaborate with team members, experts, and users to avoid surprises
11. Focus on the goal: maximum value to the user within cost and schedule

KEY PRINCIPLES EXPANDED

These principles are the fruit of some of the author's own painful and expensive lessons learned the hard way. Working with these principles in mind will reduce the likelihood that you will make a costly and avoidable data mining error. Learn them; live them.

Key Principle Number One

Choose the right people, methods, and tools for your data mining effort

We place this principle first because it is the most important to the success of a data mining effort. Further, the three choices listed are in order of importance. If you have to compromise on something, it should not be the skill sets of the people involved in the mining effort.

It is the aggregate skill set possessed by the team as a whole that will generate your success.

Once the team has been put together, choosing the proper mining methods is the next most important. Even people who really know what they're doing are less likely to be successful if the methods that they employ are not appropriate to the problem. By methods, we mean the mining goals, data sources, general methodology, and work plans.

Assuming that the right people and the right methods have been selected, the next most important item is the choice of appropriate tools. Fortunately, people well-versed in the procedures for conducting a data mining effort can often be successful even when they don't have the best toolsets. This is because many data mining activities rely on the analytic skills of the miner more than they rely on the efficiency provided by good tools.

Key Principle Number Two

Make no prior assumptions about the problem

This involves taking an agnostic approach to the problem. Assumptions are actually restrictions on what constitutes a reasonable hypothesis. Since you will not be a DE, you shouldn't have any of these. Often things that haven't been discovered about the problem space are unknown precisely because prior assumptions prevented people from perceiving them. If you make certain assumptions about what are viable solutions to a problem, you insure that certain approaches will not be carefully explored. If one of these excluded solutions is actually the solution for which you are mining, you will not discover it. Taking an agnostic approach to a data mining activity will initially leave the door open to undiscovered facts about the domain. If you don't have a solution at hand, it makes sense to at least consider approaches that might initially appear unpromising.

One of the implications of principle number two is that DEs are often not the best people to carry out a data mining effort. The reason for this is that they already have a large collection of assumptions, many held unconsciously, about what's going to work and not work in the problem space. These assumptions will prevent them from investigating avenues of analysis that they "know won't work." A data mining effort led by a DE can be expected to discover all the things they already know about the problem space, and not much else. Someone not an expert in the problem will investigate areas an expert would let pass unexamined. It is generally much better to have someone who knows more about data mining than the problem space to be the technical lead on a data mining activity. The DE certainly is a necessary part of the team, but not as the leader.

Key Principle Number Three

Begin with general techniques that let the data determine the direction of the analysis

For problem areas that are not well understood, begin the project by pursuing several lines of general investigation. For example, initially employ two or more different analytic methods, toolsets, etc. Rather than putting all the eggs into one analytic basket, this holds open multiple lines of investigation long enough to determine which is likely to produce the best result. With this known, subsequent effort can be focused on that one best choice.

I refer to this as the *funnel method*, because work begins with a broad analytic attack, progressively narrowing as the problem is more fully understood. This method also provides a good way to make use of multiple team members, each using a different method and working in parallel until problem understanding is achieved. When that occurs, all of your working capital can shift over to the method found most likely to bear fruit in your problem domain.

Key Principle Number Four

Don't jump to conclusions; perform process audits as needed

This refers to a phenomenon that occurs often in data mining efforts, and is usually (though not always!) manifested by an inexperienced data miner. It is not unusual for an amazing analytic miracle to occur, a silver bullet that solves the problem. It is often the case, however, that huge breakthroughs on really hard problems are the deceptive fruit of some analytic mistake: some data have been mislabeled, ground truth has accidentally been added to the data set, or some data conditioning error caused an experiment to produce erroneous results.

The damage is usually limited to some embarrassment on the part of the claimant, but the real danger is that word of a breakthrough will find its way to a decision maker who will take it at face value. This can derail a data mining effort and at the very least, you'll have some explaining to do.

When results from a significant experiment differ radically from expectations, the proper approach is to perform *a process audit*: a thorough examination of the experiment to determine the facts. The most common errors are related to data preparation and use as follows:

1. Inappropriate data have been added to a training set (e.g., ground truth).
2. Validation has been done on the same data that was used to create the model (training data).

3. The data set has somehow been poisoned by additions and/or deletions in such a way that it misrepresents the problem.

Key Principle Number Five

Don't be a one widget wonder; integrate multiple paradigms so the strengths of one compensate for the weaknesses of another

There is no perfect data mining tool or application; every tool and application is going to have certain strengths and weaknesses. There will be aspects of the problem a particular tool handles well, and others it does not handle well. This means that if you rely entirely on one or two tools to attack a complex data mining problem you'll probably not do the best job on all aspects of the problem.

An industry phrase for an analyst who relies entirely on one application is "a fool with a tool" (FWAT). The final product of an FWAT will consist of all the things their preferred tool does well, and none of the things it doesn't.

Key Principle Number Six

Break the problem into the right pieces; divide and conquer

A divide and conquer approach is often the key to success in difficult data mining problems. One of the factors that make some data mining problems difficult is the presence of several subproblems, not all of which can be addressed by a single approach. For example, if the data contain disparate items from multiple sources that are at different levels of precision/accuracy, or are in very different forms (such as a mixture of nominal and numeric data), using multiple tools might be the only viable approach.

When a problem has these local disparities, it makes sense to consider breaking it into pieces and deploying different methods against the pieces. This allows the use of the best tool on each component of the problem. Just as you wouldn't fight a battle against a tank brigade using only infantry, you don't want to use a single approach against a problem that has multiple modes or aspects that require different approaches. Instead, divide and conquer: break the problem into appropriate pieces and attack them individually with methods suited to the various data terrains (Fig. 3).

An additional benefit of problem segmentation is the ability to parallelize work by having different problem segments worked separately by different analysts. This can sometimes shorten the overall project schedule, and can keep staff usefully engaged, should there be slack periods in the project schedule.

Finally, it is often possible to automate the process of segmenting a difficult problem into natural chunks using unsupervised learning methods such as clustering. It is often the case that some chunks will be the hard part of the problem, and others the easy parts. Separating these allows elementary methods to handle the easy problem instances, with more computationally complex methods being used only when necessary.

Automation can make a big difference in data mining activities, but its limitations must be recognized. Automation is good for handling rote tasks that humans don't do well, such as building histograms, computing correlation measures, grinding out bulk computations, doing clustering and matching, sifting through large quantities of data to perform repetitive statistical tests, and so on. But when it gets down to actually trying to squeeze the last bit of information out of a complex problem space, some reworking of the data is going to be required. By *reworking the data* we mean applying

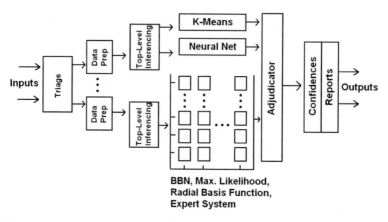

Fig 3 Multi-paradigm architecture.

some mathematical transform, alternate normalization, or synthesis of altogether new features by combining some of the old. All of these provide fresh views of the problem space that can make information not yet extracted more accessible to your tools.

Key Principle Number Seven

Work the data, not the tools, but automate when possible

If you've run a data mining problem through several spirals and have not made sufficient progress, at some point you will begin thinking about new things to try. Questions that pop up in this situation are: Do I need to modify my tools? Is there some perfect collection of parameter settings for my modeling software that will produce large improvements? (There are times when this is exactly what is called for, but it is usually not when you are running low on tricks. This leads to planless tinkering, which is addressed in key principle number eight.)

When faced with the question of whether to work the tools or work the data, the correct answer is almost always work the data. This is because the information you are looking for is not in the tools; it is in the data. Experience has shown over and over again that in mining of all sorts, data mining and otherwise, you are more likely to get increased value from better dirt than you are from a better shovel. Resorting to data mining by twiddling dials on a tool is a lot like doing your taxes by rolling dice: it's just not the best approach.

Data mining is subject to the law of diminishing returns. Obvious patterns and principles are discovered early, but as information is mined from a data set, the rate of discovery will slow. The natural temptation when you're in the hunt for information with automated tools is to speed things up by tweaking the tools to get them to act more effectively against the data (changing settings and parameters, recalibrating them, adjusting sensitivity levels, configurations, vigilance factors, etc.). This will work for a while, but at some point it will stop bearing fruit. It is important to realize when this stage has been reached, and the experienced data miner will switch from working the tool to working the data.

If you are quite sure that you've done everything with the data that makes sense, tweaking tools is worth a try. But to give it a passable chance of success, you should automate. The number of random experiments you can try manually with a tool is relatively small, and you are probably searching a large space of possible parameter settings. A better approach is to select a small data set, and then create some kind of a script that rapidly tries ranges of settings. Recognize, though, that solutions obtained in this manner often generalize poorly. This is to be expected, given that the solution

was obtained by gaming the sensitivity of your tools to find just the right arcane configuration for this particular training set.

Key Principle Number Eight

Be systematic, consistent, and thorough; don't lose the forest for the trees

It is very easy when you get into the heat of the information chase to begin trying long sequences of ad hoc experiments, hoping that something good will happen. When experimentation is run in an ad hoc manner, the risk is that the experimentation will not be systematic, won't adequately cover the problem space, and will miss discoveries by leaving parts of the problem unexplored. Documentation and other methods designed to reduce errors also tend to suffer. When operating in an ad hoc manner, it's easy to begin focusing on minutiae in the data, and lose sight of the fact that principled analysis is much more likely to be effective against a difficult problem than is luck. You don't choose a career by flipping coins, and you can't conduct good data science that way either.

Key Principle Number Nine

Document the work so it is reproducible

Just as in software engineering and hardware engineering, configuration management and version control is absolutely essential in data mining projects. In some ways it's even more important to apply good documentation standards and audit control to data mining efforts, because these are by nature experimental: procedures for reproducing particular processes don't yet exist. I've had the experience of making valuable discoveries in complex data sets, and then becoming so excited that I go into ad hoc mode before carefully documenting how I initially got them. Unless new processes are immediately documented, there is the very real possibility that you will be unable to reproduce the original breakthrough. This is a very frustrating position to be in: you know that the gold nugget is there; you've seen it and touched it but you can no longer find it.

To avoid this, when I do data mining work I keep a little notepad window open on my desktop so I can document the details of experiments as I perform them: what input files were used, what tool settings were made, what data conditioning sequence was applied, etc. This helps me reproduce any results obtained.

However, the best way to document work for reliable auditing and replication is to conduct the steps from script files that are executed automatically. In this way, not only is the process completely and unambiguously documented at the moment it is conducted, but it's easy to rerun the experiment later as well if necessary.

Key Principle Number Ten

Collaborate with team members, experts, and users to avoid surprises

We are not talking about good surprises here. Most surprises in science and engineering are not good. Data miners who are not DEs will discover things that DEs already know, and this is OK. The response to amazing discoveries must include review by a DE who can assess the practical value of pursuing them, because they might be well-known facts about the domain. If no mechanism for DE feedback is in place, much time will probably be spent rediscovering and documenting things that the expert already knows.

Another situation that can arise is the discovery of patterns in complex data that are real, but have no practical value in the solution of the users' problem. I remember an activity during which I discovered a number of interesting patterns I was fairly sure had not been seen before. After devoting a lot of time and effort to the extraction and characterization of these patterns, I brought them to a DE for review. The expert pointed out that the patterns I discovered were real patterns that did exist in the data, and they were not wellknown. They also had no value because they were noise artifacts randomly created during the collection of this particular data set, and would never occur again.

You don't want to surprise the user too much. Even good surprises can have bad effects, because they disrupt plans and introduce technical uncertainty. It is important to keep both DEs and users engaged as mining work proceeds, so that as progress is made through the prototyping cycles, everyone is carried along in their understanding at essentially the same level. In this way, when the final delivery is made, everyone knows what to expect because they have seen the results unfold, and have a stake in it because they were involved. The most certain way to produce satisfied customers is to meet their expectations. Those expectations can change during the course of the project, but there won't be a surprise if everyone is engaged.

Key Principle Number Eleven

Focus on the goal: maximum value to the user within cost and schedule

Data mining activities are undertaken to satisfy user needs. Data miners who love their analytics, their tools, and their methods can become distracted when interesting patterns are found or unexpected discoveries are made. These can initiate rabbit trails that cause the effort to go off track in pursuit of things that are interesting to the miner but not helpful to the user. It's important to remember that no matter what happens during the mining effort, the goal is to provide value to the user, and to do so within the constraints of cost and schedule.

TYPE OF MODELS: DESCRIPTIVE, PREDICTIVE, FORENSIC

Like every well-designed process, data mining proceeds toward a goal. For almost all data mining efforts, this goal can be thought of as a model of some aspect of the problem domain. These models are of three kinds: descriptive, predictive, and forensic. Understanding the differences brings us to the notion of a domain ontology.

Domain Ontologies as Models

For philosophers, an ontology is a theory of being. It is an attempt to conceptualize answers to certain fundamental questions, such as: What is reality? Do things have meaning? What can be known?

In data mining, ontology has a similar meaning. Formally speaking, *an ontology for a data set* is a representational scheme that provides a consistent, coherent, unifying description of the domain data in context. Loosely speaking, an ontology for a data set is an interpretation of the data that reveals its meaning (s) by explaining its characteristics (sources, history, relationships, connotations). These representations are called *models*. Models represent ontologies in various ways: as consistent sets of equations describing data relationships and patterns (*mathematical models*), as coherent collections of empirical laws or principles (*scientific models*), etc.

When models merely describe patterns in data, they are called *descriptive models*. When models process patterns in data, they are called *predictive models*. When models discover or explain patterns in data, they are called *forensic models*. In practice, models often have elements of all three; the distinctions among them are not always clear.

The process by which scientists devise physical theories (the so-called scientific method) is a good example of a systematic development strategy for an ontology. The scientist comes to the experimental data with a minimum of *a priori* assumptions, intending to formulate and test a model that will explain the data. The scientific method is, in fact, one particular incarnation of the general data mining process.

Looking at how data has been used by scientists through history, we see an evolutionary development

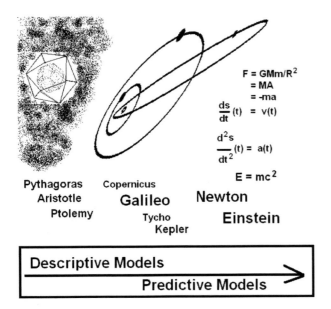

$$F = GMm/R^2$$
$$= MA$$
$$= -ma$$
$$\frac{ds}{dt}(t) = v(t)$$
$$\frac{d^2s}{dt^2}(t) = a(t)$$
$$E = mc^2$$

Pythagoras   Copernicus
Aristotle   **Galileo**   **Newton**
Ptolemy   Tycho
Kepler   **Einstein**

Descriptive Models
Predictive Models ⟶

Fig. 4 Cosmology of the solar system.

through three stages: descriptive; predictive; and explanatory use of data.

Early scientific models were long on description, short on prediction, and shorter on coherent understanding. In many ways, the maturity of a scientific discipline can be assessed by where it lies along this progression.

This is seen in its classic form in development of the cosmology of the solar system. The Pythagorean and Aristotelian models were mostly descriptive, with predictive and forensic components based mostly upon philosophical speculation. Ptolemy created a descriptive model that was useful for prediction, but it was ultimately made subservient to a philosophical model that hindered its development. It took a revolution in thought, begun by Copernicus and Galileo, and completed by Newton, to correct and extend Ptolemy's patchwork cosmology to a coherent system derivable in a rational way from first principles (Fig. 4).

The same three modes (description, prediction, and explanation) that are operative in other instances of scientific reasoning are seen in data mining. They lie in the same natural hierarchy from simplest to most complex: descriptive, predictive, and forensic data mining.

Descriptive Models

Descriptive applications are the simplest; they use data to describe its source or context. This is simple because it leaves the work of interpretation entirely to the recipient: descriptive data is what it is, and says exactly (and only) what it says. Data mining operating in this mode produces meta-data: descriptive statistics such as averages, counts, rates, charts, and plots.

Predictive Models

Predictive applications of data are somewhat more complex, in that they add to the data some external assumptions about repeatability and fidelity. Prediction is data in action, the observed facts of past experience moving into the present and future. However, prediction is almost always based upon mere correlation: when these data are observed, certain conditions often co-occur. The point is, while this might look like intelligence, it can be done quite well without having any authentic understanding of the data at all. David Hume, the British philosopher, referred to this kind of reliable coincidence as the "constant conjunction of ideas": it looks like implication or causation, but it is really an unexplained sequence for which exceptions have not yet been observed.

Forensic Models

Forensic applications are the most sophisticated data mining applications, because they interpret data in light of some context. This is an act of assigning meaning to symbolic patterns; in so doing, forensics generates semantic material from syntactic material. This is not just an enrichment process, but an elevation from one realm to another. This elevates data from the level of sense experience to understanding. This is data mining at its best.

DATA MINING METHODOLOGIES

Like any process, data mining can be carried out either haphazardly or systematically. While there is no universally accepted data mining process standard, there are several contenders for the position of de facto standard. Among these, two are preeminent, due largely to their association with widely used products: Sample, Explore, Modify, Model, Assess (SEMMA), created by the SAS Institute and supported by the tool SAS Enterprise Miner; and CRoss-Industry Standard Process for data mining, created by a consortium consisting of NCR, Daimler-Chrysler, SPSS, and OHRA, and supported by the tool SPSS Clementine.

A review of the various data mining processes that have been proposed as industry standards leaves one with the impression that underneath it all, roughly the same process is being described in different ways. This conclusion is supported by the fact that proponents of competing process standards rarely debate the merits of their favored process. Instead, they focus on how well their favored process works when applied in conjunction with their favored data mining tool. This makes sense given that the creators of the most popular processes are closely associated with tool developers.

The principal implication of all this is that, in actual practice, most data mining activities conducted by experienced analysts proceed in about the same general way: data are gathered, conditioned, and analyzed, giving descriptive models; then if desired, the results of the analysis are used to construct, validate, and field models. Each of these activities has multiple steps, requires the application of particular techniques, and has its own best practice. It is these steps, techniques, and practices that data mining process standards seek to specify.

Rather than sacrifice generality by describing the ad hoc details of just one of the competing standards, or blur the fundamentals by trying to survey them all, the following data mining process discussion will be conducted at a higher level of generality. With this done, each of the competing process standards will be seen as customizations for a particular problem type or tool set.

Conventional System Development: Waterfall Process

The standard development methodology used in many types of engineering is referred to as the Waterfall Process. In this process, projects proceed in order through a sequence of planning and development activities that culminates in the delivery of a capability specified by the user at the beginning of the effort.

This approach has some nice characteristics, and some shortcomings. On the plus side, it is inherently linear (in time), and has the look and feel of an orderly process that can be planned and managed. At each step along the way, you have some idea of how you are doing against the original plan, and how much work is left to do. It facilitates manpower and resource planning, and supports the prediction of project events. Because it has natural temporal and effort-level components, it supports cost estimation, and replanning if necessary.

On the minus side, it requires important decisions to be made at a time in the project when the least information is available. Users must fully express their requirements before work begins, and the resources required to cope with unanticipated problems and risks must be estimated in advance. Often, assumptions must be made about critical issues before they are fully understood.

In particular, since data mining has investigative activities woven throughout, the Waterfall Process is not at all natural for data mining projects. How do you schedule discovery? What skill mix do you need to implement an algorithm that doesn't exist to solve a problem you don't know about? If a discovery halfway through the project proves that a completely new approach with new goals is needed, what do you do?

A development process that can accommodate the impact of changes in problem understanding and project goals is needed for data mining: a rapid prototyping process. This and related methods are referred to as examples of Rapid Application Development (RAD) methodologies.

Data Mining as Rapid Prototyping

In practice, data mining is almost always conducted in a Rapid Prototyping fashion. Data miners using this methodology perform project work in a sequence of time-limited, goal-focused cycles (called spirals). Before jumping into the details of each step of this methodology, we begin with a summary overview of the steps that constitute a generic spiral:

- Step 1: Problem Definition
- Step 2: Data Evaluation
- Step 3: Feature Extraction and Enhancement
- Step 4a: Prototyping Plan
- Step 4b: Prototyping/Model Development
- Step 5: Model Evaluation
- Step 6: Implementation

The order and content of these steps will vary from spiral to spiral to accommodate project events. This is very different from the Waterfall Process, and addresses most of the issues that make the Waterfall Process ill-suited to data mining projects. Most importantly, rapid prototyping enables data mining researchers and developers to accommodate and benefit from incremental discovery, and holds at abeyance final decisions on some requirements until they can be settled in an informed and principled way.

The flexibility inherent in an RAD methodology does not mean that data mining efforts are undisciplined. On the contrary, using an RAD methodology in an undisciplined manner usually results in the waste of resources, and perhaps project failure. This puts the onus on the program manager and technical lead to make sure that everything done during a spiral is done for a reason, that the outcomes are carefully evaluated in light of those reasons and that the team does not lose sight of the long-term goal: satisfying user needs within cost and schedule.

A GENERIC DATA MINING PROCESS

More formal characterizations of the data mining process are discussed elsewhere in this encyclopedia. However, we will complete our informal characterization of a single spiral by reciting the process as a two-paragraph narrative:

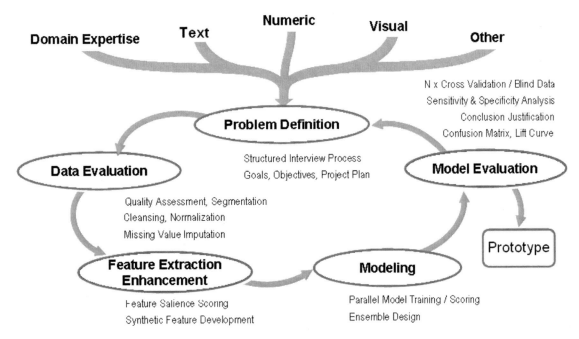

Fig. 5 Spiral methodology.

We begin by developing a clear understanding of what is to be accomplished in collaboration with the user. We then interview subject-matter experts using a (more or less formal) knowledge acquisition protocol. Next, we prepare the available data (evidence and hypotheses) for analysis. This involves inferring descriptive information in the form of meta-data (schemas), demographics (counts, ranges, distributions, visualizations), and data problems (conformation problems, outliers, gaps, class collisions, and population imbalance, all of which are covered by other entries).

Based upon this descriptive modeling work, data are repaired if necessary, and transformed for analysis. Appropriate pattern processing methods and applications are used to extract and enhance features for model construction. Appropriate modeling paradigm (s) is/are selected (e.g., rule-based system, decision tree, and support vector machine) and then integrated. The transformed data are then segmented, and models are built, evaluated, optimized, and applied. The results are interpreted in light of the goals for this spiral, and hypotheses and plans are adjusted. All work is documented and discussed with DEs.

Each of the steps in a spiral advance us around the spiral found in Fig. 5.

Each of the steps in a RAD data mining methodology will be addressed in detail in the following sections. Keep in mind that RAD is intended to be a flexible process that enables researchers and developers to accommodate both new information and changing user requirements. It is not intended, nor is it recommended, that the work pattern described here be imposed in a rigid manner because to do so would eliminate its principal advantages.

RAD SKILL SET DESIGNATORS

In later discussions of the RAD methodology, we will have occasion to discuss specific skill sets as they are tasked during the steps of an RAD effort. For our purposes in understanding the RAD methodology, it is assumed these skills will be held by specialists designated by the following titles and their abbreviations:

CE: Cognitive Engineer (the data mining analyst)

DE: DE (usually a customer/end-user having in-depth operational knowledge of the domain)

DO: DOs (usually MIS personnel who collect/manage the user data)

PM: Program Manager (manager who can make cost/schedule decisions for the effort)

SE: Software/Database Engineer (application developer)

SUMMARY

Having read this entry, you now have a deeper understanding of the fundamental principles of data mining. You understand data mining as a process of discovery and exploitation that is conducted in multiple spirals consisting of multiple steps. You have been introduced to the steps that constitute an RAD cycle. Most importantly, you can explain the relative strengths and weaknesses of conventional and RAD development methodologies as they relate to data mining projects. Now that you have a summary understanding of data mining as a structured process, you are ready to begin your study of the individual steps that comprise it.

Data Mining: Supervised Learning

Monte F. Hancock, Jr.
Chief Scientist, Celestech, Inc., Melbourne, Florida, U.S.A.

Abstract

The purpose of this entry is to address supervised learning, the most common application of data mining technology for producing operational applications. It concerns the use of data mining methods to create detectors, classifiers, estimators, and other decision support tools for users operating in complicated environments. The aspect that distinguishes this genre from the others is that here we are looking through data for instances of known patterns: patterns that have been seen before. A representative sample of the patterns of each type to be classified is available or can be generated.

GOALS

This genre section will address supervised learning, the most common application of data mining technology for producing operational applications. This type of development uses data mining methods to create detectors, classifiers, estimators, and other decision support tools for users operating in complicated environments.

Examples:

- Biometric identification (known fingerprint, known face, known voice, etc.)
- Object recognition (vehicle model classification from imagery/sound)
- Pattern matching (signal classification, e.g., AM vs. FM)
- Optical Character Recognition (OCR)
- Detection of known computer viruses

INTRODUCTION

This genre addresses problems whose solutions are instances of *supervised learning*. Supervised learning is probably the most mature application of data mining technology, with fundamental techniques that substantially predate the advent of automated computing.

The term *supervised* refers to the fact that when conducting supervised learning, we have been given ground truth assignments (the correct answer) for each of the entities being learned. The inputs to the training process consist of pairs: a feature vector containing attributes of the entity to be classified, and the answer that is to be associated with it (the ground truth). Ground truth can be obtained in a number of ways and often it is the stored outcomes for previously collected historical data. Sometimes ground truth is generated by an "oracle."

The term *oracle* refers to any mechanism, manual or automated, for determining the ground truth associated with inputs to be classified. Usually it is either a human expert who manually tags feature vectors with ground truth, or an existing classifier.

To perform supervised learning we create a training set that contains feature vectors representing objects or entities to be classified, along with ground-truth assignments for each. The goal of the learning process is the creation of an automated application that can accurately classify or infer the groundtruth of entities based upon their features.

REPRESENTATIVE EXAMPLE OF SUPERVISED LEARNING: BUILDING A CLASSIfiER

The following is an extended, detailed example that goes through the various stages of building a classifier for a supervised learning problem. It is a real, well-known problem (Fisher's Iris Problem) that is small enough to dig into. Everything done here is real and typical of how an experienced data mining expert might proceed.

PROBLEM DESCRIPTION

The problem description begins with an initial discussion with the customer and domain experts as follows:

The customer says: The problem is to build a predictive model that ingests size measurements taken from a particular type of a flower, and determine to which specific variety the flower belongs.

The data miner notes: This problem is the assignment of an entity to one of a fixed number of known

Encyclopedia of Information Systems and Technology, DOI: 10.1081/E-EIST-120053813

1	5.1	3.5	1.4	0.2	1	0.856826
2	4.9	3	1.4	0.2	1	0.200967
3	4.7	3.2	1.3	0.2	1	0.940021
4	4.6	3.1	1.5	0.2	1	0.754746
5	5	3.6	1.4	0.2	1	0.559449
6	5.4	3.9	1.7	0.4	1	0.75296
7	4.6	3.4	1.4	0.3	1	0.668683
8	5	3.4	1.5	0.2	1	0.798224
9	4.4	2.9	1.4	0.2	1	0.74738
10	4.9	3.1	1.5	0.1	1	0.912014
11	5.4	3.7	1.5	0.2	1	0.394846
12	4.8	3.4	1.6	0.2	1	0.576837
13	4.8	3	1.4	0.1	1	0.0615
14	4.3	3	1.1	0.1	1	0.874126
15	5.8	4	1.2	0.2	1	0.256284
16	5.7	4.4	1.5	0.4	1	0.156229
17	5.4	3.9	1.3	0.4	1	0.560522
18	5.1	3.5	1.4	0.3	1	0.866003
19	5.7	3.8	1.7	0.3	1	0.184352
20	5.1	3.8	1.5	0.3	1	0.206943

Appended a column of random numbers

128	6.1	3	4.9	1.8	3	0.000105
42	4.5	2.3	1.3	0.3	1	0.006435
21	5.4	3.4	1.7	0.2	1	0.007661
30	4.7	3.2	1.6	0.2	1	0.030055
111	6.5	3.2	5.1	2	3	0.03157
115	5.8	2.8	5.1	2.4	3	0.05138
5	5	3.6	1.4	0.2	1	0.053255
56	5.7	2.8	4.5	1.3	2	0.06577
109	6.7	2.5	5.8	1.8	3	0.069724
87	6.7	3.1	4.7	1.5	2	0.075649
131	7.4	2.8	6.1	1.9	3	0.077536
69	6.2	2.2	4.5	1.5	2	0.104858
84	6	2.7	5.1	1.6	2	0.106428
32	5.4	3.4	1.5	0.4	1	0.109537
112	6.4	2.7	5.3	1.9	3	0.118933
41	5	3.5	1.3	0.3	1	0.121458
51	7	3.2	4.7	1.4	2	0.127169
113	6.8	3	5.5	2.1	3	0.132538
34	5.5	4.2	1.4	0.2	1	0.134935
100	5.7	2.8	4.1	1.3	2	0.143358

Sorted all columns using random column

Fig. 1 Fisher's data set.[3,4]

Note: Measurements are in centimeters.
VID = Vector ID (merely a one-up count), Len = Length, Wid = Width, Var = Variety (Species), set. = setosa, vers. = versicolor, virg. = virginica.

categories based upon entity attributes. Therefore, this is a classification problem. The solution will be a classifier. In addition:

- The attributes are sizes, so they provide continuous numeric features.
- Visualization is often very informative when features are numeric.

Data Description: Background Research/Planning

This activity includes discussions with domain experts, research before any data has been seen.

The customer says: We will use a very famous, real data set: the Fisher's Iris Data Set. The Fisher's Iris Data Set consists of four measurements taken from each

Correlation	sepal length	sepal width	petal length	petal width	class
sepal length	1.00				
sepal width	-0.12	1.00			
petal length	0.87	-0.43	1.00		
petal width	0.82	-0.37	0.96	1.00	
class	0.78	-0.43	0.95	0.96	1.00

Pairwise Pearson Correlation Ceofficients for features and ground truth

Fig. 2 Descriptive statistics for the Fisher's Iris Data Set.

of 150 iris flowers. These data were used by Ronald Aylmer Fisher in 1936 to develop what is now called the Fisher Discriminant, a linear classification technique. The Fisher data set is balanced by class, having 50 samples of each of three iris varieties: 50 iris *setosa*, 50 iris *versicolor*, and 50 iris *virginica*.

From each flower, four measurements were taken (in centimeters): sepal length, sepal width, petal length, and petal width. The entire data set is given in a tabular form in Fig. 1 at the end of this entry.

The data miner notes:

- The problem is very lowdimensional (at most four raw features). It might make sense to consider synthesizing some additional features.

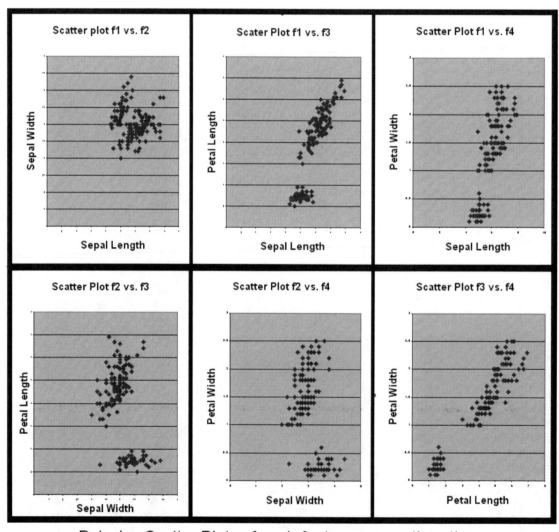

Pairwise Scatter Plots of each feature versus the others

Fig. 3 Avoidance of co-location bias.

- The number of ground-truth classes is very small (only three). This eliminates a major source of computational complexity.
- There are not very many feature vectors. Partitioning the data into more than two or three parts is probably not a good idea. Also, with few examples, the developed model might not generalize well.
- The problem is balanced by class (same number of instances of each class), so it will not initially be necessary to replicate instances, decimate instances, or modify the classifier objective function.
- It might be helpful to do some general background reading about irises to be able to get maximum benefit from future discussions with domain experts.
- Do a literature search: get Fisher's 1936 paper and his 1950 book. Check out a copy of Duda and Hart,[1] a book that describes an analysis of this data set.
- Given the size and apparent low complexity of this problem, the existing tools and infrastructure should be adequate.
- Ask the customer for access to the existing document on the problem and the data.
- Ask the customer how your classifier will be deployed. If it must be integrated with a legacy system, ask for access to system documentation and concept of operations. Ask to see the legacy system in operation and to talk with users.

Descriptive Modeling of Data: Preprocessing and Data Conditioning

This activity begins once data are received.

- **Audit the data for quality.** The preconditioning activity begins with an assessment of the syntactic quality of the data. This involves checking for formatting and alignment problems, missing data, repeated data, improper rounding (which can lead to loss of precision), and consistency with available data documentation. This process should be at least partially manual, for two reasons: first, there are some things you can only see by actually observing the data; does it "look" right? Secondly, this will help you develop some familiarity with and intuition for the problem space. However, for large data sets, most of the auditing process will have to be automated. At the very least, every datum should be range-checked, and all gaps noted.
- **Format/conform data if required.** It will probably be necessary to reformat some of the data for ingestion by the analysis tools to be used. This process should be automated to insure efficiency and repeatability. This can be a time-consuming process, and

will probably require the generation of some ad hoc software.

- **Compile descriptive statistics on entire data set.** This is the first authentic analytic activity. It is here that the miner will get the first real look at the data set as a distribution. Many databases and spreadsheets have integrated tools for computing descriptive statistics. Fig. 2 shows a sample descriptive statistics report for the four features in the Fisher's data set.
- Carry out any necessary corrections and automate if possible (gap filling, outlier detection, and processing, etc.). This process should elevate the data to analysis-ready quality.
- Randomize the order of records to avoid co-location bias. This step is not necessarily required, but should be performed if data are provided in a flat file. Data in a flat file are in a certain order for some reason, and you don't want that unknown reason biasing your partitioning operation. A simple way to order-randomize a flat file is to append a column of random numbers. By sorting the entire record on this random column, the order of the records is randomized (Fig. 3).
- **Partition the data.** Once the data are order-randomized, they can be partitioned by just grabbing blocks of sequential records. This will give a representative sample in the sense that the relative frequencies of occurrence of each class will be reflected in the resulting partitions. The Fisher's data are already balanced by class, so no special processing is required.
- In the case that certain classes have very few representatives, you might have to replicate instances of residual classes to guarantee they occur in each partition. Be careful, though, that the test file examples are not present in other partitions. This would invalidate your blind test results. For this activity, the data were divided into two, equal-sized, 75-vector partitions: TRAIN. CSV and BLIND. CSV.
- **Compute pair-wise correlations.** Using only the calibration (or training) data, compute the Pearson's correlation coefficients of each pair of features, and for each feature with the ground truth. The feature-to-feature correlations will tell you whether the features are independent, and the feature-to-ground truth correlations will provide information on the accessible information content of each feature individually. The correlations for the Fisher's data are in Fig. 4.
- Notice that the petal length and petal width are highly correlated with the ground truth class (rho of 0.95 and 0.96, respectively). This indicates these features are probably very rich in information. However, they are highly correlated with each other (0.96), so they are not independent information sources. It might make sense to use only one of them.
- **Visualize data.** Visualization allows the user to interact at an intuitive level with the data. Fig. 5 provides

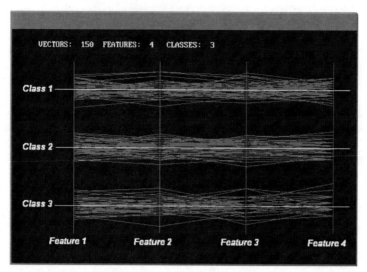

Inselberg Plot of Fisher Iris Data

Fig. 4 Pearson's correlation coefficients.

some scatter plots depicting the entire data set as one feature plotted against another. In the plot, two coherent aggregations can be seen visually. Keep in mind there is no reason to believe that the two aggregations seen in each plot are the same aggregations in each plot.

- There is also no reason to believe the two aggregations seen in any particular scatter plot are in any way related to the ground truth classes for our problem. If this happens to be the case, that is great; but it need not be. Scatter plots are helpful, but features can be correlated pair-wise without being jointly correlated. Therefore, we need to look at the data in it for native four-dimensional feature space. One way to do this is to use an Inselberg plot (Fig. 6).

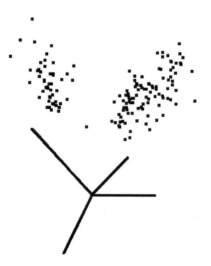

Fisher data set in its "native" four-dimensional space

Fig. 5 Visualization of feature comparisons.

- Full spatial visualization (Fig. 7) reveals that two aggregations actually exist in the higher-dimensional feature space.

Decide whether some sort of registration/normalization is needed. For example, it might be reasonable to synchronize or z-score the data. If some correction process is to be performed, compute the correction parameters from the calibration set, and not the blind set. Apply the parameters to all sets to *calibrate*. Calibration must eventually be automated since this same calibration must be applied to any data to be processed by the fielded classifier. The calibration parameters derived from the calibration set will also be used to condition blind data for processing. Perform a preprocessing data audit to minimize the chances that the data have not been inadvertently biased or degraded.

Data Exploitation: Feature Extraction and Enhancement

- **Code/quantize/transform features (if necessary).** This is usually done early on because of limitations in the available tools, but this is also done during later spirals in anticipation of improved classifier performance.
- **Compute feature correlations.** You are simply redoing the correlation computation. This is necessary because transformations and corrections that have been applied to the data will change their correlations with each other and with the ground truth.
- **Synthesize/winnow features.** This is an opportunity to combine the existing features in a nonlinear way with the hope of improving performance. This can be done in a principled way by analysis of scatter plots;

Correlation	Sepal Length	Sepal Width	Petal Length	Petal Width	Synthesized	Class
Sepal Length	1.00					
Sepal Width	-0.12	1.00				
Petal Length	0.87	-0.43	1.00			
Petal Width	0.82	-0.37	0.96	1.00		
Synthesized	-0.32	0.31	-0.42	-0.38	1.00	
Class	0.78	-0.43	0.95	0.96	-0.31	1.00

Feature-to-feature and feature to Ground Truth correlation after Z-Score Normalization

Fig. 6   Visualization of native feature space.

this is an esoteric topic that will not be addressed here. We will synthesize a new feature for the Fisher's data using the following nonlinear combination method:

$$f5 = \sqrt{(|(f1-f3)|\ |(f2-f4)|)}$$

- This is an ad hoc nonlinear transform. It is the product of the difference of the lengths and the difference of the widths. The intent is to form a nonlinear mixture of strong features (*f3* and *f4*) and weak features (*f1* and *f2*). Hopefully, this will expose some information about the ground truth, while being independent of the other features.
- We then z-score each column of data to statistically normalize the features. The new correlation matrix after normalization is in Fig. 8.
- Notice the synthesized feature is not strongly correlated with the ground truth (−0.31), so it isn't a strong feature; but neither is it strongly correlated with the other features, so perhaps it reveals some new information. Experimentation will tell whether the synthesized feature should be retained or not.

Model Selection and Development

The data are now five-dimensional, having the original four raw features and the synthesized feature. There are three ground truth classes. All indications are that this is not a difficult problem, so a very simple two-layer neural network is probably sufficient (tests show this is true), but for our illustration we choose a more powerful three-layer architecture. I typically use a few more neurons in the input layer than there are features, and about twice that amount in the hidden layer (cf. the Kolmogorov Neural Network Mapping Existence Theorem 2).[2] The output layer for this neural network has one neuron for each ground truth class, since these outputs are generating beliefs that the input is in their class. The output neuron that produces the greatest belief value determines the classification decision of the neural network.

The architecture of this neural network is depicted in Fig. 9. There are many neural network architectures; this one is called a Multi-Layer Perceptron (MLP), since the neurons that perform the transforms are arranged in layers. This neural network has three layers. Numeric data comes into each box at the bottom, is transformed, and is fed-forward to the next layer out of the top. For

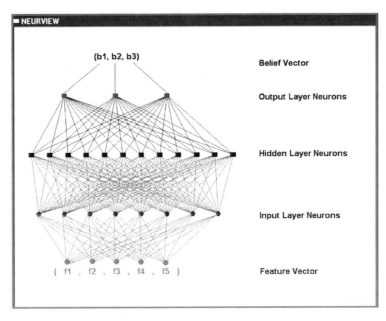

Fig. 7   Spatial visualization in high-dimensional space.

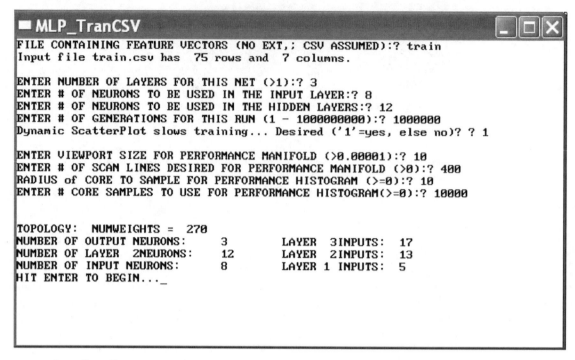

Application to train a neural network to solve the Iris problem

Fig. 8 Feature correlation after z-score normalization.

this reason, these neural networks are sometimes referred to as feed-forward neural networks.

Model Training

An MLP trainer was used to implement the architecture in Fig. 9. It used a gradient-assisted Monte Carlo method to adjust the interconnect weights to maximize an accuracy score. Total training time was less than 60 seconds. The main input display page for the trainer is shown in Fig. 10. It shows the parameters selected by the user, and states the number of neurons chosen for each layer.

```
TIME OUTPUT GENERATED:   22:57:03
DATA FILE CONTAINING SIGNATURES:
NUMBER OF SIGNATURES PROCESSED:  75
TOPOLOGY: |5|8|12|3|  NUMWEIGHTS:  270
NUMBER OF TRAINING PASSES: 1000000|
NETWORK SATURATION: 65.6872
GEOMETRIC MEAN OF CLASS PRECISIONS:  100%
PERCENTAGE OF SIGNATURES CORRECTLY CLASSIFIED:   100%
AGGREGATE NETWORK CERTAINTY OF CLASSIFICATION:  99.99986

CONFUSION MATRIX:

  1|     24      0      0
  2|      0     27      0
  3|      0      0     24
```

Fig. 9 MLP   neural network.

Model Evaluation

The neural network trainer produces certain diagnostic and performance metrics as it learns, and displays these to the user. For this training experiment, the neural network rapidly trained to 100% accuracy and very high certainty. This is not always a good thing, since over-training might have occurred. Blind testing should tell us whether the neural network generalizes or not. The performance metrics for the neural network on the training set are in Fig. 11.

The trained neural network was then used to classify the vectors in the blind set, with the results shown in Fig. 12.

This result (92%) is probably not bad for a first experiment. The confusion matrix shows we are misclassifying four class 2 vectors as class 3s, and two

```
GEOMETRIC MEAN OF CLASS PRECISIONS:  91.35967%
PERCENTAGE OF SIGNATURES CORRECTLY CLASSIFIED:  92%
AGGREGATE NETWORK CERTAINTY OF CLASSIFICATION:  85.01221%

CONFUSION MATRIX:

  1|     26      0      0
  2|      0     19      4
  3|      0      2     24
```

Results for Blind Test set: 92% of the test vectors were correctly classified

Fig. 10 Neural network training example.

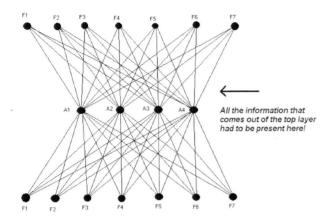

A Neural Network with a "bottleneck" compresses data

Fig. 11 Confusion matrix of training data.

class 3 vectors as class 2s. This is not surprising, since it is classes 2 and 3 that are encroaching on each other.

It appears that the classification ability of the neural network generalizes fairly well to data the machine has not seen before. If we are satisfied with the confusion matrix and speed of the neural network, we can deploy it. If not, we can perform some additional training experiments, and/or go back for another development spiral to enhance features, or try other types of neural architectures and classifiers.

SPECIFIC CHALLENGES, PROBLEMS, AND PITFALLS OF SUPERVISED LEARNING

This section describes the inherent challenges of problems in this genre, and suggests appropriate methods for addressing them.

High-Dimensional Feature Vectors (PCA, Winnowing)

The amount of time and storage required to train a classifier is a function of how difficult the problem is, how complex the classifier is, and how large the training set is. The most important factor in training set size is not the number of vectors, since the training effort is usually directly proportional to this. The real data complexity issue is the number of features in each vector.

A trainable machine is attempting to learn some relationship among the features in a training vector that determine the class to which it should be assigned. The number of possible groupings of features grows exponentially with the number of features. If training is taking too long, you will usually reduce computation time by removing a few features, rather than by reducing the number of vectors.

This super-linear growth in complexity with increasing dimension is often referred to as *the curse of dimensionality*. It presents the data miner with a difficult decision: Is the information gained by adding more features worth the performance cost? This question becomes particularly vexing when the information gain can't even be measured because training with the additional features is too time-consuming an experiment.

For reasons of efficiency in space and time, elimination of unnecessary complexity, and avoidance of numerical problems (overtraining and multicolinearity), the *best* model is usually the simplest one that gives acceptable performance (time, size, accuracy, understandability). Such a model is called *parsimonious*.

The practical value of parsimonious models makes effective feature winnowing an essential capability. One dimension reduction, principal component analysis (PCA), has been addressed earlier. We now present an example of another automated feature winnowing method, the Encoder-Decoder Network as an illustration.

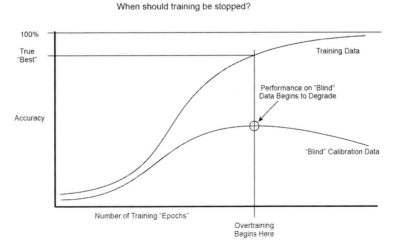

Fig. 12 Blind set classification of trained neural network.

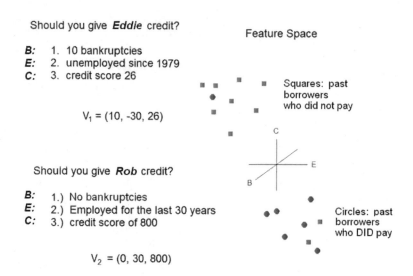

Fig. 13 Neural network bottleneck.

Many other methods can be found in the research literature.

An Encoder-Decoder Network is a neural network that has an *hourglass* architecture. The idea is simple: The neural network is trained to produce input feature vectors from a data set (these enter at the bottom) as its outputs (these appear at the top). If this is possible, it means that all or most of the information in the original vector has to be present in the output of the *bottleneck* at the middle layer. We throw away the top layer, and use the bottom two layers as a winnowing engine for this problem; in this case, reducing the dimension from 7 to 4 (Fig. 13).

Not Enough Data

Sometimes usable data is in short supply. Perhaps there are few instances available with ground truth, or some important class is underrepresented. In such a case, it might not be possible to divide the data into separate segments for training, calibration, and validation. How should we proceed?

If the data were produced by some process for which parameters are known, it might be possible to construct a simulation that can be used to generate data. This is often the case for queuing problems, such as creating a plan for scheduling elevators in a tall building, sequencing things for processing by a server bank, vehicle traffic models, etc.

If this is not possible, sometimes a replication strategy can be used: include copies or slight variants of existing data to increase the vector count (usually in an unprincipled manner). If possible, this should be done without making significant changes to the data distribution or relative proportion of ground truth classes.

Finally, a commonly used strategy is called. This strategy partitions the data into N segments, numbered 1

though N. A model is trained on all the data but that in segment 1, and blind tested on segment 1. This model is then discarded. A model is then trained on all the data but that in segment two, and blind tested on segment two. In this way, N separate models are trained and blind tested on a small holdback set. The model to be deployed is trained on all the data and the average of the results of the N blind tests provides an estimate of this model's blind performance. In the research literature, a frequently used value for N is 10.

Too Much Data

Having too much data is more of a storage problem than a data mining problem. It is usually not too difficult to select representative samples from a large corpus to obtain sets that are of a manageable size. If there is a large amount of data available for modeling, it probably makes sense to escrow some data to cover contingencies that might arise (e.g., additional blind test sets are needed).

Unbalanced Data

When building classifiers using supervised learning methods, an important but oft overlooked problem is class *imbalance*. This occurs when the ground truth classes are not represented in the same proportions. In this case, some classes occur much more frequently than others do. This causes problems because classes that are more abundant will tend to have a disproportionate effect on the training process. This can be a serious concern because it is usually the rarer, underrepresented classes that are of the most interest in data mining applications.

There are several balancing strategies. Replication (including multiple copies) of underrepresented data, and decimation (removing copies) of overrepresented data is one approach. Another is to use a simulator or some other synthesis mechanism to generate additional vectors of the underrepresented classes. Replication, decimation, and synthesis are easy to employ, but because they change the class proportions, they can bias the training data if not performed carefully.

Algorithmic methods can also be used to compensate for class imbalance. These adjust the learning algorithm so that rare classes are allowed to have a greater impact in the training process. For example, if there are twice as many class As as class Bs, the effect of class Bs in the training algorithm can be doubled. This doesn't always produce good results, but works often enough that it is worth trying.

A related method is classical *boosting*. In boosting, vectors in the training set that are misclassified are presented for learning more frequently in subsequent epochs, giving the learning machine extra practice on vectors it is missing. Boosting also addressed the imbalance problem, since underrepresented classes are more likely to be misclassified.

Overtraining

Suppose that during training, the classifier is allowed to process a semi-blind data set (vectors that are not part of the training set, but are used for diagnostics during training). A sample taken from the calibration set is often used for this purpose. As long as performance on this semi-blind set continues to improve, the training process is still learning facts about the problem that will generalize to new data.

However, as training continues, a point is usually reached where performance on the semi-blind set decreases, even though performance on the training data is continuing to improve (Fig. 14). What is going on here?

This is a phenomenon called *overtraining*. The machine is beginning to learn the idiosyncrasies of the training data; coincidences that will not generalize to other data. The machine is *overfitting* the training data, and continuing beyond this point amounts to memorizing the training set. If that's what you want to do, you should be building a database, not a classifier.

Interleaving training epochs with tests using a semi-blind set provides a practical, problem-specific means of determining when supervised training should be stopped. A typical schedule is a one-test epoch for every 100 training epochs; clearly, this is problem dependent.

Noncommensurable Data: Outliers

When processing numeric data, it often happens that different features have different ranges because of the units used to represent them. One feature might be age in years, and another feature might be annual salary in dollars. Here the age feature has a range of around 100,

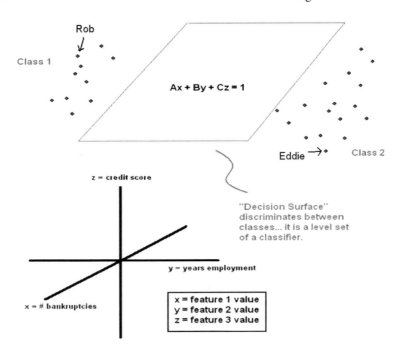

If the training set is representative of the actual problem
domain, new data points should follow the learned patterns.

Fig. 14 Overfitting the training data.

while the salary feature could have a range in the millions. This variability can cause numerical problems when building a trainable model and, most notably, loss of precision. It also makes the data impossible to plot on a scale having uniform axes.

These numeric and plotting problems can be eliminated by normalizing the features into a common range. There are several ways to do this, but some introduce ad hoc nonlinear effects (e.g., applying a log of sigmoid transform to the data).

Another approach is *amplitude normalization*, in which the values for each feature are divided by the largest value assumed by that feature. However, this becomes a problem when there are a small number of values that are much larger in absolute value than most others (e.g., a big outlier). Nearly all the data end up close to 0, with a few instances close in absolute value to 1.

A much better approach is to replace each feature value by the z-score for that feature. Using the calibration set, this is done as follows:

1. Compute the mean value, μ, for the feature.
2. Computer the standard deviation, σ, for the feature.
3. Replace each feature value with its distance above or below the mean in standard deviations:

$$Z_i = \frac{x_i - \mu}{\sigma}$$

Z-score normalization has good properties. One outlier generally has little effect on the scoring, and for many data sets (after z-scoring), almost all data will fall somewhere in the range $[-6, 6]$. An additional benefit is that, since few features should have large z-scores (say, $|z| > 6$), z-scoring provides an objective numeric test for detecting outliers. A rejection threshold can be established early in a data mining project and applied automatically; data exceeding the threshold can be clipped to the maximum or minimum values.

It is very important that data to be processed by a model trained on normalized data be normalized in exactly the same way. For example, the mean and standard deviation used for z-scoring each feature must be saved so it can be used to preprocess data for the fielded model.

Missing Features

The standard imputation techniques described earlier can be applied for filling in missing data for use in supervised learning. However, it is important to determine *why* data are missing. Getting the answer to this question reveals a lot about the domain, and the integrity of its data.

Missing Ground Truth

When ground truth is missing for some vectors, it can sometimes be filled in by reference to historical data, the use of a legacy system, or advice from an expert. A completely automated technique is to mix the untagged data with the Calibration Set, and apply a clustering algorithm. The data with missing ground truth is assigned the same ground truth as the tagged vectors with which it naturally clusters. This last method is preferred, since it is automated and repeatable.

RECOMMENDED DATA MINING ARCHITECTURES FOR SUPERVISED LEARNING

Each problem domain has its own unique aspects, some of which might require adjustments to the generic data mining process. This section addresses data mining process adjustments for this supervised learning.

Supervised learning applications ingest data tagged with ground truth and infer models capable of reproducing this tagging in unseen data. Therefore, most instances of supervised learning are *regressions*: mathematical models that fit a curve to the training data. The term *curve* here is used in a very general sense, since regressions need not have simple, one-dimensional numeric outputs that could be plotted on graph paper. A regression is much more likely to be a fit of some N-dimensional hyperplane to a complicated scatter plot (giving an estimator), or a twisted surface that winds its way between various clusters of points (giving a classifier).

Fig. 15 depicts a classification problem using three features. The scatter plot shows outcomes from previous instances of this decision problem.

Fig. 15 shows that previously, paying and nonpaying customers tend to form separate clusters in the feature space of bankruptcies, employment history, and credit score.

In Fig. 16, a two-dimensional plane serves as a decision surface; problem instances are classified based on the side of the surface on which they fall.

Training the decision model in Fig. 16 was a regression problem; find an equation for some decision surface that separates the ground truth classes. With this illustration in mind, numerous paradigms are seen to be candidates as the model for building supervised classifiers and supervised estimators.

Classifiers

- Linear Discriminant (e.g., as in the credit example given earlier)
- Neural Networks (discrete outputs: MLPs, Boltzmann machines)

VID	Sepal Len	Sepal Wid	Petal Len	Petal Wid	Var	VID	Sepal Len	Sepal Wid	Petal Len	Petal Wid	Var	VID	Sepal Len	Sepal Wid	Petal Len	Petal Wid	Var
1	5.1	3.5	1.4	0.2	*set.*	51	7	3.2	4.7	1.4	*vers.*	101	6.3	3.3	6	2.5	*virg.*
2	4.9	3	1.4	0.2	*set.*	52	6.4	3.2	4.5	1.5	*vers.*	102	5.8	2.7	5.1	1.9	*virg.*
3	4.7	3.2	1.3	0.2	*set.*	53	6.9	3.1	4.9	1.5	*vers.*	103	7.1	3	5.9	2.1	*virg.*
4	4.6	3.1	1.5	0.2	*set.*	54	5.5	2.3	4	1.3	*vers.*	104	6.3	2.9	5.6	1.8	*virg.*
5	5	3.6	1.4	0.2	*set.*	55	6.5	2.8	4.6	1.5	*vers.*	105	6.5	3	5.8	2.2	*virg.*
6	5.4	3.9	1.7	0.4	*set.*	56	5.7	2.8	4.5	1.3	*vers.*	106	7.6	3	6.6	2.1	*virg.*
7	4.6	3.4	1.4	0.3	*set.*	57	6.3	3.3	4.7	1.6	*vers.*	107	4.9	2.5	4.5	1.7	*virg.*
8	5	3.4	1.5	0.2	*set.*	58	4.9	2.4	3.3	1	*vers.*	108	7.3	2.9	6.3	1.8	*virg.*
9	4.4	2.9	1.4	0.2	*set.*	59	6.6	2.9	4.6	1.3	*vers.*	109	6.7	2.5	5.8	1.8	*virg.*
10	4.9	3.1	1.5	0.1	*set.*	60	5.2	2.7	3.9	1.4	*vers.*	110	7.2	3.6	6.1	2.5	*virg.*
11	5.4	3.7	1.5	0.2	*set.*	61	5	2	3.5	1	*vers.*	111	6.5	3.2	5.1	2	*virg.*
12	4.8	3.4	1.6	0.2	*set.*	62	5.9	3	4.2	1.5	*vers.*	112	6.4	2.7	5.3	1.9	*virg.*
13	4.8	3	1.4	0.1	*set.*	63	6	2.2	4	1	*vers.*	113	6.8	3	5.5	2.1	*virg.*
14	4.3	3	1.1	0.1	*set.*	64	6.1	2.9	4.7	1.4	*vers.*	114	5.7	2.5	5	2	*virg.*
15	5.8	4	1.2	0.2	*set.*	65	5.6	2.9	3.6	1.3	*vers.*	115	5.8	2.8	5.1	2.4	*virg.*
16	5.7	4.4	1.5	0.4	*set.*	66	6.7	3.1	4.4	1.4	*vers.*	116	6.4	3.2	5.3	2.3	*virg.*
17	5.4	3.9	1.3	0.4	*set.*	67	5.6	3	4.5	1.5	*vers.*	117	6.5	3	5.5	1.8	*virg.*
18	5.1	3.5	1.4	0.3	*set.*	68	5.8	2.7	4.1	1	*vers.*	118	7.7	3.8	6.7	2.2	*virg.*
19	5.7	3.8	1.7	0.3	*set.*	69	6.2	2.2	4.5	1.5	*vers.*	119	7.7	2.6	6.9	2.3	*virg.*
20	5.1	3.8	1.5	0.3	*set.*	70	5.6	2.5	3.9	1.1	*vers.*	120	6	2.2	5	1.5	*virg.*
21	5.4	3.4	1.7	0.2	*set.*	71	5.9	3.2	4.8	1.8	*vers.*	121	6.9	3.2	5.7	2.3	*virg.*
22	5.1	3.7	1.5	0.4	*set.*	72	6.1	2.8	4	1.3	*vers.*	122	5.6	2.8	4.9	2	*virg.*
23	4.6	3.6	1	0.2	*set.*	73	6.3	2.5	4.9	1.5	*vers.*	123	7.7	2.8	6.7	2	*virg.*
24	5.1	3.3	1.7	0.5	*set.*	74	6.1	2.8	4.7	1.2	*vers.*	124	6.3	2.7	4.9	1.8	*virg.*
25	4.8	3.4	1.9	0.2	*set.*	75	6.4	2.9	4.3	1.3	*vers.*	125	6.7	3.3	5.7	2.1	*virg.*
26	5	3	1.6	0.2	*set.*	76	6.6	3	4.4	1.4	*vers.*	126	7.2	3.2	6	1.8	*virg.*
27	5	3.4	1.6	0.4	*set.*	77	6.8	2.8	4.8	1.4	*vers.*	127	6.2	2.8	4.8	1.8	*virg.*
28	5.2	3.5	1.5	0.2	*set.*	78	6.7	3	5	1.7	*vers.*	128	6.1	3	4.9	1.8	*virg.*
29	5.2	3.4	1.4	0.2	*set.*	79	6	2.9	4.5	1.5	*vers.*	129	6.4	2.8	5.6	2.1	*virg.*
30	4.7	3.2	1.6	0.2	*set.*	80	5.7	2.6	3.5	1	*vers.*	130	7.2	3	5.8	1.6	*virg.*
31	4.8	3.1	1.6	0.2	*set.*	81	5.5	2.4	3.8	1.1	*vers.*	131	7.4	2.8	6.1	1.9	*virg.*
32	5.4	3.4	1.5	0.4	*set.*	82	5.5	2.4	3.7	1	*vers.*	132	7.9	3.8	6.4	2	*virg.*
33	5.2	4.1	1.5	0.1	*set.*	83	5.8	2.7	3.9	1.2	*vers.*	133	6.4	2.8	5.6	2.2	*virg.*
34	5.5	4.2	1.4	0.2	*set.*	84	6	2.7	5.1	1.6	*vers.*	134	6.3	2.8	5.1	1.5	*virg.*
35	4.9	3.1	1.5	0.2	*set.*	85	5.4	3	4.5	1.5	*vers.*	135	6.1	2.6	5.6	1.4	*virg.*
36	5	3.2	1.2	0.2	*set.*	86	6	3.4	4.5	1.6	*vers.*	136	7.7	3	6.1	2.3	*virg.*
37	5.5	3.5	1.3	0.2	*set.*	87	6.7	3.1	4.7	1.5	*vers.*	137	6.3	3.4	5.6	2.4	*virg.*
38	4.9	3.6	1.4	0.1	*set.*	88	6.3	2.3	4.4	1.3	*vers.*	138	6.4	3.1	5.5	1.8	*virg.*
39	4.4	3	1.3	0.2	*set.*	89	5.6	3	4.1	1.3	*vers.*	139	6	3	4.8	1.8	*virg.*
40	5.1	3.4	1.5	0.2	*set.*	90	5.5	2.5	4	1.3	*vers.*	140	6.9	3.1	5.4	2.1	*virg.*
41	5	3.5	1.3	0.3	*set.*	91	5.5	2.6	4.4	1.2	*vers.*	141	6.7	3.1	5.6	2.4	*virg.*
42	4.5	2.3	1.3	0.3	*set.*	92	6.1	3	4.6	1.4	*vers.*	142	6.9	3.1	5.1	2.3	*virg.*
43	4.4	3.2	1.3	0.2	*set.*	93	5.8	2.6	4	1.2	*vers.*	143	5.8	2.7	5.1	1.9	*virg.*
44	5	3.5	1.6	0.6	*set.*	94	5	2.3	3.3	1	*vers.*	144	6.8	3.2	5.9	2.3	*virg.*
45	5.1	3.8	1.9	0.4	*set.*	95	5.6	2.7	4.2	1.3	*vers.*	145	6.7	3.3	5.7	2.5	*virg.*
46	4.8	3	1.4	0.3	*set.*	96	5.7	3	4.2	1.2	*vers.*	146	6.7	3	5.2	2.3	*virg.*
47	5.1	3.8	1.6	0.2	*set.*	97	5.7	2.9	4.2	1.3	*vers.*	147	6.3	2.5	5	1.9	*virg.*
48	4.6	3.2	1.4	0.2	*set.*	98	6.2	2.9	4.3	1.3	*vers.*	148	6.5	3	5.2	2	*virg.*
49	5.3	3.7	1.5	0.2	*set.*	99	5.1	2.5	3	1.1	*vers.*	149	6.2	3.4	5.4	2.3	*virg.*
50	5	3.3	1.4	0.2	*set.*	100	5.7	2.8	4.1	1.3	*vers.*	150	5.9	3	5.1	1.8	*virg.*

Fig. 15 A decision problem in 3D space.

(units: centimeters)	sepal length	sepal width	petal length	petal width
Mean	5.843333333	3.057333333	3.758	1.199333333
Standard Error	0.067611316	0.035588333	0.144135997	0.062236445
Median	5.8	3	4.35	1.3
Mode	5	3	1.4	0.2
Standard Deviation	0.828066128	0.435866285	1.765298233	0.762237669
Sample Variance	0.685693512	0.189979418	3.116277852	0.581006264
Kurtosis	-0.552064041	0.228249042	-1.402103416	-1.340603997
Skewness	0.314910957	0.318965665	-0.27488418	-0.102966748
Range	3.6	2.4	5.9	2.4
Minimum	4.3	2	1	0.1
Maximum	7.9	4.4	6.9	2.5
Sum	876.5	458.6	563.7	179.9
Count	150	150	150	150

Fig. 16 Training of the decision model.

- Support Vector Machines (variants based on kernel choice)
- Likelihood Methods, Bayesian Networks (i.e., probabilistic methods)
- Random Forests (hierarchical decomposition of feature space)
- Decision Trees (many variants based upon "splitting rules")
- Nearest Neighbor Classifiers (many variants such as K-Nearest Neighbor, Restricted Coulomb Energy)

Estimators

- Linear Approximators
- Series (polynomials, Taylor Series, Fourier Series, Bezier curves, splines)
- Radial Basis Functions
- Adaptive Logic Networks
- Neural Networks (continuous outputs: MLPs)

There are many others, but these are among the most mature and commonly used. Their theories are welldeveloped, and multiple books and papers have been written about each. The common element is that all are based on some mathematical function that interpolates, approximates, or discriminates a set of *a priori* examples.

DESCRIPTIVE ANALYSIS

This section provides a summary of descriptive modeling methods and objectives for supervised learning. Recall that descriptive modeling is a preliminary analysis during which data attributes are characterized formally. This is generally done using simple analytic tools such a histograms, scatter plots, graphs/charts, and basic statistical techniques to obtain means, variances, ranges, simple correlations, and demographic/metadata.

Collectively, these constitute a characterization of the data called a *descriptive model*. There are many software applications that support descriptive analysis (e.g.,

Excel, SAS, and Oracle database products). The choice of descriptive modeling tool is often determined by data type and how the data are stored (e.g., nominal/numeric, whether it is in a database or in a flat file).

Descriptive modeling methods are of four types. For supervised methods, their greatest value lies in the depiction of relationships between ground truth and subsets of the features.

- **Meta-data model.** These provide data externals such as storage size, number of records, number of fields, data format types, and pedigree (source, age, accuracy).
- **Distributional models.** These consist of descriptive statistics such as data ranges, means/medians/modes, variances, demographics (e.g., number of items in each ground truth class), prior probabilities, tables, and charts giving summary statistics.
- **Association models.** These depict relationships among the data, such as correlation tables, association rules, network models, and relationship trees.
- **Visualizations.** These are visual depictions of the data in some feature space, such as scatter plots, histograms, graphical charts, and animations.

Technical Component: Problem Definition

These are the items that must be addressed to ensure that the data mining problem has been properly characterized. For supervised learning, it is particularly important to express these issues in terms of the ground truth.

User problems and needs being addressed

- What type of supervised learning problem is being addressed? The most common types are the classifier and estimator.

Functional project and performance goals

- A specific functional goal (what must be done) for the effort must be specified in a written form and agreed to by all parties. This should include a description of the data set used for model development, and an enumeration of the ground truth categories.
- A characterization and quantitative description of target performance levels should be in a written form and agreed to by all parties. This generally includes accuracy and error rate estimates. Performance levels need not be specified numerically for proof-of-concept or experimental efforts, but should be understood by all.

Enterprise requirements

- Keep in mind there are two kinds of success in data mining efforts; technical and business. Technical success (e.g., meeting reasonable accuracy goals) is often easier to achieve, since good technical results do not necessarily have operational value to the enterprise.
- What requirements must be met for a data mining effort to have operational value, that is, is there a business case for the project? This involves consideration of operational impact, implementation cost, user training, and performance issues traded against expected benefits.

Resources

- Project Staffing
- Cost and Schedule

In simple scenarios where modeling is done from flat files (rather than a structured repository like a database), it generally takes about 1 or 2 weeks to condition the data for modeling, and another 4–6 weeks to reach the first substantial prototype. A substantial prototype is one that implements all the desired elements of processing to a level sufficient such that the level of performance of the final, delivered model can be estimated. Once the first prototype has been evaluated, successive prototypes can often be produced in 1- or 2-week cycles.

If the data to be mined are in a relational database or data warehouse, special skill and additional work are usually needed to prepare them for modeling. This is because the database schema (organizational system) is almost always designed around the data input model (how the data arrive) and/or the data output model (how the data are accessed) rather than around an information model relevant to the data mining task. Significant elements of information will be implicit (in the relations) rather than explicit (in the "bits"), and most of these will vanish if data are extracted without a thorough understanding of the database schema.

Characterizing the operational environment (locations/software/hardware/tools/legacy integration)

- The development and operational environments should be specified.
- Any special tools and development applications should be specified.
- An integration strategy for deploying data mining applications should be developed.

Structured interviews (methodology, question lists)

- Secure a list of available, user-approved domain experts.
- Make initial contacts with experts to secure their cooperation.
- Put together a Knowledge Acquisition Plan, which includes a chief domain expert (to definitively resolve issues), a list of domain questions, and an interview schedule for discussions with domain experts.

Configuration management

Management of the data and process configuration is particularly important when using a spiral development methodology against a floating baseline and changing requirements. Two essentials are:

- Nomenclature and naming conventions for data, processes, baselines
- Documenting the workflow for reproducibility (requires automation)

Technical Component: Data Selection and Preparation

This includes common data problems (outliers, gaps, consistency, collisions, imbalance, etc.). Have a plan to detect and address the following:

- Identifying/handling outliers (statistical methods)
- Handling missing fields (weak fill values, de-gapping, gap masking)
- Handling temporal problems (aging, cycling, trends, nonstationarity, etc.)
- Checking consistency (semantic filtering)
- Handling class collisions
- Handling class imbalance (replication, decimation)

Technical Component: Data Representation

The following areas must be addressed in the project plan and some empirical experiments will be necessary. The results of this investigation will determine the nature and amount of data conditioning needed for the project. Expect changes to the project plan as these areas are addressed.

Data representation solution checklist

- Nominal vs. numeric trades
- Coding (converting nominal to numeric data)
- Quantization (converting numeric to nominal data)

Feature extraction and transformation

- Data registration
- Data normalization
- Feature synthesis

Feature enhancement

- Feature salience (discriminating power of a feature)
- Feature independence (information contribution of a feature)
- Information-theoretic transforms (making information more accessible)

Data division

- Sampling
- Stratifying
- Segmenting (creating training, calibration, validation, and holdback sets)

PREDICTIVE MODELING

This section is a summary of predictive modeling methods and objectives for supervised learning. Predictive modeling is a generic cover term that can refer to just about any sort of supervised learning application (the term *predictive* does not imply prognostication.). Recall that predictive modeling uses the results of descriptive modeling to construct applications (models) that solve enterprise problems. Predictive models are generally classifiers or estimators.

Predictive modeling (e.g., the development of a classifier or estimator) is generally done using relatively sophisticated modeling tools such as learning engines and adaptive algorithms to create models that detect/classify patterns of interest in data. The resulting applications are called *predictive models*. There are a wide range of software tools that support aspects of predictive

modeling. These range in power and complexity from relatively simple regression modelers (e.g., Excel) to very sophisticated predictive modelers (e.g., SAS). The choice of predictive modeling tool is largely driven by user performance requirements and the data distribution (e.g., required levels of accuracy and nature of the available training data).

Technical Component: Paradigm Selection

A notional decision tree for this process can be helpful. There are really only two salient issues to address here:

- What type and complexity of feature inputs are available?
- What type of decision is being made (classifier, estimator, planner, etc.)?

The paradigm is merely an algorithmic bridge that carries the user from feature space to goal space; it has to be of a type that can span the gap presented by the problem to be solved. For example, it makes no sense to use a neural network if the features are nonnumeric, and it makes no sense to use a polynomial as a classifier.

Technical Component: Model Construction and Validation

Once the paradigm has been selected, the problem of its specific architecture must be addressed. Problems that are more complicated usually require the most elaborate architectures (e.g., more layers and neurons in an MLP and higher degree in a polynomial regression). For supervised learning systems, this usually means:

Construction

- Will special tools be required (e.g., third-party applications)?
- How will the models be "trained"?

Meta-scheme development

- Will several models be built and then "bagged"?
- Will a "boosting" model be run on the results of the main model?

Technical Component: Model Evaluation (Functional and Performance Metrics)

It is important to establish the metrics for a technical project upfront in writing, and get agreement. If this is not done, trouble is inevitable. For supervised learning applications, this usually includes:

- Accuracy: %, Type I/II errors, confusion matrices, receiver operating characteristic curves, etc.
- Timeliness, utility, cost, return on investment

Technical Component: Model Deployment

Deployment mechanisms should be considered at the beginning of a data mining effort, since design decisions made during the mining process could preclude some. Will an application developed be deployed using an application programming interface, as a plug-in, using a file interface, on a menu bar, as a stand-alone process, etc.?

Technical Component: Model Maintenance

Every application deployed to an operational environment must have a maintenance plan, since normal system maintenance and version upgrades will cause the application to require adjustment and testing.

For supervised learning systems, this often means incorporating a retraining capability, automating regression testing, adding/removing features and ground truth classes, and having embedded diagnostics.

SUMMARY

This genre section has addressed supervised learning, the most common application of data mining technology for producing operational applications. It has described the use of data mining methods to create detectors, classifiers, estimators, and other decision support tools for users operating in complicated environments.

REFERENCES

1. Duda, R.O.; Hart, P.E. *Pattern Classification and Scene Analysis*; Wiley-Interscience: New York, NY, **1973**.
2. Hecht-Nielsen, R. *Neurocomputing*; Addison-Wesley, **1990**, p. 433.
3. Fisher, R.A. The use of multiple measurements in taxonomic problems., Ann. Eugenics, **1936**, *7* (2), 179–188.
4. Fischer, R.A., *Contributions to Mathematical Statistics*; John Wiley: New York, NY, **1950**.

Database Design for a Cultural Artifact Repository

Todor Todorov
St. Cyril and St. Methodius University of Veliko Turnovo, and Department of Mathematical Foundations of Informatics, Institute of Mathematics and Informatics, Bulgarian Academy of Sciences, Veliko Tarnovo, Bulgaria

Galina Bogdanova
Nikolay Noev
Department of Mathematical Foundations of Informatics, Institute of Mathematics and Informatics, Bulgarian Academy of Sciences, Veliko Tarnovo, Bulgaria

Abstract

The purpose of this investigation is to present challenges and solutions in the process of designing database from a special data. This includes data gathered in the process of digitization and organization of cultural artifacts. We present some basic steps and algorithms for development of digital archives of information gathered from artifacts, analysis, optimization, and addition of metadata for indexing of digital data, compression and data protection, prevention of data loss, and design. We investigate the methods of protection with watermarking which can be used against illegal use of data. We illustrate our methods with two such concrete archives.

INTRODUCTION

Protection and preservation of cultural heritage is particularly an actual problem today. Digitization of analog materials and the creation of digital resources in the field of cultural heritage is a major contributor to e-Europe.

Main tasks in the research are:

- Development of audio, photo, and video archive with information collected by artifacts;
- Analysis and indexing the digital data;
- Design and maintenance of digital archive;
- Compression and optimization of the archive;
- Preventing data loss;
- Development of software for adding watermark against illegal use of data;
- Development of functions for creating, formatting, and protection of samples for additional applications and web sites.

We demonstrate our methods with two projects that we have managed to successfully complete all these tasks. The project "BellKnow"[1,2] was to develop an archive containing detailed description of church bells, as well as to develop a digital archive (using advanced technologies) for analysis, reservation, and data protection. To accomplish this we have to document the main bells' characteristics: design, form, type, geometric size, decorative and artistic scheme, weight, material, state, characteristics of chime, data about the producer and owner of the bell, and estimation of its historical value. So, in case unexpected circumstances destroy a bell, the archive will store the specific details to be investigated by different specialists. Objective of the second project "Balkan wars" was the digitizing of various documentary collections and artifacts related to the Balkan wars and the creation of electronic records and various public events and publications to promote in Bulgaria and Europe, the events during this historical period for the country. Project is implemented through digitalization of historical artifacts and development of 3D digital model of some items;[3] creating a common electronic archive of documentary heritage through digitization and processing of specimens found, construction of bibliographic and full-context databases, and presenting them on the Internet.

In the second section we consider modern methods of digitization and data collection. In the third section we provide an analysis of the objects in order to determine the metadata. The fourth section contains research of advanced technologies and methods for semantic data organization.

DIGITIZATION AND DATA COLLECTION

Modern technologies have changed the way one presented the information in the archives and made possible new services that were unthinkable a few years ago. Digitization is creation of an object, image, audio, document, or a signal (usually an analog signal) from a discrete set of its points or samples. The result is called "digital image," or more specifically "digital images" of the object and "digital form of the signal."

Encyclopedia of Information Systems and Technology, DOI: 10.1081/E-EIST-120048621

The tasks of digitalization can be synthesized in certain key areas:

- Retention of funds and records—many of digitalized objects are fragile; brittle structure is influenced by weather conditions and over time their digitization is the only hope for preservation;
- Simultaneous access to materials—most objects are subject to the digitization of rare and unique items of historical past and have a priceless value; the process of digitization will allow more users to touch them;
- Conservation funds in digital formats—archives, websites, and digital libraries;
- Strengthening international exchange and promotion;
- Providing access via computer networks—easy access to digital archives, and access to records of persons with disabilities;
- Provide new opportunities to work with digitalized materials funds—all the functionality is available to users of web space to be copied, multiplied, forwarded, etc., without jeopardizing its integrity and strength;
- Full text search—digital archives' organization contributes to easier detection of the searched object among all the crowd, advanced search, as well as unification of search results;
- Classification of digital funds via metadata—entire photo metadata wealth funds may be accompanied by important information about copyright, creation date, identification number, etc.

Development of digital technology hit the storage and processing of information. Today, almost every unit of information is created digitally: digital photography, digital sound recording, digital communications, text files, videos, movies, multimedia presentations stored on digital media, etc. Storage of such digital multimedia data in digital archives was subject to the same challenges, such as archives, we know before the invention of digital computing devices.

DIGITALIZATION PROCESS

Digitizing or digitization is creating an object, image, sound, document, or a signal (usually an analog signal) by a discrete set of its points or samples. The result is called "digital presentation" of the object. Some methods of digitalization used in the project are:[2]

- TEXT, PHOTO (photographing documents)—Photographing documents and images is preferred because of the speed of digitization, accessibility,

and relatively good quality of the received digital copies;
- TEXT, PHOTO (scanning with flat scanner)—The system actually represents a scanning device which is connected to a personal computer with appropriate software components for performing the scanning process;
- VIDEO, AUDIO (digitizing analog video and stream)—The process of digital video and audio recording is done with the system that operates in real time. This is analog playback device according to media digital recording. To perform digitization adequate equipment and appropriate software process management are needed;
- 3-DIMENSION IMAGING(3D scanning)—Process of 3D scan is performed with a suitable system; The object is scanned by all the visible sides and then specific software builds a full three-dimensional representation.

We use specialized hardware tools such as:

- Digital camera—Sony Alpha DSLR-A100;
- Video-camera—Sony HDR-SR8E HD AVCHD Camcorder;
- Audio-system—PULSE11 from Bruel and Kjer;
- 3D scanner—DAVID SLS system.

3D Scanning of Historical Objects

3D scanning is a new way for protection and promotion of cultural heritage material.[3–5] 3D digital recordings have more information about the volume, shape, and structure of the surface of the object than the classic photo shooting.

3D Scanning Technology

There are a variety of technologies to digitally recreate the shape of the 3D object. Classification of 3D scanners starts with a division into two types:contact and noncontact.

Contact 3D scanners use probe to touch the surface of the object to determine the distance and hence the shape of the object.

Noncontact scanners are divided into two main types: active and passive. Active 3D scanners use radiation of some kind of light, sound, ultrasound etc., and offset the effects of this radiation, which can determine the distance to certain points of the object or its form. Passive scanners capture multiple images of an object and based on them, determine distances and spatial location of individual points on the surface of the object.

We use "structured light" technology for 3D scanning.[3]

Fig. 1 Pattern of the light emitted and reflection from the object.

Structured light 3D scanning

The technology for 3D scanning using a structured light uses light with certain patterns and according to captured impact of this model it is possible to define its shape and spatial positioning of the various items of its surfaces. The positioning of the light source (projector), the camera, and the object is schematic in the form of a triangle defined by positional parameters. This example can be seen in Fig. 1. By projecting a series of known patterns onto an object and measuring the deformation of those patterns with a camera, the position in space of each pixel can be determined through triangulation calculations. Triangular calculations are performed by specialized software, taking into account the position of the light source (projector), camera trapping effects of lighting schemes, and reflection from the surface of the scanned object. These calculations are performed in parallel for each pixel within the camera producing a depth map or "point-cloud." Fig. 1 shows vertical black and white lines designed by the projector and captured by the camera angle.

3D scanning system using structured light consists of a projector, a digital camera, and a computer system.

Basic methodology of 3D shooting is as follows:

1. Positioning System—is important and is a key point in the calculation of spatial location of points on the surface of the scanned object;
2. Calibration of the system—is also important for constructing a 3D digital model;
3. 3D scanning of the side/part of the side—the visible part of the object is scanned. To obtain a complete

Fig. 2 Working process of 3D "structured light" scanning with DAVID SLS-1 system.

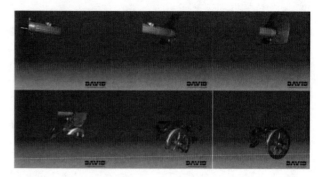

Fig. 3 3D scans of different surfaces of an object.

3D digital model of the object, all visible parts should be scanned separately;
4. Digital processing—by processing the received 3D images and combining them into a comprehensive 3D model, one can obtain the appropriate digital formats.

3D scanning of historical objects

For 3D scanning of cultural objects, we use "structured light" technology with DAVID SLS-1 system.[3,6] Fig. 2 shows the system working. The "structured light" technology requires certain conditions of controlled light and background environment.

For an example of 3D scanning and digital processing, we will show part of a 3D image of the gun "Schwarz-loze." The example shows six different 3D scans (Fig. 3) (a total of thirty four scans are required for complete coverage of the subject). Also is provided their consistent "assembly" (Fig. 4), a complete 3D image of the assembled six views with color separation for each individual scan (Fig. 5), and views from different perspectives (Fig. 6).

To build a complete 3D digital model of the example of Fig. 3, we captured 34 individual appearances of the artifact. After scan and construction of the 3D model, we add indexing textual data and the model is archived. We index the text content of the object: name, type, digitizer, date, author, archive/library number, innkeeper, brief description, copyright, etc., (necessary and explanatory data). This metadata is collected by different specialists from partner cultural and historical organizations: historians, librarians, etc., and processed by mathematicians and computer scientists. This is explained in details in.[3] Because of the specifics (file format—OBJ) of digital model we transform it to PDF or HTML format with embedded flash 3D images.

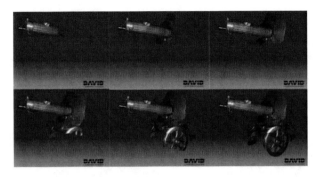

Fig. 4   Construction of 3D model.

Fig. 6   Views from different perspectives of 3D model.

ANALYSIS, OPTIMIZATION AND INDEXING THE DIGITAL DATA

Essence of Metadata

Extensible Markup Language (XML) is a markup language that defines a set of rules for encoding documents in a format which is both humanreadable and machinereadable.

The Extensible Metadata Platform (XMP) is an ISO standard for the creation, processing, and interchange of standardized and custom metadata for digital documents and data sets.

Metadata are text fields, built-in media files or additional text files (XML, XMP) for recording information on the nature of the digital resource. In other words, metadata is "data about data" describing any electronic or nonelectronic source of information on pre-established standard.

Metadata contribute to finding and sharing information. In other words, this is the last stage of information management. Once digitized (implemented in electronic form) and structured (arranged in a specific sequence and line), information is visualized in appropriate form. To fully justify the efforts of both phases scheduled for managing the information, it needs to be found and used by as many users. This is possible thanks to the metadata.

The presence of metadata with correctly placed points of connection ensures speed and accuracy of the application, and interactive user interaction.

Analysis of the objects in order to determine the metadata of selected artifacts collections and problem areas

In case of "BellKnow" archive we have the following data that should be indexed:[1,2,7]

- The main bells' characteristics: design, form, type, geometric size, decorative and artistic scheme, weight, material, state, characteristics of chime, data about the producer and owner, estimation of its historical value;
- Digital photos and video recordings of the bells while being tolled;
- The frequency spectrum of the bells during a stroke;
- The bells' frequency spectrum after transitive process;
- Charts representing the sound fade by time, sound stream, sound pressure, and other acoustic characteristics.

Modern Techniques for Intellectual Property Protection

With the development of digital technologies increasingly part of the audio, video, and any other information is available for fast, easy, and high quality copying. This fact entails the problem of protecting information from unauthorized distribution. Research in this area is considered in several aspects. One of the most important of these is steganography.[8,9] Steganography is subdealing with the concealment of information; it hides the message which should remain hidden.

Like steganography, watermark protectioncarries hidden information. However, there are significant differences between the two techniques.

Digital watermark is visible or preferably invisible to the identification code that is permanently embedded into digital data and maintains a presence in them after extracting it.[8]

Methods for image watermarking in the spatial region

In these methods, data are incorporated directly into the original image. The main advantage is that the key is not necessary to do any precondition transformations. The watermark is embedded by changing the

Fig. 5   Individual scans and a complete 3D image.

Fig. 7 Example of visual watermark.

illumination or color components. The main disadvantage is the low resistance. An example of this method is the method of Kutter.[9]

To derive the value of the embedded bit we calculate the difference between predicted and actual value of the pixels. The sign of the difference determines the value of the embedded bit. Extracting bits is done without the knowledge of the original message. The method is robust to filtering, JPEG compression, and geometric transformations.

Methods for audio watermarking using low-bit coding

By replacing the least significant bit of each sampling point by a coded binary string, we can encode a large amount of data in an audio signal.

The major disadvantage of this method is its poor immunity to manipulation. Encoded information can be destroyed by channel noise, resembling, etc. We improve robustness using by error-correcting codes.

Visual watermarking

Visible mark added in digital picture and video records (Fig. 7).

Digital Warehouse

Considering that there is a digital archive for unique Bulgarian bells, and there is lot of interesting information hidden in digital resources, we make an intelligent annotation of knowledge. A digital archive "BellKnow" is developed by using advanced technologies for analysis, reservation, and data protection, and it contains:

* The main bells' characteristics: design, form, type, geometric size, decorative and artistic scheme, weight, material, state, characteristics of chime, data about the producer and owner, and estimation of its historical value;
* Digital photos and video recordings of the bells while being tolled;
* The frequency spectrum of the bells during a stroke;
* The bells' frequency spectrum after transitive process;
* Charts representing the sound fade by time, sound stream, sound pressure, and other acoustic characteristics.

Organization of the "BellKnow" archive:[2]

* Digital data:
  * More than 3000 digital records with added digital steganographic sign (invisible watermark);

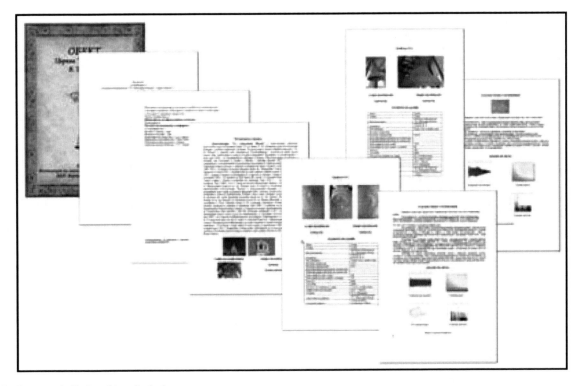

Fig. 8 Passport bells in a historical place.

o   Including photo pictures, video clips, and audio records;
o   Technical data, historical references, passports, diagrams, etc.
• Tree file structure:
• Digital files format, parameters, coding;
• Specific signature for file name;
• Additional META textual data for indexing of media files:
   o   Title (name of subject);
   o   Creator (name of digitalizer);
   o   Description (additional data);
   o   Date (date of creation);
   o   Type (type of media);
   o   Format (file format, codec, and parameters);
   o   Identifier (geographic coordinates);
   o   Rights (owner of property rights).

Organization of the archive can be separated in the following steps:

• Create archive;
• Creating own functions—actions, macros;
• Adding objects to a digital archive;
• Converting file format, codec, and size;
• Adding metadata to objects in a digital media collection;
• Adding watermark—visible and invisible.

Documentation and Passportization

Based on these and other data we prepare a passport model for each test bells.[1,2,10,11] Passports are summaries of all the information gathered about an object, in this case several sets of bells in one place. This includes photographs, historical reference, technical data, charts, and research done in the electronic version of the passport-embedded multimedia files with recorded audio and video clips (Fig. 8).

This passportization is a publication of all data collected from various studies in a document. The document includes sections in which information is divided into:

• Home page of the document and location of the bells;
• Page with a presentation of the draft study and identification of church bells in Bulgaria;
• History of the location of the bells (monastery, church, museum, etc.);
• Scheme of the bells of a given place.
• For each bell following data is included:
   o   Picture materials;
   o   Technical data shown in the next scheme (dimensions, location, type, material, year and place of creation, creator, etc.);
   o   Art Design of the bell (historical data, captions, pictures, decorations, ornaments, etc.);

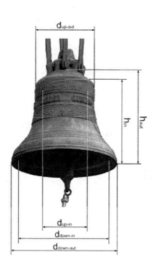

	District/Settlement	Bulgaria
	Country	Veliko Tarnovo
	Place	Preobrajenski monastery
	Coordinates	42°39'16.88" N 23°16'15.22" E
	Type	Church bell
	Material	Bronze
h_{out}	Height (outside) (cm)	45
h_{in}	Height (inside) (cm)	42
t_{low}	Max.lower thickness (cm)	3.6
t_{up}	Max. upper thickness (cm)	1
$d_{low-out}$	Lower outside diametre (cm)	54.5
d_{up-out}	Upper outside diametre (cm)	
d_{up-in}	Upper inside diametre (cm)	
	Weight (kg)	
	Condition	fair
	Pitch in the moment of stroke	
	Established tone	
	Created (year and place)	
	Creator	
	Owner	Preobrajenski monastery
	Aesthetical value	high cultural and historic value

Fig. 9 Scheme of the bell and technical data. Bell number one in Preobrajenski monastery, near Veliko Tarnovo, Bulgaria.

- o Data from sound analysis, supported by diagrams;[10]
- o Digital recording—video clips and sound recordings.

This model of passport could be used to document other bells in the future (Fig. 9).

SEMANTIC DATA ORGANIZATION

Semantic Web

The most widespread standards for the description of resources are Standard Generalized Markup Language (SGML), XML, Resource Description Framework (RDF), Web Ontology Language(OWL), etc. RDF is a framework for describing and exchanging data. It offers a modeland syntax for metadata, so that they can be used by independent components. At its core, RDF contains nodes and attached there to pairs of attributes and values. Nodes can be any Web resources (pages, servers, virtually all of which can be given Universal Resource Identifier [URI], or even other types of metadata). Attributes are properties of nodes and their values are eitheratomistic (text strings, numbers, etc.) or other resources or metadata. This mechanism allows to build boxes (labeled directed graphs), which could later be converted into XML. OWL is a Semantic Web language designed to represent rich and complex knowledge about

things, groups of things, and relation between things. OWL is a computational logic-based language such that knowledge expressed in OWL can be exploited by computer programs, e.g., to verify the consistency of that knowledge or to make implicit knowledge explicit.

We make an experimental semantic annotation, based on the current W3C Semantic Web initiative standards[12,13] of the resources in digital archive of unique bells. We use the RDF data model, because it provides a model for describing resources of bells. Digital resources have properties (attributes or characteristics of bells). RDF defines a digital resource as any object that is uniquely identifiable by an URI. OWL is a Semantic Web language designed to represent rich and complex knowledge about things, groups of things, and relation between things. OWL is a computational logic-based language such that knowledge expressed in OWL can be exploited by computer programs, e.g., to verify the consistency of that knowledge or to make implicit knowledge explicit.

Linguistic Approaches of Semantic Research

The linguistic explanation is a very essential task in our days. Basically the semantic systems are built of different types of thematic dictionaries, which explain nature (give a meaning) of the information.[7,14]

Numerous ontology dictionaries with different functions are a basis of our experimental bell ontology system. These dictionaries are made using XML/RDF/

Bell Termin Dictionary

main | search word | all of termins | advanced | show xml

advanced | add item | edit termins | detete termins | edit translate | simple xml object | show xml

List of Bell Termins

ID	termin	description	type	class	href	translate	note	edit
1	bell	music device	noun	thing, music device	campane	камбана	bell - a hollow object, typically made of metal and having the shape of a deep inverted cup widening at the lip, that sounds a clear musical note when struck, typically by means of a clapper inside.	edit
2	belfry	a bell tower or steeple housing bells	noun	thing, building	bell tower	камбанария	belfry - a bell tower or steeple housing bells, especially one that is part of a church.	edit
3	peal	a loud ringing of a bell or bells	verb	thing, verb	ring	звънене	peal - a loud ringing of a bell or bells	edit

Fig. 10 Bell term dictionary v1.1.

OWL technology to provide lexical explain and description of bell knowledge. Combination of descriptions, text explanation, and lexical rules provides basics of experimental bell ontology system.

The main tools to represent semantics are dictionaries, in which concepts are arranged in a subtype–supertype hierarchy, thus forming taxonomy.

Frequency dictionary for bell science

The main purpose of this project is to build a text-research system to create frequency dictionary from texts of bell knowledge descriptions. To construct this system are built a hierarchical datasets and WEB interface. The texts are divided into thematic headings (bell science domains).

The dictionary aims to cover big corpuses of texts that contain terms and conceptions in the field of Bulgarian bell's knowledge. Frequency dictionary is designed for large arrays of such texts. Separate phrases and words are representatives of different domains. The dictionary aims to give information on how often a particular word or phrase is used in a particular corpus of texts.

Full text search could be made with the system. After the indexing of the data, searching of the appropriate index is saved in a catalogtable. The result shows information such as: in how many files in one particular area's domain the number of words and phrases are founded. A hierarchical structure of data (tree) is used for organization of the information. The hierarchical structure of data has tables included for administration of categories and growing of the tree structure is allowed in volume and depth.

The system offers an easy and fast search, due to the hierarchy of the data. It enables introduction of many different domains and they do not influence the speed of searching. The individual tables contain only the names of domains, as well as their keys for organization

the hierarchy. The help table contains all texts of all domains, organized with the help of indexes, which enables a fast access to the relevant texts and domains. There is an option for construction of a dynamic growing of the tree of tables in depth.

Term dictionaries for bell science

For the bell science domain, more suitable dictionaries are term dictionaries. The term dictionaries present the explanation of bell knowledge in a definite corpus of texts. It is considered that the facts in the term dictionary are enough. The term dictionaries give versatile information: text context of different terms, presence/absence of define terms, relations with other terms, lexical rules, and groups of different bell domains.

Depicted is a part of XML dictionary data (Fig. 10):

```
<?xml version = "1.0" encoding = "utf-8"? >
<!DOCTYPE bdict[
<!ELEMENT item (idbt, term, description, type,
classOf, ref, transl, bnote) + >
<!ELEMENT classOf (clOf) + >
<!ELEMENT ref (href) + >
<!ELEMENT transl (bword) + >
<!ELEMENT idbt (#PCDATA) >
<!ELEMENT term (#PCDATA) >
<!ELEMENT description (#PCDATA) >
<!ELEMENT type (#PCDATA) >
<!ELEMENT bnote (#PCDATA) >
<!ELEMENT clOf (#PCDATA) >
<!ELEMENT href (#PCDATA) >
<!ELEMENT bword (#PCDATA) >
] >
<bdict >
<item >
<bdict >1 </bdict >
<term lang = "en" >bell </term >
<description lang = "en" >music device </
description >
```

```
<type lang = "en" >noun </type >
<classOf >
<clOf lang = "en" >thing </clOf >
<clOf lang = "en" >music device </clOf >
</classOf >
<ref >
<href lang = "en" >campane </href >
</ref >
</transl >
<bword lang = "bg" >камбана
</bword >
</transl >
<bnote lang = "en" >bell - a hollow object,
typically made of metal and having the shape of a
deep inverted cup widening at the lip, that
sounds a clear musical note when struck,
typically by means of a clapper inside. </bnote >
</item >
<item >
...
</item >
</bdict >
```

OWL ontologies

In recent years the development of ontologies has become very popular in different scientific areas. Ontologies have become common especially on the WorldWide Web.

Ontology defines a common vocabulary for researchers who need to share information in a domain. It includes machine-interpretable definitions of basic concepts in the domain and relations among them.

Sharing common understanding of the structure of information among people or software agents is one of the more common goals in developing ontologies.

There are a lot of definitions of ontology in the literature. Ontology is a formal explicit description of concepts in a domain of discourse called classes, properties of each concept describing various features and attributes of the concept, and restrictions on properties. If we consider ontology with a set of individual instances of classes, this results in a knowledge base.

Classes are one of the main parts of most ontologies. Classes describe the concepts in the domain.

A class can have subclasses that represent concepts that are more specific than the superclass. Properties describe features and attributes of classes and instances. In practical terms, developing ontology includes basic methodology of 3D shooting which is as follows:

1. Defining classes in the ontology;
2. Arranging the classes in a subclass–superclass hierarchy;
3. Defining properties and describing allowed values for them;

4. Filling in the values for properties for instances.

We can then create a knowledge base by defining individual instances of these classes filling property value information and additional restrictions.

The protégé platform

Protégé is a free, open-source platform that contains powerful tools to create ontologies.[15] Protégé implements a rich set of knowledge-modeling structures and actions that support the creation, visualization, and manipulation of ontologies. The environment can be extended to work as a plug-in or as a Java-based Application Programming Interface (API) for building knowledge-based tools and applications.

The Protégé platform supports two main ways of modeling ontologies:

The Protégé-Frames editor: these are tools to create ontologies that are framebased, in accordance with the Open Knowledge Base Connectivity protocol (OKBC). In this model, an ontology consists of a set of classes organized in an hierarchy, a set of slots associated to classes to describe their properties and relationships, and a set of instances of those classes.

The Protégé-OWL editor: these are tools to create ontologies for the Semantic Web, in particular in the W3C's Web Ontology Language (OWL). "An OWL ontology may include descriptions of classes, properties, and their instances. Given such an ontology, the OWL formal semantics specifies how to derive its logical consequences, i.e., facts not literally present in the ontology, but entailed by the semantics. These entailments may be based on a single document or multiple distributed documents that have been combined using defined OWL mechanisms" (see the OWL Web Ontology Language Guide).

Protégé's model is comparable to object-oriented and frame-based systems. It basically can represent ontologies consisting of classes, properties (slots), property characteristics (facets and constraints), and instances. Protégé provides an open Java API to query and manipulate models.

Using Protégé's user interface one can create classes, assign properties to the classes, and then restrict the properties' facets for certain classes. Finally Protégé is able to automatically generate user interfaces that support the creation of instances. For each class in the ontology, the system creates one form with editing components (widgets) for each property of the class.

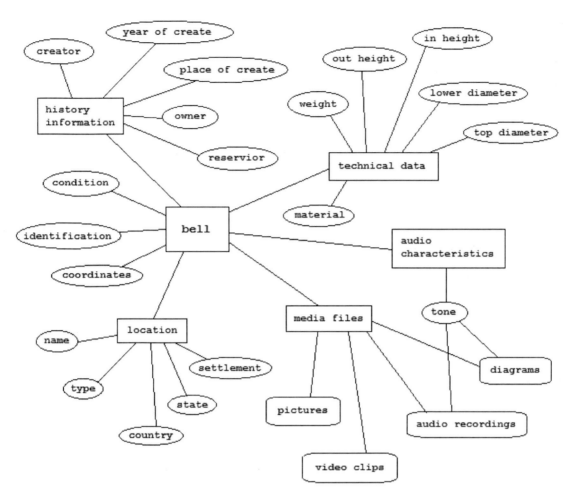

Fig. 11 Ontology basic create schema.

BellKnow Ontology

Using the information of metadata annotation we define an ontological describing the Bulgarian bells. The basic schema of these digital resources is shown in Fig. 11.

This scheme shows the basic BellKnow ontology classes (bell, history information, technical data, location, media files, and audio characteristics) and their properties. Next we will consider basic OWL ontology components and how these components are realized in the BellKnow ontology in Protégé.

An OWL ontology consists of individuals, properties, and classes, which roughly correspond to Protégé's framework objects:

Individuals—represent objects in the domain that we are interested in. For example an individual is each different bell.

Properties—Properties are binary relations between individuals. For example, the property hasLocation might link the individual Bell1AN to the individual StAleksanderNevskiCatedral, or the property hasBell might link the individual

StAleksanderNevskiCatedral to the individual Bel-l1AN. Properties can have inverses. For example, the inverse of hasLocation is isLocatationOf. Properties can be limited to having a single value—i.e., to being functional. They can also be either transitive or symmetric.

Classes—OWL classes are sets that contain individuals. For example, the class Bell would contain all the individuals that are bells in our domain of interest. Classes may be organized into a superclass–subclass hierarchy. OWL classes are built up of descriptions that specify the conditions that must be satisfied by an individual for it to be a member of the class.

We start creating ontology using 'Create New OWL Ontology' from Protégé's main menu. Next we could start building a class hierarchy using 'Classes Tab'. The empty ontology contains one class called 'Thing'. The class Thing is the class that represents the set containing all individuals. Because of this, all classes are subclasses of Thing. First we create BellKnow's main class Bell. After that we could continue building the BellKnow

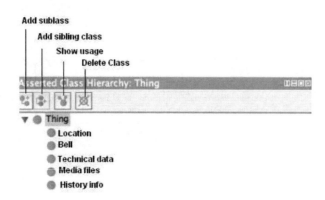

Fig. 12 Ontology properties.

ontology hierarchy by adding classes and subclasses as shown in Fig. 11.

The next step is to create OWL Properties. There are three main types of properties: Object properties, Datatype properties, and Annotation properties (Fig. 12). Object properties are relationships between two individuals. Annotation properties can be used to add metadata to classes, individuals, and properties. Using the Datatype property, we can add a restriction to the class states that all individuals of the class must meet specific restrictions. Properties may be created using the Object Properties tab.

Example properties:

*   An Object property linking the individual Bell1AN to the individual Bell1ANBeat (Fig. 13).
*   A Datatype property linking the individual Bell1AN to the data literal 140, which has a type of an xsd: float (Fig. 14).
*   An Annotation property, linking the class Bell to the data literal (string) Geogri Ivanov (Fig. 15).

We can also add additional Datatype and Range restrictions to the Properties. Finally we can use one of the key features of OWL-DL languagereasoner. It helps to test whether or not one class is a subclass of another class and whether or not it is possible for the class to have any instances.

Singing RDF Graph

An RDF statement involves a name if it has that name as subject or object. An RDF graph involves a name, if any of its statements involves that name. Given an RDF statements, the Minimum Self-contained Graph (MSG)

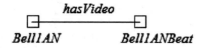

Fig. 13 Example 1.

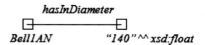

Fig. 14 Example 2.

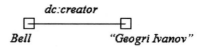

Fig. 15 Example 3.

containing that statement, written MSG(s), is the set of RDF statements comprised of the following:

*   The statement in question;
*   Recursively, for all the blank nodes involved by statements included in the description so far, the MSG of all the statements involving such blank nodes.

This definition recursively build the MSG from a particular starting statement; Theorems proved in[16,17] show that the choice of the starting statement is arbitrary and this leads to an unique decomposition of the an RDF graph into MSGs.

In[17,18] is proven that an RDF model has a unique decomposition in MSGs. The MSG definition and properties say that it is possible to sign a MSG attaching the signature information to a single, arbitrary triple composing it. Along with the signature, an indication of the public key to use for verification might be provided. By "attach" we mean by using a verification procedure. Using the same procedure more signatures can be attached to the same MSG either independently or "layered" thus providing a mechanism for countersigning.

CONCLUSION

We present some challenges related to the process of designing database from a special data.

In the survey are presented some algorithms for development of digital archives of information gathered from cultural artifacts. We investigate the methods of protection with watermarking which can be used against illegal use of data. All presented approaches are illustrated in two such concrete archives.

REFERENCES

1. Bogdanova, G.; Dimkov, G.; Todorov, T.; Noev, N. *Model of Digital Repository of Information and Knowledge—Fund BellKnow, Annual Seminar on Algebraic*

and Combinatorial Coding Theory; Ksilifor, Bulgaria, Dec 17–19, **2010**.

2. Noev, N. Organization and security of the audio and video archive for unique Bulgarian bells. Math. Balkanica N Ser. **2010**, *24* (3–4), 285–291.

3. Bogdanova, G.; Todorov, T.; Noev, N. *Digitization and 3D scanning of historical artifacts,* Международна конференция *digital preservation and presentation of cultural and scientific heritage—DiPP'13,* Велико Търново, България, Септември, 2013, 18–21, 133–138.

4. Bogdanova, G.; Noev, N.; Stoffel, K.; Todorov, T. 3D modeling of valuable bulgarian bells and churches. Math. Balkanica N Ser. **2011**, *25* (5), 475–482.

5. Cotofrei, P.; Kunzi, C.; Stoffel, K. *Semantic Interpretation of 3D Point Clouds of Historical Objects,* In the Proceedings of the First International Conference Digital Preservation and Presentation of Cultural and Scientific Heritage—DiPP'11, Veliko Tarnovo, Bulgaria, Sept 11–14, 2011, pp. 127–139.

6. *DAVID-Laserscanner,* http://www.david-laserscanner.com/.

7. Bogdanova, G.; Todorov, T.; Noev, N.; Kancheva, S. *Research on Linguistic Approaches, Used for Semantic Explanation of Bell's Knowledge,* Международна конференция *Digital Preservation and Presentation of Cultural and Scientific Heritage—DiPP'12,* Велико Търново, България, Септември 18–21, 2012, pp. 155–160.

8. Cox, I.; Kilian, J.; Leighton, T.; Shamoon, G. Secure spread spectrum watermarking for multimedia. Proc. IEEE Intl. Conf. Img. Process. **1997**, *6* (12), 1673–1687.

9. Kutter, M. Digital signature of color images using amplitude modulation. J. Elect. Imag. **1998**, *7* (2), 326–332.

10. Dimkov, G.; Alexiev, Al.; Simeonov, I.; Trifonov, T.; Simeonov, K. Acoustic Research of Historic Value Bulgarian Bells, National Conference Akustika'2008 Bulgarian, Varna Oct 24–25, 2008, Sofia Dec 05–06, 2008, Vol. 10.

11. Dimkov, G.; Trifonov, T. *Church Bells—Part of The Cultural Heritage,* MASSEE 2009 International Congress on Mathematics, Ohrid, Macedonia, **2009**.

12. Resource Description Framework, http://www.w3.org/RDF/.

13. Web Ontology Language, http://www.w3.org/TR/owl-features/.

14. Bogdanova, G.; Rangochev, K.; Paneva-Marinova, D.; Noev, N. Towards linguistics analysis of the Bulgarian folklore domain. Intl J. Inform. Techn. Knowl. **2011**, *5* (2), 119–128.

15. Bogdanova, G.; Stoffel, K.; Todorov, T.; Noev, N. *Building OWL Ontology of unique Bulgarian bells using Protégé platform,* Международна конференция *Digital Preservation and Presentation of Cultural and Scientific Heritage—DiPP'12,* Велико Търново, България, Септември 18–21, 2012, 161–166.

16. Bogdanova, G.; Todorov, T.; Noev, N. Singing individual fragments of an RDF graph of unique Bulgarian bells, ACCT'2010: Twelfth international workshop. Academgorodok, Novosibirsk, Russia, Sept. 5–11, 2010, 47–52.

17. Carroll, J. *Signing RDF Graphs,* HP technical report, **2003**.

18. Tummarello, G.; Morbidoni, C.; Puliti, P.; Piazza, F. Signing individual fragments of an RDF graph. Proc. Intl. World Wide Web Conf. **2005**, 1020–1021.

Decision Sciences

Sven Axsäter
Johan Marklund
Department of Industrial Management and Logistics, Lund University, Lund, Sweden

Abstract

This entry provides a description of the vast area of decision sciences from an operations research/ management science (OR/MS) perspective. This means that the focus is on how quantitative models can be used for improving the quality of decisions. After describing and explaining a general conceptual approach to quantitative decision modeling, some important, commonly used decision models and methods are considered in more detail. The list includes both deterministic models such as linear programming (LP), integer programming (IP), and economic lot sizing, as well as stochastic models for safety stock decisions in inventory management. Various generalizations are also discussed together with brief comments and references to other important decision modeling approaches such as game theory, multiple criteria decision making (MCDM), queuing, and simulation.

INTRODUCTION

"Decision sciences" represents a broad area of research with a common focus on advancing the understanding of decision-making processes and improving the quality of decisions, organizational as well as individual. Essentially all types of decisions fall within the realms of the field, but an emphasis is placed on various types of business-related decisions or decisions with an economic dimension. From a methodological perspective, the field contains both behavioral and quantitative modeling research. The former is often closely related to organization theory and psychology, while the latter to a large extent is synonymous with operations research/management sciences (OR/MS), and closely relates to economics, applied mathematics, and statistics. In this entry we restrict our attention to the quantitative modeling (OR/MS) area of decision sciences. The motivation is twofold: first of all, it is arguably the largest area; second, this is where our own backgrounds lie as authors.

Decision sciences research from an OR/MS perspective is usually concerned with improving the quality of decisions. This is done by describing the decision problem in a quantitative model of the real system, then use this model to generate decision alternatives and choose the best among these candidate solutions. The challenges are to model the dynamics and constraints of the underlying system with an appropriate level of detail, and to determine what criteria should be used in assessing what is the best decision. After some reflection most people find this structure intuitively appealing because it fits well with how they make their own decisions (if they are forced to dissect the situation). A set of constraints limits the choices you have and defines the possible alternatives. You then choose between these feasible alternatives according to some objective function that reflects what your goal is with the decision. In the section on "Examples of Common Decision Models and Applications," we will look at several classical models and methods that illustrate variations of this basic model structure. For the remainder of this section, we will take a closer look at the general approach for quantitative decision modeling sketched above. We will then reflect on the past development, and the future opportunities and challenges of the field.

The general approach when using quantitative models is illustrated in Fig. 1. The goal is to find good decisions for some real system. This is very difficult in many situations. Therefore we can choose to replace the real system by a quantitative model. The model seldom provides a complete description of reality; instead it serves as an approximate, simplified version of the real system. However, an advantage is that the quantitative model quite often can be optimized, that is, we can find the best decisions for the simplified version of the real system. In some cases we cannot find the optimal decisions but still some good ones, for example, by using simulation to evaluate some reasonable alternatives. Because the quantitative model does not take all aspects of the real system into account, decisions that are optimal for the model may not be optimal for the real system. However, presuming the model is a valid description of reality, it should capture the essence of the real system at an appropriate level of detail. Decisions obtained from a validated model can be expected to work well also for the real system. Thus if the model is valid, the model decisions can be implemented in the

Encyclopedia of Information Systems and Technology, DOI: 10.1081/E-EIST-120043712

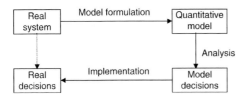

Fig. 1 Using quantitative models to improve the decision quality.

real system with good results. It is often quite difficult to design the quantitative model at the right level of detail. If the model is too simple, it may provide a poor approximation of the real system (i.e., the model has poor validity), and it may be dangerous to use the model as a basis for generating decisions to be implemented in the real system. On the other hand, if the quantitative model is too complex it may be too difficult to analyze. Thus, it becomes quite useless as a tool for helping the decision maker to make better decisions.

The approach to use quantitative models to analyze and describe reality is a cornerstone in modern science and dates back to the dawn of our civilization. However, the birth of the OR/MS field, with its focus on modeling complex decisions, is often attributed to military activities during World War II. The war effort induced an urgent need to make vital decisions about allocation of scarce resources at a scale never seen before. The United States and British military services turned to a large number of mathematicians and other scientists to do research on these decision problems, and to develop scientific methods to help solve them. After the war, the success of these efforts spurred an interest to apply the same approaches to decisions in industry and business. The dissemination was fueled by the fast industrial development following the war, and the fact that many consultants and industry people had come in contact with OR/MS methods during their military service. The fast growth of the OR/MS research field after World War II can also be attributed to the groundbreaking research achievements in OR/MS techniques that attracted talented people into the new field. A stellar example is the Simplex method for solving LP problems, originating with George B. Dantzig in 1947, see Dantzig.[1] Other important areas where much progress was done early on were dynamic programming, queuing theory, and inventory theory.

Since the early days in the 1940s, the progress of the OR/MS field of decision sciences has been closely connected to the development of the computer and information technology. The revolution in computational power due to the emergence of the digital computer, and later on the emergence of the personal computer, has made it possible to model and solve increasingly complex decision problems. Another important enabler for the development of the field is the tremendous advances

in information technology, not least in the present years. Access to an almost infinite amount of information at the press of a button, propels the opportunities for quantitative models to help decision makers evaluate information and decision alternatives. Hence, the need for quantitative decision models, embedded in user-friendly decision support systems, continues to increase as the tideway of information keeps overwhelming the decision makers. From a research perspective, easy access to new and more detailed information in combination with increased computational power creates new interesting challenges and promises an interesting future for the OR/MS area of decision sciences.

Important professional associations, which among other things host some of the most influential conferences and journals in the field, include INFORMS (http://www.informs.org), Decision Sciences Institute (http://www.decisionsciences.org), and EURO (http://www.euro-online.org).

EXAMPLES OF COMMON DECISION MODELS AND APPLICATIONS

In this section we will look closer at some commonly used quantitative decision models. The ambition is to illustrate how the general model building approach discussed above can be applied in different contexts. The models chosen are classical examples but represent a small sample of the entire field, and should not be construed as an exhaustive representation. For specific examples of OR/MS decision models applied in the library and information sciences area we refer to Kraft and Boyce.[2]

Deterministic Models

A deterministic model is characterized by the absence of randomness, meaning that all input values are known with certainty (i.e., correspond to a single outcome with probability 1). A model that incorporates randomness belongs to the class of stochastic models (see the section on "Stochastic Models"). To exemplify, consider a decision where the customer demand during next week is an important input parameter. If the demand is known to be 50 units, it is deterministic. If there is a probability of 0.5 that the demand will be 25 and a probability of 0.5 that it will be 75, the demand is stochastic (or random) with a mean of 50. The advantage of deterministic models over stochastic ones is that they are generally easier to solve, thus, larger problems may be dealt with. Clearly, in most real systems there is some uncertainty present. However, in many situations this uncertainty may be low enough for a deterministic model to be an appropriate approximation. In other situations, the inherent uncertainty may be critical for the decision and must be incorporated into the model; the choice should then fall on a stochastic model.

In this section we will consider three types of deterministic models: LP models, integer programming (IP) models, and the economic lot sizing model. Examples of stochastic models are found in the "Stochastic Models" section.

LP models

Linear programming is perhaps the most well known and most widely used decision sciences method to date. It was originally developed by George Dantzig in late 1940s, who proposed the so-called Simplex method for solving large-scale general linear programs. As the name suggests, an LP model is restricted to linear relationships between the decision variables. Programming is, in this case, synonymous with planning, thus LP can be thought of as linear planning.

Generally speaking, an LP model consists of a linear objective function to be maximized or minimized, and a set of linear constraints that limit the decision alternatives. The objective function is a linear equation of the involved decision variables and should reflect how the decision variables impact the overall decision objective. The constraints are also linear equations of the decision variables, describing logical relationships between these variables and how they consume various types of limited resources. Because of its flexibility, the LP approach has been applied to almost any decision situation conceivable, including production planning, scheduling of personnel, investment planning, marketing, logistics, supply chain management, military strategy and tactics, agricultural planning, etc. The most common type of LP application concerns decision problems of allocating limited resources to a number of competing activities in the best possible way (as defined by the objective function). To make the discussion more concrete consider the following example of a classic product mix decision problem.

A production manager who wants to maximize profits is faced with the decision problem of how much to produce of two products A and B during the upcoming planning period. The production process involves three different machines (resources). The times (resource units) to produce a batch of product A and B,

respectively, in each of the machines are specified in Table 1. One can also find the available capacity for each of the machines there, and the profit associated with each batch of product A and B sold. Demand is high so we can assume that everything that is produced can also be sold. A restriction is that previous order commitments require that at least 20 batches of product B are produced.

To formulate this decision problem as an LP, the first step is to define the decision variables, which in this case are the amounts of products A and B to be produced.

X_A = number of batches to produce product A
X_B = number of batches to produce product B

Given these decision variables, the goal to maximize total profits (Z) translates into the objective function: Max $Z = 1500X_A + 2000X_B$.

Turning to the constraints that limit the amount of product A and B that can be produced, the capacity constraints for resource 1, 2, and 3 can be expressed mathematically as:

1. $3X_A \leq 150$ (limited capacity in resource 1)
2. $1X_A + 2X_B \leq 140$ (limited capacity in resource 2)
3. $2X_A + 2X_B \leq 160$ (limited capacity in resource 3)
   Similarly, the constraint that at least 20 batches of product B must be produced can be expressed as:
4. $X_B \geq 20$ (produce at least 20 batches of product B)

Adding the non-negativity constraints, $X_A \geq 0$ and $X_B \geq 0$ (assuring that the model solution does not suggest negative production) renders the complete LP model of the product mix problem

Max $Z = 1500X_A + 2000X_B$ (maximize total profits)
Subject to

(1) $3X_A \qquad \leq 150$ (limited capacity in resource 1)
(2) $1X_A + 2X_B \leq 140$ (limited capacity in resource 2)
(3) $2X_A + 2X_B \leq 160$ (limited capacity in resource 3)
(4) $X_B \geq 20$ (produce at least 20 batches of product B)
(5) $X_A, \qquad X_B \geq 0$ (non − negativity constraint)

Note that due to constraint ([4]), the constraint $X_B \geq 0$ is redundant in this formulation and it is included solely for reasons of completeness.

Table 1 Input data for the product mix example

Resource	Production time per batch		Available capacity
	Product A	Product B	
1	3 hr	—	150 hr
2	1 hr	2 hr	140 hr
3	2 hr	2 hr	160 hr
Profit per batch	$1500	$2000	

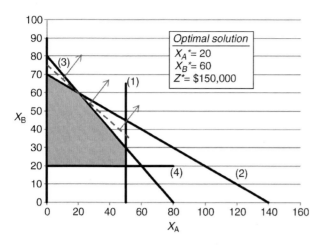

Fig. 2 Graphical solution of the product mix decision problem.

After formulating the decision model, the challenge is to solve it and determine the optimal decisions. For the present example with only two decision variables the problem can be solved graphically as illustrated in Fig. 2.

Scrutinizing the graphical representation in Fig. 2, the bold lines labeled (1)–(4) correspond to constraints (1)–(4) above when satisfied to equality. The gray shaded area corresponds to the feasible region, where all the constraints are satisfied (including the nonnegativity constraint $X_A \geq 0$). The optimal decision must satisfy all the constraints, hence the feasible region defines all decision alternatives of interest. The optimal solution is the feasible solution that maximizes the objective function. The dashed line in Fig. 2 represents the slope (or level) of the objective function, $Z = 1500X_A + 2000X_B$. To maximize Z, we increase X_A and X_B, which corresponds to parallel-shifting the dashed line in the directions of the arrows depicted in Fig. 2 (mathematically the arrows represent the gradient to the objective function). The optimal solution is the last point on the dashed line which belongs to the feasible region. From Fig. 2 we can see that this corresponds to the corner point of the feasible region where constraint (2) and (3) intersect. Solving the linear equation system defined by constraints (2) and (3) (or by inspecting the graph), the optimal solution $X_A^* = 20$, $X_B^* = 60$ is found. The corresponding objective function value is $Z^* = 150,000$. Hence, the optimal decision obtained from the LP model is to produce 20 batches of product A and 60 batches of product B, which renders a total profit of $150,000.

Clearly, LP problems of practical interest are considerably larger than the small example studied here (often including thousands or even millions of variables and constraints), which prohibits a graphical solution technique. Instead, these large-scale problems can be solved using, for example, an efficient algebraic technique called the Simplex method. This method utilizes the fact that an optimal solution to an LP problem is always found in a corner point to the feasible region (a consequence of the linearity of all equations). In principle, the method searches through the set of feasible corner point solutions in a structured fashion until a set of optimality conditions are fulfilled, and the optimal solution is found. More details about the Simplex method and other aspects of LP, such as duality and sensitivity analysis can be found in basic OR/MS textbooks such as Hillier and Lieberman.[3] For more theoretical treatment of the subject one can turn to books like Dantzig[4–6] and Vanderbei.[7]

IP models

One limitation with LP models is that the decision variables must be continuous. Hence, it is just a coincidence that the optimal solution to the product mix example above turned out to be in full batches ($X_A^* = 20$, $X_B^* = 60$) rather than fractional. If integer restrictions of the decision variables are added to an LP model, it transforms into an Integer Programming (IP) model. If some variables are allowed to be continuous while others are integer, the model is often referred to as a Mixed Integer Programming (MIP) model.

Solving a problem which contains integer variables is much more difficult than solving a LP model. The reason is that there is no longer a guarantee that an optimal solution is found in a feasible corner point solution. As a result, the number of candidate solutions to investigate increases tremendously. To avoid complete enumeration, which would severely restrict the size of the problems worth considering, much research has gone into finding good solution methods for various kinds of IP problems. One common solution approach is the family of Branch and Bound algorithms. The underlying principle with Branch and Bound is to divide a difficult problem into subproblems that are easier to solve, and then use these subproblems to bind the optimal solution. The subproblems may, for example, be linear programs. For more details about Branch and Bound techniques and other solution approaches for IP models one can turn to, for example, Wolsey.[8] For a more general introduction to IP models, including examples of formulated problems[3] is an excellent starting point.

A special case of integer-valued decision variables are binary variables, which are restricted to be either 0 or 1. The binary variables are important in decision modeling because they can be used to describe Yes/No decisions, either or alternatives, fixed charges and stepwise changes. They can also be used for representing general integer variables.

To exemplify the use of binary variables, we return to the product mix example in the "LP Models" section. After further analysis it turns out that there is a fixed

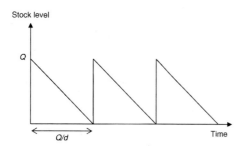
Stock level

Q

Q/d

Time

Fig. 3 Development of inventory level over time.

charge of $1000 associated with starting up production of product A. This startup cost is due to necessary configuration of machinery and special material handling equipment that needs to be acquired in case product A is produced. To incorporate this feature into the decision model, an additional decision variable is needed together with new constraints and a modified objective function.

Definition of the additional (auxiliary) decision variable:

$$y_A = \begin{cases} 1 & \text{if product A is produced} \\ 0 & \text{if product A is not produced} \end{cases}$$

The modified objective function (maximize total profits) that includes the fixed charge associated with producing product A becomes:

Max $Z = 1500X_A + 2000X_B - 1000y_A$

The new constraints must assure that y_A is binary and that the contingent decision to produce A or not (modeled by y_A), is aligned with the original decision of how much to produce of A (modeled by X_A). For the formulation, we define the parameter M to be a very large number, larger than the highest possible production of product A.

(6) $X_A - My_A \leq 0$ (X_A positive only if $y_A = 1$)

(7) y_A is binary

The complete formulation of the fixed charge product mix decision problem now amounts to the following MIP model.

Max $Z = 1500X_A + 2000X_B - 1000y_A$

Subject to

(1) $3X_A \leq 150$ (limited capacity in resource 1)

(2) $1X_A + 2X_B \leq 140$ (limited capacity in resource 2)

(3) $2X_A + 2X_B \leq 160$ (limited capacity in resource 3)

(4) $X_B \geq 20$ (produce at least 20 batches of product B)

(5) $X_A, X_B \geq 0$ (non − negativity constraint)

(6) $X_A - My_A \leq 0$ (X_A positive only if $y_A = 1$)

(7) y_A is binary

The versatility of IP models means that they can be used to describe almost any kind of deterministic decision situation with a single objective. Their usefulness in practical applications may however be limited by the computational effort involved in solving large size problems. Still, the situation is continuously improving thanks to increased computer capacity and better solution algorithms. One of the most widely used software packages for solution of large-scale IP (and LP) models is CPLEX, a product sold and developed by the company ILOG.

It may be worth noting that when dealing with reasonably large integer variables it is usually an acceptable approximation to use an LP model and then round the solution to integers (although there is no guarantee that the rounded solution is feasible). However, in case of binary variables, this approach is generally not feasible.

Economic lot sizing model

Let us now consider a simple nonlinear decision model that has been around for a long time but still is very important in production and inventory management, the so-called classical economic order quantity (EOQ) model.

Consider an inventory location that replenishes its stock of an item from an external supplier. The problem is to determine a suitable batch quantity, that is, to decide on the size of a replenishment order. This decision is mainly affected by two costs. First there is usually a fixed "ordering cost" associated with each replenishment (independent of the batch size). This cost can be due to administrative costs associated with the handling of orders and to costs for transportation and materials handling. The other important cost that needs to be considered is a "holding cost" per unit and time unit. The holding cost includes an opportunity cost for capital tied up in inventory, but may also include other costs that increase with the inventory on hand.

Our simple model assumes that the known demand is constant and continuous. Furthermore, the batch quantity is not changed over time, the whole batch quantity is delivered at the same time, and no shortages are allowed. We shall use the following notation:

h = holding cost per unit and time unit,
A = ordering or setup cost,
d = demand per time unit,
Q = batch quantity,
C = costs per time unit.

Clearly, a batch should arrive and be placed in stock just as the previous batch is depleted. The development of the inventory level can therefore be illustrated as in Fig. 3.

We wish to determine the optimal batch quantity Q^*. The relevant costs to consider in the decision model are therefore the costs that vary with the batch quantity Q. We get

$$C = \frac{Q}{2}h + \frac{d}{Q}A$$

The first term represents the holding costs, which we obtain as the average stock, $Q/2$, multiplied by the holding cost h. The average number of orders per unit of time is d/Q, and multiplying by the ordering cost A, renders the ordering costs per unit time in the second term.

It is easy to optimize the cost function. We just set the derivative with respect to Q equal to zero (as one can show that C is a convex function).

$$\frac{dC}{dQ} = \frac{h}{2} - \frac{d}{Q^2}A = 0$$

Solving for Q we get the EOQ:

$$Q^* = \sqrt{\frac{2Ad}{h}}$$

This result was first derived by Harris in Harris[9] There is also a well-known early paper by Wilson, Wilson,[10] providing the same result.

As we have discussed in the introduction, it is common to use decision rules that are based on certain simplified assumptions also in settings where these assumptions are not really satisfied. For example, in practice it is common to use the classical lot size formula also in case of stationary stochastic demand. The constant demand d is then usually replaced by the demand forecast. It can be shown that this approximation, in general, works quite well. The considered simple lot size formula has been implemented in an enormous number of inventory control systems. There are also many related models, see, for example, Axsäter.[11]

Stochastic Models

In many situations, the inherent uncertainty or randomness of decision input information is the main obstacle for making good decisions. Intuitively understanding the consequences of random behavior on the system performance is difficult for most people, including decision makers. This emphasizes the need for quantitative decision models that explicitly incorporate randomness and evaluates its consequences. Describing uncertainty and randomness mathematically involves the use of probability theory and stochastic variables. To make the discussion more concrete and to illustrate the usefulness of stochastic decision models, we will in this section look closer at the classical newsvendor model, which is

the foundation on which many stochastic inventory models are built.

Before turning to the newsvendor model, it is worth emphasizing that the complexity associated with stochastic behavior often prohibits the use of detailed analytical models. In these situations computer-based simulation models may be very useful for evaluating different decision alternatives and analyzing the dynamics of complicated stochastic systems. Particularly, modern discrete event simulation software packages with graphical interface represent a flexible and easy to use decision support tool. For further details on simulation modeling and the use of modern discrete event simulation software, one can turn to Law and Kelton[12] and Laguna and Marklund.[13] The latter also provides an introduction to analytical modeling of simple queuing systems (see also Hillier and Lieberman),[3] which represents another important area in stochastic decision modeling.

The newsvendor model

In this section we consider the classical newsvendor model. In its original form, the problem deals with a newsvendor who can buy copies of a newspaper in the morning for a certain price, and sell them during the day for a higher price. The stochastic demand during the day is known through its probability distribution. The newsvendor is not paid anything for unsold copies of the newspaper.

We shall deal with a slightly more general formulation of the problem and introduce the following notation:

X = stochastic period demand,

$f(x)$ = density of the stochastic period demand,

$F(x)$ = cumulative distribution function of the stochastic period demand, that is, the probability that the demand X is less than or equal to x,

S = ordered amount,

c_o = overage cost, that is, the cost per unit for inventory remaining at the end of the period,

c_u = underage cost, that is, the cost per unit for unmet period demand.

Let us for a moment go back to the newsvendor interpretation of the problem. The period length is then one day. Assume that the newsvendor pays 25 cents for a copy of the newspaper and sells them for 75 cents during the day. We then have $c_o = 25$, and $c_u = 75 - 25 = 50$. Note that c_u in this case corresponds to the opportunity costs for lost sales.

For a certain demand X the costs are:

$$C(X) = (S - X)c_o \quad \text{if } X \leq S$$

$$C(X) = (X - S)c_u \quad \text{if } X > S$$

Using this we can express the expected costs $C = E\{C(X)\}$ as:

$$C = c_o \int_0^S (S - x)f(x)dx + c_u \int_S^\infty (x - S)f(x)dx$$

It is relatively easy to show that the expected costs are minimized when S is chosen so that

$$F(S) = \frac{c_u}{c_o + c_u}$$

This means that the optimal S can be obtained from a very simple decision rule,

$$S = F^{-1}\left(\frac{c_u}{c_o + c_u}\right)$$

The newsvendor model has many important applications, especially when considering ordering and capacity decisions regarding products with a short selling season or product life cycle, for example, in the fashion industry. The model is also closely related to many multiperiod inventory models dealing with an infinite horizon. Assume that there are many periods and associated replenishment opportunities. The overage cost in a period is then the cost to carry a unit in stock to the next period, that is, a holding cost. Similarly, the underage cost can be interpreted as the cost for letting a customer wait to the next period, that is, a backorder cost. For overviews of different types of stochastic inventory models see, for example, Axsäter[11] and Silver et al.[14]

Other Types of Decision Models

So far we have considered two types of decision models, deterministic and stochastic models. For both types of models we have assumed a single decision maker who wants to find the best decision for a considered system as a whole. However, there may also be situations where there are several decision makers interacting (competing or cooperating). If the behavior and responses of these different decision makers are important to understand in order to make good quality decisions, the dynamics need to be incorporated into the quantitative decision model. To analyze game situations where there are several decision makers with different goals, different types of game theoretic models can be used. Such situations are very common in practice.

Let us return to the newsvendor model in "The Newsvendor Model" section. In this model we only studied a single decision maker. However, it is quite natural to extend the model to include two decision makers. We let the newsvendor have the same role as in "The Newsvendor Model" section. But the newsvendor now buys the newspapers from a supplier with a certain production cost per unit. The supplier can choose the price he wants to charge the newsvendor. In this setting both the supplier and the newsvendor want to maximize their individual profits. What decisions should be taken by the two players? Will the resulting solution be optimal for the system as a whole? It turns out that the answer to the latter question is no. However, if we change the considered "wholesale-price contract" to a "buyback contract" where the supplier pays the newsvendor for left over inventory a coordinated solution may be reached. This means that it is possible to instigate a pricing and contract mechanism so that we can let the supplier and the newsvendor optimize their individual profits and still get a solution that is optimal for the system as a whole.

We refer to Cachon[15] and Chen[16] for overviews of the literature on coordination and contracts in such systems.

An underlying assumption for all the models we have considered in this entry is that there is a single, well-defined objective for each decision maker, for example, maximizing profits, minimizing costs, etc. However, in many situations the decision maker can be faced with several different objectives that may not be aligned, or may even be in direct conflict. For example, the objective to retain the present workforce may not be aligned with maximizing profits, the objective to maximize environmental friendliness may conflict with an objective to minimize costs, etc. Modeling and analysis of decision problems with multiple (conflicting) objectives is the focus of the multiple criteria decision making (MCDM) area. A basic question when approaching these problems is whether there is a clear order of priority between different objectives or not. An associated question is how to translate different objectives into a common scale. Monetary terms may not always be the best choice. For more about MCDM one can turn to, for example, Bouyssou et al.[17]

CONCLUSIONS

In this entry we have provided a description of the broad area of decision sciences from a quantitative modeling (OR/MS) perspective. An overarching objective with most research in this field is to use quantitative models to improve the quality of decisions. This means that the model is viewed as a tool for helping decision makers to generate, evaluate, and choose good decision alternatives. With this as a starting point, we have explained the conceptual approach underlying the use of quantitative decision modeling. We have also illustrated this general approach by considering some commonly used deterministic and stochastic decision models in more detail. The model types we have discussed include LP, IP, economic lot sizing, and the newsvendor model. We have also briefly commented on extensions and other modeling approaches such as game theory, MCDM, queuing, and simulation.

Looking at the development of the field, one can conclude that it is in many ways linked to the development and wide spread use of information technology and computers. With the increasing access to vast amounts of information, there is a growing potential for making better decisions that capture the value hidden in the information flow. This accentuates the need for quantitative decision models and decision support systems to help the decision makers sort, evaluate, and process input information into concrete decision alternatives. The increasing amounts of information also suggests more complex and large size models to evaluate, which can be done thanks to the fast development in computer technology, and more efficient solution methods. Altogether one can conclude that this paints a bright and interesting future for the field. However, an important challenge, in order for quantitative decision modeling to reach its full potential, is to bridge the gap between the complex quantitative model and the decision maker. The foundations for those bridges are carefully designed software packages, and easy to use decision support tools.

REFERENCES

1. Dantzig, G.B. Reminiscences about the origins of linear programming. Oper. Res. Lett. **1981/1982**, *1* (2), 43–48.
2. Kraft, D.H.; Boyce, B.R. In *Operations Research for Libraries and Information Agencies: Techniques for the Evaluation of Management Decision Alternatives*; Academic Press: San Diego, CA, 1991.
3. Hillier, F.S.; Lieberman, G.J. In *Introduction to Operations Research,* 8th Ed.; McGraw-Hill: Singapore: 2005.
4. Dantzig, G.B. In *Linear Programming and Extensions*; Princeton University Press: Princeton, NJ, 1963/68.
5. Dantzig, G.B.; Thapa, M.N. In *Linear Programming 1: Introduction*; Springer: New York, NY, 1997.
6. Dantzig, G.B.; Thapa, M.N. In *Linear Programming 2: Theory and Extensions*; Springer: New York, NY, 1997.
7. Vanderbei, R.J. In *Linear Programming: Foundations and Extensions*; 2nd Ed.; Kluwer Academic Publishers: Boston, MA, 2001.
8. Wolsey, L.A. In *Integer Programming*; Wiley: New York, NY, 1998.
9. Harris, F.W. How many parts to make at once. Factory, The Magazine of Management **1913**, *10*, 135–136, 152.
10. Wilson, R.H. A scientific routine for stock control. Harvard Bus. Rev. **1934**, *13*, 116–128.
11. Axsäter, S. In *Inventory Control,* 2nd Ed.; Springer: New York, NY, 2006.
12. Law, A.M.; Kelton, W.D. In *Simulation Modeling and Analysis*; 3rd Ed.; McGraw-Hill: Boston, MA, 2000.
13. Laguna, M.; Marklund, J. In *Business Process Modeling, Simulation and Design*; Prentice Hall: Upper Saddle River, NJ, 2005.
14. Silver, E.A.; Pyke, D.F.; Peterson, R. In *Inventory Management and Production Planning and Scheduling*; 3rd Ed.; Wiley: New York, NY, 1998.
15. Cachon, G.P. Supply chain coordination with contracts. In *Handbooks in OR & MS,* Vol. 11; de Kok, A.G., Graves, S.C., Eds.; North Holland: Amsterdam, 2003; 229–339.
16. Chen, F. Information sharing and supply chain coordination. In *Handbooks in OR & MS,* Vol. 11; de Kok, A.G., Graves, S.C., Eds.; North Holland: Amsterdam, 2003; 341–421.
17. Bouyssou, D.; Marchant, T.; Pirlot, M.; Tsoukiàs, A.; Vincke, P. *Evaluation and Decision Models with Multiple Criteria: Stepping Stones for the Analyst*; Springer: New York, NY, 2006.

Decision Support Systems

Marek J. Druzdzel
Roger R. Flynn
School of Information Sciences and Intelligent Systems Program, University of Pittsburgh, Pittsburgh, Pennsylvania, U.S.A.

Abstract

Decision support systems (DSSs) are defined as interactive computer-based systems that aid users in judgment and choice activities. The entry focuses on the core module of DSSs, notably one that directly supports modeling decision problems and identifies best alternatives. It introduces three components of decisions: decision alternatives, preferences, and uncertainty. It presents fundamental components of a DSS: the database management system, the model-base management system, and the dialog generation and management system. It discusses an emergent class of decision-analytic DSSs, based on the sound foundations of probability theory and decision theory. Finally, it reviews issues related to user interfaces to DSSs.

INTRODUCTION

Making decisions concerning complex systems (e.g., the management of organizational operations, industrial processes, or investment portfolios; the command and control of military units; the control of nuclear power plants) often strain our cognitive capabilities. Even though individual interactions among a system's variables may be well understood, predicting how the system will react to an external manipulation such as a policy decision is often difficult. What will be, for example, the effect of introducing the third shift on a factory floor? One might expect that this will increase the plant's output by roughly 50%. Factors such as additional wages, machine wear down, maintenance breaks, raw material usage, supply logistics, and future demand also need to be considered, however, because they will all affect the total financial outcome of this decision. Many variables are involved in complex and often subtle interdependencies, and predicting the total outcome may be daunting.

There is a substantial amount of empirical evidence that human intuitive judgment and decision making can be far from optimal, and it deteriorates even further with complexity and stress. In many situations, the quality of decisions is important; therefore, aiding the deficiencies of human judgment and decision making has been a major focus of science throughout history. Disciplines such as statistics, economics, and operations research developed various methods for making rational choices. More recently, these methods, often enhanced by various techniques originating from information science, cognitive psychology, and artificial intelligence, have been implemented in the form of computer programs, either as stand-alone tools or as integrated computing environments for complex decision making. Such environments are often given the common name of *decision support systems* (DSSs). The concept of DSS is extremely broad, and its definitions vary, depending on the author's point of view. To avoid exclusion of any of the existing types of DSSs, we define them roughly as interactive computer-based systems that aid users in judgment and choice activities. Another name sometimes used as a synonym for DSS is *knowledge-based systems*, which refers to their attempt to formalize domain knowledge so that it is amenable to mechanized reasoning.

DSSs are gaining an increased popularity in various domains, including business, engineering, military, and medicine. They are especially valuable in situations in which the amount of available information is prohibitive for the intuition of an unaided human decision maker, and in which precision and optimality are of importance. DSSs can aid human cognitive deficiencies by integrating various sources of information, providing intelligent access to relevant knowledge, and aiding the process of structuring decisions. They can also support choice among well-defined alternatives and build on formal approaches, such as the methods of engineering economics, operations research, statistics, and decision theory. They can also employ artificial intelligence methods to heuristically address problems that are intractable by formal techniques. Proper application of decision-making tools increases productivity, efficiency, and effectiveness, and gives many businesses a comparative advantage over their competitors, allowing them to make optimal choices for technological processes and their parameters, planning business operations, logistics, or investments.

Encyclopedia of Information Systems and Technology, DOI: 10.1081/E-EIST-120043887

Data Mining:
Healthcare–
Decision

Although it is difficult to overestimate the importance of various computer-based tools that are relevant to decision making (e.g., databases, planning software, spreadsheets), this entry focuses primarily on the core of a DSS, the part that directly supports modeling decision problems and identifies best alternatives. We briefly discuss the characteristics of decision problems and how decision making can be supported by computer programs. We then cover various components of DSSs and the role that they play in decision support. We also introduce an emergent class of *normative systems* (i.e., DSSs based on sound theoretical principles), and in particular, decision-analytic DSSs. Finally, we review issues related to user interfaces to DSSs and stress the importance of user interfaces to the ultimate quality of decisions aided by computer programs.

DECISIONS AND DECISION MODELING

Types of Decisions

A simple view of decision making is that it is a problem of choice among several alternatives. A somewhat more sophisticated view includes the process of constructing the alternatives (i.e., given a problem statement, developing a list of choice options). A complete picture includes a search for opportunities for decisions (i.e., discovering that there is a decision to be made). A manager of a company may face a choice in which the options are clear (e.g., the choice of a supplier from among all existing suppliers). He or she may also face a well-defined problem for which she designs creative decision options (e.g., how to market a new product so that the profits are maximized). Finally, the manager may work in a less reactive fashion, and view decision problems as opportunities that have to be discovered by studying the operations of her company and its surrounding environment (e.g., how can she make the production process more efficient). There is much anecdotal and some empirical evidence that structuring decision problems and identifying creative decision alternatives determine the ultimate quality of decisions. DSSs aim mainly at this broadest type of decision making, and in addition to supporting choice, they aid in modeling and analyzing systems (e.g., as complex organizations), identifying decision opportunities, and structuring decision problems.

Human Judgment and Decision Making

Theoretical studies on rational decision making, notably that in the context of probability theory and decision theory, have been accompanied by empirical research on whether human behavior complies with the theory. It has been rather convincingly demonstrated in numerous empirical studies that human judgment and decision making are based on intuitive strategies, as opposed to theoretically sound reasoning rules. These intuitive strategies, referred to as *judgmental heuristics* in the context of decision making, help us in reducing the cognitive load, but alas at the expense of optimal decision making. Effectively, our unaided judgment and choice exhibit systematic violations of probability axioms (referred to as *biases*). Formal discussion of the most important research results, along with experimental data, can be found in an anthology edited by Kahneman et al.[1] Dawes[2] provided an accessible introduction to what is known about people's decision-making performance.

One might hope that people who have achieved expertise in a domain will not be subject to judgmental biases and will approach optimality in decision making. Although empirical evidence shows that experts indeed are more accurate than novices, within their area of expertise, it also shows that they also are liable to the same judgmental biases as novices, and demonstrate apparent errors and inconsistencies in their judgment. Professionals such as practicing physicians use essentially the same judgmental heuristics and are prone to the same biases, although the degree of departure from the normatively prescribed judgment seems to decrease with experience. In addition to laboratory evidence, there are several studies of expert performance in realistic settings, showing that it is inferior even to simple linear models (an informal review of the available evidence and pointers to literature can be found in the book by Dawes).[2] For example, predictions of future violent behavior of psychiatric patients made by a panel of psychiatrists who had access to patient records and interviewed the patients were found to be inferior to a simple model that included only the past incidence of violent behavior. Predictions of marriage counselors concerning marital happiness were shown to be inferior to a simple model that just subtracted the rate of fighting from the rate of sexual intercourse (again, the marriage counselors had access to all data, including interviews with the couples). Studies yielding similar results were conducted with bank loan officers, physicians, university admission committees, and so on.

Modeling Decisions

The superiority of even simple linear models over human intuitive judgment suggests that one way to improve the quality of decisions is to decompose a decision problem into simpler components that are well defined and well understood. Studying a complex system built out of such components can be subsequently aided by a formal, theoretically sound technique. The process of decomposing and formalizing a problem is often called modeling. Modeling amounts to finding an abstract representation of a real-world system that simplifies and assumes as much as possible about the system, and while retaining the system's essential relationships, omits unnecessary detail. Building a model of a decision problem, as opposed to reasoning about a problem in a holistic way, allows for applying scientific knowledge that can be transferred across problems and often across domains. It allows for analyzing, explaining, and arguing about a decision problem.

The desire to improve human decision making provided motivation for the development of various modeling tools in disciplines of economics, operations research, decision theory, decision analysis, and statistics. In each modeling tool, knowledge about a system is represented by means of algebraic, logical, or statistical variables. Interactions among these variables are expressed by equations or logical rules, possibly enhanced with an explicit representation of uncertainty. When the functional form of an interaction is unknown, it is sometimes described in purely probabilistic terms (e.g., by a conditional probability distribution). Once a model has been formulated, various mathematical methods can be used to analyze it. Decision making under certainty has been addressed by economic and operations research methods, such as cash flow analysis, break-even analysis, scenario analysis, mathematical programming, inventory techniques, and various optimization algorithms for scheduling and logistics. Decision making under uncertainty enhances the above methods with statistical approaches, such as reliability analysis, simulation, and statistical decision making. Most of these methods have made it into college curricula and can be found in management textbooks. Due to space constraints, we do not discuss their details further.

Components of Decision Models

Although a model mathematically consists of variables and a specification of interactions among them, from the point of view of decision making, a model and its variables represent the following three components: 1) a measure of preferences over decision objectives; 2) available decision options; and 3) a measure of uncertainty over variables influencing the decision and the outcomes.

Preference is widely viewed as the most important concept in decision making. Outcomes of a decision process are not all equally attractive, and it is crucial for a decision maker to examine these outcomes in terms of their desirability. Preferences can be ordinal (e.g., more income is preferred to less income), but it is convenient and often necessary to represent them as numerical quantities, especially if the outcome of the decision process consists of multiple attributes that need

to be compared on a common scale. Even when they consist of just a single attribute but the choice is made under uncertainty, expressing preferences numerically allows for trade-offs between desirability and risk.

The second component of decision problems is available decision options. Often these options can be enumerated (e.g., a list of possible suppliers), but sometimes they are continuous values of specified policy variables (e.g., the amount of raw material to be kept in stock). Listing the available decision options is an important element of model structuring.

The third element of decision models is uncertainty. Uncertainty is one of the most inherent and most prevalent properties of knowledge, originating from incompleteness of information, imprecision, and model approximations made for the sake of simplicity. It would not be an exaggeration to state that real-world decisions not involving uncertainty either do not exist or belong to a truly limited class. As Benjamin Franklin expressed it in 1789 in a letter to his friend M. Le Roy, "in this world nothing can said to be certain, except death and taxes."[3]

Decision making under uncertainty can be viewed as a deliberation—determining what action should be taken that will maximize the expected gain. Due to uncertainty, there is no guarantee that the result of the action will be the one intended, and the best one can hope for is to maximize the chance of a desirable outcome. The process rests on the assumption that a good decision is one that results from a good decision-making process that considers all important factors and is explicit about decision alternatives, preferences, and uncertainty.

It is important to distinguish between good decisions and good outcomes. By a stroke of good luck, a poor decision can lead to a very good outcome. Similarly, a very good decision can be followed by a bad outcome. Supporting decisions mean supporting the decision-making process so that better decisions are made. Better decisions can be expected to lead to better outcomes.

DECISION SUPPORT SYSTEMS

DSSs are interactive, computer-based systems that aid users in judgment and choice activities. They provide data storage and retrieval, but enhance the traditional information access and retrieval functions with support for model building and model-based reasoning. They support framing, modeling, and problem solving.

Typical application areas of DSSs are management and planning in business, health care, military, and any area in which management will encounter complex decision situations. DSSs are typically used for strategic and tactical decisions faced by upper-level management—decisions with a reasonably low frequency and high

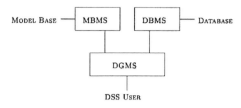

Fig. 1 The architecture of a DSS.
Source: From Sage.[4]

potential consequences—in which the time taken for thinking through and modeling the problem pays off generously in the long run.

There are three fundamental components of DSSs:[4]

- *Database management system (DBMS)*. A DBMS serves as a data bank for the DSS. It stores large quantities of data that is relevant to the class of problems for which the DSS has been designed and provides logical data structures (as opposed to the physical data structures) with which the users interact. A DBMS separates the users from the physical aspects of the database structure and processing. It should also be capable of informing the user of the types of data that are available and how to gain access to them.
- *Model-base management system (MBMS)*. The role of MBMS is analogous to that of a DBMS. Its primary function is providing independence between specific models that are used in a DSS from the applications that use them. The purpose of an MBMS is to transform data from the DBMS into information that is useful in decision making. Because many problems that the user of a DSS will cope with may be unstructured, the MBMS should also be capable of assisting the user in model building.
- *Dialog generation and management system (DGMS)*. The main product of an interaction with a DSS is insight. Because their users are often managers who are not computer trained, DSSs need to be equipped with intuitive and easy-to-use interfaces. These interfaces aid in model building, but also in interaction with the model, such as gaining insight and recommendations from it. The primary responsibility of a DGMS is to enhance the ability of the system user to use and benefit from the DSS. In the remainder of this entry, we use the broader term user interface rather than DGMS.

Although various DSSs exists, the above three components can be found in many DSS architectures and play a prominent role in their structure. Interaction among them is shown in Fig. 1.

Essentially, the user interacts with the DSS through the DGMS. This communicates with the DBMS and MBMS, which screen the user and the user interface

from the physical details of the model base and database implementation.

NORMATIVE SYSTEMS

Normative and Descriptive Approaches

Whether one trusts the quality of human intuitive reasoning strategies has a profound impact on one's view of the philosophical and technical foundations of DSSs. There are two distinct approaches to supporting decision making. The first aims at building support procedures or systems that imitate human experts. The most prominent member of this class of DSSs are *expert systems*, computer programs based on rules elicited from human domain experts that imitate reasoning of a human expert in a given domain. Expert systems are often capable of supporting decision making in that domain at a level comparable to human experts. Although they are flexible and often able to address complex decision problems, they are based on intuitive human reasoning and lack soundness and formal guarantees with respect to the theoretical reliability of their results. The danger of the expert system approach, increasingly appreciated by DSS builders, is that along with imitating human thinking and its efficient heuristic principles, we may also imitate its undesirable flaws.[5]

The second approach is based on the assumption that the most reliable method of dealing with complex decisions is through a small set of normatively sound principles of how decisions should be made. Although heuristic methods and ad hoc reasoning schemes that imitate human cognition may in many domains perform well, most decision makers will be reluctant to rely on them whenever the cost of making an error is high. To give an extreme example, few people would choose to fly airplanes built using heuristic principles over airplanes built using the laws of aerodynamics enhanced with probabilistic reliability analysis. Application of formal methods in DSSs makes these systems philosophically distinct from those based on ad hoc heuristic artificial intelligence methods, such as rule-based systems. The goal of a DSS, according to this view, is to support unaided human intuition, just as the goal of using a calculator is to aid human's limited capacity for mental arithmetic.

Decision-Analytic DSSs

An emergent class of DSSs known as *decision-analytic DSSs* applies the principles of decision theory, probability theory, and decision analysis to their decision models. Decision theory is an axiomatic theory of decision making that is built on a small set of axioms of rational decision making. It expresses uncertainty in

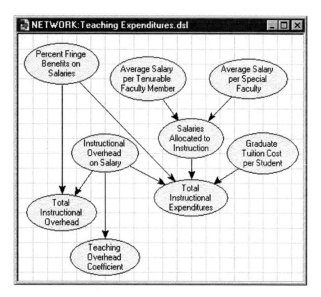

Fig. 2 Example of a BN modeling teaching expenditures in university operations.

terms of probabilities and preferences in terms of utilities. These are combined using the operation of mathematical expectation. The attractiveness of probability theory, as a formalism for handling uncertainty in DSSs, lies in its soundness and its guarantees concerning long-term performance. Probability theory is often viewed as the gold standard for rationality in reasoning under uncertainty. Following its axioms offers protection from some elementary inconsistencies. Their violation, however, can be demonstrated to lead to sure losses.[6] Decision analysis is the art and science of applying decision theory to real-world problems. It includes a wealth of techniques for model construction, such as methods for elicitation of model structure and probability distributions that allow the minimization of human bias, methods for checking the sensitivity of a model to imprecision in the data, computing the value of obtaining additional information, and presentation of results (see, e.g., von Winterfeldt and Edwards[1][7] for a basic review of the available techniques). These methods have been under continuous scrutiny by psychologists working in the domain of behavioral decision theory and have proven to cope reasonably well with the dangers related to human judgmental biases.

Normative systems are usually based on graphical probabilistic models, which are representations of the joint probability distribution over a model's variables in terms of directed graphs. Directed graphs, such as the one in Fig. 2, are known as Bayesian networks (BNs) or causal networks.[8] Bayesian networks offer a compact representation of joint probability distributions and are capable of practical representation of large models, consisting of tens or hundreds of variables. BNs can be easily extended with decision and value variables for modeling decision problems. The former denote

variables that are under the decision maker's control and can be directly manipulated, and the latter encode users' preferences over various outcomes of the decision process. Such amended graphs are known as *influence diagrams*.[9] Both the structure and the numerical probability distributions in a BN can be elicited from a human expert and are a reflection of the expert's subjective view of a real-world system. If available, scientific knowledge about the system, both in terms of the structure and frequency data, can be easily incorporated in the model. Once a model has been created, it is optimized using formal decision-theoretic algorithms. Decision analysis is based on the empirically tested paradigm that people are able to reliably store and retrieve their personal beliefs about uncertainty and preferences for different outcomes, but are much less reliable in aggregating these fragments into a global inference. Although human experts are excellent in structuring a problem, determining the components that are relevant to it, and providing local estimates of probabilities and preferences, they are not reliable in combining many simple factors into an optimal decision. The role of a decision-analytic DSS is to support them in their weaknesses using the formal and theoretically sound principles of statistics.

The approach taken by decision analysis is compatible with that of DSSs. The goal of decision analysis is to provide insight into a decision. This insight, consisting of the analysis of all relevant factors, their uncertainty, and the critical nature of some assumptions, is even more important than the actual recommendation.

Decision-analytic DSSs have been successfully applied to practical systems in medicine, business, and engineering. Some examples of applications are described in a special issue of *Communications of the ACM* on practical applications of decision-theoretic methods (Vol. 38, No. 3, March 1995). We encourage the readers to experiment with GeNIe,[10] a development system for decision-analytic DSSs developed at the Decision Systems Laboratory, University of Pittsburgh, available at http://genie.sis.pitt.edu/. As these systems tend to naturally evolve into three not necessarily distinct classes, it may be interesting to compare their structure and architectural organization.

• *Systems with static domain models.* In this class of systems, a probabilistic domain is represented by a typically large network encoding the domain's structure and its numerical parameters. The network comprising the domain model is normally built by decision analysts and domain experts. An example might be a medical diagnostic system covering a certain class of disorders. Queries in such a system are answered by assigning values to those nodes of the network that constitute the observations for a particular case and propagating the impact of the observation through the network to find the probability distribution of some selected nodes of interest (e.g., nodes that represent diseases). Such a network can, on a case-by-case basis, be extended with decision nodes and value nodes to support decisions. Systems with static domain models are conceptually similar to rule-based expert systems covering an area of expertise.

- *Systems with customized decision models.* The main idea behind this approach is automatic generation of a graphical decision model on a per-case basis in an interactive effort between the DSS and the decision maker. The DSS has domain expertise in a certain area and plays the role of a decision analyst. During this interaction, the program creates a customized influence diagram, which is later used for generating advice. The main motivation for this approach is the premise that every decision is unique and needs to be looked at individually; an influence diagram needs to be tailored to individual needs.[11]

- *Systems capable of learning a model from data.* The third class of systems employs computer-intensive statistical methods for learning models from data.[12–16] Whenever there is sufficient data available, the systems can literally learn a graphical model from this data. This model can be subsequently used to support decisions within the same domain.

The first two approaches are suited for slightly different applications. The customized model generation approach is an attempt to automate the most laborious part of decision making, structuring a problem, so far done with significant assistance from trained decision analysts. A session with the program that assists the decision maker in building an influence diagram is laborious. This makes the customized model generation approach particularly suitable for decision problems that are infrequent and serious enough to be treated individually. Because in the static domain model approach, an existing domain model needs to be customized by the case data only, the decision-making cycle is rather short. This makes it particularly suitable for those decisions that are highly repetitive and need to be made under time constraints.

A practical system can combine the three approaches. A static domain model can be slightly customized for a case that needs individual treatment. Once completed, a customized model can be blended into the large static model. Learning systems can support both the static and the customized model approach. However, the learning process can be greatly enhanced by prior knowledge from domain experts or by a prior model.

Equation-Based and Mixed Systems

In many business and engineering problems, interactions among model variables can be described by equations

that, when solved simultaneously, can be used to predict the effect of decisions on the system, and hence support decision making. One special type of simultaneous equation model is known as the structural equation model (SEM), which has been a popular method of representing systems in econometrics. An equation is structural if it describes a unique, independent causal mechanism acting in the system. Structural equations are based on expert knowledge of the system combined with theoretical considerations. Structural equations allow for a natural, modular description of a system— each equation represents its individual component, a separable and independent mechanism acting in the system—yet, the main advantage of having a structural model is, as explicated by Simon,[17] that it includes causal information and aids predictions of the effects of external interventions. In addition, the causal structure of a SEM can be represented graphically,[17] which allows for combining them with decision-analytic graphical models in practical systems.[17,18]

SEMs offer significant advantages for policy making. Often a decision maker confronted with a complex system needs to decide not only the values of policy variables, but also which variables should be manipulated. A change in the set of policy variables has a profound impact on the structure of the problem and on how their values will propagate through the system. The user chooses which variables are policy variables and which are determined within the model. A change in the SEMs or the set of policy variables can be reflected by a rapid restructuring of the model and predictions involving this new structure.[19]

Our long-term project, the Environment for Strategic Planning (ESP),[20] is based on a hybrid graphical modeling tool that combines SEMs with decision-analytic principles. The ESP is capable of representing both discrete and continuous variables involved in deterministic and probabilistic relationships. The powerful features of SEMs allow the ESP to act as a graphical spreadsheet integrating numerical and symbolic methods, and allowing the independent variables to be selected at will without having to reformulate the model each time. This provides an immense flexibility that is not afforded by ordinary spreadsheets in evaluating alternate policy options.

USER INTERFACES TO DSSS

Although the quality and reliability of modeling tools and the internal architectures of DSSs are important, the most crucial aspect of DSSs is, by far, their user interface. Systems with user interfaces that are cumbersome or unclear or that require unusual skills are rarely useful and accepted in practice. The most important result of a session with a DSS is insight into the decision problem. In addition, when the system is based on normative principles, it can play a tutoring role; one might hope that users will learn the domain model and how to reason with it over time, and improve their own thinking.

A good user interface to DSSs should support model construction and model analysis, reasoning about the problem structure in addition to numerical calculations, and both choice and optimization of decision variables. We discuss these in the following sections.

Support for Model Construction and Model Analysis

User interface is the vehicle for both model construction (or model choice) and for investigating the results. Even if a system is based on a theoretically sound reasoning scheme, its recommendations will only be as good as the model on which they are based. Furthermore, even if the model is a very good approximation of reality and its recommendations are correct, they will not be followed if they are not understood. Without understanding, the users may accept or reject a system's advice for the wrong reasons and the combined decision-making performance may deteriorate even below unaided performance.[21] A good user interface should make the model on which the system's reasoning is based transparent to the user.

Modeling is rarely a one-shot process, and good models are usually refined and enhanced as their users gather practical experiences with the system recommendations. It is important to strike a careful balance between precision and modeling efforts; some parts of a model need to be very precise, whereas others do not. A good user interface should include tools for examining the model and identifying its most sensitive parts, which can be subsequently elaborated on. Systems employed in practice will need their models refined, and a good user interface should make it easy to access, examine, and refine its models. Some pointers to work on support for building decision-analytic systems can be found in the works of Druzdzel et al.[22–25]

Support for Reasoning about the Problem Structure in Addition to Numerical Calculations

Although numerical calculations are important in decision support, reasoning about the problem structure is even more important. Often when the system and its model are complex, it is insightful for the decision maker to realize how the system variables are interrelated. This is helpful not only in designing creative decision options, but also in understanding how a policy decision will affect the objective.

Graphical models, such as those used in decision analysis or in equationbased and hybrid systems, are particularly suitable for reasoning about structure. Under certain assumptions, a directed graphical model can be given a causal interpretation. This is especially convenient in situations where the DSS autonomically suggests decision options; given a causal interpretation of its model, it is capable of predicting effects of interventions. A causal graph facilitates building an effective user interface. The system can refer to causal interactions during its dialogue with the user, which is known to enhance user insight.[26]

Support for Both Choice and Optimization of Decision Variables

Many DSSs have an inflexible structure in the sense that the variables that will be manipulated are determined at the model-building stage. This is not very suitable for planning of the strategic type when the object of the decision-making process is identifying both the objectives and the methods of achieving them. For example, changing policy variables in a spreadsheet-based model often requires that the entire spreadsheet be rebuilt. If there is no support for that, few users will consider it as an option. This closes the world of possibilities for flexible reframing of a decision problem in the exploratory process of searching for opportunities. Support for both choice and optimization of decision variables should be an inherent part of DSSs.

Graphical Interface

Insight into a model can be increased greatly at the user interface level by a diagram representing the interactions among its components (e.g., a drawing of a graph on which a model is based, such as in Fig. 2). This graph is a qualitative, structural explanation of how information flows from the independent variables to the dependent variables of interest. Because models may become very large, it is convenient to structure them into submodels, groups of variables that form a subsystem of the modeled system.[27] Such submodels can be again shown graphically with interactions among them, increasing simplicity and clarity of the interface. Fig. 3 shows a submodel-level view of a model developed in our ESP project. Note that the graph in Fig. 2 is an expanded version of the *Teaching Expenditures* submodel in Fig. 3. The user can navigate through the hierarchy of the entire model in her quest for insight, opening and closing submodels on demand. Some pointers to work on user interfaces of decision-analytic systems can be found in Wang and Druzdzel,[25] Druzdzel,[27,28] and Wiecha.[29]

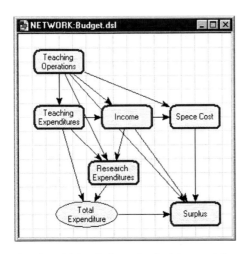

Fig. 3 A submodel-level view of a decision model.

CONCLUSION

DSSs are powerful tools integrating scientific methods for supporting complex decisions with techniques developed in information science and are gaining an increased popularity in many domains. They are especially valuable in situations in which the amount of available information is prohibitive for the intuition of an unaided human decision maker, and in which precision and optimality are of importance. DSSs aid human cognitive deficiencies by integrating various sources of information, providing intelligent access to relevant knowledge, aiding the process of structuring, and optimizing decisions.

Normative DSSs offer a theoretically correct and appealing way of handling uncertainty and preferences in decision problems. They are based on carefully studied empirical principles underlying the discipline of decision analysis, and they have been successfully applied in many practical systems. We believe that they offer several attractive features that are likely to prevail in the long run as far as the technical developments are concerned.

Because DSSs do not replace humans but rather augment their limited capacity to deal with complex problems, their user interfaces are critical. The user interface determines whether a DSS will be used at all and, if so, whether the ultimate quality of decisions will be higher than that of an unaided decision maker.

ACKNOWLEDGMENTS

Work on this entry was supported by the National Science Foundation under Faculty Early Career Development (CAREER) Program, grant IRI-9624629, by the Air Force Office of Scientific Research under grants F49620-97-1-0225, F49620-00-1-0112, and FA9550-06-1-0243 and by the University of Pittsburgh Central Research Development Fund. Fig. 2 and Fig. 3 are snapshots of GeNIe, a general purpose development environment for graphical DSSs developed by the Decision Systems Laboratory, University of Pittsburgh, and available at http://genie.sis.pitt.edu/. We want to thank Ms. Nanette Yurcik for her assistance with technical editing.

REFERENCES

1. *Judgment Under Uncertainty: Heuristics and Biases*; Kahneman, D., Slovic, P., Tversky, A., Eds.; Cambridge University Press: Cambridge, MA, 1982.
2. Dawes, R.M. *Rational Choice in an Uncertain World*; Hartcourt Brace Jovanovich: San Diego, CA, 1988.
3. John Bigelow (Ed.). *The Complete Works of Benjamin Franklin*; G. P. Putnam's Sons: New York and London, 1887, Vol. 10, 1700.
4. Sage, A.P. *Decision Support Systems Engineering*; John Wiley & Sons, Inc.: New York, NY, 1991.
5. Henrion, M.; Breese, J.S.; Horvitz, E.J. Decision analysis and expert systems. AI Mag. **1991**, Winter, *12* (4), 64–91.
6. Savage, L.J. *The Foundations of Statistics*; 2nd revised Ed.; Dover Publications: New York, NY, 1972.
7. von Winterfeldt, D.; Edwards, W. *Decision Analysis and Behavioral Research*; Cambridge University Press: Cambridge, 1988.
8. Pearl, J. *Probabilistic Reasoning in Intelligent Systems: Networks of Plausible Inference*; Morgan Kaufmann Publishers, Inc.: San Mateo, CA, 1988.
9. Howard, R.A.; Matheson, J.E. Influence diagrams. In *The Principles and Applications of Decision Analysis*; Howard, R. A., Matheson, J. E., Eds.; Strategic Decisions Group: Menlo Park, CA, 1984; 719–762.
10. Druzdzel, M.J. SMILE: Structural Modeling, Inference, and Learning Engine and GeNIe: a development environment for graphical decision-theoretic models. In Proceedings of the Sixteenth National Conference on Artificial Intelligence (AAAI-99), Orlando, FL, **1999**; 902–903.
11. Holtzman, S. *Intelligent Decision Systems*; Addison-Wesley: Reading, MA, 1989.
12. Spirtes, P.; Glymour, C.; Scheines, R. *Causation, Prediction, and Search*; Springer Verlag: New York, NY, 1993.
13. Pearl, J.; Verma, T.S. A theory of inferred causation. *KR-91, Principles of Knowledge Representation and Reasoning*; *Proceedings of the Second International Conference*, Cambridge, MA, Allen, J. A., Fikes, R., Sandewall, E., Eds.; Morgan Kaufmann Publishers, Inc.: San Mateo, CA, 1991; 441–452.
14. Cooper, G.F.; Herskovits, E. A Bayesian method for the induction of probabilistic networks from data. Mach. Learn. **1992**, *9* (4), 309–347.
15. *Computation, Causation, and Discovery*; Glymour, C., Cooper, G. F., Eds.; AAAI Press: Menlo Park, CA, 1999.
16. Heckerman, D.E.; Geiger, D.; Chickering, D.M. Learning Bayesian networks: the combination of knowledge and statistical data. Mach. Learn. **1995**, *20* (3), 197–243.

Data Mining:
Healthcare–
Decision

17. Simon, H.A. Causal ordering and identifiability. In *Studies in Econometric Method. Cowles Commission for Research in Economics*; Hood, W. C., Koopmans, T. C., Eds.; John Wiley & Sons, Inc.: New York, NY, 1953; 49–74 Monograph No. 14; Chapter III.

18. Druzdzel, M.J.; Simon, H.A. Causality in Bayesian belief networks. *Proceedings of the Ninth Annual Conference on Uncertainty in Artificial Intelligence (UAI-93)*, Morgan Kaufmann Publishers, Inc.: San Francisco, CA, 1993; 3–11.

19. Simon, H.A.; Kalagnanam, J.R.; Druzdzel, M.J. *Performance budget planning: the case of a research university;* 2000, Unpublished manuscript.

20. Druzdzel, M.J. ESP: A mixed initiative decision-theoretic decision modeling system. In *Working Notes of the AAAI-99 Workshop on Mixed-Initiative Intelligence*; Orlando, FL, 1999; 99–106.

21. Lehner, P.E.; Mullin, T.M.; Cohen, M.S. A probability analysis of the usefulness of decision aids. In *Uncertainty in Artificial Intelligence 5*; Henrion, M., Shachter, R. D., Kanal, L. N., Lemmer, J. F., Eds.; Elsevier Science Publishers: B. V.: North Holland, 1990; 427–436.

22. Druzdzel, M.J.; Díez, F.J. Criteria for combining knowledge from different sources in probabilistic models. J. Mach. Learn. Res. **2003**, *4* (July), 295–316.

23. Druzdzel, M.J.; van der Gaag, L.C. Building probabilistic networks: "Where do the numbers come from?" guest editors' introduction. IEEE Trans. Knowl. Data Eng. **2000**, *12* (4), 481–486.

24. Lu, T.-C.; Druzdzel, M.J. Causal mechanism-based model construction. *Proceedings of the Sixteenth Annual Conference on Uncertainty in Artificial Intelligence (UAI-2000)*, Morgan Kaufmann Publishers, Inc.: San Francisco, CA, 2000; 353–362.

25. Wang, H.; Druzdzel, M.J. User interface tools for navigation in conditional probability tables and elicitation of probabilities in Bayesian networks. In. Proceedings of the Sixteenth Annual Conference on Uncertainty in Artificial Intelligence (UAI-2000), Morgan Kaufmann Publishers, Inc.: San Francisco, CA, 2000; 617–625.

26. Druzdzel, M.J. Probabilistic reasoning in decision support systems: from computation to common sense. Department of Engineering and Public Policy, Carnegie Mellon University: Pittsburgh, PA, 1992; Ph.D. thesis.

27. Druzdzel, M.J. Five useful properties of probabilistic knowledge representations from the point of view of intelligent systems. Fundamenta Informaticæ **1997**, *30* (3/4), 241–254 (special issue on knowledge representation and machine learning).

28. Druzdzel, M.J. Explanation in probabilistic systems: Is it feasible? Will it work? In *Proceedings of the Fifth International Workshop on Intelligent Information Systems (WIS-96)*, Deblin, Poland, 1996; 12–24.

29. Wiecha, C.F. An empirical study of how visual programming aids in comprehending quantitative policy models (Volumes I and II). Department of Engineering and Public Policy, Carnegie Mellon University: Pittsburgh, PA, 1986, Ph.D. thesis.

EDRMS: Electronic Document and Records Management Systems

Azad Adam
London, U.K.

Abstract
This entry presents an overview of the fundamental aspects of different kinds of document and record management systems and technologies, starting off with a discussion of legislation concerning records and information. The entry then discusses fundamental components of systems, as well as presenting and explaining commonly used acronyms.

LEGISLATIVE ISSUES

Whenever any organization of any size retains information, especially when this relates to individuals, there are certain legal requirements that need to be followed regarding the recording of documents and records.

It is beyond the scope of this entry to cover all the legalities of storing information relating to individuals using electronic methods. Some important legislation need to be referred to within the United States, such as the Privacy Act 1974 and the Freedom of Information Act. In the United Kingdom, the Data Protection Act 1998 as well as the Freedom of Information Act 2000 needs to be adhered to.

Legislation—Freedom of Information Act, Privacy Act 1974, Data Protection Act 1998

The Freedom of Information Act is particularly important. Broadly speaking, under this legislation, citizens have a right to request almost any type of information from any organization within a specific time period. Needless to say, it greatly helps an organization to have an adequate document and record-keeping system in place to comply with freedom of information requests. Freedom of information laws exist in both the United States and United Kingdom.

The Privacy Act 1974 is a U. S. Act concerned with how information relating to citizens is stored and what rights they have regarding access to the information stored about themselves.

The Data Protection Act 1998 is, broadly speaking, the UK equivalent of the Privacy Act 1974 in the United States. It is concerned with how personal information relating to individuals is processed and handled.

DIFFERENCE BETWEEN DOCUMENTS AND RECORDS

The Oxford English Dictionary defines the word document as "a piece of written, printed, or electronic matter that provides information or evidence." The word record is defined as "a piece of evidence or information constituting an account of something that has occurred, been said, etc." In electronic document and records management systems (EDRMS), a record can be defined as an electronic folder consisting of one or more documents.

From the preceding definitions, where documents, that is, "written, printed, or electronic matter that provides information or evidence," are contained in a folder, all of which relate to a specific matter, or give the account over time of a specific matter, this would effectively create a record, which is "a piece of evidence or information constituting an account of something that has occurred, been said, etc."

Consider, for example, a planning or building application made to a council or municipality office. A person or organization submits a set of documents, which may include an application form, and the architect's drawings and reports. These documents would then be placed in a new folder, that is, a record, either electronic or manual, would be created to contain these documents. As the application progresses through various stages, the record concerning that particular planning application would have other documents placed in it. Thus, we have on file (electronic or otherwise) all documents that make up the record of what has happened with that particular planning application.

Another crucial difference between documents and records is that documents can change, whereas records do not and must not, change. A record is a document or set of documents, all relating to a specific matter that has occurred earlier. So, it is a record of history. As

Encyclopedia of Information Systems and Technology, DOI: 10.1081/E-EIST-120053808

EDRMS– Enterprise

451

Table 1 List of commonly used acronyms

Acronym	Actual Words
EDRMS	Electronic Document and Records Management System
EDMS	Electronic Document Management System
EDM	Electronic Document Management
ERM	Electronic Records Management
ERMS	Electronic Records Management System
DMS	Document Management System
DIP	Digital Image Processing
ECM	Enterprise Content Management
RM	Records Management
DM	Document Management

with the planning application, whenever documents are placed in the file, they become records if those documents are not subject to change. For example, the documents that make up the planning application would become a record of the planning application procedure.

A document, on the other hand, is something that could be a work in progress, which is subject to change and therefore not a record. Documents can and do become records once they are set in stone, so to speak, and do not undergo changes, that is, once those documents describe an event that has happened earlier, whether 2 minutes or 20 years ago.

ACRONYMS

The computer software that enables a computer system to store documents and records in an electronic format is referred to by many different names and acronyms. A list of commonly used acronyms is provided in **Table 1**.

Electronic Document and Records Management Systems

Electronic Document and Records Management System (EDRMS) refer to systems that are capable of handling both electronic documents and records.'

Electronic Document and Records Management

This is essentially the same as EDRMS but without the word system.

Electronic Document Management Systems

Electronic Document Management System (EDMS) mainly refer to systems that are designed primarily to deal with electronic document management.'

Electronic Document Management

This is the same as EDMS but without the word system, similar to EDRM mentioned previously. The same holds true for EDMS and EDM.

Electronic Records Management Systems

Electronic Records Management System (ERMS) refers to systems that are designed for electronic record keeping, archiving, and storage. Many of these systems also have integrated document management capabilities.

Electronic Records Management

This acronym is the same as ERMS but without the word system. As previously mentioned under EDRM, both "ERMS" and "ERM system" are the same in this text, and the acronyms are used as appropriate, for better sentence construction.

Document Management Systems

Document Management Systems (DMS) refers to systems that have been designed to manage documents. The absence of the word "electronic" would indicate that DMS is a system that is capable of managing both electronic and manual documents. However, 99 times out of 100, DMS would nowadays refer to an electronic system.

Enterprise Content Management

Enterprise Content Management (ECM) commonly refers to suites of applications, normally from one particular vendor, that are designed for content management, document management, records management, collaboration services, and workflow and Web content management as their main primary activities. An ECM system is one that has been developed and designed to manage all content, whether it be documents

Table 2 Basic components of electronic document management systems

Document Repository
Integration with Desktop Applications
Check-In and Check-Out
Versioning
Auditing
Security
Classification and Indexing
Search and Retrieval

or records, or whatever else that constitutes content within an organization.

DM and RM

Other commonly used terms are DM for document management and RM for record management. Some vendors use these terms to describe their products, for example, ACME DM or ACME RM. In other cases, these terms will simply be used as abbreviations, as already mentioned.

BASIC COMPONENTS OF EDMS

The basic components of an EDMS are listed in Table 2. With almost all commercially available EDM systems there will be functionality that will cross over into the areas of workflow, collaboration, record management, and archiving and imaging. This happens because software vendors tend to target their products at particular target audiences and will often incorporate other functionality that is needed alongside core EDMS functionality.

Document Repository

All EDM systems need to have a document repository. This is where the system stores documents that are under its management. Most commonly, the document repository will be on the hard disk of a networked server. The document repository could be in just one location on one particular server or could be distributed across many different servers. Hence, the repository should be a central store for all the documents in the organization, allowing users to retrieve them from the repository via the search and retrieval or browsing functionality.

The core idea of having a document repository could fail if users in the organization do not place documents in the repository when they are created. However, a properly implemented EDM system would ensure that documents are placed in the repository on creation. This could be achieved if users are allowed to save

documents to the repository only and, possibly, not permitted to save documents to their local hard drives or other network locations, these features being disabled at the desktop application level. For example, the Save functionality in a word processor, spreadsheet, or any other desktop application software could be configured to allow saving to the EDMS document repository only, which leads to another area of functionality known as Integration with Desktop Applications.

Besides an EDM system having a document repository, the system would also use a database of some kind to store information about the documents. This is often referred to as metadata, and will be covered in greater depth later in this section.

Folder Structures

The EDM system should allow a system administrator to set up and maintain an organized folder structure allowing for documents and files to be placed within folders according to their classification. The folder structure could be set up to follow the organizational structure, or it could be project based, representing projects within the organization, or business function based or property based. The folder structure could also be set up in a combination of the organizational structure and project-based structure, or it could be a combination of business function and property-based structure. Whichever is decided upon, the EDM system should allow a system administrator to set up and maintain a folder structure.

Integration with Desktop Applications

An EDM system needs to integrate with desktop applications, thereby allowing users to save documents straight from the application the document was created in, as mentioned in the preceding section on the document repository. The vast majority of EDM systems integrate with many popular desktop application suites such as Microsoft Office.

Check-In and Check-Out

Check-in and Check-out is a feature of EDM systems that controls who is editing a document and when it is being edited, and also ensures that not more than one person edits a document at any one time. For example, if a user needs to edit a document, it is checked out to that particular user who is thereby allowed to edit the document; other users in the organization would only be able view that document but not edit it, that is, the document is in read-only mode to everybody else except the person who has checked out the document and is editing it. When the user who has checked out the document has finished editing it, he or she can then check in the document, thereby saving the updated copy to the document repository, allowing other users to access the updated document. After a document has been updated, the system needs to keep track of the changes. This is accomplished by versioning and auditing.

Version Control

After a document has been updated, there needs to be a mechanism by which the system can keep track of the changes made to that document. This is achieved by assigning the document a version number. For example, when a document is created and first saved into the document repository, it will be assigned a version number of 1.0. After it has been updated, the document could be assigned a version number of 1.1. The next time it is updated, it may be assigned the version number 1.2, and so on. With major revisions of the document, the version number can increase by one whole increment; for example, the document version could go from 1.2 to 2.0. Besides keeping track of version numbers, the system should allow authorized users access to previous versions of the document.

Auditing

Auditing, along with version control, keeps a check on which users made changes to a document and when. The auditing feature would allow authorized users to find out the changes that have been made to the document since it was first created. For example, if a document is now in version 1.3, then the auditing feature would allow authorized users to run a report to enable them to find out when the document was first created, the date it was updated and by which user, and what were the exact changes that were made to the document when it was updated.

To sum up, auditing allows you to discover the changes that were made, when they were made, and who made them.

Security

Security is an extremely important component in a properly implemented system. Security should be tightly integrated with the system, allowing for security access permissions to be applied at different levels within the system. For example, the system should allow an administrator to apply specific security settings to an individual document, thereby specifying that certain users or a certain group of users can both read and make changes to a certain document, whereas other users may only be able to read that document but not

make any changes; still other users may not even be able to see that particular document.

An administrator of a system or a certain section of the system should also be able to set up and maintain security settings on individual files, folders, or groups of folders within the system, again allowing for read, write, or no access security permissions to be set up, as necessary.

Classification and Indexing

All documents should be classified and indexed using metadata, thereby allowing them to be easily retrieved at a later date using a search mechanism. The metadata should contain information about the document, such as the author, the document title, the date it was created, the subject of the document, and the department where the document originates, among other information. If a document is properly classified and indexed, then it can be easily found using search and retrieval mechanisms by users within the organization.

Search and Retrieval

Searching and retrieving documents is the other half of classifying and indexing documents. When documents are classified and indexed, they are placed into the EDMS document repository in a systematically organized fashion. The more intuitive the classification and indexing of documents is, the easier it will be to locate them using the search and retrieval mechanism.

A good system should offer users multiple ways in which to locate (search and retrieve) documents using a few different mechanisms, such as browsing the folder structure, a basic search, and an advanced search.

A basic search should simply allow the user to type in keywords and then retrieve all documents in which the keywords match either the metadata or the document's content. An advanced search should allow the user to search individual metadata fields, allowing them to combine the metadata fields into the search criteria, so that either all metadata field values match (known as an AND statement) or one of the metadata fields match (known as an OR statement). The advanced search should also allow the user to combine metadata search criteria as well as search for words or phrases within the document content. For example, consider the document described in Table 2. Using an advanced search, the user may want to locate all documents written by the author "Azad Adam" that contain the phrase "night sky" in the document content. The user would specify "Azad Adam" in the author search field and also the phrase "night sky" in the document content search field. The search would then return this document and all

Table 3 Example document used for OCR

Title	Short collection of Phrases
Author	Azad Adam
Subject	Phrases of the English Language
Creation Date	25/05/2006
Document Content	The quick brown fox jumps over the fence and away from the lazy dog.
	The cat sat on the mat.
	The moon in the night sky is very bright.
	The sun sets over London City.

other documents that match the search criteria in the search results.

The EDM system should also offer users the ability to browse for documents by manually going through the folder structure, just as they would browse for documents using Windows Explorer.

Optical Character Recognition

Optional character recognition (OCR) is a method used to index the typed content of documents, which then allows the typed content to be searched upon. For example, again let us consider the following short document as illustrated in Table 3. If the document's content has not been indexed using OCR, then users searching for this document would only be able to search for it based on the Title, Author or Subject fields, meaning they would have to know either some or all of the document's title or the document's subject, or the name of the author of the document in order to locate it.

If the document content has been indexed using OCR, then the content of the document would also be searchable, meaning that a user could locate the document simply by typing in the words "lazy dog" or "London" or "cat."

Indexing the document's content is a very powerful feature because users may know that they want to locate a document about a "lazy dog," for instance, but may not know the document's title, subject, or the author's name.

BASIC COMPONENTS OF RECORD MANAGEMENT SYSTEMS

The vast majority of ERMS is either used in conjunction with EDMS or contain document management functionality even though there may not be a mention of the word document in the product description. An ERMS will share some common functionality with an EDMS.

Repository

As with EDM systems, all ERM systems will need to have a repository where the records are archived.

Physically, the repository will be located on one or more networked database servers but will appear to users of the system as one central repository. Users of the ERM system should have the ability to browse the repository if their user access rights allow them to do so.

Folder Structure

The folder structure of an ERM system will exist within the repository and allows the system administrators to systematically categorize where records are archived within the system. Using a hierarchical folder structure will allow the administrator to set it up to either represent the organizational structure, business function-based structure, project-based structure, or property-based structure, or represent a combination of all four structures to facilitate the archival of records.

Classification, Indexing, and Metadata

All records in the system need to be categorized and indexed within the folder structure, using metadata to archive records in a systematic manner, and to help users to find their documents using the search and retrieval mechanisms.

Capturing and Declaring Records

An ERM system needs a method for automatically capturing and declaring records. For example, take an organization that processes forms and sends out acknowledgment letters to clients. Once they receive and process the client's form, it will become a record of the interaction with the client. The subsequent acknowledgment letter they send out will be another document that also becomes a part of the record of the interaction with that particular client.

Hence, if the system did not automatically capture and declare these documents as records, they would either not get declared as records, or it would be left to a user in the organization to manually declare those documents as records, in which case human error can and will creep into the process, resulting in their not being properly archived as records.

Retention and Disposal of Records

ERM systems need to be able to retain records for a specific length of time, depending on the nature of the records, and also dispose of them when that time limit is up. Consider a banking institution that offers members of the general public bank accounts. When customers close their accounts with the bank, the bank will be obliged to keep details of their accounts on record for a set period of time. Let us say the period for keeping accounts on record after they are closed is 7 years. Then, from the date of account closure, the system should automatically keep all the details relating to the customers and their accounts on record until 7 years later. Once the time has expired, 7 years in this case, the system should dispose of the records, either completely deleting them securely from the system or moving them to off-line storage, depending on organizational rules.

Record Security

ERM systems need to employ stringent security around the archiving of records, both for the organization's own security and to comply with legislation such as the Data Protection Act and the Privacy Act. Electronic records should be secured in such a way that only authorized users within the organization have access to them. Administrators of the ERM system should be able to easily set up and maintain record security within the system.

Managing Physical Records

An ERM should be capable of managing not only electronic records but also physical records existing in physical locations such as filing rooms and filing cabinets.

The system should be able to provide authorized users with details of where they can locate physical records and should also provide functionality for users to note on the system if they have removed records from their physical location—essentially, a type of check-out procedure for physical records stored on the system.

Search and Retrieval

As mentioned previously in the section on search and retrieval functionality regarding EDM systems, an ERM system needs to have the same search and retrieval functionality of a basic and advanced search, as well as the ability for users to browse the repository. In addition, the search mechanism needs to be able to search across

electronic records and physical records, if any, managed by the system.

A combined EDRM system should allow the use of one search mechanism, either basic or advanced, to search both documents and records and, when performing searches, should not distinguish between documents in progress or archived records. This is particularly important because if a user has a need to find information on a certain client, then there may be a number of documents that represent work in progress and a number of them that have become historic records. All of this information will be of importance to the user who will probably not know the differences between documents and records. Hence, the mechanism needs to be able to search across both documents and records, and this fact should be transparent to the user.

Auditing and Reporting

Auditing and reporting is an important feature of both records management and document management, and the system should provide functionality to allow authorized users and administrators facilities to produce audit trails concerning records and documents in terms of access and changes, dates created, dates modified, etc. Reporting facilities should be flexible enough to allow users to create bespoke reports regarding documents or records.

Compliance with Standards

Legislation such as the Freedom of Information Act, the Privacy Act, and the Data Protection Act, as well as standards such as DoD 5015.2, TNA 2002, ISO 15489, and MOREQ, are key drivers of the development of EDRM systems. Therefore, for systems to be compliant and legally accountable, both document and record management systems need to follow the relative legislation and standards that apply to both the organization and the country in which they are being implemented. Most systems from major electronic documents and records software vendors comply with one or more of these standards.

Scanning and Imaging

Facilities to scan and image paper-based documents need to be part of an ERM system because one of the main business drivers for organizations implementing these systems is the need to provide staff with instant access to centrally held information and free up space used for filing rooms.

Some ERM and EDRM systems have integrated scanning and imaging modules, allowing the organization to scan documents in batches and index them, whereas other software vendors provide scanning and imaging functionality as an optional module.

Collaboration

Collaborative services allow people and teams within the organization to communicate and share information, for example, to work on documents together. Although collaborative services are not a mandatory requirement of an EDRM system, it is certainly a very useful feature to have integrated with the system. Hence, if an EDRM system's task is to manage documents and records, then it makes sense to include functionality to encourage staff in the organization to share information and work together when necessary on relevant documents and records.

Workflow

Workflow, also referred to as business process management, is used to manage the flow of information around an organization. For example, take an invoicing system; an invoice is received through the post, gets scanned on to the system, then gets routed to accounts, may then have to go to a particular person within the accounts department for authorization, and then goes into a queue to be paid via a check run. The steps involved in the invoice being electronically routed around an organization from one person to the next are called Workflow.

As with collaboration mentioned previously, workflow is not strictly within the ambit of EDRM systems, but it is an extremely useful feature that, when properly implemented, can speed up processes, making them more efficient, eliminating the paper trail while providing accountability for each task assigned to an individual.

THE COMPLETE EDRMS

The exact functionality required of an EDRM system will differ from organization to organization, depending on their specific needs and objectives. There is, however, a core set of functionality that an EDRM system should provide. This is document management, records management, scanning and imaging, as well as some collaboration and workflow functionality.

Some vendors offer a modular approach to EDRMS, offering separate document management, records management, scanning and imaging, workflow, and collaboration software products, allowing a system to be built up as needs and requirements change and also allowing an organization to purchase just the modules relevant to their needs.

Other vendors offer products that may include both document management and collaboration as one product and then offer document and records management functionality in another product. The vast majority of vendors will have optional modules, allowing a system to be tailored to an organization's unique needs and requirements.

Whichever type of system is decided upon, it would make sense to implement one that has the capability to be scaled up in terms of both size and functionality. For example, an organization may want to implement just document management and collaboration to start with, and then, the following year, implement record management and workflow.

EDRMS– Enterprise

Enterprise Architecture: Challenges

Kirk Hausman
Assistant Commandant, Texas A&M University, College Station, Texas, U.S.A.

Abstract

This entry examines the challenges faced in applying architectural designs to an enterprise network environment. Considerations for risk management in enterprise architecture planning are provided, and the need to establish value and achieve business alignment in enterprise architecture strategies are examined.

During the months prior to the turn of the millennium, millions of dollars and tens of thousands of hours of time were spent addressing the "Y2K" issue. Until that time, programmers had designed databases and applications to handle date-years as two-digit numbers, assuming the preceding "19" to reflect the century. This was a simple oversight in planning, but one that had a tremendous potential to disrupt electronic data management. After a great deal of effort and expense, the problem was resolved in time to greet the year 2000 without significant impact, making this the largest and most widespread information technology problem ever to be corrected in time to avoid catastrophic results.

As the world has become more integrated through Internet connectivity, issues of high-level planning and strategy have an increased impact on business viability. Strategic drivers for information technology (IT) expense are not as clearly obvious as in the days before the Y2K bug, but a few guiding principles can make an equally valuable contribution to an organization's long-term operational capacity.

This entry focuses on high-level guidelines, providing a framework for detailed strategic planning. Before we delve into guidelines addressing enterprise information management, data center practices, and protective planning concerns, however, complexity issues warrant special attention. These guidelines are applicable to any organization that uses more than a handful of standalone computers storing no data of interest or worth.

COMPLEXITY

In the 14th century, a Franciscan friar called William of Ockham voiced a maxim that is widely applied today to economic, medical, and scientific endeavors. This maxim is generally known as "Ockham's razor." Commonly used as a practice for simplifying assumptions being made when observable evidence has been taken into account, the original form of Ockham's maxim is very applicable to the IT enterprise:

> "Entities should not be multiplied beyond necessity."

The renowned physicist, Albert Einstein, noted much the same in his famous statement:

> "Everything should be made as simple as possible, but not simpler."

Essentially, both statements suggest that we should always simplify whenever possible, but not oversimplify. These thoughts should be kept firmly in mind whenever an enterprise architect considers any question of implementation or strategic planning.

Sources of Complexity

A common rule-of-thumb employed by CIOs, IT directors, and other technology architects in making strategic technology decisions is that the support requirements and costs associated with technologies increase by the square of the number of similar solutions used. Thus, having two workstation operating systems will require approximately 4 times as many resources as having only a single platform; while having three standard user application suites might require as much as nine times the effort to coordinate, integrate, and update all three in comparison to an enterprise employing a single standard suite. Table 1 details a few of the potential sources of enterprise complexity that may be encountered.

The business value of IT can be affected by the complexity of its implementation. Enterprise architects must consider complexity issues not only in technology selection, but also in terms of the number of resource silos and the level of undesirable redundancy present in any enterprise that has not recently been reengineered from

Encyclopedia of Information Systems and Technology, DOI: 10.1081/E-EIST-120053817

Table 1 Common Sources of Complexity

Source	Impact
Identity management	Directory services and identity management determine almost all other aspects of an enterprise network. Commercial solutions include technologies such as SunONE, Novell's eDirectory, and Microsoft's dominant Active Directory, while open-source shops commonly employ Lightweight Directory Access Protocol (LDAP) solutions such as the common OpenLDAP service. Federated identity management solutions aid in transferring credentials across authentication boundaries, allowing disparate technologies to integrate more transparently, but they risk compromising multiple authentication systems if the IM server is compromised. Federated systems also create risk because administrative access can temporarily associate with account credentials, providing an easy mechanism for unauthorized access to protected resources.
Application stack	The application stack includes technologies such as the operating system, user suite, Web server, and many other technologies that together make up the operational environment for servers and workstations within the enterprise. Deeply integrated enterprises may make use of a single vendor's stack, such as IBM's popular WebSphere environment or the familiar Microsoft server/service/client suite of products, while the open-source LAMP stack is comprised of applications from dozens if not hundreds of sources. The basic L-A-M-P stack itself is not wedded to a particular source, as Linux has hundreds of possible sources and variations, while the Apache Web server and MySQL database platform are developed by separate vendors. Even the "P" in LAMP can reflect several options for application development—Pearl, PHP, Python, and Primate are all used interchangeably here. Without standardization, users can encounter difficulty when moving from one area of an organization to another, while update projects and upgrades become complex to plan and implement across a varied spectrum of products.
Application development	At the most fundamental level of development, the selection of programmatic style and language affects development and customization of applications used in anything other than default configurations. Selection of object-oriented programming languages, such as Java and Microsoft's. Net languages, will affect the manner in which applications access and manipulate data, compared to traditional languages such as ANSI C, FORTRAN, and COBOL. Implementation of a service-oriented architecture (SOA) development practice can add to the complexity of an enterprise as well, gaining rapid application development and deployment capability at the cost of internal consistency across all application elements. Retention of legacy applications within SOA wrappers can further increase complexity by avoiding the process of legacy software retirement. Application design and testing for multiple platforms can add tremendously to the cost of development.
Interconnectivity	Modern enterprise networks may require connectivity for external operators, partner organizations, Internet users, mobile access devices, and a wide range of implementations that fall outside the technical envelope that can be mandated within the enterprise itself. Requirements for encryption, credentials management, and even the protocols implemented for access must all take into account the potentially widely varying solutions presented here. Selection of an industry-standard platform can help mitigate this risk somewhat.
Protection	Legislative mandates may include specific requirements that must be addressed in enterprise planning, such as the Health Insurance Portability and Accountability Act (HIPAA) requirements for segregation of Protected Health Information (PHI). Complexity may also be added where access and storage mechanisms must include encryption or where access controls mandate specific protocols. Many governmental and research organizations may need to impose classification systems for Mandatory Access Controls, as opposed to the more common Discretionary and Role-Based Access Control mechanisms used in other enterprises. Careful planning is required to ensure that resource access is granted appropriately, denied to unauthorized access attempts, and reviewed regularly.

whole cloth. The issues surrounding desirable and undesirable redundancy are addressed elsewhere in this encyclopedia. Here, it is enough to recognize the need for simplification and standardization in order to provide a level foundation atop which other strategies can be constructed.

Opposition to Standardization

Whenever standardization is considered in an organization, opposition is almost guaranteed. Beyond simple issues of budgetary constraint, commonly raised issues include:

- **User familiarity**—Opponents to standardization often note existing user familiarity with the disparate technologies under consideration for replacement, and the potential disruption that may occur during transition. This is a short-term problem that may be addressed by user training and awareness as a part of the update project's requirements. The architect should, if possible, identify the platform in use by the majority of existing users, as selection of that as the new standard will reduce public outcry because proponents already exist among the user base.

- **Functionality**—Potentially the most valid complaint that may be raised is the question of functionality present in the existing solution that may be missing in a newly named standard. Mature technologies such as word processors and spreadsheet applications are beginning to converge on common features and expected functionalities, while specific advanced media manipulation software may still be required in special cases. The enterprise architect should not expect to achieve a 100% standard suite that will fulfill all users' needs. In achieving a standard platform and user suite, it may be necessary to implement limited variations based on cost or need factors. Managing the exceptions and controlling variation are challenges that must be continuously addressed. Enterprise architects who strive too hard toward total compliance may find strong opposition together with documented need opposing new standards, while those who are too flexible may find that exceptions become the de facto standard regardless of the planned end state.

- **Compatibility**—When selecting a standard platform or application suite, it is important to consider compatibility with existing file stores and application protocols. Legacy technologies may require additional interface solutions to allow operation within a standardized environment, while years or even decades of past documents and files should not be rendered unavailable due to the change. It is important to consider format-translation and accessibility requirements when selecting a new standard. Use of more common file format standards can aid in technology transitions and architectural changes.

- **Monocultures and biodiversity**—Opponents of integrated commercial off-the-shelf solutions often note the potential for a technology monoculture, where vulnerabilities in one vendor's products may compromise the entire stack. This is commonly reflected against the need for biodiversity in crops and herds to ensure that a single contagion is not able to affect the entire stock. This analogy fails under close scrutiny, however, because enterprise networks are not automatically protected by diversity as in biological farming. Viral programs capable of spreading through multiple vectors (blended threats) can pass across many different technology variations, while viruses have been written to allow cross-platform transmission as well. Unlike biological contagions, new viral programs can be created at will using simple GUI-based tools to target as many different platforms and vulnerabilities as the author desires. The advantage of desirable diversity within layers of security are addressed elsewhere, but diversity alone will not automatically improve platform and application

security—it simply complicates patch management efforts and slows large-scale disaster recovery efforts.

ENTERPRISE INFORMATION MANAGEMENT

It is important to understand the purpose of enterprise information management and enterprise information architecture so that its value becomes apparent during budgetary planning. Without executive buy-in and support, enterprise architects will find themselves in the unenviable position of being asked to work miracles while being held accountable for even the most minor glitches, all without a budget to meet an ever-growing swell of requirements that information technologies present. The value gained from architectural planning is addressed elsewhere in this encyclopedia. Here, it is enough to know that even the best plan will fail if it cannot be conveyed to stakeholders and sponsors. The architect must be not only the designer of a cohesive vision but also the herald of its virtues, to avoid being simply swept under the rug.

Sell the Value of Information

Without a comprehensive effort to plan and organize available data, an organization risks far more than simply losing data on a client, patient, or other person of interest. Poorly constructed information architectures can create barriers that oppose efforts to identify data already present, while siloed architectures that segregate resources in an undesirable manner can prevent data mining, data sharing, and other value-added capabilities of well-considered plans. Information has value as a strategic resource, because operations can come to an abrupt halt without this information. The loss of e-mail for a few hours can shut down a business for the day, while the loss of Web services can cost many thousands of dollars every minute for organizations that depend on Web access for product sales.

Companies such as Amazon, eBay, and Google are all good examples of organizations that depend on network availability simply to conduct business, while many other companies have corporate websites offering goods, services, and customer contact capabilities. Without adequate planning, valuable data and key services can be impaired if inadequately protected. An enterprise architect must identify which elements of the information architecture act as currency within the organization's operational envelope, in order to plan and negotiate for sufficient resources to identify, acquire, manage, and use information and needed information technologies. The value of IT programs must be made clearly evident to stakeholders and users alike, particularly when an architectural change creates disruption or change to the users' day-to-day experience. The architect should look for the "low-hanging fruit" that easily generates return on the initial investment, while looking down the road for longer-term benefits that might require greater planning, effort, and expense to achieve.

Avoid Drawing Fire

A popular cartoon by Bill Mauldin printed during World War II showed an illustration of an officer, standing proudly and boldly in the face of oncoming fire from the enemy while two GIs huddled in the foxhole at his feet. One of the GIs says to the officer, "Would you mind not drawing their fire while inspiring us, Sir?" This humorous aside should be kept in mind whenever a decision is made to include controversial or newly emergent technologies into enterprise planning. A network enterprise is not the place to test beta versions of new software or to implement wholesale change to meet the latest fad in computing practices, software, or information delivery.

An excellent example of drawing fire while trying to do the right thing comes from the attempt to establish the OpenDocument Format (ODF) as a mandatory requirement within the Commonwealth of Massachusetts' IT strategies. In addition to user groups voicing opposition to the change from the more familiar Microsoft Office user suite, the state found itself addressing a wide range of concerns. The strongest objections came from organizations representing persons with disabling conditions who might be barred from working with the state or accessing its offered services because of the relative scarcity of accessibility-related development applied within the open software environment, specifically the OpenOffice suite of products that was being considered for ODF document creation and management. What had seemed a simple, easy decision intended to inspire the integration of open-source solutions into governmental networks brought the state firmly into the crosshairs of some very concerned groups instead.

OUTSOURCE CAREFULLY

Outsourcing is an obvious movement within the IT arena that regularly draws fire, particularly after the economic downturn that left millions out of work. The outsourcing of jobs is a hotbed of concern during difficult economic times, while the outsourcing of data processing can present very difficult challenges as more and more legislation is enacted to impose liability and rules governing information exposure and data protection. The European Union has already enacted specific legislation that addresses the types of information that may be

transmitted outside its borders and has defined a specific listing of partner countries that may share this data. Some countries, such as China and France, have enacted legislation that restricts what information may be provided to network users accessing data from within the respective countries. Partner agreements and outsourcing efforts can become enmeshed in the politics of an organization's host country, as well as all other countries where the data is stored or processed—or even countries through which the information is transmitted.

Outsourcing should be undertaken only when necessary, with careful consideration of the laws and rules governing information and its release in all applicable countries. It is far easier to control data and address legal issues by selecting outsourcing agencies with operations within the same geopolitical region as the host organization, compared to requirements for filing a suit or recovering exposed data under a separate set of laws and rules governing information protection, privacy, and other similar hot topics. Developing legislative actions may even prevent some types of outsourcing arrangements, as in the case of the U. S. State Department's decision to eliminate ThinkPad laptops from their approved purchasing list after IBM sold the popular platform to the Chinese Lenovo Corporation. It is far easier to streamline operations locally than to outsource (particularly when considering offshore outsourcing services) and later be forced to return operations in-house, and enterprise architects should use this tool only when it is truly appropriate or necessary to avoid adding undesirable complexity to the host organization's operational environment.

PROTECT THE DATA

Being suddenly naked in public is a common nightmare but one that is not nearly as disturbing as having the sensitive or protected data of millions of clients revealed inadvertently. A number of laws pertaining to the liability of information exposure came under consideration following the spectacular data exposure of information about more than 26 million veterans and active-duty military personnel when a laptop containing this information was stolen from the home of a Veteran's Administration employee. This is not an isolated event, by any means—sensitive data from millions of clients has been exposed through loss of backup media, security compromise, and inadvertent disclosure. Credit card agencies, universities, medical facilities, and information clearing houses are common targets for identity thieves seeking useful information on large numbers of people at once.

It is not enough to plan how to handle the public reaction following data loss because many articles of

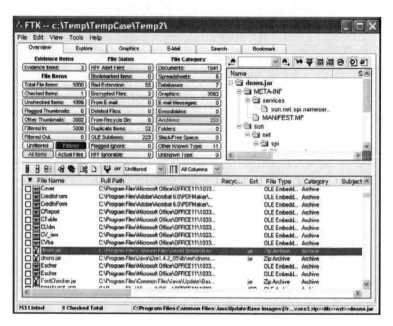

Fig. 1 The Forensic Toolkit being used on an unencrypted drive.

legislation include very strong penalties that follow automatically. The HIPAA is an excellent example of the type of legislation that may affect an organization as a result of data exposure. This act includes specific penalties, including very stiff per-item fines, whenever PHI has been disclosed. Beyond direct legal and cost factors that may affect an organization, loss of customer trust can be even more devastating to an organization. Few acts will draw public outcry as rapidly as an accidental disclosure of data that could be used for identity theft, credit fraud, or other person-affecting actions. Because of a simple household burglary, 26 million veterans and service personnel must forever monitor their credit and watch carefully lest someone misuses the stolen information.

INCLUDE SECURITY AT ALL LEVELS

An enterprise architect must include security when planning every level of the enterprise architecture. Because most computers can be booted directly from a Live CD or USB flash drive (Knoppix is a good example of a media-bootable operating system), physical access to any computer presents an attacker with almost immediate results. Security cannot be "bolted on" later; it must form the basis for enterprise defense, data encryption during storage and transport, and be deeply integrated into application development standards.

Attackers Have Tools Too

An organization's most sensitive data is readily accessible without an encrypted file system strong enough to resist tools that are available on the Internet. Many tools originally intended for law enforcement and security purposes can also be used by attackers to access sensitive information. Fig. 1 shows an example of the type of data recovery that can be conducted using the Forensic Toolkit package.

Fig. 2 shows the use of this same tool to rapidly example files of interest to an attacker after only a brief window of access to an unprotected system.

Commercial forensic suites include products such as the Forensic Toolkit, as well as offerings from Encase, Paraben, and many other vendors. Free and open-source software-developed tools also exist, such as those preinstalled on the popular Helix bootable forensic CD based on the Knoppix Linux distribution. Using tools already installed on this insert-and-run package, an attacker can examine running processes, extract stored passwords and form data, search for specific types of files, or even replicate an entire hard drive for later deep analysis. These functions are invaluable to the professional forensic investigator, but they are equally available to potential attackers seeking to bypass access control mechanisms to gain unauthorized access to protected resources.

Encrypt in Storage and Transmission

An enterprise architect must keep abreast of existing and emerging security threats and mechanisms for system exploitation and malware operation, while also remaining cognizant of physical security and user training requirements. All enterprise planning should first identify all resources and the requirements for protecting each resource before beginning implementation plans.

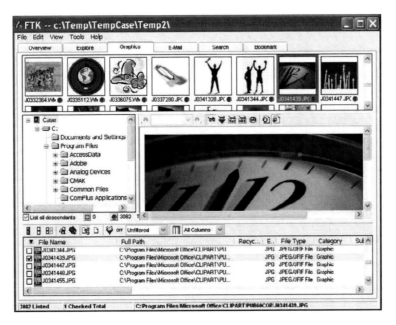

Fig. 2 The Forensic Toolkit being used to examine image files.

Encryption and data protection should be included whenever data is stored, transmitted, or processed—particularly in SOA implementations, where legacy integrated systems may not include the capability for more modern types of data transmission security or endpoint validation.

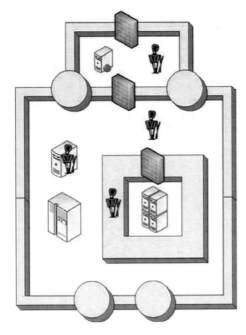

Fig. 3 A simplified network defensive strategy employing defensive applications on guard against intrusion, malware, or misuse, and firewall barriers creating a DMZ and shielded subnet.

Security Must Be Layered

Security is not only encryption, authentication, firewalls, filtering policies, runtime authorization, antivirus/anti-spam applications, or intrusion-detection systems—it is all of these and more. Security should be included at the most basic level and then layered in order to strengthen a network's defenses. Fig. 3 illustrates a simplified model of network defense including host-based and network-based defensive applications, along with firewall barriers shielding an externally exposed data management zone (or, sometimes, demilitarized zone, DMZ) as well as an internally protected shielded subnet.

An illustration of enterprise defensive concepts has much in common with early physical defenses employed to protect against invading armies. It is often said that a castle is only as secure as its least protected gate, and this same thinking must be applied when the enterprise architect is evaluating architectural plans. Most large networks are placed behind a boundary defense, as is often the case when individual business elements are allowed to maintain and update their own systems within the overall organizational network. A single unpatched or insufficiently defended system can be compromised and used to bypass boundary defenses for attacks against other systems within the protected network.

Note: One desirable complexity may be to implement devices from different vendors for defensive layering. By including products based on different technologies at the external and internal boundaries of the DMZ, for example, the same hacking toolkit cannot be used to

Table 2   PCI data security standards

Standard	Implementation
Build and maintain a secure network	Install and maintain a firewall. Do not use default settings for passwords and other security parameters.
Protect cardholder data	Protect stored data, including backup media. Encrypt data during transmission across public networks.
Maintain a vulnerability management program	Employ regularly updated antivirus software. Develop and maintain secure systems and applications.
Implement strong access-control measures	Restrict data access to least necessary. Assign a unique ID to each user. Restrict physical access to cardholder data.
Monitor and test networks	Monitor and log all network access to cardholder data. Regularly test security systems and practices.
Maintain an information security policy	Maintain clear security policies. Ensure adequate training and awareness.

Source: From MasterCard International.

bypass both barriers. Complexity can add to security when layering protections, although this only increases security—a skilled attacker can eventually bypass multiple defensive layers, whether they are constructed from a single vendor's offerings or developed using a wide assortment of products.

Conceal the Inner Workings

Like a castle, a protected network relies on standardized rules for passing through its gates. Defensive applications act as guards and turn away undesirable traffic, while ensuring that legitimate requests are passed only to the appropriate destination. Some systems may require defenses against internal threats, requiring additional layering to create shielded subnets and protected safe harbors for legacy systems or sensitive data. By exposing only encrypted Web service interfaces, external applications can interact with protected data stores and application services within these defended areas using a black-box approach. This type of defensive strategy secures even the manner in which information is arranged from easy outside observation.

Proactively Implement Standards

Many standards exist for securing information and networks, including architectural models such as CObIT and ITIL In addition to these guidelines, many industries are evolving mandated security practices that can be used to plan proactively for state defensive requirements. As one example, the Payment Card Industry (PCI) Data Security Standards provide a basic framework for protecting data related to credit card transactions (see Table 2).

Even if an organization does not employ credit card handling practices, the same standards can be applied in a proactive manner when planning for state architectural defense. If the organization later falls under the PCI

requirements, the protections will already be in place; if not, these standards remain good practices for data defense. If a public data exposure occurs, it is far better to be able to prove due diligence in attempting to defend sensitive or protected information than to be found negligent in this area. Doing nothing to prevent an exposure is certainly going to draw fire.

Look Beyond the Project

As we discussed previously, strong project management skills are vital for the CIO and any other lead architectural roles. This dictum can be misleading, however, if it is applied too thoroughly without an eye toward the big picture. Projects are discrete, with a clear beginning, identified term, and identifiable closure. Enterprise architecture may include many projects in the architectural management program, but while projects have a defined end, operational practices are ongoing and often cyclical in nature. Security, for example, is never a goal that will someday be attained once-and-for-all-time. Security is a relative state, subject to continued changes as new attack techniques are developed or personnel are moved between assignments. Tens of thousands of new viruses are released each year, along with hundreds of other potential sources of malware and network exploitation. Adding in social engineering and ever-increasing computing power, the potential threats to an organization's network become almost infinite.

Enterprise architects must plan for reactive immediate-term solutions, address existing trends and evolving requirements, while moving always toward the supportable state enterprise that is yet to exist. Selling IT projects as quick-return "low-hanging fruit" projects can create impossible expectations or unrealizable goals. The enterprise architect must also maintain awareness of the ongoing value provided to an enterprise through incremental changes and cyclic technology modernization efforts. Formal project management skills should be employed, but with an understanding that the big picture is always evolving, always moving to reveal more of the road ahead. Strategy and vision must be the ultimate drivers for all of the more finely focused implementation projects.

Align Technology and Business

The most fundamental but sometimes difficult concept to convey is the idea that technology must follow the business, and not the other way around. Many failed IT projects try to shift an organization's operations to fit a newly purchased or newly developed application. Certainly there are many very fine application suites for human resource management, accounting, inventory management, and the many other tasks necessary for a modern organization to operate. Solutions such as SAP, PeopleSoft, and Great Plains include a wide range of modules to suit the needs of different business environments, but it is not enough to select a product and then expect an organization to shift its operational processes to suit it. IT is a logistical element that supports other operational functions within an organization, and it should not be considered as more. At the same time, it must not be discounted as an afterthought or add-on to be maintained by convenience. The addition of new technologies may make new service offerings possible, if the enterprise architect can convey details of the new offering to executive staff members throughout the organization in terms that can be understood by technical lay persons.

APPLY CLEAR GOVERNANCE PRINCIPLES

An enterprise architect must be sensitive to business drivers during the full technology life-cycle process, from specification through tombstoning. Planning and procurement affect successful projects just as thoroughly as skills planning and user training. This is where a formal IT governance framework can function to improve coordination with other business elements by aligning enterprise operations with the overall organizational governance model. Governance and planning should be kept separate from functional management, as the skills and focus needed for these roles vary widely. Clear ownership and responsibility must be tied to the management of each project, while an overall vision provides guidance and coordination with the rest of the organization.

As a related matter, personnel promotion should not provide the only mechanism for incentivization, ensuring that skilled and effective technologists are not moved into management roles purely to provide recognition of their success. According to the "Peter principle," it is easy to promote individuals out of positions as a result of their excellent performance, only to find that they are unsuited to their new roles. Individuals may thus be promoted only until they reach one place beyond their peak skill level, leading to dissatisfaction and reduced operational efficiency enterprise-wide.

PLAN AHEAD AND STICK TO THE PLAN

A common maxim states that "Form follows function." While this is certainly true for sharks and submarines, it is amazing how complicated and internally inconsistent an IT enterprise can become over time. The key to a successful initiative is to have a plan and to build toward the goal, with regular checks to ensure that the goal remains valid and that efforts are achieving desired movement toward the goal's end state. Starting with modest testing will help to ensure that the new technology meets an actual need before building unwarranted expectations or creating concerns about change. With a clear plan and identified requirements, it is far easier to reach the necessary solution than when the end goal is indistinct or incompletely conveyed to the implementation staff. Above all, start at the top and build interest and support downward, to ensure that funding and reasonable expectations are in place before user requirements and preferences turn "feature creep" into a nightmare of complexity and unending revision.

COLLABORATIVE TECHNOLOGIES ARE VITAL

Collaborative technologies form the communications core, whether planning for a simple technology modernization project or a rip-and-replace total enterprise overhaul. Such technologies include e-mail, task assignment, ticket management, calendaring, virtual meeting spaces, threaded discussion boards, wikis, shared document storage, voice and video teleconferencing, voice mail, instant messaging, and a host of emerging methods for communicating and organizing groups of participants. Before a project is undertaken, it is absolutely imperative to ensure that all appropriate collaboration technologies and a formal communications plan are in place to promote communication among users, implementers, and governance roles.

REMAIN AGILE AND FLEXIBLE

Modifying architecture in production is much like trying to change tires on a moving car or performing brain surgery on oneself. Elements of the operating network environment, from data stores to authentication and Web services, may already be operating at or above optimal capacity or may be tied to divergent technologies that do not integrate well. The lead architect must be wary of

EDRMS–
Enterprise

pitfalls such as planning the reallocation of a database server that also happens to have an active Web-facing reporting utility, or a Web server that hosts small yet vital resources not identified in the initial review. Flexibility is necessary when making plans, to ensure that service disruption is minimized. This must be tempered by formal project management procedures and a firm change management process in order to avoid employing too much flexibility.

Maintaining flexibility becomes more complex during long-term planning operations, as the driving factors change from year to year as technology and regulatory mandates evolve. While wireless connectivity and mobile communication might remain a hot topic from 1 year to the next, issues of security or application development might swap places in terms of organizational priority as a result of a newly emergent threat or programming style. Because data and voice-over-IP telephony compete for the same bandwidth, network infrastructure upgrades might move ahead of technology modernization projects to ensure that adequate bandwidth is available before the new and shiny gear is connected.

AVOID TOO MUCH GOOD

Enterprise architects perform a constant juggling act to balance expenditures, resources, and requirements. Surprisingly, too much of a good thing can be as bad as lack of interest. A new SOA-based Web service coupled to an existing tried-and-true application can rapidly overrun available capacity and connectivity, if the demand exceeds the throughput of any element in the chain. New portal deployments often suffer from overly enthusiastic user interest, because users find a sudden need for expanded access to their whole team or operation as soon as the potential is demonstrated. Jumping too far, too fast can lead to problems in storage overrun, load balancing, and service availability. New technology projects should always be monitored carefully to identify overly successful solutions and apply controls or add resources to suit. The use of cloud computing hosting can help reduce the impact of suddenly vital new offerings by allowing an expansion of network and system resources at need by simply purchasing additional capacity.

Too much of a good thing can also be a problem when implementing security measures. It is easy to make layered defenses so unwieldy that users find ways to bypass controls just to perform common tasks. If the password policy calls for highly complex 14-digit passwords that change every 40 days, users may start writing down the latest version in a convenient place. Business intelligence applications often generate the same type of threat, as it is very easy to get lost in reports and dashboards showing how well operations are

performing when measured against how they were doing this morning or 10 years ago—regardless of whether this information is useful to the organization.

The same can be true of security practitioners, where the ability to log and monitor every action within the entire network can become a goal unto itself. Too much logging and data mining can sometimes get in the way of simpler updates and less flashy tasks that are fundamental to network health. Focus in the wrong area or misplaced trust in defensive technologies alone leads to vulnerable systems and a false sense of security. It is easy to miss an ongoing brute-force attack against a server hosting the company's Secure Sockets Layer-encrypted website if the fancy monitoring tools are happily logging that hits are up and encryption is in place.

PLAN ON PARTNERS

Organizations are increasingly integrating external connectivity for business-to-business partner relationships, business-to-consumer automated shipping management, and mobile workspace management. Industries may use specialized processing services or clearing houses for data management and mandatory reporting, such as in the case of caregiver integration with health insurance provider systems for billing and client account management. Services are increasingly moving to an online format, particularly with the explosion of SOA-based Web services exposing applications that could previously function only within an isolated internal network.

The savvy planner must constantly watch for opportunities and pitfalls presented by partnering solutions, and avoid being taken unawares by emerging regulatory mandates or upcoming potential mergers requiring connectivity with partner organizations. It is here that standards must be applied throughout the data center and the organization's networked resources at every stage, so that it is not a sudden scramble to implement connectivity on a truncated timetable because of a new partnership.

By planning proactively for partnerships, the lead architect can act to improve business agility as well as the potential for success in state strategic planning efforts. Although the creation of a standard Data Center Markup Language remains in a nascent state, following accepted standards such as the PCI Data Security Standards can help prepare to meet the virtual neighbors.

DATA CENTER MANAGEMENT

Internal users are most aware of changes to their desktop, but an organization is most affected by changes in the data center. Solutions implemented within the data center affect internal users, external users, partner inter-connectivity, and even the way in which the organization communicates with itself. Many of the "low-hanging fruit" projects in an enterprise are focused within the data center, where divergent authentication systems and server sprawl increase complexity and cost.

> **Tip:** Changes to the user's desktop operating system or user productivity suite are most likely to concern users, while changes within the data center are most likely to concern IT implementers. The lead architect must work to control this reaction before, during, and after planned changes to the data center. Training is critical for both technologists as well as users in order to ensure that the proper skills are in place prior to need.

CONSOLIDATION

Consolidation into a centralized or limited number of shared data centers provides the most obvious step for dealing with disparate silos of IT and expertise. By standardizing architecture and reducing administrative and procurement costs, architects can show a quick return on investment while freeing up resources for other projects. Consolidation will require not only a restructuring of technology resources, but also a realignment of planning, budgeting, and procurement compared to planning and acquisition at the individual departmental level. Cost savings are generally identifiable within the first year of operation following consolidation projects.

OPPOSITION WILL ARISE

As we discussed earlier, opposition to standardization and centralization can be varied and impassioned. Fears abound at the loss of authority and direct access by local implementers, while issues of strategic budgeting and personnel costs must be moved up the organizational hierarchy. A key factor to successful consolidation and shared service projects is to ensure that funding is managed as a budgeted expense, rather than impressed upon individual departments as a per-system or per-person cost. It is too easy to build antagonism toward a consolidation project by identifying individual business units whose per-system or per-person costs appear to be lower in direct comparison with other units, obscuring the overall reduction in cost or expansion in capability for the organization as a whole. Opt-in cost-recovery programs tend to multiply this problem, because business units with adequate resources may work to avoid sharing, while the "have nots" find themselves pooled together without sufficient funding or resources to fulfill basic requirements. Critical services

should be considered cost-of-business or commoditized operational costs and budgeted accordingly, rather than operated under outdated cost-recovery models that often create competition and conflict between organizational units within the same overall enterprise.

BENEFITS WILL BE NEAR- AND LONG-TERM

Consolidation within the data center can aid in organizational decision making through integration of cross-departmental information and increased information availability to key decision makers. Resource savings are also obvious targets for consolidation and shared service efforts, because economies of scale can be applied to common requirements such as file storage, patch control, database management, and collaboration technologies. Because these factors can be more easily tracked and maintained, overruns and shortfalls in capacity or cost can also be identified much more easily in a consolidated environment. Resource utilization is generally improved by consolidation, combining services onto more robust systems able to handle greater capacity with a similar administrative requirement.

Consolidation may not always produce direct cost savings, as the resources freed up by consolidating redundant systems and services may be used to add value and functionality elsewhere within the enterprise. Architectural leads must ensure that executives understand the value to be gained through reinvestment and reallocation following a consolidation effort. These cost savings and reallocated technologies can play a large part in moving the organization toward a more regular cycle of technology update and modernization or in adding new service options to facilitate emerging needs.

Modernization Becomes a Process

Cyclic technology refresh, update, and system modernization is a key goal when planning long-term enterprise network strategies. Consolidated resources make long-term budgetary planning possible, with a clear life cycle and maintenance strategy for both software and hardware solutions within the enterprise framework. This minimizes the impact of technology evolution, because a portion of the network can be updated each year rather than all at once or on a random basis driven by product release or technology emergence.

Consolidation and shared services can also improve service delivery by increasing the transparency between services and through a more seamless method of access for users and consumers. The "one-stop shop" becomes more efficient when service resources are well connected and built around common technologies. This ensures that clients are not greeted with a public-facing

EDRMS–Enterprise

resource site in which some elements are unavailable due to network lag or synchronization issues that may arise when integrating widely varying services into a single interface.

Boundaries Can Be Better Protected

Consolidation allows improved security by minimizing the transmission of data between services and reducing the surface area of exposure. When each information silo must possess copies of sensitive data for its own operations, the potential for accidental exposure is much greater than when data is secured within a central store that is transmitted only through tightly controlled access. Not only is it easier to maintain and update a smaller number of systems within a consolidated network, it is also easier to justify capital expenses for defensive technologies to harden the data center network and to provide adequate bandwidth for remote sites that will no longer have all resources sited locally.

CONSOLIDATION EXTENDS BEYOND CENTRALIZATION

While backups, updates, and maintenance can be performed more rapidly within a centralized site, care must be taken to avoid isolating remote sites from access to necessary services. Authentication and user provisioning for remote sites require planning and may include additional technologies to offset slow or intermittent network access. Higher-bandwidth always-on solutions such as cable modem and digital subscriber line service are reducing the dependency on demand-dial modem networks and dedicated telephony-based lines, but mobile users and remote sites may still be isolated from full-time, dependable connectivity. The lead architect must have a clear understanding of the network before moving resources to a consolidated model.

Facilities Must Be Adequate

Beyond network connectivity, consolidation projects rely heavily on adequate facilities for the consolidated hardware. Data center and server targets for consolidated services are often more robust than their departmental counterparts, requiring greater capacity for power and thermal dissipation. Soaring energy costs can create cost overruns for consolidated architectures, because ambient air movement is typically not sufficient to cool most data centers even though individual departmental servers may be able to sit in a refitted closet without a need for dedicated air conditioning. Not only do servers consume a great deal of power, they generate heat like small

toaster ovens—and they do so continuously, not just during breakfast.

It is not always possible to simply scale up power feeds and air conditioning within an existing structure, as it can lead to a very unpleasant surprise halfway through an extended consolidation effort. Capacity planning includes long-term research to ensure that the hottest months of the year are considered when evaluating capacity requirements. Layout and organization within the data center can also affect cooling and power distribution, creating hot spots or requiring renovation to strengthen floors beneath large uninterruptible power supplies.

Larger data centers may separate power and processing facilities in order to implement more efficient DC-based power distribution. Water-based cooling systems, popular with technology geeks trying to overclock their systems for maximum performance (that is, alter the settings to exceed the manufacturer-recommended maximum speed), are evolving into effective solutions for cooling large data centers, where water or oil can be used to circulate heat away from servers more efficiently and more quietly than forced-air cooling allows. Such extensive changes, however, require a wholesale shift in facilities planning as well as in server acquisition procedures.

As events have shown, facilities planning must also include factors such as potential terrorist activities and natural disasters. Data centers in the World Trade Center were completely lost as a result of the terrorist attack of September 11, 2001, while some located in the vicinity of New Orleans were literally buried in mud and sewage when levees failed following Hurricanes Katrina and Rita. Even backup sites along the Gulf Coast became unsupportable when evacuation efforts drained available fuel supplies needed to run backup power generators long-term. Organizations whose centralized consolidated resources are located in high-visibility or geographically risky locations constantly gamble on the continued performance and long-term viability of their data centers and the services they support.

Consolidation Includes the Help Desk

Another key issue to address when considering consolidation or shared services is to ensure that the help desk function is maintained. Users may not care which server holds their e-mail or how their file storage is being backed up, but they will most certainly care about how their problems can be communicated to the responsible IT professionals. Whenever human resources are consolidated, users may feel that they are losing access to their local IT support that was both responsive and directly available at need.

EDRMS—
Enterprise

An effective help desk can aid tremendously in the acceptance of consolidated services by reducing the time between user contact and effective problem resolution. While this may not be as friendly as having an IT professional in the office next door, it can go a long way toward providing user satisfaction. Failure here can close the door to projects, because users become wary of losing control or level of service. Another useful option is to retain existing support personnel in office space proximate to the consumer base, but to structure help desk functions to allow online support from any help desk operative. Users can retain the feeling of being well supported while gaining access to support skills across the enterprise by employing virtual teaming, instant messaging between support professionals, and centralized telephone and Web-based contact mechanisms for users to request help.

> **Tip:** When building interest in consolidation projects, concerns about the loss of local control can often be addressed by examining existing interdependencies. Stakeholders may not be aware that they already depend on networking, authentication, name resolution, or other services provided centrally or externally. The perceived loss of control is often merely that—a perception that control exists, without considering the interwoven nature of an enterprise network.

Consolidation Is Not Limited to Technology

Operational capability often relies on IT to such an extent that even a short time without access creates a tremendous cost or service disruption. Organizations are faced with the need to address a global marketplace, which may include requirements for maintaining data stores within specific geographic locales. Web-based services and applications are extending the full benefits of being "in the office" to a wide range of highly mobile users, which again may rely on services hosted at multiple locations. Rather than attempting to provide a full set of deep skills to all site locations, large enterprises can take advantage of remote management solutions to create a consolidated group of highly skilled professionals able to address issues arising in disparate locations. Local staff members remain necessary, as many powered-down systems still require someone to turn a key or press a button. However, businesses can reduce the number of wide-but-shallow skill sets found in remote sites and individual business units, where a single isolated support individual may be called on to perform many different tasks.

Tremendous advantages can result from standardizing technologies and implementing remote management solutions for console access, patch control, application deployment, and user support. A core group of highly skilled technical responders can address problems across a large enterprise as emerging issues are identified by help desk personnel, without requiring every site to have its own expert in security, networking, authentication, or any of the many other technologies that can be found in a modern organizational network. Although these "jacks of all trades" may enjoy jumping from one task to another, the deeper skills available with dedicated staff and trained expertise can reduce downtime and improve operational recovery windows following an incident.

Desirable Redundancy Can Be Acquired

Consolidation focuses on minimizing undesirable redundancy in service, system, or operational capability. There are times when redundancy can be desirable, and consolidation can facilitate this as well. An organization can improve its resistance to challenges by reinvesting cost savings from eliminated redundant servers, services, and personnel in desirable redundancy of key functions.

Redundancy can be desirable at many levels, including:

- **Personnel**—Load-balancing expertise within a consolidated support team reduces the impact of the loss of a key individual and allows members of the team to take vacations without risk to the organization's ability to operate in the event of an unforeseen crisis.
- **Service**—Rather than having a dozen dedicated departmental e-mail servers, an organization might instead have a centralized system able to fail-over automatically to clustered backup hardware in the event of a server crash.
- **Storage**—Where local resources may be maintained on limited hardware, centralized storage can make use of more efficient and fault-tolerant redundant array of independent disks, storage solutions capable of automatic de-duplication, single-instance storage, and a wide range of other storage management options that can allow existing storage to enjoy an extended lifetime before needing replacement or expansion.
- **Load**—High-demand user interfaces and SOA module connectivity can create high levels of demand on user-facing systems. By mirroring information and service available across multiple systems, user experience can be maintained even during periods of peak use.
- **Network**—Backup network connectivity and caching servers can reduce the load on centralized services when accessed from remote locations. Authentication services, name resolution, and even file and Web caching can all improve user access while reducing the load on the central network and data center systems.
- **Site**—A backup data center may be considered mission-critical for some organizations. When widespread disaster or extended power outages isolate an

organization's data center, a backup site outside the affected area can take over operations and provide a means for communication and organization during recovery efforts.

Automation

Automated solutions for deployment, backup, update, and patch control should be implemented whenever possible. These solutions act as a force multiplier for the available IT support staff, alleviating repetitive and cumbersome chores and allowing attention to be directed to less easily addressed issues. Standardization is absolutely vital here, to reduce complexity in system configuration across the enterprise and make automated management possible. When consolidating services into a single environment, automation strategies can reduce human administrative requirements significantly and free up resources for additional projects.

AUTOMATING UPDATES

Thousands of new viruses are released each year, requiring almost hourly updates to defensive applications protecting key data stores, e-mail gateways, and user desktops. These updates are so time-critical that they cannot be left to manual efforts at update and management, and require an automated centralized solution to provide continuously updated protection against the constant onslaught of viruses, worms, and other malicious codes (malware).

Only slightly less numerous are updates and patches to operating system and application files, which may be released on a set schedule or ad-hoc as providers add functionality or correct emergent security issues. Patch control can become tremendously unwieldy across a large distributed enterprise unless an automated patch management solution is employed. Microsoft's Windows Software Update Service is a common patch management solution used in Microsoft enterprise networks, while Linux users have similar solutions in the Up2date and Yum services that leverage native RPM package management through a comfortable user interface. Many other solutions also afford patch control capabilities such as Novell's popular Zenworks product, which is used in Netware and SUSE Linux enterprise environments.

AUTOMATING PROTECTIONS

Automation can extend beyond simple updates to include backup and restoration, such as image-based deployment systems able to wipe and reload an entire computer in a matter of minutes. In these solutions a source computer is first configured and updated with all applications installed; then the source "image" is captured. This image can then be copied to target systems, which can then be deployed in a fully ready state, without requiring extensive human action to set up and configure common settings and applications. Standardization is critical here, to reduce the number of images and the complexity of the deployment solution.

Backup solutions exist to copy files and data stores to a safe location each night, each hour, or according to whatever criterion is desired. Some of these systems provide near real-time recovery from a bare-metal hardware failure and replacement, though the network and storage requirements for constant-backup solutions can consume significant resources within the data center. By automating backup and recovery solutions, valuable information can be protected from loss or corruption. Care is required in media management and encryption of stored data to avoid accidental data exposure due to lost or stolen backups.

SUPPORTING AUTOMATION

Although automated systems can perform arduous repetitive tasks, human operational staff remains necessary even in the most heavily-automated enterprise. Logs must be reviewed regularly to ensure completion of updates and backups. Backup media should be regularly tested for recoverability, and retired on a regular schedule to protect against loss of critical data at an inopportune time. Human operators are needed in order to configure initial system images, and to ensure that patches and updates do not create problems within the test network before they are deployed to the production environment.

Enterprise architects may hear concerns from IT professionals who are afraid they may be automated out of a job, but the architect should emphasize that automation is a tool that can multiply the effectiveness of the IT professionals—not one that can remove the need for them outright. Even self-service password reset solutions, file-recovery utilities, and ad-hoc database reporting tools require configuration and management in order to provide automated results to end users.

Virtualization

Virtualization allows a single server computer to host multiple virtual servers, which function as if each were on a separate system. Each server can have its own dedicated processing power, memory allocation, and storage. Virtualization allows enterprises to bring together multiple services and standalone applications and run them all on a small number of physical servers.

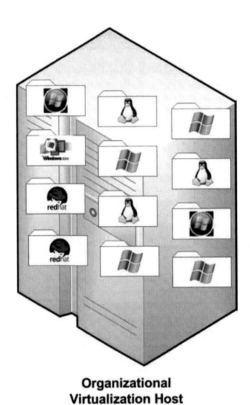

**Organizational
Virtualization Host**

Fig. 4 A simplified example of virtualization with a single host supporting multiple heterogeneousvirtual servers.

This can decrease energy costs and increase resource utilization, particularly when consolidating multiple systems that spend most of their CPU power idling. Xen, VMWare, and Microsoft are some of the vendors producing virtualization host software, many versions of which are free or provided with the server operating system at no additional charge. More robust versions of some virtualization software solutions can be used to automatically load-balance virtual systems and perform other management tasks, though these are typically commercially licensed.

MANY IN ONE

Because each virtual system functions as if installed on its own hardware, a single computer can host virtual servers of many different types (illustrated in Fig. 4). Windows, Linux, and other operating systems can be installed as virtual machines with independent operational characteristics and resources. Even the priority of resource access can be assigned, restricting less critical services to allow key services access to the lion's share of available host resources when necessary.

Virtualization is an excellent way to test consolidation procedures and to begin the data center consolidation process, because each host can remain linked to the authentication services of an organizational

unit without affecting other systems on the same host. Virtualization provides an easy mechanism for creating test networks and technology demonstrations, because multiple systems can be run side by side with provably equal resource allocations. Before diving into procurement procedures, demonstration versions of many software products can be installed on virtual servers running on existing hardware. Even a single laptop can be used to host an entire network, provided it has sufficient resources available for all operating hosts, while alternative hosts can be turned on or off at will where resource constraints apply.

VIRTUAL OPERATIONS

Because each virtual server is stored as a set of files on the host system, a backup made from a virtual server can be transported to a new host as rapidly as the media can be mounted. This can speed disaster recovery immensely, because it eliminates the need for matching hardware and lengthy configuration. Continuity of operations can also be enhanced through the use of virtualization, because a large number of virtualized hosts can be run on less expensive hardware at a backup site, with minor changes to allocated resources. Although these virtual hosts may operate at reduced efficiency, the ability to continue normal operations can be a tremendous benefit to the organization while replacement primary hardware is acquired.

Not all services can be virtualized well, particularly where the full system resources of a host computer are required for complex resource-intensive tasks. However, the ability to relocate virtual servers between hosts by simple file-transfer operations can add greatly to the effective load balancing of operational resources. Rather than trying to find more memory to fit into a physical server, a virtualized server can just as easily be moved to a different system that already has the necessary resources—taking with it all the configuration settings and even network identities of the original virtualized host. Many services developed in cloud computing environments can be automatically updated to provide additional storage, network, and processor power as needed, based on cloud hosting contractual resource allocation limits.

Plan for the Worst and Hope to Be Wrong

Consolidation, standardization, automation, and virtualization are all important considerations when planning data center operations. However, the lead architect must remain aware of internal and external threats that go far beyond whether the door is locked or the power feeds are adequate. Contingencies, fallback plans, disaster recovery, and continuity of operational planning must be

EDRMS– Enterprise

included at every step, both during consolidation activities and during ongoing normal operations.

When sunspot activity knocked out the power grid across many of the northeastern states and parts of Canada in August 2003, disaster recovery sites hours away were still within the same area of effect. During the Gulf Coast evacuation before Hurricane Rita, even sites many hours away were found to be inadequate, because fuel supplies and housing needed for relocating staff could not be found. Tsunamis, hurricanes, volcanoes, earthquakes, sunspots, and many other uncontrollable events can have a tremendous impact on an organization and the technologies needed for its continued operation.

Other problems are man-made but equally threatening, such as viruses and other malicious codes. Even defensive technologies can sometimes prove dangerous to operations, as when the popular McAfee antivirus suite incorrectly identified many business applications as a threat and quarantined or deleted application files needed for database management, business awareness, and many other functions. Recoverability must be a factor in network planning, and effective systems virtualization can speed recovery thresholds immensely.

Even concerns over the potential of threats, as in the case of severe acute respiratory syndrome or a swine flu pandemic, could lead to isolation of operational staff or facilities. By conducting proper disaster recovery and continuity of operations planning within the data center,

an organization can remain viable in times of crisis. If the business is forced to operate by running virtualized hosts on laptops from an out-of-the-way data center, at least it may still be able to maintain minimal support for key customers while its competitors are blacked out.

SUMMARY

Technology is not the solution to business requirements, but it can provide the means for an organization to remain viable and even to gain an advantage if properly directed. Standardization and a reduction in complexity are vital if an enterprise is to gain access to true economies of scale, automation, and efficient control. Although some complexity and redundancy can be desirable in order to defend a network adequately, these are areas where rapid proof of value can be found by the lead architect charged with enterprise renovation. Effective information management and data center controls can provide tremendous return on enterprise restructuring projects. Problems like the Y2K bug do not fix themselves—they are fixed by carefully guided management strategies. The reins must be firmly in hand before the next crisis arises, as it is inevitable that something will eventually go wrong. Recovery from disaster or attack is not a matter of "if" but of "when."

Enterprise Architecture: Planning

Kirk Hausman
Assistant Commandant, Texas A&M University, College Station, Texas, U.S.A.

Abstract

This entry provides an examination of elements to consider in enterprise architecture. It also identifies measures of success and common pitfalls, reviews the architectural roles and requirements, and provides considerations for formal governance and framework adoption.

Before a building can be constructed, a detailed layout of all the structural, environmental, decorative, and functional elements must first be compiled. This detailed layout, called a blueprint, ensures that adequate resources and room to expand are present and that all elements will work together in the final product. The blueprint is reviewed many times before construction begins to ensure that elements from many different disciplines will work together well—that electrical and plumbing fixtures are properly placed, that the windows and doors produce the desired effect, and that the materials specified are suitable to the environment.

Before an enterprise network can be constructed, or further developed from its existing state, a design similar to a physical construction blueprint must be created. Instead of building codes and construction methodologies, this design must identify the guidelines and strategies that will form the basis for the network architecture, along with standards and frameworks that will be used to guide its creation.

This entry focuses on the function and traits of an enterprise architect, information technology (IT) governance principles, and several architectural frameworks that can be used as templates for developing an enterprise network architectural plan.

BEYOND PLATFORM SELECTION

Many attempts at enterprise architectural planning revolve around selection of a particular technology as the standard that will be applied to purchasing choices. Such a "platform architecture" might include listings of approved hardware platforms, operating systems, desktop configurations, office productivity suites, content management and database management systems (DBMS), programming languages and development tool suites, collaboration platforms, directory and identity management solutions, and even mobile technology solutions approved for staff use or purchase reimbursement.

Architects of commercial platforms may select a particular vendor stack, such as Microsoft or IBM, for enterprise-wide standardization in order to ease integration and planning. Open-systems architects may select only a set of standards around which all purchases must be made, with minor platform or application variation allowed at the user or facility level if deemed worth the added complexity. Regardless of the particular approach chosen, selecting standardized platform architectures can provide direct benefits that are easily conveyed to stakeholders:

- Economies of scale can be gained through aggregated purchasing mechanisms spanning multiple business units that formerly purchased technologies in an ad-hoc manner using locally directed funding. Enterprise-wide licensing and per-processor licensing models can often save tremendous amounts of money compared to individual per-user licensing throughout a medium-to-large organization.
- Applications are more easily integrated and tested, depending on the level of commonality provided through platform specification. The more elements of the platform architecture are shared, the greater is the ease in initial implementation and later additions of functionality. Selecting a standard or vendor with a large body of third-party offerings allows an organization to readily adopt newly emergent technology offerings as they reach viability.
- Users and technical support staff can be more efficient throughout the enterprise, as they can gain a greater working knowledge of a smaller number of disparate solutions. This can reduce both staffing and training requirements, and allow greater mobility within an extended organization to meet marketplace agility needs. When all applications are standardized, a user trained in the standard suite of productivity

EDRMS–
Enterprise

Encyclopedia of Information Systems and Technology, DOI: 10.1081/E-EIST-120053816

applications will require very little training if he or she is transferred to another department.

- Selecting widely used platform architectures provides a greater body of community support when issues arise or when new technologies are being implemented. When problems or questions arise, it is easier to find effective solutions if the platform architecture is in common use and enjoys strong community involvement in implementation and development.

- Control is simplified because only the initial selection process must include all possible competing alternatives. After the platform architecture has been identified and detailed, selection needs only to evaluate alternatives within the identified platform's offerings.

Enterprise architecture would be greatly simplified if platform selection was its only feature. Within small, well-funded organizations, many of these "low-hanging fruit" may be plucked readily as value-for-effort. However, selection of a single platform specification to be implemented across a medium-to-large organization will rapidly encounter many stumbling blocks, often including the following:

- Many packaged applications rely on a particular set of technologies for operation. Legacy equipment such as automation and equipment control systems may rely on an embedded control technology, while other applications may only operate against a particular type of relational DBMS such as an Oracle or MySQL instance. Changing these solutions to meet newly-identified platform architectural guidelines can be problematic, requiring time, effort, and expense in acquiring alternatives that fit within the identified platform—assuming that such an alternative exists. Application virtualization systems are often tied to the fundamental architecture of the network itself, relying on the authentication and access control system to control application package assignment, deployment, and updating. The architect can address this issue by carefully identifying all such dependencies before beginning enterprise reconfiguration actions, so as to avoid mid-upgrade loss or instability of key services that can stall or terminate enterprise-wide projects.

- Replacement of existing, working systems may be beyond the budgeting ability of many organizations and business units. While there are times when a functional but expensive enterprise solution may be tossed out in favor of an alternative, the majority of businesses must enact incremental evolutionary change rather than outright revolutionary change simply because the cost of replacing everything outweighs the benefits of immediate standardization. An architect's knowledge and understanding of existing

revenue streams and any constraints on stream allocations are critical to understanding and successfully planning the scope and pace of enterprise-transforming projects.

- Changes in technology standards, development of new offerings, and the constant evolution of network threats can often outrun an established platform specification. By the time an organization can transition its technologies to meet the new standard, several new versions of an identified platform option might have been developed to add new features or close vulnerabilities not identified at the time of the original assessment. This is particularly true when dealing with governmental agencies, educational systems, and organizations with complex bureaucracies, because of the lag between specification and purchase. An identified best-in-breed at the time of original product evaluation might be woefully inadequate compared to later entries into the same application space by the time the new fiscal year rolls around and funds are available for acquisition. The architect must constantly review emerging technologies and keep abreast of changes in common technology devices, configurations, and uses.

- The scale of need and expertise may vary widely within an organization, creating a requirement for different levels of operational capability that may not be reflected by a one-size-fits-all platform specification. A commonly encountered version of this involves the dominant enterprise Microsoft platform, which includes both desktop (Access) and server (Structured Query Language Server) relational database (RDBS) solutions. Both solutions use a similar interface for query/view design and share many elements in common; however, the workgroup-scale Access application is not suited to the same level of concurrent use as its more robust Structured Query Language Server counterpart. Conversely, training to support each RDBS application differs greatly in the level of expertise required, because the workgroup product lacks many of the index, trigger, stored procedures, and other features necessary in its enterprise counterpart. Proper project management practices during the planning phase will aid in achieving an effective transformation by identifying existing solutions that are in place and compiling skills and responsibility matrices to identify available resources, both human and technological, as well as any shortcomings that must be met by acquisitions or training.

- Partner organizations may not follow the same standards, creating difficulties when the platform architecture must interoperate with that of another organization whose decisions are made along a differing standard or cycle of upgrade. This problem becomes more apparent as organizations are increasingly coupled with partners for service provision, regulatory mandate, or business opportunity. Poorly selected platform architecture or the choice of little-used technology standards can create barriers to business integration and lose opportunities for the organization well beyond simple issues of whether the solution meets an originally identified specification. This problem arises often during mergers and acquisitions when platform architecture decisions have followed different courses in the originally separate organizations. As an example, elements of the U. S. Department of Homeland Security experienced difficulties with e-mail between organizational elements when the department was created from previously separate functional organizations. Platform differences caused communications difficulties between some divisions of the new organization, even though they were all using the same underlying standard (SMTP) for e-mail. Use of common platforms and applications in architectural redesign will reduce the likelihood of poor interoperability with partner organizations or external services such as hosting or cloud computing providers. Customization of operating system, application, and service configurations beyond accepted industry standards should be kept to a bare minimum to protect both interoperability and upgrade potential.

- Individual business units or key stakeholders may be unwilling to accept the platform architectural specification. A wide range of technology preferences may factor into the local mandates provided by business-unit IT decision makers. In addition to preference, individual business units may lack the expertise and skills necessary to implement a newly specified platform standard—particularly one that differs considerably from the platform architecture currently in use. Matrices and surveys of existing resources compiled during the planning phase will help identify requirements for training to upgrade support capabilities. The platform architect should also ensure that support leadership is included in the technology council that provides change management controls, to ensure that issues are presented, considered, and addressed before initiating a change.
- Implementation of alternative standards or platform specifications without a review of service impact or analysis can compromise service availability and user capabilities, and may create push-back from user and management-level consumers in addition to technical support teams. This type of issue is common when movement to an older standard platform is necessary due to a merger between organizations and the main organization is using software versions that are older than the ones in the newly acquired organizational element. Users who have become accustomed to features and functionalities provided by the newer software may experience significantly reduced efficiency

due to a lack of certain features. Users may also feel "cheated" by being forced to roll back to the "outdated" application platform or software standard.

Certainly, these are not the only barriers to adopting a platform specification, but they illustrate clearly why the practice of enterprise architecture must take into account elements that extend beyond the range of platform specification alone. Beyond specification of a set of standards or vendor products through which the enterprise will operate, the enterprise architect must also consider integration and communications requirements, application-specific requirements, available and emergent communications protocols, business integration mandates, legislative and regulatory compliance constraints, scale and scope requirements, event management and alerting, reporting mandates, storage and architectural requirements, identity management mandates, and a wealth of other aspects.

Without guidance and consideration of these elements both in their existing form and following emergent trends, the enterprise architect may make short-term decisions that fail to provide longer-term efficiencies—in fact, some decisions can even create greater cost burdens if improperly applied. Architecture is more about plotting a course through a variety of choices than about making a particular application selection. Technical frameworks and standards must be balanced against the strategic goals of the business while minimizing the negative impact of any changes on the end user. Rather than being a goal, technology must always remain a means to facilitate user requirements.

In the end, a project that produces the desired change in technology but negatively impacts user and client service remains a failure. According to the Project Management Institute, roughly two-thirds of all projects fail. To avoid expending unnecessary effort on failure, the enterprise architect must know when to initiate a project, when to decide the time or resources are not right for a particular change, and when to call a halt to avoid spending resources on a failed effort. Always remember that sunk costs (money already spent) should not be used to determine whether to continue a failing or troubled project.

WHERE LIES SUCCESS?

Successful enterprise architecture must convey some form of advantage to the organization or it serves no purpose. While it might once have been possible for an organization to gain a competitive edge by using e-mail for internal communication or a website for user contact, these solutions are used by such a broad range of organizations that they create no operational advantage.

Although doing without them might have a negative effect, their presence alone no longer constitutes a particular competitive advantage. Enterprise architecture must provide additional value to the organization.

A few qualities that may indicate successful enterprise architecture include:

- Providing a clear upgrade path to technological progress
- Defining standards for interoperability with existing and emergent technologies
- Minimizing undesirable redundancy and optimizing fault tolerance
- Reducing risk and enhancing continuity of operations
- Reducing support and operational costs
- Improving operational opportunities for interaction and mobility
- Recognizing architecture as a valuable contribution to the enterprise

It may at first seem strange that one indicator of a successful enterprise architecture is that the architecture is recognized as valuable. However, architectural choices can have a profound effect on an organization's capabilities and opportunities for growth. An architecture that is completely in the background, which is never noticed by the users and stakeholders, may be too readily discarded as an unnecessary effort or expense during organizational changes or economic cutbacks. It is important for long-term viability that not only should good decisions be made, but that they must also be communicated to implementers and users. Successes, failures, and even near-misses should also be conveyed to primary stakeholders so that the value of the architecture remains known, identifiable, and justifiable within the overall business plan.

An enterprise architect may be aided by other architects, a change management council, or an integration competency center to ensure that all decisions that are made fit within all necessary technologies and operational mandates. However, it is the architect's vision of the enterprise that guides all policies, standards, guidelines, and specifications that will be enacted within this scope. The enterprise architect must be able to convey the value of this vision to both stakeholders and implementers, and must be able to see far enough ahead so that decisions made allow changes when necessary.

As with any project, the project manager (enterprise architect) must be selected as early in the process as possible and must be given the authority to negotiate for necessary resources and designate standards for architectural changes. There can be only one person in the role of chief architect: Effective responsibility cannot be assigned to a group.

In smaller organizations, the enterprise architect may also be the chief technologist or lead developer. This can be acceptable in a small venue, as the architect may be able to learn and consider all possible aspects of the organizational technology needs. In larger organizations, it is important to distinguish enterprise architecture from development and IT implementation. While nontechnical managerial staff members cannot be effective enterprise architects because they lack the necessary understanding of service interrelations, even effective IT professionals may be poor enterprise architects if:

- **Their personal preferences for technology specification do not provide the best opportunities for their organization as a whole.** Many organizations attempt to bypass the tendencies by placing a nontechnical individual in the chief information officer (CIO)/chief architect's position. While this may avoid the problem of IT preference, it creates a situation in which the primary decision maker responsible for architectural vision must rely primarily on the advice of others—a situation akin to sheep asking wolves to advise them. This also leads to project selection in isolation, where a change in collaboration platform might be decided on without considering the impact on related services such as an organizational intranet portal or a customer management system that leverages the collaboration platform for critical functionality.
- **Their vision lacks clarity and understanding of the needs of the organization, or changes too often to provide a useful direction.** Nothing can doom an enterprise architectural effort more effectively than a leader who does not know where the organization is going. Fuzzy goals tend to lead to unremarkable results that lack metrics for assessing success. Like a boat without a tiller, an architect without direction tends to lead nowhere. Worse, in some ways, is the architect whose vision changes with each new month's trade journals or based on which stakeholders have most recently argued their needs. An inconstant leader can cause implementers to waste valuable time jumping from project to project, at times working only to undo what has just been partially completed because the architect has just heard about the newest process-of-the-month. Nothing illustrates more how lost a leader is than such wandering in the wilderness of alternatives.
- **They are unable to convey their vision to stakeholders, implementers, or business consumers.** The most knowledgeable technologists, skilled in every aspect of their craft and instilled with the most incredibly clear vision of successful enterprise architecture, are useless if they cannot effectively convey their vision and its value to others. Many technologists eschew the "soft skills" necessary for project management, negotiation, and selling the idea of their vision and its worth to the organization. For those to

Table 1 IT maturity models

Level	Maturity	Management	Architecture
4	Value	Information improves business process and cost recovery	Processes exist to resolve strategic/tactical conflicts
3	Service	Capacity and service levels managed	Standard architecture, applied inconsistently
2	Proactive	Performance, configuration, and change management are automated	Architecture managed in some business units
1	Reactive	Basic event response, backup/recovery, and help desk	Departmental-level architectural management
0	Chaotic	No consolidation, operations are left to deployment staff	All decisions made in isolation

Source: From Gartner Research.

whom technology itself becomes the goal, conveying its value beyond existence appears unnecessary. This form of tunnel vision can doom an enterprise architectural effort to failure. The most beautiful painting in the world has no value if it is kept in the dark—so too with an architectural vision.

- **They fail to remain knowledgeable about technologies in use and in development.** While the CIO/chief architect should focus on aspects of technology that extend beyond the day-to-day implementation details, it is impossible to command the respect of information technologists charged with implementing the vision without maintaining a thorough knowledge of existing and emerging technology trends. Not only may architects miss potential opportunities, they may lose the support and input from individuals whose expertise may be the key to greater success. Buy-in from implementers within the technology service arena is often developed only in the presence of expertise on the part of the architect. While this role need not have deep expertise in all areas, the architect should be an expert in at least one area and conversant in the functions of all others in order to best gain the trust and support of other technologists. Knowledgeable architects can also bridge disparate skills as a force multiplier, producing an outcome greater than that possible by team members acting apart.
- **They fail to lead.** The worst of all possible architects are those who are so busy gathering requirements, evaluating options, negotiating with their peers, reporting to their superiors, and getting feedback from stakeholders that they never do anything. It is easy to slip into a routine so filled with the process of developing architectural guidelines that nothing is ever produced as a result. The pursuit of perfection is seductive and pointless—what must be accomplished is a solution that is good enough for business needs and good enough to allow the next generation of technologies to be managed in turn.

Many different means can be used to measure the state of architectural guidance and management within an organization. Table 1 provides a simplified maturity

model based on those offered by Gartner Research. Far too many organizations operate at the lowest levels of maturity, where decisions on architecture and implementation are missing altogether or function in chaos merely as reactions to the latest problem or need. Proactive effort and cost is generally far lower than reactive, because reactive actions include resources necessary to undo what has been done in addition to resources necessary to implement the new course of action. Without a higher level of planning, coordination, and vision, these organizations cannot take advantage of the true potential of their IT resources.

THE ARCHITECT

If a successful architecture can produce advantages, then what makes a good architect? This question is tied closely to the job the CIO/chief architect must perform in order to effectively identify, strategize, and resolve organizational needs and technology drivers that affect the enterprise. The architect is responsible for many tasks, such as:

- **Identifying data and its movement.** The enterprise architect must identify data that is being managed and maintained throughout the enterprise, along with the paths through which it is transferred, archived, or eliminated in order to properly plan for its continuity under a formal architectural style. Many times, the identification and elimination of undesirable redundancy in data stores can produce strong benefits from direct cost savings in hardware, software, and support to indirect cost savings through security of sensitive or protected data.
- **Defining technical architectural guidelines.** Standards, technology selections, protocol selections, guidelines for identity management, update management, security and recoverability statutes, computer use policy specifications, and all other aspects of the technology architecture must be coordinated by the enterprise architect in the overall vision.
- **Integrating existing resources.** The enterprise architect cannot, in almost all cases, simply throw away

everything that exists and replace it with new solutions. Embedded systems, legacy equipment, merged business units, and partner relationships may all bring different technology solutions into the enterprise. The enterprise architect must plan for the inclusion of these elements into the strategy.

- **Communicating the vision.** The enterprise architect must convey the benefits of the vision to stakeholders, the details to the implementers, and the benefits and purpose to the users. At the same time, this communication cannot be one-way. The enterprise architect must constantly be accepting useful input to be included in the evolution of the vision to encompass emerging needs and solutions.

- **Improve quality.** The results of the enterprise architect's efforts must provide value to the organization, improving the quality of IT operations. Architects whose solutions simply replace existing systems with a different version of the same thing may find it difficult to justify the continued expense without some measure of value or quality improvement. Careful metrics identified before and after each phase can aid in the identification of the value provided, requiring the architect to practice more than simple technology selection in order to be a success.

- **Program management.** Strong project and program management skills are vital to ensure that all phases of architectural reconstruction are handled in an efficient manner using well-defined strategies. In addition to maintaining technology operations, which many former IT managers are more than capable of continuing, the enterprise architect must manage numerous projects simultaneously to control costs and ensure that activities on the critical path are addressed ahead of activities with flex remaining. It is far too easy to seek "easy" projects to illustrate ongoing success to sponsors, but this can lead to missed deadlines and cost overruns when those easy projects are not ones that must be completed first to maintain overall project and program timelines.

The Chief Architect

A CIO/chief architect must be able to perform equally well in the business and technology arenas. It is here that the ability to identify business needs and shareholder expectations of value is essential in order to later convey the purpose and benefits resulting from enterprise architectural deliverables. Identifying opportunities to improve the organization through productivity, efficiency, or asset gains is as important as identifying inefficient architectures, poor buying models, and outdated solutions that are in use.

PROVIDING A PLAN

The chief architect must be able to identify the purpose of IT solutions, align them with business requirements, and communicate their value to both technical implementers as well as nontechnical stakeholders. Subordinate IT professionals at times may want to try out new solutions that have no applicability to the business environment—distinguishing new business opportunities from expensive toys is a valuable skill for the chief architect. The chief architect must be willing to simply say "no" to nonproductive projects and inefficient ways of doing business. The chief enterprise architect is rarely a popular person, as entrenched professionals with established professional and personal standing can be very influential when complaining about changes that are made counter to local preferences.

The chief architect must always be looking to identifying crises that may emerge as a result of new network threats or emerging technologies. Disaster recovery and business continuity may hinge on effective IT planning, in which good decisions and an eye on potential large-scale disruption may keep the business on track while competitors fail. Concerns about global pandemics, terrorist activities, and natural disasters all add to the scope of an enterprise architect's planning, because his decisions may determine whether an organization survives or simply ceases to exist in the worst case.

COMMUNICATING THE VISION

Chief architects must be able to see the big picture but paint it on small canvases. Translating the vision into simple, concise pieces is vital both in educating stakeholders and conveying directives to those responsible for executing planned changes. A solid business case for each primary element, along with strong project management skills that can bridge multiple projects into a cohesive program within a common framework, can aid in rapidly identifying a process gone awry or one that is being ineffectively implemented. Unhappy implementers can often be identified here, where their lack of enthusiasm may be adversely affecting project success and timeliness.

Chief architects must be as at home talking to primary stakeholders or individual users as they are comfortable communicating in the language of business or technology. They must be able to effectively convey elements of the vision at all levels of the business, but also be able to dig down to the individual details of the application of the vision so that communication can flow both ways. Ultimately, they need to be able to sell the idea to stakeholders, convey it to implementers, and document everything so that metrics can be measured against the process of change. Like all project managers, enterprise architects may spend up to 90% of their time communicating to implementers, change management functionaries, stakeholders, project sponsors, peers, and individual users.

BALANCING VALUE AND RISK

The chief architect must be able to identify value in the present architecture, as well as identify missing elements that need to be filled. Many times, some elements of efficiency can be acquired rapidly. These "lowhanging fruit" are easily obtained, and it is important to identify these for initial implementation in order to show value—but care must be taken to ensure that jumping too quickly does not incur undesirable opportunity costs, excluding opportunities for greater improvements later. Establishing clear business goals and balancing them against selected technology solutions is not a simple task, as each choice may close off other alternatives later.

Chief architects must identify metrics and goals for success and failure, while also planning and identifying risks that will arise from each step toward these goals. Cost and risk factors and various constraints must be considered during each planning phase, both at the immediate per-project level and across the entire enterprise planning process. Adding vulnerability or exposing protected data during a transitional phase may not be legally allowable under regulatory and operational mandates, while relying on a technology that is still in the incubator stage may produce an unacceptable level of risk to proofing guidelines and purchasing requirements. Security and regulatory compliance must always be considered in strategic planning to ensure that assets are not exposed to risk during transition.

The Lead Architect

In support of a chief architect, a lead architect may participate in senior management forums, serve on the change management council, or lead implementation groups in applying the strategies developed from the chief architect's vision. In small to medium enterprises, these roles are typically combined. A lead architect will often lead forums, integration competency center reviews, requirements-gathering initiatives, and other similar tasks necessary to identifying business and technology elements for integration into the overall architectural plan. This role is particularly valuable when attempting to integrate multiple cross-enterprise initiatives during mergers.

The Business Architect

Organizations that employ complex application solutions or ones with public-facing business applications such as Web shopping carts or business intelligence portals may find it necessary to assign a business architectural role. Whether combined with the chief architect's position or implemented separately, the person holding this operational role must understand and translate all business strategies and processes into requirements that can be addressed through technology selection or development.

The business architect's role may include technology planning for business-to-business, business-to-consumer, partner integration, service-oriented architecture selection, and management of heterogeneous or legacy application suites that require data gateway translation or information transfer for operation.

The Technology Architect

The technology architect role becomes necessary in organizations that employ a wide range of technological solutions, or in which application development or customization is used extensively. This role requires deep technical experience, often in one or more programming disciplines, and the technology architect acts to ensure that application development and modification are performed within the strategies detailed from the chief architect's vision.

The technology architect is responsible for guiding application design style selection, such as service-oriented, scrum, or waterfall-type development, as well as testing new techniques and technologies for potential use within the extended enterprise. Though often considered the most fun job, this role of the technology architect is not just to try out all of the new technology toys, but to be able to draw a hard line when a solution reaches end of life or is determined as falling outside the organization's needs.

Outsourced Architecture

Some aspects of enterprise architecture can be outsourced to external expertise. In general, this is done in order to gain access to skills that are not present or not present in sufficient depth within the existing human resources of the organization. When making a strategic change in storage architecture or federated identity management, outsourcing the planning roles can be effective while internal personnel are being provided the necessary training to understand a new solution's implications. During mergers and acquisitions, for instance, an outside expert may be able to begin the migration process while local IT resources are retrained into the parent organization's architecture.

EDRMS– Enterprise

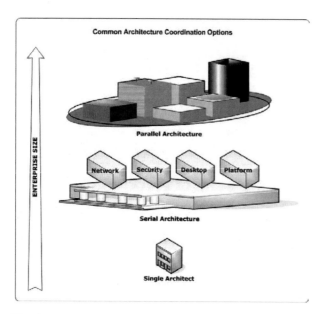

Fig. 1 Architecture coordination as enterprise size increases.

Outsourcing the developing of a strategic guide or blueprint may provide a means to save time within limited internal enterprise architect resources, or when internal political issues provide the need for an outside viewpoint to settle on one solution as the common thread for development of a strategic vision. Documentation of existing resources can also be outsourced in order to save time and to reduce the impact of internal business-unit politics on discovery and resource identification. Critical functions such as enterprise architectural change or security may be outsourced in some cases, but responsibility for services, regulatory compliance, and data protection ultimately remains with the organization.

One additional area that lends itself well to outsourcing is that of testing and compliance review. Testing new technologies for a fit within the enterprise architectural vision may be best performed by a third party in order to ensure that findings reflect technology interactions and not simply local preferences. Similarly, compliance audit and review should be performed by a dedicated or external agency in order to ensure that internal bias or simple familiarity do not cause the review to overlook areas of concern. Audit functions must not be conducted solely from within the IT organization, as it is impossible to obtain a fair and thorough report of variance when the individual reporting an issue is subordinate to the functions or personnel being assessed.

Multiple Architects

Small to medium-size enterprise architecture can easily be coordinated by a single chief architect, with additional supporting focused architects added to cover capacity shortfalls as the enterprise scope expands. This can produce an optimized architecture, capable of the most complete synthesis of homogeneous network coordination with the greatest possible reduction in data and network complexity and cost. As enterprise networks increase in size or span multiple business units with independent purchasing capabilities, the load may be distributed across multiple architects' purview, provided the organization has matured to some form of matrixed structure. A single chief architect or chief technology officer must still be identified in all cases, because someone must ultimately make choices between alternatives and be responsible for success or failure of the effort.

Distributed federated architecture for very large enterprises can be configured serially or in parallel, depending on the nature of the enterprise and its goals, as noted in Fig. 1. Serial architecture divides individual aspects of the overall architectural vision so that each element is guided by its own chief architect. Communication among the chief architectural roles creates a community environment within the coordinated guidelines dictated by each architect's contributions. This is similar to a university or corporate environment in which each business unit operates within a negotiated general vision but maintains some aspects of localized control.

Parallel architecture is more like a city, in which no common vision is implemented and each silo makes decisions for access within its own boundaries. Multiple autonomous heterogeneous silos of parallel operation yield localized responsiveness at the cost of opportunities for efficiency, much like physical city planning efforts. Parallel architectural control scenarios tend to experience large undesirable redundancies in data, hardware, and staffing requirements and do not adapt to wide-scale upgrade as well as more closely coordinated architectural forms. This is the least efficient format for large enterprise networks, as differing architectural decisions may generate standards conflict, compromise security, and create large areas of overlapping expense and operational effort.

CREATING A SYMPHONY

Federated architectural solutions, whether distributed serially or in parallel, must have a central chief architect to set basic policy and provide the highest-level vision—all other forms of federated architecture will produce conflicting internal elements and impair long-term efficiency and viability. This need is seen in many other operational arenas: Cooking, music, education, corporate control, and military strategy all rely on coordination under a designated leader in order to avoid chaos.

Without a master chef, the sous-chefs and all others working in a commercial kitchen might produce a variety of very nice dishes but would be very unlikely to create an integrated masterpiece of culinary art. A general officer in the military may rely heavily on the support of senior staff officers, but in the end must make decisions alone so that an army can move toward a single purpose. The federal Sarbanes-Oxley legislation formalized responsibilities built into the framework of corporate governance, mandating specific attention and control in the corporate sector. A master conductor must work to bring together the disparate instruments present so that an orchestra can produce a symphony—one that will differ from the same music played by the same orchestra under a different conductor's baton. Each of these scenarios represents the same need found in enterprise architecture—someone, ultimately, must hold the baton.

Governance

The art of enterprise architecture relies on similar high-level coordination to gain advantages in agility, cost reduction, and operational efficiency. The symphony that can result from effective coordinated enterprise governance depends on a clear vision, strong leadership coupled with executive buy-in and support, and an effective means of communication with those responsible for their own areas of expertise. Some assessments detail the process of enterprise architecture as follows:

1. **Creation**—Identification of the business drivers and requirements that create a need for enterprise coordination. This may be a simple need for cost-effective technology utilization, or made more complex by regulatory mandates and partner intercommunication requirements.
2. **Discovery**—Identification of the individual protocols and technologies that come together to form the executive-level vision that will guide technological development, purchase, and organization.
3. **Implementation**—Enacting changes, developing policies, communicating requirements necessary to implement the vision in actual terms.
4. **Governance**—Overseeing and managing the process that guides technology decisions, implementation actions, and all other decisions that fall within the guidelines of the technology enterprise.

However, governance is more fundamental than first appears in this process. Enterprise architecture translates business requirements into technology planning that must include strategic and operational decisions. These decisions must in turn contain decision making for capacity, cost, recovery, and survivability that must be more than theoretical abstracts. Governance is more about communicating between strategic roles (Chief executive officer, chief financial officer, CIO, business-unit leaders), operational roles (managers, partner representatives, regulatory agents), and infrastructural roles (integration competency centers, IT implementers, training staff).

Without some mechanism for governance, lines of communication and authority can become hopelessly tangled and doom the architectural effort before it has even begun. Many formal systems for IT governance exist, including:

- **Information Technology Infrastructure Library (ITIL).** Perhaps the most widely adopted standard for enterprise governance, the ITIL is a best-practice set of guidelines for operational control. Because of the level of detail in the ITIL, it can produce revolutionary change—with all of the benefits and costs that it entails. Without strong management commitment, care in training and specifying each ITIL process, and planning for a 3–5 year implementation effort, this methodology can be a bit hard to handle. As a living document, the ITIL continues to evolve to meet new challenges that follow emergent technology standards and options and is widely used in large enterprises such as governmental and multinational corporations.
- **Control Objectives for Information Technology (CobIT).** This detailed governance model produced by the Information Systems Audit and Control Association (ISACA) grew from an audit and control methodology and is also widely recognized, with a strong community supporting its continued evolution. Its sponsoring agency, together with the IT Governance Institute, produces a large number of focused-compliance guides to help CobIT apply more specifically to individual guidelines that may apply to specific industries and business sectors (Sarbanes-Oxley, COSO) and to specific technologies (zOS, Linux, SAP).
- **International Organization for Standardization/International Electrotechnical Commission (ISO/IEC) 27002.** The British governmental 7799 standard was adopted by the International Standards Organization as ISO 17799, which enjoys wide use throughout many business sectors—although it is often found combined with other governance methodologies due to the large number of translation guides that exist to bind this standard's elements with those of the other methodologies. The ISO/IEC 27002 standard has since replaced the older ISO 17799 standard, reflecting changes and more recently emergent requirements.

Many other formal systems exist for IT governance, and any sufficiently detailed system with a strong community of support and regular updates to its standards

EDRMS– Enterprise

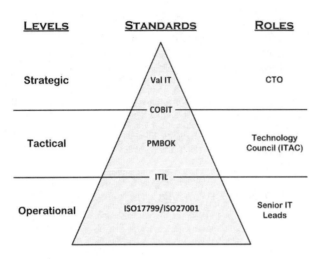

Fig. 2 An example of governance layering to address needs at different organizational levels.

could benefit the architectural process. Control objects from the ITIL, CobIT, ISO 17799, and other similar standards are aligned in many different studies, allowing organizations to use elements of those that fit best. It is vital that enterprise architects include an understanding of IT governance in their planning and vision. Few organizations of significant size will find that a single governance or control standard meets all possible needs, so methodologies are often layered at different operational levels (as shown in Fig. 2).

Architectural Models

In addition to an understanding of governance methodologies, the chief architect should also have an understanding of formal architectural frameworks that can be used as fundamental models during the architectural process. These frameworks can provide extraordinary resource, although many carry an inherent bias toward specific technological viewpoints and should be considered in that light. Formal enterprise architectural frameworks include options such as the following.

- **POSIX 1003.23.** One of the earliest formal frameworks for enterprise architecture, this standard was developed by the Institute of Electrical and Electronics Engineers as one of several standards related to software compatibility for Unix operating system variants. Because of its origins, this standard is coupled closely with Unix and Unix-like platform environments.
- **The Zachman Framework.** A widely-accepted benchmark model, this framework was developed by the Zachman Institute in order to model enterprise architecture in terms of scope, business model, system model, technology model, and other details when measured against the standard questions asked: what,

how, where, who, when, and why. As a high-level model, the Zachman Framework provides an excellent starting point for architectural theory.
- **The Open Group Architecture Format (TOGAF).** TOGAF has been developed by the Open Group, a consortium of information system vendors, software suppliers, and user organizations. It is a very detailed, extensive living document that can be used as a starting point for developing commercial platform enterprise models, though its origins couple the document itself more closely to the open systems methodology.
- **The Federal Enterprise Architecture Framework.** This framework emerged from a series of policies and guidance efforts within the U. S. federal government, aimed at providing a standard framework for planning interoperable and sustainable computing. It derives details from earlier governmental standards, including the Office of Management and Budget's EA Assessment Framework, the General Accounting Office's IT Framework, the Treasury Enterprise Architecture Framework, the Generalized Enterprise Reference Architecture Model, the Performance Reference Model, the Data and Information Reference Model, the Application-Capability Reference Model, the Technical Reference Model, and other similar frameworks. It is detailed, extensive, and continues to be updated to reflect the changing needs of governmental IT enterprises.
- **The Gartner Enterprise Architecture Framework.** Developed by Gartner Research, this framework attempts to provide a comprehensive model for the development of both commercial and open-source enterprise environments. It is divided into parts, with half of the model addressing technology, while the other half addresses business strategy and process. Although it remains less developed in terms of a body of reference guides and compliance checklists, this framework enjoys steady growth in the body of documentation and research provided by its parent organization.
- **The North American State CIO Enterprise Architecture (NASCIO).** An emerging leader in enterprise architectural planning, this model is developed by the NASCIO, which is composed of representatives of the 50 state CIOs. Coupling well with other models, this model has broad applicability throughout both commercial off-the-shelf and open-source enterprise environments. Because it is derived from ongoing state-level CIO efforts, this framework remains a living body of data.

Tip: As with governance methodologies, elements from the formal frameworks can be combined in order to better meet the needs of each enterprise's unique setting. As an example, the State of Michigan makes use of elements from both the Gartner and NASCIO frameworks in the continuing development of its Strategic Plan, with very positive results to show from this effort.

Many mappings exist between the various enterprise framework models to better allow translation and combination of their useful elements. With attention to potential source bias, they can serve as an invaluable resource when attempting to identify boundaries within an unplanned ad-hoc enterprise seeking focus.

Project and Program Management

A common fallacy encountered in many organizations is the idea that technology must drive business and operational mandates. Business goals must always drive the logical decision making that produces a technological outcome, or the technology will become an end unto itself rather than a means to facilitate business operations. Aligning these requirements is the most important task to be managed by chief architects as they develop their vision and then implement it into real-world elements. Beyond documenting requirements and technology solutions, architects must also engineer metrics and measurement criteria into each element to be able to identify and illustrate the benefits or costs incurred during implementation.

This is not, by any means, the end of the requirements for an enterprise architect. The chief architect must also plan each element with clear goals, milestones, and completion criteria before seeking or providing approval for each stage. The architect must be the final arbiter when negotiating solutions to conflicts that arise during planning, acquisition, implementation, and adoption of each change—which relies far more heavily on the project management skills of the architect than on detailed knowledge of the technologies involved. Ultimately, the architect must plan, design, guide, and monitor the ongoing fluid process of development throughout the enterprise and all of its associated business elements and technologies.

While the process of enterprise architecture never ends, individual elements must be clearly identified with a scope, planning guidelines, completion criteria, and other elements common to discrete project management. Leadership, communication, negotiation, problem solving, resolving cultural impact, meeting regulatory mandates and standards, quality control, and other aspects of formal project management play a critical role in the success or failure of a chief architect's contributions. Operational elements within small and medium-sized enterprises may not always need a formal scoping document, formal change control committees, and a detailed risk analysis for each tiny change that may be enacted. However, knowledge of these techniques is vital to knowing when they have become necessary—particularly as the enterprise scale increases.

In addition to operational technology management, the chief architect must be comfortable in some type of formal project and program management methodology. It is important that any other lead architectural roles also involve these principles, but they are imperative for the central architectural role. Note, however, that there are many different formal project management styles. General project management techniques often bring benefits beyond focused-methodology management techniques, such as those that focus closely on quality control or documentation mechanisms specific to particular technologies. More general techniques often address business drivers that may factor into long-range planning without being obvious in short- and mid-term architectural assessments.

BEYOND BASICS

The chief architect must always be looking toward identifying trends and emerging strategies that will play a part in the next cycle of enterprise evolution and the ones beyond. The architect must have an understanding of the impact of decisions made in creating and implementing the central vision, to avoid closing doors not yet even glimpsed ahead. This can at times be a journey fraught with peril, as many unanticipated consequences can arise from small differences in technology.

Language Standard

The adoption of a programming standard, such as the Java J2EE language, works very well in the resource-plentiful PC environment but may not always scale well into mainframe OS architectures, where thousands of processes may be sharing a vast but not unlimited resource pool. Even though the language can perform within both environments, the manner in which applications must operate can vary widely in such circumstances. Similarly, the selection of an object-oriented programming language (Java,. NET) can create disruption if developers have previously used a traditional language (ANSI C, COBOL), because of the fundamental differences in how these types of programming languages transfer information.

Operational Environment

Environments that must support real-time operations rely on solutions different from those required for high-volume transactional processing, distributed computing, or detailed business intelligence analytical processing. The data structures necessary to support each type of operation differ in terms of resource consumption, scalability, data throughput, metadata organization, 24/7 availability, security, recoverability, and many other factors. Beyond the data structures, user interface design, reporting, and other tools will vary widely among tasks, and decisions can have a strong impact on many of these tasks. Selection of an operating system platform, user office suite, application suite, data management solution, programming language, development suite, and all of the other elements of the technology implementation plan can amplify or negate business drivers present in each scenario.

Virtualization

The potential for technology virtualization seems almost limitless as enterprises take advantage of huge resource and storage pools, enhanced network bandwidth, and improved management utilities. Users can remotely access their desktop workstations from anywhere in the world, while server farms and their attendant power requirements are collapsing by half or better as hardware server sprawl is being channeled into a smaller number of powerful servers supporting software system emulations.

Virtual storage solutions can make use of every scrap of space throughout an entire enterprise, while others may ensure that necessary data is available on the best connected server by replicating a virtual volume throughout the enterprise. Combinations of high-performance computing strategies and service virtualization have led to the virtualization of entire network infrastructural elements into "the Cloud." These solutions promise incredible advantages in utilization, efficiency, and cost management—and the decisions made will affect their availability down the road.

Mobile Technologies

As network bandwidth and portable computing power increase, the office is leaving a physical building and becoming more a matter of availability anywhere, anytime. Weather, sports, navigation, and other personal interest data is readily at hand, while network management and server console access no longer requires anything more than a WiFi hotspot at the local coffee house or a cellular data link from the back nine at the local country club. The ability to remotely access and manipulate information that remains safe on its host system can help to alleviate business issues for corporations working across national boundaries that may restrict where information may be exported. The ability to virtually access supercomputing power from a mobile handheld device is one of the most powerful causes for change in the modern enterprise.

Service-Oriented Architecture (SOA)

As remote access and network connectivity improve, many enterprises are adopting the service-oriented approach to application development. By making use of Web service standards such as SOAP and Universal Description, Discover and Integration to pass information between applications, programmers can work simultaneously on different parts of a larger application without having to worry about using the same language or parameter-passing mechanisms. All that is required is that a set of standards is used for the information exchange itself—often a variant of the Extensible Markup Language specification. This has the short-term benefits of both rapid development and platform independence that allows a heterogeneous enterprise to take advantage of solutions developed using this methodology. However, the varied nature of development and the distributed processing potential of SOA solutions can complicate technology modernization and disaster recovery planning.

Whatever's Next

Emerging developments in optical and quantum computing offer glimpses into new mechanisms for cryptography and data mining. The synthesis of asynchronous e-mail and threaded discussion boards with synchronous chat and instant messaging systems is extending into data-based communications for voice-over-IP and teleconferencing, where a shared whiteboard can be used to share doodles across a dozen participants in a dozen different countries. These issues and more must be considered by the chief architect, so that strategies will already be planned if the new mechanisms later reach commercial viability. Built atop existing decisions, the enterprise architect must make choices that will offer several options later.

SUMMARY

In order to succeed, an enterprise needs a coordinated architectural vision. Ultimately, this requires that someone be responsible for creating the vision, presenting the implementation, and resolving the inevitable conflicts that follow change. The architect must be knowledgeable in a wide range of technologies, IT governance, existing architectural models, project management methods, and a wide range of both "hard" and "soft" skills needed to gain support and engagement in the process of turning a vision into a functional enterprise.

The architect must always be learning, looking to the future, and communicating with all involved parties. Enterprise architecture is not a goal; it is a process for implementing long-term business requirements within an environment of constant change.

BIBLIOGRAPHY

1.   The IT Infrastructure Library (ITIL), http://www.itil.co.uk.

2.   Control Objectives for IT (CobIT), http://www.isaca.org.
3.   Gartner Research, http://www.gartner.com.
4.   North American State CIOs, http://www.nascio.org.
5.   The Open Group Architecture Framework (TOGAF), http://www.opengroup.org.
6.   The Zachman Institute, http://www.zifa.com.
7.   Federal Enterprise Architecture, http://www.whitehouse.com/omb/egov/a-1-fea.html.

EDRMS–
Enterprise

Enterprise Architecture: Security

Kirk Hausman
Assistant Commandant, Texas A&M University, College Station, Texas, U.S.A.

Abstract

Considerations for layering security measures are reviewed in this entry. An examination of common enterprise threats and identification of risk management strategies are provided.

A common way of describing physical security is that "a house is only as secure as its least secure door or window." This means that an unauthorized entrance requires only one open window to provide access to the entire structure. An extended enterprise network follows the same rule: An attacker need only bypass the least secure entry point to gain access to the entire structure—unless steps are taken to isolate segments of the network and to protect information assets.

This entry addresses threats to the enterprise and some methods of mitigating these threats. Because defensive and offensive technologies continually evolve, I will not attempt to address every possible threat in specific detail, but rather to identify strategies that you can apply to your own enterprise during architecture updates. Security should form a foundation for all other architecture changes, not be layered on top of the network at some later date, and all defenses should be regularly tested and updated to meet emerging threats.

THE PROCESS OF SECURITY

Security is not a state that can be achieved once and for all time; it is an ongoing process of addressing threats to the enterprise that may arise from external attackers, internal mischief or misuse, environmental hazards, or any other vector that provides a potential undesirable change to enterprise functionality or availability. The standard view of security addresses three aspects of service and data:

- **(C)onfidentiality**—Data and services should only be available through authorized access, with unauthorized access prevented or detected and reported if controls are bypassed.
- **(I)ntegrity**—Data and services should be protected from unauthorized modification or corruption, during use and in storage.

- **(A)vailability**—Data and services should be available for use upon authorized access attempts, with outages and service interruptions monitored and reported.

Security Is like an Onion

To meet the protective goals of this C–I–A mandate, security controls should be layered to create a series of barriers against compromise, failure, or unauthorized access. Fig. 1 illustrates this type of layering, starting with leadership and vision and drilling down to implementation settings and configuration details. Attackers and undesirable events must bypass each layer in turn in order to disrupt or modify service availability or enterprise data, providing more opportunities for denial, mitigation, and alerting.

Program Rather than Project

Although individual implementation efforts may be managed as projects (limited-term, defined end goal, and criteria), the process of security is an ongoing operation and so should be managed as a program (openended, regularly reviewed, with corrective actions applied during each iteration). Security planning and review should include management of a risk register, with impact, value, and responsible parties clearly identified and communicated appropriately. This registry is a living document and must be updated at each change in standards, tech refresh cycle, change in personnel, change in partnering or hosting practices, or identification of an emerging threat.

Explain Why

Implemented security measures should not be onerous or present barriers to normal operations, or users will take action to circumvent their protective action to "just get the job done." Automation of settings management, access provisioning, and event log review can all aid in

Encyclopedia of Information Systems and Technology, DOI: 10.1081/E-EIST-120053819

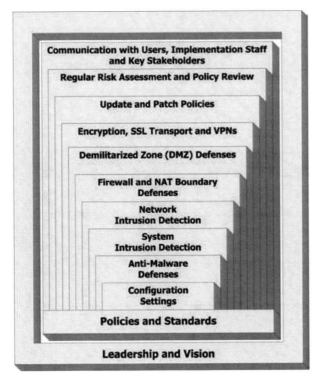

Fig. 1 A simplified structural outline of a layered defensive strategy. Note that training and communications support all other functions, while policies and standards provide a solid basis for implementation and control. Your leadership and vision will define and align protective strategies with organization requirements and mandates.

smoothing out the impact of new security measures by ensuring that standards are applied uniformly and completely. Training efforts and user awareness measures such as monthly IT newsletters are an excellent way to present the "why" of a security measure prior to its "what" and "how" implementation. Users are far more likely to avoid bypassing security measures if they understand the purpose and function of each such measure.

Standardize and Simplify

Standards and policies must apply uniformly across the enterprise, to avoid an "open window" in one area that will weaken the security stance elsewhere. As with the selection of technology and software standards, care should be taken to reduce complexity in security policies, technologies, and configuration settings across the enterprise. This aids in identification of threats, application of updates, and technical support capability.

COMMON ENTERPRISE THREATS

Uncertainty (risk) is a constant presence in the enterprise, in that directed or automated attacks may be launched from anywhere in the world or inadvertent configuration changes may compromise data availability or access controls. Power outages, storms and earthquakes, acts of terrorism or warfare, and industrial espionage are all potential threats to the enterprise that must be addressed by security and recovery practices.

Load Only in the Nursery

Malware is a generic term encompassing directly threatening software agents such as viruses and worms, as well as security-weakening agents such as Trojan horses, service proxy redirectors, and spyware such as keyboard loggers. A centrally managed malware-defense system is one of the most fundamental "must have" security technologies. The time between an unprotected system's connection to the Internet and its compromise by one of the more than 1 million identified types of malware is measured in minutes or less.

Care should be taken to ensure that new systems are loaded, fully updated, and provided an updated malware defense before exposure even to an internal organizational network. Like a newborn baby, an unprotected system is susceptible to illness passed from other systems without a strong immunity to resist electronic contagion. A shielded subnet used only for loading and updating systems can function as a nursery, to allow systems time for full configuration and malware protection before exposure to other systems.

Secure the Network

Network attacks may come in the form of denial-of-service attacks that overwhelm service availability through massed service requests, or may involve the unauthorized interception of data during transport between systems. Automated network profiling software can allow a would-be attacker to identify open service ports, unencrypted data transport endpoints, open-text protocols in use, and vulnerabilities in system defenses due to missing updates or outdated services still in use. Your security practices should include regular scanning of systems for vulnerabilities and network traffic for exposed data streams. Encryption between endpoints can aid in protecting data during transport, using solutions such as Secure Sockets Layer (SSL) website access, virtual private networking for secured access over Internet and wireless connectivity, or a public-key encryption infrastructure implementation for point-to-point encrypted data transport, as illustrated in Fig. 2.

Secure the Data

Encryption and access controls should also be applied to data during storage and backup archival processes, to

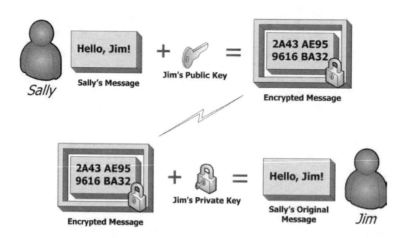

Fig. 2 An example of a public-key encrypted message transmission between Sally (the originator, with only Jim's public key) and Jim (the receiver, using only his private key). Unauthorized interception of the message, even with the public key, provides no useful data.

ensure that physical access to storage media or lost backup tapes does not expose data to unauthorized review. Mobile devices are at enhanced risk because of their small size and portability, and on-device encryption mandates are vital for devices used to conduct organizational business using data local to the device.

Backup media are also at similar risk due to size, portability, information density, and transport practices for offsite disaster recovery backup protection. Data should be encrypted on backup media to ensure that a lost tape does not lead to accidental release of sensitive or protected data assets. Data stored on file servers and in databases may also be candidates for encryption, to guard against data exposure through unauthorized access to devices and file stores.

> **Note:** Encryption of data within a relational database can have negative consequences if it is not performed properly. Because an attribute used to create a clustered index reorganizes the order of records within a table, encryption of the clustered index attribute can cause the entire table to be re-sorted every time a single value is changed, due to the re-encryption of that attribute across all records. This can create significant processor load and record-locking issues if it is not considered during application, database, and encryption planning.

Secure the Applications

Security practices must also be put into place for application development and management strategies. As with SSL requirements for Web-based access to data, reporting tools, dashboards, and other organizational services, application design must also provide internal checks and validation to protect operational continuity and function. As I have often said, applications should be made as "idiot-resistant" as possible—"idiot-proof" is an

impossible goal, because there are so many idiots who are very inventive.

Idiot resistance can be enhanced through code review and automated testing of code segments and applications, but should also include internal controls such as input validation, catching and passing failures to a secure end state, maximum allowable resource constraints, and meaningful codes for errors and unexpected termination of operations. An error page that displays information about where a failure occurred (even using cryptic numerical checkpoint values to avoid exposing details of application design) is useful when accompanied with contact information for technical support and directions for proper error reporting.

Regular review or automated monitoring of key services will allow the identification of emerging threats to the enterprise, by identifying operational characteristics outside of expected specifications. Fig. 3 provides an example of a monitoring package being used to display real-time data on a server's operations.

> **Note:** Detection of aberrant operational characteristics requires a baseline and established variance from the baseline against which to measure levels of use. This baseline must be comprehensive to cover cyclic shifts in load, such as morning start-of-day log-ons compared to midnight and weekend utilization, and updated regularly to address changes in technologies and use.

Defend the Enterprise

Because the potential attack vectors (including internal "idiots" who just hit the wrong key) are without bounds and security and defensive options are limited, it is important to prioritize threats and items listed in the risk registry. Applying Dr. Joseph Juran's extrapolated Pareto's principle, defense against roughly 80% of

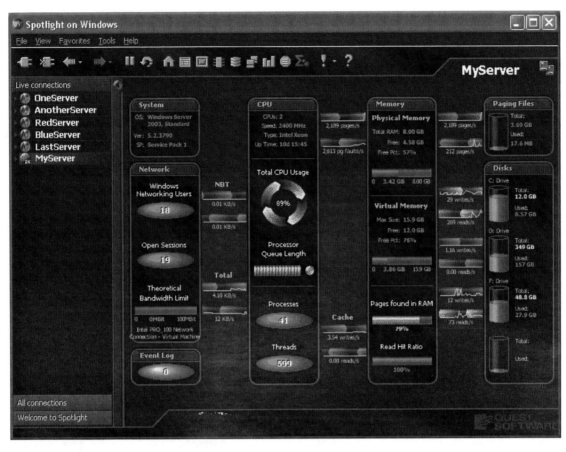

Fig. 3 An example server monitoring dashboard displaying real-time data on process load, CPU and memory use, data throughput, and storage device levels.

identified risks should fall within 20% of potential protective solutions. It is important to identify the "critical few" so as to get the greatest return on mitigation efforts, knowing that some legal and regulatory mandates are absolutes and must be addressed no matter what is required.

Malware Defense

Malware defenses and a system-load nursery are excellent starting points for securing systems against compromise. Threat signatures and antimalware applications require regular updates on a daily (sometimes hourly) basis. Centralized automated management of malware defenses is mandatory beyond a handful of supported systems, while reporting should be reviewed daily to identify compromised systems for cleansing or wipe-and-reload service. This is not an area in which to save money at the expense of quality, because the threat is continuous and includes a high probability of significantly impacting the C–I–A mandates.

Network Protection

Encryption provides a key function in protection of data transferred through and stored within the extended

enterprise. Additional services, such as intrusion detection systems, can monitor network traffic (network-based) or access and application functions within a monitored host (device-based). These systems can raise an alert when nonstandard access is identified or when specific attack signatures are detected.

Network firewalls can provide defensive "walls" around protected subnets, separating network traffic and restricting access between sub-nets based on access rules and service port constraints. Fig. 4 illustrates a firewall configured to segment a private network into protected internal services and systems and a public-facing, partially protected demilitarized zone (DMZ) subnet, separated from the external Internet by service port restrictions.

Firewall configuration management and log review should be regular and comprehensive, to ensure that changes to network resources, services, and use are properly managed to protect network resources from unauthorized access.

DEFENSE AGAINST THE UNEXPECTED

Quality and risk management disciplines attempt to address the "known known" and "known unknown"

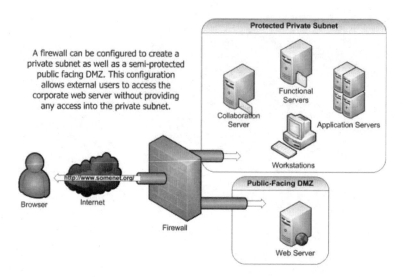

A firewall can be configured to create a private subnet as well as a semi-protected public facing DMZ. This configuration allows external users to access the corporate web server without providing any access into the private subnet.

Fig. 4 A simplified network diagram illustrating a firewall configured for constrained access between a protected private organization network, a partially protected DMZ subnet, and the public Internet.

threats to an enterprise by identifying risks, prioritizing defenses to gain the greatest protection possible using available resources, and then managing identified risks in the four standard ways:

- **Eliminating/avoiding**—Avoiding a risk by ceasing to perform a particular activity or to use a particular technology. This is not always possible or desirable.
- **Mitigating**—Reducing the likelihood of a threat's occurrence or its potential impact by changing processes or adding defenses. This is generally the most likely mechanism for addressing identified risks.
- **Transferring**—Transferring risks may consist of outsourcing a service such as backup operations or purchasing insurance to transfer financial repercussions to an external party. This practice generally has a high cost and may not protect nontangible assets such as client loyalty or a regulatory mandate with legal but nonmonetary consequences.
- **Accepting**—Some risks must simply be accepted, either due to inability to prevent or mitigate the threat or due to cost factors that make mitigation impossible. Acceptance of risk requires careful documentation of the "why" used to make this decision, and should be communicated to senior management for written approval.

Note: Keep in mind that it is possible to outsource many security functions and operations, but it is not possible to outsource responsibility.

Emergency Response Planning

In any organization, the best possible listing of all identified risks will likely miss a few. Generally, a risk registry might identify and address up to 90% of the potential (known) threats to the enterprise. The other 10% must be identified as rapidly as possible upon occurrence, through log and service review, and addressed through mitigation practices based on a well-designed action plan that is regularly tested, reviewed, updated, and communicated to all parties. The time for disaster planning is not after the emergency comes up ("Okay, the data center just disappeared into a sinkhole…who wants to discuss offsite backup media strategies first…"). It is important to build an effective response team with clear communication channels and designated responsibility well ahead of an actual emergency in order to have any chance to respond, recover, or maintain continuity of operations, rather than a simple after-action reconstruction.

Don't Forget the Little Things

The growing use of mobile, often personally owned, devices for access to organization resources requires the creation and communication of clear security policies for all devices used for business purposes. In addition to on-device encryption mandates, additional policies might include mandates for malware defenses for remote desktops or device update and on-idle automatic locking requirements. Because these devices continue to expand in variety and number, policies addressing mobile security requirements should be reviewed at least quarterly or upon the release of a new popular platform.

SUMMARY

This entry has included a review of security threats to the enterprise and examples of solutions and policies meant to mitigate the risk they present to organizational functions. Numerous regulatory and legal mandates may provide a number of "must address" constraint items in the risk registry, and should be considered first in any security prioritization efforts. Operations that depend on other functions within the organization may also play a part in determining risk priority, requiring regular review to identify changes in the organization, its functions, and technologies in use.

Enterprise Architecture: Virtualization

Kirk Hausman
Assistant Commandant, Texas A&M University, College Station, Texas, U.S.A.

Abstract

This entry examines many different types of virtualization. Identification of scenarios that may benefit from cloud computing are provided. Best practices in virtualization are reviewed.

The Greek philosopher Plato formulated the *theory of forms*, which is based on the concept that the world of experience and sensation is merely a reflection or representation of a more fundamental abstract form of reality. The modern enterprise network embodies a form of Plato's theory, creating electronic copies of physical documents that can be duplicated and re-created at will or constructing entire virtual worlds with their own physics models and constraints. Even technology is becoming more a reflection of purpose and function, compared to physical systems dedicated to a single task or purpose.

This entry will examine the virtualization of services and technologies within the extended network enterprise. While I will not attempt to rival Plato's work with a "theory of virtualization," it is worth noting the continued shift from physical representations of technology toward more fundamental abstracted forms that consume less power and provide greater flexibility than their physically bound predecessors.

VIRTUALIZED SERVICES

Virtualization of services and functions is not a wholly new concept. Answering machines, for example, provided a virtual replacement for human answering services, and have since been replaced in turn by voice mail systems. Modern enterprise collaboration systems such as the Microsoft Exchange platform with its Live Communication Server option can even take a voice message, perform automated voice recognition, and transmit the resulting text and audio to an individual's mailbox for easy review on the recipient's device of choice.

Other services, such as virtual faxes, print spoolers, and virtualized data storage reduce the technology equipment footprint within the enterprise while extending access to consumers throughout the enterprise. A single automated fax service can serve the entire enterprise, providing electronic facsimiles of documents without requiring consumables such as paper and ink cartridges and without delays involved with distribution of physical document copies.

Automated monitoring and update services allow management of maintenance and security functions without requiring direct access to individual physical systems. Such virtualized services provide a mechanism for direct support of thousands of distributed systems by a handful of support technicians, gaining efficiencies in personnel costs and user downtime. Additional support functions rely on virtualization for management over very large numbers of systems that may be distributed across many sites in a global network.

VIRTUALIZED APPLICATIONS

Virtualization of applications involves the creation of an application package that is made available to users automatically or on demand. Applications can be automatically deployed to a user's system based on role membership, ensuring that the user's desktop experience remains the same regardless of which system is used to access the enterprise network. Coupled with virtualization of user file storage using a distributed file share and/or user folder redirection, users need never worry about data and application availability. These services also allow rapid deployment of replacement or upgraded equipment, because the user experience is automatically applied to any system when the user first logs onto a new system.

Virtualized applications allow multiple versions of an application to be available simultaneously on the same system, ensuring continuity of operation for legacy applications depending on second-party add-ons or applications. For example, an older form of a Java virtual machine (JVM) might be required for Application X to operate. Users could then automatically use the older browser and the JVM when accessing Application

Encyclopedia of Information Systems and Technology, DOI: 10.1081/E-EIST-120053818

EDRMS–
Enterprise

X, but use newer versions of each during normal operations. Updates become easier in a virtualized application environment, by allowing an updated package to be uploaded onto the application virtualization server, which is then automatically downloaded to a user's system upon next use of the appropriate program or file type.

An additional efficiency provided by virtualized application environments is the potential to reduce software licensing costs by providing a reduced pool of concurrent licenses, which are claimed upon application access and freed up for reuse when the application is closed. Rather than installing an expensive application on each computer system across the network, or limiting application availability to a select group of workstations, users can be added to application virtualization groups to gain automatic package availability using a smaller pool of concurrent licenses.

VIRTUALIZED DESKTOPS

The next level of virtualization involves the user experience to include the entire desktop, encompassing the operating system and all other functions into a virtualized setting mirroring the experience of sitting at a dedicated workstation desktop environment. This is somewhat similar to older mainframe operations, when terminals provided keyboard input and returned displayed output from processes that ran entirely within the mainframe's central processing unit (CPU), memory, and storage resources.

Remote Desktop Clients

Client systems accessing virtualized desktop environments may use "dumb" terminals similar to older mainframe configurations or "thin" clients with only sufficient resources for input, output, and network communications. "Thick" clients may have local storage and applications to shift processing power from the server, while mobile computers with their own applications and configuration details may be used to access organizational services and data while limiting exposure.

Updates to a virtualized desktop environment occur at the host system, allowing rapid update to applications and system settings from a centralized data center. Remote desktop connections can be made to in-place dedicated systems for availability in mobile or remote settings, or may connect to one of many virtualized desktop sessions maintained on a powerful virtualization host residing in the data center. Virtual desktop infrastructure implementations include additional services to facilitate user reconnection to virtual desktop sessions left in operation.

A virtualized desktop environment can allow continued use of legacy desktop hardware that is no longer able to run most applications, by allowing the older hardware to function as a thin or thick client for a remote virtual desktop running on hardware with sufficient resources to support more recent applications and services. Extending the life cycle of individual systems this way reduces procurement costs and the environmental impact of computer manufacturing and disposal processes.

Virtual Appliances

Virtual appliances consist of preconfigured virtual systems with their own operating system, applications, and settings. These systems can provide an excellent mechanism for distributing entire software environments without requiring installation of packages on a host system, beyond the virtualization service itself (called a hypervisor). Demonstrations of new applications within a preconfigured virtual appliance require only a copy of the virtual hard drive files and minor network configuration to be up and running on a client's test bed.

Virtual appliances and PC-hosted virtual machines can also allow a single workstation to provide access to multiple computing platforms simultaneously. The popular Apple Macintosh system includes the Parallels virtualization environment, allowing native Windows functionality within a virtual PC hypervisor. Newer forms of Microsoft's Windows platform include the Windows on Windows virtual hypervisor for backwards compatibility in legacy applications. Use of a PC hypervisor such as the popular VMWare service can allow a single workstation to support as many different virtualized desktop configurations as system resources allow, together with options for capturing point-in-time snapshots for automatic rollback during testing and development. This can greatly reduce design time by eliminating the need to completely reload a test system each time a setting or application function is altered and by providing developers with multiple versions of operating systems, browsers, and application software suites with which to test the new application under development, without the need for individual physical hardware systems for each.

VIRTUALIZED SERVERS

Virtualization of multiple physical servers onto more powerful centralized hosts within the data center can provide significant cost savings in terms of hardware, energy, and cooling requirements. Since many servers can operate at a reduced level during off-peak hours, consolidation onto a smaller number of hosting

EDRMS– Enterprise

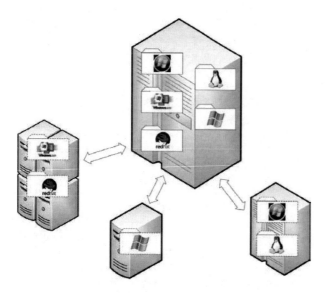

Fig. 1 An example of the portability of virtual machines across multiple hosting hardware options. Host operating systems may also vary, provided the hypervisors are compatible across all hosts.

machines can reduce the power consumed by idling systems. Each virtualized server is merely a collection of files, rather than a dedicated hardware platform with storage, CPU, and memory of its own, allowing more efficient utilization of available resources as well as portability across hardware hosts, as shown in Fig. 1.

Automatic load balancing across hosting farms can ensure that spikes in demand are met with adequate resource allocation to individual virtualized servers. Resource management requires strict policies and attention to operational thresholds in order to protect against "virtual sprawl" in the data center and alignment of dedicated resources within each host to the needs of its virtual machines. Because virtualization allows

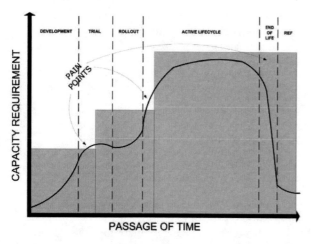

Fig. 2 A traditional application life cycle, comparing system resource availability against application resource requirements. Note that insufficiencies must be met by hardware upgrades or migration to more robust equipment.

separation of hardware and software refresh cycles, policies must also be put in place to handle software update and retirement of virtual as well as physical systems in order to properly secure the network and to limit complexity in support requirements.

VIRTUALIZED NETWORKS

Virtualization of networks beyond simple desktops and servers can afford an enterprise opportunities for modeling, testing, and defense. Construction of a test network matching the full suite of applications and services within a large enterprise can be a very costly matter, while a complete virtualized network with identical configurations and settings might be managed using only a single powerful host. Each virtual system in the test network might have reduced processing power compared to its production equivalent, but can be easily rolled back to a previous snapshot in the event of corruption or failure during test. Virtualized networks can also be used for penetration testing without concern for disruption of the production network, while "decoy" networks with automatically generated traffic and network utilization can allow would-be network attackers an environment in which their efforts are encapsulated and recorded for later review of attacking methods. These decoy networks, called *honeynets*, appear to be valid, active network environments but are actually virtual sandboxes, separate from the production network environment with only simulated use and data files present for access by an attacker.

CLOUD COMPUTING

When the network, servers, and infrastructure are virtualized and resources are made available automatically from a pool of systems, the result is termed *cloud computing*. Cloud computing is a natural extension of distributed grid processing when combined with the virtualization of services and operating systems. A cloud computing client might be allocated up to eight processors, 20 GB of RAM, 300 GB of storage, and up to four websites supported by four databases. Without needing to know the details of the location and type of these resources, an authorized user might request a new Web reporting application supported by 40 GB of storage, 4 GB of RAM, and two CPUs. Because these resource limits fall within the user's allocated constraints, the resources can be automatically provisioned without interaction with tech support.

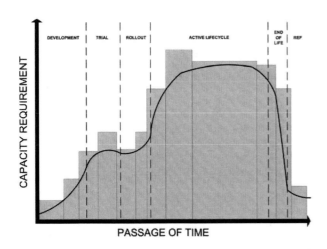

Fig. 3 A virtualized or cloud computing application life cycle, comparing system resource availability against application resource requirements. Note that incremental changes, both positive and negative, are possible through automated allocation, without requiring migration or hardware upgrade.

Comparing Cloud and Traditional Application Life Cycles

Fig. 2 illustrates a traditionally developed application, passing through the design phase, increased capacity requirements during testing, reduced requirements during rollout, and the highest resource need during its active life cycle. Pain points occur when escalating resource need exceeds available resources, requiring hardware upgrades or application migration to provide needed application host resources (represented by the dark gray boxes). Following end of life, applications retained for reference purposes continue to consume the same resources unless migrated again to other equipment.

Fig. 3 illustrates application development in a virtualized or cloud computing environment. Cloud computing resources can flex as needed, allowing the easy scaling of prototype solutions through testing and up to production levels with nothing more than an automated request for additional resource allocation. If expected capacity far exceeds actual capacity requirements, resources can be scaled back and allocated to other purposes through the same mechanism.

Types of Clouds

Because the term *cloud computing* refers to the configuration of resource availability more than a specific configuration of hardware and software, there are several common types of cloud computing that may be employed by an organization.

- **Public clouds**—These clouds are hosted on publicly accessible systems, available for Internet access from

anywhere in the world. Examples of this type of cloud include Google's Gmail and Microsoft Live Hotmail services. Most public clouds share host servers across multiple client cloud resource pools.
- **Dedicated clouds**—Like public clouds, dedicated clouds are hosted on systems available via Internet connectivity. Dedicated clouds isolate instances by restricting resource use by a particular client to a specific subset of hosting systems. Because the resources are dedicated to a particular client, these services are generally more costly than public cloud implementations.
- **Private clouds**—A private cloud is one that is typically maintained within an organization's own network, or isolated in some manner from external access. Cloud hosting services may place dedicated hardware within the organization's data center, or an organization might construct a private cloud using its own hardware.
- **Hybrid clouds**—Hybrid clouds may provide a mixture of dedicated, public, and private cloud resources. Management of disaster recovery (DR) functions, service-level agreements for resource and network availability, and other characteristics must be carefully negotiated in order to obtain the greatest value from a hybrid cloud configuration.

CLOUD FLEXIBILITY

The flexibility of resource assignment within a cloud computing environment can be very attractive to operations that require a variable amount of resources. Examples of scenarios where this availability provides greatest benefit include:

- **The bump**—This scenario, illustrated in Fig. 4, includes a sudden unexpected spike in activity. Examples include sudden surges in activity during emergencies or following the mention of a site on a popular news aggregator, causing a flood of interest outside normal access levels.
- **Cyclic surges**—This includes resources that are only necessary on a cyclical basis but are unused during other times, as shown in Fig. 5. Examples include mandatory training just before evaluation periods and end-of-month or end-of-year reporting cycles.
- **Rapid growth**—This scenario includes any application access that expands rapidly beyond expected resource requirements, as illustrated in Fig. 6. Prototypes placed into limited use may see rapid adoption enterprise-wide, or Internet information sites may experience sudden expansion of interest following initial exposure.

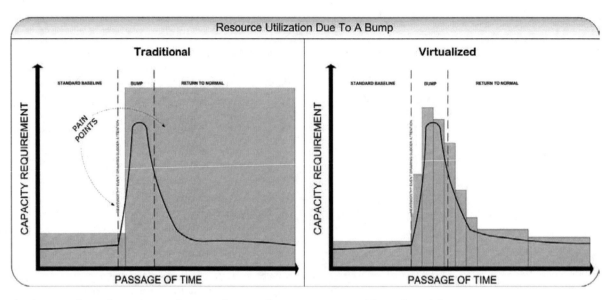

Fig. 4 A comparison of capacity requirements due to a short-term unexpected bump in activity.

BEST PRACTICES

Due to the relative newness of cloud computing, best practices continue to emerge and evolve. A few of the more common practices include:

- **Setting standards**—Cloud resource hosting services, such as the Amazon EC2 or Microsoft Azure standards, do not work well between technologies. Selection of a cloud computing standard will ensure that developed applications and services interoperate well with other cloud resources and with in-place technologies in the enterprise.
- **Controlling costs**—Because cloud service vendors scale costs based on resource allocation and

segmentation, enterprise cloud service hosting should be negotiated using the most economical model for existing and near-term requirements. Cost models include levels of dedicated resource and bandwidth availability, longer-term contracts providing a set level of resources for a fixed cost, or resource pools that may be used across a variable period of time and renewed when consumed. More complex hosting costs include per-transaction micro fees, upload/download transaction costs, incremental storage costs, and specialized costs for restrictions of data and DR backups to specific geopolitical boundaries.

- **Privacy requirements**—Contracting cloud services should include statements of where data will be stored, where DR copies may be made, and

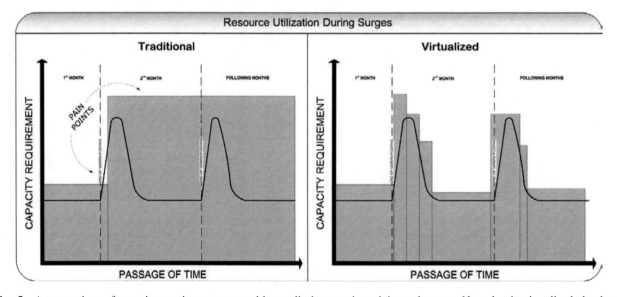

Fig. 5 A comparison of capacity requirements created by cyclical surges in activity and access. Note that in virtualized cloud scenarios, capacity can be preprovisioned to meet expected need during successive cycles.

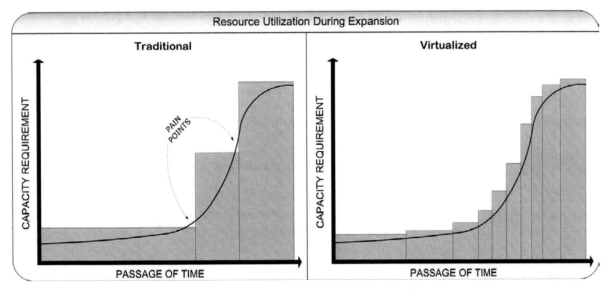

Fig. 6 A comparison of capacity requirements created by an unexpectedly rapid growth in utilization. In virtualized and cloud computing scenarios, automatic increases in capacity could be established at a particular utilization level to account for varying rates of increase.

conditions for reporting when data is exposed or transferred to new hosting facilities. Because larger hosting firms may make use of environmental cooling by moving data center operations north during summer months, requirements for legal data discovery and open records requests may fall under different legal systems. Contracts should include details regarding reporting discovery actions and other forms of external data access.

- **Compatibility**—To best use available application development skills and tools, cloud computing platform standards should be selected to integrate well with existing enterprise technologies. Mid-migration between local and cloud-hosted e-mail services, for example, is much less problematic if both services are compatible and can interoperate transparently. Because cloud services trade off flexibility and customizability for protection against potential conflict with shared resource clients, some applications may prove to be unable to migrate into the cloud and so a

standard for interoperability between cloud and local applications is mandatory.

SUMMARY

This entry has addressed the virtualization of services, applications, workstations, servers, networks, and migration of entire infrastructures into the cloud. Virtualization practices provide significant cost savings by reducing hardware, energy, and cooling costs. Virtualization provides reductions in support requirements, as well as ease of recovery following system loss or upgrade.

The steady migration of resources into the cloud reduces tech support requirements for new initiatives, and eases resource extension to meet growing or widely varying requirements. Care must be taken to ensure that virtualized resources are managed, updated, and retired just like their physical system counterparts.

**EDRMS–
Enterprise**

Ethics

Tandy Gold
Independent Executive Consultant, Sanford, Florida, U.S.A.

Abstract

Within information technology (IT) divisions and organizations, the need to execute in a competitive and complex technical environment while demonstrating personal integrity can be a significant personal and organizational challenge. Supplying concrete guidelines for those at ethical crossroads, the following excerpt from the book by Tandy Gold, *Ethics in IT Outsourcing*, explores the complex challenges of aligning IT outsourcing programs with ethical conduct and standards. Based upon the author's decades of experience in working with large firms in IT and outsourcing, this research is suitable for both veteran IT practitioners and stakeholders new to the topic. The excerpt below addresses the following ethical challenges related to IT outsourcing includes the following: (1) provides guidance on the ethical structure and execution of IT outsourcing; (2) identifies tools to concretely analyze and support the establishment of ethical program principles; (3) covers generally accepted ethical conduct and standards; and (4) describes how to align existing and new outsourcing programs to ethical standards. Based upon significant research on the economic impact of IT outsourcing at a microeconomic, macroeconomic, and corporate level, these concepts provide a comprehensive set of ethical program components that are both pragmatic and powerful.

When the minted gold in the vault smiles like the night-watchman's daughter,
When warrantee deeds loaf in chairs opposite and are my friendly companions,
I intend to reach them my hand, and make as much of them as I do of men and women like you.
—Walt Whitman, A Song for Occupation

ETHICS IN IT OUTSOURCING

An Exploration of Ethics in IT Outsourcing

This entry explores the topic of ethics in IT outsourcing within the context of the rapidly maturing body of research on business ethics. To remain grounded in reality, this inquiry includes discussion related to the ethics of movement of IT jobs overseas. While immediate monetary savings from labor arbitrage is not the only driver behind IT outsourcing, it is certainly one of the primary ones.[1] It is important to move beyond the typical IT Associations' ethical statements that focus upon the importance of simply not breaking the law or being compliant with general standards of professional conduct and courtesy.

But to take on this broader, more meaningful discussion of ethics, we must first understand the background. Therefore, we will explore two areas of inquiry.

The first is to look at the existing established framework of business ethics, as represented by the exciting, new, and rapidly growing body of academic research. The second area of discussion is to review and identify some deeply held, but nonetheless deeply untrue, macroeconomic myths fostered by the media and others. Once this groundwork has been covered, we will be able to look at ethics in IT outsourcing with the depth it deserves.

To start, let us look at the typical view of ethics within a large IT department. If you were to stop a Fortune 100 IT employee and ask about ethics, how would the person respond?

- First, ethics generally comes under the heading of compliance. Corporate ethics frequently focuses upon addressing illegalities relative to discrimination based on sex, ethnicity, sexual orientation, religion, or other personal factors. These include accounting rules of compliance, hiring rules of compliance, tax bylaws, etc.
- Second, there are corporate value statements—integrity, honesty, etc. These are of limited value if they are not modeled seriously by the firm executive leadership.
- Third, there are the more voluntary ethical alignments, such as Green IT, where negative environmental impact or *footprint* is minimized.

Encyclopedia of Information Systems and Technology, DOI: 10.1081/E-EIST-120048770

Level	Financial Equity	Transparency and Communication	Compliance	Business Model Fairness and Integrity
Micro: Individual Relationship	Are ethical as well as strict legal compliance practices followed in financial equity compensation of my team members (e.g. monetary recognition and rewards)?	Do the communications to my team reflect transparency and honesty wherever possible?	Is my team in compliance?	Can my team members feel good about their role in the company's business model (as an individual representing a fair model)?
Molar: Corporate	Is the company doing business at fair market value (selling and buying)?	Is the corporation communicating as honestly and transparently as possible in its role of corporate citizen and member of the community?	Is the firm in compliance?	Is the corporations model of business reflect basic ethical principles as interpreted by persons of integrity?
Macro: Business World	Are the normative industry business practices ethical?	Does the business environment in the industry encourage open and honest communications?	Are the national compliance laws and regulations appropriate, updated to reflect the latest technology, clear and well-enforced?	Does the national industry advocate and make clear basic ethical precepts (e.g. "first do no harm")?

Fig. 1   Three levels of business ethics.
Source: From Gold.[1]

- Finally, there is the active support of worthy causes such as charitable contributions, volunteering, and other measures of positive corporate citizenship.[1]

There is clearly a problem with this narrow ethical view. Enron, one of the corporate poster children for ethical breaches, was cited in *Fortune* magazine as a model of ethical conduct prior to its financial meltdown (see http://en.wikipedia.org/wiki/Enron).[1]

More importantly, this narrow view clearly contributes to the curious separation and marginalization of ethical conduct within the larger business context. It is not unusual for a company to double its prices only for the most economically vulnerable, voiceless customers to hold itself as a paragon of ethics. This is because at the same time it was compliant with all regulations, issued a new corporate value statement, implemented Green IT, and gave millions of dollars to a favorite charity.

With the advent of the Internet, and the new transparency it engenders, however, more and more accountability is pressuring firms to embody not only the surface but also the deeper meanings of ethics.[1]

The Business of Ethics: A New and Growing Body of Research on Three Levels of Ethical Inquiry

The growing number of publicly acknowledged ethical breaches, perhaps embodied most strongly by the bailout of the nation's banks for clear violations in good business practices, is ironically the fuel behind the increasing number of well-funded academic chairs and curriculum dedicated to business ethics. A good summary of business ethical research to date can be found at http://plato.stanford.edu/entries/ethics-business.[2]

To date, business ethics centers on three levels (see Fig. 1):[2]

1. Microethics—personal
2. Molar ethics—corporate
3. Macroethics—society as a whole

We will use the above framework to explore ethics in IT outsourcing.

MacroEthics: Debunking MacroEconomic Myths

Let us start with the reality of macroeconomic America. The United States that exists in the popular imagination

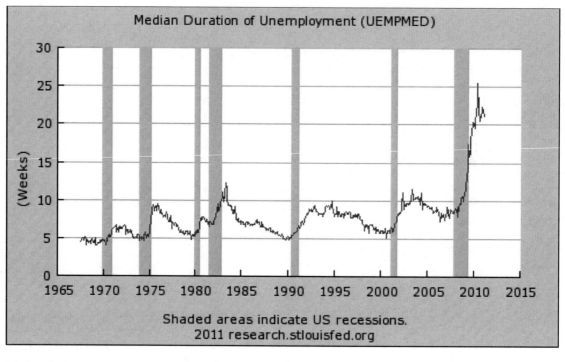

Fig. 2 Median duration of unemployment (UEMPMED).
Source: From Federal Reserve Bank of St. Louis 2011, http://research.stlouisfed.org/fred2/series/UEMPMED.[3]

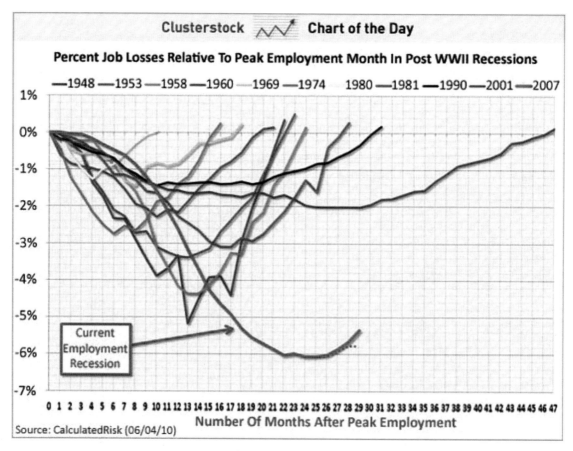

Fig. 3 Percentage of job losses relative to peak employment month in post-World War II recessions.
Source: From http://www.calculatedriskblog.com/.[4]

of the 1950s, in which anyone can grow up to be like Bill Gates, does not align with reality.

Today's economic environment is one in which more individuals are out of work, and stay unemployed for a long time (Figs. 2 and 3).

The dramatic extent to which these trends are magnified as compared to earlier recessions is not well understood or reported, but is clearly illustrated in the trend charts here. While the overall worldwide and U. S. economic stasis is alltoosadly extremely well known, there are many macroeconomic myths that must be debunked before we can have a meaningful discussion on any level of ethics. These popular myths about the UnitedStates are so dramatically opposite to our economic reality that some studies show that even professional economists donot grasp the reality.

What are the facts that are so very different from our societal truth? Listed below are the myths and the reality.

- **Myth**: The United States holds a solid economic leadership role worldwide.
- **Reality**: When standard economic indexes such as the GDP are normalized for income inequality, the United States is down to the normalized rank of 52 or 53, near Romania and Cuba. In other words, the average U.S. citizen experiences the advantages of personal wealth—in terms of income, access to health care, and access to education—as a Third World country, and not as a First World. Sadly, latest polls show that the majority of Americans perceive the United States will rapidly lose ground in worldwide economic leadership in the next few decades. Find out more at http://hdr.undp.org/en/media/HDR_2011_EN_Table3.pdf.[5]
- **Myth**: Outsourcing, including IT outsourcing, has a negative impact on the economy as a whole.
- **Reality**: Most research shows that outsourcing as a whole is actually either neutral or positive for the economy as a whole—as difficult as it can be for individuals or communities. This is true for long-term studies, such as those looking at manufacturing outsourcing since the 1950s (e.g., the excellent study by Maxim Belinkiy at UC Davis, "The Determinants of Outsourcing from the U. S.: Evidence from Domestic Manufacturing Industries, 1972–2002").[6]
- This is not too difficult to understand—it is the same principle that you may use if you *outsource* your lawn maintenance to the teenager next door. If you take that *non-core* activity and invest the time you usually spend mowing your lawn into your online business, you could generate jobs from that investment over time.
- What this macroeconomic reality does not address, of course, is the reality of individuals who are caught in the tsunami of IT outsourcing—this is discussed

further in Molar ethics. Find out more at http://mpra.ub.uni-muenchen.de/17911/1/MPRA_paper_17911.pdf.[6]
- **Myth**: Outsourcing, including IT outsourcing, is the main driver behind our existing economic downturn.
- **Reality**: The reality is that it is the extreme inequality in the United States that is causing our economic distress. It is so pronounced that even Bloomberg, the economic index, cites it as a key factor behind the lack of economic growth in the United States (http://www.bloomberg.com/news/2012-06-13/inequality-it-s-even-worse-than-we-thought.html).
- How severe is the income inequality in the United States? It is extraordinary and getting much worse over time.

Income Inequality in the United States: A Global Extreme in the Extreme, and Hurting All Americans

U. S. citizens need to know that, compared with other First World countries, our income inequality is much more pronounced, and represents a trend so longterm and far-reaching that even billionaires such as Warren Buffet have gone on record to communicate their concern.

Between 1979 and 2007 in pretax income growth:

- The top 1% increased income by 38.7% between 1979 and 2007
- The next top 4% increased income by 15.8%

Whereas, during the same time period,

- The very bottom 20% increased income only by 0.4%
- The next-to-bottom 20% increased income only by 3%

These trends coincide with a dramatic reduction in U.S. taxes on the wealthiest top 1%, from 37% in 1979, to 29.5% in 2007—a tax reduction that is more pronounced than within any other income group.[7]

Learn more at the Economic Policy Institute link http://www.epi.org/publication/taxes_on_the_wealthy_have_gone_down_dramatically/.[7]

All U.S. statistics related to income distribution as compared to other First World countries are dramatically skewed—almost beyond belief. For example, one measure that compares CEO-to-worker income provides a glimpse into the wildly skewed income distribution in America. **CEO-to-worker ratios of income in other First World countries range from 11-to-1 (Japan) to almost 50-to-1 (Venezuela). In the UnitedStates the ratio is 475-to-1! Yes—this is NOT a typo!** (http://creativeconflictwisdom.wordpress.com/2011/10/07/ration-of-

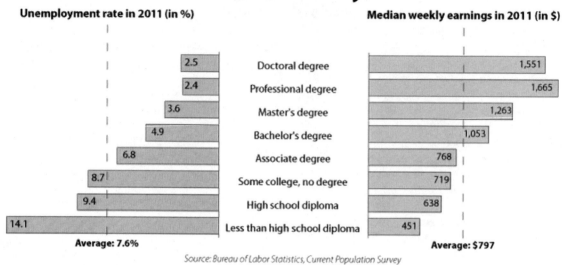

Fig. 4 Unemployment rate and median weekly earnings by education level.
Source: Bureau of Labor Statistics, Current Population Survey.

ceo-pay-to-average-worker-by-country/).[8] The topic of income inequality is too broad to examine fully here, the additional references are listed at the end of this entry.

What is clear, however, is that wealth distribution is like a game of cards in which the odds are highly stacked—to favor that lucky, elusive top 1% to 5% of Americans owning 80% or more of the total wealth (depending upon how it is defined).

Why does this hurt all Americans, even those who manage to be nearer the top of the pyramid?

The key is that wealth and income distribution is a strong predictor, at least in the United States, in determining access to higher education. As the average citizen in the UnitedStates gets poorer and poorer (as fewer and fewer amass untold amounts of wealth), the ability of our smart and deserving U. S. citizens in accessing higher education is diminished. In many ways, the focus on outsourcing, including IT outsourcing, with all of the dramatic newspaper coverage, has served to cover the much more all-encompassing, negative impact of the lack of educational access due to income inequality. In the longterm, it is this lack that will ultimately ensure the United States is a grade C player across the economics of the world stage.

Education is the great inoculator to poverty. The ongoing dramatic U. S.

recession is a poor-man's recession—income is directly related to not only higher educational attainment, but also unemployment. (Fig. 4, the U.S. Department of Labor, above).[9]

For the United States, where the per capita income is very low as compared to other First World countries, a double whammy exists—the costs of a college education

are much higher. This means one simple fact. **Fewer and fewer American citizens are able to afford higher education**.

In competitive labor market of First World countries, most of the so-called private institutions of higher learning are publically funded, and access is granted to students via national examiantions to ensure that native talent is not wasted.

Not so in the United States. **In America, it is not the smart that get to go to college, but it is the wealthy** (Fig. 5). [10]

From a macroeconomic perspective, the forecast of the UnitedStates looks bleak. As our population becomes poorer and poorer (as per the aforementioned economic trend of the rich getting richer) the resulting lack of educated workers will force large corporations to turn to other First World countries.

There is strong evidence that this is already happening, as *skills mismatch* is becoming evident in our prevailing recession. This mismatch is shown by the fact that even though the total number of U.S. open jobs is increasing (i.e., more job openings), the unemployment rate remains puzzlingly high. Although there is a debate about what this new macroeconomic development really means, a growing force of credible economists ascribe this to the fact that the U.S. job-hunting population does not have the skills to fill those jobs. If yesterday's line manufacturing job is today's computer-skilled, *knowledge worker* job, then that knowledge worker needs to have access to a college degree. The poorer we become as a nation, the fewer knowledge workers we produce.

This is another unique facet of our prevailing recession, and it validates the impassioned statement made to the United States by the prestigious organization,

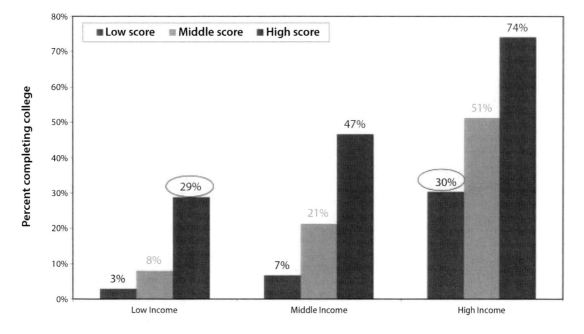

Low-scoring students from high-income families more likely to complete college than high-scoring, low-income students
College completion by income status and test scores

Note: Low income is defined as bottom 25%, middle income is middle 50%, and high income is top 25%
Source: *Fox, Connolly, & Snyder (2005).*

Fig. 5 Low-scoring, high-income students versus high-scoring, low-income students.
Source: Economic Policy Institute, http://www.epi.org/blog/college-graduation-scores-income-levels/.[10]

Organization for Economic Co-Operation and Development (OECD). The OECD believes that the future of the global labor force is to be found in the so-called knowledge worker—those individuals who, with access to higher education, are able to bring greater skills to bear to the workforce. They are in a position to know. The OECD administers a global comparative test, called Programme for International Student Assessment (PISA). PISA comparatively tests random 15-year-old highschool students in language, math, and science across the globe. The PISA test is normalized for language and culture so that worldwide educational scores can be compared.

The PISA test results show the United States as performing about average or less than average in our educational results across all nations worldwide. Rather a poor showing for an ostensible world economic leader. (Learn more at http://voices.washingtonpost.com/answer-sheet/guest-bloggers/what-international-test-scores.html).

What is scary is that there is a direct research relationship —with a gap of 15 years —between PISA test scores and gross national product. So, unless the United States improves the quality of our education as compared to the rest of the world, even our collective corporate wealth will suffer over time, as

large businesses will be forced to turn to other countries to fill the highly skilled (and educated) positions they require to be successful.

Noting this trend, OECD's PISA administrators advise...

> "Governments need to create education systems that are accessible to everyone, not just a favored few; that are globally competitive on quality; that provide people from all classes a fair chance to get the right kind of education to succeed; and to achieve all this at a price that the nation can afford. The aim is no longer just to provide a basic education for all, but to provide an education that will make it possible for everyone to become knowledge workers."[11]

The lesson seems clear—the lower the per capita income of the average U.S. worker, the lesser the higher education available to the average U.S. worker, and the poorer we all are.

For more information on the macro income inequality in the United States, refer to the facts below from Tandy Gold.[1]

- Median CEO's income has increased 430% in the last 10 years compared to the average wage income increase of 26%, and average corporate profit increase of 250%. The ratio of CEO pay to worker pay is at least 10 times (roughly) other nations.

- The gap between the wealthy few and the many poor in the United States is reaching record differences, increasing almost 20% between 1980 and 1992.
- The top 0.1% of Americans, or roughly 152,000 people, showed an increase in income of 385% between 1970 and 2009. The top 0.5% or 610,000 people showed overall increase in income of 141%, the top 1% had an increase of 90%, and the top 5% had an increase of 59%.
- The bottom 90% of Americans experienced a change of minus 1% income during the same time period.

Molar Ethics: Ethics of the Corporation

Now that we have thoroughly grounded the macroeconomic discussion in facts, not mythology, let us turn our attention to the next level of ethical inquiry. This is molar ethics, or ethics of the corporation.

We are in a time of rapidly shifting perception with a focus on business ethics, in which every day seems to bring news of a particularly smarmy, formerly hidden business-related ethical breach. This new awareness is primarily due to the influence of the Internet. Hearing about racial profiling is not quite the same as seeing a viral video of an unarmed black man being beaten by a group of policemen with a baseball bat (http://www.youtube.com/watch?v = SW1ZDIXiuS4).[12] The ubiquitous array of cameras and spyware mean a higher level of accountability for everyone—even large corporations.

Molar or corporate ethics in IT outsourcing means addressing the pink elephant in the room. That pink elephant is the constant debate about IT outsourcing and the ethical dilemma of moving jobs overseas. Let us explore this further in this section.

Unlike the inflamed fear and headlines created to sell newspapers, the results of long-term research points to either a neutral or positive impact on the economy as a whole from outsourcing, including IT outsourcing.[6]

How can moving jobs overseas help the economy as a whole? Let us take the example of a large tire company. They decide to outsource their many IT groups across the United States to a group in India. The economies of scale enjoyed by the large Indian outsourcer means the same or better quality of IT services at much, much lower prices.

It also frees up a lot of time and energy. After all, they are in the tire business, not the IT business. The money that the tire company used to invest in IT is now invested in research, creating a better, stronger, low-cost tire that will help them win market share. The success of the new tire, developed in large part due to the savings related to IT outsourcing, means that the company

can now profitably expand, adding an entirely new sales and manufacturing capability—and the jobs that go with them.

By the way, one of the core myths about IT outsourcing at the molar level that needs to be debunked is that every job is subject to outsourcing, within IT or outside of IT. This is utterly ridiculous and is another result of desperate media trying to sell newspapers, or blogs, or tweets.

The reality is that IT outsourcing is a volume play;[1]-see also http://www.ethicsinit.com. Significant business process engineering is required to make it work. It's just not worth it to either the customer or the outsourcing service provider to work with smaller businesses unless highly aggregated (again, into large numbers).

Let' us take an example. A large insurance company is implementing IT outsourcing. They must first establish secure communications with the outsourcer—some sort of satellite, across-the-ocean trunk line, or a combination of both. This is obviously costly to run and monitor unless mitigated by volume, making this an unworkable business model without large numbers (minimum 100 slots).

There is also a great deal of decision making as to what customer information is too sensitive to go overseas, and what is not, how to divide that up, and how to protect it from being mixed with the non-secure data. Security policies, technical network infrastructure, and network security must be redesigned and implemented. Small and even medium-sized companies donot want that liability and often, simply do not have those internal capabilities. The low return on investment for the outsourcer means little interest from them—they are unlikely to deal with customers that have the future capability of outsourcing a minimum of 100 roles.

Finally, IT project methodology must be completely revamped. Today (pre-outsourcing) I call my colleague Fred in Chicago, ask about his daughter's marriage, and tell him we need to launch project X. We've done this a million times and we know the drill.

Tomorrow (post-outsourcing) there is a team of resources half way around the world that I supervise. Some of those team members probably only understand every other word I utter. I probably never get to meet them in person. All my informal (read assumed and not written down) components of IT project execution must be detailed, researched, documented, transferred, and validated so that a revolving group of workers half a world away can do the work.

For a large company, these are simply the start-up costs. For small and medium-sized companies on an individual basis, they are prohibitive, too risky, or unfeasible. Despite newspaper and even some researchers parroting to the contrary, IT outsourcing has generally been limited to Fortune 500 firms, and will stay that way.

Ethics–
Fuzzy

Returning to our example of the tire company—the tire company wins—the employees are more secure, and the company's products and resultant bottom line are stronger. All is well—right?

Wrong!

What about those IT individuals who lost their job? What if everyone was doing IT outsourcing all at once nationally and there was no employment to be had, even for those who were loyal, long-term workers with great references and experience?

That is what happened with certain jobs within IT outsourcing (not all of them). Companies that did not have IT as a *core* business, such as our mythical tire company above, clearly benefited, but the individuals who were caught in the tsunami of IT outsourcing were devastated. They spent years in college learning how to code, and suddenly coders were literally a dime a dozen.

Sometimes all it takes is 100 workers—all perhaps living near each other—to devastate an entire community. Take several dozen large companies that outsource, and it can devastate a small city.[1]

Given the outrageous returns on investment in IT outsourcing, there is a clear solution. Firms can take some of the enormous profits from the outsourcing program and invest them in a robust *soft landing* program. This is not a typical separation *package*—this is an investment in supporting those IT workers not near retirement in creating a new, workable livelihood. Those near retirement can be compensated without loss. This is the core of molar ethics in IT outsourcing—not stopping the unstoppable train that is IT outsourcing, but providing a softer landing for those who are forced off that train.

This soft-landing worker investment is more than feasible, given the huge return on investment and general economics of outsourcing. How much of a return does IT outsourcing provide? Let's do the math in a given example demonstrating simple labor arbitrage. In general, if you IT outsource 10% of a 1000-person IT department in a large firm (which is typical), that is 100 people you were paying $80 an hour that can be shifted to overseas resources earning $25 per hour (as an example).[1]

Let us do the math—$80 minus $25 is a savings of $55 per hour. $55 × 40 = $2200 (savings per resource per week). $2200 times 50 weeks times 100 resources is eleven million dollars savings per year. That is a lot of tire research and development money.

There are start-up costs for IT outsourcing, sometimes very large ones, but in general the overall program savings is huge, and companies often cannot afford to maintain a completely U. S.-based IT department if their competitors aren't, just to have the same opportunity for huge returns.

In many ways, given the math, IT outsourcing is an imperative for large companies—if your competitor has this cash infusion, and you don't, it may be the lever that brings everything down.

Since there generally is no corporate structure and mechanism to step back and consider the overall ethical fairness of IT outsourcing—large firms generally don't have a department of ethics with any real business power—the outmoded approach kicks in. It's simply not sufficient to let long-term, loyal IT workers go under the old model.

Today companies try to manage the negative impressions inevitably caused by mass layoffs by hiding them; eventually they are found out by the newspapers and the community, and years of positive company relationship management may go by the wayside, simply due to inertia.[1]

Why is it that corporations are so challenged in regard to ethic, such that today entire industries serve as the butt of ethic-related jokes on late-night television?

The real drivers behind employee behavior within the typical Fortune 500 firm are informal measures of success, generally centering upon the perception of the employee by those more powerful in the company hierarchy. These measures drive the behavior of workers who need their jobs to stay financially afloat. The extent to which they compromise their own personal ethics or ideals may vary on a case-by-case basis, but within the corporation the considerations of ethics are so narrow that the more important, larger issues are simply not considered relevant. Thus the example of the paragon of corporate ethical behavior that actively preys upon the financial underclass of America, seeing nothing wrong until news coverage or Internet videos capture the fundamental dysfunction of their business model.

This is how rare, beautiful woods are run over by parking lots, the last nesting places of species are destroyed, and compromises in quality affect our general health and well-being across many industries. There simply is no measure within the corporate entity to underscore the huge relative impacts of such decisions within the narrow framework of an individual worker trying to achieve a quarterly budget.

At the most extreme, one could find ultimately see members of the U.S. Chamber of Commerce as the modern personification of evil, as we have with the 1937 photograph with Hitler, sipping tea and chillingly, ostensibly talking about efficiency.[13]

What is important to realize is that the departmental silos that are necessarily a feature of large corporations—the typical paper-stamping scenarios and hierarchies that are both necessary and ridiculous—foments and supports both a narrow focus and the out-of-control ego. Megalith human resources departments create guidelines for performance that often bear no relation to day-to-day jobs and thus create a kind of desperation for a typical worker just trying to get through a day.

Neither human resources nor the employee's manager has authority to make these measures more realistic; the employee falls through the cracks, and yet another sale is made that destroys a unique resource, compromises our health, or drains the national treasury and requires a bailout.

The rare whistleblower who bucks this trend often must deal with the resulting ridicule, including social and financial disenfranchisement.

I am convinced that in the corporate life, every employee faces at least one moment—perhaps many—when a choice must be made between doing the right thing and losing the livelihood. The lack of an ethical framework within our business culture, as clearly illustrated in the existing world economy, is threatening our very livelihoods, and sometimes in the case of ethical breaches impacting our health, our very lives.

Hitherto, the pretension was that corporate life was self-policing. Americans are slowly but surely discovering that large corporations are chock-full of the same error-prone, politically suffocating, and essentially illogical human relationships and structures that we have experienced in other institutions, starting with the first school we attended when we were very small.

That the corporate ethical model may be composed of a hodge-podge of mismatched employee incentives and half-baked, weak *corporate values* does not matter when the damage is done. The fact that these values have no application to the daily decisions of the employees does not matter when the damage to the corporate reputation is done. The opportunity is gone and the negative picture may be indelibly printed in the public mind. This is the cost of ignoring the molar ethical construct.[1]

Although a large corporation, like the questionable discount furniture store that goes under every year only to reopen under another name, may appear to suffer no consequences for public, large breaches of ethics, it is hard to measure just how many opportunities are missed or how many deals are not brought to the table. The walking away by deeply principled parties represents the unmeasured costs of a core business culture unfettered by ethical principle. The most interesting business partners, the best and strongest employees—and their creativity and pride—go elsewhere. The participation of the most principled opt out over time, and the firm is left with an abundance of the best—but these are the best swindlers, cheaters, and liars, a perfect reflection of the business model it engenders. This is how the Enron's of the world are built, at least at a leadership level.

A concept of the Ethics Project or Program Management Office (PMO), created and outlined in my book,[1] may be one way for large firms to shift the ethical culture. IT professionals are familiar with the concept of an IT PMO. The IT PMO serves as a focal point for creating IT standards across the large silos of large corporations. As an enabling platform that both requires significant investment and represents a strategic (competitive) advantage when executed with intelligence and vision, it doesn't make sense for each silo to have complete freedom of choice in IT implementation. Not only is it very expensive to implement in that manner, requiring a great deal of technical and human capital duplicative effort, but it is also unwieldy and positions the firm to be at risk when large market forces require a nimble response to a new market or technical trend.

Similarly, the Ethics PMO functions to provide ethical standards that supersede and override what may be a very narrow, and ultimately destructive, tendency to meet business goals *at all costs*. The Ethics PMO, in some ways, can be likened to risk mitigation regarding a certain kind of large institution myopia. Not long ago, a New York hospital was revealed to have a tape of a woman who collapsed in a waiting room, ultimately dying, while a hospital worker sat next to her seemingly unconcerned. A well-known and respected technology firm had a YouTube film of a worker in Iraq shooting his gun into a product, proclaiming his frustration about a financial charge for customer service in just trying to get the product to work properly.

These are two examples of an internally focused culture taken to extremes, where focus on the procedures and policies—increasingly veering away from the very customers they are serving—became so overpowering that the *raison d'être* of the entire organization became lost in the shuffle. The Ethics PMO is created to ensure that *at all costs* does not translate into bringing down the firm as a whole (Enron), incurring huge fines (pick a new firm), or an embarrassing public revelation of predatory practices.

The Ethics PMO serves to review and oversee behavior of corporate entities and serves to define and enforce ethical behavior within those entities. A definition of ethics that includes a prescriptive establishment of business principles that serve to make a firm grow in a robust way via ethical means. In addition to the obvious components of creation and support of a robust ethical culture from the top down, ethical alignment means the following:

- Actively creating a culture of objective performance accountability at all levels of the organization, most particularly including the executive level, and supporting reasonable performance goals for employees who are not constantly pressured to bend the rules to keep their jobs.
- Open sharing of non-competitive data on the impacts of IT outsourcing to debunk the negative mythology (as research suggests) and deal with it up front by addressing it as a nation or as an industry.

Ethics–
Fuzzy

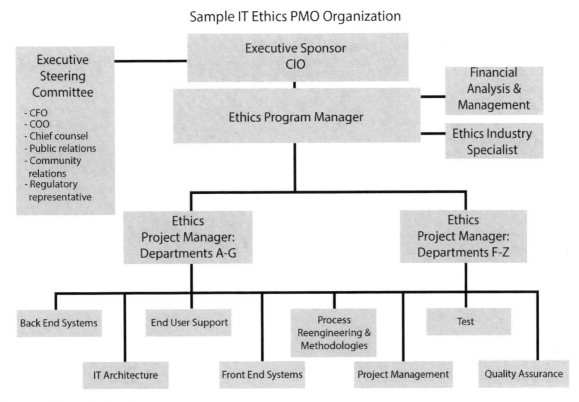

Sample IT Ethics PMO Organization

Fig. 6 Potential organization chart.
Source: Gold, T.[1]

- Participation in a robust *soft-landing* investment program for loyal, long-term IT workers impacted by IT outsourcing, actively measuring the success of the program via their return to the workforce without losing income or longevity.
- Promulgation of equal access to higher education across all income levels in the UnitedStates to support our competitive standing as a nation.

Key to the success of the Ethics PMO is placing it high enough in the organization—in other words, at peer level with other C-level officers. Fig. 6, from my book,[1] outlines a potential organization chart.

Early in the history of IT, the strategic value of IT investment was often marginalized by its frequent placement under a chief financial officer or a similar purely financial entity. While this was a workable structure for some firms, the placement was often problematic because the individuals who made decisions in IT investment tended to see IT as overhead.

Similarly, over time, the strategic investment in the reputation of a firm will prove to exceed the investment in an Ethics PMO. Unfortunately, like the firms of yesteryear that learned too late about investing strategically in IT, some firms have already sustained severe and long-lasting damage to their reputations that it will take many years to overcome.

It is the sincere wish of this author, echoing many loyal workers, that the commitment to firm growth will take a lesson from the ethical breaches of late of so many firms, and implement a robust methodology such as an Ethics PMO to ensure that their industry will not be either an active or a passive party to yet another wave of disappointing scandals and ruined economic livelihoods.

Micro: The Ethics of the Personal

Now that we have thoroughly canvassed the macro and molar (corporate) foundational ethical principles, we are finally ready to realistically turn to personal ethics, or microethics. On a personal level, as the above background makes clear, much of the challenge is how to navigate with integrity across a macro and molar landscape filled with ethical landmines.

The shifting of the workforce to incorporate legions of individuals around the world—primarily from India—into the United States has not been achieved without pain, and nowhere has this pain been greater than in the realm of the personal. Change is usually uncomfortable, but incorporating a multitude of individuals who speak another language into daily work life is certainly not the business process re-engineering (a catch-all phrase for doing business differently) of yesteryear. The sense of being invaded, of invisible borders crossed, a confusing,

Ethics–
Fuzzy

vast sea of change, and the passing of an era is difficult to avoid.

At a lunch with my peers, two men in their professional prime who work successfully for one of the fastest growing, largest IT firms, the subject turned to the impact of personal economic uncertainty. One had lost a high-paying job without warning as a result of 9–11, and the resulting 12 months of unemployment devastated his savings, retirement, and family life and also left a permanent sense of instability and vulnerability that had been completely foreign to his prior work life. The second man was caught in the housing crisis by buying a second home before the first one sold. Supporting both homes drained his resources.

Both were worried about the impact of their credit ratings on upcoming travel. Would the corporate credit card cover the long trip to India? Would their history of credit catch up with them?

These conversations would have been unheard of in the 1980s, and the 1990s before the dot-com boom, when this same group of professionals would have competed to demonstrate how quickly they could build a private wine cellar or an equivalent luxury. There is a new austerity and sense of unassailable change that informs even the so-called survivors.

In a scenario of too-rapid, uncomfortable change and the consequent fears that may result, it is tempting to apply black and white thinking or to blame—and many individuals do so. The lines of loyalty may be drawn according to color, cultural affiliation, or even conceptual support of the offshore model.

Ethical considerations aside, the winds of change tend to blow many ways, and those who hold to a particular orthodoxy of any kind tend to be most vulnerable when the winds shift. The inexorable people movement caused by the pursuit of inexpensive labor is clearly here to stay, and the pragmatic adapt. Who is to say that an individual in India is less deserving of $29 per hour for the same work for which a U.S. employee receives $55 to $80 hourly? As group membership shifts and forms, a broader definition of those who belong (us) is naturally extended.

This new austerity demands a shift in the level of personal ethical sensitivity and sense of fair play. Blanket commitment to cost savings without taking into account the human impact is as historically short lived as the tulip market craze in 16th-century Holland. At its height, historians tell us, a large estate was traded for a handful of tulip bulbs (yes, a long history of market crazes preceded our booms and busts).

The principles of ethics suggest simply that what goes around comes around. One material example is our own President Obama, one of the many children whose families were denied insurance coverage, now grown up and focusing his power upon that national debate. Who can deny him the pain of losing his mother to the denial of benefits dealt by the kind of faceless insurance bureaucracy many fear and loathe?

The bottom line is that when masses are treated unfairly and humanity is missing from a culture that consistently favors financial priorities, eventually the *wrong person*—one who comes into a position of real power—is wronged. Then the embarrassing details inevitably come to light, and the damage is done. Like the individual who is caught cheating in a hotel room or the accountant who takes a little here and there for his own use, the likelihood is that all will be revealed.

Increasingly, a self-perpetuating corporate culture that openly acknowledges that a firm is driven by financials at the expense of loyalty or even the intangible concept of concerns about employees runs the risk of becoming the company that everyone loves to hate. The damage can be incalculable, lasting, and vast. Many United States financial institutions have lost their hard-won reputations as institutions of security, careful accounting, accountability, safety, and fidelity. The shifts in the public perception may take years (if ever) to undo. When popular websites cry *boycott* based on unethical or poor business practices, the damage is done and it is too late.

Part of the challenge, of course, is that it is difficult to create an actionable set of guidelines, given the complexities. Firms are primarily financial entities, bound by laws and commitments to return on shareholder investment and alignment with industry *regulations*, but are not necessarily bound by ethics. Yet these same firms consist of individuals who can create a powerfully positive or negative individual or collective environment that in turn can further or limit business opportunity based upon the elusive quality of character.

There is an opportunity, however, to define a set of high-level ethical guidelines that reflects the reality of the new austerity and the danger of deep collateral damage to a firm's reputation. An initial set of these guidelines is outlined below and explores the impact of the promulgation of these principles. Each of these individual, microethical guidelines are explored below.

- Communications reflect the level of integrity that meets the level of austerity.
- Overt values are actively supported, not passively drawn.
- Prized values are maintained (or not maintained) bilaterally.
- The needs and consequent responsibilities of the individual are acknowledged within the whole.
- Raw abuse of power—defined as the suspension of the normal rules of business and ethics within that business—is perceived as damaging to the operations and ultimately the reputation in the broadest sense of the organization.

COMMUNICATIONS REFLECT THE LEVEL OF INTEGRITY THAT MEETS THE LEVEL OF AUSTERITY

The proverbial austerity test of being dropped in New York City's' Times Square with only a quarter to spend served as a kind of character-building exercise and is now perhaps all too real for some. Times Square is not the center of danger and crime it used to be, but the concept remains valid. Situations of financial extremes—when the relative difference of a small amount of money has huge implications—have become common. In today's new austerity, the ethics of personal conduct must reflect that reality.

One of the characteristics of the new austerity is the wide impact of financial challenges across individuals for whom the idea of struggling is completely new. Friendships may now be tested on a completely different scale, like personal cataclysms such as divorce or grave illness. The effects on friendships that stand the test, for example, of even short-term unemployment, are often hard to predict and somewhat surprising, as those who have experienced personal cataclysm know. For the so-called lucky ones, determining where and how and even how much to give to the newly disenfranchised can be painful for all parties.

In a business context, this ethical principle means that all communications and actions are crafted with the care that constrained economic circumstances demand. The impact of a bad job review or any decision to cut costs in a way that affects workers financially may have a cascading impact on a long-term career—and a family—that is dramatic and lasting. While the unscrupulous may not allow these considerations to factor into these types of decisions, it is important in a discussion of ethics to recognize these factors and to hold ourselves to a higher standard of objectivity and personal honesty.

OVERT VALUES ARE ACTIVELY SUPPORTED, NOT PASSIVELY DRAWN

Speaking personally over a 25-year career, the firms that overtly address the issues of fairness and economic impact of career management within the corporate environment are few and far between.

One company that demonstrated awareness of the ethical implications of career management on a large scale was Digital Equipment Corporation (DEC), founded by Kenneth Olsen (more familiarly, KO). I was fortunate to work for KO's DEC during the heady 1980s, when the 128 highway circling Boston was proudly labeled *America's High Tech Highway*, and MIT and other universities around Boston fed such

technology giants as Data General, Wang Computers, Raytheon, Lotus Notes Corporation, and many others.

A unique egalitarianism sensibility imbued the corporate culture at DEC. One way that the corporate culture was established at DEC was circulation of the sayings of KO. Stories circulated (probably deliberately) that served as guidelines for worker decisions. One well-known fact was that KO was one of the few Fortune 100 presidents who did not have a reserved parking space. KO walked the 10 minutes from the back of the large parking lot to the main building along with the rest of the workers.

When a computer line failed to sell, KO was said to have remarked, "Why should I fire a factory worker when some VP of marketing messed up?" KO set the tone from the top, creating a fierce loyalty that exists even today in DEC-related websites discussions and long-term relationships. Although I never had the privilege of meeting him, KO was the single most beloved leader of any firm I ever encountered. My tenure there was one of the only times I felt that ethics of compensation and the financial impact of career management decisions within a large firm was a sanctioned and even encouraged topic of conversation. I remember a certain pride of contribution that I don't see often—a sense of believing a vision, and contributing to that vision that was heady and ultimately, very productive.

Although DEC was dismantled from inside the company in parts and pieces during the early 1990s technical downturn, and the *DECies* went elsewhere after what was a shattering and very quick fall from grace, the legacy remains in the incredible technical creativity which, somewhat sadly, contributed to many other firms' profits for many years.

PRIZED VALUES ARE MAINTAINED (OR NOT MAINTAINED) BILATERALLY

Pro forma expectations of workers include loyalty and enthusiasm starting at interview, but firms often do not return that expectation and seem to go out of their way to demonstrate (despite individuals who may buck the trend, sometimes to their own peril) the opposite as a tough *willingness to go the distance* for shareholder value. Many of my earlier written contributions on this topic[1] outline the view that the savings from offshore outsourcing more than allow for generous financial compensation to loyal displaced workers.[1] In many business cultures, this is a quaint, naïve notion. But the corporate cultures that most often demand loyalty from workers are perhaps the first to fail to return that loyalty when the winds shift, and perceive their attitude as a pragmatic recognition of reality.

The cost of this so-called pragmatism may indeed be high. While few studies have been performed—almost as if the topic is radioactive—no one who has been part of an extensive layoff can minimize the impact to the ensuing organizational culture, often for years to come.

Indeed, 74% of retained employees reported impacts on their job quality and performance after layoffs; 69% said the layoffs negatively impacted the quality of the product and/or services and 87% were less likely to recommend their company to potential workers. On average, a 10% reduction in workers resulted in only a 1.5% reduction in costs.[14] A study based upon 2.5 million surveys over a 10-year period found that firms in which employee morale is high outperform their competitors. The same study compared morale and share prices for 20 companies employing almost 1 million people. Share prices for companies with high morale increased an average of 16% as compared to their industry average of 6%. Low-morale company's

share values increased only 3%.[15] Finally, the stress induced by layoffs is long term. A stress study among managers found that they reported heightened stress symptoms as long as 3 years after layoffs.[16]

The bottom line is that visionary leaders such as Ken Olsen understood that employees mirror to the customer what the company reflects to them—an immediate demonstration of "what goes around, comes around." As consumers, we know the difference between passive compliance and enthusiastic excellence in products and services. Creation of a corporate culture in which loyalty, excellence, and deep commitment to quality are nourished is a delicate process that includes the challenging components of team building and visionary leadership. To expect loyalty, excellence, and commitment not to go by the wayside without a mutual commitment to positive values and employee team welfare is unrealistic.

The Needs and Consequent Responsibilities of the Individual Are Acknowledged within the Whole.

There is a limit to group think. The price we pay for absolute obedience to a vociferous leader, no matter how charismatic, represents a failure to think outside the existing worldview needs as radical overhaul. As an example, today's marketing leadership requires a fluency with social networking and alternative media that wasn't even on the horizon 10 years ago. Tomorrow's winning business strategy and framework are just as elusive and hard to predict.

The corporate maverick, the visionary who quite doesn't see the world the same way and thus brings fresh thinking and vision still has a place. The larger a firm, the more difficult it may be to find places for these key individuals. It is a paradoxical truism of many large U. S.-based firms that individual performance accountability becomes more difficult to track as the firms grow larger.

Often within large matrix organizations different disciplines develop competitive relationships.

It is not uncommon for very large departments to act as firms in and of themselves due to their size and a corporate structure that does not share leadership below the operational management layer. This means that different groups are required to work together within that management matrix but do not share the same views, values, priorities, and measures of job performance. Credit for a job well done is based on strength of personality rather than objective contribution.

The stress of working in these constantly jockeying work cultures may cause the maverick voice to fall silent. The value of the individual—the encouragement of the new even as it may obliterate the tried and true—requires a delicate balance. It is clear no organization can survive for long without that elusive factor. From an ethical perspective, the firm must support the lone voice, even if it means an unknown in the balance of power as business processes shift and merge to incorporate the new vision.

Raw Abuse of Power—Defined As the Suspension of the Normal Rules of Business and Ethics within That Business—Is Perceived as Damaging to the Operations and Ultimately the Reputation in the Broadest Sense of the Organization

Raw abuse of power is defined as the suspension of the normal rules of business and ethics that serve as a kind of the ethical equivalent of the Generally Accepted Accounting Principles (GAAPs). While these abuses have probably been around since the first company was established, it is a sad fact in modern corporate life that we are now in a period in which power abuses are parts of our daily culture.

A TV commercial for a large institution with a highly compromised public image related how the firm helps individuals and businesses. No commercial can aid a firm known for cheating and unfair business practice. Without honesty as a foundation, no individual ethical guidelines have any meaning. My personal reaction to that commercial was, "Oh, really!?"

In an interesting historical snapshot that produced a broad impact on the world and popular U.S. culture, President Truman brought the heads of the Hollywood film studios to visit the concentration camps in Germany immediately after World War II. Most of the films they took of the camps were considered too graphic and never shown. The experience must have been truly awful and awe-filled for the majority of the studio heads possessing Jewish origins.

Truman also had many military officers underwrite the new constitutions of Europe that were carefully structured to prevent the hunger and poverty created in

Germany after World War I. These hardened men included extensive benefits to unwed mothers, the unemployed, and other economically vulnerable groups in the new constitutions. Underlying these actions was the understanding, born of hard-won experience and lives lost, that large groups of desperate individuals may foster fascism that will lead to catastrophe for all.

Additional material on applying these principles to daily life may be referenced in http://www.ethicsinit.com, or in this volume.[1]

In Sum: The Ethics of the Macro, Molar (Corporate), and Micro (Personal)

Debunking the Macrolevel mythology, we found that despite popular opinion, it is not IT outsourcing that research shows is responsible for our economic downturn, but the dramatic, ever-increasing, and highly exaggerated tendency of income and wealth to be concentrated in the hands of fewer and fewer Americans. This means that the UnitedStates will not be able to produce the knowledge workers we need to thrive, as less and less of the population is able to afford access to higher education.

Within the molar or corporate ethical context, we explored the importance of establishing an Ethics PMO,[1] empowered to enforce a more realistic and balanced implementation of profit "at any cost."

Finally, we explored microethics or ethics of the personal. It is the hope of this author that every individual within IT utilizes his or her individual power for the common ethical good. Please join the conversation at http://www.ethicsinit.com!

REFERENCES

1. Gold, T. *Ethics in IT Outsourcing;* CRC Press: May, 2012, http://www.ethicsinit.com.
2. Marcoux, A. Business Ethics. In *The Stanford Encyclopedia of Philosophy* (Fall 2008 Edition): E. N. Zalta (Ed.), CRC Press: Boca Raton, 2008, http://plato.stanford.edu/archives/fall2008/entries/ethics-business.
3. U.S.Department of Labor: *Bureau of Labor Statistics, Median Duration of Unemployment (UEMPMED),* (accessed August 2012).
4. McBride, B. , Calculated Risk Blog, http://www.calculatedriskblog.com (accessed May 2011).
5. Human Development Index Trends, *Source Human Development Indices: A statistical update 2010: United National Development Programme,* 1980–2010, http://data.un.org/DocumentData.aspx?q = HDI&id = 229 (accessed January 2011).
6. Belinkiy, M. *The Determinants of Outsourcing from the U. S.: Evidence from Domestic Manufacturing Industries, 1972–2002,* UC Davis Press: http://mpra.ub.uni-muenchen.de/17911. MPRA Paper No. 17911, posted 17. (accessed October 2009).
7. Taxes on the wealthy have gone down dramatically, Ethan Pollock and Rebecca Theiss, Economic Policy Institute, Cornell: Ithaca, N.Y. April 14, 2011 http://www.epi.org/publication/taxes_on_the_wealthy_have_gone_down_dramatically/ (accessed August 2012).
8. Creative conflict wisdom blog, Ratio of CEO Pay to Average Worker by Country, http://creativeconflictwisdom.wordpress.com/2011/10/07/ration-of-ceo-pay-to-average-worker-by-country/ (accessed August 2012).
9. *U.S. Department of Labor: Bureau of Labor Statistics, Education Pays* (accessed August 2012).
10. Gould, E. *High-scoring, low-income students no more likely to complete college than low-scoring, rich students.* Economic Policy Institute, Cornell: Ithaca, N. Y. March 9, 2012 (accessed August 2012).
11. OECD. *Lessons from PISA for the United States, Strong Performers and Successful Reformers in Education;* OECD Publishing; 2011, http://www.oecd.org/pisa/46623978.pdf
12. Rodney King tape on national news.flv, November 15, **2010** (accessed August 2012).
13. Black, E. Then They Came for the Gypsies: The Legacy of Death's Calculator, July 9, **2004** (accessed August 2012) http://www.jewishvirtuallibrary.org/jsource/Holocaust/gypibm.html.
14. Ray, B.W. *Layoffs and the Stress Response. How to Fulfill Your Potential: Blog Wired for Success, Psychology Today,* (accessed September 2009), http://www.psychologytoday.com/blog/wired-success/200909/layoffs-and-the-stress-response.
15. Sirota, D.; Mischkind, L.A.; Irwin, M. *The Enthusiastic Employee: How Companies Profit By Giving Workers What They Want Based upon Years of Research with Millions of Employees;* Wharton School Publishing: Philadelphia, 2005; http://knowledge.wharton.upenn.edu/article.cfm?articleid = 1188.
16. *Giving Employees What They Want: The Returns Are Huge, Knowledge@Wharton,* http://knowledge.wharton.upenn.edu/article.cfm?articleid = 1188 (accessed May 2005).

BIBLIOGRAPHY

1. Domhoff, G.W. Wealth, income, and power. In *Who Rules America: Power in America;* September 2005, Updated July 2011. http://sociology.ucsc.edu/whorulesamerica/power/wealth.html
2. Krugman, P. Why Does Inequality Make the Rich Feel Poorer? New York Times Blog, http://krugman.blogs.nytimes.com/2011/01/12/why-does-inequality-make-the-rich-feel-poorer (accessed January 2011)
3. Wolff, E.N. *Recent Trends in Household Wealth in the United States: Rising Debt and the Middle-Class Squeeze—an Update to 2007,* Working Paper 589, Levy Economics Institute of Bard College, http://www.levyinstitute.org/pubs/wp_598a.pdf (accessed March 2010).
4. Davies, J.B.; Sandström, S.; Shorrocks, A.; Wolff, E.N. *The World Distribution of Household Wealth, Uni-Wider*

World Institute for Development Economics Research, http://ideas.repec.org/a/ecj/econjl/v121y2011i551p223-254.html (accessed February 2008).

5. Saez, E. *Striking it Richer: The Evolution of Top Incomes in the United States* (Updated with 2008 estimates), Pathways Magazine, Stanford Center for the Study of Poverty and Inequality, Winter 2008, 6–7, http://elsa.berkeley.edu/~saez/saez-UStopincomes-2008.pdf

6. von Meyer-Gossner, M. *For Boomers Optimism and Social Conscience of brands is key, The Strategy Web*, http://www.thestrategyweb.com/study-for-boomers-optimism-and-social-conscience-of-brands-is-key (accessed April 2001).

7. Judy, M. *1 In 5 American Children Now Living In Poverty, The Human Rights Cause*, Annie E. Casey Foundation, Kids Count Databook, (accessed August 2011), http://www.care2.com/causes/1-in-5-american-children-now-living-in-poverty.html.

8. *Labor Force Statistics from the Current Population Survey—Changes to data collected on unemployment duration*, Bureau of Labor Statistics, United States Department of Labor, http://www.bls.gov/cps/duration.htm (accessed July 2011).

9. Abrams, R.; Heiser, S. *A Study in Corporate Cultures: Digital Equipment Corporation, The Reality: HeroSpeak*. Digital Equipment Corporation: 1988.

10. Abrams, R. *A Study in Corporate Cultures—Digital Equipment Corporation the Myth: A Cultural Operating Manual*; Digital Equipment Corporation: 1988, http://decconnection.org/ReesaAbrams-DIGITAL.pdf.

11. *Central Intelligence Agency, The World Factbook*, https://www.cia.gov/library/publications/the-world-factbook/docs/whatsnew.html (accessed August 2011).

Firewall Architectures

Paul A. Henry
Senior Vice President, CyberGuard Corporation, Ocala, Florida, U.S.A.

Abstract

Just a year or so ago, URL filtering was considered a nice thing to have but not a necessity; it now finds itself as a first line of defense in phishing. Two-factor authentication in the form of tokens were long considered a luxury and are now effectively being mandated by regulatory agencies for Internet banking and I expect will find their way into environments that are entrusted to secure any personal information such as that which could potentially be used in identity theft and perhaps even medical records.

PERSPECTIVE

The year 2005 can be described as a tough year for network security or, perhaps better yet, as a tough year for those who did not take network security seriously. ID theft was a hot topic for the year with breach after breach exposing the personal data of so many individuals. There is unfortunately no hard data that details specifically just how many of the data exposures actually resulted in cases of ID theft. The potential credit nightmares that the individuals will potentially face should not be taken lightly. Cleaning up your credit as a result of ID theft is time consuming, can be expensive, and even after it is cleaned up can still haunt the victim for many years. In looking at data found on the Internet in Table 1 for the first 6 months of 2005 alone, nearly 50 million individuals had their personal information exposed:

Organizations were warned that unless they got serious about security, government regulations would be imposed. With the high-profile breeches continuing to rise and setting new heights in 2005, our government took action and legislation was passed at the state level to address the issue as detailed in Table 2.

The Internet remains in flux. As organizations take measures to plug a known security hole, hackers simply first move on to easier targets, and then as the target environment dwindles they alter their tactics to enable them to continue to wreak their havoc against a new target-rich environment. This was clearly demonstrated by the decline in the number of broad-based protocol-level attacks we have witnessed as the hacking community seemed to shift its focus to the application layer. The majority of protective mechanisms in place today only offer protection by filtering on internet protocol (IP) addresses and port (serviced) numbers; it is no wonder that application layer attacks have gained in popularity. More recently, social engineering has risen dramatically in the form of phishing, again demonstrating the flexibility and or adaptability of the hacking community.

The data from the 2005 CSI/FBI crime report paints a grim picture of the state of network security:

- The damage from virus attacks continues to be the highest overall cost to organizations.
- Unauthorized access had a dramatic increase in cost and has now replaced denial of service attacks as the new second-most significant contributor to losses from computer crime.
- Although the overall losses are perhaps lower, there has been a measurable increase in the losses associated with unauthorized access to information and the theft of proprietary information.
- Website defacements/incidents have increased sharply.
- The number of organizations reporting computer crime incidents to law enforcement continues to decline. The primary reason cited is the fear of negative publicity.

In the past, many organizations have cited competitive pressure as their primary reason for choosing popularity over security in consideration of how they go about securing their networks. Time and again I have heard that although an architecture or product is inarguably more secure, a company would be giving their competitor an advantage if the company offered its customers less transparency or convenience in connecting to its network.

In light of legislation and the resulting first wave of civil penalties now being assessed, there may finally be sufficient motivation for a decisive change in how network security is viewed. Simply put, an organization's ability to mitigate the risk of the aforementioned civil penalties effectively moves network security from the

Ethics–
Fuzzy

Encyclopedia of Information Systems and Technology, DOI: 10.1081/E-EIST-120046863

Table 1 Loss or theft of personal identification information in Q1–Q2 2005

Date made public	Name	Type of breach	Number of exposed people
2/15/2005	ChoicePoint	ID thieves accessed	145,000
2/25/2005	Bank of America	Lost backup tape	1,200,000
2/25/2005	PayMaxx	Exposed online	25,000
3/8/2005	DSW/Retail	Ventures Hacking	100,000
3/10/2005	LexisNexis	Passwords compromised	32,000
3/11/2005	University of CA, Berkeley	Stolen laptop	98,400
3/11/2005	Boston College	Hacking	120,000
3/12/2005	NV Department of Motor Vehicles	Stolen computer	8,900
3/20/2005	Northwestern University	Hacking	21,000
3/20/2005	University of Nevada, Las Vegas	Hacking	5,000
3/22/2005	California State University, Chico	Hacking	59,000
3/23/2005	University of CA, San Francisco	Hacking	7,000
4/1/2005	Georgia DMV	Dishonest insider	"Hundreds of thousands"
4/5/2005	MCI	Stolen laptop	16,500
4/8/2005	San Jose Medical Group	Stolen computer	185,000
4/11/2005	Tufts University	Hacking	106,000
4/12/2005	LexisNexis	Passwords compromised	Additional 280,000
4/14/2005	Polo Ralph Lauren/HSBC	Hacking	180,000
4/14/2005	California FasTrack	Dishonest insider	4,500
4/15/2005	California Department of Health Services	Stolen laptop	21,600
4/18/2005	DSW/Retail Ventures	Hacking Additional	1,300,000
4/20/2005	Ameritrade	Lost backup tape	200,000
4/21/2005	Carnegie Mellon University	Hacking	19,000
4/26/2005	Michigan State University's Wharton Center	Hacking	40,000
4/26/2005	Christus St. Joseph's	Hospital stolen computer	19,000
4/28/2005	Georgia Southern University	Hacking	"Tens of thousands"
4/28/2005	Wachovia, Bank of America, PNC Financial Services Group and Commerce Bancorp	Dishonest insiders	676,000
4/29/2005	Oklahoma State University	Missing laptop	37,000
5/2/2005	Time Warner	Lost backup tapes	600,000
5/4/2005	Colorado Health Department	Stolen laptop	1,600 (families)
5/5/2005	Purdue University	Hacker	11,360
5/7/2005	Department of Justice	Stolen laptop	80,000
5/11/2005	Stanford University	Hacker	9,900
5/12/2005	Hinsdale Central High School	Hacker	2,400
5/16/2005	Westborough Bank	Dishonest insider	750
5/18/2005	Jackson Community College, Michigan	Hacker	8,000
5/19/2005	Valdosta State University, GA	Hacker	40,000
5/20/2005	Purdue University	Hacker	11,000
5/26/2005	Duke University	Hacker	5500
5/27/2005	Cleveland State University	Stolen laptop	44,420
5/28/2005	Merlin Data Services	Bogus account set up	9000
5/30/2005	Motorola	Computers stolen	Unknown
6/6/2005	Citifinancial	Lost backup tapes	3,900,000
6/10/2005	Federal Deposit Insurance Corporation	Not disclosed	6000
6/16/2005	Cardsystems	Hacker	40,000,000
6/18/2005	University of Hawaii	Dishonest insider	150,000
6/25/2005	University of Connecticut	Hacker	72,000
Total			49,857,830

Table 2 State laws regarding security breech notification

State	Law	Effective date
Arkansas	SB 1167	6/1/2005
California	SB 1386	7/1/2003
Connecticut	SB 650	1/1/2006
Delaware	HB 116	6/28/2005
Florida	HB 481	7/1/2005
Georgia	SB 230	5/5/2005
Illinois	HB 1633	1/1/2006
Indiana	SB 503	7/1/2006
Louisiana	SB 205	1/1/2006
Maine	LD 1671	1/31/2006
Minnesota	HF 2121	1/1/2006
Montana	HB 732	3/1/2006
Nevada	SB 347	10/1/2005
New Jersey	A4001	1/1/2006
New York	SB 5827	12/7/2005
North Carolina	HB 1048	2/17/2006
North Dakota	SB 2251	6/1/2005
Ohio	HB 104	2/17/2006
Pennsylvania	SB 721	7/1/2006
Rhode Island	HB 6191	7/10/2005
Tennessee	HB 2170	7/1/2005
Texas	SB 122	9/1/2005
Washington	SB 6403	7/24/2005

deficit column to the asset column of the organization's balance sheet.

In closing, I recall a quote from October 2000 from a friend and world-renowned security expert Marcus Ranum, which I believe is still highly relevant today: "Firewall customers once had a vote, and voted in favor of transparency, performance and convenience instead of security; nobody should be surprised by the results."[1]

FIREWALL FUNDAMENTALS: A REVIEW

The level of protection that *any* firewall is able to provide in securing a private network when connected to the public Internet is directly related to the architecture(s) chosen for the firewall by the respective vendor. Generally, most commercially available firewalls utilize one or more of the following firewall architectures:

- Static packet filter
- Dynamic (stateful) packet filter
- Circuit-level gateway
- Application-level gateway (proxy)
- Stateful inspection
- Cutoff proxy
- Air gap
- Intrusion prevention
- Deep packet inspection
- Total stream protection
- Unified threat management (UTM)

Network Security: A Matter of Balance

Network security is simply the proper balance of trust and performance. All firewalls rely on the inspection of information generated by protocols that function at various layers of the OSI model as shown in Fig. 1. Knowing the OSI layer at which a firewall operates is one of the keys to understanding the different types of firewall architectures. Generally speaking, firewalls follow two known rules:

- The higher the OSI layer the architecture requires to examine the information within the packet, the more processor cycles the architecture consumes.
- The higher in the OSI layer at which an architecture examines packets, the greater the level of protection the architecture provides because more information is available upon which to base decisions.

Historically, there had always been a recognized trade-off in firewalls between the level of trust afforded and speed (throughput). Faster processors and the performance advantages of symmetric multiprocessing

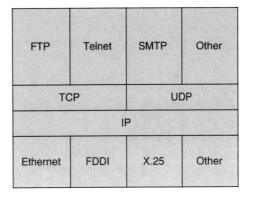

Fig. 1 OSI and TCP/IP models.

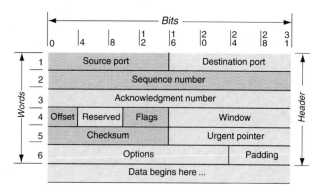

Source destination IPaddress	Source destination port	Application state and data flow	Payload
IP header	TCP header	Application level header	Data

Fig. 2   The most important fields within the IP packet.

(SMP) have narrowed the performance gap between the traditional fast packet filters and high-overhead-consuming proxy firewalls.

One of the most important factors in any successful firewall deployment is "who" makes the trustperformance decisions: 1) the firewall vendor, by limiting the administrator's choices of architectures; or 2) the administrator, in a robust firewall product that provides for multiple firewall architectures.

In examining firewall architectures, the most important fields, as shown in Fig. 2, within the IP packet are as follows:

- IP header as detailed in Fig. 3
- TCP header as detailed in Fig. 4
- Application level header
- Data-payload header

Static Packet Filter

The packet-filtering firewall is one of the oldest firewall architectures. A static packet filter as shown in Fig. 5 operates at the network layer, or OSI layer 3.

The decision to accept or deny a packet is based on an examination of specific fields as shown in Fig. 6 within the packet's IP and protocol headers:

- Source address
- Destination address
- Application or protocol
- Source port number
- Destination port number

Before forwarding a packet, the firewall compares the IP header and TCP header against a user-defined

Fig. 4   The TCP header.

table—rule base—which contains the rules that dictate whether the firewall should deny or permit packets to pass. The rules are scanned in sequential order until the packet filter finds a specific rule that matches the criteria specified in the packet-filtering rule. If the packet filter does not find a rule that matches the packet, then it imposes a default rule. The default rule explicitly defined in the firewall's table typically instructs the firewall to drop a packet that meets none of the other rules.

There are two schools of thought on the default rule used with the packet filter: 1) ease of use; and 2) security first. "Ease of use" proponents prefer a default "allow all" rule that permits all traffic unless it is explicitly denied by a prior rule. "Security first" proponents prefer a default "deny all" rule that denies all traffic unless explicitly allowed by a prior rule.

Within the static packet filter rules database, the administrator can define rules that determine which packets are accepted and which packets are denied. The IP header information allows the administrator to write rules that can deny or permit packets to and from a specific IP address or range of IP addresses. The TCP header information allows the administrator to write service-specific rules (i.e., allow or deny packets to or from ports) related to specific services.

The administrator can write rules that allow certain services such as HTTP from any IP address to view the

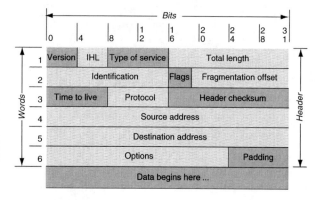

Fig. 3   The IP header.

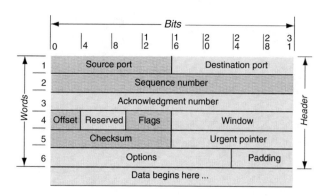

Fig. 5   A static packet filter operates at the network layer (OSI layer 3).

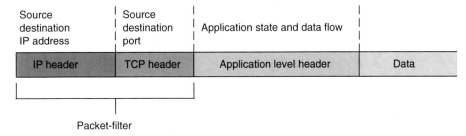

Fig. 6 The decision to accept or deny a packet is based on an examination of specific fields within a packet's IP and protocol headers.

web pages on the protected web server. The administrator can also write rules that block certain IP addresses or entire ranges of addresses from using the HTTP service and viewing the web pages on the protected server. In the same respect, the administrator can write rules that allow certain services such as SMTP from a trusted IP address or range of IP addresses to access files on the protected mail server. The administrator could also write rules that block access for certain IP addresses or entire ranges of addresses to access the protected FTP server.

The configuration of packet filter rules can be difficult because the rules are examined in sequential order. Great care must be taken in establishing the order in which packet-filtering rules are entered into the rule base. Even if the administrator manages to create effective rules in the proper order of precedence, a packet filter has one inherent limitation: a packet filter only examines data in the IP header and TCP header; it cannot know the difference between a real and a forged address. If an address is present and meets the packet filter rules along with the other rule criteria, the packet will be allowed to pass.

Suppose the administrator took the precaution to create a rule that instructed the packet filter to drop any

incoming packets with unknown source addresses. This packet-filtering rule would make it more difficult, but not impossible, for a hacker to access at least some trusted servers with IP addresses. The hacker could simply substitute the actual source address on a malicious packet with the source address of a known trusted client. This common form of attack is called *IP address spoofing*. This form of attack is very effective against a packet filter. The CERT Coordination Center has received numerous reports of IP spoofing attacks, many of which resulted in successful network intrusions. Although the performance of a packet filter can be attractive, this architecture alone is generally not secure enough to deter hackers determined to gain access to the protected network.

Equally important is what the static packet filter does not examine. Remember that in the static packet filter only specific protocol headers are examined: 1) source-destination IP address and 2) source–destination port numbers (services). Hence, a hacker can hide malicious commands or data in unexamined headers. Furthermore, because the static packet filter does not inspect the packet payload, the hacker has the opportunity to hide malicious commands or data within the packet's payload. This attack methodology is often referred to as a *covert channel attack* and is becoming more popular.

Lastly, the static packet filter is not state aware. The administrator must configure rules for both sides of the conversation to a protected server. To allow access to a protected web server, the administrator must create a rule that allows both the inbound request from the remote client as well as the outbound response from the protected web server. Of further consideration is that many services such as FTP and e-mail servers in operation today require the use of dynamically allocated ports for responses; therefore, an administrator of a static packet-filtering firewall has little choice but to open up an entire range of ports with static packet-filtering rules.

Both the pros and the cons of static packet filter considerations are detailed in Table 3.

Table 3   Static packet filter considerations

Pros	Cons
Low impact on network performance	Operates only at network layer, therefore it only examines IP and TCP headers
Low cost—now included with many operating systems	Unaware of packet payload—offers low level of security
	Lacks state awareness—may require numerous ports be left open to facilitate services that use dynamically allocated ports
	Susceptible to IP spoofing
	Difficult to create rules (order of precedence)
	Only provides for a low level of protection

Ethics—
Fuzzy

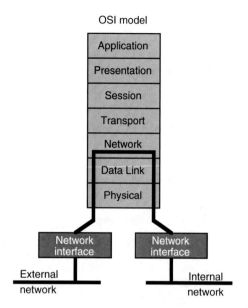

OSI model

Fig. 7 The typical dynamic packet filter, like the static packet filter, operates at the network layer (OSI layer 3).

Dynamic (Stateful) Packet Filter

The dynamic (stateful) packet filter is the next step in the evolution of the static packet filter. As such it shares many of the inherent limitations of the static packet filter with one important difference: state awareness.

The typical dynamic packet filter, as shown in Fig. 7, like the static packet filter, operates at the network layer (OSI layer 3). An advanced dynamic packet filter may operate up into the transport layer—OSI layer 4—to collect additional state information.

Most often, the decision to accept or deny a packet is based upon examination of the packet's IP and protocol headers as shown in Fig. 8:

- Source address
- Destination address
- Application or protocol
- Source port number
- Destination port number

In simplest terms, the typical dynamic packet filter is "aware" of the difference between a new and an established connection. After a connection is established, it is

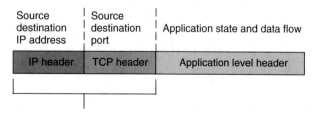

Fig. 8 The decision to accept or deny a packet is based upon examination of the packet's IP and protocol headers.

entered into a table that typically resides in RAM. Subsequent packets are compared to this table in RAM, most often by software running at the operating system (OS) kernel level. When the packet is found to be an existing connection, it is allowed to pass without any further inspection. By avoiding having to parse the packet filter rule base for each and every packet that enters the firewall and by performing this test at the kernel level in RAM for an already-established connection, the dynamic packet filter enables a measurable performance increase over a static packet filter.

There are two primary differences in dynamic packet filters found among firewall vendors:

- Support of SMP
- Connection establishment

In writing the firewall application to fully support SMP, the firewall vendor is afforded up to a 30% increase in dynamic packet filter performance for each additional processor in operation. Unfortunately, many implementations of dynamic packet filters in firewall offerings operate as a single-threaded process, which simply cannot take advantage of the benefits of SMP. To overcome the performance limitation of their single-threaded process, these vendors usually require powerful and expensive RISC-processor-based servers to attain acceptable levels of performance. As available processor power has increased and multiprocessor servers have become widely utilized, this single-threaded limitation has become more visible. For example, vendor A running an expensive RISC-based server offers only 150 Mbps dynamic packet filter throughput, while vendor B running on an inexpensive off-the-shelf Intel multiprocessor server can attain dynamic packet filtering throughputs of above 600 Mbps.

Almost every vendor has their own proprietary methodology for building the connection table, but beyond the issues discussed earlier, the basic operation of the dynamic packet filter for the most part is essentially the same.

In an effort to overcome the performance limitations imposed by their single-threaded process-based dynamic packet filters, some vendors have taken dangerous shortcuts when establishing connections at the firewall. RFC guidelines recommend following the three-way handshake to establish a connection at the firewall. One popular vendor will open a new connection upon receipt of a single SYN packet, totally ignoring RFC recommendations. In effect, this exposes the servers behind the firewall to single-packet attacks from spoofed IP addresses.

Hackers gain great advantage from anonymity. A hacker can be much more aggressive in mounting attacks if he can remain hidden. Similar to the example in the examination of a static packet filter, suppose the

Table 4 Dynamic packet filter considerations

Pros	Cons
Lowest impact of all examined architectures on network performance when designed to be fully SMP-compliant	Operates only at network layer, therefore, it only examines IP and TCP headers
Low cost—now included with some operating systems	Unaware of packet payload—offers low level of security
State awareness provides measurable performance benefit	Susceptible to IP spoofing
	Difficult to create rules (order of precedence)
	Can introduce additional risk if connections can be established without following the RFC-recommended three-way handshake
	Only provides for a low level of protection

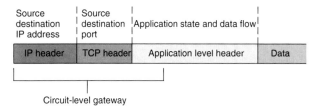

Fig. 10 The decision to accept or deny a packet is based upon examining the packet's IP header and TCP header.

way handshake to establish the connection before mounting an assault. This provides additional traffic that can be used to trace back to the hacker.

When the firewall vendor fails to follow RFC recommendations in the establishment of the connection and opens a connection without the three-way handshake, the hacker can simply spoof the trusted host address and fire any of the many well-known single-packet attacks at the firewall or servers protected by the firewall while maintaining his complete anonymity. One presumes that administrators are unaware that their popular firewall products operate in this manner; otherwise, it would be surprising that so many have found this practice acceptable following the many historical well-known single-packet attacks like LAND, "ping of death," and "tear drop" that have plagued administrators in the past.

Both the pros and the cons of dynamic packet filter considerations are shown in Table 4.

administrator took the precaution to create a rule that instructed the packet filter to drop any incoming packets with unknown source addresses. This packet-filtering rule would make it more difficult, but again not impossible, for a hacker to access at least some trusted servers with IP addresses. The hacker could simply substitute the actual source address on a malicious packet with the source address of a known trusted client. In this attack methodology, the hacker assumes the IP address of the trusted host and must communicate through the three-

Circuit-Level Gateway

The circuit-level gateway operates at the session layer (OSI layer 5) as shown in Fig. 9. In many respects, a circuit-level gateway is simply an extension of a packet filter in that it typically performs basic packet filter operations and then adds verification of proper handshaking and the legitimacy of the sequence numbers used in establishing the connection.

The circuit-level gateway examines and validates TCP and user datagram protocol (UDP) sessions before opening a connection, or circuit, through the firewall. Hence, the circuit-level gateway has more data to act upon than a standard static or dynamic packet filter.

Most often, the decision to accept or deny a packet is based upon examining the packet's IP header and TCP header as detailed in Fig. 10:

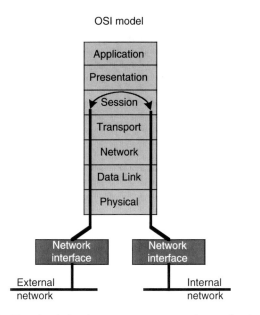

Fig. 9 The circuit-level gateway operates at the session layer (OSI layer 5).

- Source address
- Destination address
- Application or protocol
- Source port number
- Destination port number
- Handshaking and sequence numbers

Table 5 Circuit-level gateway considerations

Pros	Cons
Low to moderate impact on network performance	Shares many of the same negative issues associated with packet filters
Breaks direct connection to server behind firewall	Allows any data to simply pass through the connection
Higher level of security than a static or dynamic (stateful) packet filter	Only provides for a low to moderate level of security

Similar to a packet filter, before forwarding the packet, a circuit-level gateway compares the IP header and TCP header against a user-defined table containing the rules that dictate whether the firewall should deny or permit packets to pass. The circuit-level gateway then determines that a requested session is legitimate only if the SYN flags, ACK flags, and sequence numbers involved in the TCP handshaking between the trusted client and the untrusted host are logical.

If the session is legitimate, the packet filter rules are scanned until it finds one that agrees with the information in a packet's full association. If the packet filter does not find a rule that applies to the packet, then it imposes a default rule. The default rule explicitly defined in the firewall's table "typically" instructs the firewall to drop a packet that meets none of the other rules.

The circuit-level gateway is literally a step up from a packet filter in the level of security it provides. Further, like a packet filter operating at a low level in the OSI

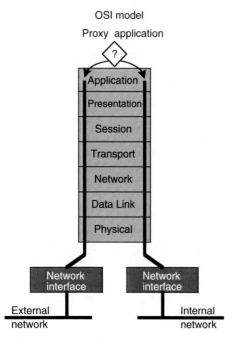

Fig. 11 The proxies examine the entire packet and can filter packets at the application layer of the OSI model.

model, it has little impact on network performance. However, once a circuit-level gateway establishes a connection, any application can run across that connection because a circuit-level gateway filters packets only at the session and network layers of the OSI model. In other words, a circuit-level gateway cannot examine the data content of the packets it relays between a trusted network and an untrusted network. The potential exists to slip harmful packets through a circuit-level gateway to a server behind the firewall.

Both the pros and the cons of circuit-level gateway considerations are shown in Table 5.

Application-Level Gateway

Like a circuit-level gateway, an application-level gateway intercepts incoming and outgoing packets, runs proxies that copy and forward information across the gateway, and functions as a proxy server, preventing any direct connection between a trusted server or client and an untrusted host. The proxies that an application-level gateway runs often differ in two important ways from the circuit-level gateway:

- The proxies are application specific.
- The proxies examine the entire packet and can filter packets at the application layer of the OSI model as shown in Fig. 11.

Unlike the circuit gateway, the application-level gateway accepts only packets generated by services they are designed to copy, forward, and filter. For example, only an HTTP proxy can copy, forward, and filter HTTP traffic. If a network relies only on an application-level gateway, incoming and outgoing packets cannot access services for which there is no proxy. If an application-level gateway ran FTP and HTTP proxies, only packets generated by these services could pass through the firewall. All other services would be blocked.

The application-level gateway runs proxies that examine and filter individual packets, rather than simply copying them and recklessly forwarding them across the gateway. Application-specific proxies check each packet that passes through the gateway, verifying the contents of the packet up through the application layer (layer 7) of the OSI model. These proxies can filter on particular information or specific individual commands in the application protocols the proxies are designed to copy, forward, and filter. As an example, an FTP application-level gateway can filter dozens of commands to allow a high degree of granularity on the permissions of specific users of the protected FTP service.

Technology application-level gateways are often referred to *as strong application proxies*. A strong application proxy extends the level of security afforded by

Table 6 Application-level gateway considerations

Pros	Cons
Application gateway with SMP affords a moderate impact on network performance	Poor implementation can have a high impact on network performance
Breaks direct connection to server behind firewall eliminating the risk of an entire class of covert channel attacks	Must be written securely. Historically some vendors have introduced buffer overruns within the application gateway itself
Strong application proxy that inspects protocol header lengths can eliminate an entire class of buffer overrun attacks	Vendors must keep up with new protocols. A common complaint of application-level gateway users is lack of timely vendor support for new protocols
Highest level of security	A poor implementation that relies on the underlying operating system (OS) Inetd daemon will suffer from a severe limitation to the number of allowed connections in today's demanding high simultaneous session environment

the application-level gateway. Instead of copying the entire datagram on behalf of the user, a strong application proxy actually creates a new empty datagram inside the firewall. Only those commands and data found acceptable to the strong application proxy are copied from the original datagram outside the firewall to the new datagram inside the firewall. Then, and only then, is this new datagram forwarded to the protected server

behind the firewall. By employing this methodology, the strong application proxy can mitigate the risk of an entire class of covert channel attacks.

An application-level gateway filters information at a higher OSI layer than the common static or dynamic packet filter, and most automatically creates any necessary packet filtering rules, usually making them easier to configure than traditional packet filters.

By facilitating the inspection of the complete packet, the application-level gateway is one of the most secure firewall architectures available; however, some vendors (usually those that market stateful inspection firewalls) and users have made claims that the security offered by an application-level gateway had an inherent drawback: a lack of transparency.

In moving software from older 16-bit code to the existing technology's 32-bit environment and with the advent of SMP, many of today's application-level gateways are just as transparent as they are secure. Users on the public or trusted network, in most cases, do not notice that they are accessing Internet services through a firewall.

Both the pros and cons in the consideration of the application level gateway are shown in Table 6.

Stateful Inspection

Stateful inspection combines the many aspects of dynamic packet filtering, circuit-level, and application-level gateways as shown in Fig. 12. Although stateful inspection has the inherent ability to examine all seven layers of the OSI model, in the majority of applications observed by the author, stateful inspection was operated only at the network layer of the OSI model and used only as a dynamic packet filter for filtering all incoming

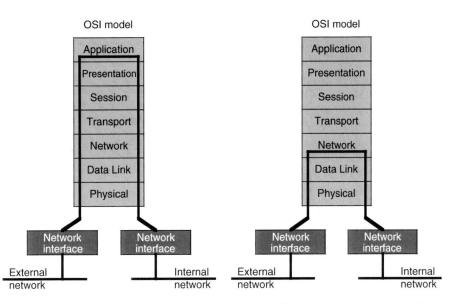

Fig. 12 Stateful inspection combines the many aspects of dynamic packet filtering, circuit-level, and application-level gateways.

Table 7 Stateful inspection considerations

Pros	Cons
Offers the ability to inspect all seven layers of the OSI model and is user configurable to customize specific filter constructs	The single-threaded process of the stateful inspection engine has a dramatic impact on performance, so many users operate the stateful inspection-based firewall as nothing more than a dynamic packet filter.
Does not break the client/server model	Many believe the failure to break the client/server model creates an unacceptable security risk as the hacker has a direct connection to the protected server.
Provides an integral dynamic (stateful) packet filter	A poor implementation that relies on the underlying operating system (OS) Inetd demon will suffer from a severe limitation to the number of allowed connections in today's demanding high simultaneous session environment.
Fast when operated as dynamic packet filter, however many SMP-compliant dynamic packet filters are actually faster	Low level of security. No stateful inspection-based firewall has achieved higher than a Common Criteria EAL 2. Per the Common Criteria EAL 2 certification documents, EAL 2 products are not intended for use in protecting private networks when connecting to the public Internet.

and outgoing packets based on source and destination IP addresses and port numbers. Although the vendor claims this is the fault of the administrator's configuration, many administrators claim that the operating overhead associated with the stateful inspection process prohibits its full utilization.

As indicated, stateful inspection can also function as a circuit-level gateway, determining whether the packets in a session are appropriate. For example, stateful inspection can verify that inbound SYN and ACK flags and sequence numbers are logical. However, in most implementations, the stateful-inspection-based firewall operates only as a dynamic packet filter and, dangerously, allows new connections to be established with a single SYN packet. A unique limitation of one popular stateful inspection implementation is that it does not provide the ability to inspect sequence numbers on

outbound packets from users behind the firewall. This leads to a flaw whereby internal users can easily the spoof IP address of other internal users to open holes through the associated firewall for inbound connections.

Finally, stateful inspection can mimic an application-level gateway. Stateful inspection can evaluate the contents of each packet up through the application layer and ensure that these contents match the rules in the administrator's network security policy.

Better performance, but what about security?

Like an application-level gateway, stateful inspection can be configured to drop packets that contain specific commands within the application header. For example, the administrator could configure a stateful inspection firewall to drop HTTP packets containing a "Put" command. However, historically, the performance impact of application-level filtering by the single-threaded process of stateful inspection has caused many administrators to abandon their use and to simply opt for dynamic packet filtering to allow the firewall to keep up with their network load requirements. In fact, the default configuration of a popular stateful inspection firewall utilizes dynamic packet filtering and not stateful inspection of the most popular protocol on today's Internet—HTTP traffic.

Do existing stateful inspection implementations expose the user to additional risks?

Unlike an application-level gateway, stateful inspection does not break the client–server model to analyze application-layer data. An application-level gateway creates two connections: 1) one between the trusted client and the gateway and 2) another between the gateway and the untrusted host. The gateway then copies information between these two connections. This is the core of the well-known proxy vs. stateful inspection debate. Some administrators insist that this configuration ensures the highest degree of security; other administrators argue that this configuration slows performance unnecessarily. In an effort to provide a secure connection, a stateful-inspection–based firewall has the ability to intercept and examine each packet up through the application layer of the OSI model. Unfortunately, because of the associated performance impact of the single-threaded stateful inspection process, this configuration is not the one typically deployed.

Looking beyond marketing hype and engineering theory, stateful inspection relies on algorithms within an inspect engine to recognize and process application-layer data. These algorithms compare packets against known bit patterns of authorized packets. Respective vendors have claimed that theoretically they are able to

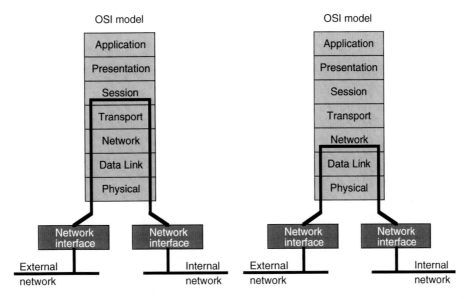

Fig. 13 The cutoff proxy initially works at the session layer (OSI layer 5) then switches to a dynamic packet filter working at the network layer (OSI layer 3) after the connection–authentication process is completed.

filter packets more efficiently than application-specific proxies. However, most stateful inspection engines represent a single-threaded process. With existing technology SMP-based application-level gateways operating on multiprocessor servers, the gap has dramatically narrowed. As an example, one vendor's SMP-capable multi-architecture firewall that does not use stateful inspection outperforms a popular stateful inspection-based firewall up to 4:1 on throughput and up to 12:1 on simultaneous sessions. Further, due to limitations in the inspect language used in stateful inspection engines, application gateways are now commonly being used to fill in the gaps.

Both the pros and the cons of stateful inspection considerations are shown in Table 7.

Table 8 Cutoff proxy considerations

Pros	Cons
Lower impact on network performance than a traditional circuit gateway	It is not a circuit gateway
IP spoofing issue is minimized as the three-way connection is verified	Still has many of the remaining issues of a dynamic packet filter
	Unaware of packet payload—offers low level of security
	Difficult to create rules (order of precedence)
	Can offer a false sense of security as vendors incorrectly claim it is equivalent to a traditional circuit gateway

Cutoff Proxy

The cutoff proxy is a hybrid combination of a dynamic (stateful) packet filter and a circuit-level proxy. In simplest terms, the cutoff proxy first acts as a circuit-level proxy in verifying the RFC-recommended three-way handshake and any required authenticating actions, then switches over to a dynamic packet filtering mode of operation. Hence, it initially works at the session layer (OSI layer 5) then switches to a dynamic packet filter working at the network layer (OSI Layer 3) after the connection-authentication process is completed as shown in Fig. 13.

What the cutoff proxy does was pointed out. Now, more importantly, we need to discuss what it does *not* do. The cutoff proxy is not a traditional circuit-level proxy that breaks the client/server model for the duration of the connection. There is a direct connection established between the remote client and the protected server behind the firewall. This is not to say that a cutoff proxy does not provide a useful balance between security and performance. At issue with respect to the cutoff proxy are vendors who exaggerate by claiming that their cutoff proxy offers a level of security equivalent to a traditional circuit-level gateway with the added benefit of the performance of a dynamic packet filter.

In clarification, the author believes that all firewall architectures have their place in Internet security. If your security policy requires the authentication of basic services, examination of the three-way handshake, and does not require breaking of the client/server model, the cutoff proxy is a good fit. However, administrators must be fully aware and understand that a cutoff proxy clearly is not equivalent to a circuit-level proxy as the

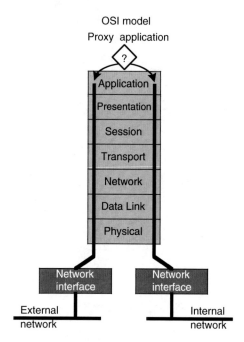

OSI model
Proxy application

Fig. 14 When considering the level of inspection, the air-gap technology offers little more protection than an application-level gateway.

client/server model is not broken for the duration of the connection.

Both the pros and the cons of cutoff proxy considerations are shown in Table 8.

Air Gap

At the time of this writing, the security community has essentially dismissed the merits of air-gap technology as little more than a marketing spin. With air-gap technology, the external client connection causes the

Table 9 Air gap considerations

Pros	Cons
Breaks direct connection to server behind firewall eliminating the risk of an entire class of covert channel attacks	Can have a high negative impact on network performance
Strong application proxy that inspects protocol header lengths can eliminate an entire class of buffer overrun attacks	Vendors must keep up with new protocols; a common complaint of application-level gateway users is the lack of timely response from a vendor to provide application-level gateway support for a new protocol
As with an application-level gateway an air gap can potentially offer a high level of security	Not verified by any recognized third-party testing authority

connection data to be written to a SCSI e-disk. The internal connection then reads this data from the SCSI e-disk. By breaking the direct connection between the client to the server and independently writing to and reading from the SCSI e-disk, the respective vendors believe they have provided a higher level of security and a resulting "air gap." However, when considering the level of inspection, the air-gap technology offers little more protection than an application-level gateway as shown in Fig. 14.

Air-gap vendors claim that although the operation of air gap technology resembles that of the application-level gateway, an important difference is the separation of the content inspection from the "front-end" by the isolation provided by the air gap. This may very well be true for those firewall vendors who implement their firewall on top of a standard commercial OS, but with the existing technology firewall operating on a kernel-hardened OS, there is little distinction. Simply put, vendors who chose to implement kernel-level hardening of the underlying OS utilizing multilevel security (MLS) or containerization methodologies provide no less security than existing air-gap technologies.

Any measurable benefit of air-gap technology has yet to be verified by any recognized third-party testing authority. Further, existing performance of most air-gap-like products falls well behind that obtainable by traditional application-level-gateway-based products. Without a verifiable benefit to the level of security provided, the necessary performance costs are prohibitive for many system administrators.

Both the pros and cons of air gap considerations are shown in Table 9.

Application-Specific Integrated Circuit-Based Firewalls

Looking at existing application-specific integrated circuit (ASIC)-based firewall offerings, the author finds that virtually all are still nothing more than VPN/firewall hybrids. These hybrids take advantage of the fast encryption and decryption capabilities of the ASIC, but provide no more than a dynamic packet filter for most Internet protocols. Although some ASIC-based firewall vendors claim to offer full layer-7 awareness and stateful inspection capabilities, a quick look at the respective vendor's GUI shows that there is no user-configurable functionality above layer 4. Although the technology might be "capable" of layer-7 inspection, the product (as delivered) provides no real administrator-configurable security options above layer 4.

The term *ASIC-based firewall* can be misleading. In fact, for most ASIC-based firewall vendors, only a small subset of firewall operations actually occurs in the ASIC. The majority of firewall functions are really

Table 10 ASIC-based firewall considerations

Pros	Cons
ASIC provides a dramatic improvement in IPSec encryption and decryption speeds	SSL VPN is gaining popularity quickly and existing ASIC-based vendors do not support SSL encryption and decryption; existing technology ASIC-based devices will become obsolete and will need to be replaced with next-generation products
ASIC fast string comparison capability dramatically speeds up packet inspection against known signatures	While this works well up through layer 4, it has not been shown to offer a benefit above layer 4 where the majority of the attacks are existing targeted
ASIC-based firewalls offer the ability to inspect packets at all 7 layers of the OSI model	No existing ASIC-based product offers administrator configurable security options above layer 4 within the respective product's GUI
ASIC firewalls are beginning to expand inspection up from basic protocol anomaly detection at layer 4 to the application layer to afford a higher level of security	Existing ASIC-based firewall inspection methodologies are signature-based and try to block everything that can possibly be wrong in a given packet; more than 100 new vulnerabilities appear on the Internet every month making this a difficult task at best

accomplished in software operating on a typical microprocessor. Although there has been a lot of discussion about adding additional depth of inspection at the application layer in ASIC-based firewalls, to date no vendor has been able to successfully commercialize an ASIC-based firewall that provides the true application awareness and configurable granularity of existing technology application proxy-based firewalls.

Application-specific integrated circuit technology is now finding its way into intrusion detection system (IDS) and intrusion prevention system (IPS) products. The fast string comparison capability of the ASIC can provide added performance to string or signature-based IDS/IPS products. There has been a substantial amount of marketing spin about the eventual marriage of a firewall and IPS embedded within an ASIC, but no vendor has successfully fulfilled on the promise. Furthermore, relying on a system that depends on knowing the signature of a possible vulnerability is a losing battle when more than one hundred new vulnerabilities are released each month.

One of the newer and more interesting ASIC-based firewall products includes an ASIC-based embedded antivirus. By design, an ASIC lends itself well to fast string comparison, which makes the ASIC a natural fit for applications such as antivirus. But do we really need faster antivirus? Typically, antivirus is limited to e-mail and a few extra seconds in the delivery of an e-mail is not necessarily a problem for most users. Therefore, one might question the trade-off in flexibility one has to accept when selecting an ASIC-based product measured against real-world performance.

Internet security standards are in a constant state of flux. Hence, ASIC designs must be left programmable or "soft" enough that the full speed of an ASIC cannot actually be unleashed. Application-specific integrated circuit technology has clearly delivered the best performing VPN products in today's security marketplace. By design, IPsec encryption and decryption algorithms perform better in hardware than in software. Some of these ASIC or purpose-built IPsec accelerators are finding their way into firewall products that offer more than layer-4 packet filtering. Administrators get the best of worlds: the blazing speed of IPsec VPN and the added security of a real application-proxy firewall.

Both the pros and cons of ASIC-based firewall considerations are shown in Table 10.

Intrusion Prevention Systems

The past 3 years has seen a rush of products to the market that claimed to offer new and exciting "intrusion prevention" capabilities. Intrusion-prevention-product vendors' claims are many and include the following:

1. Interpreting the intent of data contained in the application payload
2. Providing application level analysis and verification
3. Understanding enough of the protocol to make informed decisions without the overhead of implementing a client/server model as is done with application proxies
4. Utilizing pattern matching, heuristics, statistics, and behavioral patterns to detect attacks and thereby offer maximum attack prevention capability

Unfortunately many IPSs are still at best "born-again" intrusion detection systems with the ability to drop, block, or reset a connection when it senses something malicious. Nearly all IPS systems depend on a library of signatures of malicious activity or known vulnerabilities to compare to packets as they cross the wire. The real value of the IPS is the accuracy and timeliness of the signature database of known vulnerabilities. With BugTraq, Xforce, and others posting well over 100 new vulnerabilities each month in commercial and open-

Ethics–
Fuzzy

Table 11 IPS considerations

Pros	Cons
Provide application level analysis and verification	Existing IPS product inspection methodologies are primarily signaturebased and try to block everything that can possibly be wrong in a given packet. More than 100 new vulnerabilities appear on the Internet every month making this a difficult task
IPS is leading edge and can include heuristics, statistics, and behavioral patterns in making determinations regarding decisions to block or allow specific traffic	Network security is a place for leading-edge, not bleeding-edge solutions. The use of heuristics, statistics, and behavioral patterns are great ideas but lack the track record to be field proven as a reliable decision point to defend a network
	It is not rocket science. As the list of known signatures grows, IPS performance slows. The rate of newly discovered known bad things on the Internet is ever accelerating and, over time, could render the use of signature-based IPS unusable

source applications and operating systems, the chances of something being missed by the IPS vendor are quite high. The IPS methodology places the administrator in the middle of an arms race between the malicious hacker community (developing exploits) and the IPS vendor's technical staff (developing signatures).

The author is still of the opinion that signature-based IPS systems that rely explicitly on the knowledge of all possible vulnerabilities expose the user to unnecessary risk. Using a modern application layer firewall with a well thought-out security policy and patching all servers that are publicly accessible from the Internet could ultimately afford better protection.

Alternate IPS approaches, especially host-based approaches that rely upon heuristics, statistics, and behavioral patterns, still show promise but need to develop more of a track record for success before they should be relied upon as a primary security device. Therefore, at this point in time, the author considers IPS to be a technology to complement an existing conventional network security infrastructure, not replace it.

Both the pros and cons of IPS considerations are shown in Table 11.

Deep Packet Inspection

Deep-packet-inspection-based firewalls are still, in 2006, doing little more than comparing old outdated vulnerability signatures against traffic flow. Similar to the early days of antivirus products, someone must get hacked before the vulnerability shows up on radar. The user or administrator then must wait for the vendor to research and define a signature so they can download it to begin to have some degree of risk mitigation from the threat.

The best description I have heard of deep packet inspection is standing in front of a fire house running at full blast while trying to grab cups of water that are

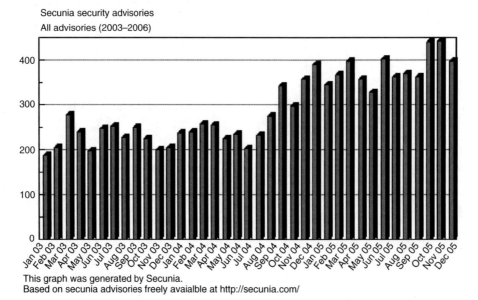

Secunia security advisories
All advisories (2003–2006)

This graph was generated by Secunia.
Based on secunia advisories freely avaialble at http://secunia.com/

Fig. 15 Secunia security advisories.

known to be bad before the stream of oncoming water has a chance to pass by you.

Although I believe this signature-based model can afford a faster response from a vendor to support a new protocol or afford fast support of additional granularity in the application controls as applications mature, I also feel that a signature-based-only model is dangerous from a security perspective. This methodology carries all of the legacy issues seen in the flawed antivirus signature-based approach. Because white space is tolerated by most applications, a little white space in the data before or after a command could logically cause the signature to fail to match the data. The hacker would then get to execute a command that the deep packet inspection firewall was supposed to prevent.

With Secunia reporting up to 100 new vulnerabilities a week as shown in Fig. 15 and vendors trying to keep up with developing new signatures to match the reported vulnerabilities, managing updates for the firewall signature database could become a daunting task.

Signature-based deep packet inspection effectively puts you in an arms race against an enemy with tens of thousands of more experienced people than you have within your organization.

Last, scalability must be considered. How long will it take to exhaust the processor resources of today's deep packet inspection firewall? In analyzing the literature

for one popular deep packet inspection firewall, it states that the initial product release will provide for 250 signatures and the total firewall signature capacity is stated at only 600 signatures. Because of the vulnerabilities reported by Gartner, there would effectively be no room for new signatures in a matter of weeks. Furthermore, the popular open-source IDS, Snort, today has nearly 4000 signatures for malicious packets. Today's deep packet inspection firewalls ship with a signature database of only 250 signatures. What about the other 3750 signatures known to define malicious packets? Deep packet inspection firewalls effectively allow a third party with no vested interest in your organization to determine or prioritize which attacks to protect you from and which attacks to not impede.

The signature-based model used by the majority of deep packet inspection offerings is simply the wrong approach. Best practices permit only those packets you define within your policy to enter or exit your network. This is a time-proven methodology and the bottom line is that it is a good common-sense approach to network security.

The lack of protocol anomaly detection is the Achilles' heel of deep packet inspection. A vendor's approach to protocol anomaly detection reveals a great deal about their basic design philosophy and the capabilities of their network security products as shown in

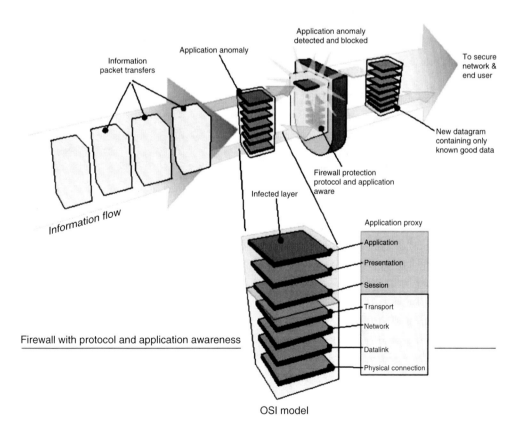

Fig. 16 Vendor's approach to protocol anomaly detection reveals a great deal about their basic design philosophy and the capabilities of their network security products.

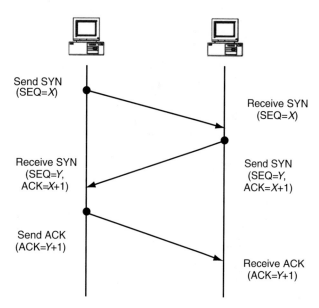

Send SYN
(SEQ=*X*)

Receive SYN
(SEQ=*X*)

Receive SYN
(SEQ=*Y*,
ACK=*X*+1)

Send SYN
(SEQ=*Y*,
ACK=*X*+1)

Send ACK
(ACK=*Y*+1)

Receive ACK
(ACK=*Y*+1)

Fig. 17 The RFC-mandated TCP three-wayhandshake is fully validated for each and every connection.

Fig. 16. The tried-and-true practice with strong application-proxy firewalls is to allow only the packets that are known to be "good" and to deny everything else. Because most protocols used on the Internet are standards-based, the best approach is to design the application proxy to be fully protocol-aware, and to use the standards as the basis for deciding whether to admit or deny a packet. Only packets that demonstrably conform to the standard are admitted; all others are denied.

Deep packet inspection firewalls, like most stateful inspection firewalls and many IDS and intrusion detection and prevention (IDP) products, take the opposite approach. Rather than focusing on recognizing and accepting only good packets, they try to find—and then deny—only the "bad" packets. Such devices are vulnerable because they require updates whenever a new and more creative form of "bad" is unleashed on the Internet. Sometimes, especially with ASIC vendors who implement these packet rules in silicon, it is impossible to make these changes at all without replacing the ASIC itself.

Another problem with the "find and deny the bad" methodology is its intrinsic inefficiency. The list of potentially "bad" things to test for will always be much greater than the pre-defined and standardized list of "good" things.

One can, of course, argue that the "find and deny the bad" approach provides additional information about the nature of the attack, and the opportunity to trigger a specific rule and associated alert. However, it is unclear how this really benefits the network administrator. If the attack is denied because it falls outside the realm of "the good," does the administrator really care which attack methodology was being employed? As many

have seen with IDS, an administrator in a busy network may be distracted or overwhelmed by useless noise generated by failed attacks.

The simplified path of a packet traversing a strong application proxy is as follows:

1. The new packet arrives at the external interface.

    Layer-4 data is tested to validate that the IP source and destination, as well as service ports, are acceptable to the security policy of the firewall. Up to this point, the operation of the application proxy is similar to that of stateful packet filtering. For the most part, the similarities end here.

    The RFC-mandated TCP three-wayhandshake (http://www.faqs.org/rfcs/rfc793.html) is fully validated for each and every connection as shown in Fig. 17.

    If the three-way handshake is not properly completed, the connection is immediately closed before any attempt is made to establish a connection to the protected server. Among other benefits, this approach effectively eliminates any possibility of SYN flooding a protected server.

    This is where vital differences become apparent. Many stateful inspection firewalls do not validate the three-way handshake to achieve higher performance and packet throughput. In the author's opinion, this approach is dangerous and ill-conceived because it could allow malicious packets with a forged IP address to sneak past the stateful firewall.

    More troubling is the "fast path" mode of operation employed by some stateful inspection firewall vendors. When "fast path" is engaged, the firewall inspects only those packets in which the SYN flag is set. This is extremely dangerous. Given the availability of sophisticated and easy-to-use hacking tools online, any 13-year-old with a modem and a little spare time can exploit this weakness and penetrate the fast-path-mode firewall simply by avoiding the use of SYN-flagged packets. The result: malicious packets pass directly through the firewall without ever being inspected. An informed network administrator is unlikely to open this gaping hole in his or her security infrastructure to gain the marginal increase in throughput provided by fast path.

2. For each "good" packet, a new empty datagram is created on the internal side of the firewall.

    Creating a brand new datagram completely eliminates the possibility that an attacker could hide malicious data in any unused protocol headers or, for that matter, in any unused flags or other datagram fields. This methodology—part of the core application proxy functionality found within strong application proxy firewalls—effectively eliminates an entire class of covert channel attacks.

    Unfortunately, this capability is not available in

any stateful inspection firewall. Instead, stateful inspection firewalls allow attackers to make a direct connection to the server, which is supposedly being protected behind the firewall.

3. Protocol anomaly testing is performed on the packet to validate that all protocol headers are within clearly defined protocol specifications.

This is not rocket science, although there is some elegant engineering needed to do this quickly and efficiently. Because Internet protocols are based on published standards, the application proxy uses these as the basis for defining what is acceptable and denies the rest.

Stateful inspection firewall vendors have tried to address this requirement by adding limited filtering capabilities intended to identify attack-related protocol anomalies and then deny these "bad" packets. Unfortunately, this approach is inherently flawed.

Most stateful inspection firewalls employ a keyword-like filtering methodology. Rather than using the RFC-defined standards to validate and accept good packets (our "virtue is its own reward" approach), stateful inspection firewalls typically filter for "bad" keywords in the application payload. By now, the problem with this approach should be evident. There will always be new "bad" things created by malicious users. Detecting and accepting only those packets that adhere to RFC standards is a more efficient and—in this writer's opinion—a far more elegant solution.

Consider the SMTP protocol as an example. A strong application proxy applies the RFC 821 standard for the format of ARPA Internet text messages (http://www.faqs.org/rfcs/rfc821.html) and RFC 822 simple mail transfer protocol (http://www.faqs.org/rfcs/rfc822.html) standards to validate protocol adherence. It also lets you define "goodness" using another dozen or so protocol- and application-related data points within the SMTP packet exchange. This enables an administrator to minimize or eliminate the risk of many security issues that commonly plague SMTP applications on the Internet today, such as:

- Worms and virus attacks
- Mail relay attacks
- Mime attacks
- SPAM attacks
- Buffer overflow attacks
- Address spoofing attacks
- Covert channel attacksIn contrast, a stateful inspection firewall must compare each packet to the pre-defined signatures of hundreds of known SMTP exploits—a list that is constantly growing and changing. This places the security professional in a virtual "arms race" with the entire hacker community. You will never be able completely filter your way to a secure network; it is an insurmountable task.

Another element of risk with filter-based approaches is vulnerability. Attackers frequently "fool" the filter simply by adding white space between the malicious commands. Not recognizing the command, the firewall passes the packet to the "protected" application, which will then disregard the white spaces and process the commands. As with any filter, if the signature does not explicitly match the packet, the packet will be allowed. No network administrator can confidently rely on such a vulnerable technology.

With the strong application proxy approach, virtually all SMTP-related attacks could be mitigated more effectively and efficiently than is possible with the filtering approach used by stateful inspection vendors.

4. The application proxy applies the (very granular) command-level controls and validates these against the permission level of the user.

The application proxy approach provides the ultimate level of application awareness and control. Administrators have the granularity of control needed to determine exactly what kind of access is available to each user. This capability is nonexistent in the implementation of most stateful inspection firewalls.

It is difficult or impossible to validate claims made by many stateful inspection firewall vendors that they provide meaningful application-level security. As we have seen, the "find and deny the bad" filter-based approaches are inefficient and vulnerable. They simply do not provide the same level of security as a strong application proxy firewall.

5. After the packet has been recognized as protocol-compliant and the application-level commands validated against the security policy for that user, the permitted content is copied to the new datagram on the internal side of the firewall.

The application proxy breaks the client/server connection, effectively removing any direct link between the attacker and the protected server. By copying and forwarding only "good" contents, the application proxy firewall can eliminate virtually all protocol level and covert channel attacks.

Stateful inspection firewalls do not break the client/server connection; hence, the attacker can establish a direct connection to the protected server if an attack is successful. Because all protection requires the administrator to update the list of "bad" keywords and signatures, there is no integral protection to new protocol level attacks. At best, protection is only afforded to known attacks through inefficient filtering techniques.

A strong application proxy elevates the art of

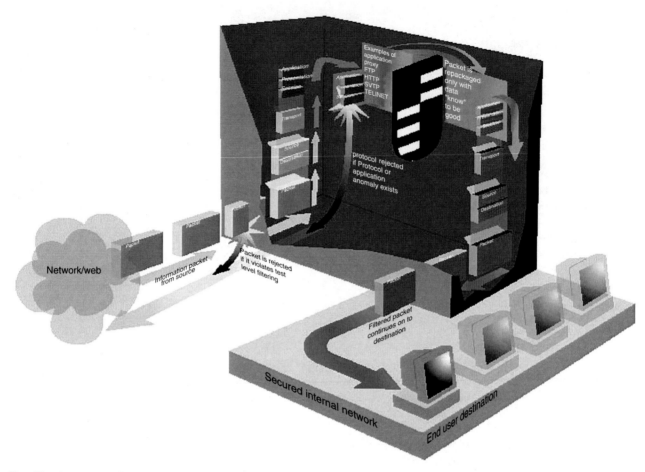

Fig. 18 A strong application proxy elevates the art of protocol and application awareness to the highest possible level.

protocol and application awareness to the highest possible level as shown in Fig. 18.

Unified Threat Management

One of the latest developments in firewalling is the UTM appliance.

IDC defines universal threat management security appliances as products that unify and integrate multiple security features integrated onto a single hardware platform. Qualification for inclusion within this category requires network firewall capabilities, network IDP, and gateway antivirus (AV) functionality. All of these security features do not need to be utilized concurrently, but need to exist in the product.

Table 12 Disparity in UTM products

	Vendor A	**Vendor B**
Operating system (OS)	Kernel-hardened OS with a strict compartmentalization approach to eliminate vulnerabilities	Patched *nix like OS. Vendor has a long history of OS vulnerabilities
Antivirus	Best of breed market leading product with ability to block over 100,000 viruses	Vendors own antivirus solution containing only 66 virus signatures
Antispam	Best of breed full featured integrated antispam solution	Single antispam signature available as an option
URL filtering	Integrated award-winning web content filtering	No on the box URL filtering
Intrusion detection and prevention (IDP) capability	Full complement of layer-7 application defenses including protocol anomaly detection and controls. Real-time user configurable alerts and user-definable actions	Layer 7 filtering through signatures available as an option

Ethics–
Fuzzy

The UTM segment of the firewall market is the fastest growing segment and has resulted in a large number of entries into the market that can, at best, be called "premature" entries.

The author regards a UTM product offering as one that also brings together best-of-breed technologies. Unfortunately for the consumer, for a vast number of product entries into this market, vendors are falling far short of utilizing best-of-breed technologies. Many vendors, to both enter the market quickly and to increase product margins, have chosen to build basic UTM functionality themselves or to use rudimentary open-source solutions (see Table 12).

When it comes to UTM appliances, caveat emptor certainly applies. I will offer six simple questions to help you in your analysis of any UTM product:

1. Is the OS hardened to the kernel level utilizing type enforcement or MLS?
2. Does the vendor have a record of zero vulnerability in the product and the underlying OS?
3. Is the on box antivirus solution a best-of-breed solution from a recognized leader?
4. Is the on the box antispam solution a best-of-breed solution from a recognized leader?
5. Is the on the box URL filter solution a best-of-breed solution from a recognized leader?
6. Is the on the box IPS based on the known good security model?

A "NO" answer to any of the preceding questions should immediately raise a red flag about the vendor's offering. Let me elaborate on why these six questions are so important.

1. To reduce costs, many vendors are simply utilizing an off-the-shelf commercial OS or a patched open-source OS, either of which comes with inherent risks. Why hack the firewall when you can simply hack the underlying OS and create a policy that allows you to do whatever you wish?
2. Would you buy a new car if you knew in advance that the product had been the subject of a few dozen safety recalls in the past year or so? It is just as important to look at the record of vulnerabilities from security product vendors at reporting websites such as CERT.
3. To reduce costs and to get to the market quickly, some vendors are utilizing sub-standard homegrown antivirus solutions or inadequate signature-based-only open-source solutions.

4. To reduce costs and to get to the market quickly, some vendors are utilizing sub-standard antispam solutions that can be little more than a handful of signatures that produce more false positives than they tend to catch real spam. Furthermore, some vendors claim to offer antispam capabilities, but it is an off-the-box option that requires additional hardware and licensing expenses.
5. URL filtering is quickly becoming a first line of defense in the battle against the zero-hour threat. Many UTM vendors are offering what ranges from giving the user the ability to write their own URL list for those that the administrator desires to block, to a static list of old outdated URLs from a substandard URL filtering product. Relatively few UTM appliances use best-of-breed URL filtering capabilities on-box.
6. Spam has grown from a simple menace to a complicated threat in a very short time. It is imperative to reduce risk by reducing spam with a comprehensive best-of-breed antispam capability onboard the UTM appliance. Again, many UTM product offerings fall short in handling antispam by the reliance on inadequate signatures or moving the antispam duties off-board and requiring additional hardware and software licensing.

The author believes that the high growth rate of the UTM firewall segment will continue for the foreseeable future. The UTM firewall fills a long-empty void in the marketplace, specifically for the small to medium enterprise that needs the ease of use and lower total cost of ownership that can be afforded by a properly architected UTM appliance.

ACKNOWLEDGMENT

This, the fourth edition of the firewall architectures text, is based on a number of related white papers I have written numerous books, white papers, presentations, vendor literature, and several Usenet news group discussions I have read or participated in throughout my career. Any failure to cite any individual for anything that in any way resembles a previous work is unintentional.

REFERENCE

1. Ranum, M.J. *The Grandfather of Firewalls. Firewall Wizard Mailing List.* October 2000.

Ethics–
Fuzzy

Fuzzy Set Theory

Donald Kraft
Department of Computer Science, U.S. Air Force Academy, Colorado Springs, Colorado, U.S.A.

Gloria Bordogna
Italian National Research Council, Institute for the Dynamics of Environmental Processes, Dalmine, Italy

Gabriella Pasi
Department of Informatics, Systems and Communication, University of Studies of Milano Bicocca, Milan, Italy

Abstract

This entry presents a definition of fuzzy set theory and an overview of some applications to model flexible information retrieval systems. The entry focuses on a description of fuzzy indexing procedures defined to represent the varying significance of terms in synthesizing the documents' contents, the representation of structured documents so as to model a subjective view of document content, the definition of flexible query languages that allow the expression of soft selection conditions, and fuzzy associative retrieval mechanisms to model fuzzy pseudothesauri, fuzzy ontologies, and fuzzy categorizations of documents.

INTRODUCTION

The objective of this entry is to provide an overview of some applications of fuzzy set theory to design flexible information retrieval systems (IRSs). The term "flexible" implies that we consider IRSs that can represent and manage the uncertainty, vagueness, and subjectivity, which are characteristic of the process of information searching and retrieval.

Consider the notions that index terms offer only an approximate and incomplete view of a document's content, that query languages (such as those incorporating Boolean logic) do not usually allow users to express vague requirements for specifying selection conditions that are tolerant to imprecision, and that a document's relevance to the user's query is a subjective and an imprecise notion. We show how imprecision, vagueness, and subjectivity can be managed within the formal framework of fuzzy set theory. This means that retrieval mechanisms capable of both modeling human subjectivity and of estimating the partial relevance of documents to a user's needs can be designed.

The retrieval process is introduced as a fuzzy multicriteria decision-making (MCDM) activity in the presence of vagueness. Documents constitute the set of the alternatives described using weighted index terms. The query specifies a set of soft constraints on the document representations that are created via indexing. The retrieval mechanism performs a decision analysis in the presence of imprecision to rank the documents on the basis of their partial satisfaction of the soft constraints.

This entry is organized as follows: in the section on "Current Trends in IR," the trends and key issues in IR are discussed. In the section on "Fuzzy Retrieval Models," an overview of the basic notions of fuzzy set theory to model flexible IRSs is presented. In the section on "Fuzzy Document Indexing," a description of the traditional fuzzy document representation is first illustrated. In addition, both a fuzzy representation of documents structured into logical sections that can be adapted to the subjective needs of a user and a fuzzy representation of HTML documents are presented. In the section on "Flexible Querying," a description of how the Boolean query language of IR can be extended so as to make it flexible and suitable to express soft constraints by capturing the vagueness of the user needs is presented. Both numeric and linguistic selection conditions are introduced to qualify a term's importance, and it is shown how linguistic quantifiers are defined to specify soft aggregation operators of query terms. In the section on "Fuzzy Associative Mechanisms," a description of how fuzzy sets can serve to define associative mechanisms to expand the functionalities of IRSs is presented. The focus of research trends in IR is on the semantic web, i.e., the capability to represent concepts and to model their semantic relationships: fuzzy sets provide notions that can be applied to this purpose allowing to model either fuzzy pseudothesauri or fuzzy ontologies and to build fuzzy categorizations of documents by fuzzy clustering techniques. In the section on "Fuzzy Performance Measures," fuzzy performance measures for IRSs are introduced and the conclusion summarizes the main contents of this entry.

Encyclopedia of Information Systems and Technology, DOI: 10.1081/E-EIST-120043233

Ethics–
Fuzzy

CURRENT TRENDS IN IR

In this section the trends and the key issues in IR are introduced.

Some of the trends in IR research run the gamut in terms of expanding the discipline both to incorporate the latest technologies and to cope with novel necessities. In terms of novel necessities, with the diffusion of the Internet and the heterogeneous characteristics of users of search engines, which can be regarded as the new frontier of IR, a new central issue has arisen, generally known as the semantic web. It mainly consists in expanding IRSs with the capability to represent and manage the semantics of both user requests and documents so as to be able to account for user and document contexts. This need becomes urgent with cross-language retrieval, which consists in expressing queries in one language, and retrieving documents written in another language, which is what commonly happens when submitting queries to search engines. Cross-language retrieval implies not only new works on text processing, e.g., stemming conducted on a variety of languages, new models of IR such as the development of language models, but also the ability to match terms in distinct languages at a conceptual level, by modeling their meaning.

Another research trend of IR is motivated by the need to manage multimedia collections with nonprint audio elements such as sound, music, and voice, and video elements such as images, pictures, movies, and animation. Retrieval of such elements can include consideration of both metadata and content-based retrieval techniques. The definition of new IRSs capable to efficiently extract content indexes from multimedia documents, and to effectively retrieve documents by similarity or proximity to a query by example so as to fill the semantic gap existing between low-level syntactic index matching and the semantics of multimedia document and query are still to come.

In addition, modern computing technology, including storage media, distributed and parallel processing architectures, and improved algorithms for text processing and for retrieval, has an effect on IRSs. For example, improved string searching algorithms have improved the efficiency of search engines. Improved computer networks have made the Internet and the World Wide Web a possibility. Intelligent agents can improve retrieval in terms of attempting to customize and personalize it for individual users. Moreover, great improvements have been made in retrieval systems interfaces based on human–computer interface research.

These novel research trends in IR are faced by turning to technologies such as natural language processing, image processing, language models, artificial intelligence, and automatic learning.

Also, fuzzy set theory can play a crucial role to define novel solutions to these research issues since it provides suitable means to cope with the needs of the semantic web,[1,2] e.g., to model the semantic of linguistic terms so as to reflect their vagueness and subjectivity and to compute degrees of similarity, generalization, and specialization between their meanings.

Key Issues in IR

Modeling the concept of relevance in IR is certainly a key issue, perhaps the most difficult one, and no doubt the most important one. What makes a document relevant to a given user is still not fully understood, specifically when one goes beyond topicality (i.e., the matching of the topics of the query with the topics of the document). Of course, this leads to the realization that relevance is gradual and subjective.

A second key issue is the representation of the documents in a collection, as well as the representation of users' information needs, especially for the purpose of matching documents to the queries at a "semantic" level. This implies introducing incompleteness, approximation, and managing vagueness and imprecision.

Finally, a key issue is how to evaluate properly an IRS's performance. Here, too, one sees imprecision.

IMPRECISION, VAGUENESS, UNCERTAINTY, AND INCONSISTENCY IN IR

Very often the terms imprecision, vagueness, uncertainty, and inconsistency are used as synonymous concepts. Nevertheless, when they are referred to qualify a characteristic of the information they have a distinct meaning.[3] Since IR has to do with information, understanding the different meanings of imprecision, vagueness, uncertainty, and inconsistency allows to better understanding the perspectives of the distinct IR models defined in the literature.

Vagueness and imprecision are related to the representation of the information content of a proposition. For example, in the information request, "find *recent* scientific chapters dealing with the *early* stage of infectious diseases by HIV," the terms *recent* and *early* specify vague values of the publication date and of the temporal evolution of the disease, respectively. The publication date and the phase of an infectious disease are usually expressed as numeric values; their linguistic characterization has a coarser granularity with respect to their numeric characterization. Linguistic values are defined by terms with semantics compatible with several numeric values on the scale upon which the numeric information is defined. Imprecision is just a case-limit of vagueness, since imprecise values have a full

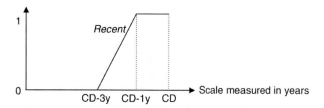

Fig. 1 Semantics of the term "recent" referring to the publication date of a scientific chapter. CD, current date; y, years.

compatibility with a subset of values of the numeric reference scale.

There are several ways to represent imprecise and vague concepts, indirectly, by defining similarity or proximity relationships between each pair of imprecise and vague concepts.

If we regard a document as an imprecise or vague concept, i.e., as bearing a vague content, a numeric value computed by a similarity measure can be used to express the closeness of any two pairs of documents. This is the way of dealing with the imprecise and vague document and query contents in the vector space model of IR. In this context, the documents and the query are represented as points in a vector space of terms and the distances between the query and the documents points are used to quantify their similarity.

Another way to represent vague and imprecise concepts is by means of the notion of fuzzy set. The notion of a fuzzy set is an extension to normal set theory.[4] A set is simply a collection of objects. A fuzzy set (more properly called a fuzzy subset) is a subset of a given universe of objects, where the membership in the fuzzy set is not definite. For example, consider the idea of a person being middle-aged. If a person's age is 39, one can consider the imprecision of that person being in the set of middle-aged people. The membership function, μ, is a number in the interval [0, 1] that represents the degree to which that person belongs to that set. Thus, the terms *recent* and *early* can be defined as fuzzy subsets, with the membership functions interpreted as compatibility functions of the meaning of the terms with respect to the numeric values of the reference (base) variable. In Fig. 1, the compatibility function of the term *recent* is presented with the numeric values of the timescale measured in years. Note that here a chapter that has a publication date of the current year or 1 year previous is perfectly *recent*; however, the extent to which a chapter remains *recent* declines steadily over the next 2 years until chapters older than 3 years have no sense of being *recent*.

In the next sections we will see how the notion of fuzzy set has been used in the IR context to represent the vague concepts expressed in a flexible query for specifying soft selection conditions of the documents.

Uncertainty is related to the truth of a proposition, intended as the conformity of the information carried by the proposition with the considered reality. Linguistic expressions such as "probably" and "it is possible that" can be used to declare a partial lack of knowledge about the truth of the stated information.

Further, there are cases in which information is affected by both uncertainty and imprecision or vagueness. For example, consider the proposition "probably document d is relevant to query q." Possibility theory,[5,6] together with the concept of a linguistic variable defined within fuzzy set theory,[7] provides a unifying formal framework to formalize the management of imprecise, vague, and uncertain information.[8]

However, the same information content can be expressed by choosing a trade-off between the vagueness and the uncertainty embedded in a proposition. For example, one can express the content of the previous proposition by a new one "document d is more or less relevant to query q." In this latter proposition, the uncertain term *probably* has been eliminated, but the specificity of the vague term *relevant* has been reduced. In fact, the term *more or less relevant* is less specific than the term *relevant*. A dual representation can eliminate imprecision and augment the uncertainty, like in the expression "it is *not completely probable* that document d fully satisfies the query q."

One way to model IR is to regard it as an uncertain problem.[9]

On the basis of what has been said about the trade-off between uncertainty and vagueness to express the same information content, there are two alternative ways to model the IR activity. One possibility is to model the query evaluation mechanism as an uncertain decision process. Here the concept of relevance is considered binary (crisp), and the query evaluation mechanism computes the probability of relevance of a document *d* to a query *q*. Such an approach, which does model the uncertainty of the retrieval process, has been introduced and developed by probabilistic IR models.[10–12] Another possibility is to interpret the query as the specification of soft "elastic" constraints that the representation of a document can satisfy to an extent, and to consider the term *relevant* as a gradual (vague) concept. This is the approach adopted in fuzzy IR models.[9,13] In this latter case, the decision process performed by the query evaluation mechanism computes the degree of satisfaction of the query by the representation of each document. This satisfaction degree, called the retrieval status value (RSV), is considered as an estimate of the degree of relevance (or is at least proportional to the relevance) of a given document with respect to a given user query. An RSV of 1 implies maximum relevance; an RSV value of 0 implies absolutely no relevance. And, an RSV value in the interval [0, 1] implies an intermediate level or degree of relevance. For example, an RSV value of 0.5 could imply an average degree of relevance.

Inconsistency comes from the simultaneous presence of contradictory information about the same reality. An example of inconsistency can be observed when submitting the same query to several IRSs that adopt different representations of documents and produce different results. This is actually very common and often occurs when searching for information over the Internet using different search engines. To solve this kind of inconsistency, some fusion strategies can be applied to the ranked lists each search engine produces. In fact, this is what metasearch engines do.[14,15]

In this entry, we analyze the representation and management of vagueness as a means of improving the flexibility of IRSs. In particular, we will focus on the modeling of vagueness and in fuzzy IR models.

The document representation based on a selection of index terms is invariably incomplete. When synthesizing the content of a text manually by asking an expert to select a set of index terms, one introduces subjectivity in the representation. However, automatic full-text indexing introduces imprecision since the terms are not all fully significant in characterizing a document's content. However, these terms can have a partial significance that might also depend on the context in which they appear, i.e., which document component.

In the query formulation, users often only have a vague idea of the information for which they are looking. Users therefore find it difficult to translate their needs into a precise request using a formal query language such as one employing Boolean logic.

A flexible IRS should be capable of providing more detailed and rich representations of documents and of interpreting vague queries in order to perform retrieval processes that tolerate, and account for, this vagueness.

FUZZY RETRIEVAL MODELS

Fuzzy retrieval models have been defined in order to reduce the imprecision that characterizes the Boolean indexing process, to represent the user's vagueness in queries, and to deal with discriminated answers estimating the partial relevance of the documents with respect to queries. Extended Boolean models based on fuzzy set theory have been defined to deal with one or more of these aspects.[16–24] Surveys of fuzzy extensions for IRSs and of fuzzy generalizations of the Boolean retrieval model can be found in Kraft et al.[9] and Bordogna and Pasi.[13]

Fuzzy "knowledge-based" models[25,26] and fuzzy associative mechanisms[27–30] have been defined to cope with the incompleteness that characterizes either the representation of documents or the users' queries. Miyamoto[31] illustrates a wide range of methods to generate fuzzy associative mechanisms.

It has been speculated that Boolean logic is passé, out of vogue. Yet, researchers have employed p-norms in the vector space model or Bayesian inference nets in the probabilistic model to incorporate Boolean logic into those models. In addition, the use of Boolean logic to separate a collection of records into two disjoint classes has been considered, e.g., using the one-clause-at-a time (OCAT) methodology.[32] Moreover, even now retrieval systems such as Dialog and Web search engines such as Google allow for Boolean connectives. It should come as no surprise, therefore, to see extensions of Boolean logic based upon fuzzy set theory for IR.

It is noteworthy that most of the research on fuzzy retrieval has been conducted by a relatively few scholars. Moreover, that research has focused upon theoretical models, focusing primarily upon text retrieval, so that precious little testing has to date been conducted.

Extensions of Fuzzy Boolean Retrieval Models

The fuzzy retrieval models have been defined as generalizations of the classical Boolean model. These allow one to extend existing Boolean IRSs without having to redesign them. This was first motivated by the need to be able to produce proper answers in response to the queries. In essence, the classical Boolean IRSs apply an exact match between a Boolean query and the representation of each document. This document representation is defined as a set of index terms. These systems partition the collection of documents into two sets, the retrieved documents and the rejected (nonretrieved) ones. As a consequence of this crisp behavior, these systems are liable to reject useful items as a result of too restrictive queries, as well as to retrieve useless material in reply to queries.[33]

The softening of the retrieval activity in order to rank the retrieved items in decreasing order of their relevance to a user query can greatly improve the effectiveness of such systems. This objective has been approached by extending the Boolean models at different levels. We shall consider those levels in order to model retrieval using an MCDM model that allows the expression of the users' queries as soft constraints and produce discriminated answers.

Fuzzy techniques for documents' indexing

The aim here is to provide more specific and exhaustive representations of each document's information content. This means improving these representations beyond those generated by existing indexing mechanisms. We shall introduce the fuzzy interpretation of a weighted document representation and then later introduce a fuzzy representation of documents structured in logical sections that can be adapted to a user that has subjective criteria for interpreting the content of documents.[17] In this same vein, we shall describe an indexing procedure for HTML documents.[34]

Definition of flexible query languages

The objective here is to define query languages that are more expressive and natural than classical Boolean logic. This is done in order to capture the vagueness of user needs as well as to simplify user–system interaction. This has been pursued with two different approaches. First, there has been work on the definition of soft selection criteria (soft constraints), which allow the specification of the different importance of the search terms. Query languages based on numeric query term weights with different semantics have been first proposed as an aid to define more expressive selection criteria.[18,21,22,24,35] An evolution of these approaches has been defined that introduces linguistic query weights, specified by fuzzy sets such as *important* or *very important*, in order to express the different vague importance of the query terms.[36] Second, there is the approach of introducing soft aggregation operators for the selection criteria, characterized by a parametric behavior, which can be set between the two extremes of intersection (AND) and union (OR) as adopted in Boolean logic. Boolean query languages have been extended and generalized by defining aggregation operators as linguistic quantifiers such as *at least k* or *about k.*[16]

As we shall see, the incorporation of weighted document representations in a Boolean IRS is a sufficient condition to improve the system via a ranking capability. As a consequence of this extension, the exact matching that is employed by a classical Boolean IRS is softened using a partial matching mechanism that evaluates the degree of satisfaction of a user's query for each document. This degree of satisfaction is the RSV that is used for ranking.

Fuzzy Associative Mechanisms

These associative mechanisms allow to automatically generate fuzzy pseudothesauri, fuzzy ontologies, and fuzzy clustering techniques to serve three distinct but compatible purposes. First, fuzzy pseudothesauri and fuzzy ontologies can be used to contextualize the search by expanding the set of index terms of documents to include additional terms by taking into account their varying significance in representing the topics dealt with in the documents. The degree of significance of these associated terms depends on the strength of the associations with a document's original descriptors. Second, an alternative use of fuzzy pseudothesauri and fuzzy ontologies is to expand the query with related terms by

taking into account their varying importance in representing the concepts of interest. The importance of an additional term depends on its strength of association with the search terms in the original query. Third, fuzzy clustering techniques, where each document can be placed within several clusters with a given strength of belonging to each cluster, can be used to expand the set of the documents retrieved in response to a query. Documents associated with retrieved documents, i.e., in the same cluster, can be retrieved. The degree of association of a document with the retrieved documents does influence its RSV. Another application of fuzzy clustering in IR is that of providing an alternative way, with respect to the usual ranked list, of presenting the results of a search.

FUZZY DOCUMENT INDEXING

In order to increase the effectiveness of IRSs, the indexing process plays a crucial role. In fact, it is not sufficient to provide IRSs with powerful query languages or sophisticated retrieval mechanisms to achieve effective results if the representation of documents oversimplifies their information content.

Vector Space, Probabilistic, and Generalized Boolean Indexing

The vector space model and the probabilistic models generally adopt a weighted document representation, which has improved the Boolean document representation by allowing the association of a numeric weight with each index term.[10,33] The automatic computation of the index term weights is based on the occurrences count of a term in the document and in the whole archive.[37–39] In this case, the indexing mechanism computes for each document d and each term t a numeric value by means of a function F. An example of F, which has the index term weight increasing with the frequency of term t in document d but decreasing with the frequency of the term in all the documents of the archive, is given by

$$F(d,t) = tf_{dt} \times g(\text{IDF}_t) \tag{1}$$

where

- tf_{dt} is a normalized term frequency, which can be defined as

$$= tf_{dt} = \frac{\text{OCC}_{dt}}{\text{MAXOCC}_d};$$

- OCC_{dt} is the number of occurrences of t in d;

- MAXOCC$_d$ is the number of occurrences of the most frequent term in d;
- IDF$_t$ is an inverse document frequency, which can be defined as IDF_t

$$IDF_t = \log \frac{N}{NDOC_t};$$

- N is the total number of documents in the archive;
- NDOC$_t$ is the number of documents indexed by t; and
- g is a normalizing function.

The computation of IDF$_t$ is particularly costly in the case of large collections that are updated online.

The definition of such a function F is based on a quantitative analysis of the text, which makes it possible to model the qualitative concept of significance of a term in describing the information carried by the text. The adoption of weighted indexes allows for an estimate of the relevance, or of the probability of relevance, of documents to a query.[10,33]

Based on such an indexing function, and by incorporating Boolean logic into the query, the first fuzzy interpretation of an extended Boolean model has been to adopt a weighted document representation and to interpret it as a fuzzy set of terms.[40] From a mathematical point of view, this is a quite natural extension: the concept of the significance of index terms in describing the information content of a document can then be naturally described by adopting the function F, such as the one defined by Zadeh[5] as the membership function of the fuzzy set representing a document's being in the subset of concepts represented by the term in question. Formally, a document is represented as a fuzzy set of terms: $R_d = \sum_{t \in T} \mu_{Rd}/t$ in which the membership function is defined as $\mu_{Rd}:D \times T \rightarrow [0, 1]$. In this case, $\mu_{Rd}(t) = F(d, t)$, i.e., the membership value, can be obtained by the indexing function F. We describe later that through this extension of the document representation, the evaluation of a Boolean query produces a numeric estimate of the relevance of each document to the query, expressed by a numeric score or RSV, which is interpreted as the degree of satisfaction of the constraints expressed in a query.

Fuzzy set theory has been applied to define new and more powerful indexing models than the one based on the function specified in Eq. 1. The definition of new indexing functions has been motivated by several considerations. First, these F functions do not take into account the idea that a term can play different roles within a text according to the distribution of its occurrences. Moreover, the text can be considered as a black box, closed to users' interpretation. Such users might naturally filter information by emphasizing certain

subparts on the basis of their subjective interests. This outlines the fact that relevance judgments are driven by a subjective interpretation of the document's structure, and supports the idea of *dynamic* and *adaptive* indexing.[17,41] By adaptive indexing, we mean indexing procedures that take into account the users' desire to *interpret* the document contents and to "build" their synthesis on the basis of this interpretation.

Fuzzy Representation of Structured Documents

We also consider the synthesis of a fuzzy representation of structured documents that takes into account the users' needs.[17] A document can be represented as an entity composed of sections (e.g., *title, authors, introduction,* and *references*). For example, a single occurrence of the term in the *title* indicates that the chapter is concerned with the concept expressed by the term, while a single occurrence in the *reference* suggests that the chapter refers to other publications dealing with that concept. The information role of each term occurrence depends then on the semantics of the subpart where it is located. This means that to the aim of defining an indexing function for structured documents the single occurrences of a term may contribute differently to the significance of the term in the whole document. Moreover, the document's subparts may have a different importance determined by the users' needs. For example, when looking for chapters written by a certain author, the most important subpart would be the *author name*; while when looking for chapters on a certain topic, the *title, abstract,* and *introduction* subparts would be preferred.

Of course, when generating an archive of a set of documents, it is necessary to define the sections that one wants to employ to structure each document. The decision of how to structure the documents, i.e., the type and number of sections, depends on the semantics of the documents and on the accuracy of the indexing module that one wants to achieve. A formal representation of a document will be constituted using a fuzzy binary relation: with each pair <section, term >, a significance degree in the interval [0, 1] is computed to express the significance of that term in that document section. To obtain the overall significance degree of a term in a document, i.e., the index term weight, these values are *dynamically* aggregated by taking into account the indications that a user explicits in the query formulation. Other nonfuzzy approaches have also introduced the concept of boosting factor to emphasize differently the contribution of the index terms occurrences depending on the document sections to the overall index term weights. However, these approaches compute *static* index term weights during the indexing process, without taking into account the user interpretation.

On the contrary, in the fuzzy approach the aggregation function is defined on two levels. First, the user expresses preferences for the document sections (the equivalent of the boosting factors), specifying those sections that the system should more heavily weight in order to take proper account of the evaluation of the relevance of a given document to that user's query. Second, the user should decide which aggregation function has to be applied for producing the overall significance degree. This is done by the specification of a linguistic quantifier such as *at least one, at least k*, or *all*.[42] By adopting this document representation, the same query can select documents in different relevance order depending on the user's indicated preferences.

An indexing model has been proposed by which the occurrences of a term in the different documents' sections are taken into account according to specific criteria, and the user's interpretation of the text is modeled.[17] During the retrieval phase, the user can specify the distinct importance (preference) of the sections and decide that a term must be present in *all* the sections of the document or in *at least a certain number* of them in order to consider the term fully significant. A section is a logical subpart identified by s_i, where $i \in 1, ..., n$ and n is the total number of the sections in the documents. We assume here that an archive contains documents sharing a common structure.

Formally, a document is represented as a fuzzy binary relation:

$$R_d = \sum_{(t,s) \in T \times S} \mu_d(t, s) \Big/ (t, s) \qquad (2)$$

The value $\mu_d(t, s) = F_s(d, t)$ expresses the significance of term t in section s of document d. A function $F_s: D \times T \to [0, 1]$ is then defined for each section s. The overall significance degree $F(d, t)$ is computed by combining the single significance degrees of the sections, the $F_s(d, t)s$, through an aggregation function specified by the user. This function is identified by a fuzzy linguistic quantifier such as *all, at least k*, or *at least 1*, which aggregates the significance degrees of the sections according to their importance values as specified by the user.

The criteria for the definition of F_s are based on the semantics of section s and are specified by an expert during the indexing of the documents. For example, for sections containing short texts or formatted texts, such as the *author* or *keywords*, a single occurrence of a term makes it fully significant in that section: in this case, it could be assumed that $F_s(d, t) = 1$, if t is present in s but 0 otherwise. By contrast, for sections containing textual descriptions of variable length such as the *abstract*

and *title* sections, $F_s(d, t)$ can be computed as a function of the normalized term frequency in the section as, for example:

$$\mu_s(d,t) = tf_{dst} * IDF_t \qquad (3)$$

in which IDF_t is the inverse document frequency of term t [see definition (5)], tf_{dst} is the normalized term frequency defined as

$$tf_{dst} = \frac{OCC_{dst}}{MAXOCC_{sd}}$$

in which OCC_{dst} is the number of occurrences of term t in section s of document d and $MAXOCC_{sd}$ is a normalization parameter depending on the section's length so as not to underestimate the significance of short sections with respect to long ones. For example, this normalization parameter could be computed as the frequency of the term with the highest number of occurrences in the section.

To simplify the computation of this value, it is possible to heuristically approximate it: during the archive generation phase, with an expert indicating the estimated percentage of the average length of each section with respect to the average length of documents ($PERL_s$). Given the number of occurrences of the most frequent term in each document d, $MAXOCC_d$, an approximation of the number of occurrences of the most frequent term in section s of document d is

$$MAXOCC_{sd} = PERL_s * MAXOCC_d$$

Term Significance

To obtain the overall degree of significance of a term in a document, an aggregation scheme of the $F_s(d, t)s$ values has been suggested, based on a twofold specification of the user.[17] When starting a retrieval session, users can specify their preferences on the sections s by a numeric score $\alpha_s \in [0, 1]$, where the most important sections have an importance weight close to 1. Moreover, users can select a linguistic quantifier to specify the aggregation criterion; the quantifier can be chosen among *all* (the most restrictive one), *at least one* (the weakest one), or *at least k*, which is associated with an intermediate aggregation criterion.

Within fuzzy set theory linguistic quantifiers used to specify aggregations are defined as ordered weighted averaging (OWA) operators.[43] When processing a query, the first step accomplished by the system for evaluating $F(d, t)$ is the selection of the OWA operator associated with the linguistic quantifier lq, OWA_{lq}. When the user does not specify any preferences on the documents' sections, the overall significance degree $F(d, t)$ is obtained by applying directly the OWA_{lq} operator to the values $\mu_1(d, t), ..., \mu_n(d, t)$:

Table 1 Normalized frequency of "genoma" in the sections of the two documents

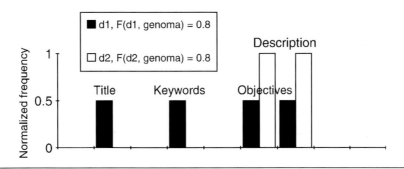

$$F(d,t) = \text{OWA}_{\text{lq}}(\mu_1(d,t),\dots,\mu_n(d,t))$$

When distinct preference scores $\alpha_1,\dots,\alpha_n$ are associated with the sections, it is first necessary to modify the values $\mu_1(d,\ t),\dots,\mu_n(d,\ t)$ in order to increase the "contrast" between the contributions due to important sections with respect to those of less important ones. The evaluation of the overall significance degree $F(d,\ t)$ is obtained by applying the operator OWA_{lq} to the modified degrees $a_1,\dots,a_n$: $F(d,\ t) = \text{OWA}_{\text{lq}}(a_1,\dots,a_n)$.

We can now briefly sketch a comparison of the effectiveness of a system adopting a simple weighted representation versus a system with this structured weighted representation. In particular, the different rankings of two documents obtained by adopting the two different representations are outlined by an example. The two documents considered in the archive of CNR research projects contain the term "genoma." Table 1 shows the normalized frequency of "genoma" in the sections of the two documents; as it can be noticed, the term "genoma" has the same total number of occurrences in both documents. Since the normalization factors are the same, by applying F as defined in Eq. 1, the significance of "genoma" in both documents gets the same value $F(d_1,\text{ genoma}) = F(d_2,\text{ genoma}) = 0.8$. Table 2 shows the significance degrees for each section in which the term "genoma" occurs. These degrees are obtained using the fuzzy representation of structured

documents; since the title and keywords sections are short texts, μ_{title} and μ_{keywords} are defined so as to take values in $\{0,\ 1\}$. After estimating that the objective section takes up averagely 30% of the documents' length, and the description section is around 40%, $\mu_{\text{objective}}$ and $\mu_{\text{description}}$ are defined.

When the user does not specify any criterion to aggregate the single degrees of the sections, a default aggregation operator is used.[16,17] Since no importance is specified to differentiate the contributions of the sections, all of them are assumed to have the same importance weight of 1. Notice that the document d_1 that contains "genoma" in the *keywords* and title sections is now considered more significant with respect to document d_2 that contains the term just in the *objectives* and *description* sections.

These results could be reversed if the user specifies that the presence of the term "genoma" in the *objectives* section is fundamental. Table 3 illustrates this situation, showing the modified degrees of significances of the sections when the user sets the aggregation criterion equal to at *least 1* and $\alpha_{\text{objective}} = 1$, $\alpha_{\text{title}} = \alpha_{\text{keywords}} = \alpha_{\text{description}} = 0.5$, and $\alpha_i = 0$ otherwise.

The fact that the user can explicate the preferences on the section and the aggregation criterion by a linguistic quantifier allows a subjective interpretation of document content and gives the user the possibility of full control on the system behavior. This is not the case

Table 2 Significance degrees of "genoma" in each section of the two documents

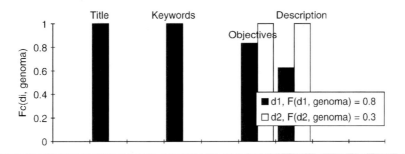

Table 3 Modified significance degrees of the term "genoma" in the documents sections

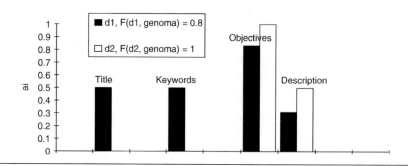

for other IR models, the probabilistic model (e.g., Bayesian updating of the probabilities as part of relevance feedback), and Rocchio's relevance feedback mechanism for the vector space model, or even the calculation of the rank for Web pages retrieved by Google using PageRank. In these models the retrieval criteria remain implicit and are not observable directly by the user.

Experimental Results

A comparison of the results produced by using the traditional fuzzy representation of documents and the fuzzy representation of structured documents can be found.[17] In this experiment, a collection of 2500 textual documents about descriptions of CNR research projects has been considered. The indexing module of the prototypal IRS named DOMINO, used for the experiment, has been extended in order to be able to recognize in the documents any structure simply by specifying it into a definition file. In this way, it is not necessary to modify the system when dealing with a new collection of documents with a different structure. The definition of the documents sections has been made before starting the archive generation phase. During this phase, it was also necessary to specify the criteria by which to compute the significance degrees of the terms in each section. Two kinds of sections have been identified: the "structured" sections, i.e., the research code, title, research leader, and the "narrative" sections, containing unstructured textual descriptions, i.e., the project description and the project objective. It has been observed that while the values of precision remain unchanged in the two versions of the system, the values of recall are higher by using the structured representation than those obtained by using the traditional fuzzy representation.

We illustrate another approach that produces a weighted representation of documents written in HTML.[34] An HTML document has a specific syntactic structure in which its subparts have a given format specified by the delimiting tags. In this context, tags are seen as syntactic elements carrying an indication of the importance of the associated text. When writing a document in HTML, an author associates varying importance to each of the different subparts of a given document by delimiting them by means of appropriate tags. Since a certain tag can be employed more than once, and in different positions inside the document, the concept of document subpart is not meant as a unique, adjacent piece of text. Such a structure is subjective and carries the interpretation of the document author. It can be applied in archives, which collect heterogeneous documents, i.e., documents with possibly different "logical" structures.

When generating an HTML document, an author exploits the importance weights associated with different subparts of the text. If characters of different fonts are used, it is assumed that the larger the font, the more important the information carried by the text. Moreover, to use boldface or italics for characters generally means the highlighting of a portion of the text. Tags constitute then indicators of the importance of documents' subparts.

An indexing function has been proposed, which provides different weights for the occurrences of a given term in the document, depending on the tags by which they are delimited.[34] The overall significance degree $F(d, t)$ of a term t in a document d is computed by first evaluating the term significance in the different document tags, and then by aggregating these contributions. With each tag, a function $F_{tag}:D \times T \rightarrow [0, 1]$ is associated together an importance weight $\mu_{tag} \in [0, 1]$. Note that the greater is the emphasis of the text associated with a tag, the greater is its importance weight. A possible ranking of the considered tags has been suggested[34] in decreasing order of tag importance. The definition of such a list is quite subjective, although based on objective assumptions suggested by commonsense. These rankings include a notion such as a larger font for the characters in a portion of text yields greater importance of that portion of text, or text in boldface or italics or appearing in a list can be assumed as having a higher importance. Of course, other orderings could be defined.

To simplify the hierarchy of the tags, we see that certain tags can be employed to accomplish similar aims, so one can group them into different classes. It is assumed that the members of a class have the same importance weight. Text not delimited by any tag is included into the lowest class. A simple procedure to compute numeric importance weights starting from the proposed ranking can be achieved. The definition of F_{tag} follows the same mechanism as the previous approach.[17] The following normalized frequency is now proposed:

$$F_{tag}(d,t) = \frac{NOCC_{tag\ dt}}{MAXOCC_{tag\ d}}$$

in which $NOCC_{tag\ dt}$ is the number of occurrences of term t inside tag in document d, and $MAXOCC_{tag\ d}$ is the number of occurrences of the most frequent term inside the tag.

Once the single significance degrees of a term into the tags have been computed, these have to be aggregated in order to produce an overall significance degree of the term into the document. In the aggregation all the significance degrees should be taken into account, so as to consider the contribution of each tag, modulated by their importance weights. To this aim a weighted mean can be adopted:

$$A(F_{tag_1}(d,t), \ldots, F_{tag_n}(d,t)) = \sum_{i=1,\ldots,n} F_{tag_i}(d,t){*}wi$$

in which $\sum_{i=1,\ldots,n} w_i = 1$. Starting from the list of tags in decreasing relative order of their importance, the numeric weights w_i are computed through a simple procedure. Assuming that tag_i is more important than tag_j iff $I < j$ (i and j being the positions of tag_i and tag_j, respectively, in the ordered list), the numeric importance weight w_i associated with tag_i can be computed as $w_i = (n - i + 1)\big/\sum_{i=1,\ldots,n} i$.

In the computation of the overall significance degree $F(d, t)$, the inverse document frequency of term t could be taken into account:

$$F(d,t) = \left(\sum_{i=1,\ldots,n} F_{tag\ i}(d,t)^{*}w_i{}^{*}g(IDF_t) \right)$$

in which the definition of $g(IDF_t)$ is given in formula (5).

FLEXIBLE QUERYING

A flexible query language is a query language that incorporates some elements of natural language so users have a simple, powerful, and yet subjective mechanism by which to express their information needs. Flexibility

can also be a characteristic of the query evaluation mechanism to allow tuning of the semantics of query's concepts with respect to the document collection, the user's subjective statement of information need, and even the user's application domain. Linguistic variables provide a suitable framework to generalize, to represent, and to manage the linguistics of the query's concepts. Thus, this approach can be used to formalize the semantics of linguistic terms introduced in a Boolean query language.

Flexible query languages have been defined as generalizations of Boolean query languages that employ Boolean logic. Within the framework of fuzzy set theory, we have the idea of a softening of the rigid, crisp constraints of a Boolean condition being strictly true (a document has a keyword) or false (the document does not contain the keyword).

A flexible query consists of either or both of two soft components. First, there can be selection conditions interpreted as soft constraints on the significance of the index terms in each document representation. Second, there can be soft aggregation operators, which can be applied to the soft constraints in order to define compound selection conditions. The atomic selection conditions for individual terms are expressed by pairs <term, weight >, in which the weight can be a numeric value in the interval [0, 1] that is used to identify a soft constraint or the weight can be a linguistic value for the variable *importance*. The compound conditions for combining terms via Boolean logic are expressed by means of linguistic quantifiers used as aggregation operators.

Query Evaluation Mechanism

Query processing within retrieval can be interpreted as a decision-making activity. Its aim is to evaluate a set of alternatives or possible solutions, in this case a set of documents, based upon some criteria or selection conditions in order to select the optimal list (perhaps ranked) of documents in response to a user's query.

In the case of a Boolean query, the alternatives are the document representations as described based on the presence or absence of index terms or keywords. The selection conditions, as expressed by terms specified in a query, define a set of constraints requiring the presence or absence of these terms within a document's representation. These conditions are expressed connected by aggregation operators, i.e., the Boolean logic operators of AND, OR, and NOT. The decision process is performed through an exact matching function, which is strictly dependent on the system query language. This decision process evaluates the global satisfaction of the query constraints for each document representation. Relevance is modeled as a binary property of the documents with respect to the user's query.

Given a fuzzy approach to retrieval, query processing can be regarded as a decision activity affected by vagueness. In fact, the query can be seen as the specification of a set of soft constraints, i.e., vague selection conditions that the documents can satisfy to a partial extent. The documents described through the significance degrees of the index terms constitute the alternatives. The query evaluation mechanism is regarded as fuzzy decision process that evaluates the degree of satisfaction of the query constraints by each document representation by applying a partial matching function. This degree is the RSV and can be interpreted as the degree of relevance of the document to the query and is used to rank the documents. Then, as a result of a query evaluation, a fuzzy set of documents is retrieved in which the RSV is the membership value. In this case the definition of the partial matching function is strictly dependent on the query language, specifically on the semantics of the soft constraints.

A wish list of requirements that a matching function of an IRS must satisfy has been proposed.[18,24] Included in this list is the separability property that the evaluation of an atomic selection condition for an individual term in a query should be independent of the evaluation of the other atomic components or their Boolean connectors. The matching function should be based solely upon a function evaluating atomic conditions. Following the calculation of these evaluations, one can then aggregate them based upon the Boolean operators in the query. It has been shown that this property guarantees a homomorphic mapping from the space of all single terms to the space of all possible Boolean queries using these terms.[44] This property has been considered widely within fuzzy retrieval models, especially in the definition of flexible query languages.

By designing the partial matching mechanism from the bottom-up the separability property is ensured. First, each atomic selection condition or soft constraint in the query is evaluated by a function E for a given document. Then the aggregation operators are applied to the results starting from the innermost operator in the query to the outermost operator by a function E^*. This E function evaluates the soft constraints associated with the query atoms on the fuzzy set R_d representing each document, where these soft constraints are defined as fuzzy subsets. The membership value $\mu_{atom}(i)$ is the degree of satisfaction of the soft constraint associated with the atomic query *atom*, i.e., $E(<atom>, d) = \mu_{atom}(F(d, t))$. In other words, E evaluates how well the term t, which has an indexing weight $F(d, t)$ for document d, satisfies the soft constraint specified by *atom*. The result of the evaluation is a fuzzy set, $\sum_{d \in D} \mu_{atom}(F(d,t))/d$ in which $\mu_{atom}(F(d, t))$ is interpreted as the RSV of document d with respect to the query atom.

The function $E^*: D \times Q \to [0, 1]$, where Q is the set of all the proper queries in the query language, evaluates the final RSV of a document, reflecting the satisfaction of the whole query. The definition of E^* depends strictly upon the structure of the query language, specifically upon the aggregation operators used to combine the atomic components. The AND connective is classically defined as the minimum (min) operator, the OR connective as the maximum (max) operator, and the NOT connective as the one-minus $(1-)$ or complement operator. These definitions preserve the idempotence property. A fuzzy generalization of the Boolean query structure has been defined in which the Boolean operators are replaced by linguistic quantifiers.[16] In this context, linguistic quantifiers are used as aggregation operators to determine the degree of satisfaction for the soft constraints. They allow to improve as well as to simplify the expressiveness of the Boolean query language.

Query Weights

To render a Boolean query language to be more user-friendly and more expressive, one can extend the atomic selection conditions by introducing query term weights.[22,23,45,46] An example of weighted query is the following: $<t_1, w_1>$ AND ($<t_2, w_2>$ OR $<t_3, w_3>$) in which t_1, t_2, and t_3 are search terms with numeric weights w_1, w_2, and w_3 in the interval $[0, 1]$. These weights are implicitly given as being equal to 1 in the classical Boolean query language.

The concept of query weights raises the problem of their interpretation. Several authors have realized that the semantics of query weights should be related to the concept of the "importance" of the terms. Being well aware that the semantics of the query term weights influences the definition of the partial matching function, specifically of the E function, different semantics for the soft constraint imposed by a pair $<t, w>$ have been proposed in the literature trying to satisfy as much as possible properties of the wish list, in particular, the separability property.

Early on, query weights were interpreted as a relative importance weight where the separability property does not hold. Two distinct definitions of E have been proposed for conjunctive and disjunctive queries, respectively.[22,47] Later, other models[23,24,46] used an interpretation of the query weights w as a threshold on the index term weight or as an ideal index term weight.[35,45]

Implicit query weights

The simplest extension of the Boolean model consists of the adoption of a weighted document representation but with a classical Boolean query language.[40] This retrieval mechanism ranks the retrieved documents in decreasing order of their significance with respect to the user query. In this case, an atomic query consisting of a single term t is interpreted as the specification of a pair $<t, 1>$ in which $w = 1$ is implicitly specified. The soft constraint associated with $<t, 1>$ is then interpreted as the requirement that the index term weight be "close to 1" and its evaluation is defined as $\mu_w(F(d, t)) = F(d, t)$. This means that the desired documents are those with maximum index term weight for the specified term t, i.e., index term weights closest to 1. This interpretation implies that the evaluation mechanism tolerates the under satisfaction of the soft constraint associated with $<t, 1>$ with a degree equal to $F(d, t)$.

Relative importance query weights

Here, query weights are interpreted as measures of the "relative importance" of each term with respect to the other terms in the query.[22,47] This interpretation allows the IRS to rank documents so that documents are ranked higher if they have larger index term weights for those terms that have larger query weights. However, since it is not possible to have a single definition for the soft constraint μ_w that preserves the "relative importance" semantics independently of the Boolean connectors in the query, two distinct definitions of μ_w have been proposed, depending on the aggregation operators in the query. This approach, sadly, gives up the separability property. Two alternative definitions have been proposed for conjunctive and disjunctive queries.[22,47] The first proposal[22] yields

  $\mu_w(F(d, t)) = wF(d, t)$ for disjunctive queries and
  $\mu_w(F(d, t)) = \max(1, F(d, t)/w)$ for conjunctive queries;
  while the second proposal[47] yields
  $\mu_w(F(d, t)) = \min[w, F(d, t)$ for disjunctive queries
  $\mu_w(F(d, t)) = \max[(1 - w), F(d, t)]$ for conjunctive queries

Notice that any weighted Boolean query can be expressed in disjunctive normal form so that any query can be evaluated by using one of these two definitions.

Threshold query weights

To preserve the separability property, an approach treating the query weights as thresholds has been suggested.[23,46] By specifying query weights as thresholds the user is asking to see all documents "sufficiently about" a topic. In this case, the soft constraint identified by the numeric query weight can be linguistically expressed as "more or less over w." Of course, the lower the threshold, the greater the number of documents retrieved. Thus, a threshold allows a user to define a point of discrimination between under- and over-satisfaction.

The simplest formalization of threshold weights has been suggested as a crisp threshold[23]

$$\mu_w(F(d,t)) = \begin{cases} 0 & \text{for } F(d,t) < w \\ F(d,t) & \text{for } F(d,t) \geq w \end{cases}$$

In this case, the threshold defines the minimally acceptable document. Due to its inherent discontinuity, this formalization might lead to an abrupt variation in the number of documents retrieved for small changes in the query weights. To remedy this, continuous threshold formalization has been suggested:[46]

$$\mu_w(F(d,t)) = \begin{cases} P(w) * \frac{F(d,t)}{w} & \text{for } F(d,t) < w \\ P(w) + Q(w) * \frac{(F(d,t)-w)}{(1-w)} & \text{for } F(d,t) \geq w \end{cases}$$

where $P(w)$ and $Q(w)$ might be defined as $P(w) = 1 + w/2$ and $Q(w) = 1 - w^2/4$.

For $F(d, t) < w$, the μ_w function measures the closeness of $F(d, t)$ to w; for $F(d, t) \geq w$, $\mu_w(F(d, t))$ expresses the degree of oversatisfaction with respect to w, and undersatisfaction with respect to 1.

Ideal query weights

Another interpretation for the query weights has been defined.[35,45] Here, the pair $<t, w>$ identifies a set of ideal or perfect documents so that the soft constraint μ_w measures how well $F(d, t)$ comes close to w, yielding

$$\mu_w(F(d,t)) = e^{\ln(k) * (F(d,t)-w)^2}$$

The parameter k in the interval $[0, 1]$ determines the steepness of the Gaussian function's slopes. As a consequence, k will affect the strength of the soft constraint *close to w*. So, the larger the value of k is, the weaker the constraint becomes. This parametric definition makes it possible to adapt the constraint interpretation to the user concept of *close to w*.[36] The retrieval operation associated with a pair $<t, w>$ corresponds in this model to the evaluation of a similarity measure between the importance value w and the significance value of t in R_d: $w \approx F(d, t)$.

Comparisons of these query weight semantics

In order to analyze the results obtained by these different semantics associated with the query weight w, let us consider the archive represented by the fuzzy sets in Table 4. The rows are the documents, the columns are the terms, and the elements are the values of the index term weights, i.e.,

Table 4 Query q (ANDed weighted pairs)

	t_1	t_2	t_4
q	1	0.6	0.2

row d_i and column t_j is the value $F(d_i, t_j)$. Let us consider the query: $q = <t_1, 1 > \text{ AND } <t_2, 0.6 > \text{ AND } <t_4, 0.2 >$, as represented in Table 5.

Table 6 yields the results of the evaluation of q for each of the query weight semantics, assuming that the AND connective is evaluated using the MIN operator.

Linguistic Query Weights

The main limitation of numeric query weights is their inadequacy in dealing with the imprecision that characterizes the concept of importance that they represent. In fact, the use of numeric query weights forces the user to quantify a qualitative and rather vague notion and to be aware of the weight semantics. Thus, a fuzzy retrieval model with linguistic query weights has been proposed[36] with a linguistic extension of the Boolean query language based upon the concept of a linguistic variable.[7] With this approach, the user can select the primary linguistic term "important" together with linguistic hedges (e.g., "very" or "almost") to qualify the desired importance of the search terms in the query. When defining such a query language the term set, i.e., the set of all the possible linguistic values of the linguistic variable *importance* must be defined. Such a definition depends on the desired granularity that one wants to achieve. The greater the number of the linguistic terms, the finer the granularity of the concepts that are dealt with. Next, the semantics for the primary terms must be defined. A pair $<t, important >$, expresses a soft constraint $\mu_{important}$ on the term significance values (the $F(d, t)$ values). The evaluation of the relevance of a given document d to a query consisting solely of the pair $<t, important >$ is based upon the evaluation of the degree of satisfaction of the associated soft constraint $\mu_{important}$.

The problem of giving a meaning to numeric weights reappears here in associating a semantic with the linguistic term *important*. The $\mu_{important}$ function is defined based on the ideal semantics of the numeric weight to yield[36]

Table 5 Each row is a fuzzy set representing a document

	t_1	t_2	t_3	t_4
d_1	1	0.9	1	0.2
d_2	0.7	0.6	0.3	0.8

Table 6 Results of query q in Table 5 referred to documents in Table 4

Query weight semantics	d_1	d_2
Ideal index term weight	0.3	0.6
Relative importance	0.8	0.6
Threshold on index term weight	0.2	0

$$\mu_{important}(F(d,t)) = \begin{cases} e^{\ln(k)*(F(d,t)-i)^2} & \text{for } F(d,t) < i \\ 1 & \text{for } i \leq F(d,t) \leq j \\ e^{\ln(k)*(F(d,t)-j)^2} & \text{for } F(d,t) > j \end{cases}$$

We see that if $F(d, t)$ is less than the lower bound i or greater than the upper bound j, the constraint is undersatisfied. The strength of the soft constraint $\mu_{important}$ depends upon both the width of the range $[i, j]$ and the value of the k parameter. The values i and j delimit the level of *importance* for the user. We note that as the value $|i - j|$ increases, the soft constraint becomes less precise. So, for the case of the ideal semantics of numeric query term weights, k determines the sharpness of the constraint in that as k increases, the constraint increases in fuzziness.

We can define the $\mu_{important}$ function based upon the threshold semantics to yield[48]

$$\mu_{important}(F(d,t)) = \begin{cases} \frac{1+i}{2} * e^{\ln(k)*(F(d,t)-i)^2} & \text{for } F(d,t) < i \\ \frac{1+F(d,t)}{2} & \text{for } i \leq F(d,t) \leq j \\ \frac{1+j}{2} * \left(1 + \frac{F(d,t)-j}{2}\right) & \text{for } F(d,t) > j \end{cases}$$

We note that this compatibility function is continuous and nondecreasing in $F(d, t)$ over the interval $[0, 1]$. For $F(d, t) < i$, $\mu_{important}$ increases as a Gaussian function. For $F(d, t)$ in the interval $[i, j]$, $\mu_{important}$ increases at a linear rate. For $F(d, t) > j$, $\mu_{important}$ still increases, but at a lesser rate. The compatibility functions of nonprimary terms, such as *very important* or *fairly important*, are derived by modifying the compatibility functions of primary terms. This is achieved by defining each linguistic hedge as a modifier operator. For example, the linguistic operators in[48] to yield

$$\mu_{very \ important}(x) = \mu_{important}(x)$$

with $i_{very} = i + 0.2$ and $j_{very} = j + 0.2$ and $\forall x \in [0, 1]$.

$$\mu_{averagely \ important}(x) = \mu_{important}(x)$$

with $i_{averagely} = i - 0.3$ and $j_{averagely} = j - 0.3$ and $\forall x \in [0, 1]$.

$$\mu_{minimally \ important}(x) = \mu_{important}(x)$$

with $i_{minimally} = i - 0.5$ and $j_{minimally} = j - 0.5$ and $\forall x \in [0,1]$.

in which i and j are values in $[0, 1]$ delimiting the range of complete satisfaction of the constraint $\mu_{important}$. With these definitions, any value $F(d, t)$ of the basic domain of the *importance* variable fully satisfies at least one of the constraints defined by the linguistic query terms.

In Herrara–Viedma[49] a query language with linguistic query weights having heterogeneous semantics have been proposed so as to benefit of the full potential offered of fuzzy set to model subjective needs.

Linguistic Quantifiers to Aggregate the Selection Conditions

In a classical Boolean query language, the AND and OR connectives allow only for crisp (nonfuzzy) aggregations, which do not capture any of the inherent vagueness of user information needs. For example, the AND used for aggregating M selection conditions does not tolerate the no satisfaction of but a single condition that could cause the no retrieval of relevant documents. To deal with this problem, additional extensions of Boolean queries have been provided, which involve the replacement of the AND and OR connectives with soft operators for aggregating the selection criteria.[33,50,51]

Within the framework of fuzzy set theory, a generalization of the Boolean query language has been defined based on the concept of linguistic quantifiers that are employed to specify both crisp and vague aggregation criteria of the selection conditions.[16] New aggregation operators can be specified by linguistic expressions with self-expressive meaning, such as *at least k* and *most of*. They are defined to exist between the two extremes corresponding to the AND and OR connectives, which allow requests for *all* and *at least one of* the selection conditions, respectively. The linguistic quantifiers used as aggregation operators are defined by OWA operators.

Adopting linguistic quantifiers more easily and intuitively formulate the requirements of a complex Boolean query. For example, when desiring that *at least two* out of the three terms "politics," "economy," and "inflation" be satisfied, one might formulate the Boolean query as

(politics AND economy) OR (politics AND inflation)

OR (economy AND inflation)

However, a simpler one can replace this:

at least 2(politics, economy, inflation)

This new query language via the nesting of linguistic quantifiers supports the expression of any Boolean query. For example the query

AND (<processing > OR <analysis >) AND <digital >

can be translated into the new, more synthetic and clear formulation:

all (<image >, *at least 1 of* (<processing >, <analysis >), <digital >).

A quantified aggregation function can be applied not only to single selection conditions, but also to other quantified expressions. Then, the E^* function evaluating the entire query yields a value in $[0, 1]$ for each document d in the archive D.

If S is the set of atomic selection conditions and Q is the set of legitimate Boolean queries over our vocabulary of terms, then the E^* function can be formalized by recursively applying the following rules

1. if $q \in S$ then $E^*(d, s) = \mu_w(F(d, t))$ in which $\mu_w(F(d, t))$ is the satisfaction degree of a pair $<t, w >$ by document d with w being either a numeric weight or a linguistic weight.
2. if $q = quantifier (q_1,\dots,q_n)$ and $q_1,\dots,q_n \in Q$ then
3. $E^*(d, \text{NOT } q) = 1 - E^*(d, q)$

in which $OWA_{quantifier}$ is the OWA operator associated with *quantifier*.

The formal definition of the query language with linguistic quantifiers with the following quantifies has been generated[16]

- *all* replaces AND.
- *at least k* acts as the specification of a crisp threshold of value k on the number of selection conditions and is defined by a weighting vector $w_{at\ least\ k}$ in which $w_k = 1$, and $w_j = 0$, for $i \leq k$—noting that *at least 1* selects the maximum of the satisfaction degrees so that it has the same semantics of OR.
- *about k* is a soft interpretation of the quantifier *at least k* in which the k value is not interpreted as a crisp threshold, but as a fuzzy one so that the user is fully satisfied if k or more conditions are satisfied but gets a certain degree of satisfaction even if $k-1$, $k-2,\dots,1$ conditions are satisfied—this quantifier is defined by a weighting vector $w_{about\ k}$ in which $w_i = \frac{i}{\sum^k i}$ for $i \leq k$, and $w_i = 0$ for $i > k$.
- *most of* is defined as a synonym of *at least $\frac{2}{3}n$* in which n is the total number of selection conditions.

With respect to nonfuzzy approaches that tried to simplify the Boolean formulations, the fuzzy approach subsumes the Boolean language, allows reformulating Boolean queries in a more synthetic and comprehensible way, and improves the Boolean expressiveness by allowing flexible aggregations.

Other authors have followed these ideas by proposing alternative formalization of linguistic query weights and flexible operators based on ordinal labels and ordinal aggregations,[52] thus reducing the complexity of the evaluation mechanism.

FUZZY ASSOCIATIVE MECHANISMS

Associative retrieval mechanisms are defined to enhance the retrieval of IRSs. They work by retrieving additional documents that are not directly indexed by the terms in a given query but are indexed by other, related terms, sometimes called associated descriptors. The most common type of associative retrieval mechanism is based upon the use of a thesaurus to associate index or query terms with related terms. In traditional associative retrieval, these associations are crisp.

Fuzzy associative retrieval mechanisms obviously assume fuzzy associations. A fuzzy association between two sets $X = \{x_1, \dots, x_m\}$ and $Y = \{y_1, \dots, y_n\}$ is formally defined as a fuzzy relation:

$$f : X \times Y \to [0,1]$$

where the value $f(x, y)$ represents the degree or strength of the association existing between the values $x \in X$ and $y \in Y$. In IR, different kinds of fuzzy associations can be derived depending on the semantics of the sets X and Y.

Fuzzy associative mechanisms employ fuzzy thesauri, fuzzy pseudothesauri, fuzzy ontologies, and fuzzy categorizations to serve three alternative, but compatible purposes: 1) to expand the set of index terms of documents with new terms; 2) to expand the search terms in the query with associated terms; and 3) to expand the set of the documents retrieved by a query with associated documents.

Fuzzy Thesauri

A thesaurus is an associative mechanism that can be used to improve both indexing and querying. It is well known that the development of thesauri is very costly, as it requires a large amount of human effort to construct and to maintain. In highly dynamic situations, i.e., volatile situations, terms are added and new meanings derived for old terms quite rapidly, so that the thesaurus needs frequent updates. For this reason, methods for automatic construction of thesauri have been proposed, named pseudothesauri, based on statistical criteria such as the terms' co-occurrences, i.e., the simultaneous appearance of pairs (or triplets, or larger subsets) of terms in the same documents.

In a thesaurus, the relations defined between terms are of different types. If the associated descriptor has a more general meaning than the entry term, the relation is classified as broader term (BT), while a narrower term (NT) is the inverse relation. Moreover, synonyms and near-synonyms are parts of another type of relationship associated by a related term (RT) connection.

The concept of a fuzzy thesaurus has been suggested,[27,31,53,54] where the links between terms are weighted to indicate the relative strengths of these associations. Moreover, fuzzy pseudothesauri are generated when the weights of the links are automatically computed by considering document relationships rather than concept relationships.[30,55]

The first work on fuzzy thesauri introduced the notion of fuzzy relations to represent associations between terms.[54,56] Let us look at a formal definition of a fuzzy thesaurus.[27,28] Consider T to be the set of index terms and C to be a set of concepts. Each term $t \in T$ corresponds to a fuzzy set of concepts $h(t)$:

$$h(t) = \{\langle c, t(c) \rangle | c \in C\}$$

in which $t(c)$ is the degree to which term t is related to concept c. A measure M is defined on all of the possible fuzzy sets of concepts, which satisfies:

$$M(\oslash) = 0$$
$$M(C) < \infty$$
$$M(A) \leq M(B) \quad \text{if } A \subseteq B$$

A typical example of M is the cardinality of a fuzzy set. The fuzzy RT relation is represented in a fuzzy thesaurus by the similarity relation between two index terms, t_1 and $t_2 \in T$ and is defined as

$$s(t_1, t_2) = M[h(t_1) \cap h(t_2)]/M[h(t_1) \cup h(t_2)]$$

This definition satisfies the following:

- if terms t_1 and t_2 are synonymous, i.e., $h(t_1) = h(t_2)$, then $s(t_1, t_2) = 1$;
- if t_1 and t_2 are not semantically related, i.e., $h(t_1) \cap h(t_2) = \emptyset$, then $s(t_1, t_2) = 0$;
- $s(t_2, t_1) = s(t_1, t_2)$ for all $t_1, t_2 \in T$; and
- if t_1 is more similar to term t_3 than to t_2, then $s(t_1, t_3) > s(t_1, t_2)$.

The fuzzy NT relation, indicated as nt, which represents grades of inclusion of a narrower term t_1 in another (broader) term t_2, is defined as

$$nt(t_1, t_2) = M[h(t_1) \cap h(t_2)]/M[h(t_1)]$$

This definition satisfies the following:

- if term t_1's concept (s) is completely included within term t_2's concept (s), i.e., $h(t_1) \subseteq h(t_2)$, then

- if t_1 and t_2 are not semantically related, i.e., $h(t_1) \cap h(t_2) = \varnothing$, then nt $(t_1, t_2) = 0$; and
- if the inclusion of t_1's concept (s) in t_2's concept (s) is greater than the inclusion of t_1's concept (s) in

By assuming M as the cardinality of a set, s and nt are given as

$$s(t_1, t_2) = \sum_{k=1}^{M} \min[t_1(c_k), t_2(c_k)] \Big/ \sum_{k=1}^{M} \max[t_1(c_k), t_2(c_k)]$$

$$nt(t_1, t_2) = \sum_{k=1}^{M} \min[t_1(c_k), t_2(c_k)] \Big/ \sum_{k=1}^{M} t_1(c_k)$$

A fuzzy pseudothesaurus can be defined by replacing the set C in the definition of $h(t)$ above with the set of documents D, with the assumption that $h(t)$ is the fuzzy set of documents indexed by term t. This yields

$$h(t) = \{(d, t(d)) | d \in D\}$$

in which $t(d) = F(d, t)$ is the index term weight defined earlier. F can be either a binary value defining a crisp representation, or it can be a value in [0, 1] to define a fuzzy representation of documents. The fuzzy RT and the fuzzy NT relations now are defined as

$$s(t_1, t_2) =$$

$$\sum_{k=1}^{M} \min[F(t_1, d_k), F(t_2, d_k)] \Big/ \sum_{k=1}^{M} \max[F(t_1, d_k), F(t_2, d_k)]$$

$$nt(t_1, t_2) = \sum_{k=1}^{M} \min[F(t_1, d_k), F(t_2, d_k)] \Big/ \sum_{k=1}^{M} F(t_1, d_k)$$

Note that s (t_1, t_2) and nt (t_1, t_2) are dependent on the co-occurrences of terms t_1 and t_2 in the set of documents, D. The set of index terms of document d, i.e., $\{t \mid F(d, t) \neq 0$ and $t \in T\}$, can be augmented by those terms t_A which have $s(t, t_A) > \alpha$ and/or nt $(t, t_A) > \beta$ for parameters α and $\beta \in [0, 1]$.

Suppose that in the definition of F we have the set T as a set of citations that are used to index documents, rather than a set of terms. In this case, a fuzzy association on citations can be defined through the fuzzy relations of s and/or nt. By using citations, a user may retrieve documents that cite a particular author or a particular reference. In addition, a keyword connection matrix has been proposed to represent similarities between keywords in order to reduce the difference between relationship values initially assigned using statistical information and a user's evaluation.[57] A new method is also proposed in which keywords that are attached to a document and broader concepts are hierarchically organized, calculating the keyword relationships through the broader concepts.

Moreover, a thesaurus can be generated based on the max-star transitive closure for linguistic completion of a thesaurus generated initially by an expert linking terms.[58] In addition, a probabilistic notion of term relationships can be employed by assuming that if one given term is a good discriminator between relevant and nonrelevant documents, then any term that is closely associated with that given term (i.e., statistically cooccurring) is likely to be a good discriminator, too.[10] Note that this implies that thesauri are collection-dependent.

On the one hand, one can also expand on Salton's[59] use of the $F(d, t)$ values. Salton[60] infers term relationships from document section similarities. On the other hand, one can manipulate the $F(d, t)$ values in order to generate co-occurrence statistics to represent term linkage weights.[61] Here, a synonym link is considered, defined as

$$\mu_{\text{synonym}}(t_1, t_2) = \sum_{d \in D} [F(d, t_1) \leftrightarrow F(d, t_2)]$$

where $F(d, t_1) \leftrightarrow F(d, t_2) = \min[F(d, t_1) \rightarrow F(d, t_2), F(d, t_1) \leftarrow F(d, t_2)]$ and $F(d, t_1) \rightarrow F(d, t_2)$ can be defined in variety of ways. For instance, $F(d, t_1) \rightarrow F(d, t_2)$, the implication operator, can be defined as $[F(d, t_1)^c \vdash F(d, t_2)]$, where $F(d, t_1)^c = 1 - F(d, t_1)$ is the complement of $F(d, t_1)$ and $\vdash$ is the disjunctive (OR) operator defined as the max; or it can be defined as min $(1, [1 - F(d, t_1) + F(d, t_2)])$. Here, a narrower term link (where term t_1 is narrower than term t_2, so term t_2 is broader than term t_1), is defined as:

$$\mu_{\text{narrower}}(t_1, t_2) = \sum_{d \in D} [F(d, t_1) \leftrightarrow F(d, t_2)]$$

Note that fuzzy narrower relationships defined between fuzzy sets can help the purpose of identifying generalization and specialization of topics, while the fuzzy similarity relationship between fuzzy sets can be of aid to identify similar topics. Thus they serve to build a labeled graph of relationships between concepts, regarded as fuzzy sets of terms, in the specific domain of the collection.

Fuzzy Clustering for Documents

Clustering in IR is a method for partitioning D, a given set of documents, into groups using a measure of similarity (or distance), which is defined on every pair of documents. Grouping like documents together is not a new phenomenon, especially for librarians. The similarity between documents in the same group should be large, while the similarity between documents in different groups should be small.

A common clustering method is based on the simultaneous occurrences of citations in pairs of documents.

Documents are clustered using a measure defined on the space of the citations. Generated clusters can then be used as an index for IR, i.e., documents that belong to the same clusters as the documents directly indexed by the terms in the query are retrieved.

Similarity measures have been suggested empirically or heuristically, sometimes analogously to the similarity measures for documents matched against queries.[33,38,62] When adopting a fuzzy set model, clustering can be formalized as a kind of fuzzy association. In this case, the fuzzy association is defined on the domain $D \times D$. By assuming $R(d)$ to be the fuzzy set of terms representing a document d with membership function values $d(t) = F(d, t)$ being the index term weights of term t in document d, the symmetric fuzzy relation s, as originally defined above, is taken to be the similarity measure for clustering documents:

$$s(d_1, d_2) = \sum_{k=1}^{M} \min[d_1(t_k), d_2(t_k)] \Big/ \sum_{k=1}^{M} \max[d_1(t_k), d_2(t_k)]$$
$$= \sum_{k=1}^{M} \min[F_1(t_k, d_1), F(t_k, d_2)] \Big/$$
$$\sum_{k=1}^{M} \max[F(t_k, d_1), F(t_k, d_2)]$$

in which T is the set of index terms in the vocabulary and M is the number of index terms in T.

In fuzzy clustering, documents can belong to more than one cluster with varying degree of membership.[63] Each document is assigned a membership value to each cluster. In a pure fuzzy clustering, a complete overlap of clusters is allowed. Modified fuzzy clustering, also called soft clustering, uses thresholding mechanisms to limit the number of documents belonging to each cluster. The main advantage of using modified fuzzy clustering is the fact that the degree of fuzziness is controlled. The use of fuzzy clustering in IR have several applications that span from unsupervised categorization of documents into homogeneous overlapping topic categories, so as to offer users an overview of the contents of a collection or to organize the results of a search into labeled groups, thus allowing users to have an immediate view of what has been retrieved. With respect to crisp clustering, fuzzy clustering allows finding a document in several labeled groups, thus reflecting distinct interpretation of document's content.

FUZZY PERFORMANCE MEASURES

One problem with the existingcriteria to measure the effectiveness of IRSs is the fact that Recall and Precision measures have been defined by assuming that relevance is a Boolean concept. In order to take into account the fact that IRSs rank the retrieved documents based on their RSVs that are interpreted either as a probabilities of relevance, similarity degrees of the documents to the query, or as degrees of relevance, Recall–Precision graphs are produced in which the values of precision are computed at standard levels of recall. Then the average of the precision values at different recall levels is computed to produce a single estimate.

Nevertheless, these measures do not evaluate the actual values of the RSVs associated with documents and do not take into account the fact that also users can consider relevance as a gradual concept. For this reason some authors have proposed some fuzzy measure of effectiveness. Buell and Kraft[46] proposed the evaluation of fuzzy recall and fuzzy precision, defined as follows:

$$\text{Fuzzy precision} = \frac{\sum_d \min(e_d, u_d)}{\sum_d e_d},$$
$$\text{Fuzzy recall} = \frac{\sum_d \min(e_d, u_d)}{\sum_d u_d}$$

where u_d is the user's evaluation of the relevance of document d (u_d can be binary or defined in the interval [0, 1]) and e_d is the RSV of document d computer by the IRSs. These measures take into account the actual values of e_d and u_d, rather than the rank ordering based in descending order on e_d.

These measures can be particularly useful to evaluate the results of fuzzy clustering algorithms.

CONCLUSIONS

This entry reviews the main objectives and characteristics of the fuzzy modeling of the IR activity with respect to alternative approaches such as probabilistic IR and vector space IR. The focus of the fuzzy approaches is on modeling imprecision and vagueness of the information with respect to uncertainty. The fuzzy generalizations of the Boolean Retrieval model have been discussed by describing the fuzzy indexing of structured documents, the definition of flexible query languages subsuming the Boolean language, and the definition of fuzzy associations to expand either the indexes or the queries, or to generate fuzzy clusters of documents. Fuzzy similarity and fuzzy inclusion relationships between fuzzy sets have been introduced that can help to define more evolved fuzzy IR models performing "semantic" matching of documents and queries, which is the prevailingtrend of research in IR.

REFERENCES

1. Tho, Q.T.; Hui, S.C.; Fong, A.C.M.; Cao, T.H. Automatic fuzzy ontology generation for semantic web. IEEE Trans. Knowl. Data Eng. **2006**, *18* (6), 842–856.

2. Sanchez, E. In *Fuzzy Logic and the Semantic Web*; Elsevier: Amsterdam, London, 2006.

3. Motro, A. Imprecision and uncertainty in database systems. In *Fuzziness in Database Management Systems*; Bosc, P., Kacprzyk, J., Eds.; Physica-Verlag: Heidelberg, 1995; 3–22.

4. Zadeh, L.A. Fuzzy sets. Inform. Control **1965**, *8* (3), 338–353.

5. Zadeh, L.A. Fuzzy sets as a basis for a theory of possibility. Fuzzy Set Syst. **1978**, *1* (1), 3–28.

6. Dubois, D.; Prade, H. In *Possibility Theory: An Approach to Computerized Processing of Uncertainty*; Plenum Press: New York, NY, 1988.

7. Zadeh, L.A. The concept of a linguistic variable and its application to approximate reasoning. Inform. Sci. **1975**, *8* (3), 199–249 parts I, II. 301–357.

8. Bosc, P. Fuzzy databases. In *Fuzzy Sets in Approximate Reasoning and Information Systems*; Bezdek, J., Dubois, D., Prade, H., Eds.; The Handbooks of Fuzzy Sets Series, Kluwer Academic Publishers: Boston, MA, 1999.

9. Kraft, D.; Bordogna, G.; Pasi, G. Fuzzy set techniques in information retrieval. In *Fuzzy Sets in Approximate Reasoning and Information Systems*; Bezdek, J. C., Dubois, D., Prade, H., Eds.; The Handbooks of Fuzzy Sets Series, Kluwer Academic Publishers: Boston, MA, 1999; 469–510.

10. van Rijsbergen, C.J. In *Information Retrieval*; Butterworths & Co. Ltd.: London, U. K., 1979.

11. Fuhr, N. Models for retrieval with probabilistic indexing. Inform. Process. Manage. **1989**, *25* (1), 55–72.

12. Crestani, F.; Lalmas, M.; van Rijsbergen, C.J.; Campbell, I. Is this document relevant? ... Probably. ACM Comput. Surv. **1998**, *30* (4), 528–552.

13. Bordogna, G.; Pasi, G. The application of fuzzy set theory to model information retrieval. In *Soft Computing in Information Retrieval: Techniques and Applications*; Crestani, F., Pasi, G., Eds.; Physica-Verlag: Heidelberg, 2000.

14. Yager, R.R.; Rybalov, A. On the fusion of documents from multiple collections information retrieval systems. J. Am. Soc. Inform. Sci. **1999**, *49* (13), 1177–1184.

15. Bordogna, G.; Pasi, G.; Yager, R. Soft approaches to information retrieval on the WEB. Int. J. Approx. Reason. **2003**, *34* (2-3), 105–120.

16. Bordogna, G.; Pasi, G. Linguistic aggregation operators in fuzzy information retrieval. Int. J. Intell. Syst. **1995**, *10* (2), 233–248.

17. Bordogna, G.; Pasi, G. Controlling information retrieval through a user adaptive representation of documents. Int. J. Approx. Reason. **1995**, *12* (3-4), 317–339.

18. Cater, S.C.; Kraft, D.H. A generalizaton and clarification of the Waller-Kraft wish-list. Inform. Process. Manage. **1989**, *25* (1), 15–25.

19. Buell, D.A. A problem in information retrieval with fuzzy sets. J. Am. Soc. Inform. Sci. **1985**, *36* (6), 398–401.

20. Kraft, D.H. Advances in information retrieval: Where is that /#*%@^ record?. In *Advances in Computers*; Yovits, M., Ed.; Academic Press: New York, NY, 1985; 277–318.

21. Buell, D.A.; Kraft, D.H. A model for a weighted retrieval system. J. Am. Soc. Inform. Sci. **1981**, *32* (3), 211–216.

22. Bookstein, A. Fuzzy requests: An approach to weighted Boolean searches. J. Am. Soc. Inform. Sci. **1980**, *31* (4), 240–247.

23. Radecki, T. Fuzzy set theoretical approach to document retrieval. Inform. Process. Manage. **1979**, *15* (5), 247–260.

24. Waller, W.G.; Kraft, D.H. A mathematical model of a weighted Boolean retrieval system. Inform. Process. Manage. **1979**, *15* (5), 235–245.

25. Lucarella, D.; Zanzi, A. Information retrieval from hypertext: An approach using plausible inference. Inform. Process. Manage. **1993**, *29* (1), 299–312.

26. Lucarella, D.; Morara, R. FIRST: Fuzzy information retrieval system. J. Inform. Sci. **1991**, *17* (2), 81–91.

27. Miyamoto, S. Information retrieval based on fuzzy associations. Fuzzy Set Syst. **1990**, *38* (2), 191–205.

28. Miyamoto, S. Two approaches for information retrieval through fuzzy associations. IEEE Trans. Syst., Man Cybernet. **1989**, *19* (1), 123–130.

29. Murai, T.; Miyakoshi, M.; Shimbo, M. A fuzzy document retrieval method based on two-valued indexing. Fuzzy Set Syst. **1989**, *30* (2), 103–120.

30. Miyamoto, S.; Nakayama, K. Fuzzy information retrieval based on a fuzzy pseudothesaurus. IEEE Trans. Syst., Man and Cybernet. **1986**, *SMC-16* (2), 278–282.

31. Miyamoto, S. In *Fuzzy Sets in Information Retrieval and Cluster Analysis*; Kluwer Academic Publishers: Dordrecht, 1990.

32. Sanchez, S.N.; Triantaphyllou, E.; Kraft, D.H. A feature mining based approach for the classification of text documents into disjoint classes. Inform. Process. Manage. **2002**, *38* (4), 583–604.

33. Salton, G.; McGill, M.J. In *Introduction to Modern Information Retrieval*; McGraw-Hill: New York, NY, 1983.

34. Molinari, A.; Pasi, G. A fuzzy representation of HTML documents for information retrieval systems. In Proceedings of the IEEE International Conference on Fuzzy Systems, New Orleans, September, 8–12, 1996; Vol. 1, 107–112.

35. Cater, S.C.; Kraft, D.H. TIRS: A topological information retrieval system satisfying the requirements of the Waller–Kraft wish list. In Proceedings of the Tenth Annual ACM/SIGIR International Conference on Research and Development in Information Retrieval, New Orleans, LA, June, 1987; 171–180.

36. Bordogna, G.; Pasi, G. A fuzzy linguistic approach generalizing Boolean information retrieval: A model and its evaluation. J. Am. Soc. Inform. Sci. **1993**, *44* (2), 70–82.

37. Salton, G.; Buckley, C. Term weighting approaches in automatic text retrieval. Inform. Process. Manage. **1988**, *24* (5), 513–523.

38. Sparck Jones, K.A. In *Automatic Keyword Classification for Information Retrieval*; Butterworths: London, U. K, 1971.

39. Sparck Jones, K.A. A statistical interpretation of term specificity and its application in retrieval. J. Doc. **1972**, *28* (1), 11–20.

40. Buell, D.A. An analysis of some fuzzy subset applications to information retrieval systems. Fuzzy Sets Syst. **1982**, *7* (1), 35–42.

41. Berrut, C.; Chiaramella, Y. Indexing medical reports in a multimedia environment: The RIME experimental approach. In *ACM-SIGIR 89*; Boston, MA, 1986; 187–197.

42. Zadeh, L.A. A computational approach to fuzzy quantifiers in natural languages. Comput. Math. Appl. **1983**, *9* (1), 149–184.

43. Yager, R.R. On ordered weighted averaging aggregation operators in multi criteria decision making. IEEE Trans. Syst. Man Cybernet. **1988**, *18* (1), 183–190.

44. Bartschi, M. Requirements for query evaluation in weighted information retrieval. Inform. Process. Manage. **1985**, *21* (4), 291–303.

45. Bordogna, G.; Carrara, P.; Pasi, G. Query term weights as constraints in fuzzy information retrieval. Inform. Process. Manage. **1991**, *27* (1), 15–26.

46. Buell, D.A.; Kraft, D.H. Performance measurement in a fuzzy retrieval environment. In Proceedings of the Fourth International Conference on Information Storage and Retrieval, Oakland, CA, May 31–June 2; **1981**; *16*, 56–62 ACM/SIGIR Forum (1).

47. Yager, R.R. A note on weighted queries in information retrieval systems. J. Am. Soc. Inform. Sci. **1987**, *38* (1), 23–24.

48. Kraft, D.H.; Bordogna, G.; Pasi, G. An extended fuzzy linguistic approach to generalize Boolean information retrieval. J. Inform. Sci. Appl. **1995**, *2* (3), 119–134.

49. Herrera-Viedma, E.; Lopez-Herrera, A.G. A model of an information retrieval system with unbalanced fuzzy linguistic information. Int. J. Intell. Syst. **2007**, *22* (11), 1197–1214.

50. Paice, C.D. Soft evaluation of Boolean search queries in information retrieval systems. Inform. Technol.: Res. Develop. Appl. **1984**, *3* (1), 33–41.

51. Sanchez, E. Importance in knowledge systems. Inform. Syst. **1989**, *14* (6), 455–464.

52. Herrera, F.; Herrera-Viedma, E. Aggregation operators for linguistic weighted information. IEEE Trans. Syst. Man Cybernet. Part A: Syst. Hum. **1997**, *27* (5), 646–656.

53. Neuwirth, E.; Reisinger, L. Dissimilarity and distance coefficients in automation-supported thesauri. Inform. Syst. **1982**, *7* (1), 47–52.

54. Radecki, T. Mathematical model of information retrieval system based on the concept of fuzzy thesaurus. Inform. Process. Manage. **1976**, *12* (5), 313–318.

55. Nomoto, K.; Wakayama, S.; Kirimoto, T.; Kondo, M. A fuzzy retrieval system based on citation. Syst. Control **1987**, *31* (10), 748–755.

56. Reisinger, L. On fuzzy thesauri. In *COMPSTAT 1974*; Bruckman, G., Ed.; Physica Verlag: Vienna, Austria, 1974; 119–127.

57. Ogawa, Y.; Morita, T.; Kobayashi, K. A fuzzy document retrieval system using the keyword connection matrix and a learning method. Fuzzy Set Syst. **1991**, *39* (2), 163–179.

58. Bezdek, J.C.; Biswas, G.; Huang, L.Y. Transitive closures of fuzzy thesauri for information-retrieval systems. Int. J. Man Mach. Stud. **1986**, *25* (3), 343–356.

59. Salton, G. In *Automatic Text Processing: The Transformation, Analysis and Retrieval of Information by Computer*; Addison Wesley: Boston, 1989.

60. Salton, G.; Allan, J.; Buckley, C.; Singhal, A. Automatic analysis, theme generation, and summarization of machine-readable texts. Science **1994**, *264* (June 3), 1421–1426.

61. Kohout, L.J.; Keravanou, E.; Bandler, W. Information retrieval system using fuzzy relational products for thesaurus construction. In Proceedings IFAC Fuzzy Information, Marseille, France, 1983; 7–13.

62. Salton, G.; Bergmark, D. A citation study of computer science literature. IEEE Trans. Prof. Commun. **1979**, *22* (3), 146–158.

63. Bezdek, J.C. *Pattern Recognition with Fuzzy Objective Function Algorithms*; Plenum Press: New York, 1981.

Index

Abacus, 41

Abstraction
  Data Center Edition for Windows Server
      2008, 236–237
  definition, 235–236
  hypervisors, types 1 and 2, 236
  Microsoft's .NET framework, 236
  toolkits, 236
  Virtual Server product, 236

Accelerated life testing (ALT), 71

Access control, VNC systems
  attack.c program, 1077–1078
  authentication messages, 1076
  ClientInitialization messages, 1077
  protocol version number, 1076
  ServerInitialization messages, 1077
  WinVNC registry, 1078–1079

Accountable Care Organizations (ACOs), 375

Acknowledgment (ACK) frame, 2

Acquisition, cyberforensics
  bit-for-bit forensic imaging, 281
  cloud accounts, 282
  redundant array of inexpensive disks
      (RAID), 281–282
  and smart phones, 282

Active operating system fingerprinting,
  585–586

Adaptive route planning, 836

Address Resolution Protocol (ARP), 590

AddRoundKey step, 272

Ad hoc networks
  Bluetooth, see Bluetooth technology
  communication, 853
  delay, 1
  IEEE 802.11 standard, 1–2
  literature, 852–853
  network topology, 853–854
  node configuration, 854–855
  taxonomy, 854–856
  throughput, 1

Administrative controls framework
  assigned security responsibilities,
      653–654
  baseline, 652
  business associate contracts, 659
  contingency planning, 657–658
  detective controls, 752–753
  documentation, 659
  evaluation, 658–659
  information access management, 655–656
  operational records, 652
  personnel/security, 751
  policies and procedures, 651
  preventive controls, 751–752
  security awareness and training, 656
  security incident procedures, 656–657
  security management process, 652–653
  standards and guidelines, 651
  workforce security, 654

Adobe Integrated Runtime (AIR), 242

Advanced encryption standard (AES)
  Blackberry, 196
  candidates for, 14–16
  cracking device, 17
  data encryption standard (DES), 14–15
  elements, 13
  FIPS, 13
  impacts, 17–18
  Kerckhoff's assumption, 13

NIST, see National Institute of Standards and
      Technology (NIST)
  process, 14
  proprietary algorithm, 13
  Rijndael algorithm, 16–17

Advanced Micro Dynamics Virtualization
    (AMD-V), 201

Advanced Research Projects Agency (ARPA),
    181

Advanced Research Projects Agency Network
    (ARPANET), 182

AES, see Advanced encryption standard (AES)

Age distribution chart, 305

Aggregation (AGG) functions and rules,
    390, 394

Agreed service time (AST), 806

AI, see Artificial intelligence (AI)

Aircraft vibration alerts, 328–329

Air Force Office of Scientific Research and
    Development, 184

Air-gap, 524

Air Traffic Information System (ATIS), 111

Alavi and Leidner's scheme
  coding and sharing, 826
  community view, 827
  expert finder system, 826
  networks creation, 826–827

Algebra, see Boolean algebras

AlohaNET, DARPA-funded project, 235

Alzheimer's disease, 171

Amazon
  identity federation, 239
  Internet commerce, 90
  Simple Storage Service (S3), 188–190, 207

Amazon Web Services (AWS), 167

American National Standards Institute (ANSI)
  American National Standards (ANS), 20
  conformity assessment, 20–21
  hallmarks, 20
  industry sectors and services, 19
  international standards activities, 20
  standards panels, 21
  U.S. standardization system, 19

American Productivity and Quality Center
    (APQC), 814

American Recovery and Reinvestment Act
    (ARRA), 648

American Society for Cybernetics, 290

American Society for Information Science and
    Technology (ASIS&T), 693

Amplitude normalization, 416

Analysis, cyberforensics
  data exfiltration review, 283–284
  deterministic analysis, 285–286
  file system review, 284
  hash matching review, 285
  internet history review, 283
  keyword search review, 285
  probabilistic analysis, 286
  recycle bin history review, 284
  registry review, 284
  scheduled jobs review, 285
  system logs review, 284
  USB activity review, 285
  volatile memory review, 285

Analytical center of excellence (ACE), 628

Analytics, Healthcare informatics
  analytical center of excellence, 628
  business vs. clinical analytics, 621–622
  capabilities, 619
  costs control, 618
  healthcare costs, lowering of, 624–626
  healthcare outcomes, 626–628
  health sciences ecosystem, 618
  information technology, 618
  levels of reporting, 619–621
  nursing care, 624
  organizational performance, 622–623
  quality and safety, 624

Android Software Development Kit, 194–195

ANN, see Artificial neural networks (ANNs)

ANN-based NLP
  cognitive models and, 55
  function approximation, 53
  implications, 55–56
  inscrutability, 53
  literature on, 60
  local representation, 56–57
  meaning representation, 59–60
  mental states transformations, 54
  noise tolerance, 53
  physical symbol system hypothesis (PSSH),
      54
  research paradigms, 56
  sequential processing, 58–59
  strands of development, 54
  subsymbolic position, 54–55
  symbolic NLP, 52

ANSI-Accredited Standards Committee
    (ASC), 20

Anything-as-a-Service (XaaS), 207–208

Apple iPhone, 106, 194

Application developers, standards
  Asynchronous JavaScript and XML (AJAX),
      222
  Extensible Markup Language (XML), 223
  ICEfaces Ajax Application Framework,
      222–223
  JavaScript Object Notation (JSON), 223–224
  Linux, Apache, MySQL and PHP (LAMP),
      224
  Linux, Apache, PostgreSQL and PHP
      (LAPP), 224
  purpose, 222

Application-level gateway, 520–521

Application Programming Interface (API), 860

Application programming interfaces (APIs),
    195, 835

Application security, 216–217
  advantages, 26
  commercial off-the-shelf software (COTS),
      25
  cyber-security attack, 26
  development life cycle, 22–24
  outsourced development services, 26
  production, 25
  Web applications threat, 22

Application service providers (ASPs), 870

Application-specific integrated circuit-based
    (ASIC)
  advantage, 524
  intrusion detection system (IDS), 525
  intrusion prevention system (IPS), 525
  IPsec and VPN, 525